THE WORKS OF STEPHEN CHARNOCK

The Works of
STEPHEN CHARNOCK

Volume V

Truth and Life

THE BANNER OF TRUTH TRUST

THE BANNER OF TRUTH TRUST
3 Murrayfield Road, Edinburgh EH12 6EL
P.O. Box 621, Carlisle, Pennsylvania 17013, U.S.A.

*

Reprinted from Volume Five of the
Works of Stephen Charnock, published by James Nichol in 1866

First Banner of Truth Trust edition 1997

ISBN 0 85151 724 2

*

Printed in Great Britain by
The Bath Press, Bath

THE COMPLETE WORKS

OF

STEPHEN CHARNOCK, B.D.

With Introduction

BY REV. JAMES M'COSH, LL.D.,

PROFESSOR OF LOGIC AND METAPHYSICS, QUEEN'S COLLEGE, BELFAST.

VOL. V.

CONTAINING:

MISCELLANEOUS DISCOURSES, INDEXES, &c.

EDINBURGH: JAMES NICHOL.

LONDON: JAMES NISBET AND CO. DUBLIN: G. HERBERT.

M.DCCC.LXVI.

CONTENTS.

DISCOURSES.

CONTENTS.

DISCOURSES.

A DISCOURSE OF THE NECESSITY OF CHRIST'S DEATH.

Ought not Christ to have suffered these things, and to enter into his glory?—LUKE XXIV. 26.

THE words are an answer of our Saviour's to the discourse of two of the disciples who were going to Emmaus, ver. 13. He came *incognito* to them while they were discoursing together of the great news of that time, viz., the death of their master, whom they acknowledge 'a prophet mighty in deed and word before God and all the people,' ver. 19; confirmed by God to be so by miracles, and confessed to be so by the people. Yet they questioned whether he were the Messiah that should redeem Israel, and erect the kingdom so much promised and predicted in the Scripture. They could not tell how to reconcile the ignominy of his death with the grandeur of his office, and glory of a king. And though they had heard by the women of 'a vision of angels' that assured them 'he was alive,' yet they do not seem in their discourse to give any credit to the report, but relate it as they heard it; though both by what they said before, ver. 21, that they had 'trusted that it was he that should have redeemed Israel,' and also by the sharp reproof Christ gives them, ver. 25, 'O fools, and slow of heart to believe all that the prophets have spoken!' we may conclude that they thought it a mere illusion, or a groundless imagination of the women. Christ, to rectify their minds, begins with a reproof, and follows it with an instruction, that what they thought a ground to question the truth of his office, and the reality of his being the Messiah, was rather an argument to confirm and establish it, since that person characterised in the Old Testament to be the Messiah was to wade to his glory through a sea of blood, and such sufferings in every kind as cruel and shameful as that person in whom they thought they had been deceived, had suffered three days before; and afterwards discourseth from the Scripture that his death, and such a kind of death, did well agree with the predictions of the prophets; and therefore, 'beginning at Moses and all the prophets, he expounded unto them in all the scriptures the things concerning himself.' He might well sum up in two or three hours' time (wherein we may suppose he was with them) most of those testimonies which did foretell his sufferings for the expiation of sin. The proposition which he maintains from Moses and the prophets, is in the text, 'Ought not Christ to have suffered those things?' which is laid down by way of interrogation, but equivalent to an affirmation; and he backed, without question, his discourse with many reasonings for the confirmation of it, to reduce them from the distrust they had to a full assent to the necessity of his death, in order to his own glory, and consequently theirs; the foundation of his own exaltation, and the redemption of mankind, being laid in his being a sacrifice.

Ought not?

1. It is not said, it is convenient or becoming. As it was said of his baptism, Matt. iii. 15, 'It becomes us to fulfil all righteousness.' His baptism had more of a convenience than necessity.* He might have been the Messiah without subjecting himself to the ceremonial law, or passing under the baptism of John. But it was impossible he should be a redeeming Christ without undergoing an accursed death. No sin was expiated merely by his submission to the yoke of legal rites, or the baptismal water of John; all expiation of sin was founded only in his bloody baptism.

2. It is said, *he ought.* Not an absolute, but a conditional *ought;* not his original duty as the Son of God, but a voluntary duty as the redeemer of man. He voluntarily engaged at first in it, and voluntarily proceeded to the utmost execution, yet necessarily after his first engagement. Necessity there was, but not compulsion. All necessity doth not imply constraint, and exclude will. Paul must necessarily die by the law appointed to all men, but willingly he 'desires to be dissolved, and to be with Christ.' God is necessarily holy and true, yet not unwillingly so. Angels and glorified souls are necessarily holy by their confirmation in a gracious and glorious state, yet voluntarily so by a full and free inclination; necessary by the decree and counsel of God, necessary by the engagement and promise of Christ, necessary by the predictions and prophecies of Scripture.† All which causes of necessity are linked together, because the restoration of man required such a suffering; therefore it was from eternity decreed by God, embraced by Christ, published in Scripture. It was ordained in heaven, and set out in the *manifesto* of the Old Testament; so that if this death had not been suffered, the counsel of God concerning redemption had been defeated, the word and promises of Christ violated, and the truth of God in the predictions of the prophets had fallen to the ground. The decree of God was declared in many prophecies before the execution; and this will of God is an evidence of the necessity of it.‡ Why did he ordain it, if it were not necessary to so great an end? Though the end, the redemption of man, was not necessary, yet when the end was resolved on, this, as the means, was found necessary in the counsel of God. The natural inclination and will of Christ, as man, did startle at it, when he desired that this cup might pass from him. It was contrary to the reason and common sense of men. How, then, should that infinite Wisdom, that wills nothing but what is unquestionably reasonable, have determined such a means, if it had not been necessary for his own glory and man's recovery? But both the Father and the Son were moved to it by the height of that good will they bore to the fallen creature.

These things, ταῦτα. Every one of those severe and sharp circumstances. The whole system of those sufferings, not a dart that pierced him, not a reproach that grated upon him, but was ordained; every step he took in blood and suffering was marked out to him. Since Christ was to die for the reparation of man, for the expiation of sin, it was necessary that his death should be attended with those particular sharpnesses that might render his love more admirable, the justice of God more dreadful, the evil of sin more abominable,

* Daillé, Serm. de Resurrect. de Christ, p. 226. † Gerhard in loc.

‡ Daillé, Serm. de Resurrect. de Christ, p. 226.

and the satisfaction itself more valuable. The intenseness of his love had not been set off so amiably in a light and easy death, as in a painful and shameful suffering; and though the greatness of his merit and the fulness of his satisfaction did principally arise from the dignity of the suffering person, yet some consideration might be also had of the greatness of his suffering. Not only his death, as he was considered equal with God, but his shameful death in the circumstance of the cross, is a mark of his obedience and a cause of his exaltation, Philip. ii. 8. Both were regarded in the crown of glory, and that high dignity wherein he was instated, so that the sum of Christ's speech amounts to this much: be not doubtful whether the person so lately suffering, whom you account so great a prophet, were the Messiah. You clearly may see in the prophets that nothing hath been inflicted on him but what was predicted of him; so that it is not merely the malice of man that hath caused those sufferings; that was only a means God in his infinite wisdom used to bring about his own counsel. He was not forced to what he suffered, but willingly delivered up himself to perform the charge and office of a Redeemer, which could not else have been accomplished by him; and that glory which you expected, was not by the order of God to be conferred upon him till he abased himself to such a passion. He will have a glory to your comfort, though not answering your carnal expectations. Be not dejected, but recover your hopes of redemption which you seem to have lost, and let them be rectified in the expectation, not of an earthly, but an heavenly, glory.

Observe,

1. The nature of Christ's sufferings, *these things.*
2. The necessity, *Ought not Christ to suffer?*
3. The consequence, *and to enter into his glory.*

There are two doctrines to be insisted on from these words:

1. There was a necessity of Christ's death.
2. Christ's exaltation was as necessary as his passion.

For the first, there was a necessity of the death of Christ. It was necessary by the counsel of God, Acts ii. 23; 'Him being delivered by the determinate counsel and foreknowledge of God, Acts iv. 28. It was not a fruit of second causes, which God only suffered by a bare permission, but it was a decree of his will fixed and determined, and that before the world began, an irrevocable decree God made to deliver his Son to death for the sins of men, and according to this counsel he was in time delivered, and by the merit of his death hath reconciled to God all those that believe in him.

In handling this doctrine, I shall shew,

(1.) What kind of necessity this was.
(2.) That it was necessary.
(3.) The use.

1. What kind of necessity this was.

Prop. 1. His death was not absolutely necessary, but conditionally.

(1.) It supposeth, first, the entrance of sin. There was no necessity that sin should enter into the world. There was no necessity on man's part to sin. Though he was created with a possibility of sinning, yet not with a necessity; he was created mutable, but not corruptible: 'God made man upright,' Eccles. vii. 29. His faculties, as bestowed upon him, stood right to God. He had an understanding to know what of God was fit for him to know, a will without any wrong bias to embrace him, and affections to love him. God permitted him to fall, the devil allured him to sin, but neither the one nor the other did immediately influence his will to the commission of his crime. There was no necessity on God's part that sin should enter; though his wisdom thought good to permit it, yet there was no absolute necessity that it should step up in the world. He might have fixed man, as well as the holy angels, in an eternal purity; he might have enlightened the mind of man by a particular act of grace at the first proposal of the temptation by the devil, to discern his deceit and stratagem, and so might have prevented man's sin as well as permitted it. Had not sin entered, there had been no occasion for the death of the creature, much less for the death of Christ. The honour of God had not been invaded; there had been no provoked justice to satisfy, nor any violated law to vindicate. Some indeed there are* that think the incarnation of Christ had been necessary without the entrance of sin, because they consider God of so holy a nature that it had been impossible for him to be pleased with any creature, though the work of his own hands, so that neither angels nor men could have stood one moment in his sight without beholding him in the face of a mediator. Several had anciently imagined† that if man had continued in obedience till the time appointed for his confirmation, then Christ would have been incarnate, and man have become one mystical person with him for his confirmation, as the angels were confirmed by him; but none assert the death of Christ but upon supposition of sin. All sacrifices for sin imply the guilt of sin antecedent to them; but after man had transgressed the rule by his disobedience, and thereby made himself incapable of answering the terms of that righteous law which God had set him, the death of Christ became as necessary as his incarnation, for the righting the injured law and satisfying offended justice, and the conveyance of mercy to the creature, with the honour of God and preservation of his rights. As Christ's rejoicing from eternity, 'in the habitable parts of the earth,' supposeth the creation of the world in the order of God's decree, Prov. viii. 31, so the eternal counsel of God, for the making his Son a sacrifice, supposeth the rise of sin and iniquity in the world. Had not man run cross to the preceptive will of God, he had enjoyed the presence of God without a sacrificed mediator, and would have had an everlasting communion with him in happiness; but after sin entered upon the world, there was need of a propitiation for sin. An infinitely pure God could not have communion with an impure creature. It was not fit a sovereign majesty should make himself savingly known to his creature without a propitiatory.

(2.) It supposeth death to be settled by God as the punishment of sin. Some question whether it were absolutely necessary that death should have been threatened upon the breach of the law. It is true, as the law depends upon the will of the lawgiver, so doth the punishment. And it is in his liberty, if you consider him as an absolute sovereign, to annex what penalty he pleaseth; yet, as all laws are to spring from righteousness, so all punishments are to be regulated by righteousness and equity, that a punishment deserved by the greatest crime should not be ordered as the recompense of offences of a lighter nature. But in the case of transgressions against God, no penalty less than death, and eternal death, could, according to the rules of justice, have been appointed. It is certain sin doth naturally oblige to punishment: it is senseless to imagine that a law should be transgressed without some penalty incurred. A law is utterly insignificant without it, and it is inconsistent with the wisdom of a lawgiver to enact a precept without adding a penalty. If, therefore, a punishment be due to sin, it is requisite, according to the rules of justice and wisdom, to proportion the punishment to the greatness of the offence. I say this is the rule that

* Bacon's Confession of Faith, at the end of his Remains, pp. 117, 118.
† Jackson, vol. ii. quart. p. 191.

righteousness requires. And it is as natural that a crime should be punished suitably to its demerit as that it should be punished at all. Why doth any fault deserve punishment, but because there is an unreasonableness in it, something against the nature of man, against the nature of a subject, against the authority of the lawgiver, against the order and good of a community? The punishment therefore ought to be as great as the damage to authority by the crime. To order a punishment greater than the crime is tyranny; to order it less than the crime is folly in the government: unrighteousness in both, because there is an inequality between the sin and the penalty. Now, such is the excellency of God's nature, and so inviolable with his creature ought his authority to be, that the least offence against him deserves the highest punishment, because it is against the best and most sovereign being. It seems therefore to us that God had not acted like a righteous governor if he had not denounced death for the sins against him; the offence being the highest, the punishment in the order of justice ought to be the highest. What could be supposed more just and reasonable than for God to deprive man of that life which he had given him, that life which man had received from the goodness of his Creator, and had employed against his authority and glory? As his sin was against the supreme good, so the punishment ought to be the depriving man of his highest good. The vileness of the person offending, and the dignity of the person offended, always communicate an aggravation to the crime. The sin of man, being infinite, did, in the justice of God, merit an infinite punishment. And this is not only written upon the hearts of men by nature, that it is so, but that it is deservedly so, Rom. i. 32, 'that they are worthy of death.' The justice of God in inflicting death for sin is as well known as his power and Godhead, and the justice of it is universally owned in the consciences of men when they are awakened. Adam, when he sinned, did not think the offence of so great a weight, but his roused conscience presented him with those natural notions of the justice of God, and sunk him under the sense of it, till God had revived him by a promise.

(3.) It supposeth that, after man's transgression, and thereby the demerit of death, God would recover and redeem man. There was no necessity incumbent upon God to restore man after his defection from him and rebellion against him. As God was not obliged to prevent man's fall, so he was not obliged to recover man fallen. When he did permit him to offend, he might have let him sink under the weight of his own crimes, and left him buried in the ruins of his fall. He might for ever have reserved him in those chains he had merited, and have let him feed upon the fruit of his own doings, without one thought of his delivery, or employing one finger of that power for his restoration, whereby he had brought him into being; for the restoration of man was no more necessary in itself than the first creation of him was. As God might have left him in his nothing without producing him into being, so he might have left him in his contracted misery without restoring him to happiness. Nor was it any ways more necessary than the reducing the fallen angels to their primitive obedience and felicity. The blessedness and happiness of God had no more been infringed by the eternal destruction of man, than it was by the everlasting ruin of devils. Upon the supposition that God would save sinners after his justice was so fully engaged to punish them, no way in the understanding of man can be thought of, but the sufferings of the creature, or some one for him, to preserve the justice of God from being injured. Though the thoughts of some differ in other things, yet not in this. All say it was not simply necessary that man should be freed from his fallen state. But since God would not hurl all men into the damnation they had deserved, and treat them as he did the devils in the rigours of his justice, this way of the death of his Son was the most convenient way;* and indeed necessary, not necessary by an antecedent necessity (for there is no such necessity in God respecting created things), but a consequent necessity upon a decree of his will, which being settled, something else must necessarily follow as a means for the execution of that decree; as supposing God would create man to be Lord of the creature, and return him the glory of his works, it were then consequently necessary that he should create him with rational faculties, and fit for those ends for which he created him; but the creation of man in such a frame is not of absolute necessity, but depends upon the antecedent decree of his will, of creating such a creature as should render him the tribute of his works. So it is not necessary that God should free man from the spot of sin, and the misery contracted thereby, and reduce him from damnation to felicity; but since he determined the redemption of him after the violation of the law, which he had confirmed by the penalty of death, God could not without wrong to his justice and truth freely pardon man, because he is immutably righteous and true, and cannot lie; and since he is so righteous a judge that he can no more absolve the guilty than he can condemn the innocent, Exod. xxxiv. 7, his justice was an invincible obstacle to the pardon of sin, though men had implored his mercy with the greatest ardency and affection, unless this justice had been satisfied with a satisfaction suitable to it, *i. e.* infinite as the divine justice is infinite; and since neither man nor any other creature, being all of a finite nature, were able to give a full content to the justice of God, a necessity is then introduced of some infinite person to put himself in the place of the fallen creatures, clothe himself with their nature, and suffer in it the penalty they had merited, that they might be exempted from that which, by the transgression of the law, they had incurred.

(4.) It supposeth Christ's voluntary engagement and undertaking of this affair first. There could be no necessity upon God to redeem, nor any necessity upon Christ to be the Redeemer; but after his consent, which was wholly free, his promise engaged him to performance. He was free from all bonds till he entered into bond; he was at liberty whether he would be our surety; no compulsion could be used to him: John x. 18, he had 'power to lay down his life.' It implies a liberty either of laying down his life or not; a liberty of choice whether he would die for man or no. He had power if he pleased to avoid the cross, but he undertook it, 'despising the shame,' Heb. xii. 2. And after having once undertaken this charge, it was necessary for him to suffer. As it is in the liberty of a man's choice whether he will engage himself in bonds for an insolvent debtor, yet when he is entered into suretyship, both his own honesty and the equity of the law necessitates him to stand to his engagements, and pay the money he is bound for, if the debtor be still insolvent;† so after Christ hath promised payment for bankrupt man, he could not retract both in regard of his truth, and in regard of the tenderness which first moved him to it. He could not violate his promise, nor deny his contract; both the order of his Father and his own righteousness did not permit him to cast off this resolution. Though it was naturally voluntary, yet it was morally necessary; and therefore often when he speaks of his sufferings to his disciples, he puts a *must* to them: Mat. xvi. 21, John iii. 14 '*must* suffer many things,' '*must* be lifted up.' And his prayer from a natural inclination of the human nature, that this cup might pass from him, *if it were possible*, not being granted, shews it to be morally impossible,

* Petav. Theol. tom. iv. lib. ii. cap. 13, sect. 10.
† Daillé, Serm. de Resurrect. de Christ, p. 226.

after it was determined, that we could be saved any other way. God's not answering his own Son, manifests an impossibility to divert his death without our eternal loss. Had not that promise been past, if Christ had been incarnate, he might have lived in the world with glory and honour; he might have come, not as a surety, but as a lawgiver and judge; but after that promise made by him to his Father, and that the Father had by the covenant of redemption 'laid upon him the iniquities of us all,' and Christ on his part had covenanted to 'take upon him the form of a servant,' Philip. ii. 7, and to be 'made under the law,' Gal. iv. 4, he did owe to God an obedience as our surety according to the law of redemption, as well as an obedience to the moral law as a creature, by virtue of his incarnation. Had he been incarnate without such a promise of suffering, he had not been bound to suffer unless he had sinned; for, having no spot, neither original nor actual, he had stood firm upon the basis of the first covenant. But the obligation to the obedience of suffering was incumbent upon him by virtue of the compact between the Father and himself. Had he been incarnate without that precedent compact, he had owed an obedience to God in his humanity as a creature; but as he was incarnate for such an end, and was, pursuant to the law of redemption, made under the moral law, he owed an obedience to both those laws, an obedience as a creature, an obedience as mediator, as a son owes obedience to a father by virtue of his relation of a son; but if this son be bound apprentice to his father, he owes another obedience to him as a servant by virtue of the covenant between them; the duty of obedience as a servant is superadded to that of a son; so the necessity of obedience as a surety was added to the necessity of obedience as a creature in regard of Christ's humanity, so that this necessity is only consequent, and supposeth at first the voluntary engagement of Christ. For indeed his sufferings could not be of infinite merit for us except they had been voluntarily undertaken by him.* If his sufferings took their worth and value from his person, they must likewise have their freedom and election from his person. Whatsoever punishment, reproach, and trouble the fury of wicked men brought upon him, was not suffered by an absolute necessity, but conditional, after the engagement of his will.

Prop. 2. All things preceding his death, and all circumstances in his death, did not fall under a necessity of the same kind. Upon the former supposition, his death was necessary, and could not be avoided. Death was threatened by God as a sovereign; it was merited by man as a malefactor, and was necessary to be inflicted by God as a judge and governor. And by virtue of this threatening, and his engagement in suretyship, it was necessary that he should suffer, not as an innocent person, but under the imputation of a sinner; a reputed sinner, though he were perfectly innocent in his own nature: 1 Cor. v. 21, he was 'made sin for us.' Yet Christ, in his humiliation, did undergo some things which were not immediately necessary to our redemption. We might have been redeemed by him without his being hungry and weary. But this was mediately necessary to our redemption, in manifesting the truth and reality of his human nature. We might have been redeemed without the piercing of his side, and the letting out the water in the *pericardium*. But this was convenient to shew the truth of his death. These were necessary by virtue of God's decree, manifested in the prediction of the prophets, to be done unto him. But his incarnation and passion to death were immediately necessary to our recovery and the atonement of sin. We could not have been redeemed unless he had satisfied justice; justice could not be satisfied but by suffering; suffering could not have been under-

* Bilson on Christ's sufferings, p. 286.

gone unless he had been incarnate. A body he must have prepared for suffering; nor could he have suffered for us unless he had been incarnate in our nature.

2. Thing. To demonstrate this necessity. Having declared what kind of necessity this is, we may now demonstrate this necessity.

1. To suffer death was the immediate end of the interposition of Christ. The principal end of his undertaking was to right the honour of God, and glorify his attributes in the recovery of the creature; but the immediate end was to suffer, because this was the only way to bring about that end which was principally aimed at in Christ's interposition, and God's determination concerning him. Death being denounced as the punishment of sin, Christ interposeth himself for our security, with a promise to bear that punishment in our stead for the procuring our exemption from it; therefore, what punishment was of right to be inflicted on man for the breach of the law, was, by a gracious act of God, the governor of the world and guardian of his laws, transferred upon Christ, as putting himself in our stead. His first interposition was for the same end with his death, but his death was evidently for our sins. It was for them 'he gave himself,' Gal. i. 4; they were our sins which 'he bare in his own body on the tree,' 1 Peter ii. 24; 'for our iniquities he was wounded, and for our transgressions he was bruised,' Isa. liii. 5; our health was procured by his stripes, and therefore intended by him in his first engagement. He offered his person in our stead, which was able to bear our sin, and afford us a righteousness which was able to justify our persons; he offered himself to endure the curse of the law in his own body, and fulfil the righteousness of the law in his own person; he would be united with us in our nature, that he might make the sins of our nature his own in suffering for them, and give to us what was his, by taking to himself what was ours; he took our stripes that we might receive his medicine. This, therefore, being the end of his first undertaking, was necessary to be performed; for Christ is not yea and nay, 2 Cor. i. 19, one time of one mind, and another time of another, but firm and uniform in all his proceedings, without any contradiction between his promise and performance.

That this was the end of his first interposition is evident,

(1.) By the terms of the covenant of redemption incumbent on his part. What God demanded was complied with on the part of Christ. The demand of God was the offering of the soul, because upon that condition depends the promise of his exaltation and seeing his seed: Isa. liii. 10, 'When thou shalt make his soul an offering for sin, he shall see his seed;' or as others, 'When his soul is put an offering for sin.' The word אשם is properly a sin-offering, and his soul is the matter of this offering, as well as the spring and principle of the offering himself to God. It was upon this condition only he was to see his seed; he had had no seed, *i. e.* none had been saved by him according to this covenant, unless his soul had made itself an offering for sin. This death of Christ was the main article to be performed by him; this was the eye of Christ fixed upon in the offering himself in the first transaction to do the will of God: Ps. xl. 6–8, 'Burnt-offering and sin-offering hast thou not required. Lo, I come; I delight to do thy will,' Heb. x. 7, 8. The will of God for a satisfaction by sacrifice. The will of God was the demand of something above all legal sacrifices; for he had no pleasure in those which were offered by the law, wherein Christ complies with God; and it was something which was not to fall short of, but surmount those legal offerings. The denial of any pleasure or content in them implies a demand of a higher pleasure and content than all or any of them could afford. To this Christ gives his full consent, and offers himself, according to the will of God, to be a sacrifice, and puts himself in the place of those sin-offerings wherein God had no pleasure; as if he should have said, A sin-offering, Lord, thou wilt have, and one proportionable to the greatness of the offence; since none else can be suitable to an infinite majesty, I will be the sin-offering, and answer thy will in this; and therefore the apostle infers, Heb. x. 10, that the offering the body of Christ for our sanctification, our restoration, was the particular will of God in this affair, which will Christ particularly promises in that eternal transaction to perform: Gal. i. 4, 'Who hath given himself for our sins, according to the will of God.' And, indeed, God could not have been said to enter into his rest at the foundation of the world without this transaction, as he is said to do, Heb. iv.; for foreseeing that an universal stain and disorder would overspread the world by sin, that the glory which would naturally issue to him from the creatures would meet with an obstacle from it, and no way be left for the glorifying of any other attributes after sin but his power and justice in the due and righteous punishment of the creature, he could not take any pleasure in the works of his hands, had not the second person stood up as a sacrifice of atonement to purify the bespotted world, rectify the disorder, and render a content to the justice of God, that all the other attributes of God in the creation might have their due glory perpetuated and elevated. It was in this one person, and that by his blood, that God found the best way and method to gather together those things which sin had scattered, Eph. i. 7, 10. And the first promise in paradise after the fall, of the bruising the serpent's head, in having the seed of the woman's heel bruised by the serpent, intending thereby his death (as is cleared up by considering the revelations of God afterwards), shews that this was fixed in him, since it is most likely it was the second person appeared to Adam and made that promise. This was the first promise to man, founded upon this covenant of redemption.

(2.) The command that Christ received to die, manifests his interposition for this end. He was made under the law, and his death is called 'obedience,' Philip. ii. 8.* Obedience implies a command as the rule of it. Obedience to the moral law engaged him not to die for us; it had bound him over to death, had he been a transgressor of it; but considered in itself, it obliged him not, being innocent, to suffer death for those that were delinquents. Obedience, therefore, in regard of his death, must answer to a particular command of God, flowing from some other act of his will than what was formally expressed in the moral law. Such a command he received from his Father, to lay down his life, John x. 18; which supposeth the free proffer of himself to a state of humiliation for such an end as dying. Had it not been obedience to a command, God had not been bound to accept his offering. Though in itself, and its own nature, upon the trial of God it would have been found sufficient, yet it had been a just exception, 'Who hath required this at your hands?' If he had not offered himself to this purpose, he had not been God's voluntary servant; and if he had not received a law in order to the performance of what he offered, he had not been God's 'righteous servant,' as he is called, Isa. liii. 11, there being no rule whereby to measure his righteousness in this act. The concurrence of both these made his death necessary and acceptable. Though, as I said before, this command of dying for us was not formally any command of the moral law, yet after once he had received this order, and obliged himself to the performance of it, the moral law obliged him to the highest manner of performing this, *i. e.* with the highest love to God and his neighbour, whose nature he had taken, and thereby became our kinsman. Since God was

* Cocc. de Fœd. cap. v. p. 117.

dishonoured and man damaged by sin, his love to the glory of God and the salvation of man were to be with the greatest intenseness; and this the moral law enjoins in all acts we undertake for God.

(3.) If he had not interposed himself for this end, he could not have suffered. Since God passed such a judgment on him, and laid upon him the iniquities of us all, there must be some precedent act of Christ for this end; for it was not just with God to force any to bear the punishment of another's sin. The justice of God, in his dealings with man, is regulated by his own law; he inflicts nothing but what his law hath enjoined. To punish without law, and a transgression of it, is injustice. No law of God ever threatened punishment to one in every respect innocent. Christ, by a free act of his own, put himself into the state of a reputed nocent, and by his interposition for us, as a surety, was counted by God as one person with us; as a surety and a debtor are, in a legal and juridical account, as one person, and what the debtor is liable to in regard of that debt for which the surety is bound, whether it be a pecuniary or a criminal debt, the surety being considered as one person with him, is to undergo. Christ's substituting himself in our stead was to this end, that the sins of those that God had given him might be imputed to him; for he proffered himself to make his soul an offering for sin. It could be no sin of his own; sin he did not, sin he could not. It must be another's sin, transferred upon him in a juridical manner; transferred, I say, upon him, not by any transfusion of our sins into Christ by way of inherency, but by imputation, without which he could not be a sufferer. For what reason, what justice had there been to expose one to suffering, that was wholly innocent, and had no sin, neither by inherency nor imputation? How could any be liable to punishment, that could not in any manner be regarded as guilty? To be under judgment, supposeth a man's own crime, or the crimes of others. Since God, therefore, 'made him to be sin for us,' 2 Cor. v. 21, and could not in justice make him so without his own consent; his consent, then, in the first offer of his mediation, was to be made sin for us, *i.e.* to bear our sins. He offered himself for the same end for which God accepted him, and for which God used him. Pursuant to this offer of himself, he was made under the law, and put into such a state and condition, by his investing himself with the human nature, as that the law might make its demands of him, and receive the penalties which were due by it for the offence.

Add to this, the giving of some to Christ to save, John xvii. 18, vi. 39, which presupposeth the obligation of Christ to death; for after sin, the law being to be vindicated, and justice glorified, God's committing some to him to save, presupposeth his engagement to satisfy the law and justice on their behalf.* It was for this end also he came to the hour of his death, John xii. 27; and his prayer to his Father, to 'save him from this hour,' had been groundless, if he had not passed his word to his Father to enter upon that hour. What need he have prayed to his Father to save him, who might have saved himself, if there had been no antecedent obligation to undertake this task?

He thus interposing himself for this end, it was necessary he should die. For,

[1.] Else none could have been saved from the foundation of the world. Some were saved before his actual death upon the cross. God was the God of Abraham, Isaac, and Jacob; but 'God is the God of the living, not of the dead,' Mat. xxii. 32. They therefore lived in his sight before the actual oblation of Christ upon the cross; but they could no more have been saved

* Cocc. de Fœd. cap. v. pp. 118. 119.

without the credit of this death of Christ in our nature, than the fallen angels could have been saved. The reason they are not saved, is rendered by the apostle, Heb. ii. 16, because Christ took not their nature; his taking our nature therefore, and dying in it, is the cause of any man's salvation that lived after his coming; his promise of taking our nature, and dying in it, is the cause of the salvation of any that lived before. The apostle's reasoning would not else stand good; had Christ assumed the angels' nature, they would have been saved; had not Christ then assumed our nature, we could not have been saved; and had he not promised to assume our nature, none could have been saved. He could not have been called the Captain of the salvation of all the sons that are brought to glory, whereof many were before his coming, Heb. ii. 10. They must have been saved upon the account of that future death, or else there must be some other name besides that of Christ whereby they were saved; but that there is not, Acts iv. 12. Faith had not always been the way of salvation. Christ had begun to be a mediator and redeemer at the time of his death, and not before; and so had not been in that relation 'the same yesterday, to-day, and for ever.' Had he not died, he could not have been set out with any good ground before his coming as an object of faith. The promises of him had wanted their due foundation, the predictions of him had been groundlesss; and, consequently, the faith and hope of the ancient believers had been in vain. It is certain, all that were saved, were saved upon the account of his death; for the merit of his death might have an influence before it was suffered, it being a moral, not a natural, cause of salvation; as many times a prisoner is delivered upon the promise of a ransom before the actual payment of it.

[2.] Since some were saved before upon the account of his future death, had he not died, God had been highly dishonoured. Had not Christ performed his promise of suffering, and thereby satisfying the justice of God, God, having saved many before his incarnation upon the credit of this promise, had received a manifest wrong. It would have argued a weakness in him to lay such stress upon that which would not be full and secure, which would never have been accomplished. God had not been omniscient, but had been deceived in his foreknowledge, had his expectations been frustrated. For what was the reason God saved any before, but upon the credit of this ransom, which was promised to be paid in time, and his foreknowledge, that when the term came, the surety would not be wanting to discharge himself of his promise? Had not, then, Christ really suffered, and accomplished what he had promised, God had suffered in his honour, and all things could not have been said to be present to him; he would have been deceived. As if a prisoner be delivered upon the promise of a ransom, and the ransom be not paid according to agreement, the person that hath delivered the prisoner suffers in point of wisdom in trusting a person that hath not been as good as his word, and is defeated of that which is in justice due to him. Again, since God had admitted some to happiness before the actual suffering of Christ, had not Christ performed what he had actually undertaken, God must have renounced either his justice or his mercy; his justice, had he let sinners go unpunished, and then he had denied in part his own name, which is 'by no means to clear the guilty,' Exodus xxxiv. 7; or else he must have punished sin in the persons of those whom he had already brought to happiness; and had he done so, how had the honour of his mercy suffered, in turning them out of that felicity wherein he had always* placed them! Some, therefore, make the remission of the sins past before the coming of Christ not to be properly a full pardon, bnt a passing by, the full remission not

* Qu. 'already'?—ED.

being to be given till the actual payment was made; and indeed the word the apostle useth in that place, Rom. iii. 25, is different, πάρεσις, a passing by, a word not used for pardon in all the New Testament, but ἄφεσις. Had not Christ suffered, there had been nothing of the righteousness of God manifested in the remission of sins which were past; the end of God had been frustrated, it being his end, in the death of Christ, 'to declare his righteousness for the remission of sins that are past, to declare at this time his righteousness,' *i.e.* what his righteousness was in passing by sins before committed, to declare that he pardoned no sins before, without an eye to this satisfactory death of his Son; but that in all his former proceedings he kept close to the rules of his infinite justice. Now, had not Christ died according to his engagement, God had highly suffered in his honour, his omniscience had been defeated; God had been deceived in the credit he gave, his righteousness had not been manifested, his justice had suffered, or his mercy to his poor creatures had been dammed up for ever from flowing out upon them.

2. The veracity of God, in settling the penalty of death upon transgression, made it necessary for redemption. God passed his word that death should be the punishment of sin, Gen. ii. 17; the veracity of God stood engaged to make this word good upon the conditions expressed. The sentence was immutable, and the word that went out of God's mouth must stand; had it been revoked without inflicting the punishment, the faithfulness and righteousness of God, in regard of his word, could not have been justified: 'God cannot lie, or deny himself,' Titus i. 2, 2 Tim. ii. 13; his truth is not a quality in him, but himself, his essence. Had he, then, after so solemnly pronouncing, without any reverse, that the wages of sin should be no less than death, been careless of his own word, and left sin unpunished, God had made a breach upon his own nature, and had infringed his own happiness; for a lie or falsity is the fountain and original of all evil and misery. Supposing God had other ways to deal with man (though it is beyond the capacity of man to imagine any other way of God's government of him, or any intellectual and rational creatures, than by a law, and a penalty annexed to that law, which otherwise would have proved insignificant), yet after his wisdom had settled this law, and the threatening had passed his royal and immutable word, it was no longer arbitrary, but necessary by the sovereign authority, that either the sinner himself, or some surety in his stead, should suffer the death the sinner had incurred by the violation of the precept; we must either pay ourselves, or some other pay for us, what we stand bound in to the justice of God. Impunity had been an invasion of God's veracity, which is as immutable as his nature; since, therefore, the inflicting of death upon transgression was the real intent of God, upon the commission of sin death must enter upon man, otherwise God would be a disregarder of himself, and his threatenings a mere scarecrow.

(1.) Had God violated his word, he had rendered himself an unfit object of trust. He had exposed all the promises or threatenings he should have made after man's impunity to the mockery and contempt of the offender, and excluded his word from any credit with man. Had God set man right again by a mere act of mercy, without any regard to his word past, and inflicting any punishment upon the offender, though he had made man more glorious promises than at the first, he would have had little reason to trust God. If he had found God unfaithful to himself in the word of his threatening, he could not have concluded that he would have been true to the word of his promise, but might reasonably have suspected that he would falsify in that as he had done him in the other. Had his truth failed in the concerns of his justice, it had been of little value in those of his mercy. He might be as careless of the honour of the one as of that of the other. If a man fail of his word in one thing, there is little reason to believe him in another. The righteousness of God would as little have engaged him to fulfil his promise, as it did engage him to fulfil his threatening. God would have declared himself by such an act, not willing to be believed, not worthy to be trusted, feared, loved, because regardless of his truth and righteousness. And by the same reason that he denied himself fit to be trusted, he would deny himself to be a God, because he would thereby have acknowledged a weakness incompatible to the nature of the Deity. How could any trust him who had denied himself, by restoring a life to him, without righteousness and truth on his part? It had rather been an encouragement to them to disown him to be any fit object for their confidence, since the great ground of trust among men is their faithfulness to their word. Upon the supposition of God's restoring the creature, the doing it by the intervention of a satisfaction was very necessary to fix the creature's confidence in God; for when he sees God so righteous and true that he will not do anything against the rules of his truth and justice, he hath the more ground to believe God after a satisfaction made, that he will preserve the honour of his wisdom in approving and accepting that satisfaction, and his truth in promising, declared upon it.

(2.) Had God violated his word, he had justified the devil in his argument for man's rebellion. The devil's argument is a plain contradiction to God's threatening. God affirms the certainty of death, the devil affirms the certainty of life: Gen. iii. 4, 'Ye shall not surely die.' Had no punishment been inflicted, the devil had not been a liar from the beginning. God would have honoured the tempter, and justified the charge he brought against him, and owned the envy the devil accused him of, and thereby have rendered the devil the fittest object for love and trust. As the devil charged God with a lie, so, had no punishment been inflicted, God would have condemned himself, and declared Satan, instead of a lying tempter, to be the truest counseller. He had exposed himself to contempt, and advanced the credit of his enemy, and so set up the devil as a God instead of himself. It concerned God, therefore, to manifest himself true, and the devil a liar; and acquaint the world that not himself, but the evil spirit, was their deceiver, and that he meant as he spake.

(3.) Suppose God might have altered his word, yet would it consist with his wisdom to do it at that time? It was the first word of threatening that ever went out of his lips to man; and had he wholly dispensed with it, after he had fenced his precept with such a penalty, and seen such a contradiction in his new created subject to his truth, authority, and righteousness, such a daring contempt of his rich and manifested goodness, he had emboldened the apostate creature in his sin, and encouraged him to a fresh rebellion as soon as ever he had been set right again by an infinite mercy, without any mark of his justice. Men would have thought God had either been mistaken in the reason of his threatening, and had settled a penalty too great for the offence, or had wanted power to maintain his authority in inflicting the due punishment, had he indulged man in this sin. What influence could any of his precepts have had upon the souls of men, if he had so lightly passed by the transgression of his law? Would he not have been less secured in the rights of his authority for the future, than he had been for the time past? Would not man have been encouraged to have run the same risk of disobedience, in hopes of an easy pardon, and continued the attempt which he had begun in his first apostasy, to have freed himself from all the orders of the divine law, to have been his own rule? How could a just sense and awe of

God have been preserved in the minds of men, when they should have thought God like one of themselves, and as false to his own righteousness as they had been to his authority? Ps. l. 21. This certainly would have been the issue, had man been set up in his former state without inflicting that punishment upon the human nature, which had been so righteously denounced, and so highly merited, by the disingenuity of man. Man had been more tempted by this to sin than he could have been by the devil, and when he had been brought to an account for his second transgression, he would have excused himself by God's indulgence to him for the first; and, indeed, God's denial of his truth in this, would seem to be a sufficient apology for after offences.

(4.) Therefore God, for the preservation of his truth and righteousness, accepts of a surety to bear the just punishment for man. Since God had enacted, that if man sinned he should die, upon man's apostasy God must either eternally punish him to preserve his truth and justice, or neglect his own law, and change it to discover his mercy. These things were impossible to the nature of God; he must be true to his nature, and true to his word. If justice should destroy, what way was there to discover his mercy? If mercy should absolutely pardon, without the due punishment, what way was there to preserve the honour of his truth? The wisdom of God finds out a means to preserve the honour of his truth in the punishment, and discover the glory of his mercy in a pardon, not by changing the sentence against sin, but the person; and laying that upon his Son, as a surety, which we in our own persons must have endured, had the rigour of the law been executed upon us, whereby his righteousness and veracity are preserved by the punishment due to the sinner, and the honour of mercy established by the merit of our Saviour. Death was threatened by the law, but there was no exclusion of a person by that law, that should offer himself to stand in man's stead under the punishment. Man had been for ever irrecoverably miserable, had such a clause been inserted, and would have been without hope as much as the devils. And therefore, saith a learned author of our own,* this acceptance of a surety for us was not an abrogation of the law, for then there could be no execution of the sentence upon wicked men and unbelievers for their sins against it (where no law is, there is no transgression; and where no transgression, no just execution); but it was a merciful relaxation or condescension of the sovereign lawgiver, by his infinite goodness and wisdom, to find out an expedient for the good of the fallen creature, with the preservation of the rights of those divine perfections engaged in the threatening. God was not prejudiced, or his immutability impaired, by a change of the person suffering, as long as the penalty threatened was inflicted. Though there was a translation of the penalty, yet there was not a nulling of the penalty; the person was changed, not the punishment; death was threatened, death was inflicted. Death was threatened, not so much to the person of Adam, as the human nature, whereof he was the head, and regarded the descendants from him; death was suffered by the human nature, though in another person; death was threatened to Adam as the root of all in him; death was suffered by Christ, as the mystical head of all in him by faith, so that, as in Adam sinning, all sinned that were in his loins as in their root, Rom. v. 12, 14, 18, so it may be said, that in Christ suffering all believers suffered, his sufferings being imputed to them by virtue of that union they have with him. Besides, God having created the world for the displaying his divine perfections in Christ, 'for whom all things were created,' Col. i. 16, had in his eternal counsel decreed the death of Christ as a surety for man; and this threatening, as well as the creation, being pursuant to this

* Burges of Justificat. part ii. p. 84.

eternal counsel, did not exclude, but rather include, the surety, though it be not expressed.

3. The justice of God made the death of Christ necessary for our redemption. Christ, in his coming, respected the glory of God's righteousness, for he substituted himself as a sin-offering, instead of those insufficient ones under the law: Heb. x. 8, 'Sin-offering thou wouldst not; lo, I come to do thy will,' *i. e.* the will of the divine justice as well as divine mercy, for in the legal sacrifices both were expressed; justice in the death of the beast, whereby man was taught what he had merited, and mercy in substituting the beast in his room. Christ came to do that in the room of a sin-offering, which the legal sin-offerings were not able to effect. The command of the Father did chiefly respect this satisfaction of justice. It principally required of him the laying down his life, and making his soul an offering for sin, John x. 18. And this it was which his obedience did principally respect, whence it is called an 'obedience to death,' Philip. ii. 8. Death is an act of justice. After the command was given, with the sanction of it, the authority of God in enacting it, and the justice of God in adding the penalty to it, were contemned, and man could not well be reduced to his order without a reparation of the damage done to the authority and justice of God. How could God be the judge of all the earth, doing right, Gen. xviii. 25, had he suffered such a manifest wrong to himself to go unpunished? Justice had as loud a cry for condemnation, as mercy could have for any stream of compassion. The sanction of the law was irrevocable, unless God had ceased to be immutable in his justice as well as his truth. God can do whatsoever he will, but he can will nothing against his goodness and righteousness.* God had derogated from his own righteousness, if he had not recompensed the sin of man. For as justice requires punishment, so it requires the greatest punishment for the greatest offence. Satisfaction must then be given in such a manner as the justice of God in the law required. It must be then by suffering that death it exacted as due to the crime, which must be done by the person sinning, or some other capable to do it in his stead, and answer the terms of the law, between whom and the sinner there might be such a strait union, as that there might be a mutual imputation of our sins to him, and his sufferings to us. That he might suffer, justice was to impute our sins to him; that his sufferings might be advantageous, mercy and justice were to impute his sufferings to us.

I shall lay down under this three propositions.

(1.) It seems to be impossible but that justice should flame out against sin. There is the same reason of all God's attributes. It is impossible that the goodness of God should not embrace and kindly entertain an innocent creature, for then he would not be good. It is impossible his mercy in Christ should refuse a penitent believer; then he would not be compassionate. It is impossible he should look upon sin with a pleasing† countenance; then he would not be holy. It is impossible that he can be false to his word; then he could not be true. It is impossible that he should not act wisely in what he doth; then he would be foolish. Shall we deny the same rights to his justice, that we acknowledge to belong to the other perfections of his nature? Why should not his justice be as unchangeable and inflexible as his goodness, mercy, truth, and wisdom? Shall we acknowledge him firm in the rest, and wavering in this? Justice is as necessary a perfection pertaining to him as the governor of the world, as his wisdom, or any other glory of his nature. Had God acted the part of a just governor, if he had suffered

* Dr Jackson.

† Qu. 'pleased'?—ED.

those laws to be broken with impunity, whereof he was the guardian as well as the enactor? Is there not a double reason of punishment accruing to him, both as he is the offended party and the rector of the world? And what is justice, but a giving to every one his due, reward to whom reward belongs, and punishment to whom punishment is due? If God had pardoned where punishment was due, it had been an act of mercy, but what had become of his justice? If God be not just in everything he doth, he is unjust in something, and then doth iniquity, which is utterly impossible for the divine nature; he neither will nor can do iniquity, Zeph. iii. 5. This is an inseparable property of the divine nature. What should his creatures judge of him, if he were utterly careless of vindicating his law, and did totally abstain from evidencing his holiness to his rational creatures? Is his holiness only to be manifested in precepts, and not demonstrated in punishments? If his love to righteousness be essential to him, the exercise of that righteousness upon suitable objects is necessary. His love of righteousness flows from his nature as righteous: Ps. xi. 7, 'The righteous Lord loveth righteousness.' It is not only an act of his will, but of his nature; it is not *so* natural to him as heat is to the fire, that doth necessarily scorch and burn, without any influence of a free and rational principle. There is a liberty of the divine will to order those acts of his justice in convenient seasons. God acts in all things according to his own nature, and cannot act below himself and the rectitude of it. The first foundation of all his actings towards his creatures is in his will. As upon the supposition that God would create man (which it was free for him to do or not to do, and so depended only upon his will), he could not, according to the rectitude of his own nature, but create him upright, otherwise he had denied his own holiness; so, upon the supposition of man's sinning (the prevention or permission of which depended upon his will), he cannot but punish him, because otherwise he had denied his justice, and seemed to have approved of the disorder man had introduced into the world; and if he had not punished it in the degree it merited, there had seemed to be some abatement of that hatred which was due to the unrighteousness of it; for so much as a punishment is lessened, so much less doth the detestation of the crime appear. The power of God is not limited hereby; his own holiness and truth, and the righteousness of his nature, bound him.* Doth any man deny the power of God, in saying he cannot forget his creature? Would it not be a weakness in him to be capable of lying? Is it not an imperfection to be capable of doing any thing unjust? And what would it be but injustice in the Judge of all the earth to let sin go unrevenged? It is rather an argument of strength and virtue, whereby he cannot renounce the rectitude of his nature.†

[1.] This seems to be a general and a natural notion in the minds of men. God hath settled it as an immutable and eternal law, and engraven it upon the hearts of men, that sin is to be punished with death. What other sentiment could be expressed by the universal practice of sacrificing beasts, and, in some places, men, for the expiation of their sins, implying thereby a necessity of vindictive justice, that God would not leave sin unpunished, without a compensation from the sinner himself, or some other in his stead? And therefore they thought the blood of man, the best of the creatures, a means to avert the stroke they had merited from him themselves. What other foundation could there be of all those sacrifices than a conscience of sin, and a settled notion of the vengeance of God? For that which they principally, or only, respected in those sacrifices, was the justice of God. Upon this account it was probably that the apostle so positively asserts, Rom. i. 32,

* Daillé, de la Resurrect. de Christ, p. 358. † Turretin, de Satisfac. p. 300.

that they 'knew that they were worthy of death.' They sufficiently expressed it in subjecting other creatures to the stroke of death in their stead, to pacify the offended deity, acknowledging thereby, that he could not pardon sin without a satisfaction. This was learned by them in the school of nature, not by the revealed will of God; or if it were handed to them by tradition from Adam, it had so near an alliance with an universal principle in their own consciences, that it met with no opposition or dispute, the practice of it being almost as universally spread, as the notion of the being of a God, since we scarce find a nation without the sacrificing animals for the appeasing the divinity they adored.

[2.] The holiness of God seems necessarily to infer it. Since justice is nothing else but the testimony or expression of God's hatred of sin, it must be by consequence unavoidable, unless the sin committed can be wholly undone, which is impossible; or his justice be appeased some way or other. If God did not punish sin, how could his hatred of it be manifest? His creature could not discern any aversion in him from it, without the interposition of vindictive justice; for that perfection of God's nature, which requires that he should have an implacable detestation of sin, requires also that the sinner, remaining under guilt, should be perpetually punished. If God cannot but hate all the workers of iniquity (Ps. v. 5, 'Thou hatest all the workers of iniquity'), he cannot but punish them. The holiness of God is not only voluntary, but by necessity of nature; were it only an act of his will, he might love iniquity if he pleased, as well as hate it. How could it be said of him by the prophet, Hab. i. 13, that he is 'of purer eyes than to behold evil, and cannot look upon iniquity,' if his purity had been only from choice, and a determination of the indifferency of his will, and not from his nature? It is not said, He *will not* look on iniquity, *i. e.* with affection, but he *cannot.* God cannot but be holy, and therefore cannot but be just; because injustice is a part of unholiness. And upon the holiness of God, Joshua asserts the Israelites' sins in themselves unpardonable: Josh. xxiv. 19, 'He is a holy God, he is a jealous God, he will not forgive your transgressions, nor your sins.' He is jealous of the honour of his perfections; his holiness and jealousy stand as bars against forgiveness, without some means for preserving the honour of them; his holiness and jealousy, whereby his justice and wrath are sometimes expressed, are linked together, and are nothing else but the contrariety in the nature of God, which is infinitely good and righteous, to the nature of sin, which is evil and unrighteous, whereby he is inclined to detest it.* All hatred is a desire of revenge; and the stronger the hatred, the more vehement the inclination to revenge. The loathing of sin being infinite in God, as he is the rector of the world, and so necessary a perfection of his nature, that without it he would not be God; the inclination to punish it, and thereby highly manifest his hatred of it, necessarily follows that perfection. A will to punish sin is always included in an hatred of it. Now, if the hatred of sin be as essential to God as his love to his glory, punishment must follow it. There is a certain connection between the one and the other. This hatred must necessarily be evidenced by some acts, according to the greatness of the evil. How shall it be testified, but by punishment? If he doth not punish, how shall we certainly know but that it pleaseth him? By his bare precept we cannot, if he suffers it to be violated at the pleasure of men without rebuke; we may then judge him to be a negligent governor, and one that hath no regard to his own command, and cares not whether his creature observes it or no. Hatred cannot be discovered without some expressions of aversion. What signs can those be, unless God's denying his

* Amyraut, des Religions, p. 309.

communications to his creature, and a positive inflicting of evil? If a governor hates a disorder never so much, if he expresseth it not, whereby the offending person may be sensible of his hatred, it is as much as no hatred; for, *Idem est non esse, et non apparere*. What would all his prohibitions of sin amount to, if he did not punish the commission of it? He that cannot but prohibit sin, cannot but punish sin. God cannot but prohibit sin, because he cannot but hate it, it being contrary to his holy nature. The commands of God are not bare acts of his will, but of his wisdom and righteousness. If they proceeded from bare will, without any regulation by his wisdom and righteousness, he might command things contrary to the law of nature, and the necessary relation of a creature to himself. So neither is his hatred of sin only a free act of his will, but necessarily results from the rectitude of his nature. If it were only an act of his will, as the creation of the world, he might as well love sin as hate it; as he might as well have neglected the creation of the world as performed it, and let the several creatures remain in their nothing, as well as have brought them into being. But it flows from the righteousness of his nature (Prov. xv. 9, 'The way of the wicked is an abomination to the Lord'), and consequently so doth his justice, which is an expression of this hatred, otherwise God would be unjust to his own holiness.

(2.) Hence it follows, that this justice must be satisfied before man could be restored. The justice of God was the bar in the way, and must be removed by punishment. Christ could not have brought one son to glory, had he not first been 'made perfect by suffering,' Heb. ii. 10. The wrath of God for the violations of the law, was the flaming sword that guarded paradise from being entered into by guilty man. This was becoming God as the governor of the world, in which capacity he is considered in punishment. It became not God to do anything unjustly or inordinately. It was an intolerable thing that the creature should despoil God of his honour, and withdraw itself from that indispensable subjection it owed to its creator. It became God to restore that order by punishment, which had been broken by sin.

Let us consider,

[1.] Justice had at least an equal plea with mercy. If mercy pleaded for pardon, justice as strongly solicited the punishment of the sinner. The remission of the offence would appear more charitable; but the vindicating the public laws, and punishing the offence, would appear more righteous. It was not convenient the creature should be utterly ruined as soon as ever God had displayed his power in creating it, nor was it convenient the creature should be emboldened in sin by a free act of pardon, after so high and base an act of disingenuity. What could mercy plead on the behalf of the creature, that justice could not as strongly plead on the behalf of God? If the ruin of the creature be argued to move compassion, the dishonour of God on the other side would be argued to excite indignation. If the nature of God, as love, 1 John iv. 8, be pleaded by mercy, the nature of God, as righteous and a consuming fire, Heb. xii. 29, would be opposed to it by justice. His mercy would plead, It were not for his honour to let his enemy run away, just after the creation, with the spoil of the best of his works. His justice would reply, It was fit the judge of the world should do right, and be the protector of his righteous law. If his mercy inclines him to will our salvation, justice would not permit him to leave sin unpunished, and his laws trampled in the dust. Had mercy been discovered without preserving the rights of justice, when the whole nature of man fell, God had been but a half governor of the world, and exercised but one part of government.

[2.] Justice seems to have a stronger plea. (1.) The highest right falls on the side of justice. That had been declared and backed by his truth, when mercy was not yet published upon the stage of the creation. The righteous and just nature of God had been signified to man, and his veracity brought in to second it, Gen. ii. 17. No notion of pardoning mercy had yet been imprinted upon the mind of man, or revealed to him; so that God was not so much concerned in honour to shew mercy, which stood single, as I may say, and lay hid in the nature of God, without the appearance of any perfection to back and support it. Had man stood, the veracity of God had stood on the side of his goodness (for we may suppose a promise of life implied, if man continued in obedience, as well as a threatening expressed, if he fell into rebellion). But when men broke the precept, the whole force of God's truth fell on the side of justice. There being not a syllable of pardoning grace uttered in any promise before the sin of man, the truth of God had no part at that time to take with mercy; so that there were greater engagements at that time, from the manifestation of God's nature, for the making good his justice, than for the demonstration of his mercy.

(2.) Mercy could principally plead the good of the creature, justice principally insisted on the honour of God. Mercy might solicit the liberty of God's will, but justice might strongly challenge the holiness and rectitude of God's nature to support it. The creature was fallen under the hatred of God and penalty of the law, and rendered itself an unfit object of love by its rebellion and filthiness.

(3.) Besides, the wits and consciences of men cannot frame so many arguments for the necessity of mercy, in regard of God, as for the necessity of his justice. Mercy is wholly a free act, but justice is a debt due to a sinful creature. The necessity of mercy to a fallen creature, in regard of God, cannot possibly be asserted with any reason. For it would then be asserted on the behalf of devils more than men. I say, the necessity, for perhaps something may be said for the congruity of God's shewing mercy to man rather than to devils. Justice respects merit caused by the righteousness or unrighteousness of men,* according to which God immutably carries himself in rewarding or punishing of them, and never doth reward or punish any but according to their merit; but the mercy of God doth not at all respect merit, or any work done by man, but is busied wholly in giving freely, and offering graciously to man those things he hath not deserved.

(4.) Again, justice had stronger arguments from the rectitude of God's nature. Justice might argue, If God did righteously judge sinners to everlasting death, then if he had not judged them to everlasting death, he had done unjustly, being unmindful of the rectitude of his own nature. And if he should not now, after sin, inflict eternal death, but wholly lay aside his threatening, he would do unjustly; for those being contrary acts, one of them must needs be unjust. Who could call that a righteous government, wherein laws should be made with the greatest wisdom, and be broken with the greatest impunity?

(5.) Again, consider, though mercy be essential to God, yet mercy must not be unjustly exercised. The fallen creature, indeed, was an object of both: as *miserable*, he was an object of mercy; as *criminal*, he was an object of justice. But being first criminal before he was miserable, he was first the object of justice by his crime, before he was an object of mercy by his misery. Had he been miserable without being culpable (which was impossible, in regard of the goodness of God), he had then been an object of com-

* Zarnov. de satisfact. Christi, part i. cap. ii.

passion only. But falling under justice first, it was not fit mercy should wholly despoil justice of its rights.

(6.) Again. Man, as miserable by the fall, is not the object of mercy. For what mercy could pardon an obstinate rebel? And how could man have been otherwise, without some supernatural operation upon him? Mercy could not challenge any footing to exercise itself about man, till he had confessed and bewailed his crime, and been sensible, not only of his misery, but of his offence. It is not honourable for God to exercise mercy upon those that continue in their enmity; this seems to be clearly against the rectitude of the divine nature; this had been a favouring of the crime as well as the criminal. Had he been sensible of and sorrowful for his misery, without a true grief for his offence, this had been an act of love to himself, but had had in it nothing of a true affection to God. After man had contracted in his nature an enmity against God, how could he have acquired a true repentance flowing from an affection to God? Repentance for a fault against a prince, and enmity against a prince, are inconsistent. How should man have attained this quality of himself, any more than the devils have done, of whose repentance we read not one syllable in the Scripture, who are left to those habits of malice and aversion from God, which they had superinduced upon themselves? And if devils, who were creatures of greater understanding, and more sensible of their misery, because they fell from a greater happiness than man, were morally impotent to this, can we think that man had a stronger bias in his will after the revolt from God, to return again to God? Besides, repentance is made a gift of God, 2 Tim. ii. 25; and the Spirit that gives repentance, is a fruit of Christ's death; and the repentance itself is made a fruit of Christ's exaltation, due to him upon his death, Acts v. 32. To strengthen this, it may be considered that when God came to examine Adam, as a judge, about his crime, there is not a syllable that savours of any true repentance issues from him, Gen. iii. 8–10, &c., whatsoever he might exercise after the promulgation of the gospel-promise.

[3.] Consider, if there had not been a tempering of these two perfections towards man, one of them had remained undiscovered to the world. Justice only could have appeared in the creature's suffering, mercy only could have appeared in the creature's restoration. Mercy could not have been discovered by the condemnation of the creature, nor justice by the mere salvation of the creature. Had there been no punishment, or a light one below the demerit of the creature, there had been no demonstration of the highest glory of his holiness in the hatred of sin, or of the highest glory of his justice in the punishment of sin. Had the punishment due to the creature been inflicted upon him, the creature had been utterly destroyed, and mercy had been for ever obscured; and had mercy solely acted about the creature, justice had been wronged. Justice therefore must be one way or other righted, that the streams of his grace might flow out to man, since, after man's fall, justice had stopped all commerce of God with man, because sin had rendered him unfit for the communications of God. As the nature of compassion must be satisfied in acting about a miserable creature, and the love God bore to man as his creature manifested; so the nature of justice must be satisfied for the injury done, and the hatred of God to man as a sinner discovered. And this must be satisfied either by the creature's bearing the punishment, or compensating the injury, for that properly is satisfaction. God's justice could not have come off with honour without it; for since he was engaged by his word to have sin punished, would not God have been unjust had he laid by all consideration of his justice and holiness in this case? Had justice been glorified upon the person of the sinner, mercy would have lost the manifestation of itself, and have had no objects to exercise itself about; had mercy been glorified in bringing man to a happy state, without any punishment, after so base a breach of his law, where had been the demonstration of the unchangeable holiness of God, and the exactness of his justice? God therefore appointed a Mediator, in whom he might act as a righteous judge for the punishment of sin, according to his law, that his dreadful majesty might be more feared; and a tender father according to the necessity of his creatures, that his love might be commended, as a wise governor tempering both together. And therefore God, foreseeing the fall of man, elected some to eternal glory, but in Christ as the means, Eph. i. 4, not as the meritorious cause of election, but as the means and foundation of the execution of it, that the glory of his grace might issue out in the preservation of the rights of his justice, maintained by the blood of his Son, in whom we have redemption, ver. 6, 7, and without this way we cannot see how the glory of God had been preserved. God had made the world for his glory, and the communication of his goodness. After the world was polluted and disordered by sin, the justice of God, by annexing such a penalty to the law, stood as a bar in the way of any kindness to the creature, unless some way might be found out to preserve the honour of that justice. Shall God in a moment lose all the glory of his creation? Did he make the creatures, whose fall he did foresee, only to punish and damn them; and that the glory of his other perfections, save that of his justice and holiness, should be spoiled by it? His glory therefore must be preserved; that could not be if the glory of his justice or mercy were wholly lost. To preserve it, therefore, Christ is substituted in our room, and the Captain of salvation made perfect through sufferings, which was most becoming God, as he was Lord of all, and his glory the end of all, Heb. ii. 10. His love not permitting him to leave the world under the curse, nor his justice to leave sin without punishment, both those necessities are provided for by the wisdom of God; a wonderful temperament wrought, whereby sin is punished in the surety, and impunity secured to the believing sinner.*

[4.] This satisfaction must be by death, because death was threatened. Since it was the judgment of God that sin was worthy of death, God had contradicted his own judgment and holy wisdom, if he had remitted it without death, or punished it with less than death. God established our propitiation in the blood of Christ, 'to declare his justice,' Rom. iii. 25.† If justice had required less than death, it had been unjust to have demanded so much as death, for then he had demanded more than was due. Sin could not be expiated by a less punishment than it had merited, but that was death. Besides, the love of God to his Son would not have permitted him to expose him to a cursed and cruel death, merely to shew his justice implacable, had it not really been in itself implacable without it, as the most transcendent means to discover the incomprehensible purity of his nature. Certainly, that God who would not do the least injustice to the meanest of his creatures, would not have delivered up his Son to so shameful a death, and took so many counsels about it, and made it the principal work of his wisdom in all ages of the world, to order all things for the execution of it, if justice could have been contented with less than death, and remission of sin could have been granted by the pure mercy and bounty of God, at least after the threatening. Could justice have been satisfied at a lower rate than death, the Father would have answered the request of his Son when he prayed so earnestly that this cup might pass from him; nor would death have been exacted of him, if a drop of his blood had been a sufficient payment to the demands

* Daillé sur iii. Jean, p. 330.

† εἰς ἔνδειξιν, for a demonstration of his justice.

of justice. The suffering death had been superfluous, and the imposing death upon him had been an unrighteousness in God; and his giving himself up to death, without any necessity, had been an injustice to himself. Could a few drops of blood have satisfied justice, it might have been satisfied without any blood at all, as well as with a punishment beneath what the law demanded. The effusion of one drop of blood cannot pass for a punishment of sin, when death for it was required by the law, so that it could be no less than death.

Prop. 3. None could satisfy the justice of God but the Son of God incarnate.

[1.] Let us remove those things that might be supposed capable to do it. Nether could man do it for himself, nor any intellectual or rational creature do it for him, nor any observances of God's institutions do it, so that it must necessarily fall upon some one above the rank of creatures. Some divine person only was capable to undertake it and effect it. There is a necessity of satisfaction to the law, both by paying obedience to every tittle of it, and by enduring the penalty for the transgression of it. God stands so much upon the honour of his law, that the heavens shall be folded up, and the earth shaken out of its place, before one point of the law shall be disregarded, Mat. v. 18. Some one therefore must repair the breach made upon it, and restore the honour of it. Let us see if anything else could.

(1.) Man was unable to do it for himself. It must be done either by active or passive obedience, by doing or suffering; but was man capable of either as a full compensation to God? Man by sin fell in his person, and with all that he had, under the curse of the law, Gal. iii. 10; and what was under the curse, and by sin was forfeited, could not remove the curse. Man may be considered as a sinful creature or a gracious creature. A sinful creature cannot satisfy; for being a sinner in that satisfaction, he doth offend the holiness of God, and heap new provocations before the eyes of his justice instead of pacifying it. A gracious creature cannot, for that supposeth satisfaction first, whereby justice is moved to take away the bar that locks up the treasures of grace from being dispensed to man. A man might be gracious after a satisfaction, but not before; besides, grace is finite, for whatsoever is in a finite creature is finite; its effects therefore cannot be of an infinite value.

(1.) Man could not effect it by offering something to God, or by doing something equivalent to the offence.

1. Man had nothing to give. What was there he could call his own, since he was a creature, especially since as an offender he had forfeited what was his by right of creation? Had man the world to give? How came he by it? Was it created by him or for him? If not by him, it was none of his own; he was but a steward to manage all for the use of his Lord and true proprietor. Can a steward recompense his lord for the wrong done to his honour, by offering to his master those goods which are his own already, and which the steward was only entrusted with? The world was none of man's to give; he never had it as an absolute lord by right of an independent propriety, nor was it possible he should, since he was not either the creator or preserver of it; and neither man, nor any other creature in the world, could possibly be brought into a state independent on God, so that man held as a feudatory *in capite* of God. But suppose it had been his own, he had forfeited all by his rebellion; for his sake, for his sin, the earth was cursed by the sovereign Lord of it, Gen. iii. 17; and a thing cursed in all the parts of it could not be fit for an oblation to the divine Majesty.

2. Nor could his repentance be a compensation. Bare grief for an offence

is not a compensation for an injury done to man, much less for an affront of so high a nature offered to God. But we find no such thing in man at the time wherein he fell from the top of his felicity to the gulf of misery. If he who had a sense of the happy state he had lost, and the miserable condition he had contracted, was more for excuses than relentings, how can a penitent posture be found by nature in any of his descendants? Gen. iii. 9–13. If there were any blushes in him, they were occasioned more by the discovery of his crime than by the sense of the crime itself; and he was troubled more at his loss than at his offence, and so might relent that he was miserable, not that he was criminal; and so it was a repentance as it respected himself, not as it respected the honour of his Lord; and such a repentance is to be found in hell, but is unable to break those chains wherein they are held. How should man come by a repentance? Can he break himself into a true contrition? What stone was ever heard to melt itself? Is not captive man fond of his sin, in love with his chains? And how can he by nature attain that which is so contrary to what he is by nature mightily delighted with? The least spark of grace is above the power of corrupted nature. How should man, then, come by this repentance? Must it not be a melting spark from heaven lighting upon his soul, that must produce so kindly a work in a forsaken creature? Would it have consisted with the wisdom of divine justice to seize upon the forfeiture, to withdraw from man supernatural grace, and presently to restore it without any regard to the vindication of the honour of that justice? Besides, suppose man had been able to repent of himself, and had actually performed a repentance of the right stamp, what would this have signified, since no such thing was required as the condition the righteousness of God exacted in the law? That demanded not repentance, because it gave not liberty to any crime. It challenged an exact and perfect obedience, complete in all circumstances, of man in his uprightness; and, in case of failure, left man to the severity of the penalty he had incurred Not a drop of repentance was allowed as any part of legal obedience. That was introduced upon a change of the dispensation from legal to evangelical. 'The law is not of faith,' and as little of repentance, 'but the man that doth them shall live in them,' Gal. iii. 12. Besides, if repentance and faith in the mercy of God could have razed out the sin of Adam, and broken in pieces the chains of eternal death, could we think that God should be at the expense of the blood of the promised seed? What need had there been of a sacrifice to appease God, if he had been already appeased by the relentings of man? What a vanity had that been, to go about the taking away that which the faith and repentance of Adam had already removed!* The wisdom of God would not do anything useless and in vain. Faith and repentance could never change the nature of God's righteousness, but must first suppose some satisfaction made to justice, and then step in as conditions; and the one as an instrument apprehending and applying mercy obtained by some other means, not the efficient or meritorious cause, no more than the looking upon the brazen serpent was the efficient or meritorious cause of the cure, but only the means. But how can we think man after his fall should have either faith in the mercy of God, or repentance, which flows from a sense of mercy, when no mercy had been revealed to him? He found nothing of it in the law; and though he might apprehend such a perfection in God by the consideration of his own nature, yet since he had never seen any miserable object to draw out such a perfection, it is a question whether he knew any such quality to be in himself or no, and therefore could not conclude any such perfection to be in God, since there was not the least revelation of it, and therefore could

* Zarnov. de Satisfact. part i. cap. iv. pp. 14, 15.

have no footing for any such exercise of faith and repentance till the discovery of mercy in the promised seed.

3. Nor could any after obedience to the law be a compensation for the offence. For,

(1.) Man had not power of himself after his fall to obey. He had by his revolt lost that original righteousness which enabled him to a conformity to the law: Gen. iii. 10, 'I was afraid, because I was naked.' His corporeal nakedness could be no more the cause of fear after, than it was before, his sin; but he was naked, *i. e.* stripped of the image of God, and his primitive integrity. Man cannot now do any work commensurate to the precepts of the law. In everything he comes short of his duty; and therefore, being defective in what he ought to do by the law of creation, cannot satisfy for the injury done to God in the state of corruption: 'How shall a man be just with God? If he will contend with him, he cannot answer him one of a thousand,' Job ix. 2, 3. God requires an obedience to the law, not according to our measure, but according to his own righteousness, which is perfect; and this no sinful creature can arise to of himself. If any man were able to offer God a spotless obedience, free from any defect the law could find in it; by whose strength would he do it? Not by his own; for since he was a sinner, he hath been without strength. To be *sinners*, and to be *without strength*, are one and the same, Rom. v. 6, 8. From whom, then, should he have this strength? From the Creator? How can he then satisfy God by that which is God's already? It is as if when a man had wronged a prince, he should satisfy him for the injury by a sum taken out of the prince's exchequer. Indeed, man is not willing to obey any command of God; there is nothing in his nature but an enmity against God and his law, Rom. viii. 7, and therefore no complete will to give God any satisfaction, or pay him any obedience. The will is naturally enslaved to sin, and under the power of vicious habits, sins always, never obeys perfectly, but in the moment of a material obedience offends God, comes short of what the law requires. Till the will of man be changed, he cannot be willing with a complete will to obey God; and the will cannot be changed before a satisfaction be made, because it is not reasonable that the punishment of sin, which was a spiritual as well as eternal death, and consisted in leaving the soul under the power of those ill habits it had contracted, which are indeed the death of the soul, as diseases are the death of the body, should be taken off till some satisfaction were made. Man can no more free himself from this spiritual death, than he can free himself from the death of the body; and we have no reason to think God would do it before a satisfaction, for then the law he had enacted would be wronged by himself. Well, then, man hath not power to obey God: Job xiv. 4, 'Who can bring a clean thing out of an unclean? not one;' *i. e.* saith Cocceius, Who can change an unclean thing into a clean? Is there not one? Yea, and but one; Christ only can do it.

(2.) Supposing man had power to obey the law, and that perfectly, yet this was due to God before the sin of man, and therefore cannot be a compensation for the sin of man. After obedience will not make amends for past crimes; for obedience is a debt due of itself, and what is a debt of itself cannot be a compensation for another. What is a compensation, must be something that doth not fall under the notion or relation of a debt due before, but contracted by the injury done. Obedience was due from man if he had not sinned, and therefore is a debt as much due after sin as before it; but a new debt cannot be satisfied by paying an old. As suppose you owe a man money upon a bond, and also abuse him in his reputation, or some other concern; is there not a new debt contracted upon that trespass, a debt of reparation of him in what you have wronged him? The paying him the money you owe him upon bond, is not an amends for the injury you did him otherwise. They both in law fall under a different consideration. Or when a man rebels against a prince of whom he holds some land, will the payment of his quit-rent be satisfactory for the crime of his rebellion? So obedience to the law in our whole course was a debt upon us by our creation; and this hath relation to the preceptive part of the law, and to God as a sovereign: but upon sin a new debt of punishment was contracted, and the penalty of the law was to be satisfied by suffering, as well as the precepts of the law satisfied by observing them. And this was a debt relating to the justice of God, as well as the other to the sovereignty of God. Now, how can it be imagined that man, by paying the debt he was obliged to before, should satisfy the debt he hath newly contracted? The debts are different: the one is a debt of observance, the other a debt of suffering, and contracted in two different states; the debt of obedience in the state of creation, the debt of suffering in the state of corruption; so that the payment of what was due from us as creatures, cannot satisfy for what was due from us as criminals. All satisfaction is to be made in some way to which a person was not obliged before the offence was committed; as men wronged in their honour, are satisfied by some acts not due to them before they were injured. So that all men taken together, yea, the creatures of ten thousand worlds, cannot, by obedience to the preceptive part of the law, satisfy for one transgression of it; because, whatsoever they can do, is a debt due from themselves before. When men fell from God, and entered into league with the devil, they laid themselves at the foot of God's righteous wrath, and sunk themselves into the desert of eternal death, and so stood in another relation to God than as subjects; and God might require a reparation for the past disobedience, and security for obedience for the future; unless man could perform this, he must lie bound in chains of darkness. What compensation could man make for what was past, or what security could he give for time to come? Some other, therefore, must interpose, whose suretyship God would accept; who could give a satisfaction to God, as pleasing to him as sin had been displeasing, and offer to God what was not due to him before; who was able to perform what he undertook, and whose security for what was due for the future, might be esteemed valid; and therefore it must be some divine person, that was not bound in his own nature to those terms of obedience, which were necessary to this satisfaction.

(3.) Supposing man had power after his fall to obey, and that obedience were not due before, yet could not his obedience be compensatory for the injury by sin. Because being a finite creature, whatsoever obedience he could pay could not be infinite, and so not proportioned to an infinite majesty. Since the sin of man is infinite, in regard of the person offended, who is an infinite and eternal Being, and thereby debased below the meanest of his creatures, in the reflection that every sin casts upon him, as being not worthy to be beloved and obeyed; and that which doth satisfy must be as great as the demerit of the crime (for it must be proportionable to the disgrace and damage accruing to God by sin); this a finite creature cannot do: for though obedience is an honour paid to an infinite person, as well as sin a contempt of an infinite person, yet the offence is always aggravated by the person offended, as an injury done to a prince is by the dignity of his person and the greatness of his authority; but the satisfaction is measured from the capacity of the subject offending, which is finite, and not commensurate to the greatness of a wronged God. Nor can our obedience and holiness be counted infinite, because they are the fruits of an infinite Spirit in us;* for by the same reason all creatures should be accounted infinite, because they are the works of an infinite power. The Spirit infuseth the habits of obedience and holiness, and excites them; but the creature, and not the Spirit, exerciseth them, the soul doth obey and believe, &c., so that though they are the Spirit's *efficiently*, yet they are the creature's *subjectively*. Besides, though the Spirit dwells in believers, yet he is not hypostatically united to them, as the divine nature of the second person was to the human. The Holy Ghost and the soul do not make one person; if so, the acts of the new creature would be subjectively infinite, as the mediatory acts of Christ were, because his person, which was the subject of them, was infinite. So that our obedience cannot be infinite; and, indeed, the best obedience any mere creature is able to pay, cannot be so honourable to God as sin is debasing, because by our obedience we honour him according to his nature, as far as our capacity reacheth, and give him no more than his due, and acknowledge him as he is the most excellent Being, the most rightful sovereign; but in sin we prefer every thing before him, do what we can to ungod him, fight against his sovereignty, snarl at his holiness, dare his justice, and render him so vile, as if he were not fit to be ranked above, or with any of his creatures in our hearts; and what rate of obedience is able to render God a satisfaction for so great a contempt and audaciousness? All the obedience a subject can pay to a prince, can never be esteemed in value equal to the contempt, which an endeavour to destroy his person, and pull down his statues, and trample his picture in the dirt, doth cast upon him. Sin is of a higher order in the rank of evils, than the works of righteousness are in the rank of good.†

(2) Nor could man give a full satisfaction by suffering, so as to obtain a restoration to happiness. He is as unable to suffer out his restoration, as he is to work it out. His sufferings would be as finite, in regard of the subject, as his obedience; but the glory he had stained, and the justice he had wronged, were the glory of an infinite God; and the sufferings of a finite creature, though lengthened out to eternity, could not be a compensation to an infinite glory disgraced by sin. Alas! the wrath of an incensed God is too fierce and heavy for the strength of a feeble man to break through. But suppose it were possible for a man that had committed but one crime against God, and afterwards repented of it, and retained no more affection to that sin or any other, by suffering torments for some millions of years, to make a compensation for that one sin; yet how is it possible for men, whose natures are depraved, and have nothing of a divine purity in them, to satisfy by suffering, since they suffer, not only for sin, but in a sinful state, and are increasing their sins while they are paying their satisfactions. No suffering of any that retain their rebellious nature can be a satisfaction to the majesty of God, so as to free such a creature from suffering, while that nature remains, and he loves that sin for which he is punished, though he hath not opportunity to commit it. Besides, since man by nature is 'enmity against God,' Rom. viii. 7, God's judicial power would not render him amiable to the sinner, nor suffering inspire him with a love to his judge; if he should therefore suffer multitudes of years, without any certain hope of recovery, could he be without a hatred of God? So, then, all the time he would be suffering he would be highly sinning; and still sinning would increase the debt of suffering instead of diminishing it. A creature, while a creature, in every state is bound to love God; but no fallen creature can do it without a change of nature. Besides, if a man be not able to satisfy by suffering for one sin, how is he able to satisfy for numberless? Every

* Polhill of the Decrees, p. 188.

† Lessius.

new sin increaseth our obnoxiousness to God, both in its own nature, and as it is a virtual approbation of all former sins, at least of the same kind; now he that cannot pay a farthing, or a shilling, or make satisfaction for a small sum, is not able to make a recompence for millions. And though a man might begin his satisfaction by suffering, where would he end? Since he cannot give one infinite in value, he must give one infinite in time, and then he would be always paying, and never coming to a period of payment; for when you have in your thoughts run along the line of eternity, you would have further to go than you have gone; for in looking back you may find a beginning, but in looking forward you will never find an end; the further you look, still more remains to come than is past.

To conclude this. The church of old saw her utter inability any way to make a propitiation for sin but by God himself: Ps. lxv. 3, 'Iniquities prevail against me; as for our transgressions, thou shalt purge them away,' תכפרם. Our iniquities are too strong for us, we cannot make an atonement for them; but thou shalt be the Messiah, thou shalt propitiate by the Messiah, who is typified by the legal propitiatory, and therefore the same name is given to Christ: Rom. iii. 25, 'a propitiation,' or the propitiatory for our sins. Since the first age of the world to this day, wherein so many ages are run out, there is not one man to be found that ever was his own ransomer, or paid a price for his own redemption.

(2.) No creature is able to do it for us. All creatures are nothing in their original; there could be then nothing of dignity in a mere creature to answer the dignity of the person offended. The plaster would be too narrow for the wound. The whole creation of creatures was of a finite goodness, and nothing to the honour due to so great a majesty. If a creature could satisfy, it could not be by his own strength, but by a great deal of grace conferred upon him, so that he had not paid what was his own to God, but what was God's own already. No creature but must be sustained by the grace of God, that he may not fall into utter ruin while he is satisfying. Angels themselves could not do it but by grace; and the more any creature should do by the grace of God, the more he would be obliged by God, and the less compensate him. Again, it must be one creature, or a multitude of creatures. How one mere creature could satisfy for a numberless number of men, every one of them foully polluted, cannot well be conceived by common reason. One creature can only be supposed to be a sufficient ransom for one of the same kind. There could not be a dignity in any creature to answer the dignity and equal the value of all mankind. If a multitude of creatures were necessary, there must be as many creatures satisfying as were creatures sinning; so God would lose one species of creature to restore another, or an equal number of creatures to them that were redeemed. But indeed no creature could satisfy if the wrong was infinite; and by the rights of justice the satisfaction is to be proportioned to the greatness of the injury and the majesty of the person injured. Those being infinite, no creature was able to manage this affair and bring it to a happy period, because no creature but is finite, and cannot be otherwise than finite, infiniteness being the incommunicable property of the Deity; therefore neither man nor any angel was able to effect it.

1. Not man. This is clear. All men were sunk into the gulf of misery, and he that was unable to redeem himself, could not pretend to an ability to redeem another: Ps. xlvii. 7, 'None of them can by any means redeem his brother, nor give to God a ransom for him.' All that a man hath is not of so much worth as the soul of man; so that no man can pay a sufficient price for the redemption of his captive brother. All human nature could not have shewn a valuable sacrifice. Consider him as man, he is worse than

nothing and vanity. How shall God have a satisfaction for an unexpressible evil, from that which is worse than nothing? Can the drop of a bucket repair an infinite damage? But consider him in a state of rupture with God, and you find him, by his uncleanness, much more unfit for so great a task. It had been too much a debasing the majesty of God, had one mere man been sacrificed for others as a sufficient price of redemption, as if he had been equal in dignity to the offended majesty of God. And what advantage could it have been to the rest of mankind, since the sacrifice would be as corrupt and unclean as those that needed it? No such thing as an innocent mere man can be found, since Adam's revolt, in all those ages which have run out since; all were sunk into the common gulf, all come short of the glory of God, Rom. iii. 23. All were destitute of the image of God, and become filthy; every one without exception, Ps. xiv. 3. And could the sacrifice of rebels redeem rebellious creatures? Could anything morally impure content God, when a maimed beast was not thought fit for his altar? A polluted sacrifice, overgrown with uncleanness and corrupt imaginations, would rather have provoked than pacified him. But suppose an innocent man could be found out, stored with all the holiness of men and angels; yet how can we conceive that the holiness of that man should please God, as much as the sin of Adam displeased him? Such a person in his obedience would only have given God his due; whereas by sin, man robbed God of his holiness, more dear than many worlds, and unconceivable numbers of men and angels.

2. Nor could angels be a sacrifice for us; because they were not of the same nature with the offending person. And the apostle intimates that the redemption is to be made in the same nature that transgressed, when he excludes the fallen angels from the happiness of redemption, because Christ took not upon him the angelical nature, Heb. ii. 17. Though the angels were innocent, yet they were creatures and finite; nor were they the offending nature. And though they transcend man, both in the dignity and holiness of their nature, yet they come infinitely short of the dignity of God, who was injured. They are not pure in his sight, with such a purity as is commensurate with the infinite holiness of their Creator: Job iv. 18, 'He chargeth his angels with folly.' They would fall and vanish from their glory if they were not supported by the grace of God. By angels is not meant prophets, messengers God sends to men; for he speaks of persons distinct from them that dwell in houses of clay: but the prophets were of this latter number. And that he means the good angels is evident, by giving them the title of his angels, his servants, as peculiarly belonging to his service. He proves man not to be just and pure in God's sight, *à majori*, because he chargeth the angels with folly. There had been nothing in the argument to say, man is not more pure than his Maker, because the devils are not. Angels were creatures, and therefore had not a holiness adequate to the holiness of God. What proportion was there between a finite, mutable holiness, and that which is immutable? Though angels were innocent, yet in their own nature they might cease to be so. They had not strength enough to bear and break through an infinite wrath; they could not satisfy, so as to effect redemption, till their satisfaction had been completed, which could not have been even in an endless eternity. What is finite in nature, can never become infinite in nature; one cannot pass into another. If one sunk a number of them into hell, how could one angel, or a number of them, answer for the multitude of sins charged upon the world? So great also is the malignity of sin, and so great an injury to the majesty of God, that it cannot be compensated by all the services and sufferings of saints and angels. But suppose angels had

been capable to be sacrifices for us, and so our redeemers, it had not been agreeable to the wisdom of God to confer that honour upon a creature, to be the redeemer of souls, which would mount a step higher than the bare title of creator, and thereby glorify a creature above himself.

To conclude this. The most excellent satisfaction and sacrifice becomes the dignity of an injured God, and such a satisfaction, that there cannot be imagined a greater by a creature; but whatsoever satisfaction can be given by men or angels, is not so great as may be imagined and apprehended by a creature; for such an one may be imagined as may proceed absolutely holy from the person offering, and be attended with an immutable innocence, without any possibility of a charge of folly, which is a condition above a created state. God was made lower than any creature by sin; and therefore such a satisfaction was suitable, as might render God infinitely higher than any creature, and demonstrate the highest and most glorious perfections of his nature. This was wrought by the death of the Son of God, and could not have been evidenced in that height by the death of any creature.

3. Ceremonial sacrifices, under the law, could not be sufficient for this affair. The Jews, indeed, did rest upon them; thought that, if not by their own virtue, yet by the virtue of God's institution, they purged away their sin, Isa. i. 13, 14. But,

[1.] This was against common reason. Common reason would conclude, that the sin of a soul could never be expiated by the blood of a beast, and that a nature so inferior could not be a compensation for the crime of a nature so much superior to it. The prophet spake but the true reason of mankind, when he asserted, that the Lord would not be pleased with thousands of rams, or ten thousands of rivers of oil, nor the first-born of the body be a satisfaction for the sin of the soul, Micah vi. 6, 7. The first-born and fruit of a man's own body was too low, much more the first-born of a beast. The soul was the principal in sin, and what fitness had a corporeal blood to make amends for the crime of a spiritual nature? A rational sacrifice only was fit to be an atonement for the sin of a rational being. The brutish nature was not the human, there was no agreement between the nature of man and that of a bullock. The transgressing nature was to suffer, the soul that sins, that shall die, Ezek. xviii. A beast had no communion in nature with man, whereby it might respect the sinner, nor any worth in itself, whereby it might respect God, nor any willingness or intention for such an end. Can any think sin so light, as to be expiated by such pitiful mean blood? The remedy ought to be suited to the disease and the party afflicted.* The sin consisted in rebellion and hatred of God; the remedy then must consist in perfect righteousness, exact obedience, and intense love to God; all which beasts were uncapable of. A man must put off his own reason, and have very debasing apprehensions of the perfections of God, if he thinks infinite holiness scorned, infinite justice provoked, infinite glory rifled, can put up all upon the offering brutish blood, that knows not why and to what end it is offered. It was too base a thing to be thought to bear a proportion to an infinite offended nature. What should the flesh and blood of goats signify to a spiritual nature, with which it had no agreement? Ps. l. 13. It was not agreeable to the wisdom of God. A wise earthly lawgiver would not think the life of a beast to be a fit recompence for the capital crime of a malefactor. The wisdom of God knew that they were unproportioned to the end of an expiatory sacrifice. And was it not inconsistent with this perfection, for God to be contented with so vile a thing, after such terrible thunderings from mount Sinai, and giving the law with so much solemnity? What

* Turretin. de Satisfact., pp. 240, 241.

a ridiculous thing would all that ado appear to be, if a beast's blood were powerful enough to quench the force of those flames, and put to silence the thunders of the divine fury, if the transgression of any part of it might be washed away by so cheap an offering? Besides, the same wisdom surely would not let man, the most excellent creature, be beholden to brutes for the merit of righteousness, nor could they be agreeable to the justice of God in the law, which required the death of the party offending. If all the beasts of Lebanon were sacrificed, and the cedars cut down for wood for the burnt-offerings, all could not be a sweet-smelling savour before God. There is an infinite disproportion between this kind of satisfaction and the divine majesty. With God only is plenteous redemption, Ps. cxxx. 7, 8; with God, not in the blood of beasts, but in the true sacrifice, and ransomer; yet with God, and not then manifested to the world.

[2.] The repetition of those sacrifices shewed their imperfection and insufficiency. It is from this head the apostle argues their weakness and impossibility to take away sin, Heb. x. 1-4. There was after them a remembrance of sin; the offerer was not so bettered by them, but still he had need of new ones to keep him right with God. Had any thing been perfected by them, they had ceased, only the new application of an old sacrifice had been required; but there was no ground for an after application of a past sacrifice upon new sins, because the efficacy of the blood ceased as soon as it was shed and sprinkled, so that multitudes of them could not constitute an inexhaustible treasure of reconciliation and merit. The variety of them manifested that there was nothing firm in them. As many medicines shew their own inefficacy, so the many sacrifices and purifications did evidence that a firm and efficacious propitiation was to be sought elsewhere. If the great annual sacrifice, the most solemn one in that whole institution (of which you may read, Levit. xvi. 29, xxiii. 27), could not effect it, much less could sacrifices of a lower dignity. It is from the repetition of this great sacrifice Paul argues the insufficiency of it. This was the most solemn sacrifice, because it was offered by the high priest himself, and for all the people, and the blood sprinkled in the holy of holies. A less sacrifice could not have a larger virtue than the greatest, yet the repetition of this shewed its imperfection.

[3.] God never intended them for the expiation of sin by any virtue of their own. The majesty of God, that sin fought against, was infinite; the sacrifice then must be infinite; but none of those sacrifices under the law were so. Why then did God constitute them? Not with any intention to purge away the sin of the soul, but the ceremonial uncleanness of the flesh: Heb. ix. 13, 14, 'The blood of bulls sanctifies to the purifying the flesh.' The apostle compares those and the sacrifice of Christ together, shewing that one purified only the flesh, the other the conscience. It was not a moral guilt they were intended to remove, but a ceremonial, as when one was defiled by touching a dead carcase or a leprous body, which was in estimation a defilement of the body, not of the soul. It was a guilt judged so by God, not by any law of nature, but a positive law, an arbitrary constitution, which punished it not with death, but with a suspension from communion till it were expiated by a sacrifice; and therefore God might settle what compensation he pleased of a lower nature, for that which was not a moral guilt, for there was nothing in those ceremonial impurities which might waste the conscience, or be accounted a dead work, ver. 14, or infect the soul.* But as to moral crimes, they were rather the confessions than expiations of them. And, indeed, God often discovered their weakness, and that they

* Turretin. de Satisfac., pp. 237, 238.

could not give him rest, or recompense the injury received by sin: Isa. lxvi. 1, 'Where is the house that you build me, and where is the place of my rest? For all those things have my hands made, and all those things have been, saith the Lord.' By the house or temple, is meant all the Jewish economy, and the lump of sacrifices; all those things, though God appointed them, and though they had been used and performed, God had no rest in. They neither satisfied his justice, nor vindicated the honour of his law, nor could they ever take away sin, Heb. x. 11. And, therefore, the only wise God never instituted them for that end, unless we will say he was deceived in his expectations, and mistaken in the end of his appointments. God therefore rejected them, not only upon the hypocrisy of the offerers (as sometimes he did), but upon the account of their own nature, being unable to attain the end of a propitiatory sacrifice, Heb. vii. 18. They were disannulled for the weakness and unprofitableness of them. Though they had been practised for so many ages, yet not one sin had been expiated by them in that long tract of time.

[4.] God did therefore appoint them to prefigure a more excellent sacrifice, able to do it. The vileness and poorness of a beast appointed for sacrifice might admonish the Jews that such light things were insufficient for so great a work as the taking away of sin, the wrath of God, and eternal punishment, and redeeming the soul of man (more precious than all the beasts of the field or birds of the air); they must needs conceive sin was too foul to be washed away with such blood; and this would naturally lead them to conceive that they prefigured a sacrifice more excellent and sufficient for those ends. They were but shadows, Heb. x. 1, and did typically respect a crucified, dying Christ as the substance; and what virtue they had was not in and from themselves, but from their typical relation to that which they shadowed. They signified the sacrifice of Christ, by whose blood, in the fulness of time, the sins that were past were to be expiated, Rom. iii. 25; and as shadows received what value they had from their substance. They did not as shadows purge away any sin, but represent that which should. The shadow of a man shews like a man, but hath not the virtue and power of a man, whose shadow it is, to act what he doth. They easily might collect from them that they were not able to expiate their sins themselves, that it must be done by death, and by the death of some other, not the offender, but of one too that was innocent, and whose sacrifice might be of perpetual virtue; and this those shadows signified to any inquisitive mind.* And the Scripture evidenceth this, the will of God was the reparation of mankind; and when those were insufficient for it, Christ steps in as the great sacrifice wherein God had pleasure, to do this will of God, viz., man's restoration in a way congruous to the honour of God, Heb. x. 6-8. So that what pleasure God had in the institution of legal sacrifices, did not arise from anything in themselves, nor was terminated in them, but in this sacrifice, more excellent than the sacrifice of worlds of creatures.

[2.] Since all these were insufficient, some other must be found out to effect it. And this was Christ only, the Son of God. To fancy a satisfaction below the demerit of the offence, and disproportioned to the injury committed, is to wrong the wisdom and justice of God, and to vilify God in such low thoughts of his nature. That only can be properly called a satisfaction, which is suited to the majesty of God, and is equivalent to the sin of man. Now, since none else were able to offer to God anything for the reparation of his glory, there must be something offered to God, which is greater

* Mornæ, Cont. Inst. p. 168, &c.

than everything that was not God. There was therefore a necessity of some divine person to give that satisfaction which was necessary for the honour of God; that, as a father saith, there might be as much humiliation in the expiation as there was presumption in the transgression. If God would have accepted a satisfaction less than infinite, he might as well have pardoned sin without a satisfaction at all.

(1.) Christ was the fittest, and only capable of effecting it. He was more excellent than all the creatures of the lowest and highest rank put together. There was none whose merit and dignity could equal the greatness and infiniteness of the injury done to God by sin. None could compensate the blackness of the offence with such a greatness of satisfaction. And indeed we cannot imagine that God would expose his Son to so cruel a death, were it not necessary or highly convenient for his honour, or that the Son himself would have taken such a task upon his shoulders, to redeem man in a way of perfect justice. The death of Christ was necessary, our redemption could not else have been in the most perfect manner. None but a divine person could offer a price of redemption worthy of God. His person was infinite, and therefore was able to compensate an infinite injury. He was the prime male in the world, and therefore called the first-born of every creature, Col. i. 15, *i.e.* the basis and foundation of the whole creation.* He was innocent; he was free from everything that might render him an unsavoury sacrifice. He was like us, and in that had what was necessary for a sacrifice, but sin excepted; and in that he wanted what would have made him incapable of effecting our redemption. It was necessary that we should have such a surety and satisfier as was not only innocent, but immutably so, that could not by any means be bespotted by sin; and that the apostle intimates, Heb. vii. 26, 'holy, harmless, undefiled, separate from sinners,' and from sin. Had he only been holy, without being immutably so, the election of God had not stood firm; for since God chose some to bring to glory, and that in Christ, it had been a tottering and uncertain resolution, had the perfecting the redemption of his chosen ones depended upon the transactions of a mutable person, that could not eternally secure himself from offending. Had it been possible for the Redeemer to sin, it had been possible for the absolute decree of God to become vain, and of no effect. He had also strength to do it; his own arm brought salvation, Isa. lxiii. 5. He paid God that which he was not bound to pay; he paid an obedience as man, which was not due from him as God. He was made subject to the law, Gal. iv. 4; not, he was subject to the law by his nature, but made so by his incarnation. He was the fittest, in regard of his being the second person in the Trinity.† It was not fit the Father should suffer, he is regarded as the Governor of the world; who should then have been judge of the satisfaction, whether it had been sufficient or no? Was it fit the Father should have appeared before the tribunal of the Son? Nor was it so fit that the Spirit of God should undertake it; because, as there was a necessity of satisfaction to content the justice of God, so there was a necessity of applying this satisfaction, and quickening the hearts of men to believe and accept it, that they might enjoy the fruits of this sacrifice. The order of the three persons had then been disturbed; and that person whereby the Father and the Son execute all other things, had changed his operation.

He was fit, in regard of both natures in union.‡ Since neither man nor angel could do this business, and there is no nature above theirs but the

* Davenant *in loc.*

† Amyrald. sur Heb. vi. p. 156, 158, much changed.

‡ Ferii Orthod. Scholast. cap. xxii. sect. 3, p. 223.

divine, it must be the divine nature and human together: human, because man had sinned; divine, because the satisfaction should equal the offence. Here they are both in conjunction; the substance of the satisfaction is made in the human nature suffering, and the value of the satisfaction is from the divine. Had he not been mortal, he could not have undergone the punishment sin had merited; and had he not been divine, he could not have given a reparation equivalent to the damage by sin; he was man to perform it, and God to be sufficient for it.

(2.) The honour of God was most preserved and elevated thereby. This way mercy did not invade the rights of justice, nor justice trespass upon the bowels of mercy; both contain themselves in their own spheres. Mercy was preserved from being injured by seeing man solely punished, and justice was preserved from being wronged by seeing man solely pardoned. Thus was the nature of God glorified, without one attribute clashing against the other. Justice could not so well have been declared without the death of Christ, he was therefore set forth εἰς ἔνδειξιν, Rom. iii. 25. To declare his righteousness, as an index of justice, to point to every head and part of it in the nature of God. In this way God saved us as a judge, a lawgiver, and a king, Isa. xxxiii. 22; as a judge in the manifestation of his righteousness, as a lawgiver in the vindication of his holiness, as a king in the demonstration of his sovereignty, in such a way as that his justice is cleared, his law righted, and his sovereignty acknowledged. His hatred of sin was more clearly manifested, and his truth in his threatenings made good and established, and sinners more obliged to God, and engaged upon the account of ingenuity to a greater abhorrency of sin, and a fear and love of God, which, by the suffering of any creature, could not have had so strong a foundation in them. God set a high value upon his law; it was his royal law; and had it been wholly neglected, the royalty of God had not only been violated, but his holiness and righteousness had been disparaged, which shone forth in the law, and made up the whole frame of it; and since death was required by the law, death must be suffered, that there might be an agreement between the threatening and the suffering, the punishment and the justice of God, which required it. We may reasonably think it had been a greater act of wisdom to make no law, than to let it be violated always, without preserving the honour of it.

The doctrine of the death of Christ is the substance of the gospel.* Though there be many doctrines in it besides that, there is no comfort from any of them without the consideration of the cross of Christ; for, though God be merciful in his own nature, yet since sin hath made a separation between God and his creature, it is impossible to renew any communion with him, without a propitiation for the offence. We see, then, Christ is the only meritorious cause of our justification; nothing that we can do can satisfy God, we must be wholly off from ourselves and our own righteousness, as to any dependence on it, and act faith in the death of the Son of God, if we would be secure here in our consciences, or happy hereafter.

As to suffer death was the immediate end of the interposition of Christ; and the veracity of God in settling the penalty of death did require it; and the justice of God made the death of Christ necessary for our redemption; so,

4. It was necessary in regard of the offices of Christ.

(1.) For his priestly office. The reason that he was to be made like his brethren, subject to the law, and the penalties and curse of it, with an exception of sin in his own person, was, that he might be a faithful and merciful high priest. Heb. ii. 17, 18, 'Wherefore in all things it behoved him to

* Amyraut, Sermons sur l'Evangile, Sermon 3.

be made like unto his brethren, that he might be a merciful and faithful high priest in things pertaining to God, to make reconciliation for the sins of the people;' faithful to God for the expiation of the guilt of sin, merciful to men for the succouring them in their miseries by sin; faithful to God in that trust committed to him, to satisfy God for the guilt of sin, that his anger might be averted, and the sinner received into favour, and therefore he was made like to them in the curse, though not in the sin; which was necessary for his being a merciful high priest. This qualification of compassion could not result in such a high manner from anything so well as from an experimental knowledge of the miseries we had contracted; and this must be by a sense and feeling of them. No man is so affected with the wretched state of men in a shipwreck by beholding it in a picture, as when he sees the ship dashed against the rocks, and hears the cries, and beholds the strugglings of the passengers for life; nor is any man so deeply affected with them upon sight, as upon feeling the same miseries in his own person. That makes a man's compassions more readily excited upon seeing or hearing of others in the like state. Now, had not Christ run through the chief miseries of human life, and the punishment of death, he had not had that experimental compassion which was necessary to qualify him for this priesthood. It was by being made perfect through sufferings that he became the author of eternal salvation, Heb. v. 10. It was a thing becoming God as a just and righteous sovereign, in bringing many sons in glory, to make the Captain of their salvation perfect through sufferings, Heb. ii. 10; 'it became him, by whom and for whom are all things.' It became God, as the sovereign of all things, to have his justice vindicated, and, as the end of all things, to have the glory of his attributes exalted. Had not Christ suffered, he had not been a perfect Saviour, neither faithful to God nor merciful to man, because without blood justice had not been satisfied, and so sin, the great hindrance of salvation, had not been expiated. If he were a priest, he must have a sacrifice. A priest and a sacrifice are relatives. A priest is not properly a priest without a sacrifice, nor a sacrifice properly a sacrifice without a priest. Being settled a perpetual priest, Ps. cx. 4, he must have a perpetual sacrifice. Now, having nothing worthy of God's regard but himself, he sacrificed himself. No other sacrifice could have been perpetual in its efficacy, and consequently without a perpetual sacrifice he could not have been a perpetual priest. He as a priest purged our sins, but by himself as a sacrifice: Heb. i. 9, by his own blood as an offering, he entered into the holiest as a priest, Heb. ix. 12. He could not have entered into heaven to act as a priest there without blood, and no blood was fit to be brought in there but his own. There had been else no analogy between him and the legal priests, who were to enter into the most holy place with blood, and never without it. He could not have been an interceding priest unless he had been a sacrificing priest, because his sacrifice is the ground of his intercession. His intercession is not a bare supplication, but a supplication with unanswerable arguments, a presenting his atoning blood, which he carried with him into the holy place when he went to appear in the presence of God for us; whence the apostle, speaking of his advocacy, joins it with his propitiation, 1 John ii. 1, 2. His propitiation on earth and his advocacy in heaven complete him a priest for ever. The one is the foundation of the other. Without it, Christ had been a bare petitioner in heaven, and would have had no ground for any plea against the demands of justice.

(2.) For his kingly office. The first thing he was to do for our reconciliation, was the offering his soul for sin, Isa. liii. 10. Upon this article did all the promises of his mediatory exaltation depend; so that nothing of the dignity promised could be rightly claimed, or reasonably expected, by him, without the performance of this main and necessary condition, which himself had consented to in the first agreement. For consenting to this undertaking, upon the condition of the promise of his exaltation, he implied that he would not expect any exaltation, unless he performed the condition required on his part, of making his soul an offering for sin; and therefore, without such an oblation, could not justly demand the making good the promise to him. There was an *ought to die*, and then *to enter into glory* by the way of death, as a price to be paid for the restoration of our nature to that happiness from whence it fell; his obedience to death was to precede, his exaltation to a throne and dominion was to follow; he was not to sit down on the right hand of the Majesty on high till he had purged our sins by himself, Heb. i. 3; nor had he been Lord of the dead and living unless he had died, Rom. xiv. 9. The royalty, not only over those whom he had redeemed from sin, but over the good angels, was granted him as a recompence for his sufferings, Philip. ii. 8, 9, and the conquest of the evil angels was by his death; for in his cross he triumphed over principalities and powers, Col. ii. 15. The change of laws in the church, which is a part of royalty, was to follow this sacrifice of himself, which is understood in Cant. iv. 6, 'Until the day break, and the shadows fly away, I will get me to the mountains of myrrh.' The removing the shadows of the law was to follow his being upon the mount Moriah, the place of his sufferings, there being an allusion in the word מור, *myrrh*, or *Moriah*. Nor had the Spirit been sent into the world, unless his death had preceded: John vii. 39, 'The Holy Ghost was not yet given, because Jesus was not yet glorified.' This rich treasure could not be dispensed till the acceptation of this sacrifice, till his glorification; and he could not have a mediatory glory till he had offered his mediatory sacrifice. It is the Lamb slain that hath seven eyes and seven spirits, Rev. v. 6; power to prefer his people, and power to send the Spirit to them for their supply. Besides, the Spirit could not have come as a comforter without it, because the consolations he shoots into the soul are drawn out of this quiver. Without his death, we had not had a propitiation for sin, the mysteries of divine love had lain undiscerned in darkness; since we cannot be renewed without the Spirit (because the nature of man was depraved by his fall, whereupon justice denied the restoration of original righteousness), justice must be satisfied, and God reconciled, before mercy could restore it. Justice must be appeased, before it would consent to the return of that favour which had devolved into its hands by forfeiture; so great a gift as the Spirit, the author of renewing grace, was not like to be bestowed upon us by God, while he remained an enemy. The gift of the Spirit is therefore ascribed to the purchase of Christ's death.

(3.) There was some necessity of it for his prophetical office. His death was the highest confirmation of his doctrine. This was not indeed the only cause, nor the principal cause, of his death; if it were, his death would differ little in the end of it from the death of martyrs. Besides, if he had suffered death chiefly for this, what need was there of his undergoing the curse, and groaning under the desertion of his Father? There was no absolute necessity of his death for the confirmation of his doctrine, since the miracles he performed were a divine seal to assure us of its heavenly original; therefore he directs the Jews to his works, as a means of believing him to be from heaven, John x. 38. Yet in his death he set forth a perpetual pattern of that obedience, meekness, love to God and man, and trust in his Father, above what any creature had ever been able to propose to us. He taught us in his life by the words of his mouth, and in his death instructed us by the exemplary exercise of his graces, and the voice of his blood, 1 Peter ii. 21. He taught us the highest part of obedience to the utmost, by performing the exactest and sublimest part of obedience to his Father; and, therefore, after he had discoursed to his disciples of his death and departure, he adds the reason of it, 'That the world may know that I love the Father; and as the Father gave me commandment, even so I do,' John xiv. 31; that the world might know that he loved the glory of the Father, who was so merciful as to be willing to remit sin, yet so just, as not to remit it without a sacrifice.

5. The death of Christ was necessary upon the account of the predictions and types of it in the Scripture. Had not Christ suffered, all the predictions had been false, and the types to no purpose. In this the veracity of God was engaged, not only in making good the threatening of death discovered to the first man, in inflicting what was threatened, but in the way of redemption by his Son. This was not only truth to his own resolve, as he had determined it, but truth to his word, as he had published it. God having decreed and declared the redemption of mankind, and the death of the Messiah as the medium, could not appoint then another way, because his counsel had not only pitched upon redemption as the end, but the death of Christ as the means; and there could be no change in God. Had there been a change in the end, and had God altered his purpose for man's redemption, he had obscured and lost the glory of all those attributes which sparkled in it. There could be none in the means; if so, it must have been for the better or worse. The better it could not be; for no way of so great a sufficiency could be found out as this, nor could any sacrifice of a higher value be thought of. Nor could it be worse; for he could not have pitched upon any deficient way but he would have testified himself weary of, and changed in, his end for which he appointed those means. This necessity of his death, Christ, in his discourse with his staggering disciples, confirms by the exposition of all the Scriptures, which contained the things concerning himself, beginning at Moses, *i. e.* at the books of Moses, and all the prophets, Luke xxiv. 27; which he testifies again, ver. 43, naming the Psalms also as particularly containing things that concerned his person and death. Moses discovered it by types, as he was the minister of settling them, and by prophecies, as he was the amanuensis to write some of them. The prophets declared it in express words, they spake it all with one mouth; and their chief prophecies centred in this, that Christ should suffer: Acts xxvi. 22, 23, 'Saying none other things than what Moses and the prophets did say should come; that Christ should suffer.' And the apostle Peter excludes none of the prophets from speaking of those things which were to be done in the latter days, Acts iii. 21; and that this was the design of the Spirit in them, to testify of the sufferings of Christ, 1 Peter i. 11.

(1.) Predictions. We shall speak of a few.

[1.] The first promise: Gen. iii. 15, 'It shall bruise thy head, and thou shalt bruise his heel;' speaking to the serpent of the seed of the woman, which was to defeat all his devices. The Messiah here, as the seed of the woman, was promised to Adam to break the serpent's head, *i. e.* to take away sin and eternal death from man, which the devil had introduced, by the subtle contrivances of his head, into the world; for he was to take away the strength, power, and wisdom of the devil, signified by the head. The way whereby he was to do it was by having his heel bruised, viz., the heel of his humanity, by suffering. For as he was the seed of the woman, having human nature, he was to be bruised, he was to feel the power of the devil (now, the power of the devil was the power of death, Heb. ii. 14), yet so to feel the power of the devil as not utterly to sink under it; for not his head, but his heel, was to be bruised, *i. e.* his flesh, not his wisdom and chief design for the redemption of man. He was only to be bruised, not destroyed, or to see corruption; so that his death and resurrection are here predicted. And by suffering his heel to be bruised by the serpent, he was to break the serpent's head, *i. e.* through death to destroy him that had the power of death, Heb. ii. 14. And we know the death of Christ was the conquest of the devil. Sufferings are necessary;* for there can be no conquest of the devil but by a satisfaction performed to the righteousness of the law; for his whole empire consisted in the curse of the law; and the law, after sin, required death, called therefore a 'law of sin and death,' Rom. viii. 2. The devil was the jailor, having the power of death; the law must be satisfied before the prisoner be freed from the jailor's power. The value of those sufferings is declared,† because his bruise cannot wholly destroy the seed, nor hinder him from bruising the serpent's head. He could not by suffering bruise the serpent's head, unless he had been innocent, and from his innocence derived a dignity and worth to his sufferings; and this no fallen creature could do. Again, he must be innocent; for if he had been under the power of the devil, he could not have bruised his head. And since he was to overcome the devil by having his heel bruised, it signifies his suffering for those sins which were the foundation of the empire and dominion of the devil. Adam might well understand this conquest of the devil to be the death of the seed, because after this promise he was taught to sacrifice; and the sacrifices, he was presently taught (as may be well conjectured by the skins of beasts, viz., of sacrificed beasts, wherewith God clothed him), as a comment upon this promise, shewed him in their death what he had deserved, and in what manner he was to expect his redemption, so lately promised him. And surely the wisdom and goodness of God would not teach him the way of sacrificing, without acquainting him with the reason and end of sacrifices, which the Scripture mentions as a means to make man accepted with God, Gen. iv. 7; to purge away sin, 1 Sam. iii. 14; and to make reconciliation for it, Ezek. xlv. 17. And Adam, having more natural knowledge after his fall than all his posterity have had since, might easily know by reason that the blood of beasts was too weak and vile to make an atonement for his late offence, which had brought so much misery upon him, and thereby was manifested to be infinitely offensive to God, and therefore more offensive to him than the blood of beasts could be pleasing. This he could not but know, that those sacrifices 'could not make him that did the service perfect as pertaining to the conscience,' as the expression is in Heb. ix. 9. And Adam, being the high priest, as head of all, could not but know that those sacrifices were offered for sin; because this was the end of the appointment of a priest, and the chief part of his office, as well as the end of the sacrifice: Heb. v. 1, 'Every high priest is ordained for men in things pertaining to God, that he may offer sacrifices for sin.' Let us further consider. The end of this promise was to defeat the devil, and to comfort Adam after his revolt from God, and thereby his falling under the vindictive justice of God, and to cheer him up before he should hear his own sentence, which was pronounced, Gen. iii. 17–19. So that Adam could not reasonably understand this promise any other way for his comfort, than that this promised seed should take away sin and the death threatened for it; otherwise it had been but little comfort to Adam to see himself ruined beyond any hopes of recovery, and to hear only of the destruction of his enemy. But in this promise Adam saw the sentence of death respited, because the seed of the woman was promised, which necessarily included the continuance of his life, else there could have been no seed of the woman. This also signifies

* Cocc. in Gen. iii. 15. † Cocc. in Gen. iii. 15.

to us that the sufferings of Christ were intended for a satisfaction of the violated law and provoked justice; for if sin and death were to be taken away by Adam's imitation of this promised seed when he should appear, Adam could take no comfort in the promise, unless he had been sure to live to see this promised seed in the flesh. How could he imitate as an example the promised seed whom he was never to see in the world, but was to return to dust long before the appearance of it in the world? And it was necessary Adam should behold this seed in the flesh, if the breaking of the fetters of sin and hell were to be brought about only by his imitation of this seed. Again, to bruise the serpent's head cannot reasonably be understood of a confirmation only of the promised mercy (which some make the end of the death of Christ). There was no need of bruising the heel barely for a confirmation of this mercy; for that was confirmed by the unalterable promise and will of God. And no question but Adam thought it sufficiently valid, since he received it from the mouth of God himself, and had so late an experience how true God was to the word of threatening. There is no other thing left, then, as the end of this bruising the heel, but to render mercy triumphant without any wrong to justice, and to vindicate the honour of the law, and, in a way of righteousness, not only of sovereign dominion, to defeat the serpent and restore the fallen creature.

[2.] Another prediction is Psalm xxii. All the circumstances of his passion are here enumerated: sufferings, revilings, contempt by men, the desertion of God, his agonies, the parting his garments; and, at last, the propagation of the gospel and the calling of the gentiles are here predicted. The Jews understood it of the body of the Jewish nation;* but the design of the psalmist is to set forth a particular person, who is distinguished from the wicked crew that oppressed him, and from those that favoured him, whom he calls his brethren, and distinguisheth himself from the congregation wherein he would praise God, ver. 23; and upon the death of this person the world was to be gathered in to God: ver. 27, 'All the ends of the world shall remember, and turn unto the Lord;' agreeable to the prediction of our Saviour, that when he should be lifted up, he would draw all men after him. Here is the prediction of the very words he spake upon the cross, when he lay under the imputation of our sins, and cried out, under the sense of his Father's wrath, ver. 1, 'My God, my God,' &c. The miserable condition he was brought to, ver. 6, as a worm and no man, exposed to such a state of misery, and to be of no more account than the most contemptible animal, a worm. The word *worm*† comes of תולע, which signifies the grain which gave a scarlet dye, because the colour proceeded from a worm enclosed in that grain. Our Saviour was as a worm crushed to tincture others with his blood. The very gesture of the people when they reviled him, wagging their heads, ver. 7, and Mat. xxvii. 29; the reproaches they belched out against him, ver. 8, Mat. xxvii. 43, 'He trusted in God, let him deliver him;' the sharpness of his death, ver. 14, 'I am poured out like water, all my bones are out of joint;' a distortion and racking of all his bones, effusion of his blood, dissolution of his vital vigour (like wax melted) under the sense of God's wrath, an expression used, Ps. lxviii. 2, to shew the greatness of God's wrath against sin and sinners; his extreme thirst, ver. 15, 'My tongue cleaveth to my jaws;' the manner of his death by crucifixion, ver. 16, by piercing his hands and his feet, shewing it to be a lingering and painful death, which manner of death is also prophesied, Zech. xii. 10, 'They shall look upon me whom they have pierced,' which the ancient Jews understood of the Messiah,

* Dr Owen on Heb., vol. i. Exercit. pp. 217, 218.

† תולעת. Vermillion colour is derived of *vermis*.

and is a proof that the Messiah was to be pierced or digged into. And this place is cited as a prediction of the death of Christ, John xix. 37, Rev. i. 7; and as the manner of his death, so the excellency of his person is described there. The same person is a God to pour out the Spirit, and a man to be pierced; he works wonders as God, and suffers wonders as man.

[3.] The whole 53d of Isaiah is a prediction of this. He was to be rejected of men, wounded for our transgressions, to have our sins laid upon him by God, to bear iniquity, to be led as a sheep to the slaughter, to make his soul an offering for sin. This is so plain that the Jews anciently understood it of the Messiah;* but the latter Jews, to evade it, have fancied a double Messiah, one a sufferer, another a triumpher, the sufferer of the tribe of Ephraim, the triumpher of the tribe of Judah; but where doth the Scripture mention a Messiah of the tribe of Ephraim? It always fixeth his descent from the house of David, of the tribe of Judah.

Many other prophecies there are of this: Zech. xiii. 7, 'I will smite the shepherd,' and Dan. ix. 24, the 'Messiah shall be cut off, but not for himself;' he shall be counted the wickedest man, and put to death as the greatest malefactor, who hath no crime of his own to merit death, but his death shall be for the good of mankind. And the ends of it are expressed, ver. 24, to finish transgression, and make an end of sin, and to make reconciliation for iniquity, and to bring in everlasting righteousness, and to seal up the vision and prophecy; to finish transgression, or restrain it; to abolish sin in regard of the guilt of it, and restrain it from accusing us before God, and procuring the condemnation of us; to make an end of sin, or seal up sin, covering it, that it shall no more appear against us, as the writings of the Jews were rolled up, and sealed on the back side, that the writing could no more be seen; to make reconciliation for iniquity, to expiate iniquity (a word belonging to sacrifices), to take away the obligation of sin (and it is observable, that all the words used in Scripture to signify sin, are here put in, פשע, עון, חטאה, to shew the universal removal of them, as to any guilt, by the death of Christ), and to bring in everlasting righteousness. As righteousness was lost by the first Adam, so it was to be restored by the second, to make us for ever accepted before God. And to seal up the vision and prophecy, to accomplish all the visions and prophecies in the appearance of his person, and performance of his work. All prophecies pointed to him, and centered in him; and the end of his coming and excision was to deliver us from sin, and introduce such a righteousness as might be valuable for us before God. And then he was to be a prince, when he had been a sacrifice, and cut off for the sins of the people. As the time approached for the coming of this promised seed, God made clearer revelations of the death of the Messiah, and his chief design in it. And this is such a testimony of a dying Messiah, by the hands of violence, and for those great ends which the Christian religion affirms, that the Jews, with all their evasions and obstinacy, know not how to get over it.

(2.) The second thing is the types. There were several types of Christ in the Old Testament, both in the persons of men and the ceremonies of the law. No one type, no, nor all together, could fully signify this great sacrifice. The figure hath not what the truth hath.† The image of a king represents not all that the king hath or is. Moses was a type of the Messiah, who was to be raised up like to Moses, Deut. xviii. 15. Moses, put into an ark, was exposed to the mercy of the Egyptians on the land, and the crocodiles in the river, and after that advanced to be chief governor of Israel; Jonah,

* Pugio fidei. part iii. distinct. i. cap. x. § 4, 5, and distinct. iii. cap. xvi.

† Theodoret.

buried three days in the belly of the whale; Noah, penned up in an ark, to become the father of a second generation; Joseph, cruelly put into a pit, and sold by his brethren, and afterwards lifted up to a throne, to be the preserver of his spiteful brethren,—these, it is likely, had all some relation, as types, to Christ. It would be endless to mention all; let us consider in general.

[1.] Sacrifices. These were practised by all nations, as well Gentiles as Jews, and from a notion that they did pacify their offended deities. Heathen authors give us a full account of their sentiments in this case; and the Philistines, neighbours to the Jews, declare this as their sense in their trespass offering, they would return to God after they had felt his hand, 1 Sam. vi. 3–5. The common notion of all heathens was, that they were offered to God for a propitiation for sin, and either for preventing the judgments they feared, or removing the judgments they felt.

(1.) These sacrifices could not arise from the light of nature. Being universally practised, they must arise from the light of nature, common to all men, or from some particular institution derived to all men by tradition. The light of nature could not be any ground for the framing such an imagination in men's minds, that God should be appeased by the blood of irrational creatures. The disproportion of them both to the offence, the offender, and the offended person, hath been seen and spoken of by the wiser sort of the heathens themselves. Natural light would rather have dictated to them that their devout prayers, deep repentance, and hearty reformation would have been more efficacious to avert the anger of God than the cutting the throat of a bullock or lamb, and pouring out the blood at the foot of their altars. They could no more suppose that such offerings should appease an offended God, than the cutting off a dog's neck, or the crushing a fly before the statue of a prince would have appeased the anger of their injured sovereign. And none could think but the killing a worm, and offering it to the prince, had been as well or more sufficient to have mitigated his wrath, than the killing a thousand cattle had been to allay the wrath of God, in regard of the proportionableness of a worm to the one, greater than that of all the beasts in the world to the other. The light of nature would not instruct the heathens barbarously to take away the lives of men, and offer them for the expiation of their sins. For that teacheth us to love one another, as being descended from one root, and being of the same stamp. Besides, had any law of nature obliged men at any time to bloody sacrifices in such a nature, it would have obliged them still. No law of nature is razed out by the gospel, but more cleared; and whatsoever is due to God by the law of natnre is more improved by the Christian religion. Natural light would be able to make more objections for the forbearance of such a practice, than arguments for the preserving it in the world.

(2.) They must be therefore from institution. And since the practice hath been so universal, and the head of it can less be traced than the head of the river Nilus, it must be supposed to descend from the first man by tradition, and carried by his posterity to all the places which they first peopled, and so continued by their descendants. Bloody sacrifices seem to be instituted just after the fall. How should Adam be clothed with the skins of beasts? Gen. iii. 21. If it be meant that God only taught him to clothe himself with the skins of beasts, it implies a giving him order to slay beasts, and most probably first in sacrifice, and ordering him to take the skins for clothing, which in the Levitical service were appropriated to the priests. For food it is probable they were not killed; the food then appointed was the herb of the field, even after the fall, Gen. iii. 18. And the objection against this, that there were but two of a kind, male and female, created, and therefore if two beasts of the same kind had been slain, a species had been destroyed, is of no validity. For the story of the creation mentions not such a parsimonious creation, nay, it is more probable there were more than two of a sort created. However, sacrifices began early. Abel is the first we plainly read of, Gen. iv. 4. He brought of the firstlings of his flock, and Cain brought of the fruit of the ground, an offering to the Lord. They may not be out of the way who think that there was a crime in the matter of Cain's sacrifice, it not being a bloody one. No doubt but he had seen his father offer to God the fruits of the earth, as well as the bodies of beasts, and might think that the offering those fruits of the ground (the tilling whereof was his proper employment) was sufficient, that there was no need of blood for the expiation of his sin. He seems to stand upon his own righteousness, and offer only what was an acknowledgment of God's dominion and lordship over the whole world, as if he had only been his creature, and not an offending creature. It was not inconsistent with a state of innocence for a man to make such acknowledgments to God, as the Lord of creation and the Benefactor of man. But after the fall there was not only the dominion of God, but his justice, to be acknowledged, which was best signified in a way that might represent to man the demerit of his offence and the justice due to him, which could not be by the offering of fruits, but by the shedding of blood, without which there is no remission.

(3.) If then they were from the special institution of God, they must be figures of something else intended. For since we find an universal sentiment in the practisers of them among the Gentiles, that they were for expiation, and that common reason could not find ground enough to fortify such an opinion in them; and that the Scripture, the ancientest book in the world, gives us an account of their ancient practice and divine institution; they could not be instituted by God, as the prime means of appeasing him, for that could not be congruous to the nature of God. There was no proportion between the justice of God and them, nor between them and the sin of man. But the most reasonable conclusion would be, that they were ordained to signify some other thing or sacrifice intended for the expiation of sin; that they were typical of the death of some one able to bear the punishment and purge the transgression. Since they could not purge the conscience, they must be concluded to be types of something that should have a sufficiency and an actual efficacy to this end. And this the heathens might have guessed from reason and the universal practice, that they were shadows of something else, though they could not have imagined the true person they were shadows of.

To sum up, therefore, the account the Scripture gives us of them, we must consider * that after Adam's revolt, and contracting death and the curses of the law by that apostasy, there was a necessity of maintaining the honour of the law, and God's own veracity in the commination, and satisfying his provoked justice, which must be done by that nature which had offended. Upon this account, and for this end, the second person, the Son of God, voluntarily exposed himself, and stood as a screen between the consuming fire and the combustible creature. Hereupon the sufferings of the Son of God were mutually agreed upon, the particular sufferings appointed and determined, and the time when he should be incarnate, and expose himself to that which the criminal should have endured, was settled, and the redemption, the design of those sufferings, declared by promise; and because the time would be long before his coming to suffer, and the faith of men might

* Owen, Heb. vol. ii. Exercit. p. 61.

languish, God kept it up by lively representations of those sufferings, and the end of them, in the death of sacrificed beasts. Not that they should rest upon them, but use those shadows as props to their faith in the promised seed, till the fulness of time should come. All those sacrifices were a rude draught, or initial elements or rudiments, to teach the world what was to be done with a full efficacy by the person appointed to it. Whence the apostle calls them 'the rudiments of the world,' Col. ii. 20. And so they were a copy of what was resolved in heaven from eternity, to be fulfilled in time, for the expiation of sin. They all had relation to Christ. They were to be without blemish, and dedicated wholly to God, as things that were to perish for his glory; and being burnt, and the smoke ascending to heaven, God might, as it were, partake of the oblation, as the Scripture testifies: Gen. viii. 21, 'And God smelled a sweet savour,' viz., from Noah's sacrifice. So Christ offered himself as a holocaust to the Father, as the antitype of those victims that were wholly to be consumed by fire. And this blood speaks better things than the blood of Abel's sacrifice, or the blood of all the sacrifices shed from the very first; for this pacifies an angry God, purges a guilty conscience, and breaks the chains of hell and damnation. There is no question to be made, but the believers among the Jews did apprehend the heel of the promised seed bruised in every sacrifice; they could not else offer them in faith. As mathematicians measure the greatness of the stars, which are above their reach, by the shadows of the earth, which are within their compass, so did they, upon the view of those sacrifice-shadows, apprehend the virtue and efficacy of the grand oblation.* As those that did understand Christ in the manna did also eat Christ in the manna, 1 Cor. x. 3, 4, so those that did apprehend Christ in the legal sacrifices, were also sprinkled with the blood of Christ. Thus was Christ a lamb slain from the foundation of the world, not only by purpose and decree, but significatively and typically in all the ancient sacrifices. I might here instance in the two anniversary goats, Levit. xvi., one offered, the other devoted to the wilderness; in the red heifer, Num. xix., burnt upon the day of expiations, both eminent types of the death of Christ; as also in the passover or paschal lamb, the blood whereof sprinkled upon the posts was of no necessity in itself for the Israelites' preservation from the destroying angel, nor had any intrinsic virtue in it to procure their security. The angel, no doubt, had acuteness of sight enough to discern the houses and persons of the Israelites from those of the Egyptians.† We cannot justify the wisdom of God in this conduct, if we refer it not to Christ, as a representation of that great miracle of redemption to be wrought by him for the true Israelites, when he should come to free man from a bondage worse than Egyptian. This is the true Lamb of God, that hath the virtue and vigour of all that whereof the paschal lambs had but the image and shadow. Let me add the observation of one,‡ the command of God, that the bones of the paschal lamb should not be broken, signified that the redeemer of the world should die such a death wherein the breaking of bones was usual. Yet that that circumstance should not be used in his death, and therefore that that order of not breaking the bones of the paschal lamb, is cited by John, as if it had been literally meant of him and not of the lamb: John xix. 36, 'That the Scripture should be fulfilled, a bone of him shall not be broken.' I might also instance in that eminent type of the blood of Christ, the blood of the sacrifice sprinkled upon the altar, book of the law, vessels of the sanctuary; after which the elders of Israel ate and

* Mares. contra Volkel. lib iii. cap. xxxiii. p. 389.
† Daillé sur 1 Cor. v. 7. Serm. xx. p. 381.
‡ Pearson on the Creed, p. 408.

drunk in the presence of God, no longer exposed unto his anger, Exod. xxiv.; commented upon by the apostle, Heb. ix. 19, 20.

[2.] Isaac's death was a type of the death of Christ. Of his death; for he was, in the purpose of his Father, upon the command of God, cut off. And Isaac, bearing the wood, did prefigure the manner of the death of Christ, viz., such a death wherein the bearing the wood was customary.* As in crucifying, the offenders bore the cross to the place of execution, and Christ did his. And a type also of the resurrection of Christ; for it was the third day from the command of offering him that Abraham received him to life as new born, and raised from the dead, Gen. xxii. 4, and that in a figure of some nobler sacrifice and resurrection, Heb. xi. 19. Moriah was the place appointed by God where Abraham was to offer his son, Gen. xxii. 2, in one part whereof was the temple and the tower of David; another part of the mount was without Jerusalem, and was called Calvary, upon which Isaac was to be sacrificed, as Jerome tells us from the Jewish tradition. Now, upon Abraham's readiness to offer his son Isaac, God binds himself by an oath, that in his seed all the nations of the earth shall be blessed, Gen. xxii. 16–18. In his seed, as dying, and to be offered up, and rising again, as Isaac did in figure. God now binds himself by an oath to do that to Abraham which he had before promised to Adam; the intent of which oath the apostle, Heb. vi. 13, 19, 20, refers to the settling of Christ as redeemer, and more positively affirms this seed to be Christ, Gal. iii. 10. This oath to Abraham was pursuant to that promise to Adam, which expressed the bruising of the seed of the woman; and now God by oath appropriates this seed to Abraham (as being singled out from the rest of the world), from whom the Messiah should descend. God obliged himself to bless the world by one of the seed of Abraham to be offered up really, as Isaac was in figure. And by his hindering him from sacrificing Isaac, and shewing him a ram, he intimates that there would be some interval of time before the blessed seed should be offered. And the words which Abraham speaks, Gen. xxii. 8, 'God will provide himself a lamb for a burnt-offering,' seem to be a prophetic speech of the death of this great sacrifice, though Abraham might not at that time know the true meaning of that speech, no more than many of the prophets knew what they prophesied of, 1 Peter i. 11; and the mount Moriah is concluded by that prophecy, ver. 14, 'In the mount of the Lord it shall be seen,' to be the place of the appearance of this seed: in the mount the Lord Jehovah shall be seen, the particle *of* not being in the Hebrew text, which was the place afterwards of the sufferings of Christ.

1. Let us here see the evil of sin. Nothing more fit to shew the baseness of sin, and the greatness of the misery by it, than the satisfaction due for it; as the greatness of a distemper is seen by the force of the medicine, and the value of the commodity by the greatness of the price it cost.† The sufferings of Christ express the evil of sin, far above the severest judgments upon any creature, both in regard of the greatness of the person, and the bitterness of the suffering. The dying groans of Christ shew the horrible nature of sin in the eye of God; as he was greater than the world, so his sufferings declare sin to be the greatest evil in the world. How evil is that sin that must make God bleed to cure it! To see the Son of God haled to death for sin, is the greatest piece of justice that ever God executed. The earth trembled under the weight of God's wrath when he punished Christ, and the heavens were dark as though they were shut to him, and he cries and groans, and no relief appears; nothing but sin was the procuring meritorious cause of this. The Son of God was slain by the sin of the lapsed

* Pearson on the Creed, p. 416.

† Charron.

creature; had there been any other way to expiate so great an evil, had it stood with the honour of God, who is inclined to pardon, to remit sin without a compensation by death, we cannot think he would have consented that his Son should undergo so great a suffering. Not all the powers in heaven and earth could bring us into favour again, without the death of some great sacrifice to preserve the honour of God's veracity and justice; not the gracious interposition of Christ, without becoming mortal, and drinking in the vials of wrath, could allay divine justice; not his intercessions, without enduring the strokes due to us, could remove the misery of the fallen creature. All the holiness of Christ's life, his innocence and good works, did not redeem us without death. It was by this he made an atonement for our sins, satisfied the revenging justice of his Father, and recovered us from a spiritual and inevitable death. How great were our crimes, that could not be wiped off by the works of a pure creature, or the holiness of Christ's life, but required the effusion of the blood of the Son of God for the discharge of them! Christ in his dying was dealt with by God as a sinner, as one standing in our stead, otherwise he could not have been subject to death. For he had no sin of his own, and 'death is the wages of sin,' Rom. vi. 23. It had not consisted with the goodness and righteousness of God as Creator, to afflict any creature without a cause, nor with his infinite love to his Son to bruise him for nothing. Some moral evil must therefore be the cause; for no physical evil is inflicted without some moral evil preceding. Death, being a punishment, supposeth a fault. Christ, having no crime of his own, must then be a sufferer for ours: 'Our sins were laid upon him,' Isa. liii. 6, or transferred upon him. We see then how hateful sin is to God, and therefore it should be abominable to us. We should view sin in the sufferings of the Redeemer, and then think it amiable if we can. Shall we then nourish sin in our hearts? This is to make much of the nails that pierced his hands, and the thorns that pricked his head, and make his dying groans the matter of our pleasure. It is to pull down a Christ that hath suffered, to suffer again; a Christ that is raised, and ascended, sitting at the right hand of God, again to the earth; to lift him upon another cross, and overwhelm him in a second grave. Our hearts should break at the consideration of the necessity of his death. We should open the heart of our sins by repentance, as the heart of Christ was opened by the spear. This doth an *Ought not Christ to die?* teach us.

2. Let us not set up our rest in anything in ourselves, not in anything below a dying Christ; not in repentance or reformation. Repentance is a condition of pardon, not a satisfaction of justice; it sometimes moves the divine goodness to turn away judgment, but it is no compensation to divine justice. There is not that good in repentance as there is wrong in the sin repented of, and satisfaction must have something of equality, both to the injury and the person injured; the satisfaction that is enough for a private person wronged is not enough for a justly offended prince; for the greatness of the wrong mounts by the dignity of the person. None can be greater than God, and therefore no offence can be so full of evil as offences against God; and shall a few tears be sufficient in any one's thoughts to wipe them off? The wrong done to God by sin is of a higher degree than to be compensated by all the good works of creatures, though of the highest elevation. Is the repentance of any soul so perfect as to be able to answer the punishment the justice of God requires in the law? And what if the grace of God help us in our repentance? It cannot be concluded from thence that our pardon is formally procured by repentance, but that we are disposed by it to receive and value a pardon. It is not congruous to the wisdom and righteousness

of God to bestow pardons upon obstinate rebels. Repentance is nowhere said to expiate sin; a 'broken heart is called a sacrifice,' Ps. li. 17, but not a propitiatory one. David's sin was expiated before he penned that psalm, 2 Sam. xii. 13. Though a man could weep as many tears as there are drops of water contained in the ocean, send up as many volleys of prayers as there have been groans issuing from any creature since the foundation of the world; though he could bleed as many drops from his heart as have been poured out from the veins of sacrificed beasts, both in Judea and all other parts of the world; though he were able, and did actually bestow in charity all the metals in the mines of Peru: yet could not this absolve him from the least guilt, nor cleanse him from the least filth, nor procure the pardon of the least crime by any intrinsic value in the acts themselves; the very acts, as well as the persons, might fall under the censure of consuming justice. The death of Christ only procures us life. The blood of Christ only doth quench that just fire sin had kindled in the breast of God against us. To aim at any other way for the appeasing of God, than the death of Christ, is to make the cross of Christ of no effect. This we are to learn from an *Ought not Christ to die?*

3. Therefore, let us be sensible of the necessity of an interest in the Redeemer's death. Let us not think to drink the waters of salvation out of our own cisterns, but out of Christ's wounds. Not to draw life out of our own dead duties, but Christ's dying groans. We have guilt, can we expiate it ourselves? We are under justice. Can we appease it by any thing we can do? There is an enmity between God and us. Can we offer him anything worthy to gain his friendship? Our natures are corrupted, can we heal them? Our services are polluted, can we cleanse them? There is as great a necessity for us to apply the death of Christ for all those, as there was for him to undergo it. The leper was not cleansed and cured by the shedding the blood of the sacrifice for him, but the sprinkling the blood of the sacrifice upon him, Lev. xiv. 7. As the death of Christ was foretold as the meritorious cause, so the sprinkling of his blood was foretold as the formal cause of our happiness, Isa. lii. 15. By his own blood he entered into heaven and glory, and by nothing but his blood can we have the boldness to expect it, or the confidence to attain it, Heb. x. 19. The whole doctrine of the gospel is Christ crucified, 1 Cor. i. 23, and the whole confidence of a Christian should be Christ crucified. God would not have mercy exercised with a neglect of justice by man, though to a miserable client: Lev. xix. 15, 'Thou shalt not respect the person of the poor in judgment.' Shall God, who is infinitely just, neglect the rule himself? No man is an object of mercy till he presents a satisfaction to justice. As there is a perfection in God, which we call mercy, which exacts faith and repentance of his creature before he will bestow a pardon, so there is another perfection of vindictive justice that requires a satisfaction. If the creature thinks its own misery a motive to the displaying the perfection of mercy, it must consider that the honour of God requires also the content of his justice. The fallen angels, therefore, have no mercy granted to them, because none ever satisfied the justice of God for them. Let us not, therefore, coin new ways of procuring pardon, and false modes of appeasing the justice of God. What can we find besides this, able to contend against everlasting burnings? What refuge can there be besides this to shelter us from the fierceness of divine wrath? Can our tears and prayers be more prevalent than the cries and tears of Christ, who could not, by all the strength of them, divert death from himself, without our eternal loss? No way but faith in his blood. God in the gospel sends us to Christ, and Christ by the gospel brings us to God.

4. Let us value this Redeemer, and redemption by his death. Since God

was resolved to see his Son plunged into an estate of disgraceful emptiness, clothed with the form of a servant, and exposed to the sufferings of a painful cross, rather than leave sin unpunished, we should never think of it without thankful returns, both to the judge and the sacrifice. What was he afflicted for, but to procure our peace? bruised for, but to heal our wounds? brought before an earthly judge to be condemned, but that we might be brought before a heavenly judge to be absolved? fell under the pains of death, but to knock off from us the shackles of hell? and became accursed in death, but that we might be blessed with eternal life? Without this our misery had been irreparable, our distance from God perpetual. What commerce could we have had with God, while we were separated from him by crimes on our part, and justice on his? The wall must be broken down, death must be suffered, that justice might be silenced, and the goodness of God be again communicative to us. This was the wonder of divine love, to be pleased with the sufferings of his only Son, that he might be pleased with us upon the account of those sufferings. Our redemption in such a way, as by the death and blood of Christ, was not a bare grace. It had been so, had it been only redemption; but being a redemption by the blood of God, it deserves from the apostle no less a title than riches of grace, Eph. i. 7. And it deserves and expects no less from us than such high acknowledgments. This we may learn from *Ought not Christ to die?*

A DISCOURSE OF THE NECESSITY OF CHRIST'S EXALTATION.

Ought not Christ to have suffered these things, and to enter into his glory?—LUKE XXIV. 26.

WE have already spoken to the first part of this scripture, and from thence declared the necessity of Christ's death; the next is his exaltation. His sufferings were necessary for the expiation of our sin, and his exaltation necessary for the application of the merits of his death. Some add the particle *so*, and so to enter into his glory; but that is not in the Greek, though it may be implied, for the entrance of Christ into his glory was to be by the way of suffering.

Observe by the way, the great grace of God, that makes often the diffidence of his people an occasion of a further clearing up of the choicest truths to them. Never did those disciples hear so excellent an exposition of the Scriptures concerning the Messiah from the mouth of their Master, as when their distrust of him had prevailed so far. Glory he was to enter into. By this glory is not meant only his resurrection; that was not his glory, but the beginning of his exaltation, a *causa sine qua non;* it freed him from mortality, and invested him with immortality, but was not the term, but a necessary means of his glory (as the fetching Joseph from prison was a necessary antecedent to his elevation on a throne; he could not be a governor while he was a prisoner). By his resurrection, he was prepared for it; by his ascension, he was possessed of it; his resurrection was an entrance into his glory, but not the consummation of his felicity. *His glory.* It is called his as distinguished from the glory belonging to any other; thus he distinguisheth a glory peculiarly his own from the glory of his Father, and the glory of the holy angels, when he mentions his coming to judgment in all those glories: Luke ix. 26, 'When he shall come in his own glory, and in his Father's, and of the holy angels;'* in the mediatory glory, in the glory of the Father, the glory of his Godhead, as he is equal with God; in the glory of the whole creation, the angels being the top of it; or in the glory of all the administrations of God, the glory of God as Creator, creation being attributed to the Father; the glory of the holy angels, by whose disposition the law

* Sterry of the Will, p. 244.

was given, in the glory of the legal administration; in his own glory, the glory of the gospel administration, as judging men according to those several degrees of light they were under, the light of nature, that of the law, and the more glorious of the gospel, his glory.

(1.) As having a peculiar right to it.

[1.] In regard of his designation to it by his Father. He calls it a glory given by God, John xvii. 24. His glory, as promised him by the Father, and covenanted for by himself. He was to be the first-born, higher than the kings of the earth, Ps. lxxxix. 29. His glory, as by gift he was to have 'dominion from sea to sea, and from the river to the ends of the earth. They that dwell in the wilderness shall bow before him; and his enemies shall lick the dust. For he shall redeem the soul of the needy from deceit and violence. His name shall endure for ever: men shall be blessed in him; and the whole earth was to be filled with his glory,' Ps. lxxii. 8, 9, 14, 17, 19.

[2.] In regard of his purchase of it, all this was his glory. It is generally said that Christ had a title to glory, by virtue of the union of the divine nature to the human. It is true, had Christ been only incarnate for no other end but to take our flesh, glory had of right belonged to him from the beginning, by virtue of that union; but in regard of that economy of God for redemption by blood, and the covenant passed between them consisting of such articles, it was not his incarnation, but his passion invested him with a right to claim it; he was to fulfil his charge before he was to have the fruition of his reward. His glory was promised to him, not as assuming our flesh, but as suffering in our flesh, and making his soul an offering for sin, and being incarnate for this end. Glory belonged not to him till his death had been actually suffered, and declared valid in the sight of God. The satisfaction of his Father by him was to precede his Father's satisfaction of him, Isa. liii. 11. His obedience to death gave a *wherefore* to his exaltation: Philip. ii. 9, 'Wherefore God also hath highly exalted him.' The right to it may be measured by the order of conferring it; it was not conferred till he 'had purged our sins,' Heb. i. 3, and therefore the right to claim it was not till he had performed what was due to his Father.

(2.) As being the first subject of glory, as being the spring of glory to all that were to be glorified. As Adam, the head of mankind, was the first subject of God's rich gifts to his reasonable creature, so was Christ the first subject of God's glorious grace, and gifts to and for his redeemed creature. Others have a glory from him as private persons, Christ hath this glory as a public person, as a second Adam, and so it is his glory peculiar to him, and incommunicable to any else, as being the only and singular head, the one and only public person in the charge of redemption. As his sufferings were peculiarly his, wherein neither men nor angels could be partners with him, so is the glory peculiarly his. As he trod the wine-press alone, so he alone hath right to the crown, and whoever else wears a laurel wears it as his member, not as a head.

Let us consider the connection: 'Ought not Christ to suffer those things, and to enter into his glory?' It is argued whether there was a meritorious connection between the sufferings of Christ, and his glory, *i. e.* whether this glory was merited by his suffering.

1. Some say his sufferings were not meritorious of his own glory; though his exaltation followed upon his passion, yet it was not merited by it. His cross was the way to his crown, but not the deserving cause of his crown; he merited by his sufferings a glory for us, but not for himself; and the act of God whereby it was conferred, is expressed by a word, ἐχαρίσατο, Philip. ii. 9, 'given him,' or freely given him, 'a name which is above every name,'

which signifies an act of grace and not of debt. As he did not fulfil the law for himself, but for us, that he might redeem us from under the curse of the law, by being made a curse for us; and therefore is said to be given to us, Isa. ix. 6, or for our sakes, not to himself or for his own sake; so he acquired nothing for himself by his death but what he had possession of before, *quoad divinitatem* and *quoad humanitatem;* for all power both in heaven and earth was conferred upon him before his death, Mat. xi. 27. All glory,* say they, would have flowed down upon his humanity at the instant of his conception, as the glory of the husband is conferred upon the spouse at the first moment of marriage; but God, by a special dispensation, detained it till he had accomplished his work in the lowest degree of his humiliation; God suspended his concourse, as he did to the fire, which hindered it from exercising its proper quality of burning upon the three children; but this work being performed, and the suspension taken off, his glory could not but naturally fill his humanity, as the quality of fire would return to its natural course upon removing the stops; and therefore, to assert any merit for himself, is a disparagement of, and an impeachment to, his glorious union; and for those places which are alleged for his merit of it, as Philip. ii. 8, 9, Heb. i. 9, and also the text, they shew the order of conferring it, rather than the merit of it, that his glory followed his passion, not that his passion merited his glory;† his glory rather seemed to be a necessary consequent of God's acceptation of his death, and a testimony of heaven's approbation of it. As the occasion of his death was the fall of man, so the moving cause of his death was the redemption of man, not the exaltation of the name of Christ primarily and immediately. For our sakes he slid down from heaven into our nature; for our sakes he bore that burden the law and wrath of God had cast upon him; it was for us that he combated with death, and forced our enemies out of their fortresses. And so by this voluntary submission and humiliation, he came to his former dignity; for if he came to an higher dignity than he had before, it had been evident that he was obedient for himself, not for others.

2. Others say, Christ did merit this glory for himself. The oil of gladness was poured upon his humanity, wherein he had fellows, because he had loved righteousness, Heb. i. 9. *Therefore* is a causal particle, not only of the final cause, but the moral, efficient, or meritorious cause. He did by this merit an exaltation at the right hand of God, above all the choirs of angels. It was indeed due upon his suffering, yet called grace,‡ because the whole design of redemption, in the pitching upon Christ, and the sending him, was an act of free grace in God to us; as it was grace to accept his interposition for us, so it was grace to promise him this glory, and set this joy before him for his encouragement in his sufferings;§ and as it was free grace to unite the flesh to the person of the Son of God, so it was of grace that there was a continuation of demonstrating the glory of the Deity in the same flesh. Yet, after his sufferings, the glory of Christ may be said to be a merited reward, because his glory was not improportionable to his sufferings; he merited the dispossession of the devil, and merited therefore the transferring that power upon himself, to manage for the honour of God, which the devil had usurped over man in rebellion against God. A man may have a double title to an inheritance, by birth and by some signal services done, whereby what was due to him by birth may be due to him by merit; as when a province flies into rebellion against the lawful prince, he

* Donn, vol. i. p. 108. Alvarez de Incarnat. † Suarez.

‡ As was noted before in the word ἐχαρίσατο, Philip ii. 9.

§ Coccei. de Fœdere, sect. cvi.

sends his eldest son with an army to quell those tumults; his arms prove successful, and the rebels are reduced to obedience. Doth he not merit a title to that inheritance by his sword, which was due to him by his birth? Indeed, Christ did not merit his first mission, no more than the prince's son merited his being sent for the reduction of the rebels; nor did he merit his first unction and habitual grace. This belonged to the perfection of the soul of Christ, and fitted him for his mediatory work in our nature; he could not have wanted this without prejudice to the work of redemption, and to our salvation, which was the end of it, though this was necessarily consequent upon an admission of Christ's mediation, and a necessary article in the covenant of redemption, yet it was the act of God's free grace. Nor must we think that this glory was the motive to Christ to engage him first in this undertaking, but pure grace to us; for what attractives could there be in our nature to make this divine person assume it? Or what glory could be conferred upon the humanity, that could allure the Deity to embody itself in it? Could the promise of an honour to be conferred upon an angel, if he would enclose himself in the body of a fly or other insect, move him to link his own nature with that for ever, since he enjoyed before a higher honour in his own nature than could be conferred upon him upon such a conjunction? It was the grace of Christ that moved him when he was rich to become poor, not that he might be the richer by that poverty, but we: 2 Cor. viii. 9, 'For you know the grace of our Lord Jesus Christ, that, though he was rich, for our sakes he became poor, that we through his poverty might be rich.' Yet Christ may be said to merit this mediatory glory for himself; the Holy Ghost was a meritorious fruit of the sufferings of Christ, and why not that glory then which was necessary to the sending the Holy Ghost, whose coming he had purchased? The very sending the Holy Ghost was a great part of his glory; and we must remember, that whatsoever was merited by Christ, was not merited by virtue of his humanity singly considered, but as having the Deity in conjunction with it; and why might not so great a person merit at the hands of God?

3. Let this be as it will, yet the sufferings of Christ were a cause of his glory, or a way to his glory, by mediatory compact. For as he was by that bound to pay an obedience he was not obliged to before, so was the Father by that obliged to give him a glory proportionable to his work, and a glory distinct from the glory of the Deity. The waters were to come into his soul, Ps. lxix. 2; he was to drink of the brook in the way, therefore should he lift up his head, Ps. cx. 7. This order did God require for the exalting of him, combat before triumph. This glory could not be conferred upon him before his suffering. If he had enjoyed it from the beginning, by virtue of the hypostatical union, his body had been impassible, incapable of suffering, and so could not have been a sacrifice for our sins. His triumphant laurel grew upon the thorns of his cross, and received a verdure from his dying tears. The palms spread in his way at his entrance into Jerusalem, a little before his suffering, are by some regarded as an emblem of this, it being the nature of that plant to grow higher by the weights which are hung upon it, for so did our Saviour rise more glorious by his pressures. There was a worthiness in his death to entitle him to the fruition of glory: Rev. v. 12, 'Worthy is the Lamb that was slain to receive power, and riches, and wisdom, and strength, and honour, and glory, and blessing.' Worthy to receive power for silencing the oracles of the devil, power to conquer his enemies; riches, to pour out upon his friends; wisdom, to govern his empire; strength, to execute his orders; worthy to be honoured, adored, blessed by all. And this glory he challenged as due by virtue of his sufferings, John xvii. 1. It was fit he

should be lifted up above death after he had so obediently suffered, and be instated in the empire of the world after he had so magnificently redeemed it. The necessity of his sufferings is here described, and also the necessity of his glory. *Ought not* is to be referred to both,—ought he not to suffer, ought he not upon those sufferings to enter into glory? How did he suffer? As man. He entered into glory as man; as man he suffered, as man he was glorified. His divine nature was impassible, and also unglorifiable by any addition of glory to it. His death was necessary for us, so was his glory. He died in a public capacity as a surety for mankind; he was exalted in a public capacity as the head of those he died for. As he offered himself to God for us upon the cross, so he entered into heaven to appear in the presence of God for us upon his throne, Heb. ix. 24.

The doctrine to be hence observed is this,

Doct. The exaltation of Christ was as necessary as his passion.

As it was necessary for him to reconcile us by his death, so it was necessary for him to reinstate us in happiness by his life, Rom. v. 10. Reconciliation is ascribed to his death, salvation to his life in glory. He could not have been a Saviour without being a sacrifice; he could not have applied that salvation without being a king; he was to descend from heaven clothed with our infirmities, to suffer for our crimes. He was to ascend to heaven, invested with immortality, to present our persons before God, and prepare a glory for every believer.

In the handling this doctrine I shall shew,

I. The necessity of this glory.

II. The nature of it.

III. The ends of it.

IV. The use.

I. The necessity of this glory.

First, Upon the account of God.

1. In regard of his truth, the truth of his promise; his promise *to* him, his promises *of* him.

(1.) His promise to him, to Christ. God's truth was engaged for his glory, as the Mediator's truth was engaged for his suffering; and therefore that was as necessarily to be conferred upon him, as the other was to be endured by him. As the ignominy of the cross was an article on his part, so the honour of a crown was an article on God's part. Upon the making his soul an offering for sin, did depend all the promises made to him of his headship over the church, dominion over the world, manifestation of his Deity, propagation of his kingdom, and subjection of his enemies. Without the performance of what he promised, he could not claim one; and upon the performance of what he promised, he could claim all, and his claim could meet with no demur in the court of heaven, so long as God was true to his word. Christ was to surrender himself as a surety for man to the wrath of God, and God was to surrender the government of the world into the hands of Christ. His visage was to be marred, and he was to sprinkle many nations by his blood, Isa. lii. 14, 15; and then kings should shut their mouths at him. Kings in power, kings in wisdom, should be astonished at his growth, and submit to his sceptre. As he was to suffer for many nations, so he was to judge among many nations, Micah iv. 3. He was not to see corruption, his soul was not to be left in hell, Ps. xvi. 10, 11; 'Thou wilt not leave my soul in hell, neither wilt thou suffer thine Holy One to see corruption,' &c., Acts ii. 27, 28. Christ articled with God to go into the state of the dead, but not to be left there; he was to pass into the grave, but not to be invaded by the rottenness of it; he was to be shewn the paths of life, *i.e.* to be restored to another life, to be possessed of a fulness of joy, that was to follow his resurrection, after the ignominy of his death and the agonies of his spirit. As he was to have a fulness of spirit in the world, so he was to have a fulness of joy in his glory. As his grace was to be so great as not to be measured, so his glory was to be so great as not to be bounded; and as his death was to be of a short duration, not fully the term of three days, so his pleasures were to be of an endless duration, pleasures for evermore. And all this glory was to flow from the presence of God, whom his human soul was for ever to behold and converse with, with infinite pleasure: 'In thy presence is fulness of joy.' His whole exaltation, which consisted principally in a manifestion of his Deity and Sonship, was passed by a decree of God, and published to him as Mediator: Ps. ii. 7, 'I will declare the decree, the Lord hath said unto me, Thou art my Son, this day have I begotten thee;' which is interpreted of his resurrection, Acts xiii. 33, which was the first powerful declaration God issued out to the world of his being his Son, Rom. i. 4. Upon which account Peter tells us he was foreordained, both to his sufferings and glory, before the foundation of the world, 1 Peter i. 20, 21; he was to inherit the spoils of his enemies, and take for his own what was before Satan's prey as a reward; and that for the pouring out his soul to death, Isa. liii. 12, he was to see his seed upon the making his soul an offering for sin, Isa. liii. 10; then also his days were to be prolonged. What! to a miserable and infirm life? No, but to such a one as should endure to eternity, wherein is included, not only his resurrection, but his glorious state. How could he see his seed, if he remained in the fetters of death? or behold them with comfort, if he should enjoy an immortality in as infirm a body as he had in the time of his humiliation? The sight of his seed was to follow his investiture in glory, and was a part of it; then it was that nations should run unto him, Isa. lv. 5. All those promises were made to him as incarnate, and making himself an oblation; for, as God, he was not the subject of any promise. He was to bear our iniquities on the cross, and then to live triumphantly upon a throne. Christ pleads this, John xvii. 1, 'The hour is come; Father, glorify thy Son;' the hour of my passion, the hour of thy promise. I am willing to undergo the one, and just now ready to drink of the brook in the way; be thou ready, O Father, according to thy promise and oath, wherein thou stoodest obliged to perform the other part, my glorification; and particularly the manifestation of my deity, upon which all the other parts of my exaltation depend. Ver. 5, 'And now, O Father, glorify me with thy own self, with the glory which I had with thee before the world was;' which was not the glory of his humanity (which was not in being before the world was), but the glory of his divinity in the full unveiling of it, that it might shine brighter before the eyes of men. It had indeed before been obscured in the form of a servant in the time of his life, in the repute of a criminal at the time of his death; but now he prays that he might be manifested to be what he really was, a person that had a glorious existence before the world was, and that had no need to come down and take the nature of man for any advantage to himself. Now, as God promised him a glory, and Christ pleads the promise, so God performed it; and therefore his ascension is expressed by God's receiving him up into glory, as well as by his own act of entering into it: 1 Tim. iii. 16, 'received up into glory,' 'Ανελήφθη, recovered again unto glory; for it was impossible God should be false to his eternal purpose, and his repeated promise.

(2.) His promises or predictions of him. So that his exaltation was necessary to justify the prophecies of it, which were not the predictions of one or two of the most eminent of the prophets, but that which all of them, one way or other, spake of ever since the world began, Acts iii. 21. Isaiah is the plainest of all, and many things to this purpose are inserted in his prophecy: Isa. iv. 2, 'In that day shall the branch of the Lord be beautiful and glorious, and the fruit of the earth shall be excellent and comely.' As he is the fruit of the earth, he shall be excellent in his humanity; and as he is the branch of the Lord, he shall be acknowledged in his divinity; or, as he is the branch of the Lord in his conception by the Holy Ghost, and the fruit of the earth in his birth of the virgin, he shall be glorious in the world. And this was to be for his service, and as the servant of God: Isa. lii. 13, 'My servant shall be exalted and extolled, and be very high;' which relation of service he had not in the divine nature, but his mediatory function; and so glorious was his life to be, and so long the duration of it, after he should be taken from prison and from judgment, that it should be past the declaration of any creature: Isa. liii. 8, 'Who shall declare his generation?' And it is very clear, in Ezek. xvii. 22, 'I will also take of the highest branch of the high cedar, and will set it; I will crop off from the top of his young twigs a tender one, and will plant it upon a high mountain and eminent,' &c. This is not meant of Zerubbabel, under whom the people had not such a signal rest, nor did his empire extend so far as to shadow the fowl of every wing, the people of every nation. Christ was a plant of his Father's setting, a young twig in his humbled, a tall cedar in his exalted, state; planted in the highest mountains, eminent above all the rest; *i.e.* even he was to be cut off, but not for himself, Dan. ix. 26; not to himself, say some;* his cutting off shall not be without a second springing up in a resurrection. And when he is the Son of man, he was to be brought with the clouds of heaven, with the angels which attended him at his ascension, before the Ancient of days, and that near to him; and so welcome he was to be upon his approach, as to be presented with the dominion of the whole world, Dan. vii. 13, 14, which is not to be understood of his coming at the day of judgment, but his coming after his oblation. He comes not here to judge man, but to be judged by his Father; and upon being found to have performed the part of the Son of man, he hath a kingdom both extensive and everlasting bestowed upon him, which should not be destroyed by the subtleties or force of his enemies; a present only worthy of the Son of God. Again, he received not his power at the day of judgment, but upon his resurrection and ascension after his death; but this expresseth the first investiture of this power in him. This glory was prophesied of a thousand years before the accomplishment:† Ps. lxviii. 17, 18, 'Thou hast ascended on high.' The whole design of the psalm manifests it, as well as the citation of it by the apostle, Eph. iv. 8. Joseph was not taken from prison to live his former life of slavery, but a princely life upon a throne, and rule the whole kingdom next to the sovereign prince; so Christ was not to live the same life after his resurrection that he had done before in his sweats and combats, and to endure the contradictions of sinners against himself; but was to be advanced to a place suitable to his greatness, upon the right hand and throne of his Father.

2. Upon the account of righteousness and goodness.

(1.) In regard of his innocence, he was a real innocent, though a reputed criminal; innocent in himself, guilty only as standing in our stead; holy, harmless, undefiled, separate from sinners, Heb. vii. 26, as if there were not words enough to express his purity, he being most holy and undefiled. It doth not seem to consist with the justice of God for him so to give his life for us as never to reassume it. He was a person more excellent than the whole

* Sennert. de Idiotis. linguar. orient., canon xxviii. p. 25.

† Daillé de l'Ascension, p. 431.

world of men and angels. He being a divine person, his life was incomparably more excellent than the lives of all mankind. Surely God, that loved him so dearly, would not have given so glorious a life for the salvation of men, to be swallowed up in the grave without a happy restoration of it. It doth not seem to consist with the wisdom, love, or justice of God to give so excellent a life for the saving ours, if it were not again to spring up to a glorious state out of the ashes of mortality. Was not his death the fruit of his innocence? Was it equal that he should be held in the bands of that, or walk in the world under the load and burden of a mortal body, any longer than the expiation of our sins required? * If this had been, had not a fundamental law of God, which orders immortality and happiness to perfect holiness, been violated, which is impossible?

(2.) In regard of the near alliance to himself. Did it consist with equity to let that person who was equal with himself in regard of the divine nature; that person who was in the form of God, as well as in the form of a servant, Philip. ii. 6, 7; that nature which was so gloriously united to a nature infinitely above the angelical, to corrupt in the grave and crumble to dirt and filth? to be a banquet for worms that had been a fragrant sacrifice to God? Or could it be counted equity to have raised him to no better a life than that miserable one he led before, his agonies in the garden, and his gaspings on the cross? Had it not been an unrighteousness to himself, as well as to his Son? Surely that a flesh which had the honour to be the temple of God, a branch of the Lord, the powerful conception of the Holy Ghost, that had the glory to be personally united to the Son of God, to live and subsist in him, should not be glorified after it was raised again, seems to be against all the laws and rules of goodness and righteousness.

(3.) In regard of the work he had performed. How could justice forbear to deliver the surety, after he had paid so much that it was impossible, upon an exact scrutiny, to find a farthing wanting? How could it be agreeable to goodness to continue a person under the chains of death, or the lighter fetters of an infirm and earthly life, who was not liable to more punishment, nor capable of performing a greater service in this world than what he had already done? It was the interest of satisfied justice to raise him from death; and was it not as well the interest of remunerative righteousness to exalt him to be the head of that church he had so dearly purchased? Coul' goodness continue him a little lower than the angels, who had performed a task that would have broke the back and cracked the heart of the whole angelical nature to accomplish? If God rewards as a righteous judge, 2 Tim. iv., a reward below an exaltation above all the angels had been disproportioned to so deep a humiliation, to so punctual, and in all respects a voluntary and unconstrained, obedience. Was it congruous to the goodness of God to let so signal an obedience, more excellent than the obedience of millions of worlds of angels, pass away without as signal a reward? That so sharp a cross, endured by an innocent with so much affliction and freeness, should not be succeeded by a crown as glorious as the cross was ignominious? In equity he was to be placed far above principalities and powers, the revolted rabble of devils, and their companions bad men, since he had so gloriously conquered and routed those armies of hell, Col. ii. 15, and above the corporations of the standing angels, since he had so graciously confirmed them, Eph. i. 10, by whom those blessed spirits commenced masters of a greater knowledge of the perfections of God than they had by the whole creation for four thousand years. There was all the reason that so incomparable a victory should be attended with as glorious a triumph.

* Daillé sur Resurrect. de Christ. p. 361.

(4.) In regard of the glory which redounded to God from this work. All that was done tended to the restoring of God's honour in the casting out the prince of the world from his usurpation, demolishing idolatry, and restoring the worship of God upon pure and spiritual principles. God received more glory by his mediation than by all the works of his hands, the glory of his grace in his mission, the glory of his justice in his sufferings, and the glory of his wisdom in the whole dispensation, which was a new glory that never accrued to him before, nor could ever be brought into his exchequer by any other way than this. By this the bar to God's resting and rejoicing in his work was removed, the bands of sin were broken off, a carnal Adam changed into a spiritual, the defaced image of God restored, the world formed into a second and more noble creation, and the kingdom of God established in the world by the conquest and spoiling of the revolted spirits. If God were glorious by creating a world, he was more glorious in the redemption of the world. It was reasonable Christ should be advanced to the highest pitch of glory, suitable to that degree of emptiness to which he had abased himself for this end,* that he should triumphantly be settled in the most glorious and majestic place of the empire of God, and have not only the highest place of residence, but the greatest height of authority over men and angels, having made peace between God and the creation, and between one part of the creation and another; that as he died once with a pure zeal for the glory of God, he might live in a new state to a further exaltation of him; for so he doth: Rom. vi. 10, 'In that he lives, he lives unto God,' to gather his people, to glorify them, and be glorified by them. As there was a glory brought to God by Christ in his low estate, so there was a further glory to be brought to him in his exalted estate, according to the voice of the Father to him: John xii. 28, 'I have both glorified my name, and will glorify it again.' As he had glorified it in the doctrine and miracles of Christ, so he would glorify it again by his passion and resurrection, sending the Spirit, propagating the gospel, and setting him upon the throne as the judge of the world. This glorifying God was the argument Christ pleaded for his assistance and exaltation in the prophet (Ps. lxix. 7, 'Because for thy sake I have borne reproach, shame hath covered my face'), that the faith of the saints in the divine promises might not be enfeebled by any carelessness of God towards him, ver. 6. And near the time of his death he pleads it in his own person, that he might be in a state to carry on that glory he had begun to bring to God, to the highest degree: John i. 17, 'Glorify thy Son, that thy Son also may glorify thee.' Christ was to do more service for God in heaven than he did on earth, and glorify his Father after his Father had glorified him, *i.e.* by a particular application of his death to men, by the virtue of his intercession, though indeed the foundation of all that glory was laid upon the cross by his satisfaction. Had God been good to the Redeemer, if he had given him less than a crown for a cross, a reward for the work effected by his suffering? And had he been righteous and good to himself, if he had put Christ into a state below that which should capacitate him to perfect the remains of that honour of his name, which were further to be extant in the world? What capacity could we imagine him to have if he had lain under the feet of death, or sat languishing on the footstool of the earth in a feeble immortality? A throne was due for the glory he had gained, and a throne was fit for the glory he was yet to effect.

3. Upon the account of love to Christ. His paternal affection to his Son required not only a deliverance of him from the jaws of death, but the putting such a crown upon his head, by which he might be known by all to be his

* Faucheur, in Acts ii. 9, p. 109.

Son, whom he embraced with an ardent affection.* God would not love his Son according to his own greatness, if he did not manifest it to the world with the most signal marks and ensigns of authority. And surely after he had vanquished his Father's wrath, and triumphed over the enemies of his honour, he could expect no other than the strong effluxes of his Father's love in the highest expressions of it. What could hinder him from resting in his bosom, when all the wrath excited by the transgressions of the law was calmed, and the Redeemer came out victorious from that furnace of wrath wherein he had been enclosed. Wrath thus being quenched by his sufferings, there was no room for the exercise of any other affection to him than that of love; and no testimony could be given proportionably to such an affection, but the highest degree of honour conferred upon him. The Father loved him because he laid down his life, John x. 17; and the same affections would be more strongly manifested after he had laid it down, and prompt him to shew him greater works than those which had been wrought in the world, that the world might marvel, John v. 20. He would manifest him to be the partaker of all his counsels, that nothing of authority should be denied him, nothing of knowledge concealed from him. These were the signal demonstrations of the Father's love, expected by our Saviour.

Secondly, It was necessary on the account of Christ himself.

(1.) In regard of his nature.

[1.] As it was of an heavenly original: He came down from heaven, Job iii. 13. He was that holy thing born of the virgin, but as overshadowed by the power of the highest, Luke i. 35. He was not born by the force of flesh and blood, according to the law of creation settled in old Adam; he was an heavenly man, or the Lord from heaven, 1 Cor. xv. 47, and therefore was immortal in the true and original constitution of his nature.† And though he lived in a veiled condition to fulfil the charge which he undertook, and which could not otherwise be accomplished, yet, after the completing of it, he could not be retained in the bands of death, but must necessarily return by the law of his own nature to his true and original condition, and lead an heavenly and glorious life, suitable to the principle whereby he was formed.‡ All things are ordered by God in places suitable to their nature; heavy things are placed lowest, lighter things highest; and if for the good of the universe they remove out of their proper place contrary to their natures, as soon as ever the occasion which obliged them to such a motion is over, they return to the place of their former settlement proportionable to their nature. As air, whose place is above the earth, when it is enclosed in the bowels of the earth, and there increased by vapours, will find its way out by an earthquake, to that place which God hath settled for it; stones descend, and water flows down to its proper place, as soon as the let is removed; so, though Christ, for the good of mankind, stepped into the world, yet when he had effected that business, he must necessarily take his flight to heaven, his proper place. When that which obliged him to come upon the earth was ceased, and he had no more to do here, upon that occasion of the expiation of our sin, heaven, that was the principle of his original, was to be that of his rest and abode. As earth was assigned to the first man, who was earthly, for an habitation, so heaven was the proper element of repose for the second man, who was heavenly. It was most convenient that an earthly man should be lodged in the earth, and the Son of God have his seat where the throne of his Father was.§ It was not fit that any creature should be above the person of the

* Amyrald, Symbol. Apostol. p. 169. † Daillé, Melan. part ii. p. 631.

‡ Daillé sur l'Ascens. de Christ. p. 434, somewhat changed.

§ Faucheur, in Act. i. 9, p. 109.

Son of God, what nature soever he had assumed, and therefore his exaltation above the angels was due also upon that account.

[2.] As his body was changed by the resurrection. Since after his resurrection his body was made immortal, and had new qualities conferred upon it, whereby it had acquired an incorruptible life;* as our bodies shall at the resurrection be incorruptible and spiritual, 1 Cor. xv. 42, 44; it was not fit it should make any long stay in a place of corruption and misery; and that so excellent a person should have an habitation in a world of men and beasts. A corrupted place was not convenient for an immortal body; nor an earth, cursed by God, suitable to an unstained nature, that had nothing further to do here by himself. But seeing it was the most perfect body, it was convenient it should be taken up into the most perfect place, and ascend above all bodies.† Indeed, while he had a body of such a mould as ours, and furnished with the same earthly qualities and infirmities with ours, his abode in the world was somewhat suited to his body as well as to his work; but when he had put off his grave-clothes, and was stripped of that old furniture, and enriched with new and heavenly qualities, heaven was the most proper place for his residence. Again, had the earth been a proper place for him, it was not fit the Divinity should stoop to reside in the proper place of the humanity, but the humanity be fetched up to the proper place of the Deity, where the Deity doth manifest itself in the glory of its nature. The lesser should wait upon the greater, and the younger serve the elder.

[3.] As the greatest part of his exaltation consisted in the manifestation of his Deity. It was not fit so great a conqueror and Redeemer, who was God as well as man, should have his deity still under the veil of our flesh, after he had accomplished so great a work. Indeed, he hath our flesh united in heaven to his divine nature, but his divine nature is not veiled by it, as it was here. Now, had his deity been manifested here below in that vast brightness and splendour which was proper for it, the sons of men had been undone, and met with their ruin instead of their recovery; for who can see God and live? Exod. xxxiii. 20, 'No man can see my face and live.' Heaven was therefore the only place where this could be manifested in that illustrious manner which it ought to be, though earth was the place for the powerful effects of it. I say, then, it was not fit the glory of his deity should have been longer overshadowed by the veil of his humanity; and it could not have broken out in its clearness without not only dazzling our eyes, but consuming our beings, in that state we are. The brightness of an angel is too great an object for weak man, without the shadow of some assumed body, much more the brightness of the Son of God; and what need was there of his being veiled for us still, when he had done all that was necessary to be effected in that veil of infirmity he had wrapped himself in?

(2.) It was necessary upon the account of Christ, in regard of his offices. Had not Christ been glorified, the offices conferred upon him by his Father could not have been executed; his prophetical, priestly, and royal functions could not have been exercised, to which he was chosen by God, and without which he could not have been a Saviour to us. He had been a sacrifice, without being a priest; a king, without possessing a throne; a prophet, without a chair to teach in; at least none of these offices could have been managed in a way worthy of himself, unless he had been in a glorious condition, and his humanity in a glorious place.

[1.] It was necessary for his prophetical office. As he did but begin to exercise his priestly office in his death, and began to execute his royal func-

* Faucheur, in Act. i. 9, p. 109.

† Savonarola, Triumph. cruc. lib. iii. cap. 19.

tion in his miracles, so he did but begin to manage his prophetical office in his life: Heb. ii. 3, 'Salvation began to be spoken by the Lord.' His death was a consecration to a further exercise of his priestly office, his signs and wonders the first essays of his kingly, and his own teachings the first rudiments of prophecy. After his ascension he did, as the Sun of righteousness, spread the wings of his grace, and flew about the world in the illuminations of hearts, Mal. iv. 2. As it is with the sun, so was it with Christ, the nearer the earth in the winter of his humiliation, the less force he had for the production of fruits, but the higher he mounted in heaven the more vigorous. The beams of the sun shot from heaven make us distinguish those things which we mistook in the dark, and the rays of Christ, after his ascension, manifested the difference between truth and error. Then the living waters of the sanctuary grew high, Ezek. xlvii. 3–5, and what was before but a drop of knowledge in Christ's beginning to teach, became an unfathomable sea of knowledge in Christ's effusion of the Spirit at his ascension.

[1.] Without this ascension, his doctrine had not had a perfect confirmation. As his divine Sonship was declared in part in his resurrection, Rom. i. 4, so his doctrine met with a confirmation in that manifestation of him to be the Son of God; but as that was but the first step to a manifestation of his person, so it was but the first degree of the manifestation of his doctrine. The more complete justification of his doctrine was cleared by his elevation to heaven; it then appeared that he did (as he said himself) declare the words of God; that as his humiliation discovered him to be a man, his exaltation and the fruits of it discovered him to be a divine prophet of a greater dignity and richer influence than all that went before him. He had been unjustly charged, in the delivery of his doctrine, with the crime of blasphemy, and very few were persuaded either of the divinity of his person or the heavenliness of his doctrine. By his ascension God declared him to be a prophet sent by him, and that prophet whereof Moses spake, Acts xxi. 22; he acknowledged him to be really what he reported himself to be, one with the Father, having a perfect knowledge of the Father, one speaking the words of God, and acting according to the order of God. Had what he asserted of himself been false, he had been so far from being advanced to heaven, that he had been hurled down to the bottomless pit for his imposture. God would not by any act, much less by the conferring so great a glory, have contributed credit to a lie. But God hath decided the controversy between him and the Jews, his accusers, and cast them by, owning him in the quality of his Son, and the great prophet, whereby he had entitled himself among them. What greater testimony can there be than God's putting all power into his hands, giving him the keys of death and hell, the power of opening the seals, and slaying by the words of his mouth? Thus God recommended his doctrine, and by lifting him up to heaven, set him there as a Sun to free the world from the blackness of error, wherewith the night had filled it.

[2.] Without this the apostles could not have been furnished with gifts for the propagation of his doctrine. Those weak men could not have gone about so great a work without a mighty furniture and magazine of divine eloquence and vigorous courage; to give this was not his immediate work as Mediator, and in the economy of the divine persons pertained to the Holy Ghost. It was necessary, therefore, that he should, as high priest, enter into the holy place, and appear before God with the blood of his eternal sacrifice, that the treasures of the Spirit might be opened, and that that divine flame might issue out from thence to inspire them with abilities for so great an undertaking. This he had not had power to do, unless he had been glorified, John vii. 34, 'The Holy Ghost was not yet given, because Jesus was not yet glorified.' He could not before invest his officers with a transcendent power, because he was not mounted to a full execution of his own office. It was after this he erected the Christian church among the Gentiles as well as Jews, completed the rule of faith in the writings of the apostles, which was to endure to the end of the world. Without this glorification, he had not been the universal teacher of the mysteries of salvation, nor qualified the apostles for the propagation of his doctrine. But by this means he exercised his office, not only among the Jews, as the minister of the circumcision, but among all nations of the Gentiles, as the chief doctor and prophet of the world, by the publication of the gospel and the grace of the Spirit.

[3.] Nor could the apostles without this have had any success. They had nothing of a worldly stamp and beauty that could persuade people to an entertainment of their doctrine. They had not the wealth and grandeurs of the world to offer them, nor could allure them by earthly empires and conquests, as Mahomet did his followers. To preach a crucified God would be justly thought an extravagance and the fruits of a frenzy; but when they should hear not only of his resurrection, but the possession of a glory, from so many witnesses upon whom they could fasten nothing of distemper, an end would be put to their astonishment.* His crucifixion could not appear so irrational to them, as the news of an exaltation, whereby the ignominy of the cross was changed into the glory of a crown, would appear amazing. Since the Spirit could not come unless Christ were glorified, it was impossible that without this glorification of the Redeemer, and consequently the effusion of the Spirit, that those delegates of Christ could publish the gospel with such power, resist such violences, triumph over such oppositions; and impossible for men to have believed or regarded what they said, since their doctrines were so contrary to the common maxims of the world, which had been so long strengthened by education and custom, the strongest chains next to corrupt nature. As the ascension of Christ gave the apostles (the spectators of it) courage to publish the greatness of our Saviour with boldness, as before they had denied him with cowardice in his humiliation, so it made way for the entrance of his doctrine into the belief of the hearers, which otherwise they would have been ashamed to entertain, had it not been backed with so great an argument, and testified by such witnesses, and seconded by such miracles, against which they could have no exception. Without this, those main truths of the gospel upon which the Christian religion depended, and which are the life and soul of it, as the redemption of man, the justification of believers by the blood of his sacrifice, had wanted a ground for the manifestation of them, and all the comforts of the gospel been frustrate. Men could have had no apprehension of such things without an accomplishment of his glory. Hence it was that so often Christ assured his disciples while he was instructing them, in the time of his life, of the great works they should perform, and the success they should meet with after his departure. His doctrine had been more obscure, and lost much of its clearness, had he stayed below.

[4.] Heaven alone was a fit seat for him wherein to exercise this office. It was no more convenient for him to be placed on earth, who was to disperse his light into the understandings of men, and scatter ignorance in all parts of the world, than for the sun to have been placed on the earth for the spreading its beams into all climates of the world. An earthly seat was fit for an earthly prophet; but was it fit for him who was constituted by God, not only a prophet to the Jews, but to all the nations and tribes of mankind; whose doctrine was not to be confined to the narrow limits of Jerusalem or Judea,

* Amyraut. in Tim. p. 224.

but extend to all parts of the world?* What though the dusty earth bore his body in the days of his humiliation, while he was laying the foundation of those truths which were to sound in every quarter! Yet when he came to be installed the sole doctor and teacher of the whole world, it was not fit he should be placed in any sphere lower than that of heaven, whence he might make his voice known both to heaven and earth, to men and angels, and convey his instructions to those blessed spirits who were yet to learn more of the mysteries of divine wisdom, Eph. iii. 10, and also to the multitudes of the Gentiles, as well as to the small number of the lost sheep of the house of Israel.

(2.) Necessary it was for his priestly office. Though he was a priest by authority in the days of his humiliation, yet he was not fully installed in the perpetual exercise of this office, till his 'sitting at the right hand of God,' Ps. cx. 1, 4; and when he was declared harmless, and undefiled, and separate from sinners, though sacrificed for them, and thereupon made higher than the heavens, and by that declared to be the Son of God, then he was as his Son consecrated a 'priest for evermore,' Heb. vii. 26, 28.

[1.] He had not done the whole work of a priest had he remained upon the earth. As the legal high priest had not been a complete high priest, and fulfilled every part of his office, had he not entered into the holy of holies, so neither had Christ performed the whole work of a priest had he remained upon earth and not entered into the heavenly sanctuary, to appear or be manifested in the presence of God for us, Heb. ix. 24. It was not enough for the legal high priest to cut the throat and pour out the blood of the sacrifice in the outward tabernacle, and offer it upon the altar on the day of the annual expiation,† but he was to pass within the veil, to present the blood of the victim to the Lord, and sprinkle it towards the propitiatory, Lev. xvi., and upon his return to publish the atonement and reconciliation to the people; so that there had been no analogy between the type and antitype, if our Saviour after his oblation on earth had not in the quality of a priest passed into the heavens, as through the veil which separated the heavenly sanctuary from the outward court. It was necessary therefore that the true high priest should advance into the true sanctuary, into heaven itself (figured by that legal place), where God hath his residence among the true cherubims and angels of glory; that he should sprinkle this mercy-seat, and present before the throne that blood which he had shed upon the cross, till the time that, the number of his elect being completed, he is to return out of the sanctuary, *i. e.* descend from heaven to earth to pronounce the sentence of their general absolution, and gather them to himself in the glory of his kingdom. By his own blood he entered into the holy place, having obtained eternal redemption for us, Heb. ix. 12. This entering into the holy place with the blood of the sacrifice was the main end of the sacrifice, and a necessary act of the high priest, and appropriate to him alone. The end why it was offered in the temple was, that it might be presented in the sanctuary; so while Christ disposed himself to those sufferings which he was to undergo for the expiation of our sins, it was necessary he should be upon the earth; but after he had offered himself a sacrifice upon the cross, it was no less necessary for him to ascend in person, and carry the treasures of his blood with him, to be laid up in that repository, to be sprinkled in the heavenly places, and remain for ever as a mark in the true sanctuary, as a treasure of perpetual merit. The legal priest was also to burn incense in the holy place. By incense in Scripture is frequently meant prayer. If Christ be not then an intercessor in heaven,

* Daillé sur l'Ascension de Christ, p. 435, somewhat changed.

† Faucheur in Acts, vol. i. p 111.

there is no analogy between the type and the antitype. This intercession, a great part of his priestly office, could no more have been managed but in heaven than the oblation, the first part of his office, could have been performed anywhere but on earth. Had he therefore remained upon the earth after the shedding of his blood, he had not fully executed his office, but had performed it by halves, and that which he had performed on earth had been without strength, without performing the other in heaven; for then it was that he was made an high priest for ever after the order of Melchisedec, Heb. vi. 20 and a minister of the sanctuary, Heb. viii. 1, 2. He is hence called the high priest of our profession, Heb. iii. 1, as performing all the duties, and enjoying all the privileges really, which the legal high priest did perform and enjoy figuratively. Without this glorious translation, he could not really in his own person have carried his blood into the sanctuary, nor appeared in the presence of God for us, nor have opened heaven for those that are his followers.

[2.] Heaven only was fit to be the residence of so great a priest. As he was a priest, it was fit he should have a sanctuary; as he was the great priest, it was fit he should have the highest sanctuary; as he was the everlasting priest, it was fit he should have an everlasting sanctuary; as he was an undefiled priest, it was fit he should have an undefiled sanctuary; as he was a priest constituted and consecrated in a special manner by God, and not by man, as Aaron and his posterity were, it was fit he should have a special sanctuary, which Aaron and his posterity had not; as he was to appear in the presence of God for us, it was fit it should be in a place where God doth manifest himself in the glory of his deity. Now, no place but heaven can challenge all those qualities. It was very convenient and necessary that he who was the high priest according to the order of Melchisedec, a blessing as well as a sacrificing priest, distributing spiritual and heavenly blessings to his people, should not be seated in an orb inferior to that place whence those blessings were to receive their original, and flow down upon the world. And since he was a priest not designed for one particular nation, nor consecrated only for such a spot of land as Judea, but for the whole world, it was necessary that he should be in such a place where all may address themselves to him that stand in need of the exercise of his office, and from whence he may behold all with those compassions which are annexed to his priesthood. It was necessary also that he that made the reconciliation for men should reside with God (who had been offended, and now was reconciled) to preserve it firm and stedfast, since while the world doth last there are daily so many breaches made to forfeit it.

[3.] It was necessary for his kingly office. It was fit that he that had done so great a work, and had merited so great a crown, that was exalted to be a prince and a saviour, and had received an heavenly authority and power to give repentance and forgiveness of sins, Acts viii. 31, should also be received into heaven till the time of the restitution of all things, Acts iii. 31, till all things be restored to their due order.

[1.] It was necessary for his triumph. Indeed, for the beginning of the exercise of his prophetical charge, there was a necessity of his residence among men for the divulging some truths and counsels of his Father; and while he was to conflict with his enemies with sweat and blood, it could not well be but in the field of battle wherein the enemies were; but when he came off with victory, he could not conveniently triumph in the place of battle, or reign as a king suitably to his grandeur upon the dunghill of the earth.* It was fit he should sit in triumph at the right hand of his Father, to end

* Amyraut. in Tim. p. 213.

and complete the fruits of his victory : Ps. cx. 1, 'Sit thou at my right hand, till I make thine enemies thy footstool.' As he had not been in a capacity to reign had he continued as a subject under the dominion of death, so he could not exercise the office of a king so commendably as upon the throne of his Father. Heaven only was a palace fit for the residence of the King of kings.

[2.] It was necessary for his government. As heaven is the fountain of providence, so it was fit that the king, into whose hands God committed all judgment, the power and government of the world, should sit upon a throne in heaven; and it was not congruous that he that was made the head of principalities and powers, the governor of the angelical spirits, should have a meaner dwelling than the greatest of his subjects, and as low as the vilest of his vassals. The wisdom of God hath disposed all causes in an order superior to those effects which depend upon them ;* the heavens are above the earth, because the earth is influenced by them ; and the sun above the earth, because the earth is enlightened by it. It was no less necessary, according to the order of God's wisdom, that he who was made by God his viceroy both in heaven and earth, and had the management of all things conferred upon him, should be lodged in a place superior to those things he was to govern, from whence he might send forth his directions to all his subjects. And though he had by his death given his enemies a mortal wound, and stripped the devil of the right he had acquired by the sin of man, yet, in the order of divine wisdom, the possession he had of the world was not to be taken away, and men reduced to the sceptre of this great king, but in a way convenient to the nature of man. Those gifts, therefore, which were necessary for the reduction of him, could only be dispensed from heaven; it was therefore necessary for Christ in person to ascend thither, to give out his commission, and enable his servants with gifts, whereby to 'wound the head of his enemy,' Ps. lxviii. 18, 21. It was fit that an eternal King should have an everlasting palace; that a King constituted in a special manner by God, should have a palace not made with hands; that he who was put into the possession of all nations, Ps. ii. 8, and had a grant of all the kingdoms of the world to be his own, Rev. xi. 15, that was not to rule in a corner of the earth, and sway the sceptre in places that could be included in a map, should have his throne fixed in any part of the world but the glorious heaven. An earth defiled by that sin he hated, and an earth yet too much filled with those enemies he had conquered, was not a place convenient for the perpetual residence of so great a monarch. It was most fit also that he who was ordained the Judge of the whole world, and confirmed in that office by his being raised from the dead, Acts xvii. 31, should be taken up into that sovereign court of heaven, and come in majesty from thence to execute that charge. All the ends of his government and triumph could not have been answered without this glory; he could not have reigned in the midst of his enemies unless he had been placed above them, nor conducted his church to an happy immortality, unless he had had a possession of that heaven he was to conduct them to.

3. As this glory was necessary on the account of God, and on the account of Christ, so it was necessary on our account also,

(1.) That God's choice acceptance of his sacrifice for us might be manifested. The acceptance of it by God was in part manifested by his resurrection; but the infinite pleasure he took in it, and the fragrancy of that savour he smelt from it, had not been testified to the world had he given him only the recompence of an earthly life and glory. Indeed, his resurrection

* Daillé, vingt Serm. p. 435.

is an attestation of the truth and fulness of his satisfaction, for he rose again for our justification, Rom. iv. 24. He cannot be considered as our propitiation but in the state of his resurrection. No man is freed legally and justly from prison till he hath paid his debts; so then the resurrection of Christ is an argument that his payment was commensurate to the debt; but the glorious exaltation of Christ is an argument of the high acceptableness of it to God. Who can doubt of his satisfaction after his resurrection? and who can doubt of the infinite content God took in his obedience after he had crowned him with so immense a glory, and established him a prince and a priest for ever at his right hand? God hath not only declared himself satisfied, but satisfied with an incomparable pleasure. God made a diligent search into him, to see whether he was without spot, and perfect in his person and works: Dan. vii. 13, 'And they brought him near before him,' *i. e.* the Son of man before the Ancient of days. As persons and things are brought near to be tried and diligently inspected, so was Christ brought near to God in a judicial way, that God may pass a judgment upon him and his work; and upon a strict view he was so ravished with his obedience, that he conferred upon him a dominion, glory, kingdom, that all people, nations, and languages should serve him, an everlasting dominion, a dominion that passes not away, &c., ver. 14. Such a multitude of expressions used in this donation do signify the mighty pleasure of God in him, as if (to speak after the manner of men) God had been grieved that there was not more to confer upon him. As by the resurrection of Christ God declared himself by the title of a God of peace, Heb. xiii. 20, so in the ascension of Christ he declared himself a God of all grace to us, 1 Pet. v. 10. He declared himself reconciled to us by raising Christ from the dead, and he hath declared himself a God of all grace in calling us to an eternal glory by Christ, because the glory Christ hath is a pledge of that glory believers shall have as a fruit of God's high acceptance of him. This is the cordial Christ gives his disciples, and assures them they had reason to rejoice in the midst of their worldly calamities at his going to his Father, if they well understood it, John xiv. 28. It is indeed a clear evidence that God hath an inconceivable pleasure in him; he would not otherwise have suffered him to enter heaven, but would have thrust him back again upon the earth. In his death there is a satisfaction, and in his glory the highest testimony of it. Without a glorious entrance into heaven, his resurrection with his continuance upon earth had not been so clear a witness of God's high value of his sufferings; but now by his glorified state it must be concluded that his death was not the common fate of mankind, but highly meritorious, since God hath rewarded him with so great an honour as the government of men and angels; I say it must be concluded, not only that it was a death proportionable to what the justice of God required, but an infinite purchase of whatsoever happiness the creature wanted.

(2.) That the Spirit might have a ground to comfort us. Since the end of the Spirit's coming is to comfort us, and the principal argument whereby he comforts us is the high value of his death with God, and the acceptance he meets with in heaven, there had been little or no ground for him to build his comfort upon without the ascension of Christ to glory. How doth the Spirit demonstrate the sufficiency of Christ's righteousness? Not because he was raised, but because he goes to his Father, and is seen no more here: John xvi. 10, 'He shall convince the world of righteousness, because I go to the Father, and you see me no more.' His resurrection is the first corner stone of comfort, because it was a necessary antecedent to his glory. But had he been only raised to an earthly life, our joy had been but a twilight mixed with darkness, and the arguings of the Spirit for our cheering been somewhat disputable, and wanted much of that efficacy which now they have. This going to the Father, which includes a glory, was the spring whence the Spirit was to draw those waters of consolations he was to pour into our souls. Had Christ remained upon the earth, the Spirit had not come; but if he had, the breasts of consolation had been very lank, and little could have been drawn out by us. Some jealousies would have remained, we could not have fully answered the accusations of our sins, our own consciences would have had some racks, and we should have felt sometimes some griping doubts. If God had appeared reconciled by the raising him, yet he would not have appeared highly pleased with us without his glorious translation. We might have had some comfort in peace with him, but seen no appearance of favourable and gracious smiles in his countenance. Our Saviour lays a stress upon that of seeing him no more here, viz., in that state wherein he was before, or in a state without a glory. This, in his account, was a sufficient argument of the value of his death with God. Could we behold him here in the flesh, we might discard all our hopes of standing before God in a glorious eternity as vain imaginations; but when ye shall see me go to my Father, and maintain my interest in his favour, you may conclude that God is not only pacified, but hath lofty thoughts of grace towards you. Without this his going to the Father, the cordials of the Spirit would have wanted their due temper, and had not found any relish in our guilty consciences.

(3.) That there might be an irresistible ground of faith. If the Spirit had wanted a ground of comfort, our faith had wanted a ground of reliance. As faith respects the person of Christ, it had been subject to staggering; it could have had no assurance that he had truly the dignity of the Son of God if he had remained in the condition of a man upon the earth.* As faith respects the death of Christ, though it might have concluded an expiation of the crimes, yet not a fulness of merit to procure a complete felicity, if he had had no other sphere but the rude earth to spend his immortal life in. And less confidence still had belonged to faith as it respects the word and promise of Christ; for how could we imagine he could prepare mansions for us in heaven, if he had never stepped from the earth? or restore us to paradise, a place of bliss, that could not find the way back to that heaven from whence he said he descended to redeem us? We could not have concluded that his death had been a ransom if his word had been false; and his word had had no credit with us if he had not returned to that heaven to which he affirmed he always had a right. He could never bring us to that place to which he could not restore himself. Had he not risen, we should have thought him no higher than a mere man; nay, an impostor, and his death a punishment of his own crime. Had he not risen, we should have regarded him as no other than a conquered captive of death among the rest of mankind; and had he, after his resurrection, resided in the corrupted earth with our flesh, could we have imagined it to be the flesh of God, any more than we could have conceived it so had it remained under the power of death? His glory hath given assurance and courage to our faith, which had been very languishing, or rather nothing at all, had he stayed on earth; nor could we have had any hopes ever to have attained the happy vision of God in heaven. Had the Redeemer abode on this side that place of glory, we had been without a pledge of so great a felicity; nor could our souls have been carried out with those noble affections suitable to the extraction of them. Our love to Christ had been directed by a knowledge of him after the flesh, 1 Cor. v. 16, and therefore had mounted no higher than a carnal affection.

* Daillé, Melan. part i. p. 143, &c.

We should have had no ground for those refined and spiritual affections, and lifting our hearts to heaven, which are the ennoblement of our spiritual natures. Without this entrance into glory, there had been no foundation for the superstructure and exercise of any grace in a lively and delightful manner; and without it, and the acknowledgment of it, all falls to the ground.

But now there is a ground for all, since,

[1.] Satisfaction is declared to be full. The validity of the price is not to be scrupled, since we are assured of the weight of his glory. Shall we doubt of the sufficiency of that, after the assurance of so many jewels in his crown? What is all his glory but a return of his blood, and an approbation of the value of it for the ends for which it was shed? His appearance in heaven could not have been glorious, had not his oblation on earth been satisfactory. For our sins being in the nature of debts, Mat. vi. 12, and the justice of God in the law in the nature of a creditor, to which we are responsible, Gal. iii. 10, his death was the payment, his resurrection the acquittance, but his glory the fullest testimony that God can give that he is satisfied, and remains so. So that there is no room for any doubt of eternal redemption purchased, since his entrance into the holy place, with the blood of his sacrifice, Heb. ix. 12. His exaltation assures man that he hath appeased God.

[2.] And therefore all enemies are removed out of the way. His triumph had not been just if his victory had not been full. The law would have resisted his elevation, and stopped his way to the throne, if it had anything to object against him. This glory manifests that all the enemies which stood with drawn weapons between him and his throne are removed out of the way, the obligation against us cancelled, the devil disarmed by the taking away sin, upon which his power was founded; 'principalities and powers' spoiled of their prey, Col. ii. 14, 15; justice appeased, the law fulfilled, sin expiated, death vanquished; all those are sealed to us by his entrance into glory, and God's hanging 'the keys of death and hell' at his girdle, Rev. i. 18.

[3.] Heaven is assured. As our bond against us is evidenced to be cancelled, so God hath entered into a bond by this act towards Christ, whereby he doth acknowledge that he, as it were, owes heaven to every believer upon the account of the surety, and hath manifested his reality by beginning the payment of it in the glory of his person. For in setting Christ 'at his right hand in heavenly places,' all believers were virtually set there, Eph. ii. 6. As his resurrection assures us of the fulness of the payment of our debt, so his glory assures us of the fulness of the merit of our happiness. Had he lain in the grave, our hopes would have remained wrapped up with him, and mouldered to dust with his body; or, after his resurrection, had he remained on the earth, our hopes had aspired no higher than the place of his residence.* But when we do not only see him rising victoriously from the horrors and corruptions of the grave, but mounted into an incorruptible glory, we have reason to believe we shall, by his power, enjoy that glory we believers breathe after. For as he did not rise to live for himself, and expose his members to a perpetual captivity under death, so he hath not received his glory to reign for himself, and leave his members grovelling in the mire of the earth; but both the intention of God in conferring it, and the design of Christ in receiving it, was, that all united to him in grace might be joined with him in glory, to see and enjoy, according to their measures, the glory God hath given him, John xvii. 24. Now had Christ stayed in a miserable world, though he had not lain in a corrupting grave, we could not have concluded our debt to have been paid to divine justice, nor expected the benefits he had promised, nor upon any ground elevated our hopes, hearts, or affec-

* Faucher in Act. vol. i. p. 62.

tions to heaven; there had not been those comfortable encouragements to duty, nor those delightful motives to any acts of religion. But now his admission into glory spirits our faith, erects our hopes, expels our fears, stifles our jealousies and doubts, and fixes wings to a spiritual love, by giving us not only a demonstration of the fulness of his satisfaction, but the overflowing redundancy of his merits for our happiness, and a pledge of an eternal and glorious life.

To sum up all, and in that the whole scheme of the Christian religion and doctrine in short, let us consider, since it was the common condition of the sons of Adam to have rebelled against God, and, after that revolt, were no more able to stand in the presence of God's consuming justice than straw and stubble before the fury of a flame, there was a necessity for some other person to make way for our return by appeasing that justice which was exasperated against us. Though this person were found out, and kindly and courageously undertook, and as faithfully, and to a full content of justice, performed it in the most perfect manner, yet there could be no assurance of it without some signal testimony of the gratefulness of the person and the accomplishment of the undertaking. His continuance in the world would have nourished rather some jealousies of the imperfection of his person and passion, than assurances of their acceptation with God. His exaltation, therefore, was a necessary sign that he had fulfilled righteousness and disarmed justice, conquered death and hell, and opened the gates of heaven. Since he suffered as our surety, his glory would manifestly be conferred on him because he so suffered, and therefore it would respect our interest; and though by the efficacy of his death, had he only risen again, we had been freed from those torments that remain after death, yet had he not been glorified in heaven, we could not have been restored to the happiness of that paradise we had lost, no more than our bodies could have been delivered from the darkness of the grave, had he himself remained under the chains of death. We should have wandered about the earth without a supreme felicity, though without a smarting punishment. But by his glory we have a certain evidence that we are not only freed from the dominion of death, but made heirs of life, and have a pledge in our hands that we shall enjoy it. If we have a union with him by faith, and a communion with him in the power of his death, there is no doubt but we shall have a communion with him in the felicities of his heavenly glory; and to such a confirmation of our faith and hope was an entrance into his glory necessary. This doctrine is the highest comfort in the Christian religion; and without this, and a share in it, what comfort can we expect in the deplorable, and, I may say, stupefying dispensation we are now under?

Second thing. The nature of this glory. It was a great glory. As he was filled with the Spirit without measure above all the prophets, for the performing his mediatory function, so he was instated in a glory without stint above all the angels for the application of the fruits of his mediation; as great a glory as a creature united to the person of the Son of God was capable of receiving. As he had the Spirit without measure, so he had a glory without end. God did *super-exalt* him, as the word signifies, Philip. ii. 9, ὑπερύψωσε, as he was set at the right hand of God, which was granted to no mere creature, and had a name above every name. Christ consisted of two natures, divine and human; let us see how these were glorified.

1. His deity was glorified.

(1.) This could not properly have any addition of intrinsecal glory. To enter into glory doth suppose a temporary exclusion or absence from glory, as to be advanced supposeth some meaner state, as the term from whence that advancement is. Now, the Deity was never empty of any essential glory; nor could that be advanced, because it, being infinite, was not capable of any higher degree, but was above all alteration. The substance and properties of that nature, which always remain the same, are incapable of abasement and elevation. We may as well conclude a diminution of the essence of God, as a decrease of the essential glory of God. The divine nature cannot ascend, any more than it can descend, because of its filling all places by its immensity; so neither can it be humbled or exalted; but the person that consists of both natures may be said to descend and ascend, to be humbled and exalted, because that person which was glorious in heaven manifested himself on earth by the assumption of our nature, and ascended to manifest himself in heaven in our nature, which he had assumed on earth. The Deity then had no new glory by the entrance of Christ into heaven, as it had no essential disgrace by his humiliation on earth; for that nature is immutable and infinite, free from any change. If the divine nature might be essentially less than it was, it might wholly cease to be what it was; all diminution is a degree of destruction.

(2.) There was a manifestation of the glory of this divine nature of Christ. The divine nature, while it was wrapped up in the rags of our infirm flesh, wanted that reputation which was due to it from man; and in this respect Christ is said to 'empty himself,' as the word ἐκένωσε, which we render 'made himself of no reputation,' signifies, Philip. ii. 7. He that was sovereign became a subject, as the seed of the woman, to the law of nature, subject as an Israelite to the law of Moses, subject as a man and our surety to the penal infirmities belonging to the human nature, as weariness, hunger, thirst, death. And as the divine nature seemed to be humbled in being obscured under the veil of our flesh, so it is glorified in breaking out with most resplendent rays in the Son. As he was humbled in the form of a servant, so he was exalted in appearing in the form of God. 'In the same sense that we say Christ as God was humbled, in the same sense we may say Christ as God is glorified; but it is certain that Christ, who was equal in regard of his deity with his Father, did humble himself to the form of a servant', Philip. ii. 7, 8.* As the divine nature may be said to be humbled by suffering an eclipse, so it may be said to be glorified by emerging out of it, as the sun may in a sort be said to enter into a glory, or reassume its glory, when it scatters a dark cloud which muffled it, and strikes its warm and clear beams through the air. There is nothing here of a glory added to the sun, but a glory exerted by the sun, which before lay in obscurity, under a thick mist; and when God is said to be glorified by men, we must not conceive any addition of intrinsic glory to God, but an acknowledgment of that glory he displays in his works of creation, providence, and redemption. So the exaltation of Christ was not the conferring a new glory upon the divine nature, but the outshinings of it in the sacred vessel of his humanity, and surmounting those mists wherewith before it had been clouded. It was then a manifestation of him as the Son of God, and a discovery of that relation he had to the Father from eternity, which was not only clouded in the days of his flesh, but all the time of the Old Testament, and was not known, at least in such a measure and clearness, as in the discovery of the gospel. Therefore he prays, John xvii. 1, 'Father, glorify thy Son;' discover this prerogative of Sonship, that I am the only begotten of the Father, of the same essence with thee, and not a mere man, as the world accounts me. Therefore the resurrection of Christ, which was the first step to his glory, is called a new nativity of him as the Son of

* Jackson, vol. iii. fol. 314.

God in regard of his manifestation: Acts iii. 33, 'In that he hath raised Christ from the dead, as it is also written in the second psalm, Thou art my Son, this day have I begotten thee;' as his resurrection was a confirmation of his eternal generation, and consequently of his deity, and therefore Christ adds in his prayer, John xvii. 5, 'Glorify me with thy own self,' *i. e.* in a way of equality with thyself. As the Father did not in the time of his humiliation treat him as a son, but as a servant, as a sinner, as one he was angry with, he was exposed to the violences of men, as if he had been utterly neglected and abandoned by his Father; he desires therefore that he might have that glory he had with God before the world was, that he might be treated and declared to be the Son of God, equal to the Father in power and majesty; and that this might be manifested both in heaven and earth, in heaven to the angels, and in earth to Jews and Gentiles. And thus he 'sat down on the right hand of the Majesty on high,' as 'the brightness of the Father's glory, and the express image of his person,'* all which is not an addition of glory, but a manifestation of glory; for Christ, John xvii. 1, desires the Father to glorify himself as his Son, that he might glorify him as his Father. Now the glory Christ brought to God was not a new accession of any glory to the nature of God, but a displaying the glorious perfections of his nature to the sons of men. So the glory of Christ's deity is the springing of it out of that obscurity wherewith it was masked, and a breaking out from under the cloud of his humanity in a glorious lustre. And after he was clothed with 'a vesture dipped in blood,' his name was manifested to be 'the Word of God,' Rev. xix. 13, *i. e.* he was manifested to be the Word of God, after and upon the account of his death, and his glory was sensible as the glory of the only begotten Son of God.

(3.) There was a manifestation of the glory of his deity in and through his humanity. As it had been obscured in the humanity while he was humbled, so it breaks out in the humanity when that nature is glorified, as a candle in a dark lantern doth through the transparent horn or crystal, when the obscuring plate is drawn aside. This glory he prayed for: John xvii. 5, 'Glorify me with the glory I had with thee before the world was.' The glory he had as God before the world was, was not impaired, and therefore is not that which he here desires; his humanity was not glorified before the world was, that had no existence till it was formed in the womb of a virgin. We must therefore understand it of the glory of his deity, to be extended to his humanity, to capacitate it for those offices which were to be performed in it. He was to be the guardian of his church as Mediator, and the Judge of the world; but his humanity could not know the names of all his people he was to guide, unless informed by his divinity. As man, he is to execute judgment, John v. 27, which he could not do unless he knew the inwards of men, and viewed their thoughts; nor could his humanity do this, unless instructed by his divinity. This knowledge is not originally from the human nature, but by revelation from the divine; the government of the world, of angels, and men, could not be managed by him as the Son of man, unless his humanity were enlivened, and thoroughly influenced by the divinity as he was the Son of God; so that Christ here desires another manner of glory in regard of manifestation than was before, a derivation of that glory to his humanity. He doth not say, *Glorify me with that glory which my humanity had with thee before the world was;* but which *I*, *my divine person*, had with thee: that that glory which I had with thee from eternity, according to my divine nature, may be derived upon the human nature, to fashion it for those great ends for which it is designed. I see no reason to understand

* For so Camero refers the word *sat down* to the ἀπαύγασμα, Heb. i. 3.

it of the glory of his humanity, which he had before the world was, by the predestinating decree of God; for then there would be no peculiarity in Christ's prayer to himself, for every assured believer may pray the same, Lord, give me that glory which I had with thee before the world was, viz., in thy decree. But no such expression fell from the lips of Moses, David, Paul, or any of those most triumphant in the assurances of everlasting happiness. It must be some expression of glory peculiar to the Son of God, and therefore a manifestation of the glory of the deity in his humanity in another manner than before, since that person that was the Son of God was now also the Son of man. Now this was no addition of glory to his deity, but a new mode of manifesting that glory which the human nature had before the world was, which never was exerted in such a manner before. It was a real addition of glory to his humanity, but a new way, or manner of manifestation of his divinity.

2. His humanity was really and intrinsecally glorified. There was a glory conferred upon his humanity by the grace of union with the second person in the blessed trinity; this was at the first conception in the womb of the blessed virgin. A greater glory than this can no creature have, to be 'called the Son of God,' Luke i. 35. There was also a glory bestowed upon it by the communication of unmatchable perfections to his soul, a fulness of the Spirit, a spotless sanctification, and an infallible knowledge of God, and of those truths he was to reveal. But now his humanity did ascend up where his person was before, and our nature was carried up to sit with him in the same court, where he had been glorious before in his deity. 'He ascended far above the highest heavens,' Eph. iv. 10, into that place where God represents himself in the greatest majesty to angels and glorified spirits. He descended to assume our nature, he ascended to glorify our nature. The humanity was taken into perpetual society and conjunction with the deity at the first assumption of it; but by his exaltation the eternal subsistence of it in the deity was confirmed; and by the translating it to heaven, assurance was given that it should never be laid aside, but be for ever preserved in that marriage knot with the divinity. It was so enlarged and spiritualised, as to be a convenient habitation for the fulness of his deity to reside in, and exert its proper operations: Col. ii. 9, 'In him dwells all the fulness of the Godhead bodily;' not dwelling as if imprisoned, but to break forth in all its glories and graces; not formerly dwelling in it, but now dwells. There is a way of the presence of the deity with the humanity above all those manners of the presence of God with angels and men; it dwells in it, and acts in it, as a soul in its own body it is clothed with, so that the humanity is the humanity of the Son of God, and heightened to be the sacred vessel of the fulness of the Godhead. That nature wherein the person of the Son of God was 'made lower than the angels, was crowned with glory and honour,' Heb. ii. 7. That nature wherein he was raised, was set 'at God's right hand in heavenly places,' Eph. i. 20, and in that nature, as well as in the divine, the person of the Son of God had a sovereign authority granted to him. Thus the humanity was glorified above all the reach of any human understanding. The glory of the saints is not to be fathomed by the conceptions of men, much less the glory of Christ, the exemplar of all the glory they are to have.

The humanity of Christ, consisting of two principal parts, body and soul; both were glorified.

(1.) His body. As his sufferings were in order to his glory, so the part wherein he suffered was to enjoy a glory. 'Enter into his glory,' *i. e.* a glory due to him for his sufferings, therefore due to every part wherein he suffered.

This being an essential part of the human nature, is not laid aside; the knot between this and his deity remains for ever indissoluble; it remains still as to its substance, though enriched with new qualities, being stripped of the mutability and mortality to which it was subject on earth. As in his descent the deity was emptied of the manifestation of its glory, so in his exaltation, his body of its natural infirmities. The image of the first Adam, except the substance, was razed out, and was actually framed in the second Adam; there was not a destruction of the body, but a transfiguration of it, and his body is no more changed in regard of the substance by its translation into heaven, than it was in his transfiguration on the mount; nor changed in its lineaments, but in its qualities: Mat. xvii. 2, 'His face did shine as the sun;' the substance remained, but changed into a glorious appearance; he had the same lineaments in Tabor as he had at the foot of the mount. Peter could not else have distinguished him from Moses and Elias. Had he not been stripped of his infirmities, he had still, even in heaven, been in some sort lower than the angels, which he was designed to be only for a time, Heb. ii. 7, βραχύ τι, 'a little while,' a short space, in the time of his humiliation.

[1.] His body is therefore of a spiritual nature, in opposition to infirm flesh. Flesh in Scripture is sometimes taken so: Ps. lxxviii. 39, 'He remembered that they were but flesh,' *i. e.* infirm and perishing flesh. The natural bodies of the saints shall, at the resurrection, be changed into spiritual, 1 Cor. xv. 44; much more is the body of Christ in glory, since it is the pattern according to which the body of the saints shall be copied and fashioned, Philip. iii. 21. His state in the world is called 'the day of his flesh,' Heb. v. 7; his state above is a spiritual state, as being free from the infirmities and clogs of the flesh. Flesh he hath still, but more suited to that heaven which was his original; an heavenly, no longer an earthly, image, 1 Cor. xv. 48, 49; like turf or wood, that loses its drossy and foggy qualities, when heightened into a pure flame, or minerals heightened into spirits. His body was spiritual after his resurrection, it could pass in a short moment from one place to another, Luke xxiv. 31. As his body rose, so it ascended, and remains a spiritual body, or as one calls it, organized light.

[2.] It is therefore bright and glorious. If the righteous are to 'shine as the sun in the kingdom of their Father,' Mat. xiii. 43, the head of the righteous shines with a splendour above that of the sun, for he hath a glory upon his body, not only from the glory of his soul (as the saints shall have), but from the glory of his divinity in conjunction with it. The glory of his divinity redounds upon his humanity, like a beam of the sun, that conveys a dazzling brightness to a piece of crystal. There was an interruption of this glory while he was in the world, though the human nature then was united with the divine. But this interruption was necessary for those acts which he was to perform in our stead, for the satisfaction of God and the discharge of his office. Had the glory of the divinity broke out upon his body, he had not been capable of suffering. What mortal could have stood before him, much less laid hands on him? What mortal durst have accounted him a blasphemer, an impostor, and have exercised any violence against him, had his divinity so fashioned his humanity? But now it is, as it was in his transfiguration, Mat. xvii. 2; the glory he had then *in transitu* wrought an alteration not only in his body, but in his garments, which could not be of the most splendid, as not suiting his present state of humiliation, yet they 'became shining, exceeding white as snow, so as no fuller upon earth can white them,' Mark ix. 3; much more must that firm and perpetual glory in heaven have the same influence upon his refined body, that hath cast off those corruptible qualities which hung upon it on earth, and doth more excel in glory that body he had on earth, than the glory of the sun surpasseth that of a glow-worm. It is such a glory as would dazzle mortals to behold it; for if his glory upon mount Tabor cast Peter into an ecstasy, what effect would his glory upon his throne work upon a moral nature? Whence it follows that there must be a mighty change of the bodies of the glorified saints, to capacitate them for the beholding this glory of Christ, the intent views whereof are part of their happiness, John xvii. 24.

[3.] His body is immortal. His body now lives, and shall live for evermore: Rev. i. 18, 'I am he that lives, and was dead; and behold, I am alive for evermore, Amen;' which is confirmed by him with a solemn *Amen*. A corruptible body is not fit to be admitted to sit down upon the throne of the Father in heaven. The promise that secured to him, in the state of his humiliation, a speedy resurrection from the grave, and an impossibility of seeing corruption, Ps. xvi. 10, is as valid as ever. That body that was not dissolved to dust by the power of the grave, cannot sink into nothing in the glories of heaven. The union of the Godhead to it preserved it here, and the perpetual confirmation of that union preserves it for ever above. His body lives an indissoluble life, death shall never more lay hands on it; he hath no more sufferings to endure, or satisfactions to make to the demands of the law. Men and devils cannot touch him in his person, though they do in his mystical body. He is above the reach of all temptations, all wrath from his Father, all violences from men, and therefore his glorious body is not in such a state as to be ground between the teeth of communicants, or eaten by rats and mice, or in any part of it dropped upon the ground, and buried again in the dust or mire, as the bread in the supper may. If that were really the body of Christ, the body of Christ would be then so treated, as consisted not with the glory it is now possessed of.

(2.) As his body, so his soul, the principal part of the humanity, was glorified. That suffered in agonies and sorrows: 'His soul was sorrowful, even to the death,' Mat. xxvi. 38. That also enters into glory; and indeed the body cannot be rightly glorified without the glory of the soul; for the glory of the body is but the reflection of the glory of the soul in any creature.

[1.] He hath an unspeakable joy in his soul. Ps. xvi. 11, 'Thou wilt shew me the path of life: in thy presence is fulness of joy; at thy right hand are pleasures for evermore.' It is Christ's triumphing in the consideration of his exaltation, and taking pleasure in the fruits of his sufferings; 'thou wilt shew me the paths of life.' God hath now opened the way to paradise, which was stopped up by a flaming sword, and made the path plain by admitting into heaven the head of the believing world. This is a part of the joy of the soul of Christ; he hath now a fulness of joy, a satisfying delight instead of an overwhelming sorrow; a 'fulness of joy,' not only some sparks and drops, as he had now and then in his debased condition; and that in the presence of his Father. His soul is fed and nourished with a perpetual vision of God, in whose face he beholds no more frowns, no more designs of treating him as a servant, but such smiles that shall give a perpetual succession of joy to him, and fill his soul with fresh and pure flames. Pleasures they are, pleasantness in comparison whereof the greatest joys in this life are anguish and horrors. His soul hath joys without mixture, pleasures without number, a fulness without want, a constancy without interruption, and a perpetuity without end. And having a fulness of joy, he hath a fulness of knowledge in his soul; he increased in wisdom in his soul, as he did in stature, and that as really in the one as he did in the other, Luke ii. 40; his humanity had not the knowledge of all things in his humiliation, his soul had one thing revealed to it after another. But in his exaltation his soul is endowed with all the treasures of wisdom and knowledge. He knows now the time of judgment, since he is constituted the Judge of the world, whereof his resurrection was an assurance to men, and no less an assurance to himself, Acts xvii. 31, since by his resurrection, the first step of his exaltation, God judged him a righteous person, and acknowledged him his Son with power, that had redeemed a world, whereby there was an evidence also that by him he would judge the world. Among other infirmities of his nature, his soul hath put off that of ignorance. Nothing that is a treasure of knowledge is concealed from it; he hath the knowledge of God's decrees concerning his people: Rev. i. 1, God gave the revelation of all to him; no other person opens the book, or is acquainted with the counsel of it, Rev. v. 5–7. This knowledge he hath in his humanity, as he is the lion of the tribe of Judah, and the root of David. This revelation is to him as Mediator, in his human nature, distinct from that knowledge he had as God. As his mediatory glory is distinct from that essential glory he had as God, so there is a revealed knowledge to him, distinct from that knowledge he had as God. There was a necessity that Christ, in his human nature, should understand the secrets of God, since he was in that nature to be the executor of the counsels of God; and this is another part of the glory of his soul.

(3.) His person was glorified. His divine nature being glorified in a manifestation, and a new manner of manifestation, and his human nature being glorified by an accession of new qualities to it, his person then was glorified. As his person was the prime subject of humiliation in taking upon him the form a servant, so it was the prime subject of exaltation and glory. His person was the *subjectum quod*, and his human nature the *subjectum quo*. In regard of his person he is glorified, as in regard of his person he was humbled; the same person 'that was rich became poor,' 2 Cor. viii. 9. He that was rich and he that was poor was one and the same person. Howsoever riches and poverty were distinct conditions, and divinity and humanity were distinct natures, yet they were the conditions and they were the natures of one and the same person, who is both rich and poor in regard of different states, as well as immortal and mortal, existing from eternity and born in time in regard of different natures, eternal as God and born as man, above all suffering and violence as God, exposed to suffering and violence as man. The person that was crucified was the Lord of glory, 1 Cor. ii. 8; the person that was crucified and suffered entered into glory; it was the person of Christ therefore wherein this glorious exaltation did terminate. As the deity was not emptied, nor could be, but obscured in the assuming our flesh and investing himself in the form of a servant for the performance of those mediatory acts in his humiliation which were necessary for our redemption, so the deity could not be exalted but by displaying itself, and discharging that disguise of infirmities wherewith it was clouded. Nor could the exaltation of his human nature, simply considered, be for the happiness and comfort of his people, for as man barely considered he could not be the king of angels and governor of the church; he could not, as man barely considered, direct the angels in their needful messages, or relieve the church in her great distresses; for the humanity was neither omniscient nor omnipotent, nor could be. It is impossible humanity can become a deity, and a creature inherit the incommunicable perfections of the Creator; but as the deity is in conjunction with the humanity, and doth make use of the humanity, and act in and by it, he is capable of performing those things which were necessary, as Lord of the world and head of the church. The actions Christ doth perform, as sitting at the right hand of God, are the acts of him as man; but the principle of those acts is his divine nature as he is God. The glorious exaltation of Christ is therefore the exaltation of his person, for those ends which were necessary for the good of the believing world.

(4.) This glory which Christ entered into was a mediatory glory. The glory Christ was advanced to was not the essential glory of God, for this he always possessed; this was communicated to him in the communication of the essence, and inseparable from him. As being God, he had all the prerogatives of God; but it was a mediatory glory conferred upon his person, as the first-born of every creature; such a glory as the humanity, so dignified by the divine nature's assumption of it, was capable of. The humanity being a creature, was not capable of a divine and uncreated glory. The glory Christ hath as God is the same with the glory of the Father, but the glory Christ hath as mediator is peculiar to him as a person consisting of a divine and a human nature; therefore it is in the text called *his glory*, in a way of peculiarity belonging to him as a sufferer; for the divine nature was not capable of an addition of glory, nor the human nature capable of the infinite perfections of the divine. In regard of his essential glory, he was the Son begotten; in regard of his mediatory glory, he was the heir appointed, Heb. i. 2. He is appointed heir in order after his sufferings, as he was appointed mediator in order to his sufferings, Heb. iii. 2. He was mediator by a voluntary designation, so he was heir by a voluntary donation. His glory was given to him upon condition of suffering, and conferred upon him after his suffering; but he was from eternity the Lord of glory, and Son of God by a natural generation. The one belonged to him by birth, the mediatory by office; the one is natural to his person, the other is the reward of his sufferings: Philip. ii. 8, 9, 'Wherefore God hath exalted him,' viz., because of his obedience to death. In the essential glory, he is one with the Father; in his mediatory glory, he is lower than the Father, as being his deputy and substitute. His essential glory is absolute, his mediatory glory is delegated, judgment is committed to him, John v. 22. The essential glory is altogether free, and hath no obligation upon it; the mediatory glory hath a charge annexed to it (for he is 'ascended far above the heavens, that he may fill all things,' Ephes. iv. 10), an office of priesthood to intercede, and a royal office to gather and govern those that are given to him by his Father. His essential glory he would have enjoyed, if he had never undertaken to be our ransom; yet without his sufferings for us, he had never had the glorious title of the Redeemer of the world. As God had been essentially glorious in himself, if he had never created a world; but he had not then been so manifest under the title of Creator. This glory was, nevertheless, properly neither divine nor human; not divine, because, considered as man [he] was a creature, and a divine glory is incommunicable to any creature; considered as God, there could be no addition of glory to him.* This is said to be given him as that which he had not before; not a human glory, for as man only he was below it, and was not a subject capable of it. A mere man was unable to govern and judge the world. To be head of the church, and judge of the universe, are titles that belong to God, and none else; but it was a mediatory glory proper to the person of Christ, and both natures as joined by the grace of union for the work of mediation. Now though Christ, in regard of his divine nature, was 'equal with his Father,' Philip. ii. 6, yet in the state of mediator and surety for man, his Father was 'greater than he,' John xiv. 28; and in this state he was capable of a gift and glory from the Father, as from one that was superior to him in that condition; as it hath been recorded in history, that a king equal, nay, superior, to another prince, hath put himself under the ensigns of that prince inferior to him, and received his pay; as he puts himself in such a

* Rivet in Ps. cx. p. 300, col. 1 changed.

military state, he is inferior to that prince he serves as his general. And what military honour may be conferred upon him for his valour and service, is an honour distinct from that royal dignity he had before as a sovereign in his own territories. So is this name given to Christ 'above every name,' Philip. ii. 9, *i. e.* a glory surpassing that of all creatures, the potentates of the earth, or seraphims of heaven, which was a distinct glory from that which he had, as one with the Father, before his incarnation and passion, and had possessed if he had never suffered. But this glory mentioned by the apostle was given him upon his sufferings. It was not therefore a name in regard of his eternal generation, as some interpret it;* for the particle *wherefore*, in the beginning of ver. 9, puts a par to any such interpretation, it referring this glory as a consequent upon his humiliation to the death of the cross. It was therefore a mediatory glory, whereby the authority of God was conferred upon him, not absolutely and formally, as though he were then made God, but as to the exercise of it as mediator in that human nature which he had so obediently subjected to the cross for the glory of the Father and the good of the creature.

(5.) This mediatory glory consisted in a power over all creatures; for it was such a 'name as was above every name, so that at the name of Jesus every knee shall bow, and that every tongue shall confess that Jesus Christ is Lord, to the glory of God the Father,' Philip. ii. 10, 11. He had the same power committed to him which the Father hath; his throne is the highest, being the same with that whereon the Father sat, Rev. iii. 21, a throne of government and dominion. His commission is extensive, a power as large as the confines of heaven and earth: Mat. xxviii. 18, 'All power is given me both in heaven and earth. A power over hell is also put into the patent: Rev. i. 18, 'And have the keys of hell and death.' His right to this was conditionally conferred upon him at the first striking of the agreement between the Father and himself, Isa. liii. 10–12. He promised upon his oblation for sin, to 'divide him a portion with the great,' and he should 'divide the spoil with the strong.' This was acknowledged due to him upon his resurrection, which, being an owning of the validity of his performance, was an acknowledgment of the justice of his claim; and to this that in Mat. xxviii. 18, refers, 'All power is given to me.' But the solemn investiture was not given him till his ascension. God put the sceptre in his hands when he used that form of words, Ps. cx. 1, 'Sit thou at my right hand till I make thy enemies thy footstool;' for in the apostle's sense, to sit at the right hand of God and to reign, are one and the same; for what is 'sitting at the right hand of God till his enemies be made his footstool,' is 'reigning till all enemies be put under his feet,' 1 Cor. xv. 25. At his resurrection he was stripped of his servile garb, at his ascension he put on his royal robes, at his session on the right hand of God he was crowned, and began the exercise of his royal dignity.

[1.] He hath all power in heaven. Power in the treasures of heaven, power over the inhabitants of heaven.

(1.) Power in the treasures of heaven, of sending the Comforter: John xv. 26, 'The Comforter whom I will send,' which was sent in his name, John xiv. 26. His power was first in heaven, then in earth; his power on earth could not have been manifested without a power first in heaven; by his power in heaven he gathered his people on earth. When God had given us the greatest gift, his Son, for the honour of his mercy, he gives the greatest gift next to him, viz., that of the Spirit, for the honour of his Son's mediation. As Christ, in the evangelic economy, acted for the honour of the

* Ambrose.

Father, so doth the Spirit in the same economy for the honour of Christ: John xvi. 14, 'He shall glorify me.' He is therefore called the Spirit of Christ. He is also said to have 'the seven spirits of God,' Rev. iii. 1. *Seven* is a scriptural number of perfection; he hath the full power of the gifts and graces of the Spirit to bestow upon the church, and fill his mystical body with. By this it was evident that as a mediator he had a mighty power with God, since the first fruits of his exaltation was the effusion of a comforter for us, a second advocate on earth. This being the fruit of his mediation, and given to him as mediator, was a full confirmation not only of the virtue of his death, but the powerful continuance of it still in heaven, not only that it was accepted for us, but that the virtues and fruits of it should be perpetually distributed to us. This power of the Spirit was given to Christ immediately upon his ascension, as the purchase of his sufferings, and the reward of his conquests: Ps. lxviii. 18, 'Thou hast ascended on high, thou hast led captivity captive, thou hast received gifts for men.' By his solemn investiture, he was settled in a power over the treasures of God, and gave out that in abundance which before was communicated in some few drops; the heavens are opened, and a golden shower comes down upon the world. In a sensible and apparent manner, he received this Spirit before for himself, for he had it without measure, he received it before, when he entered upon his office, to fit him for his mediation, he now receives this power as mediator upon his ascension, and as a steward for his people, to distribute this rich revenue of God for the greatening of his church; upon his ascension he received it to give out to those he had left behind him in the world, Ps. lxviii. 18. 'Received gifts for men,' Eph. iv. 8; it was then the donative of the Father to Christ, that it might be Christ's donative to us.

By the way, we may take notice of another argument for the necessity of the exaltation of Christ in heaven, since the Spirit being an heavenly gift, it was not fit he should be sent by a person that was not possessed of heaven; and it being the purchase of the mediator, and to be sent in his name, it was convenient the mediator should be in heaven, and have a more glorious residence than in the earth, before the mission of so great a gift.

(2.) Power over the inhabitants of heaven. In his incarnation, in the days of his flesh, he was lower than the angels; in his ascension, he is made higher by the shoulders than the loftiest of them, and this in regard of his office as mediator, for as God he had an essential superiority above them before; the superiority over them as he was God he had by nature, the superiority over them after his humiliation he had upon the execution of his mediatory office. The angels that had their residence in heaven were to bow to him, yield obedience to him, as he was God-man, for so he was exalted as *Jesus*, as one that had 'suffered death,' Philip. ii. 9. They were to give him an adoration which pertained to God, and, according to this divine order, they pay him actual adorations before his throne as 'the Lamb of God,' Rev. v. 11–13, and they are put in subjection to him as their head, not only for a time but for ever, in this world and that which is to come, Eph. i. 21, to order, direct, and commission them for the ends of his mediation, according to that compassionate sense he hath in his glory, of the infirmities and distresses of his people. He is Lord of all of them to this purpose; one hath not the privilege to stand before God, and another subject to run upon his errands in the world, but all are subjected to the sceptre of Christ, to be used by him at his pleasure in his service. And in this respect he received all power, first in heaven, then in earth; 'things in heaven' are first gathered, after that 'things on earth,' Eph. i. 10. The holy angels were all subjected to him upon his exaltation by one entire donation, the promise of making him their head was fully accomplished; whereas there is to be a revolution of time to the end of the world, before things in earth shall be gathered to him, before all his elect shall submit to his sceptre, and his enemies be debased to his footstool. But upon his advancement, as there was an actual donation of them by his Father, so there was an entire submission of them in one body to him. The whole corporation of those blessed spirits waited upon him in his entrance into heaven to his coronation, according to the will of their God, and his God, who had given them a precept to 'worship him,' Ps. lxviii. 17, 18, and that in a military posture as their general, noted by the word *chariots*, which were used chiefly in war and warlike triumphs.

[2.] Power in earth over all creatures: 'There is nothing left that is not put under him,' Heb. ii. 8. All things are given him by God, to be in subjection either voluntary or constrained. He is Lord of all the creatures as God-man, because all the creatures were made for man; and Christ being the Lord of all mankind, is also the Lord of all the creatures that were made for the use and benefit of man.* He is therefore 'the first-born of every creature,' Col. i. 15; the right of primogeniture is conferred upon him, and so he became Lord of all; as Adam, in regard of his dominion over all earthly creatures, might be said to be the first-born of them, though himself is created after them. His power upon earth consisteth in this, that all the worship of God is to be done in his name; our supplications for the supply of our wants, our acknowledgments for the receipt of his blessings, must be presented 'in his name,' John xvi. 26, Eph. v. 20. He is made a priest to offer our sacrifices and incense of prayers; he is the channel through which God conveys all the marks of his kindness to us; he hath power as a prince 'to give repentance' as the means, and 'remission of sin' as the privilege of those that are given to him, Acts v. 31. He hath a name above every name in the earth; no person was ever so famous, none ever was adored by so many worshippers, none worshipped with so much fervency, none ever had so many lives sacrificed for his glory, and acknowledgment of his mediation and person. His glory hath extended one time or other over the whole world. It is a power that hath given check to the power of kings, and silenced the reason of philosophers; it hath put to flight the armies of hell, and been celebrated by the songs of angels; no name was ever so glorious, no power ever so great.

The third thing I should come to is,

III. The end of his glory. As his sufferings were necessary for us, so was his glory; as it was needful he should die to redeem us, so it was needful he should enter into glory to bless us. There are two great things accrue to us by Christ, *acquisition* of redemption, and *application* of redemption; the one is wrought by his death, the other by his life; the one by his elevation on the cross, the other by his advancement on his throne. It is there he hears us, and from thence he purifies us; had not Christ entered into glory, we had wanted the application of the fruits of his death, and so his incarnation and passion had been fruitless.

I shall name only two, one consequent upon the other.

1. The sending the Spirit. Indeed, since there could be no grace and sanctification without the Spirit, we must suppose that the Spirit was given before the coming of Christ. In the old world, the Spirit did strive with men, and the Spirit of God was in and upon the prophets, and the holy men in the Old Testament; but it was communicated in weaker measures, in

* Sabund. Tit. 263, 550.

scanty drops, not in that abundance till the instalment of Christ; it was then shed abundantly through Jesus Christ, Titus iii. 6, whence our Saviour is said, after his ascension, not to drop upon persons, but to 'fill all things,' viz., by his Spirit, Eph. iv. 10. The Spirit was in the world before, as light was upon the face of the creation the three first days, but not so sparkling and darting out full beams till the fourth day of the creation of the world. The full effusion of the Holy Ghost was reserved for the time and honour of Christ. He was communicated to the Jews anciently for working miracles and uttering prophecies; but the Jews tell us, that after the death of Zechariah and Malachi, the Spirit of God departed from Israel, and went up. So that afterwards miracles were very rare among them, and therefore, when the disciples at Ephesus, of the Jewish race, Acts ix. 2, said they had not heard whether there were any Holy Ghost or no, it is not to be understood that they had not heard that there was such a person, for that they believed, but they knew not whether the Holy Ghost, which departed away after the death of Malachi, was restored again in the gift of prophecy and miracles. The golden shower of the Spirit for grace and gifts was not to be rained down upon the world in so full and sensible a manner till the coronation of Christ, as only at some public solemnities of princes the conduits use to run with wine. Hence Christ flatly tells his disciples, that it was expedient for him to go, that the Comforter might come, which was not to come till after his departure; and particularly by his mission: John xvi. 7, 'Nevertheless, I tell you the truth, it is expedient for you that I go away; for if I go not away, the Comforter will not come unto you; but if I depart, I will send him to you;' and this he avers as a certain truth. Indeed, Christ received the Spirit for himself at the first inauguration and entrance into the exercise of his office at his baptism, but not fully to convey it to his people, but upon his coronation, and full investiture with all power. Then he received 'the promise of the Spirit,' Acts ii. 33, *i. e.* he obtained the full execution of the promise in the full effusion of the Holy Ghost, when he had entered into the sanctuary not made with hands. The purchase of it was a fruit of his death, but the mission of it was consequent upon his exaltation; by his death, in satisfying the justice of God, he removed that bar which had been upon those treasures, and broke the seal from the fountain, that the waters of divine grace might be poured out upon men; by his death he merited it, by his glory he possessed it, and then made the effusion of it, and that for the good of his people.* 'It is expedient for you:' it was not only for his honour that he went to heaven, but for our advantage, that our faith might be perfected, our hope elevated, and every grace strengthened and refined. Now the Spirit was sent to this end, to carry on the work of Christ in the world, and to apply the redemption he had wrought. He was to 'bring things to remembrance, whatsoever Christ had said to them,' John xiv. 26; he was 'not to speak of himself,' John xvi. 13. He was not to be the author of a new doctrine in the church, but to impress upon men what Christ had taught, and what he had wrought by his passion. He is therefore called 'the Spirit of truth,' *i. e.* teaching and clearing up to the minds of men, that truth which Christ had taught and confirmed by his blood, and to raise the superstructure upon that foundation Christ had already laid. He was to declare only what he heard, John xvi. 13, 14; to act the part of a minister to Christ, as Christ had acted the part of a minister to his Father; to glorify Christ, *i. e.* to manifest the fulness of his merit, and the benefits of his purchase; for he was to receive of Christ's, *i. e.* the things of Christ, his truth and grace, and manifest them to their souls, and imprint upon them the comfort of both. This Spirit being

* Pont. part v. Medit. xvii. p. 324.

then a fruit of the glory of Christ, is an abiding Spirit for those ends for which he was first sent, John xiv. 16. The permanency of the Spirit is as durable as his glory. Christ must be degraded from his exaltation, before the Spirit shall cease from performing the acts of a comforter and advocate on earth.

2. Consequent upon this was the communication of gifts for the propagation and preservation of the gospel. Christ was to raise a gospel church among the Gentiles, to apply the fruits of his death. This he could not do without receiving gifts to bestow upon men. These gifts were not to be received by him, till his finishing his work; and this work could not be declared to be completely finished without his advancement to the right hand of his Father, Ps. lxviii. 17. He received them with one hand, and distributed them with the other; he handed them to the world, as they were conveyed to him by his Father in his glory. 'He ascended up far above all heavens, that he might fill all things,' Eph. iv. 10; all the world with the knowledge of himself, all kinds of men with gifts; officers with abilities; private Christians with graces. His glory is the foundation of all Christianity; by those gifts of the Spirit to men, he rescues men from a spiritual death, and plants them as living trees in the garden of God. By those we find our hearts linked to him in love, panting after him with desires, and aspiring to the happiness of heaven, where he is. All the channels through which he pours the waters of life upon the world, were cut and framed by his hands. The Spirit is called the seven spirits in the hand of Christ, and joined with the seven stars, Rev. iii. 1, as being distributed by him in the seven states and periods of the church, to the end of the world.

There might be more named, but they may come in in the Use, to which we may now proceed.

IV. *Use.*

I. Of information.

1. How groundless is the doctrine of transubstantiation. 'And to enter into his glory,' after his suffering. Had there been such a thing as his daily descent to earth in the sacrifice of the mass, it had been a very proper season to have intimated such a notion to his disciples in this discourse; he might have had a very fair occasion to say, Wonder not at the sufferings of your Redeemer; he ought not only to suffer those things, but you shall see him every day a sufferer in the sacramental wafer. As often as a priest shall be the consecrator, you shall crush his body between your teeth, and see him suffer a thousand times, not by the hands of violent men, but between the teeth, and in the stomachs of impure creatures. No such thing is here spoken of; it is 'enter into his glory.' He was to be a sufferer but once, and then be received into glory; his glory was to follow his sufferings. By this doctrine his daily sufferings would follow his glory, would be together with his glory. He would be a sufferer on earth, while he were glorified in heaven; and while he sits at the right hand of his Father, his body would be corrupted in the foul stomachs of some men, as bad as devils, at one and the same time. Is this a glory his human body entered into, to be frequently degraded to a lodging in an impure stomach, among the dregs of the last nourishment which was taken in, to pass from thence to the draught, and be condemned to the dungeon of putrefying jakes? Would not this be worse than his sufferings on the cross, which were but temporary, and more loathsome and ignominious than all the reproaches he suffered on earth? This is a dealing with the Mediator as the heathens did with God, in changing his glory into a corruptible image. This is inconsistent with that glory he

is entered into after his sufferings; there is a repugnancy between his sitting upon a throne, and being subject to the accidents of material things on earth. As Christ was silent in any such doctrine, so were the angels at his ascension (Acts i. 10, 11, 'This same Jesus, which is taken up from you into heaven, shall so come in like manner as you have seen him taken up into heaven'), when they had a fit occasion to mention it; especially when they mention his coming so again for the comfort of the disciples that were spectators of it. They mention, not a coming every day in body and soul in the wafer, into their mouths, but only of a visible and glorious coming again in the same manner as he ascended. As he hath entered into glory, so the heavens receive him, and contain him, till the time of the restitution of all things. His body is too glorious to pass into the mouths and stomachs of man, and undergo those various changes with their nourishments.

2. How greatly is our nature dignified! He is entered into glory with our nature, and hath lifted up our flesh above the heavens, and hath in this glorified our very dust. In that nature wherein he suffered, in the same nature he hath ascended into the most glorious part of the creation of God, above the highest heavens. The humanity of Christ, and in that our nature, was not taken up for a time, but for ever. It was debased for a short space: Heb. ii. 7, 'Thou madest him a little lower than the angels;' or, 'Thou hast made him lower than the angels for a short time.' But he is advanced for ever: 'Thou hast crowned him with glory and honour.' The Redeemer is always to wear our nature; it is never to be out of fashion with him. How glorious is this for us, that the Son of God should take our nature, our dusty humanity, all our infirmities except sinful, to clear our natures from all penal infirmities, to transform our clay (if I may so say) into virgin wax, and wear it as a pledge that the members of his body shall at length be brought to him! Our nature now hath, by Christ's assumption of it, an affinity with the divine, which that of the glorious angels hath not in such a manner. Our nature, not theirs, was assumed, and remains united to the person of the Son of God. It is advanced to the right hand of God, sits upon the throne with God. The angelical nature is below the throne, stands about it, but is not advanced to sit upon it. Our nature hath not only now a dominion over the beasts, as at the first creation, but a principality above and over the angels, Eph. i. 21. By creation we were made a little lower than the angels; by this union of the divine, and the exaltation of the human nature of the Son of God, our nature is mounted above theirs. It was then made as low as earth, it is now advanced as high as heaven; yea, above the heavens. Our nature was before at the foot of the world, the world is now at the foot of our nature.

3. How pleasing to God is the redemption of man! Christ's glorious advancement speaks a fragrancy in his satisfaction to God, as well as a fulness of merit for men. There was a good pleasure in his mission, there was a sweet savour in his passion; for since he is crowned with glory upon a throne, that so lately suffered ignominiously upon a cross, what can the consequence be but that his obedience to death was highly agreeable to the mind of God, and afforded him a ravishing delight! For without his receiving an infinite content by it, it is not possible to imagine he should bestow so glorious a recompence for it. We have his word for a testimony of his delight in the service he designed: Isa. xlii. 1, 'Behold my servant, in whom my soul delights.' We have his deed for an evidence of the pleasure he took in the service he performed, by putting the government into the hands of the Mediator, and giving him power over the angels, and setting him at his right hand as his Son. He hath testified what a ravishing sense he hath of the

redemption he wrought, and of that death whereby he completed it. He took more pleasure in him as the Redeemer than in all the angels in heaven. The apostle challengeth all to produce any one angel to whom God spake so magnificent a word, 'Sit thou at my right hand, till I make thy enemies thy footstool,' Heb. i. 13. 'To which of the angels said he so at any time?' He is proclaimed to the angels as an object of worship as he is brought into the world, Heb. i. 6, as he is the heir appointed as well as he is the heir begotten; as 'he hath by inheritance obtained a more excellent name than they.' He hath now a glorious empire over the angels, as Mediator in his humanity, which he had before in his deity, as God blessed for ever. He enters into his glory as Adam into the possession of a world, with a dominion over all the works of God. Had not every part of his work in the world administered a mighty pleasure to God, there had not been a hand reached out to have lifted him to glory; but he went up 'with a shout,' Ps. xlvii. 5,—with the applause of God and acclamations of angels. No shouting had been in heaven, no chariot sent from thence to fetch him, no attribute of God had bid him welcome, had any been disgraced by him. There had been a gloominess and disorder instead of a jubilee, nor could he ever have sat down upon the throne of the divine holiness, had not the holiness of God, the most estimable perfection of his nature, been highly glorified by him.

4. How terrible should the consideration of the glory of Christ be to the unregenerate and unbelievers! The greatness of God's pleasure in the redemption performed by our Saviour, testified by this his exaltation, argues a wrath as terrible against those that lightly esteem him. What greater provocation than to set our judgment against the judgment of God, and to think him not worth glory by our disesteem, who hath deservedly entered into a glory above all creatures. It is far worse to despise a Saviour in his robes than to crucify him in his rags. An affront is more criminal to a prince upon his throne, than when he is disguised like a subject and masked in the clothes of his servant. Christ is entered into glory after his sufferings; all that are his enemies must enter into misery after their prosperity. As there is the greatest contrariety in their affections, so there will be the greatest distance in their conditions. Such cannot be with him where he is in glory, because they are contrary to him. What prince upon his throne and in his majesty would admit into his presence base and unworthy criminals, but to punish them, not to cherish them? Impure persons are not fit to stand before a prince's throne. The sight of Christ in glory is the happiness of believers, not to be communicated to the wicked. Those that will not bow to him must bend to him; if they will not bend to him in his glory, they must fall under his wrath, and be parts of his conquest in his anger, if they will not surrender to him upon his summons from his throne of grace. What a folly is it to kick against that person, before whom, one time or other, all knees must bow, either voluntarily or by constraint, and render him an active or a passive honour! Philip. ii. 10, 11. Since he had a power joined with his glory, that power will as much be exercised against his enemies as for his friends. As the one are to sit upon his throne, so the other are to be made his footstool; and whosoever will not be ruled by his golden sceptre, shall be crushed by his iron rod.

Use 2 is of comfort. The great ground of almost all discomfort is a wrong and imperfect notion of the death, and especially of the exaltation, of Christ, and his sitting at the right hand of God. Sorrow filled the disciples' hearts, because they apprehended not the reason and ends of Christ's departure from them, John xvi. 5, 6. Had they considered whither he was to go, and for what, they would not have been dejected.

(1.) By his glory the justification of believers is secured. As all believers did make a satisfaction to God in the death of Christ, so they are all discharged by God in the resurrection and ascension of Christ. Christ having a full discharge by his entering into glory as a common person, all those whose sins he bore have a fundamental discharge in that security of his person from any more suffering. As he bore the sins of many as a common person in the offering himself, and thereby satisfied for their guilt, so he receives an absolution as a common Head for all those whose guilt he bore in his sufferings. The glory he entered into secures him from any further lying under the burden of our sins, or enduring any more the penalties of the law for them; for as he suffered, so he was acquitted, and entered into glory as our surety and representative: Heb. ix. 27, 'As it is appointed unto all men once to die, and after that the judgment, so Christ was once offered for the sins of many; and unto them that look for him, shall he appear without sin unto salvation.' As judgment is appointed for all men as well as death, and they receive their final and irreversible judgment after death, so Christ, by his exaltation, is judged perfect, fully answering the will and ends of God; and shall not appear any more as a sacrifice in a weak and mangled body, but in a glorious body, as a manifestation of his justification, fitted for the comfort of those that look for him. Upon the score of this judgment passed upon him by God in our behalf, he is to appear at length for salvation. If he suffered for us, his sufferings are imputed to us; and if his exaltation be an approbation of his sufferings for us, then the validity of his sufferings for our justification is acknowledged by God's receiving him into glory; for as in his death all believers were virtually crucified, so in his justification (whereof his exaltation is an assurance) all believers have a fundamental justification. It was for the purging, not his own but our sins, that he 'sat down at the right hand of the throne of the Majesty on high,' Heb. i. 3; and therefore he sat down as justified for us. The reason of his advancement was the expiation performed by him. As long therefore as the glory of Christ holds, the reason of that glory holds, *i.e.* the stability of his expiation, and consequently the security of our justification upon faith. The glory Christ is dignified with adds no value to his sufferings, but declares the value of them; as the stamp on bullion declares it to be of such a current value, but adds no intrinsic value to what it had before. In Christ's death, the nature of his sacrifice is declared; in his resurrection, the validity and perfection of his sacrifice is manifested; in his glorious ascension, the everlasting virtue of that sacrifice is testified. All three, eyed by faith in conjunction, secure our justification, and render a perpetual repose to the conscience. His throne being for ever and ever, the virtue of his sacrifice, upon the account of which he was placed in that throne, is incorruptible; and therefore there is no room for dejection and jealousies of the sufficiency of the ransom, after so illustrious a recompence received by him. Had he not indeed entered into glory, we had but a weak assurance of a discharge from the Judge.

(2.) Hence there is a perpetual bar against the charge our sins and Satan may bring against us. As Christ suffered for us, so he entered into glory for us. He suffered in the notion of a redeemer, and he is ascended up into heaven under the notion of an advocate. He sits not there as a useless spectator, but as an industrious and powerful intercessor. The end of his being with the Father is to be an advocate: 1 John ii. 1, 'We have an advocate with the Father;' and the office of an advocate is to plead the cause of a client against a false and unjust suit. He drew up the answer upon the cross to the bill sin had put in against us, and in his glory he pleads and makes good that answer. He merited on the cross, and improves that merit on his throne, and diffuseth his righteousness to shame the accusations of sin. It was through the blood of the covenant he rose; it was through and with the blood of the covenant he entered into the holy place, to carry the merit of his death as a standing monument into heaven. He fixes the sight of it always in the eye of God, and the savour of it is in his nostrils, so that as the world, after the savour of Noah's sacrifice, should no more sink under the deluge, so a believer in Christ should no more groan under the curses of the law, though he may smart in this world under the correction of a Father. We have great enemies: the devil tempts us, and corruptions haunt us, and both accuse us. To whom do they present their accusations, but to that Majesty, at whose right hand the Redeemer hath his residence? Whence must the vengeance they call for ensue, but from that Majesty, upon whose throne a suffering Saviour sits in triumph to answer the charge, and stop the revenge? Since he suffered to tear the indictment, hath he entered into glory to have it pieced together again and renewed? As he bowed down his head upon the cross to expiate our sins, so he hath lifted it up upon the throne to obviate any charge they can bring against us. This is a mighty comfort to a good and clear conscience in the midst of infirmities, that Christ is ascended into heaven, and is on the right hand of God, angels, authorities, and powers, evil ones as well as good, being made subject to him; evil ones by force, and good ones voluntarily; and therefore secures those from any charge of evil angels that are baptized into his death, and have 'the stipulation of a good conscience towards God,' which is the apostle's reasoning, 1 Peter iii. 21, 22.

(3.) The destruction of sin in a perfect sanctification is hereby assured, since his glory is a pledge of the glory of believers. It is an earnest also of all the preparations necessary to the enjoyment of that glory, but a perfect holiness is the only highway to happiness. A Redeemer in glory will at length 'present to himself a glorious church,' Eph. v. 27; glorious without spot, smooth without wrinkles, sound, without blemish, like to himself. The resurrection of Christ, the beginning of his exaltation, is the foundation of the sanctification of every believer. The power which raised him, and set him in heaven, was an earnest of the power that was to be exerted to raise and work in those that were to be his members, and fix them in the like condition, Eph. i. 19, 20. Christ being risen and exalted for their justification, was an assurance that the same power should be employed for doing all works necessary in a justified person. As in his death they were crucified with him, and by virtue of his resurrection raised from their spiritual death, so by virtue of his exaltation they shall at last cast off their grave-clothes, and, like Elijah, be wholly separated from a dusty mantle. All that are chosen by God shall pass into a conformity to the image of his Son, Rom. viii. 29. What did Christ enter into glory for, and receive a power, but to destroy the strength of that in the heart, the guilt whereof he expiated by his blood, that as he appeased the anger of God and vindicated the honour of the law by removing the guilt, he might fully content the holiness of God by cleansing away the filth? As he had a body prepared him to accomplish the one, so he hath a glory conferred upon him to perfect the other, that as there is no guilt shall be left to provoke the justice of God, so there shall be no defilement left to offend his holiness. The first-fruits of this glory therefore was the mission of the Holy Ghost, whose proper title is a 'Spirit of holiness,' in regard of his operation as well as his nature, and whose proper work is to quicken the soul to a newness of life, and mortify by his grace the enemies of our nature. He is not entered into glory to be unfaithful in his office, unmindful of his honour, negligent of improving the virtue of his blood in purging the souls that need it and desire it. No doubt but *Father, sanctify them through thy truth*, sounds as loud from his lips upon his illustrious throne as it did upon earth, when he was approaching towards the confines of it, John xvii. 17. He did not utter those words upon the borders of his kingdom, to forget them when he was instated in it. What he prayed for in his humiliation, he hath power to act in his exaltation; and therefore, since his desires for the sanctification of his people were so strong then, his pursuit of those desires, and his diligence to obtain them, will not languish now in his present state. His peremptory desire, John xvii. 24, that all his people might be with him, implies a desire for the perfection of that grace which may fit them to be with him.

(4.) An assurance from hence of an holy assistance in, and an honourable success of, all afflictions and temptations. He entered into glory, but after his suffering, and therefore went not into glory without a sense of his sufferings. He entered into glory in the same relation as he suffered: he was a sufferer for us, and therefore ascended into heaven for us. He hath therefore a sense of what sufferings he endured for us, as well as of what glory he enjoys for us. The sense he bears in him still is therefore for our sakes. It is that human nature wherein the expiation was made on earth that is now crowned with glory in heaven; that human nature, with all the compassions inherent in it, with the same affections wherewith he endured the cross and despised the shame, with the same earnestness to relieve us as he had to die for us; with the same desire to supply our wants as he had to redeem our persons. He forgets not in his glory what he was in his humiliation, nor is unmindful of them in their misery whom he intends to bring to glory. He remembers his own sufferings, and for what he suffered, and how he hath left a suffering people behind him. He cannot mark out a mansion in heaven for any one remaining upon earth, but he remembers what condition he left them in, and what present misery attends them. To that end he went to heaven to prepare a place, and order the mansions for reception, John xiv. 2. His head is not more gloriously crowned than his heart is gloriously compassionate. His passion was temporary, but his compassions are as durable as his glory. While he left the infirmities of his body behind him, he took his pitying nature with him to wear upon his throne: he is 'touched with a feeling of our infirmities,' Heb. iv. 15. Indeed, he cannot but be touched with them, because before his glorious entrance he felt them. To think there is a glorified head in heaven, is a refreshment to every suffering member on earth; and such a glorified head that can as soon forget his own glory as any part of his suffering body. And as to temptation from the devil, this glory gives an assurance of a complete victory over him at last. That devil that was repulsed by him in the wilderness, wounded by him on the cross, chained by him at his resurrection, and triumphed over at his ascension, cannot expect to prevail. He that could not overpower our Head, while he was covered with the infirmities of the flesh, cannot master him, since all power is delivered to him in heaven and earth; and while the head is in glory, it will protect and conduct the members. He that wanted not wisdom and strength in the form of a servant to defeat him, doth not want it upon the throne of a conqueror to outwit and crush him. He can, and will, in due season, as well silence the storms of hell, as in the days of his infirm flesh he did the waves of the sea and the winds of the air. The members cannot be drowned while the head is above water.

(5.) An assurance of the making good all the promises of the covenant accrues from hence. If he suffered death to confirm them, he will not enjoy his glory but to perform them. 'The sure mercies of David' were established at his resurrection, and at his ascension put into his hands to be distributed by him; by those (though his resurrection is only named as being the beginning of his exaltation) God assures us that he shall die no more, but live to dispense those blessings he hath purchased, and accomplish those covenant promises in his glory, which he sealed by his blood, which are sure mercies, declared sure by his seal, and by his possession. The end of his exaltation is not cross, but pursuant to the end of his passion. It is upon the account of his being a 'faithful witness,' that he is the 'prince of the kings of the earth,' Rev. i. 5. It is a strong argument that he will be exact in his glorious condition to honour the truth of God in the performance of his promises, since he hath been so exact in the ignominious part of his work, to remove that which barred the way to the accomplishment of them, viz., satisfying that justice which protected the covenant of works, that mercy might act by a covenant of grace towards men.

(6.) Hence there is an assurance of the resurrection of our bodies; he began to enter into glory when he was raised, and his resurrection was in order to his further glorification. He was exalted to bring death, among the rest of his enemies, under his feet, and therefore his entrance into glory completes the conquest of it, 1 Cor. xv. 25, 26. It is not so much an enemy to his person now, since he hath surmounted it, but an enemy to his mystical body, and therefore is to be conquered in it. As Adam in his fall was the spring of death to all that descend from him, so Christ in his advancement is the fountain of life to all that believe in him. Hence is he called 'a quickening Spirit,' 1 Cor. xv. 45, so that he hath the same efficacy to give life, as Adam had to transmit death to his posterity, ver. 20–22. As it was not only the soul of Christ, but the body, was exalted, so our bodies shall be raised, since they are sanctified by Christ as well as our souls. He redeemed not one part of us, but our persons, which consist both of body and soul. There is no ground to imagine that when the head is raised, the members should always remain crumbled to dust, and covered with grave-clothes. He rose as our head, otherwise we could not be said by the apostle to 'rise with him,' Col. ii. 12. The glorious resurrection of Christ, indeed, is not the meritorious cause of our resurrection (for all the merit pertains to his humiliation), but the seal and earnest and infallible argument of it. He did not only rise for himself, but for his members, and their justification, Rom. iv. 25, and therefore for their resurrection; for there is no reason death, the punishment, should remain, if guilt, the meritorious cause of it, be removed. He rose for our justification declaratively, *i.e.* his resurrection was a declaration of our fundamental justification, because justice was thereby declared to be satisfied, which would else have shut us in the grave, and locked the chains of death for ever upon us. It is by this, the first step of his entrance into glory, we have an assurance that the graves shall open, bodies stand up, and death be swallowed up in victory.

(7.) Hence ariseth an assurance of a perfect glorification of every believer. The heavens receive him *till*, and therefore *in order to*, 'the restitution of all things,' Acts iii. 21, the full restoration of all things into due order, and therefore a full freedom of the regenerate man from sin and misery. As the apostle argues in the case of the resurrection, 'if Christ be risen, we shall rise,' 1 Cor. xv. 13; so it may upon the same reason be concluded, that if Christ entered into glory, believers shall enter into glory; for as from the fulness of his grace we receive grace for grace, so from the fulness of his glory we shall receive glory for glory; and the reason is, because he entered into glory as the head, to take livery and seizin of it for every one that belongs to him. He entered as a forerunner, to prepare a place for those that were to follow him, and was crowned with glory as he is the Captain of salvation, Heb. ii. 9; so that this glory was not possessed by him merely for himself (for he was glorious in his deity before), but to communicate to our nature which he bore in his exaltation. As immortality was given to Adam, not only for himself, but to derive to his posterity, had he persisted in a state of innocence; so the second Adam is clothed with a glorious immortality, as the communicative principle to all believers. As God, in creating Adam the root of mankind, did virtually create us all, so in raising and glorifying Christ, the root of spiritual generation, he did virtually raise and glorify all that were his seed, though their actual appearances in the world, either as men or believers, were afterwards. As the resurrection of Christ was an acquittance of the principal debtors in their surety, so the advancement of Christ was the glorification of his seed in the root. When the head is crowned with a triumphant laurel, the whole body partakes of the honour of the head; and a whole kingdom has a share in a new succession of honour to the prince. As those that believe in Christ shall sit with him upon his throne, Rev. iii. 21, so they shall be crowned with his glory; not that they shall possess the same glory that Christ hath (for his personal glory as the Son of God, and his mediatory glory as the head of the church, are incommunicable, it hath an authority to govern joined with it, which the highest believer is uncapable of), but they shall partake of his glory according to their capacity, which he signifies by his desire and will: John xvii. 24, 'That they may be with him where he is, and behold his glory;' not only *with him* where he is, for so in a sense devils are, because, as God, he is everywhere, but in a fellowship and communion with him in glory. He is exalted as our head, whereby we have an assurance upon faith of being glorified with him. Had he stayed upon earth, we could have had no higher hopes than of an earthly felicity, but his advancement to heaven is a pledge that his members shall mount to the same place, and follow their Captain; in which sense his people are said to 'sit together with him,' Eph. ii. 6. And herein is the difference between the translation of Enoch into heaven, the rapture of Elias in a fiery chariot, and the ascension of Christ: they were taken as single persons, he as a common person. Those translations might give men occasion to aspire to the same felicity, and some hopes to attain it upon an holy life, but no assurance to enjoy it upon faith, as the ascension of Christ affords to his members. And further, the glory of Christ seems not to be complete till the glorification of his members; his absolute will is not perfectly contented, till his desire of having his people with him be satisfied, John xvii. 24. The departed saints are happy, yet they have their desires as well as fruitions, they long for the full perfection of that part of the family which is upon earth. Christ himself is happy in his glory, yet the same desires he had upon earth to see his believing people with him in glory, very probably do mount up in his soul in heaven; and though he fills all in all, and hath himself a fulness of the beatific vision, yet there is the fulness of the body mystical, which he still wants, and still desires. The church, which is his body, is called 'his fulness,' Eph. i. 23. It is then his glory is in a meridian height, when he 'comes to be glorified in all his saints' about him, 2 Thes. i. 10. The elevation then of the Head, is a pledge of the advancement of believers in their persons, and a transporting them from this vale of misery to the heavenly sanctuary. His death opened heaven, and his exaltation prepares a mansion in it; his death purchased the right, and his glory assures the possession.

Use 3. Of exhortation.

Meditate upon the glory of Christ. Without a due and frequent reflection upon it, we can never have a spirit of thankfulness for our great redemption, because we cannot else have sound impressions of the magnificent grace of God in Christ. It is the least we can do, to give him a room in our thoughts, who hath been a forerunner in glory, to make room for us in an happy world.* As the ancient Israelites linked their devotion to the temple and ark at Jerusalem, the visible sign God had given them of his presence, ought we not also to fix our eyes and hearts on the holy place which contains our ark, the body of the Lord Jesus? The meditation on this glory will keep us in acts of faith on him, obedience to him, 'lively hope' of enjoying blessedness by him, 1 Peter i. 21. If we did believe him dignified with power at the right hand of his Father, it would be the strongest motive to encourage and quicken our obedience, and fill us with hopes of being with him, since he is gone up in triumph as our head; it would make us highly bless God for the glory of Christ, since it is the day of our triumph, and the assurance of our liberty.

(1.) It will establish our faith. We shall esteem Christ fit to be relied upon, and never question that righteousness, which hath so great an advancement to bear witness to the sufficiency of it. Since his obedience to death was to precede the possession of his glory, that being now conferred, evidenceth his obedience to be unblemished. It gives us also a prospect of that glory which shall follow our sufferings for him, which is very necessary for the support and perfection of our faith.

(2.) It will inspire us not only with a patience, but a courage, in suffering for the gospel. By this the apostle encourageth Timothy to endure hardness: 2 Tim. ii. 8, 'Remember that Jesus Christ, of the seed of David, was raised from the dead.' The elevation of Christ is a full confirmation of the gospel, and all the doctrines contained therein. Who can faint under sufferings for that, that seriously reflects, and sees the ignominy of the cross turned into the honour of a crown? If his humiliation was succeeded by an exaltation, the members may expect the same methods God used to the head. What shame can it be to confess, yea, and die, for one that is so highly advanced, especially when, in that advancement, we have a communion with him? A conformity to him in suffering, will issue in an honour in the same place. If he entered as a forerunner, then all that are to follow him must go the same way, to mount to a like honour.

(3.) It will encourage us in prayer. From this topic Christ himself raised the disciples' hopes of speeding in their petitions: John xiv. 12, 13, 'Because I go to the Father, whatsoever you ask in my name, that will I do;' for so some join the words. He was glorified as a priest, not only because he was one, but that he might be in a better capacity to exercise the remaining part of his office. The perpetuity of his priesthood is a great part of his glory; and it is a part of this office to receive and present the prayers of his people, Rev. viii. 3. How cheerfully may we come to him, who is entered into the holy of holies for us, if we had sensible apprehensions of his present state! A dull frame is neither fit for that God that hath glorified Christ, nor fit for that Christ that is glorified by him.

(4.) It would form us to obedience. Since the humanity is in authority next to the deity, it would engage our obedience to him, to whom the angels are subject. The angels, in beholding his glory, eye him to receive his commands; and we, in meditation on it, should be framed to the same posture. Christ, by his death, acquired over us a right of lordship, and hath laid upon us the strongest obligation to serve him. He made himself

* Daillé vingt serm. p. 443.

a sacrifice, that we might perform a service to him: Rom. xiv. 9, 'He both died, and rose, and revived, that he might be Lord both of the dead and living.' By his reviving to a new state and condition of life, his right to our obedience is strengthened. There is no creature exempt from his authority, and therefore no creature can be exempt from obedience to him. Who would not be loyal to him who hath already received a power to protect them, and a glory to reward them?

(5.) It would alienate our affections from the world, and pitch them upon heaven. The thoughts of his glory would put our low and sordid souls to the blush, and shame our base and unworthy affections, so unsuitable to the glory of our head. If we looked upon Christ in heaven, our 'conversation' would be more there, Philip. iii. 20, 21; our hearts would 'seek' more 'the things which are above,' Col. iii. 1; we should loathe everything where we do not find him, and think on that heaven where only we can fully enjoy him. It would make us have heavenly pantings after the glory of another world, and disjoint our affections from the mud and dirt of this. This would elevate our hearts from the cross to the throne, from the grave to his glory, from his winding-sheet to his robes. If we think on him mounted to heaven, why should we have affections grovelling upon the earth? It is not fit our hearts should be where Christ would not vouchsafe to reside himself after his work was done. If he would have had our souls tied to the earth, he would have made earth his habitation; but going up to the higher world, he taught us that we should follow him in heart, till he fetched our souls and bodies thither to be with him in person.

(6.) It would quicken our desires to be with Christ. How did the apostle long to be a stranger to the body, that he might be in the arms of his triumphant Lord! Philip. i. 23. How did Jacob ardently desire to see Joseph, when he heard he was not only living, but in honour in Egypt! And should not we, upon the meditation of this glory, be enflamed with a longing to behold it, since we have the prayer of Christ himself to encourage our belief that it shall be so? What spouse would not desire to be with her husband in that glory she hears he is in? What loving member hath not an appetite to be joined to the head? There is a natural appetite in the several parts of some animals, as serpents, &c., to join themselves together again. No nature so strongly desirous to join the several parts, as the same spirit of glory in Christ, and of grace in his members, is to join head and members together. The thoughts of his glory would blow up desires for this conjunction, that we may be free from that sin which hinders his full communications to us, and by pure crystal glasses receive the reflections of his glory upon us.

(7.) It would encourage those at a distance from him to come to him, and believe in him. What need we fear, since he is entered into glory, and sat down upon a throne of grace? If our sins are great, shall we despair, if we do believe in him, and endeavour to obey him? This is not only to set light by his blood, but to think him unworthy of the glory he is possessed of, in imagining any guilt so great that it cannot be expiated, or any stain so deep that it cannot be purified by him. A nation should run to him because he is glorified, Isa. lv. 5. The most condescending affections that ever he discovered, the most gracious invitations that ever he made, were at those times when he had a sense of this glory in a particular manner, to shew his intention in his possessing it. When he spake of all things delivered to him by his Father, an invitation of men to come unto him is the use he makes of it, Mat. xi. 27, 28. If this be the use he makes of his glory to invite us, it should be the use we should make of the thoughts of it to accept his proffer. Well, then, let us be frequent in the believing reviews of it. When Elisha fixed his eyes upon his master, Elijah, ascending into heaven, he had a double portion of his spirit. If we would exercise our understandings by faith on the ascension and glory of the Redeemer, and our hearts accompany him in his sitting down upon the throne of his Father, we might receive from him fuller showers, be revived with more fresh and vigorous communications of the Spirit; for thus he bestows grace and gifts upon men.

A DISCOURSE OF CHRIST'S INTERCESSION.

My little children, these things I write unto you, that ye sin not. If any man sin, we have an advocate with the Father, Jesus Christ the righteous.—1 JOHN II. 1.

THE apostle having, in the latter verses of the former chapter, spoken of the extensiveness of pardon, ver. 7, 9, subjoins, ver. 8, 10, that yet the relics of sin do remain in God's people. But though all sin that was pardoned, was pardoned upon the account of the blood of Christ, which had a property to cleanse from all sin, and that confession of sin was a means to attain this forgiveness purchased by our Saviour's blood, yet men might suck in the poisonous doctrine of licentiousness, believing that upon their confession they should presently have forgiveness, though they walked on in the ways of their own hearts. And, on the other side, many good men might be dejected at the consideration of the relics of sin in them, which the apostle asserts, 1 John i. 8, 10, that no man was free from in this life. In this verse, therefore, the apostle prevents those two mistakes, which men might infer from the former doctrine, that we may not presume by the news of grace, nor despond by a reflection on our sin.

I. Presumption, on the one hand, in these words, 'My little children, these things write I unto you, that you sin not.' Though I have told you that forgiveness of sin is to be had upon confession, yet the intent of my writing is not to encourage a voluntary commission.

II. Dejection and despair, in these words, 'If any man sin, we have an advocate with the Father.' If you do commit sin, you must not be so much cast down, as if the door of mercy were clapped against you; no, there is an agent above to keep it open for every one that repents and believes. Here, then, the apostle treats of the remedy God had provided for the sins of believers, viz., the advocacy of Christ, who having laid the foundation of our redemption in the satisfaction made to God by his blood, resides in heaven as an advocate to plead it on our behalf. This, saith one,* is the sum and scope of the whole gospel; he that believes this can never despair; he that believes it not, is ignorant of Christ, though he hath the whole doctrine of the gospel in his memory. The word Παράκλητος signifies an *advocate, comforter*, or *exhorter;* it is only in this place used of Christ, but of the Spirit it is used, John xiv. 16, John xvi. 7, and in both places rendered

* Ferus *in loc.*

Comforter. And παράκλησις, a word of affinity to this from the same root, is rendered, 1 Thes. ii. 3, *exhortation.* Some* tell us, that because the advocates among the Romans and Greeks were the most eloquent orators, therefore the Jews commonly called the most eminent doctors among them paracletes. The word is used by the Jews,† who derived it from the Greeks, for one that intercedes with a prince, either to introduce or restore a person to his favour. The Syriac uses the same word פרקליטא, derived from the Greek word, though it seems to have some affinity with the word פרק, which signifies to redeem or deliver. The word is used to express an advocate by another author,‡ where he tells us, that it is necessary for him that would be consecrated to the Father of the world, to make use of his Son, the most perfect advocate, both for the remission of our sins, and the communication of happiness to us; where the word παράκλητος cannot be taken for a comforter, but an advocate or solicitor, because the Son of God procures the not remembering of sins, as well as the supplying of us with all good. And the same author, in another place, ascribes the purging of sin to the λόγος θεοῦ, a term whereby Christ is signified in Scripture. § The same word which, when serving to express the Holy Ghost, is translated *comforter*, is here, when used of Christ, translated *advocate.* The Spirit is a persuasive advocate for God among men, as Christ is an eloquent advocate by the rhetoric of his wounds with God for men. Christ is both an advocate and a comforter. He owns himself a comforter, as well as the Spirit: John xiv. 16, 'I will pray the Father, and he shall give you *another* Comforter,' implying that he was a comforter as well as the Spirit. He is a comforter of man in the name of God, and advocate with God in the behalf of man.

Let us consider the words distinctly; *we*, we apostles, we believers.

1. *Not only we apostles.* The intercession of Christ is not so narrowed. He sits not in heaven only to plead the cause of twelve men; he doth indeed manage their concern; and if they which are specially commissioned by him, and are to judge the world, need him in this relation, much more do others.

2. But *we believers.* It is the same *we* he speaks of in the first chapter; *we* that have our sins pardoned, *we* that have fellowship with God, *we*, as distinguished from all the world: ver. 2, 'Who is a propitiation for our sins, and not for ours only, but for the sins of the whole world;' where the *we* (the apostle speaks of) that have an interest in this advocate, are differenced from the world. His propitiation belongs in some sort to the world, his intercession to his church, to those that are children new begotten by the Spirit. Upon the cross as a man he prayed for his murderers; but in his mediatory prayer, John xvii. 9, he prays 'not for the world,' but those given him out of it.

3. *We in particular.* Every one who hath the like precious faith hath the like powerful advocate; he means the children he writes to, and every one of them. It had not been any preservative against dejection, had not this advocate belonged to them, and every one of them. 'If any man sin,' let him be what he will, rich or poor, high or low, one as well as another belongs to this advocate. Every believer is his client; he makes intercession for them 'that come unto God by him,' Heb. vii. 25, and therefore for every one of those comers.

We have, not *had*, as if it were only a thing past; nor *shall have*, as if it were a thing to come, and expected, but *have*, ἔχομεν, in the present tense, which notes duration and a continued act. We *have* an advocate, *i. e.* we

* Mede, Fragment. Sacra, p. 104.
† Camero. p. 179.
‡ Philo Judæ, vitâ Mosis.
§ Critica, p. 158, Christus, λόγος.

constantly have; we have him as long as his life endures. And another apostle tell us, 'he ever lives to make intercession.' He is at present an advocate, always an advocate; and in particular, for every one that comes to God by him; and for every one of them, he is an advocate as long as he lives, which is for ever; we have him not to seek, but we have him this instant in the court, with the Judge, before the tribunal where we are to be tried.

An advocate. It is a metaphor taken from the Romans and Greeks. The proper office of an advocate is to defend the innocency of an accused person against his adversary.* In that notion doth the apostle take it here; he mentions Christ as an advocate in the cause of sin, which is a charge of the law. An advocate stands in opposition to an accuser, and his work is in opposition to the charge of the accuser. Satan is the accuser, sin the charge. Christ stands by to answer the accusation, and wipe off the charge by way of plea, as the office of an advocate is to do.

Advocate. It is not *advocates.* It seems John was ignorant of the intercession of saints and angels. This was a doctrine unknown in the primitive time. John knew but one, but the Romanists have made a new discovery of many more. Multitudes of saints and angels in this office for them; and they never canonise a saint but they give him his commission for an advocate, as if they mistrusted themselves since their apostasy, or feared the affection or the skill of him the primitive Christians trusted their cause to. It had been as easy a matter for the apostle to have wrote *advocates* as *advocate;* it had been but the change of a letter or two, and the cause had been carried. This apostle, to whose care Christ bequeathed the blessed virgin when he was upon the cross, would not have waived her right had there been a just claim for her. We find them urging the distinction of mediators of *redemption* and mediators of *intercession;* they acknowledge the sole honour of the first to belong to Christ, but link colleagues with him in the second. The Holy Ghost here nulls any title but his to either, since the same person who is called our *Advocate* in the text is called our *Propitiation* in the next verse. As there is but one Redeemer, so there is but one Intercessor; and the right of his intercessory power flows from the sufficiency of his propitiatory passion. The intercession of this one advocate, Jesus Christ, brought all the glorified saints to heaven; and he can by the same office secure every believer to the end of the world, without needing the interposition of any that he hath introduced before them. He is not yet tired in his office, nor are the multitude of his clients too numerous for his memory to carry, so that he should need to turn any of them over to weaker heads.

With the Father. As the first person in order, and the conservator of the rights of the Deity, not only with God, where God is, but with God as the object of his intercession, and with God as a Father. 'With the Father.'

(1.) Not with an enemy. Little hopes then that he should succeed in his suit. An enemy may lay aside his anger, and he may retain it. The pressing an enemy with importunities many times makes his fury seven times hotter. But it is with the Father, one reconciled to us by the price of the Redeemer's blood. No, nor with a judge, a term as affrighting as that of a father is refreshing. Thus Christ phrased it before his departure: John xiv. 16, 'I will pray the Father;' not I will pray the Judge. The apostle puts it in the same term Christ had done before him.

(2.) It is not said with *his Father.* It is no mean advantage for the son of an offended prince to espouse the suit of a rebel. The affection of the father might encourage the solicitation of the son; but this had not been a

* Tertullian, Apolog. cap. ii. p. 23.

sufficient cordial. The relation of a son might make him acceptable to his father for himself, but not for the criminal. Christ might have been dear to God in the place of a Son, but we might have still been hateful to him upon the account of our rebellions.

(3.) Nor is it said, with *your Father*. Had God been only our Father, and an angry Father, and standing in no such relation to the advocate, we might have had reason to hang the wing. The title of a father is often without the bowels of a father.

(4.) But with *the Father*, a father both to the advocate and client. To the advocate, by an unspeakable generation; to the client, by an evangelical creation; a Father in all respects, not only by general creation, but special adoption and spiritual regeneration; one of paternal tenderness as well as title, and possessing the compassions as well as the relation of a father. *The Father* respects both. As Christ ascended to God as his Father and our Father, John xx. 17, so he intercedes with him as standing in such a capacity both to him and us. Christ treats not with him as a Judge only, but as a Father. As a Judge, God's justice was satisfied by the death of Christ; but the end of his advocacy is upon the account of this satisfaction, to excite the paternal bowels of God towards his people. The object of the oblation was God as a judge or governor; the object of intercession is God as a Father, an advocate with the Father. The first was a payment to justice, and the other is the solicitation of mercy. This title of Father assures us of the success of his intercession.

Jesus Christ the righteous. Now he specifies this advocate, together with his necessary qualification. The words righteous and righteousness, both in the Hebrew and Greek (*Δίκαιος, Δικαιοσύνη*; צדיק, צדקה), are sometimes taken for mercy and charitableness. The words following may favour the interpretation of righteous in this sense, for it was the compassion of Christ that moved him to be our propitiation, and his charitable temper is not diminished by the things that he suffered; but I would rather take *δικαιος* in the proper sense, for *just*. Mercy without righteousness in the world is but a foolish pity, and may support a world of unrighteousness. The honesty and righteousness of an advocate upon earth is of more value and efficacy for his client with a just judge than all his compassion. In this sense of holy or righteous doth Peter use the word: Acts iii. 14, 'You have denied the Holy One and the Just,' where *just* is opposite to an unrighteous murderer; and 1 Peter iii. 18, 'Christ also hath once suffered for sin, the just for the unjust,' where the righteousness of the surety is opposed to the unrighteousness of the criminal for whom he suffered. This is the comfort, that he is as righteous for an advocate as the Father is for a judge, that he is as holy as we are unholy. Our sin rendered us hateful, but the righteousness of the advocate renders him such as it became him to be for us, whose advocate he is, Heb. vii. 26.

He may be said to be righteous;—

(1.) In regard of his admission to this office. He was righteously settled in it. Every man cannot thrust himself into a court to be an advocate in another's cause; it is not enough to be entertained by the client, but there must be a legal admission to that station in the court. Christ was legally admitted into this office; he had God's order for it: Ps. ii. 8, 'Ask of me.'

(2.) In regard of the ground of his admission, which was his loving righteousness: Heb. i. 9, 'Thou hast loved righteousness,' &c., 'therefore God, even thy God;' thy God and thy Father, whom thou didst serve, and rely upon in the office of mediation, 'hath anointed thee,' or inaugurated thee in the chief office of trust 'above thy fellows.' Unction was a solemn investiture of the high priests among the Jews in that honour and function. This anointing of Christ to the perpetual office of high priest (whereof this of his intercession is a considerable part, and the top-stone) was upon the account of the vindicating the rights of God, the honour of his law by his death. He loved righteousness above his fellows, and therefore is advanced to the highest office above his fellows. He is such an one who hath made a complete satisfaction, and hath upon that account been entertained by God, and settled 'an high priest for ever, after the order of Melchisedec.' He was anointed as being most holy in finishing transgression, making reconciliation for iniquity, and bringing in everlasting righteousness,' Dan. ix. 24. His holiness, manifested in all these, preceded his unction to that unchangeable priesthood which is exercised in heaven solely in his intercession, Heb. vii. 24, 25, 28.

(3.) In regard of his person. No exception against his person or his carriage, to weaken any motion he should make. The known unrighteousness of an earthly advocate is rather a ruin than support to the client's cause managed by him. Christ is righteous, therefore the Father cannot be jealous of his intruding upon his honour, or presenting any unbecoming suit to him; and because righteous, therefore fit to be trusted by us with our concerns. He can neither wrong the Father nor his people; righteous towards God in preserving his honour, righteous towards us in managing our cause. And this righteousness was manifested in his being a propitiation for sin, whereby the righteousness of God was glorified, and the righteousness of the creature restored. This being without sin rendered him fit to be a sacrifice, 1 John iii. 5, which also renders him fit to be an intercessor. A guilty person is not a proper advocate for a criminal, nor can he well sue for another who needs one to sue for himself.

(4.) In respect of the cause he pleads, viz. the pardon of sin; which, upon the account of his being a propitiation for sin, he may rightly lay claim to. It is a just thing for him to plead, and a just thing for God to grant: 1 John i. 9, he is 'just to forgive us our sins, and to cleanse us from all unrighteousness.' Remission and sanctification, the great matters of Christ's plea, are righteous suits. He hath a sufficient price with him, whereby he may claim what he desires; and a price so large, that is not only a sufficient compensation to God for what he doth desire for his people, but is equivalent to a world of sins.

(5.) Upon the account of his righteousness in all these respects, he must needs prevail with God. This the apostle implies; he represents him as an Advocate, and as righteous, for the comfort of believers that through a temptation fall into sin, which could be none at all if the efficacy of his intercession were not included in this of his righteousness. Because he is righteous in his admission, in the foundation of his office, in his person, and the matter of his plea, he is worthy to be heard by God in his pleas; and since he wants nothing to qualify him for this office, he will not want entertainment with the Father in any suit he makes. And since his propitiation is sufficient for the sins of the whole world, we need not question the prevalency of his intercession for them that believe. If it hath a sufficiency for such multitudes, it must have an efficacy for those few that do comply with the terms of enjoying the benefit of it. The righteousness of the person of our Advocate, renders his intercession grateful to God and successful for us.

The foundation of this discourse, or the reason of it, is, ver. 2, 'He is the propitiation for our sins; not for ours only, but for the sins of the whole world.' He hath expiated our sins, and appeased the wrath of God which flamed against us.

[1.] Not only for our sins who now live, but for the sins of all believers in the past and succeeding ages of the world, as well as the present. His propitiation, in the virtue and efficacy of it, looks back upon all believers, in every age since the foundation of the world; and looks forward to every believer to the last period of time. The apostle's following discourse in this chapter evinceth that he restrains the efficacy of this expiation to believers, that manifest their faith by their holiness, and walk in his commands.

[2.] Or he is the propitiation, not only for the sins of us Jews, but for the Gentiles also.

[3.] Or he is a propitiation for the whole world in point of the sufficiency of the sacrifice and infinite value of his blood. The malignity of them that refuse it doth not diminish the value of the price, nor the bounty and grace that offers to them the benefits of it upon believing.

We may now thus paraphase the whole:

These things I write to you, not that you should sin upon a presumption of pardon after the confession of your crimes, and from God's readiness to forgive imagine you have a grant of liberty to offend him with the greater security. No; but that you should, out of an ingenuous principle, fly from all occasions of offending a God of such boundless mercy. Yet if any of you that walk in communion with God do fall through the infirmities of the flesh, and the strength of a temptation, be not so dejected as to despair, no, though the sin may happen to be very heinous; but let them consider that they have a gracious and righteous Advocate with the Father in heaven, even with that Father whom they have offended, to plead their cause, and sue out a pardon for them. And remember also that this Advocate is the very same person who, in the days of his flesh, did expiate sin and reconcile God by his bloody passion, and made so full an atonement as that it was sufficient not only for the sins of the present age, but of the whole world; and hath been efficacious for the blotting out the sins of all former believers before his coming. And to this Advocate you must address yourselves by faith, for you must know him, *i.e.* believe in him, which is implied in verse the third.

We see here a description of the office of Christ in heaven:

1. The office itself, an office of *advocacy*.

2. The officer, *Jesus Christ the righteous*, described,

(1.) In his person and inauguration, *Jesus Christ*. The Messiah, the Anointed, to this as well as any other part of his work.

(2.) Qualification, *righteous*. Righteous in his person, office, actions, cause.

3. The court wherein he exerciseth this office, in heaven *with the Father*. His Father, our Father, a Father by affection as well as creation.

4. The persons for whom, *we*. Us believers, us sinners after believing, every one of us: if *any man* sin.

5. The plea itself, *propitiation*.

6. The efficacy of this plea, from the extensiveness of this propitiation, *for the whole world*.

Several observations may be drawn hence:

1. The doctrine of the gospel indulgeth no liberty to sin: 'These things write I unto you, that you sin not.' Not that sin should not reign in you, but that sin should not be committed by you. Some understand that not the act of sin, but the dominion of sin, is here chiefly intended by the apostle.* But the contrary is manifest; the term *sin* must be taken in the same sense in the whole sentence. But when he saith, 'if any man sin,' he means it of an *act* of sin, or a fall into sin; and therefore the former words, 'I write unto you, that you sin not,' must be understood in the same sense. For if

* Mestrezat, 1 Jean ii. 1, 2, p. 237.

any man be under the empire of sin, and gives the reins to lusts of his own heart, he is not the subject of Christ's intercession. Christ is an advocate for none but those that are in communion with him, and walk in the light, as appears by the connection of this with the former chapter. If any such person fall into a sin, Christ is an advocate for him: 'if any man sin,' *i.e.* any man of these I have before described, 1 John i. 7. No sin must be indulged; it is the breath of the devil, the filth of the man. One sin brought death upon mankind, violated the divine law, deformed the face of the creation, wrecked the soul, inflamed the wrath of God; every sin is of this nature, and therefore must not be practised by us. Not to hate sin, not to resolve against it, not to exercise ourselves in an endeavour to avoid every act of it, is inconsistent with a believer. It is not to receive, but to abuse and profane, the gospel.

2. Believers, while in the world, are liable to acts of sin. *If any man;* he supposeth that grace may be so weak, temptation so strong, that a believer may fall into a grievous sin. While men are in the flesh, there are indwelling sins and invading temptations; there is a body of death within them, and snares about them. The apostle excludes not himself; for putting himself, by the term *we*, into the number of those that want the remedy, he supposeth himself liable to the disease: 'We have an advocate with the Father.'

3. Though believers do, through the strength of the flesh, subtlety of the tempter, power of a temptation, and weakness of grace, fall into sin, yet they should not despair of succour and pardon: 'If any man sin, we have an advocate.' Such a total despondency would utterly ruin them; despair would bind their sins upon them. Be not only cast down under the consideration of the curses and threatenings of the law, but be erected by the promises of the gospel, and the standing office of Christ in heaven.

4. Faith in Christ must be exercised as often as we sin: 'If any man sin, we have an advocate.' What is it to us there is an advocate, unless we put our cause into his hand? Though we have a faithful attorney in our worldly affairs, yet upon any emergency we must entertain him, let him know our cause, if we expect relief. Though Christ, being omniscient, knows and compassionates our case, yet he will be solicited; as, though God knows our wants, he will be supplicated to for the supplies of our necessities. Though he understands our case, he would have us understand it too, that we may value his office. Faith ought therefore to be exercised, because by reason of our daily sins we stand in need of a daily intercession. *If any man sin;* it implies that every man ought to make reflections on his conscience, lament his condition, turn his eye to his great Advocate, acquaint him with his state, and entertain him afresh in his cause. Though he lives for ever to make intercession, it is only for 'those that come to God by him' as their agent and solicitor, for those that come to the judge, but first come to him as their attorney.

5. Christ is not an advocate for all men, but only for them that believe, and strive, and watch against sin; for those that are invaded by it, not for those that are affected to it; for those that slip and stumble into sin, not for those that lie wallowing in the mire. He doth not say simply, 'If any man sin,' as holding up in that expression every man in the world; but '*And* if any man sin,' by that copulative particle linking the present sentence with the former chapter, signifying that he intends not this comfort for all, but for those that are in fellowship with God, and strive against temptation. Intercession, being the application of the propitiation, implies the accepting

the propitiation first. Christ in his mediatory prayer excludes all unbelievers: John xvii. 9, 'I pray for them; I pray not for the world.' For them! For whom? For those that 'have believed that thou didst send me,' ver. 8. He 'lives for ever to make intercession for those that come to God by him;' so that the coming to God by him is previous to the intercession he makes for them.

6. The proper intendment of this office of Christ is for sins after a state of faith. He was a priest in his propitiation to bring God and man together; he is a priest in his intercession, to keep God and man together. His propitiation is the foundation of his intercession, but his intercession is an act distinct from the other. That was done by his death; this is managed in his life. His death was for our reconciliation, but his life is for the perpetuating that reconciliation: Rom. v. 10, 'If any man sin, we have an advocate.' If any man sin that hath entered into a state of communion with God, let him know that this office was erected in heaven to keep him right in the favour of the Judge of all the world. We should quickly mar all, and be as miserable the next minute after regeneration and justification as before, if provision were not in this way made for us. In the first acts, faith eyes the propitiation of Christ, and pitches upon his death. Christ, as dying, is the great support of a soul new come out of the gulf of misery and terrors of conscience. In after acts, it eyes the life of Christ, as well as the death, taking in both his propitiation and intercession together.

7. No man can possibly be justified by his own works. We have an advocate, Jesus Christ the righteous. He directs them not to any pleas from their former walking in the light. If our justification be not continued by virtue of our own works after conversion (for though they are works proceeding from renewed principles, and are the fruits of the operation of the Holy Ghost, spring from a root of faith and love, and are directed in the aim of them to the glory of God, yet one flaw spoils the efficacy of all in the matter of justification); I say, if our justification be not continued by works after conversion, which have so rich a tincture on them, much less is it procured by works before conversion, wherein there is not a mite of grace. Our justification, in the first sentence of it, and also in the securing and perpetuating our standing before God, depends not in the least upon ourselves, but upon the mediation of Christ for us. If justification and pardon owe their continuance to Christ, they much more owe their first grant solely to the mediation of Christ.

8. Therefore observe further, that nothing of our own righteousness, or graces, or privileges, are to be set up by us as joint advocates with Christ before the tribunal of God in case of sin. The apostle saith not, If any man sin, let him plead his former obedience, let him plead his habitual grace, let him plead his adoption, and by that challenge the renewing of God's paternal affection. Let him plead his present repentance. He strikes off our hands from all these by that one word, 'We have an advocate, Jesus Christ the righteous.' We must enter no plea but what Christ doth enter, and that is only his propitiation. The apostle hints not any matter of the plea of this advocate but this one. Those that set up their own satisfactions, penitential acts, their humiliation, remorse, or their other glittering graces, mightily intrench upon the honour of Christ, and his standing office in heaven. They may be of some use in the accusations of our own consciences, but not before God's tribunal. It is certain our own righteousness sticks as close to us as our enmity to God. Nay, a secret confidence in it is the great citadel and chiefest fort and strength wherein our enmity against God and his righteousness lies. There is no man but is more willing to part with his sin than to

part with his righteousness; and there is nothing we find more starting up in us in the actings of grace than the motions of spiritual pride. We would be eking out the merits of Christ, and be our own advocates. We would not let him manage the cause upon his own account, and by this we spiritually injure Christ in the work of mediation, as much as the papists do in setting up glorified saints and angels with him; may I not say, worse, since an unspotted angel and a perfected saint is a more meet mate for him than a spotted righteousness and grace?

9. Christ is a person in the Godhead distinct from the Father: *advocate with the Father.* The Father and the advocate are here distinct. A judge and an advocate are different persons, have different offices, are exercised in different acts. The Father is considered as the governor, and the advocate as a pleader.

10. How divine is the gospel! 'Sin not.' 'If any man sin.' It gives us comfort against the demerit of sin, without encouraging the acts of sin. It teaches us an exact conformity to God in holiness, and provides for our full security in Christ, a powerful advocate. No religion is so pure for the honour of God, nor any so cordial for the refreshment of the creature.

The doctrine I shall handle is this: Christ is an advocate with the Father in heaven, continually managing the concerns of believers, and effectually prevailing for their full remission and salvation upon the account of the propitiation made by his death. We shall see,

I. That Christ is an advocate, in some general propositions.
II. What kind of advocate he is.
III. How he doth manage this advocacy and intercession.
IV. That he doth perpetually manage it.
V. That he doth effectually manage it.
VI. That he doth manage it for every believer.
VII. The use.

I. In general, Christ is as much an advocate as he is a sacrifice, as God is as much a governor as he was a creator. As we say of providence, it is a continued creation, so of intercession, it is a continued oblation. As providence is a maintaining the creation, so this intercession is a maintaining the expiation, and therefore is by some called a presentative oblation. The heathens had some notice of the necessity of some mediator or intercessor, either by tradition from Adam, from whom the notion of a mediator might as well be transmitted as the notion of expiation of guilt by bloody sacrifices. But while they retained the carcase, they lost the spirit of it; and while they preserved the sentiment of the necessity of an advocate, they framed many wrong and unserviceable ones. They dubbed their heroes, and men that had been benefactors to them in the world, with this title after their death, and elevated them to be intermediate powers between God and them. Some of those demons are fancied to carry up their prayers to God, and back their prayers with new supplications;* others brought gifts from God. Some handed their petitions and pleaded for them; others brought the answers of their prayers and relieved them, which the apostle alludes to: 1 Cor. viii. 5, 6, 'For though there be that are called gods, as there be gods many, and lords many; but to us there is but one God, the Father, of whom are all things, and we in him; and one Lord Jesus Christ, by whom are all things, and we by him.' As they had many gods, so they had many mediators between themselves and those particular gods; but, saith he, 'To us there is but one God,' the principal cause, 'and one Lord Jesus Christ,' the procuring cause

* Apuleius de Deo Socratis, p. 426.

of all things, by whose suit we are what we are, and enjoy what we have. This intercession of Christ was ancient; it is as ancient as his first undertaking our suretyship, by virtue of which the vengeance the sinner had merited was deferred. He 'upholds all things by the word of his power,' Heb. i. 3, or his powerful or prevailing word, when they were ready to sink; not only as God by the word of providence, but as mediator by his word of intercession, that the guilty sinner might not be dealt with by the rigours of justice, but in the tenderness of mercy. As he was fore-ordained a sacrifice, so he was fore-ordained an advocate; as he was a lamb slain, so he was an advocate entertained, from the foundation of the world. His sacrifice, though not performed, could not have a credit with God, as it had, but his pleas upon the credit of that sacrifice must be admitted also. Thus were believers of old saved by him, and redeemed in his pity, as he was 'the angel of the presence' of God, Isa. lxiii. 9, *i.e.* in the phrase of the New Testament, 'appearing in the presence of God for them,' Heb. ix. 24, noting the manner of his intercession. He did, as an undertaker for them, interpose for their salvation; he 'bare them, and carried them all the days of old,' alluding, I guess, to Aaron the high priest bearing the names of the twelve tribes in the breast-plate of judgment upon his heart when he went into the holy place to intercede for the people, Exod. xxviii. 29. He was an advocate for them to whom the credit of his propitiation did extend; but that did extend to those that believed before his coming in the flesh; to them therefore his intercession extended also. It was then indeed an intercession upon credit; it is now an intercession by demand, since the actual offering himself a victim.

1. This office of advocacy belongs to him as a priest, and it is a part of his priestly office. The high priest was not only to slay and offer the sacrifice in the outer part of the tabernacle, on the anniversary day of expiation, but to enter with the fresh blood into the sanctuary, and sprinkle it seven times, to shew the perfection of that expiating blood which was figured by it, Lev. xvi. 14. In the blood was the expiatory virtue: Lev. xvii. 11, 'It is the blood that makes an atonement for the soul;' yet the high priest did not perform his office complete, till he had sprinkled the blood of the sacrifice with his finger on the mercy seat; he was also to bring a censer full of burning coals from off the altar, and incense in his hands, and put it upon the fire before the Lord, within the veil, that the cloud in the incense might cover the mercy seat, Lev. xvi. 12, 13. As the high priest going into the holy of holies after the sacrifice, was a type of Christ's ascension after his passion on the cross; so the blood he was to sprinkle was a type of that blood, and the incense he was to kindle, a figure of the prayers of Christ after his entering into heaven.* Incense in Scripture frequently signifies prayer, and prayer is compared to incense. As the high priest's office was to enter into the sanctuary with this blood and incense to intercede for the people, and obtain a blessing for them, so it pertained to the office of Christ, as a priest, not only to enter with his own blood, but with the incense of his prayers, as a cloud about the mercy-seat, to preserve by his life the salvation he had merited by his death. Christ entered into heaven as a priest, and in that capacity 'sat down on the right hand of the throne of the Majesty in the heavens,' Heb. viii. 1, and was settled 'an high priest for ever,' by a solemn oath, Ps. cx. 4. There is therefore some priestly act, which he hath a capacity and an obligation, by virtue of his office, to perform for ever, all the time he stays in heaven, till his second appearing (as the high priest, all the time he was in the holy of holies, was performing a sacerdotal act), which is not the act of sacrificing, that was done by him on earth (as the sacrifice was slain

* Amyraut sur Heb. ix. p. 74.

without the veil). Nothing but intercession can answer to that type, which is called an appearing for us, as a proxy or attorney, in the presence of God, Heb. ix. 24, otherwise there is no priestly act for him to do; and so his being a priest would be an empty title, a name without an office. God's oath would be insignificant, if there were not some priestly act to be performed by him, as well as a priestly office vested in him. Being a priest, therefore, he must have something to offer, even in heaven; which cannot be a new sacrifice, for that was but once to be done. It must be therefore the presenting his old, his body wounded, which is nothing else but this which we call intercession; a presenting to God this sacrifice of himself, and pleading the virtue of it in every time of need. The apostle tells us our salvation depends upon his intercession, and his intercession upon his priesthood, Heb. vii. 24, 25. Our salvation depends not simply upon his living for ever, for that he had done if he had never come upon the earth to redeem us, but upon his living for ever in an unchangeable priesthood; the end of which unchangeable and everlasting priesthood is intercession. As our salvation depends not upon God's living for ever, for God had lived for ever had we been damned; but upon God's living for ever as a reconciled God, and entered into covenant. As he was a priest upon the cross to make an expiation for us, so he is our priest in the court of heaven, to plead this atonement, both before the tribunal of justice and the throne of mercy, against the curses of the law, the accusations of Satan, the indictments of sin, and to keep off the punishment which our guilt had merited.

2. This, therefore, was the end of his ascension, and sitting down at the right hand of God. In his incarnation, he came from the Father to acquaint us with his gracious purposes, and how far he had agreed with God on our behalf; and at his ascension he went from us to the Father, to sue out the benefits he had so dearly purchased. He drew up an answer upon the cross to the bill, that sin by virtue of the law had drawn against us, and ascended to heaven as an advocate to plead that answer upon his throne, and rejoin to all the replies against it. When his offering was accepted, he went to heaven to the supreme Judge, to improve this acceptation of his sacrifice, by a negotiation which holds and continues to this day. Heb. ix. 24, 'Christ is entered into heaven;' for what end?' 'To appear in the presence of God for us;' but may he not appear for us at first, and afterwards cease from it? No: *now* to appear for us. He entered into heaven long since, but he appears for us this instant. *Now*, as if the apostle should have said, while I am writing, and you are reading, in this, in that instant, Νῦν, is he appearing for us as a public person. Though there be a change in his condition, from a state of humiliation to a state of exaltation, yet there is no change in his office: Heb. viii. 1, 2, 'He is set down as a priest on the right hand of God,' 'a minister of the sanctuary,' or of holy things, λειτουργὸς τῶν ἁγίων, as a performer of a divine office for men. As Moses, forty days after his conducting the Israelites out of Egypt (the type of our redemption), ascended the mount, while his redeemed people were in a conflict with Amalek, to pray for them as a type of Christ, so Christ himself, forty days after his resurrection, which was an evidence of our deliverance from spiritual slavery, ascended up into heaven, to lift up his head there as our advocate, for assistance to be granted to us against our spiritual enemies. As this intercession is the true design of his eternal life as a priest; and since the apostle lays it down as a manifest truth, witnessed by all the prophets, Acts iii. 21, that there is to be a restitution of all things, and that the heavens receive Christ till that restitution; it will follow that he sits there in order to that restitution; not as an idle spectator, but a promoter of it by

the efficacy of his mediation; and no other order did he receive from his Father after his resurrection, being declared the begotten Son by his resurrection, but to ask, for that follows just upon the declaration of his being his Son, Ps. ii. 7, 8, which is interpreted in the New Testament of his resurrection. Asking was all required of him for the enjoying his reward, of which the advantage of his people in enjoying the fruits of his death, is none of the meanest part in his own account, since it was 'the joy set before him.' His mediation kept the world from ruin after man's fall, and his intercession promotes the world's restoration after his own passion.

3. This advocacy is founded upon his oblation. He is our advocate, because he was our propitiation; the efficacy of his plea depends upon the value and purity of his sacrifice. He is an intercessor in the virtue of his blood. The apostle, therefore, speaking of his intercession, Heb. vii. 24, considers it with a respect to his sacrifice: ver. 27, he could not have interceded as a priest, if he had not offered. As the high priest could not enter into the holy of holies, till, by the slaying of the sacrifice, he had blood to carry with him, so the true High Priest was not to be admitted to solicit at the throne of grace, till he had satisfied the tribunal of justice; so that a propitiation and his advocacy are not one and the same thing (as the Socinians affirm), but distinct: the one is the payment, the other the plea; one was made on earth, the other is managed in heaven; the one was by his death, the other by his life; the one was done but once, the other performed perpetually; the first is the foundation of the second. Because he paid the debt as our surety, he was fit to plead the payment as our attorney; what he finished on earth, he continually presents in heaven. By shedding his blood, he makes expiation; by presenting his blood, he makes intercession; in the one he prepares the remedy, and in the other he applies it. They are not the same acts, but the first act is the foundation of the second, and the second hath a connection with the first.

4. The nature of this advocacy differs from that intercession or advocacy which is ascribed to the Spirit. The Spirit is said to 'make intercession for us,' Rom. viii. 26; and he is in a way of excellency called the Comforter, which we heard is the same word in the Greek with this word which is here translated advocate. Christ is an advocate with God *for us*, and the Spirit is an advocate with God *in us*, John xiv. 17. Christ is our advocate, pleading for us in his own name; the Spirit is an advocate, assisting us to plead for ourselves in Christ's name. Christ pleads for us in the presence of God, the Spirit directs us to such arguments as may be used for pleas for ourselves. The Spirit doth not groan himself, but excites in us strong groans, by affecting us with our condition, and putting an edge upon our petitions, and strengthening us in the inward man, Eph. iii. 16. The Spirit is an advocate to indite our petitions, and Christ is an advocate to present them. Some distinguish them that Christ is an advocate by way of office, and the Spirit by way of assistance; but certainly the Spirit is an advocate by way of office to counsel us, as Christ is an advocate by way of office to plead for us; and the Spirit is as much sent to do the one in our hearts, as Christ was called back to heaven to do the other for our persons. The Spirit is an intercessor on earth, and Christ is an intercessor in heaven. Again, as there are two courts we are summoned to appear in, the court of the supreme Judge and the court of the Judge's deputy, our own consciences, Christ clears us by his plea at God's bar, and sets us right with the offended Father. The Spirit, as Christ's deputy, being sent in his name, clears us at the bar of our own consciences. Christ answers the charge of the law in the court of God's justice, and the Spirit answers the accusations of sin in the court of God'

deputy. The one pleads for our discharge above, the other pleads for our peace below; and the voice of God's Spirit is as mighty in us, as the voice of Christ's blood is mighty for us.

II. Thing. What kind of advocate Christ is.

1. An authoritative advocate. He intercedes not without a commission and without a command. God owns himself as the cause of his drawing near and approach to him: Jer. xxx. 21, 'I will cause him to draw near, and he shall approach unto me,' both in his first mediation and his following intercessions. He manages not an intercession merely in a way of charity, but in a way of authority, as a person entrusted by God, and dignified to this end; not only as our friend, but as a divine officer; as an attorney may manage the suit of his kinsman, but not only as being related to his client, but as being admitted by the court into such an office. Christ is not only admitted as one of kin to us, but commissioned as mediator for us. This was promised, that he should be 'a priest upon his throne,' Zech. vi. 13. The commission takes date from the day of his resurrection; when he was declared to be the begotten Son of God, he had an order to ask, Ps. ii. 8. This charge was given him at his solemn inauguration, and was to precede all the magnificent fruits of it. God settles Christ a priest and intercessor, while he commands him to ask the heathen for his inheritance; which connection the apostle confirms: Heb. v. 5, 'Christ glorified not himself to be made an high priest, but he that said unto him, Thou art my Son.' But the priesthood doth not appear to be settled upon Christ by any other expression than this, 'Ask of me.'* The psalm speaks of his investiture in his kingly office; the apostle refers this to his priesthood, his commission, for both took date at the same time; both bestowed, both confirmed, by the same authority. The office of asking is grounded upon the same authority, as the honour of king. Ruling belonged to his royal office, asking to his priestly. After his resurrection, the Father gives him a power and command of asking, and obligeth himself to a grant of what he should ask. The same power that admits him to be an advocate, assures him he should be a prevailing one; the obligation to give is as strong as his order to ask. As his death was the end of his incarnation, so his intercession was the end of his ascension; his dignity in heaven was given him for the exercise of this particular office, Heb. vii. 25. As he had his life from God, so he had it for this end, to make intercession. He had a command to be a sufferer, and a body prepared him for that purpose; so he had likewise a command to be an advocate, and a life given him, and a throne prepared for him at the right hand of God to that end. The like commission is mentioned Ps. lxxxix. 26, 'He shall cry unto me, Thou art my Father, my God, and the rock of my salvation;' and this after his exaltation, ver. 24, 25. Yet for the full completing of it, ver. 27, the matter of his plea is there mentioned, 'Thou art the rock of my salvation,' the foundation, the first cause, of all thy salvation I have wrought in the world, being the first mover of it, and promising the acceptance of me in the performance of what was necessary for it. As he hath authority to cry to God, so he hath an assurance of the prevalency of his cry, in regard of the stability of the covenant, the covenant of mediation, which shall stand fast with him, or be faithful to him: 'and my mercy I will keep for him for evermore,' ver. 27. The treasures of my mercy are reserved only to be opened and dispensed by him; and the enjoying of his spiritual seed for ever, and the establishing of his own throne thereby, is the promised fruit of this cry, ver. 28. Christ indeed was a surety by authority, but by a greater right

* Rivet. in Ps. ii. 8.

an advocate. That he was accepted in the capacity of a surety, was pure mercy; it was at God's liberty whether he would accept a surety for us, or accept Christ for our surety; but after he had accepted him, upon the doing of his part in the work of redemption, he hath a right to the application of redemption, and consequently to the office of advocate, to see right done us, to see our debts discharged, and to put justice in mind of the full payment he hath made. He hath a right to it, a commission for it, a command to discharge it; he is as much bound to intercede as he was to sacrifice, for it is as much belonging to his priestly office as the other.

2. He is a wise and skilful advocate. Every advocate must understand the law of the state and the cause of his client, that he may manage it to the best advantage. This advocate hath an infinite knowledge as God, and a full and sufficient knowledge as man. His deity communicates the knowledge of our cause to his humanity, and excites the compassion of his nature. He knows the sincerity of his clients' hearts, their inward groans and breathings which cannot be expressed. He knows our cause better than we do ourselves, he needs not the representing our own cause from ourselves: 'He needs not that any should testify of man, he knows what is in man,' John ii. 25. He understands the best and the worst of our cause; he hath a clear view of all the flaws in it better than they are visible to ourselves. If he had no more skill and knowledge of us than what our outward expressions might furnish him with, he might mistake the business of a stammering spirit, and on the other side be imposed upon by the voluble expressions and flourishing gifts of others; he might be cheated by the hypocrisy of some, and mistake the concerns of his own people, who often mistake themselves, and are not able to express their own wants; but it cannot be so with him; 'he knows all things,' he knows those that love him and those that hate him, John xxi. 17. He understands our cause, he understands the law according to which he is to plead, the articles of agreement between the Father and himself, and he understands the fulness and redundancy of his own merit. He uses arguments proper to the cause he pleads, and drawn from the nature of the person he applies himself to. When he meets with the church in weakness and distress by potent adversaries, and would have the Jews delivered and the temple rebuilt, he solicits God as *the Lord of hosts*, Zech. i. 12. When he finds his people in danger of sin and temptation, he petitions God under the title of *holy*, John xvii. 11. When he would have promises performed to them, he appeals to the *righteousness* of the Father, John xvii. 25; it being part of his righteousness to fulfil that word which he hath passed, and make good the grant which so great a redeemer merited. He pleads the respects he had to the divine will in the exercise of every part of his office, both of priest and prophet: Ps. xl. 9, 10, a prophetic psalm of Christ, 'I have not hid thy righteousness within my heart, I have declared thy faithfulness, and thy salvation; I have not concealed thy loving-kindness and thy truth from the great congregation.' The adding *thy* to every one of them is emphatical: it was *thy* righteousness I had commission to declare, *thy* faithfulness I had order to proclaim, *thy* mercy I had a charge to publish; *thou* wert as much interested in all that I did as I myself was. I shall be counted false and a liar, thou wilt be counted unjust and cruel, if all be not fulfilled as I have spoken. Since it was thy rule I observed, and thy glory I aimed at in declaring it, disgrace not thyself and me in refusing the petition of such a supplicant, who believes in my word which I gave out by thy authority. Surely as Christ observed the will of God upon earth, so he is wise to intercede for nothing but according to those rules he observed in his humiliation, which was whatsoever might honour and manifest the righteous-

ness, faithfulness, salvation, truth, and loving-kindness of the Father. This is a part of his wisdom, to plead for nothing but what he hath the nature of God to subscribe to his petitions, and back him in them. It is not for the honour of an advocate to undertake a cause he cannot bring to pass, nor will any wise man engage in a suit which he hath not some strong probability to effect. Our Lord, in whom are hid all the treasures of wisdom and knowledge, stands more upon his honour than to undertake a cause he cannot accomplish.

3. He is a righteous and faithful advocate. He is as righteous in his advocacy as he was in his suffering. His being without sin rendered him fit to bear our sins on the cross: 1 John iii. 5, 'He was manifested to take away our sins, and in him is no sin;' and it renders him fit to plead for the pardon of our sins upon his throne. As he was manifested to destroy the works of the devil, so he is exalted to perfect the conquest by his intercession. If he had sin, he could not be in heaven, much less a pleader there. God tried him, and found him faithful in all his house, in all his own concerns, and the concerns of his people, which are his spiritual temple. The altar of incense, which was overlaid with pure gold all about the sides of it, Exod. xxxvii. 26, and set before the ark of the testimony, Exod. xl. 5, signified the purity of his soul, and his freedom from any kind of corruption in those pleas he makes in the holy of holies above, where 'he ever lives to make intercession for those that come to God,' Heb. vii. 25. But in what state? Ver. 26, an high priest, 'holy, harmless, undefiled, separate from sinners.' He lives in heaven a pure person, fitted by his purity to such an office. The words refer not to Christ's life in the world,* but to his life in heaven; 'separate from sinners' in regard of communion in their sins, but not in regard of compassion to their miseries. He hath nothing of his own concerns to divert him from our business; as he had no sin of his own to suffer for in the world, so he hath no sin of his own to solicit the pardon of in heaven. He having an incomparably righteous nature, will be exactly righteous in his office. After Christ's resurrection, when he had finished his work on earth, and was to begin it in heaven, God saluted him with a great deal of kindness: Ps. ii. 7, 'This day have I begotten thee.'† God regarded him as his only begotten Son, of the same holy and righteous nature with himself; justified him as his righteous servant, and thereupon gives him a power of asking; so that the prevalency of his intercession depends upon the righteousness of his person, and the righteousness of his cause; he pleadeth his own righteousness, which carries with it a necessity of having sin pardoned; which the righteousness of God is as ready to remit, as the righteousness of Christ was to purchase the remission of it. Whatsoever Christ intercedes for is righteous; if it were unrighteous, it were not fit to be moved to God; this would be to endeavour to persuade him to an unworthy act, contrary to his nature. If any proposal of his were unrighteous, Christ would be false to God, and his own principles, in making and defending such a motion. This would be to destroy all the ends of his coming, and design of his death, which was to declare the righteousness of God, advance it in the world, and in the souls of men. If Christ should undertake an unrighteous cause, what ground of confidence and security could any righteous man have in him?

4. He is a compassionate advocate. His compassion to us is joined with his faithfulness to God in his priestly office, Heb. ii. 17; so that, if he be not tender to believers in misery, he is not faithful to God in the exercise of

* As Crellius well notes.

† Upon which the Chaldee hath this note, *Purus es acsi hac die crexvissem te.*

his office. His intercession springs from the same tenderness towards us as his oblation, and both are but the displaying of his excessive charity. His compassion to us was a lesson he learned, together with obedience to God, by his sufferings, Heb. v. 8. He learned how necessary obedience was to God, and how grievous the misery of man was; and being instructed in one as well as the other, his pity to us had as deep an impression as his sense of obedience to the divine will. And since one part of his obedience was to make way for the opening the treasures of his mercy, he cannot be obedient to his Father without being merciful to us. He was exposed to such a condition as wrested from him strong cries for himself, that he might send up strong cries for us in our misery. He was a man of sorrows, that he might be a man of compassions. He indeed had pity of old; for with such an affection he redeemed the Israelites, Isa. lxiii. 9. His compassions are not lessened by an assumption of our humanity, but an experimental compassion gained in his human nature, which the divine was not capable of, because of the perfection of impassibility. By a reflection upon his own condition in the world, he is able to move our cause with such a tender feeling of it, as if he had the smart of it present in his own heart and bowels. The greatest pity must reside in him, since the greatest misery was endured by him in our nature; what he had a real feeling of on earth, he must have a memorative feeling of in heaven. He cannot forget above what he experimented below, since one part of his priestly office, in suffering, was to fit him for a more faithful and merciful exercise of the other part in his intercession; not an affliction was laid upon him but was intended to compose his heart to a sympathising frame with his people: Heb. iv. 15, 'We have not an high priestwhich cannot be touched'; (two negatives affirm it strongly). Not a taste of bitterness in any temptation he endured, but was more deeply to engrave in his heart a tenderness to us; nor can those compassions in him be equalled by any creature; no angel nor man can be touched with such a sense as he is, because no angel nor man ever smarted under such extremity as he did. Our pity to ourselves cannot enter into comparison with his pity to us. With what a sense of his disciples' condition did he pray for them upon earth! John xvii. The glory of heaven hath made no change in his judgment and affections; he hath the same will in heaven that he had on earth; the same human will, and therefore the same human compassions in league with his divine. He was God-man on earth, man to suffer for us, and God to render that suffering valuable; he is God-man in heaven, man to pity us, and God to render that compassion efficacious for us. This fits him for a zealous prosecution of our cause in heaven. His intercession receives a sharper edge from the things which he suffered; the taste that he had of the infirmities of men, and the wrath they are obnoxious unto, warms his heart, and strengthens his pleas, and makes him a more zealous solicitor at the throne of divine grace; as an earthly advocate that had drank deep of the same cup, and had had the same suit for himself as he hath for his client, better understands the cause, and is able to manage it with a deeper sense, than if he had never felt the like misery. Our advocate was framed in the same mould with us in regard of his nature, and was cast into the same furnace of wrath which we had merited; and thus knowing the miseries of man, not by a bare report, but experience of the heaviness of the burden, is more careful to solicit the liberty and absolution of every comer to God by him from the sentence that hangs over them; and the greater their miseries are, the more are his compassions exercised. The more deplorable the misery is, the greater object of pity the person is that feels it; and to exercise compassion, when the object stands most in need of it, is very agreeable to a compassionate nature, such as Christ's is; and therefore, if he had so much pity to procure the redemption of the Israelites from a temporal and bodily captivity, much more will he be careful to free believers from the spiritual captivity they groan under, since in that condition they are more suitable objects of compassion than any man can be under a mere bodily and temporal affliction. And therefore, whenever the knowledge of our condition comes to his humanity by the assistance of his divinity, we cannot have a more powerful solicitor than the experimental sense he hath in his own breast and bowels. To conclude, he is a compassionate intercessor, because he was a great sufferer, as compassionate to us as he is valuable with God; his merit for us is not greater than his pity to us.

5. He is ready and diligent. He is never out of the way when the cause should be heard; he always sits at the right hand of the Father, who is the judge of the world, and is never out of his presence. When Stephen, Acts vii. 55, 'saw the heavens opened, he saw Christ standing at the right hand of God,' in the posture of an advocate and protector, as sitting is the posture of a prince and a judge. He times his intercession for the church according to the providential state of the world, Zech. i. 11, 12. He had sent out his messengers to view the state of the earth, who, upon their return, brought him word that it was in peace and rest; upon which news he petitions for the restoring of Jerusalem. He would not let slip the opportunity of such an argument, that the church, the seat of the divine glory on earth, should be in misery, when the world, wherein God did less concern himself, flourished in peace and prosperity. Shall the enemies of the church be in a better condition than the people thou hast entrusted with thy law? His messengers brought him an exact account of things, and he is diligent to take hold of the first occasion to solicit the security or restoration of his people. Now that the princes of the earth have nothing of war to hinder them, put it into their hearts to deliver thy people and rebuild thy temple. It is one property of Christ to be 'of quick understanding in the fear of the Lord,' Isa. xi. 3; to be sensible of anything that may promote the honour and worship of God, or may obstruct and lessen it. His sense is as quick as his understanding, and readily interposeth for whatsoever may conduce to the manifestation of the attributes of God, which is the foundation of his fear in the world. He is ready to put in a plea for us to the Father, and is more studious of our welfare, and to bring us off, than we are ourselves. In the midst of his dolours he gave us an evidence of it. Though his disciples were so careless and senseless of his present condition that they fell asleep, when they had most need to watch both for him and themselves; yet, after his reproof for their negligence, he frames an excuse for them from the consideration of their weakness, before they could apologise for themselves: Mat. xxvi. 41, 'The spirit is willing, but the flesh is weak.' He lays it upon the infirmities of their flesh, though it was also the security of their spirits, as appears by his reproof. Is he not as ready to plead the same for us in his glory? He is always ready at the throne of grace to give out grace and mercy in a time of need, Heb. iv. 16. We have no reason to fear his absence from that throne of grace we solicit in our necessities. He is passed into the heaven, seated there in a perpetual exercise of this office, to entertain all comers at all times; and can no more be sleepy than he can be cruel, no more cease to be diligent than he can be bereaved of his compassions.

6. He is an earnest and pressing advocate. When an advocate hath much business for himself, it will cool him in the affairs of his client: Christ hath once offered up himself, and being thereupon advanced, has no need to offer up himself again. He is secure from any further suffering in his per-

son. He hath nothing to do for himself; but all his ardency is employed for his people, which is the reason rendered why he 'lives to make intercession for the comers to God by him,' Heb. vii. 25, compared with ver. 27, 'He needeth not daily, as those high priests, to offer up sacrifice, first for his own sin, and then for the people's; for this he did once, when he offered up himself.' He needs not any solicitousness for himself, as before the time of his death; he hath nothing now to blemish his happiness, and divert his affections from the concerns of his people. He hath no strong cries now to put up for himself. All his affections run in another channel. His whole soul is put to pawn in the business, as the word signifies in Jer. xxx. 21, 'He hath engaged his heart to approach unto me, saith the Lord.' He hath undertaken it with the greatest cordialness of spirit. His expostulation speaks his earnestness of old: Zech. i. 12, 'O Lord of hosts, how long wilt thou not have mercy on Jerusalem?' Like an expression we use when we would rouse a drowsy person in a time of danger, and snatch him out of the fire; as if Christ thought the mercy of God too sleepy, and earnestly jogs it to awaken it, and spurs it on to manifest itself. 'How long wilt thou;' thou who hast an affection to the captives, an affection to me, their solicitor; thou who hast mercy to pity them, and power to rescue them; thou who knowest that the set time of their captivity is at an end, and hast faithfulness to be as good as thy word? The seventeenth of John is a map of his carriage in heaven, how he presses his Father for his people. When he prayed for himself, it is 'Father, if it be thy will, let this cup pass from me.' It is then '*Not as I will, but as thou wilt;*' but for his disciples' glory and salvation it is, *I will*, ver. 24, as though he were more a judge than an advocate, and had more a right to a sovereign dominion than that of a plea. What did the censer full of burning coals of fire from the altar,* which the high priest was to carry within the veil, into the holy of holies, Lev. xvi. 12, 13, represent, but the ardency of the affections in the soul of Christ, when he presents the incense of our prayers to his Father in heaven? The names of the tribes of Israel were to be not only upon the high priest's shoulders, Exod. xxviii. 12, but also upon his breastplate, ver. 29; near his heart when his face is towards them, and as near his heart when, in desertion, his back is turned upon them. They are next his heart all the time he is in the holy of holies. Great affections cannot be without earnestness in their cause. He desired not more earnestly to be baptized with his bloody baptism on earth than to complete all the fruits of it in heaven. He was not more vehement to shed his blood than he is to plead it. No man is more solicitous to increase the honour and grandeur of his family, than Christ is to secure the happiness of his people. Our prayers for ourselves, when tinctured with the greatest affection, cannot be so fervent as his pleas for our souls are at the right hand of his Father; for to what purpose did he carry up those human affections to heaven, but to express and act them in their liveliness and vigour for us and to us?

7. He is a joyful and cheerful advocate. He hath not a sour kind of earnestness, as is common among men; but an earnestness with a joy, as being the delight of his heart. When he prayed in the garden for himself, he was in an agony; but in his mediatory prayer, a model of his intercession in heaven, he was in a cheerful frame, John xvii.; for it was his prayer after the most comfortable sermon he ever preached to his disciples, wherein he had heaped up all the considerations that might be capable to elevate their hearts; and he makes this use of it in the end, John xvi. 33, that they should 'be of good cheer' at his victory, because he hath 'overcome the world.'

* Amyraut sur Heb. ix. p. 83.

And in this frame he puts up this mediatory prayer immediately, to signify to them both the matter and manner of his intercessions in heaven for them, and that he doth rejoice in putting up these requests above, as well as he did when he presented them at times before, as is intimated: ver. 13, 'These things I speak in the world, that they might have my joy fulfilled in themselves;' that they might have such a joy in the considerations of it, and in the receiving thy favour, as I have in the petitioning for them. Certainly he doth as well rejoice in the habitable parts of the earth, since he hath laid so great an obligation upon it, as he did formerly in the prospect of what he was to do for it. His death was sweet to him after his resurrection; the very remembrance of it was a pleasure, in which sense some understand that: Jer. xxxi. 25, 26, 'I have satiated the weary soul, and I have replenished every sorrowful soul. Upon this I awaked, and beheld; and my sleep was sweet unto me.' It is certain some passages in that chapter are applied to Christ's time, as ver. 15, the weeping at Ramah was a prediction of the slaying of infants by Herod, Mat. ii. 17, 18; and ver. 22, the 'creating a new thing in the earth, A woman shall compass a man,' is generally understood of the conception and incarnation of Christ. And the expression in ver. 25 seems to be too magnificent to be understood of any other prophet than that in whom the weary find rest; and the consideration of the success of his incarnation and passion make his sleep, *i. e.* his death, pleasant to him at his awaking or resurrection. His pleading, therefore, for the fruit of his death cannot be bitter or distasteful to him; he delights as much in the exercise of this office as he did in the first undertaking of it and consecration to it. Since he accounted his priesthood an honour when God called him to it, he will not think it disgraceful when his people own it, and desire the exercise of it in their behalf.

8. He is an acceptable advocate. He hath an active joy in his intercession, a passive joy in his acceptation. He is the favourite of the court wherein he pleads, acceptable to the judge in his person, acceptable to him in his office, acceptable to him in the suits he manages. His intercession is nothing else but the presenting to God the sacrifice which restored to him the pleasure of his creation, gave him a rest, and continues it. The savour of that sacrifice in heaven which was offered on earth is grateful to the judge of the world. It is as sweet to God as the Levitical incense, the type of it, can be to man, mentioned Exod. xxx. 34–36, and reserved for the service of the temple, a composition of the sweetest and most aromatic simples. How much sweeter is the advocacy of Christ to God than the most fragrant scents can be to us! In the presence of God he meets with a fulness of joy: Ps. xvi. 11, 'Thou wilt shew me the paths of life, and shew me in thy presence a fulness of joy, and pleasures at thy right hand for evermore.' So Cocceius reads it. It is to be understood of his mediatory pleasure he hath in his being in the presence of God, or appearing in the presence of God for us, Heb. ix. 24. You know that psalm is to be understood of Christ, which is evidenced by ver. 10, applied to him Acts ii. 31, Acts xiii. 35. 'Thou wilt shew me the path of life;' thou wilt bring me into glory, as the head of the believing world, of those saints and excellent ones in whom my delight hath been; in this presence I shall have fulness of joy, in the reflections upon my obedience, and the plentiful effusions of thy grace upon the account of it. Pleasures flow with a full and perpetual torrent from the right hand of God by the mediation of Christ. It is as if he should have said, I shall have a fulness of joy after my bitter passion, in the contemplation of thy pleased countenance to the sons of men; and thy right hand shall communicate spiritual blessings upon the account of this passion, which shall be the delight

of my soul. All this thou wilt shew me after my resurrection, to testify how acceptable my mediation hath been to thee. Since God constituted him a priest by an irreversible oath, an oath he would never repent of, Heb. vii. 21, and thereby confirmed him in an 'unchangeable priesthood,' ver. 24, as he hath an unchangeable office, so he hath an endless acceptation. He that never will repent of fixing him in it, will never repent of his exercising of it. As God is infinitely pleased with this office, so he is infinitely pleased with the execution of the charge; and the presenting his death for any soul is inexpressibly grateful to the reconciled judge. His deity adds a value and efficacy to his intercessions in heaven, as it did to his passion on earth.

9. He is the sole advocate. Those of Rome distinguish between mediators of redemption and mediators of intercession; the first they appropriate to Christ, in the other they make angels and saints his companions, and thereby snatch the glory from Christ to confer it upon a creature. But since our High Priest alone hath the honour to sit at the right hand of God, he alone hath the honour of this office of advocacy. 'To which of the angels,' or saints, 'did he at any time say, Ask of me, and I will give thee the heathen for thine inheritance?' The office and power of asking belongs to him who is the begotten Son. Since Christ trod the wine-press alone, he solicits our cause alone, intercession being founded upon propitiation; he, therefore, that is the sole propitiator, is the sole intercessor. He only hath the right to plead for us, who had the right to purchase us. As God never gave any commission to redeem us to any other, so he never gave a commission to any other to appear for us in that court. The entering into the holy of holies with the perfuming incense, was annexed to the honour of the chief priesthood, which had any of the inferior priests, or any soul alive, usurped, they had incurred the pains of death. It is a disparagement to Christ to interest any creature in it, as though he wanted some other favourite to give him a full credit with the Father, and some monitors to excite his affections to us; or as though the suits he had to manage were so numerous, that he wanted a multitude of clerks to draw up for him the petitions he had to present. It is our Saviour's prerogative to be 'the first and the last,' Rev. i. 11; as he was the first that stepped up to keep the world from perishing by the hand of justice, so he will be the last in securing it; as he was the first in purchasing, so he will be the last in completing, that the whole work of redemption may be ascribed to him alone. As he is the sole author of it by his passion, so he will be the sole finisher of it by his intercession.

III. Thing. How Christ doth manage this advocacy and intercession.

In general. Christ as God, essentially considered, doth not intercede in heaven. He that intercedes by way of petition, wants the blessing of that person he intercedes with, and in that respect is inferior to him. He no more intercedes in heaven as God, than he prayed on earth as God. His intercession as well as his passion belongs indeed to his person; and as his Deity is in personal union with his humanity, so his prayers and intercessions may be called the intercessions of God, as well as his blood was called the blood of God. As the human nature suffered, and the divine nature made it valuable, so the human nature intercedes by way of motion, and the divine nature makes it prevalent. The person of the Son of God suffered, but only in the human nature, the divine not being passible; so may we not say the person of the Son of God intercedes, but the human nature only supplicates? He is our advocate, as he was our propitiation.

1. Christ is not an advocate in heaven in such a supplicating manner as he prayed in the world. This servile way of praying, as they call it, because

it was performed by Christ in the form of a servant, is not agreeable to his present glorious estate. It is as unsuitable to his state in heaven, as his prayers with strong cries were suitable to his condition on earth. Such 'prayers and supplications, with strong cries and tears,' belong only to 'the days of his flesh,' Heb. v. 7, *i. e.* the state of humiliation, wherein he was encompassed with the infirmities of the flesh; but such a posture becomes him not in heaven, where he is stripped of all those natural infirmities and marks of indigence. Though such a kind of petitioning is not inconsistent with his humanity as joined to his divinity, and making one person (if it were, he could not then have supplicated in the world, as he did in the garden; for his humanity was joined to his divinity in that humbled, as well as in his exalted state. He was God in the days of his flesh when he lived amongst mortals, as well as now in the days of his glory); yet his praying with so deep a humiliation as he did in this lower region of the earth, is inconsistent with his glorified state in heaven; for if the glory of heaven wipes tears from the eyes of his members, it doth certainly from the eyes of the Head. Nor is it a supplication in the gesture of kneeling, for he is an advocate at the right hand of God, where he is always expressed as *sitting*, and but once (as I remember) as *standing*, and that was in the case of Stephen, Acts vii. 55. This some of the fathers and others call a servile manner of praying, and say that it was not convenient for the Father to require it of Christ in his elevated state, nor for the Son to perform it.

2. Yet it may be a kind of petition, an expressing his desires in a supplicatory manner. Though he be a king upon his throne, yet being settled in that royal authority by his Father, as his delegate, he is in regard of that inferior to the Father, and likewise in the economy of mediator. And also as his human nature is a creature, he may be a petitioner without any debasement to himself, to that power, by whose authority he is settled in his dignity, constituted in his mediatory office, and was both made and continues a creature. Though God 'hath put all things under him,' yet he did not put himself under him, but remains in his full authority, 1 Cor. xv. 27. His divine nature in union with his human, is no argument against it, for then he should not have petitioned on earth. He was then the same person in his disguise that he is now in glory. There are promises made to him which are not yet accomplished; enemies to be made his footstool, which are not yet brought into that lowest degree of subjection. Divine promises are to be turned into petitions; the heathen are promised to be his inheritance, but asking was ordered to precede the performance. Ps. ii. 8, שאל signifies to desire and wish, as well as to ask. There are some things still of want, though not in Christ personal, yet in Christ mystical, till the church be fully completed. He is an high priest in heaven, and it is the office of a high priest to pray for those for whom he hath offered the sacrifice. Why should asking, by way of desire or petition, be more uncomely when there is yet something of indigence, than praising after supplies, which Christ doth in heaven; if we understand those words of Christ, Ps. lxix. 30, 'I will praise the name of God with a song, and will magnify him with thanksgiving,' after he should be set on high? And Ps. xxii. 25, 'My praise shall be of thee in the great congregation, and I will pay my vows before them that fear him.' Both which psalms, upon perusal, you will find prophetic of Christ. And himself expresseth, that what he was to do in heaven for the accomplishment of the promise of the Spirit which he had made to them, was to be by way of prayer: John xiv. 16, 'I will pray the Father, and he shall give you another Comforter.' He speaks of an asking or praying (for the word signifies both the one and the other), not in this life, but after his ascension, for

the first and necessary fruit of his death, viz., the Comforter. He evidenceth hereby, that his glory should not cloud his mercy, and the cares of their concerns; his love should be stronger than death or glory, and he would not rest till he had obtained of infinite goodness what was necessary for them. This he would do by way of asking, which inclines to a petitionary way when a boon is desired.

3. It is such a petition as is in the nature of a claim or demand. It is not a petition for that which is at the liberty of the petitioned person to grant or refuse, but for that which the petitioner hath a right to by way of purchase, and the person petitioned to cannot in justice deny. An advocate is an officer in a court of judicature, demanding audience and sentence in a judicial way. So that this intercession of Christ is not a bare precarious intercession;* for as when he was in the world he taught as one having authority, and not as the scribes, Mat. vii. 29, so in heaven he intercedes as one having authority by virtue of his mediatory power, and not as an ordinary supplicant. He hath a right to demand. On earth, indeed, he had only promises of assistance to put in suit; but in heaven he pleads the conditions performed on his part, upon which the promises made to Christ become due to him. It is now, 'Father, I have glorified thee upon the earth; now glorify me with thy own self,' John xvii. 4, 5. He pleads for his people as they are the gift of his Father, and as they have received his words, ver. 8. He pleads his own commission as one sent, ver. 23. He minds the Father of the covenant between them both, as God gave him a command what he should do in the world, which was no other but an injunction to perform those conditions which had been agreed upon, and that will of God expressed in the covenant of redemption, which is called the will of God, Heb. x. 7. Christ, having done this will, mediates for the performance of the conditions God was bound to by this covenant, and claims the performance of them *jure pacti*, as a debt due to his meritorious obedience on the cross; so that it is not a *desire* only in a way of charity, but a *claim* in a way of justice, by virtue of meriting, and a demand of the performance of the promise. There were promises made by God to Christ as our head and representative 'before the world began,' Tit. i. 1, 2, and 2 Tim. i. 9, when he was fore-ordained to suffering, 1 Pet. i. 20. Eternal life was 'promised before the world began.' To whom could this promise of so long a date be made? Not to any creature, since it was before any creature had a being. Therefore to Christ; not for himself, who was the eternal Son of God. This promise and this grace, given us in Christ, he sues out by his intercession as a feoffee in trust for us; and it being added, 'which God, that cannot lie, promised,' gives us an intimation of the manner of Christ's pleading, in calling the truth of God to witness the validity of the promise which he pleads. It seems to be in an expostulatory manner, as we find it before his incarnation: Zech. i. 12, 'How long, Lord?' which was upon the account of his future incarnation; for which reason he that is called the angel, ver. 12, who was the angel of the covenant, is called 'the man,' ver. 10. So the expostulation of Elias with God is called particularly intercession, Rom. xi. 2; and Rev. iii. 5 intimates it by way of claim, 'He that overcomes, I will confess (ἐξομολογήσομαι) his name before my Father;' I will confess him plainly and clearly, and claim him as one that belongs to me. His advocacy for us is a confession of our interest in him, our owning of him, by virtue of which confession or claim we are set right in the court of God, as those for whom he hath shed his blood.

4. This intercessory demand or asking is accompanied with a presenting

* Mares. contra Volkel, lib. iii. cap. xxxviii. p. 378.

the memorials of his death. It is a commemoration of the sacrifice which he offered on earth for our expiation; and the whole power of intercession, with the prevalency of it, is wholly upon this foundation. It is a presenting the efficacy of his death, the virtue of his blood, the pleasure of God in the sacrifice offered by him. It is by the displaying the whole merit of his passion that he doth solicit for us. Intercession is not properly a sacerdotal act, without respect to the sacrifice. It was with the blood of the sacrifice that the high priest was to enter into the holy of holies, and sprinkle it there. The same blood that had been shed without on the day of expiation was to be carried within the veil. What was done typically, Christ doth really: first give himself a sacrifice, and then present himself as the sacrifice for us. The apostle shews us the manner of it, Heb. xii. 24. The blood of Christ is a speaking blood, as well as the blood of Abel; it speaks in the same manner as Abel's blood did, though not for the same end.* As the blood of Abel, presenting itself before the eyes of God, was as powerful to draw down the vengeance of God as if it had uttered a cry as loud as to reach to heaven; so the blood of Christ, being presented before the throne of God, powerfully excites the favour of God by the loudness of its cry. He speaks by his blood, and his blood speaks by its merit. The petitions of his lips had done us no good without the voice of his blood. He stands as a lamb slain when he presents the prayers of the saints, Rev. v. 6, 8, with his bleeding wounds open, as so many mouths full of pleas for us; and every one of them is the memorial and mark of the things which he suffered, and for what end he suffered them, as the wounds of a soldier received in the defence, and for the honour of his country, displayed to persons sensible of them, are the loudest and best pleas for the grant of his request. If the party-coloured rainbow, being looked upon by God, minds him of his covenant not to destroy the world again by a deluge, Gen. ix. 14–16, much more are the wounds which Christ bears, both in his hands, feet, and side, remembrancers to him of the covenant of grace made with repenting and believing sinners. The look of God upon those wounds, whereby so great an oblation is remembered, doth as efficaciously move him to look kindly upon us, as the look upon the rainbow disposeth him to the continuance of the world. If our Saviour had not a mouth to speak, he had blood to plead; and his blood cries louder in heaven for us than his voice did in any of the prayers he uttered upon earth; for by this his performance of the articles on his part is manifested, and the performance of the promises on God's part solicited. When he sees what the Redeemer hath done, he reflects upon what himself is to do. The blood of Christ speaks the tenor of the covenant of redemption made with Christ on the behalf of sinners.

5. It is a presenting our persons to God, together with his blood, in an affectionate manner; as the high priest, when he went into the holy of holies, was to bear the names of the children of Israel in the breastplate of judgment upon his heart, Exod. xxviii. 29, to which the church alludes in her desire that she might be 'set as a seal upon the heart' of her beloved, Cant. viii. 6; and perhaps an allusion may be also in Rev. iii. 5, confessing the names of the victorious sufferers before his Father, bearing their names visibly before him. The persons of believers are his jewels, locked up in the cabinet of his own breast, and shewed to his Father in the exercise of his priestly office.

IV. The fourth thing. That Christ doth perpetually manage this office.

* Daillé sur le Descent d'Esprit, serm. i. 461.

The first evidence is in the text, 'We *have* an advocate;' we have at this present; we have an advocate actually remembering us in his thoughts, and presenting us to his Father; we in this age, we in all ages, till the dissolution of the world, without any faintness in the degrees of his intercession, without any interruption in time. He never ceases the exercise of this office, so far as it is agreeable to that high and elevated state wherein he is. As there are continual sins of believers in all ages of the world, so there are constant pleas of the advocate. This epistle was written many years after the ascension of Christ; some think in the time of John's banishment in the isle of Patmos, some think after; yet at that time he owns himself to have a share in the benefit of this intercession. The term *we* is inclusive of himself. Christ is an intercessor for us in the whole course of our pilgrimage. All the time that we have any need of him, his voice is the same still, 'I will that they behold my glory which thou hast given me,' till they are wafted from hence to a full vision of it. This is the true end of his heavenly life, and his living for ever there: Heb. vii. 25, 'Seeing he ever lives to make intercession for them.' He lives solely to this purpose, to discharge this part of his priesthood for us. His advocacy is, like his life, without end. As he died once to merit our redemption, so he lives always to make application of redemption. He would not answer the end of his life if he did not exercise the office of his priesthood. It would not be a love like that of a God, if he did not bear his people continually upon his heart. He was the author of our faith by enduring the cross, and the finisher of our faith by sitting down at the right hand of God, Heb. xii. 2. He will be exercised in it as long as there is any faith to be finished and completed in the world. His oblation was a transient act; but his appearance in heaven for us is a permanent act, and continues for ever. His mediatory glory is not consummate, though his personal be. He hath yet a mystical self to be perfected, a fulness to be enriched with. He cannot be intent upon this without minding the concerns of, and putting up pleas for, his people; for they are one with him, 'the fulness of him that fills all in all,' Eph. i. 23. There can be no cessation of his work till his enemies be conquered, and his whole mystical body wrapped up in glory. If he had finished this part of his function, we should have had him here again before this time, with all his train of angels, to put an end to the present state of things, as the high priest stayed no longer in the holy of holies than was necessary for the atoning their sins, expecting the felicity of an acceptation, that he might bring the welcome news of it to the people that waited without. As soon as he hath reduced all the elect to an happy state, he will come again, for 'the heavens receive him' only till 'the restitution of all things' is completed, Acts iii. 21; and then 'he shall come with a shout,' 1 Thes. iv. 16, all the angels in heaven triumphing and applauding the accomplishment of redemption.

It is necessary it should be so.

1. Because it is founded upon his death. As his oblation is of eternal efficacy, so his advocacy hath an everlasting virtue. It is an 'eternal redemption,' Heb. ix. 12, and therefore an eternal intercession. This the apostle signifies in the text by arguing from his propitiation to his advocacy; he is at present an advocate with an uninterrupted plea, because he is at present a propitiation in the efficacy of his passion. There was an end of his actual suffering when he expired, but no end of the virtue of his sacrifice; and therefore no end of his intercession, which depended not upon his death simply considered, but upon the value of it. It is in the virtue of this he pleads; since the virtue of his blood is perpetual, the plea grounded upon that virtue, and which is nothing but the voice of his blood, is of the same duration.

There can be no end of the intercession of his person till there be an exhausting of the merits of his death; the one must fail in its strength before the other cease in its plea; his blood must be a speechless blood before he can be a silent advocate. As the continual sacrifice typified the continual virtue of the Redeemer's death, so the perpetual burning incense signified the perpetuity of his intercession; and no less was signified by the sprinkling the blood of the sacrifice upon the mercy-seat, which was not wiped off, but stuck there, as a visible mark, and remained as a continual solicitor for the continuance of grace and favour to the people.

2. The exercise of this office must be as durable as the office itself. His priesthood is for ever, therefore the act belonging to his priesthood is for ever. He was more particularly constituted an high priest 'after the order of Melchisedec' when he entered into heaven 'as a forerunner for us,' Heb. vi. 20, where he abides an high priest continually, Heb. vii. 3; made so 'not after the law of a carnal command,' or a command to be abrogated, but 'after the power of endless life,' ver. 15, 16; and 'confirmed by the oath of God a priest for ever,' ver. 21; and therefore exerciseth his function of a priest for ever. Not of sacrificing himself, because he lives for ever, and cannot die again, but of interceding, since no other act belonging to the priesthood can be exercised in that glorious and endless state he hath in heaven but this of intercession, which must be without intermission, because it is the only act of that office which he can perform. It is not said he is a man for ever, but a priest for ever, which is a name of an office, and implies an exercise of the office. He is not called a priest for ever in regard of his life, but in regard of his function for which he lives. His mouth cannot be stopped by God, because he was constituted by the irreversible oath of God. God cannot deny himself, and destroy his own solemn act. He is a priest for ever, without repentance on God's part; he must therefore perpetually mind his office, the neglect of it else would cause repentance in God for exalting him to so high a dignity, and be a reflection upon divine wisdom, to settle one in this excellent place that were too weak for it, or too careless in it, that should bear only the title, and neglect the work; it would be a cause of repentance in God at the expending so much grace to no purpose. This advocate, as he bears the name of priest, so he appeared clothed with a priestly robe: Rev. i. 13, 'He had a garment down to the feet, and girt about the paps with a golden girdle,' which was the habit of the high priest under the law. As he is an everlasting priest, so he manages an everlasting intercession. He was too faithful in discharging his part on earth, to be negligent of performing his office in heaven; he did not embrace so great an honour to be idle in it, and neglect the work and duty that his place called for.

3. This was both the reason and end of his advancement. The intercession he made for transgressors was one reason why God would 'divide him a portion with the great,' Isa. liii. 12; 'because he made intercession for the transgressors.' This is alleged as one reason, among others there mentioned, of his glorious exaltation, which intercession is most evident to us in his last prayer, John xvii., wherein he prays for all that should believe on him. And also upon the cross, when he prays for his murderers: 'Father, forgive them, for they know not what they do,' Luke xxiii. 34. An act so pleasing to God as to be the motive to give him the division of the spoil of the strong, cannot but be perpetual. Will Christ, who always did what was pleasing to God on earth, discontinue that which is so delightful to the bowels of his mercy? He cannot look upon his own glory, the robe he wears, the throne he sits on, the enemies prostrate at his feet, but he must reflect upon the reason of his present state, and be excited to a redoubling his solicitations for his people.

He would be no longer glorious than he were an advocate. The superstructure cannot stand when the foundation moulders. Since he was anointed with the oil of gladness above his fellows, because he loved righteousness and hated iniquity, he cannot be unmindful of promoting the destruction of the one and the perfection of the other. A perpetual action will be the result of these perpetual qualities; and being anointed a priest for these qualities, he will act as a priest for the glory of them, which can be no other way but by intercession. It was the end of his advancement: Heb. x. 12, 'But this man, after he had offered one sacrifice for sins, for ever sat down on the right hand of God.' The antithesis is made between him and the legal priests; they stood at the altar every day offering the same sacrifices, but this (not *man* as it is in our translation, but rather to be supplied with *priest*) this priest, having finished his work on earth, sat down for ever, viz. as a priest, on the right hand of God, and never leaves the place. Other priests stood, as not having finished their sacrificing work, but were to repeat it again; this priest sits, as having finished his sacrificing function, and having attained the glory due to his person. His sitting down is not mentioned only as a point of honour, but of office; he sat down as one that had offered a complete sacrifice in the nature of a priest, and sat down for ever to exercise his priesthood at the right hand of God. This verse, compared with the other, would not else have a full sense; and the words following second it, ver. 13, he sat down 'expecting till his enemies be made his footstool,' expecting the full fruits of that sacrifice in the complete subjection of his enemies, and consequently the full felicity of himself and his friends; and all this time of expectation he is suing out the promise of God to him, asking that inheritance which was assured him in the covenant between them, Ps. ii. 8. This is the reason of his sitting down for ever to exercise his priesthood for ever in the presence of the King and Judge of all the earth. He is always in the presence of his Father in the dignity of his person and fulness of his merit, continually spreading every part of his meritorious sacrifice in the view of God. The high priest entered into the holy of holies but once a year, but this high priest sits for ever in the court in a perpetual exercise of his function, both as a priest and a sacrifice. And since his own sacrifice for sins offered on earth was sufficient, he hath nothing to do perpetually in heaven but to sprinkle the blood of that sacrifice upon the mercy-seat. He is never out of the presence of God; and the infiniteness of his compassions may hinder us from imagining a silence in him when any accusations are brought in against us. The accusations might succeed well were he out of the way; but being always present, he is always active in his solicitations. No clamour can come against us but he hears it, as being on the right hand of his Father, and appears as our attorney there in the presence of God to answer it, as the high priest appeared in the holy of holies for all the people.

V. Thing is, the efficacy of this intercession. The efficacy of it is implied in the text, both in the person of our advocate, *Jesus Christ;* in his quality, *righteous;* in regard of the work he had wrought on earth, *propitiation;* in the object of his intercession, and the place, *with the Father*. He is an advocate to the Father; not only *to* him at a distance, but *with* him. The constant presence of a favourite with a king, of a princely son with a royal father, is a means to make his intercessions of force with him. He is an advocate, and he is constantly with the Father in that capacity. A letter from a friend is not so successful as a personal appearance for gaining a suit. If his death were meritorious, his prayer must be so too, as being put up in virtue of his meritorious blood; and though we are reconciled by his death, yet we are saved by his life, with a *much more*, Rom. v. 10; not formally in regard of merit, for that was the effect of his death, but in regard of application of that merit, the end for which he lives, to render it efficacious to us, as it had been in his passion valuable for us. If he separated himself to death to procure it, he will employ the authority and dignity of his life to finish and apply it. As none offered so noble a sacrifice, so none lives a more powerful life. As when he was on earth never man spake as he spake, so, now he is in heaven, never did any man or angel plead as he pleads. If 'whatsoever we ask in his name' we shall receive, John xvi. 23, surely whatsoever he asks in his own name will not be refused.

1. This was typified.* The strength of his mediation was signified by the horns, ordered by a special precept to be made upon the four corners of the altar of burnt-offerings, Exod. xxvii. 2, and also upon the altar of incense, Exod. xxx. 2. As the brazen altar signified the strength of his death, so the golden altar signified the excellency of his intercession, horns in Scripture being an emblem of strength, power, and dignity. And perhaps his feet of brass wherewith he is described, Rev. i. 15, when he appears to John in a priestly garb, signifies his irresistible standing before God in the exercise of that office. Much more may be said of him, as it was of Jacob, Gen. xxxii. 28, 'As a prince he hath power with God,' by his death and intercession, as well as power with men by his Spirit, and prevails in all when he pleases.

2. It was prophesied of Christ, Ps. xxi. 2, 'Thou hast given him his heart's desire, and hast not withholden the request of his lips.' This psalm seems to be a comment upon part of the second psalm, or rather a dialogue between Christ and the Father, Christ speaking ver. 1, and the Father promising him a full victory, ver. 8, which is a prophetical triumph of the church after the victory gained by the passion of Christ. And of the Messiah, the Chaldee and some of the Jews understand it. The expressions in the psalm are many of them too illustrious to be meant of David, as ver. 4, 'length of days for ever and ever,' which cannot be understood of David in his royalty as a mortal man. God had given Christ the right of asking, and grants him whatsoever he asks; he bestows upon him whatsoever he desires, and refuseth nothing that he sues for. The good of his people is the desire of his heart, and the request of his lips, and nothing is refused that his heart wishes, and his lips move for. This, of the efficacy of his intercession, is the salvation he rejoices in. The pleasing and favourable countenance of God is that which makes him exceeding glad. He would have little content in the rest of his glory without this power of prevalency with his Father. Since his intercession for his church is for his own mystical glory, it must be successful, or his own glory would be in part defective, since it is linked with that of his church, which is yet behind. As Christ glorified the Father, so the Father is reciprocally to glorify the Son, John xvii. 4, 5, which is by giving him a power of asking, and engaging himself to a facility of granting. A promise of granting was annexed to the command of asking: Ps. ii. 8, 'I will give.' He should not be so ready to request as the Father would be liberal to bestow. He was promised a mighty encouragement till he had set judgment in the earth, and wrought a perfect deliverance for his people, Isa. xlii. 4. It is to this contrite person that he would look perpetually favourably, Isa. lxvi. 1, 2. It is that person by whom the ceremonial law was to be torn in pieces to whom God promised to look.

3. God never denied him any request which he put up upon the earth for the divine glory and his people's good, and Christ himself acknowledges its

* Lightfoot, Temple, cap. xxxiv. p. 198, 199.

John xi. 42, 'I know that thou hearest me always.' He did but groan in his spirit without moving his lips, ver. 38; and how soon did his groans rise into hallelujahs: ver. 41, 'Father, I thank thee that thou hast heard me.' As soon as ever he sighed, he had an occasion of praise. He was heard in all his petitions in the world, Heb. v. 7, εἰσακουσθεὶς, heard to purpose; while he was in the days of his flesh encompassed and pressed with the infirmities of our nature, much more will he be heard in the days of his glory. He was not indeed heard for himself at the time of his suffering, so as to have what he begged formally granted; for in that prophetic psalm, Ps. xxii. 3, he complains that he had cried all the day, and God heard him not. His prayer that the cup might pass from him was *in specie* denied him. That prayer proceeded from a natural fear and horror of an accursed death as he was man, and is therefore said to be in the days of his flesh, when he had our natural infirmities about him, which was not also an absolute desire, but conditional. 'If it were possible,' *i. e.* if it were not prejudicial to the glory of God and the salvation of his people; yet in this also he was heard; for though he was not delivered from death, he was supported in it. The death was to be suffered, and yet to be conquered; and afterwards his bloody passion was changed into a spiritual and glorious life by a resurrection. He was heard ἀπὸ εὐλαβείας; a deliverance from his fears and horrors was granted, that he might with courage proceed on in his suffering. Christ sometimes prayed as mediator, and for things in order to his mediatory work, as when he prayed for the raising of Lazarus, that by so great a miracle his doctrine might be propagated, and the faith of his disciples strengthened: John xi. 40, 42, It was for the glory of God, and that they might believe that God had sent him. In this Christ was never in the least denied, and to this that speech of his success, 'Thou hearest me always,' refers. He utters this confidence and assurance in the hearing of the people, 'that they may believe that thou hast sent me.' Thou hearest me always, when what I desire tends to the propagation of the gospel doctrine, and the faith and advantage of that people to whom and for whom thou hast sent me. But in those prayers he puts up from human affections, and the innocent inclinations of nature, as that in the garden which he put up from a human sense, yet with a condition; and that upon the cross, which he puts up as a man subject to the laws of charity; though he was not formally answered, yet he was not absolutely denied, because he did not absolutely beg, but with a condition expressed or implied. It was not possible that cup should pass away from him according to the determination of things and the predictions of the prophets, without a manifest alteration of purpose in God, breach of his word, and the utter ruin and devastation of mankind. And for that prayer upon the cross, Luke xxiii. 34, 'Father, forgive them; they know not what they do,' a condition is implied, viz. if they did repent and believe. It cannot be supposed that he prayed for their pardon without their repentance, whether they repented and believed or no; and indeed the motive that he urgeth implies a condition, 'they know not what they do,' implying that when they came to be sensible, and to know with an inward penitent practical knowledge what they had done, that they had crucified the Lord of life, God would pardon them, which without doubt he would, according to the tenor of his own promise. But to consider rightly that petition of his in the garden, the refusing his request upon the account of the impossibility of the passing away of the cup, doth strongly conclude the efficacy of his intercession in heaven. The reason why he was not answered was because such a grant had been inconsistent with the redemption of his people; and upon the same reason he will be answered in every suit in heaven, because he doth everything pursuant to the redemption and full felicity of believers. He intercedes not there, as he prayed sometimes on earth, as a man, but as a mediator. If anything were denied him on earth because the refusal conduced to the advantage of his elect, it necessarily follows that he will have all things granted him in heaven which are for the glory of God, the happiness of his people, and the fulness of their redemption. The same reason God hath now to allow his pleas, which before he had to refuse them. The necessity of his death for redemption was the cause of the refusal. The accomplishment of redemption, which is that he now intercedes for, cannot be denied him upon the same account, but he will always carry the cause he sues for. As to that petition upon the cross, he was answered in it. Many of those whose hands were red with his blood, had their hearts afterwards filled with repentance, and their heads crowned with pardon; and if his prayer upon the cross was so efficacious for some of his bloody persecutors, shall it have less force in heaven for his affectionate friends, since it is for those that believe, and not for the world, that he there intercedes? John xvii. 9. If he were heard always, as himself asserts, before he had offered that sacrifice, much more in heaven, since he had completed it, and is now suing out his own right after he had paid God his. If his prayers were so prevalent here before he had accomplished his task of suffering, his intercession is much more prevalent above, since his sufferings are at an end, which are the ground of his intercession.

Now this intercession must needs be efficacious, if you consider,

(1.) His person.

[1.] The greatness of it. A person in the form of God, infinitely more excellent than all the tribes of angels; a person so great, that all the creatures in heaven and earth, and millions of worlds cannot equal him, they being less to him than a grain of sand to the glorious sun. It cannot be said of all creatures that ever were made, or of all that ever God can make, that in them all dwells the fulness of the Godhead bodily; as it is said of Christ, Col. ii. 9, he is not as the highest angel, that must cover his face, and stand before the throne, but the man, God's fellow, sitting upon the throne with him, Zech. xiii. 17; applied to Christ, Mat. xxvi. 31. He is equal with God, and therefore cannot be refused by God. As his divine nature gave value to his satisfaction, so it gives efficacy to his intercession. His agonies in the garden, and his gaspings upon the cross, were rendered by the greatness of his person mighty to reconcile us, and by the same, his pleas in heaven are rendered successful to save us. His humanity being in conjunction with his divinity, is the instrument, that receives all its virtue from the Deity. Though he doth not intercede with God, as himself is God, because in that respect he is equal with God, but as mediator in his human nature, yet his intercession as man receives a power and dignity from him as God, which causes the prevalency of it. What there was of humility and supplication in his prayers upon earth, proceeded from his human nature; what there was of authority and efficacy in his mediatory interpositions, proceeded from his divine nature. He was bound to die as he was man, taking upon him our sins; he had a right to have his death accepted, as he was God assuming and sustaining our nature. It is a privilege due to the greatness of his person to have his suit granted, as it is his duty, as the high priest of his church, to present it in the holy of holies. The infinite worth of his prayers results from his divine nature, as well as the infinite worth of his passion; and being the intercessions of a divine person, they are as powerful as his sufferings were meritorious. In regard of this greatness of his person, God seems to stand in an admiring posture at the approach of Christ to him: Jer. xxx. 21, 'Who is this that hath engaged his heart to approach unto me?' and presently the decree passes out for the confirming the fruits of his mediation in the fullest manner: ver. 22, and 'ye shall be my people, and I will be your God,' taking them as his own propriety, and giving himself to them as their portion. Nothing can be denied to so great a person. We know the suits of princes meet with greater success than those of peasants. In the same capacity that Christ performed his oblation, he manages his intercession; it was 'through the eternal Spirit,' the strength of his deity, he offered up himself to God; and so through the eternal Spirit, the strength of his deity, he presents his supplications to God.

[2.] His near relation to the Father. As there was to be a respect to him in regard of the greatness of his person, so there was an affection due to him in regard of the nearness of his relation. It is against the rules of justice to deny him his requests, because of his obedience, and against the rules of goodness to deny him his respects,* because of his alliance. As he was from eternity begotten by the Father, and his particular delight, his person cannot but be very acceptable to God. It is upon this relation his consecration to his eternal priesthood is founded, which he exerciseth in this administration: Heb. vii. 28, 'The word of the oath makes the Son,' *i.e.* priest, 'who is consecrated for evermore.' Upon the account of this relation he had the power of asking, and the privilege of obtaining: Ps. ii. 7, 8, 'Thou art my Son, ask of me.' It is this relation enters thee into this honour and glory; this prerogative had not been granted but as thou art my Son; and when he went into heaven, to appear in the presence of God for us, he was entertained as a Son-priest, not only as a priest in relation to us, but as a Son in relation to his Father: Heb. iv. 14, 'We have a great high priest that is passed into the heavens, Jesus the Son of God;' and the text implies that he manages his advocacy in heaven with God as a Father, rather than with God as a Judge: 'advocate with the Father.' He appeals to God in heaven under the title of a Father, as God considered him in all his expressions to him in the world as his Son: 'This is my Son, in whom I am well pleased; this is my Son, hear him;' carrying himself in all ways of paternal tenderness to him while he was upon earth, which cannot but be as strong now he is in heaven. He always considered him in the capacity of his Son, as well as our surety. As Christ was placed in this office as a Son, so he doth manage it as a Son; in the same capacity he was placed in this function, he doth exercise this office. Now what can render his intercession more efficacious than his relation? If Moses, a man, could screen a people from divine anger, and cool the wrath of a provoked God, by interposing between God and the offenders, so that God should say to him, 'Let me alone, that my wrath may wax hot against this people, and I may consume them at once,' Exod. xxxii. 10; and when Moses would not silence his cry, God at length would silence his wrath, ver. 14;—if Moses, who was dignified only with a glorious title of his friend, with whom he spake face to face, had so great a power, how forcible must be the interposition of that person, who hath the more illustrious title of that of his Son? What suit can be cast out of the court that is presented by a beloved Son, of whom he hath signally pronounced that in him he is well pleased, and well pleased with whatsoever he doeth? Denials would be an argument of displeasure, not of a well-pleasedness; it would then be a Son with whom I am displeased, if any plea he makes be rejected as invalid. To whom should he grant anything if he refused his Son, and his Son upon the same throne with himself, and put a slur upon him in the face of the whole host of

* Qu. 'requests'?—ED.

heaven? If an earthly father knows how to give good gifts to his children that ask him, a heavenly Father doth much more, and most of all to an only-begotten and only beloved Son, for whose sake he loves all his other children. It is a consideration that discovers the sincerity and tenderness of divine mercy. Had not God intended to hear him in all his requests for us, he would never have appointed one so nearly allied to him to plead our cause; one that he could not deny without some dishonour to so near a relation, and a reflection upon his own affection, as he might have done to some inferior person. God would not love his Son according to his own greatness, if he did not express it in the most signal marks of his favour.

[3.] The special love God bears to his person for what he hath done in the earth, and doth yet in heaven. Could there have been any increase of the Fatherly affections to him, his person had been more endeared to God after he had performed so exact an obedience. After he had triumphed over the enemies of his Father's honour, he might challenge as a reward the most sprightly sparklings of his Father's affection. What could hinder the grant of his suit, when the flames of that wrath in his Father's breast, which was an hindrance to any request, were quenched? Since justice was silenced, no other voice could be heard but that of tenderness and love, which was the spring of that power he gave him after his conflict; power in heaven as well as in earth, Mat. xxviii. 18, which may comprehend a power with God as well as power over angels; a power with God, not over God. Though the relation of a son be endearing, yet, when the quality of obedience is added to the dearness of that relation, it enlarges and inflames paternal affection, and renders the Father more inclinable to grant any request that is made to him by such a person; as a king will listen more to the petitions of a son who had done him signal service, and brought by his achievements a renown and honour to his name and government, than to a son barely in the relation of a child, without testifying the same affection and obedience in such eminent enterprises. If the Father had so special a care of Christ in the management of his office in the world, as to uphold him in his arms, as Sanctius saith the word אתמך signifies, Isa. xlii. 1, and support him in the depth of his misery; much more delight hath he in him now in heaven, since he hath brought that honour to him, that no created men or angels were ever capable to offer him. He will not be insensible of so great an obedience, or stain that glory he hath given him for it, by denying anything he presents to him. How can God express a greater affection to him, than by committing the government of the world into his hands? And as the apostle argues in our case, Rom. viii. 32, from his delivery of his Son up for us to an assurance of the free gift of all things else, so it may in this, since he hath put the sceptre for a time into his hands, and from a boundless affection invested him in the government of the world, how shall he refuse him anything in the confines of it, since he hath during this state of things committed all judgment and power or rule to him? John v. 22. If his intercession upon earth for transgressors was a motive to God to clothe him with so great a glory, as hath been before mentioned from Isaiah liii. 12, his intercession in heaven (every way as delightful to him) would excite him to confer a greater glory on him, were it possible for him to be elevated to a throne of a higher pitch. The one hath as mighty an influence upon his affections as the other, and there is the same reason of both. There is an intimate union and an affectionate communion between the Father and the Son in heaven in regard of this advocacy: 'Believe me that I am in the Father, and the Father in me,' John xiv. 11, which he speaks upon a discourse of his ascension, ver. 2, 3, and to encourage them to ask in his name after his going to the Father, ver. 13. Believers have not only an advocate with the Father for them, but the person that was offended is now united to them in their advocate by an indissoluble league and communion, and unalterable affection. And as whatsoever we ask in his name should be, 'that the Father might be glorified in the Son,' ver. 13, so whatsoever Christ sues for is for the same end, which must needs in the very act of it fix him more strongly in that affection, which was due to him upon the account of his eternal alliance and his unspotted obedience.

2. It must needs be efficacious in regard of the pleas themselves, the matter of them.

(1.) The matter of his plea is holy. It is, as was said, that the Father might be glorified in the Son in regard of his holiness and righteousness, and it is included in the text, by the epithet *righteous*, 'Jesus Christ the righteous'; righteous in his person, righteous in his office as an advocate, both in the pleas he makes, and the manner of managing them. He is 'holy, and harmless, and undefiled,' as an high priest, Heb. vii. 26. All his petitions are as himself, unspotted, his suit is as holy as his nature; if there be no guile in his mouth, there can be no iniquity in his plea. Our prayers are of themselves rejected because of their impurity, Christ's intercession is accepted because of its perfection. If a sinful Jacob prevailed with God, much more must a perfectly holy Jesus, presenting nothing to God but what is becoming the purity and mercifulness of his own nature to grant. If his blood were 'without blemish,' 1 Peter i. 19, his intercession must be without spot, because the one is the sole foundation of the other.

(2.) It is nothing but what he hath merited. He doth not desire as a bare supplicant, but pleads in a way of right and justice. What he sues for is due to him from God's truth, because of his promise, and from God's righteousness, because of his merit. So that his suit is put up *ratione meriti, ratione juris*, he intercedes for no more than he hath purchased, and may demand as a due debt. It is necessary God should render what he owes unto that person that hath merited of him; he would be unrighteous if he did not, or put a note of insufficiency upon the sufferings of his Son. What he pleads for in heaven, is nothing but what he sued for on earth, John xvii. 4, 5, upon the account of his glorifying his Father, *i. e.* rendering to him what was due by agreement between them; no doubt but the same argument is used by him in heaven; the matter of his plea is what he hath merited, viz., pardon of sin, sanctification, continuance of justification, all which he sued for in that chapter. The Father hath acknowledged it already a just demand, for by his raising him from the dead, he hath given his approbation of all the acts of his life, not only to his death, whereby he merited, but to his prayers, whereby he supplicated for those things which he now solicits for in heaven, upon the account of the glory he did by his incarnation and passion bring to God. No plea can prevail against him, since he hath conquered his enemies, wiped out the guilt of sin by his sacrifice, condemned sin in the flesh, led captivity captive; and all this not by a mere strength, but by a legal right; having satisfied the rigours of the law, prevailed at the tribunal of justice (which was the sharpest tug and hardest conquest), all which God hath subscribed to, by setting him 'at his right hand, far above principalities and powers,' Eph. iv. 8. Yet, in as legal a way as he merited it, he might sue out the fruits of his merit. Shall he not much more prevail at the throne of grace by his intercession, since the mouth of justice, which gave life and strength to all suits against us, is perfectly stopped by the merit of his death? It hath nothing to except against the issues of mercy upon the perpetual pleading of that merit; what he doth sue for is rather short of, than outweighs his merit. An infinite merit deserves infinite blessings, but all the blessings he solicits for are finite in themselves, though proceeding from infinite grace, and purchased by a payment of infinite value. God cannot be unjust to detain the goods and the price paid for them; Christ must have his death and sufferings given back again and uneffected, which is impossible, or else have the fruits of his death given to him and to those for whom he suffered.

(3.) Whatsoever he pleads for is agreeable to the will of his Father. The will of Christ whereby he intercedes, is the same with the will of the Father with whom he intercedes; and when the will of an eternal mercy and the will of an infinite merit meet together, what will not be the fruit of such a glorious conjunction? As on earth he did nothing but what he saw the Father do, John v. 19, 20, so he intercedes for nothing but what he knows the Father wills. What he did on earth was not without, but with, his Father's will; what he doth in heaven hath the same rule. As they were joint in the counsel of reconciliation and peace, which was 'between them both,' Zech. vi. 13, so they are joint in the counsel of advocacy and intercession, which is between them both, the one as the director, the other as the solicitor. Their wills are in the highest manner conformable to one another, and the will of the Father as much known by the soul of Christ in heaven as it was on earth. He asks nothing but he first reads in the copy of his Father's instructions, and considers what his will was. He reads over the annals of his Father's decrees and records; he does nothing but what he sees the Father do; he takes the copy of all from his Father, and whatsoever Christ doth, the same doth the Father also. They have but one will in the whole current of redemption, so that he can plead nothing in regard of the persons for whom he appears, and the good things he desires for them, but it is according to the will of God. When he came into the world, he came 'not to do his own will,' *i. e.* only his own will, 'but the will of him that sent him;' and when he returned, he went up, not to do his own will, but the will of him that accepted him. The persons were given him by God for the ends which he intercedes for; the words Christ gave them were first given him by God; and this will of God, and his people receiving his words, he urgeth all along as an argument for the grant of his prayer, John xvii. 8, 9. His intercession is in some sort a part of his obedience as well as his passion; by his obedient suffering he learned a further act of obedience, Heb. v. 8, which could not be practised here but in heaven. The apostle seems to refer this obedience to that part of his office as high priest in heaven after the order of Melchisedec, which he discourseth of in that chapter. His whole advocacy is but pursuant to that command given him by his Father, of losing none of those that God had given him, but 'raising them up at the last day,' John vi. 39. What he doth in heaven is in a way of obedience to this obligation, and conducing to this end. There is not an answer of prayer which is the fruit of his advocacy, but the design of it is 'that the Father may be glorified in the Son,' John xiv. 13. As he glorified his Father on earth by his suffering, so he glorifies the same attributes by his intercession in heaven; it is for the glory of divine grace that the one purposed and the other acted, Eph. i. 5, 6. If he gives blessings for the glory of his Father, he then in his suit urgeth the glory of his Father as an argument to obtain them. God must then be an enemy to his own glory, if he be deaf to his Son's suit; and since the Advocate's plea is suitable to the Father's will, he cannot reject the will of his Son without offering violence to his own will. They are both one in will and one in affection. His human will cannot desire anything in opposition to the divine. Though he desired the passing away of the cup here, which was not agreeable to the divine will, yet it was without any sin, because with submission to the divine will; but since he is stripped of our infirmities, and hath no furnace of wrath any more to suffer in, there cannot in his intercession be so much as a conditional dissent from the divine will. What Christ acts now is upon that foundation which he laid here according to God's instructions. Christ had not come had not God sent him; the world had not been reconciled had not God employed him upon that errand. The whole plot was laid by him; it was his own purpose. Should God deny anything which was founded upon this his will, he would be mutable and deny himself; deny his own act and deed in denying the fruits of that work which was designed and cut out by himself. The intercession of Christ concurring with the eternal design of God, with his will, with the good pleasure of it, and being for the glory of his grace, he must be beloved in and for that very act of mediation, and consequently prevalent in it. To conclude: it was God's will to make any of you children, and he took a pleasure in purposing and effecting it, Eph. i. 5; and will he stop his ears when the wants of those children are presented to him for supplies by their mighty Advocate, who acts nothing but what is agreeable to the eternal pleasure of his Father's will?

(3.) In regard of the foundation of his intercession, his death. His intercession must be as powerful as his satisfaction. As he was a mighty surety for the discharge of men's debts, so he is a mighty intercessor for the salvation of men's souls, because his intercession is in the virtue of his satisfaction: he is an advocate, but by his propitiation; both are linked together in the text. His intercession being founded upon his death, his death may as soon want its virtue as his intercession its efficacy. If his blood is incorruptible, which must be concluded from the antithesis, 1 Peter i. 18, 'We are not redeemed with corruptible things, but with the precious blood of Christ.' If his blood be incorruptible, as being precious in the eyes of God, his intercessions are undeniable, as having an equal value in God's account. If his blood hath the same virtue now, which it had when it was first presented to God, his pleas must have the same virtue with his blood; as the one was owned, the other cannot be refused. There is a necessary connection between the perfection of the one and prevalency of the other. If his sacrifice be perfect, his plea upon it must be prevalent; if his plea be not prevalent, it must conclude the imperfection of his sacrifice. A *fiat* must be set upon all his petitions, since he hath finished his passive obedience. What greater rhetoric can there be in the tongues of men and angels than in the tongue of Christ? Yet all his eloquence cannot be so powerful as that of his gaping wounds. His blood hath the same efficacy in heaven that it had on earth; it speaks the same things, and must meet with the same success. His merit must be deficient before his intercession can be successless; and his blood will not want a voice while his death retains a satisfactory sufficiency. Having by his bloody obedience silenced justice, that it cannot put in any exception, he hath nothing to do but to solicit mercy, prone enough to bestow all good upon those that love him and believe in him.

(4.) In regard of the persons he intercedes for. They are those that are the special gift of God to him, as dear to the Father as to Christ: John xvii. 9, 'They are thine;' thine as well as mine; thine before they were mine; thine in purpose, mine by donation. There is a likeness in the love the Father bears to his people to that love which he bears to Christ. It is the argument Christ himself uses for the grant of what he desired in that intercessory model: John xvii. 23, 'That the world may know that thou hast loved them as thou hast loved me;' not that the Father might have a rise for his affection, but an occasion for the manifestation of his affection in the view of the world. And though Christ doth pray the Father, yet he intimates how easily his prayer for them would be granted; because, saith he, 'the Father himself loves you': John xvi. 26, 27, 'At that day you shall ask in my name: and I say not unto you, that I will pray the Father for you; for the Father himself loves you, because you have loved me.' Do not think the Father is so full of revenge that he must be earnestly pressed to be merciful to you. I do not say I will pray the Father for you, he of himself is inclinable to embrace you with the tenderest affection; he hath, for your love to me, a particular kindness for you. It is as if a favourite should say, I will entreat the king for you, but I need not; for he bears you such an affection because you are my friend, and belong to me, that he will, from his own inclination, be ready to do you all good. Christ doth not here deny his intercession for them, which before he had promised them, but would have them in their dependence consider not only his suing for them, but fix their mind upon the Father's love to them, and assure themselves there is nothing but they may expect from his immense bounty and infinite affection. The Father himself loves you in the greatness of his majesty; he hath as deep a stamp of affection to you as I myself have, and as you know I have manifested to you. The persons he intercedes for are those whom the Father loves, those whom the Father hath given him, those whom God hath justified, those for whom himself is a propitiation, those for whom he 'died and rose again;' for, Rom. viii. 33, 34, since they were the persons for whom he was intended as a sacrifice, and for whose good his glorious resurrection and exaltation were designed, there is no doubt but his intercession shall be accepted for them. When the love of the Father to the advocate, and his love to his clients, meet together, what a glorious success must be expected from such an intercession!

(5.) It is evidenced by the fruit of it.

[1.] Before his sacrifice. The text intimates it; as he was 'a *propitiation* for the whole world,' *i. e.* for all ages of the world, so he is an *advocate* in all ages of the world. How could the execution of God's vengeance upon the world for sin, at the first commission of it, have been prevented, but by the interposition of the Son of God? He interposed then by virtue of a promise to offer himself a sacrifice, he interposeth now by virtue of his actual performance. If it were so prevalent as to support the world for so many ages, in the midst of that abundance of mire and dirt which should overflow it, and to save those that should believe in a promised Messiah, it is much more powerful to save those that believe in a sacrificed and conquering Messiah. For as he was a lamb slain from the foundation of the world, so by the same reason he was an advocate pleading from the foundation of the world. The credit of his plea is the same with that of his passion; as he was a sufferer by promise from the foundation of the world, so he was an intercessor by virtue of that promise.* There is the same reason of his intercession upon the credit of his future suffering, as there was for the pardon of sin upon the credit of his future passion. Those that were saved before, were saved upon the account of his life as well as we; as they were reconciled by his death as well as we. For God made not several ways of salvation, one for them and another for us, Acts xv. 8, 9, 11. They were 'saved by faith;' by the same grace, by the same grace of Christ. And his future death being a sufficient ground from the foundation of the world for the pardon and salvation of those that believed in him, because it was not possible, in regard of the greatness of his person, and faithfulness to his trust,

* Ursin.

that he could fail in the performance of the condition required of him, and God knew he could not; and besides his own stedfast resolution, and his ability to accomplish his undertaking, God having given him promises of his omnipotent assistance; upon those accounts, Christ might with confidence be, even before his coming, a powerful advocate for those that laid hold upon the promise by faith. Though he was not actually installed in all his offices, yet he exercised them, if I may so speak, as a candidate; as a king he ruled his church; as an angel he guided his Israel; as a prophet he sent the prophets of the Old Testament, and revealed his will to them. So though he was not a perfect priest till he was a propitiation for sin by the oblation of himself as a grateful victim to God, because propitiation could not be made without blood, yet upon the account of the promise of his suffering he did exercise that part of his priesthood, whereupon the sins of many were pardoned. God was then a pardoning God, and a God blotting out iniquity; and whenever Christ interposed himself for his people, he was answered with 'comfortable words,' Zech. i. 13. And though it be said, that Christ upon his ascension went 'to appear in the presence of God for us,' Heb. ix. 24, this excludes not his former intercession in heaven. He tells the disciples that he went to heaven to prepare a place for them, yet the place is said to be 'prepared before the foundation of the world,' Mat. xxv. 34. He interceded before as a promiser, he intercedes now as a performer; and if his intercession then was graciously answered with comfortable words, his intercession now hath a ground to meet with a no less acceptable entertainment.

[2.] After his sacrifice, in the first fruit of it, the mission of the Holy Ghost. God gave a full proof and public testimony of the vigour of his interposition, in that abundance of the Spirit which he poured forth upon the apostles at the day of pentecost; and his sending the same Spirit to dwell in the hearts of believers, and the gracious operations of this Spirit in the hearts of men, are infallible evidences that his intercession is still of the same force and efficacy. He had acquainted his disciples before that he 'would pray the Father, and he should give them another Comforter,' John xiv. 16. We find not any prayer of Christ for the Spirit upon record while he remained upon the earth. He prayed for this Spirit after he went to heaven; for he seems to speak of it as that which was to be acted by him after his going from them; and, saith he, the Father will 'send the Comforter in my name,' ver. 26, *i. e.* as a fruit, and a manifestation of the great interest I have in him. This was so great a pledge of the prevalency of this advocacy, that a greater could not be given. As soon as ever he was at God's right hand, and had put up his petition for it, before he could be well warm in his throne, he received 'the promise of the Holy Ghost,' Acts ii. 23, *i. e.* that Holy Ghost which had been promised, the richest gift, next to that of his Son, that could be presented to man. As the apostles had but little hopes after his death of his being a redeemer, till they saw the truth of his resurrection, so they might have as little expectations of his mighty power in heaven after his ascension, till he gave them this token of it in the mission of his Spirit. The Spirit, indeed, was in some measure sent before, when he was an advocate designed (the live coal, which seems to be an emblem of the Spirit, was taken from the altar, a type of Christ, Isa. vi. 6), but much more richly poured out when he was an advocate installed. The Old Testament had some drops, and the New Testament full effusions and showers. Though all the blessings of the new covenant are the fruits of Christ's death and intercession, yet the first fruit of it was the Holy Ghost, as the person who by office was to convey to us, and work in us, the blessings of the covenant sealed and settled by the blood of the Redeemer; and therefore the promise of the Spirit is the first promise of the new covenant: Ezek. xxxvi. 25-27, 'I will sprinkle clean water upon you, a new spirit will I put within you, and I will put my Spirit within you.' This was the first thing Christ solicited for when he came to heaven, as the first blessing of the new covenant. And though he gave his disciples in his prayer, John xvii. an essay whereby they might well imagine what should be the substance of his petitions in his state of glory, yet he tells them not positively of any particular thing, but of this of the Comforter, 'I will pray the Father, and he shall give you another Comforter.' This was the first boon he begged after his ascension; this was granted him, and with this the riches of heaven and the blessings of eternity to pour down upon us, which the apostle notes, Titus iii. 6, when he speaks of the shedding of the Holy Ghost abundantly and richly by the Father, but through Jesus Christ our Saviour, as the choicest witness of the irreversible validity of our Saviour's intercession with the Father; so that we may as well conclude in this case as the apostle doth in a like case of the love of God, Rom. viii. 32, 'He that spared not his own Son, but delivered him up for us all, how shall he not with him also freely give us all things?' So, since the intercession of Christ hath been so efficacious for a gift of so great a value as the Holy Ghost, wherein the gift of whatsoever was great in heaven was virtually contained, should it not be a warrant of assurance to us that nothing will be denied to the solicitation of one that, in his very first request, hath been so inexpressibly successful?

VI. Thing is the particularity of this intercession. Christ is an advocate for believers only, and for every one in particular.

1. For believers only. It is their peculiar privilege. It is not every name he takes into his lips, Ps. xvi. 4. The names of those that hasten after another God, that own another God and another mediator, he would not offer their drink-offerings, or back them by any solicitation of his own for acceptance. He would deny them, and not assert them for his clients, nor be an high priest for them, to offer any of their sacrifices; for those that believe not in him as mediator, disown that God by whom he was sent for the redemption of the world; and therefore he disowns, in his mediatory prayer, the whole unbelieving impenitent world: John xvii. 9, 'I pray not for the world, but for them which thou hast given me.' It is not agreeable to his wisdom to intercede for those that reject him. He is an advocate, but only for those that entertain him. He manages no man's cause that is not desirous to put it into his hands. Advocates manage the business only of those that enter themselves their clients. As he prayed not for the world on earth, so much less doth he in heaven. No person hath an interest in his intercession, but he that, by faith, hath an interest in his satisfaction. Though his death was the remedy of our evils in a way of satisfaction to divine justice, yet the application of this remedy by the act of his priesthood in heaven is only to those that repent and believe; in the text, 'We have an advocate with the Father,' *we* that walk in communion with God. Though he be a propitiation for the world, if any should take it extensively, yet he is not an advocate for the whole world, but for those that separate themselves from the world by believing on him.

2. For every believer particularly. The text intimates, 'We have an advocate,' every one of us, 'if *any man* sin.' Sin is a particular act of a person, and this advocacy is for every particular sin that the accuser can charge the criminal with. Advocates answer every particular charge against every particular person that is in the roll of their clients.

There is, indeed, an intercession for the church in general in the time of its sufferings. So he interceded for mercy on Jerusalem and the cities of Judah in the time of the Baylonish captivity, Zech. i. 12. What the high priest did in a shadow, that doth our high priest in the substance; when he went into the holy place, he bore the names of 'all the tribes of Israel upon his breast,' Exod. xxviii. 29; and when our Saviour was preparing to sacrifice himself, and afterwards to ascend into the heavenly sanctuary, he prayed not only for those that were then with him, the whole church at that time, but the whole lump, even to the end of the world, were then presented to God by him: John xvii. 20, 'Neither pray I for these alone, but for them also which shall believe on me through their word,' comprehending them all in one mass in that intercessory prayer. And though he did not particularly name every one of them, yet since his divine understanding was furnished with omniscience, he knew them all distinctly in their successive appearances and varieties of conditions in the world. But his pleas in heaven are particular, according to the particular persons he solicits for, and the particular necessities wherewith they are encumbered. It was for Peter's person in particular he prayed when he was on earth, and for preservation of that particular grace of faith to recover from under the temptation that was ready to invade him: Luke xxii. 31, 32, 'But I have prayed for thee, that thy faith fail not;' 'thee,' his person, and 'thy faith,' his case. He is an high priest over the house of God, Heb. x. 21, and therefore over every member of the house and family; upon which the apostle founds his exhortation to every one to draw near with a true heart, and in full assurance of faith. Men pray in particular for themselves and others, and Christ hears in particular: 1 John v. 14, 'And this is the confidence that we have in him, that if we ask anything according to his will, he hears us.' The Son of God, of whom he was speaking, hears us in particular what we request in particular; and as he hears us he pleads for us; he offers 'the prayers of all saints,' Rev. viii. 3, and therefore of every saint upon every occasion with a particular plea and incense of his own. There is not one but he keeps in his remembrance, nor one request but he presents to his Father, though not by an oral expression of every man's name and cause, yet by some distinct way of representation of them and their wants to God, not so easily conceivable by us in this state of obscurity and darkness. As the devil is an accuser in particular, and cannot well be supposed to accuse all in the gross, so Christ stands particularly to excuse them, and frustrate the indictment. They were given to him in particular, and he pleads for them as given to him, and as they were the propriety of his Father, John xvii. 6, 9, 10, 11. God knows all his own in particular, and Christ hath a care of them in particular. Christ hath a charge of every one's person; he is to raise every one of them at the last day; he is to give an account of every one's case. Again, he intercedes for those that 'come to God by him,' Heb. vii. 25; but those that believe come not in the gross to God by Christ, but by a particular act of faith in every one; and for every such comer, Christ lives for ever to make intercession for them. As he saves every comer to God by him in particular, so he doth particularly use the means of salvation for them, *i. e.* his intercession. He hath his life for ever, and his standing office of advocacy for ever, to make a distinct suit for every one upon his application to God by him in the methods of that court where he exerciseth this function. And as every believer owns Christ in particular, so Christ will confess them by name plainly and clearly: Rev. iii. 5, 'I will confess his name before my Father;' every individual person will be named by him at last in his final sentence, nd every individual person is named by him in his intercessory office; the name is confessed, the grace owned, and the merit of the Redeemer pleaded by him as an advocate before his Father. He is entered into the holy of holies, with all the names of those that belong to him upon his breast.

VII. Thing. What doth Christ intercede for? In general, his intercession for believers is as large as the intent of his death for them. Whatsoever privilege he purchased for them upon the cross, he sues for upon his throne. His intercession is the plea, upon the account of his satisfaction, which was the payment.

He intercedes for the church in all its states and conditions. As soon as ever the news of the state of the world, and the condition of his church in it, is brought to him by the angels, his messengers, Zech. i. 11, 12, and the seventy years of captivity in Babylon were expired, he presently expostulates with God for the withdrawing his hand, and restoring their freedom. There is not any weapon formed against the church blunted, any design hatched against his people abortive, any seasonable rescue, any discovery and defeat of clandestine and hellish works of darkness, but they are fruits of the diligence and industry of our Advocate, and the benefits of his intercession. Let the profane world look upon them as products of chance; let natural religion regard them as works of common providence; let us look upon them in their true spring and their proper channel. Since God grants all things upon the account, and acts all things by the hands, of a mediator, all things flow to us through the intercession of Christ. Since all things were purchased for us by the sacrifice of Christ, he is an advocate to sue out what he merited for us as a surety; and since the mission of the Spirit was the first fruit of this office after his taking possession of heaven, it must needs follow that all the works which the Spirit began and doth accomplish in the soul, are fruits of it also. Therefore Christ said, John xvi. 14, 'He shall receive of mine, and shew it unto you.' He shall take of *mine*, what is mine by purchase, what is mine by plea, what is mine by possession, and shew it unto you. The casting out the accusations of Satan from the court of justice, the casting them out of our own consciences, the pardon of our transgressions, the healing of our natures, our support against temptations, perseverance in that grace any have, and perfection of that grace any want, and at last the perpetual residence of our souls with him, are procured by him as an advocate, as well as purchased by him as our surety.

1. Justification.

(1.) He is an advocate in opposition to an accuser.

In the matter of justification, the Scripture represents God as a judge and Christ as an advocate, pleading his blood and death; and when we come for justification, we come 'to God as the judge of all,' listening to the voice of that blood of Jesus, 'the mediator of the new covenant:' Heb. xii. 23, 24, 'Ye are come to God, the judge of all, and to Jesus, the mediator of the new covenant, and to the blood of sprinkling, that speaks better things than the blood of Abel.' We come to God as a judge, and also 'to the blood of sprinkling,' whereby he was appeased, of which 'the spirits of just men made perfect' are a full testimony. To this blood we come, as it is a blood of sprinkling, in regard of its imputation to us; and as it is a speaking blood in regard of its solicitation for us. Our triumphant justification by God, the apostle places upon this as the top-stone in the foundation. He first lays it upon the death of Christ; next, with *a rather* on the resurrection of Christ; and lastly, with an *also* upon his intercession: Rom. viii. 33, 34, 'It is God that justifies, who is he that condemns? It is Christ that died, yea, rather, that is risen again, who is even at the right hand of God, who also makes intercession for us.' Justification by God, as opposed to condemnation, is ascribed to Christ and to his intercession as completing it, and putting the last hand to it. In the title of an advocate, there is respect to judicial proceedings.* In the method of this proceeding, God is considered as a judge, man as the arraigned criminal; Satan is the accuser: Rev. xii. 10, 'The accuser of the brethren,' who brings in the indictments of sin, pleads the righteousness of the law, solicits for judgment upon his accusation, and the execution of the curse due to the crime. Our own consciences may be considered as the witness, and the law as the rule, both of the accusation brought in, and of the judgment demanded. Christ is considered as an advocate in opposition to Satan the accuser, pleading the efficacy of his merit against the greatness of our crimes, and his satisfaction to justice by the blood of his cross against the demands of the law, whereby the sentence of condemnation due to us as considered in ourselves is averted, and a sentence of absolution upon the merit and plea of our advocate is pronounced, and Satan cast out, and this upon an universal rule of righteousness, which suffers not that which is either a criminal or pecuniary debt to be twice paid. And in the text, wherein it is said, 'we have an advocate with the Father,' in case of sin, the Father is implied to be the sovereign judge, sin to be the crime, and Satan, though not mentioned, to be the accuser; and this advocacy is there expressed to be, not for preventing sin, to which Satan excites us, but the pardoning sins committed, for which Satan accuses us, procuring an acquitting sentence for us from the Judge of all the earth, and indemnity from the punishment merited by our crimes, but stopped by his plea. As Christ appeared as an advocate against Satan when he would be Peter's winnower,—Luke xxii. 31, 32, 'I have prayed for thee,'—so he appears as an advocate against Satan when he steps up as our accuser. Now, the intercession of Christ being opposite to the accusations of the devil, as one would reduce us under the actual execution of the legal sentence, so the other hath a contrary effect, pleading for our justification by the application of his righteousness to us, and the acceptation of it for us, that we may stand clear before the tribunal of God.

(2.) Besides, Christ's blood speaks contrary, or puts up contrary demands to what Abel's blood laid claim to. The blood of Abel pierced heaven with its cries, and solicited a condemning vengeance on the head of Cain; the blood of Christ, on the contrary, must then cry for justifying grace on the person of every believer, otherwise it would not speak better things than Abel's blood did, but the same things: that called for punishment, this for pardon; that desired the death of the murderer, and this sues out the life of the rebel.

(3.) And further consider, since this blood is a speaking blood, it shews that the intercession of Christ is managed in the virtue of his blood. The same thing therefore which was the end of the effusion of his blood, is the end of the solicitation or elocution of his blood. His blood was shed for the expiation of sin, and 'bringing in an everlasting righteousness,' that sinners might not be condemned, Dan. ix. 24; his intercession is for the application of this propitiation, that believers might be justified. Christ pleads the propitiation made by his blood, and accepted, according to the rule of application, by the faith of the repenting sinner.

(4.) Again, if Christ prayed for this on earth when he prayed for his glory, he solicits for it also in heaven when he prays for his glory: John xvii. 1, 'Father, glorify thy Son.' He prays for his resurrection, ascension, sitting at the right hand of God; not only as it was his own personal concern, but as it was terminative for his believing people, as verse 2 intimates; and, ver. 10, he expresses himself to be glorified in them. Now, as he died for

* Mares. contra Volkel, lib. v. cap. iv. pp. 8, 9.

the pardon of our sins, so he rose again for our justification; as he therefore desired his resurrection, so he desired it for the same end for which it was intended and promised, viz. our justification, and therefore virtually begged our justification in the petition for his glory. Now, since he hath gained the request as to his own person, and as to a fundamental justification in his resurrection, and exaltation in heaven, yet it not being perfectly accomplished in all the ends of it, he moves still by his intercession for the actual justification of every one that comes, furnished with the gospel condition, to God by him.

Upon the whole we must consider, that though our propitiation made on the cross by the blood of Christ be the meritorious cause of our justification, yet the intercession upon the throne made by the same blood of Christ, as a speaking blood, is the immediate moving cause, or the *causa applicans*, of our justification, as Illyricus phraseth it. The propitiation Christ made on the cross, made God capable of justifying us in an honourable way; but the intercession of Christ, as pleading that propitiation for us, procures our actual justification. The death of Christ accepted made justification possible, and the death of Christ, pleaded by him, makes justification actual. Righteousness to justify was brought in by him on the cross, and righteousness justifying is applied by him on his throne. Our justification was merited of God by his death, the merit of it acknowledged by God at his resurrection; and is conferred on us, when we believe, by his intercession. When a soul believes, Christ recommends him to God as a performer of the condition of the new covenant, and thereupon pleads his death for him, and demands his actual admission into that favour which was purchased. And thus by him as our living Advocate, exercising his priesthood in heaven, we 'receive the atonement,' Rom. v. 10, 11.

2. Daily pardon. This is principally intended in the text: 'If any man sin'—if any one of those that walk in the light, in communion with God and Christ, which cannot be without justification—'If any man sin, we have an advocate,' *i.e.* in case of sin after justification. We contract daily debts by committing daily sins, and there is not a day but we merit the total removal of justifying grace, that God should revive the memory of his former justice, and cancel the grants of his lately conferred mercy. And how could we avoid it, if Christ did not renew the memory of his propitiation before his Father, which first procured our admission, and is only able to maintain our standing? Every sin brings in its own nature an obligation to punishment, that is guilt. Sin and guilt are inseparable; that which hath no guilt is no transgression. This intercession of Christ answers the obligation which every sin brings upon us, as well as it did answer all the obligations at our first coming into the presence of God. It is upon every sin he doth exercise this office, and by his interposition procures our pardon thousands of times, and preserves us from coming short of the full fruits of reconciliation at first obtained by him, and accepted by us. He that had been stung a second time by the fiery serpent, must have had a fresh influence of the brazen one for his cure, as well as the first time he was wounded. As sin daily accuseth us by virtue of the law, so Christ daily pleads for us by virtue of his cross; sin charges us before the tribunal of justice, and Christ by his intercession procures our discharge from the chancery of mercy.

3. Sanctification. As he is a priest set on the right hand of the throne of the Majesty on high, he preserves the stability of the better covenant, the new covenant, and perpetuates the fruits of it: justification, in blotting out the memory of our sins; and sanctification, in writing the law in our hearts, Heb. viii. 1, 6, 10, 12. He is the author of our first sanctification

by his intercession, as the first fruits of it was the sending that Spirit by whose powerful operations the soul is reformed according to the divine image; and he is the author of our repeated sanctification by the exercise of his advocacy. He is an advocate in case of sin, in regard of the guilt, that it should not remain upon our persons; in regard of the power, that the contagion of it should not seize upon our vitals; in regard of the filth, that it might not remain to unfit us for a fellowship with the Father and himself. His intercession in heaven is a continuation of that intercession on earth, whereby he testified his desire that we might be 'kept from the evil' while we resided in an infectious world: John xvii. 15, 'Keep them from the evil,' and 'sanctified through his truth,' while we are upon an earth full of lying vanities, ver. 17. The end of his intercession is not for sharpness of wit, a pompous wealth, a luxurious prosperity, or a lazy peace; such things may be hurtful; but for faith, holiness, growth, wherein we can never be culpable. His intercession is not employed for low things, but for such as may fit us for an honour in another world. Mortification of sin, and holiness of conversation, are therefore called 'things above, where Christ sits at the right hand of God,' Col. iii. 1 compared with ver. 5, &c.: things which come from above by virtue of that session of Christ at the right hand of God, and the office he doth there exercise, which the apostle explains to be a mortification of our members which are upon the earth; and since the great reason of his exaltation is his hating iniquity and loving righteousness, the end of his exaltation and of his intercession in that state, is to manifest the same disposition in the perfect expulsion of sin, and the full implantation of righteousness in us. The same dispositions which animated him to a dying on the cross here, do animate him to his intercession above, which is nothing else but a presenting his death, and a presenting not only his death, but all the motives which moved him to it, and the ends he aimed at in it. He is 'manifested to take away sin,' 1 John iii. 5; manifested in his humiliation on earth, manifested in his exaltation in heaven, to take away sin, sin in the filth as well as sin in the guilt. What he designed in the one, he designs in the other; the same end he aimed at in dying, he aims at in interceding. Since he is an advocate in the virtue of his blood, he is an advocate for the ends of his blood. He will not let sin continue in his members, which he came to wash off by his blood. As long as his love to righteousness and his aversion from sin continues in him, so long will he be acting in heaven, till he hath in the highest manner manifested to the full his affections to the one and disaffection to the other, by utterly dispossessing out of the hearts of his people what he hates, both root and branch, and perfecting what he loves, in all the dimensions of it. He doth not only sue out our pardon, but sue out a grant of those graces which are necessary preparatories and concomitants of pardon. The end of his intercession is no doubt the same with that of his exaltation, which is not only for forgiveness of sin, but repentance, Acts v. 31, which includes the whole of sanctification. All the holiness believers have here is a fruit of this advocacy; the communication of that power which subdues corruption flows from it. Christ, by his intercession, receives all from his Father, that, as a king, he may convey all necessary supplies to us. But we must consider, that though Christ doth intercede for the sanctification of his people, yet it will not follow that any of them are at present perfect, and totally free from the relics of corruption. This is not intended by him in this life, any more than when he prayed for Peter, he desired not that he should be kept wholly from falling, but that his faith should be kept from totally failing. Sin is likewise suffered to continue in the best here, that men should not think that the acceptation of their persons doth arise from their own works and holiness, but from the sweet savour of the Mediator's sacrifice continually presented in heaven. Yet perfection in grace will be the final issue of this advocacy. If grace should never be perfected, Christ would never be fully answered in his intercession, and so this office of his in heaven would want a manifestation of its true power and value.

4. Strength against temptation. We have an enemy industrious to entrap us, and we have an Advocate as industrious to protect us, who will either solicit for a reasonable strength to resist his invasion, or strength to improve it to our spiritual advantage, if he suffers the temptation to meet with some success in its attempt. Satan desires to sift us: Luke xxii. 31, ἐξῃτήσατο, *he hath desired*, or *asked and begged with earnestness*, for so ἐξ, being added to αἰτέω, signifies; and our Advocate is ready to stop the full proceedings of so fierce a solicitor. The seed of the woman, the mystical seed, shall overcome their enemies 'by the blood of the Lamb,' Rev. xii. 11; by his blood shed upon the cross, by his blood presented in heaven, which cries for vengeance against the great seducer of mankind, and prevails to the casting him down. If strength against temptations were not procured by it, Christ's office of advocacy would lose a great part of its end. It was in kindness to us he was so advanced, not an advocate for himself personal, but for himself mystical, *i. e.* for believers; in the text, 'we have an advocate.' It were little kindness to us, if we should lie grovelling in the dust, upon every inroad our enemy makes against us, and sink under every shot that comes from the mount of his battery. It is this intercession that renders us either immoveable against his assaults, or after a foil victorious in the issue of the combat. Christ doth not solicit for such a strength whereby a temptation may be wholly successless, but whereby it may not be wholly victorious. He prayed for Peter against Satan, that his faith might not fail, but he did not pray positively that the temptation might wholly fail. He implies by that expression, Luke xxii. 32, 'When thou art converted, strengthen thy brethren,' that he should fall so foully as that not a grain of grace should be visible in him; but he should appear like one in an unregenerate state, so that his return should be as a new conversion. So that though he prayed not for a prevention of his fall, yet he prayed for a recovery of him after his fall, by implying that he should be converted. His intercession is not always for keeping off a temptation from us, for he many times suffers fierce ones to invade us for gracious ends, both for his own glory and our good; but he solicits that a temptation may not utterly sink us, and mortify our grace. So that, according to that model in the case of Peter, Christ sues not so much against a temptation, as for your faith; for if that keep up, a temptation will fall like a bullet against a brazen wall. He is content we should be in an evil world, but not satisfied unless we be preserved from the evil, or rescued from it after it hath assaulted us; and therefore a believer's courage hath a support in the greatest temptation. Christ opposes his petition against the demands of Satan; the first-born of every creature sets himself against the head of the wicked world; the seed of the woman against the seed of the serpent, and the serpent himself; as he defends us against his accusations before God, so he succours us in his temptations of our own persons.

5. Perseverance in grace. This follows upon the other. His prayer for the not failing of Peter's faith, is an earnest that the same petition is continually put up by him for all that believe in him. For since the Scripture is written for our comfort, this part of it would be little for our comfort, if he were not as well concerned in the standing of every believer as of Peter; why should he wish him, when he was converted, to strengthen his brethren, if he had not intended it for a standing example of comfort to his

church? The objection, that Christ did not intend to pray for the perseverance of any but Peter, would have split all the arguments Peter could have used from this carriage of Christ to him for the strengthening of others. How could he strengthen his brethren in faith, if they had not been his brethren in Christ's prayer, for their perseverance, as well as he in his faith? It is principally for the continuance of our standing, that his intercession is intended, if we may judge of what he doth in heaven by that prayer on earth, which was the model of his intercession in heaven, in which this petition for his Father's keeping us 'through his own name,' and keeping us 'from the evil,' and furthering our progress in sanctification, takes up much of the time, John xvii. 11, &c. Certainly he hath the same language in heaven as he had then on earth; he would else leave out a main head in his petitions above, which this prayer below was intended to present us with a pattern of, and so there would be no agreement between his carriage in heaven and the pledge he gave us on earth. It would have been but a fawning and dissembling affection, to desire this in his disciples' hearing, and never solicit the same cause when he went out of their ken. No; our Saviour hath given evidence of a choicer and more durable affection than to give occasion to any to think, that he should be regardless of that in his glory, which he was so mindful of at the time of his approaching misery. What he was earnest for then, he is as desirous not to be defeated of now; and for him to desire that his people should be kept from evil, and yet that they should sink under the greatest evil of a total apostasy, would argue the small credit his suit hath with the Father, and would shew that his advocacy is as impotent to secure us as our inability to preserve ourselves. Since Christ doth therefore concern himself for the perseverance of his own, his intercession is as powerful in that as in any other thing. If it meet with a failure in any one part, we are not sure of its successfulness in any at all. If his merit be of an infinite value, his advocacy is of a sovereign efficacy. There is no question to be made, but those for whom he formerly merited, and those for whom he at present solicits, shall endure to the end: the gates of hell are as unable to prevail against the latter as they were to weaken the power of the former. Did he by his propitiation procure our admission into God's favour, in spite of the enemies of our salvation? and shall he not, by his intercession, maintain our standing in that favour, in spite of the enviers of our first admission? This is a choice fruit of the intercession of Christ. Upon this score he lays Peter's preservation from a total and final apostasy: 'I have prayed for thee, that thy faith fail not,' Luke xxii. 32. He doth not say, Peter, there is such a principle in thee that is able to stand; thy own free will and the strength of thy grace shall bring thee off, and preserve thee from that precipice. No; 'I have prayed': there lies our security. The least grain of true grace, though as small as a mustard seed, stands better settled by the support of Christ's intercession against the most boisterous winds of Satan than the strongest grace can of itself, by the power of free will, against the least puff of hell. The instability of our minds would shake it, and the relics of our corruption extinguish it, without this.

6. Acceptation of our services. As this advocate preserves our graces, so he presents our services, and by his intercession maintains life in the one and procures credit for the other. He is as powerful a solicitor for the acceptance of our duties as he was a grateful sacrifice for the expiation of our sins, and a mighty redeemer for the liberty of our persons. Our prayers are both imperfect and blemished, but his merit applied by his intercession both purifies and perfects them. Our Advocate, by his skill, puts them into form and language according to the methods of the court of heaven, as an

attorney doth the petition and cause of his client, and by his interest procures a speedy hearing. Our works are no more the cause of the recording our petitions than they are of the justification of our persons. Though our prayers are not entertained without some holiness in them, yet they are not entertained without a greater holiness than ours to present them. When Christ tells his disciples that he had ordained them to bring forth fruit, he adds a clause to prevent their imaginations of meriting the answer of their prayers by the present of their fruits, that whatsoever they asked they must expect only to obtain in his name, John xv. 16. As they are ours, though attended with never so much fruit, they may be rejected; as he makes them his by his intercession, they cannot be non-suited. He is the altar upon which our sacrifices ascend with a grateful fume before the God of the whole world: Isa. lvi. 7, 'They shall be accepted upon my altar.' He is the altar, that hath much incense to add or bestow upon the prayers of the saints, Rev. viii. 3, *i.e.* a mighty quantity of merit and power of intercession, to give a sweet savour to our spiritual sacrifices, that they may be acceptable to God, not by themselves, but by Jesus Christ, 1 Pet. ii. 5, alluding to the office of the high priest under the law, who, after he had offered the sacrifice without the veil, took both his hands full of those aromatic drugs, of which the incense was composed without the veil, and put them in a censer of gold full of fire, and covered the propitiatory or mercy-seat with the fume of it. Nothing that we can offer is agreeable to God, without it comes through the hands, and with the recommendation of, our powerful advocate so beloved by him. The fire he fetches from the golden altar makes them to fume up, and render a pleasing scent before the mercy-seat. He is our Aaron in this part of his priesthood in heaven, bearing the iniquity of our holy things, Exod. xxviii. 38, when he presents himself in the sanctuary on high for the interest of his people. This he implies in the prophetic psalm, Ps. xvi. 4, when he declares he 'will not offer the offerings of those that hasten after another God, nor take their names into his mouth;' he intimates thereby that he doth present the offerings of those that believe in him as the only mediator, and pronounces their names with a recommendation of them before God, as such as are parts of his mystical body, such as have owned him and performed the condition of faith, such persons 'in whom is all his delight.' It is from this consideration of Christ's being passed into heaven as a high priest that the apostle exhorts the Hebrews not only to 'hold fast their profession,' but to 'come boldly to the throne of grace,' with an assurance of acceptance and obtaining grace in their necessity, Heb. iv. 14, 16. And indeed, having such a lieger in heaven, we may boldly venture to that throne which his propitiation on earth, and his appearance in heaven, render a throne of grace.

7. Salvation. This is the main end of his intercession, Heb. vii. 25; he saves us 'to the uttermost,' or to all kind of perfection, noting the kind of salvation as well as the perpetuity of time, and this by interceding. Thus the apostle's argument runs; he is able to save, because the end of his life is to intercede, and the end of his intercession is to save. The immediate end of his death was satisfaction respecting God; the immediate end of his intercession is salvation respecting us. He lives there to sue out for us the possession of that which he died here to purchase. We are therefore said to be 'saved by his life,' as we are said to be reconciled by his death, Rom. v. 10; not simply by his life, for no man is said to preserve another merely as he is a living man, but as his life is active for another in managing some means of preservation for him. Christ saves us by his life, *i.e.* by that life

which he lives, which is a life of intercession. As he did not reconcile us simply by his death, but by his death as a sacrifice, so he doth not save us simply by his life, but by his life as an accepted advocate. The expiation of our sins was made by him on the cross, and the happiness of our souls is perfected by him on his throne. He took our nature that he might die for us, and possesses a throne above that he might live to save us. This part he managed in that model of his intercession on earth, John xvii.; after he had prayed for what was necessary for them during the length of their pilgrimage, viz., sanctifying grace and preservation from evil, he puts forward in the upshot for the happy entertainment of them in heaven: verse 24, 'Father, I will that they be with me where I am.' When he comes to this period, he demands it in a way of more authority than what he had sued for before, to shew that his desire would be utterly unsatisfied without the grant of this. All that which he had sued for before was with respect to this top-stone of salvation and glory. After this demand he concludes his prayer, as having no more after the completing of their happiness to beg for them. As, after he had finished the task of his humiliation, and had ascended to heaven, he had no more need to pray for himself, so when he hath brought all his people to the possession of that happiness with him, he leaves off any further pleading for them, because they are in the fullest ocean of felicity. Christ would be an unsuccessful advocate, and consequently an impotent propitiator, if any believer, after all his wading through the mire of this world, should fall short of a comfortable reception and mansion above.

Use 1. Of information.

(1.) Here is an argument for the deity of Christ. If he be a prevailing advocate for such multitudes of believers, preserving them in the favour of God by his intercession, it evidenceth his person to be infinitely valued by God, which would not be if his person were not worthy of an infinite love; and he could not be worthy of an infinite love were not his passion of an infinite value; and his passion could not mount to so high a value were not his person infinitely valuable, for the worth of his death depends upon the eminency of his person.

Besides, as an advocate, he presents every man's cause before the Father, and puts in for every one a memorial of his death, to preserve them in a justified state, and maintain that grace which would else be destroyed by a deluge of corruption. He must needs be God, that knows every person in that multitude of those that sincerely believe in him, that hears all their petitions, and understands all their more numerous griefs and burdens, inward and outward sins, those inward agonies of spirit, those mental as well as oral prayers, and all those in those distant places where every one of those persons reside, and knows whether their supplications be in sincerity or hypocrisy. He that knows all those is endued with omniscience, and must needs be God. He could not be a sufficient advocate if he did not understand every man's cause, to present it before the Judge of the world; and without omniscience he could understand little or nothing. He could only understand what is outwardly declared, not what really the cause is. He must depend upon the declaration of his client, as advocates do, and so be often deluded by false representations, as they are. He could not, without omniscience, take care of all his clients; to have so many clients whose cases to present every day would be his burden and perplexity, and render heaven a place of trouble to him, not of glory. Were he a mere man, it could not be conceived how it were possible for him: but how easy is all this to one possessed of a deity!

(2.) Hence is a ground to conclude the efficacy of his death. His intercession is an argument for the perfection of his sacrifice. The virtue of his passion is the ground of his plea; and therefore, if he had not perfectly satisfied God, he must have offered himself again (Heb. x. 14, 'By one offering he hath perfected for ever them that are sanctified'), and repeated the sacrifice before he could have begun his advocacy. Had his death been destitute of merit, there had been no room for his appearance as a justifier of our cause at the throne of grace. He could not have been a prevailing pleader if he had not first been an appeasing propitiator. His standing up as a solicitor for us had been of little efficacy, if the atonement he made on the cross had not been first judged sufficient. The high priest must be punctual to the prescriptions of the law in the sacrifice without, before he could enter with the blood of it into the holy of holies. If our faith be shaken at any time with the doubt of the validity of his death, let us settle it by a reflecting upon his advocacy. This verifies the virtue of his passion more than all miracles that can be wrought in his name.

(3.) See the infinite love of God in Christ; of God, that he should appoint an advocate for us. If we were left to ourselves and our own pleas, our least sins would ruin us. There are daily sins would sink us to hell, were it not for this daily intercession. And this love is further enhanced in appointing, not an angel, or one of the highest cherubims most dear to him, but his own Son, the best and noblest person he had in all the world, to this office of advocacy for a company of worms; one that is equal with himself in glory, and is equal with himself in the distinct knowledge of all our cases, better acquainted with them than we ourselves; and one equal to us in our nature, experimentally acquainted with all our burdens and grievances. How great also is the love of Christ, who, when he was properly our judge, takes upon him to be our advocate; when he hath a mouth to condemn us, and a wrath to consume us, he binds the arms of his wrath, and employs his tongue to solicit our cause and procure our mercy! He is not only an advocate for himself and the glory promised him, but for an unworthy sinner, for those penitents he hath yet left behind him in the world. He remembers them as well as himself. As Satan never appears before God but he hath some to accuse, so Christ never appears before God but he hath some to defend.

(4.) How little ground is there to dream of such a thing as perfection in this life! If we stand in need of a perpetual intercession of Christ in this life, we have not then a perfection in this life. Intercession supposeth imperfection. Those that pretend to a state here totally free from sin, conclude themselves mounted above the need of any to interpose for them. It is in the case of sin that this advocacy is appointed; not in the case of sin unjustly, but justly charged; for it is not *if any man be accused of sin*, but *if any man sin* really. The interposition of an advocate always implies a charge against the client, but in the text it implies a charge that hath a true, and not a mistaken, foundation. Sin is as durable as this world, because Christ's intercession endures to the end of the world. 'He ever lives to make intercession,' *i. e.* till the end of this state of things. If believers did not sin after they were united to Christ and justified, an advocacy for them would be of no necessity. The settling Christ in this office implies that God had no intention to render men perfect in this life. If we were arrived to such a state, we had no more need of Christ's further mediating for us than the blessed angels have. After the restitution of all things, and the consummation of the elect, Christ no longer acts the part of a mediator, but God shall be all in all. Nor can it be said that some may be perfect in this life, though all are not; and for those that are short of such a state, indeed, the advocacy of Christ is necessary. There is little probability for this from the text. The apostle puts himself in the number, 'If any man sin, *we* have an advocate'; not *you*, as excluding himself from having any need of it. The consideration of what apostle it was that speaks thus would damp any presumptions of perfection. Was it not he that had the honour to lie in his master's bosom, and to be blessed with the greatest share in the Redeemer's affections? that disciple whom he appointed to be the host and guardian of his own mother, the dearest thing to him as man he left behind him in the world; and the apostle to whom he was resolved, and did afterwards make known, the various revolutions in the church to the end of the world in the book of the Revelations? If any could be supposed to be settled in a sinless and perfect state in this life, he might; but he disowns any such eminency, and looks upon himself in that state as to have need of entertaining this common advocate in his cause.

(5.) Hence it follows that the church is as durable as the world. *We have*, is the time present, but it takes in the future ages. 'He ever lives to make intercession for those that come to God by him.' There will always then, as long as the world doth endure, be some comers to God. If his intercession run parallel with the duration of the world, there will always be some in the world, whose necessities are to be represented by him to his Father.

(6.) If Christ be an advocate, the contempt or abuse of his intercession is very unworthy. It is an abuse of it when men presume upon it to sin wilfully against knowledge, and then to run to him to interpose for their pardon. This is a profanation of the holiness of this advocate, as though he were settled in this office to beg a licence for our crimes, to sue for impunity to impenitence; when, indeed, they are sins of infirmity, not sins of contempt, without remorse, that he interposeth for: 'If any man sin.' And his interposition is to comfort us under our burdens, not to encourage us in our iniquities.

Unbelief is also a denial of the sufficiency or necessity of his intercession, since it is a slighting of that propitiation which is the ground of it.

A total neglect of prayer is also a contempt of it. If there should be no service, he would have no matter to perfume by his obedience. We should frustrate that part of his priesthood which consists in intercession, and render him an empty-handed priest, to be full of merit to no purpose. An unreasonable dejectedness in good men is no honouring of it; to walk disconsolately, as though there were none in the upper region to take care of us and mind our cause. Hath Christ lost his power, his eloquence, his interest in his Father? Is the value of his sufferings abated, the market fallen? Hath God utterly discarded the righteousness of his Son? Hath God repented of sending his Son to suffer? Are our Saviour's pleas distasteful to him? Is Christ, that was carried triumphantly to heaven, now of no account there? or hath the Redeemer thrown off all thoughts of us, all care for us? One would think some of those things are happened, since Christians walk so feebly, with heads hanging down, as if no person concerned himself above in their affairs. At least a stranger would admire to hear them talk of an advocate, and walk as dejectedly as if there were none at all. It is a dishonour also to it when men, after sin, betake themselves to vows or alms for their solicitors, and not to the sacrifice and advocacy of Christ.

(7.) If Christ be our advocate, it is a dishonourable thing to yoke saints as mediators of intercession with him. The Romanists tell us that Christ is the mediator of redemption, but the saints are also mediators of intercession; though, to give them their due, they say that the prayers of saints and angels prevail not by the sole virtue of their own merit, but receive their spiritual validity from the merit of Christ. What need, then, of invocating saints, since their intercessions for us will do us no good without the intercession of Christ, and his pleading his merit for us? None had authority to offer the incense upon the altar of gold but he that offered the sacrifice upon the altar of brass. When the high priest went to burn incense in the holy place, he was attended with none of the people, nor any of the priests; not a man nor angel appears with Christ in heaven as an intercessor to present the services of any. As they shed none of their blood for us, so have they no blood to sprinkle in heaven. Those that have no merit to purchase for themselves, have no merit to apply to others. He only that hath satisfied for us, hath the authority to intercede for us. Christ only that is our Redeemer can be our advocate. The glorified saints have been brought into heaven by his grace, not to receive our services, but rejoice in his salvation. They are co-heirs with him in his inheritance, not co-officers with him in his function. To yoke him with saints is to apprehend him very unmindful of his office or lazy in his solicitations, that he needs a spur from those that are about him. It is to strip him of his priestly garments, and put them upon his inferiors; and it is as great a sacrilege to rob him of the honour of his advocacy as to deny him the glory of his death.

The text strikes off men's hands from such an invasion; it intimates that the right of intercession belongs only to him who hath made the propitiation; but that was made by Christ alone, without any saints to tread the winepress with him; and therefore the advocacy is managed by Christ alone, without any saints to assist with him at the throne of grace. Since they shed no blood to pacify the wrath of God for our sins, they have no right to present our prayers for acceptance at his throne. The apostle, Heb. xiii. 7, when he speaks to them to follow their faith, had a fair occasion, had he had a knowledge of the truth of it, to mention it; he adviseth them to imitate the saints, not to invocate them. He proposeth their example to them on earth, when he might as well have added also their intercessions in heaven. He had had as good a ground to wish them to present their prayers to them which were glorified, if those spirits had been in a capacity to do them such a kindness. He would not have been guilty of such an omission, as not to have minded them of their duty, and increased their comfort, had such a thing been known to him. And whence the assertors of this doctrine had the revelation we may easily conclude, since those that were enlightened from heaven never mentioned a syllable of anything so dishonourable to the Redeemer.

(8.) If Christ be our advocate, how miserable are those that have no interest in him! He is an advocate for all that walk in communion with God, that walk in the light; those that walk otherwise are under the condemnation of the law, not under the propitiation and intercession of Christ; they have the injured attributes of God, and slighted blood of Christ, to plead against them, not for them. If Christ did not pray for the world here, he will not plead for the world in heaven, John xvii. 9. He is introduced in those prophetic psalms, praying that those that wish him evil may be 'confounded, and put to shame,' Ps. xl. 14; and that the indignation of God might be poured out upon them, and his 'wrathful anger take hold of them,' Ps. lxix. 21, 24; and indeed, at his first settlement in this office, the power of asking was conferred upon him, as well for the ruin of his enemies, as for the security of his believing friends: Ps. ii. 8, 9, 'Ask of me, and I shall give thee the heathen for thine inheritance;' and what follows? 'Thou shalt break them with a rod of iron.' Breaking his enemies is a fruit of his asking. Impenitent men are so far from having an interest in his intercessions for mercy, that they have a terrible share in his pleas for wrath.

And himself doth solemnly publish in his speech to his Father, Ps. xvi. 4, that he will 'not take their names into his lips that hasten after another god' by idolatrous services. If it be a misery to want the prayers of a Noah, Daniel, Job, or a Jeremiah, Jer. xi. 14, what a horrible misery it is to want the prayers of the Saviour of the world, and to have the pleas of Christ directed against them? As the blood of Christ speaks better things than the blood of Abel, for those on whom it is sprinkled, so it speaks bitterer things for all such as by unbelief and impenitence trample upon it. It is a mighty misery to want so powerful a patronage.

Use 2 is of comfort. His design in uttering his prayer on earth, the model of his intercession, was for the joy of his people: John xvii. 13, 'These things speak I in the world, that they may have my joy fulfilled in themselves;' that they might have a joy in his absence, in the assurance of his faithful managing their cause above, by remembering how earnest he was for them below, that this joy might be fulfilled in them, *i. e.* that they might have a full and permanent joy; as much joy proportionably in having me their advocate, as I have in undertaking and managing the office for them. We should draw forth the comfort of this function he exerciseth. As a propitiation, he turned the court of justice into a court of mercy; and as an advocate he keeps it firm in that change he made by his passion. To this we may ascribe the firmness of the divine reconciliation, and the fruit of it, the non-imputation of our daily sins. It is the top of our comfort that he is in heaven a pleader, as it was the foundation of our comfort that he was once on earth a sufferer. There is not the meanest beggar that is a believer, but he hath a greater favourite to manage his cause with God than any man can have with an earthly prince. It is a thousand times more comfort that he is an advocate in heaven than if he were a king visibly upon earth. He is above, to prevent all evils, which can there only receive their commission, to procure all blessings, which there only find their spring. What reason of discouragement, when we have one in heaven to be our advocate, one so acceptable to the Father, one that hath given such proofs of his affections to us, one that is both faithful and earnest in our cause, and one that it is no disparagement for the Father to listen to? What could comfort itself, saith one,* wish more for her children, had she been our mother, than to have so great a person our perpetual advocate at the right hand of God? His death is not such a ground of assurance as this, because that is past; but when we consider how the merit of his death lives continually in his intercession, all the weights of doubts and despondency lose their heaviness; faith finds in it an unquestionable support.

(1.) There is comfort in the perpetuity of this intercession. He is as much a perpetual advocate as he is a perpetual propitiation. Till there be a failure in the merits of the one, there can be no interruption in the pleas of the other. The blood that was sprinkled on the mercy-seat in the holy of holies was not to be wiped off, but to remain there as a visible mark of the atonement. As the high priest went not into the holy of holies to look about him, and feast his eyes with the rarities of the place, but to perform an office for the people that stayed without all the time he remained before the mercy-seat, so is Christ entered to 'appear in the presence of God for us,' Heb. ix. 24, to appear all the time of his residence there. He is not silent, but is always pleading in the strength of his sacrifice for the benefits purchased by it. He hath (that I may so say) little else to do where he is but to intercede. When he was in the world, and had a glory due to him to petition for, he doth it not without intermixing more suits for his people than for himself,

* Dr Jackson.

John xvii. His love is not cooled by his being in heaven. There is little of his own glory behind to solicit for. His zeal and earnestness runs in one channel for his people, and is more united. He was dead, but his love did not die with him; he now lives, and his affections live with him, and he lives for evermore: Rev. i. 18, 'I am he that lives, and was dead; and, behold, I live for evermore.' His life had been little comfort without the end of his life. He lives in that nature wherein he died; he lives for ever, as well as he died once in the office of a redeemer. He interceded for all believers when he was alive, John xvii. 19. If it be a great comfort to have a stock of prayers going for us among our friends, it is a greater to have Christ praying for us, and to consider he prayed 1600 years ago, and hath never left pleading one moment since he sat down on his throne. Christ's power cannot be weakened, his eloquence cannot grow dull and flat; his interest is not decayed; the righteousness of God endures for ever; he repents not of his contrivances for man's salvation; he is to this day pleased with the interposure of his Son on our behalf; the laws of heaven are unchangeable; our Advocate is in high esteem there, and his thoughts of us the same as ever they were.

(2.) There is comfort in the prevalency of it. The perpetuity assures us of the prevalency of it. If the appearance of the rainbow in the cloud be a memorial to God to withhold his hand from ever drowning the world, as he promised Noah, Gen. ix. 16, the suffering person of his Son being perpetually before him every moment of an endless eternity, will not suffer him to be forgetful of the covenant of grace sealed by the blood of so great a person. He that remembered Abraham in the case of Lot, some time after Abraham had done praying, Gen. xix. 29, cannot be unmindful of those for whom he hath a perpetual solicitor before his eyes. Can any man lose his cause that hath so powerful an advocate as a deserving Son with a gracious Father, who hath affection to us to edge his plea, and interest enough in the Father to prevail for our good? His prayers above are not less, but rather more prevalent (if any difference may be supposed) than they were here below. As there were no sinful infirmities in his nature, so there were none in his prayers on earth; but there were natural infirmities, as hunger, thirst, sleep, which might give some interruption to the constancy of actual prayer; but there can be none in his intercession, since all his natural infirmities were dropped at his resurrection. He is the watchman and advocate of Israel, that 'never slumbers nor sleeps.' He pleads not as Moses for the Israelites, or as an Israelite for himself, but as the angel and head of the covenant. As by his sacrifice, so by his plea, he frees them from a state of condemnation: Rom. viii. 34, 'Who is he that condemns? it is Christ that died, yea rather, that makes intercession for us.' No blessing he pleads for but we shall obtain. The Father can refuse him nothing; we cannot want help till the Father has discarded all affection to his Son, and declares himself mistaken in the judgment he discovered of the greatness of his merit at his resurrection and ascension. Certainly, if we shall have whatsoever we ask in his name for ourselves, John xvi. 23, he will obtain whatsoever he asks in his own name for us.

(3.) Hence ariseth comfort to us in our prayers. We cannot doubt of success as long as Christ hath faithfulness. The office of the priests under the law was to receive every man's sacrifice that was capable of presenting one, and refuse none. Christ, as an advocate, hath it incumbent upon him to receive our spiritual sacrifices, and he doth receive them, and present them with more mercy, because he transcends them in faithfulness and compassion.

We are many times dejected at the remembrance of our prayers, but the concern that Christ hath in them is a ground to raise us. We have an advocate that knows how to separate the impertinences and follies which fall from the mouths of his clients; he knows how to rectify and purify our bills of requests, and present them otherwise than we do. How happy a thing is it to have one to offer up our prayers in his golden censer, and perfume our weak performances by applying his merit to them! Satan distracts our prayers, but cannot blemish Christ's intercession. When we cannot present our own case by reason of diseases and indispositions, we have one to present our cause for us that can never be distempered, who is more quick to present our groans than we are to utter them. Besides, all prayer put up in his name shall be successful, John xvi. 23. The arguments we use from Christ's merits are the same fundamentally upon which the plea of Christ in heaven is grounded; and if God should deny us, it were to deny his Son, and cast off that delight he expressed himself to have in the merit of his death; but God loves that mediation of his Son, and that this work of his should be honoured and acknowledged. And though we had no promise to have our own prayers heard, yet there is no doubt but he will hear the prayers of Christ for us, for them he hears always, John xi. 42.

(4.) Hence ariseth comfort against all the attempts and accusations of Satan, and the rebellion of our own corruption. He foresees all the ambushments of Satan, searcheth into his intention, understands his stratagems, and is as ready to speak to the Father for us, as he was to turn his back and look Peter into a recovery at the crowing of the cock. The devil accuseth us when we fall, but he hath not so much on his side as we have. All his strength lies in our sinful acts, but the strength of our advocate lies in his own infinite merit. Satan hath no merit of his own to enter as plea for vengeance. When he pleads against us with our sins, Christ pleads for us by his sufferings, and if our adversary never cease to accuse us, our advocate never ceaseth to defend us. How comfortable is it to have one day and night before the throne to control the charge of our enemy, and the despondencies of our souls, that Satan can no sooner open his mouth, but he hath one to stop and rebuke him, who hath more favour in the court than that malicious spirit, and employs all his life and glory for our spiritual advantage, who will not upon such occasions want a good word for us. And as to our corruptions, he is in heaven to make up all breaches. His blood hath the same design in his plea that it had in the sacrifice, which was to purify us, Titus ii. 4. The difficulty of any cause doth not discourage him, but honours both his skill in bringing us off, and the merit of his blood, which is the cause of our restoration. Upon every occasion he steps in to plead with the holiness of God, and pacify the justice of God for our greater as well as lighter crimes. While therefore we feelingly groan under our spiritual burdens, let us not be so dejected by them, as cheered by the advocacy of our Saviour.

Use 3, of exhortation.

(1.) Endeavour for an interest in this advocacy. It is natural for men to look after some intercessor with God for them. When the Israelites were sensible of their sin in speaking against God, they desired Moses to be their mediator: Num. xxi. 7, 'Pray unto the Lord for us.' Behold here a greater than Moses to be the patron of our cause.

To this purpose,

[1.] We must have a sincere faith. This is absolutely necessary for an interest in Christ's priesthood, Heb. vii. 24. It is only for 'those that come to God by him.' He hath not a moral ability to save or intercede for any but such. That is clearly implied. If 'able to save those that come unto

God by him, seeing he ever lives to make intercession for them,' then able to save none else: it is restrained only to such. It is a foolish imagination to think Christ prays for unbelievers, because he prayed on the cross for those that murdered him. There is a great difference between his prayer then and his intercession in heaven.* That upon the cross was as he was a holy man, and would both shew his own charity to his enemies, and set us a pattern of it to ours; but in his mediatory prayer put up by him as God-man, John xvii., a copy of what he doth to this day in heaven, he doth not pray for the world, but for those that believe on him, ver. 19, 20, and therefore it is plain that he doth not pray for them that will not believe on him. Faith only gives an interest in the prayers Christ made on earth, or suits he urgeth in heaven.

[2.] We must have a sincere resolution of obedience. Such are the subjects of Christ's intercession. The apostle had prefaced it so in the chapter before the text, and applies the cordial to such only as wallowed not in a course of gross sins. Those that 'walk in darkness' he excludes from any fellowship with him in any of his offices, 1 John i. 6. It is a fellowship with the Son as well as with the Father that he understands it of, ver. 3. The comfort of this intercession belongs not to those that wilfully defile themselves, but to those that abhor sin, and yet may fall through the violence of a surprising temptation. And after he had laid down this comfortable doctrine in the text, he closes it with a limitation to strike off the hands of any bold and undue claim to it: ver. 3, 'Hereby do we know that we know him, if we keep his commandments.' Hereby we know that we know him to be both our propitiation and our advocate, if we bear a sincere respect to all the discoveries of his will. Christ did not offer himself as a sacrifice, nor stand up as an advocate to countenance our sins, and free us from the debt of obedience, but to excite and encourage us the more, and that in a comfortable way, assuring us of pardon for our defects through him. Trust in him and obedience to him are the sole fee he requires of us for his care and pains.

(2.) Have a daily recourse to this advocate and advocacy. It is necessary because of our daily infirmities, and our imperfect services. We know not how to plead our own cause, nor do we understand the aggravations of those accusations that may be brought in against us. It is necessary that we should fly to one who always is present in the court to appear for us. Every man is ready to engage any person that hath the ear and interest of the judge on his side. Every man is to lift up his eye to this advocate: 'If any man sin, we have an advocate.' The *having* is little without employing. The more we exercise faith in his intercession, the more communion we have with the advocate, and the more sanctification will increase in us: John xvii. 17, 'Sanctify them through thy truth.' His prayer there for sanctification is a standing notice to us whence sanctification is to be fetched, viz. from heaven by virtue of this intercession. In our shortest ejaculations, as well as our extended petitions, let us implore him under this title. No man under the law was to offer the meanest offering, though a pigeon, by his own hand, but the hand of the priest appointed to it by divine order. In all distresses, infirmities, and darkness in this world, we should get up to that mountain of myrrh, and to the hill of frankincense, Cant. iv. 6 (which is, as some understand it, a speech of the church), to the passion of Christ, which was bitter like myrrh, to the intercession of Christ, which is sweet like incense. Our whole life, till everlasting glory be ready to receive us, should be a life of faith in his death and intercession.

(3.) Let our affections be in heaven with our advocate. Though the

* Camero de Ecclesia, p. 229.

people of Israel were barred from entering into the holy of holies with the high priest when he went to sprinkle the blood on the mercy-seat, yet they attended him with their hearts, continued their wishes for his success, and expected his return with the notice of his acceptation. Since Christ is entered into the holy place, and acts our business in the midst of his glory, we should raise our hearts to him where he is, and link our spirits with him, and rejoice in the assured success of his negotiation. Though a man be not personally present with his advocate in the court, yet his heart and soul is with him. The heart is where the chief business is. Let us not keep our hearts from him, who employs himself in so great a concern for us.

(4.) Glorify and love this advocate. If Christ presents our persons and prayers in heaven, it is reason we should live to his glory upon earth. If he carries our names on his breast near his heart as a signal of his affection to us, we should carry his name upon our hearts in a way of ingenuous return. We should empty ourselves of all unworthy affections, be inflamed with an ardent love to him, and behave ourselves towards him as the most amiable object. This is but due to him, as he is our advocate.

A DISCOURSE OF THE OBJECT OF FAITH.

Let not your heart be troubled: ye believe in God, believe also in me.—
JOHN XIV. 1.

OUR Saviour in the foregoing chapter, having discoursed of his death by the treachery of Judas, and upon his interruption by Peter's vaunt of his affection to him, having predicted his cowardice, could not but possess the hearts of his disciples with a wonderful trouble. What could be the first reflection upon this alarm, but a fear of the consequences of so sad a separation, and a distrust of themselves? Their Master would be removed from them by the treason of one of their own college, John xiii. 21, and to a place whither they could not at present follow him, ver. 36. They must lose that ravishing converse they had so long a time enjoyed with him; they saw themselves ready to be exposed to the fury of his and their ill-willers in Judea; they should want the support they had in his presence; they could not imagine how they should bear up against temptations, since the fall and apostasy of Peter, one of the most clear-sighted and resolute of their associates, was in such plain words foretold in their hearing: ver. 38, 'The cock shall not crow till thou hast denied me thrice.' Christ, knowing the agitation of their spirits, proposeth remedies both to calm their present fears, and arm them against future troubles; and in this chapter mixes several cordials together, suited to their present and future condition. The grand remedy is prescribed to them in the text, which is both a *preface* and a *thesis*, which he strengthens in his following discourse, 'Let not your heart be troubled: ye believe in God, believe also in me.' I know what troubles those discourses have raised in your spirits; give not way to them, there is a remedy as great as the distemper, and far greater than the cause of your fears; faith will quell all. You think you have cause to be troubled, but if you rightly understood the whole affair, you would find cause of confidence and rejoicing; you have a remedy in your trust in God, a trust which your fathers have successfully practised, and yourselves have been religiously bred in; you believe in the power, goodness, and faithfulness of God; keep that hold still, but take with you also an additional support. Believe also in me, as the person designed in all the promises, from the first to Adam to the last in the prophets, as that person in whom you shall see the evidences of the power, mercy, and goodness of that God you and your fathers have hitherto relied upon.

Let not your heart be troubled. The word ταρασσέσθω signifies properly a commotion of water, which rages, swells, and flings up mud and slime from the bottom; or the disturbance of an army when it is out of rank and order; and thence translated to signify perturbations and fear in the heart of man, when the rest and quietness of the mind is interrupted.

Be not troubled. Entertain no rage or fear in your spirits, do not think I have deceived you, let not your hearts swell with any disdain of me, because your carnal expectations are frustrated. We find in many places that they expected their Master's erection of a worldly empire, wherein they hoped to be his favourites, and settled in some great employments, as ministers of state; and now, at the upshot, finding him to predict nothing but his own death, his leaving of them behind him to endure sufferings and persecution, and all their grand expectations in a moment defeated, they might have an occasion to find storms in their spirits, raking up all the mire and dirt to fling in his face, as if he had been some impostor; well, saith he, 'Let not your heart be troubled, believe in me' as firmly as you have believed in God, and in the issue you will find I have not deceived you, but acted according to the directions of that God in whom you believe; your faith in me shall no more make you ashamed, than your faith in God hath done.

Observe,

1. The best of God's people are apt to be overwhelmed with an ungrounded sorrow. A sorrow for sin never wants ground, but a sorrow for other things often doth. Ignorance and heedlessness is frequently the cause of commotions in the minds of good men. These had heard in the whole course of Christ's ministry enough to waylay their fears, and prepare them for this hour; they had heard him more than once speaking of his death, yet a fond conceit of obtaining an earthly grandeur by him made them little to regard it. They had seen the power of God shielding him from the power of his enemies, and illustrious in the miracles he had wrought before their eyes, and might have fortified themselves with considerations against any dejection, till they had seen the issue. But their inadvertency, regardlessness, and ignorance, not only gave way to, but fomented, their inward storms.

2. How apt is man to be troubled oftentimes at that which conduceth to his happiness! They are troubled at Christ's death and departure, which in themselves were the only means appointed by God for their felicity; that which was to render them happy did in their own account render them miserable. Had they known the design of it, it had rather been matter of joy to see their sins expiated, and an incensed God reconciled to them upon the surest and most irreversible terms, and to be assured that mansions should be prepared for them in heaven; but short-sighted men perceive not the secrets of divine wisdom in its paths in the world, which are double to what they apprehend, Job xi. 6.

3. How tender is Christ to remedy the troubles of his people! In his dying posture he seeketh not their assistance of him, but neglects himself to cheer up them; he gives them some drops of those comforts here, whereof they were to have floods hereafter. He shews them now what he was to do in heaven, to order affairs in such a manner as to expel their troubles. What he was so ready to do when his calamitous condition might have excused him from so friendly an office, he will be more ready to do since he hath nothing to obstruct him. What was his office on earth, is still his office in heaven; 'Let not your hearts be troubled,' is his language from the place of his glory; and while he retains his compassions, he will issue out his consolations.

4. How gracious is our Redeemer, to take occasion, from unbelieving

distrusts, to pour out his choicest cordials! Nothing so admirable was ever published to the world as the doctrine that had dropped from his lips to his followers. He had acquainted them that redemption was the design of his coming; he had again and again assured them of his Father's and his own love to them; yet you see their corruption shoots up its head above their grace; their unbelieving fears seem to give the lie to all he had formerly acquainted them with; yet he doth not manifest any marks of indignation, and strike them down at his foot, as he did shortly after those that came to apprehend him, but comforts them without checking them; and, which is more astonishing, takes occasion from hence to utter something more magnificent and cordial than he had ever done before: he takes occasion, from the workings of hell in them, to give them a clearer appearance of heaven, and opens that place of glory for them, which was quickly after opened for himself. His discourses after this, in this and the following chapters, bear a general eminency, and are more full of refreshments, than any before; he now rains down manna upon them, and gives them that incomparable promise of the Spirit to be their comforter; after this evidence of their distrustful fear, he seems to open all the repositories in heaven to make a cordial for them. What could be done more to quell fear, and encourage faith, unless he had wafted them immediately to glory, and exchanged their faith for that eternally triumphant affection of love which shall reign in heaven?

5. Christ doth not remove the cross from his people, but comforts them under it. He doth not retract anything he had said before, which gave life to their fear and sorrow, as many tender persons do when they see others startled and grieved at their resolves; but he bears up their spirits, while he holds the cross upon their shoulders, and is as forward in comforting them as the matter he had treated of was apt to disquiet them. That which he useth to repel their fears is, 'Ye believe in God; believe also in me.' The word πιστεύετε in our translation is, in the first place, in the indicative mood; in the latter, in the imperative. But the text is read various ways. Some read it,

1. You believe in God, you do also believe in me;* both in the indicative mood; as much as to say, Since you do believe in us both, this your faith in God, and in me, will be a sufficient bulwark against all your fears. Others read it,

2. Believe in God, believe also in me; both in the imperative, commanding this act upon those two objects. Others read it,

3. Believe in God, and you do then also believe in me; the first in the imperative, the second in the indicative; *i. e.* If you believe in God rightly, you cannot but believe in me; for there is no true faith and trust in God but in and through the Mediator.

The matter is not great which way we read it; either thus, 'Believe in God, believe also in me,' as ordering both; or, 'You do believe in God, believe also in me,' as allowing the first by way of concession, and ordering the latter; both do suit the occasion of his discourse.

You believe in God. You believe in God as the creator, preserver, and governor of all things.† This is natural to all, to acknowledge God, to own him one way or other as an object of trust in extremity, which is evidenced by the common approach to him, and calling upon him in cases of exigence; but this is not all that is meant here. But, further, you believe the promises of God in Moses, the Psalms, and prophets; you believe all that is spoken of the Messiah, by whom he hath promised to justify and save his

* Erasm. *in loc.*

† Grot.

people. Thus you have the same faith your fathers had before you, and you do not only believe the authority of God speaking, by an act of your understanding, but you do embrace those promises by a consent of will, and rely upon him for the performance of them, that he will bring forth the Messiah for those great ends and purposes for which he is promised.

Believe also in me. I do not go about to turn you from your confidence in God, but to establish it; you must, besides this, repose yourselves in me. You believe God to be true and merciful, and you believe the promises he hath made of the Messiah; you must believe in me also; you must believe that I am the person designed in all those promises to be that Messiah; you must believe that I am he, as he expresseth it, John xiii. 19, that very seed of the woman that was to bruise the serpent's head, and rest yourselves in me as that Messiah; and that fear which hath reigned in the hearts of men, from the first moment of Adam's fall, will expire in the spirits of all those that have a true and sincere faith in me; for in me they will behold their restoration. If you believe God making those promises, you must also believe me to be the matter of them. I am the person which was the centre of them, that person by whom your enemies are to be destroyed, your judge to be pacified, your pardon to be purchased. Before, a general faith in the promise of God, that there should be a Messiah, was sufficient for you; this you have, and this your fathers had; and you believe in God, promising this Messiah, and rest upon him for the accomplishment of this promise; but now, since this promise is accomplished, and the Messiah is come, your faith must be more particular; you must believe me to be an all-sufficient Saviour, and must believe in me for the remission of sin, and the eternal mansions which I am going to prepare for you. You must firmly believe that I am the person sent by God in that capacity and office, whatsoever storms you shall see raised against me, and whatsoever black clouds you shall see me wrapped in.

Believing here notes not only an assent, but a recumbency, 'believe in me.' You do not only believe God, but believe *in* him, *i. e.* rely upon him for what he hath promised. You must not only believe me to be the Messiah, but rely upon me for those things God hath promised to be done by the Messiah. *Believe in me, i. e.* believe in me as mediator, and rely upon me for all the fruits of my mediation.

Believe in me. As you believe God is constant in his promises, so believe also that I will not forsake you, though I be absent from you. So that Christ brings them here to himself as mediator, as well as to God the fountain of salvation, and proposeth himself here as an object of faith, in conjunction with the supreme Deity. Nothing would make the poor disciples so dejected as to see him hanging on a cross whom they expected upon a throne; and nothing but a consideration of him to be the Messiah, and a great faith in him, could support them under so unexpected a disaster.

Observe,

1. By way of caution, that this Scripture is no argument against the deity of Christ, because our Saviour doth here distinguish God from himself.

By *God* here is meant the *Father;* and by calling the Father God, the Son is no more excluded from the deity than when Christ is called God, as he is Rom. ix. 5, 'Christ, who is over all, God blessed for ever,' the Father is excluded. Christ doth here assert his own deity in the substance of the command, in making himself an object of faith in conjunction with God, and as necessary for the support of the soul as God himself. He orders faith in himself in the same manner as he orders it in God: John v. 17, 'My Father works, and I work;' as my Father works, so I work, because of the unity of essence; so as you believe in God the Father, believe in me also the Son.

2. It is necessary to believe Christ to be the Messiah. This is the first thing to be believed in the Christian religion, that Jesus is the Christ, the Saviour of the world. The apostles directed their discourses generally to prove this, Acts ii. 36, ix. 22, xviii. 5; and the great *medium* to prove it by was his resurrection after his death; and for not believing this, the Jews are pronounced by Paul judgers of themselves, as 'unworthy of eternal life,' Acts xiii. 46. Cornelius, before he heard Peter, believed that there would be a Messiah; but after the hearing of Peter's declaration of Christ's death and resurrection, he was to exercise a particular faith in him; and if he had not, his former faith had stood him in no stead, because he would have despised the revelation of God. How can he be said to believe God in his promise, that believes him not in his performance? I am afraid there is too much unbelief of this amongst us; we are brought up in the profession of Christ, and our faith in him is of no better a stamp than an education faith; we understand not upon good grounds that this Christ is the Messiah promised from the foundation of the world.

3. Only faith in God, through the Mediator, can bear up the heart in troubles. This is the ballast that can keep the soul steady in a stormy sea. 'Fear not, but believe,' said Christ, as the proper remedy, Luke viii. 50. Faith makes not ashamed, it doth elevate the heart above all that would depress it. It breeds a great and courageous spirit, and makes men willing to want the satisfactions of the flesh for the delights of heaven. To come believingly is to come boldly in a time of need, Heb. iv. 16. Faith is dignified with a title of confidence, and with that of a full assurance, Heb. x. 22. This was that whereby God dispelled the cloud of fear from Abraham: Gen. xv. 1, 'Fear not, Abraham,' the wrath due to sin upon the revolt of man, I am sufficient to bring forth the promised seed; I will be thy shield against the terrors of wrath, and I will be the reward of thy faith and obedience in a glorious salvation. It was not a carnal fear, or a fear of some temporal evil, for this speech was after his victory over the kings that had conquered and plundered Sodom, after he had been blessed by so great a type of Christ as Melchisedec was; the fear of Abraham was occasioned by his want of a child, and a seed wherein the nations of the earth were to be blessed, as appears by his answer, ver. 2, that promised seed, that was to change the curse of sin into a blessing; this seed is promised him, ver. 4, 5, and then Abraham believed, *i. e.* all his fears vanished, and he relied upon God for the performance of this.

4. All our comforts are fetched from above. Christ sends them not here to the waters of the earth, to quench the heat of their troubles; he directs not their eyes downwards, but upwards, to God and himself. It is a scanty relief that is fetched from a man's self, and from the uncertainty of the world in shaking troubles; one God in the one Mediator out-balanceth all those things whence men commonly gather their supports. It is as much as if he had said, You have fancied great things to yourselves, you thought to have had great employments under that earthly royalty you imagined I should be possessed with; and no doubt but I should have had a regard to such friends as you are, that have followed me in my perplexed condition, had such a kingdom been designed me; but I would not have your souls so mean and low: take a higher flight, nourish yourselves with hopes of a purer glory, and more durable mansions which I am going to prepare for you; a temporal grandeur will only stupefy your fears, not stab them to the heart, but the consideration of what I propose to you will perfectly despatch them.

In the text you see,

1. An act: 'believe in God.'
2. The object: 'In God,' 'in me.'
3. The fruit and effect of it: 'Let not your heart be troubled.'

I shall speak of the object, and the doctrine resulting thence will be,

Doct. God and Christ are in conjunction, the true and proper object of faith. Read it which way you will, this is the result of it; he doth not discourage their faith in God, but encourageth that, together with faith in himself. Every act hath something about which it is exercised; faith is an act of the soul, it must therefore have an object upon which it is terminated. God is the object of faith according to his present dispensation, which is the manifestation of himself as a reconciled God through a mediator. As he is a God of grace and peace, he is an object of faith, and trust, and joy; but grace and peace are not manifested, not given forth, not multiplied simply by the knowledge of God, but also of Jesus our Lord: 2 Peter i. 2, 'Grace and peace be multiplied unto you through the knowledge of God, and Jesus our Lord.' Not by the knowledge of God alone, nor by the knowledge of Christ alone, but of God in the mediator Christ, in whom only he is known to be our God in the covenant of grace, the spring of all our comfort, the knowledge of God and Jesus our Lord, *i. e.* the knowledge of God in Jesus our Lord, Ἓν διὰ δυοῖν, as Rom. i. 5, 'grace and apostleship,' *i. e.* grace of apostleship.

God is not the object of faith now as creator; he was so in the state of man's rectitude, and could not be considered by the creature in any other notion; but in our lapsed state God is not only considered as creator, but as the offended Majesty, and consequently as judge, and we cannot behold him but encompassed with scorching flames about his throne. He that exerciseth faith in God merely as creator, understands not the present condition of human nature, the malignity of his own provocations, nor the glorious perfections of righteousness, veracity, justice, which are essential to the Deity. Though the fall of man did not null the relation of God as creator, which stands irreversible, yet it added another relation to him, that of a judge, and cracked in pieces all grounds and props of a trust in him for the expressions of kindness, and set up only the expectation of a mighty revenge, according to his threatening. You find no other sentiments in Adam after his rebellion, not the least mite of a trust in God, though he had newly come out of the hands of God, and the relation of a creator was fresh and flourishing; and why any of his posterity should have other sentiments than he had, in this single relation, I cannot conceive any ground from the revelation of God; he beats the hands of the creature off from expecting any salvation from him upon that account. Isa. xxvii. 11, 'It is a people of no understanding: therefore he that made them will have no mercy on them, and he that formed them will shew them no favour.' It is spoken upon the wasting of Jerusalem, and laying it desolate; yet, he adds for their comfort, that in that day he would gather them, and they should worship the Lord in the holy mount at Jerusalem. As he was their creator, or under the notion of a creator, they must expect nothing from him, since they were a people of no understanding, as all men in Adam are, who being in honour, and understanding not, *i. e.* not walking according to the knowledge they had, became like the beasts that perish; but what they were to expect from him was, as he was God Redeemer, expressed by the worship of him in the holy mount at Jerusalem, alluding to the ceremonial worship, a type of Christ, the way whereby men were to come to God, and blessings to be conveyed from God to them. He would not be the object of their expecting faith, nor of their religious worship as Creator, but as God Redeemer. And though Peter speaks of 'committing of souls to God, as unto a faithful Creator,' 1 Peter iv. 19, it is not to be understood of God in the first creation, but the second; and the attribute *faithful* annexed to Creator, evinceth it; for though faithfulness be a perfection of the Deity, yet it is not apparent in the act of creation. In relation to that act, it is the powerful, wise, good creator; but faithfulness respects the promise and covenant of grace. As righteousness is a fit attribute for a judge,—and so God is called, when he is spoken of under that title, 2 Tim. iv. 8,—so powerful is a fit attribute of the Creator, as considered in the first material creation of the world. How had God engaged himself in creation to preserve the soul of man, but in a way of obedience! Suffering was not to be expected in a state of innocence, and it is the committing of our soul to God in a suffering state that the apostle speaks of. His engagements to this purpose are, in his promises, made pursuant to the covenant of grace, but he is called Creator here, in regard of the new creation, as he is called 'the Creator of Israel, and their King,' Isa. xliii. 15, as he is their Holy One, sanctifying them through his grace. He is no more the Creator of Israel in a way of appropriation, if you consider him so in the first creation, than he is of the fallen angels and the beasts of the earth; but as he formed them into a church, he was peculiarly their Creator. But this creation respected the Messiah, and so doth this in Peter respect Christ, in whom all the promises, wherein God's faithfulness lies at pawn, are *yea and amen*. He is the Creator of believers, as they are sons of the promise; and therefore Calvin inclines to interpret the word translated *creator* here as *possessor;* and the word doth sometimes, in heathen authors, though rarely, signify preserver or restorer.* Yet is not the title of God as Creator excluded from an object of trust, for since Christ hath restored in part the soul to the image of God, which it had by creation, it may expect from God as Creator a faithfulness to his own image, and his service, but not singly as Creator, but in conjunction with the Redeemer.

I shall lay down some propositions for the clearing of this.

I. God is the object of faith.

God is the principal object of faith and trust. The whole revelation in Scripture tends to the knowledge of God. Why did God create, but that he might be known to be omnipotent and good? Why did God send Christ, but that he might be known to be merciful and gracious? Whatsoever is revealed in the word, and concerning Christ in particular, hath a direct tendency to God, and the knowledge of him, and this practical duty which follows thereupon: John xvii. 3, 'This is life eternal, to know thee, the only true God, and Jesus Christ, whom thou hast sent.'

1. God in his attributes. He is an object of faith as made known to us, but he is made known to us in some perfections of his nature, as encouragements to approach to him, and ground our hopes in him; and he is an object of faith in every one of his distinct attributes, in his power, wisdom, goodness, and righteousness, according to our several occasions and circumstances; for he is the object of faith as he is a God in covenant, our God; and he is our God in every attribute which makes up that glorious nature; and those perfections of his nature were made known in Christ, that he might be known not only speculatively, but fiducially. The name of God was in him, Exod. xxiii. 21, in that Angel of the covenant. Whatsoever was knowable of God was unveiled in Christ, as the exact and perfect medium wherein we may have a prospect of God; there was more of wisdom, and more of power discovered in uniting the Godhead to the manhood; more of good-

* Stephanus in verbo Κτίζω.

ness, grace, righteousness, holiness, which are all attractives to seek God, and lay hold upon him, than made known any other way; and all were discovered to promote that great doctrine of faith preached by Christ and the apostles.

2. Particularly the veracity of God is the first object, or ground of faith. He is not the first object of faith in any attribute, but his veracity. As God creates the world as powerful, and punisheth the wicked as he is just, and pardons sin as he is merciful, and provides for all as he is good, so he is believed on as true in the first motion of the soul to him. The first act of faith considers God as true in his promise, and powerful to accomplish it: 'This is life eternal, to know thee, the only true God, and Jesus Christ whom thou hast sent,' John xvii. 3. 'Αληθινός, signifies *verax*, as well as *verus;* not only true in thy nature, but true in thy word; 'the only true God' in Jesus Christ, in whom there was the performance of the first and greatest promise made in paradise; by the same figure spoken of before, ἓν διὰ δυοῖν. As in loving God, we have his goodness for the immediate object; in hoping in him, we centre in his power; so in our first assent to him we fix our eye upon his truth.* For when any declaration is proposed as from God, the first act is an inquiry whether it be from God, or no; when the result of that inquiry is this, that God speaks and declares this, the assent to it is moved by the consideration of the truth of God; for to a belief of any thing that is offered, there is necessary first an evidence that the declarer is not deceived, and that he will not willingly deceive others. In the believing that God cannot be deceived, faith respects the certainty of his knowledge; in believing that he will not deceive, and so making his word the object of our reliance, faith respects the certainty of his faithfulness and veracity. The promise is the object of trust; the reason why I trust the promiser, is his fidelity and constancy to his word. That is not faith which respects not either a command, promise, or threatening, in all which the faithfulness and veracity of the person urging the precept, or uttering the threatening, or making the promise, comes first into consideration. But justifying faith respects chiefly the promise; hence believers are called 'the children of the promise,' Rom. ix. 8, Gal. iv. 28, because by faith they entertain the promise; and as it is an *assent*, it hath for its object the unerring truth of God; and as it is a *consent* and reliance, it still principally eyes the same for the accomplishment of what he hath engaged to do for us in his word; and the first language of faith in receiving the testimony of Christ, is a testifying, or 'setting to the seal that God is true,' John iii. 33; that he hath been as good as his word, and makes good what he promised to our first parents, and repeated several times since in other language.

3. But faith doth ultimately centre in the Deity. God himself, in his glorious nature, is the ultimate object whereinto our faith is resolved. The promise, simply considered, is not the object of trust, but God in the promise; and from the consideration of that we ascend to the Deity, and cast our anchor there. 'Hope in the word' is the first act, but succeeded by hoping in the Lord: Ps. cxxx. 5, 7, 'In his word do I hope;' that is not all; 'but let Israel hope in the Lord.' That is the ultimate object of faith, wherein the essence of our happiness consists, and that is God. God himself is the true and full portion of the soul. If it be asked, why we believe God?† the answer is, because he is true. If it be asked, why God is true? the answer is, because he is God, and cannot be God unless he were true. No further answer can be given. In this the soul doth acquiesce as a full

* Suarez, vol. viii. p. 65. † Ibid. p. 64.

resolution; so that, though faith in the first act respects the truth of God, yet it is ultimately resolved into the Deity itself.

4. It particularly centres in the Deity as the author of redemption (Ps. cxxx. 7, 8, 'Let Israel hope in the Lord, for with him is plenteous redemption; and he shall redeem Israel from all his iniquities'), and takes away all the oppressive and provoking guilt of the soul by that redemption, which, like a vast ocean, knows no bounds. As God was the first in forming the design of creation, so he was the first in laying the platform of redemption, and appointing Christ to be a sacrifice for the expiation of our sins, and ransom of our souls. As our thanksgivings are to be directed to him, as he is the 'God and Father of our Lord Jesus Christ,' Eph. i. 3, so is our faith. This was the title he assumed; and he is 'the Father of glory,' in being 'the God of our Lord Jesus Christ,' ver. 17. He was the orderer of all those glorious acts Christ did, and that purchase he made. He is the God of our Lord Jesus Christ, not in regard of his divine nature, wherein there is not a superiority of power, though a priority of order, Christ in regard of his divine nature not being inferior to, but equal with, God; but in regard of his mediatory office, as he was the ambassador of God, and his righteous servant acting by his commission and authority, according to his particular instructions, and in regard of the covenant between them. He is said to be the God of Christ, as he is said to be the God of Abraham, not in regard of his creating him, but in a more special manner, as being in covenant with him. Now faith looks through the ambassador to the prince that employs him, and through the servant to the Lord that sends him, and to the person that first proposed the terms of the covenant, and revealed his everlasting purpose of saving sinners by Christ. Faith looks beyond the time of Christ's conversing in the flesh, and sealing the covenant by his blood. It looks to the everlasting platform of it in the bosom of the Deity; beyond the beam of it in the incarnation and death of Christ; beyond the first promise of it in paradise, Hab. i. 13, 'Art thou not from everlasting, O Lord my God, my Holy One?' The prophet looks back to the everlasting springs of it in the heart of the Deity, and pierceth to the first point of the resolve, and thence concludes we shall not die. It was not barely the eternity of God he considers there; for that simply considered might be an argument for the restoration and sanctification of devils, as well as Israel; but God from everlasting, as his God and his Holy One, as resolving upon a covenant of grace, and to be a sanctifier of his people; and from thence his faith draws a conclusion of an impossibility of dying, and a certain assurance of enjoying life. And the apostle's faith looked to Christ as the medium, 'by whom are all things,' but to the Father, 'of whom,' by whose authority, 'all things are,' 1 Cor. viii. 6. Faith doth not stick only in Christ, but mounts up to the Deity, as the fountain and spring of all. 'He that believes on me, believes not on me,' saith Christ, 'but on him that sent me,' John xii. 44. Not on me chiefly, not on me solely; it must pierce through the veil to the original wisdom that contrived, and the original authority that enacted, and the grace which inspired every action of the Mediator. God is the ultimate object of faith in all our considerations of Christ; to this purpose he was raised, 'that our faith and hope might be in God,' 1 Peter i. 21, that it might not stick immoveably in Christ, Rom. iv. 24, but be as a ladder to get up, and clasp about the Highest and the Ancient of days. In Christ we see first the smiles of God, in him we see the tender voice of his bowels, in him we feel the lively and affectionate motions of his heart. When we have fixed on Christ, faith rests not there, but ascends ultimately to God, as the great promoter of this design, by whose authority all was transacted, and

before whom all is to be finished, as to him who set out this propitiation for sin, and keeps in his own hand the royalty of pardoning iniquity.

II. Christ is the object of faith. God alone was the object of trust in the state of innocence, and under the covenant of works. The covenant, 'Do this, and live,' being established between God and man without a mediator, none could be the object of trust for the performance of the promise upon condition of obedience, but God in the simplicity of his own being, without any other relation. But under the covenant of grace, which is settled in a mediator, 'Believe this, and live,' Christ the mediator is an object of faith, though God be still the ultimate object; because we believe in him, that he will give us life and salvation for the merit of this mediator, in whom we believe first.

1. Therefore Christ is the immediate object of faith, as he by whom all the counsels of redemption were executed, as he who assumed our nature, to suffer in it for the satisfaction of divine justice, and was raised again to transact our affairs, and manifest the value and infinite fulness of that satisfaction. We cannot look upon God under any other notion than that of an incensed governor and judge, if we well apprehend the condition of lapsed man. Unless we behold him in and through a mediator, the terrors of his majesty would confound us; we dare not look him in the face because of our vileness as sinners. We must first, therefore, fasten our eyes upon the mediator, and then upon God. The mercy of God in pardoning sin is that which faith exerciseth itself about; the satisfactory death of Christ, upon the account of sin to be pardoned, must be the first and immediate object of faith. Christ must first be known, because the riches of divine grace are knowable and manifested only in him; God speaks not a word of mercy out of this propitiatory. Faith being an applying the reconciliation and mercy obtained, it must consider and believe the satisfaction of divine justice, whereby it was obtained. Before any man can think to stand before the face of God's justice, and be admitted into the secret delights of his mercy, and riches of his grace, he must consider this mediator as appeasing God, and consider the voice of God proclaiming himself appeased in his Son, Mat. iii. 17. We are first to believe and rest upon the strength and value of this sacrifice, and with this in the hands of our faith, go to God with a further act of faith, for an application to us of what was purchased for us. It is *by him* we believe in God, 1 Peter i. 21; we must first, therefore, believe *in him*. The faith, therefore, that justifies, is called 'the faith of Christ,' Gal. ii. 16; and in other places it is called a 'coming to God by Christ,' Heb. vii. 24. It is, therefore, first a coming to Christ to bring us to God. We cannot 'come to the Father but by him,' as he speaks in the same chapter where the text is, ver. 6, pursuant to the doctrine he had laid down in the first verse; and must first, therefore, come to him as 'the way, the truth, and the life.' It is in him, and 'by the faith of him, that we have access with confidence,' Eph. iii. 12. There must first be a coming to him to be inspired with confidence; he that will come to the holy of holies must pass through the veil. Thus Christ is brought in in the prophet proclaiming himself the object of faith: Isa. xlv. 22, 'Look to me, and be you saved, all the ends of the earth.' It is that person is introduced speaking, to whom every knee should bow; that person in whom we have righteousness and strength; that person in whom all the seed of Israel should be justified, ver. 23–25. It is in him we can find all things necessary for our deliverance from the ruin sin hath brought upon us, whatsoever is necessary to restore us to the happiness we have lost. In him is righteousness, to remove our variance with God; and sanctification, to clear us from what may be offensive to

the eyes of his holiness; and therefore the apostle, 1 Tim. i. 1, calls Christ 'our hope,' *i. e.* the object of our hope, as God is called 'the fear of Isaac,' Gen. xxxi. 53. The Israelites' worship was directed towards the tabernacle and temple where the ark was placed, their thoughts were to be fixed on that; so all the motions of our souls must be directed to Christ, and in and by him to God. And therefore faith, in regard of this immediateness of it, is appropriated to Christ as the proper and proxim object, and called faith in the Lord Jesus Christ, in regard of his mediating and reconciling us; whereas repentance respects God immediately, who hath been offended by us, and therefore called 'repentance towards God,' Acts xx. 21.

2. Christ was always, in the times of the patriarchs, the object of faith; and the immediate object, though not so distinct as now.

He was the immediate object of their faith. As he is the object of faith now, as actually destroying the works of the devil, so he was the object of faith then, as potentially bruising the head of the serpent. The object was always the same, though diversified; they believed in the Messiah to be incarnate. Those that lived in the days of his flesh, believed in his present incarnation and passion; those that lived after, believed in him as dying and rising. The faith was the same for substance, the same for object, only differenced in point of time—future, present, past.

(1.) It is clear of David: Ps. cx. 1, 'The Lord said unto my Lord.' He calls him his Lord, that was his Son, Luke xxii. 44. Observe, when he speaks of God, or the Father, or the Deity, singly considered, it is *the* Lord; but when of Christ, it is *my* Lord, a more particular application and appropriation of the one than of the other.

(2.) It is as clear of Moses: Heb. xi. 26, 'Esteeming the reproaches of Christ greater riches than the treasures of Egypt.' What esteem could he have of the reproach of Christ, if he never knew or believed anything of him? Upon what account should he refuse so great an earthly honour, to be treated as the son of Pharaoh's daughter, but upon some higher account than the hopes of enjoying an earthly Canaan, not a better land in itself than Egypt, which was counted the fruitfullest spot in the world? It was certainly the promise of the seed wherein all nations should be blessed, and which he might be twitted with by the Egyptians.

(3.) It is plain of Abraham. The gospel was preached to him in that promise, 'In thee shall all the nations of the earth be blessed,' Gal. iii. 8. Abraham in some sort understood it as God preached it; it cannot be thought God should preach the gospel to him, and he understand nothing of gospel in it; and as it was preached to him to raise his faith, so it was entertained by him with a suitable act of faith; he eyed the Mediator in it, who was to bless all nations, and remove the curse which Adam had brought upon his posterity. He is called the father of us all in regard of his believing: Rom. iv. 16, 'The father of us all,' of all the believers among the Romans, who were not all of Jewish extraction; so the apostle understands that promise made unto him, thou shalt be the father of many nations, *i. e.* of many believers among nations; he should be a copy and pattern of their faith, which could not well be, if he had not the same object of faith that they were afterwards to have, and had not for substance the same prospect of Christ. He did see the day of Christ in that promise, and was glad, John viii. 56. That which was the matter of his joy must be the object of his faith; if he rejoiced in the day of his appearing, he believed in the person who was to appear in that day. Joy is so far from being without a belief, that it is a branch that springs from that root.

(4.) Enoch pleased God by faith, and walked with him. Two cannot walk together unless they be agreed. But there was no agreement between God and lapsed man but in the reconciling mediator; for God out of the promised seed was as terrible then as God out of Christ is now.

(5.) By faith Abel offered a sacrifice, Heb. xi. 4. It must be a belief in the person signified by that sacrifice. God was not the object of his faith barely as Creator; the first threatening of death, which he could not well be unacquainted with, put a bar to that; but it must be a faith in God as a promiser, and so had the matter of the promise, 'the seed,' for its object. It was such a faith whereby he believed God to be a rewarder, ver. 6, which he could have no prospect of but in the redeeming declaration. It was such a faith upon which God pronounced him righteous, which could not be as he stood upon his natural corrupted bottom. He looked for a righteousness in and by that which was represented by his sacrifice, and he obtained a witness from heaven that he was righteous. It is very likely his sacrifice was accompanied with petitions for the hastening the appearance of that seed, and thanksgivings to God for making that gracious promise, and performing those acts of grace after the fall, which necessary attendants were neglected by Cain. It cannot be supposed that Abel could be ignorant of the promise, unless we can suppose Adam so forgetful of it, as never to mention that which could be his only support in his removal from paradise. He that knew the delights of his original state, cannot be imagined to slight a cordial so necessary to keep up his spirits in his exiled condition. The reflection upon his former state must needs fill his mind with a sense of the curse he at the present lay under; and this would by consequence mind him of the remedy God had provided for it; and with what pleasing eye could he look upon his children whom he had brought into that misery, without putting, as I may speak, like a tender nurse, some of the cordial into their mouths?

(6.) That Adam exercised a faith immediately upon this object, the promised seed, is not difficult to represent to you from Gen. iii. 20, 'And Adam called his wife's name Eve, because she was the mother of all living.' כל חי, of all living, in the singular number, or the mother of him that was to enliven all that were to be enlivened; of that latter Adam, who was to be made a quickening Spirit; of that person who was to communicate life to the world; or if we understand it of all living in the plural number, he includes himself then.* But she could not be the mother of him according to an animal life, but as one to be spiritually quickened and restored by the seed of the woman. He gave this name to his wife just after the sentence of death and returning to dust pronounced upon him, ver. 19; and had he been possessed only with an horror of that sentence, he would rather have called her the mother of all dying than of all living; and the name Eve signifying life, shews that he did not so much in this name respect her as a mother, but that life which was to be brought forth into the world by her seed, that restoration promised; and giving her this name just after the sentence of returning to dust, he doth evidence his faith in that seed whereby man that was sentenced to death should live again. The Holy Ghost placing this imposition of a new name upon her (who was before called *isha*, woman) just after the sentence of death, is not without an intimation that Adam looked beyond the sentence of death, to the promise made before of bruising that enemy whose subtlety had brought upon him that judgment, and laid hold on that promise to support him against the sentence of returning to dust. Such a relation to the promise it must have; we can hardly think

* Heideg. Vit. Patriar, vol. i. Coccei Disput. Selec. disp. ix. sec. 12. Pareus in Gen. iii. 20.

that Adam in the state of his fall, and under so gracious a word of deliverance, should be guilty of so great a pride, as, in a vaunt and contempt of the divine sentence, to call her the mother of all living, who had brought death upon the world. How could he call her the mother of all living, when he had just before heard that he was to return to dust, if he had not respected a better and a higher life than that short one he was to pass in the world, and respected also the cause of it? Had he respected only an animal life, he might as well have called himself the father of all living, since we find the name of Abraham and Sarah changed upon the giving the promise. But without question he had respect in this to the Messiah, who was to be the seed of the woman, in appropriating this title to her.* And she might be called the mother of all living in regard of her faith, as Sarah is called the mother of all believing women; 1 Peter iii. 6, because the promise mentioning only 'the seed of the woman' and not of the man, might give her occasion first to exercise a faith in it before Adam did. Besides, that particle *and*, *And* Adam called his wife Eve, &c., linking it with what went before, ver. 19, wherein death was pronounced, shews that he considered the promise of restoration as his support in that state; so that the Messiah in the promise, or the seed of the woman to bruise the serpent's head, was the immediate object of his faith.

(7.) Eve also expresseth her faith in this seed: Gen. iv. 1, when Eve bare Cain she said, 'I have gotten a man from the Lord.' It is true the word את is sometimes the note of other cases as well as the accusative; as Exod. i. 1, 'with Jacob,' where it is the same particle, את, and Gen. v. 22, 'Enoch walked with God,' את; and some interpret it 'from the Lord,' *i. e.* by God's gift and favour; others, 'with the Lord;' others, 'a man, the Lord.' It doth not seem to be any straining of the text to render it 'a man, the Lord,' as respecting the promised seed in her son, the first seed God was pleased to give her, giving him the name Cain,† as if he were the person that were to repossess them again of paradise, and restore them to their happy estate. As a little before Adam had manifested his faith in the name Eve, which he gave to his wife, and the reason of it, so in the birth of Cain there might be as fit an occasion for manifesting the faith of Eve; and it is very probable there might be something more in it than barely an acknowledgment of a mere child from God, and some regard to the promise, since we find no special remark upon any name presently after, but what did refer to that promise, as that upon Noah, of whom Lamech said, Gen. v. 29, 'This same shall comfort us concerning our work and toil of our hands, because of the ground which the Lord hath cursed,' for the return of the sons of men (adds Jonathan); which doth evidently point to that promised seed whereby he expected the curse to be taken off the ground; and though they both erred in their conception of the persons, yet it was a sign they bore a sense of the promise in their minds, and that Eve bore Christ in the womb of her faith, though Cain, whom she bore in the womb of her body, was not that special seed. This particle את, between two nouns, grammarians say, doth specify the person or thing spoken of; as Ezek. xxxiv. 23, 'I will set one shepherd over them, even David my servant.' And it is to be considered that an ancient paraphrast, Jonathan ben Uzziel, who best understood the idiom of the Hebrew language, explains it so; 'a man, the Lord.' And the objection against this interpretation, that Eve erred in her imagination of the birth of the promised seed to be like the birth of other men, signifies not much; so did Lamech in the birth of Noah, yet his speech cannot be denied to have some respect to the promise; and why

* Ainsworth *in loc.* † So Fagius, Luther, Cocceius, Schindler, Foster.

may not both their errors be very well ascribed to the vehemency of their longing (which argued the greatness of their faith) and the obscurity of the revelation? That there should be such a seed, was manifest to them from the truth of God; but the manner how this seed should be brought forth into the world, whether of a virgin, was hid from them, and not revealed till many ages after. I do not see any inconvenience in thus interpreting this place; as if Eve should have said, I have gained that very man, the Lord; that divine person promised to be the conqueror of the serpent, that hath been the cause of bringing this misery upon us.

(8.) All those that believed under the law had their faith pitched upon the Messiah. We may easily perceive by the whole eleventh chapter to the Hebrews that the substance of faith was always the same, and therefore the object of faith was in the gross, confusedly or distinctly, the same. Upon this account, all believers from the beginning of the world may be called Christians.* Whatsoever the ceremonies of the church might be, their faith had the same foundation, was of the same tenure. Upon the promised seed it was pitched, and the bruising of the serpent, and removing of the curse by it, was longed for. The whole mystery of prophecy was designed for the encouragement and support of this faith. Eating and drinking are metaphors to signify faith in its applicatory act. This the ancients are said to do; they ate Christ in the manna, and drank Christ in the rock, 1 Cor. x. 3, 4. They came to God as a rewarder. That was as necessary to be considered by them as the existence of a God is to be believed by them, Heb. xi. 6, not as a rewarder in a way of nature; they could not but know Adam's fall to be a discouragement to such expectations; but in a way of grace, according to the promise made to Adam after the fall. This Messiah the church perpetually held under all the corruptions of ages and the abuses of the watchmen, and would not let him go, Cant. iii. 4. They had the same fruits of faith under the law, and therefore the same substantial object of faith as we have under the gospel. All that were justified and saved had the sentence of justification pronounced upon them on no other account than we have, which Paul labours to evidence in several places, especially Rom. iv., throughout the whole chapter, in the examples of Abraham and David. Their justification was by faith, which faith was 'imputed to them for righteousness;' and what that faith was, the apostle plainly deciphers: ver. 23, 24, 'It was written for us, to whom it shall be imputed, if we believe on him that raised up Jesus our Lord from the dead.' If his faith were of another kind and had another object, God alone, and not God in Christ, it could not have been so positively said it was written for our sakes. It is a faith in God through Christ that is imputed to us under the gospel for justification. It was a faith in God through the Messiah that was imputed to them. It was imputed to them, it shall be imputed to us; the same faith pitched upon the same object. It would not be any strong arguing in the apostle that Abraham and we should be alike justified by faith, if our faith and his were not the same, and embraced not the same object. All that were sanctified were perfected by Christ, Heb. x. 14. If any man came to the Father, they came by him, because 'no man comes to the Father but by' that true and living way, John xiv. 6. They anciently embraced the promises, Heb. xi. 13. What! With the neglect of the first root promise, to which all the other promises were but appendixes or comments upon it? Could they embrace the comments, and act faith upon nothing of the text? It was an heavenly inheritance they expected, 'for they confessed themselves strangers and pilgrims on the earth;' and ver. 10, 'they looked for a city, whose builder

* As Eusebius saith, Histor. lib. i. cap iv.

and maker is God:' a city having foundations, *i. e.* an immutable state, which they could not do if they had not exercised their faith about that first promise, which took off the execution of the first threatening, and promised the ruin of that enemy which had ruined their health they had in the first creation; and could all this be without a faith in that Messiah who was to be the worker of those glorious things, who was indeed the author and finisher of faith; the author of it, or the foundation of it, in the ancient Israelites, in the types and figures; and the finisher and completer of it in his appearance in the flesh and bloody passion, wherein he laid the top-stone?

This may be further cleared if we consider,

1. Sacrifices in themselves could be no content and satisfaction to them, nor the proper object of their faith. They could not but be sensible of too great a burden to be taken off from them and supported by the weakness of a lamb; they could not but be sensible of too deep a stain to be washed off from them by the blood of a little kid, or a greater quantity of it in a heifer. Could they possibly imagine that brutish blood could open the gates of heaven, and eat through those bars that justice had fixed upon them, or the smoke of the carcase of a slain beast could sweeten the stench of their sins? It is an injury to the faith of those worthies so highly celebrated, Heb. xi., to think that it fell so flat, and was drowned in the blood and bowels of the beasts, and mounted no higher than the smoke of their entrails, that they expected no higher expiation, and no higher contentment, as the issue of these things. Though some of those worthies 'wandered about in sheep-skins and goat-skins,' Heb. xi. 37, yet their faith was not wrapped up in the skins of lambs or hides of heifers, since they had so often heard by the prophets that those things were not pleasing to God in themselves, that he did not 'eat the flesh of bulls and drink the blood of goats,' Ps. l. 13. Though they knew God true to perform his promise, and merciful to pity their miseries, yet they knew him to be of a pure and spiritual nature, above any delight in a ceremonious pomp, and too just to be appeased by an herd of consecrated animals. The groans and repeated desires of the ancient saints for the 'consolation of Israel,' that 'the salvation of Israel would come out of Sion,' their hungry waitings for God's salvation, manifested that those things were thought too weak by them to ease them of their burdens, to procure the good things they felt the need of. If their faith had been confined to those sacrifices, if it had here taken its rest, and laid its head at ease upon a pillow of beasts' skins, what ground was there for those groans, those ardent desires for another kind of salvation, even when they were in the most prosperous and flourishing condition, tasting every day of the milk and honey of Canaan, and settled in a ceremonious worship of God's institution? Surely their faith ascended above the blood and smoke of the sacrifices to the throne of the Messiah. Sacrifices were the gospel in a rough draught, not with the perfect lineaments.

2. They could not but apprehend some mystery in these ceremonies, and use them as assistances of their faith, and as means to conduct it to the right object. They could not but apprehend them to be rather the representations of the true object of faith than to be the proper object themselves. It can hardly be imagined that all the Israelites stuck in the shell of sacrifices and ceremonies, that their eyes were terminated to the outward pomp and bloody offerings, without any respect to some mystery in them; they could not but conjecture that those types were significant of some great work to be done.* It could never enter into the understanding of rational men that all that corporeal worship was enjoined for itself, and that those multi-

* Amyr. Moral. tom. iv. pp. 128, 129.

tudes of ceremonies were without a signification of something to them. When there were such perpetual orders about the tabernacle, the meanest utensils of it, the ark, and propitiatory, the cherubims to overshadow it, the shew-bread, the sacrifices, the scapegoat, it was known to them that all those had a respect to the expiation of sin, and therefore must represent some other greater thing, which might be sufficient for the expiation, since they could not but judge those things too feeble to attain so great an end of themselves; or else they must have very unworthy and unbecoming notions of God, and very slight imaginations of the deep taint original sin had left upon their natures, with which we cannot imagine that the minds of believers could be possessed. They knew that God was infinitely wise, that in everything that he did and ordered there was something to be understood by them: could they think that the passage through the Red Sea was intended only to deliver them, and had no further aim, since God could have delivered them many other ways, struck the enemy dead upon their march, or enabled the Israelites to overcome them in a plain fight? The wiser at least might well think that the manna, rock, the serpent lifted up in the wilderness for the healing of the people, and many other actions of God among them, had something mysterious in them, though they could not discern every lineament of that mystery. Did they not all tend to the encouragement of their faith, pursuant to the first promise, and was the design of them altogether unknown to those for whose sake they were appointed? If they were all baptized in the Red Sea, can we think that all were ignorant of something of the spiritual meaning of it? 1 Cor. x. 1–4. Did they eat Christ in the manna, and drink Christ in the rock? Did they eat the spiritual meat and drink the spiritual drink (for that is the apostle's assertion), and did all of them eat and drink it unspiritually, without any understanding of the general spiritual signification of it? 'Our fathers,' saith the apostle, speaking to the Gentile Corinthians. The Israelites were not the Corinthians' fathers according to the flesh, but their fathers in faith. The faith then the Israelites had in the type must respect the antitype, Christ, upon whom only the faith of the Corinthians was pitched. That could not be the same faith that had two different objects, as distant from one another as heaven from earth. Can a faith in the Messiah, and a faith terminated only in corporeal manna, and the liquid waters of a rock, be accounted a faith equally great and of the same kind? The nature of faith, as well as any other act of the soul or body, is quite changed by the object about which it is conversant. The mystery of those things could not be altogether unknown to so many thousands. Would God not hide from Abraham the thing which he would do about Sodom, since Abraham should become a mighty nation, and that God knew that he would command his children and his household after him to keep the way of the Lord? Gen. xviii. 17–19. And would God totally hide the mystery veiled under those things from Moses, whom he had appointed the conductor of this people under him, one who had an excellency above all prophets, to be known by God face to face? Deut. xxxiv. 10; *i. e.* saith Maimonides, to have an apprehension of things bestowed upon him above what any of the prophets which followed him in Israel had, and one that the Spirit of God in the history associates with God himself as the object of the Israelites' faith after the deliverance at the Red Sea, as a type of Christ.* Exod. xiv. 31, 'They feared the Lord, and believed in the Lord, and in his servant Moses;' for so the words run in the Hebrew, believed *in* the Lord, and *in* Moses, as implying a mystery. Can we think the mystery was wholly obscured from him? Was not his mind enlightened to some apprehensions of

* More Nevoch. part ii. cap. xxv.

what was couched under all those things? Surely it was, and he would not conceal it to himself and veil it from all his people. The gospel was preached to the Israelites while they were in the wilderness: Heb. iv. 2, 'Unto us was the gospel preached, as well as unto them; but the word preached did not profit them, not being mixed with faith in them that heard it.' They had the word preached to them, and that word was the gospel; Christ therefore, that is the substance and marrow of the gospel, was preached to them; preached to them in the types, manna, and the rock, and the serpent lifted up; preached to them in the promise of Canaan. And who were those it was preached to? The Israelites in the wilderness; it was to them to whom God sware that they should not enter in his rest, to them who had grieved him forty years, and whose carcases fell in the wilderness. And why did they not enter into his rest? Because they believed not, Heb. iii. 17–19. And what was that which they did not believe? That we may not think it was only the promise of entering into the land of Canaan that they thus discredited, he tells us that it was the gospel that they did not believe. The gospel they rejected, by their murmuring against manna and Canaan. Those therefore that did believe among them believed the gospel, pitched upon Christ, who is the marrow of the gospel. They saw Christ in the manna, and Christ in the pleasant land promised them; Christ in the blood of the sacrifices: the whole was the Christian religion in its rough draught. If the gospel were thus preached to them, Christ was the object of faith. Would God preach the gospel to them wholly in vain, so that no act of an evangelical faith should be exercised by any of them? Would he be at such pains to send forth a vain sound so many ages, one after another, to people to whom he would give no understanding, not to a man of them, in some measure of what he meant by it? It cannot be supposed that the gospel should be preached to them in all those figures, without a gospel faith exercised by some of them upon that which was represented by those shadows; they had else been in vain and to no purpose to them.

3. The object of their hope and trust under all that dispensation was the Messiah, and their faith was expressed by waiting and trusting. Jacob upon his death-bed breathes out his soul in longing for God's salvation, or God's Jesus,—Gen. xlix. 18, 'I have waited for thy salvation, O Lord,'—and that in a very remarkable manner. Our interpreters refer it to a prediction of Samson, who was of the tribe of Dan, who was afterwards a deliverer of the Israelites, and say that Jacob's prophetic foresight of the dangers of that tribe made him break out into such a pathetic expression. But did not the other tribes conflict with dangers as well as Dan? Why should Jacob have such an eruption of soul in his speaking of this tribe more than of any other, which were more considerable, and were to undergo as great sufferings as this? Besides, Jacob speaks not of Dan as afflicted, but as victorious, ver. 16, 17; he should judge his people, and as a serpent overthrow the rider. Jacob had certainly an higher consideration. And therefore some of the ancient rabbins* thus paraphrase the words: When Jacob foresaw Gideon and Samson to be the deliverers of his posterity, he saith, I do not so much expect the salvation by Gideon, nor the deliverance by Samson, which are temporal and created salvations; but I expect that redemption which thou hast promised in thy word to come to Israel, that salvation which shall be for ever. The occasion of this sudden ejaculation of Jacob will easily clear the thing. He had been speaking of Dan, ver. 16, 17, and likens him to a serpent by the

* Jonathan Ben Uzziel and Targum Hierosolymit. *in loc.*

way, an adder in the path, that bites the horse heels so that his rider should fall backwards. Probably the speaking of Dan as a serpent, and his subtlety, minded him of the trick the serpent played our first parents, who is described, Gen. iii. 1, by the quality of the subtlest of all the beasts of the field; and then breaks forth into an high expression of faith in that salvation which God had promised against that serpent. If this were not the occasion of it, why did he not utter the same expression upon a very fit occasion, when he had spoken before of the tribe of Judah, and of Shiloh's coming of that tribe? ver. 10. But upon this occasion only, and no other in his whole prophecy, doth he breathe out his soul in such an expression. He kept this promise of the seed of the woman, and salvation by him, as a *depositum* in his heart, fed upon it all his days, and makes a solemn confession of his faith in him in his dying posture. The psalmist ardently expected it, as those that watch for the morning, tired with a gloomy and tedious night: Ps. cxxx. 6, 'My soul waits for the Lord, more than they that wait for the morning; I say, more than they that watch for the morning.' The repetition speaks the vehemency of his faith. It was after he had spoken of forgiveness of sin being with God, ver. 4, he expresseth his waiting: ver. 5, 'I waited for the Lord; my soul waits for the Lord.' Because it is a soul mercy I desire, in his word do I hope; in that first promise of the Messiah, and all the promises of pardon and propitiation built upon that foundation. 'I wait more than they that watch for the morning:' when the sacrifices are to be continued in the temple, my soul waits for that Messiah who is to bring forth a plenteous redemption, that Lord who is to redeem Israel from all his iniquities.* I wait for him in these sacrifices more than those do for the morning, wherein they are appointed to offer their sacrifices. The object of their waiting was the same with that of Simeon, Luke ii. 25, the consolation of Israel; and that consolation was the Lord Christ, ver. 26. It was the promise made to the fathers that they hoped in; that hope of the promise for which Paul was accused and set before a tribunal, which was his hope in Christ, Acts xxvi. 6, 7. *Waiting* and *hope* are the words whereby faith is expressed in the Old Testament. Faith respects things present or past, hope respects things future and to be exhibited; they believed the promise of the Messiah, and hoped for the accomplishment of it. Since Christ was the object of their hope, he was also the object of their faith. Since faith is the root of hope, nothing can be waited for but what is believed to be certainly and infallibly to come to pass. Their salvation, propitiation of their sins, redemption of their souls, they expected from Christ; and therefore their faith must be pitched upon him before he came.

2. The second part of the proposition was, that though Christ was the immediate object of the faith of the ancients, yet he was not so distinct an object as now.

(1.) They could not have a distinct knowledge, because the revelation was dark, both in the obscurity of the prophecies wherein it was signified, and the shadiness of the ceremonies wherein it was represented; and from this obscurity they had many extravagant imaginations of an earthly Messiah,—not in the contemptible form of a servant, but in the royal posture of a prince, with a magificent attendance, to break the Roman yoke. Because as the spiritual glory of the Messiah was signified, so it was obscured also, by those earthly terms; and indeed they could not well have understood those spiritual mysteries without the expressions of them in terms suited to their sense.

(2.) The mercy of God and the incarnation of the Messiah they had a know-

* Chaldee Paraphr. *in loc.*

ledge of, but not so clear of his death. The mercy of God was the distinct object of their faith. That was fully revealed to secure them against the fears of justice, and revealed to be brought about in and through the Messiah. Their faith in that was distinct, as appears Ps. cxxx. 3, 4; and the publican's address was supported by the simple consideration of the mercy of God, Luke xviii. 3; but the particular methods of the discovery of this mercy, in and by the Messiah, they were ignorant of. Yet a Messiah incarnate they were clear in, and as such he was represented as a distinct object of their faith; and thus they considered his person and glory, and their hearts longed for him.* They knew by the first promise that he would be an extraordinary person, and by the titles God had given him of his righteous servant, that he should be an holy person, that he should be in high favour with God, because he was styled the Branch, and the Branch of righteousness, Zech. vi. 12 and iii. 8, Jer. xxxiii. 15. That he was to be a king upon a glorious throne, and a priest of a more excellent order than Aaron, even according to the order of Melchisedec, they could not be ignorant of; and a prophet whose words they were not to refuse upon the peril of their souls. Such oracles of him were plainly delivered; but what was the religion he should settle by virtue of his prophetic office, or the conquests he should make, or the government he should establish as a king, or the sacrifice he should offer as a priest, they did not clearly understand. Christ in all those offices was wrapped up in types; they had only the rough draught of a picture, the light and colours were not yet added; the virtue of all lay hid in a dispensation of shadows. Though they trusted in God for a mediator, yet they understood not the manner of the administration of this office, only they expected a clearness of knowledge, a firm peace, and a salvation by him. They had a faith in the gross, embraced the promise, saluted the things promised afar off, and rested upon the wisdom of God to clear up all in time, and bring all about that his grace had assured them of. We are not certain that anything besides his incarnation and some kind of suffering was revealed to Adam: his incarnation, in his being called the seed of the woman; and his suffering, in the bruising of his heel by the serpent, Gen. iii. 15. But whether he understood that he was to redeem them by death from the expression of his bruised heel, or did collect it from the sacrifices instituted as a representation of this way of redemption, and a support to his faith in it, we have no assurance. But that he did understand a salvation and redemption of him and his posterity to be wrought by that seed, is evident by the promise. God doth not usually make a promise to people, but he gives them some understanding of that promise which may conduce to their refreshment; the promise would be otherwise useless. Had not Adam had some understanding of the intent of the promise, his despair could not have been remedied, he could not with any heart have performed worship to God, which consists in prayer and thanksgiving; nor have taught his posterity to worship, if he had not understood something of the intent of the promise, which he did, as appears by Abel's sacrifice. And we cannot think that he omitted the worship of God till the time of Seth, when the Scripture speaks of it again, which was about a hundred years; and that he had no children between is easily gathered from Gen. iv. 25, wherein Eve calls him a seed instead of Abel. But yet the representations he and his posterity had were at the best but like a bright cloud which kept off the heat of divine wrath, and shed some rays upon them, not a clear sunshine. The glory of Christ was in the bud, and not so visible; as the glory of a flower is hid in the bud till it comes openly to display itself, and then it refresheth every sense. They could not have such a distinct view,

* Amyraut, Moral. tom. iv. pp. 120, 121.

and therefore their faith could not so distinctly exercise itself about every part of this Messiah as ours may. They saw the Messiah as we do a man at a distance, or in a disguise; we see him to be a man, but know not what man, we discern not his distinct features and lineaments; they saw him as the Israelites saw Moses his face through the veil, not in all its splendour and glory. This indistinct faith being caused by an imperfect revelation, did not prejudice their interest in the saving grace of the Messiah; for God is so righteous as not to require a faith but what is proportioned to the revelation he vouchsafes. They were members of Christ with their faith in the gross under Moses, as well as we with our more particular faith under Paul and the apostles.

(3.) Our faith must be more distinct. While the revelation was in the gross, a faith in the gross was sufficient. But for us who have a clearer revelation, a more distinct faith is required, proportioned to the measure and circumstances of the discovery. When they saw the throats of the sacrifices cut by the priest, they might know that they were typical; but how exactly in every part they answered to the antitype, neither did they know then, nor we now; but since we are not under types, but clear manifestations, since the fulness of time is come and the veil is rent in twain, since Christ hath passed through the veil of the shadow of death to his throne of glory, a confused faith will not serve our turn. God, in regard of his veracity, mercy, and goodness, was the distinct object of their faith, Christ, a more obscure one; now one is as distinct as the other. Therefore Christ says, 'Believe also in me,' in the same manner, and as distinctly as you did believe in the mercy and truth of God. The former revelation was not intended to draw out a faith from them as explicit as ours ought to be, but was intended to confirm us who should live in and after the fulness of time, that by the consideration of the ancient predictions, and comparing them with the after transactions, we should have our faith strengthened by them. This is clearly expressed by Peter: 1 Peter i. 12, 'Unto whom it was revealed, that not unto themselves, but unto us, they did minister the things which are now reported unto you.' By all these obscure revelations anciently, we have certain evidence of the truth of those things declared to us in the gospel.

3. Christ is the immediate object of faith in his person. 'Believe also in me,' that I am the great person appointed by God for the redemption of the world. Christ in this speech directs them to himself, not to a promise; it is not, Believe in this or that promise, but in me. As faith in God centres in the Deity, so faith in Christ centres in his person. Promises may be a ground, yet they are not the object of a justifying faith, nor are they in any sort objects of faith in themselves; but in regard of the good things promised in them, as they contain in them the grace of God, and the blessings of the mediation of Christ, they direct us to Christ, as the proclamation and promise of a prince directs and encourageth the rebels to come into his presence, and supplicate his pardon. Faith is called a coming to Christ, Mat. xi. 28, which rather notes his person than his doctrine. It is not a faith simply in his Godhead that is required by him, for so he is the object of faith in the same manner as the Deity is; nor simply in his manhood, for so he is no more the object of faith than another man may be, but Christ in his person, God-man. Christ must be believed in as God gives him; God gives his person first, and then his benefits; the benefits bestowed upon us are consequential to the gift of his person to us: Rom. viii. 32, he first delivered him for us, and then with him gives us all things. The blessings expected are not the object of our faith, but Christ, by whom those benefits were purchased, and by whom they are conveyed to us. God gave him as

his only-begotten Son, a person, not a doctrine; though he did not give him without giving him orders what doctrine to publish. As God gave him, so we are to believe in him; believe in him, and believe on the Son, John iii. 16, 36. We can never apply ourselves to him as the Son of God without a consideration of his person; we are sanctified by faith that is in him, Acts xxvi. 18, not faith in his word severed from his person; and, indeed, there can be no true faith in Christ, if he be not considered in the excellency of his person. The apostle therefore, in the beginning of the Hebrews, an epistle written to draw off the Jews from their ceremonies to the Messiah, proposeth him, Heb. i., in his dignity and grandeur. As the Deity in its excellency is the ultimate object, so Christ in his eminency is the immediate object of faith. Faith respects Christ dying and meriting by his death, which it cannot do unless it considers him in the excellency of his person above that of a simple man, even the Son of God sanctified for us. His merit, had it been finite, would have been insufficient for the weight of our souls and the burden of our sins, without the greatness of his person. He is not only man: then he might have fallen as the first Adam did, and left us in the same or a worse condition; he is not only God: then he could have performed no obedience to the law, as being not concerned in it as a subject, but as a lawgiver; nor could he have offered any satisfaction to God, as being uncapable of suffering in the Deity; but God and man, fit to repair the honour of God and the fallen state of the creature. Since Christ as crucified is the object of faith, what significancy would his sufferings have without the consideration of the other, which puts so high a value upon his passion, and communicates so rich an efficacy to it? We are to believe in Christ for the remission of sin, which is obtained not so much by the sacrifice, as by the quality of the sacrifice. The Jews searched for their expiation in the bowels of beasts, uncapable to make an atonement for them. The nature of the sacrifice must be first considered, and that we cannot have a prospect of in the value and merit of it, till we fix the eye of our faith upon the greatness of his person, who was thus made a sacrifice for us. Indeed, to consider Christ barely in his person attracts our love more than our recumbency; to consider him barely in his passion without the excellency of his person, would excite neither faith nor love, but grief and horror; to consider him as suffering for us, would attract our love in a way of gratitude; but to consider him as suffering for us; without considering the ability of his person to relieve us by that suffering, would be too weak to elevate our faith to him. Reliance always respects ability as well as goodness and affection; faith therefore respects the person of Christ immediately, but not absolutely in himself, but as he stands in relation to the Father, as his Son and his servant.

4. Therefore, Christ as sent by God is the object of faith, as sent to such an end as redemption. Faith rests upon Christ as a gift, upon God as the donor. There is little comfort in all that Christ did and suffered, unless we respect him as one sent by his Father; it is this fastens our faith on him, and possesses our souls with a confidence in him; this is the magnifying emphasis he himself sets upon his disciples' faith, in his solemn pleas in heaven, if we may judge of them by the pattern of them he gave us on earth: John xvii. 8, 'They have believed that thou didst send me.' Christ as sent is the object of faith, since the love of God in sending Christ is urged as the encouragement to faith, John iii. 16. Though faith pitcheth upon Christ's propitiating blood, yet it is under this consideration, that he was set forth by God for such an end: Rom. iii. 25, 'Whom God hath set forth to be a propitiation through faith in his blood.' This is necessary

to the formal condition of faith in its closing and justifying act, without which it would be a lifeless and comfortless thing, for faith justifies us before God as a judge; but can any thing be confidently and comfortably pleaded by a criminal, who doubts the judge's approbation of it? The allowance of God as a judge upon the propitiation of Christ heartens faith in its act; it would wholly droop, nay, not go a step, if it did not see God's authority in Christ's action and passion; it considers Christ not only as a Redeemer, but a Redeemer by commission, and carries God's commission to Christ in its hand in every address to the throne of grace for justifying mercy. If a pardon be proclaimed to those that shall come to such an inferior magistrate, no man would come but upon the strength of the declaration of the supreme authority which made that proclamation, and can only make it valid for a rebel's safety. This is so necessary a part of the object of faith, that no true grounded and well-built faith can be without it. When our eyes have respect to the Holy One of Israel, we must look to our maker, Isa. xvii. 7. I question whether if an Israelite bitten by a fiery serpent had looked upon the brazen one, lifted up on the pole, only to contemplate the figure, and the ingenuity of the artificer, without considering the end for which Moses had set it up in relation to his cure, and the divine appointment of it, he would have found from it any remedy for his distemper; natural influence it had none, and moral influence supposeth a suitable apprehension in the spectator. I am sure an ancient so paraphraseth Numb. xxi. 8, 9, 'When he looks upon it, he shall live: he shall live, if his heart be directed to the name of the word of the Lord;'* and so ver. 9, 'When he looked upon the brazen serpent, and his heart was intent upon the name of the word of the Lord, he did live.' His look was to be not only to the elevated serpent, but to the divine authority that ordered it.

5. Christ in all his offices. 'Believe also in me,' without any limitation or restriction to this or that particular office. If faith pitch upon the person of Christ, and the person of Christ as authorised by God, it embraceth Christ with all his offices, because his person is invested with them; and the same authority which settled him in one, conferred upon him the rest. True faith rests upon his person as commissioned, and receives him in the extent of his commission; and therefore in every office distinctly, to be given up to his rule, sit under his instructions, and eat and drink of his sacrifice. His person is not separated from his offices, nor his offices from one another; nor is there a distinct commission for each of them. As faith takes God with all his perfections, so it takes Christ with all his dignities; as when we believe in God, we believe in him with all his attributes, so when we believe in Christ, we believe in him with all his excellencies; as you believe in God, believe also in me. You do not take God to be your God, only in his power, or mercy, goodness, or faithfulness, or wisdom, but in all; so you must not take me to be Messiah, anointed for you to a priesthood only, but to a kingly and prophetical office. Christ is proposed whole, and therefore must be taken whole; God doth not offer him in pieces, but entire; he is not a priest without being a king, nor a prophet without being a king and a priest. As faith is exercised for justification, Christ is considered as a priest; as it is exercised for an understanding of God, he is considered as a prophet; as it is exercised for sanctification, to put down the dominion of sin, and relics of corruption, he is considered as a king, advanced to put all enemies under his feet. Our necessities require such acts of faith upon his distinct offices; we are full of guilt and filth, and we must have Christ as our priest to secure us by his sacrifice from the merit of our guilt, and wash us by his blood

* Jonathan Targum *in loc.*

from the defilements of our filth; we are beset and inlaid with darkness, and we must have Christ by his wisdom to shew us the way, and conduct us in saving paths; we are possessed with a stubbornness and impotency, and we must believe in Christ as a king to quell our enmity, and strengthen our weakness by his power. The ingenuity of faith speaks this language: Since Christ is a priest to sacrifice for me, it is but reasonable he should be my prophet to teach me, and my king to govern me; that as I live by his blood, I should walk by his rule; receive every ray of light, suck in every spiritual direction, as well as feed upon the juice of his sacrifice.

6. Yet, Christ as crucified is the more immediate object of faith. He had spoke of his death in the foregoing chapter, which was the occasion of their sorrow; and now he speaks of their believing in him: 'You believe in God' as a living God, 'believe also in me' as a dying Saviour. We are to receive Christ as God doth offer him to us, as a redeemer from eternal death, and the purchaser of eternal life: and this he doth in the quality of a sacrifice satisfying for our sin, and meriting our life: Rom. iii. 25, he is set out as a propitiation; as one in whom God is well pleased. It is faith therefore in his blood that justifies, ver. 24; not faith in his precept, nor faith in his miracles, nor abstractedly faith in his person, but faith in him as bathed in his own blood, and rolling in his own gore. The other parts are but conductors of faith to this bath, wherein it washes the soul; to this throne, whereon faith sits triumphantly, and never sparkles with such a life, as in this. Faith in the latitude of it, extends to all parts of Scripture; and as it is a general faith, is exercised about precepts, promises, and threatenings; but in its acts about those objects, it is not a justifying faith, but only as it respects Christ, and Christ too in the very act of expiating sin by his satisfactory death on the cross; as the soul of a man doth exercise itself in vegetation and sense, yet a man is not said to be a rational creature by those acts, or by those powers of the soul, but by the soul, as it is rational.

(1.) This was proposed as the formal object in the first promise, Gen. iii. 15, as having his heel bruised by the devil, as well as bruising the devil's head. This promise was the great charter of our redemption, and the foundation of the faith of Adam's posterity for several ages. It was indeed spoke to the serpent, but for the sake of man; a threatening to the tempter, and a promise to the tempted, and an argument of terror to the first, and support to the latter. Christ is here proposed for men's comfort under the notion of a conqueror, but yet under the notion of a sufferer; his passion in his heel was to precede his breaking his enemies' head; so his sufferings are first to be eyed by faith before his victory. The devil could not be overcome, and stripped of his power, but by a satisfaction to the broken law, which could not be only by observing the precept, without suffering the penalty. The devil's authority was built upon the curse of the law, which must be endured before the devil could be turned out of his palace. It was upon the cross that principalities and powers were stripped of their dominion, and exposed in triumph, Col. ii. 15. And in this promise, though the seed of the woman be proposed to their faith as one to be bruised, yet not as one to be conquered, but as prevalent and triumphant, bruising the enemy in the head and vital part, while himself is only bruised in the heel, a part remote from the heart, and more remote from the head. The ancients therefore, in sucking the sweet juice of this gracious word, could not but consider Christ as combating, as well as conquering; the Messiah suffering something from the serpent, as well as defeating and surviving him.

(2.) Christ under this notion was proposed in all the Jewish sacrifices. As the promise was a publication of Christ to faith in a suffering condition, so the sacrifices were a publication of Christ to sense in the kind of his sufferings in a dying posture. It was more than once expressed to the Israelites that sacrifices were appointed for the atonement of sin; they must be exceeding blind, if they could persuade themselves that any such expiation of sin could be wrought by any value in the blood of a beast, that that could bear a proportion to the injured honour of God, and the broken tables of the law; they could not but conceive something mysterious in them; and the more inquisitive, it is like, perceived some analogy between the type, and the thing signified by it. They might read something of a suffering Messiah in them for the atonement of their sins; but they could never be instructed by the dying groans and heart-blood of beasts to fancy such a triumphant Messiah as they did, without being exposed to a calamitous condition. It is certain, Christ as a sacrifice was proposed in all those sin-offerings; they were all but legal shadows of the good things to come by the great sacrifice, Heb. x. 1. Our faith ought not less to pitch upon Christ as a crucified sacrifice offered to God, than theirs was to look to him under that consideration in every beast, in every lamb slain, and offered upon the altar. He was not shadowed in those sacrifices in the glories of his person, the miracle of his resurrection, the triumphs of his ascension, and his honours at the right hand of God, but in the agonies of his bitter passion, represented by the strugglings and dying gasps of the slain victim; these sacrifices had no analogy but with his death.

(3.) This was proposed by the apostles in their teaching. It was Paul's practice among the Corinthians: 1 Cor. ii. 2, he 'determined to know nothing among them,' *i. e.* to make known nothing as the object of the faith he invited them to, 'save Jesus Christ and him crucified.' His design was to manifest Christ in the glory of his person, in the excellency of his natures, in the end of his coming, but more especially as crucified, being under that consideration the fountain of their salvation, and most proper for the exercise of their faith. And when he heard of the Galatians' departure from the truth, he wonders at it, since Christ had been evidently set forth crucified among them, Gal. iii. 1. It was an astonishment to him that they should imagine to find a remedy for their guilt, a sanctuary for their souls, a screen against the justice of God, anywhere else but in the cross of Christ. Christ as crucified was in all their preaching proposed as the object of faith, security from punishment, and way to happiness. Believing in Christ is called eating of the altar, Heb. xiii. 10, *i. e.* of the sacrifice which had been offered on the altar, the apostle speaking in legal terms. In some sacrifices part was burnt upon the altar, and part reserved for a feast for the offerer and his friends. They ate it in the relation of a sacrifice; and Christ can be fed on by faith only under the consideration of a sacrifice, as a dying sacrifice, before he be considered as a living Saviour.

(4.) Under this consideration will the faith of the Jews pitch upon him, when God shall be pleased to convert them. Christ as pierced is to be looked upon: Zech. xii. 10, 11. 'They shall look upon him whom they have pierced.' They that did actually pierce him shall so look upon him with an eye of faith, planted in them by the Spirit of grace; and he that was pierced for their sins shall be seen and owned by them. It is a look of belief, not a bodily look. They shall look upon him so as to rest in him: they shall look upon him as pierced, as their predecessors did look upon the serpent lifted up in the wilderness, with a reliance on the promise of God, that they should have the restoration of their health, and the expulsion of their venom by it. He will be acknowledged in the great intent of his death, which was to take away sin.

(5.) That is the object of our faith, which is God's object in justifying a sinner. But God in his justifying act particularly looks upon this blood: Rom. v. 9, 'Being now justified by his blood.' He speaks of God's act of justifying as he doth in the expression of God's act in saving us. In the act of justification, God looks upon the sinner as bedewed and sprinkled with this blood. He crosses not one of our debts without first dipping his pen in this blood. Christ therefore as dying, and paying the price of his precious blood for our redemption, is the immediate object of faith. Christ as risen is an object of faith successively to this. The payment of a debt is really the ground of the justification and security of him for whom that debt is paid. The acquittance is only the declaration of the payment, if the debtor should be questioned afterwards. It was this sacrifice God took the sole pleasure in: Heb. x. 8, 'Offerings for sin thou wouldst not, neither hadst pleasure therein;' not in any offered by the law, which the apostle adds in a parenthesis, intimating thereby that this great offering was the delight of the soul; and in this offering of the body of Christ his whole will for our sanctification centred, as it follows ver. 9, 10. Our faith must therefore bear some parallel with the pleasure and will of God, and wrap itself up in the same object. The blood of Christ is that whereby we are justified, for we are pronounced justified by God upon the account of a righteousness answering the law; but Christ as a king and Christ as a prophet did not answer either the precept or penalty of the law, but Christ as a priest. This therefore whereby God justifieth is considered by faith in its going out for justification. This only can expel fears, and be a ground of the greatest consolation. This was that God's heart was chiefly set upon. This was that he called him out to perform. He had never been a king nor a prophet had he not acted the part of a priest, nor had God justified any but upon that account of his sacrifice. It was in this office God confirmed him for ever with so much delight as to engage himself by oath to the perpetuating of it. He was not so solemnly by oath invested in the other two.

(6.) Nothing else of Christ can be the immediate and primary object of our faith, but his death. Nothing else but the priestly office of Christ and his propitiation, and atonement he hath made for sin (and thereby delivered us from the wrath to come), can be the formal object of faith in its first application. There are many things in Christ that faith afterwards considers, and that are worthy of our deepest inquiries and meditations; but this only is considered in the first application. What did the poor stung Israelites consider in their looking upon the brazen serpent? Did they consider it only as the figure of a serpent, or let their minds run out upon the excellency of the figure, the skill of the artificer, and the curiosity of the workmanship? These indeed to a sound man would have been a delightful employment; but as soon as ever he had been bitten, he would have laid aside all such thoughts, and cast his eye upon it, according to the intent of its elevation on the pole for the cure of his disease. What did the poor malefactor consider in his distress when he ran to the horns of the altar? He considered it only as a place of refuge, and not as a place of worship. A man in the first act of faith considers himself guilty before God, and in danger of eternal fire, under the dreadful displeasure of God by reason of his transgression of the law; he considers himself a breaker of that law, and consequently under the threatening and curse of it, and wishes for security from that fire: his conscience, by virtue of a violated law, flasheth in his face. That therefore which prompts a man in this condition to go to Christ, is the belief and hope of a sure deliverance by him. His great intendment is justification, freedom, and deliverance, and therefore he eyes Christ as a deliverer, and in that posture and method wherein he was a deliverer, *i. e.* as hanging upon the cross. Indeed, afterwards, when the soul comes to consider its own ignorance and pollution, and longs for sanctification, then its faith goes out to Christ as a prophet to instruct him, and as a king to defeat his enemies in him. But to a soul sensible of the guilt of sin, and racked by the horrors of conscience, what is most convenient to be proposed? Would you set forth Christ in his glories as a king that must be obeyed? This strikes the soul dead. What would his answer be? The more able to damn me for my disobedience. A king, say you, to be obeyed? What is this to me that have disobeyed him, that find no power in myself to obey him; and if I could, I cannot, upon a diligent scrutiny, find any merit in that obedience? But if there were, how can I wipe off my former scores, and pacify God for my manifold past errors, and please his offended holiness? Would you propose Christ as a prophet to teach him his duty? What is this to the curse? How shall I be rid of my guilt? How shall I escape punishment? But propose Christ as a priest and sacrifice: set him forth in his priestly attire, with the streams of blood issuing from him for the expiation of guilt. This will make a soul that hath all the flames of hell about his ears listen. Here is an offer of Christ in a suitable capacity to the present state and wants of a sinner. What is the language of a poor soul at first? How can I endure wrath? How can I satisfy justice? The proposal of Christ as having undertaken this work for him, and becoming sin in his stead, is the only proportionable remedy. It is then, and not till then, that the soul clasps about him. Here I find the satisfaction of my soul, where God found the satisfaction of his justice. This contents me under the charge of a violated law, the dread of an incensed God, the tortures of an enraged conscience. Here I find a surety satisfying my debts, bearing my punishment, and interposing his shoulders between me and the wrath merited by me; here I find that which pacifies God and pacifies me. This gives rest to the soul. The day of atonement among the Israelites, which typified this great saving expiation by the death of the Messiah, is called, not God's Sabbath, but your Sabbath, Lev. xxiii. 32. Here, and here alone, is the rest that faith finds in its first search. Christ as a king and Christ as a prophet did not merit, and therefore Christ as a king and Christ as a prophet are not considered in the first act of seeking after justification; but Christ as meriting, and therefore Christ as a priest and a sacrifice. As a king he rules, as a prophet he instructs, as a priest he merits. Christ did not profit us but as dying, and all the benefits we have by him were radically in his death. Hereby he satisfied the curse of the law, which was the only bar to our restoration to happiness. This was the main thing he was to do by articles drawn between the Father and himself, so that upon this account this death, or Christ as dying, is the main object of faith.

(7.) Nothing can continue, and keep life in faith afterwards, but Christ considered as dying. Since there are slips and new pollutions, faith, in all its acts for continuance of justification and repeated pardons, goes afresh to the embraces of the cross, and pleads the merits of Christ's wounds and agonies; it looks upon the Lamb of God as taking away the sins of the world, and begs the favour of God for the merits of Christ.

As Christ dying is the object of the first act of faith, so he is the encouragement to a continuance of faith; for he hath in so high a manner evidenced himself merciful and faithful in this, that there is no doubt of his mercifulness and faithfulness in everything that concerns us after. He hath declared himself worthy of our most fixed reliance on him, and that he will not stick at lesser things, since he hath undertaken and finished so great a task as that of suffering. From his priesthood faith takes spirit and heart to go to him as king and prophet, which it could never do if it did not first receive encouragements from hence, and first pitched upon it; for, as I said before, as all the after benefits of Christ are radically in his death, so all the after acts of faith upon Christ in any other condition are radically in his first act of faith upon Christ as a sacrifice, which first act gives life to all the exercises of faith upon Christ in another capacity afterwards.

To conclude. The death of Christ, as it is satisfactory to God, is the object of faith; as it is of infinite efficacy and perpetual force, it is the object of a triumphant faith and hope. The righteousness of Christ in his death is to be considered in all this. If we take him as a sacrifice, we must take him as a spotless sacrifice; if as a priest, as an undefiled one, separate from sinners, as well as for sinners. We cannot believe in Christ without taking in his righteousness, as we cannot behold the sun without beholding its light.

7. Christ, as risen and exalted, is the object of faith. He is the immediate object of faith as dying, the triumphant object of faith as rising. His sacrifice was in his death, but the value and virtue of that sacrifice was manifest by his resurrection. Had Christ left his body in the grave, and had sins committed before been pardoned upon the atonement he made by his death, yet the sacrifice ceasing and corrupting, it had not been of everlasting efficacy. If God, as raising Christ from the dead, is the object of faith,—Rom. iv. 24, 25, 'If we believe on him that raised up Jesus our Lord from the dead, who was delivered for our offences, and raised again for our justification,'—then Christ, as raised by God, is the object of faith also. He was raised from the grave for our justification, as well as delivered to the cross for our offences. As in his death in our stead he bore the curse of the law, so in his resurrection as a common person we received our acquittal from the hands of the judge. Though his resurrection was not meritorious of our justification, yet it was a declaration of the efficacy of his death, and consequently of our discharge. Faith must eye that whereby we are justified. Now, though we are justified by Christ's death as the meritorious cause, yet we are justified by his resurrection as the perficient cause. Had his death been supposed to be fully meritorious without a resurrection, it had freed us from death by cancelling the bond; but his resurrection instates us in life by God's gracious acceptation, and makes the redemption complete, which else had been but a partial one; nay, none at all. To the one we owe our freedom from death; to the other, our investiture with eternal life and glory. To the one we owe our righteousness; to the other, our sonship. It is by his resurrection from the dead we are begotten to a lively hope, 1 Peter i. 3; it is upon him, therefore, as raised, that our faith must be settled. Had he not risen, we had been still in our sins; not a mite of our debts had ever appeared to have been paid, 1 Cor. xv. 17. His death had been insufficient for our happiness without his resurrection. His resurrection was an evidence that he could save others, since he was delivered himself, and that his Father would save the members, since he had raised the head. Had he not been raised, faith in his death had had no ground. It had been an unaccountable thing to believe in him that lay under the power of death, and had not sufficient strength to shake off the bands of it. This is the key that unlocks to us the whole design, end, and sufficiency of his death, and renders faith in him as crucified more easy. Everything in Christ, everything promised by him, is very credible. Nothing can be matter of any difficulty to faith, since this of his resurrection is perfected. Faith is, therefore, called 'the faith of the operation of God,' Col. ii. 12, noting the object of faith, and not the efficient cause of it; not because God works it in us (though that be

true, yet it is not the sense of the place), but a faith of that energy and mighty power of God put forth in the raising Christ from the dead. It was by this act, whereby he fulfilled his past promises, that he gives us security for the performance of future ones. 'For as concerning that he raised him up from the dead, now no more to return to corruption, he saith in this wise, I will give you the sure mercies of David,' Acts xiii. 34. What were those sure mercies of David given in this? The fulfilling of the promise made to the fathers, ver. 32, 33; the promise of an everlasting covenant, Isa. lv. 3, whence this is cited. That grand promise God made to Adam, and in him to all his posterity, was fulfilled in this act of Christ's resurrection. The bruising the serpent's head, the blessing all nations in the seed of Abraham, the bringing in an everlasting righteousness, were declared thereby to be fulfilled. Hereby was the efficacy of his death cleared to all the world, in his being eased of the burden of our sins, which bowed down his head upon the cross. Hereby it was manifest that his blood was the blood of the everlasting covenant, Heb. xiii. 20; a blood established and settling the covenant of grace for ever, and making it truly everlasting. As our redemption was not in its meridian glory till his resurrection, so neither is our faith in its full strength and vigour, but as eyeing this together with his death.

Use 1. If God and Christ in conjunction be the proper object of faith, here is an argument for the deity of Christ. If he be a mere creature, how can he assert himself an object of faith in conjunction with the eternal God? It would be the highest invasion of the right and authority, and affront to the perfection and sufficiency of God, to make himself equal with God as the object of our faith, if he were not equal with God in the dignity of his nature. He doth everywhere propose himself in this consideration to us: John vi. 29, 'This is the work of God, that you believe on him whom he hath sent.' It is not a belief *of* Christ, but a belief *in* Christ, or *on* Christ. To believe a person is one thing, and to believe on him is another. We believe Paul and Peter, but are never said to believe in Paul or in Peter. The devils cannot but believe what Christ saith to be true, but they do not believe in him. To be believed in or relied upon for salvation and pardon is proper only to the deity, and a flower of his crown. If Christ were a mere man, though in the highest throne of excellency and holiness as a creature, as indeed he is, yet he could not be an object of our trust and faith without an offence to God, a violation of his precept, and contracting his curse. He doth expressly threaten to lay his curse upon every one that makes flesh his arm or confides in man, because that is a departure from the Lord, Jer. xvii. 5; and promiseth a blessing to them that trust in the Lord and make him their hope, ver. 17. If he be liable to the curse that puts his trust in man solely for worldly advantage, much more he that puts his trust in a mere man for an eternal salvation. He pronounceth a curse on them that put their trust in man, but a blessing on them that put their trust in his Son the Messiah: Ps. ii. 12, 'Blessed are all they that put their trust in him.' If Christ were a mere man, we are cursed by God for trusting in him; if blessed for putting a confidence in him, then he is more than a man, the true God. He that was obedient to his Father would never have ordered such an act wherein we should be accursed by the Father. God would never have backed this proposition of faith in Christ, asserted by Christ himself, and preached by the apostles, with the seal of so many miracles, and justified that which he had cursed before. He would never have cast the crown from his own head, or made another partner with him, had he not a dignity in his own nature equal with God. If God our Saviour and Jesus Christ be the joint objects of hope, 1 Tim. i. 1; if those that believe in him shall not be ashamed, Rom. ix. 33, it is a blasphemy to say he is a mere man, a mere creature, and not God, since a sovereign prerogative of God is ascribed to him. We should otherwise meet with a curse rather than a blessing by relying on him.

2. The difference between the law and the gospel. The law orders a trust in God, but utters not a syllable of a restoring mediator upon the entrance of sin, and therefore exacts not from us such a kind of faith as this, which is necessary for our happiness since we are all fallen. The law cannot order such an act but it must also present the object of that act; it speaks nothing of the latter, and therefore enjoins nothing of the former. It represented God as a sovereign and judge, not as a merciful pardoner; as a revenger upon transgression, not as a redeemer and restorer. The law is therefore insufficient to save us; our happiness is wrapped up solely in the gospel; we have no safety but in the arms of a mediator. Faith is wholly a gospel grace and a new covenant duty.

3. Comfort. 'Believe also in me.' What doth this signify but that our faith in Christ will be as effectual for our good as our faith in God? He was too faithful to his Father to invade his rights, and too merciful to us to put us upon a fruitless act; his joining himself with God as the object of faith, shews that our faith in him will be as prevalent as our faith in God, and our happiness be as mount Sion, not to be shaken; for 'he that believes in him shall not be ashamed,' Rom. ix. 33. He had never commanded us to believe in him as we do in God, if he had not had an office to relieve us; it intimates, that both God and the mediator are in conjunction for our salvation and felicity. Do we believe God to be merciful, powerful, gracious? The mediator also hath as tender a compassion to pity us, and as sovereign a grace to heal us; he hath as ardent a love to bless us, and as infinite a power to rescue us; he hath as overflowing a peace to quiet us, and as everflowing a goodness to relieve and perfect us. If they are jointly to be respected by our faith, they are joint also in the answering the expectations of our faith: John x. 30, 'I and my Father are one;' one in saving, one in preserving, one in perfecting; for it is spoken in relation to the perpetual preservation of his people to salvation, 'none shall pluck them out of my hand, none shall pluck them out of my Father's hand.' We grasp them both by faith, and they grasp one another's hand for our safety; we lay hold both on the Father and the Son by an act of faith, and both Father and Son lay hold on us by an act of particular affection; as we own them, so they will prove in the end joint Saviours to our faith. As they are one in power, so they are one in the cares of the flock. Christ would never else have ordered us to pitch our faith as strongly and fully upon him as upon the Father.

Again, 'believe also in me.' He requires a true faith, as true in him as in God, but not an equal measure of faith in all. If we have not a faith of such a stature and growth as that of Paul or the other apostles, yet if it have the same mien and lineaments, it will not be ineffectual. The serpent was to be looked upon, but not by all with an equal clearness of sight; some eyes were dimmer, some clearer; a look was sufficient, though but a weak one. A blear-eyed Leah might have been cured by a look, as well as a sharp-sighted Rachel. Believe in me, close with me, though your hands may not be equally strong to hold fast as others are. No one's spirit is always in an equal degree of health, and an even complexion; the wheels do not always move with an equal swiftness; reflections on a state of sin, and the blackness of transgressions, sometimes make us shrink and tremble; the wonderful greatness of God's mercy, like the light of the sun, sometimes dazzles and blinds our eye. Yet if we believe in him with all these palsies, it will go well with us. It is 'believe in me,' not ordering all faith to be of the same elevation.

4. Let us examine our faith by the object. Many will speak carelessly, and many will boast confidently, of their faith and trust in God, and scarce ever think or speak of Christ, separating that which God hath joined. What warrant have we to trust in God, singly considered, without a mediator? As it is eternal life to know him, not in the simplicity of his own being, but as he makes himself visible in a mediator, John xvii. 3, so it is to believe in him in the same manner. As our knowledge of God, with an ignorance of Christ, so our faith in God, with an unbelief in Christ, will never entitle to an eternity of happiness. No act of faith is right that doth not virtually and implicitly take in Christ together with God. Our Saviour speaks it here in relation to the troubles of his disciples' hearts for their outward condition, and the misery they expected by his departure from them. You have been educated in a reliance on God, and the expectations of a Messiah: believe me to be the person, and believe in me as the great undertaker and accomplisher of your happiness. We have a prospect of troubles, soon we may feel the smart of them; we believe in God as the sovereign of the world, let us see whether we eye at the same time Christ as the king set upon the holy hill of Sion for the protection as well as the government of the church. We have a great deal of ignorance. We believe in God as the Father of lights; do we also believe in Christ as a prophet to instruct us, and a Sun of righteousness to enlighten and heal us with his wings? We believe in God as infinitely merciful; do we also believe in Christ, as a priest settled for ever to make an atonement by his sacrifice, and perpetuate the application of it by his intercession? We have no warrant to exert one act of faith on the one without the other. By faith in God singly, without a mediator, we neither obey God nor secure ourselves. Since the object of faith is Christ as dying, true faith must eye the motive which persuaded Christ to die, and have the same motive in itself, viz., the hatred of sin and the love of righteousness; the hatred both of guilt and filth, and a desire to vindicate the righteousness of God. The hatred of sin is therefore necessary in our compliance with Christ, and therefore believers are called his fellows, Heb. i. 9; not only fellows in his glory, but in his disposition; in the integrity of it, not in the degrees of it. Faith fastens upon Christ as the gift, upon God as the donor; it considers the greatness of the gift, and with ravishments ascends to a confidence in the giver. It reads God's heart in Christ, sees the glory of God in the face of Christ, and mounts up to clasp about him who hath issued out the knowledge of himself in such a full spring of mercy and grace. It looks upon Christ as a propitiator, and upon God as a father. Faith hath recourse to the atoning blood of Christ, and by that blood to God. The goodness of faith consists chiefly in the object it is placed upon; as all acts receive their goodness from the object, as well as from the principal end and circumstances.

5. Exhortation. Let us observe his order. We do believe in God, that is taken for granted. There is indeed a natural confidence that all men have explicitly or implicitly in God: 'He is the confidence of all the ends of the earth,' Ps. lxv. 5, This is not sufficient; a faith in Christ as mediator, a belief of it, a reliance on him in that capacity, together with a walking according to the rules of his prophetic office, is the whole of the Christian religion. This is every man's duty, as much his duty to believe in Christ as to believe in God. It is enjoined with the same authority, 'believe also in me;' it is a command as well as an invitation. Not believe, if you will, but you must believe in me as well as in God, if ever you have a security

against trouble, here or hereafter. To believe is not only our privilege, but our duty; not to believe, is not only our misery, but our sin; it is not a matter of indifferency. Christ had a command from God to die for us, and we have a command from himself to believe in him. God will have every one confess to the glory of the Father that 'Jesus is the Lord,' Philip. ii. 11. God in him hath discovered the wonders of his mercy, justice, and wisdom, and without believing in him, we disown God in the glory of those discovered perfections: 'He that honours not the Son, honours not the Father that hath sent him,' John v. 22, 23. He that believes not in the Son, believes not in the Father, whatever vain imaginations he wraps himself in; he that believes not in Christ satisfying, believes not in the Father satisfied. As God goes out to us in him, our return must be by him to God. God was the judge, Christ the mediator; we must first go to the mediator to be conducted to the judge for our sentence of absolution. We have offended the sovereign lawgiver; we must first believe in him who is the repairer of the honour of the law. Our standing is not secure by absolute mercy; mercy through Christ only saves us; it breathes in no other air. We must first lay hold of the strength of God before we can be at peace with him, Isa. xxvii. 5. Take hold of Christ, who is the power as well as the wisdom of God, 1 Cor. i. 24.

1. All our salvation comes in by believing in Christ. We can have no satisfaction but in this way; we cannot answer the terms of the law but by our surety, nor the demands of the gospel but by our faith in him. Do not our own hearts often disquiet us? Doth not the perfect law amaze us? Doth the devil never accuse us? Do our own consciences never charge us? Where can we find a peace for ourselves, a discharge against the law, and an answer to Satan, but by faith in him who hath vindicated the law, conquered our enemy, and hath blood enough to besprinkle our consciences with an eternal peace? Paul had tried all other ways that were of vogue in the Jewish church, but met with nothing that could have a just pretence to be a competitor with Christ. With what joy did Andrew meet Peter with the news, 'We have found the Messiah'? John i. 41. Nothing can contribute such a measure of peace and joy to the soul as faith in Christ. There is not, indeed, an ear to be gleaned anywhere else; all is laid up in that garner. God cannot now save us in a way of absolute mercy, since he hath settled the method of our salvation by faith in his Son; it would be against his truth, his wisdom, and also against the honour of his obedient Son. If he would save one by absolute mercy, why not more, why not all? What need, then, of his Son's sufferings to make the purchase?

2. We cannot believe any promise without believing in Christ. As the promises are confirmed and conveyed to us, so must our faith be exercised about them; there is not a promise that is yea and amen, *i. e.* firm and irreversible, but in Christ, 2 Cor. i. 20. It is in Christ; it is in Christ that our faith must be exercised in every promise, upon the promise in Christ, upon Christ in the promise; we else believe and depend upon them without their confirmation. No man will depend upon a deed and conveyance without the seal; look first to the seal, and then, and not till then, will the promise pour out comfort to the soul.

3. He only is fit to be the immediate object of our faith. As he is the mighty God, and the Prince of peace, as well as a Son given, Isa. ix. 6; as he made a suitable compensation for the offenders in regard of the human nature, which had committed the trespass, and as he made a sufficient compensation in regard of the divine nature, which had been injured by sin. Infinite justice was satisfied by an infinite person. He only is fit to be the

immediate object of our faith whose shoulders bore the weightiest burdens, whose head bowed under the sharpest curses, whose soul drunk down the bitterest potions in our stead. He had all the fitness to answer the demands of God, and all the fulness to answer the indigencies of man; he hath an office, and himself furnished both with ability and compassion for the execution of it; he hath a wisdom not to be ignorant of what he is to do, and an integrity not to be false in it. Let us, therefore, according to his own order, believe in him in conjunction with God.

1. Solely. *In me*, without joining any created thing in me. We must strike off our hands from all other purchases but that of the pearl. It is not Believe in me and your own righteousness, though it appear in the utmost glory; not Believe in me and your own hearts, though they smile upon you never so kindly. You believe in God. It doth not follow, believe in me and your own righteousness; believe in me and in saints; in Abraham, Jacob, David, or Elijah; but believe in me alone, without the conjunction of any thing less than a Deity. No other Lamb but this was slain from the foundation of the world. This is the only seed of the woman that was wrapped up in the promise. None else was the centre of the prophecies, the subject of the promises, the truth of the types; none in conjunction with him, none in subordination to him in the work of mediation and satisfaction. He only is the first-born among many brethren. As the eye seeks for no other light than that of the sun, and joins no candles with it to dishonour the sufficiency of its beams, so no created thing must be joined with Christ as an object of faith. This is a dishonour to the strength of this Rock, which is our only foundation, this is to undervalue the greatness of the gift, and the wisdom of the giver. It is a folly to seek for security anywhere else. Who would join the weakness of a bulrush with the strength of a rock for his protection? Who would fetch water from a muddy pond to make a pure fountain in his garden more pleasant? All other things are broken reeds under the most splendid appearances. Address yourselves only to him, to find a medicine for your miseries, and counsel in your troubles. Believe in him as the power of God under the weight of your guilt. Believe in him as the wisdom of God under the darkness of your ignorance. He alone is sufficient for our redemption by the allowance of God, and therefore the sole object of faith in conjunction with God. Let us live a life of faith only in him, as Paul did, Gal. ii. 20. This is the vital juice and nourishment of faith; it languisheth when it applies to any thing else. We cannot trust him too much, nor ourselves too little. God trusted him alone, therefore should we; he puts no trust in his saints, Job xv. 15; not in the highest glory of their saintship. Nothing else comes up to the exactness of the law, nor bears proportion with the holiness of God's nature.

2. Believe in me wholly. Not in a part or a piece of me, not in any one particular action of Christ. Nothing of Christ can be well spared by us; he is full and rich, and not any of his fulness or riches but are of use to us. He is necessary in every capacity; the merchant would have his whole pearl, not a part; nothing of Christ is vain and fruitless. God hath given us nothing in the creation but what we may use for his glory; he hath stored Christ as a redeemer with nothing but what we may use for our comfort. We must take whole Christ in his sufferings as well as Christ in his glory; Christ with his sceptre as well as Christ with his salvation. True faith will lay hold on every word, on every promise, on every particle of Christ, as the vine will upon every stick in the support which is set for it.

3. Constantly believe in me. Not for a time and a spurt, by fits and starts; as you always believe in God, so always believe in me; as you do

not cast God off from being your confidence, so do not in the least waive me from being your hope. Upon all occasions when storms arise in the world, believe in me as your protector, as your conductor; when racks appear to be set up in your consciences, believe in me as your peace-maker; when corruptions creep up and defile you, believe in me as a refiner. The woman of Canaan would not leave her faith in him, though he spoke a word sour enough to make her turn her back in sorrow upon him. Let not an act of faith be exercised in God, but let there be a mixture of an equal quantity of faith in the Mediator. The word spoken to us doth not profit us unless mixed with faith; nor do any of our returns to God please him unless mixed with faith in the Redeemer. Whenever we exert a particular act of faith in God, let us exert a particular act of faith in Christ too; not look upon the one without the other, nor embrace the one without the other. We are as constantly to honour the Son as to honour the Father.

Let us therefore frequently meditate on this object of faith, view every wound of a dying Saviour; it will increase our faith in him, add a new life to our faith in God. Our faith is feeble, and our souls languish under spiritual burdens, because we do not look to him as lifted up upon the cross. Our addresses to God are faint, fearful, and disturbed, because our eye is not fixed upon the Mediator, who hath changed God from the frightful garb of a judge to the pleasing aspect of a father. By such acts upon this object, our faith will receive a new spirit, a fresh boldness, a pleasant liveliness.

Let us consider him in his person, in his promises, in his offices, in his mediation, in his sacrifice, and in the righteousness of all, and we shall find what is here spoken by way of command, to be exemplified in a powerful operation in our hearts, which will make us echo back again, Our hearts are not troubled, O Lord, since we believe in God, and believe also in thee.

A DISCOURSE OF AFFLICTIONS.

And ye have forgotten the exhortation, which speaketh unto you as unto children, My son, despise not thou the chastening of the Lord, nor faint when thou art rebuked of him. For whom the Lord loveth he chasteneth, and scourgeth every son whom he receiveth. If ye endure chastening, God dealeth with you as with sons: for what son is he whom the father chasteneth not? But if ye be without chastisement, whereof all are partakers, then are ye bastards, and not sons. Furthermore, we have had fathers of our flesh, which corrected us, and we gave them reverence: shall we not much rather be in subjection to the Father of spirits, and live? For they verily for a few days chastened us after their own pleasure, but he for our profit, that we might be partakers of his holiness. Now no chastening for the present seemeth to be joyous, but grievous: nevertheless, afterward it yieldeth the peaceable fruit of righteousness unto them which are exercised thereby.—Heb. XII. 5–11.

The apostle, after having drawn a catalogue of those illustrious souls that had manifested a choice faith upon several occasions, descends in this chapter to press the believing Hebrews to an exercise of patience and faith under those pressures they should meet with in their Christian course, where he proposeth first to them the example of Christ, ver. 2, 3; next, the exhortation of the Holy Ghost, drawn from Prov. iii. 11, 12, 'My son, despise not the chastening of the Lord; neither be weary of his correction: for whom the Lord loveth he corrects, even as a father the son in whom he delighteth;' which, being an instruction concerning the nature and use of afflictions God sends upon us, the apostle applies to the particular case of the Hebrews, but discourseth in general of the author, subjects, and ends of the afflictions God exerciseth his children with. 'Have you forgotten the exhortation which speaks to you as to children?' Have you lost the remembrance of what God saith in that exhortation by his wisdom, Prov. iii., where he commends his goodness, and shews the obligation you have to listen to him, by vouchsafing you the name of children, the greatest glory and the highest comfort of a creature? Have you, saith he, forgot this? Have you not the intent of it in your minds and memories, in your hearts and considerations? The apostle discourses here of the necessity and advantages of afflictions. In ver. 5, he orders us not to despise the chastening of the Lord, nor to despond under it: 'Faint not when thou art rebuked of him.' This he backs with many motives in the following verses. Μὴ ὀλιγώρει, do not make a light account of afflictions.

1. One motive is in the word chastening (παιδεία), which signifies the instruction whereby a child is brought to the knowledge of things profitable for him, which being it is not effected in that age, subject to extravagancy, without stripes as well as words, the word is therefore used for the discipline which attends such instruction.

2. Another motive is from the author of afflictions, the Lord: despise not the chastening of the Lord.

Observations.

1. It must be our great care not to make slight of afflictions, nor to be too much dejected under them. The smart will keep us from despising an affliction in itself; but we make light of it when we are careless of improving it for the ends for which God inflicts it. We may be sensible of the pain, when we are not sensible of the profit which may accrue to us by it. God forbids here two extremities; the one an excess, the other a want of courage. Both dishonour God, the one in his sovereignty, the other in his goodness and love; and both are injurious to the sufferer, as he rebels against the one, and loseth the sweetness of the other. We should receive the afflictions God sends with a humility without despondency, with a reverence without distrust, and keep ourselves from either fearing too much, or not fearing God enough. Mix reverence with confidence, adore the hand which we feel, and rest in the goodness which he promiseth. This is the way to reap the fruit of afflictions.

2. All afflictions, let them be from what immediate causes soever, are from the hand of God. Whether they come from man, as loss of goods or other calamities; whether they be sicknesses, griefs, &c.; they are all dispensed by the order of God for one and the same design, viz., our instruction. Human reason doth not believe this. Some think they come by chance, or look only to second causes, and regard them not as wholesome instructions from God, and the orders of his providence.

1. This should stop any impatient motions. It is fit we should be of the psalmist's temper, 'hold our peace, because God hath done it,' Ps. xxxix. 9. Shall the clay formed say to him that formed it, Why didst thou thus? We should rather say as Eli, 1 Sam. iii. 18, 'It is the Lord; let him do what seemeth him good.' Especially since an infinite wisdom is joined with the sovereign authority of God, and when we are not able to understand the reason of his conduct, we ought to acquiesce in his will and in his wisdom, and stop the motion of any passion, by a humiliation under his hand.

2. It teacheth us to whom to have recourse. That hand that strikes can only cease striking. When David had stilled impatience, he awakens his prayer: Ps. xxxix. 10, 'Remove thy strokes from me: I am consumed with the blows of thine hand.' If Shimei casts a stone at David, it is the Lord that bade him; if the humours of our bodies rise against us, it is God that arms them, and it is he must be sought to for redress. He only can disband what force he raises. It is our comfort there is a sovereign power to whom we can make our moan in our addresses, and that our sovereign that struck us is ready to heal us.

3. How sweet is God towards his children groaning under any affliction! 'My son, despise not,' &c. He calls them his sons, his children, sweetening in the name whatsoever is rigorous in the suffering. He gives them a title whereby he manifests that he doth share in their grief, hath a resentment of their trouble. What father is there on earth, unless he hath lost all natural affection, who doth not sympathise in the suffering of his children?

All the bowels of earth, met together in one combined tenderness, are not to be compared to the yearning bowels of heaven. Afflictions are not always sent by God in anger with his creatures, but sent by God as a Father.

(1.) Hence it is easy to conceive that neither the intentions of God, nor the issue of a suffering, can be any other than happy to those that are the children of God, since he gives the name of child, and son, to every one that he doth instruct as a Father by correction.

(2.) It will teach us to have a sense of the sufferings of others. The argument to press this exhortation is taken from the impulsive cause, the love of God; and the word translated *chasten*, signifies such a chastisement as a father gives his son, or a master his scholar.

Observation,

(1.) The afflictions of believers are effects of divine love. 'For whom the Lord loves he chasteneth, and scourgeth every son whom he receiveth': Rev. iii. 19, 'As many as I love, I rebuke and chasten.' They are not acts of divine revenge, whereby God would satisfy his justice; but of divine affection, whereby he communicates his goodness, and draws the image of his Son with more beauty and glory. They are the acts of God, but not of a sleepy and careless God, but a wise and indulgent Father, who takes all the care, both of instruction and correction, to train you up to his will and likeness. God indeed afflicts other men who are not in the number of his beloved children. There are scarce any among the sons of men that pass their life in a continual prosperity, exempt from all kind of affliction; and all these evils are from God as the governor of the world. Yet though there be no difference between the sufferings of one and the other, and though the sufferings of believers are often more sharp than those of carnal men in outward appearance, yet there is a vast difference in the motives of them. Love makes him strike the believer, and fury makes him strike the unregenerate man. The design of the correction of the one is their profit, not their ruin; the strokes upon the other are often the first fruits of eternal punishment.

(1.) Then the world is much mistaken in judging the afflictions of believers to be testimonies of God's anger and hatred. God acts towards the world as a lawgiver and judge, but towards those that he hath renewed and adopted in the quality of a father. And who would judge of the hatred of a tender father by the corrections he inflicts upon a child that is so dear to him? Believers suffer by God not simply as he is a judge, but as he is *Paternus Judex*. There is a combination of judge and father. God doth not intend revenge on them; for though they are afflicted for sin, yet the principal aim is to prove them, reform them, that they may be worthy of a blessed inheritance. 'Lazarus whom thou lovest is sick,' was the speech of his sister to Christ. They were fearing, thinking that Christ's love was departed with Lazarus his health.

(2.) No man hath then any reason to fancy himself the object of God's love for an outward prosperity: Eccles. ix. 1, 'No man knows either love or hatred by all that is before him.' God doth not always love those whom his providence preserves in health and ease. Such a conceit proceeds from an ignorance of another life, and too great a valuation of the things of this world. Temporal goods, credit in the world, outward conveniences, and an uninterrupted health, are effects of God's patience and common goodness, but not of his affection and choicest love. They are the marks of his affection, when, by his grace, they are made means to conduct us to a better inheritance; but how often are they pernicious to us by reason of our corruption and ill usage of them! How often doth the health of the body destroy that of the soul, and the prosperity of the flesh ruin that of the spirit! How often do riches and honours link our hearts to the earth, and expel any thoughts of an heavenly paradise! How often doth a portion in this world make many slack their endeavours for a portion in heaven! How often do they hinder our sanctification, which is the only means to an happy vision of God!

(3.) How should this move us in our afflictions to a carriage pleasing to God! This is the motive the apostle uses to press his exhortation in the former verse, neither to despise the chastening of God, nor despond of his care. Why should we despise that which is dispensed by love? Who would not be willing to satisfy a friend in his desire, which they are assured love is the motive of, though their prudence is not so exact as that we can absolutely trust it? Should we not with greater care consider the chastisements which the love of God, both good and wise, doth ordain by providence? Is not the love, the motive of suffering, a sufficient ground to prevent distrust and discouragement? Why should any distrust him by whom he knows he is afflicted? That correction which frights us is a work of his love, not of his hatred. Should we not, therefore, wait with faith for an happy issue of that chastisement which we suffer? If we be once thus affected, we shall receive afflictions with a temper answerable to God, and improve them for those holy ends for which God sends them. We should also bear them patiently, since they are not for the reparation of the holiness of the law and the satisfaction of his justice, but to prove the soul and fit it for heaven. It is not the love of the criminal, but the love of the laws, which causes a judge to condemn and punish him. No wise man ever said that a prince did punish malefactors because he loved them, or that God makes the wicked suffer eternal punishment in hell because he loves them. It necessarily follows that, therefore, the chastisements God doth inflict are not properly punishments of the same nature with those God doth ordain for unbelievers. We have reason, therefore, to bear them with patience. It is inexcusable to murmur at an act of love. Use, then, a religious reason in the consideration of this. When the father scourgeth, the child cries, and then he thinks his father hates him. It is but the error of his childhood, and when he comes to reason he will regard it as a false opinion. When a physician hath lanced you, and given you a bitter potion, you never had any suspicion that he hated you; you have received all his charitable offices, and thought him more worthy of a reward than a rebuke. Why should not our carriage be so to God?

2. Observation.

No righteous man in the world is, or ever was, free from sin. He scourgeth every son whom he receiveth. Sin is the cause of afflictions. Were we free from sin, we should be free from scourges. Afflictions cease not till sin be quite destroyed, which will not be in this world. Justice finds enough in every believer in the world to punish, and mercy finds enough to pardon.

(1.) It is against this, then, that we should turn our aim. What Satan would make us vent in impatience against God, let us manifest in a hatred of that which is the true cause of all the evils which in general or particular we suffer. Let us strike that as much as God strikes us; and it is but grateful reason, since it is the best way whereby we can shew our love to God, who, in his strokes upon us, shews his love to us. Let us take no rest till we have put that to death which God only hates. It is the death of sin, and not the death of the soul, God designs in afflictions.

(2.) It is, upon this account, an argument for patience. While our disease remains, why should we think ill of the physician for using means for a cure? If he did not use the means, though sharp, we then should have most reason to accuse him of a want of pity. What father would not be counted very tender, that should lance his child himself when he saw there was need for it? Sin puts God upon a necessity of scourging; his goodness and wisdom will not suffer him to do anything but what is necessary and expedient. Now, ver. 7, the apostle exhorts them to a patient bearing the hand of God, because he deals with them as a father with his sons in a way of reward afterwards. As parents caress those children, they see quiet after punishment. If ye endure chastening, God deals with you as sons. God προσφέρεται, offers himself to you as a father to his sons. Or rather, the apostle doth render the comfort in the former verse more efficacious to the Hebrews, and makes application of what is contained in that truth which he hath cited out of the Proverbs, in the former verse: that yet, if they endure chastisement, God treats them as children; and, being men are apt to think that a troublesome affliction is inconsistent with the love of God, the apostle contradicts such a thought by the question, 'What son is there whom the father chasteneth not?' And he goes further, verse 8, and draws another conclusion: that we should be so far from thinking that to be afflicted is a sign of our not being the children of God, that on the contrary he affirms that not to be chastised is a sign that a man is not of God's family: verse 8, 'If you be without chastisement, whereof all are partakers, then are ye bastards, and not sons.' For if the Lord scourgeth every son whom he receives, it is clear that he whom he leaves without chastisement is not a true and legitimate son, but a stranger, a bastard, *i. e.* one that is not of the family, but takes only the name and quality, without any right to it.

Observation 1. God, in chastening believers, treats them as children. *If*, here, is as much as *when*: 'if you endure chastening,' *i. e.* when you endure chastening; as Lev. xix. 5, *if* you offer a sacrifice of peace-offering, *i. e.* when you offer a sacrifice. So John xiv. 3, 'If I go and prepare a place for you,' *i. e.* when I go and prepare a place for you. Since God hath commanded men expressly in his word to chastise their children, and hath engraved such a disposition in the hearts of mankind, and authorised such a carriage by his law, we must not think it strange that God, who is wisdom, goodness, and love, should exercise in his family such a just, and holy, and wholesome discipline. And as none can say that a tender father, when he chastiseth his child, deals with him as with an enemy, so none can affirm the same of God; and though affliction be an evil in itself, and sharp to the child that suffers it, yet if you compare it with the good it procures, it is not an evil, but an experienced good. Compare the lives of those children that have not been without the correction of their parents or strangers to the lives of those that have been left to themselves without it, and the advantage of the one and miseries of the other will easily appear: Prov. xiii. 1, 'A wise son hears the instruction of his father.' *Hear* is not in the Hebrew. A wise son is the instruction or chastisement of his father. The Jews have a proverb, If you see a wise child, be sure that the father hath chastised him.* God deals in this manner with his children, and there is need of it, for though the regenerate are freed from the slavery of sin, yet while they are clothed with flesh, the flesh will lust against the Spirit; and God not only chastises us for our infirmities, but to prevent them; and since the love which he bears us, and the salvation which he procures by his chastisements, doth infinitely surpass the affections of the best and tenderest fathers, and the best fruit we can draw from their

* Drusius.

discipline, we may well confess that no father in the world can be said to deal as a father with his children so as God doth with the believer. He offers himself to do a father's office: he is the world's sovereign, but a believer's father. As he is the governor of the word, he treats men righteously in his judgments; as he is the Father of believers, he treats them graciously in his afflictions.

Here is a great comfort, if God deal with you as with children in his striking of you. His wisdom and his goodness is infinite; he doth nothing but what is just and reasonable, and is guided by a fatherly affection in all that he doth: his blows are healthful. If David would account it a kindness if the righteous would smite him, and count his rebukes as an excellent oil, Ps. xli. 5, how much more ought we to have the same sentiments of the chastisement of God. Good men may mistake in their rebukes, God cannot. He is too wise to be deceived, and too good not to make even his strokes become an excellent balsam. He doth not assault us as enemies, nor only as criminals, but as children; not to punish us in his fury, but to refine us, to make us fit for him to take pleasure in, to make us more like him in the the frame and temper of our souls. This is the end of a tender father's chastising his children, and this is the end of God. We should receive his corrections therefore, not so much as a punishment as a favour, since he strikes not as an enemy to destroy, but as a father to correct; not only as a God of righteousness, but as a God of tenderness.

Observation 2. No child of God but is one time or other under his correcting hand. The apostle makes a challenge to all to shew one in that relation privileged from it: 'What son is there whom the Father chasteneth not?' None of those mentioned among the believing Hebrews in the foregoing chapter were without this smart: Noah had an affliction in a child, Gen. xii. 10, Abraham and Jacob were afflicted with famine, Isaac by an Esau, Moses fain to fly for his life, Job suffered the loss of his goods, Hezekiah a dangerous sickness. To be under afflictions, then, is to travel in the road of all that have gone before. And the apostle goes further, ver. 8, and affirms that not to be chastised is a certain sign of no right to a membership of his family: 'But if you be without chastisement, whereof all are partakers, then are you bastards, and not sons.' This is an argument from the antithesis, they are bastards, and not sons, who are not corrected. Bastards, not, saith Grotius, those whom the father of the family hath begot, but those that an adulterous mother would obtrude upon him as part of his family, which he rejects from any paternal care of instruction and discipline, as having no part in his inheritance, no right to his goods, not born of his seed, which is the word. By this the apostle signifies,

(1.) That all the true children of God are under his discipline. If they are not, they are no parts of his family. He that is left without it, is not in the number of those he owns for his children. Hereby he strengthens what he had spoken before, that God deals with those he afflicts as children; whence it follows, that there is no child of his but he doth at one time or another afflict. This is one of the clauses of the covenant God hath made with us in Jesus, which he doth peculiarly insert, when he owns himself our God and Father: Ps. lxxxix. 32, he would visit them with a rod, but not take away his loving-kindness. In the New Testament, God promiseth spiritual blessings. In the Old, when he promised most temporal blessings, his people were not exempt from his discipline. In the New Testament, it is more express, that through afflictions we must enter into the kingdom of heaven. His only Son must suffer, and so enter into glory.

(2.) That those that are not under his discipline are not his children.

Afflictions therefore are so far from being discouragements, that where there is an evidence of grace in the heart, they are rather marks of adoption. We might well doubt of a relation to him if he took no care of us; that we were not his sheep if he used not his crook to pull us unto him. Let us then receive his chastisements without regret, since he manifests his care of us in them, and regards us with the eyes and heart of a father. If we were wholly strangers, he would abandon us, and leave us as persons he knew not. His paternal rod is for his children, his rod of iron for his enemies. But now in the ninth verse, and the following verses, the apostle exhorts them to a reverence of God under his chastising hand. The argument is *a minori ad majus*: ver. 9, 'Furthermore, we have had fathers of the flesh which corrected us, and we gave them reverence: shall we not much rather be in subjection to the Father of spirits, and live?' And he urgeth the exhortation, (1.) from the right of God: he is the Father of spirits; (2.) from his intention, which is our spiritual profit, ver. 10; (3.) from the issue: it is as much our advantage in the event as it was in his intention, ver. 11. The fathers of our flesh have corrected us, and we gave them reverence; how much rather ought we to be subject to the Father of spirits, who chasteneth us that we may live? The two persons which the apostle compares together, viz. God and man, have this in common: one and the other is a father, one and the other chasteneth, one and the other is carried out to it by love, one and the other designs advantage; but as there is this resemblance, so there is a great difference: man is but the father of the body, the more ignoble part of our natures, that which we have common with beasts; God is the Father of our spirits, the more noble part, and that which makes us properly men. More submission is therefore due to him, who confers more upon us, than to them who confer less. The love which fathers bear to their children is a passion, and many times is not regulated by reason; but the love of God is a true love, not mingled with any imperfection either of excess or defect, and therefore doth nothing but with the justest reason. Again, earthly fathers aim at the good of their children, but their ignorance is so great that often they mistake it; but the knowledge of God is as perfect as his love, who always chastiseth his people for their true good, and therefore a greater submission is due to him.

(1.) How glorious is the condition of a true believer! He is the child of God: 1 John iii. 1, 'What manner of love is this, that we should be called the sons of God!' It is an argument of great love to give his people so honourable and dear a title, to call himself their Father, as well as their God. It is not so strange that he should call all the pure spirits in heaven his children, as that he should call those that have defiled his image by that title; that he should own himself a Father to them that are by nature children of wrath, slaves to Satan, sold under sin, that have nothing in them to please him by nature, but are fit objects of his wrath and curse. Wonderful love, that God should not think it a dishonour to him to be called our Father! And hence it is reason we should carry ourselves to him in all his dispensations as children to a father, that we should comfort ourselves in this relation in all the sufferings we encounter. If he be our Father, what should we fear? Nothing passes in the world without his order; no evil arrives to us without his will. Every affliction is the rod of his hand. The very thought that God is our Father should sweeten any grief.

(2.) God is the creator of souls. By spirits are meant the souls of men; some understand it also of spiritual gifts, the graces God infuseth into the souls of his people. Both are good motives to that submission unto, and reverence of God, the apostle urgeth. Most interpreters run the first way.

The antithesis requires that we should understand by this expression that God is the creator of souls, because it is opposed to the fathers of the flesh. God is called the God of the spirits of all flesh, Num. xvi. 22. As by the flesh the apostle means the body, the material and visible part of our natures; so by the spirit he means the soul, the spiritual and invisible part of our being. As for the body, man engendered it; as for the soul, God only formed it; as in Eccles. xii. 7, 'Then shall the dust return to the earth, and the spirit shall return to God that gave it;' where by the dust is meant the body, and by the spirit the soul. The body was formed of the dust of the ground, Gen. ii. 7; but the soul was breathed in by God. It is the spirit that gives life and sense to the parts of the body, which otherwise are without sense and motion; and God is said to form the spirit of man, Zech. xii. 1, and challengeth to himself the particular forming of the soul: Isa. lvii. 16, 'The soul which I have made.' God, indeed, forms the body too by the hand of nature, by the intervention of second causes which he employs; but the soul he forms without any other cause but his own will. The first manner of acting by nature in the production of the body is not sufficient to demonstrate God the Father of it, no more than he can be called the Father of beasts and plants, which are produced by his powerful providence, as well as the bodies of men; but the second manner of acting in the production of an immortal and spiritual substance is sufficient to demonstrate God the Father of spirits, as they also are called the children of God, because God immediately created them, and clothed them with an immortal nature. The apostle, therefore, hath good reason to call men which have begot us the fathers of the flesh; because, though the wisdom and power of God in his providence acts in our conception and generation, yet it is also the work of man, who acts as a second cause; but the production of the soul is purely by the will and power of God, without the action of any creature. Hence it follows that the soul is immortal; for since it doth not depend in its original upon matter, it doth not in its subsistence, neither after death hath separated the body from it. It follows also that the reasonable soul is more excellent than the bodies which we receive from earthly fathers; and therefore we owe more submission and reverence to God and his chastisements than to those who have been only the fathers of our bodies, which the interrogation intimates, 'Shall we not much rather be in subjection to the Father of spirits, and live?'

(3.) 'And live;' or that we may live. This is an argument from the reward of a patient suffering. The apostle seems tacitly to refer to the promise of life to children that honour their parents. As a temporal life was promised to them, so a spiritual and eternal life is promised to those that are patiently obedient under the hand of God. As in Israel those that slighted the rebukes of their parents were stoned without pity, so will God handle those that kick against his discipline, and make no profit of his rod. Corrections cause life, not meritoriously, but instrumentally. If we, therefore, own God as a Father, we ought to carry ourselves to him as our Father. If we desire an happy and eternal life, we must subject ourselves to his hand, acknowledge the righteousness of his discipline, and, by how much the paternity of God is more excellent, our submission ought to be the more reverential. In ver. 10, the apostle urgeth the exhortation further, from the manner of God's proceedings with us, different from that of earthly fathers, and from his aim in it: 'For they for a few days chastened us after their own pleasure; but he for our profit, that we might be partakers of his holiness.' This he doth by comparing of the heavenly Father and the earthly father with one another, and acquaints us that it is the aim of God, in those afflictions which seem most bitter, to reduce us to that holiness which we have lost in Adam.

1. They verily for a few days chastened us. Either death deprives them of their authority, or the growth of their children exempts them from suffering under it. Parents only take care to correct their children during the weakness of their childhood, when, by ignorance and inexperience, they are incapable to conduct themselves. They have, therefore, need of their parents to form their spirits, and make those impressions upon them whereby they may govern themselves the rest of their lives. But when they are arrived at years of discretion, they are left to govern themselves according to their own reasons, without using the rod to supply the defect of their understanding; so that the corrections of earthly parents are but for few years, a little time.

Observation.

1. Hereby appears the advantage of God's discipline above that of earthly parents. God continues his care to us all our lives upon the earth, as long as we have need; exercises a greater providence over us than earthly parents over their children.

2. Hereby the apostle comforts us. It is but a little time that God subjects us to chastisements; only that part of our life which we are to pass on earth, which is but a small time to that eternity wherein we shall be exempt from suffering; bears infinitely less proportion to eternity than the least instant doth to all the time from the creation to the end of the world; so that the time of a believer's chastisement is shorter than that of children under their parents. And herein is the kindness and love of God apparent, who deals more favourably with his children in regard of the time of their correction than the best father in the world can do.

2. The motive of, and rule that parents too often follow, in their chastising their children, 'after their own pleasure.' They have often a greater regard to their own passions than their children's advantage, correct oftener in humour than with reason. Having no other law but their own will, their judgment is apt to be deceived, whereby it happens that their corrections often injure their children instead of advantaging them, whatsoever their intention may be, and that either by mistake of the nature of things for which they chastise them, or the indiscreet measure and manner of their chastening.

(1.) Mistaking the nature of the things for which they chastise their children. Fathers endeavour to form their children to that which they judge best and most profitable for them in this life; but their judgments are often mistaken, as a covetous parent, that acknowledges no other happiness than wealth, will instill such instructions into his child to think nothing unjust that is profitable and enriching; an ambitious man will endeavour to imprint the sentiments of worldly honour upon his children; a superstitious parent will correct his child for not conforming himself to that mode of worship he is himself addicted to. Thus parents often use their power to extinguish good principles in their children, and discourage beginnings of virtue in them.

(2.) Mistaking the measure. How often are good parents transported with choler in the corrections they inflict? Others, through a fond indulgence, altogether neglect it, and give the reins to the follies of their children. But the chastisements God inflicts are otherwise; he hath a perfect knowledge of all things, is subject to no passion, never afflicts but when there is need, never chastiseth his own but for their good. God, being infinitely wise, cannot err in his judgment of what is convenient for us; he is not biassed by weak affections. David acknowledged this wisdom of God: Ps. cxix. 71, 'It is good for me that I have been afflicted, that I might learn thy statutes.' He is wise, and foresees an evil we are apt to run into, and prevents it by affliction; sends Paul a thorn in the flesh, not so much to correct a present default as to prevent it, 2 Cor. xii. 7, that he might not be lifted up above measure. Sometimes he afflicts to make their graces apparent. God afflicted Job in his goods, in his person, that the truth of his faith and patience might be seen in the midst of his sufferings, to the praise of God. He sends not temptations unless there be need, and that the trial of faith may be found to praise and honour, 1 Peter i. 6, 7. Other parents use their arbitrariness often, and not their wisdom. God's afflictions are sovereign acts, but not separated from wise and gracious intentions. But the apostle explains the particular profit which God aims at, 'That we might be partakers of his holiness;' to refine their dross, and purify them for himself, and render them fit for the place wherein dwells nothing that is unclean. Earthly parents correct their children that they may learn useful arts and manners in the world: an external profit chiefly they aim at; sometimes they correct that their vices may be imitated; God, that his holiness may be communicated here, and blessedness hereafter. This seems to be an exposition of what he meant by *live* in the former verse. This preserves us, and renders us partakers not only of holiness, but of *his* holiness; the holiness which he approves, which he commands, and hath some resemblance and conformity to his own. In the same sense we are said to be partakers of the divine nature, 2 Peter i. 4, whereby we have a portraiture of the nature and holiness of God drawn in our souls by the Spirit. It is not that we may possess the holiness of God, but partake of the holiness of God. The lineaments of his image, formed in us by the gospel and by afflictions, are as the beams and sparks of his holiness. The original is in God, the picture of it in the believer; as light is in the sun, but some splendour of it in the glass upon which it shines. This God works by afflictions, whereby he makes us exercise ourselves more in repentance; weans us from the flesh, that would alienate us from God; cleave faster to Christ by faith, who is the spring of holiness; more earnestly thirst to draw of the fountain, and pursue those things that are heavenly. Parents correct their children to bring them to an imitation of their manners; God corrects his to bring them to an imitation of his holiness. They chastise to make their children like them; and God, to make his children conform to him.

(1.) Then afflictions are not always punishments; they are not inflicted for satisfaction for sin. God aims at our profit. A judge regards not the profit of a criminal when he condemns him to punishment, but only the honour of the law; and to repair the offence done to the law by the violation of it, and satisfy that justice which hath been violated. But God aims at the advantage of the believing sufferers, and makes them smart to make them gracious and glorious, to impart to them the highest excellency a creature is capable of.

(2.) A great argument there is from hence to love God even for afflictions. 'In all things give thanks,' saith the apostle. In these there is great reason to give thanks, in regard of their fruit. An earthly father transmits his inheritance to his son, but not his internal endowments; but God communicates his holiness to his children by these means.

(3.) How patiently should we bear them! The majesty of God above earthly parents, and his gracious aim and wise conduct of them, doth oblige us to this duty. He never strikes but with reason, never strikes his children but for their good. Happy blows should be received without murmuring. It is a welcome weapon that hath more of balsam than smart, a blessed sword that breaks the imposthume. That which is not only profitable, but necessary, calls not only for our patience, but our willing embracing when God doth wisely inflict it; besides, they are short, they are of no longer duration than this life. There might be reason to complain much if it were an eternal smart, but it is only for a little time.

(4.) We should endeavour to answer the intention of God. To form ourselves to that holiness he aims at, to embrace every motion of the Spirit in our afflictions. To that purpose the rod hath a voice, the Spirit hath a voice; both must be listened to.

And because it is a hard matter to be without complaints, the apostle still urgeth it further, and prevents the ground of complaint, which is the sharpness of a rod, and sets the smart and fruit in opposition one to another: ver. 11, 'Now no chastening for the present seems to be joyous, but grievous; nevertheless, afterwards it yields the peaceable fruit of righteousness to them that are exercised thereby.' It is confessed they are grievous, but it is in appearance only. They seem so; but as a beautiful face under a frightful mask, as a bitter potion, that gripes, but purgeth. This is an argument taken from the fruit of correction, and amplified by concession of the objection; I confess suffering is grievous, but wholesome. The end and issue of it is to be considered. A rational creature in all things should mind the end as well as the means. The end makes a vast difference between things. Because the trouble and grief which is in every chastisement makes our flesh to apprehend it is an evil, the apostle distinguisheth between what is troublesome and what is desirable, between the pain and the fruit; and draws an argument of patience from the effect.

[1.] All afflictions are grievous to the flesh. God doth not expect we should be Stoics, to be without sense or grief. Christ himself hath set us a pattern of it; he shed tears for the death of his friend Lazarus, and shed drops of blood at the approaching of his sufferings: 'his soul was sorrowful, even to the death;' he was 'tempted in all things like to us, yet without sin.' It is no sin to grieve under, to complain of suffering, without murmuring. If we have not a sense of the grief, we can never be capable of the profit of affliction. Without some grief, affliction would leave us worse than it finds us. As we ought to hear God when he speaks, so we ought to fear God when he strikes. At first the trouble of a chastisement doth wholly possess our spirits, it makes us mistake the end of it, we cannot sometimes in our pressures imagine that a root so bitter should bear a joyful fruit; as the griping physic afflicts the patient so much sometimes, that he scarce thinks of the good which will issue from it. David often is full of complaints while he is under an affliction, and seems often to have no sense of anything but the present trouble, but afterwards he hath no sentiments but of the gracious fruit: 'In faithfulness thou hast afflicted me.' 'It is good for me that I have been afflicted.' 'Thy rod doth comfort me.' After experience manifests a truth which the present grief will not often give us leave to consider.

[2.] Though afflictions be grievous, the fruit is gracious to a believer. Experience corrects the false judgment we have while we are under a stroke. Indeed, afflictions of themselves are rather a means to cool our affections to holiness, to extinguish in our minds the sparks of godliness, and make us despond and distrust the grace of God; but God in his sovereign wisdom doth so dispose and manage them, that he makes them end in a happy fruit. By the grace of God they break off those inclinations we have to the world, quicken our prayers, awaken us out of our lethargies, put us upon a review of ourselves. The strings of an instrument yield a different sound when they are stretched, from what they did when they were slack. It is a fruit of righteousness, holiness, and sanctification, which he had spoken of in the former verse; also righteousness, which is a peaceable fruit; as when it is said, the 'incorruptible crown of glory,' 1 Peter v. 4. It is as much as to say, the glory which is a crown incorruptible, so a righteousnes which is the spring of peace and serenity of conscience: Isa. xxxiii. 17, 'And the work of righteousness shall be peace; and the effect of righteousness, quietness and assurance for ever.' It yields the fruit of righteousness, as being a means that brings us nearer to God, in communion with whom that peace doth consist. It brings us to seek in God and Christ the true remedy of all our evils; and by this means, the trouble of our souls is calmed, and an assurance of the grace of God promoted. The joy of the Holy Ghost is often strongest in us when afflictions are sharpest upon us: 1 Thes. i. 6, 'Having received the word in much affliction, with joy of the Holy Ghost.' And though it be not always so with a believer, yet after the affliction hath wrought kindly, and done its work, God comes in with comfort and joy; as cheering cordials follow bitter physic. They bring forth the fruits of righteousness, not as the efficient cause, but the means.

1. Let us then make a right judgment of afflictions. Let us not think God intends to destroy when he begins to strike. We are often in the same error the apostles were in when they saw Christ walking upon the waves in the dead of the night, and terrors of a tempest, coming to succour them, they imagined he was a spirit coming to mischief them, Mark vi. 47–49. The flesh makes us think God often to be our enemy when he is our friend. But as Christ cried out to them, 'Fear not, it is I,' so the apostle doth to believers here. Fear not; though the smart be grievous, the fruit is peaceable; if the flesh suffer, it is for the good of the spirit. The issue will declare, that 'all things work together for the good of them that love God,' Rom. viii. 27.

2. Let patience and faith have their perfect work. Affliction makes the beginning sad, patience will make the success glorious. Had the Israelites believed God's promise of deliverance, they had not murmured at the Red Sea. God brought them to the Red Sea to deliver them from the Egyptians, and made all their fears end in joy and triumph. The more we trust God, the more he is concerned in our welfare; the more we trust ourselves, the more he doth to cross us. The committing our way to the Lord renders our minds calm and composed: Prov. xvi. 3, 'Commit thy way to the Lord, and thy thoughts shall be established.' God hath always 'an eye upon them that fear him,' Ps. xxxiii. 18, 19; not to keep distress and affliction from them, but to quicken them in it, and give them as it were a new life from the dead, new fruit from the rod. God brings us into straits, that we may have more lively experiments of his tenderness and wisdom. We should submit our way to the guidance of God's wisdom, with an obedience to his will and a reliance on his goodness; and then the success will be gracious in this life, and glorious in that which is to come,—a peaceable fruit of righteousness in earth and heaven. Wait upon God, being he is a God of judgment: Isa. xxx. 18, 'For the Lord is a God of judgment; blessed are all those that wait for him.' He goes judicially to work, and can best time the execution of his will. God hath as much wisdom to bring an affliction to a good issue, as he hath love at first to inflict it.

A DISCOURSE OF THE REMOVAL OF THE GOSPEL.

Remember from whence thou art fallen, and repent, and do the first works; or else I will come unto thee quickly, and remove thy candlestick out of his place, except thou repent.—Rev. II. 5.

These words are part of the epistle of Christ, as king and governor, to the church of Ephesus, and they contain a severe threatening after a charge and indictment brought in against that church. The bill is preferred against them by Christ, who is described, ver. 1, to be him 'that holds the seven stars in his right hand, and walks in the midst of the seven golden candlesticks.' He holds the stars in his hand to shew his tenderness, in his right hand to shew his power, and he walks among the candlesticks to shew his care over them and his love to them. Before he brings the charge, he takes notice of what was praiseworthy in that church, and gives them the commendation of their patience under persecution and zeal for his glory, vers. 2, 3. But, alas! the case was changed, their zeal was cold, and their love was flatted: ver. 4, 'she had left her first love.' Ephesus was a mart-town of Asia, famous for Diana's temple, Acts xix. 28, which brought resort and consequently wealth to her from all parts of Asia and Greece.

I have formerly noted that the condition of the church in the several states of it is described in these epistles. Crocius discourseth of them to this purpose,* whence our Dr Moor might take his rise for that ingenious and rational piece he hath writ upon these epistles in this sense. The design of this book is to predict what should happen to the church in all ages till the conclusion of time; and what is spoken here to these seven churches seems to be greater than can well suit these places in Asia while they remained Christian. The conversion of the Jews seems to be intimated to be brought to pass in the Philadelphian state, to which we probably are approaching, after a smart trouble: Rev. iii. 5, 'I will make those that are of the synagogue of Satan, which say they are Jews, and are not, but do lie; behold, I will make them to come and worship before thy feet;' those that are of the Jewish synagogue, which he calls the synagogue of Satan, being blinded by the God of this world to keep up that worship which God hath rejected, which are indeed Jews in the flesh and by circumcision, but are not so in

* Epist. Dedicat. ante Syntag.

spirit; or it may be meant of some people that pretend to be of the Jewish race, or practising the Jewish rites, that shall in that state of the church give up their names to Christianity. And for Laodicea, it is argued that the epistle cannot be meant of local Laodicea, because that is reported to be swallowed up by an earthquake in the time of Nero, before the writing of this epistle. And it is that state of the church which shall be before the day of judgment, and therefore fitly put in that term of Laodicea, which signifies in the Greek, the people's judgment, or the judgment of the people. The church of Ephesus is understood by him to be the first and apostolical condition of the church, or perhaps not that primo-primitive, but the state of the church immediately succeeding it. It is true the primitive church was fired with zeal and ballasted with patience; she had a courage to assert the truth, and a meekness to bear her troubles, and detected those false apostles that would join works with the righteousness of Christ in justification. But after the death of the apostles, yea, and in the life of Paul, there were some that made disturbance, would have blended the gospel doctrine and worship with legal ceremonies. And when the head of that great founder of the Gentile church was laid, coldness in Christianity and corruption in doctrine crept in.

Doct. 1 How unwilling is the nature of man to be guided by the word of Christ! Men will be mixing their own wills and wisdom with the wisdom and will of God. Error could not else have crept in so soon while the memory of the apostles lasted. The church of Ephesus was the first state of the church next to the primitive, and this gave strong provocations to God to take away the gospel from her.

2. Christ takes an account both of the good and evil works of a church. One makes him not overlook the other; he will not cocker any for their good, or spare them in their evil. He sweetens his reproof here with a commendation, like oil that makes way for a sharp nail. He reckons their labour, patience, sense of his dishonour, their discovery of seducing spirits, the circumstances of their zeal for his name, and constancy and unweariedness in it. He sees our good grain and beholds our chaff; he take notices of our decreases and of our decays.

3. Grace doth not privilege sin. Though he takes notice of their worth, yet he charges them with their crime. Christ takes more notice of the sins of his people than of the sins of others. Others' sins are enmities: he expects no other from them; their sins are unkind, and more affect him. Their professions, mercies, covenants, assistances, privileges, require a suitable walk. Judas his betraying Christ did not so much trouble him as Peter's denial of him. We do not read that he thought of Judas after he had betrayed him, but he would look back upon Peter whilst he was exposed to the danger of his life, and approaching to a contest with death and wrath. Christ will be terrible in the assembly of his saints: he will not endure the dustiness of his golden candlestick.

We may see here,

1. The disease: ver. 4, 'Thou hast left thy first love.'

2. The issue of it, if it were not cured: the removal of the candlestick.

3. The cure, which consists

(1.) In consideration, 'Remember.'

[1.] Of their present condition, fallen.

[2.] Of the term of their apostasy: whence thou art fallen. Reflect upon your present condition and your former state, and compare them one with another.

(2.) In contrition, 'repent.'

(3.) In reformation; and 'do thy first work,' write after thy former copy. This method of cure was to be observed, otherwise Christ would take away the golden candlestick.

'Do thy first work;' reduce thyself to the form of primitive Christianity; away with all mixtures in worship, chillness in discipline, looseness in practice.

Doct. Reformations are reductions of things to their original pattern and first institution. When Christ would reform the abuses in marriage, he doth not bring them to the practice of their fathers and the practice of their posterity, but measures both that of their own and that of their ancestors by the first rule, 'In the beginning it was not so,' Mat. xix. 18. We are usually swayed by customs in morals, and precedents in politicals, when custom and prescription alter not the nature of unrighteousness and unreasonableness. True reformations are reductions of things to reason and reduction of things to Scripture.

'I will remove thy candlestick out of his place.' I shall not trouble you with the different interpretations of it. There was a candlestick within the tabernacle, Heb. ix. 2, which had seven branches, wherein lamps were continually presented lighted. The candlestick represented as a type the gospel church, and the lamps the gospel in it, and the oil to supply the lamps the gifts of the Spirit for the preservation and propagation of the gospel. An allusion is made in this place to the candlestick in the ancient tabernacle. Some think the candlestick with the seven golden branches represented the seven planets, but with what reason I understand not, since the branches of the candlestick were all equal, but the planets are of a different light and magnitude. The chief intention of the ancient tabernacle was to represent and signify future things. The seven particular churches allude here to the seven branches of that candlestick, seven particular churches or seven states of the church, all parts of the universal. The chief concern of the candlestick was the light in it, without which, as the tabernacle had been a place of darkness, so is the world without the gospel.

By removing the candlestick is therefore to be understood the removing of the gospel, and so an unchurching of them. Candlestick may be here put for the light in it, by a metonomy of the subject for the adjunct.

We might observe,

1. A nation, people, or church, that have been eminent for the owning the ways and truths of God, may have great decays in their affections, and greatly apostatize.

2. Apostasy in a church is followed with a removal of the gospel.

3. The removal of the gospel is the saddest judgment that can happen to a nation.

We may put the two last together, and so I shall insist on this doctrine.

Doct. God doth often remove the gospel upon provocations, as the severest judgment he can inflict upon an unworthy people. Apostasies have been very frequent. Everything under the sun is subject to alteration and corruption. Faith is not a hereditary thing like a standing patrimony. Children do not always tread in the steps of their ancestors; what they receive only by education, they will easily part with upon some carnal interest, some smiling or frowning temptation. Some have observed that the purity of the gospel hath scarce lasted in a city or province to the third generation. The gospel in the honour of it may remain longer, but usually some error, some mixtures, have deformed it. Good corn is scarcely sown but the devil is as ready to sow his tares.

I shall premise,

1. The gospel shall not be removed out of the world, while the world endures. Sion, the universal church, hath a promise of stability; the gospel therefore, whereby she is constituted a church, shall be perpetually in her. The shutting the gate of the sanctuary after the Lord's entering into it, Ezek. xliv. 2, is expounded by some, of the everlasting dwelling of the Lord in the gospel church, and never departing from it, as he had done from the temple of Jerusalem. The promise of Christ assures it: Mat. xxviii. 20, 'I will be with you always, even unto the end of the world.' Not with the persons of the apostles, who were to expire, but with the doctrine of the apostles, which was to endure; though the apostles die in their bodies, yet they live in their doctrine.

2. The gospel hath been, and still may be, removed from particular places. No particular church but may be unchurched, because no particular church hath a promise of stability. There is no entail of God's favour to any particular church in the world. The gospel is a candle, and the church is a candlestick; both candle and candlestick are moveable things, not an entailed inheritance. Many nations have had their day of grace set, and are now benighted. Jerusalem had a season wherein to know the things that concerned her peace, Luke xix. 42. She finds nothing now but sorrow and exile. There is a time when the Spirit strives, and there is a time when the Spirit turns his back, and ceaseth any longer wrestling. Sometimes God doth both unchurch and unnation a people, sometimes he removes the gospel, and continues a nation in being; but this is rare, to continue providential mercies when his most excellent truth is departed. But in such cases he gives them up to strong delusions, who would not render themselves at his summons; he continues the substance, while he removes the efficacy by withdrawing his Spirit; and then the gospel is like a carcase without a soul: Isa. vi. 9, 10, 'They shall hear and not understand.'

I shall observe this method in handling this doctrine. I shall shew,

I. The gospel has been removed, a nation hath been unchurched.

II. It is the greatest judgment.

III. The Use.

I. That a nation has been unchurched, and the gospel has been removed.

1. The Jews are an eminent instance. They had the gospel in a type, while they enjoyed the ceremonies; they had the gospel unveiled, while they had the presence of Christ among them. God gave them anciently some evidences of the possibility of it. The law was near being quite removed from them, when upon their idolatry, the two tables were broken by Moses, which a little before had been received from God. When the ark was put into the temple, at Solomon's dedication of it, though it was lodged there without any intention in the people to remove it, yet the staves whereby it was carried were continued in it, 1 Kings viii. 8, 9, so that it was ready for a removal at any time; to shew, say some, that if the ark were abused and the testimonies slighted, it should be taken from them.

(1.) Consider, they were a people that had the greatest titles. They were called by his name, Jer. ii. 2, 3. They were his peculiar treasure, they were called God's son, his first-born, his spouse, his portion, inheritance, his delight; yet he hath flung this treasure out of his coffers, disinherited his first-born, cast his children out of his house to be fugitives about the world; his spouse is divorced from him, and his inheritance laid waste. No child was more endeared to a father, no wife more to a husband, than those people to God; yet how is that Jerusalem, which was his delight, now a den of thieves?

(2.) Consider the privileges they enjoyed. They were a people cherished in his bosom, walled about with miracles, protected by him in person; he marched before them as their general, and conducted their motions, Exod. xiii. 21. He was their lawgiver, and penned their statutes, whereby they were to be governed, with his own hand; he spake to them from heaven (which he did to no other nation); he was their caterer, and provided manna for them in their necessity, and fed them by miracle. He was their bishop to settle them a church, and their prince and magistrate to form them into a state; not only their religion, but their civil government was the birth of the wisdom of heaven. He put his oracles as a treasure into their hands, Rom. iii. 2. The covenant, ark, pot of manna, were committed to them; he planted them a noble vine, culled them out from all the nations of the earth, whereby they were made the delights of heaven, and the admiration of the rest of the world. He made them his garden, they cost him more than all the nations beside, and he seems to have no care of any part of the earth besides them, Ps. cxlvii. 19, 20. The world had his alms, and they the inheritance; the rest of the world were his Ishmaels, and they his Isaacs; and which is observable, his first thoughts seem to be, to have the gospel confined only to them in that covenant which he makes with Christ, which is represented in the manner of a treaty between the Father and the Son. He seems to pitch no further than Israel, 'in whom he would be glorified,' Isa. xlix. 3, till Christ complains of the narrow limits, and gains a larger portion for himself. The terms are then enlarged: ver. 6, 'It is a light thing that thou shouldest be my servant to raise up the tribes of Jacob, and restore the preserved of Israel; I will also give thee for a light to the Gentiles.' The promises of the Messiah made to Abraham and Jacob were often with an addition of clearness renewed to them by the prophets. He chose them of all nations, of whom his Son the Saviour of the world should be born, with whom he was first to treat. His personal ministry was designed for them, to the lost sheep of the house of Israel only he was sent, that nation he in person solicited, over them he wept, and for them he prayed, Mat. xv. 24. Those that were to carry the gospel into other parts of the world, were selected out of that nation; and though they used him so ill, yet he was indulgent to them, sent his Spirit upon the apostles first at Jerusalem; seemed to have little care of the Gentiles. How long after was it that Peter scrupled to treat with them? But since they have proved false to God, and forgot the Rock of their strength, he exposed them to the fury of a Roman army, tore up the foundations of their government, demolished their temple, caused the land he had infeft them in to spue them out, scattered them over the face of the world as a spectacle of his vengeance, and a standing monument what the case will be of any nation that walks unworthily of the gospel.

(3.) Consider the multitude of strange providences they had. He delivered them, to the amazement of all round about them; they were a happy people, in being a people saved by the Lord, Deut. xxxiii. 29. They saw more of his wonderful providences than all the world ever since hath done: he put himself out of the ordinary course of providence in their favour; he spread their tables in the wilderness, and filled their cup; no good thing they could have a mind to, but they had for asking; the sun must stand still in heaven to light them to the gaining a victory, if Joshua desire it; they had upon all occasions immediate direction from the ark. What favour did they find from Cyrus after they had been captivated? A hundred thousand were set at liberty by Ptolemy, after they had been enslaved by his father. When they proved false to God, and played the harlot upon every high hill, and under every green tree, how was their temple and city destroyed, and after some revolution of time repaired; and that by their enemies, as some observe, contrary to all the rules of policy, since the re-edifying their temple, and the repairing the walls of their city, might be encouragements to them to rebel, they being a people that had so often forced their necks out of the conqueror's yoke. And often when the temple wanted repairs, God stirred up the hearts of their enemies to send supplies out of the Roman provinces to beautify it, that as God had at first enriched them by the jewels of the Egyptians, he would maintain their wealth by the assistance of the other Gentiles. And when Pompey entered into their temple, where there was a treasure in the vessels, and instruments of gold, amounting to about nine millions of money (a strong temptation to a generous person), yet God so ordered it, that he could see nothing there but a cloud. They never were conquered (which you know was often), but God raised them up some patrons. Yet notwithstanding all these providences whereby God so miraculously owned them, and all the dangers from whence he so powerfully delivered them, they are now pulled up by the root, persecuted by man, abandoned by God, 'the generation of his wrath,' Jer. vii. 29. Of a tender Father he has become their enraged enemy, and flings vengeance down upon those heads which before he crowned with mercy. No spiritual dew falls upon these mountains of Gilboa. Those that were as plessant to God as the 'grapes in a wilderness' to a thirsty traveller, Hosea ix. 10, are of as little regard as a bramble. Their names are a detestation in nature, and a hissing to the Gentiles. God sometimes embraced the Jews without taking the Gentiles, and now hath received the Gentiles with rejecting the Jews.

2. The seven churches of Asia, to whom these epistles are written, are another instance. How do their places know them no more as once they were! Not only their religion, but their civil politeness is exchanged for barbarism. They have lost their ancient beauty for a Turkish deformity. Mahomet's horse hath succeeded in the place of the gospel dove. The blasphemies of the Alcoran sound where the name of Christ hath been called upon. The triumphant banners of an impostor advanced where the standard of the gospel had been erected. Christ had a great company of votaries in those places when the ancient Britons were under the empire of Satan, but now he seems to have sowed those places with salt, and made them barren. No courageous Athanasius, or silver-tongued Chrysostom, or lofty Nazianzen to be found in those places. He hath translated the gospel into other parts, and multiplied children in those places which before were barren. We might instance also in the church of Rome, a church whose faith was spoken of throughout the whole world; and how is the truth and purity of religion discarded, true faith dwindled into implicit, the righteousness of Christ changed for impotent and feeble merit; pilgrimages, oblations, self-chastisements advanced instead of the virtues of the cross; whole countries made drunk with the wine of her fornication; the glory of the gospel gone, a mere echo only remaining, the end of a voice, and no reality! They are given up to strong delusions to believe a lie.

II. Thing. That the removal of the gospel and unchurching a nation is the greatest judgment. Can there be a greater judgment than to have the word of God removed, to want a prophet to instruct and warn, when the law shall perish from the priest, and counsel from the ancient? This God threatens as the greatest, Ezek. viii. 26. And the church complains of it as the sorest: Ps. lxxiv. 9, 'We see not our signs, and there is no more any prophet among us.' It was the greatest token of God's anger, when his glory went up from the cherubims, Ezek. ix. 2. *A loco placationis.* How much more terrible is the shaking off the dust of the feet of God against a people, than the shaking off the dust of the feet of an apostle! What greater evidence can there be of a father's indignation against a disobedient son, than not only to disinherit him but disdain to speak to him, or send to him any notice of his mind and will? The misery of the old world was summed up in this, 'My Spirit shall not always strive with man,' Gen. vi. 3; and then are the flood-gates of heaven opened. The shutting up the book of mercy is the opening the book of justice, the unstopping the vials of wrath; this, this is the very dregs of vengeance.

1. The gospel is the choicest mercy, and therefore the removal of it the sharpest misery. The gospel is so much the best of blessings, as God is the best of beings. This is the sun that enlightens the mind, this is the rain that waters the heart. Without this, we should sink into an heathen, brutish, or devilish superstition. By this, the quickening Spirit renews the soul, and begins a gracious and spiritual life in order to a glorious and eternal one. It is by this our souls are refined and our lusts consumed. Without it we are without help, and without hope; without it we have no prospect of a world to come, nor any sight of the paths that lead to happiness. This is the foundation of the peace and joy of our spirits here, this is the basis of our hopes of happiness hereafter. This is a pearl of great price; this is the glory and honour of a church, people, or person. This only instructs us to save our souls. Your trades may gain and preserve an estate, your bread may nourish your bodies, this only can fatten and prop your souls; had we the law only, which yet is the law of God, we should still find it weak through the flesh, it cannot now save us, though the observance of it might have made our father Adam happy. It is the gospel only that is strong to save through the Spirit. The law could bless an innocent man, but the gospel only restores a guilty man. When the candlestick, the gospel, therefore, is removed, the light is removed which is able to direct us, the pearl is removed which is able to enrich us. In the want of this is introduced a spiritual darkness, which ends in an eternal darkness. As the gospel is compared to heaven, and so called the kingdom of heaven, and a people in the enjoyment of it are said to be 'lifted up to heaven,' Mat. x. 23, so in the want of it they are said to be cast down into hell, so that what resemblance there is between heaven and the means of grace, that there is between the want of them and hell, both are a separation from God by divorce between God and a people.

2. It is made worse than those judgments that are accounted the severest. Plagues, wars, famine, are lighter marks of divine anger than this. God, upon several provocations of the Jews, sent enemies to waste their habitations and ravage their country, plagues to diminish their inhabitants, yet they were still his people; but when he takes the word and ordinances from them, they are Lo-ammi, not my people, Hosea i. 9. God may take notice of a people under the smartest afflictions, but when he takes away his word, he knows a people no longer. A father may scourge a child and yet love him, but when he takes away his treasure, his food, from his child, he can no longer be said to love him, he breaks the bands of all relation and natural affection. This judgment is compared to, and yet made worse than, a famine of bread. What more terrible than famine, that hath forced parents against the ties of natural affection to devour their children, and children to feed upon the lean flesh of their parents! What more terrible than famine, that hath rendered carrion, dung, rats, serpents, the refuse of nature, a delicious food in that extreme necessity! What more dreadful than this, that brutifies the nature of man, and necessitates them to horrid and abominable actions! Yet this is made a light thing in comparison of the other: Amos viii. 11,

'Behold, the days come, saith the Lord, that I will send a famine in the land, not a famine of bread, nor a thirst for water, but of hearing the word of the Lord.' In what bitter gall doth God here dip his pen! I will not send so light a judgment, I have a worse scourge for them. When God sent the Jews into captivity, he sent prophets to attend them while they were under the Chaldean power. The remains of them in the land had Jeremiah and Baruch. The captives in Babylon had Daniel, Ezekiel, Esdras; after the captivity they had Zechariah, Haggai, Malachi; but in this judgment threatened against Israel, none at all; they were to be without a prince, or a priest, Hosea iii. 4 (for the word signifies both), without a sacrfice, without Ephod and Teraphim. As the soul surpasses the body in excellency, so a soul famine exceeds a bodily famine. The want of spiritual is more dreadful than the want of corporeal food; this makes us weak, and that makes us wicked; this pines away the strength of the body, that drives out the health of the soul; this may be a means to make us seek the Lord, but that leaves us groping in the dark. We may live in our souls by the influence of the word, when we have not bread to convey strength to our bodies, but how must the soul languish when it is deprived of spiritual food to nourish her! Isa. xxx. 20. How doleful would it be to have the ground parched by the sun, the sky emptied of clouds, or the bottles of heaven stopped close without venting a drop of refreshing rain. But how much more deplorable is this judgment than the withholding the clouds from dropping upon our earth, or the sun from shining upon our fruits.

3. When the gospel departs, all other blessings depart with it. When the great charter is taken away, all the privileges depending upon it are snatched away together with it. When God departs, judgments succeed. When the glory of God was gone up from the first cherub to the threshold of the house, Ezek. ix. 3, the angels are commanded to execute the destructive sentence against the city, ver. 4, 5.

(1.) The honour and ornament of a nation departs. When a man departs from his house, the hangings are taken down, the furniture removed, and the walls left bare. Length of days are the blessings of wisdom's right hand, riches and honour the treasures of her left hand, Prov. iii. 16. She departs not from any, to leave her hands, and the blessings of her hands, behind her.

(2.) The strength of a nation departs. The ordinances of God are the towers of Sion. The temple was not only a place of worship, but a bulwark too. The ark was often carried with the Israelites into their camp, because there their strength lay; and when David was chased away by his son Absalom, he takes the ark of the tabernacle as his greatest strength against the defection of his son and subjects. When the gospel goes, God continues no longer the protector of a people. When a man hath packed up his wares, and removed them, he cares not much what becomes of the house he hath left, which, while he is in it, he will defend to the utmost. When the ark was taken by the Philistines, what a rout is there among the Israelites, thirty thousand of them slain; Eli, the High Priest, breaks his neck; his sons fall in the battle; and the strength and glory were departed from Israel, 1 Sam. iv. The flourishing condition of the seven churches withered when the candlestick was removed. When the things of Jerusalem's peace were hid from their eyes, the destruction of their city followed, so that one stone was not left upon another, because they knew not the time of their visitation, Luke xix. 42, 44. Then the Roman eagles clapped their wings in judgment upon them; then did the armies of the enemies bring desolation upon the points of their swords; then was the temple filled with the blood of the worshippers, which had been formerly consecrated in a way of mercy by the blood of sacrifices; then were carcases heaped one upon another, and the survivors led in chains to a miserable captivity, or a disgraceful death. What a wasted wilderness is that land now, deprived of that ancient fruitfulness whereby it afforded maintenance to such multitudes, which in David's time were about one hundred and thirty thousand fighting men, yet thought by some not much bigger than Yorkshire! When the gospel of peace removes, eternal peace goes with it, temporal peace flies after it; and whatsoever is safe, profitable, prosperous, takes wings and attends it.

4. God hath no other intention in the removing the gospel, and unchurching a nation, but the utter ruin and destruction of that nation. Other judgments may be medicinal; this is killing. Other judgments may lance and let out the corrupt matter; this opens a passage for life, soul, and happiness. Other judgments are but scourges; this is a deadly wound. In other judgments, God may continue a Father; in this, he is no other than an enemy and a destroyer. Other judgments are upon our backs; but this is in our bowels. Other judgments may be for conversion; this takes away the means of conversion. The torments of hell are not inflicted for the conversion of the damned, nor the setting of the gospel sun for the conversion of a nation. Other judgments may be *nubecula cito transitura*, as the Father's speech was of the storm in Julian's time; but this is a covering the heavens with blackness, a pulling the sun out of the firmament. A deluge of other judgments may lift the ark higher, but this overthrows it. Other judgments may have their period; this is hardly reversed. Not one of the seven churches restored to their former beauty to this day. This is an absolute shutting the gates of heaven against a people, and entailing upon them death and curses.

5. This judgment is accompanied with spiritual judgments, which are the sorest. The pounding of the jewel is far worse, and of greater loss, than the breaking the casket. The judgment of being given up to our hearts' lusts, to sensuality, pride, hardness of heart, delusions to believe a lie, are the sorest judgments; they are like poison in the soul, that will never leave till it hath eaten out the vitals. There shall then be no divorce between men and their idols: Hosea iv. 11, 'Your daughters shall commit whoredom, and your spouses shall commit adultery,' *i. e.* spiritual adultery and idolatry. When the check of idolatry is gone, the fury of that lust will rage.

III. *Use.* Doth God often remove the gospel upon provocations, as the severest judgment he can inflict upon an unworthy people? Then,

1. Be afraid of this judgment. How do we know but that God hath limited the preaching of the gospel, and the standing of the candlestick in this and that place, only for a time; and when that is expired, it may be carried to another place? We see it hath been so with others. If he hath not spared the natural branches, nor the church next the primitive, nay, those churches where the gospel was planted by the apostles, what reason have we to think he should spare us, who have long ago discarded primitive discipline, and are in a fair way to throw away primitive doctrine after it? Is England better than Jerusalem and Ephesus? Are the privileges we enjoy a bar to the removal of it? Are our privileges greater than those churches which were planted by the apostles had? Yet the hand of God hath shaken them off. Did not the Jews oppose their descent from Abraham, to whom the promises were made, and the glory of their temple, as an invincible shield against all the threatenings of destruction by the prophets, as though God had been shut up in their temple, and so enamoured on the beauty of that

structure, that he could not have the heart to leave them? But are they not rejected, and the Gentiles received in their room? Is not that which was once the glory of their nation, and the wonder of the world, many an age since fallen to the ground and mouldered to dust? What though the gospel be not yet gone? That sin may lie at the door which is meritorious of its departure. God's patience doth still last, but will it always last? The gospel may shine bright one day, and be eclipsed the next hour. The Jews might say with confidence, 'Our temple yet stands,' till they heard the report of the Roman eagles marching towards them. The sun shone very bright that day Sodom was burned. The preaching the gospel in a plentiful manner is a sign of judgment when there is unfruitfulness under it. Was not the gospel preached to Jerusalem by the best preachers of it that ever were, the Son of God, and the apostles after him, not many years before the destruction of that city? God is quick in his judgments when the gospel is contemned. The black, red, and pale horse—plague, war, and famine—followed just upon the white horse, to cut off such as would not be conquered by him that sat on him, Rev. vi. 2, &c. The sun shines brightest many times when it is nearest setting. I must confess I am of the opinion that the gospel will never be perfectly and totally taken away from these western parts of the world. It hath borne up its head for many ages within the scent of Rome, in those of Piedmont, notwithstanding all endeavours to extinguish it. The slaying of the witnesses, or the two prophets, which perhaps is not far off, is not a corporal, but a political death. Their dead bodies would not then be suffered to lie in the streets three years and a half (which we must understand by the three days and a half, Rev. xi. 9); and the resurrection of them, the returning of the spirit of life into them, is not to be meant of the resurrection of their bodies, but the resurrection of their offices; which political slaying is to be not long before the fall of the tenth part of the city, *i. e.* Rome, that city being the tenth part in greatness now of what it was anciently. And before the fall of Babylon the everlasting gospel shall be published with more efficacy than in many years before, ver. 13; and therefore I think the gospel will never totally depart, though it may for a while be much obscured. And I cannot but mind you of an observation a Jewish writer hath of the lamps in the temple,* that though some of them went out in the night, yet the western lamp was always found burning. The lamps were representations of the gospel, and this might signify the perpetuity of the gospel in the western parts of the world, when we see it is extinguished, or at least burns very dim, in most of the eastern parts. Yet a great eclipse, I fear; the interposition of a black moon between us and the sun, an antichristian smoke out of the bottomless pit to darken the sun and the air. In the description of the Sardian church, Rev. iii. 1–3, which is the state of the church where we are, Christ speaks of decays coming on them with some sharp scourge, but doth not threaten the removal of the candlestick. And may we not have just reason to fear it? to fear, I say, a judgment like this of removing the gospel, the removal of it in part? Bethel, when Jacob laid his head there, was a place where angels went up and down in vision; afterwards it was changed into Bethaven, where calves and devils were worshipped, when Jeroboam swayed the sceptre.

(1.) Is not our profaneness a just ground of our fear? Is there not more wickedness found amongst us, where the glorious gospel hath shined, than among them that live under the fogs of the Turkish Alcoran? Have not our fruits been grapes of Sodom and clusters of Gomorrah? Have not many,

* Kimchi, in 1 Sam. iii., edit. by Lightfoot, Temple, chap. xiv. se. v. p. 83.

that have been lifted up to heaven by the presence of the gospel, walked as if they had the seal of hell in their foreheads? A fulness of iniquity makes the harvest ripe, and fit for the sickle, Joel iii. 13. Why may we not fear the clouding of the gospel, as well as we have heard of Moses his breaking of the tables of the law, when he found a people given to luxury, sensuality, and idolatry? When Eli the priest is remiss, and Phinehas his son is profane; when there is little care of the true worship of God, and no censures for profaneness of life, is not the fruit of this an *Ichabod*, 'the departure of the glory from Israel'? 1 Sam. iv. 21. What can be expected, when the punishment of profaneness is neglected, and the practice of piety hath been discouraged? When the Jewish vineyard brought forth wild grapes, God commanded the clouds to rain no more upon it, Isa. v. 6.

(2.) Is not the slighting of the means of grace a just ground of this fear? When reformations have not answered calls, nor improvement answered mercies conferred; when we have fought against God with his own gifts, and contemned that rich mercy we cannot want without ruin. Doth not every man's observation witness, that this contempt of the gospel hath been a national sin in those frequent and repeated endeavours to suppress the purity of it, and tire out the professors thereof: and as a great man saith, they had rather part with the gospel, than part with a rag. And is it not to be observed, that in many of those places where the gospel was powerfully preached in our memories, the very sense of it seems to be worn out? What can be expected, when children throw a precious commodity in the dirt, but that the parents should take it away and lay it in another place, and lash them too for their vanity? God will not obtrude the gospel long against men's wills. When the Gadarenes desired Christ to depart from their coasts, Christ granted their wish and turned his back. When there is no delight in the word, Sabbath, gospel, then comes a famine of the word, Amos viii. 5. After Christ had pronounced a woe upon Bethsaida, Mat. xi. 21, though he came afterwards to the town and had the opportunity of curing a blind man, he would not do it in the town, and commanded him, after he was restored, not to go into the town, nor tell it to any inhabitants of it, Mark viii. 22, 26. He would spill no water upon that ground he had cursed. We shall know God, 'if we follow on to know the Lord.' If we then neglect the knowledge of God, which is the end of the gospel, to what purpose should means of knowledge continue among us? God will not suffer the waters of life to run there, where he sees they will altogether run waste. The gospel hath too much worth, and the honour of God is too much interested in it, to leave it exposed to the injuries of men, without revenging it.

(3.) And what shall I say of the barrenness of the church's womb? How few real converts are there brought forth of the church's womb, and nursed upon the church's knees? God seems to have written barrenness upon her womb, and dryness upon her breasts. Doth not ignorance sway, where before the gospel triumphed? When the ground yields but a faint increase, and answers not the cost and labour of the husbandman, he lays it fallow. The abatement of the powerful workings of the Spirit, is a presage of a removal or dimming the light in the candlestick. When God withdraws gifts from his ministers, and the Spirit from the hearers, it is a sign he will take away that lamp, into which he will pour no more oil.

May we not add to this, the apostasy of the age? Where is the old primitive spirit, I had almost said puritan spirit, that sincere love to all the truths of the gospel, that valuation of all its ordinances? What generous designs are taken up to glorify and propagate it? Here is pride and worldliness, lik l ‿araoh's lean kine, devour the fat ones of spiritual duties. How seldom have we a sense of God, an estimation of Christ, when we speak of him!

(4.) And may not the errors in the nation step in as the occasion of our fears? Not little petty errors, but errors about the foundation, when the doctrine of justification is not only denied, but scoffed at; a doctrine which, as it was owned or opposed, was deservedly accounted in the first times of the Reformation, *articulus stantis et cadentis ecclesiæ.*

(5.) What should I speak of the divisions amongst us? These preceded the ruin of the Jews, and made way for the fall of the seven churches in Asia. By these did Rome grow to that height, as to put a veil upon the gospel, and in most places to extinguish it. The concord of the ancient Christians was the cause of the flourishing progress and increase of the gospel; when they began to scuffle, their feuds rose to such a height, as threw down the candle which gave them light, and ruined that which the union of the former Christians had strongly built. When children fall out and fight about the candle, the parents come and take it away, and leave them to divide* their differences in the dark.† We may justly fear, God will take away that light which we quarrel by, instead of walking and working by.

(6.) May we not consider also the death of the ablest ministers as a sad prognostic? Sometimes, indeed, the removal of signal instruments portends a nearness of some great appearance of God. When the people were upon the skirts of Caanan, first Aaron and then Moses are snatched away; but there were others to succeed in their room: a zealous Phinehas was left behind Aaron, and a courageous Joshua succeeded Moses. Many good men may do things offensive to God, and the work of their generation, for which cause God will not let them live to see the blessings he is bringing upon a people. But, alas, it is often a sign of an approaching judgment. When the Lord gives out his word, 'great is the company of them that publish it,' Ps. lxviii. 11; when the Lord will remove his word, small is the company of them that publish it, till at last not one labourer may be left, because God will not have a harvest to gather in, but leave the place as a wild field to ravenous beasts and the fowls of the air. Methuselah is taken away just before the deluge; and Ambrose his head was scarce cold in his grave before the Goths invaded and wasted Italy. It was observed by the Jews, that while they were in God's favour, before the sun of one righteous man set, the sun of another righteous man did arise. Before Moses' sun set, Joshua's sun arose; before Eli's sun set, Samuel's sun arose; and this, they say, is the meaning of that place, 1 Sam. iii. 9, that before the lamp of God went out, the spirit of prophecy came upon Samuel. Is it thus with us? Doth a new spring equal the old stock that are gone? How few do possess a prophet's spirit among them that wear a prophet's garment!

We may well therefore fear an eclipse of the gospel, and many eyes may not see the emerging of it out of that eclipse. It is worth our consideration, that when the spies that were sent to Canaan returned, and gave a good report of the land, the common multitude would not believe them, they would return back to Egypt; and though they had been lashed for their murmuring, yet after this provocation, and the slighting the good land, and the perfection of the deliverance in the possession of Canaan, God swore the destruction of that generation, Numb. xiv. 21–23 (though because of the word passed he did not deprive their posterity of the enjoyment of the promised land); and God never left, till he had swept away that generation, before the people came to Canaan.

Use 2. If the removal of the gospel be so great a judgment, we have

* Qu. 'decide'?—Ed.

† Fuller.

reason to bless God for its continuance so long among us. What a grace is it, that God hath drawn us out of the depths of error and folly, wherein other nations have been plunged so long a time! How mercifully hath God indulged us that which thousands of heathens have wanted, and do to this day! Many in the world never enjoyed it, and many that have had it have now lost it. We have been like Gideon's fleece, wet, while most of the world have been dry. He hath nourished us with heavenly manna, making it to fall every day at our gates, without putting us to much labour to gather it. That ever God should vouchsafe a light to direct us, who are descended from a race of first pagan, and then popish idolaters, plunged in superstition! How criminal will our ingratitude be, if we have not lively resentments of his immense goodness! God hath yet rained upon us, and not upon many of our neighbours, who are under the thickness of popish fogs. We are yet in the way where his blessings be, and where his heavenly manna often falls. How deplorable would our case have been, if we had been starved for want of food! Had the sun been extinguished, and the stars put out, and our residence had been in a gloomy and dolesome world, ignorance might have bemisted our minds, and an implicit faith, we know not in what, have hoodwinked us to damnation; our Bibles might have been as sealed books, and a crime as bad as atheism so much as to peep into the word of God. Traditions might have been mingled with the oracles of God, whereby the wisdom of God would have been blemished; the merits of Christ might have been mated with the merits of men, whereby the grace of God would have been dimmed, and worship given to idols and images, whereby the glory of God would have been rifled. What a ravishing mercy is it, that our brains have not been knocked out by St Peter's successor! that God hath hitherto continued our preservation, when the seal of the fisher had ratified our destruction! Antichristianism leaves men in thick darkness. It is the gospel dispels our ignorance, and disperseth the beams of saving knowledge. It is this which rescues you from despair, by shewing you the doctrine of justification, which heathens could never attain to, and antichristianism would fain expunge out of the world. It is the gospel acquaints you with the fulness of the satisfaction of Christ; whereas antichristianism would fright you with a pretended fire of purgatory, to empty your purses, and defeat your heirs. The gospel teaches you to worship God only; whereas antichristianism would divert your prayers to saints, perhaps to St Garnet and St Fawkes, saints of a new stamp, and saints of so bad a hue, that a sober man would never admit to be his servants. It is the gospel that fills you with peace, that settles you upon the basis of an infinite satisfaction of the Redeemer, that elevates you in a sincere belief, not only above the fears of a pretended purgatory, but of a real hell. It is the gospel that puts you upon a real sanctification, a mortification of lust by the power of Christ's death, and the grace of his Spirit, not by bodily torturings, whereby the soul may be rendered unfit for its proper function in worship. It is the gospel that directs us in an inward holiness of heart, and frees us from being painted tombs and gilded sepulchres. How much ought we to bless God for the continuance of this gospel among us!

3. It should teach us to improve the gospel while we enjoy it. The time of the gospel revelation is the time of working. Good entertainment and good improvement invites the gospel to stay; ill usage drives it out of doors. God hath allowed us his gospel, and set his candlestick among us, but not left it to our discretion to do with it what we please; he hath given it to us, as he did the angel to the Israelites, to comfort and conduct them, Exod.

xxiii. 20, 21; but with a caution not to despise and provoke him, because his name was in him.* Let us improve the gospel dispensation to the getting a gospel nature. It is not enough to be within the visible ark; so was a cursed Ham. Let us not receive the grace of God in vain, but adorn the gospel by a gospel spirit and a gospel practice, and walk as children of light. Let us not trample it under our feet, but put our souls under the efficacy of it, and get from it the foretastes of a heavenly and everlasting life. Let us not loiter while the sun shines, lest we be benighted, bewildered, and misled into quagmires and puddles by some *ignis fatuus*. We cannot command the sun to stand still and attend our pleasure; it will go its course according to the word of its governor, and listen not to the follies of men, nor stay for their loiterings. Let not an antichristian principle reign in your hearts; implicit faith is against the improvement of the gospel; there is as much of it in practice in England as there is of principle in Rome. How many believe as their church, or churchmen believe, without being able to render a reason why they do so? The gospel was given for every man to study and embrace, to embrace knowingly, not blindly. If we do not increase in knowledge and grace by it, we anticipate the judgment of God; we remove that from us voluntarily which God accounts the removal of judicially to be the most deplorable misery. If we do not improve and hold fast what we have received and heard, the coming of Christ in a way of revenge will be sudden, like a thief in the night, and we shall not know what hour he will come upon us till we feel the stroke; I mean not by death, but some sore scourge, for so he speaks to the church of Sardis, the state wherein the church is at this day, Rev. iii. 3.

4. Let us prevent by repentance and prayer the removal or eclipse of the gospel. The loss of your estates, the massacring of your children, the chains of captivity, are a thousand times more desirable than this deplorable calamity. Estates may be recovered, new children raised, fetters may be knocked off, new houses may be reared upon the ashes of the consumed ones, the possession of a country regained, but it is seldom the gospel returns when carried away upon the wings of the wind. God indeed is interested in the preservation of religion and a church, but not in this or that particular church, not among this or that particular people; rather than want one, he will raise up stones to be children to Abraham. As he will not have his blessings abused, so he will not have his gospel extinguished in all parts of the world, or all parts of this western world. But doth this secure us from any great eclipse? What if God will not remove his gospel? may he not suffer many to be infected with popery? May not many of your friends, children, be tainted with this leprosy, that may prove incurable in them? What if there be a likelihood that it will not endure long? If it shall enter upon the stage must we not therefore endeavour to prevent it? Prophecy is the rule of our foresight, precept is the rule of our duty. What if God will not remove the gospel, may he not bring a sharp persecution? Is not the enemy at our door; the rod shaken over our heads? Have we not gathered the twigs of it ourselves, and formed a scourge for our own backs? Did we not first let in the serpent's head, and what should we expect but that he will get in his whole body? What can we expect but that God should begin his judgments at his own house, and scrape the sides of his sanctuary that have been defiled with so much filthiness? Let us therefore meet God in an humble reforming posture, and lay hold on his strength; consider where we left him, and do our first work, whence we are fallen, and fallen by our own fault and peevishness, fallen from a zeal for

* Claud de Nopces, p. 179.

God, a national endeavour for the propagation of the gospel. Let us desire him, as the disciples that were going to Emmaus did Christ, Luke xxiv. 29, 'Lord, abide with us, for the evening begins to come, and the day is far spent.' Our Saviour did so, and gave them his blessing before he vanished again out of their sight. God may deal so with us, and leave some notable blessing with us, till he comes again to pitch his sanctuary in the midst of us for evermore, as the promise is, Ezek. xxxvii. 28.

Let us therefore seek to him, chiefly to him, only to him; he only can remove the candlestick, he only can put his hand as a bar upon the light; men may be instrumental, but it is Christ only removes the candlestick, and he only can maintain it against the puffs of men and devils. He hath the enemies in a chain, and the full command of their breath. Place no confidence in men, some may have some power to give relief, and will not; others may have will to help, and cannot. If we maintain our feud with God, he will bid the gospel go, and it shall go; if we make our peace with him, he will bid the gospel stay, and it shall stay. As he hath angels to bring, so he hath angels to carry away the everlasting gospel. Remember the threatening in the text is not absolute, there is an *else* and an *except* to mitigate it. 'Remember from whence thou art fallen, and repent, and do thy first works; or *else* I will come unto thee quickly, and remove thy candlestick out of his place, *except* thou repent.'

A DISCOURSE OF MERCY RECEIVED.

Thy vows are upon me, O God: I will render praises unto thee. For thou hast delivered my soul from death: wilt not thou deliver my feet from falling, that I may walk before God in the light of the living?—Ps. LVI. 12, 13.

This psalm was penned by David when he was in a notable affliction, when the Philistines took him in Gath. David had fled from the fury of Saul to Abimelech, otherwise Achish, king of Gath, a city of the Philistines, 1 Sam. xxi. 10, 12, 13, where he changed his behaviour. Whether this was penned at the same time that the 34th Psalm was, or before, is uncertain. Perhaps before; for it is said, 'When they took him in Gath.' Though David fled thither for the preservation of his life, yet being known to be that famous person who had been celebrated in the songs of the Israelites, as slaying his ten thousands in the slaughter of Goliath, 1 Sam. xxi. 11, he might perhaps be apprehended as a suspected person, coming thither upon design; or else from desire to revenge themselves upon him for the slaughter of Goliath, who was their countryman and citizen; for he was of Gath, 1 Sam. xvii. 23. And some appearance there is that it was this, by Achish his speech to his servants: 1 Sam. xxi. 14, 'Lo, you see the man is mad; wherefore have you brought him to me?' Howsoever it was, he was in some trouble; yet still keeps his faith and hope as an anchor fixed on God: ver. 3, 'What time I am afraid, I will trust in thee.' And his assurance of deliverance upon his prayer: ver. 9, 'When I cry unto thee, then shall mine enemies turn back: this I know; for God is for me. In God will I praise his word; in the Lord I will praise his word. In God have I put my trust: I will not be afraid what man can do unto me.' And stirs up himself to thankfulness upon the remembrance of former mercies: ver. 12, 'Thy vows,' &c.; and to confidence for future: ver. 13, 'For thou hast delivered,' &c.

You have here,

1. The commemoration of former mercies: 'Thou hast delivered.'
2. The confidence of future: 'Wilt not thou?'
3. The end of all: 'To walk before God in the light of the living.'

Vows. 'Thy vows are upon me, O God.' Passively, vows made to God, not by God; or the obligations of those vows and prayers which I have made, and upon which I have received answers. Sacrifices of thanksgiving were called vows, as having been vowed to God upon the want, and to be paid upon the receipt, of mercy: Lev. i. 1, 'If the sacrifice that is offered be a vow.' Thy vows are upon me; the fruit of my vows, so that I stand indebted to God for the return of praise.

'Thou hast delivered.' He understands some great danger, wherein he had sunk, had not God stood by him. And from a greater mercy, the deliverance of his soul from death, argues for a less, the keeping his feet from falling.

'That I may walk before God in the light of the living.' By light of the living is meant life, which is called being enlightened with the 'light of the living,' Job xxxiii. 30. Sometimes eternal life in heaven: John viii. 12, 'He that follows me shall not walk in darkness, but shall have the light of life.'

'To walk before God.' To walk obediently in the sight of God, with a respect to his presence; a walking unto all well-pleasing. This is the last argument in the psalm, whereon he builds his strongest plea, as if he knew not what to urge if this should fail him; as if he should have said, Lord, I have had experience of thy wisdom in contriving, thy power in effecting, thy mercy in bestowing deliverance upon me, thy goodness in answering my vows and prayers. 'Thou hast delivered from death,' a danger as great and unavoidable as death itself. O Lord, art thou not the same that thou wert? Art thou not still as wise to design, and as gracious to confer further mercy? Wilt thou not as certainly also deliver my feet from falling? The one contains his experience, the other the inference or conclusion he draws from it.

Doct. 1. Mercies received, are in a special manner to be remembered.

2. Mercies received are encouragements to ask, and strong grounds to hope for the mercies we want.

For the first, mercies received are in a special manner to be remembered. This has been the method of God's people. David entitles Psalm xxxviii., 'A psalm to bring to remembrance his afflictions,' much more then his comforts: Ps. lxxvii. 10, 11, 'I will remember the years of the right hand of the Most High; I will remember the works of the Lord.' Paul remembered a manifestation of God to him fourteen years before, 2 Cor. xii. 1. If God treasures up our tears, much more should we treasure up his mercies; as lovers keep the love tokens of those they affect. God hath a file for our prayers, we should have the like for his answers. He hath a book of remembrance to record our afflictions, and believing discourses of him, Mal. iii. 16; why should not we, then, have a register for his gracious communications to us? Remembrance is the chief work of a Christian; remembrance of sin to cause a self-abhorrency: Ezek. xx. 43, 'There shall you remember your ways, and loathe yourselves.' The remembrance of God for a deep humility: Ps. lxxvii. 3, 'I remembered God, and was troubled.' Remembrance of his name for keeping his law, Ps. cxix. 55. Remembrance of his judgments of old for comfort in afflictions, Ps. cxix. 52. And remembrance of mercy for the establishment of faith: Isa. lvii. 11, 'Of whom hast thou been afraid, and hast not remembered me?' It is observed by some that Shushan, the royal seat of the Persian, was pictured upon the east gate of the temple, to mind them of the wonder of Purim, Esther ix. 26; the deliverance they had in that place from Haman, by God's ordering Mordecai's advancement. Jacob changed the name of Luz into Bethel, that the new name might be a memorial of God's comfortable apparition to him, both to himself and his posterity, Gen. xxviii. 19.

They are to be remembered, because,

1. They are the mercies of God. They are dispensed out of the treasury of his goodness, wrought by the art of his wisdom, effected by the arm of his

power. Christ evidenced this by praying to his Father for the mercies he wanted, by blessing him as the fountain of any mercy received. The great dominion Christ hath is from God; it is first, 'Ask of me,' Ps. ii. 8; yea, though wrought by means. The woman doth touch the hem of Christ's garment, but the healing virtue springs from Christ. Men may spread their nets, toil and labour nights, and days, and years, and catch nothing, unless Christ sends the fish into the net, Luke v. 5, 6: 'Our works are in the hands of God,' Eccles. ix. 5. Though our works, yet in God's hand, he pours forth his blessing, he gives success. The first link of the chain of mercy is in God's hand. If we do not then remember them, and him in them, we deny his providence and goodness, and pay that to the servant which is due to the Lord: 'We should remember his love more than wine,' Cant. i. 4; his love in mercies more than the choicest delights of earth. No gift so small, but is a messenger from the great God, and hath the badge of his name upon it.

2. Mercies purchased by Christ. Mercies dear bought by the best blood that ever was in the world. The print of Christ's nails are upon every one of his blessings, the least as well as the greatest. 'Ye are not your own, ye are bought with a price,' 1 Cor. vi. 19. You and your bodies, and the preservation of your bodies, you and what you have, you and your mercies, and your comforts, are all purchased by another, and freely conferred upon you; worthy, therefore, of remembrance.

3. Mercies beneficial to us. We should certainly remember those things whereof we carry the sensible marks upon us.

2. How we should remember them.

(1.) Admiringly and thankfully. We should observe God's mercies, not only as works, but as wonders: Ps. lxxvii. 11, 'I will remember the works of the Lord; surely I will remember his wonders of old,' to admire them and the author. Old antedated mercies, as well as fresh, should fill us with new astonishments; not a speculative but an elevating remembrance, to cry out with raised spirits, how great God is: ver. 13, 'Who is so great a God as our God!' Paul never looked back upon God's mercies in his conversion, without a new admiration: 1 Tim. i. 12, 'I thank Jesus Christ, our Lord, who hath enabled me.' This was not enough; it was a peg too low for so great a mercy, till he rises up into an high doxology, ver. 17, 'Now unto the King eternal, immortal, invisible, the only wise God, be honour and glory for ever and ever.' What an heaven sparkles here in Paul's language, so like that of glory! Shall we not have thankful frames in the remembrance of them, when we should stand ready with praise to meet every mercy in its first motion: Ps. lxv. 1, 'Praise waits for thee in Sion.' Mercy in its first step should not find us a minute without a thankful frame. As God waits for an opportunity to be gracious, we should wait with praise in our mouths to be thankful to him; a volley of praise should stand ready to meet a shower of mercy. They did not think amiss, that asserted a main part of religion to consist in admiration; this had been the work in innocency. Many other duties have been introduced by a fallen state; this is an entrance into a state of innocency, by reassuming the duty of that state, an entrance into the state of heaven by beginning the work of it; this is the eternal religion. Not a bullock nor a goat was to be killed for a man's own table in the wilderness, but they were to bring it 'to the door of the tabernacle, and offer an offering to the Lord;' if not, they were accounted murderers, Lev. xvii. 3, 4. God must be acknowledged in all.

(2.) Affectionately. What a deep print of love did the kindness of Christ stamp upon many whose diseases he cured upon the earth! We then rightly remember them, when they raise choice affections to God in us. It was God's promise: Hosea xiii. 4, 'Yet I am the Lord thy God from the land of Egypt; thou shalt know no other god but me.' Love no god, acknowledge no god but me, because I have brought you out of the land of Egypt, and maintained you by a constant succession of merciful streams of benefits. We begin to love God by the knowledge faith gives us of him; but the experience of his mercy renders him more amiable, and the consideration of it should render our love more lively. Our very common mercies should not be thought of without affection, much less our spiritual. The deliverance of our bodies from death deserves a return of love, much more the redemption of our souls. Remember them warmly, so as to kindle a flame of love. That is not properly remembered, that works not a suitable impression in the review of it; he rather forgets his sin, that remembers it without a disaffection to it; and he his mercies, that thinks of them without being raised in affection to God by them.

3. Obediently and fruitfully. David, upon the remembrance of it, would walk before God in the land of the living. They are given to encourage us in his service, and should be therefore remembered to that end. Rain descends upon the earth, not that it might be more barren, but more fertile. We are but stewards; the mercies we enjoy are not our own, and therefore to be improved for our Master's service. Great mercies should engage to great obedience. God begins the Decalogue with a memorial of that mercy in bringing the Israelites out of Egypt: Exod. xx. 2, 'I am the Lord thy God, which brought thee out of the land of Egypt.' How affectionately doth the psalmist own his relation to God as his servant, when he considered how God had loosed his bonds: Ps. cxvi. 16, 'O Lord, truly I am thy servant; thou hast loosed my bonds!' the remembrance of thy mercy shall make me know no relation but that of a servant to thee. When we remember what wages we have from God, we must withal remember that we owe more service, and more liveliness in service, to him. Duty is but the ingenuous consequent of mercy. It is irrational to encourage ourselves in our way to hell by a remembrance of heaven, to foster a liberty in sin by a consideration of God's bounty. When we remember all that we have or are is the gift of God's liberality, we should think ourselves obliged to honour him with all that we have, for he is to have honour from all his gifts. It is a sign we aimed at God's glory in the begging mercy, when we also aim at God's glory in the enjoying of it. It is a sign love breathed the remembrance of mercy into our hearts, when at the same time it breathes a resolution into us to improve it. It is not our tongues, but our lives must praise him. Mercies are not given to one member, but the whole man. Thanks without obedience is but flattery; it is but Hail, master, while we crown him with thorns.

(4.) Humbly. Remembrance of free mercies should not be attended with a forgetfulness of our own sinfulness, nor increase our pride, but our humiliation. When Peter saw so great a stock of fish driven into the net, he had the lowest thoughts of himself: Luke v. 8, 'He fell down at Jesus's knees, saying, I am a sinful man, O Lord.' What a gracious frame is that, when the remembrance of mercy brings us upon our knees to a humble confession of sin! Kindness makes wicked men more proud, and good men more broken. We are usually as lead melted in the fire of affliction, and hardened in the fresh air of prosperity, and grow inactive; but let it be otherwise.

(5.) In the circumstances. As circumstances adorn our actions, so they beautify God's mercies, the manner, the time, &c. Every line in mercy owns God as the author, as well as the whole mass. Mercy beaten to pieces, as spice, will yield a sweeter scent than in the lump. Remember what misery preceded the mercy; as it made the mercy the sweeter, so it will make the remembrance of it more savoury: Hosea ii. 15, 'I will give her her vineyard from thence;' that is, from the wilderness; 'then shall she sing as in the day of her youth.' 'Thy heart shall meditate terror,' Isa. xxxiii. 18. Thou shalt consider what thy troubles were, and what the frame of thy heart was, and what thy vows and resolutions were in thy distress. It is good to call to mind what desires, what fervency in prayer, there was before the mercy came, and upon the remembrance of the mercy to act the same fervour over again.

6. Argumentatively and fiducially. But this leads to the next observation.

Doct. 2. That mercies received are encouragements to ask, and ground to hope, for the mercies we want. In spiritual blessings it certainly holds; they are earnests of other blessings of the same kind; and, as it were, obligations wherein God binds himself to bestow greater blessings hereafter. They are but further confirmations of his promise for encouragement of our faith. As 'whatsoever is written in Scripture is for our comfort and our hope,' Rom. xv. 4, so as much as God hath performed of Scripture to us is for the same end.

In temporal mercies. God intends them to his people as means to settle their faith faster on him, and make them trust him in future exigencies. When God commands Jacob to remove to another place, he puts him in mind how he was with him when he fled from the face of his brother Esau, Gen. xxxv. 1. It is an argument Moses used to God when he was in a great anger against the Israelites: Num. xiv. 19, 'Thou hast forgiven this people from Egypt until now;' *i. e.* thou hast preserved them, notwithstanding their murmurings. Upon this argument, though Moses had used others before, God presently answers, 'I have pardoned according to thy word.' How ready was God to yield to motions of mercy, when his former kindness to them was pleaded! Paul doth thus act faith on God: 2 Cor. i. 10, 'Who hath delivered us from so great a death, and doth deliver.' What is the consequence? 'In whom we trust that he will yet deliver.' And the psalmist makes this a medium to tie his two petitions together: Ps. iv. 1, 'Hear me when I call: thou hast enlarged me when I was in distress; have mercy upon me, and hear my prayer;' and expresseth his confidence, from his experience of former deliverances, that he should have a quick answer at any time: ver. 3, 'The Lord will hear me when I call upon him.' For,

1. There is as great an ability in God, when we are in need of new mercies, as there was when he gave former ones; nay, as much as there was from eternity. He is not a God whose arm is shortened, that is not what he was, or shall ever cease to be what he is: Isa. lix. 2, 'Is my hand shortened at all that I cannot redeem, or have I no power to deliver?' He is always, *I am that I am.* There is no diminution of light in the sun no more than there was at the first moment of its creation, and the last man upon the earth shall enjoy as much of it as we do now. No more doth the Father of lights lose by imparting it to others. Thus we light many candles at a torch, yet it burns never the dimmer. Standing waters may be drawn dry, but a fountain cannot. God is a spring, this day and to-morrow, Jehovah unchangeable. The God of Isaac is not like Isaac, that had one blessing and no more; he hath as much now as he had the first moment that mercy streamed from him to his creature, and the same for as many as shall believe

in Christ to the end of the world; nay, the more we receive from God in a way of faith, the more God hath for us. A believer's harvest for present mercies is his seed-time for more. The more mercies he reaps, the more hopes of future mercy he hath. God's mercies, when full blown, seed again and come up thicker. Can the creature want more than the everlasting fountain can supply? Can the creature's indigency be greater than God's sufficiency? What an irrational way of arguing was that: Ps. lxxviii. 20, 'He smote the rock, that the waters gushed out; can he give bread also? can he provide for his people?' as if he that filled their cup could not spread their table, as if he that had a hidden cellar for their drink had not a secret and as full a cupboard for their meat. Do we want mercies for soul and body? Look to the rock whence former mercies were hewn: the same fulness can supply again.

2. There is as much tenderness in God as there was before. His power is more unquestionable with us than his goodness. We think his compassions come short of his ability. We question more his will than his strength: Mat. viii. 2, 'If thou wilt, thou canst make me clean.' If thou wilt, thou canst give me mercy as well as before. You may be sure Christ will speak still the same language, *I will.* I will give thee spirituals and temporals, so far as are good for thee. His bowels can no more be straitened than his arm is shortened; his compassions fail not, Lam. iii. 22. All his attributes are alike essential to him. As he cannot but be God, so he cannot but be powerful, he cannot but be true. His truth lies in pawn for the constancy of his good will to them that trust in him. Let your condition be what it will, there is some promise to suit it. There is a condition for faith to beg, and his truth is engaged to make good one promise as well as another. He is a Father, a tender Father, surpassing in tenderness all natural affections. No kind father doth ever tell his child, I will do no more for you. The heavenly Father will not, who delights more in giving than we do in receiving. God's love is not as ours, a sudden passion, but a resolve of eternity.

3. There is the same ground to beg and believe for mercies we want, as there was for the mercies we have received. We are under the same covenant, the influence of the same mediator. Should not our faith be more abundant, since we have more evidences of the graciousness of God, the prevalency of the Mediator, and stability of the covenant? Was it not upon this account you did plead with God for what you had before? Were not your arguments drawn from God's name, his covenant, his Son? They are arguments that can never want a force while God is God; they are as unanswerable as ever. Will God disown his name, deny his promise, overlook his Son? Doth the covenant reach only to those mercies we have received? Did Christ purchase no more? Then indeed our expectations may dolefully flag; we may take our leaves of ever hoping for mercy from him. But his promise is for this life, all the parts of it, and for that which is to come. It hath been tried millions of times, and always found sound: Ps. xii. 6, 'The word of the Lord is as silver tried in a furnace of earth, purified seven times;' seven times, multitudes of times, seven being a number of perfection. It hath been tried in many furnaces of affliction. It is an everlasting covenant: God's name is his self, and endures for ever. The blood of Christ is of infinite value. The Mediator is the same yesterday, to-day, and for ever; the same in his affection to his people; the same in his prevalency with God. The plea therefore upon this account is as firm for all mercies and for all times. Christ's blood was slain to pay for the mercies you have received. The mercies we expect to eternity are conveyed to us this way, so are the mercies we expect in time. The believers of old had what they

had upon these accounts. These arguments have always been used, and have been of force to prevail; the same arguments shall always be used, and have the same efficacy. The covenant, the blood of the covenant, reacheth far beyond what we have, though it be never so great, in this world.

4. One mercy in spirituals is to no purpose without further mercies. God would not lay a foundation, and not build upon it. He is not light and uncertain in his actions. He knew before he gave the first spiritual mercy what charge you would be to him. He sat down and counted all, and he cannot be disappointed, since nothing can happen but what he did foresee. To what purpose should one forgive a debtor a part of the debt, and lay him in prison for the remainder? To what purpose should God begin to heal a leprous soul, and take away a part of the disease, if he did not intend to master all, and expel the *fomes* of it? To what purpose hath God given Christ to any, if he did not intend freely to give all things necessary with him? Rom. viii. 32. All temporals are but dross and dung in comparison of him. Has God been at so much charge for you at the expense of his Son's blood, and did he not stick there? What, then, can limit the mercy of God? Upon these accounts, then, former mercies, especially spiritual, are good arguments to plead with God, and good grounds of hope and trust in him for future ones.

Use 1. Take heed of forgetting mercies received. Keep a catalogue of mercies to quicken your love, wind up your thankfulness, and encourage your faith. We can remember ourselves when we pray for mercy, and forget God when we receive it, and the mercy itself not long after. We cannot profit by mercies unless we thankfully remember them: direct rays convey not so much warmth without reflecting back upon the sun. God remembers the kindness of our youth to him, Jer. ii. 2. Why should not we remember the tenderness of his grace to us? Great comforts must be especially remembered; they come but seldom. Paul had but one special rapture in fourteen years. Let every new mercy call the old to mind. The mercy of the lamb put them in mind of his mercy to Moses, and the Israelites, Rev. xv. 3. 'Bless the Lord from the fountain of Israel,' Ps. lxviii. 26, *i. e.* from the very first mercy. Remember also the impressions God makes upon your souls under the influence of your mercies. Keep them alive and fresh; it is a way to procure more from God when he beholds such valuations of them.

Let us observe, therefore, God's motions to us in mercy, and see how he walks with us, and our motions to God in duty, to see how we walk with him, especially in the mercies which are fruits of prayer. Hannah called her son which she had received as an answer of prayer, *Samuel*, that in the hearing the name she might remember God's kindness.

(1.) Without a remembrance of them, we shall be very apt to distrust God, and abate in our love. The death of our experiences is the resurrection of our distrust. When we write mercies in the sand, the next wind makes the letters invisible, and our fears terrible. When the Israelites forgot that power that had provided for them, their corruption took heart to express itself in murmuring: Ps. lxxviii. 19, 'Can he spread a table in the wilderness?' If you remember the time when you were cast down in sorrow, and found God raising you up and embracing you in the arms of a tender love, such a remembrance would not easily admit jealousies of him into the room with it, unless you have ceased to be his followers and given him cause to withdraw his care. God breaks not with us till we break with him. When David had drawn a catalogue of God's former mercies towards him, he concludes it with a 'Surely goodness and mercy should follow me all the days of my life,' and takes up resolutions to stick to God in holy affections, 'and I will dwell in the house of the Lord for ever,' Ps. xxiii. 6.

(2.) Without a remembrance of them we cannot so well improve them. If we do not remember what talents of mercy we have, how can we employ them? What account can we give to the supreme Lord of whom we received them? An account there must be, for God cannot be conceived in reason to be careless whether his blessings were improved, and regardless whether the fruit of his mercy lost or not. We are accountable for the mercies received by our ancestors that we have the knowledge of, much more for our own. God brings an indictment against Eli for sinning against the first mercy to Aaron: 1 Sam. ii. 27, 'Did I plainly appear to the house of thy father when they were in Egypt, in Pharaoh's house?' The debt due from our fathers must be paid by the heirs; as we enjoy the profit of them, it is fit we should pay our great Creditor, much more for those immediately bestowed upon us, superadded to what is derived by succession. How can we do either without remembrance? If we forget them, we must needs forget the hand that gave them, and the gratitude we owe for them, and hereby not only become false to our Creator ourselves, but make his mercies prove false to the end for which he sent them. The end of every mercy is to glorify God: Ps. l. 15, 'I will deliver thee, and thou shalt glorify me;' what glorifying God with forgetfulness of what he wrought for us?

(3.) Without a remembrance of them, we shall not so easily resist temptations. An ingenuous spirit under a sense of mercy could not easily lend an ear to an enticing temptation, and be drawn to do wickedness and sin against the author of his mercy. 'Shall I thus requite the Lord, who hath made and established me?' Moses intimates the forgetting this to be the ground of their unworthy usage of God, Deut. xxxii. 6. Have I thus learned Christ? Did mercy drop any such instruction into me to sin? If I had not been a subject of his mercy, I had not now lived to be tempted; and shall I live by that mercy to embrace a temptation? 'Since thou hast given us such a deliverance as this, shall we again break thy commandments?' saith good Ezra, chap. ix. 13. The goodness of God is to lead us to repentance; how would the remembrance of it strengthen us against a temptation!

Use 2. Make use of former mercies to encourage your trust for the future. Was it God's end in giving us mercies to encourage our jealousies of his faithfulness or our hopes of his goodness? It is fit we should trust God upon his bare word, much more upon a trial of him. If we can say, God hath delivered, and therefore he will deliver, why may we not with as good reason say, We have trusted God, and will trust him still? We have not only heard how faithful and good he is, but we have also seen, known it, found him to be so. If, after the knowledge of his name, we trust him not, we have a frame contrary to that which should be in all believers: Ps. ix. 10, 'They that know thy name will put their trust in thee.' If we trust him not after mercies received, he may well reproach us for our jealousy. What! Did I ever fail you? did you seek my face in vain? have you found me false to you? nay, have I not been good to you above your expectations? What iniquity then is there in me, that you should have any suspicious thoughts of my goodness? With what haste doth David catch at Goliath's sword when Abimelech told him there was none but that in the tabernacle: 1 Sam. xxi. 9, 'There is none like that, give it me,' as having experienced God's former kindness by it. Moses would shew the rod of God, the rod whereby he had wrought wonders, when he prayed for the discomfiture of Amalek, Exod. xvii. 9, as if no mercy could be denied him, when the rod in his hand pleaded the power and kindness of God so many times manifested by it.

And Jehoshaphat's prayer is all made up of pleas from ancient mercy and promises. If we do not improve mercies this way,

1. God loseth his glory by us. It is an unreasonable thing, if we will not believe him for his word, yet not to believe him for the work's sake: John xiv. 11, 'Believe me for the very work's sake.' God must be of very low esteem with us if he cannot be trusted for his word and deed too. Has God given us many a mercy, and shall we have such dishonourable thoughts as not to trust him? What excuse is there for distrust against the constant stream of his care?

2. We lose the sweetness of mercy. Every mercy looks two ways: it satisfieth our present want, and is a pledge of a future store. Every flower of the field, every passage of providence in the whole course of our lives, may yield honey and sweetness. David could never consider how God had been his help, but he had a new frame of joy in God: Ps. lxiii. 7, 'Because thou hast been my help, therefore in the shadow of thy wings will I rejoice.'

Whenever we find our souls dejected, let us remember God's dealing with us, and, with the psalmist, check them: Ps. xlii. 11, 'Why art thou cast down, O my soul?' What, O my soul, that hast had so many rich mercies out of the storehouse of God's free grace and favour, 'why art thou disquieted within me? Hope thou in God, for I will yet praise him who is the health of my countenance and my God.'

A DISCOURSE OF MORTIFICATION.

For if ye live after the flesh, ye shall die: but if ye through the Spirit do mortify the deeds of the body, ye shall live.—ROM. VIII. 13.

THE apostle having before spoken of justification by Christ, and shewed the necessity of sanctification, whereby we indeed resemble the holiness of God, which he shews to be wrought by the Spirit of God, which is the band of communion between saints and Christ, who raises them both from sin here and the grave hereafter; and that we are not debtors to the flesh, that we should follow the suggestions of that, but to the Spirit, to observe his inspirations; he then in the text backs his exhortations with a threatening and a promise: a threatening to excite our industry, and a promise to prevent our dejection. You must not imagine you shall be justified without being sanctified; for if you live after the flesh, you shall fall under that eternal death which is due to sin; but if you follow the motions of the Spirit, and endeavour to quench the first sparks of sin, the death of your bodies shall be an entrance into the happy life of your soul.

Flesh. Some, by flesh, understand the state under the law; others, more properly, corrupted nature. Ye shall die, without hopes of a better life. But if you mortify the deeds of the body: the deeds of the body of sin, which is elsewhere called the body of death; the first motions to sin and passionate compliances with sin, which are the springs of corrupt actions. Corrupt nature is called a body here, morally, not physically; it consisting of divers vices, as a body of divers members. 'Ye shall live;' ye shall live more spiritually and comfortably here, and eternally hereafter.

In the words we may observe,

1. A threatening: 'If ye live after the flesh, you shall die.'

2. A promise: 'If you through the Spirit do mortify the deeds of the body, ye shall live.' In the promise there is, 1, the condition; 2, the reward.

In the condition,

1. The act: mortify.

2. The object: the deeds of the body. 1. The cause: the body. 2. The effects: the deeds.

3. The agents: ye and the Spirit. The principal, the Spirit; the less principal, ye; both conjoined in the work: ye cannot do it without the

Spirit, and the Spirit will not do it without your concurrence with him, and your industry in following his motions,

From the act we may observe,

1. Sin is active in the soul of an unregenerate man. His heart is sin's territory; it is there as in its throne before the Spirit comes. Mortification supposes life before in the part mortified. We call not a stone dead, because it never had life. Justification supposeth guilt, sanctification filth, mortification life, preceding those acts.

2. Nothing but the death of sin must content a renewed soul. The sentence is irreversible: die it must. No indulgence to be shewn to it, no lighter punishment than death; not the loss of a member, but the loss of its life. The axe must be laid to the root, and the knife must be held to the throat. The devils are restrained by the power of God from many sins, which cannot therefore be said to be mortified. As nothing but the death of Christ would satisfy the justice of God, so nothing but the death of sin must satisfy the justice of the soul.

3. 'Do mortify.' The time present. Whence observe, as sin must have no pardon, so it must have no reprieve. No such mercy must be extended to it, as to give it a moment's breathing. Dangerous enemies must be handled with a quick severity. If we do not presently kill sin, it may suddenly suck out the blood of our soul.

4. 'Do mortify.' It notes a continued act. It must be a quick and an uninterrupted severity. The knife must still stick in the throat of sin, till it fall down perfectly dead. Sin must be kept down though it will rage the more, as a beast with the pangs of death is more desperate.

From the object observe,

1. Mortification must be universal; not one deed, but deeds, little and great, must fall under the edge, the brats must be dashed against the wall. Though the main battle be routed, yet the wings of an army may get the victory. There are evil dispositions, depraved habits, corrupt affections; we should not spare a nest of vipers when we find them, being all equally injurious.

2. All actual sins are but the sproutings of original. The body signifies corrupt nature, deeds are the products of it; all the sparks issue from the furnace within; the body gives nourishment to the members, and the members bring supplies to the body. There are outward and inward deeds, acts of the mind, which though not acts of the natural body, yet are acts of the body of sin, Gal. v. 19, 20, hatred, envyings, acts which the soul may perform separate from the body.

3. The greatest object of our revenge is within us. Our enemies are those of our own house, inbred, domestic adversaries; our anger is then a sanctified anger when set against our own sins. Our enemy has got possession of our souls, which makes the work more difficult. An enemy may better be kept out, than cast out when he has got possession. Sin is within us, and is always present with us, Rom. vii. 21; it lies in ambush for us in the best duties, and starts out upon every occasion when we would do good; it would cut off all correspondencies with heaven; it is in our reason, in our affections; it encamps in us, round about us, and easily besets us, Heb. xii. 1.

From the agents, *ye, the Spirit*, observe,

1. Man must be an agent in this work. We have brought this rebel into our souls, and God would have us make as it were some recompence by endeavouring to cast it out; as in the law, the father was to fling the first stone against a blasphemous son. We must not be neuters in this work,

nor lookers-on. It will not be done without, though it cannot be done simply by us: it will not be done without our concurrence, though it cannot be done without a supernatural operation.

2. *Ye*, all of ye. It is a universal duty for the subject, as well as the object.

(1.) Ye carnal men, there is no precept given to you to sin, and therefore it is not your duty to sin. The life of sin is your misery, and the mortification of sin is your happiness, as well as your duty.

(2.) Ye renewed and justified persons, regeneration doth not privilege sin, or exempt from the mortifying work. Election, and consequently the fruits of it, is to holiness, not from it, Ephes. ii. 4. Vocation and sanctification, whereof mortification is the first step, are perspective glasses to see to the top of election. Though ye have mortified, yet still do it.

3. Through the Spirit. (1.) Mortification is not the work of nature; it is a spiritual work. Every man ought to be an agent in it, yet not by his own strength. We must engage in the duel, but it is the strength of the Spirit only can render us victorious. The duty is ours, but the success is from God. Every believer is *principium activum*, but the Spirit is *principium effectivum*. We can sin of ourselves, but not overcome sin by ourselves; we know how to be slaves, but are unable of ourselves to be conquerors. As God made us first free, so he only can restore us to that freedom we have lost, and doth it by his Spirit, which is a Spirit of liberty.

(2.) The difficulty of this work is hereby declared. The difficulty is manifested by the necessity of the Spirit's efficacy. Not all the powers on earth, nor the strength of ordinances, can do it; omnipotency must have the main share in the work. The implantation of grace in the heart is called creation, the perfection of grace is called a victory, both belonging to an almighty power.

From the promise, observe,

1. Heaven is a place for conquerors only: Rev. iii. 21, 'To him that overcomes, will I grant to sit with me on my throne.' He that will be sin's friend, cannot be God's favourite. The way to eternal life is through conflicts, inward with sin, outward with the world. There must be a combat before a victory, and a victory before a triumph.

2. The more perfect our mortification, the clearer our assurance of glory. The more sin dies, the more the soul lives. The sounder our lives are, the more sensible we are that we do live. The more the enemy flies, the more certainty of an approaching victory.

3. Mortification is a sure sign of saving grace. It is a sign of the Spirit's indwelling and powerful acting, a sign of an approach to heaven.

Doct. The doctrine to be hence insisted on is this: Mortification of sin is an universal duty, and the work of the Spirit in the soul of a believer, without which there can be no well-grounded expectations of eternal life and happiness.

I do not intend a full discourse of mortification, but in pursuance of a former exhortation of resemblance to the holiness of God, to which this work is necessary. We cannot resemble God till that which is the hindrance to this resemblance be taken away; and as our deformity is pared off, we come nearer to our original pattern. And, therefore, I shall only shew, in short, what this mortification is, and how we may judge of ourselves, whether we are mortified or no, and that without it there can be no hope of heaven.

I. What mortification is.

1. It is a breaking the league we naturally hold with sin. Since we were upon ill terms with God, we have kept a constant correspondence with

his enemy; and the union between sin and the soul is as strait as that between the flesh and the bones, or the flesh and the blood, blood being in every part of the flesh, and sin in every part of the soul. In regard of this union, sin is called flesh, because of its incorporation with flesh. The union between sin and the soul is naturally as great as the union between Christ and a believer, and expressed by the similitudes of marriage, Rom. vii.; body and members, root and branches, as well as the other. It is political too, as between king and subjects. Sin is therefore said to have dominion, to make laws, whence we read of the law of the members. In regard of this, mortification is expressed by the term of having 'no fellowship with the unfruitful works of darkness,' Ephes. v. 11; a breaking of the conjugal knot. The acquaintance and familiar correspondence with sin are broken off, the communion between sin and the soul is at an end, the common interest wherein they were linked together is divided; *Res tuas tibi habeto*, the form of the ancient divorce is all the welcome sin hath: Isa. xxx. 22, 'Thou shalt say unto it, Get thee hence;' or with Ephraim, 'What have I to do any more with idols?' Hosea xiv. 8. It looks now upon its former favourite as an enemy. Sin's yoke, that was light, is now burdensome; nothing so much desired as the shaking it off; and that is the object of our antipathy, which before had been the object of the choicest favour. In this regard it is called a denying of lust, Titus ii. 12; a stopping the ears against the importunities of it, and refusing all commerce and cohabitation with it.

2. A declaration of open hostility. As leagues between princes are not broken but a war ensues, the ways of sin are rejected, the dominion of sin opposed, the throne of sin assaulted. The soul is in arms to chase out this usurper, and free itself from its tyranny; and sin up in arms to reduce its subject to its ancient obedience. And here behold that irreconcileable and tedious war, without a possibility of renewing the ancient friendship, and which ends not but with a total conquest of sin. This hostility begins in a bridling corrupt affections, laying a yoke upon anything that would take part with the enemy. It cuts off all the supplies of sin, stops all the avenues to it; which the apostle expresseth by 'making provision for the flesh,' Rom. xiii. 14, &c.; a turning the stream which fed sin another way. As anger is a degree of murder, and he that hates his brother is a manslayer, so he that hates sin, and proclaims a war against it, hath killed it *affectu*, though not *actu;* he hath attained one degree of mortification when his anger against it is irreconcilable, like the anger of those that quarrel about a crown, which cannot be ended but by the death of one of the pretenders.

3. A strong and powerful resistance, by using all the spiritual weapons against sin which the Christian armoury will afford, the list of which magazine we have, Ephes. vi. 13, 14, &c.; at the hearing of the word, setting his sin in the front, that the arrows of God may pierce it to the heart, and the two-edged sword may cut the sinews of it asunder; improving baptism, which is a burial with Christ, to which end the apostle mentions it, Rom. vi. 2, 3; sending up strong cries for the assistance of heaven, as Paul did when he had that thorn in the flesh, 2 Cor. xii. 7; redoubling his messages to heaven for a quick supply.

The apostle expresseth this reluctancy against sin by two emphatical words: 1 Cor. ix. 27, 'I keep under my body, and bring it into subjection;' *ὑπωπιάζω*, *δουλαγωγέω*, 'I keep under.' The word signifies to take hold of or to grip an adversary, as wrestlers do when they would give their antagonist a fall, and lay him flat with the earth; or to beat and pound, as wrestlers anciently did with their plummets of lead; whence *ὑπώπια*, a word derived from this in the text, signifies putrified wounds. And the other word, *δουλαγωγεῖν*, signifies to lead captive; to subject the body to serve God, not lusts; to lead it as a slave, not to endure it as a master; a bringing the affections into order, that they may not contradict and disobey the motions of the Spirit and sanctified reason.

4. A killing of sin, expressed in the text by mortifying or putting to death; and, Col. iii. 5, by νεκρώσατε, mortify; but the word signifies to reduce to a carcase; that though, like a carcase, it may retain the shape, lineaments, and members that it had living, yet it hath not the life, strength, and motion it had before. And it is called a crucifying, Gal. v. 24, which comprehends all the acts which preceded the crucifying of Christ, which was done with the greatest spite, as much as could be. The same measures, the same proportions, the same eagerness of spirit are observed; a total deafness to the cries and complaints of sin, as that of the Jews to the groans of the Lord of life; a crucifying it, notwithstanding all it would give in exchange. It is called in Scripture by the name of revenge, which ends not without the destruction of the hated person, and sometimes not with it. Every day there is to be a driving a new nail into the body of death, a breaking some limb or other of it, till it doth expire.

II. The second thing is, how we may judge of our mortification.

1. Negatively.

(1.) All cessation from some particular sin is not a mortification. A non-commission of a particular sin is not an evidence of the mortification of the root of it. Indeed, a man cannot commit all kinds of sin at a time, nor in many years; the commands of sin are contrary, and many masters commanding contrary things cannot be served at one and the same time. Pride commands to lavish, and covetousness to hoard. All sins have their times of reigning in a wicked man, as all graces have their particular seasons of acting according to the opportunities God gives. Hazael abhorred the thoughts of that cruelty the prophet foretold that he should act: 'What, am I a dog?' 2 Kings viii. 12, 13. Yet that sin lay hid by him as Joash by Jehoiada, hoping for the time to play its part and act Hazael as a slave to it. The cessation of a member from motion at present, is no argument either of the death of the body or the mortification of that member.

[1.] A cessation from one sin may be but an exchange. It may be a divorce from a sin odious to the world, and an embracing another that hath more specious pretences; as a man may forsake one harlot, and fall in league with another. Some sins do not so much affright the conscience, and those may be entertained when a frowning conscience scares a man from some more abominable. Lusts are divers, Titus iii. 3; a man may cast off the service of one master, and list himself in the service of another; he changes his lord without changing his servility. A man cannot be said to be clean because he has risen out of one sink to drench himself in another.

[2.] This cessation may be from some outward gross acts only, not from a want of will to sin, did not some log lie in the way. There may be speculative pride, ambition, covetousness, uncleanness, when they are not externally acted; which is more dangerous, as infectious diseases are when they are hindered by cold from a kindly eruption, and strike inward to the heart, and so prove mortal. The pollutions of the world may be escaped when the pollutions of the heart remain. A man may be a fine, garnished, and swept house, and yet an habitation for seven devils worse than reigned there before. The apostle's command for cleaning reaches to the filthiness of the spirit as well as that of the flesh, 2 Cor. vii. 1. We say of the soul, *Anima est ubi amat, non ubi animat;* so we may of sin. The bias of the soul may run strongly to that sin in affection and pleasure, from the outward acts of which it abstains. It is most dangerous for the house when the fire burns inward. A man may be sooner cured of an outward scald than an inward heat, which, when it comes to a hectic fever, is incurable.

[3.] It may be a cessation from a sin merely because of the alteration of the constitution. Every age hath particular sins which it inclines men to; some sins are more proper to young men, which the apostle calls therefore 'youthful lusts,' 2 Tim. ii. 22. Lust reigns in young men, but its empire decays in an old withered body; some plants which grow in hot countries will die in colder climates. Ambition decays in age when strength is wasted, but sprouts up in a young man, who hath hopes to live many years and make a flourish in the world. A present sickness may make an epicure nauseate the dainties which he would before rake even in the sea to procure. There is a cessation from acts of sin, not out of a sense of sin, but a change of the temper of his body.

[4.] A cessation from acts of sin may be forced by some forethoughts of death, some pang of conscience, apprehension of hell, present sense of some Scripture threatening, or some sharp and smarting affliction, some signal judgment of God inflicted upon one or other of the companions in sin, which are all of themselves but a kind of force, they being the scourges wherewith God sometimes lasheth a man from the present act of sin. As a present pain in one part of the body may take away a man's stomach to his food, but when the pain is removed, his appetite returns to him; so while a man is upon the rack, and God accusing him, he takes no pleasure, tastes no sweetness, in sin; but after these horrors are off, he feeds as heartily as before, nay, sometimes hath a greater stomach, as men after a fit of sickness eat more plentifully, to recover the strength which before they lost by the distemper.

[5.] A cessation from acts of sin may be for want of an occasion, for want of time, place, and materials. A man's will is not against sin, but he wants an opportunity. This is not from mortifying grace within, but from a providential operation of God, in withholding the materials necessary for the commission of sin. Who will say the sins of drunkenness, gluttony, and oppression, committed by men on earth, are mortified in them when they are in hell? They want materials, not a nature nor an affection, to commit the same, were they again upon earth. Grace lies idle many times for want of objects to exercise itself about; so doth lust in the heart, like a snake starved with cold, till heated by a temptation. A man's condition in the world is not a sign of this mortification; there may be grasping and ambitious thoughts in a cottage. Prodigality may be in a poor man's wishes, though not in his power; yea, and sometimes there is more prodigality in a poor man's unnecessary expense of a penny, than in another's throwing away a pound.

(2.) Restraints from sin are not mortification of it. Men may be curbed when they are not changed; and there is no man in the world but God doth restrain him from more sins, which he hath a nature to commit, than what he doth actually commit. He often hedgeth up the way with thorns, when he doth not alter the heart by grace, and doth by his providence hinder the execution of the sinful motions, when he doth not root out the wickedness that lies secretly in the nature. It was an act of God's providence to restrain Abimelech: Gen. xx. 6, 'I withheld thee from sinning against me.' These restraints are mercies God would have us bless him for, but not evidences of mortifying grace.

[1.] Mortification is always from an inward principle in the heart, restraints from an outward. A restraint is merely a pull back, as a man is hindered from doing a mischief by a stronger power. But mortification is from a strength given, a new mettle put into the soul, both a courage and strength to resist it; there is a 'strength in the inward man,' Eph. iii. 16. In a renewed man, there is something beside bare considerations to withhold him, something of antipathy which heightens and improves those considerations, whereby the soul is glad of them, because the edge and dint of them is against sin; whereas a man barely restrained would fain stop the entrance of such thoughts, or when they are entered, would turn them out of doors again. They are things merely put into him, that have no welcome, neither do they change the will, but put a little stop, to alter the method of proceedings. Mortifying grace finds something in the nature, as there is in the nature of a fountain, to work out the mud when dirt is cast in to infect it.

[2.] True mortification proceeds from an anger with, and a hatred of, sin, whereas restraints are from a fear of the consequents of sin; as a man may love the wine, which is as yet too hot for his lips. But mortification proceeds from an anger, a desire of revenge. Hence sin is called an abomination to a good man as well as to God; which signifies an intense and well-heated anger. It is not only a passionateness, which upon some disappointment in sin, or a tasting the bitterness of it, may be vented against it, which is short-lived, and quickly allayed, as the sea after a storm; but it is a rooted revenge, which is the sweetest passion, and accomplished by many projects and contrivances. A man tastes a sweetness in giving blow after blow to sin, as before he took a pleasure in, and had friendship with it.

[3.] Mortification is a voluntary, rational work of the soul; restraints are not so. The devil hath nothing of his nature altered, but hath as strong an inclination to sin as ever, though the act he intends is often hindered by God. As in the case of Job, his malice was as great before to do him a mischief; but God puts a bar upon him, and refuses him a licence, Job i. 10. Now if that grace which hinders be no more than what a devil hath, it no more argues a man mortified than the devil's forbearance of sin argues him mortified, and recovering his angelical state.

2. We may judge of our mortification positively.

(1.) When upon a temptation that did usually excite the beloved lust, it doth not stir, it is a sign of a mortified state; as it is a sign of the clearness of a fountain, when after the stirring of the water the mud doth not appear. Peter's sin seems to be self-confidence, but it was a sign of a greater mortification of it, that when Christ pressed him to declare his love in that demand, John xxi. 15, 'Lovest thou me more than these?' he would not vaunt his love to Christ to be greater than the rest of his brethren's. His answer goes no further than, 'Yea, Lord, thou knowest that I love thee,' without adding 'more than these.' As it is with a man that is sick, set the most savoury meat before him, which before he had a value for, if he cannot taste it, and his appetite be not provoked by the sight, it is an argument of the strength of his distemper, and where it is lasting, of his approaching death; so when a man hath a temptation to sin, decked and garnished with all the allurements the devil can dress it with, and he hath no stomach to close with it, it is a sign of a mortified frame. It is a sign of the power of sin, when upon the fair offer it makes, and the alluring baits it lays, the affections to it are presently stirred; it is an evidence of a co-naturality and a mighty agreement between that sin and the heart, when upon every spark it takes fire; it is a sign a man was filled with all unrighteousness, and had not only a few loose corns about him; so on the contrary, when upon the least motion of temptation, that was wont to have the gates open for it, the affections rise against it, and upon the least alarm all run to the walls to defend them and forbid the entrance;

it is an evidence of the weakness of that lust that kept before a correspondence with such temptations, and the greater evidence it is when the temptation is high and yet vigorously resisted; as when a spring-tide is high and blown in with the wind, it is an argument of the strength and firmness of the bank to keep it out from entering upon the ground; whereas when a man is carried away by every temptation, as marsh ground is drowned at every tide, it is a sign that there is no mortifying grace at all, but a great friendliness between sin and the heart. None will question the deadness of that tree at the root which doth not bud upon the return of the spring sun; nor need we question the weakness of that corruption which doth not stir upon the presenting a suitable temptation.

(2.) When we meet with few interruptions in duties of worship. The multitude of such diversions, and an easiness to comply with them, is a sign of an unmortified frame; as it is the sign of much weakness in a person, and the strength of his distemper, when he is not able to hold fast anything, or when the least blow or jog makes him let go his hold. In duty we are to lay fast hold on God, Heb. vi. 18, and join ourselves to the Lord, Isa. lvi. 3; it is a weak union when every puff of wind is able to separate us. When the starting of sin in us doth easily turn us from our course, it argues either our credulity to believe its enticements, or our affection to love its allurements; and also the force and strength of sin; as the frequent starting of an enemy from woods and fastnesses to obstruct our passage, is a sign of some strength remaining, and of more than some few scattered troops, rather some well-bodied army. The more there is of a man's self, flesh, unspiritualness in any service, the more there is of an unmortified temper. The sprouting up of such fruits argues much juice and sap at the root, especially when the eruptions of sins are more numerous and vigorous than the resistances of them. But when the heart can run its race in a service with some freedom, and the interruptions from the flesh are few and languishing, it is a sign it hath met with a weakening wound; they are rather gasps of corruption than any strong attempts.

(3.) When we bring forth the fruits of the contrary graces, it is a sign sin is mortified. It is to this end that sin is killed by the Spirit, that fruit may be brought forth to God; the more sweet and full fruit a tree bears, the more evidence there is of the weakness of those suckers which are about the root to hinder its generous productions. Believers are called vines, and olives planted in a fair soil, and God the husbandman, who waters and dresseth, prunes, and cuts off the luxuriant branches that he may have fruit, and 'fruit meet for him,' John xv. 1, 2. The more fruit is brought forth, the greater sign that the soul is purged, and whatsoever is an enemy to that fruit is cut off and weakened. The more nature doth rise to the exercise of acts proper to it, the more the strength of the disease that oppresses it is wasted. Every exercise of grace is both a discovery of the weakness of sin, and a fresh blow given to it for the wounding of it.

III. The reasons why there can be no expectation of eternal life without mortification, are,

1. An unmortified frame is unsuitable to a state of glory. There must be a meetness for a state of glory before there be an entrance into it, Col. i. 12. Vessels of glory must be first seasoned with grace. Conformity to Christ is to fit us for heaven. He descended to the grave, and there laid his infirmities, before he ascended into heaven; so our sins must die before our souls can mount. It is very unsuitable for sin's drudges to have a saint's portion. A fleshly state is unfit for a spiritual life. All men are under the power of the devil or under the power of Christ. The world lies ἐν τῷ

πονηρῷ, under the power of the devil, 1 John v. 19.* He that hath the wicked spirit ruling in him, and not cast out, with all his accomplices, by the Spirit of God, cannot hope to have a friend's privilege, but an enemy's punishment. A fleshly palate cannot relish an heavenly life: Mat. xvi. 23, 'Thou savourest not the things that be of God.' Where there is no savour of God in this world, but only of what is contrary to God, there cannot be a savour of him in another world. Every vessel must be emptied of its foul water before it can receive that which is clean. No man pours rich wine into old casks.

2. God cannot in any wise delight in an unmortified soul. To delight in such would be to have no delight in himself and his own nature; the less the degrees of our mortification, the less God doth delight in us. He hath no pleasure in wickedness; the more maims, diseases, rottenness any have, the less pleasure there is. Sin is a mire; the more miry we are, the less can God embrace us, Ps. v. 4. It is a plague; the more it spreads, the less will he be conversant with us. The more of a swinish, viperous, serpentine nature, the less of God's affections. Sin represents us more monstrous in God's eyes than the filthiest things in the world can do in man's. To keep sin alive is to defend it against the will of God, and to challenge the combat with our Maker.

3. Unmortified sin is against the whole design of the gospel and death of Christ, as though the death of Christ were intended to indulge us in sin, and not to redeem us from it. That sin should die, was the end of Christ's death; rather than sin should not die, Christ would die himself. It is an high disesteem of Christ to preserve the life of sin in spite of the death of the Redeemer, and if we defend what he died to conquer, how can we expect to enjoy what he died to purchase? It is a contempt of his death not to look after that mortifying grace, which was the purchase of so deep a passion. The grace of the gospel of God doth more especially teach this lesson, Tit. ii. 4, 'to deny ungodliness and worldly lusts.' Grace in God was the motive to him not to account the blood of Christ too dear for us, and therefore should teach us not to account the blood of our sins too dear for him. The tenor of the gospel is, that a man without mortification has no interest in Christ, and therefore no right to glory, Ps. v. 4. It is an inseparable character of them that are Christ's, that 'they have crucified the flesh with the affections and lusts,' *i.e.* they are Christ's that are under the power of his death, not they that only hold the opinion of his death, or they are Christ's that are truly planted into the likeness of his death, Rom. vi. 5.

IV. The use; of exhortation.

Let us labour to mortify sin. If we will not be the death of sin, sin will be the death of our souls. Though the allurements of sin may be pleasant, the propositions seemingly fair, yet the end of all is death, Rom. v. 21. Death was threatened by God and executed upon Adam; death must be executed upon our sins, in order to the restoration of the eternal life of our souls. Love to everlasting life should provoke us, fear of everlasting death should excite us to this, the two most solemn and fundamental passions that put us upon action. 'Why will you die?' was God's expostulation, Ezek. xxxiii. 11; Why should thou, O my soul, for a short vanishing pleasure, venture an eternal death? should be our expostulation with ourselves. This would be a curing our disease, bringing our soul into that order in part which was broken by the fall; by this the power of that tyrant that first headed and maintained the faction against God would be removed, and the soul recover that liberty and life it lost by disobeying of God. This would conduce to our

* Camero.

peace. We have then a sprouting assurance when we are most victorious over our lusts: after every victory, God gives us a taste of the hidden manna, Rev. ii. 17. Unmortified lusts do only raise storms and tempests in the soul; less pains are required to the mortification of them than to the satisfaction of them. Sin is a hard taskmaster; there must be a pleasure in destroying so cruel an inmate. Gratitude engages us; God's holiness and justice bruised Christ for us, and shall not we kill sin for him? An infinite love parted with a dear Son, and shall not our shallow finite love part with destroying lusts? We cannot love our sins so much as God loved his Son: he loved him infinitely. If God parted with him for us, shall not we part with our sins for him? He would have us kill it because it hurts us; the very command discovers affection as well as sovereignty, and minds us of it as our privilege as well as our duty. And to engage us to it, he hath sent as great a person to help us as to redeem us, viz. his Spirit; he sent one to merit it, and the other to assist us in it and work it in us, who is to bring back the creature to God by conquering that in it which hath so long detained it captive. And therefore to this purpose,

1. Implore the help of the Spirit. Whenever we set seriously upon this work at any time, let us apply ourselves to the Spirit of God, as one in office to this end, as being a Spirit of holiness not only in his nature but in his operations, Eph. i. 13, Rom. i. 4. The Father and the Son are not so often called holy as the Spirit, who is called the Holy Spirit and the Holy Ghost, not that he is more holy than the other persons, but in regard of his office to work holiness in the hearts of men. As Jehoshaphat upon the assault from the enemy cried unto God for deliverance, so upon any arming of our corruptions we should cry to the Spirit for assistance; he doth as much delight to be our auxiliary on earth, as Christ doth to be our advocate in heaven. The neglects of application to him are the cause of our miscarriages; we are half persuaded to a sin before we beg strength against it.

2. Listen to the convictions of the Holy Spirit. The work of the Spirit is to convince, by shaking the soul out of its carnal lethargy. As the Spirit gives a strong alarm at the first conversion, whereby the soul sees the strength of its enemy, and the greatness of its danger, its own impotency and inability to contest with it, so upon carrying on the degrees of mortification, there are various alarms to put us upon a holy watchfulness against the projects of sin. Listen to these convictions which come in by the word, which is the ministration of the Spirit, and in respect to the spiritual energy of it is called spirit, John vi. 53.

3. Plead the death of Christ. The end of his death was to triumph over sin. As to take away the guilt of sin, he was the righteousness of God; so to take away the dominion of sin, he is the power of God: his expiation of sin, and his condemnation of it, were twisted together in his sacrifice, Rom. viii. 3. 'For sin,' or a sacrifice for sin, 'condemned sin in the flesh': and the consideration of his death, and the end of it, would inflame us to desire not to be under the power of a condemned malefactor. A consideration of his death, and that sin had its hands imbrued in his blood, would awaken our love to him, and an indignation against his enemy.

4. Let us often think of divine precepts. The frequent meditation on the law of God would excite our endeavours after a principle more conformable to the purity of that law. God's commands establish not men's humours, neither do they gratify men's lusts, but are suited to the holy nature of God, a conformity to which ought to be our aim in mortification.

5. Let us be jealous of our own hearts. Venture not to breathe in corrupt air, for fear of infection. There is a principle in the heart naturally dis-

posed to take fire upon the spark of a temptation. A strict watch in a city hinders foreign correspondence and intestine treachery.

6. Let us often think deeply of the corruption of our natures, how loathsome it is to God, and this will make it loathsome to us. The more it is abominated, the more it is mortified; the supplies of it are cut off, its attempts discovered. When Paul considered his misery by the body of death, it strengthened his resolution of serving God with the law of his mind, Rom. vii. 24, 25, which must needs be accompanied with a strong resistance of the law of his members.

7. Let us bless God for whatsoever mortifying grace we have received, though never so little. When we pay him in praise what we receive of him, it is the way to have more from him. David grew hot against Nabal after he had received his churlish answer, 1 Sam. xxv., and resolved the murder of the whole family, which he had no authority to do; but God prevents him by Abigail's intercession; he blesses God for the success of it, in hindering his intentions. And as God prevented his sin, so, after his thanksgiving, he took away the occasion of his evil resolution, by calling Nabal, ten days after, into another world, ver. 38; and gives him further occasion of praise, ver. 39. A little strength, owned as the gift of God, shall be backed with more. Praising God for what we receive, as well as praying for what we want, is a means to promote the mortification of our sins in order to eternal life.

A DISCOURSE PROVING WEAK GRACE VICTORIOUS.

A bruised reed shall he not break, and smoking flax shall he not quench, till he send forth judgment unto victory.—MAT. XII. 20.

WE need not take our rise higher than verse 17, where the quotation out of Isa. xlii. begins, where you find God like a herald proclaiming his Son to the world under the name of his servant: Mat xii. 18, 'Behold my servant, whom I have chosen; my beloved, in whom my soul is well pleased: I will put my Spirit upon him, and he shall shew judgment to the Gentiles.' It contains, (1.) His election of him: God chose, called him to his mediatory office; (2.) The agreeableness of the person to God: he did wholly acquiesce in him, and deposit in his hand the concerns of his glory; (3.) The ability and assistance God gave him, 'I will put my Spirit upon him;' (4.) The work he should do, 'he shall shew judgment to the Gentiles.' Verse 19, his coming is set down; not with pomp or noise, 'he shall not strive, nor cry, neither shall any man hear his voice in the streets.' The meekness and tenderness of his carriage, 'he shall not cry.' *Palam noluit fieri hominum vitia*, as Grotius; he shall not be contentious with the people, of which a sign is, an immoderate raising of the voice, and clamour against them.

Take notice hereof,

1. The Object.

(1.) A bruised reed. Jerome takes it for a musical instrument made of a reed, which shepherds used to have, which, when bruised, sounds ill, and is flung away by the musician, as disdaining to spend his breath upon such a vile instrument that emits no pleasant sound. But Christ will not cast off poor souls that cannot make so good music in God's ears as others, and answer not the breathings of the Spirit with that life and vigour, but he will take pains with them to mend them. Bruised reeds, such as are convinced of their own weakness, vanity, and emptiness.

2. The smoking flax of the wick of a candle, wherein there is not only no profit, but some trouble and noisomeness. Though the soul is noisome by reason of the stench of its corruptions, yet he will not blow out that expiring fire, but blow it up and cherish it; he will not rigidly oppress and throw off those that are weak in grace, and faith, and hope, but he will heal them,

nourish them, inflame them. Maldonate interprets it, that though he walk in the way where bruised reeds lie, he will step over them, and not break them more; he will not tread upon a little smoking flax that lies languishing upon the ground, and so put it out with his foot, though it hurts the eyes with its smoke, and offends the nostrils with its stench. Smoking souls that have some weak desires and fumings towards heaven, some small evaporations of their spirits towards God, he shall not quench them. The Chaldee paraphrase, Those meek or gracious ones which are like a bruised reed, shall not be broken by him.

2. The act. He shall not break; not quench, *litotis* or *meiosis;* he shall mightily cherish, support the reed, inflame the flax.

3. The continuance of it, 'till he send forth judgment unto victory.' In Isaiah it is, 'till he bring forth judgment unto truth;' *vere judicabit*, so Menochius, so the Septuagint hath it; but Matthew alters it, and instead of truth puts victory.

Judgment is taken several ways. For,

1. Wisdom: Isa. xxx. 18, 'The Lord will wait that he may be gracious, for the Lord is a God of judgment;' *i.e.* of wisdom to give in the most convenient season.

2. Righteousness: Isa. lix. 9, 'Judgment is far from us, neither doth justice overtake us;' *i.e.* there is no holiness in us.

3. Overthrow of a Christian's enemy: John xii. 31, 'Now is the judgment of this world, now shall the prince of this world be cast out,' now shall the devil be conquered; Isa. xlii. 3, 'He shall bring forth judgment unto truth;' *i.e.* he shall govern in righteousness. Now Christ's government being chiefly in the souls of men, he shall assist and encourage that which is the better; as governors ought to be encouragers of the good, and discouragers of the bad. Matthew explains this, and shews the consequence of this government; if it be in truth, it will make the better part victorious. Some by judgment understand the gospel, the new evangelical law: ver. 4, 'The isles shall wait for his law;' so Christ will not rest till he makes the gospel glorious, and advances it in the world above the lusts and idolatries of men, which then overflowed the world. Some by judgment understand grace, which is the draught and copy of the gospel drawn in the soul; and both those senses the words will bear. The words in Isaiah seem to bear the first sense, 'the isles shall wait for his law;' the other seems most consonant to Matthew, 'and in his name shall the Gentiles trust'; *i.e.* he will make their faith victorious. The effect of this judgment, or evangelical law, should be the victoriousness of grace and faith. Implanting grace in the heart is the main design of the gospel; and grace is nothing else but a moulding the soul into the form of that law and doctrine of Christ. As Christ will make the gospel glorious above all the carnal reasonings of men, so he will make grace, which is the end of the gospel, victorious above all the corruptions of men. In this latter sense we shall now handle it; Christ shall make those beginnings of grace and infused habits to obtain a perfect conquest. By his governing of it, he shall make the conquest over corruption perfect; or if κρίσις be taken as the physicians use it, for the κρίσις of a disease, he shall make the κρίσις end in victory, and nature the conqueror over the disease.

Doct. True though weak grace shall be preserved, and in the end prove victorious.

Seeds of grace, though mixed with a mass of corruption, cannot be overcome by it, as gold cannot be altered in its nature by the dross, or transformed into the nature of the rubbish in which it lies. Grace is surely weakest at the first infusion, when it is newly landed in the heart from heaven; when the devil and wickedness of man's nature have taken the alarm, and drawn together all the armies of hell to hinder its progress; yet though it be thus, in so weak a condition, indisposed to make a stout resistance, having got but little footing in the heart, and a man's own inclinations not well reconciled to it, nor his evil apprehensions and notions fully exterminated, and the predominant corruptions that held the empire before, having received but their first wound, and being much unmortified, and grace also as yet but in a strange soil, not naturalised at all, yet is grace then so strong, that all the legions of hell cannot totally worst it. Though it be like a grain of mustard-seed newly sown, yet it springs up into a mighty tree; for as the weakness of God is stronger than men, so is the weakness of grace stronger than sin in the event and issue. The meanest grace is above the highest intellectual parts, as the smile of a sunbeam is more powerful to chase away the grim and sour darkness of the night, than the sparkling of a diamond. According to the degrees of its growth, its effects are wonderful; as a small spark, by a breath of wind growing into a flame, may fire and consume a spacious and stately building. The weakest grace by degrees shall have strength, Zech. xii. 8, which is meant of the Jews' strength at their conversion; 'He that is feeble shall be as David,' who was a mighty man of valour, and when a stripling laid Goliath in the dust, but in the strength of Christ; for the 'house of David shall be as God, as the angel of the Lord before him,' *i. e.* Christ that descended from David. In the text, you see God assures us that Christ shall perform this; therefore let us see what engagements are on God's part, and what also on Christ's part, to effect this business, which will be sufficient demonstration of this truth.

In general. Grace hath great allies; the greatest power that ever yet acted upon the stage of the world had a hand in the birth of it. Should we see all the states of the world engaged in bringing a person to a kingdom, and maintaining him there in his right, we could not rationally think that there were any likelihood they should be baffled in it.

The Trinity sat in consultation about grace; for if there were such a solemn convention held about the first creating of man, Gen. i. 26, much more about the new and better creating of him, and raising him somewhat above the state of a man. The Father decrees it, Christ purchaseth it, the Spirit infuseth it; the Father appoints the garrison, what grace shall be in every soul, Christ raiseth this force, and the Spirit conducts it. The Trinity have an hand in maintaining it; the Father purgeth out corruption, the Son washes, and the Holy Ghost sanctifies; all this is but the carrying on the new creature: Titus iii. 4–6, 'But after the kindness and love of God our Saviour appeared, not by works of righteousness, &c., but according to his mercy he saved us, by the washing of regeneration, and renewing of the Holy Ghost, which he shed on us abundantly through Jesus Christ our Saviour'; 'God our Saviour,' *i. e.* God the Father. The Father is the author of salvation from sin, Christ the purchaser, the Spirit the conveyer. There is a special relation between the Trinity and grace; the Father is said to beget us, John i. 13. and we are said to be the seed of Christ, Isa. liii. 10, and born of the Spirit, John iii. 6. That, therefore, which hath so strong a relation cannot perish.

1. The Father, who is the first root of grace in his good will and pleasure. Though Christ merited the fruits of election, yet he did not merit election itself, for Christ himself is a fruit of that first election.

(1.) In respect of his attributes. Grace will engage God's assistance. Every grace is part of the divine nature, because it is an imitation of one or other of the divine attributes, and exemplifies the divine perfections in its operations: 1 Peter ii. 9, 'But you are a chosen generation, a royal priesthood, a holy nation, a peculiar people; that you may shew forth the praises of him who hath called you out of darkness into his marvellous light.' Shew forth the praise of God, ἀρετὰς, the virtues of God. Grace in all the parts of it doth glorify one or other attribute of God; humility his power, contentedness his sufficiency, watchfulness his omniscience, prayer his sovereignty, repentance and sorrow for sin his justice, faith his love and truth, a fiduciary reliance on his word, his wisdom, &c.

[1.] The love of God is engaged in it. The riches of his grace was the motive to work grace in the heart. Goodness made him bring light into the world, and it is the same motive makes him bring grace into the soul. It is called God's workmanship, his *poem*, Eph. ii. 10, ποίημα, about which he spent more skill than about all other things. As usually men are more lofty in a poem than in prose, and enrich it with the sublimest fancies, and diligently observe their numbers and measures; so is God exact in the production of the new creature, which is rather his ποίημα than ἔργον, as if it were not so much the work of his hands as the work of his heart; for, as ver. 18, his soul was pleased in Christ, so in all things which make to the glory of Christ. His soul, it notes an high joy which we find not expressed of the creation; and therefore his heart is chiefly set upon grace, as that which he chiefly designed Christ to purchase, and Christ to implant.

Well, then, did God's love give his Son to die for thee, to purchase that grace? And will not the same love engage his power to preserve and perfect that grace? Shall his common love to his creature cause him to provide for sparrows, and will he neglect his children? Shall he provide for his children, and not stand by to second that which gives them the denomination of children? Shall their hairs be numbered, and not one fall to the ground without the will of God? Hairs, I say, which are inconsiderable, of which there is no miss, no endangering of life by their fall; and shall grace be thrown to the ground by corruption, which brings down with it the life and happiness of a Christian, and the glory of God? No; the weakest grace hath a certain interest in the love of God, because the weakest is the birth of that love; as the child that is crying in the cradle is as much related to the father as the son stoutly working in the shop.

[2.] The power of God. It is not in a bare moral, but physical way, that grace is brought into the soul. If power must be employed in raising the body, less surely will not serve the turn to raise the soul, which is a far more noble and excellent work. Can it be possibly thought that when Satan, the strong man, had possession of the soul, well provided for defence, had a great interest in the affections and love of a man, making no laws, enjoining no commands but what were suitable for and pleasant to flesh and blood, that ever grace of itself could have dispossessed him, and wrested this empire out of his hands? Surely it must be the power of God that did it, else so strong an enemy, so mighty a prince, could never have been overcome, so well beloved a governor could never have been overthrown. God is the strength of the soul; all the contrivances and stratagems against the flesh are from him: 2 Cor. iii. 5, 'Our sufficiency is of God: we are not sufficient of ourselves,' λογίσασθαι, 'to think,' *i. e.* to come to some certain resolution, as men do when they sum up their particular accounts, or state our own affairs; and when this is done, we cannot will it, or put it in execution without him; therefore, Philip. ii. 13, 'He works in us both to will and to do, and that of his good pleasure,' εὐδοκίας, love and power is put together. It would be derogatory to God if that should be totally overcome, which his immediate power is the cause of, put on by his special love; for it would either argue a want of love, or a want of sufficiency to maintain it. But it is not thus; for the same power which brought us to God, keeps us from being drawn from him: 1 Peter i. 5, 'If kept by the power of God through faith,' then that faith is also kept by the power of God; that faith whereby we overcome the invasions of Satan, and repel his fiery darts; that faith whereby the corruptions of the heart are resisted and expelled by its purifying act; for faith purifies the heart instrumentally, Acts xv. 9.

[3.] The holiness of God. Men are said to be like God, not in power, infiniteness, omniscience, &c., but in holiness, which is the attribute most cried up in heaven, Isa. vi. 3, an attribute which God doth most magnify, as swearing by it, Ps. lxxxix. 35, which he doth not particularly and expressly by any other attribute; an attribute which he is so tender of. For what is the cause of that justice which employs his power in punishing offenders, but his holiness and hatred of sin? Grace hath its print from God, and is conformity to the holiness of God, as appearing in his law. It is the image of God; there is an harmony and proportion of all graces in the soul to those perfections of holiness which are in God, as there is of the members of the body of a child to its father; in respect of this likeness men are said to be the children of God. It may better be said of grace than it was said of the soul by the heathen, *Scintilla divinæ essentiæ*, or, as the Jews say, souls were the shavings or chips of the throne of glory. Graces are the drops of God's perfections, they are so exact an image of him. In respect of this likeness to God's holiness, gracious souls that have escaped the corruptions of the world through lust, do partake of the divine nature, 2 Peter i. 4. It is called a bearing 'the image of the heavenly,' 1 Cor. xv. 48. Not that God bestows anything of the divine essence upon the soul, but an image and representation of himself, just as a golden seal conveys to the wax the image engraven on it, but not the least particle of its matter, the wax remaining wax, though under another form and figure. This likeness is a likeness to God in his highest perfection, viz., his holiness, which runs through all, and may be applied to all the attributes, as holy power, &c., and herein grace excels the perfections of the whole creation put together, for all the creatures are not so like to God as grace makes the soul. And how can we imagine anything, wherein we can be more like to God, than in that which is the highest excellency and perfection of God? Now seeing grace hath so near a relation to God, and God doth so delight to see this in his people, that all his end is to make them like him, in a completing of holiness in them in heaven, and that this is that which Christ must do at the last, present them holy and blameless without any spot, will he neglect that which is so dear and like to him, and suffer his own image to be wholly crushed under feet by corruption, his basest enemy?

[4.] The wisdom of God. The weakest grace is the birth of his eternal counsel: Eph. i. 4, 'chosen us that we might be holy.' If thou hast any grace, though never so mean, thou wert from eternity given by God to Christ; and Christ purchased this grace for thee, else the Spirit would never have infused it into thee, for the Spirit receives of Christ, and shews it unto you; there was a decree passed in heaven for all that grace thou hast. Therefore, that which made God at first resolve upon it, and made him send such a force and brigade into thy soul, will cause him to perfect it to a complete victory: Philip. i. 6, 'Being confident of this very thing, that he which hath begun a good work in you, will perform it until the day of Jesus Christ.' The apostle was confident that because God had begun it, he would perfect it. What ground should he have for this confidence, if weak grace could be totally overcome? God being unchangeable in his counsels and decrees, if any saint whom he hath purposed to save should be totally drawn from him, it would argue God changeable, that his will was altered, or weak, that his power was extinguished or unwise, that his counsel was rashly undertaken. But surely his love, being founded upon his counsel, admits of no change. Besides, God doth infuse grace into those souls which are naturally and morally most incapable of it. The most rugged pieces he smoothes, the darkest souls he enlightens, the greatest enemies he makes friends, and would he begin this work to have it presently spoiled? God, before he meddled with any soul, foresaw what contests and conflicts of sin and the devil there would be against him. He counted all the cost and charges, and all the pains he was to take. And it doth not consist with the wisdom of God to lay aside this undertaking, nor with the patience of God not to endure the brunt, when he foresaw every stratagem of the devil against such a soul when he first set up the standard in it. The gospel is called the manifold wisdom of God, Eph. iii. 10; and surely all the effects of it, and this of grace in the heart, which is the chief effect and design of it, is an act of God's wisdom; and should this, which is the birth of his manifold wisdom, be suppressed?

[5.] The glory of God. God's end in everything is his glory, and that which grace aims at is the glory of God. As God minds himself and wills himself, the chief good, so doth grace mind and will God as the choicest and supreme happiness. Those graces which maintain the hottest fight against corruption, and are the strongest and most active legion, have a peculiar objective relation to God, as love to him, faith in him, desire for him. Those graces which are exercised about man, and the duties of the second table, have not so great an interest in this quarrel. Now, is it for the honour of God to let that which is his best friend in the world be totally suppressed? Would not his honour suffer in it? The two sisters thought it a good argument to prevail with Christ to come and help Lazarus when they sent him word, 'He whom thou lovest is sick;' and Christ himself took an argument from his friendship to raise him, 'Our friend Lazarus sleeps.' And is it not as good an argument with God to come in for relief of languishing grace, when you send him word how hard it is beset?

(2.) Christ is engaged in this work. The promise in the text manifests that Christ was ordered by his Father to it, his Father having promised it upon his proclaiming him his chosen servant.

Christ is engaged as,

[1.] A purchaser. He died to 'redeem us from all iniquity, and to purify unto himself a peculiar people, zealous of good works,' inward works as well as outward, Titus ii. 14. He gave himself that we might be without filth, and at last without spot, wrinkle, or blemish: Eph. v. 25–27, 'Christ loved the church, and gave himself for it, that he might sanctify and cleanse it with the washing of water by the word, that he might present it to himself a glorious church,' not an imperfect church, 'not having spot or wrinkle, or any such thing,' anything like them, 'but that it should be holy and without blemish.' To sanctify and cleanse by degrees, to perfect it by wiping out all the spots and smoothing the wrinkles, and making it highly beautiful, fit to be presented to himself as his eternal spouse. If these spots and blemishes should keep their standing, it would argue that it was not Christ's purpose in the giving himself to remove them, or that his gift was not equivalent to so great an end, and sufficient to attain it, or else that he had since repented of his intent; but none of those will hold. This scripture assures us he gave himself for this purpose. The Father hath exalted him at his right hand for it, and his compassions work powerfully in his bowels, even in heaven. He was of the same mind after his ascension, when Paul wrote this epistle. Therefore he is said 'by one offering to perfect for ever them that are sanctified,' Heb. x. 14; that is, that one offering was of such infinite value, that it perfectly purchased the taking away of sin, both in the guilt, filth, and power, and was a sufficient price for all the grace believers should need for their perfect sanctification to the end of the world. There was the satisfaction of his blood for the removal of our guilt, and a treasure of merit for the supply of our grace. Though glory was due to him even from the moment of his incarnation, as he was the Son of God, yet he would not enter into it and sit down at the right hand of the Majesty on high, till he had purchased grace and all the measures of it for his people, and that by himself, by the laying down his life as the price for it: Heb. i. 3, 'When he had by himself purged our sins, sat down at the right hand of the Majesty on high.' Sat down when? Not till he had purged, *i. e.* made atonement for our sins, and paid for whatsoever holiness or purging grace his people should want. His blood was so valuable that the treasures of God were dealt out to believers before his coming upon the credit of his bond; much more will they be so after his coming upon God's actual receipt of the price, and our Saviour's sitting down at the right of God to see the grace he purchased given out. Upon this account Christ hath a care of the weakest saint as well as of the most glorious angel, because he died to purchase the weakest believer, not the highest angel, who stood in no need of it. If Christ bought us, we belong to the purchaser, which is the apostle's inference: 1 Cor. vi. 19, 20, 'Ye are not your own, ye are bought with a price;' not our own governors, not our own keepers. The possession the Holy Ghost hath of us, making us his temples, is by virtue of this price. If Christ died that his people might have grace, and that it might be powerful, shall lust trample upon that which Christ hath so dearly bought? Was it a light thing for which he endured all the torments upon the cross, and will he now make no matter of it? If he purchased us, and grace for us, when we were enemies, will he not preserve it in us since we are his friends? Shall he be at the expense of his richest blood to buy it, and spare his power to secure it? Is the right of his purchase of so low a value with him as to suffer it to be usurped by his greatest enemy?

[2.] An actual proprietor and possessor by way of

(1.) Donation from his Father. Every believer is God's gift to Christ as mediator for this end, to give eternal life to them, and every one of them: John xvii. 2, 'That I should give eternal life to as many as thou hast given me,' which eternal life is the knowledge of God, which includes all grace. And they were given to him that they might be perfect, one, as the Father and the Son are: John xvii. 11, 'Keep through thy own name those whom thou hast given me, that they may be one, as we are.' He gave them with an intent that they should be one in as high a manner as the creature is capable of. This was the end both of God's giving and Christ's keeping, for the particle ἵνα may refer to *keep* or to *given*. If they be not at last one, the end of God's giving must be frustrate, and the petition of Christ not heard. Christ will not undervalue his Father's gift. We prize even small tokens from a friend we love. Because our Redeemer valued this gift, he accepted of it, and took it into his own possession; and because he loves his Father, he will answer the ends of this donation. Christ calls those his sheep by virtue of this donation, John x. 16. Our being his sheep by virtue of this gift, will be as much a reason to preserve us in faith as it was at first to confer it on us. The same is as valid for preserving as for first conferring, and that is the Father's gift.

(2.) He is proprietor and possessor by the conquest of every gracious person, and whatsoever was contrary to grace. As our Redeemer was to purchase us by his death at the hand of God's justice, so he was to rescue us by his power from the fury of our hellish oppressor. As he was to appease the justice of God, so he was to deface the works of the devil: 1 John iii. 5, 'He was manifested to take away our sins;' ver. 8, 'For this purpose was the Son of God manifested, that he might destroy the works of the devil.' As God's justice is so perfectly pacified as never to renew the curses of the law against a believer, so is the devil so thoroughly subdued as never to repair the ruins of his works. Did Christ rise as a conqueror out of the grave, to let sin and Satan run away with the fruits of his victory? Shall he overcome the powers of hell, and triumph over them, to let the devil rob him of the honour of his achievements by regaining his loss? Shall that man of his right hand, whom God hath made strong for himself, that we might not go back from him, Ps. lxxx. 17, be made weak again by man's own corruptions and the devil's repossession? Should grace truckle under the devil's works, and the standard which was set up in the soul when it was first snatched from the power of darkness be pulled down, what would become of the glory of our Redeemer's death, and the honour of his victory? What a disparagement would it be, to have that which he paid so great a price for, which was the special gift of his Father, the acquest of the travail and sweat of his soul, wrested out of his hand by an enemy he hath subdued, condemned upon the cross, and triumphed over at his ascension! No, this will never be. Christ and the Father are one in operation, and whom God delivers from the power of darkness he translates into the kingdom of his dear Son, not to return under the government of a hated devil, and makes them 'meet to be partakers of the inheritance of the saints in light,' Col. i. 12, not to be partakers of the inheritance of the devils in darkness. Neither the Father nor the Son will lose the fruit of their pains.

(3.) By mutual consent and agreement. He hath possession of them by God's gift, and their own choice: John x. 27, 28, 'My sheep hear my voice, and I know them, and they follow me: and I give unto them eternal life, and they shall never perish, neither shall any man pluck them out of my hand.' Believers are his sheep in his hand; he knows them with a knowledge of affection, and therefore will be careful of their feeding, growth, and safety. On the other side, they hear his voice, answer his call, and believe in him, and own him for their Lord and proprietor. They follow him, he calls them; they hear his voice, he knows them; they follow him, he gives unto them eternal life, a life never to perish, either by their own wills or the wolves' violence. Against both those, Christ in this promise, as their owner, secures them. Against their corruptions; they shall not perish, viz., by a corruptive principle in themselves; here he removes from them all inward causes of destruction. Against outward violence; neither shall any man, no, nor devil, pluck them out of my hands, οὔτις. By this promise he holds us safe in his own possession against the encroachments of our lusts, and the rapine of the devil. They chose him for their guardian, and cast all their care upon him, and follow his conduct, and he takes care of them to give them eternal life, and to mind the weakest as well as the strongest of his sheep. He hath them in his hand. They apprehend him, and are apprehended by him, that they may attain the same end of the race with him, the resurrection of the dead, viz., a state of perfection: Philip. iii. 11, 12, 'If by any means I may attain unto the resurrection of the dead. Not as though

I had already attained, or were already perfect; but I follow after, if that I may (καταλαβῶ) lay hold of that for which [for which end] I am apprehended of Christ Jesus.' Apprehended, or laid hold on by Christ, a metaphor from those that run a race, that take hold of another to draw him after to win a prize as well as themselves. Christ lays hold on believers, and they follow him. Will Christ be easily persuaded to let go the hold of his own right? will he throw them out of his hand? That would be changeableness and unfaithfulness after his promise. Shall any pluck them out of his hand? That would be weakness. Faith cleaves to Christ, and Christ to faith. Faith hands Christ into the heart, and gives him possession; Christ takes the heart as his own propriety,—Eph. iii. 12, 'That Christ may dwell in your hearts by faith,'—and engageth himself by promise that both he and his Father shall abide there, John xiv. 23. Will any gracious heart cast Christ out of his lodging? He that knows the sweetness of their company can never desire to have their room. Doth Christ dwell in the heart to let sin pull his house down about his ears? Will he suffer the devil to bring in hell-fire to burn up his dwelling? It is his own house, the church and every member of it, Heb. iii. 6. Will he not hinder the decays of it, and repair the beams and walls; yea, the very tiles and pins? Shall he not brush down the cobwebs, and sweep out the dust? The heart is his field; will he not gather in his wheat, and burn up the tares at last?

[3.] Christ is a steward and officer, appointed by God to this purpose, to take care of every believer and his grace. How is he the surety of the covenant, and of a better testament? Heb. vii. 22. How can it be a better testament, if it may be broken, and prove as weak as the first? He is bound for the performance of the articles of it, whereof those are the two standing parts of this agreement: Jer. xxxii. 40, 'I will not turn away from them, to do them good: but I will put my fear in their hearts, that they shall not depart from me.' That God will not turn away from us to do us good, and that we shall never depart from him; and our perpetual cleaving to him doth depend upon his putting his fear into our hearts, and is the end of it. This never departing is the end why God puts his fear into our hearts. And Christ being a surety of this testament, is to look to both parts of it, that both what concerns God's part, and what concerns ours, may be made good.

Here it is to be considered, that,

(1.) Christ had a charge from the Father to this purpose.

[1.] He had charge concerning what he was to do for them. He had a charge to redeem them, and a charge to govern them; he hath a charge to relieve them, and a charge to perfect them.

1. He had a charge to redeem them. The copy of it you may see: Isa. xlix. 9, 'That thou mayest say to the prisoners, Go forth; to them that are in darkness, Shew yourselves.' He was to call them out of their prisons, knock off their fetters, bring them out of darkness into a marvellous light.

2. To be their governor was as much in his commission as to be their Redeemer, for, ver. 10, 'They shall not hunger nor thirst; neither shall the heat nor sun smite them; for he that hath mercy on them shall lead them, even by the springs of waters shall he guide them.' So also in Isa. iv. 6, where by heat, &c., is meant all troubles and inconveniences in a Christian life. They should not be wasted by fiery temptations, nor left in a forlorn condition. And the reason is, because that Christ, that Holy One, to whom God speaks, ver. 7, that Redeemer that called them out of a state of darkness and captivity, was to lead them in his hand, and have his eye upon them, and guide them by the springs of water, that they might have a fulness of the Spirit, and all refreshings and supplies of grace necessary for their

present condition. By water, alluding to the river out of the rock, which followed the Israelites in the wilderness; and by the heat and sun, to the fiery serpents, and the plague at that time. Christ here had the conduct of those redeemed captives committed to him, and was not to rest satisfied with conferring the first grace in the conversion of them, but to provide all things for their future security as well as their present freedom. And Isa. xlii. 3, when God proclaimed him his servant, this was in his commission, to have a special care of the bruised as well as the standing reed; of the smoking as well as the flaming flax; of the infant grace as well as the adult; and, indeed, the charge is chiefly for them.

3. He hath a charge to receive them: John vi. 37, 'All that the Father gives me shall come to me: and him that comes to me I will in no wise cast out.' Ver. 38, 'For I came down from heaven, not to do my own will, but the will of him that sent me.' He was in no wise to cast them out. It is a *meiosis;* he was affectionately to entertain and shelter them. And that he might make it as firm as possible could be, he tells us it was not only his will, but his office, and that he was under a necessary as well as voluntary obedience to his Father in this case. It was a part of God's will and charge to him, upon the sending him into the world, to receive very kindly any that come to him, though the most feeble and crippled believers that came upon crutches. As he was to receive kindly those that came, so it implies that he should receive them as often as they came, and that in any exercises of faith they should find fresh welcomes. Though their faith were very feeble, it should not be denied entertainment, but be highly caressed. So that Christ was ordered here to entertain every comer, as well as to die for them, and charged upon his obedience not to discountenance any that come, come when they will, and as often as they will.

4. He hath a charge also to perfect them, not to lose one of those God hath given him: John vi. 39, 'Τοῦτο δέ ἐστί τὸ θέλημα τοῦ πέμψαντός με πατρὸς;' 'That of all which he hath given me, I should lose nothing, but should raise it up again at the last day.' This is my Father's absolute and immutable will; and he hath sent me to perform this will, that of every person he hath given me, μὴ ἀπολέσω ἐξ αὐτοῦ, lose nothing of it, not the meanest, weakest person. Not one mite or grain of grace should be lost, but I should raise it up all at the last day. It was not the bare raising up that was the charge God gave unto Christ, but the raising up to eternal life, ver. 40, with that perfection of holiness and grace which God expects as the end of all his dispensations; otherwise it cannot be a raising up to eternal life in such a completeness as God intended in his charge. This charge not to lose any, but to raise them up fit to be presented unto God, without blemish, doth include all means and methods in subserviency to this end. And in this charge they are all implied to be looked after by Christ. Christ would be no friend to his Father should he slight his Father's orders. If he should fail of being a perfect Saviour, where would be his love and obedience to God? It is as impossible for an elect person to perish as it is for Christ, who is one with the Father, to act contrary to his Father's will. For since they are given to him, and that on purpose to receive eternal life by him, they must be preserved; and all that which prepares them to be vessels of glory, must be secured from a total and final miscarriage, or else Christ breaks his trust, disobeys his Father, and frustrates his expectations of a rest and satisfaction in him. (2.) A charge which Christ must give an account of. Officers are to give an account of the management of the trust reposed in them; so is Christ of every believer's soul. Our Saviour is in several places called God's servant. Servants are to give an account to those that employ

them; and it is part of the faithfulness of a servant so to do; and Christ's faithfulness is to be glorified. He is 'a merciful and faithful high priest,' Heb. ii. 17; faithful to God, as well as merciful to us; and faithful to God in being merciful to us. And by giving account of his mercy to us, he gives an account of his faithfulness to God. God expects all to be returned to him in that perfection and conformity to Christ which he designed when he first made the deed of gift of them to Christ. He will see whether a man be lost by comparing the number of his sanctified ones with the names written in the book of life. Some model of this account we have: Heb. ii. 13, 'Here am I, and the children which thou hast given me.' When he shall deliver up his charge, and all be numbered, he will tell his Father of the faith of his people, as he did John xvii. 6, 8, 'Thou gavest them me; and they have kept thy word. They have received the words which thou gavest me, and they have believed that thou didst send me.' This is the confession he will make of men before God and his angels, when he delivers up the kingdom to his Father. Will Christ be found tardy in his accounts? What could he answer if any one given to him should be missing? How could he say he hath kept them in his Father's name, and lost none, if any should miscarry, as he did, John xvii. 12, which is a copy of what will be said at the last?

[2.] As he hath a charge, so there is a power conferred on him to perform that charge.

(1.) A power of authority. He hath a power over death and hell to this end: Rev. i. 17, 18, 'Fear not; I am he that lives, and was dead: and, behold, I am alive for evermore, Amen; and have the keys of hell and death.' The giving the key is a mark of authority, and is a ceremony used in investitures into office. Christ hath the keys of death and hell delivered to him by God, and he hath them to prevent the fears and unbelief of his people; for such a use he makes of them here: 'Fear not.' By hell and death are meant all kinds of evils which were the bitter consequents of sin. Sin opened the mouth of death and the gates of hell; they are the only things which can possibly prevail against a believer to hurt him. Will not Christ keep those fast locked up, never to send them out upon a believer for his destruction? And if Christ hath the keys of hell and death, he hath also power to keep his people from that state which will necessarily run them into hell and death. All the power Christ hath given him over all flesh is in subserviency to the performing this charge: John xvii. 2, 'As thou hast given him power over all flesh, that he should give eternal life to as many as thou hast given him,' ἐξουσίαν; not only a power over those given to him to give them eternal life, but a power over all flesh, all the corruptions of men and devils, in order to this end of giving eternal life to every believer, 'to as many as God hath given him;' so that there is not one believer, no, not the weakest, but all the power God hath put into the hands of all flesh is with a design that it should be used for his security; as if God should say, Son, look to it; if any one that I have given to thee miss of eternal life, since I have given thee power over all flesh for their sakes; if any sinful or natural flesh deprive them of this life, it is for want of thy exercising the power I have granted thee to this purpose. Will Christ be unfaithful not to exercise his power to the right end? No. Much less will he abuse his power over all flesh to an end quite contrary to that for which it was given him. And Christ doth so exercise his power; for those righteous judgments and just reproofs of men in the world, they are for the sakes of the meek of the earth: Isa. xi. 4, 'With righteousness shall he judge the poor, and reprove with equity for the meek of the earth.'

(2.) Power of ability. Christ had the Spirit upon him, to bring forth judgment to the Gentiles, and judgment unto truth or unto victory, Isa. xlii. 4. This rich *depositum*, his jewels, laid up in the hand of Christ, are more highly valued by God than to be entrusted with a weak and feeble keeper.

Ability in respect of,

[1.] Strength to lay the foundation of our security. God made him strong for himself for attaining the ends he proposed: Ps. lxxx. 17, 'Let thy hand be upon the man of thy right hand, upon the Son of man, whom thou madest strong for thyself. So will not we go back from thee.' The death and mediation of Christ is the strongest preservation against apostasy. God made Christ strong for his own glory, to purchase a people that should keep their standing with him, and not fall as Adam did. The effect of the hand of God being upon Christ, and the strength he had to go through in his work, was to keep his people's wills and hearts close to God. This is the issue and inference the psalmist makes of it. What might in Adam's or angels' hands miscarry, never shall in his.

[2.] Assistance in this business to hold his people secure. Though God gave them to Christ as his charge, yet not wholly to leave them in Christ's hands, and take no care of them himself. Though they were safe enough in Christ's hands, yet the Father, to shew his care of them, and tenderness towards them, would have the keeping of them too, and would have fast hold as well as his Son, to assist his Son in it: John x. 29, 30, 'My Father, which gave them me, is greater than all (greater than Christ in his office of mediation), and no man is able to pluck them out of my hand. I and my Father are one.' God would have his hand upon them to assist Christ in it, to give him the highest security for their happiness. 'I and my Father are one:' one in resolution, affection, power, ability, and consent in this business; one in holding of my sheep; we both have our hands upon them. It is strange that any should perish that are grasped both by the Father and the Son. What power is able to do it, since the Father is greater than all, all men and devils, corruptions and temptations, and falls in with his greatest assistance to enable Christ in this business?

(3.) Of knowledge and wisdom. He is the wisdom of the Father; in him are hid all treasures of wisdom and knowledge, for the advantage of those persons designed in his commission. The all-wise God would never have put so great a concern as his own glory in his people's security into unskilful hands, and have disparaged his own wisdom in the choice of an unfit steward. He hath the book of God's decrees delivered to him, therefore called the Lamb's book of life, and there he finds every name written, Rev. xxi. 27, and he hath their names written in heaven before him: Heb. xii. 23, 'To the general assembly and church of the first-born which are written in heaven.' There is a commerce between Christ and his Spirit, so that by the Spirit he knows the state of every believer; their offices depend upon one another. Christ is the treasurer of grace, the Spirit the conveyer of it. He receives of Christ's and shews it unto us. Christ knows what goes out, and he knows to whom the Spirit hands it; knows the mind of the Spirit. He searches and listens to know the Spirit's mind, what it would have, what is fit to give to the soul. The Spirit intercedes in us; Christ intercedes for us. Christ knows the voice and mind of his own Spirit, and the Spirit knows the will of our Redeemer; for he 'makes intercessions for us according to the will of God,' Rom. viii. 27. So he cannot but know our state, because he hath a faithful Intelligencer, the same that is our faithful Comforter, and watcheth over us to take care of us. The catalogue of the gifts he had is reckoned up: Isa. xi. 2, 'And the Spirit of the Lord shall rest upon him, the spirit of wisdom and understanding, the spirit of counsel and might, the spirit of knowledge and of the fear of the Lord.' All his wisdom, and knowledge, and counsel, and understanding, are managed by the fear of the Lord, which is put last, as that which is the end of all the rest, viz., faithfulness to God. The fear of the Lord is the beginning of wisdom in us, and the top of wisdom in Christ. His wisdom and knowledge is to fit him for his faithfulness; as ver. 3, 'and shall make him of quick understanding in the fear of the Lord,' in all the methods of obedience to his charge; and God gave him the tongue of the learned, that he should know how to speak a word in season to them that are weary, Isa. l. 4, *i. e.* that are weary under sin, and apprehensions of wrath, and power of corruptions. The wisdom God gives him is principally for this end.

(4.) The sufficiency of treasure for it. Christ hath a ministerial fulness to this end: 'it pleased the Father that in him should all fulness dwell,' Col. i. 16. The issues of this fulness are our reconciliation to God, and the presenting us holy, unblameable, and unreprovable in God's sight, *i. e.* in such a state that his infinitely pure eye should find no fault in us, ver. 20–22. These are the effects of this fulness, and therefore are the end. Though the condition be put in, ver. 23, 'if you continue in the faith grounded and settled,' it doth not signify that our continuance in faith depends upon our own wills. It is frequent in Scripture to put into promises those conditions which in other places are promised to be wrought in us; so that all those promises of life upon our continuing and holding out to the end, do not weaken this, that our preservation is the effect of this fulness, because those conditions are promised in other places, and are parts of the covenant of grace, for the performance of which this fulness was given to our Saviour. Our completeness and perfection doth depend upon that fulness of the Godhead which dwells in him bodily: Col. ii. 9, 10, 'For in him dwells all the fulness of the Godhead bodily.' It is a ministerial fulness, whereby he is made sanctification to us as well as righteousness, 1 Cor. i. 30. He is made to us sanctification, and as much sanctification, and as perfect sanctification, as righteousness, or wisdom, or redemption; so that if any of those be perfect, as our righteousness and redemption, our sanctification also shall be perfect, though it be never so weak at present. The oil first poured upon Christ's head, as well as that upon Aaron the type, runs down to the skirts of his garments, and anoints all the other members. God poured out this grace first upon Christ, and through him upon all believers. There is as much a dependence of the grace in our hearts, not only in its birth, but in its continuance, upon this fulness of grace in Christ, as there is of light in the moon or air upon that in the sun; and there is a constant efflux of it from him to expel the darkness of sin, as there is of light from the sun to conquer the darkness in the air. And indeed, were it not maintained by a constant influence of Christ's fulness, we should quickly have no more grace left than Adam just after his fall, and should prove as very bankrupts as the worst of sinners. The sun is not able to dry up a drop of sea-water that lies in the midst of the sand, which the sea every minute rolls upon and preserves; neither can the flesh the least grace, while the fulness of Christ flows out upon it to supply it.

(5.) The perpetuity of this office. The continuance of Christ for ever in an unchangeable priesthood, makes him able to save to the utmost in spite of all men and devils: Heb. vii. 24, 25, 'But this, because he continueth for ever, hath an unchangeable priesthood: wherefore he is able,' &c. If he continues for ever in his office, he will then be for ever able to perform the business pertaining to the office, which is to save to the utmost, εἰς τὸ παντελὲς, perfectly, both in respect of the *terminus a quo*, from which he saves, and the *terminus ad quem*, to which salvation tends; from all kind of sins and corruptions, though never so powerful; but it continues for ever, none can deprive him of his office, because none can deprive him of his life. God neither can nor will, because he hath consecrated him by an oath to be a priest or officer upon this account for ever. And this office being conferred upon him on purpose for the salvation of believers, the ends and effects of this office are of as long a continuance as the office itself; for if Christ did not perform the end of his office, it would be but an empty title. And this life which is for ever, Christ doth intend to use for the standing and perfection of the weakest grace; so that as long as that endures, the grace and happiness of a Christian stands immoveable: John xiv. 19, 'Because I live, ye shall live also.' You shall live a spiritual life here, and an eternal life hereafter; all my life shall be employed for you, to communicate a gracious life to you, and preserve it in you, till it come to be swallowed up in a life of glory with me for ever. If the spring of Christ's life fail, then, and not till then, may the stream of ours. Grace cannot be destroyed while Christ's life is continued, which will be for ever: Rev. i. 18, 'I live for evermore.' A creature under the full beams of the sun cannot be cold till the light and heat of the sun be extinguished.

(6.) Honour. By this God encourageth Christ in this business; Christ hath his honour to this end. Places of trust among men are places of honour. Will Christ be careless of his own happiness and glory? He 'was exalted to give repentance, and forgiveness of sin,' Acts v. 41. The grace of repentance is only mentioned; but, by consequence, all the rest which accompany remission of sins are intended. What was the reason he had so great a glory conferred upon him? Because 'he loved righteousness, and hated iniquity,' Heb. i. 9, Ps. xlv. 7. Because he maniftested this love and hatred by vindicating the righteousness of God, and setting up an everlasting righteousness, and taking away iniquity. Now, this disposition of loving righteousness and hating iniquity, must needs be as powerful in him in heaven as it was before; nay, he must needs love this disposition the better, which was the cause of so great an exaltation. And if this disposition was the reason of his advancement, should this disposition languish in him, his very advancement would decay with it. If it were the reason why he was exalted, it must then follow that he was exalted that he might still love righteousness and hate iniquity, and διὰ τοῦτο may imply so much; for this end, for the exercise of this, he was anointed with the oil of gladness above his fellows. Since therefore this affection continues in him, is it possible he should endure to see that iniquity which he hates prevail over that righteousness which he loves, after he hath planted one in the heart, and subdued the other? The apostle prays, 2 Thes. i. 11, 12, 'That God would fulfil the work of faith with power, that the name of our Lord Jesus Christ may be glorified in you.' The name of Christ is glorified in a believer when the work of faith is fulfilled with power. It makes his crown shine the brighter. What hopes then have the devil and corruption of ever regaining their former standing in a believing soul? None, till the glory of Christ becomes vile in his own eyes.

3. As there is a charge and office given by God to Christ, and an ability to perform, so there is a compliance of Christ with it; which appears,

(1.) In his faithfulness in the discharge of it to this end. He promiseth this; he promised it to his Father in their agreement, else he had never been sent; he promises it to us. In John vi. 39 there is God's charge to him, that he should lose nothing of what he had given to him, but raise it up. In verse 40 there is one absolute promise, 'I will raise them up at the last day,' *i.e.* every believer; where he engageth himself to be faithful in the performance of God's will. He hath given a full evidence of it already, in finishing the work God gave him to do upon the earth: John xvii. 4, 'I have glorified thee on earth, I have finished the work which thou gavest me to do;' for he appeals to God for his faithfulness in this particular. And he will be no less faithful in finishing the work which is to be yet done by him in heaven in the behalf of his people and their graces, for such a work he hath to do: Heb. xii. 2, a finisher of faith, in his sitting at God's right hand. His faithful care extends to all his subjects, even the weakest as well as the highest believer, as God's providence doth to every creature, the lowest worm as well as the highest angel. They are all one in Christ, whether Jew or Gentile, bond or free, Gal. iii. 8. They are all one to him, for he is faithful in the exercise of his office to every one.

(2.) In his affection (and that a strong one) to this office, besides his faithfulness; such as,

[1.] His stirring compassions to weak grace. These were great in him before the assumption of our nature: Exod. xxxiii. 2, 3, 'I will send an angel before thee, for I will not go up in the midst of thee, for thou art a stiff-necked people, lest I consume thee in the way.' They will give me so many provocations that I shall be as a consuming fire, as God must needs be in a way of justice when he treats with a sinful people himself. But I will send an angel. What angel was this? It is called his presence, ver. 14. Isaiah puts them both together, chap. lxiii. 9, and calls him the angel of God's presence or face. Jesus Christ, the messenger of his favour, he shall go up, for he hath compassion; therefore it is said, Isa. lxiii. 9, 'In his pity he redeemed them.' The antithesis doth easily manifest this sense. He shall go up with thee, and he shall not consume thee, though thou art a stiff-necked people, because he is a mediator, and hath undertaken to satisfy my consuming justice; and being designed by assuming of your nature to be kin to you, hath great compassions towards that nature; his delights are among the sons of men. For God here is considered as a judge, and the angel of his presence as a mediator. The government of them by Christ is here appointed for their security, which they could not have under the immediate government of God. His compassions are in some sense greater now than they were then, since he hath been made like unto us, and compassed with our infirmities, and hath learned obedience (the necessity of obedience to the mediatory law) by the things which he suffered. Infirmity is the object of compassion, and the more pressing the infirmity is, the more stirring is the pity. As God pities the more when he 'remembers they are but dust, and knows their frame, Ps. ciii. 13, 14, so doth Christ know thy frame, thy believing frame, how weak it is; thy sinful frame, how strong it is; he knows thy enemies and he knows thy indigence, and how unprovided thou art of thyself to make a stout resistance, and this awakens his compassion. As the sickly, faint child, hardly able to go, and not the strong one, is the object of the Father's pity, the weaker thy faith, which lies mixed with a world of strong corruptions, the more will Christ be affected with thy case, and pity that grace of his own which suffers under them; for to this end his heart was stored with bowels to be exercised upon such occasions. He cannot have a greater object of pity than his own grace at the lowest ebb, nor a fitter opportunity to shew what a priest he is, how merciful to man in his misery, how faithful to God in his interest, which was the end of his being 'clothed with our infirmities,' Heb. ii. 17. That very sin which he hates, which is a burden, a grief, a trouble to him, shall rather excite than damp his compassion. It shall draw out his bowels to thy person and thy grace, and his anger only against thy sin. If he hath any compassions in heaven, they are for those that are his own, and for that grace which he loves when it is shot at by powerful corruptions.

[2.] A choice love to the weakest believers and their grace. The having a seed is the greatest article that he insisted on in his first agreement with God in this mediatory work. He was satisfied with the promises of it, for all the satisfaction he was to give to God by his blood: Isa. liii. 10, 11, 'He shall see his seed, and the travail of his soul, and shall be satisfied;' and in his last prayer, John xvii., he prays more for his people and their graces than for himself, to shew that his seed lay then nearest his heart, and that his soul travailed most with them. And shall that which he had an entire affection for in the first agreement between his Father and himself be slighted now after all his agonies, pains, sweat, and blood to gain it? When he was in the flesh, he admired not the buildings of the temple, had no fondness for the pomp of the world or the splendour of a prince's court. No; the faith of the centurion was the matter of his wonder, that of a Canaanitish woman, and the penitent love of a converted harlot the object of his affection, the revelation of God to babes and sucklings the subject of his thanksgiving. He had more desire to recover a little languishing grace to its former vigour than to preserve his life. When he was near his sentence of condemnation, he would in that extremity look back upon Peter to inspire him with a new strength after his fall, and by rallying his scattered graces make him victorious, who had been so miserably baffled by his corrupt fears. Would it be correspondent to the sincere love of Christ to let that which is his special favourite lie grovelling in the dust, wounded to death by sin, his hateful enemy?

[3.] His delight in believers and their graces. The very first grace acted by a new convert causes a jubilee in heaven. Christ, as it were, makes a feast in heaven when the lost sheep is found, and calls upon all the angels to congratulate with him for the recovery of it. Surely he will never have this joy turned into sorrow, these graces rifled and routed by the devil, and so give him occasion to laugh or scoff both at himself and the angels for their too forward joy. He was glad even of sad occasions contrary to his nature, when they might further the increase of a little faith. When Lazarus was dead, he was glad he was not there in the time of his sickness to hinder the death of a friend he loved, because by his raising him again his disciples might be confirmed in faith, and gain a greater power against their frequent doubts and unbelief: John xi. 15, 'I am glad for your sakes that I was not there, to the intent that you may believe.' If Paul calls the Philippians his joy and crown, because he instrumentally converted them, believers then are Christ's joy and crown, because he effectually died for them. Will Christ have his joy torn from his heart, his jewels rifled from his crown, and his crown plucked from his head? What was that joy of his which he desires of his Father to be 'fulfilled in his disciples,' John xvii. 13, but the sanctification of his people which he prays for? The very discourse of the fruitfulness of his saints' graces cheers his heart: John xv. 11, 'These things I have spoken to you, that my joy might remain in you,' *i.e.* that I might rejoice in you. He delights in the beauty, *i.e.* the graces of his queen: Ps. xlv. 11, 'So shall the king greatly desire thy beauty.' And will he not increase his own pleasure by increasing the spiritual beauty and graces of a believer? He doth boast of believers which are his heritage, Ps. xvi. 6, 'The lines are fallen to me in pleasant places, yea, I have a goodly heritage.' And can we think he will not improve it? It must be more pleasure to enjoy it flourishing than to possess it wasted. And Christ doth not repent of any undertaking of his for the happiness and security of his people: Hos. xiii. 14, 'I will ransom them from the power of the grave; I will redeem them from death: O death, I will be thy plagues; O grave, I will be thy destruction: repentance shall be hid from mine eyes.' It is the speech of Christ triumphing over death. That it is meant of Christ, the word פדע, to redeem with a price, and גאל, to redeem *jure affinitatis*, do evince. It includes the conquest of all other enemies, as the apostle descants upon it, 1 Cor. xv. 55–57. Sin and the curses of the law, of this he would not repent; 'Repentance shall be hid from my eyes;' I will cast away any motion to it, that it shall never come more in my sight. If he rejoices in this redemption, he will also in the effects of it upon the hearts of his people. These affections are unchangeable as his office. If that be perpetual, Heb. vii. 24, the qualifications necessary to that office must be as perpetual as his office itself. 'Christ is the same yesterday, to-day, and for ever,' Heb. xiii. 8. The same in credit with his Father, faithfulness to his charge, affection to his people, ability for his office, fulness of his person, virtue of his blood, compassions to his weeping, gasping new creature, and his hatred of that which doth oppress it. And when there is such a combination in the heart of Christ, and the end of all is the good of these poor bruised reeds his believing creatures, can we think it possible that those affections should be idle? And if they be excited, as undoubtedly they will, they will attain their ends, being all armed with a mighty power for the effecting of them.

Well then, let us act faith upon these engagements of Christ, and say with him in the psalm, Ps. xlviii. 14, 'This God is our God for ever and ever, he will be our guide even unto death,' and beyond death too. It is his office to guide by his counsel here, those that he will bring to glory hereafter. Lord Jesus, direct us by thy counsel here, as parts of thy charge, and bring us to glory as vessels of thy mercy, to be filled with everlasting riches of grace; cherish our bruised reeds, and inflame our smoking flax.

[4.] The author of grace. He keeps this treasure in his own hands. He is so choice of it, that he never entrusted an angel to bestow it. Angels were employed to strengthen him both after his temptation and in his agony; they are ministering spirits to the heirs of salvation, but they have not the custody of that which brings them into a state of heirship. He employs none but his Spirit to be his attorney and deputy in the world to this purpose, which Spirit is sent in his name, John xiv. 26. What it bestows, it receives from Christ, and doth it by his order: John xvi. 14, 'He shall glorify me,' in doing my work, for 'he shall receive of mine, and shew it unto you. All things that the Father hath are mine, therefore said I, that he shall take of mine, and shew it unto you.' To his glory, and by communication from him, all the saving light in our understanding, that vital principle in our will, those supernatural impressions upon our affections, are all handed to us from Christ by the Spirit, and wrought in us by our Redeemer's order. It is all his work by his proxy. The Father is the fountain of grace, Christ the treasurer, the Spirit the dispenser. It was his prerogative to be the author of faith, when he endured the cross and despised the shame: Heb. xii. 2, 'Looking unto Jesus, the author and finisher of our faith, who, for the joy set before him, endured the cross, despising the shame, and is set down at the right hand of the throne of God,' that he might thereby be the author of faith. And he will not lose the other part of his royalty to be the finisher of it, for that is his title too, and he performs this by sitting at the right hand of the throne of God. There he sits upon a throne of grace, to distribute grace upon every emergency, to finish that faith which is the weakest, and because it is the weakest, needs most assistance for its relief and perfection, and wants his greatest care for the support of it: Heb. iv. 15, 16, 'Let us therefore' (*i.e.* because we have not an high priest which cannot be touched with the feeling of our infirmities) 'come boldly to the throne of grace, that we may obtain mercy, and find grace;' *εἰς ἔυκαιρον βοήθειαν*, an emphatical word, *καιρὸς*, signifies season, without the addition of the adverb *ἐ̃υ* in the composition. He gives out mercy from thence for the remission of sin, and dispenseth grace for a seasonable help. It is then most seasonable, when habitual grace is weakest in itself, and its enemy strongest. If he would be the author of faith by his death, because of the joy set before him, he will be no less the finisher of it by his life, because of the joy possessed by him. This being his work since his return to glory, his care to look after both the supporting and completing bruised and imperfect faith is greater, because hereby he shews more of his art (as masters reserve the completing of a work to themselves for the honour of their own skill), and manifests more of his faithfulness to God, which is more evident in the perfection of a thing, than the first draught of it. And perhaps this may be meant by that expression, 'he learned obedience by the things which he suffered; and being made perfect, he became the author of eternal salvation unto all them that obey him,' Heb. v. 8, 9. He learned by his sufferings the necessity and the acceptableness of obedience to God in this mediatory work, and therefore will not be wanting to that part of faithfulness and obedience, which is still due, in being the author of eternal salvation, by his being made perfect in heaven, as he was the author of faith by his being humbled upon the earth. And indeed that grace which he gives is eternal life, for so he calls it, John xvii. 2, 3. What he calls eternal life, which he had power to give, he calls, ver. 3, 'the knowledge of God, and Jesus Christ whom God had sent.' The knowledge of God in Christ, a gracious, affectionate knowledge of faith, spiritually to know him as sent by God for such great ends, is faith and eternal life. Though it be but a bud in this world, subject to storms and winds, mixed with much ignorance and doubts, yet it is life, and eternal too. For there is no essential difference between grace and glory, but only in degree; therefore Christ saith so frequently in John, 'I give unto them eternal life;' I give, not I will give, but I give at present; and he that believes hath eternal life, not shall have; for grace is a preserving principle, which shall overpower the corruptive principle of sin. If this knowledge of God in Christ, implanted in the soul, should perish, it cannot then deserve the title Christ gives it. And indeed it is not agreeable to the wisdom of God, and the honour of his Son, to cast about so much, and contrive the sending of Christ, to bestow only a perishing gift, and to let the honour and fruit of his Son's death, his gift of grace, depend upon the mutable will of man.

Well then, to be the author and finisher of faith, are his two titles combined together; and therefore where he is the author, he is engaged to be the finisher of the weakest grace. The smallest star receives its light, and the preservation of it, from the sun, as well as of the greatest magnitude.

[5.] The exemplar and pattern of grace. God set up Christ as the great standard or standing copy, according to which all believers should be framed and wrought just like him: Rom. viii. 29, 'Whom he did foreknow, he also did predestinate to be conformed to the image of his Son, that he might be the first-born among many brethren.' To the image of his Son; not to the image of the most glorious man that ever was in the world. Not to Enoch, that signal walker with God; nor Noah, the only loyal preacher of righteousness in his time; nor Abraham, God's friend and the believers' father; but his own Son, who was free from all taint of sin. As his perfect purity made him fit to be a sacrifice to take away sin, 1 John iii. 5; to be an advocate to plead against sin, 1 John ii. 1, 'Jesus Christ the righteous;' so also to be the idea according to which all believers should be framed. Now the weakest habitual grace is an inchoative conformity to Christ as well as the strongest, and as well as that which is perfected in heaven, and hath in its own nature all the parts of that grace which is in Christ; as an infant in his body hath the lineaments of his father, as well as the grown son: 1 John xvi., 'And of his fulness have all we received grace for grace.' Grace in us suited to that grace which is in Christ, as some well express it; as the paper receives the image of every letter set in the press. The highest believer in the world was not wrought according to a more exact mode than the lowest. The meanest branch of God's affectionate foreknowledge is conformed to Christ, and the highest cannot have a more excellent pattern. The Spirit, in drawing grace in the soul, fixeth his eye upon Christ in every line he draws, and forms the lineaments of habitual grace in some proportion to that original. Here we are said to be *συμμόρφοι*, of the same spiritual form and shape, with the image of his Son. It is therefore called 'a forming of Christ,' Gal. iv. 19; 'a changing into the same image,' 2 Cor. iii. 18, *μεταμορφούμεθα*, metamorphosed from our natural into a spiritual shape, from glory to glory; from grace, glory begun, to glory, grace perfected. There is not only the shape of Christ, as a limner draws the picture of a man, but not the intellectual or moral endowments; but in this draught of grace in some measure there is. Believers are therefore said to have 'the Spirit of Christ,' Rom. viii. 9; the same dispositions of holiness, &c., which were in Christ; the same mind which was in Christ, Philip. ii. 5; and to be 'partakers of Christ,' Heb. iii. 14, not of a part of Christ; partakers of his purchase, of his grace, of his nature; and that by faith, by holding the beginning of our confidence, our first ground of faith, and our first act of faith, stedfast to the end; and are called his brethren, not by the human nature (for so all men are), but by a nature like his. Now the end of this conformity being that Christ might have brethren, and many brethren, can we imagine he would have one brother among the sons of men, if this conformity to Christ were to be preserved by our own power? Certainly that tempter who would have deprived us of a Saviour, by making him to cast himself down from the pinnacle of the temple, would quickly deprive us of his image, by hurling it down from the pinnacle of our hearts, and dashing all the dirt of hell upon it; and so the end of God in this absolute will of conforming us to Christ, being thereby to make him the first-born among many brethren, would be frustrate. For if any one true believer, thus conformed to Christ, might totally and finally fall, then a second and a third might, and all till you come to the last man of them. And if we were left to our own care, we should as certainly lose this image as Adam did in innocency. Can we preserve our spiritual life without this constant influence of God's grace, when we cannot our natural, without an uninterrupted stream of his providence; and when Adam did not will to preserve himself without the influx of God's grace preserving him in the integrity of his nature?

Well then, will Christ suffer one to perish who hath the same nature, spirit, and mind which he himself hath? Will he endure that his own picture, limned by the art of his Spirit, with the colours of his own blood, in so near a resemblance to him, that he hath not his image again in any thing in the world besides it; and this drawn for his own glory, that he might be a head among many brethren; will he suffer so excellent a piece as this to be torn in pieces, in contempt of him, either by flesh or devils ?

[6.] As the head and husband of believers, by virtue of union with them. Union in all bodies is the ground of stability. There is no straiter union in the world than that of Christ to believers; it is therefore compared to all kinds of members, natural and political, to shew the firmness of a believer's state upon all accounts. He is the head, believers the members; he is the root, they the branches; he the husband, they the wife. The bands of this union are, on Christ's part, the Spirit; on our parts, faith and love. The greatness of the person he sends to bind it close on his part, shews the high delight he hath in it; and shall he not as much delight in continuing this union by preserving that faith and love which knits us to him ? Christ's delight shall not be quenched, nor the Spirit's operation prove fruitless.

This will further appear by shewing what kind of union this is.

(1.) It is a marriage union, and as a natural union of head and members. Both are discoursed on together by the apostle: Eph. v. 28-30, 'He that loves his wife, loves himself. For no man ever yet hated his own flesh; but nourisheth and cherisheth it, even as the Lord the church. For we are members of his body, of his flesh, and of his bones.' Where, exhorting husbands to love their wives, he sets Christ as a copy to enforce it upon them. And ver. 32, he seems to intimate, that his whole discourse, wherein he began to speak of the love of Christ to the church, from ver. 25, did refer to this: 'No man ever yet hated his own flesh, but nourisheth it,' ἐκτρέφει, provides for it, and θάλπει, clothes it, and beautifies it, and defends it against the injuries of the weather. So doth Christ nourish the graces of his people, and protects them against the temptations of Satan. What prince would without resistance see a traitor wrest his beloved queen from his arms, and cut her throat ?

The apostle from this passes to mix both those unions together, and illustrates one by the other: ver. 30, 'We are members of his body, of his flesh,' &c., alluding to Eve's being taken out of Adam's side. And not only the church in general, but every believing member, 'We are members of his body;' we believers, and every one of us. It being thus, it is impossible Christ can do any other than nourish and cherish his own body, and every member of it, his own spouse. For in doing so, he loves himself, ver. 28, as a head, a husband, his mystical self, and his own honour, which is concerned in his spouse: 'No man ever yet hated his own flesh.' Whatsoever is implanted in our nature as a perfection of it, is eminently in God; now since he hath twisted with our nature a care of our own bodies, this care must be much more in the nature of Christ, because he hath a higher affection to his mystical body than we can have to our natural, for he is set here as the exemplar, and originals are always more excellent than the copied draughts. Would not every man improve both the beauty and strength of his own body, take care to preserve it from wounds, and to heal them when they are received, and not suffer the flesh to be mangled, unless it be for the security of the whole ? This would be a hatred of his own flesh, which never any man in his right wits was guilty of. Shall Christ then let spots always defile his body, and wounds putrefy it for want of curing ? Shall he let sin within, and the devil without, gnaw, slash, and cut his members, and stand by unconcerned ? Will he suffer the least member of his body to be torn from him by his enemies ? Shall our affectionate Redeemer, that hath taken upon him to be our head, and to cause this union, and delights in it, be the first that shall do such an unnatural act, and be worse natured to his body than the wickedest man in the world is to his ? Men do not use to cut off a finger for every wart or wen, or for every wound that hath putrefaction in it. Christ doth not cut off believers for their infirmities, he would then cut off his own members. Men rather use diseased parts with more tenderness, because they stand in more need of it. Christ therefore will much more cherish the affected part, and chase the disease away. Certainly believers, being members of his body, he must naturally care for their state, especially for that grace which is the band of union, and the vital spirit in all its members. Will he ever suffer that to decay for want of food? Christ hath not only the name, but the affection, of a head; and it is his office by union (and not only so, but his nature), as well as his Father's charge, to be careful of the preservation of his members. Shall he feel what is done against his people by persecutors? And will he not be much more sensible of what the flesh, that grand tyrant and persecutor of his people's graces, doth against his body, as well as what the lesser and more extrinsecal enemies execute?

Obj. But if it be said, that there is no doubt of Christ's faithfulness to us while we continue faithful to him; but we may cast off Christ from being our husband, and we being not natural, but mystical members, may cut off ourselves;—

Ans. Against this the covenant secures: Jer. xxxii. 40, 'I will make an everlasting covenant with them, that I will not turn away from them, to do them good; but I will put my fear in their hearts, that they shall not depart from me.' The fear he hath put into our hearts, keeps us from ever departing from him. Besides, there is a stronger stay, 'God will not turn from us, to do us good,' even the highest good, all the good he can. God stores us with habitual grace, and stands by it. It is God's keeping close to us, secures us from turning our backs upon him. Again, Christ's love to keep, is armed with gracious omnipotency to effect it, which no husband in the world hath over his wife, nor any man over any members of his body.

(2.) It is so strong a union intensively, that Christ and a regenerate man become one spirit: 1 Cor. vi. 17, 'But he that is joined to the Lord is one spirit,' κολλώμενος, glued; one spirit, as if they had but one soul in two bodies. What the Spirit doth in Christ, it doth also in a believer, according to the capacity of his soul. The same Spirit, which was the immediate conveyer of grace to the human nature of Christ, is so to us. Christ had an essential holiness in respect of his Godhead, but a derivative holiness as man. And this derivative holiness proceeded from the Spirit in him without measure, which we have in our measures. And by virtue of this union, by the same Spirit whereby you become one spirit with Christ, not only that grace which is in you and the greatest apostle are the same, but that grace which is in you and our great Mediator the man Christ Jesus, are of the same nature and original. As the light of the sun and the light of a star are the same, but they differ in degrees, not essentially; and as we say of souls, *animæ sunt pares dignitate*, though the actions are not the same, because of the indispositions of the organs, and the predominancy of some particular humour. It is the same Spirit in Christ and a believer, as it is the same soul in dignity, which is in an infant and a man of the most refined parts. It is more here, for it is the same Spirit, in respect of his person, which makes Christ very near of kin to us. This Spirit must either desert Christ or us, before this union can be dissolved: not Christ, for he had it in the world not by measure, and he is yet anointed with the oil of gladness above his fellows; not us, because the promises of Christ cannot be broken; this being the top-stone of the comfort of believers, in sending this Comforter, that he was to abide for ever.

(3.) This union of the soul to Christ is strengthened by the union of Christ to the Father: John xvii. 23, 'I in them, and thou in me, that they may be made perfect in one;' εἰς ἕν, into one. First, the Father in Christ, and then Christ in believers; so that whatsoever fulness, strength, grace, the Father gives to Christ by virtue of his union with him, and which is communicable to his members, the same hath the soul by virtue of its union with Christ. And both these unions, that of the Father with Christ, and that of Christ with us, are for the perfection of all those that should be with him to the end of the world, even the weakest as well as the strongest; for it refers to ver. 20. But we must understand this, not of that essential union between the Father and the Son, as they are one essence, but of the union of the Father to Christ as mediator, in respect of the Father's influence upon him, and assistance of him. Christ being the medium of our union with God, both the Father's union with him, and his with us, are for our perfection. Because, whatsoever grace Christ hath, by virtue of his union with the Father, is to be communicated to us according to our capacity, or employed for us according to our necessity. And from this union it is that God loves believers as he loves Christ: ver. 23, 'That the world may know that thou hast loved them, as thou hast loved me.' Christ himself made no question but the Father loved believers as he loved him their head, *amore similitudinis*, not *æqualitatis;* but Christ would have the world know it, and themselves know it too, and therefore would have them sanctified, and at last perfected. From this passage, I think, this will plainly follow, that as Christ cannot miscarry because of his union with the Father, whereby he hath a continual influence from him, so neither can a believer by virtue of his union with Christ, which invests him in the same love which the Father bears to Christ.

Methinks the apostle refers to this passage: Col. iii. 3, 'Our life is hid with Christ in God.' Our life is hid with Christ by virtue of our union with him, as Christ is in God by union with the Father; Christ in God, and our life in Christ. The flesh then and the devils may as well pull God out of heaven, and overthrow the security of Christ, and pull him from the right hand of the Father, as rob a true believer of his spiritual life, or pull grace, which is Christ formed in the heart, out of the soul of a new creature.

(4.) From this union with Christ doth result a communion with him, which secures grace in a believer's heart. A communion with him in his death, and from thence a perfection. So the apostle argues: Rom. vi. 5, 6, 'If we have been planted together in the likeness of his death, we shall be also in the likeness of his resurrection: knowing this, that our old man is crucified with him, that the body of sin might be destroyed,' &c. If we are planted with him in the likeness of his death for the destruction of the body of sin, we shall grow up with him in the likeness of his resurrection for the perpetual life of grace; for by our dying with him we are freed from sin, *i. e.* from serving sin, and yielding up ourselves to it. And this communion in his death will introduce a communion with him in his life: ver. 8, 'Therefore, as Christ, being raised again, dies no more,' so a Christian being regenerate, and raised from a death in sin, which spiritually answers to a resurrection of the body, cannot spiritually die again, ver. 9–11; for Christ formed in the heart dies no more there, than Christ exalted in heaven doth. And after an exhortation, that they should not obey sin in the lusts thereof, whereby he shews what this communion with Christ in his resurrection is, not a total freedom from sin, but a not obeying sin in its lusts and motions; not reverencing the commands of it, as if it were our lord; not yielding ourselves to its service, but to the service of God, ver. 12, 13; which is a good comment upon those places which some have made an erroneous use of, and from which they do at this day cry up an absolute perfection in this life, 1 John iii. 9: 1 John v. 18, 'Whosoever is born of God doth not commit sin: for his seed remains in him, and he cannot sin because he is born of God.' He cannot morally, because of the seed of God and strong habit of grace, fed by union to and communion with Christ. I say, after this exhortation, this is the final inference the apostle makes: ver. 14, 'Sin shall not have dominion over you, for you are not under the law, but under grace,' *i. e.* by virtue of your being in the covenant of grace, united to the mediator of that covenant, who as surety hath satisfied the law for you, and brought it about that you are no more under the law, but under grace; and having a communion with him in his death and resurrection, you are in the same stable state inchoatively as Christ himself is, and you will be at last perfectly so in heaven. For that is the strength of the apostle's reasoning, as you will find perusing that chapter at your leisure, viz., to shew that it was impossible that any one that was in the covenant of grace should abuse that grace to a licentiousness in sin, and a devoted affection to it, because if he had been once planted into that likeness of Christ's death, he is freed from sin, and will be planted in the likeness of Christ's resurrection; and therefore it will be impossible for him to be under the reign of sin. And to encourage them to keep up their standing against sin, he assures them that sin shall have no dominion over them; as nothing makes a man fight more courageously in a battle than to be sure of victory. Union cannot be without communion; for while the members are united to a living, sound head, there will be an influx of animal spirits whereby they shall partake of life and motion. The spirit from our mystical head will be working in us, providing for us, and standing by us for our mystical preservation.

Well, then, sum up this together, that this union is a marriage union, and that thereby we become the body of Christ, yea, and are acted by the same Spirit; add the union of the Father with Christ, as well as that of Christ with us, and the communion both of his death and resurrection resulting from this union; and if those be not strong enough to hold and secure a true believer, though he have but little strength, he may then, and not till then, totally and finally fall away.

[7.] An advocate of grace in respect of his intercession. Christ's office being that of an advocate, doth ascertain this truth. An advocate is so to plead his client's right, that he may gain the victory over his adversary in the suit. Christ being an advocate that always entertains a good cause, will certainly so manage it that grace shall at length prove victorious.

(1.) The concerns of grace are the principal subject of his intercession.

[1.] Our standing in grace. Our first access by faith is the immediate fruit of his reconciling us. But our actual salvation, and all the methods of it, are the fruits of his life: Rom. v. 2, 'By whom also we have access by faith into this grace wherein we stand, and rejoice in hope of the glory of God.'

The apostle in that verse mentions three things:

1. Our access by faith.

2. Our standing in this grace, whereunto we have access.

3. Our joy in the hopes of all the fruits of it. All which are ascribed not only to his death, but to his life, and the two last principally to that, ver. 10. 11. By his death, he takes away the partition wall between God and us, built on our parts by sin, and on God's part by the hand of justice. By his life, he preserves this access free and open, and secures the wall from ever being built up again to hinder our access, which would be if sin should prevail; for if sin builds it on our part, justice could not but rebuild it on

God's part, were it not for the life of Christ, which doth as much maintain our standing, as his death did work our reconciliation, otherwise the apostle could not have put a *much more* to it. For by this life of Christ we can joy in God as our friend, who was formerly our enemy, because by Christ thus living we receive the atonement, *i.e.* it is continually applied to us: ver. 11, 'by whom we have now received the atonement, ἐλάβομεν, *aorist*, just now,' the fruits of the atonement; and by this constant application of the atonement, our standing is secured with joy; for in receiving the atonement made by his death from him now living, we receive all the other fruits of his purchase. Hence he is said to prepare heaven for us, *i.e.* by keeping up the favour of God towards us, that when we come we may have the kindest reception, just as he doth make us meet below for the inheritance of the saints in light by his Spirit.

[2.] Our progress in sanctification. The keeping his seed from the evil, and preserving of them, is the main matter of all that prayer, John xvii. 15, 'Keep them from the evil,' ἀπὸ τοῦ πονηροῦ; from the devil, the head of sin, from all sorts of evils, evils within and evils without; which implies not only a desire negatively, that they might not be hurt by evil, but also that they might overcome it, and be improved by it. And that no believer should be discouraged, and think himself out of Christ's thoughts, he presents to his Father the whole generation of them to 'the end of the world,' ver. 20. He holds up here all his seed, as it were, in his hand, as those to whom he would have those petitions then put up, answered in time, to every one of them, weak and strong, to the very last man that should give up his name to him; every one that should believe through the apostles' word, their word ministerially, because committed to them to be delivered down by them from age to age, so that the same gospel being now preached in the world, and producing the fruit of faith in any soul, entitles him to the benefits of this prayer. In his recovery of Peter by his prayer on earth, he sets a pattern of what he would do for all his people in heaven: Luke xxii. 32, 'But I have prayed for thee, that thy faith fail not: and when thou art converted, strengthen thy brethren,' which is evidenced by those words, 'when thou art converted,' &c. Tell them that the rallying of thy routed faith was by the prevalency of my prayer, and that they may expect the like from me in their temptations; that their faith shall not fail, but rather get a surer standing, as indeed Peter's did, who, though he so shamefully denied his Master under the power of the temptation, yet was the most forward afterwards to confess him in the teeth of his adversaries. As Paul's conversion was a pattern to after-ages of the power of his grace for the turning the most giant-like sinners, so was this a pattern of the force of his intercession for the preservation and further sanctification of oppressed believers. These words, 'strengthen thy brethren,' would be of little force if it were not a leading case, and that Christ intended to make it a rule of court for the comfort of his people that are like Peter, having the revelation of Christ from God, and not from flesh and blood.

[3.] The keeping the covenant firm in both the parts of it, as the foundation of both these. Therefore in the solemn appearance of God in prophetic visions, relating to the gospel dispensation, both before the manifestation of Christ and since, the throne of God is encircled with a rainbow. But the place I would consider is Jer. xxx. 21, 22, 'And their governor shall proceed from the midst of them; and I will cause him to draw near, and he shall approach unto me: for who is this that engageth his heart to approach unto me? saith the Lord. And you shall be my people, and I will be your God.' God causeth Christ to draw near, and gives him a power of mediating: 'I will cause him to draw near;' Christ accepts it; 'he shall approach unto me.' Who? 'Their governor,' that 'shall proceed from the midst of them.' God then breaks out into a delightful astonishment at this approach of Christ to him as a surety and advocate, so that he gives out all blessings upon his asking, 'Who is this that hath engaged his heart?' ערב את לבו, hath pawned his heart, hath become a surety in his heart; so the word is used and translated, Gen. xliv. 32, ערב את הנער, thy servant hath 'become a surety for the lad;' and likewise Prov. vi. 1, 'If thou be surety for thy friend.' This is that which makes the covenant firm, and preserves the knot between God and us. Ver. 22, 'You shall be my people, and I will be your God;' I understand it of the mediation of Christ in general, but with a particular application to his intercession, as being a great part of that mediation, and the principal, if not the only, continued act of it. Now as long as those engagements of his heart, those affections, remain, he hath liberty as a surety to approach to God, which he will always have; and as long as God delights in it, as here he doth even to admiration, so long shall believers be God's people, and he their God. Certainly such an answer doth Christ receive upon every act of his intercession, even a covenant answer; God saith, that poor, weak, believing soul whom thou dost plead for shall be mine, one of my people, and I will be his God, and I will do what thou wilt for him.

(2.) His intercession seems to be appointed by his Father for this end, the support and happiness of those that believe in him; which appears not only in that fore-mentioned place of Jeremiah, wherein God would cause him to approach to him for the keeping the covenant stable between God and his people; but in Ps. ii. 8, 'Ask of me, and I shall give thee the heathen for thine inheritance, and the uttermost parts of the earth for thy possession;' which is Christ's patent for this office of advocate, and granted him after his resurrection, intimated in those words, 'Thou art my Son, this day have I begotten thee.' As Christ did not die for himself, or rise again for himself, but as a public person, so he hath this power of asking, and promise of receiving upon asking, as a public person, as a king and governor, as he is styled in Jer. xxx. 22, and as he is set King upon his holy hill of Sion, *i. e.* king in his church. If he had then this grant of asking, as a public person, and as king in his church, it must then be employed for those who are his church, his voluntary subjects, those for whom he died and rose again. If his asking were designed as a means to come to the possession of his inheritance, the possession of the Gentiles, by the same reason it is also designed as a means for the improvement of his inheritance; for those that are chiefly his heritage in the world, his garden in the wilderness, so pleasant to him, Ps. xvi. 6, that if he can make it more pleasant for asking he will not stick at it, and God will do it for him. For the large promise made him implies both the preservation and improvement of his inheritance, to make it comfortable to him. This power of asking was chiefly designed for believers, as appears by the use the psalmist makes of it, of exhortation to the powers of the world, ver. 10, 11, 'to serve him;' but of exultation in the latter end of ver. 12 to believers, 'Blessed are all they that put their trust in him.' If it were not designed by God for them, and for every one of them (all they), and to be employed for them chiefly, they would be no more blessed than others. And this blessedness doth consist in justification and sanctification, for 'blessed is the man whose sins are forgiven,' Ps. xxxii. 1; and Christ blesseth us 'by turning us away from iniquity,' Acts iii. 26.

(3.) Christ doth ask this blessing of grace in particular, for every believer n particular, which still adds a strength to this truth. Christ's living for ever to make intercession for us is the reason rendered why he is able to 'save to the utmost,' Heb. vii. 25. It is εἰς τὸ παντελὲς, *ad omnimodam perfectionem*, so Camero; perfection of parts here, perfection of degrees hereafter. If he lives for ever to make intercession for the perfect salvation of his people, he doth consequently intercede for all those things which may promote the perfection of their salvation, and consequently for their graces, which are necessary to it. Therefore the habit of grace shall be actually and perpetually preserved, otherwise Christ's intercession would be in vain. And this he doth in particular for every believer. They were given to him in particular, they come to God by him in particular, and he saves them in particular; therefore he intercedes for them in particular, even for all those that come unto God by him. As they come, he intercedes for them; as a great master of requests, he receives the petitions of every comer, and presents their particular cases to his Father with a good and powerful word of his own; so he prayed for Peter in particular, Luke xxii. 32, 'I have prayed for thee (and for thy grace too), that thy faith fail not.' It is probable Christ prayed for all, it seems to be implied; Satan had an aching tooth at every one of them; Ἐξητήσατο, he hath earnestly desired you to sift you as wheat. He prayed particularly for their faith, that it might not be conquered, because this being the fundamental grace, if this stands all the rest keep up their heads. His intercession is for everything which may preserve, and against everything which may destroy. Not only for the preservation itself, but for the particular means of it: John xvii. 17, 'Sanctify them through thy truth: thy word is truth.' Do it by thy word, where he intercedes for the keeping up a gospel in the world in subserviency to this end, viz., their sanctification. Do it by thy truth, that incorruptible seed, that eternal gospel, eternal in the duration of the effects of it. So that thy standing, and all the means of it, the habit and the very acting of thy faith, the impressions made upon thy soul by any particular truth, are the fruits of Christ's intercession. I cannot imagine that a person that Christ doth in so particular a manner intercede for in all his concerns, can fall totally and finally.

(4.) He intercedes more fervently (if there be any degrees at all in his affection in heaven above what he had here) in heaven than he did upon the earth. If he, upon the earth, did pray so earnestly to his Father to keep them, and that a little before his death, when the sorrows of death and the grave, the contest he was to have with his Father's wrath, began to stare him in the face; when he had a foresight of all those bruises his soul was shortly to suffer, which, if anything, might reasonably divert his thoughts, and damp his affections from praying for others; when he hath conquered all this, and hath no more death to suffer, no infirmity of the flesh to clog him, not the least eclipse of his Father's countenance so dreadfully to groan under, he will rather be more fervent than cold in his suit. Shall he pray against the indulged sins of his enemies under the anguish of death, and not against the lamented and troublesome corruptions of his friends in the triumphs of glory? Shall he pray for his murderers under the horror of his Father's wrath, and not plead for the support of his people's graces in the arms of his Father's love? Hath he not more encouragements to plead strongly for them since he sits upon a throne of grace, than when he suffered upon a cross by justice? He stood at his death as a guilty person charged with the guilt of others; but in heaven he pleads as a righteous advocate, freed from all that guilt which was then charged upon him. Hath he not more engagements? Shall not the esteem of his purchase, the value of his Father's gift, honour of his conquest, consent of his people, credit of his office, obedience to his Father's charge, elevated affection, delight in his people's graces, care of his image, relation of a husband, straitness of union; shall not all these inflame his spirit with a zeal in his plea beyond the power of a control, were there a possibility of any?

(5.) His intercession now must be every jot as prevalent, if not more, than his prayer upon earth. If he prevailed at the tribunal of God's justice by his satisfaction, which was the sharpest conflict he could ever enter into, shall he not much more prevail at the throne of God's grace by his intercession? If his death were powerful to procure a perfect righteousness for our justification, his intercession will keep pace with it to apply that and perfect grace for our sanctification. Will not Christ be successful in one as well as the other, and as good at finishing the work in heaven as he was at finishing his work on earth, especially when his finishing his work on earth is the foundation of the continuance of that work of his intercession; being first a propitiation and then an advocate? It will certainly produce as perfect effects for the perfection of the weakest believer, as his death upon the cross did for his reconciliation, which is to 'present us holy, unblameable, and unreprovable in God's sight,' Col. i. 22.

How strongly grounded his intercession in heaven is, and what arguments he doth use, see John xvii. 11, 12: 'And now I am no more in the world, but these are in the world, and I come to thee. Holy Father, keep through thy own name those whom thou hast given me, that they may be one, as we are. While I was with them in the world, I kept them in thy name: those that thou gavest me I have kept, and none of them is lost, but the son of perdition.' I am no more in the world, corporally, but those are in the world. I shall leave those behind me in a world of temptation and misery. 'I come to thee.' I shall shortly ascend to thee. Now, 'Holy Father, keep through thy name,' &c. Here we have,

(1.) God's relation to himself, and to his people. Father, not My holy Father. The relation reaches not only to the intercessor, but the persons pleaded for. Christ in heaven pleads with God as a Father, our Father.

(2.) God's holiness. Holy Father; not merciful, powerful Father, or righteous Father, as afterwards. Grace is an image of God's holiness, and therefore is the most proper attribute of God to be used as an argument for the preservation of it.

(3.) The gift of God. Keep those whom thou hast given me, which he urgeth twice. Thou gavest them me to redeem and sanctify; not wholly to part with them, but to be presented to thee again in a better state. I had never had them but by thy donation. Thou didst not give them to me that they might perish, but that they might be kept. Keep, therefore, thy own gift, that they may be returned to thee in a better state. Thou gavest them me, and they are still thine. Neglect not thy own, because thou art immutable in thy counsel and affection.

(4.) The end why God gave them to Christ. That they may be one, as we are. Ἵνα, the causal particle, may refer either to δέδωκας or τήρησον. If the end, Father, why thou didst give them to me, was that they might be one, as we are, keep them, therefore, till they attain this end in perfection, that thy aim may not be frustrated.

(5.) God's past preservation of them. I have kept them through thy name. Though I have been in the world with them, and have kept them, it was through thy strength; and in my present petition I desire no greater a strength than what already thou hast exerted for their preservation.

(6.) His own obedience to God. Those whom thou gavest me, I have kept. He lays a stress upon God's donation and his own faithfulness. I have been obedient to thee in the keeping of them, because they were thy gift. Wilt thou command me to keep that which thou thyself wilt neglect and slight? Wilt thou be careless of that charge thou gavest me such strict orders to preserve? Shall my faithfulness to thee in that charge outstrip thy mercifulness to them and care of their standing?

(7.) The success of his care. None of them is lost. This charge thou gavest me, not to lose any. I have hitherto performed it. Not one son of election, but only that of perdition, which was given to me as my attendant, not my charge. The *but*, or εἰ μὴ, doth not weaken this assertion of Christ. As Camero and others observe, εἰ μὴ is not by way of exception, but opposition. He was not of the number of those given to Christ, but of another rank of society, as Gal. ii. 16, 'A man is not justified, εἰ μὴ, but by the faith of Jesus Christ,' where faith is set in opposition to works in justification; not at all by works, but only by faith. So Mat. xxiv. 36, 'Of that day and hour knows no man, no, not the angels in heaven, but, εἰ μὴ, my Father only.' The Father is set in opposition to men and angels, not excepted as either man or angel. So Judas here is set in opposition to those that were given to Christ, not excepted as a lost part of that number. I have been the larger in it that it may serve for a little use of what hath been spoken. It will be a good pattern of prayer. Arguments may be fetched from those topics so far as will suit us to plead with God in our case, and there is scarce any of these considerations which have been delivered but may be turned into an argument in prayer.

Now sum up all this. Doth Christ plead for our standing in grace and progress in sanctification, and live for this end? Did he set Peter up as a pattern of what he would do in this case? Is the covenant kept firm by his mediation, and covenant-answers procured by his intercession? Is it appointed by God for this very end, viz., the blessedness of his people? Doth he present every man's case in particular, and intercede for his grace in particular, and what truth shall make impressions on him? Is there some reason to think he is more fervent in it now than he was upon the earth? To be sure, no less. Are the arguments he uses very strong? Then the standing even of the weakest grace is sure. Before that can fall, God must change his end in giving his Son a power to ask; Christ must leave pleading, or his arguments must lose their strength. But as Ambrose said to Monica concerning Austin, who remained in his natural condition notwithstanding his good education and his mother's prayers, It is impossible that a son of so many prayers should perish, so may I say of grace, It is impossible a child of so many, so fervent, so powerful intercessions, in all circumstances, can ever, either totally or finally, perish.

3. The Spirit is engaged in this business. The reason why God puts his Spirit into the heart is to preserve us from departing from him, Jer. xxxii. 40. As Christ was true and faithful to God in the end of his coming, so will the Spirit be faithful to God in the end of his being put into the heart. It is the same Spirit which, being upon Christ, enabled him to the performance of his charge, Isa. xi. 1, 2, and made him of quick understanding in the fear of the Lord, to establish him in faithfulness and obedience to God in his mediatory work. The same Spirit is in us, to establish us in the fear of God, to keep that principle of God's fear put into our hearts alive. And as the Spirit performed his office fully upon the human nature of Christ, so it will not be deficient in us according to our measure. Consider the Spirit every way, and this work of preserving grace will appear to be his business. What Christ doth by his proxy may well be interpreted to be his own act.

(1.) His mission. If Christ were not to break the bruised reed, surely no messenger sent by him is to do it. 'The Spirit is sent by the Father in his Son's name,' John xiv. 26. He is sent 'by Christ from the Father,'

John xv. 26; with his Father's consent and commission. There is a conjunct authority, sent by commission from both, sent to supply Christ's place upon earth. Christ's business in part was to keep his people, and he wanted one to do it after his departure; therefore prays his 'Father to keep them in his name,' John xvii. 11. In answer to this prayer, the Spirit is sent; therefore sent by the Father and Son in subserviency to this end of preserving his people, and comes himself with an intention to answer this end, and perform the covenant. If both concur in sending him, his mission must be in order to the fulfiling what was agreed upon by the three persons, and more particularly by the Father and Son in the mediatory covenant, for they would never send one that should go contrary to the covenant they were engaged in.

(2.) His titles. He is called

[1.] A Comforter: John xiv. 16, 'I will pray the Father, and he will give you another Comforter.' The Comforter, κατ' ἐξοχήν. Such another Comforter as I have been unto you, and in some respects better; a more spiritual Comforter. It was expedient that Christ should go away, that this Comforter might come: John xvi. 27, 'Nevertheless I tell you the truth, it is expedient for you that I go away; for if I go not away, the Comforter will not come unto you.' I tell you the truth; I must deal plainly with you; I have a great desire the Comforter should come, and if I go not away, he will not come; intimating thereby that it was a greater blessing to have the Comforter with them than Christ in person. What comfort could they have in this declaration, and what expediency in it, if the Spirit did not mind the same end in keeping and preserving us as Christ did? It had been no ways expedient. Better a thousand times Christ had never gone, and the Comforter never come, if it were not for the same end which Christ minded in the world. The ends of Christ were to give 'the oil of joy for mourning, the garment of praise for the spirit of heaviness, that they might be called trees of righteousness, the planting of the Lord, that he might be glorified,' Isa. lxi. 3. As this was the work of Christ, so this is the work of the Spirit as a comforter, to make the heart grow up in fruit to the glory of God.

[2.] An abiding Comforter: John xiv. 86, 'That he may abide with you for ever.' He must abide with us in the capacity wherein he is sent, *i. e.* as a comforter. His comfort would signify little if it did not meet with the main trouble which pesters us, *i. e.* the fear of miscarrying and not continuing to the end. Oh, I am afraid that this little spark may be quenched by the floods cast out of the dragon's mouth, that this little faith may be wounded to death by some strong temptations. I doubt it will quickly gasp its last. I have but a little oil in the cruse; it will soon be wasted, and I shall die. These kind of thoughts every believer hath more or less. The chosen vessel and the greatest instrument for God that ever was, found such fears clambering up in him: 1 Cor. ix. 27, 'I keep under my body, lest that by any means I myself should be a castaway.' The Spirit therefore must be a comforter to mate this grand trouble, and melt this gloomy cloud which doth so often darken the strong as well as the weak believer; and truly every one's experience can testify that when such thoughts do creep up, some hopes also start up with them from the Spirit, like a covenant rainbow with a shower; and one thing which, as a comforter, he is to convince the world of (and the best part of the world too, even those that are convinced of unbelief, sinfulnesss, and the necessity and sufficiency of the righteousness of Christ) is, that the prince of the world is judged and condemned, his works dissolved, and that he shall never more have power over believers to ruin them, John xvi. 11. He is to abide with us to that end and purpose for which he came into our hearts, and that was to bring us to God; therefore his abiding with us is to keep us with God. If our first conversion were the work of the Spirit, and our standing in it our own, we should be more beholding to ourselves than to the Spirit, because a good condition stable is a greater blessing than a good condition mutable. If the Spirit stand only as a careless spectator, to see how we would steer our course, without putting his hand to the helm, what good would his abiding with us do? If a man have a great business to do, the presence of a multitude of men will do him no good unless he hath assistance from them. By the Spirit's abiding with us is meant, not the remaining of his person without his operations. As when God's promises to be present with us, he doth not mean his essential presence, for that cannot but be present, whether he promiseth it or no, but his gracious presence. The Spirit abides with believers not only in moving them, for so he abides with wicked men, but efficaciously moving, not only in their first conversion, but in their growth and progress.

The use is,

1. Matter of information;

2. Of comfort;

3. Of duty.

1. Information.

(1.) The doctrine of the possibility of a total and final apostasy of a regenerate man after grace infused is not according to truth. You see upon what pillars the doctrine we have asserted stands. Whence it follows that the contrary doctrine of the apostasy of a regenerate man is against the whole tenor of the covenant of grace, against the attributes of God engaged in it and about it, against the design of Christ, the mediator of it, against the charge committed to him, against the ends of the Spirit's mission and abiding with us.

The question then may be thus stated, whether that vital principle or habit of grace put into the heart by the powerful operation of the Holy Ghost at the conversion of the soul be not perpetually preserved and cherished by the same Spirit, so that it never dies; and that therefore a regenerate man, endued with this vital principle, neither can nor will, by reason of this implanted inworking of the Spirit, fall from faith and serve sin, so as to give himself up wholly to the commands of it. The question is not, whether we shall persevere if grace doth continue, as the contrary-minded assert, and accordingly gloss upon the scriptures alleged for it. Such a question would be ridiculous. It is as much as to ask whether a man shall live to-morrow if his life remain in him, or whether the sun shall shine to-morrow if its light continues; and is as much as to say, a man shall persevere if he doth persevere. But whether the habit of grace, the fear of God, faith, the new creature, new man, or howsoever you will term it, be not so settled in the soul as that it shall never be totally removed. Some affirm that it may. Satan was of this persuasion (though he has since discovered himself more orthodox), when he tells God to his face, Job i. 8–11, 'Put forth thy hand now, and touch all that he hath, and he will curse thee to thy face;' that smart afflictions would divest Job of that uprightness God so signally applauded in him, as a none-such in all the earth. The chief ground is, that they lay all, both conversion and preservation, upon the will of man, not grace.

I shall therefore lay down,

[1.] Some propositions for explaining it.

It is acknowledged that,

(1.) The operations of grace may be interrupted. As long as there are two laws, one of sin in the members, another of grace in the mind; as long as there are two principles in a grand contest, flesh and spirit; as long as our knowledge is imperfect, and our love but of a weak growth, the operation of both cannot be perfecter than the nature of their principle. The vigour of our gracious actions is often enfeebled by the power of the flesh, that we do many times the evil we hate, and omit that good we love. And we cannot deny but that our acts flow oftener from a corrupt than a renewed principle; yea, and those actions which flow from grace are so tinctured with the vapours of the other principle, that they seem to partake more of the impressions of the law of sin than of the law of the mind; so that our perseverance is not to be measured by the constant temper of our actions, but from the permanency of the habit. The acts of grace may be suspended by the prevalency of some sinful distemper, as the operations of natural life are in an epileptic or apoplectic paroxysm. Hence it is that we find David so often praying for quickening grace, according to the promise, upon a sense of the flagging of his grace.

(2.) The comfort of our grace may be eclipsed. We may lose the sense of it without losing the substance. An actual communion may be lost, upon a sinful fall, till actual repentance, when the union is not unloosed. A benumbed member is knit to the body, though it hath not its wonted vigour and active heat. Mutual comfort may be suspended between man and wife, though the conjugal knot be not dissolved. Believers may be separated from Christ's smiles, but not from their relation to Christ and being in him. Comfortable interest may be interrupted, when radical interest receives no damage. A leper under the law was hindered of actual enjoyment of his house, but not deprived of his legal title to it.

(3.) Relative grace cannot be lost. Every regenerate man being the son of God by a double title, that of regeneration and adoption, can never cease to be his son. The relation of a son to a father is indissoluble. It can never be that he that is once a son can become no son; the relation is firm, though the affection may be on both sides extinguished. The relation we have to God as his children, is knit with that other of heirs. The apostle made no doubt of the truth of that consequence: Rom. viii. 17, 'If children, then heirs, and heirs of God.' And he was afterwards of the same mind: Gal. iv. 7, 'And if a son, then an heir of God through Christ.' If it be objected, True, unless a believer disinherit himself by an undutiful and contemptuous carriage. But he cannot, unless he should cease to be a creature; for the same apostle doth as positively affirm in a triumphant manner, that no other creature, under which believers themselves are comprehended, can separate from the love of God: Rom. viii. 38, 39, 'I am persuaded that neither death, nor life, nor angels, &c., nor any other creature, shall be able to separate us from the love of God which is in Christ Jesus our Lord.' And the other apostle comes in as a witness, that a son of God, so born, can never be guilty of such a contemptuous carriage habitually as may end in a disinheriting of him, because the seed of God, whereby he was born, remains in him as the band of his relation: 1 John iii. 9, 'His seed remains in him, and he cannot sin, because he is born of God.' His being born of God is the rock against the flood of sin, because he is born of God, and makes it eternally true that such an one is the son of God. Who ever did, or ever will, hear of a son of God by those two titles in hell? It seems not congruous to divine wisdom to make any his heirs that he saw he should disinherit. No wise man would do so, if he were conscious of all future events, and did sincerely adopt a person. And shall the all-wise God be represented weaker than man?

(4.) The habit of inherent grace cannot be lost. A believer hath eternal life in actual possession in the seed, and in reversion in the harvest, John vi. 54. It is plain: 1 Peter i. 23, 'Being born again, not of corruptible seed, but of incorruptible, by the word of God, which lives and abides for ever.' It is called an incorruptible seed in opposition to corruptible, both in its own nature and the effects produced by it. But this seed of the word being incorruptible, raises effects according to its nature. The antithesis is express: we are not born of corruptible seed, which is of a perishing nature, but of an incorruptible seed. The seed of our regeneration is incorruptible; the word, the instrument, is unchangeable; the Spirit, the efficient cause which manages the word, and thereby infuseth the seed, abides for ever. All these causes agreeing in one attribute of incorruptible, must needs produce an effect suitable to the nature of them. It is indemonstrable that so many incorruptible causes should centre in a corruptible effect, and be combined together to produce an ephemeron, a thing that may have no longer life, according to this opinion, than the day it is born in. Further, the connection of those words with those ver. 17, &c., import as much. He exhorts them to pass the time of their sojourning here in fear, not servile, but filial: ver. 17, 'Forasmuch as you know that you were not redeemed with corruptible things.' Be encouraged to all holy and humble obedience, since you are fully assured of your perfect redemption, &c. As the blood of Christ doth not purchase a corruptible redemption, so neither doth the grace of Christ work a corruptible regeneration. As the blood of Christ was incorruptible blood, by virtue of the hypostatical union, and in regard of the efficacy of it to our redemption, so is grace an incorruptible seed, by reason of the believer's union with the Son of God, its production by the Spirit of God, and in regard of that incorruptible word whereby it is both begotten and maintained in us. The habit of grace attends the soul to heaven, and for ever. The vital principle was not extinct in David by his gross fall, since we find him not praying for salvation, but the joy of it; not praying for the giving the Spirit, but not taking it away from him, which he had by his sin deserved to be deprived of: Ps. li. 11, 12, 'Take not thy Holy Spirit from me: restore unto me the joy of thy salvation.' And also for greater degrees of sanctification, and cleansing his heart from its filthiness and falseness. Grace may indeed, like the sun, be under an eclipse, but its internal light and heat cannot expire.

(5.) Though grace be oppressed, yet it will recover itself. It is indeed sometimes overtopped by temptation (as a fountain which, being overflowed by the torrent of a neighbouring river, is covered while the flood lasts, that a man knows not where to find it; but, after those great waters are slid away, the fountain bubbles up as clearly as before), yet it works all that while under that oppresssion, though not perceived. It will rise again by virtue of a believer's union with Christ. As a bough bent down by force, yet by virtue of its union to the body of the tree, will return to its former posture when the force is removed. The sap in the root of a tree, which the coldness of the season hath stripped of its leaves, will, upon the return of the sun, disperse itself, and, as it were, meet it in the utmost branches, and renew its old acquaintance with it. Shall the divine nature in the soul be outstripped by mere nature in the plants? Grace can never be so blown out, but there will be some smoke, some spark, whereby it may be re-kindled. The smoking snuff of Peter's grace was lighted again by a sudden look of his Master. Yea, it may, by a secret influence of the Spirit, gather strength to act more vigorously after its emerging from under the present oppression, like the sun, more warm in its beams after it hath been obscured by fogs.

Peter's love was more vigorous after his recovery. Christ implied it, when he acquainted him with his danger, that he who had not strength to keep his faith from falling, should, after his rising, have strength both for himself and his brethren: Luke xxii. 32, 'When thou art converted, strengthen thy brethren.'

[2.] Let us see what inconveniences and reflections upon God do follow from their doctrine. Their denial of this truth is grounded upon their denial of election, and on the supposed resistibility of grace, by the will of man.

(1.) It evacuates all the promises of God, and concludes them to be empty, vain things, as if they were made by God in mockery, and to sport himself in deceiving his creature.

[1.] It frustrates the glory he designs by the promises. Doth God promise his presence with the church to the end of the world? and doth it consist with infinite wisdom to make an absolute promise concerning an uncertainty? It is possible, according to this doctrine, that God might not have so much as one sincere worshipper, one faithful servant, in the whole earth; not one immediately capable of his gracious presence. What would become of the glory he intended to himself by all the promises of redemption and sanctification, and those praises and admirations he expects from men, when, according to this doctrine, it is possible there might not be one to give him the glory due to his name, if it were left to their natural wills, whether they would receive the grace offered them, or continue in it if they do receive it? For if one saint may fall away, notwithstanding the covenant of grace, the truth of God, and the strength of Christ, why may not another, and a third, till there be not the appearance of one sincere Christian? What certainty then had there been of a church in the world for God to be present with? What certainty of any admirer of his grace to eternity? Nay, what certainty that any would have received it, had it been left wholly to their natural wills? The Scripture intimates otherwise by representing man to us as dead in sin and enmity against God, one that cannot receive the things of God, &c. May a man be said sincerely to worship God one hour that doth cast dirt upon him the next, as the peasants in Germany deal with their St Urban, the patron of their vines? Is that a worship intended by his promises, that might not endure the space of one minute, but be succeeded by the grossest despites and rebellions? Is that fear put into the heart, that they might never depart from him, of no greater prevalency than to come to so sudden a period, and produce no better effects? Is so slight, so short-lived a worship, fit for the great God by so many declarations in Scripture to promise himself from his creature? No better it would be if it were left only to the creature's corrupt will, and the management of that natural enmity which is in the heart. Is the holiest soul in the world, without assisting and preventing grace, so sure of the immoveableness of his own will, among so many blustering storms and temptations, or flesh-pleasing snares and allurements?

[2.] It frustrates the promises made to Christ. Is it consistent with the faithfulness of God to be careless of all the agonies, groans, and blood of his Son? Our Saviour might have bled and died, and not seen one grain of seed, but lost all the travail of his soul, if this doctrine be true. Will God, according to these men's fancies, make no greater account of his oath? Ps. lxxxix. 33–36, 'My covenant will I not break, nor alter the thing that is gone out of my lips,'—that the seed of his servant David, the Messiah, as the Jews understand it, should endure for ever, and his loving-kindness he would not utterly take from them, nor suffer his faithfulness to fail. This, though sworn but once by his holiness, is enough for an eternal obligation upon God, and a perpetual ground of faith to us. 'The pleasure of the Lord' was promised, to 'prosper in his hand,' Isa. liii. 10; it was to 'break through'* all opposition, and overcome all invaders. Is it a way to glorify his faithfulness to Christ, to take the pleasure, the object of his pleasure, the fruit of his death, out of the hands of Christ, and put it into the hands of free will? The promise is, that his pleasure should prosper in his hand,—not in our hands, not in the hands of natural will.

[3.] It frustrates the comfort of the promises to us. Doth not this doctrine give the lie to that blessed apostle, who was wiser in the mysteries of the gospel than the whole world besides? Doth it not accuse him of arrogance, when by a divine inspiration he confidently persuades himself and all other believers that neither 'angels, nor principalities,' &c., 'should separate them from the love of God'? Rom. viii. 38, 39. Doth God in the Scripture pronounce those actually blessed that put their trust in Christ, the Messiah? Ps. ii. 12, 'Blessed are all they that put their trust in him.' How can it deserve the name of blessedness, and in all of them too, if the faith of any one that sincerely believes in him could be totally and finally lost? Could they be blessed even while they have faith, since the comfort and happiness of any particular act of faith would be overwhelmed by the tormenting fears of the possibility and probability of their losing the habits of it? It is not only probable, but certain, to be lost, if its preservation depended upon no other hand but the slight hold of our own will. Adam in innocency fell under a covenant of works; and we should as soon lose our habitual grace under a covenant of grace, did not our stability depend upon a supernatural and divine power promised in it. This doctrine therefore wipes off all the oil of gladness from believers' hearts; and, contrary to Christ's commission, clothes them with the spirit of heaviness instead of the garments of praise.

(2.) It darkens the love of God. Are the products of infinite love so light as these men would make them? Is not his love as immutable as himself? Can there be decays in an eternal and unchangeable affection? Can any emergencies be unknown from eternity to his omniscience? How then can the fountain of kindness be frozen in his breast? Shall not that everlasting love, which was the only motive to draw the believer at the first conversion to him, be as strong an argument to him to preserve the believer with him? Jer. xxxi. 3, 'I have loved thee with an everlasting love, therefore with loving-kindness have I drawn thee.' It was love in the choice; but by the expression *loving-kindness*, it seems to be increased in the execution. What is it then that should make it run as fast backward till it dissolve into disaffection? Was there a love of benevolence towards them in appointing them to be heirs of salvation, when they lay like swine in the confused mass and mire of the corrupt world? And is there not a love of complacency in them, since he hath pardoned them according to the riches of his grace, renewed them by the power of his word, and sealed them by the Holy Spirit of promise? Is it likely this everlasting love should sink into hatred, and the glorious fruits of it be dashed in pieces at one blow by a sudden change? To what purpose did he lay the first stone of thy redemption, and bring the blood of his Son and thy soul to kiss each other? Was it not that he might be your God in covenant with you? It was so in the type, the deliverance from Egypt: Lev. xxvi. 45, 'Whom I brought forth out of the land of Egypt, that I might be their God.' Much more in the antitype, the deliverance from Satan. Could the kindness of God be so illustrious if it did not make the

* יצלח *à* צלח *perrumpere.*

permanency of his gifts a great part of the benefit of them? Can these men then fancy infinite tenderness so unconcerned as to let the apple of his eye be plucked out, as to be a careless spectator of the pillage of his jewels by the powers of hell, to have the delight of his soul (if I may so speak) tossed like a tennis-ball between himself and the devil? Which must be the consequence of this doctrine, if a renewed man be at one time in the hands of God, and presently after in the hands of the devil. Is this easy parting with them like the affection of a mother to her sucking infant? How much less suitable is it to the kindness of God, which infinitely surmounts the other!

(3.) It disgraceth his wisdom and power. Doth this doctrine support the honour of God's wisdom, in contriving ways so admirable for the restoration of his creature, that may be lost in a moment? Is it congruous to infinite wisdom, set on work in man's recovery, to make a covenant that should be more uncertain than the former? Which should be if it depended only upon the voluble and inconstant temper of the creature's corrupt will for the making it good. The former was less likely to be violated by a nature filled with integrity, than this by a nature stuffed with iniquity. Is it consistent with the honour of this attribute, to have his wonderful designs, wherein he intended to make known his manifold wisdom, puffed away by a breath of sin and Satan? Was God subject to error or ignorance in not foreseeing what events might happen before he obliged himself by promise; or to dissimulation if he did not foresee, and notwithstanding all these contrivances and preparations, not absolutely intend, the salvation of any one man, but leave it to themselves whether they would be saved or no? It disgraceth his power. Where can any safety be expected if not in our Redeemer's hand? Shall his power be beaten out of breath by the wrestling of the devil? None, say these men, shall pluck them out of God's hand while they remain there, but they may depart themselves; as though that promise, John x. 28, did not provide against their inward corruption as well as external violence. But the promise is exclusive of all ways of destruction: 'They shall not perish,' *οὐ μὴ ἀπόλωνται*, two negatives to strengthen it, according to the custom of the Greeks. And it is not, as it is translated, *no man*, but *οὐχ ἁρπάξει τις*, *not any one*. If they depart, they perish; but because they shall not perish, against which the promise secures them, therefore they shall not depart. If they may be overcome against the will of God, and against his promise, it may be inferred that the devil is superior to God, and that God hath not power, or wants will, to make good his promise of perseverance to them. As there never was, so there never will be, any violation of his faithfulness, or breach made upon his power. Had God let them lie in their sins, no objection could be made; but since by such an admirable power he had snatched them from the clutches of the prince of darkness, doth it consist with his wisdom or goodness to throw them away, or to let them fall out of his hands into the power of their old oppressor?

(4.) It sets God at great uncertainties as to the object of his love. If a renewed man be discarded from God's favour, and lose the habit of grace because he commits a sin which deserves death, he would upon every sin be cashiered, because every sin deserves death by the rigour of the law, Rom. vi. 23; and the whole life of a Christian would be nothing else but an interchange of friend and enemy, son and no son. Nay, there could not be a moment fixed, wherein it could be said of any godly man in this life, that he were in God's favour, and had the habit of grace, because there is not a moment but man is guilty of some sin or other, of infirmity at least. If it be said, it is meant only of those sins that waste the conscience; these, we say, cannot live in the constant practice of a regenerate man. But suppose he be overtaken, is he then cast out of favour, *i. e.* out of God's everlasting love? I would demand, if he be, what brings him in again? Good works afterwards? Alas! there is not one of them but is mixed with that which deserves eternal death. Can they bring us into favour, which need something themselves to make them accepted? Can a menstruous rag look so amiable in the eyes of God, as to introduce us into a forfeited favour? Is it our Saviour's merit? That is as sufficient to keep our knot with God indissoluble, as it is upon every breach to renew it; for the merit of Christ is greater than the demerit of sin. If every act of unbelief did destroy faith, might it not be destroyed and revived an hundred times a-day? For what is the course of the best Christian, but a mixture of faith and unbelief? It is true the bent of the heart stands right in faith; but there are frequent starts of unbelief. Now, according to this doctrine, there would be so many blottings out, and so many writings again of their names in the book of life every day. A man may be, in their sense, in God's favour, and out of it, many times in a day; one moment in a state of salvation, the next in a state of damnation; and so run in a circle from salvation to damnation all the year long. Is this uncertainty like the stability of mountains and hills, a greater than which God promises? Isa. liv. 10, 'The mountains shall depart, and the hills be removed, but my kindness shall not depart from thee, neither shall the covenant of my peace be removed, saith the Lord, that hath mercy on thee.' God provided such a covenant of peace that might not be removed, that he might not be at such constant removes in his kindness as these men would make him. Is it not unworthy to make such a representation of the all-wise and immutable God, as if he were daily caressing his creatures, and daily repenting of those gifts of effectual calling, which the Scripture asserts to be without repentance? Rom. xi. 29. Repentance of any design is an effect of weakness of judgment as well as mutability of will.

(5.) It doth the rather set God at uncertainties, because it doth subject the grace of God to the will of man. It hangs the glory of God's grace, in all the motions of it, and the efficacy of the promise, upon the slipperiness of man's will and affections. It makes the omnipotent grace of God follow, not precede, the motions of men's will; to be the lacquey, not the leader, either in converting or preserving; which is at the best to make the glory of his grace as volatile as a feather, at the best sometimes up, sometimes down; the soul this moment embraced by God with the dearest affections, the next cast out as a vessel wherein is no pleasure, and the succeeding moment admitted to fresh communications; this hour the temple of the Holy Ghost, the next an habitation for dragons and satyrs, the will of man giving one time the key to the Spirit, the next time to the devil; one time as clean as a saint, another time as foul as a fallen angel. So that a Christian's life would be spent in nothing but ejectments and repossessions between God and the devil, and the grace of God beholding for its residence in the heart only to the humour of the will. Is it reasonable thus to subject the fruits of the great undertaking of Christ to the lottery of fancy, and to take the crown from the head of grace, to set upon the scalp of our corrupt will?

(6.) It frustrates the design and fruits of election. The seduction of believers by false prophets, with their train of great signs and wonders, which our Saviour concludes impossible,—Mat. xxiv. 24, 'There shall arise false Christs, and false prophets, and shall shew great signs and wonders; insomuch as, if it were possible, they should deceive the very elect,'—is according to this doctrine very easy and natural. One start of the fancy completes it. The impossibility of their embracing, or at least persisting in damnable errors, is founded upon the eternal choice of them by God, and his decree for their preservation. It was the entry of their names into the Lamb's book of life, that preserved his followers from the contagion in the universal apostasy of the Romish church : Rev. xiii. 8, 'All that dwell upon the earth shall worship him, whose names are not written in the book of life of the Lamb.' If believers could totally and finally fall away from Christ, why is it impossible for them to be deceived by damning errors, accompanied with such wonders, that might stupefy the reason of the wisest natural men, and the elect too, did not their election make it impossible ? 'The very elect.' But it is laid upon a higher score than their own wisdom, and depends upon that golden chain of electing love, which neither the wit of man, nor malice of devils, the terrors of afflictions, nor pleasures of temptations, are able to break, Rom. viii. 38, 39.

(7.) It frustrates the fruits of Christ's mediation and offices. Was it not the design of his coming, according to the ancient promise, that all nations should be blessed in him, in the seed of Abraham, which seed he was ? According to this doctrine it is uncertain at the best, whether any one person should be blessed by him or no. If the gates of hell could prevail against one real member of Christ, they might against a second and a third, till he should not have one member to enjoy a blessing by him. Grace infused is as the 'holy fire upon the altar, which descended from heaven,' Lev. vi. 12, 13. And as it was the priest's office, so it is the office of Christ the antitype, to feed it morning and evening by his Spirit, with fresh fuel for its continual support. According to this doctrine, the offices of Christ signify nothing but with the consent of the will of man. The death of Christ might be wholly an unprofitable sacrifice. The intercession of Christ in heaven would signify nothing, since they can persevere without him, and notwithstanding his intercession can fall away. This is to unpriest Christ, and destroy the end of his living for ever. His prophetical office fares no better, because they make the efficacy of it depend upon their will ; and the teaching of Christ, like the sibyls' writing upon leaves, may be blown away by the next wind. It robs Christ of the key of government, by making every man his own governor in this affair, and denying Christ the sovereign throne in the wills of men. His government would be exercised only in punishing, since none left wholly to themselves but would prove obstinate rebels. He might be a priest without a people to sacrifice for, an advocate without a client, a prophet without a disciple, and a king without a subject, and so be insignificant in the fruits of all his offices.

(8.) It disparageth the work of the Spirit. As if the Spirit of God did tincture the soul with so weak a colour as might be easily washed off by the next shower ; as if he did only strew, not sow the seed of grace, easily to be blown away by the next puff of wind or devoured by fowls. Are the divine image and workmanship of heaven, the products of infinite power, wisdom, and love, of so slight a make as the embracers of this doctrine would fancy? Is the Spirit too weak to hold, or is he unwilling ? Would Christ ever send so uncertain a comforter as he would be unless he did abide with us? Would Christ, after laying so strong and rich a foundation for the redemption of his people, send a deputy that should build so weakly and work so slightly upon it ? The Spirit was to glorify Christ, John xvi. 13. How? Certainly, as 'Christ glorified the Father,' John xvii. 4. But Christ glorified the Father by finishing the work which was given him. Therefore the Spirit will glorify Christ in the same manner by finishing the work he is sent to do ; as the Father is not imperfect in his choice, nor Christ in his purchase ; so neither will the Spirit be imperfect in his conduct. The very end why God puts the Spirit into the heart, is to preserve the believer from going back from God. What is called 'putting the fear of the Lord into us, that we might not depart from him,' Jer. xxii. 40, is called putting a new heart and a new spirit: Ezek. xxxvi. 26, 'And I will put my Spirit within you, and cause you to walk in my statutes, and you shall keep my judgments and do them;' and a putting his own Spirit within them to preserve and assist that new habitual grace, for it is to cause them to walk in his statutes. It is not only a cleansing them from their filthiness, and then leaving them to be their own guides, but it is a putting a contrary principle into them; and the end of putting this spirit into them, is that they 'should live till they be placed in their own land, in the heavenly Canaan,' Ezek. xxxvii. 14, and be settled there in the work of admiration, and blessing God for his faithfulness in performing this covenant; 'then shall ye know,' by a full experience, 'that I the Lord have spoken, and performed it.' I know some understand it of their deliverance from the Babylonish captivity; but the words methinks seem to be of a higher import, and the deliverance from Babylon was typical of redemption by Christ, Jer. xxiii. 6–8, speaking of the days of the gospel, 'The Lord lives that brought up the seed of Israel out of the north country.' I leave you to judge; however take it as an allusion. The Spirit will be no more false to God in not answering the end of his being put into the heart, to cause us to walk in his statutes, than Christ was or can be false to God in not answering the end of his designation to the mediatory office. This doctrine doth quite subvert the end of the Spirit's coming, and being put into the heart of a renewed man, and makes all its work a slight and superficial business.

For a close, then, of this. This doctrine stands firm, I hope. Though it be possible and probable, and I may say certain, that the habit of grace in a renewed man, considered abstractedly in itself without God's powerful assistance, would fall, and be overwhelmed by the batteries of Satan and secret treacheries of the flesh, yet it is impossible it should wholly fall, being supported by God's truth in his covenant, his power in the performance, held up by the intercession of Christ, and maintained by the inhabitation of the Spirit. Our wills are mutable, but God's promise unchangeable; our strength is feeble, God's power insuperable; our prayers impotent, Christ's intercessions prevalent. Our sins do meritoriously expel it, but the grace of God through the merit of Christ doth efficiently preserve it. If therefore believers fall totally and finally, it must be by themselves, or by the industry of some external agent.

(1.) Not by themselves and their own wills. Not as considered in themselves, but as their wills are the proper subject and seat of this habitual grace. They are made 'willing in the day of his power,' Ps. cx. 3; and they are continued willing by the influence of the same power, for the day of his power endures for ever. They will not depart out of Christ's hand, because it is the chief part of this grace to determine their wills, and to bring down every high imagination which might pervert their wills, to a subjection to Christ, and fix them upon God as the chief good, and last end. Hence being his sheep, and knowing him for their shepherd, they are said to hear his voice, and follow him; so that this perseverance is not a forced and constrained work. They cannot totally fall by their own wills, they are renewed and strengthened; nor by their own corruption, that is subdued and mortified by the Spirit of God, which is continually in arms against it; and if, when it was in its full strength, it could not hinder the power of God's grace in conversion, surely when it is thus impaired, and only some relics of it (though, alas! too, too much) abiding, it can less resist the power of the same grace in our preservation.

Again, not by their own wills, for it is here that grace sets its throne, and establisheth the heart. Neither doth that life which is hid with Christ in God depend upon the levity of our wills; it being an abiding life, it hath an influence upon our wills to preserve them in a due bent, wherein they are set by the Spirit.

(2.) Not by any external agent.

[1.] Not by God. The counsel of his election stands firm, and they are heirs by an immutable covenant. Though God by reason of his omnipotent sovereignty might justifiably take grace away, and we deserve it, yet morally, in regard of the immutability of his righteousness and truth, he will not. Chist will not do it; he died to purchase it, and lives for ever to preserve it. The Spirit will not do it; the end of his coming and indwelling is to maintain it.

[2.] Not by the devil; for 'he that is in us is greater' and stronger 'than he that is in the world,' 1 John iv. 4, in all the allurements and affrightments of the world. Not by his temptations; they shall either be intercepted or resisted by an assisting grace stronger than their author's malice: 1 Cor. x. 13, 'God is faithful, who will not suffer you to be tempted above what you are able, but will with the temptation also make a way to escape, that you may be able to bear it.'

[3.] Not by the world. If the God of the world cannot do it, the world itself shall not be able. Christ hath 'conquered the world' for us by his death, John xvi. 23, and hath given us 'power to conquer it by our faith,' 1 John v. 4.

Use 2. Matter of comfort.

This doctrine of the preservation of grace is the crown of glory, and sweetness of all other privileges. We should in the midst of regeneration, justification, adoption, droop and be Magor-missabibs, tormented with fears of losing them. It is the assurance of this that makes believers come to Sion with songs and everlasting joy upon their heads. Premise this I must; this comfort belongs only to those that have true grace; see therefore whether you can find any serving-work upon your hearts towards God, before you entitle yourselves to the comfort of this doctrine.

(1.) Our state by redemption and regeneration is better than Adam's by creation, in respect of permanency, though not by present integrity. God keeps us safer in a state of imperfection, than Adam was in all his innocence. Adam had a better nature, and a stronger inherent power conferred upon him by creation; he was created after God's image, but he defaced and lost it, and afterwards begat in his own likeness, not in the likeness of God, whereof he was stripped. He had a natural power, but no supernatural assistance. We have no natural power, but we have a supernatural help. Our supernatural assistance confers upon us a better state than his natural power did, or could do upon him. We are kept by the power of God to salvation, and he was to be kept by his own; he was to stand by the strength of nature, we by the strength of grace: Rom. v. 2, 'Grace wherein you stand, through faith;' 2 Cor. i. 24, 'By faith you stand.' Grace is as immutable as nature changeable. He was under the government of his own free will; it is our happiness to be under the conduct of the Son of God by his Spirit: Rom. viii. 14, 'As many as are led by the Spirit of God, they are the sons of God;' and that by virtue of a charge, a privilege never allowed to Adam nor angels, who, being their own keepers, were soon their own destroyers. He had a natural power to stand, but without a will; we have a gracious power to will, and the act of perseverance conferred upon us. He had a power to stand, precepts to stand, promises to encourage him to stand, but not one promise to secure him from falling; we have both a supernatural help, and an immutable promise that the fear of God should be put into our hearts to this end, to preserve us from falling, Jer. xxxii. 42. By Christ we have not only words of grace to encourage us, but the power of grace to establish us; not only precepts to persevere, but promises that we shall, otherwise the promise could be no surer than that annexed to the covenant of works. If the condition of it might be as easily lost as the condition of Adam's covenant, then would it lose its end, which was to ensure the promise or covenant to all the seed: Rom. iv. 16, 'Therefore it is of faith, that it might be by grace; that the promise might be sure to all the seed.' Adam was under a mutable covenant, and we under an everlasting one. Adam had no reserve of nature to supply nature upon any defect; we have out of Christ's fulness, grace for grace, John i. 16; grace for the supply of grace upon any emergency. The manner whereby we stand is different from the manner of his standing; he stood in dependence on his original righteousness, which being once lost, all the original virtues depending on that were lost with it. Our state is secured in higher hands. Christ is made wisdom, &c.: 1 Cor. i. 30, 'But of him are you in Christ Jesus, who of God is made unto us wisdom, righteousness, sanctification, and redemption;' all which are dispensed to us in the streams, but reserved in him as the fountain. He is made all those to us, not we to ourselves. Adam's life was hid in himself; ours with Christ in God, Col. iii. 3. Our life is as secure in Christ's, as Christ's is secure in God. Christ's hand, and his Father's bosom, is not to be rifled by any power on earth. Heaven is no place to be pillaged by the serpent. Which state, then, is best? Our nature is restored by the second Adam, fundamentally better; not at present so bright as his, but more permanent. The mutability of the first Adam procured our misery; the strength of the second preserves our security. So that a gracious man is better established in his little grace, by the power of God, than Adam in his flourishing integrity by the strength of his own will.

(2.) The state of a regenerate man is as secure as the state of the invisible church, and more firm than that of any particular visible church in the world. You stand upon as good terms as the whole assembly of the first-born, and upon a surer foundation than any particular church: Ps. cxxv. 1, 'They that trust in the Lord shall be as mount Sion, which cannot be removed, but abides for ever.' They shall he impregnable; as stable as that mountain of the Lord's house which was to be established on the top of the mountain, Isa. ii. 2, alluding to that temple built upon mount Moriah, of a steep ascent, firmer than all the worldly powers and strongest monarchies, compared to mountains in Scriptures. Particular churches may fall. How is the glory of many of them vanished! Particular believers shall not, because their standing is in Christ, by virtue of that covenant whereof Christ is mediator, and of that promise made to the whole body, wherein the interest of every member is included: Mat. xvi. 18, 'The gates of hell shall not prevail against it.' Neither the power nor policy of hell; gates being the seats of judgment and magazines of arms. The visible church is only so by profession and privileges; an invisible member is so by nature and union. Appearance will expire when nature shall abide. The mystical body of Christ, and every member of it, can no more die than the natural body of Christ can now, or any member of that. No member of Christ's fleshly body did or shall see corruption. The knot between the soul and the body is natural by the band of vital spirits; the knot between a true member and Christ is supernatural. The second person in the Trinity, being united to the body of Christ, kept it from corruption. The third person in the

Trinity keeps the union between Christ and a mystical member from dissolving, which no particular church in the world, as a church, can lay claim to. Though Christ may discard a particular church, yet not a particular elect person, because of that agreement between his Father and himself concerning those given to him. But we read not of any whole nation or church in the world given to Christ as such, and in such a manner as a particular person is. There is a difference between God's electing a people to have the gospel preached, and his electing a person to have the gospel wrought in him. The standing of any particular church is not for itself, but for the elect in it. When God chooseth a nation to be under the preaching of the gospel, it is for the sakes of his elect ones sprinkled among them; and that church stands as long as there are elect persons among them to be brought in. When the number is gathered into God's fold, the gospel is removed thence, because of the rejection of it by the rest. These two elections, of persons and matters,* the one to grace, and the other to the enjoyment of the ministry of the gospel, are mixed together by the apostle in his discourse, Rom. xi. Some places must be understood of the one, and some of the other. When the election is said to be void, it is meant of the election of a nation, as the Jews are called God's chosen people; when it is said to stand, it is meant of the election of a person: as when we say, man is mortal, and man is immortal, it is in different senses, both true: mortal, according to his body; immortal, in respect of his soul.

(3.) Comfort against the weakness of grace. This is the proper comfort of this doctrine. It is, and ought to be, a matter of trouble that our grace is so weak; it should not be a matter of murmuring and despondency. We have reason to mourn that our graces are not strong; we have reason to rejoice that we have any at all. Little grace is enrolled in heaven. Not a weak member of the invisible church, but hath his name written there, Heb. x. 23. How glimmering was the disciples' faith, yet our Saviour bids them, in all that weakness, 'Rejoice that their names were written in heaven,' Luke x. 20. Could their names have been blotted out again, the joy he exhorts them to could not have dwelt with such a ground of fear. As the least sin beloved brings us into alliance with the devil, so the least grace cherished entitles us to the family of God; for it is but a rough draught with blots, of what God had fairly drawn in the glorified saints. The weakest grace gives a deadly wound to sin, and a sure, though not so highly comfortable a title to so abundant an entrance into heaven as a stronger. Do not therefore seek your torment, where you should find your comfort.

[1.] The foundation of weak grace, and the hopes of it, is strong. Every new creature hath not an equal strength, but every one hath an equal interest in the covenant, and as sure a ground of hope, as the highest. The design of God was to make the new covenant secure from the violations of the creature: Jer. xxxi. 31, 32, 'I will make a new covenant with the house of Israel; not according to the covenant I made with their fathers, which my covenant they brake, though I was an husband to them.' He would make a covenant stronger than to be broken by them. That covenant was perpetual, in regard of God, for he continued a husband to them, and did nothing to dissolve the knot. This is not to be broken by a person in covenant. If it could be broken, it would be the same with the other covenant, though not in terms, yet in the issue. Now true grace depends upon this covenant: ver. 23, 'I will put my law into their inward parts, and write it in their hearts.' Besides, this covenant and the blessings of it are settled upon

* Qu. 'nations'?—ED.

believers, and every one of them, as an inheritance : Isa. liv. 9, 10, 'I have sworn that I will not be wroth with thee: for the mountains shall depart, and the hills be removed ; but my kindness shall never depart from thee, neither shall the covenant of my peace be removed, saith the Lord that hath mercy on thee ;' and that by oath. It could not have been made over in surer terms. Mountains, the stablest parts of the creation, that cannot be blown away by storms, shall depart at the end of the world, this covenant shall not. It proceeds not only from love, but kindness, which is love spread with a choicer affection. It is a covenant of peace, wherein their reconciliation with God, and the blessings following from it, are settled upon them, and that as an heritage: ver. 17, 'This is the heritage of the servants of the Lord ;' and lest they should fall, or lose their righteousness, the latter clause secures them, 'and their righteousness is of me, saith the Lord.' Whether you understand it of the righteousness of justification or sanctification, it amounts to the same thing. This is the sure mercies of David. So that thou hangest upon a covenant settled fast by the promise and oath of God, and cemented in every part by the Mediator's blood. God never yet broke his word. It depends upon promise ; eternal life was promised before the foundation of the world: Titus i. 2, 'In hope of eternal life, which God, that cannot lie, promised before the world began.' To whom ? To Christ, and in him to all the elect, of what size or stature soever, babes as well as strong men. God had time to consider all that unconceivable eternity before Christ came, and yet he never repented of this promise of eternal life, because he cannot lie, which the apostle lays an emphasis upon. When Christ came, all his actions and speeches upon record were pursuant to the confirmation of this promise. The Lamb, in whose bosom you are carried, was slain from the foundation of the world in the decree of God, and voluntary designation of himself. Was there not a long time to consider ? and did he not repent of it all that time ? and will he now, since he has paid all the price for your grace, and the continuance of it ? Can a little time, sixteen hundred years since Christ was in the flesh, make any alteration in God's counsel and Christ's design, which eternity could not ? Besides, the root is strong though the branch be weak ; buds draw sap from the root, as well as the forwarder fruit. The least splinter of wood in a tree is a part of the tree. The least atom, though never so small, is a part of the world. Every one in Christ is a part of Christ, and hath a share in the promise made to him. Is there any distinction or difference made in the covenant between weak and strong ? The babe in Christ is as well within the verge of it, as the most compact Christian. Never then sadden your souls if you find true grace in yourselves, when you are within the arms of an everlasting covenant. The grace which lies smoking in the chaff hath fire in it, as well as that which flames.

[2.] All grace, now triumphant, was weak at first. The highest began in a seed, a little seed. The waters of the sanctuary, whereby the propagation of the gospel in the world, and the operation of it in the heart, is figured ; I say, those waters which will perfectly purify the soul, did at first reach but to the ankles, Ezek. xlvii. 3–5, after that to the loins, and afterwards arise to the height of waters to swim in. Till you read of any grace in Scripture without its mixtures, do not despond. Moses had his encomium of God's familiar, yet though he struck the rock through faith, he struck twice through unbelief, when indeed he was only to speak, not strike, Numb. xx. 8, 11, which God interprets unbelief, ver. 12. Abraham, who is honoured with the noble title of father of the faithful, had a distrust of God's promise : Gen. xii. 2, 3, 'I will make of thee a great nation, I will bless thee ;

I will bless them that bless thee, and curse them that curse thee;' therefore he deals with his wife to call herself his sister for fear of his life in Pharaoh's court, Gen. xii. 12; and after much more experience of God's truth, in the court of Abimelech, Gen. xx. 11.

[3.] Your stock is sure. Your grace is weak, but the stock in Christ's hands for supply is full. He keeps it in his own hands. He knows our necessity better than we do, and measures supplies by his own wisdom, not by our desires; for 'he feeds them with judgment,' Ezek. xxxiv. 16, *i.e.* he will govern them wisely; for so that place may be understood. It is our happiness that, though we have little in possession, we have much for our necessity. It is our happiness that it is laid so high that we cannot reach it but by faith, that we have it not in our hands to squander it away. Were it in our own hands, it would quickly be out of them, and we not have a mite left. The covenant with us was founded upon that made with Christ: Isa. lix. 21, 'This is my covenant with them, saith the Lord; My Spirit that is upon thee, and my words which I have put in thy mouth, shall not depart out of thy mouth, nor out of the mouth of thy seed, nor out of the mouth of thy seed's seed, saith the Lord, from henceforth and for ever.' 'This is my covenant with them,' *i.e.* made with us in Christ. 'My Spirit that is upon thee,' &c. As long as Christ hath the Spirit by virtue of that everlasting mediatory covenant, so long shall the Spirit, and the fruits and power of the gospel, be in the hearts of his people. 'The words in the mouth of his seed' depend upon 'the word put into his mouth,' and 'the Spirit put upon him.' The covenant was made with Christ, not for himself, but for his seed, and his seed's seed; made with them, but founded upon him. It was for their sakes the Spirit was put upon him, for their sakes that words were put into his mouth; for their sakes for whom he sanctified himself, John xvii., even for the sakes of those weak disciples he then prayed for. The words put into his mouth were not bare words, but attended with spirit; not mere professions, but operative. And this was to abide upon him for them henceforth and for ever; for he calls it a covenant with them, yet turns and speaks to one person. It must, therefore, be for them that this person is endowed with the Spirit; otherwise it was not a covenant with them.

[4.] Christ's charge extends to this weak grace. It was for this reason he hath the order given him in the text by his Father; not for the standing reed, or flaming flax, though that is included. The weakest is here committed to him, and therefore is as much under his care. To what purpose hath Christ this order, if the weakness of grace were a ground of despondency? It is a ground of humiliation, but not of distrust. The gardener that regards all his ground, watcheth over the tenderest plants. Our keeper riseth early to look after the tender grapes and pomegranate buds, Cant. vii. 12. That which is feeble is as much under his conduct as that which is vigorous. He was ordered to be a shepherd, whose office is to attend the weak motions of the new fallen lambs. His bosom is appointed a place for them. He gathereth them by his arms, *i.e.* converts them by his power, and was to carry them in his bosom: Isa. xl. 11, 'He shall feed his flock like a shepherd; he shall gather the lambs with his arm, and carry them in his bosom, and shall gently lead those that are with young.' If you can go, he is to guide you gently; if you cannot, he is to bear you tenderly, not on his shoulders, merely by strength, but in his bosom, with a tender affection. He is not only the shepherd, but bishop of our souls, 1 Peter ii. 25; and our conversion to him makes us part of his diocese: 'You are returned to the shepherd and bishop of your souls.' In all your weakness, he was ordained by God for your help: Ps. lxxxix. 19, he 'laid help upon one that is mighty;'

mighty to preserve his power, and mighty to use it. Help supposeth persons most in need of it, as the objects to whom it is to be afforded. Every new creature hath not an equal strength, but they have an equal interest in the Redeemer's death and merit; and the weakest may seem more under his care than the strongest, because they stand more in need of that office which he is entrusted with and delights to exercise.

[5.] He delights in this charge. It was his delight to do the will of God; yea, and his meat and drink to cherish the beginnings of grace in the Samaritan woman, John iv. 34, because it was his Father's work. Surely it was no small part of the joy set before him, that upon his dying he was to be invested with a power to perform his Father's charge. He will not therefore refuse to embrace the feeblest saint. He knew how well the soul of his Father was pleased with his undertaking this care of the smoking flax, as the words intimate: Mat. xii. 18, 'My beloved, in whom my soul is well pleased;' pleased with that which Christ was to do, whereof that in the text is a part. God takes particular notice of the beginnings of grace, and Christ's affection runs in the same channel with his Father's; yea, he regards the very trembling degrees of it. He overlooks all the philosophers of Athens, who boasted themselves to be the grandees in learning, and records only two new converts, Acts xvii. 34: Dionysius, who for all his ability and justice in judging controversies, had never had his name set down there but for his faith, and Damaris, a woman. He joins a woman with a judge, to shew that he takes notice of the weakest faith, as well as that which is joined with the strongest parts. This great man is mentioned only upon the account of his faith. See also how he overlooks the infirmities of Job: Job ii. 3, 'Hast thou considered my servant Job?' though he knew them as well as his graces, and doth not only approve of him and defend him, but makes his boast of him. He makes a public proclamation with joy in the very teeth of the devil, though he had so many pure angels about him, that one would think he should have spoken of with applause, as well as of a poor mortal. Was Job's grace very strong? What means, then, that multitude of impatient expressions scattered in the book?

[6.] He will therefore be faithful in it. His faithfulness is more illustrious in regarding the more troublesome parts of his charge, as the fidelity of a friend or servant is more evidenced by the difficulty than facility of his trust. When he knew how weak we are, and how apt to swerve, had he not been resolved to relieve us, he had never sent his Spirit to abide with us for such an end. The apostle assures us that the care lies upon him still to confirm us to the end: 1 Cor. i. 8, 'Who shall also confirm you to the end, that you may be blameless in the day of our Lord Jesus:' in the day, not before; expect not grace to be triumphant till then. Wherein the faithfulness of God also bears a part, ver. 9; and surely those Corinthians were none of the strongest, when the apostle doubts whether he should write to them as spiritual or as unto carnal. The weakest is his seed, and he will not lose it. You cannot value your security more than Christ values the honour of his office; and it being his Father's pleasure that he should exercise it, it doth more affect him than the desires of your security can affect you. Suppose he himself had no love to grace, yet you cannot doubt but that he hath so much respect to his Father as not to displease him by a neglect of that which he solemnly committed to him as a pledge of his affection, and a testimony of his confidence in him. He will also be faithful to his own glory; but the 'fulfilling of the work of faith with power' is for the glory of his name, 2 Thes. i. 11, 12. It is one part of the glory he reserves to himself, to be admired not only by them that believe, but in them at the last day, ver. 10;

admired in the admirable conduct of their faith through all weaknesses and difficulties.

[7.] He has given evidences of this faithfulness. He never yet put out a dim candle that was lighted at the Sun of righteousness.

(1.) It was his course in the world. He found some smoking flax in the ruler: John iv. 47–49, 'Come down and heal my son; come down ere my child die.' He thought Christ could cure his son. There was some fire of faith, but not unless he came to his house, and that before he died too, as if Christ could not recover him by a word, and could not restore him after his breath was expired. Christ, according to his office of not quenching smoking flax, complies with him; so Mat. vii. 32. Their faith thought Christ could cure their friends, but not unless he laid his hands upon them, yet he grants their requests. He easily complies with a weak faith, when he loves to put a strong one to its shifts; as he did in the repulse he gave to the woman of Canaan, whose faith afterwards he applauds with admiration, 'O woman, great is thy faith!'

(2.) It was his disposition after his resurrection, Luke xxiv. 13. He meets with two disciples going to Emmaus, who seem to have thrown away all their faith and hope in him, and to be upon the brink of the sin against the Holy Ghost: ver. 21, 'We trusted that it had been he that should have redeemed Israel.' The next words in course were like to have been, But we think him an imposter. But doth Christ with indignation cast them off, as though he would have no more to do with them? No; he takes pains to enliven their faith, and takes occasion from their weakness to renew their strength; and that in so eminent a manner, that it seems to be one of the most excellent sermons that ever he preached, a comment upon the whole Scripture concerning himself, ver. 27. Beginning at Moses, he went through all the prophets, and expounded all the Scriptures concerning himself. He filled their heads with knowledge, and inspired their hearts with life.

(3.) After his ascension too. He takes notice of a little strength in Philadelphia, Rev. iii. 8, and opens a door for it that no man can shut. Well, did our Redeemer ever yet disappoint a trembling faith, or let a limping grace go from him without a blessing? It is too late surely for him to begin now at the close of all things, when the world is almost at an end.

[8.] Therefore you may in the weakest state expect assistance. The weakest grace hath a throne of grace to supply it, a God of grace to delight in it, a Mediator of grace to influence it, a Spirit of grace to brood upon it. Though our grace be weak, yet the grace of all these are sufficient to preserve us. The weakest grace in Christ's hand shall stand, when the strongest nature without his guard shall fail. It is not our hold of Christ so much preserves us, as Christ's hold of us; though the faith we hang by be a weak thread, yet Christ hath a strong hand. Had you the grace of a glorified saint, you could not maintain it without his help, and that is sufficient to conduct through the greatest storms into a safe harbour. The 'preserved in Christ' is the happy title of those that are sanctified by God the Father, as Jude speaks, 'To them that are sanctified in God the Father, and preserved in Jesus Christ, and called.' His mercy is in the heavens; his righteousness as the great mountain, stable; his title issuing from thence is, the preserver of man and beast, Ps. xxxvi. 5, 6. And shall not that which is more valued by him than man and beast, that which is the cause of his keeping up the world, be preserved by him? 'Fear not, thou worm Jacob,' Isa. xli. 14, 'I will help thee, saith the Lord, and thy Redeemer, the Holy One of Israel.' What hath more need to fear than a worm, that is liable to be trod on by every passenger? What hath more reason to fear than a creeping grace in itself? Yet what hath less reason to be afraid, when backed by such a mighty power? It is a weakness, but fortified by an almighty strength; it hath a power which neither Adam with all his nature, nor the holy angels before their confirmation, were ever possessed of.

Well, then, the weaker thy grace the faster let thy dependence be on Christ, and then thou wilt be more secure by that exercise of faith than by the strongest grace without it. A small vessel, managed by a skilful pilot, may be preserved in a rough sea, when a stronger, left to itself, will dash in pieces.

(4.) Comfort against corruptions. Indwelling and easily besetting sin is that which makes a believer hang down his head. Oh this enemy within me that I cannot conquer! surely I shall one day die by the hand of Saul. It is our unbelief and the ignorance of the great transaction between God and Christ, and the tenor of the covenant of grace, which is the ground of all the practical doubts about this doctrine, as well as the notional disputes against it. Every member, though it hath boils and scabs, is as much a member of the body as the soundest, till it be cut off, and that it shall not hath been the design of the whole discourse to prove. Christ doth not cut it off, but heal it. Is it not a part of the covenant of grace to heal our backslidings? Hosea xiv. 4. When he finds a disease, he cures us by the application of his blood, for the end of his stripes was that we might be healed, Isa. liii. 5. And though God hath a piercing eye to see every sin, and the malignity of every circumstance, yet the motion of his eye that way is not to destroy, but to heal: Isa. lvii. 18, 19, 'I have seen his ways, and will heal him, though he walked frowardly.' We speak not now of a course of gross sins. No true believer can be guilty of that; there is a great difference between fouling the feet in the mire, and a total wallowing in it like a swine with delight and pleasure.

Therefore consider that,

[1.] Christ's charge extends to this too. Is his charge not to break the bruised reed? He is by the same reason to provide against that which would break it. Is he not to quench the smoking flax? Then he is also to prevent the extinction of it by any other cause. The charge cannot be supposed only to tie his own hands from doing it. Such a comfort would be of a small value while we were endangered by powerful enemies. But this charge arms him with a commission, and lays a necessity upon him to prevent the breaking and quenching of it by any other hand, and therefore obligeth him to withstand that which is most able and most likely to do it, viz., indwelling sin. Though the devil be our great external enemy, yet this is our greatest internal, without whose assistance the keenest arrows of the devil would be shot at rovers, and be uncertain in their effects. Christ, therefore, undertaking the work, undertakes every part of the charge, and this among the rest. The conquest of this in the soul was the reason of the oblation of himself: Titus ii. 14, who gave himself for us, not only to redeem from iniquity, but to purify a people peculiar to himself. Is it agreeable to the wisdom of Christ to neglect the main end of his undertaking, which was 'to make an end of sin'? Dan. ii. 4. What end is there if it recover its loss, and regain its empire in a believing soul? It were in vain for him to go to heaven to prepare mansions for believers, and send his Spirit to prepare them for those mansions, if corruption should get a full head, which would incapacitate them for ever possessing those mansions. Would he be worthy of the name of Saviour, yea, and Salvation, a title God conferred upon him in the past ages, if he should not save those that have the mark of God upon them from that corruption, without which deliverance they could not enjoy any real benefit of his purchased salvation? You have no reason to question his power, and as little to suspect his faithfulness. The distrust of either is an unworthy reflection upon that God that chose him for his work and upheld him in it. Infinite wisdom and immutable goodness would never have pitched upon a person, for the restoration of mankind, of a dubious fidelity. This were to disparage his wisdom, sully the glory of his mercy, and render the designs of his goodness insignificant. Shall not this great person be thought fit to be trusted by us against our enemies, when we have both his own word and his Father's for his willingness and ability, whom God thought fit to trust with a power against the greatest enemy he had in the world upon his own single promise? It is unworthy for us to nourish jealousies of so great a Redeemer, when God that sent him never had cause to have the least suspicion of him. Let me then beg this of any despondent soul, not to distrust the Redeemer's faithfulness, till you meet with a person of more unblemished fidelity to confide in.

[2.] He has an enmity against your corruptions. Sin hath done more wrong to God than ever it did to us. Can it be thought, then, that he should let so injurious an enemy reign in the hearts of any that love God, and are beloved by him. Your hatred against it cannot be so great as his, because you cannot arrive to an equality of holiness with him. The greater the holiness, the greater the hatred of anything contrary to it. Our high priest is 'holy, separate from sinners,' and therefore 'made higher than the heavens,' Heb. vii. 26. Separate from sin too, in all kinds of affection. Letting sin reign in them for whom he is a priest is inconsistent with the holiness of his office. Had he not had an indignation against sin, and a pity to the sinner, he would have spared both the trouble of coming and the pains of dying.

[3.] His residence in heaven is an evidence that this corruption shall be destroyed. The heavens must receive him till the time of the restitution of all things. Acts iii. 21, 'Αποκατάστασις, τελείωσις; so Hesychius. Till the time of the perfection of all things. His being there is an evidence that things shall be restored to a perfect state. It was promised by God from the beginning of the world, all the prophecies were designed to declare it, that those things deformed by the devil should be restored to their primitive lustre. Things cannot be restored till sin be destroyed, grace fully completed, Satan put out of all dominion; in a word, all his enemies put under his feet. And we have the greatest assurance of this; for God hath repeated it again and again by all the prophets from the beginning of the world, as if God's thoughts run upon nothing else but this, and the spirit of prophecy was nothing else but 'the testimony of Jesus' (as indeed it is not, Rev. xix. 10), a witness of what Christ was to do. He hath the government to restore things. If everything is to be restored, believers certainly shall not be left out. It was his main design to expel unbelief and sin out of the hearts of his disciples by his gracious exhortations when he was in the world; much more will he do it by his power conferred upon him since his resurrection, and possessed by him upon his ascension. He sits king in heaven to restore this.

[4.] It is his glory to conquer them. The stronger our corruptions are, the firmer ground hath Christ to glorify his strength in our weakness. If they were not so strong and sin so foul, redemption would not appear so plenteous. His office is chiefly exercised about those. When those are fully conquered in all the elect, his office ceaseth, and the kingdom is to be resigned to the Father. Till then he is a shepherd, and in that respect his office is to find his sheep out when they wander, and bring them home. If he came to seek that which was lost, it is no less for his honour to preserve that which he hath found. The choicer the thing, and the stronger the opposition, the more glory accrues to the preserver of it. Is it for his honour to begin a work in thee, and start back from it? Is it likely he would ever have struck a stroke at those hard hearts of ours, if he did not intend to make thorough work with them? He never yet did any work by halves, and shall he begin now?

[5.] It is already condemned by him. God condemned sin in the flesh by the sacrifice of Christ: Rom. viii. 3, 'And for sin condemned sin in the flesh.' As at his death there was a general condemnation of sin in its nature, so upon faith in this sacrifice, our faith in his blood, there is a particular condemnation of sin in its power, as an unrighteous thing, and not fit, by reason of its malignity, to have a standing there. He condemned it by his holiness in the law, by his justice in the death of Christ, and by his mercy in the renewing of thy nature, which is always accompanied with a condemnation, and in part an execution, of sin. When the guilt of thy sin was pardoned, the power of thy sin was condemned. As the pardon of the one will not be reversed, so neither shall the condemnation of the other. If it be condemned by our Saviour in his flesh, it will be conquered in us by his Spirit; for whatsoever was done by Christ as mediator in his person, was an evidence of what he would do by his Spirit in his members, according to their capacity. Hence they are said to be crucified, risen, ascended, and to sit in heavenly places with him, not only virtually in him as their head, but spiritually in themselves. Shall a dying, gasping sin overpower a living, thriving grace? Sin, therefore, shall be conquered. The Father, by his Spirit, will purge away the worms and suckers which may hinder the growth and ripening of the fruit: John xv. 2, 'Every branch that bears fruit, he purgeth it, that it may bring forth more fruit.' If a branch, though small, he will take care to remove the hindrance to its fruitfulness. God foresaw what infirmities thou wouldst have, before he gave Christ this commission; and Christ foresaw them before his acceptance of the charge. If their prescience could not stop God in his gift, nor cool Christ in his acceptance, why should it now? But,

(1.) This conquest is by degrees. It is victory promised in the text; therefore a conflict is implied, and must be endured. Victory doth not attend the beginning of a war just at the heels. Some time must be allowed between the smoke and flame. Christ must not quench the smoke; but grace may smoke, and only smoke for a while. His charge is to keep that which is committed to him, not presently to overthrow its enemies. He will eye his authority and instructions, as he is God's servant; for as he hath 'received a commandment from his Father,' John xiv. 31, so he acts. He will not perfect it in an instant, but at length he will. Light, and a fulness of it, is sown for the righteous. It is but sown; time must be allowed between that and the harvest. The new creation is no more than the old was, perfected at once. Can you expect your Saviour should make quicker work with you than with his disciples when he was upon the earth? It was his pleasure not to reduce them presently to a perfect state. Neither can we expect more than our Saviour prayed for, which was not that you should be without foils to your faith, but without the failing of your faith. He did not desire his Father presently to take them out of a world of sin, or sin presently from them, but to preserve them under it from being conquered by it. God works to will and to do, but of his own good pleasure; not as we please, but as himself pleaseth.

(2.) Yet while they do continue, the love of God to thee is not hindered by them. The incorruptible seed, which is his own, will more prevail to draw out his love than thy infirmities to engage his hatred against thee. When Christ hung upon the cross, with all the sins of believers about him, God did not withdraw his love from him, because of that righteousness, holiness, and love to God found in him; yet he withdrew his comfortable presence, to shew his hatred of sin. As God dealt with the head, so he will with the members. Especially if your hearts begin to hanker after any sin, though he hath engaged not to take away his loving-kindness from you, yet he may withdraw his comfort till you have repented of your sin. He may chastise you with rods, but will not suffer his faithfulness to fail. He will, as a mother, raise you when you fall, but whip you for falling, to cause you to take more heed. Christ seems to have had as much reason to cast off his disciples as ever he had to cast off any believing soul since. None could ever forsake him in such extremity as they did, for his person will never be in the like straits again. Yet, having once loved them, he loved them to the end, and after the end, after his resurrection, as appears by viewing the story. And it is to be observed, that though their unbelief, ignorance, and pride did often fume from them in the presence of their Master, yet Christ mentions none of them in his prayer to his Father; only their grace: John xvii. 6–8, 'They have kept thy word; they have believed that thou didst send me.' They had indeed received the word of God, but it was lodged in souls very muddy.

(3.) While they do continue, God by his wisdom and grace draws profit to you from them. The very stirring of one sin is sometimes the ruin of another; a gross sin sometimes is the occasional break-neck of spiritual pride. The high thoughts Peter had conceived of himself upon the confession of Christ, were not scattered till he had as shamefully denied him as before he had gloriously confessed him. The thorn in the flesh of that great apostle, whether it was an outward temptation or inward corruption, kept him upon his level, from being 'lifted up above measure.' Thus doth Christ make good his charge by ordering things so by his wisdom, that that which would in itself quench the smoking flax is an occasional means to inflame it. The fogs, which threaten the choking the sun, make his heat more vigorous after the dispersion of those vapours. Neither can sin, because it hath no positive being, be excluded from the number of those things which, by the overruling grace of God, are ordered to our good, Rom. viii. 28, though it be not so in its own nature, since the penmen of Scripture spake not alway according to the rules and terms of philosophy.

For a close, therefore, of this. Perhaps it is our own fault that our corruptions are no more shattered. God hath given you success against some sin; but have your hearts been as much elevated in praise for it, as they were before fervent in prayer? If corruption gather strength, charge not God with want of love, but yourselves with want of thankfulness. Prayer procures mercy, but praise is a means to continue it. As we must depend upon his strength for a victory, so we must acknowledge his strength in our success, else he may withdraw his power, and our enemies may thereupon reassume new life, and assault us with a greater courage. Again, let not anything you have heard of the faithfulness and power of Christ make you neglect your duty. Let Asaph be your pattern, Ps. lxxiii., who, after a strong conflict with sin, had an assurance that God would guide him by his counsel to glory, ver. 24. This makes him not lazy, but quickens him into a resolve that it was good, and good for him too, 'to draw nigh to God,' ver. 28. God is ready with his counsel to guide us, but we must be ready with our petitions.

Use 3. Matter of duty.

(1.) How should men labour to get into a state of grace! To get within the verge of Christ's commission, into such a security which may at last bring them to an eternal triumph over death and hell! Security of estate, and security of person and interest, is the main intendment of men in the world. But security of soul is least in men's thoughts. Should not this latter be as seriously minded? Were there a strong tower wherein they might be infallibly preserved in the time of hostile invasion, and be out of the reach of the enemy's battery, how greedy would men be to get under the shelter! Such a strong tower is the name of the Lord, and those that put their trust in him shall be safe both against open invasions and secret stratagems: Prov. xviii. 10, 'The name of the Lord is a strong tower: the righteous runs into it, and is safe.' By the name of the Lord, the Jews understand in this place, and in many other, the Messiah appointed for the security of the righteous. Methinks every natural man should run with all haste into his closet, fall upon his knees, and not rise till he hath that grace which is by God's order the subject of Christ's tender care. Methinks he should cry and groan, sigh and pray, till he have at least some smoking flax. There is no medium; we must either be under the conduct of Christ, or the government of the devil. If we are in our natural state, we are not enrolled in Christ's family. There is nothing for Christ, but enough for the devil to make victorious. Smoking grace shall grow into a flame of love, and smoking sins into a flame of wrath. Smoking grace is under his care, and smoking sins under his vengeance. As at the last Christ shall come to be admired in all them that believe, *i.e.* in the conduct of them through grace to happiness, so he shall be admired too in the vengeance he shall take upon all them that obey not the gospel, 2 Thes. i. 8, 10.

(2.) Examine whether you have grace or no. It is not lost time to inquire whether you have this victorious principle. Put those questions to your souls: Have I a sincere resolution to discard my former sin? Do I most abhor my darling lusts? Is the burden of this body of death my greatest grief? Have I valuations of Christ above all the world? Would I rather be under the gracious government of Christ, than be the greatest prince in the world without it? Do I esteem God my chief good, and delight in spiritual converse with him, above thousands of gold and silver? Have I a relish of the things of God above all the pleasures of sense? Is the knowledge of God, and excitation of my affections towards him, my chief light? Try it by its activity. It is a true maxim, *Operari sequitur esse*, to be without operation is not to be. If there be not the operation, there is not the essence of grace. It is impossible so active a being as that should lie idle in the soul; there will be smoke, strong desires, ascents upwards, and aims at an heavenly region, though sometimes it be hindered in its direct ascent by the violence of the winds, as the smoke is. Every creature is active in that which concerns its welfare; grace therefore will be as active as any natural thing whatsoever, according to its degrees, because it is a divine communication, a participation of the divine nature. It being more noble, and of a choicer extraction, than any other creature, it will be more active to resist the invasions of the devil, and to move towards God as its chief end.

Only take these cautions:

[1.] Judge not of thy want of grace by the not acting of that grace which formerly was very vigorous. One grace may for a time cease to act so sensibly, to give way to the powerful operations of another. John Baptist did decrease, that Christ might increase. Graces have their particular seasons to traverse the stage of the soul; sometimes love, sometimes hope, sometimes patience, humility, faith, and dependence, sometimes sorrow for sin, sometimes joy, &c.

[2.] Grace may be sometimes oppressed by a temptation, and so may cease a sensible acting, but it will recover itself by degrees.

[3.] If you find upon a diligent search that you have true grace, take heed of nourishing jealousies of God, and unbelieving doubts of the care of Christ over you. We indeed often have our fears of ourselves upon the clouding of our evidences; and when we have reason to question the truth of our grace, we have very good reason to question our standing also. Though we have a clear prospect of our grace, and know it to be true, yet there may be fears in us of what might have been, had we not this security in Christ's commission. As a man upon a high tower, though hemmed in with strong battlements, and sure that he cannot fall, yet when he looks down he cannot but have some horror and chillness in his blood at the apprehension of what might be if he had not that protection.* Neither do I discourage fears in ourselves, and fears of those things which may weaken our hopes of salvation, for those the apostle joins with a confidence in God: Philip. ii. 12, 13, 'Work out your salvation with fear and trembling, for it is God which works in you both to will and to do.' Fear yourselves, but have confidence in God, a believing fear without an unbelieving jealousy of God's neglect of you; for all doubts of the stability of the covenant, and the perpetual tenderness of God, are brats of a natural Pelagianism. Breathe not your unbelieving fears in the face of Christ; it is a wrong to his commission, a disparagement to his Father's wisdom, as if he had placed so great a trust in feeble hands, and a virtual accusing of God and Christ of the greatest falsity imaginable, whereby we make him more base and deceitful than the worst of men; an affronting the main tenor of the covenant of grace, and making the work of redemption to bear no better fruits than that of creation. How languishing will be our love to God, while we have unworthy suspicions of him, that he should love us this day, and be an enemy to us to-morrow! Can we love a man this day that we fear will the next be our deadly enemy? Let the time spent in such jealous thoughts and complaints of God be spent in duty. Would it not be a trouble to a loving husband to have his wife complain of her fears of his casting her off after the marriage-knot, and reiterated promises and assurances of his affection? Would she not better engage his affections by a performance of all offices of love and duty towards him?

[4.] Let not this doctrine encourage any remissness in our known duties. Let none encourage themselves to a freedom in sin, and presume upon God's preservation of them without the use of the means. No; the electing counsel upon which this victory is founded, chose us to the means as well as to the end. He that makes such a consequence, I doubt whether ever he was a Christian. I may safely say, that any person that hath a settled, resolved, and wilful remissness, never yet was in the covenant of grace, since that promiseth such a fear of God in the heart which is incompatible with a resolved laziness in duty. It is a new heart and a new spirit, not a lazy heart, that is the intendment of the covenant. The same will which is the seat of grace can never be the settled seat of the neglects of God. God hath promised a victory; but the very promise of victory implies a war, and commands as well as encourages a standing to our arms. Victories are never gained by sleep and laziness; camps may be beat up, and throats cut, if guards be neglected. He that is not under the influence of the doctrine of grace, never had the truth of habitual grace in him. He that hath not learned the lesson which the grace or gospel of God teacheth, to 'deny ungodliness and worldly

* Thes. Salm. de Persever.

lusts,' &c., Titus ii. 11, 12, was never any proficient in Christ's school, never had any work of grace. It is the nature of grace to be active. It is a divine principle, security a diabolical; darkness and light cannot blend together in intense degrees, Christ and Belial cannot shake friendly hands. Security is never the effect, but the disease, of grace, the death of holiness, and the life of sin. That grace which assures us to the end, will make us conscionable in the means to attain it. A partial security is also very dangerous in a Christian: it will kill our comfort, though it may not destroy our souls; it will impair the beauty of grace, though not its being. Would any but a madman under a distemper neglect the means to restore his healthfulness, because he were sure to live so long a time?

[5.] Admire the grace of God. How much are we beholding to the grace of God, which is at an hourly expense upon us! As his providence is called a continual creation by the efflux of his power, so our preservation in the new state is a continual regeneration by the influence of his grace. God, in giving thee grace, hath given thee more than if he had given thee all the glory of the world. All other things are managed only by a common providence, this is put more immediately under Christ's charge. By giving thee this, which is a peculiar part of his commission, he hath given thee such a guardian, such an advantage, which could never have been gained by a confluence of all the honours in the world. It is a standing miracle in the world, that all the floods of temptations should not be able to quench this little heavenly spark in the heart; that it should be preferred from being smothered by the steams of sin which arise in us; that a little smoking flax should smoke and burn in spite of all the buckets of water which are poured upon it. To see a rich jewel in a child's hand, with a troop of thieves about him snatching at it, and yet not able to plunder, would raise an astonishment both in the actors and spectators, and make them conclude an invisible strength that protects the child, and defeats the invaders. Thus God perfects his strength in our weakness, and ordains matter for praise in the mouths and hearts of babes and sucklings.

[6.] Acknowledge thy standing and thy present victories only to be by the grace of God. Give the grace of God its due praise. God hath fixed our standing in Christ, and entrusted and charged him with our preservation, that grace might triumph in the whole Christian pilgrimage, till we come to the land of rest; that nothing may be heard either in heaven or earth, but the acclamations of grace, grace. 'God put no trust in his saints,' Job xv. 15; in some other person therefore, as the head of them. The ground of our perseverance is not in ourselves then, since God puts no trust in us, but in another, in the mediator.

We cannot beat men too much off from themselves; and therefore to strengthen this, take these grounds:

(1.) Grace in its own nature is not immutable, nor independent. Immutability is not intrinsecal to grace; neither is it, nor can it be, the essential property of any creature, though never so high. It is a natural perfection belonging only to God. The habit of grace is called an incorruptible seed; not that it is so in its own nature (for it is a creature, and therefore defectible; for mutability is as much belonging to the essence of a creature, as immutability to the essence of God. As it is impossible God should be mutable, so it is impossible a creature should be in its own nature immutable); but grace is immortal in respect of that omnipotent power which doth attend the principle, and spreads its warm wings over it, as the Spirit over the world, to bring it to a perfect beauty and order out of the chaos. If grace did not depend upon God in its preservation, but were unchangeable in its own nature, it might be counted as perfect as God, whose only prerogative it is to be independent and immutable in himself. The heathens could say, there was no τὸ ὄν, no *ens*, but God; in him we have our being, and in him only we have our firm and stable being.

(2.) The same power that doth create, is necessary to preserve. There is little difference between creation and conservation: the one gives *primo esse*, the other *porro esse*. The wisdom and power of God is as eminent in the preservation and government of the world, as in the rearing of it. We are no more able to preserve grace, than we are to create it. We cannot preserve our own thoughts, which are the natural products of our minds, much less so rich a treasure as grace, which is purely supernatural, and in the midst of so many pirates which endeavour to rob us of it. As the first habitual grace is by the operation of God's grace in us, so the daily preservation of it is by his assisting grace, which in a sweet way, and yet efficacious, keeps grace in its station, and carries on the soul to further degrees. As it is the preserving power of God maintains the world, so the auxiliary grace of God maintains grace, and all the exercises of it in the heart, which could not else be kept up by all the power of men's wit or will. As the influence of the sun is necessary to all natural productions, preservation and maturity of them, so is the influence of Christ necessary to all productions and preservations of grace. The righteousness whereby we are justified, and whence our habitual grace doth spring, is laid up in Christ, and our strength too: Isa. xlv. 24, 'In the Lord have I righteousness and strength.' Righteousness to justify us, and strength to preserve us; and as he is our Redeemer, laying thereby the foundation of the new creation, so he is our strength whereby it is preserved: Ps. xix. 14, 'O Lord, my strength, and my Redeemer.' The former part of the psalm is by the apostle, in the Romans, applied to the times of the gospel. Our redemption and our strength, our righteousness imputed, our righteousness inherent, and our strength, are the effects of the same cause; so that we can no more be our own strength than be our own redeemers, nor be our own strength no more than our own righteousness. When Paul complains of his temptation, God answers him that his grace should be sufficient for him; not the habitual grace in Paul, but the assisting grace of God, 2 Cor. xii. 9. Hence it is that the saints in Scripture desire so often God to help them, which they need not, if their inherent grace were sufficient to preserve them.

(3.) The standing of those who are in their consummate state in glory, is only by grace as the chief cause. The good angels and blessed souls are confirmed in that state by a superabounding grace; for by nature they are mutable. Was it the contemplation of the face of God that kept the angels firm in that state? What is the reason some of the angels fell, who contemplated God's face at the creation as well as those that stood? Or is it that they see no good which they want, being advanced the highest of any creatures? Was not this the case of the fallen angels? What good did they want which was proper to a created state?* Besides, confirmation is *positivus effectus*, a positive effect, and therefore must have a positive cause, a privative cause not being sufficient to produce a positive effect. Or do the good angels and glorified saints continue firm to God, because they know that, if they sin, they should be eternally miserable? But this doth not become a blessed state, to avoid sin for fear of punishment, rather than love of righteousness. Besides, the happiness of heaven could not be eternal, nor the joy pure, that is mixed with those fears of falling and losing it. Or is it from an affection to the pleasure of the place? Such a self-principle

* Bradw. de Causa Dei. l. ii. c. xv.

becomes not the purity of that state. But though their inherent grace, the contemplation of God, and delight in him, may be some means of their standing, and methods God useth, yet those are not sufficient of themselves. It is God in his incomprehensible grace which preserves them. It is an excellent speech of a holy man of our neighbour nation: 'I am sure if my feet were in heaven, and Christ should say, Defend thyself, I will hold thee no longer; I should go no farther, but presently fall down in many pieces of dead nature.'* If you could find one saint that in that place of glory ascribes the beginning or perfection of his salvation to himself, then glory in yourselves too. But not till then, and I am sure you never will.

(4.) If all this be true, much less can the best grace in this world preserve itself, because at best in itself it is weaker than its adversaries. No sooner is grace put into the heart, but all the powers of hell are in arms against it, and would murder the new-born heavenly nature. Now it being a creature weak and imperfect, it cannot be so powerful in operation, as to resist the force of a stronger being, and a subtle and insinuating adversary. Were there no devils to assault, I do not understand how this principle, so weak in itself, were able to make head against the deceitfulness of our own hearts. It is the Spirit steps in to quell those destroyers, and brood upon his own work in the soul. What! Was it Peter's strength, or God's grace in him, that made the difference between him and Judas, between Paul and the rest of the persecuting pharisees? It is from God's faithfulness that we are established and kept from evil: 2 Thes. iii. 3, 'But the Lord is faithful, who shall establish you and keep you from evil.' If God, not ourselves; it is true we will, but God works that will in us. We work, but the grace of God works that work in us, and for us. If by grace we are what we are, it is by grace we do what we do, and that of God's good pleasure, not our merit. Our sufficiency is of God, not of ourselves. Our fruitfulness depends upon our abiding in Christ. What can dust and ashes do against principalities and powers? What man is able, without the grace of God, to wrestle with an experienced devil? A smoking flax would quickly be blown out or expire after a little blaze, if God did not cherish it; a bruised reed would be trod in the dirt, if he did not secure it. A gracious man depends upon God, as the steel doth upon the loadstone in the air, which, if once separated, will be carried down with its own weight, and be reduced to a motion proper to its nature. If God should withdraw his grace from us, the grace in us would not preserve us from falling as low as hell; for of itself it is far more insufficient to preserve us, than the strength which angels and Adam had was to preserve them. We are preserved not by any inherent power in ourselves, but by the constant touches of God upon our wills, whereby he keeps our wills fixed to him.

Let not, then, our free will usurp the praise which is due only to God's grace.

(1.) There is danger in it. To ascribe thy standing or victory to thyself, is an usher to some scurvy and deplorable fall. When we confide too much in ourselves, God leaves us to our own foolish confidence, to reduce us to our proper dependency on him. Peter's boasting of the power of his own grace was a just cause of his being left to himself, that he might be sensible of his own weakness, and the true ground of his security. If we do fall, it is not for want of faithfulness in God, but for want of thankfulness in us.

(2.) It is our sin. So much as we ascribe anything to our own strength, so much we rob grace of its glory. We provoke the Lord to jealousy, who will not have the glory due to his name ascribed to the creature.

(3.) The contrary is our advantage. The acknowledgment of our depend-

* Rutherford's Letters, p. 184.

ency on God is the way to be preserved; the more we give God the glory of his grace, the more will he give us the comfort of it.

[7.] Let the falls of others that seem stronger than you make you more thankful, and more compassionate. If they make you more thankful, they will make you more compassionate. Though you may be engraven with more lively characters of God's image, and in an higher manner like to God, yet grace is to be acknowledged that kept temptations from overcoming you. Let not your pride, but your praise, take encouragement from thence. Think not yourselves better, because you are victorious while others are defeated, but God more gracious to you. The continuance of his assisting grace was the cause of your success, as the withdrawing of it was the cause of the other's defeat. If this too much natural corruption be indulged, it is a ground to fear we may shortly be his successors in the like fault, or a worse.

Be more compassionate to others: Gal. vi. 1, 'If a man be overtaken in a fault, you which are spiritual restore such an one in the spirit of meekness; considering thyself, lest thou also be tempted.' Let the faults of others teach us to exercise the grace of humility in our hearts, and carriage towards them. Make not the breach wider by our censures, which is too wide already by Satan's power. Restore with meekness, not proud censoriousness; by a dove-like meekness, like that of our Saviour; the case may shortly be our own, and we may stand in need of his assistance for our restoration. To pity or help a gracious man in such a case, is to assist Christ in his charge, and be his seconds in his duel against the devil, and will be kindly accepted by him. God commanded in the law to help a beast, if they saw it in a ditch. It is unnatural to let an infant lie on the ground, and not lend a hand to lift it up; much more to let an infant grace, the birth of God and charge of Christ, to lie grovelling in the earth by the power of sin.

[8.] Despise not therefore small grace in any. Is Christ to have a special regard to smoking flax and bruised reeds? Is it fit we should be of a temper contrary to our Saviour in despising that which God hath ordered him to regard? Must that be the object of our laughter, which is the object of Christ's tenderest care? Is that to be the subject of our scorn, which is one of the chief parts of his commission to take care of? Can he be thought to be regenerate, who is of a disposition so contrary to him who ought to be his pattern? If God's soul be well-pleased with Christ's care of small grace, he must abominate any temper so opposite to his own and that of his Son. It is a pride and a scorn like to that of devils, not a spirit like that of God. As the least sin in others must not draw our affection, so the weakest grace in others must not lie under our contempt. Would you tread upon a diamond because it is little, or slight a star bigger than the whole earth, because it seems a little twinkling spark in your eye? Let us look to it, then, that we disesteem not that in another which is of more worth than the whole mass of the ungracious world. It is a gallant disposition not to be offended with that smoke which doth not offend the Redeemer's eye.

[9.] Stand fast. Leave not off till you gain a full victory, till judgment be brought forth to victory. It is necessary. He that is not at last victorious was never any soldier under Christ's pay, or inspired with Christ's spirit. Men may think they stand fast, and are, in a prosperous way to victory, when they are not: 1 Cor. x. 12, 'Wherefore, let him that thinks he stands fast take heed lest he fall.' There must, therefore, be much watchfulness and wariness used. Though this doctrine stands firm, yet such exhortations must be used. The word of Christ to Peter, that his faith should not fail, was as firm as a rock; yet, Mat. xxvi. 40, 41, 'He saith unto Peter, Watch and pray, that you enter not into a temptation;' he stirs him up particularly to his watchful guard, though there were two others besides that had not that assurance from his mouth, that their faith should not fail, as Peter had. Paul promiseth the Corinthians, in the name of God, 1 Cor. x. 13, 14, that God would not suffer them to be tempted above measure; must they therefore stand idle, and suffer themselves to be carried down the stream of a temptation, and leave God wholly to do his work? No; ver. 14, he draws an argument from this promise to exhort them to do their duty, 'Wherefore, my beloved, flee from idolatry;' fly, not creep, not go, not walk. Promises are not to encourage our laziness, but quicken our industry. Let not the charge, then, brought against Ephraim fall upon us, that 'our goodness is like a morning dew,' Hosea vi. 4. When men begin in the spirit, and end in the flesh, the end will be both dreadful and shameful. An eternal crown is entailed upon a constant faithfulness. Our running in a race near to the end will be insignificant, if then our antagonist get the start of us. It is by this constancy we come nearest the name of God, which is, 'I am that I am,' unchangeable in perfections, and immutable in goodness. Our actions should be suitable to the reward promised, which is not for a day or two, but for eternity. We must hold on and wrestle till we get the blessing. Without continuance, we lose our pains, and the fruit of them, our crown. Run not slowly; but that you may obtain, let your eye upon the crown; you will never else run swiftly, because not cheerfully. But, withal, means must be used to stand fast in grace and gain a victory.* God doth not preserve a Christian by force, or compel him to keep his standing, as he doth establish the earth, or the heavens; but by rational means, by promises and precepts suitable to the condition of a rational and voluntary agent, and proposing affective and alluring arguments to encourage him in his course; yet he leaves not the success barely to this, and the operation of our own wills, but attends it with the supernatural power of his Spirit, suitable to the manner of our first conversion, which was not by violence, but by the proposals of the gospel, and the salvation promised in it, wherein a secret power of the Spirit was exerted upon the heart, enlightening the mind, and inclining the will, and drawing it with the cords of a man in a way of love, to a compliance with the gospel promise. So, likewise, in the preservation and progress of grace, there is still a secret working of the Spirit of God with outward exhortations and admonitions to perseverance, thereby keeping up the new habit and new heart in us, quickening it by outward means and rational ways suited to the judgment and reason of the new creature; and thus keeping his hand upon the will, he moves it to such ends for which he first touched it, and draws it on from one degree unto another, till it comes to perfection.

Therefore we must not make use of this doctrine to neglect the means God hath appointed for the establishing and completing of grace; since God acts with us as rational creatures, we are not only passive but active subjects in this work. John assures the believers that the unction in them should preserve them from soul-destroying errors. There is this passive perseverance: 1 John ii. 27, 'As it hath taught you, ye shall abide in him.' Must they therefore be careless? No; ver. 28, he backs it with duty on their parts, 'Wherefore, my little children, abide in him; that, when he shall appear, we may have confidence;' abide in him that certainly abides in you. There is scarce a promise in the whole book of God to encourage us, but is somewhere or other attended with a precept to quicken us.

Means.

(1.) Look well to sincerity. This is the blood and vital spirit which runs through the veins of every grace, without which it is not what it seems to

* Camero de Eccles. p. 227.

be. Faith is not faith unless it be unfeigned, and what may seem to be love is not so unless it be sincere. Sincerity is that principle in the heart which complies with the quickening grace of God, as the vital spirit in a plant doth with the beams of the sun, which doth not only make it stand, but grow against the injuries of the weather. It was God's manner long ago to have a special respect to sincerity: Job viii. 20, 'Behold, God will not cast away a perfect man, neither will he help the evil-doer;' לא ימאס. He will not despise or turn away himself. If a sincere man falls, he will reach out his hand to lift him up, as the antithesis manifests. The word being in the Hebrew, he will not take the evil-doer by the hand, לא ביד יחזיק, implying that he doth hold the other, and raise him up. It is our sincerity in withstanding the sins and temptations of the world, that the promise of perfect sanctification is made to: Rev. iii. 4, 5, 'Thou hast a few names in Sardis which have not defiled their garments; and they shall walk with me in white:' they shall be clothed in white. An allusion to the Jewish custom of admitting the priests into their office, by clothing them with white as a badge of their office and continuance in the priesthood. 'Job held fast his integrity,' Job ii. 3; and that was a means to preserve and recover him. Uncompounded things are least subject to putrefaction, whereas mixed bodies easily ferment and corrupt. Sincerity can never be feeble, because the spirit of power always attends it: 2 Tim. i. 7, 'For God hath not given us the spirit of fear, but of power, of love, and of a sound mind.' The apostle couples them both together. A single respect to Christ in the midst of shaking persecution, is both an evidence of the strong touch of the heart by the Spirit, and a preservative against apostasy; as the standing right of the needle in the compass, in the midst of the winds which toss the ship, manifests its powerful touch by the loadstone, and is a means to direct it in its course and preserve it from a wreck.

(2.) Get a stock of spiritual knowledge, and actuate it often. The grave, considering Christian will stand, when the hot-headed professor, like horses of the same temper, will jade and sink under the rider in a few miles. Men whose religion consists rather in a commotion of their passions than a judicious and considerate determination of their wills, will quickly flag; hot beginners are not durable; violent motions, either in naturals or morals, are not perpetual; get the experience of every truth you hear. Experimental knowledge is the true ballast of the soul, when mere sound and air is a rolling and moveable thing. Mere head professors are as light as a cork dancing upon every dash of water. An experimental taste of the grace of God, viz., that grace of Christ which produceth a coming to him, is a means to be built up a spiritual house: 1 Peter ii. 3–5, 'If so be you have tasted that the Lord is gracious.' It must be a taste, not only the hearing of a sound; it is not enough to be sound in judgment, but spiritual in taste, Col. i. 23. Skilful musicians, who understand the delicacy of the airs in a tune, will chain their ears to the sound, when an unskilful person will listen and stare a while, and run away. Our valuations of God are according to the degrees of our knowledge; and our cleavings to him, according to the degrees of our estimations of him. Actuate it often; let thy knowledge sink down to thy will, and lie ready by thee, to bring forth new and old upon any exigency. The forgetting the precepts and promises of God is the cause of fainting, Heb. xii. 5: 'Wisdom and knowledge shall be the stability of thy time and strength of salvation,' Isa. xxxiii. 6. As this makes the kingdom of Christ stable in the world, so it will the kingdom of grace in our souls. Get, therefore, and actuate a knowledge of the tenor of the covenant, the substance of the promises, the nature and ends of Christ's mediation: 'Be strong in the grace that is in Christ,' 2 Tim. ii. 1, 3 ; have a right understanding of the covenant of grace which is manifested in and by Christ, of the stock of grace stored up in Christ. This will make you endure hardship as the soldiers of Christ; this will make you high-spirited in the acting of your faith and pleas before God, without which both your faith and prayers will be very faint and languishing.

(3.) Rest not in small degrees of grace. It is true, weak grace will keep close to Christ; Philadelphia with her little strength kept Christ's words, Rev. iii. 8; yet that pretended grace that always remains in the same posture, may well be suspected as a counterfeit. He that stands at a stay in what he supposeth to be grace, never had grace in truth. It is impossible anything should be without its essential properties, and it is an essential property of grace to grow; it would not else be the seed of God and an immortal principle. He that hath grace, finds such a pleasure and excellency in it, that he can but have little acquiescence in himself without exercise of it. If you do not strengthen your grace, you will make way to strengthen your doubts. Though weak grace will carry a man to heaven, it will be just as a small and weak vessel surprised by a shattering storm, which, though it may get to the shore, yet with excessive hardships and fears; such will sail through a stormy sea, and have a daily contest with stormy doubts ready to overset their hopes ; whereas a stout ship, well rigged, will play with the waves in the midst of a tempest, and at last pass through all difficulties, without many fears, into its haven. We are not perfect here. Perfection is a title peculiar to the blessed: Heb. xii. 23, 'The spirits of just men made perfect.' Yet we must press forward towards it, to attain the resurrection of the dead, Philip. ii. 11, *i.e.* such a perfection of holiness which shall be the state of glorified souls. When this is our mark, we shall have a further progress in the degrees of grace, and by that means be nearer to a complete victory. Though a man cannot reach the sun in shooting, yet if he aim at it, he shall mount his arrow higher than if he aimed at a shrub.

Well, then, let our aims be at the highest degrees. He is so far from gaining strength that doth not aspire to a further conquest, that he is in danger to be beaten out of what he hath, and lose the things which he hath wrought. To take up our rest beneath it, is a sign that neither the hatred of sin, our enemy, nor the love of God, our friend, were ever sincere and well rooted. Not to arrive to a complete victory is our weakness ; not to aspire to it is our sin ; for it answers not the design of Christ's coming, which was not only that we might have life spiritual and eternal, but an abounding life: John x. 10, 'I am come that they might have life, and that they might have it more abundantly.' Not a decreasing life, or one that stands at a stay.

(4.) Study much your exemplar and copy. That hope whereby we expect to become like Christ in an eternally happy state, must be formed by no lower copy than that of Christ himself: 1 John iii. 3, 'He that hath this hope, (*i. e.* to see him as he is) purifies himself, as he is pure ;' not as the saints are pure, as Abraham, Noah, Job, Daniel. He that steers himself only by the lower exemplars, will be more subject to imperfect draughts and failings than he that endeavours to form his soul and life according to the original. He that sets the best copy to imitate, will exceed others who propose lower patterns, though he may not yet come near the original. The apostle directs to study Christ much, who is the foundation of our standing: Heb. xii. 3, 'Consider him that endured such contradictions of sinners against himself, lest you be wearied and faint in your minds;' consider him as the author and finisher of your faith ; consider him in his patience on the cross, despising the shame, and the success of his heroic temper, and this will inspire you with a holy courage under the contradictions of corruptions and temptations against your grace. This is our duty: Mat. v. 48, 'Be you therefore perfect, as your Father which is in heaven is perfect.' Christ himself commands it when he exhorts them to mount above publicans in their duty, and not to conform themselves to the low patterns of the world. Some translate it, *You shall be perfect*, enforcing thereby the strength of the command; as men, when they would impose anything by the stress of their authority, say, *You shall* do such a thing, instead of saying, *Do* such a thing. Be as resolute and vigorous in all your duties to God, as he is in all his notes of mercy and goodness to you.

(5.) Be conscientious in the performance of holy duties. A fire which for a while shoots up to heaven will faint both in its heat and brightness, without fresh supplies of nourishing matter. Bring fresh wood to the altar morning and evening, as the priests were bound for the nourishment of the holy fire, Lev. v. 12. God in all his promises supposeth the use of means. When he promised Hezekiah his life for fifteen years, it cannot be supposed that he should live without eating and exercise. It is both our sin and misery to neglect the means. Therefore, let an holy and an humble spirit breathe in all our acts of worship. If we once become listless to duty, we shall quickly become lifeless in it. If we languish in our duties, we shall not long be lively in our graces. The loss of the stomach is a sign of the loss of health. If we would flourish, we must drink of those waters which spring up to everlasting life. If we desire our leaves should prosper, we should often plant ourselves by the rivers of waters; we must be where the sun shines, the dews drop, and the Spirit blows. If you find yourselves growing into a slothful temper, check it betimes, and recall to your minds the pleasure you have had in your lively and warm converses with God in any duty, and how delightful afterwards both the beauty and comfort of your graces were. Liveliness in action is a sign of the continuance of health, and liveliness in duty an evidence of the continuance of grace. Let them all be performed in the strength of Christ. It is not means or ordinances bring judgment to victory, but Christ in them.

[1.] Attend upon the word and sacraments. As the word was the seed whence grace did spring, so it is the channel through which strength and nourishment is conveyed. It is the seed whereby we are begotten, 1 Peter i. 23, and the milk whereby we are nourished, 1 Pet. ii. 2. If the stomach to our spiritual food grow weak, the vigour of our grace will quickly begin to gasp.

[2.] Prayer. This is the chiefest duty, and that which makes all others more vigorous in their tendency to their end. Our Saviour breathes out strong cries, though he had the strongest assurances of a victorious success, Heb. v. 7. Promises of perseverance should be the guides of our prayers. We may pray most comfortably for that which we are sure to speed in. The Spirit which is sent to comfort us in our fears of miscarrying, is a spirit of supplication as well as a spirit of grace, Zech. xii. 10. Where it is most a spirit of grace, it will be also most a spirit of supplication. To talk of a gracious man that neglects prayer, is as great nonsense as to tell us of a living man that doth not breathe. We in all our distresses make our application to those that have power in their hands. It is God only draws us to Christ, and keeps us with him. It is Christ that is ordered to bring forth judgment unto victory. To him therefore we must be petitioners. He gives us first the grace of desire, that he may with the more honour confer the mercy he intends us. Our Saviour sets us a pattern in praying to the Father to preserve and keep us, John xvii. We must not therefore be negligent in our desires of it, or distrustful of the success, especially when we have encouragements by Christ's petition for the same thing, who was never denied by his Father any request for his people. You have many arguments to use: Ps. lxviii. 28, 'Strengthen, O Lord, what thou hast wrought for us.' Let thy power preserve what thy power did work. It is as much to the glory of thy omnipotent love to second thy own work with thy own strength, as it was to begin it. To what purpose, O God, wert thou pleased to work it, if thou wilt not maintain it? The arguments of God's glory are most prevalent. They were so in the mouth of Moses. Plead the same believingly, and thou wilt find the same success. It is for the glory of God you should be victorious: 'He which stablisheth us with you is God,' 1 Cor. i. 21. Shall we think to stand without seeking to the author of our standing? And that you may pray boldly, believe it to be a thing belonging to you by virtue of Christ's purchase as well as your reconciliation and adoption. If you can but pray, you are sure to succeed in the conquest; and you can never want pleas for standing till God cancel the bond of his everlasting covenant, and depose Christ from his office of an advocate. Plead these then. God cannot deny his own bond, nor resist the exercise of an office of his own erecting.

(6.) Exercise grace much. Graces, as soldiers, well exercised, are more fit to engage an invading enemy. Muster them up often, and see thy strength, but behold it with humility, prayer, and thankfulness. Living bodies grow stronger by moderate exercise, and many things grow rusty and unfit for want of use. Graces are compared to armour, Eph. vi., and armour is the better for use. Frequent blowing up this fire will make it stronger in itself, and more comfortable to us.

[1.] Faith. It was by faith that out of weakness the ancient worthies were made stronger, Heb. xi. 24. It was this made Abraham the father of the faithful, and it will make all the children mighty men of valour, Rom. iv. 24. It is a mighty expression, Ps. cxlvii. 11, 'The Lord taketh pleasure in them that fear him: in those that hope in his mercy;' as if the delight and content of his being were maintained by this grace. He takes pleasure to relieve and pleasure to support them. Mercy cannot be so hard-hearted as to deny assistance to that faith that clings about it. Should God do so, he would cast off that pleasure. You can never offend him by the straitest clasping, or pain him by too close embraces. The faster you hold him, the less power will indwelling sin or watchful Satan have to drag you from him, for the more you hold him, the more he holds you. You do not only apprehend him, but are apprehended by him. A sling and stone, with faith in the name of the Lord, will be more successful to pierce the head of Goliath with his whole army of Philistines, than if you did march clothed with Saul's armour. Faith will do more than all the arms and ammunition of moral philosophy, so much furbished and trimmed up in our day. It is to faith all the victorious acts of a Christian, through the whole Scripture, are ascribed. Faith quencheth the fiery darts of the devil; faith purifies the heart from inward corruptions; faith wrestles with principalities and powers; faith gets the victory over the world; faith preserves us by engaging God's power for us; and faith in all this contest never leaves us till it lands us in heaven. It is the prime piece in the Christian armour whereby we gain the victory, and therefore there is such an emphasis set upon it, as if though a man had all the rest and wanted this, he would be foundered in all his attempts: Eph. vi. 16, 'Above all taking the shield of faith;' as if all other pieces, though very gallant and strong, were nothing to this to keep off the darts of the enemy. It is a grace worthy the exercise. Other graces may fail, and the soul recover; but if faith fail, all is gone. The acting of all our graces depends upon the strength and acting of our faith. The stronger our faith, the greater our stability; the weaker our faith, the more tottering our standing. If the soul could at the first go out to God in acts of faith, when its corruptions had the first blow given them, and found success, much more encouragement hath it to launch out to Christ and renew the same faith, since the wounds upon its lusts are both more numerous and deeper.

[2.] Patience. I mean not patience under afflictions, but a patient waiting; there is need of patience to uphold us in a course of obedience, and need of it also to strengthen our expectations of reward: Heb. x. 36, 'Ye have need of patience, that after ye have done the will of God, you may receive the promise.' God in the course of his providence seems sometimes to turn the back of his promise upon us; there is need of a patient waiting, till it turn again and march towards us. He sometimes lets loose the devil upon us, and then we fear the waters will swallow up our souls, and that our spiritual enemies will utterly defeat us; there is need of patience, till God pulls back the chain whereby he holds our enemy. Christ accomplisheth the most glorious things by degrees; as he doth not give all grace in a moment, so he doth not perfect it in a moment. Patience must endure in the whole military exercise. We cannot lay it aside till we gain the victory. It is as necessary as faith, to entitle us to the inheritance of the promises of perseverance and victory: Heb. vi. 12, 'Through faith and patience inherit the promises.' Without it, we cannot believe in hope against hope; without it, we can never run our race, Heb. xii. 1.

[3.] Love. Love adds weight to the soul, and suffers not the affections easily to be divorced from the endeared object. The holy angels are fixed in their standing by grace as the principal cause, by the purity of their love as the internal principle. An intelligent and purified love will not forsake a choice object. The iron mixed with drossy particles runs not so quick, nor sticks so close to the loadstone, as the refined and best tempered steel. Men embrace not the truth as truth for want of faith, and they fall from it for want of love: 2 Thess. ii. 10, 'They receive not the love of the truth.' They receive the truth, but not the love of the truth. The purer our love, the faster we shall stick to that rock which is our strength. God is the strength of those that love him: Ps. xviii. 1, 'I will love thee, O Lord, my strength.'

[4.] Humility. God gives grace to the humble; then surely the greatest supplies of grace in our deepest exercises of humility. We should find the very workings of God's grace more powerful in us, in the very exercises of this grace. Christ finds those most strangers to him, that are most proud of themselves. He that is not sensible of his own weakness, is never like to have recourse to another for strength. To trust in our grace, is to make our grace a god, because the principal object of the creature's trust is God, and it belongs to him to be so as the highest good. Now to make our inherent grace the chief object of our trust, is to own it to be as good as God, and as sufficient as God to keep its standing. A conceit of our strength may make us seem bigger, but in reality it makes us weaker. All the humours in the soul run to the boil of pride. Fearfulness of ourselves is a good prologue to a firmness in God, it will make us more strongly lay hold of his power, and more earnestly plead his faithfulness. Exercise it most after the conquest of a temptation; then it is our time to take heed of spiritual pride, we may else overcome one temptation, and sink under another. Pride after a victory gives the enemy an opportunity of success, upon a new assault with a fresh recruit. Humility is as necessary to preserve us after a conquest, as faith was to arm and strengthen us for it.

(7.) Frequently renew settled and holy resolutions. A soldier unresolved to fight may easily be defeated. True and sharpened courage treads down those difficulties which would triumph over a cold and wavering spirit. Resolution in a weak man will perform more than strength in a coward. The weakness of our graces, the strength of our temptations, and the diligence of our spiritual enemies, require strong resolutions. We must be 'stedfast and unmoveable,' and this will make us 'abound in the work of the Lord,' 1 Cor. xv. 58. Abundant exercise in God's work will strengthen the habit of grace, increase our skill in the contest, and make the victory more easy and pleasant to us. Let them be believing, humble resolutions in the strength of God's grace, with a jealousy of yourselves; not a vaunting resolution in the strength of your own wills, a fear of ourselves, but a confidence in God. David bound himself to God with a hearty vow, depending upon his strength: Ps. cxix. 106, 'I have sworn, and I will perform it, that I will keep thy righteous judgments.' 'I have sworn,' &c., but not in his own strength, for, ver. 107, he desires God to quicken him, and to accept the 'free-will offering of his mouth,' ver. 108, *i.e.* the oath which proceeded from a free and resolved will. God will not slight, but strengthen the affectionate resolutions of his creature. We cannot keep ourselves from falling, if we first keep not our resolutions from flagging.

(8.) Look often back upon your state under convictions, and the first state of conversion. Measure your present complexion by your former temper. Cast up your accounts often, and see whether you thrive or decay, and renew your former dispositions. It is our Saviour's counsel: Rev. ii. 5, 'Remember from whence thou art fallen, and do thy first works;' which cannot be done without reflection upon thy wonted delight in God, thy desires for him, and the sweet communications dispensed by him. Inquire into the cause of thy decay. This is a necessary attendant upon this act of remembrance, for it is not a bare simple act of memory Christ commands, but a diligent inquisition by a practical remembrance. A timely observance of the cause of our loss, will prevent many future ones; without this act, the devil will creep in and finish his business before we are aware. It is a pleasure to reflect upon the time of danger wherein we have been, and to recount the methods God used in our delivery, and the resolutions we then entertained: Isa. xxxiii. 18, 'Thy heart shall meditate terror,' *i.e.* thou shalt consider what thy troubles were, what the frame of thy heart was, what terrors thou hadst in thy distress; for it is spoken of the gospel times, when they shall 'see the King in his beauty.' So likewise it is useful to recall to our memory what desires, what fervency in prayer, what holy vows there were in and upon us, when we were under a wounded spirit, and act the same fervours over again. This would restore and inflame the heart more in duty, and enable thee for the contest, by calling into thy assistance the supplies of all the habitual grace thou hast had since those firsts heats. Remember then the strength of thy appetite to the word; how your zeal did glow, what sprightliness in your affections, with what devotion your prayers were winged, with what stoutness your faith did breathe, how high it did climb, with what detestation you entertained the motions to sin, with what courage you entered into the lists of temptations, how quick and nimble your obedience was, what a freshness and verdure was upon all your graces. Remember those, and do the same works.

(9.) Cherish any breathing of the Spirit. Man is unable to keep his knowledge and evangelical impressions upon himself without the Spirit: 2 Tim. i. 14, 'That good thing which was committed unto thee, keep by the Holy Ghost which dwells in us.' If we cannot keep the knowledge and form of sound words agreeable to that affection in man whereby he desires knowledge, much less can we preserve grace in us, which is more stomached by corrupted nature. Men have a natural desire to know, but no natural desire to be gracious. Christ promised the Spirit to abide with us, and shall we slight his harbingers which come to prepare the way for a more powerful residence ? We can never prize the assistance of the Holy Ghost, if we neglect the auxiliary force he sends us. Those heavenly motions are the Spirit's orders. How can we expect to gain the victory, when we neglect the directions and conduct of our great general ? Perseverance is no more to be ascribed to our own wills, than our first conversion. As without the Spirit we could never by the power of our own wills turn to God, so without the continuance of his efficacy, the will would never keep with God, but would start from him. We are forgetful creatures, therefore need a monitor ; stupid creatures, therefore need a quickener. The main reason of our falls is a non-attendance to those motions ; for we cannot ascribe them to the Spirit's carelessness, but our own. We cannot suppose him negligent in his office, but ourselves in our duty. Grace cannot live, if you neglect this oil put into the lamp to preserve it from expiring. The Spirit's motions are the physic he uses for the removal of that which endangers the health of our grace, and cordials to strengthen the languishing spiritual nature to a recovery of itself. Neglect him not, therefore, but when you find him turning his back, withdrawing his motions, and beginning to grieve, do what you can to delight him. Beg, pray, cry, with an holy imitation of David, 'Lord, take not thy Holy Spirit from me,' Ps. li. 11.

(10.) Take frequent views of glory. An heavenly conversation will quicken our graces, enliven our duties ; while the vigour of both is kept up, the heart cannot flag in the ways of God. Can a man be lazy in a duty, when he considers he must pray, hear, meditate, walk for heaven ? The heat of our graces will be more purer and more durable, when we approach nearest, and lie closest under the sunbeams. Glory in the eye will encourage grace in the heart, and quicken a resolution against temptations, and contempt of the foolish pleasures and enticements of the world, as the glory set before Christ made him despise the shame of the cross.

I might add more ;—

(1.) Look to the first flagging of thy heart, thy first remissness in religious duties. Slothful proceedings become not fervent beginnings.

(2.) Be much in the duty of mortification. Shake off every weight, Heb. xii. 1, that may weaken thee in thy course. Those that are to run a race, or go to a battle, carry not burdens with them.

(3.) Entertain wise considerations of the worst that may happen in your Christian course. Prepare against the worst, though it may never come upon you. Consider the fury of persecutors, the diligence of the devil, the multitude of temptations, and what promises are suited to elevate you above them.

(4.) Remember the promise. This will stay us in our wavering : Heb. x. 23, 'Let us hold fast the profession of our faith without wavering ; for he is faithful that promised.'

A DISCOURSE OF THE SINFULNESS AND CURE OF THOUGHTS.

And God saw that the wickedness of man was great in the earth, and that every imagination of the thoughts of his heart was only evil continually.—GEN. VI. 5.

I KNOW not a more lively description in the whole book of God, of the natural corruption derived from our first parents, than these words; wherein you have the ground of that grief which lay so close to God's heart, ver. 6, and the resolve thereupon to destroy man, and what was serviceable to that ungrateful creature. That must be highly offensive which moved God to repent of a fabric so pleasing to him at the creation, every stone in the building being, at the first laying, pronounced good by him; and upon a review, at the finishing of the whole, he left it the same character with an emphasis, 'very good,' Gen. i. 31. There was not a pin in the whole frame but was 'very beautiful,' Eccles. iii. 11; and being wrought by infinite Wisdom, Ps. civ. 24, it was a very comely piece of art.* What, then, should provoke him to repent of so excellent a work? 'The wickedness of man, which was great in the earth.' How came it to pass that man's wickedness should swell so high? Whence did it spring? From the imagination. Though these might be sinful imaginations, might not the superior faculty preserve itself untainted? Alas! that was defiled. The imagination of the thoughts was evil. But though running thoughts might wheel about in his mind, yet they might leave no stamp or impression upon the will and affections. Yes, they did. The imagination of the thoughts of his heart was evil. Surely all could not be under such a blemish: were there not now and then some pure flashes of the mind? No, not one; every imagination. But granting that they were evil, might there not be some fleeting good mixed with them; as a poisonous toad hath something useful? No, only evil. Well, but there might be some intervals of thinking, and though there was no good thought, yet evil ones were not always ruling there. Yes, they were continually; not a moment of time that man was free from them. One would scarce imagine such an inward nest of wickedness, but God hath affirmed it; and if any man should deny it, his own heart would give him the lie.

Let us now consider the words by themselves.

* Περικαλλὲς τεχνούργημα.—*Euseb. Præpar. Evang.*

יצר, imagination, properly signifies *figmentum*, of יצר to afflict, press, or form a thing by way of compression. And thus it is a metaphor taken from a potter's framing a vessel, and extends to whatsoever is framed inwardly in the heart, or outwardly in the work. It is usually taken by the Jews for that fountain of sin within us. Mercer tells us it is always used in an evil sense.* But there are two places (if no more) wherein it is taken in a good sense: Isa. xxvi. 3, 'whose mind is stayed;' and 1 Chron. xxix. 18, where David prays, that a disposition to offer willingly to the Lord might be preserved in the 'imagination of the thoughts of the heart of the people.' Indeed, for the most part it is taken for the evil imaginations of the heart, as Deut. xxxi. 21, Ps. ciii. 14, &c. The Jews made a double figment, a good and bad; and fancy two angels assigned to man, one bad, another good; which Maimonides interprets to be nothing else but natural corruption and reason.† This word *imagination* being joined with *thoughts*, implies not only the complete thoughts, but the first motion or formation of them, to be evil.

The word *heart* is taken variously in Scripture. It signifies properly that inward member, which is the seat of the vital spirits; but sometimes it signifies, 1, the understanding and mind: Ps. xii. 2, 'With a double heart do they speak;' *i. e.* with a double mind, Prov. viii. 5. 2. For the will: 2 Kings x. 30, 'All that is in my heart;' *i. e.* in my will and purpose. 3. For the affections; as, 'Thou shalt love the Lord thy God with all thy heart;' *i. e.* with all thy affections. 4. For conscience: 2 Sam. xxiv. 5, 'David's heart smote him;' *i. e.* his conscience checked him. But heart here is used for the whole soul, because (according to Pareus his note) the soul is chiefly seated in the heart, especially the will, and the affections her attendants; because, when any affection stirs, the chief motion of it is felt in the heart. So that, by the 'imaginations of the thoughts of the heart,' are here meant all the inward operations of the soul, which play their part principally in the heart, whether they be the acts of the understanding, the resolutions of the will, or the blusterings of the affections.

Only evil. The vulgar mentions not the exclusive particle רק, and so enervates the sense of the place. But our neighbour translations either express it as we do, *only*; or to that sense, that they were *certainly*, or *no other than evil.*

Continually. The Hebrew כל היום, all the day, or every day. Some translations express it *verbatim* as the Hebrew. Not a moment of a man's life, wherein our hereditary corruption doth not belch out its froth, even from his youth, as God expounds it, Gen. viii. 21, to the end of his life.‡

Whether we shall refer the general wickedness of the heart in the text to that age, as some of the Jesuits do, because, after the deluge, God doth not seem so severely to censure it; or rather take the exposition the learned Rivet gives of it, referring the first part of the verse, 'And God saw that the wickedness of man was great in the earth,' to those times, and the second part to the universal corruption of man's nature, and the root of all sin in the world; the Jesuits' argument will not be very valid, for the extenuation of original corruption, from Gen. viii. 21. For if man's imaginations be evil 'from his youth,' what is it but in another phrase to say they were so 'continually'? But suppose it be understood of the iniquity of that age, may it not be applied to all ages of the world? David complains of the

* Alii rectiùs dicunt non esse יצר nisi in malum. Merc. in loc.

† יצר־סמוך יצר הרע יצר הטוב *Maimon. More Nevoch.* par. iii. cap. 22. *Amam. Censur. in locum.*

‡ Rivet. in Gen. exercit. 51.

wickedness of his own time, Ps. xiv. 3, Ps. v. 9; yet St Paul applies it to all mankind, Rom. iii. 12. Indeed, it seems to be a description of man's natural pravity, by God's words, after the deluge, Gen. viii. 21, which are the same in sense, to shew that man's nature, after that destroying judgment, was no better than before. Every word is emphatical, exaggerating man's defilement. Wherein consider the universality,

1. Of the subject, 'every man.'
2. Of the act, 'every thought.'
3. Of the qualification of the act, 'only evil.'
4. Of the time, 'continually.'

The words thus opened afford us this proposition:

That the thoughts, and inward operations of the souls of men, are naturally universally evil, and highly provoking.

Some by *cogitation* mean not only the acts of the understanding, but those of the will, yea, and the sense too. But indeed that which we call cogitation, or thought, is the work of the mind; imagination, of the fancy.* It is not properly thought till it be wrought by the understanding, because the fancy was not a power designed for thinking, but only to receive the images impressed upon the sense, and concoct them, that they might be fit matter for thoughts; and so it is the exchequer wherein all the acquisitions of sense are deposited, and from thence received by the intellective faculty. So that thoughts are *inchoativè* in the fancy, *consummativè* in the understanding, *terminativè* in all the other faculties. Thought first engenders opinion in the mind; thought spurs the will to consent or dissent; it is thought also which spirits the affections.

I will not spend time to acquaint you with the methods of their generation. Every man knows he hath a thinking faculty, and some inward conceptions, which he calls thoughts; he knows that he thinks, and what he thinks, though he be not able to describe the manner of their formation in the womb, or remember it any more than the species of his own face in a glass.

In this discourse, let us first see what kind of thoughts are sins.

1. Negatively. A simple apprehension of sin is not sinful. Thoughts receive not a sinfulness barely from the object. That may be unlawful to be acted which is not unlawful to be thought of. Though the will cannot will sin without guilt, yet the understanding may apprehend sin without guilt; for that doth no more contract a pollution by the bare apprehension, than the eye doth by the reception of the species of a loathsome object. Thoughts are morally evil when they have a bad principle, want a due end, and converse with the object in a wrong manner. Angels cannot but understand the offence which displaced the apostate stars from heaven, but they know not sin *cognitione practicâ*. Glorified saints may consider their former sins, to enhance their admirations of pardoning mercy. Christ himself must needs understand the matter of the devil's temptation; yet Satan's suggestions to his thoughts were as the vapours of a jakes mixed with the sunbeams, without a defilement of them. Yea, God himself, who is infinite purity, knows the objects of his own acts which are conversant about sin; as his holiness in forbidding it, wisdom in permitting, mercy in pardoning, and justice in punishing. But thoughts of sin in Christ, angels, and glorified persons, are accompanied with an abhorrency of it, without any combustible matter in them to be kindled by it. As our thoughts of a divine object are not gracious, unless we love and delight in it, so a bare apprehension of sin is not positively criminal, unless we delight in the object apprehended. As a sinful object doth not render our thoughts evil, so a divine object doth not

* Cartes. Princip. Philos., part i. sect. ix.

render them good, because we may think of it with undue circumstances, as unseasonably, coldly, &c. And thus there is an imperfection in the best thought a regenerate man hath; for though I will suppose he may have a sudden ejaculation without the mixture of any positive impurity, and a simple apprehension of sin, with a detestation of it, yet there is a defect in each of them, because it is not with that raised affection to God, or intense abhorrency of sin, as is due from us to such objects, and whereof we were capable in our primitive state.

2. Positively. Our thoughts may be branched into first motions, or such that are more voluntary.

1. First motions: those unfledged thoughts and single threads, before a multitude of them come to be twisted and woven into a discourse; such as skip up from our natural corruptions, and sink down again, as fish in a river. These are sins, though we consent not to them, because, though they are without our will, they are not against our nature, but spring from an inordinate frame, of a different hue from what God implanted in us. How can the first sprouts be good, if the root be evil? Not only the thought formed, but the very formation, or first imagination, is evil. Voluntariness is not necessary to the essence of a sin, though it be to the aggravation of it. It is not my will or knowledge which doth make an act sinful, but God's prohibition. Lot's incest was not ushered by any deliberate consent of his will, Gen. xix. 33, 35, yet who will deny it to be a sin, since he should have exercised a severer command over himself than to be overtaken with drunkenness, which was the occasion of it? Original sin is not *effectivè* voluntary, in infants, because no act of the will is exerted in an infant about it; yet it is voluntary *subjectivè*, because it doth *inhærere voluntati*. These motions may be said to be voluntary negatively, because the will doth not set bounds to them, and exercise that sovereign dominion over the operations of the soul which it ought to do, and wherewith it was at its first creation invested. Besides, though the will doth not immediately consent to them, yet it consents to the occasions which administer such motions, and therefore, according to the rule, that *causa causæ est causa causati*, they may be justly charged upon our score.

2. Voluntary thoughts, which are the blossoms of these motions: such that have no lawful object, no right end, not governed by reason, eccentric, disorderly in their motions, and like the jarring strings of an untuned instrument. The meanest of these floating fancies are sins, because we act not in the production of them as rational creatures; and what we do without reason, we do against the law of our creation, which appointed reason for our guide, and the understanding to be τὸ ἡγεμονικὸν, the governing power in our souls.

These may be reduced to three heads.

I. In regard of God. II. Of ourselves. III. Of others.

I. In regard of God.

1. Cold thoughts of God. When no affection is raised in us by them. When we delight not in God, the object of those thoughts, but in the thought itself, and operation of our mind about him, consisting of some quaint notion of God of our own conceiving; this is to delight in the act or manner of thinking, not in the object thought of; and thus these thoughts have a folly and vanity in them. They are also sinful in a regenerate man, in respect of the faintness of the understanding, not acting with that vigour and sprightliness, nor with those raised and spiritual affections, which the worth of such an object doth require.

2. Debasing conceptions, unworthy of God. Such are called in the

heathen 'vain imaginations:' Rom. i. 21, διαλογισμοῖς, their reasonings about God; who, as they 'glorified not God as God,' so they did not think of God as God, according to the dignity of a deity. Such a mental idolatry may be found in us, when we dress up a god according to our own humours, humanize him, and ascribe to him what is grateful to us, though never so base: Ps. l. 21, 'Thou thoughtest that I was altogether such an one as thyself;' which is a grosser degrading of the Deity than any representation of him by material images; because it is directly against his holiness, which is his glory, Exod. xv. 11; applauded chiefly by the angels, Isa. vi. 3; and an attribute which he swears by, Ps. lxxxix. 35, as having the greatest regard to the honour of it. Such an imagination Adam seemed to have, conceiting God to be so mean a being, that he, a creature not of a day's standing, could mount to an equality of knowledge with him.

3. Accusing thoughts of God, either of his mercy, as in despair; or of his justice, as too severe, as in Cain, Gen. iv. 13. Of his providence: Adam conceited, yea, and charged God's providence to be an occasion of his crime: Gen. iii. 12, 'The woman whom thou gavest to be with me.' His posterity are no juster to God, when they accuse him as a negligent governor of the world: Ps. xciv. 11, 'The Lord knoweth the thoughts of man, that they are vanity.' What thoughts? Injurious thoughts of his providence, ver. 7, as though God were ignorant of men's actions; or, at best, but an idle spectator of all the unrighteousness done in the world, not to regard it though he did see it. And they in the prophet were of the same stamp, that said in their hearts, Zeph. i. 12, 'The Lord will not do good, neither will he do evil.' From such kind of thoughts most of the injuries from oppressors, and murmurings in the oppressed, do arise.

4. Curious thoughts about things too high for us. It is the frequent business of men's minds to flutter about things without the bounds of God's revelation. Not to be content with what God hath published is to accuse him, in the same manner as the serpent did to our first parents, of envying us an intellectual happiness: Gen. iii. 5, 'God knows that your eyes shall be opened.' Yet how do all Adam's posterity long after this forbidden fruit!

II. In regard of ourselves. Our thoughts are proud, self-confident, self-applauding, foolish, covetous, anxious, unclean, and what not?

1. Ambitious. The aspiring thoughts of the first man runs in the veins of his posterity. God took notice of such strains in the king of Babylon, Isa. xiv. 13, 14, when he said in his heart, 'I will exalt my throne above the stars of God, I will ascend above the heights of the clouds, I will be like the Most High.' No less a charge will they stand under that settle themselves upon their own bottom, 'establish their own righteousness, and will not submit to the righteousness of God's appointment,' Rom. x. 3. The most forlorn beggar hath sometimes thoughts vast enough to grasp an empire.

2. Self-confident. Edom's thoughts swelled him into a vain confidence of a perpetual prosperity; and David sometimes said, in the like state, that he should never be moved.

3. Self-applauding. Either in the vain remembrances of our former prosperity, or ascribing our present happiness to the dexterity of our own wit. Such flaunting thoughts had Nebuchadnezzar at the consideration of his settling Babylon, the head and metropolis of so great an empire: Obad. 3, 'That saith in his heart, Who shall bring me down to the ground?' Dan. iv. 30, 'Is not this great Babylon, that I have built for the house of the kingdom?' &c. Nothing more ordinary among men than overweening reflections upon their own parts, and 'thinking of themselves above what they ought to think,' Rom. xii. 3, 4.

4. Ungrounded imaginations of the events of things, either present or future. Such wild conceits, like meteors bred of a few vapours, do often frisk in our minds. (1.) Of things present. It is likely Eve foolishly imagined she had brought forth the Messiah when she brought forth a murderer: Gen. iv. 1, 'I have gotten a man the Lord' (as in the Hebrew, איש את־יהוה), believing (as some interpret) that she had brought forth the promised seed. And such a brisk conceit Lamech seems to have had of Noah, Gen. v. 29. (2.) Of things to come, either in bespeaking false hopes, or antedating improbable griefs. Such are the jolly thoughts we have of a happy estate in reversion, which yet we may fall short of. Haman's heart, Esther vi. 6, leaped at the king's question, 'What shall be done to the man whom the king delighteth to honour?' fancying himself the mark of his prince's favour, without thinking that a halter should soon choke his ambition. Or perplexing thoughts at the fear of some trouble which is not yet fallen upon us, and perhaps never may. How did David torture his soul by his unbelieving fears, 1 Sam. xxvii. 1, that he should one day perish by the hand of Saul! These forestalling thoughts do really affect us. We often feel caperings in our spirits upon imaginary hopes, and shiverings upon conceited fears. These pleasing impostures and self-afflicting suppositions are signs either of an idle or indigent mind, that hath no will to work, or only rotten materials to work upon.

5. Immoderate thoughts about lawful things. When we exercise our minds too thick, and with a fierceness of affection above their merit; not in subserviency to God, or mixing our cares with dependencies on him. Worldly concerns may quarter in our thoughts, but they must not possess all the room, and thrust Christ into a manger; neither must they be of that value with us as the law was with David, sweeter than the honey or the honeycomb.

III. In regard of others. All thoughts of our neighbour against the rule of charity: 'Such that imagine evil in their hearts, God hates,' Zech. viii. 17. These principally are, 1, envious, when we torment ourselves with other's fortunes. Such a thought in Cain, Gen. iv. 5, upon God's acceptance of his brother's sacrifice, was the prologue to, and foundation of, that cursed murder. 2. Censorious, stigmatizing every freckle in our brother's conversation, 1 Tim. vi. 4. 3. Jealous and evil surmises, contrary to charity, which 'thinks no evil,' 1 Cor. xiii. 5. 4. Revengeful; such made Haman take little content in his preferments, as long as Mordecai refused to court him, Esther v. 13; and Esau thought of the days of mourning for his father, that he might be revenged for his brother's deceits: Gen. xxvii. 41, 'Esau said in his heart,' &c.

There is no sin committed in the world but is hatched in one or other of these thoughts. But beside these there are a multitude of other volatile conceits, like swarms of gnats buzzing about us, and preying upon us, and as frequent in their successions as the curlings of the water upon a small breath of wind, one following another close at the heels. The mind is no more satisfied with thoughts than the first matter is with forms, continually shifting one for another, and many times the nobler for the baser, as when upon the putrefaction of a human body, part of the matter is endued with the form of vermin. Such changeable things are our minds in leaving that which is good for that which is worse, when they are inveigled by an active fancy, and Bedlam affections. This 'madness is in the hearts of men while they live,' Eccles. ix. 3, and starts a thousand frenzies in a day. At the best, our fancy is like a carrier's bag, stuffed with a world of letters, having no dependence one upon another; some containing business, others nothing but froth.

In all these thoughts there is a further guilt in three respects, viz. 1, delight; 2, contrivance; 3, reacting.

1. Delight in them. The very tickling of our fancy by a sinful motion, though without a formal consent, is a sin, because it is a degree of complacency in an unlawful object. When the mind is pleased with the subject of the thought, as it hath a tendency to some sensual pleasure, and not simply in the thought itself, as it may enrich the understanding with some degree of knowledge. The thought indeed of an evil thing may be without any delight in the evil of it, as philosophers delight in making experiments of poisonous creatures, without delighting in the poison as it is a noxious quality. We may delightfully think of sin without guilt, not delighting in it as sin, but as God by his wise providential ordering extracts glory to himself, and good to his creature. In this case, though a sinful act be the material object of this pleasure, yet it is not the formal object, because the delight is not terminated in the sin, but in God's ordering the event of it to his own glory. But an inclination to a sinful motion as it gratifies a corrupt affection is sin, because every inclination is a malignant tincture upon the affections, including in its own nature an aversion from God, and testifying sin to be an agreeable object; and without question there can be no inclination to anything without some degree of pleasure in it, because it is impossible we can incline to that which we have a perfect abhorrency of. Hence it follows that every inclination to a sinful motion is *consensus inchoatus*, or a consent in embryo, though the act may prove abortive. If we think of any unlawful thing with pleasure, and imagine it either *in fieri* or *facto esse*, it brings a guilt upon us as if it were really acted; as when, upon the consideration of such a man's being my enemy, I fancy robbers rifling his goods and cutting his throat, and rejoice in this revengeful thought as if it were really done, it is a great sin, because it testifies an approbation of such a butchery, if any man had will and opportunity to commit it; and though it be a supposition, yet the act of the mind is really the same it would be if the sinful act I think of were performed; or when a man conditionally thinks with himself, I would steal such a man's goods, or kill such a person, if I could escape the punishment attending it, it is as if he did rob and murder him, because there is no impediment in his will to the commission of it, but only in the outward circumstances; nay, though it be a mere *ens intentionale* or *rationis*, which is the object of the thought, yet the act of the mind is real, and as significant of the inclination of the soul as if the object were real too: as if a man hath an unclean motion at the sight of a picture, which is only a composition of well-mixed and well-ordered colours; or at the appearance of the idea of a beauty framed in his own fancy, it is as much uncleanness as if it were terminated in some suitable object, the hindrance being not in the will, but in the insufficiency of the object to concur in such an act. Now, as the more delight there is in any holy service, the more precious it is in itself, and more grateful to God, so the more pleasure there is in any sinful motion, the more malignity there is in it.

2. Contrivance. When the delight in the thought grows up to the contrivance of the act (which is still the work of the thinking faculty). When the mind doth brood upon a sinful motion to hatch it up, and invents methods for performance, which the wise man calls artificial inventions, Eccles. vii. 29, חשבנות, so a learned man* interprets διαλογισμοὶ πονηροί, Mat. xv. 19, of contrivances of murder, adultery, &c. And the word signifies properly, reasonings. When men's wits play the devils in their souls, in inventing sophistical reasons for the commission and justification of their

* Dr Hammond on Mat. xv. 19.

crimes, with a mighty jollity at their own craft, such plots are the trade of a wicked man's heart. A covetous man will be working in his inward shop from morning till night to study new methods for gain;* and voluptuous and ambitious persons will draw schemes and models in their fancy of what they would outwardly accomplish: 'They conceive mischief, and bring forth vanity, and their belly prepares deceit,' Job xv. 35. Hence the thoughts are called the 'counsels,' 1 Cor. iv. 5, and 'devices of the heart,' Isa. xxxii. 7, 8, when the heart summons the head, and all the thoughts of it, to sit in debate as a private junto about a sinful motion.

3. Reacting sin after it is outwardly committed. Though the individual action be transient, and cannot be committed again, yet the idea and image of it remaining in the memory may, by the help of an apish fancy, be repeated a thousand times over with a rarefied pleasure, as both the features of our friends, and the agreeable conversations we have had with them, may with a fresh relish be represented in our fancies, though the persons were rotten many years ago.

Having thus declared the nature of our thoughts, and the degrees of their guilt, the next thing is to prove that they are sins.

The Jews did not acknowledge them to be sins,† unless they were blasphemous, and immediately against God himself. Some heathens were more orthodox, and, among the rest, Ovid, whose amorous pleasures one would think should have smothered such sentiments in him.‡ The Lord (whose knowledge is infallible) 'knows the thoughts of men that they are vanity, Ps. xciv. 11; yea, and of the wisest men too, according to the apostle's interpretation, 1 Cor. iii. 20. And who were they that 'became vain in their imaginations,' but the wisest men the carnal world yielded: the Grecians, the greatest philosophers, the Egyptians their tutors, and the Romans their apes? The elaborate operations of an unregenerate mind are fleshly, Rom. viii. 5, 7. If the whole web be so, needs must every thread. 'The thought of foolishness is sin,' Prov. xxiv. 9 (*i.e.* a foolish thought, not objectively a thought of folly, but one formally so); yea, 'an abomination to God,' Prov. xv. 26. As good thoughts and purposes are acts in God's account, so are bad ones. Abraham's intention to offer Isaac is accounted as an actual sacrifice, Heb. xi. 17, James ii. 21; that the stroke was not given was not from any reluctance of Abraham's will, but the gracious indulgence of God. Sarah had a deriding thought, and God chargeth it as if it were an outward laughter and a scornful word: Gen. xviii. 12, 15, 'Therefore Sarah laughed within§ herself, saying,' &c. Thoughts are the words of the mind, and as real in God's account as if they were expressed with the tongue.

There are three reasons for the proof of this, that they are sins.

1. They are contrary to the law, which doth forbid the first foamings and belchings of the heart, because they arise from an habitual corruption, and testify a defect of something which the law requires to be in us, to correct the excursions of our minds: Rom. vii. 7, 'I had not known lust, except the law had said, Thou shalt not covet.' Doth not the law oblige man as a

* 2 Pet. ii. 14, *καρδίαν γεγυμνασμένην ταῖς πλεονεξίαις*, a heart exercised in covetous practices.

† Kimchi in Ps. lxvi. as quoted by Grotius in Mat. v. 20.

‡ 'Ut jam servaris bene corpus, adultera mens est,
Nec custodiri, ni velit, illa potest.
Nec mentem servare potes, licet omnia claudas:
Omnibus occlusis intus adulter erit.'
—*Ovid. Amor*. l. iii. Eleg. iv. v. 5, &c.

§ במעהא *in visceribus suis*, Targum.

rational creature? Shall it then leave that part, which doth constitute him rational, to fleeting and giddy fancies? No; it binds the soul as the principal agent, the body only as the instrument. For if it were given only for the sensitive part, without any respect to the rational, it would concern brutes as well as men, which are as capable of a rational command and a voluntary obedience, as man without the conduct of a rational soul. It exacts a conformity of the whole man to God, and prohibits a deformity, and therefore engageth chiefly the inward part, which is most the man. It must then extend to all the acts of the man, consequently to his thoughts, they being more the acts of the man than the motions of the body. Holiness is the prime excellency of the law, a title ascribed to it twice in one verse: Rom. vii. 12, 'Wherefore the law is holy, and the commandment holy, just, and good.' Could it be *holy*, if it indulged looseness in the more noble part of the creature? Could it be *just*, if it favoured inward unrighteousness? Could it be *good*, and useful to man, which did not enjoin a suitable conformity to God, wherein the creature's excellency lies? Can that deserve the title of a *spiritual* law, that should only regulate the brutish part, and leave the spiritual to an unbounded licentiousness? Can *perfection* be ascribed to that law which doth countenance the unsavoury breathings of the spirit, and lay no stricter an obligation upon us than the laws of men? Mat. v. 28. Must not God's laws be as suitable to his sovereignty, as men's laws are to theirs? Must they not then be as extensive as God's dominion, and reach even to the privatest closets of the heart? It is not for the honour of God's holiness, righteousness, goodness, to let the spirit, which bears more flourishing characters of his image than the body, range wildly about without a legal curb.

2. They are contrary to the order of nature, and the design of our creation. Whatsoever is a swerving from our primitive nature is sin, or at least a consequent of it. But all inclinations to sin are contrary to that righteousness, wherewith man was first endued. Man was created both with a disposition and ability for holy contemplations of God; the first glances of his soul were pure; he came every way complete out of the mint of his infinitely wise and good Creator; and when God pronounced all his creatures good, he pronounced man very good amongst the rest. But man is not now as God created him, he is off from his end, his understanding is filled with lightness and vanity. This disorder never proceeded from the God of order; infinite goodness could never produce such an evil frame; none of these loose inventions were of God's planting, but of man's seeking: Eccles. vii. 29, 'God made man perfect; but they have sought out many inventions.' No; God never created the intellective, no, nor the sensitive part, to play Domitian's game, and sport itself in the catching of flies. 'Man that is in honour, and understands not' that which he ought to understand, and thinks not that which he ought to think, 'is like the beasts that perish,' Ps. xlix. 20; he plays the beast, because he acts contrary to the nature of a rational and immortal soul. And such brutes we all naturally are, since the first woman believed her sense, her fancy, her affection, in their directions for the attainment of wisdom, without consulting God's law, or her own reason, Gen. iii. 6. The fancy was bound by the right of nature to serve the understanding. It is then a slighting God's wisdom to invert this order, in making that our governor which he made our subject. It is injustice to the dignity of our own souls, to degrade the nobler part to a sordid slavery, in making the brute have dominion over the man, as if the horse were fittest to govern the rider. It is a falseness to God, and a breach of trust, to let our minds be imposed upon by our fancy, in giving them only feathers to dandle, and

chaff to feed on, instead of those braver objects they were made to converse withal.

3. We are accountable to God, and punishable for thoughts. Nothing is the meritorious cause of God's wrath but sin. The text tells us, that they were once the keys which opened the flood-gates of divine vengeance, and broached both the upper and nether cisterns, to overflow the world. If they need a pardon—Acts viii. 22, 'If perhaps the thought of thy heart may be forgiven thee'—(as certainly they do), then, if mercy doth not pardon them, justice will condemn them. And it is absolutely said, Prov. xii. 2, 'That a man of wicked devices,'* or thoughts, 'God will condemn.' It is God's prerogative, often mentioned in Scripture, to 'search the heart.' To what purpose, if the acts of it did not fall under his censure, as well as his cognisance? He 'weighs the spirits,' Prov. xvi. 2, in the balance of his sanctuary, and by the weights of his law, to sentence them, if they be found too light. The word doth discover and judge them: Heb. iv. 12, 13, 'It divides asunder the soul and spirit,' the sensitive part, the affections, and the rational, the understanding and will; both which it doth dissect, and open, and judge the acts of them, even the thoughts and intents, ἐνθυμήσεων καὶ ἐννοιῶν, whatsoever is within the θυμὸς, and whatsoever is within the νοῦς, the one referring to the soul, the other to the spirit. These it passeth a judgment upon, as a critic censures the errata even to syllables and letters in an old manuscript. These we are to render an account of (as the Syriac renders those words, ver. 13, *with whom we have to do*). Of what? Of the first bubblings of the heart, the motions, and intents of it. The least speck and atom of dust in every chink of this little world is known and censured by God. If our thoughts be not judged, God would not be a righteous judge. He would not judge according to the merit of the cause, if outward actions were only scanned, without regarding the intents, wherein the principle nad end of every action lies, which either swell or diminish the malignity of it. Actions in kind the same, may have different circumstances in the thoughts to heighten the one above the other; and if they were only judged, the most painted hypocrite might commence a blessed spirit at last, as well as the exactest saint. It is necessary also for the glory of God's omniscience. It is hereby chiefly that the extensiveness of God's knowledge is discovered, and that in order to the praise or dispraise of men, 1 Cor. iv. 5, viz., to their justification or condemnation. Those very thoughts will accuse thee before God's tribunal, which accuse thee here before conscience, his deputy: Rom. ii. 15, 16, 'Their thoughts the mean while (*i. e.* in this life, while conscience bears witness) accusing or excusing one another, in the day when God shall judge the secrets of men;' *i. e.* and also at the day of judgment, when conscience shall give in its final testimony, upon God's examination of the secret counsels. This place is properly meant of those reasonings concerning good and evil in men's consciences, agreeable to the law of nature imprinted on them, which shall excuse them, if they practise accordingly, or accuse them, if they behave themselves contrary thereunto. But it will hold in this case, for if those inward approbations of the notions of good and evil will accuse us for our contrary practices, they will also accuse us for our contrary thoughts. Our good thoughts will be our accusers for not observing them, and our bad thoughts will be indictments against us for complying with them.† It is probable the soul may be bound over to answer chiefly for these at the last day; for the apostle chargeth Simon's guilt upon his

* איש מזמות. A man of thoughts, *i. e.* evil thoughts, the word being usually taken in an ill sense.

† Non solum opus, sed mali operis cogitatio pœnas luet.—*Hieron.* in Hosea vii.

thought, not his word, and tells him pardon must be principally granted for that, Acts viii. 22. The tongue was only an instrument to express what his heart did think, and would have been wholly innocent, had not his thoughts been first criminal. What, therefore, is the principal subject of pardon, would be so of punishment; as the first incendiaries in a rebellion are most severely dealt with. And if (as some think) the fallen angels were stripped of their primitive glory, only for a conceived thought, how heinous must that be which hath enrolled them in a remediless misery?

Having proved that there is a sinfulness in our thoughts, let us now see what provocation there is in them, which in some respects is greater than that of our actions. But we must take actions here *in sensu diviso*, as distinguished from the inward preparations to them. In the one there is more of scandal, in the other more of odiousness to God. God, indeed, doth not punish thoughts so visibly, because, as he is governor of the world, his judgments are shot against those sins that disturb human society; but he hath secret and spiritual judgments for these, suitable to the nature of the sins.

Now thoughts are greater in respect,

1. Of fruitfulness. The wickedness that God saw great in the earth was the fruit of imaginations. They are the immediate causes of all sin. No cockatrice but was first an egg. It was a thought to be as God, Gen. iii. 5, that was the first breeder of all that sin under which the world groans at this day; for Eve's mind was first beguiled in the alteration of her thought, 2 Cor. xi. 3. Since that, the lake of inward malignity acts all its evil by these smoking steams. Evil thoughts lead the van in our Saviour's catalogue, Mat. xv. 19, as that which spirits all the black regiment which march behind. As good motions cherished will spring up in good actions, so loose thoughts favoured will break out in visible plague-sores, and put fire unto all that wickedness which lies habitually in the heart, as a spark may to a whole stock of gunpowder. The 'vain babblings' of the soul, as well as those of the tongue, 'will increase to more ungodliness,' 2 Tim. ii. 16. Being thus the cause, they include virtually in them all that is in the effect; as a seed contains in its little body the leaves, fruit, colour, scent, which afterward appear in the plant. The seed includes all, but the colour doth not virtually include the scent, or the scent the colour, or the leaves the fruit. So it is here, one act doth not include the formal obliquity of another; but the thought which caused it doth seminally include both the formal and final obliquity of every action, both that which is in the nature of it, and in the end to which it tends. As when a tradesman cherisheth immoderate thoughts of gain, and in the attaining it runs into 'many foolish and hurtful lusts,' 1 Tim. vi. 9, there is cheating, lying, swearing, to put off the commodity; all these several acts have a particular sinfulness in the nature of the acts themselves, besides the tendency they have to the satisfying an inordinate affection, all which are the spawn of those first immoderate thoughts stirring up greedy desires.

2. In respect of quantity. Imaginations are said to be *continually* evil. There is an infinite variety of conceptions, as the psalmist speaks of the sea, 'wherein are all things creeping innumerable, both small and great,' and a constant generation of whole shoals of them; that you may as well number the fish in the sea, or the atoms in the sunbeams, as recount them.

There is a greater number in regard of the acts, and in regard of the objects.

1. In regard of the acts of the mind.

(1.) Antecedent acts. How many preparatory motions of the mind are there to one wicked external act!* Yea, how many sinful thoughts are twisted together to produce one deliberate sinful word! All which have a distinct guilt, and, if weighed together, would outweigh the guilt of the action abstractedly considered. How many repeated complacencies in the first motion, degrees of consent, resolved broodings, secret plottings, proposals of various methods, smothering contrary checks, vehement longings, delightful hopes, and forestalled pleasures in the design! All which are but thoughts assenting or dissenting, in order to the act intended. Upon a dissection of all these secret motions by the critical power of the word, we should find a more monstrous guilt than would be apparent in the single action, for whose sake all these spirits were raised. There may be no sin in a material act, considered in itself, when there is a provoking guilt in the mental motion. A hypocrite's religious services are materially good, but poisoned by the imagination skulking in the heart that gave birth unto them. It is the wicked mind or thought† makes the sacrifice (a commanded duty), 'much more an abomination to the Lord,' Prov. xxi. 27.

(2.) Consequent acts. When a man's fancy is pregnant with the delightful remembrance of the sin that is past, he draws down a fresh guilt upon himself; as they did in the prophet, in reviving the concurrence of the will to the act committed, making the sensual pleasure to commence spiritual, and, if ever there were an aching heart for it, revoking his former grief by a renewed approbation of his darling lust: Ezek. xxiii. 3, 19, 'Yet she multiplied her whoredoms in calling to remembrance the days of her youth,' &c.; ver. 21, 'The lewdness of her youth.' Thus the sin of thoughts is greater in regard of duration. A man hath neither strength nor opportunity always to act, but he may always think, and imagination can supply the place of action; or if the mind be tired with sucking one object, it can with the bee presently fasten upon another. Senses are weary till they have a new recruit of spirits; as the poor horse may sink under his burden, when the rider is as violent as ever. Thus old men may change their outward profaneness into mental wickedness; and as the psalmist remembered his old songs, Ps. lxxvii. 5, 6, so they their calcined sins in the night with an equal pleasure. So that you see there may be a thousand thoughts as ushers and lacqueys to one act, as numerous as the sparks of a new lighted fire.

2. In regard of the objects the mind is conversant about. Such thoughts there are, and attended with a heavy guilt, which cannot probably, no nor possibly, descend into outward acts. A man may in a complacent thought commit fornication with a woman in Spain, in a covetous thought rob another in the Indies, and in a revengeful thought stab a third in America, and that while he is in this congregation. An unclean person may commit a mental folly with every beauty he meets; a covetous man cannot plunder a whole kingdom, but in one twinkling of a thought he may wish himself the possessor of all the estates in it. A Timon, a *μισάνθρωπος*, cannot cut the throats of all the world; but, like Nero, with one glance of his heart he may chop off the heads of all mankind at a blow. An ambitious man's practices are confined to a small spot of land, but with a cast of his mind he may grasp an empire as large as the four monarchies. A beggar cannot ascend a throne, but in his thoughts he may pass the guards, murder his prince, and usurp the government. Nay, further, an atheist may think there is no God, Ps. xiv. 1, *i. e.*, as some interpret it, wish there were no God, and thus in thought undeify God himself, though he may sooner dash heaven and earth in pieces

* *Ἂν δὲ σαυτὸν ἔνδοθεν ἀνοίξῃς ὦ ἄνθρωπε, ποίκιλον καὶ πολυπαθὲς ταμεῖον κακῶν εὑρήσεις καὶ θησαύρισμα*, &c.—*Plutarch. Moral.* p. (mihi) 500.

† בזמה, with a wicked thought.

than accomplish it. The body is confined to one object, and that narrow and proportionable to its nature; but the mind can wing itself to various objects in all parts of the earth; where it finds none, it can make one; for fancy can compact several objects together, coin an image, colour a picture, and commit folly with it when it hath done; it can nestle itself in cobwebs spun out of its own bowels.

3. In respect of strength. Imaginations of the heart are *only*, *i. e.* purely evil. The nearer anything is in union with the root, the more radical strength it hath. The first ebullitions of light and heat from the sun are more vigorous than the remoter beams; and the steams of a dunghill more noisome next that putrefied body than when they are dilated in the air. Grace is stronger in the heart operations than in the outward streams; and sin more foul in the imagination of the thoughts of the heart than in the act. In the text the outward wickedness of the world is passed over with a short expression; but the Holy Ghost dwells upon the description of the wicked imagination, because there lay the mass, Ps. v. 9. Man's inward part is very wickedness, קר בם הוות, a whole nest of vipers. Thoughts are the immediate spawn of the original corruption, and therefore partake more of the strength and nature of it. Acts are more distant, being the children of our thoughts, but the grandchildren of our natural pravity; besides, they lie nearest to that wickedness in the inward part, sucking the breast of that poisonous dam that bred them. The strength of our thoughts is also reinforced by being kept in, for want of opportunity to act them; as liquors in close glasses ferment and increase their sprightliness. Musing, either carnal or spiritual, makes the fire burn the hotter, Ps. xxxix. 3; as the fury of fire is doubled by being pent up in a furnace. Outward acts are but the sprouts; the sap and juice lies in the wicked imagination or contrivance, which hath a strength in it to produce a thousand fruits as poisonous as the former. The members are the instruments or 'weapons, ὅπλα, of unrighteousness,' Rom. vi. 13; now the whole strength which doth manage the weapon lies in the arm that wields it, the weapon of itself could do no hurt without a force impressed. Let me add this too, that sin in thoughts is more simply sin. In acts, there may be some occasional good to others, for a good man will make use of the sight of sin committed by others to increase his hatred of it; but in our sinful thoughts there is no occasion of good to others, they lying locked up from the view of man.

4. In respect of alliance. In these we have the nearest communion with the devil. The understanding of man is so tainted, that his wisdom, the chiefest flower in it, is not only earthly and sensual (it were well if it were no worse), but devilish too, James iii. 15. If the flower be so rank, what are the weeds? Satan's devices and our thoughts are of the same nature, and sometimes in Scripture expressed by the same word, νοήματα, 1 Cor. ii. 11, 2 Cor. x. 5. As he hath his devices, so have we, against the authority of God's law, the power of the gospel, and the kingdom of Christ. The devils are called 'spiritual wickednesses,' Eph. vi. 12, because they are not capable of carnal sins. Profaneness is an uniformity with the world, and intellectual sins are an uniformity with the god of it, Eph. ii. 2, 3. There is a double walking, answerable to a double pattern in verse 2: 'fulfilling the desires of the flesh,' is a 'walking according to the course of this world,' or making the world our copy; and 'fulfilling the desires of the mind,' is a 'walking according to the prince of the power of the air,' or a making the devil our pattern. In carnal sins Satan is a tempter, in mental an actor; therefore in the one we are conformed to his will, in the other we are transformed into his likeness. In outward, we evidence more of obedience to his

laws; in inward, more of affection to his person, as all imitations of others do. Therefore there is more of enmity to God, because more of similitude and love to the devil; a nearer approach to the diabolical nature, implying a greater distance from the divine. Christ never gave so black a character as that of the devil's children to the profane world; but to the pharisees, who had left the sins of men to take up those of devils, and were most guilty of those high imaginations which ought to be brought into captivity to the obedience of Christ.

5. In respect of contrariety and odiousness to God. Imaginations were only evil, and so most directly contrary to God, who is only good. Our natural enmity against God, Rom. viii. 7, is seated in the mind. The sensitive part aims at its own gratification, and in men serving their lusts they serve their pleasures: Titus iii. 3, 'serving divers lusts and pleasures.' But the τὸ ἡγεμονικὸν, the prince in man, is possessed with principles of a more direct contrariety; whence it must follow that all the thoughts and counsels of it are tinctured with this hatred. They are indeed a defilement of the higher part of the soul, and that which belongs more peculiarly to God. And the nearer any part doth approach to God, the more abominable is a spot upon it; as to cast dirt upon a prince's house is not so heinous as to deface his image. The understanding, the seat of thoughts, is more excellent than the will; both because we know and judge before we will, or ought to will only so much as the understanding thinks fit to be willed; and because God hath bestowed the highest gifts upon it, adorning it with more lively lineaments of his own image: Col. iii. 10, 'Renewed in knowledge after the image of him that created him,' implying that there was more of the image of God at the first creation bestowed upon the understanding, the seat of knowledge, than on any other part; yea, than on all the bodies of men distilled together. *Father of spirits* is one of God's titles, Heb. xii. 9; to bespatter his children then, so near a relation, the jewel that he is choice of, must need be more heinous. He being the Father of spirits, this spiritual wickedness of nourishing evil thoughts is a cashiering all child-like likeness to him. The traitorous acts of the mind are most offensive to God; as it is a greater despite for a son to whom the father hath given the greater portion to shut him out of his house, only to revel in it with a company of rioters and strumpets, than in a child who never was so much the subject of his father's favour. And it is more heinous and odious if these thoughts, which possess our souls, be at any time conversant about some idea of our own framing. It were not altogether so bad if we loved something of God's creating, which had a physical goodness and a real usefulness in it to allure us; but to run wildly to embrace an *ens rationis*, to prefer a thing of no existence, but what is coloured by our own imagination, of no virtue, no usefulness, a thing that God never created, nor pronounced good, is a greater enmity, and a higher slight of God.

6. In respect of connaturalness and voluntariness. They are the imaginations of the thoughts of the heart, and they are continually evil. They are as natural as the estuations of the sea, the bubblings of a fountain,* or the twinkling of the stars. The more natural any motion is, ordinarily the quicker it is. Time is requisite to action, but thoughts have an instantaneous motion.† The body is a heavy piece of clay, but the mind can start out on every occasion. Actions have their stated times and places; but these solicit us, and are entertained by us at all seasons. Neither day nor night, street nor closet, exchange or temple, can privilege us from them; we meet

* Αὐτόχθονας πηγὰς τῆς κακίας.—*Plutarch. Moral.*

† Τάχιστον μὲν νοῦς, διὰ παντὸς γὰρ τρέχει.—*Thales. (Diog. Laert.)*

them at every turn, and they strike upon our souls as often as light upon our eyes. There is no restraint for them; the laws of men, the constitution of the body, the interest of profit or credit, are mighty bars in the way of outward profaneness, but nothing lays the reins upon thoughts but the law of God; and this man is 'not subject to, neither can be,' Rom. viii. 7. Besides, the natural atheism in man is a special friend and nurse of these; few firmly believing either the omniscience of God, or his government of the world, which the Scripture speaks of frequently as the cause of most sins among the sons of men, Isa. xxix. 15, Ezek. ix. 9, Job xxii. 13, 14. Actions are done with some reluctance, and nips of natural conscience. Conscience will start at a gross temptation, but it is not frighted at thoughts. Men may commit speculative folly, and their conscience look on, without so much as a nod against it; men may tear out their neighbours' bowels in secret wishes, and their conscience never interpose to part the fray. Conscience indeed cannot take notice of all of them; they are too subtle in their nature, and too quick for the observation of a finite principle. They are many,—Prov. xix. 21, 'There are many devices in a man's heart,'—and they are nimble too; like the bubblings of a boiling pot, or the rising of a wave, that presently slides into its level. And as Florus saith of the Ligurians,* the difficulty is more to find than conquer them. They are secret sins, and are no more discerned than motes in the air without a spiritual sunbeam; whence David cries out, Ps. xix. 12, 'Cleanse me from secret sins,' which some explain of sins of thoughts, that were like sudden and frequent flashes of lightning, too quick for his notice, and unknown to himself. There is also more delight in them; there is less of temptation in them, and so more of election, and consequently more of the heart and pleasure in them when they lodge with us. Acts of sin are troublesome; there is danger as well as pleasure in many of them; but there is no outward danger in thoughts, therefore the complacency is more compact and free from distraction; the delight is more unmixed too, as intellectual pleasures are more refined than sensual. All these considerations will enhance the guilt of the inward operations.

The uses shall be two, though many inferences might be drawn from the point.

1. Reproof. What a mass of vanity should we find in our minds, if we could bring our thoughts, in the space of one day, yea, but one hour, to an account! How many foolish thoughts with our wisdom, ignorant with our knowledge, worldly with our heavenliness, hypocritical with our religion, and proud with our humiliations! Our hearts would be like a grot, furnished with monstrous and ridiculous pictures; or as the wall in Ezekiel's vision, Ezek. viii. 5, 10, portrayed with every form of creeping things and abominable beasts; a greater abomination than the image of jealousy at the outward gate of the altar. Were our inwards opened, how should we stand gazing both with scorn and wonder at our being such a pack of fools! Well may we cry out with Agur, Prov. xxx. 2, 'We have not the understandings of men.' We make not the use of them as is requisite for rational creatures, because we degrade them to attendances on a brutish fancy. I make no question, but were we able to know the fancies of some irrational creatures, we should find them more noble, heroic, and generous *in suo genere*, than the thoughts of most men; more agreeable to their natures, and suited to the law of their creation: Ps. x. 4, 'God is not in all his thoughts.' How little is God in any of our thoughts according to his excellency! No; our shops, our rents, our backs and bellies, usurp God's room. If any thoughts of God do start up in us, how many covetous, ambitious, wanton, revengeful

* Major aliquanto labor erat invenire, quam vincere.—*Florus*, lib. ii. cap. iii.

thoughts are jumbled together with them! Is it not a monstrous absurdity to place our friend with a crew of vipers, to lodge a king in a stye, and entertain him with the fumes of a jakes and dunghill? 'A wicked man's heart is little worth,' Prov. x. 20; all the peddling wares and works in his inward shop are not valuable with one silver drop from a gracious man's lips. It was an invincible argument of the primitive Christians for the purity of the Christian religion above all others in the world, that it did prohibit evil thoughts.* And is it not as unanswerable an argument that we are no Christians, if we give liberty to them? What is our moral conversation outwardly but only a bare abstinence from sin, not a disaffection? Were we really and altogether Christians, would not that which is the chiefest purity of Christianity be our pleasure? and would we any more wrong God in our secret hearts than in the open streets? Is not thought a beam of the mind, and shall it be enamoured only on a dunghill? Is not the understanding the eye of the soul, and shall it behold only gilded nothings? It is the flower of the spirit.† Shall we let every caterpillar suck it? It is the queen in us. Shall every ruffian deflower it? It is as the sun in our heaven; and shall we besmear it with misty fancies? It was created surely for better purposes than to catch a thousand weight of spiders, as Heliogabalus employed his servants.‡ It was not intended to be made the common sewer of filthiness, or ranked among those ζῶα πάμφαγα,§ which eat not only fruit and flesh, but flies, worms, dung, and all sorts of loathsome materials. Let not, therefore, our minds wallow in a sink of fantastical follies, whereby to rob God of his due, and our souls of their happiness.

2. Exhortation. We must take care for the suppression of them. All vice doth arise from imagination.‖ Upon what stock doth ambition and revenge grow, but upon a false conceit of the nature of honour? What engenders covetousness, but a mistaken fancy of the excellency of wealth? Thoughts must be forsaken as well as our way: Isa. lv. 7, 'Let the wicked forsake his way, and the unrighteous man his thoughts,' &c.; we cannot else have an evidence of a true conversion; and if we do not discard them, we are not like to have an abundant pardon; and what will the issue of that be but an abundant punishment? Mortification must extend to these; affections must be crucified, Gal. v. 24, and all the little brats of thoughts which beget them, or are begotten by them. Shall we nourish that which brought down the wrath of God upon the old world, as though there had not been already sufficient experiments of the mischief they have done? Is it not our highest excellency to be conformed to God in holiness, in as full a measure as our finite natures are capable? And is not God holy in his counsels and inward operations as well as in his works? Hath God any thoughts but what are righteous and just? Therefore the more foolish and vain our imaginations are, the more are we 'alienated from the life of God,' Eph. iv. 17, 18. The Gentiles were so, because they 'walked in the vanity of their mind;' and we shall be so if vanity walk and dwell in ours. As the tenth commandment forbids all unlawful thoughts and desires, so it obligeth us to all thoughts and desires that may make us agreeable to the divine will, and like to God himself. We shall find great advantage by suppressing them. We can more easily resist temptations without, if we conquer motions within. Thoughts are the mutineers in the soul, which set open the gates for Satan. He hath held a secret intelligence with them (so far as he knows them) ever

* Apud nos et cogitare peccare est.—*Minucius Felix.*

† Ἄνθος τῆς ψυχῆς.—*Plat.*

‡ Lampridius.

§ Arist. Histor. animal. lib. viii.

‖ Mirandul. de Imaginat. c. vii.

since the fall, and they are his spies to assist him in the execution of his devices. They prepare the tinder, and the next fiery dart sets all on a flame. Can we cherish these, if we consider that Christ died for them? He shed his blood for that which put the world out of order, which was accomplished by the sinful imagination of the first man, and continued by those imaginations mentioned in the text. He died to restore God to his right, and man to his happiness, neither of which can be perfectly attained till those be thrown out of the possession of the heart.

That we may do this, let us consider these following directions, which may be branched into these heads: 1, for the raising good thoughts; 2, preventing bad; 3, ordering bad when they do intrude; 4, ordering good when they appear in us.

1. For raising good thoughts.

(1.) Get renewed hearts. The fountain must be cleansed which breeds the vermin. Pure vapours can never ascend from a filthy quagmire. What issue can there be of a vain heart but vain imaginations? Thoughts will not become new till a man is in Christ, 2 Cor. v. 17. We must be holy before we can think holily. Sanctification is necessary for the dislodging of vain thoughts, and the introducing of good: Jer. iv. 14, 'Wash thy heart from wickedness,' &c.: 'how long shall thy vain thoughts lodge within thee?' A sanctified reason would both discover and shame our natural follies. As all animal operations, so all the spiritual motions of our heads, depend upon the life of our hearts as the *principium originis*, Prov. iv. 23. As there is a law in our members to bring us into captivity to the law of sin, Rom. vii. 23, so there must be a law in our minds to bring our thoughts to the obedience of Christ, 2 Cor. x. 5. We must be renewed in the spirit of our minds, Eph. iv. 23, in our reasonings and thoughts, which are the spirits whereby the understanding acts, as the animal spirits are the instruments of corporeal motion. Till the understanding be born of the Spirit, John iii. 6, it will delight in, and think of, nothing but things suitable to its fleshly original; but when it is spiritual, it receives new impressions, new reasonings and motions, suitable to the Holy Ghost, of whom it is born. A stone, if thrown upwards a thousand times, will fall backward, because it is a forced motion; but if the nature of this stone were changed into that of fire, it would mount as naturally upward as before it sunk downward. You may force some thoughts toward heaven sometimes, but they will not be natural till nature be changed. Grace only gives stability: Heb. xiii. 9, 'It is a good thing that the heart be established with grace,' and prevents fluctuation by fixing the soul upon God as its chief end; and what is our end will not only be first in our intentions, but most frequent in our considerations. Hence a sanctified heart is called in Scripture a 'stedfast heart.' There must be an enmity against Satan put into our hearts, according to the first promise, before we can have an enmity against his imps, or anything that is like him.

(2.) Study Scripture. Original corruption stuffs us with bad thoughts, and Scripture-knowledge would stock us with good ones; for it proposeth things in such terms as exceedingly suit our imaginative faculty, as well as strengthen our understanding. Judicious knowledge would make us 'approve things that are excellent,' Philip. i. 9, 10; and where such things are approved, toys cannot be welcome. Fulness is the cause of stedfastness. The cause of an intent and piercing eye is the multitude of animal spirits. Without this skill in the word, we shall have as foolish conceits of divine things as ignorant men without the rules of art have of the sun and stars, or things in other countries which they never saw. The word is called a lamp to our feet, *i. e.* the affections, Ps. cxix. 105; a light to our eyes, *i.e.* the understanding: Ps. xix. 8, 'Enlightens the eyes.' It will direct the glances of our minds, and the motions of our affections. It enlightens the eyes, and makes us have a new prospect of things. As a scholar newly entered into logic, and studied the predicaments, &c., looks upon everything with a new eye, and more rational thoughts, and is mightily delighted with everything he sees, because he eyes them as clothed with those notions he hath newly studied. The devil had not his engines so ready to assault Christ, as Christ, from his knowledge, had Scripture-precepts to oppose him. As our Saviour by this means stifled thoughts offered, so, by the same, we may be able to smother thoughts arising in us. Converse, therefore, often with the Scripture, transcribe it in your heart, and turn it *in succum et sanguinem*, whereby a vigour will be derived into every part of your soul, as there is by what you eat to every member of your body. Thus you will make your mind Christ's library, as Jerome speaks of Nepotianus.*

(3.) Reflect often upon the frame of your mind at your first conversion. None have more settled and more pleasant thoughts of divine things than new converts when they first clasp about Christ, partly because of the novelty of their state, and partly because God puts a full stock into them; and diligent tradesmen, at their first setting up, have their minds intent upon improving their stock. Endeavour to put your mind in the same posture it was then. Or if you cannot tell the time when you did first close with Christ, recollect those seasons wherein you have found your affections most fervent, your thoughts most united, and your mind most elevated, as when you renewed repentance upon any fall, or had some notable cheerings from God; and consider what matter it was which carried your heart upward, what employment you were engaged in, when good thoughts did fill your soul, and try the same experiment again. Asaph would oppose God's ancient works to his murmuring thoughts; he would remember his song in the night, *i.e.* the matter of his song, and read over the records of God's kindness, Ps. lxxvii. 6–12. David, too, would never forget, *i.e.* frequently renew the remembrance of those precepts whereby God had particularly quickened him, Ps. cxix. 93. Yea, he would reflect upon the places too where he had formerly conversed with God, to rescue himself from dejecting thoughts: Ps. xlii. 6, 'Therefore will I remember thee from the land of Jordan, and of the Hermonites, from the hill Mizar.' Some elevations surely David had felt in those places, the remembrance whereof would sweeten the sharpness of his present grief. When our former sins visit our minds, pleading to be speculatively reacted, let us remember the holy dispositions we had in our repentance for them, and the thankful frames when God pardoned them. The disciples, at Christ's second appearance, reflected upon their own warm temper at his first discourse with them in a disguise, to confirm their faith, and expel their unbelieving conceits: Luke xxiv. 32, 'Did not our hearts burn within us, while he talked with us by the way, and while he opened to us the Scriptures?' Strive to recollect truths, precepts, promises, with the same affection which possessed your souls when they first appeared in their glory and sweetness to you.

(4.) Ballast your heart with a love to God. David thought all the day of God's law, as other men do of their lusts, because he inexpressibly loved it: Ps. cxix. 97, 'O how I love thy law! It is my meditation all the day.' Ver. 113, 'I hate vain thoughts, but thy law do I love.' This was the suc-

* Lectione assidua et meditatione diuturna pectus suum bibliothecam Christi fecerat.—*Jerome*, Ep. iii.

cessful means he used to stifle vain thoughts, and excite his hatred of them. It is the property of love to think no evil, 1 Cor. xiii. 5. It thinks good and delightful thoughts of God, friendly and useful thoughts of others. It fixeth the image of our beloved object in our minds, that it is not in the power of other fancies to displace it. The beauty of an object will fasten a rolling eye. It is difficult to divorce our hearts and thoughts from that which appears lovely and glorious in our minds, whether it be God or the world. Love will, by a pleasing violence, bind down our thoughts, and hunt away other affections.* If it doth not establish our minds, they will be like a cork, which, with a light breath and a short curl of water, shall be tossed up and down from its station. Scholars that love learning will be continually hammering upon some notion or other which may further their progress, and as greedily clasp it as the iron will its beloved loadstone. He that is winged with a divine love to Christ will have frequent glances and flights towards him, and will start out from his worldly business several times in a day to give him a visit. Love, in the very working, is a settling grace;† it increaseth our delight in God, partly by the sight of his amiableness, which is cleared to us in the very act of loving, and partly by the recompences he gives to the affectionate carriage of his creature; both which will stake down the heart from vagaries, or giving entertainment to such loose companions as evil thoughts are. Well, then, if we had this heavenly affection strong in us, it would not suffer unwholesome weeds to grow up so near it. Either our love would consume those weeds, or those weeds will choke our love.

(5.) Exercise faith. As the habit of faith is attended with habitual sanctification, so the acts of faith are accompanied with a progress in the degrees of it. That faith which brings Christ to dwell in our souls will make us often think of our inmate. Faith doth realise divine things, and make absent objects as present, and so furnisheth fancy with richer streams to bathe itself in than any other principle in the world. As there is a necessity of the use of fancy while the soul is linked to the body, so there is also a necessity of a corrective for it. Reason doth in part regulate it; but it is too weak to do it perfectly, because fancy in most men is stronger than reason.‡ Man being the highest of imaginative beings, and the lowest of intelligent, fancy is in its exaltation more than in creatures beneath him, and reason in its detriment more than in creatures above him; and therefore the imagination needs a more skilful guide than reason. Fancy is like fire, a good servant, but a bad master; if it march under the conduct of faith, it may be highly serviceable, and, by putting lively colours upon divine truth, may steal away our affections to it. 'Faith is the evidence of things not seen,' viz., not by a corporeal, but intellectual eye; and so it will supply the office of sense. It is 'the substance of things hoped for;' and if hope be an attendant on faith, our thoughts will surely follow our expectations. The remedy David used, when he was almost stifled with disquieting thoughts, was to excite his soul to a hope and confidence in God, Ps. xlii. 5; and when they returned upon him he used the same diversion, ver. 11. 'The peace of God,' *i.e.* the reconciliation made by a mediator between God and us believingly apprehended, will 'keep (or garrison) our hearts and minds' (or thoughts) against all anxious assaults both from within and without: Philip. iv. 5, 7, φρουρήσει τὰ νοήματα ὑμῶν. When any vain conceit creeps up in you, act faith on the intercession

* Æneas oculis semper vigilantis inhærit.
Ænean animo noxque diesque refert.—*Ovid. Her. Ep.* vii.

† Ὁ δὲ ἔρως βιαίον τι ἐστὶ—*Lucian. Dialog.* Πτερωθεῖσα οὐρανίῳ ἔρωτι.—*Chrysost.*

‡ Mirand. de Imaginat. c. xi. xii.

of Christ; and consider, Is Christ thinking of me now in heaven, and pleading for me, and shall I squander away my thoughts on trifles, which will cost me both tears and blushes? Believingly meditate on the promises; they are a means to 'cleanse us from the filthiness of the spirit,' as well as that of the flesh, 2 Cor. vii. 1. If the having them be a motive, the using them will be a means to attain this end. 'Looking at the things that are not seen' preserves us from 'fainting,' and 'renews the inward man day by day,' 2 Cor. iv. 16, 18. These invisible things could not well keep our hearts from fainting, if faith did not first keep the thoughts from wandering from them.

(6.) Accustom yourself to a serious meditation every morning. Fresh-airing our souls in heaven will engender in us a purer spirit and nobler thoughts. A morning seasoning would secure us for all the day.* Though other necessary thoughts about our calling will and must come in, yet when we have despatched them, let us attend to our morning theme as our chief companion. As a man that is going with another about some considerable business, suppose to Westminster, though he meets with several friends on the way, and salutes some, and with others with whom he hath some affairs he spends a little time, yet he quickly returns to his companion, and both together go their intended stage. Do thus in the present case. Our minds are active, and will be doing something, though to little purpose; and if they be not fixed upon some noble object, they will, like madmen and fools, be mightily pleased in playing with straws. The thoughts of God were the first visitors David had in the morning, Ps. cxxxix. 17, 18. God and his heart met together as soon as he was awake, and kept company all the day after. In this meditation, look both to the matter and manner.

First. Look to the matter of your meditation. Let it be some truth which will assist you in reviving some languishing grace, or fortify you against some triumphing corruption; for it is our darling sin which doth most envenom our thoughts: Prov. xxiii. 7, 'As a man thinks in his heart, so is he.' As if you have a thirst for honour, let your fancy represent the honour of being a child of God and heir of heaven. If you are inclined to covetousness, think of the riches stored up in a Saviour, and dispensed by him; if to voluptuousness, fancy the pleasures in the ways of wisdom here, and at God's right hand hereafter. This is to deal with our hearts as Paul with his hearers, to catch them with guile. Stake your soul down to some serious and profitable mystery of religion; as the majesty of God, some particular attribute, his condescension in Christ, the love of our Redeemer, the value of his sufferings, the virtue of his blood, the end of his ascension, the work of the Spirit, the excellency of the soul, beauty of holiness, certainty of death, terror of judgments, torments of hell, and joys of heaven.† Why may not that which was the subject of God's innumerable thoughts, Ps. xl. 5, be the subject of ours? God's thoughts and counsels were concerning Christ, the end of his coming, his death, his precepts of holiness, and promises of life; and that not only speculatively, but with an infinite pleasure in his own glory, and the creatures' good to be accomplished by him. Would it not be work enough for our thoughts all the day, to travel over the length, breadth, height, and depth of the love of Christ? Would the greatness of the journey give us leisure to make any starts out of the way? Having settled the theme for all the day, we shall find occasional assistances, even from worldly businesses; as scholars, who have some exercises to make, find helps in their

* Intus existens prohibet alienum.

† The heads of the Catechism might be taken in order, which would both increase and actuate our knowledge.

own course of reading, though the book hath no designed respect to their proper theme. Thus, by employing our minds about one thing chiefly, we shall not only hinder them from vain excursions, but make even common objects to be oil to our good thoughts, which otherwise would have been fuel for our bad. Such generous liquor would scent our minds and conversations all the day, that whatsoever motions came into our hearts would be tinctured with this spirit and savour of our morning thoughts; as vessels, having been filled with a rich wine, communicate a relish of it to the liquors afterwards put into them. We might also more steadily go about our worldly business if we carry God in our minds; as one foot of the compass will more regularly move about the circumference when the other remains firm in the centre.

Secondly. Look to the manner of it.

First, Let it be intent. Transitory thoughts are like the glances of the eye, soon on and soon off; they make no clear discovery, and consequently raise no sprightly affections. Let it be one principal subject, and without flitting from it; for if our thoughts be unsteady, we shall find but little warmth: a burning glass often shifted fires nothing. We must look at the things that are not seen, 2 Cor. iv. 18, σκοπούντων, as wistly as men do at a mark they shoot at. Such an intent meditation would change us into the image, 2 Cor. iii. 18, and cast us into the mould, of those truths we think of; it would make our minds more busy about them all the day, as a glaring upon the sun fills our eyes for some time after with the image of it. To this purpose look upon yourselves as deeply concerned in the things you think of. Our minds dwell upon that whereof we apprehend an absolute necessity. A condemned person would scarce think of anything but procuring a reprieve, and his earnestness for this would bar the door against other intruders.

Secondly, Let it be affectionate and practical. Meditation should excite a spiritual delight in God, as it did in the psalmist: Ps. civ. 34, 'My meditation of him shall be sweet: I will be glad in the Lord;' and a divine delight would keep up good thoughts, and keep out impertinencies. A bare speculation will tire the soul; and without application, and pressing upon the will and affections, will rather chill than warm devotion. It is only by this means that we shall have the efficacy of truth in our wills, and the sweetness in our affections, as well as the notion of it in our understandings. The more operative any truth is in this manner upon us, the less power will other thoughts have to interrupt, and the more disdainfully will the heart look upon them if they dare be impudent. Never, therefore, leave thinking of a spiritual subject till your heart be affected with it. If you think of the evil of sin, leave not till your heart loathe it; if of God, cease not till it mount up in admirations of him. If you think of his mercy, melt for abusing it; if of his sovereignty, awe your heart into obedient resolutions; if of his presence, double your watch over yourself. If you meditate on Christ, make no end till your hearts love him; if of his death, plead the value of it for the justification of your persons, and apply the virtue of it for the sanctification of your natures. Without this practical stamp upon our affections, we shall have light spirits, while we have opportunity to converse with the most serious objects, We often hear foolish thoughts breathing out themselves in a house of mourning, in the midst of coffins and trophies of death, as if men were confident they should never die, whereas none are so ridiculous as to assert they shall live for ever. By this instance in a truth so certainly assented to, we may judge of the necessity of this direction in truths more doubtfully believed.

(7.) Draw spiritual inferences from occasional objects. David did but wistly consider the heavens, and he breaks out into self-abasement and humble admirations of God, Ps. viii. 3, 4. Glean matter of instruction to yourselves, and praise to your Maker, from everything you see; it will be a degree of restoration to a state of innocency, since this was Adam's task in paradise. Dwell not upon any created object only as a virtuoso, to gratify your rational curiosity, but as a Christian, call religion to the feast, and make a spiritual improvement. No creature can meet our eyes, but affords us lessons worthy of our thoughts, besides the general notices of the power and wisdom of the Creator. Thus may the sheep read us a lecture of patience, the dove of innocence, the ant and bee raise blushes in us for our sluggishness, and the stupid ox and dull ass correct and shame our ungrateful ignorance, Isa. i. 3. And since our Saviour did set forth his own excellency in a sensible dress, the consideration of those metaphors by an acute fancy would garnish out divine truths more deliciously, and conduct us into a more inward knowledge of the mysteries of the gospel. He whose eyes are open cannot want an instructor, unless he wants a heart. Thus may a tradesman spiritualise the matter he works upon, and make his commodities serve in wholesome meditations to his mind, and at once enrich both his soul and his coffers; yea, and in part restore the creatures to the happiness of answering a great end of their creation, which man deprived them of when he subjected them to vanity. Such a view of spiritual truths in sensible pictures, would clear our knowledge, purify our fancies, animate our affections, encourage our graces, disgrace our vices, and both argue and shame us into duty; and thus take away all the causes of our wild wandering thoughts at once. And a frequent exercise of this method would beget and support a habit of thinking well, and weaken, if not expel, a habit of thinking ill.

2. The second sort of directions are for the preventing bad thoughts. And to this purpose,

(1.) Exercise frequent humiliations. Pride exposeth us to impatient and disquieting thoughts, whereas humility clears up a calm and serenity in the soul. It is Agur's advice to be humbled, particularly for evil thoughts, Prov. xxx. 32. Frequent humiliations will deaden the fire within, and make the sparks the fewer. The deeper the plough sinks, the more the weeds are killed, and the ground fitted for good grain. Men do not easily fall into those sins for which they have been deeply humbled. Vain conceits love to reside most in jolly hearts, but 'by the sadness of the countenance the heart is made better,' Eccles. vii. 3, 4. There is more of wisdom or wise consideration in a composed and graciously mournful spirit, whereas carnal mirth and sports cause the heart to evaporate into lightness and folly. The more we are humbled for them, the more our hatred of them will be fomented, and consequently the more prepared shall we be to give them a repulse upon any bold intrusion.

(2.) Avoid entangling yourselves with the world. This clay will clog our minds, and a dirty happiness* will engender but dirty thoughts. Who were so foolish to have 'inward thoughts that their houses should continue for ever,' but those that 'trusted in their riches'? Ps. xlix. 6, 11. If the world possess our souls, it will breed carking thoughts; much business meets with crosses, and then it breeds murmuring thoughts, and sometimes it is crowned with success, and then it starts proud and self-applauding thoughts. 'Those that will be rich fall into many foolish and hurtful lusts,' 1 Tim. vi. 9, such lusts as make men fools; and one part of folly is to have wild and senseless fancies. Mists and fogs are in the lower region near the

* Lutea felicitas.—*Aug. de Civ. Dei.* l. x.

earth, but reach not that next the heavens. Were we free from earthly affections, these gross vapours could not so easily disturb our minds; but if the world once settle in our hearts, we shall never want the fumes of it to fill our heads. And as covetous desires will stuff us with foolish imaginations, so they will smother any good thought cast into us, as the thorns of worldly cares choked the good seed and made it unfruitful, Mat. xiii. 22. As we are to rejoice in the world as though we rejoiced not, so, by the same reason, we should think of the world as though we thought not. A conformity with the world in affection is inconsistent with a change of the frame of the mind, Rom. xii. 2.

(3.) Avoid idleness. Serious callings do naturally compose men's spirits, but too much recreation makes them blaze out in vanity. Idle souls as well as idle spirits will be ranging. As idleness in a state is both the mother and nurse of faction, and in the natural body gives birth and increase to many diseases by enfeebling the natural heat, so it both kindles and foments many light and unprofitable imaginations in the soul, which would be sufficiently diverted if the active mind were kept intent upon some stated work. So truly may that which was said of the servant be applied to our nobler part, that it will be wicked if once it degenerates into slothfulness in its proper charge, Mat. xxv. 26, 'Thou wicked and slothful servant.' As empty minds are the fittest subjects for extravagant fooleries, so vacant times are the fittest seasons. While we sleep, the importunate enemy within, as well as the envious adversary without us, will have a successful opportunity to sow the tares, Mat. xiii. 25, whereas a constant employment frustrates the attempt, and discourageth the devil, because he sees we are not at leisure. Therefore, when any sinful motion steps in, double thy vigour about thy present business, and the foolish impertinent will sneak out of thy heart at this discountenance. So true is that in this case, which Pharaoh falsely imagined in another, that the more we labour the less we shall regard vain words, Exod. v. 9. As Satan is prevented by diligence in our callings, so sometimes the Spirit visits us and fills us with holy affections at such seasons, as Christ appeared to Peter and other disciples when they were a-fishing, John xxi. 3, 4, and usually manifested his grace to men when they were engaged in their useful businesses or religious services. But these motions (as we may observe by the way) which come from the Spirit are not to put us out of our way, but to assist us in our walking in it, and further us both in our attendance on and success in our duties. To this end look upon the work of your callings as the work of God, which ought to be done in obedience to him, as he hath set you to be useful in the community. Thus a holy exercise of our callings would sanctify our minds, and by prepossessing them with solid business, we should leave little room for any spider to weave its cobwebs.

(4.) Awe your hearts with the thoughts of God's omniscience, especially the discovery of it at the last judgment. We are very much atheists in the concern of this attribute, for though it be notionally believed, yet for the most part it is practically denied. God 'understands all our thoughts afar off,' Ps. cxxxix. 2, as he knew every creature which lay hid in the chaos and undigested lump of matter. God is in us all, Eph. iv. 6, as much in us all as he is above us all, yea, in every creek and chink and point of our hearts. Not an atom in the spirits of all men in the world but is obvious to that all-seeing eye, which 'knows every one of those things that come into our minds,' Ezek. xi. 5. God knows both the order and confusion of them, and can better tell their natures one by one than Adam named the creatures. Fancy then that you hear the sound of the last trumpet, that you see God's tribunal set, and his omniscience calling out singly all the secrets of your heart.

Would not the consideration of this allay the heat of all other imaginations? If a foolish thought break in, consider, What if God, who knows this, should presently call me to judgment for this sinful glance? Say with the church, Ps. xliv. 21, 'Shall not God search this out?' Is it fit, either for God's glory or our interest, that when he comes to make inquisition in us, he should find such a nasty dunghill and swarms of Egyptian lice and frogs creeping up and down our chambers? Were our heads and hearts possessed by this substantial truth, we should be ashamed to think what we shall be ashamed to own at the last day.

(5.) Keep a constant watch over your hearts. David desires God to 'set a watch before the door of his lips,' Ps. cxli. 3: much more should we desire that God would keep the door of our hearts. We should have grace stand sentinel there especially, for words have an outward bridle: they may disgrace a man and impair his interest and credit; but thoughts are unknown if undiscovered by words. If a man knew what time the thief would come to rob him, he would watch. We know we have thieves within us to steal away our hearts; therefore, when they are so near us, we should watch against a surprise, and the more carefully, because they are so extraordinary sudden in their rise and quick in their motion. Our minds are like idle schoolboys, that will be frisking from one place to another if the master's back be turned, and playing instead of learning. Let a strict hand be kept over our affections, those wild beasts* within us, because they many times force the understanding to pass a judgment according to their pleasure, not its own sentiment. Young men should be most intent upon their guard, because their fancies gather vigour from their youthful heat, which fires a world of squibs in a day (which madmen and those which have hot diseases are subject to, because of the excessive inflammation of their brains), and partly because they are not sprung up to a maturity of knowledge, which would breed and foster better thoughts, and discover the plausible pretences of vain affections. There are particular seasons wherein we must double our guard, as when incentives are present that may set some inward corruption on a flame. Timothy's office was to exhort younger as well as elder women, 1 Tim. v. 2, and the apostle wisheth him to do it with all purity or chastity, *ἐν πάσῃ ἁγνείᾳ*, that a temptation lying in ambush for him might not take his thoughts and affections unguarded. Engage thy diligence more at solitary times and in the night, wherein freedom from business gives an opportunity to an unsanctified imagination to conjure up a thousand evil spirits; whence perhaps it is that the psalmist tells us, Ps. xvii. 3, God had 'tried him in the night,' and found him holy. The solitary cave tainted Lot with incest, Gen xix. 30, who had preserved himself fresh in the midst of the salt lusts of Sodom. In ill company, wherein we may be occasionally cast, there is need of an exacter observation of our hearts, lest corrupt steams which rise from them, as vapours from lakes and minerals, being breathed in by us, may tincture our spirits, or as those *μιάσματα*, which (as physicians tell us), exhaling from consumptive persons, do by inspiration steal into our blood and convey a contagion to us. And though, above all keepings and watchings, we are to keep and watch our hearts,† because 'out of them are the issues of life,' Prov. iv. 23, yet we must walk the rounds about our senses and members of the body, as the wise man there adviseth, ver. 24: the mouth, which utters wickedness, the eyes, ver. 25, which are brokers to make bargains for the heart, and ver. 26, the feet, which are agents to run on the errands of sin. And the rather must we watch over our senses, because we are naturally

* *Θηρια τῆς ψυχῆς.*—*Plato.*

† Cellulam mearum cogitationum pertimescebam.—*Hieron.*

more ready to follow the motions of them, as having had a longer acquaintance and familiarity with them before we grew up to the use of reason. Besides, most of our thoughts creep in first at the windows of sense. The eye and the ear robbed Eve of original righteousness, and the eye rifled David both of his justice and chastity.* 'If the eyes behold strange women, the heart will utter perverse things,' Prov. xxiii. 33. Perverse thoughts will sparkle from a rolling eye. Revel rout is usual where there is a negligent government. 'He that hath no rule over his own spirit is like a city that is broken down, and without walls,' Prov. xxv. 28, where any thieves may go in and out at pleasure.

3. The third sort of directions are for the ordering of evil thoughts, when they do intrude; and,

(1.) Examine them. Look often into your heart to see what it is doing; and what thoughts you find dabbling in it call to an account; inquire what business they have, what their errand and design is, whence they come, and whither they tend. David asked his soul the reason of his troubled thoughts: Ps. xlii. 11, 'Why art thou disquieted, O my soul?' So ask thy heart the reason why it entertains such ill company, and by what authority they come there, and leave not chiding, till thou hast put it to the blush. Bring every thought to the test of the word. Asaph had envious thoughts at the prosperity of the wicked, Ps. lxxiii. 2, 3, which had almost tripped him up, and laid him on his back. And these had blown up atheistical thoughts, that God did not much regard whether his commands were kept or no; as though God had untied the link between duty and reward, and the breach of his laws were the readiest means to a favourable recompence: ver. 13, 'I have cleansed my hands in vain.' But when he weighed things in the balance of the sanctuary, by the holy rules of God's patience and justice, ver. 17, he sees the brutishness of his former conceits: ver. 22, 'So foolish was I and ignorant, I was as a beast before thee;' and, ver. 25, he makes an improvement of them to excite his desire for God, and delight in him. Let us compare our thoughts with Scripture rules. Comparing spiritual things with spiritual, is the way to understand them; comparing spiritual sins with spiritual commands, is the way to know them; and comparing spiritual vices with spiritual graces, is the way to loathe them. Take not, then, anything upon trust from a crazy fancy; nor, without a scrutiny, believe that faculty whereby dogs dream, and animals perform their natural exploits.

(2.) Check them at the first appearance. If they bear upon them a palpable mark of sin, bestow not upon them the honour of an examination. If the leprosy appear in their foreheads, thrust them, as the priests did Uzziah, out of the temple; or as David answered his wicked solicitors, Ps. cxix. 115, 'Depart from me, ye evil doers: for I will keep the commandments of my God.' Though we cannot hinder them from haunting us, yet we may from lodging in us. The very sparkling of an abominable motion in our hearts is as little to be looked upon, as the colour of wine in a glass by a man inclined to drunkenness. Quench them instantly, as you would do a spark of fire in a heap of straw.† We must not treat with them. Paul's resolve is a good pattern, not to confer with flesh and blood, Gal. i. 16. We do not debate whether we should shake a viper off our hands. If it be plainly a sinful motion, a treaty with it is a degree of disobedience; for a putting it to the question whether we should suckle it, is to question whether God should be obeyed or no. If it savour not of the things of God, hear not its rea-

* Plotinus describes thoughts thus: τῶν ἔξω πρὸς τ' ἔνδόν ὁμοιότης καὶ κοινωνία.—*Ænead*, lib. i. Cor et oculi sunt proxenetæ peccati.

† Hic Annibal virtute, non morâ frangitur.

sons, and compliment it with no less indignation than our Saviour did his officious disciple upon his carnal advice: 'Get thee behind me, Satan,' Mat. xvi. 22, 23. Excuse it not, because it is little. Small vapours may compact themselves into great clouds, and obstruct our sight of heaven; a little poison may spread its venom through a great quantity of meat. We know not how big a small motion, like a crocodile's egg, may grow, and how ravenous the breed may prove. It may, if entertained, force our judgment, drag our will, and make all our affections bedlams.* Besides, since the fancy is that power in us upon which the devil can immediately imprint his suggestions, and that we know not what army he hath to back any sinful motion, if once the gate be set open, let us crush the brat betimes, and fling the head over the wall, to discourage the party. Well, then, let us be ashamed to cherish that in our thoughts, which we should be ashamed should break out in our words or actions. Therefore, as soon as you perceive it base, spit it out with detestation, as you do a thing you unexpectedly find ungrateful to your palate.

(3.) Improve them. Poisons may be made medicinable. Let the thoughts of old sins stir up a commotion of anger and hatred. We feel shiverings in our spirits, and a motion in our blood, at the very thought of a bitter potion we have formerly taken. Why may we not do that spiritually, which the very frame and constitution of our bodies doth naturally, upon the calling a loathsome thing to mind? The Romans' sins were transient, but the shame was renewed every time they reflected on them: Rom. vi. 21, 'Whereof you are now ashamed.' They reacted a detestation instead of the pleasure: so should the revivings of old sins in our memories be entertained with our sighs, rather than our joy. We should also manage the opportunity, so as to promote some further degrees of our conversion: Ps. cxix. 59, 'I thought on my ways, and turned my feet into thy testimonies.' There is not the most hellish motion, but we may strike some sparks from it, to kindle our love to God, renew our repentance, raise our thankfulness, or quicken our obedience. Is it a blasphemous motion against God? It gives you a just occasion thence to awe your heart into a deeper reverence of his majesty. Is it a lustful thought? Open the flood-gates of your godly sorrow, and groan for your original sin. Is it a remembrance of your former sin? Let it wind up your heart in the praises of him who delivered you from it. Is it to tempt you from duty? Endeavour to be more zealous in the performance of it. Is it to set you at a distance from God? Resolve to be a light shining the clearer in that darkness, and let it excite you to a closer adherence to him. Are they envious thoughts which steal upon you? Let thankfulness be the product, that you enjoy so much as you do, and more than you deserve. Let Satan's fiery darts inflame your love rather than your lust, and, like a skilful pilot, make use of the violence of the winds, and raging of the sea, to further you in your spiritual voyage. This is to beat the devil, and your own hearts, with their own weapons; who will have little stomach to fight with those arms wherewith they see themselves wounded. There is not a remembrance of the worst objects but may be improved to humility and thankfulness; as St Paul never thought of his old persecuting, but he sank down in humiliation, and mounted up in admirations of the riches of grace.

(4.) Continue your resistance if they still importune thee, and lay not down thy weapons till they wholly shrink from thee. As the wise man speaks of a fool's words, Eccles. x. 13, so I may not only of our blacker, but our more

* Ex hinc nota est infirmitas mea: quia multo faciliùs irruunt abominandæ phantasiæ quám discedunt.—*Kemp. de Imit. Chr.* lib. iii. cap. xx.

aerial fancies. 'The beginning of them is foolishness,' but if suffered to gather strength, they may end in 'mischievous madness;' therefore, if they do continue, or reassume their arms, we must continue and reassume our shield: Eph. vi. 16, 'Above all, taking the shield of faith,' ἀναλαβόντες, *taking up again.* Resistance makes the devil and his imps fly, but forbearance makes them impudent. In a battle, when one party faints and retreats, it adds new spirits to the enemy that was almost broken before; so will these motions be the more vigorous if they perceive we begin to flag. That encouraging command, James iv. 7, 'Resist the devil, and he will fly from you,' implies not only the beginning a fight, but continuance in it till he doth fly. We must not leave the field till they cease their importunity, nor increase their courage by our own cowardice.

(5.) Join supplication with your opposition. 'Watch and pray' are sometimes linked together, Matt. xxvi. 41. The diligence and multitude of our enemies should urge us to watch, that we be not surprised; and our own weakness and proneness to presumption should make us pray, that we may be powerfully assisted. Be as frequent in soliciting God as they are in soliciting you; as they knock at your heart for entrance, so do you knock at heaven for assistance. And take this for your comfort: as the devil takes their parts, so Christ will take yours at his Father's throne; he that prayed that the devil might not winnow Peter's faith, will intercede that your own heart may not winnow yours. If the waves come upon you, and you are ready to sink, cry out with Peter, 'Master, I perish,' and you shall feel his hand raising you, and the winds and waves rebuked into obedience by him. The very motions of your hearts heavenward at such a time is a refusal of the thought that presseth upon you, and will be so put upon your account. When any of these buzzing flies discompose you, or more violent hurricanes shake your minds, cry out with David, Ps. lxxxvi. 11, 12, 'Unite my heart to fear thy name,' and a powerful word will soon silence these disturbing enemies, and settle your souls in a calm and a praising posture.

4. A fourth sort of directions is concerning good motions; whether they spring naturally from a gracious principle, or are peculiarly breathed in by the Spirit. There are ordinary bubblings of grace in a renewed mind, as there are of sins in an unregenerate heart; for grace is as active a principle as any, because it is a participation of the divine nature. But there are other thoughts darted in beyond the ordinary strain of thinking, which, like the beams of the sun, evidence both themselves and their original. And as concerning these motions joined together, take these directions in short:

(1.) Welcome and entertain them. As it is our happiness, as well as our duty, to stifle evil motions, so it is our misery, as well as our sin, to extinguish heavenly. Strange fire should be presently quenched, but that which descends from heaven upon the altar of a holy soul* must be kept alive by quickening meditation. When a holy thought lights suddenly upon you, which hath no connection with any antecedent business in your mind (provided it be not unseasonable, nor hinder you from any absolutely necessary duty, either of religion or your calling), receive it as a messenger from heaven, and the rather because it is a stranger. You know not but you may entertain an angel, yea, something greater than an angel, even the Holy Ghost. Open all the powers of your souls, like so many organ-pipes, to receive the breath of this Spirit when he blows upon you. It is a sign of an agreeableness between the heart and heaven when we close with, and preserve, spiritual motions. We need not stand long to examine them; they are evident by their holiness, sweetness, and spirituality. We may as easily discern them as we

* Θυσιαστήρια τοῦ Θεοῦ.—*Polycarp. Epist. ad Phil.*, terms holy persons.

can exotic plants from those that grow naturally in our own soil, or as a palate, at the first taste, can distinguish between a rich and generous wine, and a rough water. The thoughts instilled by the Spirit of adoption, Gal. v. 22, are not violent, tumultuous, full of perturbation; but, like himself, gentle and dove-like solicitings, warm and holy impulses, and, when cherished, leave the soul in a more humble, heavenly, pure, and believing temper than they found it. It is a high aggravation of sin to 'resist the Holy Ghost,' Acts vii. 51. Yet we may quench his motions by neglect, as well as by opposition, and by that means lose both the profit and pleasure which would have attended the entertainment. Salvation came both to Zaccheus his house and heart, upon embracing the first motion our Saviour was pleased to make him. Had he slighted that, it is uncertain whether another should have been bestowed upon him. The more such sprouts are planted and nourished in us, the less room will stinking weeds have to root themselves, and disperse their influence. And for thy own good thoughts, feed them and keep them alive, that they may not be like a blaze of straw, which takes birth and expires the same minute. Brood upon them, and kill them not, as some birds do their young ones, by too often flying from their nests. David kept up a staple of sound and good thoughts; he would scarce else have desired God to 'try and know them,' Ps. cxxxix. 23, had they been only some few weak flashes at uncertain times.

(2.) Improve them for those ends to which they naturally tend. It is not enough to give them a bare reception, and forbear the smothering of them; but we must consider what affections are proper to be raised by them, either in the search of some truth, or performance of some duty. Those gleams which shoot into us on the sudden, have some lesson sealed up in them to be opened and learned by us. When Peter, upon the crowing of the cock, called to mind his Master's admonition, 'he thought thereon, and wept,' Mark xiv. 72; he did not only receive the spark, but kindled a suitable affection. A choice graff, though kept very carefully by us, yet if not presently set, will wither, and disappoint our expectation of the desired fruit. No man is without some secret whispers to dissuade him from some alluring and busy sin: Job xxxiii. 14–17, 'God speaks once, yea, twice, that he may withdraw man from his purpose;' as Cain had by an audible voice, Gen. iv. 7, which, had he observed to the damping the revengeful motion against his brother, he had prevented his brother's death, his own despair, and eternal ruin. Have you any motion to seek God's face, as David had? Let your hearts reply, 'Thy face, Lord, will I seek,' Ps. xxvii. 8. The address will be most acceptable at such a time, when your heart is tuned by one that 'searcheth the deep things of God,' 1 Cor. ii. 10, and knows his mind, and what airs are most delightful to him. Let our motion be quick in any duty which the Spirit doth suggest; and while he heaves our hearts, and oils our wheels, we shall do more in any religious service, and that more pleasantly and successfully, than at another time, with all our own art and industry; for his injections are like water poured into a pump to raise up more; and as Satan's motions are not without a main body to second them, so neither do the Spirit's go unattended, without a sufficient strength to assist the entertainers of them. Well then, lie not at anchor when a fresh gale would fill thy sails, but lay hold of the present opportunity. These seasons are often like those influences from certain conjunctions of the planets, which, if not (according to the astrologer's opinion) presently applied, pass away, and return not again in many ages. So the Spirit's breathings are often determined, that if they be not entertained with suitable affections, the time will be unregainable, and the same gracious opportunities of a sweet intercourse may be for ever lost; for God will not have his Holy Spirit dishonoured in always striving with wilful man, Gen. vi. 3. When Judas neglected our Saviour's advertisement, John xiii. 21, the devil quickly enters and hurries him to the execution of his traitorous project, ver. 27, and he never meets with any motion afterwards but from his new master, and that eternally fatal both to his body and soul.

(3.) Refer them, if possible, to assist your morning meditation; that, like little brooks arising from several springs, they may meet in one channel, and compose a more useful stream. What straggling good thoughts arise, though they may owe their birth to several occasions, and tend divers ways, yet list them in the services of that truth, to which you have committed the government of your mind that day; as constables in a time of necessary business for the king, take up men that are going about their honest and lawful occasions, and force them to join in one employ for the public service. Many accidental glances (as was observed before) will serve both to fix and illustrate your morning proposition; but if it be an extraordinary injection, and cannot be referred to your standing *thesis*, follow it, and let your thoughts run whither it will lead you. A theme of the Spirit's setting is better than one of our own choosing.

(4.) Record the choicer of them. We may have occasion to look back upon them another time, either as grounds of comfort in some hour of temptation, or directions in some sudden emergency; but constantly as persuasive engagements to our necessary duty. Thus they may lie by us for further use, as money in our purse. Since Mary kept and pondered the short sayings of our Saviour in her heart, Luke ii. 19, 51, committing and fitting* them as it were in her commonplace book, why should not we also preserve the whisperings of that Spirit who receives from the same mouth and hand what he both speaks and shews to us? It is pity the dust and filings of choicer metals, which may one time be melted down into a mass, should be lost in a heap of drossy thoughts. If we do not remember them, but like children are taken with their novelty more than their substance, and like John Baptist's hearers, rejoice in their light only for a season, John v. 35, it will discourage the Spirit from sending any more; and then our hearts will be empty, and we know who stands ready to clap in his hellish swarms and legions. But howsoever we do, God will record our good thoughts as our excusers, if we improve them; as our accusers, if we reject them. And as he took notice how often he had appeared to Solomon, 1 Kings xi. 9, so he will take notice how often his Spirit hath appeared to us; and write down every motion whereby we have been solicited, that they may be witnesses of his endeavours for our good, and our own wilfulness.

(5.) Back them with ejaculations. Let our hearts be ready to attend every injection from heaven with a motion to it, since it is ingratitude to receive a present without returning an acknowledgment to the benefactor. As God turns his thoughts of us into promises, so let us turn our thoughts of him into prayers. And since his regards of us are darted in beams upon us, let them be reflected back upon him in thankfulness for the gift, and earnestness both for the continuance and increase of such impressions; as David prayed that God would 'not take his holy Spirit from him,' Ps. li. 11, which had inspired him with his penitential resolutions. To what purpose doth the Holy Ghost descend upon us, but to declare to us 'the things which are freely given us of God'? 1 Cor. ii. 12. And is it fit for us to hear such a declaration without a quick suitable reflection? Since the Comforter is to bring to our remembrance what Christ both spake and did, John xiv. 26, it

* *συμβάλλουσα. Συμβάλλων, συναρμόζων—Hesych.*

must be for the same end for which they were both spoken and acted by him, which was to bring us to a near converse with God. Therefore when the Spirit renews in our minds a gospel truth, let us turn it into a present plea, and be God's remembrancers of his own promises, as the Spirit is our remembrancer of divine truths. We need not doubt some rich fruit of the application at such a season; since without question the impressions the Spirit stamps upon us are as much according to God's will, Rom. viii. 27, as the intercessions he makes for us. Therefore when any holy thought doth advance itself in our souls, the most grateful reception we can bestow upon it will be to suffer our hearts to be immediately fired by it, and imitate, with a glowing devotion, the royal prophet in that form he hath drawn up to our hands: 'O Lord God of Abraham, Isaac, and of Israel our fathers, keep this for ever in the imagination of the thoughts of the heart of thy servant, and prepare my heart unto thee,' 1 Chron. xxix. 18. This will be an encouragement to God to send more such guests into our hearts; and by an affectionate entertainment of them, we shall gain both a habit of thinking well, and a stock too.

A DISCOURSE OF THE CHURCH'S STABILITY.

And of Sion it shall be said, This and that man was born in her; and the Highest himself shall establish her.—Ps. LXXXVII. 5.

THE author of this psalm, and the time when it was penned, are uncertain. Some think it was composed after the return of the Jews from Babylon, upon the erection of the second temple, and designed to be sung in their constant public assemblies; others think it was composed by David when he brought the ark to Sion as the repository for it, till the building of the temple, wherein it might honourably rest. It seems, whoever was the author, to be ecstatical. The penman breaks out into a holy rapture and admiration of the firmness and stability of the church. It is also prophetical of the Christian church, of the glory of it, the largeness of its bounds, and perpetual duration. The Jews ridiculously interpret it of literal Jerusalem, in regard of the excellency of its climate, the goodness of the air, being seated in the middle or navel of the earth, and the seat and spring of all the wise men, accounting all fools that were to be found in other parts. It is true, others were not wise with a wisdom to salvation; they were not instructed in the high mysteries of religion by God as those people were; but was there not learning among the Greeks, and wisdom among the Chaldeans, and a ripeness in mechanic arts among the Tyrians, which lived in the same climate with the Jews? It can by no means be understood of the material Jerusalem and Sion, that was ruined by the Babylonians, and though re-edified, yet afterwards subverted by the Romans, and the remainders of it at this day become a stable for Mahomet; and the bringing in those nations mentioned, ver. 4, overthrows any such interpretation, which never were enrolled in the registers of Sion, nor became votaries to the true religion while the walls of that place were standing in their glory. Sion was the place whence the law was to come, Micah iv. 2, a law of another nature than that which was uttered with thunders from mount Sinai. Sion was the place where the throne of Christ was to be settled, where he was to be crowned king, Ps. ii. 6, and where he was to manage the sceptre, and 'rule in the midst of his enemies,' Ps. cx. 2; and therefore it is here celebrated as the figure of the Christian church, of that city which Abraham expected, 'whose builder and maker is God, Heb. xi. 10; and the Christian church is particularly called by this name of mount Sion, Heb. xii. 21, and believers are called the sons of Sion, Joel ii. 23. The psalmist speaks,

1. Of the great love the Lord bears to Sion, ver. 2.
2. Of the glory of the promises made to her, ver. 3.
3. Of the confluence of new inhabitants to her, ver. 4.
4. Of the duration and establishment of her, ver. 5.

Ver. 1. *His foundation.* The foundation of God, *i. e.* that which God hath founded, that Jerusalem which is of God's building, is seated in the holy mountain. The city was built before Jehovah conquered Canaan; but God is said to be the founder of it in regard of that peculiar glory to which it was designed, to be the rest of his ark, the place of his worship, the throne of the types of the Messiah, the seat whence the evangelic law was to be published to all nations, and the Messiah revealed as the redeemer and ruler of the world.

In the holy mountains. Jerusalem was seated upon high mountains. The palace of the kings was built upon Sion, and the temple, the house of the Most High, was built upon Moriah, and encompassed with mountains round about, Ps. cxxv. 2, an emblem of the strength and stability of the church. 'Holy mountains;' not that there was any inherent holiness in them more than in the other mountains of the earth,* or that they were naturally more beautiful and stately than other mountains, but because they were separated for the worship and service of God, and had been ennobled by the performance of a worship there before the building of the temple. It was upon Moriah that Isaac was designed for a sacrifice, and the most signal act of obedience performed to God by the father of the faithful. It was there also that David appeased the wrath of God by sacrifice, after it had issued out upon the people in a plague, for the numbering of them; and the very name *Moriah* hath something sacred in it, signifying either *God teaching* or *God manifested*, which name might be given it by God with respect to the manifestation of Christ, who was to come during the standing of the second temple.

Ver. 2. *The Lord loves the gates of Sion.* By *gates* in Scripture is meant the strength, or wisdom, or justice of a place. Gates were the magazines of arms, and the places of judicature. He had manifested his love to her in choosing that city before all the cities of Israel and Judah wherein to place his name, and have his worship celebrated; and that place in Jerusalem particularly where his law should be given by the Spirit to the apostles on the day of Pentecost; and to apply it to the gospel church, it signifies the special respect God bears to her, above all the rites, observances, and ceremonies of the Judaic institution. It was in this gospel church, the true Sion, that he 'desired to dwell,' and will 'remain for ever,' Ps. lxviii. 17, which is a prophetic psalm of the gospel times, and the ascension of Christ.

1. The stability of the church is here asserted.† The church is not built upon the sand, which may fall with a storm, nor upon the waters, that may float with the waves, nor spread out as a tent in the desert, that may be taken up, and carried away to another place, but upon a mountain, not to be removed: Ps. cxxv. 1, 'Mount Sion cannot be removed.' It is built upon a rock, the Rock of ages, upon a mountain which is not shattered by waves

* Daillé Melange, part ii. page 354. † Geierus in loc.

or shaken by storms; upon Christ, who hath the strength of many mountains in himself.

2. The necessity of holiness in a church. What though the church be a mountain for strength and eminency, have the honour and privilege of sacraments, and be the ark of the oracles of God, it is not established unless it be a holy mountain. Holiness is the only becoming thing in the house of God. As it is consecrated to the glory of God, so it must be exercised in things pertaining to the glory of God. As the foundation is holy, so ought the superstructure to be. There was no filth in the framing it; there must be no filth in the continuance of it.

Ver. 3. He speaks with some kind of astonishment of the glorious things spoken of her, or promised to her, and concludes it with a note of attention, or a mark of eminency, *Selah;* ver. 3, 'Glorious things are spoken of thee, O city of God.' No place enjoyed an equal happiness with Jerusalem while it remained faithful to its founder. It maintained its standing in the midst of its enemies; no weapon formed against it was able to prosper. Heaven planted it, and the dews of heaven watered it; it had a continual succession of prophets; the best kings that ever were in the world swayed the sceptre in it; it was blessed with more miraculous deliverances than any part of the universe; the nations that loved it not yet feared its power, and feared the displeasure of its guardian. It was here the Son of God delivered the messages of heaven by the order of his Father; it was here the Spirit first filled the heads and hearts of the apostles, in order to the conversion of a world from idolatry to the sceptre of God. But more glorious things are spoken of the spiritual Sion than of the material Jerusalem; that had Christ in the flesh, and the gospel-church hath Christ in the Spirit. He went from thence to heaven, but he comes from heaven to visit them with his comforts; he hath left the walls of Jerusalem in its ruins, but he hath not, he will not leave his spiritual Sion fatherless and comfortless; John xiv. 18, his Spirit abides for ever with his church. Glorious things are spoken of it, when he pronounced it impregnable, and that the gates of hell, the power and policy of all the apostate angels and their instruments, should not prevail against her; when he assured her he would be present with her, not to the end of an age or two, but till the period of time, the consummation of the world; privileges that material Jerusalem could never boast of. Whatsoever countries have been applauded for secular excellencies, or been famous for wisdom, none can claim such elogies as gospel Sion, where God hath declared his will, published himself a God of salvation, placed the laws of heaven, and poured out that wisdom which comes from above. These are glorious things, above human experience, above human desires.

The glorious things mentioned of the gospel-church are in ver. 4, where he speaks of the enlargement of her bounds, the increase of her inhabitants, and the numerous muster-rolls of those that shall list themselves in her service: 'I will make mention of Rahab and Babylon to them that know me. Behold Philistia and Tyre, with Ethiopia: this man was born there.'

The time shall come when those nations that are most alienated from the profession of truth shall come under her wing, and pay allegiance to her empire. Strangers shall be brought into her bosom, not only Philistia and Tyre, nations upon her confines, but Egypt and Ethiopia, nations more remote. Nations born and bred at a distance shall be registered as born from her womb, and nursed in her lap; distance of place shall not hinder the relation of her children; and when God shall count the people of foreign nations, he shall set a mark upon every true believer, and reckon him as one born in Sion, a denizen of Jerusalem, though not a Jew in the flesh.

I will make mention of Rahab and Babylon to them that know me; or rather among them that know me,* or for them that know me, ליֹדְעָי. I will remember them as persons enlightened by me, and acquainted with me.

The psalmist reckons up here nations that were greatest enemies to the church, Rahab or Egypt, for so Egypt is named, Isa. li. 9, her ancient enemy, Philistia her perpetual invader. *Rahab* signifies pride or fierceness; the fiercest people shall be subdued to Sion by the power of the gospel; Egypt, the wisest and learnedest nation, the most idolatrous and superstitious; men that rest in their own parts and strength shall cast away their idols; Babylon, the strongest and most powerful empire, the subjects of which the Scripture often describes as luxurious, cruel, proud; Tyre, the greatest mart, whose citizens were the greatest merchants; the Ethiopians, the posterity of cursed Ham, whose souls are blacker than their bodies; men buried in sin, benighted with ignorance, poisoned with pride; the most fierce and envenomed enemies shall be brought in by an infinite grace, and make up one body with her, and shall be counted as related to her by a new birth, and be made members of her by regeneration; this is properly to be born in Sion: 'This man was born there.' As without regeneration we have not God for our father, so neither have we Sion or the church for our mother. This is the great privilege we should inquire after, without which we are not in God's register. This second birth God only approves of; he enrols no man in the number of the citizens of Sion, nor endows them with the special privileges of it upon the account of their first, wherein they lie buried in the corruption of Adam, and are citizens of hell, not of Jerusalem. Again, this second birth is never without the knowledge of God: 'Among those that know me.' Ignorance is a bar to this enrolment; he is no man that is not a rational creature, and he no regenerate man that hath not some knowledge in the great mysteries of God in Christ.

In ver. 5. 1. The honour of Sion is described by her fruitfulness.

1. In regard of the eminency of her births, she is not wholly barren; she hath her births of men, and worthy men. The carnal world hath not exceeded the church in men of raised intellectuals; Sion hath not been a city of fools. Dionysius the Areopagite hath been her production, as well as Damaris a woman. Kings also have been nursed at her breasts, that they might be nursing fathers to her by their power; but the honour of Sion consists in the inward change it makes on men, dispossessing them of the nature of wolves for that of lambs, rendering them the loyal subjects of God instead of his active enemies. It is the glory of Sion that this or that man born in her was changed to such principles and such affections, that all the education and politeness of the most accomplished cities in the world could not furnish them with.

2. In regard of the multitude of them; 'this and that man,' of all sorts and conditions, and multitudes of them, so that 'more are the children of the desolate than of the married wife.' The tents were prophesied to be enlarged, the curtains of the habitations of Sion to be stretched out, and her cords to be lengthened, to receive and entertain that multitude of children that should be brought forth by her after the sacrifice of the Son of God, Isa. liv. 1, 2; for that exhortation follows upon the description of the death and exaltation of Christ, Isa. liii.

2. The happiness of Sion. 'The Highest himself shall establish her.'

(1.) Security in her glory. 'Establish her.'

(2.) The author of that security and perpetuity; 'the Highest;' and that

* De Dieu *in loc.*

exclusive of any other. 'The Highest himself;* all that are not the most high are excluded from having a share in the establishment of the church.

It is a work peculiar to him. It is not the excellent learning, strength of the wise or mighty men that are born in her, that doth preserve her, but God alone. He spirits and acts them; means God doth use in bringing in inward grace, means he doth use in settling the outward form: but such means that have in reason no strength to effect so great a business, means different from those which are used in the establishment of other kingdoms, whereby the hand that acts them is more visible and plain than the means that are used.† It is not the wit of man, which is folly, nor the strength of man, which is weakness, nor the holiness of man, which is nothing, can claim the honour of this work. God himself picks stones out of the quarry, smooths them for the building, fixeth them in their places. He himself is the only architect; his wisdom contrives it, his grace erects it, his power preserves it, and accomplisheth his own work. It is the highest; none higher to overpower him, none so high as to check and mate him.

Shall establish her. This cannot be meant of the literal or local Sion (though that indeed was preserved while the legal service was to endure, excepting that interruption by the Babylonish captivity, but now Mahomet's horse tramples upon it, and it retains none of the ancient inhabitants), but of the true mystical Sion, the gospel state of the church, which shall continue in being, as Christ the head of it hath settled it, till time shall be no more. Other kingdoms may crumble away, the foundations of them be dissolved; but that God which laid the foundation of Sion, and built her walls, will preserve her palaces, that the gates of hell, the subtlety of heretics, the fury of tyrants, the apostasy of some of her pretended children, all the locusts and spawn of the bottomless pit, shall not be able to root her up.

Shall establish her. The word כונן signifies the affording all things necessary for defence, increase of victory, preparations of it, the knitting of it.

Doct. The gospel-church is a perpetual society, established by the highest power in heaven or earth.

It shall continue as long as the world, and outlive the dissolution of nature; she shall bring forth her man-child (maugre all the vigilancy of the dragon), which shall be caught up to God and his throne; and though she be forced to fly into the wilderness, yet a place is prepared for her habitation, and food for her support during that state, no less than twelve hundred and sixty days, or years, and this by no weaker, no meaner a hand than that of God himself: Rev. xii. 3, 6, 'Where she hath a place prepared of God.' That hand that catches up Christ the man-child into heaven, that hand that sets him upon the throne of God, provides meat for the woman in the wilderness. The head and the body have the same defender, the same protector, the same hand to secure them.‡ Or by *man-child* is meant the whole number of the believers, which were more numerous before she went into a wilderness-condition, the Scripture using often the singular for the plural, and the Holy Ghost expressing himself here according to the property of the woman, which is to bring forth one at the same time. The figure of the church notes stability; it is 'four-square, and the length is as large as the breadth,' Rev. xxi. 16. 'The length, breadth, and height of it are equal;' the most perfect figure, noting perfection and duration. So it was described in the prophecy, Ezek. xlviii. 16, exactly four thousand five hundred measures on each side. All belonging to this city or church is reckoned by the number twelve, a

* Coccei. in loc. † Folang. ‡ Ribera in loc.

square number, equal on all sides; twelve gates, twelve foundations, twelve tribes of Israel, twelve apostles, twelve stones to garnish it, Rev. xxi. 12–14, &c. A four-square figure is an emblem of unchangeable constancy. Things so framed remain always in the same posture, cast them which way you will, and among some of the heathens was reckoned as a divine figure;* and the character of a virtuous man in regard of his constancy was τετράγωνος.

The shutting of the gate of the new temple, Ezek. xliv. 2, after the God of Israel had entered in by it, is interpreted by some of the everlasting dwelling of the Lord in the church of the gospel among his people, and never departing from it, as he had done from the first temple.† None shall enter in to deface it, none shall prescribe new laws to it, none shall trample upon it. When God enters into the Christian church, he shuts the door after him; his presence never departs from it; his gospel shall never be rooted out of it. The church hath a security in its foundation, as being 'built upon a rock,' Mat. xviii. 16. It hath an assurance of preservation by the presence of the God of Israel, of 'Christ in the midst of her,' Mat. xxviii. 19, 20. 'The tabernacle of Sion shall not be taken down; not one of the stakes thereof shall be removed, neither shall any of the cords thereof be broken;' and that because 'the glorious Lord shall be a place of broad rivers and streams to it,' Isa. xxxiii. 20, 21.

The enemies of the church shall be consumed, that God may have his due praise. *Hallelujahs* are never sung with the highest note till the wicked and idolatrous generation be rooted out of the earth. *Hallelujahs* were never used, as the Jews observe, till the consummation of all things by the setting the church above the tossing of the waves, and the destruction of its troublers; when the glory of the Lord should endure for ever, and God rejoice in his works, Ps. civ. 31, 35. And therefore, when the blood of his children is avenged by his justice upon his enemies, and the smoke of antichrist riseth up before him, and the kingdom of God is for ever settled, *Hallelujah* is pronounced and repeated with a loud voice, Rev. xix. 2, 3, 6. Such a time will be, and God will establish and secure his church till he hath perfected his own and her glory.

This stability the church hath had experience of in all ages of the world: and it will always be said in her, Ps. xlviii. 8, 'As we have heard, so have we seen in the city of the Lord of hosts, in the city of our God; God will establish it for ever.'

In the handling this doctrine, these four things are to be done.

I. The explication. II. The proof that it is so. III. Why it must needs be so. IV. Use.

I. Explication.

1. This stability must not be meant of any particular church in the world. Particular churches have their beginnings, progresses, and periods. Many churches, as well as many persons, have apostatised from the faith; many candlesticks have been broken in pieces, and yet the candle not blown out, but removed and set in another socket. Particular churches have been corrupted by superstition and idolatry, rent by heresies, and scattered by persecutions. What remains are there of those seven churches in Asia which were the walk of Christ, Rev. ii. 1, but deplorable ruins? There is no absolute promise given to any particular church that it shall be free from defection. The church of Rome, so flourishing in the apostles' time, was warned to be humble, lest it became as much apostate as that of the Jews, Rom. xi. 21, 22. Nay, there are predictions of almost an universal apostasy:

* The Arcadians made *Jovis signum quadrangulum (Pausanias de Arcadicis).*

† Lightfoot, Temple, cap. xxxviii. p. 252.

'All the world wondered after the beast,' Rev. xiii. 3, 'and worshipped him,' ver. 8. And just before the coming of Christ, it will be difficult to find a grain of faith among the multitude of chaff, Luke xviii. 8. There is not one place which was, in the primitive times, dignified with truth, but is now deformed by error. Yea, the universal church hath been forced by the fury of the dragon, though not to sink, yet to fly into the wilderness and obscurity, yet hath been preserved through all changes in the midst of thos desolations and deserts. It is not, indeed, so fixed in one place but the cords may be taken up, the stakes removed, and the tents pitched in another ground. It is spread through the world wherever God will set up the light of his gospel. Sion hath stood, though some synagogues of it have been pulled down; it hath, like the sun, kept its station in the firmament, though not without eclipses and clouds to muffle it. The church is but one, though it be in divers countries, and named according to the places where it resides, as the church of Ephesus, the church of Sardis, &c., which all are as the beams of the sun darted from one body, branches growing from one root, streams flowing from one fountain. If you obstruct the light of one beam, or lop off one branch, or dam up the stream, yet the sun, root, fountain remains the same. So though the light of particular churches may be dim and extinguished, the beauty of them defaced, yet the universal church, that which is properly Sion, remains the same; it remains upon Christ the rock, and is still upon the basis of the covenant; it is still God's church, and God is her God. When a people have forfeited their church privileges by barrenness and wantonness, and God in justice strips them of their ornaments, he will have another people, which he will form for his glory and fit for his residence. The gospel shall never want an host to entertain it, nor a ground to be made fruitful by it: Mat. xxi. 43, 'The kingdom of God shall be taken from you, and given to a nation bringing forth the fruits thereof.' The kingdom of God is not destroyed when it is removed, but transplanted into a more fruitful soil. While Christ hath a body in the world, he will find a Joseph of Arimathea to embalm it, and preserve it for a resurrection. When the glory of the Lord goes off from one cherub, it will find other cherubims whereon to settle, Ezek. x. 4, 18. That glory which had dwelt in the material ark of the sanctuary departs from thence to find a throne in that chariot which had been described, Ezek. i. Nay, the departure of God from one church renders his name more glorious in another.* The rejection of the carnal Israel was the preamble to the appearance of the spiritual Israel; and the kingdom of the Messiah was rendered more large and illustrious by the dissolving of that church that had confidence in the flesh, trusted in their external rites, and patched the beauty and purity of divine worship with their whorish additions; just as the mortification of the flesh gives liveliness to the spirit, and the pulling up noisome weeds from a garden makes room for the setting and flourishing growth of good plants.

2. Though God unstakes the church in one place, yet he will not only have a church, but a professing church in another. 'It shall be said of Sion, This and that man was born there.' It shall be said of Sion by God; it shall be said of Sion by men. If Christ confesseth none before his Father but such as confess him before men, Luke xii. 8, shall he ever want employment? Shall the world ever be at that pass as to bear none that profess him, and so none to be owned by him at the right hand of his Father? Shall he by whom all things subsist, have none to acknowledge their subsistence by him? The world may be the inheritance of Christ, but scarce counted his possession, if there were not in some parts of it a body of sub-

* Rivet in Hos. i. x. p. 518.

jects to justify their allegiance to him in the face of a persecuting generation. Indeed, when the church was confined to the narrow limits of the carnal Israel, the profession of the truth was contracted to a few, though the faith of it might be alive in others; only Caleb and Joshua among the whole body of the murmuring Israelites in the wilderness asserted the honour of God, and maintained the truth of his promise, though the belief of it might sparkle in the hearts of others under the ashes of their fears, that hindered their discovery of it to others. It was another time reduced to one, and Elijah only had the boldness to make a declaration of the name of God, though there were seven thousand who had retained their purity, while they had lost their courage to publish it, 1 Kings xix. 18. But in the Christian church, since the number of elect are more, the profession will be greater in the midst of an universal apostasy of pretenders: Rev. xiii. 18, 'All that dwell upon the earth shall worship him,' *i.e.* the beast, 'whose names are not written in the book of life of the Lamb.' If their election be a preservative against an adoration of the beast, it is also a security against the denial of any such worship, and an encouragement to profess the name of Christ when they shall be brought upon the stage.

This profession may lie much in the dark, and not be so visible as before; as a field of corn overtopped by weeds, looks at a distance as if there were nothing else but the blue and red cockle and darnel, but when we come near we see the good grain shews its head as well as the weeds; but a professing people there will be one where or other. It is a standing law of Christianity, that a belief in the heart should be attended by confession with the mouth, Rom. x. 9. And the church is a congregation of people sounding the voice of Christ, as he was preached and confessed by the apostles. While there are believers, there will be professors in society together; some ordinances settled in being during the continuance of the world, as the supper, 1 Cor. xi. 6, implies a society, as the seat of the administration; baptism is a ceremony of admission into a society; the supper, a feasting of several upon spiritual viands. Officers appointed imply a body professing some rules, Mat. xxviii. 20. To what purpose are all these settled during the continuance of the world, if they were not somewhere to be practised till that period of time; and how can they be practised without a confederation and society? Without such a body all the ordinances and rules of Christ would be in vain, and imply as little wisdom in enacting them, as a want of power in not keeping up a society in some part of the world to observe them according to his own prescriptions. There will therefore, be, in some part or other of the world, a church openly professing the doctrine of truth.

3. This church or Sion shall have a numerous progeny. The spiritual Israel shall be 'as the sand of the sea, which cannot be measured or numbered,' Hosea i. 10, which was the promise made to Abraham, Gen. xxii. 17, and renewed in the same terms to Jacob, Gen. xxxii. 12. The church is a little flock in comparison of the carnal world, yet it is numerous in itself, though not in every place; for sometimes there may not be above three found to withstand the worship of a golden image; yet in some one or other place of the world, and successively, it shall be numerous; he will not lose the honour of the feast he hath prepared, though those that are invited prefer their farms and oxen before it, but will find guests in the highways; he will spread his wings from east to west, and 'in every place incense shall be offered to his name,' Mal. i. 11. The church is compared to the morning, Cant. vi. 10, which from small beginnings in a short time fills the whole hemisphere with light; and the promises concerning it run all that way. 'The hills were to be covered with the shadow of it;' 'her boughs are to be sent out to the sea, and her

branches to the river,' Ps. lxxx. 10, 11. It was to spread itself 'like a goodly cedar, and be a dwelling-place to the fowl of every wing,' Ezek. xvii. 23. Yea, a numberless multitude from all nations, kindreds, people, and tongues, are to stand before the throne, and before the Lamb, 'clothed with white robes, and palms in their hands,' Rev. vii. 9, adorned with innocency, and crowned with victory. No monarchy ever did, ever can so far stretch her bounds; nor hath the sun seen any place where it hath not seen some sprinkling of a church. Every kingdom hath met with unpassable bounds, but the ensigns of Christ have not been limited. The church was once crowded up in a narrow compass of Judea, but since that her territories are enlarged; her ensigns have flourished over many countries, Rahab, Tyre, Ethiopia, the vast circuit of Asia, and the deserts of Africa have been added to her empire; her progeny shall be hereafter as numerous as it hath been. When the devices of antichrist shall be more seen and perceived, they will be more nauseated; and many with Ephraim shall say, 'What have I to do any more with idols?'

II. Second thing. That God has hitherto established Sion.

1. It is testified by its present standing, when other empires have sunk by age or violence.

God hath promised the stability and eminency of the mountain of the Lord's house above all the mountains, the strongest power, and most compacted empires of the world, sometimes signified to us by that title, Isa. ii. 2. And in the midst of his destroying plagues, and his milder anger with the church, she hath a charter of security: Jer. xxx. 11, 'Though I make a full end of all nations, yet will I not make an end of thee.' Further, the reasons why kingdoms and nations are pulled up by the roots and utterly wasted, is not only because they are inveterate enemies, but refuse her easy chains, and decline her service: Isa. lx. 12, 'The nation and kingdom that will not serve thee shall perish; yea, those nations shall be utterly wasted.' The warrant for the execution of such is as firmly sealed by heaven, as the patent for the church's preservation; it is repeated with an emphasis. The persecuted church hath still been lifted up, when the Assyrian, Persian, and Greek monarchies have fallen in pieces, and left no footsteps of their grandeur. The prosperity of worldly kingdoms is no better than a fire of straw that blazeth and vanisheth; it hath but the brittle foundation of human policy, and an establishment by a temporary providence. The everlasting covenant and the basis of divine truth and love cannot be claimed by any but the church. Not a kingdom can be pitched upon in all the records of history that hath maintained its standing and triumphed over its enemies, and subsisted at such a rate, and by unusual and unheard-of methods, as the church hath done. Those that have been best guarded by laws, hedged in with the best methods of government, and armed with a strong power to protect them, have found something or other rising from their bowels, or enemies' power to procure their dissolution. But the church, though dashed against so many rocks, has yet floated above the deluge of those commotions that have sunk other societies. The kings of the world could never yet boast of a full conquest of her, or brag that she hath been subjected to the same condition with themselves. She hath borne up her head in the midst of earthly revolutions, and met with her preservation or resurrection where carnal interests have found their funeral. Those that have set their feet upon the church's breasts, or spilt her blood, have found their poison where they imagined they should find their safety. The Babylonish empire, which was God's rod for the correcting his people, saw herself in the chains of her enemies that night she had been sacrilegiously carousing healths in the sacred vessels of the temple, Dan. v. 3, 30; and the Jews enjoyed a deliverer, where the Babylonians felt the force of a conqueror. Many such fatal periods may be reckoned up, both in sacred and human story, either for not protecting or persecuting that which is so dear to the Highest, who hath established her.

2. No society but the church ever subsisted in the midst of a multitude of enemies. Has she not been like a little flock in the midst of many wolves, which, though they sucked the blood of some, yet could never reach the head or heart of the whole? The devil hath attacked her, without vanquishing her; shaken her, without ruining her. The biting of the serpent, according to the ancient promise, may bruise the heel, but not the head, and make an incurable wound in the mystical body. She hath been preserved in a hating world in spite of the enmity of it, by a divine wisdom that hath not regulated itself by the methods of flesh and blood. His feeding the Israelites in the wilderness was a figure of what he would do to his church, and he hath accomplished it to the gospel church as really as he did to the ancient Israel. While she hath been in a wilderness these twelve hundred years, and I hope somewhat upwards, she hath not wanted her manna, nor her rock; she hath been fed in her straits, and preserved in her combats; and as Christ reigns, so the church lives, and hath her table spread in the midst of her enemies. What is eleven hundred years' continuance of the Venetian government to so many thousand years' preservation of the church in the midst of atheism, paganism, antichristianism, ever since it was first born and nursed in Adam's family; and this hath been when her friends have forsaken her, when her enemies have been confident of her ruin, when herself hath expected little else than destruction, when she hath thought sometimes in her straits her God ignorant of her; when hell hath poured out a flood, the carnal earth hath sometimes found it their interest to help her, though their enmity were irreconcileable against her, Rev. xii. 16. The subtilty and power of her enemies, that have found success in their other projects, have met with an unforeseen baffle when they have armed against her. Men of the greatest abilities have proved fools when they have exercised their wit against her. Ahithophel's wisdom was great when on David's side, and changed to folly when he shifted sides against him. A secret blast hath been upon the projects of men when they have turned against her upon secular interests. In the greatest judgments which have come and shall come upon the world, when wonders shall be shewn in the heavens and in the earth, blood, fire, and pillars of smoke, when 'the sun shall be turned into darkness, and the moon into blood,' Joel ii. 30, 31; yet God will have a mount Sion and a Jerusalem, some 'that call upon his name,' ver. 32. Not the malice of her enemies shall impair her, because of God's power, nor the common judgments of the world under which others sink shall extinguish her, because of God's truth: ver. 32, 'As the Lord hath said.' Whence comes all this, but from God's having been her 'dwelling-place in all generations'? Ps. xc. 1. He was so to her from the time of Abraham to the introduction of his posterity into Canaan; he hath sheltered her as an house doth an inhabitant, or the ark did Noah in the midst of many waters. In all generations, Sion hath been impregnable; for he that is her dwelling-place hath formed the mountains, and 'from everlasting to everlasting is only God,' ver. 2; and though one generation pass and another comes, he is the same dwelling-place, and never out of repair, never will want repair; and therefore it is an astonishment that the devil, after so long an experience, should be such a fool as to engage in new attempts, when he hath found so little success in his former, and hath had so many ages to witness the baffles he hath received. What a fool is he, to think that her

defender should be conquered by a revolted angel, that lies under an everlasting curse!

3. The violences against her, which have been fatal to other societies, have been useful to her. This bush hath burned without consuming, and preserved its verdure in the midst of fire; not from the nature of the bush, but the presence of Him that dwelt in it. It hath not only subsisted in the bowels of her enemies, but hath been established by means of the violence of men, and grown greater in the midst of torments and death. She hath not only out-grown her afflictions, but grown greater and better by them. The last monarchy, composed of clay and iron, clay for its earthly and miry designs, and iron for its force and violence, is the immediate usher of the kingdom of God, that shall never be destroyed, but stand for ever, Daniel ii. 41, 44.

(1.) She hath been often increased. Persecution hath lopped off some branches of the vine, but have been found more sprouting up instead of them that were cut off. Her blood hath been seed, and the pangs of her martyrs have been fruitful in bringing forth new witnesses. We have scarce read of more sudden conversions to Christianity, though indeed more numerous, by the preaching of the word, than by the shedding the blood of Christians. Eminent professors have sprung out of the martyrs' ashes. The storms have been so far from destroying her, that it hath been the occasion of spreading her tents in a larger ground. Saul's winnowing the church blew away some of the corn to take rooting in other places, Acts viii. 3, 4, like seeds of plants blown away by the wind, which have risen and brought forth their kind in another soil; and it is no more than hath been predicted, Daniel xii. 1, 4, such 'a time of trouble that never was since there was a nation,' should be the time when 'many should run to and fro, and knowledge should be increased.' While other societies increase by persecuting their enemies, this increaseth by being persecuted herself: it 'grows as a vine,' Hosea xiv. 7. Though it be cut, the cutting hath contributed to its thriving. This rose-bush hath not only stood in the wind which hath rooted up other oaks, but the fragrancy of it hath been carried by that wind to places at a greater distance. When Antiochus commanded all the books of the Scripture in the hands of any to be burned, they were not only preserved, but presently after appeared out of their hidden places, as they were translated into the Greek tongue, the language then most known in the world, and made public to other nations. Truth hath been often rendered by such proceedings more clear and glorious. The persecution of Sion's head, the Captain of our salvation, to death, was the occasion of the discovery of the gospel to the whole world. He was the great seed, that being cast into the ground became so fruitful as to spread his branches in all corners of the earth, John xii. 24. And that persecution which I suppose remains yet to be acted, and which will be the smartest, shall be succeeded by the clearest eruption of gospel light, wherein the gospel shall recover its ancient and primitive glory. The slaying of the witnesses shall end in an evangelical success, Rev. xi. 9, 10, &c. The world 'shall give glory to the God of heaven,' ver. 13; 'The kingdoms of the world shall become the kingdoms of Christ,' ver. 15; Christ shall more illustriously reign, ver. 17; the temple of God shall be opened in heaven, ver. 19. The spiritual Israel as well as the national, the antitype as well as the type, have multiplied under oppression;* and, like an arched building, stood firmer by all the weights that have been designed to crush her.

(2.) She has often been refined by the most violent persecutions of her enemies.

She hath not only survived the flames that have been kindled against her,

* Decay of Christian Piety, p. 23.

but, as refined gold, come out more beautiful from the furnace, left her dross behind her, and hath been wrought into a more beautiful frame by the hand of her great Artificer. Like the sand upon the sea shore, she hath not only broke the force of the waves, but been assisted by them to discharge her filth, and been washed more clean by those waves that rushed in to drown her. She hath been more conformed to the image of her Head; and made fitter to glorify God here, and to enter into the glory of God hereafter. The church is to 'cast forth her roots like Lebanon,' Hosea xiv. 5. The cedar by its shakings grows up more in beauty as well as strength, and the torch by its knocks burns the clearer. Though the number of her children might sometimes decrease through fear, yet her true offspring that have remained, have increased in their zeal, courage, and love to God. Apostates themselves have proved refiners of them that they have deserted: Daniel xi. 35, 'And some of them of understanding shall fall to try them, and to purge and make them white.' The corn is the purer by the separation of the chaff; thus hath she grown purer by flames, and sounder by batteries.

4. When she has seemed to be forlorn and dead, God has restored her. When Israel was at the lowest, a decree issued out in Egypt to destroy her males and root out her seed, deliverance began to dawn; and when a knife was at her throat at the Red Sea, and scarce a valiant believer found among a multitude of despairers, God turned the back of the knife to his Israel, and the edge to the throat of the enemies. When the whole church as well as the whole world seemed to be at its last gasp, God preserved a Noah as a spark to kindle a new world and a new church by. When Jerusalem was sacked, the city destroyed, the people dispersed into several parts of the Babylonish empire, without any human probability of ever being gathered again into one body, yet she was preserved, restored, recollected, brought out of the sepulchre, resettled in her ancient soil, and recovered her beauty; which can be said of no other society in the world but this, whose deliverance and restoration hung not upon the will and policy of man, but upon the word of God, who had limited their captivity to seventy years, and promised a restoration. The blessing of God to Abraham and Sarah is set out as a ground of faith and comfort for the church's restoration and increase: Isa. li. 1–3, he will 'comfort Sion, and comfort all her waste places; and make her wilderness like Eden, and her desert like the garden of God, that joy and gladness may be found therein,' as well as he did enliven the dead body of Abraham and the barren womb of Sarah. When the church hath been so low that men have despaired of seeing any more of her than her ashes, God hath produced a new remnant, he hath reserved a tenth to return, Isa. vi. 13; and from the hidden womb of the earth brought forth a new succession by the vigorous influence of the Sun of righteousness. And after the last attempt and success of the antichristian state, when they are jolly and merry at the church's funeral, Rev. xi. 10, they shall soon be amazed at her resurrection, ver. 11; as much as the high priests were at the resurrection of Christ, for the church can no more lie in the grave than her Head, the mystical body no more than the natural. His resurrection was an earnest of this, and this the accomplishment of that. Little difference in the time of their grave state; three days the natural body lay, three days and an half only the mystical shall lie before a full revival.

5. God never wanted instruments for his church in the due season. If Abel be butchered by Cain, God will raise up Seth in his place to bring men to a public form of worship, Gen. iv. 26. If Nebuchadnezzar be the axe to hew down Jerusalem, Cyrus shall be the instrument to build her up; when his time is come, he will not want an Ezra and Nehemiah to rear her walls,

nor be wanting to them to inspire them with courage and assist their labour, in spite of the adversaries that would give checkmate to the work. If Stephen be stoned by the Jews, he will call out Paul, an abetter of that murder, to be a preacher of the gospel, and he that was all fire against it shall become as great a flame for the propagation of it: one phœnix shall arise out of the ashes of another. When Arianism like a deluge overflowed the world, the church wanted not an Athanasius to stand in the gap and be a champion for the truth of the deity of Christ. When enemies rise up against the church from all quarters to afflict it, God raised others from all quarters to defend it, Zech. i. 19, 20. Yea, those that have been the instruments to support the antichristian state against her, by giving their power and strength to the beast, shall turn their arms against that which they supported, to 'make her desolate, eat her flesh, and burn her with fire,' Rev. xvii. 12, 13, 16. It is the same Christ that is king in his church, and the Spirit is not dispossessed of his office to furnish men with gifts for the defence and increase of it; he is still a spirit of government in magistrates, and the spirit of fire in ministers, for the church's interest. Now, since the church hath maintained its standing longer than any other empire, and that in the the midst of its enemies, and hath been both increased and refined by the violences used against her, since she hath been so often restored and never wanted instruments for the rearing and protecting her, who can doubt whether the Highest hath not, and whether the Highest will not, establish her and cover her with his mighty wings?

III. The third thing, Why it must needs be so.

1. It is necessary for the honour of God. Those societies may moulder away, and those religions grow feeble, which have drawn their birth from the wisdom of man and been settled from the force of man, but a divine work must needs have a divine establishment. It is so,

(1.) If you regard it as his main design in the creation of the world. Can we think God made the world for the world's sake, that he pitched tabernacles here for a few creatures that could spell from all his works but a few and little letters of his name? Could the bare creation shew to man so much as his back parts? The most glorious perfections of his nature could never be visible in a handful of creatures, though never so glorious, no, nor in multitudes of worlds of a more beautiful aspect, without the discovery of the gospel and the settling a gospel church. How should we have known his patience, been instructed in his mercy, have had any sense of his grace, or understood the depths of his wisdom, or heard the voice of the bowels of his love, so as they are linked together in his nature? If God created the world for his glory, he created it for his highest glory: a bare creation, without a redeemed company of creatures, could never have given us a prospect of the great glory of his nature, nor have answered the end of God, which was the manifestation of his perfections. His wisdom broke out in the frame of all creatures, giving them life and motion; but his eye, when he made the world, was upon the manifestation of a greater wisdom which then lay hid in his bosom, and was not to be discovered but in the publishing the gospel, Eph. iii. 9, 10. The wisdom that broke out in the creation was but a scaffold whereon in time his wisdom in the glory of a church peculiar to himself should appear. All things were created for Christ as well as by him, for him and his glory as mediator and as head of the church, and therefore for the glory of his body. And his end in sending Christ was to 'gather all things together in him,' those things which are in heaven as well as those which are on earth, Eph. i. 10; and in order to that end he works all things: ver. 11, 'He works all things according to the counsel of his own will.' This counsel and will of appointing Christ was the spring and rule of all his works, and therefore of creation, as well as the rest succeeding it. He that would upon occasion give the richest parts of the world for the ransom of Sion, as Egypt, Ethiopia, Seba, Isa. xxiii. 43, may well be thought to create those and other nations to lay a foundation for her. We know that soon after the creation the rest of God was disturbed by the entrance of sin, which could not come unexpected, unforeseen, and unpermitted. There had not then been any ground of rejoicing in the habitable parts of the earth, Prov. viii. 31, if he had not designed something else. But he provided in his counsel another rest, and in order to that suffered this first in the bare creation to be spoiled: Sion he chose, and Sion he desired as his rest for ever, wherein he would dwell, Ps. cxxxii. 13, 14. The end of God in creation was not certainly only to make a sun or stars, an earth bedecked with plants, and man, a rational creature, only to contemplate these works, but to render him the acknowledgments of his power and wisdom.* As a limner lays his chief design in the midst of the cloth, and fills the void places with many other fancies to beautify and set off his work, but those were not in his first intention, but his main design was the draught in the middle, surrounded with the rest. Now, when man by sin had made himself uncapable of performing the work he had to do, God orders things so as to have a rest, to have a people to acknowledge him. Hence, perhaps, the forming of such a people is called by the term of a new creation, not only as it is an act of creative power, but as it was the chief design of the exerting his power in the creation of the world. 'His foundation is in the holy mountain,' Ps. lxxxv. 1; and shall the chief of his counsel be the conquest and triumph of Satan? Shall he, at the closing up of the world, be defeated of his main contrivance? Surely if there were a greater opposition to Sion than ever there was, he would exert a greater strength than ever he did not to be crossed in his principal aim.

(2.) As he hath been the author and builder of Sion. Great kings have a particular care of the cities they have founded, for the honour and preservation of their name, and a testimony of their magnificence; with what choice privileges do they use to endow them! With what strong garrisons do they use to secure them in time of danger! And shall not the great God perpetuate that which he hath formed for his glory, to which he hath given a peculiar denomination of the City of God?† Nebuchadnezzar cannot be more industrious to enrich Babylon, which he had built by the might of his power, than God will be to perpetuate Sion, which he hath built for the honour of his majesty. God was the architect of this city, and gave the model. Christ was the builder of this city, and raised the structure: Heb. iii. 3, 4, He, *i. e.* Christ, built the house, 'and he that built all things is God.' God laid the platform of all things, much more of that which is dearer to him than all things. He laid the foundation of it by his Son; whereas the Jewish synagogue was formed by the ministry of Moses. He hath poured upon her greater treasures of knowledge, a fuller measure of the Spirit than he did before, that the knowledge of precedent ages was nothing in comparison of that which he lighted on the gospel Sion, in the fulness of time. The Spirit hath formed the church in the womb of the world, as he formed Christ in the womb of the virgin. The natural and the mystical body of the Son of God have the same author and original; not a stone fitted to be a part in composing this temple, but was culled out and polished by

* Charron. iii. Verit. lib. iii. cap i. p. 16.

† Called by that title four times in the 48th Psalm, 1, 2, 8, 14, whence the psalmist concludes the establishment of her.

God, 1 Peter iii. 5. He that laid the corner stone, fixeth the 'lively stones' to become a 'spiritual house.' *Are built;* not built themselves; it is his house, because he built it, as well as his house, because he dwells in it, and rules it as the master of the family. Though the whole fabric of nature is God's work, yet the church is peculiarly, and by way of distinction, called his work: Hab. iii. 2, 'revive thy work;' and every stone in it is called his jewel: Mal. iii. 17, 'my jewels;' made so by his power, in working a real change; for by nature they were as unfit as the common pebbles of the earth. He is therefore peculiarly called the Creator of Israel, Isa. xliii. 15. As he hath maintained a creation revolted from him, notwithstanding all the provoking sins of men, so he will maintain a creation dear to him, notwithstanding all the bloody contrivances of men. Sion's inheritance is secured, because it is 'a branch of God's planting,' Isa. lx. 21. Things are preserved by the same means whereby they are first settled. Is it not, then, for the honour of God, to be the establisher of that, by the power of his might, whereof he hath been the founder by the strength of his arm. He made not use of the riches, power, and wisdom of the world, to lay the foundation of Sion; but as the Jews, he wrought, as it were, with a trowel in one hand, and a sword in the other, and erected her walls against the force and policy of hell and earth; and as he founded it without worldly advantages, and against the stream of corrupt nature, he knows how to preserve it, when the wit and strength of the world are contrary to it. It would be too low a conceit of the wisdom and power of God, to imagine that he should undertake so great a work, to be baffled in the end he designed to himself. His wisdom is as much concerned in honour to work wonders for the preservation of Sion, as his power was employed at first miraculously to lay the first corner stone of her.

(3.) As he hath been the preserver and enlarger of her to this day. Men think themselves concerned in honour to perfect those which they call their creatures, and often regard one act of kindness as an engagement upon them to successive acts of the like nature. It is not for the honour of any man to stand by a friend a long time, and to enjoy the glory of assisting him, and desert him at the last pinch. God set up the church after the fall in Adam's family, rather than create a new world to create a new church; he raised up Seth to propagate it, when Abel was taken off by the bloody hands of his brother; he preserved it in Noah's family in the midst of a corrupted and degenerate world, and settled it upon the foundation of the gospel in both. Upon the first promise in the family of Adam, Gen. iii. 15; upon the sweet-smelling sacrifice offered by Noah, Gen. viii. 20–22; not upon the symbol or type, the blood of the beasts, but upon the thing signified by it; and the preservation of the world promised after that sacrifice, was chiefly in order to the preservation of a church in it, as the creation of the world was in order to the erecting it; and therefore the rainbow, settled then as a sign of the covenant for the world's preservation from a flood of waters, is made the sign of the everlasting covenant of peace both in Ezekiel, chap. i. 28, and in the Revelation, chap. iv. 3, as a sign he would preserve his church from the multitude of waters, from the rage of the people, signified by waters in the prophetic part of Scripture, and from the floods that the devil should cast out against her. And thence it is that this covenant of her establishment is compared with that covenant God swore to Noah, and the faith of the church strengthened by reflection upon that, Isa. liv. 9. After this settling it in Noah, he fixed it in Abraham, and cleared up the promise of the Messiah with a greater evidence than to the ages before. He multiplied it in the fleshly Israel, and enlarged the bounds of it to a whole nation. After that, he takes away the partition wall, and spreads her confines to the possession of the Gentiles, that 'the sons of Japhet might dwell in the tents of Shem,' according to his promise, Gen. ix. 27; out of the forlorn Gentiles, as stupid as stocks and stones, he raiseth up children, a great posterity, to Abraham. Those that he employed in the erecting Sion, and establishing the law that went out from her in the rubbish of the Gentiles, he struck off from all human assistances, all strength and power in themselves, when he commanded them not to depart from Jerusalem, but to wait there for a 'power from on high,' before they ventured to be witnesses to him, and publish his name not only in the uttermost parts of the earth, but in Jerusalem, the city where they were to abide, or in any part of Judea, Acts i. 4–8. They were not to speak a word of him in their own strength, or in any strength less than a power from heaven, which was to be given them by the sending the Spirit; and this he calls 'the promise of the Father,' as signifying his purpose to enlarge his church, as well as build it at the first, by himself and his own power. It is this, the promise of the Father, our Saviour there pitches their faith upon, and it is this our faith should be established in, in all conditions of the church.

Now hath God thus reared up a church out of the ashes of man's original apostasy, settled it among the murmuring and ungrateful Israelites that industriously longed for the garlic and onions of Egypt, as weary of the greatness of his mercy to them, and propagated it to the idolatrous Gentiles, filled with all unrighteousness, as bad as bad could be, as is described Rom. i. 29–31? To what purpose was the enlarging the church's patent, if he did intend the footsteps of her should ever be rooted out of the world? He picked out the weakest, poorest persons as the matter of it, that he might shew his own honour in preserving it; he hath yet supported her all the while she hath carried the cross of her Lord; he hath sent his Spirit to frame a succession of new materials for her. How fruitless would all this be, if he should let hell waste the temple erected for heaven? What! did he gather and enlarge the church only to make it a richer conquest, and a fatter morsel for the devil? How vain would his former kindness appear, if he should let it utterly sink as long as the world endures! It cannot be imagined, with any semblance of reason, that God hath taken all this care about the nursing and growth of the church from small beginnings, to let his darling be a prey to the mouth of lions, and be of no other use than to fatten his enemies.

(4.) In regard of the cost and pains he hath been at about Sion. Did the creation of the world ever cost him so much? Was there one tear, one groan, one sigh, much less the blood of the Son of God, expended in laying the foundation of it? When the matter of it was without form and void, the beauty of it was not wrought with a washing with blood. When God established the clouds above, and strengthened the foundations of the deep; when he gave the sea his decree, and appointed the foundations of the earth, the Son of God was by him, rejoicing in the habitable parts of the earth, and his delights were among the sons of men, Prov. viii. 28, 29, 31. Not bleeding and dying. But this he must do; he must take human nature, be bruised in his heel by the serpent, and be a sacrifice himself, make an atonement for sin, before a stone for the building of spiritual Sion could be framed and laid.

What pains have been taken also in the effecting it! The birth of the church was a work of greater power than the fabric of the world. A few words went to the rearing of that. In the revolution of six days, it was set upon its feet; but many a year was God in travail before Sion was brought forth. There was an enemy as potent as hell to deal with in setting it in Adam's family after man's apostasy; the corrupt nature, that had then got the possession of the world, to contest with. The world must be drowned, to bring it to a second nativity and establishment in Noah. The forming the church of the Jews was not without some pangs of nature; what signs and wonders, and great terrors, were wrought in its bringing forth out of Egypt, and striking off the chains of her captivity! Deut. iv. 34. What fire, blackness, darkness, tempest, that made a convulsion in the souls of those that were to be her materials! Heb. xii. 18, 19. And the bringing forth the Gentile church, and enlarging the cords and stakes of Sion, was preceded by the darkening the sun, the trembling of the earth, the opening of the graves, the suffering of that which was dearest to God himself.

No power was ever employed so signally in the affairs of any worldly concern as in the settlement of Sion. The devouring waves of the Red Sea have been made her bulwarks, and the sand, the grave of her enemies, hath been a path for her passage. The sun hath forgotten his natural race, to gaze upon her victories, Josh. x. 13. Angels have been commissioned to be her champions, and fight her battles, 2 Kings xix. 35. The whole host of heaven have been arrayed to fight for Sion on earth. The merciless nature of the fire hath been curbed, to preserve her children, when she seemed to be reduced to a small number; and the mouths of hunger-starved lions have been bridled for the same purpose, Dan. vi. 22. The proudest enemies to her have been vanquished by frogs and lice; and tyrants, that would lay their hands upon her, have been made, to their disgrace, a living banquet for worms, the vilest creatures, Acts xii. 23.

And indeed, after the malice of the devil had usurped God's right in the creation, and had drawn the chiefest of his sublunary creatures into an apostasy with himself, no less than an infinite power could be engaged against the greatest of created powers, if God would not forego his own honour, in suffering himself to be deprived of the fruit of his works. No less than infinite power could erect a church in the world. That God might have the fruit of his creation, he ordered this power to appear, struck down the gates of hell, sent his Son to rescue his honour, and his Spirit to polish stones for his temple. Every one that is fitted for this building, had almightiness at work with him before he was formed, Eph. i. 19, 20. Every stone was hewed by the Spirit, and the image of God was imprinted by a divine efficacy. Shall the fruit of so much power, and the mark of his own image, want an establishment? God would seem to be careless of the treasures of his own nature, wherewith he hath endowed her. Shall all this cost and pains be to no purpose? Were the gates of hell taken down to be set up again more strongly? and the chargeable counsels of God to be puffed away by the breath of Satan? Doth it consist with his wisdom to let Sion fall out of his hands into the power of her old oppressor? Men are more desirous to preserve the estate they have gotten by sweat, than that which is left them by inheritance, and are most careful in settling that which hath cost them more treasure and more labour. Jacob sets a value upon the portion he got with his sword and bow, Gen. xlviii. 22; no less will God upon that Sion he hath wrested out of the world by the might of his arm.

(5.) In regard of faithfulness, his veracity is engaged.

[1.] In regard of faithfulness to Christ the head. The Spirit was promised to Christ: Acts ii. 33, 'Having received the promise of the Holy Ghost;' *i.e.* the Holy Ghost promised to him by the Father. He received that which was promised; his receiving it from God implied the Spirit's being promised to him by God. To what end was this Spirit given him, and sent by him? 'To convince the world of righteousness,' John xvi. 10, an effect necessary to the building of Sion. For this end he received it, for this end therefore it was promised to him. The promise would be vain, the performance of the promise, in the mission of the Holy Ghost, would be to no purpose, if the end for which he was promised, and for which he was sent, were not performed; if there should not be a perpetual number convinced of, and embracing that righteousness of Christ, which hath been manifested by his going to the Father.

God also promised him a great posterity after his 'making his soul an offering for sin,' Isa. liii. 10, 11. A seed that he should see, therefore stable and perpetual, because always visible to him. A posterity was to follow his sacrifice, his cross was to give them being, and his blood was to give them life. God pawned his word upon the condition of his death; the condition was performed to the full satisfaction of God, his truth therefore hath no evasion, no plea to deny the performance of the promise in raising up a multitude of believers in the world, and such a multitude as shall always be seen with pleasure by him, as good and sound children, and the travail of the mother's womb, are by the parents. The truth of God is obliged by Christ's exact performance of the condition, as well as by the particular respect he hath to the glory of it; it was for the church Christ 'gave himself,' Eph. v. 25. It is necessary therefore that God should preserve and establish a church for him to the end of the world; that Christ might not, by any default of his Father, lose the end and design of his death, there shall be a generation of believers, a little seed lying in the midst of all the chaff, so God promised: Ps. lxxii. 17, 'His name shall be continued, ינין, as long as the world.' His name shall be propagated in a perpetual birth of children, it shall be found while the sun in the heaven keeps its station.

[2.] In regard of faithfulness to the church itself. How doth the word sparkle with promises to Sion in all her concerns! He hath promised an indissolvable marriage, the fixing a knot that shall never be untied: Hosea ii. 19, 'I will betroth thee unto me for ever, and that in judgment, righteousness, loving-kindness, mercy, faithfulness.' A marriage that shall never end in widowhood, so that judgment, righteousness, loving-kindness, mercy, faithfulness must first fail, before the church meet with an entire dissolution; *i.e.* God and the glorious perfections of his nature shall fail, before the church be forsaken and left to her enemies. She is no less assured of continual supplies and nourishment, and that by no meaner a hand than that of God himself: Isa. xxvii. 3, 'I the Lord do keep it, I will water it every moment, I will keep it night and day.' (Nor a meaner dew than himself, Hosea xiv. 5.) Also without the failing her a minute; he would water her with doctrine to preserve her verdure and increase her growth. He would be her guardian night and day, in the darkness of adversity, in the sunshine of prosperity, so that Satan should not outwit, nor the craft and subtilty of heretics waste her; for it refers to ver. 1, wherein God promiseth her to punish 'the piercing serpent, the crooked serpent,' that by various windings and turnings insinuates himself to the destruction of men. And he adds, ver. 4, 'Fury is not in me;' he lays by his anger against her, as considered in apostate nature; the fury of hell shall not prevail where the anger of God is pacified, but her enemies shall be as briers and thorns before him. He hath a consuming fury for her enemies, though he hath none for his vineyard. Protection is in no less measure promised, and that not a temporary one, nor a bare defence, but with the ruin of her enemies, and treading them down as straw is trodden down for the dunghill: Isa. xxv. 10, 'In this mountain shall the hand of the Lord rest.' By *hand* is meant his power, and by *rest* is meant the perpetual motion of it for her, and that against the most furious, malicious, and powerful of her enemies: Mat. xvi. 18, 'Against the gates of hell,' against the wisdom of hell, gates being the seat of council; against the censures and sentences of hell, gates being the place of judicature; against the arms of hell, gates being the place of strength and guards. When Christ secures against hell, he secures against all that receive their commission from hell; neither hell itself, nor the instruments edged and envenomed by hell, shall prevail against her; she is secured for her assemblies in one part or other, when they gather together to hear the law, and to sacrifice: 'And I that am the Lord thy God, from the land of Egypt, will yet make thee to dwell in tabernacles, as in the days of solemn feasts,' Hosea xii. 9; it is a promise to the church; it was never yet, nor appears like to be performed to the ten tribes as a nation, but to their posterity, as swallowed up in, and embodied with, the Gentiles. The conquest of her enemies is secured to her, Ps. cx. 1. The promise is made to Christ of making 'his enemies his footstool;' but made to him as David's Lord, and consequently as the Lord of his people, as King in Sion, and therefore made to the whole body of his loyal subjects. And all those things are of little comfort without duration and stability, which is also secured to her: Hosea vi. 3, 'His going forth,' *i.e.* the going forth of God in the church, 'is prepared as the morning,' נכון, stable; his appearance for her, and in her, is as certain as the dawning of the morning light at the appointed hour. All the clouds which threaten a perpetual night cannot hinder it; all the workers of darkness cannot prevent it; the morning will dawn whether they will or no. Her duration is compared to the most durable things, to that of the cedar, the most lasting of all plants. Three times it is compared to Lebanon in the promise, Hosea xiv. 5–7. The cedar never rots, worms eat it not. It is not only free from putrefaction itself, but the juice of it preserves other things. Numa's books,* though of paper, yet dipped in the juice of cedar, remained without corruption in the ground 500 years. How shall that God, who always remembers everything, yea, the meanest of his creatures, forget his own variety of expressions and multiplied promises concerning his Sion?

(6.) In regard it is the seat of his glory. It is 'the branch of his planting, the work of his hands, that he might be glorified,' Isa. lx. 21. His glory would have a brush, if Sion should sink to ruin. He sows her for himself, Hos. ii. 23; speaking of the church in the time of the gospel, not to the devil, to sin, to the world, but to his own glory. As husbandmen sow their fields for their own use, to reap from them a fruitful crop; and therefore till the harvest be in, they take care to make up the breaches, and preserve them from the incursions of beasts. Though God hath an objective glory from all creatures, yet he hath an active glory only from the church. It is Israel, the house of Aaron, and those that fear the Lord, that the psalmist calls upon to render God the praise of the eternity of his mercy, Ps. cxviii. 2–4. He forbids the profane and disobedient world to take his covenant in their mouth, Ps. l. 16. None do, none can truly honour and acknowledge him but the church; therefore the apostle, in his doxology, appropriates the glory that is to be given to God as the object, to the church as the subject: Eph. iii. 21, 'Unto him be glory in the church by Jesus Christ throughout all ages, world without end.' So solemn a wish from so great an apostle, that it *should* be, amounts to a certainty that it *will* be. There cannot be a glory to God in the church throughout all ages, without the continuance of the church in all ages. God will have a revenue of glory paid him during the continuance of

* Sanct. in loc.

the world; there shall therefore be a standing church during the duration of the world; while he therefore expects a glory from the midst of his people, he will be a wall of fire round about them, and keep Sion, one where or other, in a posture to glorify him. What is the apostle's motive to this glory? It is not a remote power, such as can act, but will not; but a power operative in the church, in doing those things for her which she could never ask, nor think for herself: ver. 20, 'Now to him that is able to do exceeding abundantly above all that we ask or think, according to the power that works in us.' God hath a greater glory from the church than he can have from the world; he therefore gives her more signal experiments of his power, wisdom, and love, than to the rest of the world. He had a glory from angels, but only as Creator, not as Redeemer, till they were acquainted with his design, and were speculators of his actions in gathering a church in the world. The church therefore was the original of the new glory and praise the angels presented to God: 'Glory in the church by Christ.' Musculus thinks that is added to distinguish it from the Jewish church, which was settled by the ministry of Moses; as much as to say, God had not so much glory by the tabernacles of Jacob, as he hath by the church as settled by Christ. Or, *by Christ* notes the manner of the presenting our praise, and the ground of the acceptance of our praise. God accepts no glory but what is offered to him by the hand of Christ; and Christ presents no glory but what is paid him by the church. It is the church, then, and the gospel-church, that preserves the glory of God in the world. If the church therefore ceaseth, the glory of God in the world ceaseth. But since God hath created all for his own glory, separated a church out of the world for his glory, appointed his Son the head of it, that he might be glorified, his church therefore is as dear to him as his glory, and dear to him in order to his glory; in establishing it, therefore, he establishes his own honour and name. It shall therefore remain in this world to glorify him, afterwards in another to glorify him, and be glorified by him.

(7.) In regard that it is the object of his peculiar affection. Establishment of a beloved object is inseparable from a real affection. By this he secures the spiritual Sion, or gospel-church, both from being forsaken by him, or made desolate by her enemies, because she was *Hephzibah*, Isa. lxii. 4, *my delight*, or, *my will is in her*, as if he had no will to anything but what concerned her and her safety. As men engrave upon their rings the image of those friends that are dearest to them, and as the Jews in their captivity engraved the effigies of their city upon their rings, to keep her in perpetual remembrance, so doth God engrave Sion 'upon the palms of his hands,' Isa. xlix. 16, to which the Holy Ghost seems to allude. He so loves his Israel, that he who will be commanded by none, stoops to be commanded by them in things concerning his sons, Isa. xlv. 10. Not only ask of me what you want, but command me in the things that are to come; the pleas of my promises of things to come, and your desires to bring them forth as the work of my hand, shall be as powerful a motive to me as a command from a superior is to an obedient inferior; for it is to things to come, such things that God hath predicted, that he limits their asking, which he calls also here a commanding of him. There was a real love in the first choice; there is an intenseness of love in the first transaction: Jer. xxxi. 3, 'I have loved thee with an everlasting love; therefore with loving-kindness have I drawn thee.' His love, which had a being from eternity, is expressed by words of more tenderness, when he comes to frame her; loving-kindness, as if his affection seemed to be increased, when he came to the execution of his counsel. According to the vigour of his immutable love will be the strength of her immutable establishment. This promise is made, not to the church in general, but to all the families of the spiritual Israel, ver. 1. Men are concerned in honour for that upon which they have placed their affection. Shall there, then, be decays in the kindness of that God, whose glory it is to be immutable? Is it possible this fountain should be frozen in his breast? Was there not a love of good will to Sion to frame her, to pick out their materials when they lay like swine in the confused mass and dirty mire of a corrupt world? Is there not also a love of delight, since he hath refined and beautified her, by imparting to her of his own comeliness, Ezek. xvi. 14. Is it likely this affection should sink into carelessness? and the fruit of so much love be dashed in pieces? Can such tenderness be so unconcerned, as to let the apple of his eye be plucked out? to be a lazy spectator of the pillage of his jewels by the powers of hell? to have the centre of his delight tossed about at the pleasure of men and devils? Shall a mother be careless of her suckling child? How then can that God, whose tenderness to the church cannot be equalled by the bowels of the most compassionate mother to her infants? Surely God is concerned in honour to maintain against a feeble devil, and a decrepid world, that which is the object of his almighty affection.

(8.) In regard of the natural weakness of the church. No generous prince but will think himself bound in honour to support the weaker subject; no tender parent but will acknowledge himself obliged in affection to take a greater care of the weaker than the stronger child. The gardener adds props to the feeblest plants, that are most exposed to the fury of the storms, and have least strength to withstand them. The powers of the world have always been the church's enemies; the wise have set their reason, and the mighty their arms against her; the devil, the god of this world, is so far from being her friend, that Sion hath been the only object of his spite. He contrives only floods to drown her, or mines to demolish her. Her own friends are often so darkened or divided, that they cannot sometimes for ignorance, and will not other times for peevishness, hit upon, and use the right means for her preservation. It is an honourable thing, then, for that God who entitles himself 'the Father of the fatherless,' to shew his own power and grace in her establishment. The fatherless condition of the church is an argument she hath sometimes used to procure the assistance she wanted: Hosea xiv. 3, 'With thee the fatherless finds mercy.' And the weakness of Jacob, urged by the prophet, excited repentance in God, and averted two judgments which were threatened against that people, Amos vii. 2, 3, 5, 6. It is no mean motive to him to help the helpless, this opportunity he delights to take; when there was no man to help, no intercessor to plead, then 'his own arm brought salvation.' When he saw no defenders, but all ravishers, no physicians, but all wonders, then should the Spirit of the Lord lift up a standard, Isa. lix. 16, 19.

To conclude; if Sion, the gospel church, were not of as long a duration as the standing of the world, God would lose the honour of his creation, after the devil, by sin, had made the creatures unuseful for those ends to which God had appointed them by his first institution. The wisdom of God had been blurred, the serpent would have triumphed, the kingdom of God had been dissolved, the enemy would have enjoyed a remediless tyranny, had not God put his hand to the work, and erected a new kingdom to himself out of the ruins of the fall. And since God was pleased to take this course, rather than create a new world, and hath laid the foundation of a new kingdom by drawing some out of that common rebellion the human nature was fallen into, and that he might do it with honour to himself, hath sent his Son upon that errand, by his blood to bring back man to God, and his Spirit to make men fit for a communion with him, and hath backed his affection to the church with so much cost and pains for her welfare. If, after all this, God should desert his church, the dishonour of God's wisdom, the loss of the fruit of all his cost and pains, the weakness of his affection, or of his power to perform his promise, and the ruin of his glory intended by those methods, would be the issue, which would be attended with the triumph of his revolted creature and greatest enemy. This would be, if God should cease picking out some men for his praise, and keeping up his name and royalty in the earth.

2. It is for the exercise of the offices of Christ that Sion should be established. He is prophet, priest, and king, which are all titles of relation. Prophet implies some to be instructed, a priest some to offer for, and a king some to be ruled; put one relation, and you must necessarily put the other. If there were no church preserved in the world, he would be a nominal prophet without any disciples, a king without subjects, and a priest without suppliants to be atoned by him upon earth. Now Christ is the 'wonderful Counsellor, the everlasting Father,' and 'the government is laid upon his shoulders.' To what end? 'To order and establish the kingdom of God,' Isa. ix. 6, 7. All the strength and vigour he had, as it was from God, so it was intended for God: Ps. lxxx. 17, 'Thou madest the Son of man strong for thyself.' And the reason is, because, though God hath given up the administration of things to Christ, yet he hath not divested himself of his right, nor can; for God is the chief Lord, and the relation of creatures not ceasing, the relation of Lord and Creator cannot cease. And therefore, since the right of God continues, the grant of the uttermost ends of the earth to be the inheritance and possession of Christ, includes not only a gift, but an office, to preserve, protect, establish, and improve his possession for those ends for which he had the grant, and to prevent all that may impair it. As he had a right and strength, by the order of God, to rear it, so he hath an office and power to establish it, as well as to erect it; and Christ is 'the same' in all his offices, 'yesterday, to-day, and for ever,' Heb. xiii. 8; the same in credit with God, in faithfulness to his office, the virtue of his blood, the force of his arm, and compassions to bleeding Sion.

(1.) It is his part, as a prophet, to establish it in doctrine. It is his part externally to raise his truth when it lies gasping in the rubbish of error, and refine his worship when it is daubed with superstition and idolatry. Internally to clear the understanding to know his truth, quicken the will to embrace it, rivet the word in the conscience, and inflame the affections to love and delight in it. Certainly the promise of the abiding of his Spirit implies the efficacy of his operation while he abides. He is to provide against the subtilty and rapine of foxlike heretics, that they spoil not the tender vine, Cant. ii. 15; and to furnish the church with gifts for the preserving and increasing her. The perpetual exercise of this prophetical office he promised them, when he gave the apostles a charter for his presence 'to the end of the world,' Mat. xxviii. 20; which was in relation to their ministry and their office of teaching. Since he promised his presence with his ministry to the end of the world, he will have a church to the end of the world, to enjoy the benefit of that promise to be taught by them. It consisted not with the wisdom or faithfulness of Christ to promise a perpetuity to that, if he knew it were to be cut short before the end of the world. And this himself also assures the church of in all its variety of states: Rev. ii. 1, 'These things saith he that holds the seven stars in his right hand, who walks in the midst of the seven golden candlesticks.' Not only seven stars at one time, or seven golden candlesticks in being together, but in all the successions of the church to the consummation of the world. And as he describes himself by this title when he speaks of the church of Ephesus, which was the first state of the church, not only assuring her of his holding her star, and walking by her candlestick, but all the rest that were to follow, so he doth renew the same expression in part when he speaks of the church of Sardis, which is the rising of the church from the apostasy wherein it had been covered in the Thyatirian state: Rev. iii. 1, 'These things saith he that hath the seven spirits of God, and the seven stars.' The seven spirits of God signifies the gifts for the building and perfecting the church still in the hand of Christ, which should be in a more plentiful way poured out than for some time before, as they were in the first reformation. He is still, therefore, as a prophet, walking in the church in all ages; not only in the first foundation of it by the apostles, but in the reformation of it, after it had been buried in superstition and idolatry. And at the restoration of the church in the world, there shall be 'a pure river of water, as clear as crystal, proceeding from the throne of God and the Lamb,' Rev. xxii. 1, *i. e.* pure doctrine, without any mud and mixtures.

(2.) It is his part as a priest to establish it in the favour of God, and look to the reparations of his temple. The church is his temple. A temple is the proper seat and the proper care of a priest. He is 'a priest still upon his throne,' Zech. vi. 13, and that for ever. As he hath therefore something to offer, so he hath always some for whom he offers. Who are they but his church? His prayer on earth, John xvii., was but a model or draught of his intercession in heaven; one part of it is for preservation of them 'through the truth' of God, John xvii. 17. The keeping up the gospel in the world, in order to a sanctification of some, is the matter of his intercession, which is one part of his priestly office. And we cannot imagine his plea for his church to be weaker on his throne, it being also a throne of grace, than it was for his enemies when he was upon a cross of suffering. The compassions annexed to his priesthood remain still, Heb. iv. 15. If his office be perpetual, the qualifications necessary to that office are as durable as the office itself, as long as there is any object for their exercise. To what purpose are his compassions, if he should not pity her for whom they were designed, and for whose behoof he was furnished with them? He cannot be faithful to God in his office, if he be not merciful and tender to Sion in her distresses. He certainly pities her as he would himself, were it possible he should be in an infirm condition. He must lose his soul before he can lose his pity; and the church must cease to be his body, before she can cease to be the object of his compassions. He hath the same sentiments now that he had when he called to Paul from heaven, Acts ix. 4. It was not then, Why persecutest thou *mine*, but 'Why persecutest thou *me?*' Nor is it so now; as the relation continues the same, so doth the compassion, so do his sentiments, so do his cares. To what purpose doth he as a priest sit upon a throne of grace, if he did not shew grace to his Sion against the cruel designs of her enemies? As God pities us when he remembers our frame, Ps. ciii. 13, 14, so no question doth Christ, when he remembers Sion's oppressions, as a distressed child is the object of the father's pity. Add to this, that since the death of Christ was one part of his priestly performance, and that the virtue of his sacrifice is as eternal as his priesthood; what a disparagement would it be to him, and the virtue of his death, if ever the world, while it stood, should be void of the fruits of it? There can be no moment wherein it is not valid to expiate the sins of some men, and therefore not a moment wherein the world shall be without a Sion, whose sins are expiated by it. Should the standard of Sion be snatched away and torn by the powers of darkness, what would become of the glory, what would become of the virtue of the Redeemer's death? Would God consecrate him so solemnly by an oath to be a priest to so little purpose? How could it be for ever, if the execution of that office should be interrupted by the cessation of a church, as long as the world stands upon its pillars? Would it not be an empty title, if the end of it were not performed? We cannot imagine the falling of Sion, but we must question the merit of his death, the truth of his exaltation, the strength of his intercession, the faithfulness of his office, and the sincerity and candour of his compassions.

(3.) It is his part as a king to establish Sion in being, and govern her. The prophets always testified that 'of his government there should be no end.' If the church should cease for one moment in the world, what subjects would he have to govern here? Can he be a king without a kingdom, or a governor without subjects, to bear a voluntary and sincere witness to his name? If he be king in Sion, he will also have a Sion to own him, and a Sion to rule in; not only a conquest of the serpentine brood and infernal powers was promised, but the total and perpetual victory, Gen. iii. 15. 'The seed of the woman was to bruise the serpent's head.' When the head is bruised, there is no more wisdom to guide, or force to spirit the arm and the other members of the body. It was a promise made not only of Christ to man, but of a complete victory to Christ, that he should outwit the serpent's wisdom, and utterly discomfit the serpent's power. If the conquest were not perfect and perpetual, it could not be called a spoiling of principalities and powers, as it is Col. ii. 15, but an interruption or temporary check, whence they might rescue themselves. He is therefore said to 'still the enemy and the avenger,' Ps. viii. 2,* *i. e.* make them utterly silent, not knowing what firm counsels to take, or what successful orders to give. And it being his end to destroy the works of the devil, the destroying the works must be the root of the being and preservation of the church. Did Christ then rise as a conqueror out of the grave, and sit down as king upon his throne, to let the devil and the world run away with the fruits of his victory? Will he be so injurious to himself as to let his throne be overturned by his enemies? and to let the adversary of Sion repossess himself of that which he hath been so powerfully and successfully stripped of? Christ, being king, cannot be chased out of his kingdom, nor wants power to keep it from being utterly wasted. To be the governor of Sion was as much in his first commission as to be her redeemer, Isa. xlix. 10. He was to feed and guide his flock, which is often in Scripture put for ruling. Christ, as king, will never leave beating up the quarters of hell till he hath utterly routed their force, and made the partizans of it his footstool, and thereby established Sion beyond the fears of any tottering. Therefore, when he speaks of the church of Smyrna, which was to have a sore conflict with the devil, and feel the smart of him for ten days, understanding those ten ancient persecutions of the church, he assumes a new title for her encouragement: Rev. ii. 8, 'These things saith the first and the last, which was dead and is alive.' I was the first that lifted you and embodied you for the war, and I will be the last to bring up the rear; I was first in raising you, and I will be the last in preserving you. Fear not the terror of those persecutions, though they be to blood and death; I was used so; I was dead, but I am now alive, and I live for my church, to behold her battles, to procure her victory, and to crown those that shall fall in the fight against her enemies. Christ, in encouraging

* I make no scruple to understand the whole psalm of Christ, since the apostle hath interpreted part of it of him, Heb. ii.

them to suffer for him, assures them of the security of a church; the devil should not waste the whole, but cast some of them into prison, not all, and that for their refining: ver. 10, 'The devil shall cast some of you into prison, that you may be tried.' Christ lives still, and acts as king for the security of Sion, and preserving a generation to serve him, till the time comes that is promised, Rev. xxii. 3, that 'there shall be no more curse, but the throne of God and of the Lamb shall be in it,' and then 'his servants shall serve him' with a full security from all trouble.

3. The foundation of Sion is sure. It is founded upon Christ, the corner stone. Christ is called the foundation, 1 Cor. iii. 11. The apostles are the foundation, Eph. ii. 20. Christ is the foundation personally, the apostles doctrinally; Christ meritoriously, the apostles ministerially; the apostles in regard of the publication of the doctrine, Christ in regard of the efficacy of the doctrine, whereby the church is established.

(1.) The church is engrafted in Christ, united to him, one with him; the parts of it are reckoned as his seed: Ps. xxii. 30, 'A seed shall serve him; it shall be accounted to the Lord as a generation.' As if they had sprung out of his loins, as men naturally did from Adam's; that as Adam was the foundation of their corruption, so shall Christ be the foundation of their restoration. They shall be looked upon as the children of Christ, and Christ as their Father, and, as father and children, legally counted one.

The church is his own body, Eph. v. 29, 30. In loving and establishing the church, he loves and establisheth himself. Whatsoever is implanted in nature as a perfection, is eminently in God. Now, since he hath twisted with our natures a care of our own bodies, this care must be much more in the nature of Christ, because his church is as nearly united to him as our members to the flesh and the bones; and he hath an higher affection to his mystical than we can have to our natural bodies. Christ will no less secure and perfect his own body, than a man would improve the beauty and strength of his natural body, to preserve it from wounds, from being mangled or scarified, unless it be for the security of the whole. If he did not do it, it would be a hatred of his own flesh, which never any man in his right wits was ever guilty of. The eternity of Christ is made the foundation of the church's establishment: Ps. cii. 27, 28, 'Thou art the Son,* and thy years shall have no end. The children of thy servants shall continue, and their seed shall be established before thee.' There could be no strength in the argument, without union and communion with him. The church is settled upon him as a foundation, and therefore is of as long a duration as the foundation upon which it stands; the conjunction is so strait, that if one fails, the other must, especially since, as Christ is the head, the church is his fulness, Eph. i. 22, 23. Sion cannot be complete but in him, and Christ cannot be complete without her. A foundation is of little use without a superstructure; a building falls not without a discredit to the foundation upon which it stood. Sion's completeness depends upon the strength of Christ, and Christ's mystical completeness depends upon the stability of Sion; he will not leave himself an imperfect and empty head.

(2.) It is founded upon the covenant: upon that which endures for ever, and shall survive the funeral of the whole world. Heaven and earth shall pass away, but the church is founded upon that which shall not pass away, 1 Peter i. 23, 'The word of God,' &c. Not such a word as that whereby he brought forth light in the world, and formed the stars at the creation; a word that engaged him not to the perpetuating of it.† This covenant is more firm than the pillars of heaven, and the foundations of the earth. The stars

* Qu 'same'?—Ed.

† Turretin, Sermons, p. 330.

of heaven shall dissolve, the sun shall be turned into darkness, the elements shall change their order for confusion; but the church, being founded upon an eternal and immutable covenant, shall subsist in the midst of the confusions and flames of the world: Isa. liv. 10, 'The mountains shall depart, and the hills be removed, but my covenant of peace shall not be removed.' It is more established than the world. The apostle clearly intimates it in his commendation of Abraham's faith, when he tells us, 'he looked for a city which hath foundations,' by virtue of the promise of a numerous seed, Heb. xi. 9, 10, as if the world had no foundation in comparison of the church. It is beyond the skill of hell to raze up the foundation, and therefore impossible for it to beat down the superstructure. Adam fell under the strength of the serpent's wit, but he could by no promise lay claim to stability, as the church can by an immutable covenant for her support.

IV. The use. 1. Information.

1. If the church hath a duration and stability, then ordinances and ministry are perpetual. Ministers may be thrust into corners, clapped up in prison, hurried to their graves, but the sepulchres of ministers are not the graves of the ministry. A ministry and a church, ordinances and a church, cannot be separated; they run parallel together to the end of the world; for Sion cannot be supposed without divine officers and divine institutions; the one cannot be established without the other. Christ 'walks in the midst of the seven golden candlesticks,' Rev. ii. 1, in the seven states of the church, to the end of the world.* As there are seven states of the church, so there are seven stars in the hand of Christ for all those states; the ministry have the same support, the same guardian as the church herself. What was in the Ephesian and primitive state, is also in the Sardian state, the state of the church rising from corruption of doctrine and ordinances: Rev. iii. 1, 'These things saith he that hath the seven spirits of God, and the seven stars.' Christ hath still stars to shine, and seven spirits to gift them; *hath* at present, not *had; hath* in the state we are, which seems to be the end of that Sardian state. It is true, the church is in a wilderness condition, and hath been so for above twelve hundred years; but hath she yet seen her funeral? No; she hath a place for her residence, and food for her nourishment, and both provided for her by that God that framed her, by that God that stood by her in the pangs of her travail, and sheltered her man-child from the fury of her enemies: Rev. xii. 6, 'And the woman fled into the wilderness, where she hath a place prepared of God, that they should feed her there a thousand two hundred and threescore days.' They should feed her; she is not starved in the desert, she hath manna to comfort her, her caterer to provide her food, and some to administer the banquet of the word and sacraments to her. For any member of Sion to deny a ministry, and deny ordinances, and therefore to neglect them, is to conclude her dead in a grave, and not living in a desert, utterly famished and not fed. Though there be a smoke in the temple, a cloud and obscurity, the truths and ordinances of God not so clear, so efficacious as they have been, as some understand Rev. xv. 8, or as they shall be, yet there is a temple still. A smoke in the temple supposeth a temple standing, and ordinances in it; the obscurity of a thing nulls not the being of it, nor a cloud upon the sun the stability and motion of it. He that denies a church, a ministry, and divine ordinances in it, must first charge Christ with falsehood, when he promised to be with them to the end of the world: Mat. xxviii. 19, 20, 'Alway, even to the end of the world.' Not to sustain their particular persons to the end of the world, but

* I do not question but that the whole is prophetical; it would not else be called mystery, as it is Rev. i. 20, were it meant of those particular churches.

their doctrine, in a succession of some to teach and baptize by virtue of authority from him; for to that doth the promise and command refer, and not unto the continuance of the apostolical dignity, or of their extrordinary gifts of miracles, but the duration of their standing work till the top-stone were laid with the loud acclamations of grace, grace. The church shall no more want a ministry in the desert, than she wanted a prophet in Babylon.

2. The doctrine of the establishment of every member of Sion is clearly confirmed. He that establisheth Sion counts up every man that was born in her. Every child of Sion is in the same state and under the same promise as Sion herself. The promise of stability to Sion is not to be understood of the firmness of her palaces, but the duration of her inhabitants; as when God is said to build a house, it is not to be understood of the rearing the walls, but increasing the family: Exod. ii. 21, 'God made them houses,' *i. e.* gave them children. Every renewed man, every one truly born in Sion, stands upon the same foundation of the covenant, hath the same charter with Sion herself, and therefore upon a surer ground than any particular society of men in the world: Ps. cxxv. 1, 'They that trust in the Lord shall be as mount Sion, which cannot be removed, but abides for ever.' He is upon a better foundation of security than the church at Ephesus or Smyrna, Pergamos, or Sardis, which have lost their footing, and their places know them no more. A believer enjoys other privileges with Sion; but the patent runs here for his stability in the favour of God, and runs high by removing all fears in the negative, 'cannot be removed,' and confirming all confidence in the affirmative, 'abides for ever.' No name writ upon God's hand, no name presented on Christ's breast, shall be razed out, no fruit of his death shall be lost, no devil shall steal from him any part of his purchase. As he hath blood enough to redeem them, so he hath power enough to preserve them; the same blood that is the cement of Sion, the same hand that built her, the same head that influenceth her, secures every one of her true-born children. They are all in the same posture and upon the same foundation with Sion herself.

3. How great is the folly of Sion's enemies! They judge of her by the weakness of her worldly interest, and not by the almightiness of her guardian. They stand against a God, that, in decreeing the stability of Sion, decreed the ruin of her opposers, and can with as much ease effect it as resolve it. The stone which is the foundation of this kingdom shall break in pieces the image of all worldly glory, the policy of all worldly wisdom, and the force of all worldly power, Dan. ii. 35, 44, 45. It shall make the mountains of the world as a level, and dust underneath it. Chaff may as well stop the wind, and force it to another quarter; stubble may as well quench the fury of the flames, as the enemies of Sion be victorious over the God of Sion. As he hath a 'fire in Sion' to warm her, so he hath a 'furnace in Jerusalem' to consume her enemies, Isa. xxxi. 9; a fire to burn his people's dross, but a furnace to dissolve his enemies' force. Pharaoh is an example to all generations, to warn them not to struggle with those whom God resolves to patronise. How did he further his own destruction by his hardness, and the deliverance of the oppressed by his fury! How often is the violence of her enemies the occasion of the manifestation of God's glory, and the settling Sion's security! Had not Pharaoh been so furious, God had not manifested the glory of his power, nor his Israel enjoyed so miraculous a safety. It is true, the church is weak, but the arm that holds her is the strongest in heaven and earth. Her outward interest is small, but her interest is twisted with that of her Lord. An enemy shall find more mischief from mud walls, under the protection of a valiant arm, than from stone walls under the guard of an infant. How foolish is it for a man to think to break a rock with his

fist for hurting his shins, whereby he bruiseth his hands as well as his legs! How foolish is it for men to beat the bushes about a lion's den, whereby they will be sure to rouse him! God dwells in Sion. From thence he 'roars' to the 'shaking of heaven and earth,' the powers of the world, when he will manifest himself to be 'the hope of his people, and the strength of the children of Israel,' Joel iii. 16.

4. What a ground is here for prayer! This sets an edge upon prayer. No petition can more comfortably, no petition can more confidently, be put up, than for Sion's establishment. Prayers for particular persons, or for ourselves, may want success; but supplications for Sion never miscarry. They have the same foundation for an answer that Sion had for her stability, viz., the promise of God. They are agreeable to that affection which shall never be removed from her. How believingly may we cry out, 'Be it unto Sion according to thy word!' There is no fear of a repulse. Whatsoever God denies, he will not deny that for which he hath so often engaged himself. It may be for the good of the church that so great a person as Paul should lie in chains, and his fetters conduce 'to the furtherance of the gospel,' Philip. i. 12; but it can never be for the interest of Sion, or for the interest of Sion's God, that she should be crushed between the teeth of the lions, and that which he hath redeemed by the blood of his Son, be a prey to the jaws of the devil. God hath entitled Sion by the name of 'a city not forsaken,' Isa. lxii. 12. And as we have his promise for her settlement, so we have his command for our earnestness: ver. 7, 'And give him no rest, till he doth establish Jerusalem a praise in the whole earth.' And he prescribes us to back that by our prayers, which he had promised: ver. 1, 'For Jerusalem's sake, I will not rest, till the righteousness thereof go forth as brightness.' Our desires in this case are suited to his resolves, and run in the same line with his immutable decree; he will have no rest in himself, nor he would have no rest from us, till this be accomplished. We cannot call upon God with a greater confidence for anything than for that church that shall outlive the funeral of the world, and survive the frame of nature that shall lie in ashes.

5. What a strong ground is here for trust! Look not so much upon the condition of Sion's walls as upon her foundation; not upon her present posture, as upon her promise-charter; not upon her as a weak vine, but under the hand of the Highest as the vine-dresser. Look not upon the feebleness of the flock, but upon the care of the shepherd; nor upon the fierceness of the lions, but upon the strength and affection of her guardian.

(1.) Let not our faith rest upon appearances. Flesh will then make a wrong judgment of God. Providences are various, and should our faith be guided only by them, it would have a liveliness one moment, and faint the next. As the promise is the stability of the church, so it is only the stability of our faith. The authority of the word is the life of our faith, and not the sense of any particular providence in the world. A faith built upon protecting providences is a sensitive faith; a faith built upon the promise is a spiritual faith.

(2.) Yet the experiences God hath given us hitherto of the continuance of the church may be called in to bear witness to the truth of the promise. He hath before conducted his Israel into Canaan, when Pharaoh meditated their utter ruin, or their continuance under his chains. He fed them with manna, and watered them with a rock in a desert, that afforded no earthly assistance. The preserving the vine could never be ascribed to the vine itself, in which there is no strength, nor to the foxes, in whom there is no pity; but to the keeper of the vineyard. We have reason, therefore, to trust God, but not at all to trust man. Is it from man or from God that the church hath subsisted so long in the world, a little flock in the midst of many wolves, among enemies more numerous than her friends? What a small number hath the church had in any age to mate the multitude of her enemies, what wisdom to countermine their policy, and what power to repel their force? The church is not weaker now than it hath been. The sons of Sion were always sheep. Sheep have not the strength of lions to resist, nor the swiftness of eagles to fly away from danger. The danger cannot be greater than it hath been. There were always dragons that spat out their venom, and lions that opened their mouths against her. The devil never wanted diligence, nor the world enmity, to overturn her. Could she for one moment have subsisted in the midst of so many furies, had not God been her shield and glory? Call to mind how often God hath healed her diseases and bound up her wounds. Let us rest in that promise, which hath so often been made good by his power, which he hath in many ages displayed upon as great occasions of danger as Sion can be in. Let us live believingly under his wings, and fear not our own weakness or our enemies' strength.

(3.) We have greater ground of confidence than the church of Israel had. In the day of Israel's trouble by Shalmanezer, the prophet comforts the church in her anguish by the consideration of the Messiah, who was to assume the government, though many years after, Isa. viii. 22, ix. 1, 6. Shall a promise, that was to stay so many ages for performance, be a ground of trust and confidence to a tottering church then? And shall not the staggering church have more ground to rest, since the Messiah is made the head of the corner, and hath the keys of hell and death delivered to him? What a base thing is distrust, then, against so many assurances of stability, and the experience of a multitude of ages. Grasp the promise, plead it earnestly, shew God his written word which he hath sent from heaven; he never yet disowned it, nor ever will. Methinks the voice, God is able to deliver Sion, sounds too much of distrust. If we know no more than God's power, we know not so much as the devil doth; he knows his power, and he knows his promise. Let us therefore first eye the promise, which God loves, and the devil fears, and then call in his power to back his word.

(4.) Regard not man. Too much eye upon him implies too little upon God, as if God's word were not enough to create and support a confidence, without the buttresses of secular strength. All dependence on man is either upon a broken reed, that cannot support itself, or a piercing reed, that wounds instead of healing, Isa. xxxvi. 6. It is a dishonour to God, and provokes him to lengthen a misery and retard a deliverance. The nearer Sion comes to a final settlement, the more God will act by himself, either without instruments, or in a more signally spiriting instruments, that himself shall be more visible in them than themselves. 'The Highest himself shall establish her.' If he be the Highest, he is fit to be trusted by us; if he will do it himself, it is fit we should couple none with him. The nearer the time comes wherein God will appear himself, the more we should depend upon him himself; the exercise of faith should be strongest, when the promise, the object of faith, is nearest its meridian. Let us be more careful to keep our faith from sinking, and let God alone to keep his church from sinking.

Use 2. Of comfort. The church's patent is singular; the greatest worldly society could never shew the fellow of it: 'The Highest himself shall establish her.' There is not such a clause in the settlement of any nation. Why should we be afraid, then, of the joint conspiracy of men or devils. He that hath laid the foundation, can and will preserve the superstructure, not only because he formed it, but because he hath promised it. When Christ would reveal to John the future condition and conflicts of the church to the end of the world, he appears like a conqueror, with all the ensigns of authority and power about him, Rev. i. 13–16. He hath 'eyes like a flame,' to pierce his enemies; 'feet like brass,' to crush them; 'a two-edged sword out of his mouth,' to pierce them; and this while he is in the midst of the seven candlesticks; the several alterations and periods of the church to the end of the world, to preserve and cleanse them.

1. Here is comfort in the confusions and troubles of the world. The shaking of heaven and earth were the harbingers of the appearance of Christ for redemption, and laying the corner-stone of Sion, Hag. ii. 7. The same methods will be used when he shall come to lay the top-stone, and complete all the fruits of redemption, Luke xxi. 25, 26, 28. The confusion of the world is the restoration of Sion. A storm or rushing mighty wind preceded the plentiful effusion of the Spirit upon the apostles, for the blowing the gospel into every corner, Acts ii. 2. Never were the disciples in so hopeless a condition as before the resurrection of Christ, the ground of the church's stability. They then expected to see his face no more. What commotions and thunders are described in the Revelation before the New Jerusalem comes down from heaven, and God pitch his tabernacle among men! But he suffers not those commotions to be raised in the world by the ministering angel till the servants of God be sealed in the forehead, for their preservation in those confusions which shall be the ruin of their enemies, Rev. vii. 2, 3. The ark may shake with the motion of the oxen, but it cannot fall. Noah's ark may be tossed by the waves that drown the world, but not sink, and at last 'rest upon the mountains of Ararat,' Gen. viii. 4, of ארר and רטט, *i.e.* the curse of terrors, the removal of fears. Christ came not to the disciples but in the fourth watch of the night, and that when the ship was tossed by the waves, and was tugging against a contrary wind, Mat. xiv. 24, 25. It is no hardship for Sion to be in a boat beaten by the sea, when Christ walks upon the waters, and bids her 'be of good cheer,' saying, 'It is I, be not afraid.' An earthquake preceded the deliverance of Paul and Silas out of prison, Acts xvi. 26; and lightnings, and voices, and thunderings, earthquake, and great hail, shall accompany the opening of the temple of God in heaven, and the manifestation of the ark of the testament in that temple, Rev. xi. 19.

2. Here is comfort in persecutions. Persecution is yet for a while the lot of the church; a sea and a wilderness are yet the passage to Canaan. The first promise to Abraham of a numerous seed, was with the comparing it to 'the dust of the earth,' Gen. xiii. 16; dust that is trampled upon, dust that is removed by a puff of wind. But the next was by comparing it to 'the stars in heaven,' Gen. xv. 5, that are bright, and fixed, and have their orderly motions. Before the introduction of the Philadelphian state of the church, or brotherly state (which it is likely we are not far from), the promise of glory to them that overcome intimates a combat, and the promise of Christ's confessing the names of such before his Father implies a time before the period of the Sardian state, wherein the church is to bear a signal testimony to the truths of Christ in the way of a conflict, Rev. iii. 5. The glorious state of the church at the resurrection of the witnesses shall be preceded by such a calamity as shall be the terror of the godly, and the triumph of an enemy devoted to a sudden and unexpected destruction, Rev. xi. 9–12.

Persecutions make way for Sion's stability. Never was she firmer and purer than in the time of the apostles, and those immediately following them, when the witnesses for the truth, to the loss of their blood, were as numerous as the survivors. She was then, when the flood was cast out against her, 'clothed with the sun, and crowned with a crown of twelve stars,'

Rev. xii. 1, 2. Such troubles now may dim the outward splendour, but increase her inward spirit, and refine her to that temper she was in in the primitive ages of Christianity. Prosperity was never much the church's friend. Poison was flung in her dish when she gained an earthly felicity, and the fondness of great ones. Her stability consists not in this, but in the graces and spirit of Christianity. That which established her head established the body. Her Captain ascended not from mount Olivet till he had suffered on mount Calvary. The church was never described so glorious in her outward attire as her greatest enemy, that is clothed in scarlet and decked with gold, Rev. xvii. 4. Sion's glory is internal: Ps. xlv. 13, 'The King's daughter is all glorious within.' All those persecutions that are yet to come upon her shall not demolish her walls. The rigours of her enemies, and the treasons of her pretended friends, have not yet expelled her out of the earth. She hath not yet sunk, though her masts have been sometimes cut close to the deck, and her visible pilots flung overboard into the sea; and shall she sink when she is not far from an entrance into the harbour? She hath been 'a brand plucked out of the fire,' Zech. iii. 2. She was plucked out of the furnace of Babylon, and shall be plucked out of the furnace of mystical Babylon. Though she should be mown down as grass by the scythe of her enemies, yet the presence of Christ shall be as rain upon her, to make her sprout and spread after all her afflictions, Ps. lxxii. 6. Though she had been in the midst of the fire, she never yet was, nor ever will be, consumed. She hath had joy in her disgraces, and greatness by her flames. She hath always had a God to inspire her with vigour, to sustain her weakness, and prop her by his arm, and hath often swam to a safe harbour in a tide of her own blood. Is not that God still a sufficient defence, and the promise a sufficient charter against the violence of the world: 'The Highest himself shall establish her;' himself by his own arm, and himself by his own methods.

3. Here is comfort in the deepest designs of her enemies: 'The Highest himself shall establish her.'

If he be the Highest, and employs himself as the Highest, there is none so high as to overtop him, none so high as to outwit him. Though their union be never so close, and their projects never so deep, yet God's being with the church is curb enough for them, and comfort enough for Sion: Isa. viii. 9, 'Associate yourselves together, O ye people, &c. Take counsel together, and it shall come to nought; speak the word, and it shall not stand; for God is with us.' God's presence with Sion blows away all. God was with the ark in its captivity, and made it victorious in its chains. It crippled Dagon, the Philistines' idol, 1 Sam. v. 4, and made them return it to their disgrace, which they thought they had seized upon to their honour. While God is a strength to the poor, 'the branch of the terrible shall be brought low, and their blast be but as a storm against a wall,' Isa. xxv. 4, 5. He can hasten their ruin by their own subtilty, and catch them in their own net, Ps. xxxv. 8; or he can turn them to glorify the church as much as they hindered her, Isa. xxv. 3. They are sometimes compared to bees, Ps. cxviii. 12, Isa. vii. 18; and he can make them afford honey as well as a sting. They are bees for their wrath, and bees for their weakness, and many times bees for her profit. Sometimes he makes 'the house of Jacob as fire, and the house of Esau as stubble before him,' Obad. 18. It is not more natural to the serpent's seed to spite the church, than it is natural to God to protect her; their malice cannot engage them so much in attempts against her, as God's promise engageth him in the defence of her. What can weakness do against strength, folly against wisdom, hell against heaven, and a fallen Lucifer against the highest God?

4. Here is comfort to expect the glory of the church: 'The Highest himself

shall establish her.' 'The mountain of the Lord's house shall be lifted up on the the top of the mountains,' Isa. ii. 2. In the last days it shall be more glorious than any mountain dignified by God: above mount Sinai, where the law was given, the terrestrial mount Sion, where the temple was built; mount Moriah, where Abraham had a type of the death and resurrection of Christ; mount Horeb, where Moses by prayer discomfited Amalek; and mount Pisgah, where Moses had a prospect of Canaan. Abraham's conquest of the four kings, Gen. xiv., seems to be a figure of the church's victories, when the captive *Lots* should be rescued, and Sodom itself should be something better for Sion. Then shall Christ meet her as King of Salem, King of Peace, with the blessing of the most high God. Then shall he, as he did at the feast in Cana, turn the church's water into wine. 'Idols shall be utterly abolished,' Isa. ii. 18; dross and mixtures in doctrine and worship purged out: Rev. xxii. 1, 'The river of the water of life shall be as clear as crystal, proceeding from the throne of God, and of the Lamb;' 'the everlasting gospel preached,' Rev. xiv. 6; called *everlasting*, because it shall never more be clouded and obscured by the foolish inventions of men. 'There shall be no more sea,' Rev. xxi. 1. The troubles of Sion, signified by a stormy sea, shall cease, and 'a new heaven and a new earth' be created. There shall be multitude of conversions: Rev. xi. 15, 'The kingdoms of the world shall become the kingdoms of Christ.' The breath of the Lord shall come in to many, and make them 'stand upon their feet,' Ezek. xxxvii. 9, 10. There shall be a greater presence of God in ordinances, for the earth 'shall shine with his glory,' Ezek. xliii. 2. Holiness shall sparkle in her, for 'the glory of the Lord shall be upon her,' Rev. xxi. 11. His holiness to purify her, and his power to protect her. Persecutions without and divisions within shall cease. Satan shall be bound, his force restrained; he shall not wander about with his cloven foot, Rev. xx. 3. The 'sea of glass,' which was mingled with fire, with the fire of worldly persecutions, with the fire of intestine animosities, shall be as 'clear as crystal,' Rev. xv. 2, Rev. xxii. 1. He will then have magistrates no longer carrying on the interest of the god of this world, but the interest of the church, whom he calls his princes, Ezek. xlv. 8; his, because set up by a more immediate providence; his, because acting designedly and intentionally for his glory; no more pinching his people, and making a prey of his Sion, but laying down their crowns at the foot of his throne; and, to complete all, there shall be a perpetuity in this spiritual prosperity; only between the beginning and completing it, Satan shall be let loose, but for a little season, Rev. xx. 3; and after this it shall not have one blow more from hell, but the devil must for ever give over nibbling at her heel. Now the church never yet found such a state suitable to those promises and predictions. Some great thing remains to be accomplished, which the world hath not yet seen, nor the church experienced; but that truth that will not lie, that truth which cannot lie, has assured it: 'The mystery of God shall be finished,' Rev. x. 7. The church hath hitherto been gasping in the fire and in the water. She has lived, but as wrapped in a winding-sheet. The saints under the altar have cried a long time for the vengeance of the temple to recompense their blood. There is a time when this Lazarus, that hath lain begging at the door of the rich and mighty, shall be mounted up to a better state. Sion shall enjoy a resurrection, and fling off all badges of a funeral, for 'the Highest himself shall establish her.'

Third use of exhortation.

1. Take heed of apostatising from Sion; from the doctrine and worship of Sion.

If God shall establish her, stability is not to be found out of her. To depart from her, is to leave a firm rock to find security in a quicksand; to leap out of a stout ship in a storm, to expect a preservation in the waves; to turn our backs upon heaven, to seek ease in the bowels of hell. The altar at Damascus is cast down, and Jeroboam's altar is demolished, when that at Jerusalem stood. To stay in Sion, is to be exposed to the gunshot of men and devils; to run from her, is to seek to the devil for protection, and run into the mouth of all the artillery of God, that is set for the establishment of Sion. If we are Christians, no force nor violence should separate us from her.

2. Let us love Sion. There is nothing the Scripture uses more as an argument to separate our affections from the world than the uncertainty and fading nature of it. The perpetuity, then, of the church should be a motive to place our affections there, where they shall never want an object, and which we cannot love without loving her head and her establisher. The Jews in Babylon would rather forget themselves than their city and temple, Ps. cxxxvii. 5, 6. Our affections to gospel Sion should be more tender, since God hath poured out more of his Spirit upon her, and she is more amiable in his eye. That which the Jews so much affected is perished. But the true Sion is eternal, and shall flourish for ever. The Highest himself hath an establishing affection to her. Let our affections to her equal the malice of the enemies against her, since we have greater incentives to love her than they can have to hate her. While others cry, 'Raze, raze it even to the ground,' let us at least testify our affections, and if we have not her standing walls to love, let us not estrange our tenderness from 'her very dust,' Ps. cii. 14. There is a pleasure to be taken in her stones, because they shall be again set in their place, a favour to be shewn to her dust, because it shall be again compacted and enjoy a resurrection. For the Highest that hath promised to establish her, will not desert her in her ruins: ver. 16, 'When the Lord shall build up Sion, he shall appear in glory.' We have therefore more ground to favour her dust than to admire the proudest palaces.

3. Let us desire the establishment of Sion more than our own private establishment.

It is the sign of a gracious spirit, to 'look not only on his own things, but the things of others,' Philip. ii. 4. And what things of others should be regarded, if the things of Christ and his spouse be overlooked? No private person hath any promise of establishment but as he is a denizen of Sion, as one born in her. In desiring therefore the welfare of Sion, we wish and make way for the establishing of ourselves; our interests are common with hers. Her prosperity therefore should be the first and last of our wishes. When we wish the stability of Sion, we wish the honour of God, the continuance of his worship, the glorifying his name which is deposited in that cabinet. The glory of God cannot flourish if the church perish. How base then are those, that if they can swim in a worldly prosperity, care not if the church be drowned in tears and blood; that clothe themselves and regard not her nakedness; that provide an earthly Canaan for themselves, and care not what desolate desert Sion sits weeping in!

4. Let us endeavour the establishment of Sion. It is a grateful thing to a prince to favour his favourite. Let us be as forward to enlarge her territories, as the devil and his instruments are to increase the suburbs of hell. The Highest himself will establish her by himself; we must therefore take those methods which are agreeable to the chief preserver. A compliance with the enemies of God was never the way to secure the interest of Sion. A divine work in a divine way will meet with divine assistance. To contribute to the establishment of Sion is a work honourable in itself, since it is

the work of God himself; it is an imitation of the highest pattern. In this we are associates and co-workers with God. For the Highest himself shall establish Sion.

A DISCOURSE UPON THE FIFTH OF NOVEMBER.

The enemy said, I will pursue, I will overtake, I will divide the spoil; my lust shall be satisfied upon them; I will draw my sword, my hand shall destroy them. Thou didst blow with thy wind, the sea covered them: they sank as lead in the mighty waters.—EXOD. XV. 9, 10.

AN anniversary commemoration of a memorable deliverance falling upon this day, hath caused a diversion of my thoughts, to look back not only upon a mercy never to be forgotten, but to look forward to that deliverance which is to come, parallel to this in the text. Israel was a type of the church, Pharaoh a type of the church's enemies in all ages of the world, both of the spiritual enemy Satan, and of the temporal, his instruments.

The deliverance was a type of the deliverance that Christ wrought upon the cross by his blood; also of that Christ works upon his throne, the one from the reign of sin, the other from the empire of antichrist.

This was the exemplar of all the deliverances the church was to have. As the Assyrian should 'lift up a staff against Jerusalem, after the manner of Egypt,' so the Lord should lift his rod up for them 'upon the sea, after the manner of Egpyt,' when 'the yoke shall be destroyed because of the anointing,' Isa. x. 26, 27, when the power of the enemies shall be destroyed by the strength of Christ. The Lord himself makes it his pattern in those victories he is to gain for his people. When he calls upon his arm to 'awake as in the ancient days,' when he 'cut Rahab, and wounded the dragon, and made the depth of the sea a way for the ransomed to pass over,' Isa. li. 9–11, then 'the redeemed of the Lord shall come with singing unto Sion;' the song of Moses, while they stand upon a sea of glass, a brittle, frail, and stormy world, Rev. xv. 3. And our Redeemer makes this his pattern and rule when he comes to tread the wine-press in wrath, and make them drunk with his fury, that then he would 'remember the days of old, Moses and his people, when he divided the water before them, to make himself an everlasting name,' Isa. lxiii. 1, 2, 11, that his power may be as glorious in the latter as it was in the former, and all deliverances of the church from the beginning to the end be knit together to be an everlasting matter of praise to his name.

This historical narration is to have a more universal accomplishment; the deliverance from Egypt is promised to be fulfilled a second time, and God would act the same part over again, as also their deliverance from Og king of Bashan, after the ascension of Christ: Ps. vi. 22, 'The Lord said, I will bring again from Bashan, I will bring my people from the depths of the sea.' This is after he had ascended, ver. 18; when he came to 'wound the head of his enemies,' ver. 21. So Isa. xi. 15, 'The Lord shall utterly destroy the tongue of the Egyptian sea; and with his mighty wind shall he shake his hand over the river, and shall smite it in the seven streams; and make men go over dry-shod.' Nilus with its seven streams was the glory of Egypt, and Rome with its seven hills is the glory of the papacy, Rev. xvii. 9. So

Zech. x. 10, 'I will bring them again out of the land of Egypt, and they shall pass through the sea with affliction, and the depths of the river shall dry up.' Pharaoh and his army cannot revive and stand up in their former ranks, but there shall be deliverances with resemblances to that, when the enemies shall be as arrogant and furious as Pharaoh, and the church as dejected and straitened as Israel.

The text is a part of Moses his song; a carmen, ἐπινίκιον, a song after victory, a panegyric; the praise of God, attended with dancing, at the sight of the Egyptian wrecks, ver. 20.

1. It was then real; the Israelites then sang it.

2. It is typical; the conquerors of antichrist shall again triumph in the same manner, Rev. xv. 3.

3. It was an earnest of future deliverance to the Israelites. When God appeared for them in their first exit, he would not fail in that work which should conduce so much to his glory; it was a pledge that his purchased people should pass over, and be planted in the mountain of his inheritance, ver. 16, 17. There is in the words,

1. A description of the enemy.

2. His defeat.

The enemy is introduced laying his counsel, and vaunting his resolution, by an elegant climax, and orderly proceeding: 'I will pursue, I will overtake, I will divide the spoil; my lust shall be satisfied,' &c. They laid the foundation deep in counsel, built their resolves high in power, and then applaud themselves in their insolence.

I will pursue. Had he no reflections upon his former successless attempts to keep the Israelites in slavery? Or could he with any reason hope to reduce them with his baffled strength to that yoke which had been broken by a powerful arm? Had he not reason freshly to remember his own inability to remove one of the plagues sent upon them, to promote Israel's rescue? Was that high arm which brought them out of Egypt broken, God's weapons blunted, his magazine of plaguing ammunition wasted, and his strength too feeble to preserve those he had by a strong hand redeemed? These things be obvious to Pharaoh's thoughts. Yet, I will still pursue. How heady and rash are the church's enemies! Infatuation is the usher to destruction. When you find the church's enemies lose their wits, you may quickly expect they will lose their strength and lives.

I will divide the spoil. He promiseth them this victory before the conflict, encourages his soldiers with hopes of the prey, which was the recovery of their jewels, which the Israelites had borrowed by God's order, and the Egyptians had lent them by a secret impression, and the flocks and herds of the poor Israelites to boot.

How great is the pride of the church's enemies! They strut without thinking of a superior power to curb them, and promise themselves the accomplishment of their designs, without fearing the check of providence. Thus did Sisera's mother triumph in a presumptuous hope before a victory, Judges v. 30, and sing *Te Deum* before a conquest. *Ventosa et insolens natio,* is the title Pliny gives the Egyptian nation.

My lust shall be satisfied upon them. תמלאמו נפשי, my soul shall be satisfied. How revengefully do they express themselves! They apprehend themselves cheated of their jewels by the Israelites: such an apprehension would increase rage and animosity.

I will draw my sword, my hand shall destroy, תורישמו ידי, my hand shall disinherit them. I will reduce them like a company of fearful fugitives, by brandishing a drawn sword, that they shall quickly return to their former bondage, and become the perpetual inheritance of the Egyptians. How secure are the church's enemies! The sight of a glittering sword, and an edict for a return, they thought, would quell their spirits. It is true they had to deal with an unarmed people, unprovided for defence, whose late slavery had rendered them unfit for military exercises, an unequal match for a numerous and disciplined army. But what if they were? Had they not the same power to protect them in their march, which had brought them out of their bondage? This the enemies never reflected on. Pride and security are always twins.

In ver. 10 you have their defeat. The sea quenched the fire of their rage, and laid flat the towers of their proud confidence. God blows with his wind, the strong east wind, Exod. xiv. 21, a strength added to its natural fierceness, which made the meeting of the floods more swift and fierce. Some think thunders and lightnings burst out of the pillar of fire in the cloud, when 'God looked upon them,' Exod. xiv. 24.

They 'sank like lead,' suddenly, easily, irrecoverably; they were lashed before, now executed. Other plagues had a mixture of patience, this is a pure cup of the indignation of God.

The defeat is described,

1. By the author: 'Thou didst blow.'

2. Instrument: 'Thy wind, the sea;' wind and the sea conspire together against the enemies, when God orders them.

3. Victory, or success of this order: 'The sea covered them; they sank like lead in the mighty waters.'

General observations.

1. The greatest idolaters are the fiercest enemies against the church of God. It is the Egyptian is the enemy. No nation had more and more sordid idols.* The Persians adored the sun, the greatest benefactor to the world, in the rank of inanimate creatures; other nations several stars, but none did so much abuse the reason of man as that accursed nation. Onions, garlic, cats, oxen, flies, and crocodiles; those dunghill creatures were their adored deities. And how much better adoration is the swaddling clouts of our Saviour, or the straw which was in the manger, or the tail of the ass he rode upon, and so many splinters of the cross, which, if put together, would make a Colossus! For this, among the rest, may the church professing such worship be called spiritual Egypt.

2. The church's enemies are not for her correction, but her destruction: 'I will pursue; my hand shall destroy them.' They breathe out nothing but slaughters; 'My hand shall destroy them;' down with it, down with it even to the ground, and 'men are famous as they can lift up axes upon the thick trees,' Ps. lxxiv. 5.

3. How desperate are sometimes the straits of God's Israel in the eye of man! How low their spirits before deliverance! They here behold a deep sea before them and a raging enemy behind them; hear a confused noise of women and children in the midst of them; feel the pantings of their own hearts, and perhaps see a consternation in the faces of their governors; they see themselves disarmed of weapons, lying almost at the mercy of an oppressor with a well-furnished army; they repent of what God had done for them, and are more ambitious of slavery than liberty; quarrel with Moses, (and, as one of their historians saith, were about to stone him), Exod. xiv. 10–12. Without doubt they then thought him a liar, and it is likely had no more honourable thoughts at that time of God; for when they saw the happy success in the miraculous overthrow of the Egyptians, then 'they be-

* Ægyptii diis fœcundi.—*Hieron.*

lieved God and his servant Moses,' Exod. xiv. 31, as if they gave credit to neither of them before. They had a pillar of fire and a cloud, the chariot of God, a greater argument to establish them than the preparation of their enemies to terrify them. But what a faithless creature is man under the visible guard of heaven, and so far naturally from living by faith that he will hardly draw establishments from sense!

4. God orders the lusts of men for his own praise. He had forced Pharaoh to let the people go; he had stopped the streams of his fury; when he removes his hand and pulls up the dam, Pharaoh returns to his former temper with more violence, thereby giving occasion for God's glory in his own destruction. He serves himself of the desperate malice of his enemies, to make his wisdom and other attributes more triumphant.

5. The nearer the deliverance of the church is, the fiercer are God's judgments on the enemies of it, and the higher the enemies' rage. The former plagues were but small gashes in the Egyptian state; but when the time approached of the Israelites' perfect deliverance, then the firstborn in every house, the delight and strength of the parents, is cut off; and at the completing of it, the glory, power, and strength of Egypt buried in the sea. The fuller beams of mercy on the one are attended with more scorching darts of judgment on the other.

6. All creatures are absolutely under the sovereignty of God, and are acted by his power in all their services. 'Thy wind': all are subject to his conduct, and are the guardians of his people, and the conquerors of his enemies. How easy is it for the arm of Omnipotency to demolish the strongest preparations against his Israel, and with a blast reduce their power to nothing! The sea suffers violence to preserve his people, and the liquid element seems transformed into a wall of brass. God can make the meanest creatures ministers of his judgments, raise troops of flies to rout the Roman army, as it was in Trajan's siege of the Agarenes.

7. By the same means God saves his people, whereby he destroys his enemies: the one sank, the other passed thorough. That which makes one balance sink makes the other rise the higher. The Red Sea was the guardian of Israel and the executioner of Egypt, the Israelites' gallery to Canaan and the Egyptians' grave. The cloud that led the Israelites through the Red Sea blinded the Egyptians; the waters that were fifteen cubits high above the mountains kept the ark from dashing against them, whereby Noah might be endangered, and drowned the enemies, though never so high according to human stature.

8. The strength and glory of a people is more wasted by opposing the interests of the church than in conflicts with any other enemy. Had the Egyptian arms been turned against any other enemy, they might have prospered, or at least retired with a more partial defeat, or saved their lives though under chains; but when they would prepare them against God's Israel, they meet with a total defeat where they expected victory, and find their graves where Israel found their bulwarks: the choicest of their youth, the flower of their nobility, the strongest of their chariots and horses, at one blow overthrown by God.

9. We may take notice of the folly of the church's enemies. Former plagues might have warned them of the power of God, they had but burned their own fingers by pinching her, yet they would set their force against almighty power, that so often had worsted them; it is as if men would pull down a steeple with a string.

But the observations I shall treat of are,

1. When the enemies of the church are in the highest fury and resolution, and the church in the greatest extremity and dejection, then is the fittest time for God to work her deliverance fully and perfectly. When the enemy said, 'I will pursue, I will overtake, I will divide the spoil,' &c., then 'God blowed with his wind,' then 'they sank.'

2. God is the author of all the deliverances of the church, whosoever are the instruments. 'Thou didst blow with thy wind; who is like unto the Lord among the gods?'

1. For the first, When the enemies of the church are in the highest fury, &c. Great resolutions against God meet with great disappointments. The church's straits are the enemies' hopes, but God's opportunity. When their fury is highest, God's love is nearest.

1. There are four seasons on the part of the enemy God takes hold of:

(1.) Flourishing prosperity. Here is Pharaoh in the head of a gallant army, the Israelites in a pound, at his mercy. The Egyptians' prosperity is a forerunner of their destruction, the adversity of the other of their salvation. Haman is in the top of his favour when the Jews are marked out for slaughter, and then himself is marked out for ruin. Prosperity, like rain, makes the weeds of pride and atheism to grow up, and then they are fit matter for God's sickle to cut down. When 'the clusters of the vine of the earth are ripe,' full of an outward glory and sweetness, then 'the angel thrusts in his sharp sickle,' Rev. xiv. 18. There is an ἀκμὴ set them. When 'the great city is clothed in fine linen, purple and scarlet, decked with gold and precious stones,' Rev. xviii. 16, and come to the highest point of its glory and prosperity, then shall God thicken the clouds of his vengeance, and bring their riches to nought in one hour.

(2.) Swelling pride: 'I will pursue,' &c. Pride is provoking, because it is a self-deifying, and sets up the creature as God's mate. God stands upon his honour, and loves to attack those that would equal themselves with him. Pride sunk the glory of the fallen angels into misery, and so it will that of the serpent's seed. This is the immediate forerunner of destruction, Prov. xvi. 18. Men have their hairy scalp, the prime of their strength, and pride of their hearts, when God wounds them, Ps. lxviii. 21. Egypt was become Rahab, pride itself, as the word signifies, and so God called it by that name, Isa. li. 9. When Egypt mounted to Rahab, to the top of pride, then God cut it. When the dragon bristled, and erected his stately head to seize upon the prey, then God wounded him, put an end to Egypt's pride and the Israelites' fear. He loves to beat down the pride of the one, and raise up the lowliness of the other. When Herod will assume the title of a god, given him by the acclamations of the people, an angel shall immediately make him a banquet for worms, Acts xi. 22, 23. When Sennacherib had prospered in his conquest of Judea, had taken many strong towns, closely beleaguered Jerusalem, thundered out blasphemies against God, and threatenings against his people, then comes an angel, makes an horrible slaughter in a night, sends him back to his own country, where, after the loss of his army, he lost his life by the hands of his own children. A greater pride cannot be expressed than what the apostle predicts of the man of sin, and that hath been extant for some time in the world: 2 Thes. ii. 4, 'Who opposeth and exalteth himself above all that is called God,' in additions to the word, clipping the institutions of God, and adding new, and canonizing new mediators of intercession; who sits in the temple of God in a profession of Christianity, shewing himself that he is God, assuming the name of God and the title of God in being called *most holy*. And perhaps it will yet amount to a higher step than it hath yet done before he be consumed by the brightness of the Lord's coming, since all that yet lets and hinders is not taken out of the way. The higher the pride, the nearer the fall. When Goliath shall defy the God of Israel, a stone from a sling, thrown by the hand of David, our great David the antitype, shall lay him vomiting out his soul and blasphemies on the earth. We are many times more beholding to the enemies' insolence than our own innocence: Deut. xxxii. 27, 'Were it not that God feared the wrath of the enemy,' *i. e.* in their pride, lest 'their adversaries should behave themselves strangely, and say, Our hand is high,' a sinful Israel should not have so many preservations.* When they will 'ascend into heaven, and exalt their throne above the stars of God;' when they will 'ascend above the heights of the clouds, and be like the Most High; then shall they be brought down to hell, to the sides of the pit,' Isa. xiv. 13–15. The highest towers are the fairest marks for thunder, and the readiest tinder for the lightning of heaven. When Tyrus had set her heart as the heart of God, then would God defile her brightness, and make her die the death of them that are slain in the midst of the sea, Ezek. xxviii. 6–8.

(3.) Eager malice. Nothing would satisfy the Egyptians here but the blood of the Israelites. 'My hand shall destroy them;' they were under a cruel bondage, attended with anguish of spirit, before God began their rescue. The serpent's seed have the same principles of craft and malice sown in their nature, that are resident in his; ever since the beginning, he endeavoured to shape men into the same form and temper with himself; their rage would raze out the very foundation of Israel, and not suffer the name to be had any more in remembrance,' Ps. lxxxiii. 4. They love to be drunk with the blood of the saints, and are no more satisfied with blood than the grave with carcases; they repair their arrows, and watch for an opportunity to discharge them, and never want poison but opportunity. This is God's time to deliver. When Pharaoh would pollute the land with the blood of the Hebrew males, and ordain them to be dragged from the womb to the slaughter, then God raises up himself to attempt the rescue of Israel; yet he bears with his insolence, punisheth him, but not destroys him. But when he would be still stiff against a sense of the multitude of plagues, and a greater mercy of patience in them; when he would arm for the field against that God the smart of whose force he had felt, and resolves to destroy or bring back the Israelites upon the point of his sword, God would then bear no longer, but make the water his sepulchre. When Haman designs the ruin of the Jews, procures the king's commission, sends despatches to all the governors of the provinces, sets up a gibbet for Mordecai, and wants nothing but an opportunity to request the execution, he tumbles down to exchange his prince's favours for an exaltation on the gallows, Esther vi. 4, vii. 10. When the serpent increased his malicious cruelty, and cast out a flood against the church, God makes the earth, the carnal world, to give her assistance, and repel the force that Satan used against her: Rev. xii. 15, 16, 'The earth helped the woman.' When 'multitudes shall gather together in the valley of decision,' then shall 'the Lord roar out of Sion, and be the hope of his people, and the strength of the children of Israel,' Joel iii. 14, 16. And when spiritual Egypt shall make a war against Christ, who sits upon the white horse, and combine all their force for the destruction of his people, then shall the beast and the false prophet be taken and brought to their final ruin, and their force be broken in a lake of fire, as that of Egypt was in a sea of water, Rev. xix. 19, 20. The time of their greatest fierceness shall be the time of Christ's fury; he will strike them sorest when he finds

* Trap on Exod. p. 9.

them cruellest; their rage shall rouse up his revenge. When the men of Sodom, to which the antichristian state is likened, shall be resolutely bent to wickedness, they shall be struck with blindness, and that blindness succeeded by destruction; then will God set bounds to the outrageous waves, and snatch the prey out of the teeth of the lions.

(4.) Confident security. 'I will divide the spoil, my lust shall be satisfied upon them.' God lets the enemy 'come in like a flood' and torrent, with a confidence to carry all before him, before he 'lifts up a standard against him,' Isa. lix. 19. Then shall the Spirit of the Lord stir up himself gloriously in the principles and actions of his people, and the Redeemer shall come to Sion. God will set his force against their confidence, and break their impetuousness by his own power. When the enemies of the church think they have entangled it in such a snare, reduced it to so low a condition as to be secure of her ruin with a blast and puff, then God will 'arise and set her in safety from them that puff at her,' Ps. xii. 5. This will be the case of Babylon, when she shall say, 'I sit as a queen, and am no widow, and shall see no sorrow,' then 'shall her plagues come in one day, death, and mourning, and famine,' for then God will stir up his strength to judge her, Rev. xviii. 7. It is in the time of the antichristian polity, and mutual congratulations, with the highest security for their happy success, triumphing over the dead bodies of the witnesses, that they shall stand again upon their feet (the same persons, if politically dead, others witnessing the same doctrine, if they were corporeally dead), and damp all their mirth and triumph, and turn their security into fears; then shall glory be given to the God of heaven, and the ark of his testament be seen in his temple, and the power of the Lord be magnified, Rev. xi. 10, 11. When they shall all be gathered together to the battle of the great day of the Lord, the place is called *Armageddon*, Rev. xvi. 14, 16, &c., חרם and גדון. A cursed troop, an army under God's *anathema*, when they have the greatest confidence. When Jerusalem shall be penned up by a siege, it shall be 'a cup of trembling in the hands of her enemies,' Zech. xii. 2. Fear shall seize upon them in the midst of their confidence. The sun was risen upon Sodom just before the devouring shower of fire and brimstone. With what derision would they have entertained any messenger, that should have assured them of such a shower in so clear a day! No doubt but the Egyptian horses went prancing into the sea, and their riders confident of catching their prey; when they saw the waters congealed, they had not the least suspicion but that the division of the sea was made in their favour, till the chariot wheels were taken off, and the waters ready to roll upon them, Exod. xiv. 23, 25.

2. As something on the part of the church's enemies forwards the deliverance, so there is some regard God hath to the church's straits: *cum duplicantur lateres, venit Moses.* It is God's usual method to let the church be in great distress before he commands deliverance. The distress of the church was great in the concern of this day, though it was not sensible, the deliverance being known near as soon as the danger.

The church is to be in the depths of the sea before she be fully delivered, Ps. lxviii. 22. The Jews were to pass through the sea with affliction before the pride of Assyria should be brought down, and the sceptre of Egypt depart away; after that, he would strengthen them in the Lord, and they should walk up and down in his name, Zech. x. 11, 12. The sharpest pangs precede deliverance; it was so when Christ came in the flesh, it will be so at every new rising of Christ in his Spirit. When things were at a low ebb; when the sun set in the greatest darkness of error, idolatry, and profaneness; when the Jews, the only spot of ground God had, was as a wilderness, almost barren of any grace; when the great predictions of the prophets were unminded, and less understood; when Urim and Thummim had ceased, and the spirit of prophecy was shut up: then Christ comes in the fulness of time to work an universal relief for mankind. When the day of vengeance is in the heart of the Redeemer, he shall look and find none to help, he shall wonder to find none to uphold; therefore his own arm shall bring salvation, Isa. lxiii. 5.

This has always been God's method. With his Son, the powers of darkness had their hour, and triumphed when they had laid him in the grave, before he was raised by the glory of his Father. The witnesses must be killed by the hand of their enemies, before they stand upon their feet, and ascend up into heaven, in the sight of their adversaries, Rev. xi. 7. When the church shall walk in darkness, 'grope for the wall like the blind, mourn like doves, look for salvation, and it shall seem far off,' then will the Lord 'put on a helmet of salvation on his head, and the garments of vengeance for clothing, and be clad with zeal as a cloak,' Isa. lix. 9, 10, 11, 17. The break of day is ushered in by a thicker darkness than that which clouded the night before. The sharpest persecution that ever the church had, was in the time of Diocletian, a little before Christianity was to rule his empire in the exaltation of Constantine. Abraham was in hardship, out of his country, when he received the promises of the Messiah; and Israel in the wilderness, when the oracles of God were delivered to them. Confusion of the church precedes always the communication of light.

The reasons of the doctrine are these.

1. This makes for God's glory. The creature cannot in this condition challenge any share in the honour of the deliverance, or pare off so much as a splinter of his glory. Had the Israelites been armed, and drawn into a strong battalion, and so defeated the Egyptian army, the victory would rather have been challenged by them than ascribed to God; but neither the strength of their multitude nor the wisdom of their guides were able to protect them. Counsel failed, and heads were feeble. Then did God get himself a name, when they were upon the point of a remediless ruin. It was manifest the name of the Lord got David the victory, since he encountered unarmed with Goliath, who could have crushed him like a fly had he been in his fingers.

The time of the church's depression is the time of God's exaltation. He waits for the extremity to lift up himself. When paleness is upon the face of his people, when the cedars of Lebanon hang their heads, when the church's beauty seems a lamentable deformity, and Sharon is like a wilderness, then will God arise, Isa. xxxiii. 9, 10. God never builds up Sion, but he ordains all things in a method for his appearance in the greatest glory: Ps. cii. 16, 'When the Lord shall build up Sion, he shall appear in his glory,' that is, when the church is destitute, ver. 17.

(1.) God exalts his power. His right hand then becomes 'glorious in power,' Exod. xv. 6. He loves to appear in his dress as a Creator, when there is no fitness in the subject to answer his end but what he bestows upon it. When Jerusalem becomes 'a rejoicing, and her people a joy,' it is an act of creating power: Isa. lxv. 18, 'For, behold, I create Jerusalem a rejoicing.' When the creature can give them not the least assistance, then will they be sensible of God's unbounded sufficiency, and their own necessary dependence. God never had too little help from his creature in a deliverance; he hath sometimes complained of too much, and disbanded some of the church's forces, as in the case of Gideon, Judges vii. As Christ rules in the midst of his enemies, so doth God's power most visibly in the midst of distresses. A physician's skill is most conspicuous when the disease is most dangerous and most complicated, and nature at the lowest ebb. It is more glory to God to quench the fire in its fullest rage than to extinguish it in its first smoke and sparkles. God loves the fairest mark to shoot at, and will rather down with Goliath than with the ordinary Philistines, grapple with the great rather than with a light danger, that the Lord may appear to be 'a man of war,' Exod. xv. 3. As God shews his mercy in his people's redemption, he will shew his strength in their conduct, Exod. xv. 13. He that made this deliverance a standing monument of his power, entitles himself by it: Isa. xliii. 16, 'Thus saith the Lord, which makes a way in the sea, a path in the mighty waters.'

(2.) His kindness to, and care of, his people. When the straits are remediless, and the counsels whereby the projects are laid not to be defeated by human skill; when God seems to have forgot, then in a seasonable deliverance he shews himself the careful watchman of Israel. When the ship is in a raging storm, and Christ asleep, he will leave his own ease to keep his word and content his people. When the church thinks God hath forgotten his mercies, and they have forgotten their dependence; when the misery is so pressing that there is no faith of a deliverance left: then Christ comes, when faith is scarcely to be found upon the earth, Luke xviii. 8, to exalt his mercy in the depths of their misery, and work terrible things they looked not for, Isa. lxiv. 3. The Israelites would not have understood God's care in their protection without this or the like strait. God had a new opportunity to shew his watchfulness over them, to turn the cloud, which went before them as their guide, behind them for their defence, Exod. xiv. 19. The scoffs of the enemy at the church's misery are God's motive to help her: 'I will restore health to thee, because they called thee an outcast,' Jer. xxx. 17. It is in straits we see God's salvation, not man's: Exod. xiv. 13, 'Stand still, and see the salvation of the Lord.'

(3.) His justice. He lets the church be encompassed with miseries, and the enemies in a combination against her, that he may overthrow them at once. God makes a quicker dispatch with the Egyptians when they were united than when they had assaulted Israel with a smaller body. His righteousness gets glory at one blow, when he makes them to lie down together, Isa. xliii. 17. His justice is unblemished in striking when their wickedness is visibly ripe; the equity of it must needs be subscribed, that when the enemy's malice is greatest, when they have no mixture of compassion, it is the clearest righteousness to crush them without any mixture of mercy. God brings things to that pass that he may honour both his justice and mercy in the highest; that the black horses and the white horses may march firm together, Zech. vi. 6; the black horses that brought death and judgment northward to Babylon, where the church was captive; the white horses that followed them, and brought deliverance to his people: the one to be instruments of his judgments, the other of his mercies. God loves to glorify those two attributes together; he did so in the redemption of mankind by the death of his Son, and he doth so in the deliverance of his church. There is a conformity of the church to Christ in her distress, that there may be a conformity of God's glory in temporal to his glory in eternal salvation. God singles out a full crop to be an harvest for both. A wicked man is said to be 'waited for' by the sword, Job xv. 22. God attends the best season for revenge, when mercy to the one shall appear most glorious, and vengeance on his enemies most equitable, and all disputes against his proceedings be silenced.

2. It makes to the church's advantage. God had a work to do upon mount Sion and on Jerusalem, before he would 'punish the stout heart of the king of Assyria, and the glory of his high looks,' Isa. x. 12. His end shall

be attained in the correction of his church, before his glory shall be exalted in the destruction of her enemies. There are enemies in the hearts of his people to be conquered by his grace, before the enemies to her peace and prosperity shall be defeated by his power. He will let them be in the fire, till, like gold, they may have a purer honour in a brighter lustre.

(1.) Humiliation is gained hereby. God would not presently raze out the Canaanites, lest the wild beasts should increase upon them, Deut. vii. 22. Too quick deliverances may be occasions to multiply the wild beasts of pride, security, and wantonness in the heart; humility would have but little footing. There is need of a sharp winter to destroy the vermin before we can expect a fruitful spring. Without humiliation, the church knows not how to receive nor how to improve any mercy. The enemies hasten their own ruin by increasing the measure of their sins, and Israel's deliverance by being instruments to humble their hearts. The sooner the plaster hath drawn out the corrupt matter, the sooner it is cast into the fire. God hereby prevents the growth of weeds in that ground he intends to enrich with new mercies.

(2.) A spirit of prayer is excited. Slight troubles make but drooping prayers; great straits make it gush out, as the more the bladder is squeezed the higher the water springs. We hear not of the Israelites crying to the Lord after their coming out of Egypt, till they had a sight of the formidable army: Exod. xiv. 10, 'They were sore afraid: and the children of Israel cried unto the Lord.' Prayer gains mercies, but scarce springs up free without sense of distress. We then have recourse to God's power, whereby he is able to relieve us, when we are sensible of our own weakness, whereby we are unable to relieve ourselves. Men will scarce seek to God, or trust him, while any creature, though but a reed, remains for their support; they are destitute before they pray, or believe God regards their prayers: Ps. cii. 17, 'He will regard the prayer of the destitute, and not despise their prayer.' Distress causes importunity, and God will do much for importunity's sake, Luke xi. 8.

(3.) Discovery of sincerity. Hereby God discovers who are his people, and who are not; who are in the highest form of Christianity, and who are not in the school, or at least but in the lowest form. He separates the good corn from the useless chaff. No question but there were some among the Israelites that, in this extremity, acted faith upon the remembrance of the wonders God had wrought for them in Egypt before their departure. Certainly they did not all murmur against Moses. Were there no Calebs and Joshuas that followed God fully in a way of faith and submission? Their faith and courage had not been conspicuous without this extremity. Thunderings and lightnings, and terrible things in righteousness, are to prove us, whether the fear of God be before our faces that we sin not, Exod. xx. 18, 20. God separates the dross. You never know a new building without pulling down, to separate the rubbish and rotten rafters from the sound materials. Abraham was put upon hard work, the imbruing his hands in the blood of his only son, to prove his integrity. When God sees his sincerity, he diverts the blow; not only delivers him from his grief, his son from his danger, but renews the promise of the Messiah to him as a reward. Deliverance then comes when God hath separated the corn from the stubble.

(4.) A standing encouragement for future faith. When the straits are greatest from whence God delivers us, there is a stronger foundation for a future trust. When the distress is inconsiderable, faith afterwards will be more feeble. A large experience heartens and strengthens faith in the promise. When gloomy clouds are blown over, the brighter and thinner will not be much feared. When we see the sun melt the thickest over our heads, we shall not doubt its force to dissolve the lesser vapours which may afterwards assemble. When the ship hath escaped a raging storm, we shall not doubt it in a less. God often puts them in mind of their deliverance in the Red Sea, to strengthen their faith and dependence on him. It must needs be an establishment to faith, for deliverances from great straits are some kind of obligation on the honour of God. When the Israelites had provoked God by murmuring, and wished they had died in Egypt, and not in the wilderness, Moses intercedes with this argument, The Egyptians shall hear of it, from whom God brought up Israel with a strong hand; and it would disparage God's power, and tax him with an inability to bring his people into the land he intended. Then God grants their pardon, Num. xiv. 13, 14, 15.

(5.) Engagement to future obedience. It is upon this account God prefaceth the law with his mercy in delivering them out of Egypt. The strongest vows are made in the greatest straits. Many obligations there are when the extremity forces us to cry. When we are in the jaws of death, God may have his terms of us; when we are at some distance, we will have our own. The lower a person is, the more readily will he bend to any condition; hope of deliverance will make him stoop. And when God snatches his people as firebrands out of the fire, they are more obliged to him from common ingenuity, and must be more ashamed of breaking their vows than if their mercies were of a great alloy. If common patience leads to repentance, a rescue from an amazing danger is a stronger cord to draw us to repentance and obedience. And it is certain that when the church in sincerity makes vows to God, it will not be long before God puts her into a condition to pay them, and furnish her with incentives to a holy ingenuity.

(6.) The greater thankfulness. The more straitened, the greater thankfulness for enlargement. As we hear not of the Israelites' prayers, after they came out of Egypt, till they were in the pound, so we read of none of their songs, though they had matter enough for them, in their first departure, till God had dashed in pieces the enemy, and 'thrown the horse and the rider into the sea.' Then, and not till then, had they a deep sense, how 'glorious God was in holiness, fearful in praises, doing wonders,' Exod. xv. 11. Great mercies unveil God's face more to the view of his people. When Israel inherits great salvation, then the Lord shall inherit the praise of Israel. When we have less mercies, we take little notice of the author. God hears the language of but one of our bones; but when he 'delivers the poor from him that is too strong for him, and spoils him, then all my bones shall say, Lord, who is like unto thee?'

(7.) To prevent future mischief to the church. The destruction of the greatest enemies is a disarming the less. God, by this destruction, struck a terror into those nations, upon whose confines Israel was to march into Canaan, who, without so remarkable a rebuke of providence, would have been desirous to finger some of their prey. Then 'trembling took hold of the mighty men of Moab. All the inhabitants of Canaan did melt away; fear and dread fell upon them by the greatness of the arm of God, that they should be as still as a stone, till they passed over the river,' Exod. xv. 15, 16. Their present deliverance was a passport for their future security in their journey; and no enemies troubled them in the way but those upon whom God had a mind to shew his power.

How doth God deliver when the season is thus?

1. Suddenly. They sank like lead in the mighty waters, which quickly reaches the bottom. Judgment comes like lightning. Death and hell are said to 'ride upon horses,' Rev. vi. 8. They are too swift for God's enemies, and will easily win the race of them. Destruction comes, 'as travail

upon a woman with child,' 1 Thes. v. 3. How suddenly did God turn the Assyrian camp into an Aceldama, overthrow a powerful army, and make their tents their tombs in the space of a night! He will dash them 'in pieces like a potter's vessel,' Ps. ii. 9, all in bits at a stroke. He comes suddenly; he 'rides upon a cherub,' Ps. xviii. 10. But because the motion of an angel is not so intelligible, he adds another metaphor from the nimblest of sensible things; 'he flies upon the wings of the wind,' to assist his people in extremity. The enemy comes like a 'whirlwind,'* and God comes forth as a 'whirlwind of fury,' Jer. xxx. 23. The whirlwind of his judgments shall be as quick as the whirlwind of their malice; a continual whirlwind, when the other is vanishing; it 'shall fall with pain upon the head of the wicked,' when the other shall be as fruitless as a snowball against a wall of brass. The enemy beholds him not till he be upon him; for the 'clouds are as dust under his feet,' Nahum i. 3, and obscure his appearance, as the raising the dust doth the march of a troop. He comes unawares upon them in a cloud. The execution is sudden. They shall be 'cut down as grass,' Ps. xxxvii. 2, which this moment faceth the sun, triumphing in its natural bravery, and the next moment is cut off from its root with one shave of a scythe. He quencheth them as tow is quenched in water, Isa. xliii. 17, as the snuff of a candle is quenched by being bruised by the fingers. He cuts them off as foam, the excrement of the water, Hosea x. 7, which bursts in pieces like a bubble, on the sudden. Vengeance comes upon Tyre and Sidon swiftly and speedily, Joel iii. 4. Tyre comes of צוּר, which signifies to afflict, to straiten. Sidon of צדה; the word signifies to pursue. All persecutors are threatened in Tyre and Sidon with a swift destruction. God delays the time to try the faith and patience of his people, to make the expected deliverance more sweet and welcome, and mercy more singular. He may have some of the seed of Christ in the loins of some of his enemies. But when he doth draw his sword, he gives a sudden blow before the enemy fears it, or his people expect it. The Jews in Babylon, when the chains of their captivity were unloosed, were like those that dream, they could scarce believe they were freed when the enemy felt himself punished. In all other plagues, God sent Moses as an herald, with warning to Pharaoh; but in this God surprised him, and hurried him to destruction, without giving him any caution. Like 'chaff that the tempest carrieth away, and is seen no more,' Job xxi. 18: so shall the plagues of spiritual Egypt 'come in one day,' Rev. xviii. 8; yea, 'in one hour,' ver. 17. And the church shall be like a lily, which, by the assistance of the dew, flourisheth in the morning, when over night it looked as if it were withered.

2. Magnificently. Sometimes in deliverance God puts the frame of nature in confusion. 'He melts the mountains, cleaves the valleys, as wax before the fire, and as waters poured down a steep place,' Micah i. 4, *i. e.* he wastes the strength and riches of his enemies when he comes to judge. When he appears in the generation of the righteous, he shall appear in such glory, as to make the adversaries in great fear, and strike a terror into them, Ps. xiv. 5. God will perform it in a prodigious and unusual way. God might have taken off the wheels of the Egyptian chariots before they had entered the gap of the sea, and hindered them from approaching so near his beloved people; he might have afflicted their hands with the palsy, and rendered them incapable to manage their weapons; or might have sent a spirit of emulation among them, and made them sheathe their swords in one another's bowels. But though this had secured his people, it would not have rendered his operation so illustrious, as the making that which was a means

* 'They came out as a whirlwind to scatter me.'—Hab. iii. 14.

of his people's security to be his enemies' destruction, and the waters at once indulgent to the Israelites, and severe to the Egyptians. He magnifies his judgments and mercies by one and the same stroke, and drowns the enemies in the sea, whereby he delivers the Israelites. So he preserved Daniel in the midst of those lions which devoured his accusers. The more contrary things are to an eye of reason, the fitter subjects they are for the exaltation of God. As Christ, the head, so the church, the body, is raised out of the grave by the glory of God the Father, Rom. vi. 4. His right hand shall find his enemies, Ps. xxi. 8; his right hand shall teach him terrible things, Ps. xlv. 4. Then shall he come with a shout, as one refreshed with wine, recruited with new spirits, and risen from sleep, Ps. lxxviii. 65. He calls upon all creatures to be assistant to Cyrus in the design of his people's deliverance, Isa. xlv. 8. He will perfect it by a way of creation, ('I have created righteousness' to deliverance) with the manifestation of his, and he makes things serve against their natural order appointed by God. Thus, when God shall appear for the final overthrow of spiritual Egypt, he shall come with voices, thunders, and lightnings, an earthquake out of the temple, and appear as magnificently in the garb of a judge as he did on Sinai in that of a lawgiver, Rev. xvi. 19, and make the ten horns, which were the support of the beast, to be the instruments of her desolation, Rev. xvii. 16.

3. Severely. They sank to the bottom like lead in the mighty waters. God sends out the greatest judgments against those that deal sharply with his people, greater than against any other part of the world, Zech. vi. 6. The black horses, the instrument of the execution of his anger, were sent towards Babylon, where his people were in captivity; but the bay horses, of a mixed colour, noting a mixture of mercy and judgments, are sent towards other parts of the world, to walk, not to run, signifying the patience of God to those parts which had not yet oppressed his people. God deals not so smartly with those, as with them that are enemies to Israel. In such concerns he answers his people 'by terrible things in righteousness.' When he appears as a God of salvation to his people, he appears terrible in his righteousness to his enemies: Ps. lxv. 5, 'By terrible things in righteousness wilt thou answer us, O God of our salvation.' His judgments shall be as terrible as they are righteous. The executioners of his vengeance ride upon horses, to shew their readiness to any warlike engagement; upon red horses, of a bloody colour, to shew the severity of their commission against the enemies of God, Zech. i. 8. He will pay all arrears together, that they shall be forced to say, God is true to the word of his threatening, as well as that of his promise; as the Amalekites, in Samuel's time, paid the scores of their ancestors in the time of the Israelites' travel through the wilderness: 1 Sam. xv. 2, 'I remember that which Amalek did to Israel, how he laid wait for them in the way when they came up from Egypt.' So when God reckons with Babylon for all the blood of the saints and prophets,—Rev. xviii. 20, 'The blood of all the prophets and saints that were slain upon the earth, shall be found upon her skirts, and avenged on her,'—he gives unto her the cup of the wine of the fierceness of his wrath; all that she hath done shall come into his remembrance, Rev. xvi. 19. And how severe it shall be is expressed, Rev. xiv. 19, 20; she shall be cast into the great wine-press of the wrath of God, as grapes bruised with the greatest strength, and crushed in pieces, both skin and stones. And to express it more sensibly to our understandings, he speaks of the flowing of the 'blood out of the wine-press into the horses' bridles,' by the space of a thousand and six hundred furlongs, two hundred miles; not that we should understand it literally, but the Spirit of God is so particular in describing the height of the deluge of blood to the

bridles of the horses, the length of the flood to the space of two hundred miles, to set before our apprehension the severity of the wrath that shall be poured out upon them. And as God never repented of his judgments upon Egypt, so never will he of those which are to come upon Babylon.

4. Universally, and therefore severely. 'The horse and the rider did God cast into the sea;' the chariots, the host, and the chosen captains were drowned there, Exod. xv. 1, 4. The waters covered the enemy, there was not one of them left, Ps. lx. 11, Exod. xiv. 28. Not a messenger to carry back the news; their floating bodies and wrecks were the first that gave notice of the defeat to their remaining countrymen. God throws off all tenderness, his bowels are silent, he strikes like a wrathful enemy, lanceth not like a tender chirurgeon; so shall it be with the partners of their sins, every man that worships the beast and his image, shall drink of the wrath of God, which is poured out without mixture into the cup of his indignation, and whoever receiveth the mark of his name, Rev. xiv. 9–11. The sun, the political power that defends it, shall be darkened; the rivers, whereby their traffic and riches come into them, shall be dried up; all that have any dependence on them, recourse to them, stand in the defence of the power of Egypt, shall fall under the indignation of God.

5. Totally, irrecoverably. They sank as lead. God will make an utter end; affliction shall not rise up a second time, Nahum i. 9, 10. He overtakes them when they are drunk in the height of their pleasure, while they are making their confederacies against the church, while they are folden together like thorns, they shall be devoured like stubble fully dry. Ποιήσει τὴν ἐκδίκησιν: Luke xviii. 7, 'He will avenge his own; he will avenge them speedily;' he will act so as if wrath were his only and proper work; he will do it to purpose, and perfectly. The Egyptian carcases lay as trophies of the victory, Exod. xiv. 30. Their former plagues had something of patience; punishment was inflicted, but life preserved; judgments sent, but, upon promise of reformation, quite removed. Now patience folds her hands, and stands spectator, while justice opens hers, and becomes a sole actor; mercy runs on the side of Israel, and wrath marcheth without any impediment against the Egyptians. As they like lead, so irrecoverably shall Babylon fall like a millstone in the depths of the sea, and shall be found no more at all; all her mirth and jollity shall for ever cease, Rev. xviii. 21–23. When things fall to the bottom of the sea, they are entombed there for ever; no skill can restore them to their former station; when judgment turneth the key, and locks them in, there is no more opening the door.

6. And all this justly. Pharaoh had commanded that the Hebrew male children should be exposed to the mercy of the river, to find their death in the water as soon as they had breathed in the air, Exod. i. 22; and God makes them perish in that element to which they had adjudged the harmless infants. Now God pays the law-maker and his counsellors with the same coin, and makes the malefactors food for the inhabitants of the deep, who had before fed the crocodiles with the blood of the innocent. God shall reward Babylon as she hath rewarded his people, and double unto her the cup she hath filled for others, Rev. xviii. 6. Upon this account shall praise be given to God, that he hath given them blood to drink who have shed the blood of his saints and prophets, Rev. xvi. 6. 'Thou art righteous, O Lord, because thou hast judged thus.' As she hath kindled fires to consume the witnesses of Christ, so God shall kindle a fire to consume her, Rev. xvii. 16: 'She shall be utterly burnt with fire,' Rev. xviii. 8. Some think Rome will at length be consumed with fire from heaven. She is indeed spiritual Sodom, Rev. xi. 8; and as she answers it in carnal and spiritual sins, she may par-

take of the same visible and spiritual judgments. Whether the punishment will be the same for kind I know not, but certainly it will be such a kind of punishment whereby the judgments of God shall be read, both in proportion and kind of it, as a retaliation for her sins; and the Scripture speaks of fire coming down from God out of heaven upon the last enemies of the church that shall afflict the beloved city, alluding to the fire upon Sodom, and that which descended upon the persecutors of Elijah, Rev. xx. 9.

7. Wisely. He cuts off the spirits of princes, as he took off the wheels of the Egyptian chariots, Ps. lxxvi. 12, either by infatuating their counsels, or turning them as the rivers of waters into other channels. He stripped the Egyptians first of their wealth, and now spoils them of their strength; he kept a bridle upon the waters till the enemies were got into the midst of them, and then commands the sea to swallow them up in the depths of her bowels. When men lay their counsels deep, second them by an invincible strength, have almost brought them to their imagined period ready to bring forth, God disappoints their hopes, baffles their counsels, renders their projects frothy, raiseth a storm and blows the ship from its harbour, contrary to its intended course, and glorifies his wisdom by overthrowing their designs when they have brought them to a birth. He watches upon the evil, to divert it from the innocent object upon the malicious actor. As God watches for the fittest season to bring evil upon his people, Dan. ix. 14, he will be as diligent to watch for the fittest opportunity to bring judgment on his enemies. God hath promised vengeance, but he hath reserved the knowledge of the 'due time' to himself, when he will make their foot to slide, Deut. xxxii. 35. Every mercy is then most seasonable. Usually God lets men bring the ball almost to the goal, and then kicks it from them, and them from it; and the wisdom of God hath been, and will be, glorious in the overthrow of the remaining enemies of the church, in making them which were horns to defend the beast to be carpenters to ruin him, Rev. xvii. 16.

Use 1. Of comfort. How dear is the church to God! When God was engaged in the deliverance of his people, he sinks the strength of Egypt rather than one hair of the Israelites' heads should perish; they went safe over, while no man or horse of the enemies escaped. God gave Egypt for Israel's ransom, Isa. xliii. 3; and the sea should have drowned the whole land, rather than the enemies have hurt his people. So did the contrivers of the powder plot come to destruction, when not one hair of a head was lost, or one splinter of the place they intended was shaved off, by the prepared gunpowder. God sits in heaven and laughs at the little petty designs of men, Ps. ii. 4. God that is infinite to countermine them, infinitely powerful to defeat them, hath them in derision. Christ in glory mocks at the folly of earth-worms. The decree of God, which settles Christ a king, assures him a kingdom, and secures his people as it did his person, Ps. ii. 7. God is 'a sun and shield,' Ps. lxxxiv. 11; a shield to defend them, and a sun to extinguish the fire of the enemy's fury by shining upon it. God values no nation for the security of his people. The Babylonians, a warlike nation, shall sink under the army of Cyrus, for the restoration of the captive Jews: Isa. xliii. 4, 'I will give men for thee, and people for thy life.' He had given Egypt for their ransom before, and Ethiopa and Seba in the time of Asa; and still, in after ages, God was of the same mind. God is as gracious to his people as terrible to his enemies; he is light to the one, when he is fire to the souls and bodies of the other, Isa. x. 17. Christ still sits the Watchman of Ephraim with God, Hosea ix. 8. He inspects his church, and waits to bring the day of visitation upon his enemies. The covenant is of special force with God to move him to deliver his people: Isa. lxiii. 8, 'He said, Surely they are my people; so he was their Saviour.' It seems to refer to the deliverance from Egypt. Shall I have so little regard to the league I have entered into with their fathers, as to be unconcerned in their misery? There is hope in Israel till God forgets his covenant, and Christ strip himself of the name of a Saviour. Christ hath his priestly habit in heaven for his people, but eyes as flames of fire, quick and piercing, to consume the very hearts of his enemies, and feet like fine brass to trample upon them, Rev. i. 13–15. He is the Lion of the tribe of Judah, to tear his enemies, as well as a Lamb slain, to expiate the sins of his people. He hath meekness for his friends, and terrible majesty for his enemies: Ps. xlv. 4, 'In thy majesty ride prosperously, because of meekness.' His kindness to his people makes him ride in majesty against the others. God will not be at rest till he hath revenged the cause of his people. Egypt will be drowned, Babylon will fall, Rev. xviii. 2. Christ can have no satisfaction without it. The executioners of his judgments in the north country, which was Babylon, lying northward from Jerusalem, do quiet his Spirit, both as tending to the glory of his justice and the manifestation of his mercy to his people, Zech. vi. 3. Christ will stain his garments in the blood of Edom and Bozrah, Isa. lxiii. 2, 3: Edom, the posterity of Esau; Bozrah, a city of Moab, types of the church's enemies. The Jewish doctors, by Edom in the prophets, understand Rome. Christ sits in heaven till his enemies be made his footstool. All the time of his sitting, God is acting and preparing things for a final issue. There is a strong cry of blood, and a file of prayers; the one will be revenged, and the other will be answered. Their own pride and cruelty witness against them. God hath a noise of petitions every day for a full end; a combined importunity will prevail. But clouds now hang over us; a gloomy storm seems to threaten us. God may indeed blow over the cloud. Our Saviour hath the command of the storms and winds in heaven, as well as he had upon the earth. The pillar of the cloud, which hath hitherto conducted us, may be our guardian in the rear to defend us. But yet, if he doth suffer them to prevail, they shall be but as whisks to brush off the dust, wisps of straw to cleanse the filthy pot. You know what is to be done with them when their work is done. Their language indeed is, Let Sion be defiled; but they understand not the counsel of the Lord, who in time will make the horn of Sion iron, and her hoofs brass, Micah iv. 11. Though the beasts that ascend out of the bottomless pit do kill God's people, Rev. xi. 7, yet, even in this victory of theirs, Satan himself shall be overcome. As when Christ was taken out from among the living by Satan's means, it was but for a time, but himself was cast out for ever, so, after this victory, the church shall overcome, Rev. xi., and God shall break the head of the leviathan in the waters; and when he doth, by his wisdom, contrive ways of salvation, he will, by his power, execute them, and save in such a way as may most glorify himself, and witness that the salvation was the immediate work of his arm: Hosea ii. 7, 'I will save them by the Lord their God.'

2. Remember former deliverances in time of straits. In our plenty of mercies, we should not be unmindful how near we were to the pit, nor let the impression of God's power, wisdom, and mercy wear off from our hearts. The Israelites were apt to forget the most signal mercies, though they had seen them, and had more sensibly tasted the sweetness of them than their posterity. God, therefore, often puts them in mind of them; the Lord that brought them out of the land of Egypt, out of the iron furnace, Deut. iv. 20: Hosea xii. 9, 'I the Lord your God from the land of Egypt.' It was the more fit to be remembered by them, because many of them were fitter subjects for God's wrath with the Egyptians than for his delivering-

kindness, since she committed whoredoms in Egypt in her youth, *i. e.* had been guilty of the Egyptian idolatry, Ezek. xxiii. 3. Unmindfulness of former experiences may make you hopeless of future deliverances. The remembrance of former mercies is a ground of confidence in God for the like mercies for the future. God recalls to his people's minds, in their afflictions, the memorable defeat of the Moabites by his sole power, in the time of Jehoshaphat's reign; they should, from that deliverance, hope for as great from the hands of God in their straits. And, Zech. x. 11, God would have them consider their deliverance at the Red Sea as a ground of hope in the time of their distress.

3. Thankfully remember former deliverances. If we have not some praise for God, we may suspect ourselves. It is observed that the city Shushan, the royal seat of the Persian monarchy, was portrayed upon the east gate of the temple,* not because of the Persian command, or because of their fear of that king, as some think, but to have a thankful remembrance of the wonderful deliverance of Purim, which was wrought in Shushan, Esth. ix. 26. If it had been only by the Persians' command, it would have been defaced after the fall of that monarchy, which held but thirty-four years after the building of the second temple. The 136th Psalm is a good copy, where is a threefold exhortation to thankfulness in the beginning, and one at the end; and in the record of every mercy, the burden of every verse is, 'his mercy endureth for ever.' How should we imitate the psalmist! He broke the teeth of the invincible leviathan in '88, and sent a strong wind to disperse the fleet, 'for his mercy endureth for ever.' God prevented the dreadful blast of gunpowder, 'for his mercy endureth for ever.' God sent the light of the gospel into England, and freed it from the yoke of antichrist's tyranny, 'for his mercy endures for ever.' God hath been a wall of fire about Ireland, in the protection of it, 'for his mercy endureth for ever.' Let mercy receive the praise of what our own wisdom and power could not effect. The way to overcome the same enemies we fear, is to praise God for what he hath before acted against them. The strength of a people consists in praises, as well as praying: Ps. viii. 2, 'Out of the mouths of babes and sucklings hast thou ordained strength;' in the evangelist, 'thou hast perfected praise,' Mat. xxi. 16. The more hallelujahs we put up, the more occasion God may give us for them. If we have any fears of the overflowing deluge God formerly delivered us from, our non-improvement of those deliverances, the fruits whereof we enjoy this day, may strengthen our fears. When Israel was idolatrous in Jeroboam's reign, yet God delivered them from the Syrians, because he saw their affliction was bitter, and there was no helper; yet when they did not thankfully improve it to a reformation, God denounced judgments against them for their idolatry: 2 Kings xiv. 26, 27, 'The Lord said not that he would blot out the name of Israel;' so that he had not yet denounced it, for he waited to see the improvement of this mercy. But before the end of Jeroboam's reign, by the prophet Hosea, who began to prophesy in his time, he declared their final captivity, from whence they are not restored to this day. Praise for former mercies is a means to gain future ones; the music of voices in Jehoshaphat's camp, praising the beauty of holiness, was a prologue of a deliverance from a formidable army, 2 Chron. xx. 21, 22, and more successful than the warlike music of drums and trumpets.

4. Exercise faith on the power of God manifested in deliverances in the time of straits. It is not for want of ability in God, but for want of faith in us, that we at any time go groaning under misery. Faith would quiet the soul. When David relied upon God, and found by experience God sus-

* Lightfoot, Temple, cap. iii. p. 9.

taining him, he would not then be afraid of ten thousand, Ps. iii. 5, 6. Let that be our carriage which is recorded of the Israelites after this memorable defeat: Exod. xiv. 31, 'They believed the Lord, and his servant Moses.' We must never expect to see God's arm bare without faith in him. Christ can do no great work where unbelief is predominant. Unbelief doth not strip God of his power and mercy, but it stops the streams and effluxes of it. Unbelief against experience is a double sin. It is gross when against a bare word, worse when against the word confirmed by a witness. Israel was past thoughts of any relief in this strait, but expected to perish by the hand of their enemies, yet God brought them into straits in mercy, to bring them out of straits with power. He makes their distress a snare to their enemies, and a scaffold for their faith. That deliverance ought to be a foundation for our trust in God, though bestowed upon another nation; yet not so much upon them as a state, but as a church, and a type of those future ones under the gospel which are yet expected. Well, then, trust upon this foundation. Great trust in God is a sort of obligation upon God. Men, out of generosity, will do much for them that depend upon them. Dependence on God magnifies his attributes; this will bring deliverance, whereby God will magnify himself. Do not distrust him, till you meet with an enemy too strong for him to quell, a Red Sea too deep for him to divide, an affliction too sturdy for him to rebuke, an Egyptian too proud for him to master; then part with your faith, but not till God hath parted with his power, which he hath formerly evidenced.

5. Expect and provide for sharp conflicts. God brings into straits before he delivers. Another deliverance is yet to come; the church's distresses are not come to a period; Babylon hath another game to play. The right of the devil to tyrannise over the mystical body was taken away at the death of the head, yet he still bruiseth Christ's heel, and bites, though he cannot totally overcome. As long as Christ's enemies are not made his footstool, as long as there is the seed of the serpent in the world, as long as Christ's members want a conformity to the head, Satan's pinches must be expected; as long as the beast is in being, he will make war with the followers of the Lamb; his power is to continue forty-two months, to make war with the saints, and to overcome them, Rev. xiii. 5, 7. Forty-two months, of years; it is like the time is not expired. One thousand six hundred and twenty years, which make forty-two months; no ending since he first had his power. When his time draws near to an end, he will bite sharpest. This deliverance from Egypt is yet again to be acted over, and that must be at the end, when the whole Israel of God shall be freed from Antichrist, the antitype of Pharaoh.

6. Yet let us not be afraid. Apostasies may be great. There will be but two witnesses; not two in number, but in regard of the fewness of those that shall bear testimony to the doctrine of Christ. There may be no advocate for the church. Sion may be an outcast, cast out of the affection of many that served or favoured her; but the sharpest convulsions in the world are presages of an approaching redemption, Luke xxi. 28, and the gospel will shine clearer, as the sun doth after it hath been muffled with a thick cloud. The words in the mouths of the witnesses will be most killing and convincing. Fear not a natural above a supernatural power. Was not all the church God had in the world in as low a condition at the Red Sea? Not a soul that we read of exempt (or but few, as Job, and some few others in other parts), yet the church was then delivered for a pattern, to shew forth the power of God in the ages to come. What though there may be a want of instruments? Are not all instruments outlived by God? Has God dismissed the care of his people? Is he not always the church's guardian?

He must be dethroned before he can be disarmed. While heaven is too high for human hands to reach, the church is too well guarded for them to conquer. Fear not, till Christ lets his sceptre fall out of his hands, and ceases to rule in the midst of his enemies, and flings away the keys of death and hell; fear not till God strips himself of his strength wherewith he is clothed; he is clothed with strength, Ps. xciii. 1. Though there be little strength in the church, there is an almighty one in their confederate. It is no matter what the enemy resolves against what God ordains. Pharaoh intended to destroy, God intended to deliver. God will have his will, and Pharaoh's lust goes unsatisfied. When the enemies are most numerous, God shall darken their glory and strength, and then shall he be the hope and strength of his people, Joel iii. 14–16. The valley of Achor, the valley of the sharpest trouble, shall be a door of hope, Hosea ii. 15. That God that can create a world out of nothing, can create deliverance when there is no visible means to produce it. What can be too hard for him that can work without materials, that can make matter when it is wanting, and call non-entities into being? He created the world with a word, and can destroy the sturdiest men in the world with a look. The strongest devil trembles before him, and the whole seed of the serpent is but as the dust of the balance before the breath of his mouth. He looked the Egyptian host into disorder, and their chariot wheels into a falling sickness, Exod. xiv. 24. He created the world by a word; he restored Jerusalem by a word, Isa. xliv. 26, 27, dispirited Egypt by a look. There is no need of an arm; a word, and a look of omnipotency, will be efficacious both for the one and the other; one royal edict from him will perform it: Ps. xliv. 4, 'Thou art my King, command deliverance for Jacob.' He hath authority as a king, engagement as the church's king. As he hath right of dominion, so he hath an office of protection, which the church of right may claim. And is it Jacob that wants deliverance? Be not afraid, but sanctify the Lord of hosts himself, Isa. viii. 12, 13. To trust in his power is to sanctify his name, and regard him as the sovereign of all creatures, and the Lord of hosts. If we sanctify his name by relying on his power, he will sanctify his name by engaging his power.

7. To this end study the promises God hath made to his church, and what predictions are upon record. It is a title of the faithful, that they are such as keep the sayings of the book of the Revelation, Rev. xxii. 9. The angel that came to John owns himself his fellow-servant, and of the prophets, and those that keep the sayings of that book. See God's bond, and behold his witness; compare the promise, the prophecy, and performance. See his mercy in making them, his truth in performing them; let these be as the Hur and Aaron to support the glory of God in our souls. This will be a matter of praise, and furnish us with arguments to spread before God. Daniel first looked into the book for the set time of the Jews' return from Babylon, Dan. ix. 2, and took his rise for pleas from thence. You may have need of this food; a divine promise is the best cordial at a stake or gibbet, or when a sword is at your breast.

8. When a time of straits comes, wait patiently upon God. Let not hope sink when reason is nonplussed by storms, and sees nothing but wrecks. Wait upon God in the way of his judgments, Isa. xxvi. 8, in his storms as well as calms. God waits to be gracious, and therefore we should wait to be gratified. Not to wait, is to be partners in that sin which brought destruction upon the church's enemies, viz. pride. It concerns God more in point of his glory to hasten deliverance in its due time, than us in point of security; but there is as much danger in coming too soon as too late. By waiting, we imitate the highest pattern, who waits with patience for the refor-

mation of his enemies, and Christ, who waits for the total victory. The longer God keeps the church at any time under the enemy's chains, the sweeter will be his mercy to the one, and the severer his justice on the other. The Israelites waited, and God followed Pharaoh with plagues, as he followed them with burdens, and took his time to cut off their oppressors, with most glory to himself, and most comfort to them. The vision hath its appointed time. Impatience will not make God break the chains of his resolves, but patience will bring down the blessing with great success, and big with noble births. God is not out of the way of his wisdom and grace, and we can never keep in our way but by patience in waiting; by this we give him the honour of his wisdom; by too much hastiness we check and control him, and will not let him be the master and conductor of his own blessings. We many times get more good by waiting than we do by enjoying a mercy. Such a posture keeps the soul humble and believing, whereas many times, when we receive a mercy too hastily with one hand, we let go faith and humility with the other. Sincere souls have the strongest and most heavenly raptures in a time of waiting: Isa. xl. 31, 'They mount up with wings like eagles.'

9. In times of such straits, be found only in a way of duty. If our straits should ever prove as hard as the Israelites' at the Red Sea, *i.e.* have something of a resemblance to their case, let us follow Moses his counsel to them: Exod. xiv. 13, 'Stand still, and see the salvation of the Lord.' Let us not anticipate God's gracious designs. If we will have our finger where God only will have his arm, God may withdraw this arm, and leave us to the weakness of our own fingers. Let them that want a God to relieve them use sinful and unworthy shifts for their deliverance. If any success be found out of the way of duty, it may be attended with a curse, and want that favour of God which only can sanctify it. We may purchase a present deliverance with a more durable plague at the end of it, because we forfeit that favour which only can work a real freedom. Sinful ways do not glorify God, but disparage him. Our actions at such a time particularly should adorn the gospel, not discredit it, for it is by the sword of his mouth that such enemies will be destroyed, and every sword cuts best when it is sharpest and cleanest, not when it is blunt and rusty. Not but that lawful means may, nay, they must be used. Noah, though he went into the ark by God's command, and was not to stir out without his order, yet he sets open the windows, and sends forth a raven and a dove, to bring him notice when the waters were dried up. It is a foolish thing to offend God, who only can help us in our straits, and by our sin to hold his sword in his sheath, which, upon our obedience, would be drawn for our relief. We know not how soon we may need him, and our distress be such, that none but he can bring salvation. Let no sin be a bar in the way.

10. Be much in prayer. Israel cried unto the Lord before God did relieve, Exod. xiv. 10. The persecuted church cried, travailing in birth, and found a security both for herself and her offspring, Rev. xii. 2, &c. The distress of the time is an argument to be used: Ps. cxxiii. 3, 4, 'Have mercy upon us, Lord, for we are exceedingly filled with contempt.' When enemies are high, and access to God free, it is an high contempt of God not to use the privilege he allows us, and it is to trust in an arm of flesh rather than an arm of omnipotence; to think him either inexorable or unable. And for encouragement, consider you have Christ armed against his spouse's enemies, and provided with merit to make her prayers successful. Our prayers may at last be turned into praises, and we may say with David, Ps. ix. 6, 'O thou enemy, destructions are come to a perpetual end.'

A DISCOURSE OF DELIGHT IN PRAYER.

Delight thyself also in the Lord ; and he shall give thee the desires of thine heart. —Ps. XXXVII. 4.

This psalm in the beginning is a heap of instructions. The great lesson intended in it is placed in verse 1 : 'Fret not thyself because of evil doers, neither be thou envious against the workers of iniquity.' It is resumed, verses 7, 8, where many reasons are alleged to enforce it.

Fret not.

1. Do not envy them. Be not troubled at their prosperity.

2. Do not imitate them. Be not provoked by their glow-worm happiness to practise the same wickedness, to arrive to the same prosperity.

3. Be not sinfully impatient, and quarrel not with God, because he hath not by his providence allowed thee the same measures of prosperity in the world. Accuse him not of injustice and cruelty, because he afflicts the good, and is indulgent to the wicked. Leave him to dispense his blessings according to his own mind.

4. Condemn not the way of piety and religion wherein thou art. Think not the worse of thy profession because it is attended with affliction.

The reason of this exhortation is rendered, ver. 2, 'For they shall soon be cut down as the grass, and wither as the green herb ;' amplified by a similitude or resemblance of their prosperity to grass. Their happiness has no stability ; it hath, like grass, more of colour and show, than strength and substance. Grass nods this and that way with every wind. The mouth of a beast may pull it up, or the foot of a beast may tread it down. The scorching sun in summer, or the fainting sun in winter, will deface its complexion.

The psalmist then proceeds to positive duties, ver. 3.

1. Faith. Trust in the Lord. This is a grace most fit to quell such impatiencies. The stronger the faith, the weaker the passion. Impatient motions are signs of a flagging faith. Many times men are ready to cast off their help in Jehovah, and address to the god of Ekron, multitudes of friends or riches ; but trust thou in the Lord, in the promises of God, in the providence of God.

2. Obedience. Do good. Trust in God's promises, and observance of his precepts, must be linked together. It is but a pretended trust in God where there is a real walking in the paths of wickedness. Let not the glister of the world render thee faint and languid in a course of piety.

3. The keeping our station. Do good. Because wicked men flourish, hide not thyself therefore in a corner, but keep thy sphere, run thy race, 'and verily thou shalt be fed,' have everything needful for thee. And now because men delight in that wherein they trust, the psalmist diverts us from all other objects of delight to God as the true object : 'Delight thyself in the Lord ;' place all thy pleasure and joy in him. And because the motive expresseth the answer of prayer, the duty enjoined seems to respect the act of prayer as well as the object of prayer ; prayer coming from a delight in God, and a delight in seeking him. Trust is both the spring of joy and the spring of supplication. When we trust him for sustenance and preservation,

we shall receive them; so when we delight in seeking him, we shall be answered by him.

1. The duty. In the act, 'delight;' in the object, 'the Lord.'

2. The motive: 'he shall give thee the desires of thy heart;' the most substantial desires, those desires which he approves of. The desire of thy heart as gracious, though not the desire of thy heart as carnal; the desire of thy heart as a Christian, though not the desire of thy heart as a creature. *He* shall give; God is the object of our joy, and the author of our comfort.

Doct. Delight in God, in seeking him only, procures gracious answers; or, without cheerful prayers, we cannot have gracious answers.

There are two parts: 1, cheerfulness on our parts; 2, grants on God's part.

1. Cheerfulness and delight on our parts. Joy is the tuning the soul. The command to rejoice precedes the command to pray: 1 Thes. v. 16, 17, 'Rejoice evermore, pray without ceasing.' Delight makes the melody; prayer else will be but a harsh sound. God accepts the heart only when it is a gift given, not forced. Delight is the marrow of religion.

1. Dulness is not suitable to the great things we are chiefly to beg for. Gospel discoveries are a feast, Isa. xxv. 6. Dulness becomes not such a solemnity. Manna must not be sought for with a dumpish heart. With joy we are to draw water out of the wells of salvation, Isa. xii. 3. Faith is the bucket, but joy and love are the hands that move it. They are the Hur and Aaron that hold up the hands of this Moses. God doth not value that man's service, who accounts not his service a privilege and a pleasure.

2. Dulness is not suitable to the duty. Gospel duties are to be performed with a gospel temper. God's people ought to be a willing people, Ps. cx. 3, נדבת, a people of willingness, as though in prayer no other faculty of the soul had its exercise but the will. This must breathe fully in every word, as the spirit in Ezekiel's wheels. Delight, like the angel, Judges xiii. 20, must ascend in the smoke and flame of the soul. Though there be a kind of union by contemplation, yet the real union is by affection. A man cannot be said to be a spiritual king if he doth not present his performances with a royal and prince-like spirit. It is for vigorous wrestling that Jacob is called a prince, Gen. xxxii. 28.

This temper is essential to grace. Natural men are described to be of a heavy and weary temper in the offering of sacrifices, Mal. i. 13. It was but a sickly lame lamb they brought for an offering, and yet weary of it; that which was not fit for their table they thought fit for the altar.

In the handling this doctrine I will shew,

I. What this delight is.

II. Whence it springs.

III. The reasons of the doctrine.

IV. The use.

I. What this delight is. Delight properly is an affection of the mind that springs from the possession of a good which hath been ardently desired. This is the top-stone, the highest step. Delight is but an embryo till it come to fruition, and that certain and immutable; otherwise, if there be probability or possibility of losing that which we have present possession of, the fear of it is as a drop of gall that infects the sweetness of this passion. Delight properly is a silencing of desire, and the banquet of the soul on the presence of its desired object.

But there is a delight of a lower stamp.

1. In desires. There is a delight in desire as well as in fruition, a

cheerfulness in labour as well as in attainment. The desire of Canaan made the good Israelites cheerful in the wilderness. There is an inchoate delight in motion, but a consummate delight in rest and fruition.

2. In hopes. Desired happiness affects the soul; much more expected happiness: Rom. v. 2, 'We rejoice in the hope of the glory of God.' Joy is the natural issue of a well-grounded hope. A tottering expectation will engender but a tottering delight. Such a delight will madmen have, which is rather to be pitied than desired; but if an imaginary hope can affect the heart with some real joy, much more a hope settled upon a sure bottom, and raised upon a good foundation. There may be joy in a title as well as in possession.

3. In contemplation. The consideration and serious thoughts of heaven do affect a gracious heart and fill it with pleasure, though itself be as if in a wilderness. The near approach to a desired good doth much affect the heart. Moses was surely more pleased with the sight of Canaan from mount Pisgah than with the hopes of it in the desert. A traveller's delight is more raised when he is nearest his journey's end, and a hungry stomach hath a greater joy when he sees the meat approaching which must satisfy the appetite. As the union with the object is nearer, so the delight is stronger. Now, this delight the soul hath in duty is not a delight of fruition, but of desire, hope or contemplation, *gaudium viæ*, not *patriæ*.

1. We may consider delight as active or passive.

(1.) Active, which is an act of our souls in our approaches to God, when the heart, like the sun, rouseth up itself, as a giant to run a spiritual race.

(2.) Passive. Which is God's dispensation in approaches to us, and often met with in our cheerful addresses to God: Isa. lxiv. 5, 'Thou meetest him that rejoiceth and works righteousness.' When we delightfully clasp about the throne of grace, God doth often cast his arms about our necks, especially when cheerful prayer is accompanied with a cheerful obedience. This joy is, when Christ meets us in prayer with a 'Be of good cheer, thy sins are forgiven,' thy request granted. The active delight is the health of the soul, the passive is the good complexion of the soul. The one is man's duty, the other God's peculiar gift; the one is the inseparable property of the new birth, the other a separable privilege. There may be a joy *in* God when there is little joy *from* God; there may be gold in the mine when no flowers on the surface.

2. We may consider delight as settled or transient, as spiritual or sensitive.

(1.) A settled delight. In strong and grown Christians, when prayer proceeds out of a thankfulness to God, a judicious knowledge and apprehension of God. The nearer to God, the more delight; as the motion of a stone is most speedy when nearest its centre.

(2.) A sensitive delight. As in persons troubled in mind there may be a kind of delight in prayer, because there is some sense of ease in the very venting itself; and in some, because of the novelty of a duty they were not accustomed to before. Many prayers may be put up by persons in necessity without any spiritual delight in them; as crazy persons take more physic than those that are healthful, and observe the spring and fall, yet they delight not in that physic. The pharisee could pray longer, and perhaps with some delight too, but upon a sensual ground, with a proud and vaunting kind of cheerfulness, a delight in himself, when the publican had a more spiritual delight; though a humble sorrow, in the consideration of his own vileness, yet a delight in the consideration of God's mercy. This sensitive delight may be more sensible in a young than in a grown Christian. There is a more sensible affection at the first meeting of friends, though more solid after some converse; as there is a love which is called the love of the espousals. As it is in sorrow for sin, so in this delight; a young convert hath a greater torrent, a grown Christian a more constant stream. As at the first conversion of a sinner there is an overflowing joy among the angels, which we read not of after, though without question there is a settled joy in them at the growth of a Christian. An elder son may have a delight in his father's presence more rooted, firm, and rational, than a younger child that clings more about him with affectionate expressions. As sincerity is the soul of all graces and duties, so this delight is the lustre and embroidery of them.

Now, this delight in prayer,

1. It is an inward and hearty delight. As to the subject of it, it is seated in the heart. A man in prayer may have a cheerful countenance and a drowsy spirit. The Spirit of God dwells in the heart, and love and joy are the first-fruits of it, Gal. v. 22. Love to duty, and joy in it; joy as a grace, not as a mere comfort. As God is hearty in offering mercy, so is the soul in petitioning for it. There is a harmony between God and the heart. Where there is delight, there is great pains taken with the heart; a gracious heart strikes itself again and again, as Moses did the rock twice. Those ends which God hath in giving are a Christian's ends in asking. Now, the more of our hearts in the requests, the more of God's heart in the grants. The emphasis of mercy is God's whole heart and whole soul in it, Jer. xxii. 41. So the emphasis of duty is our whole heart and whole soul. As without God's cheerful answering a gracious soul would not relish a mercy, so without our hearty asking God doth not relish our prayer.

2. It is a delight in God, who is the object of prayer. The glory of God, communion with him, enjoyment of him, is the great end of a believer in his supplications. That delight which is in prayer is chiefly in it as a means conducing to such an end, and is but a spark of that delight which the soul hath in the object of prayer. God is the centre wherein the soul rests, and the end which the soul aims at. According to our apprehensions of God are our desires for him; when we apprehend him as the chiefest good, we shall desire him, and delight in him as the chiefest good. There must first be a delight in God before there can be a spiritual delight or a permanency in duty: Job xxvii. 10, 'Will he delight himself in the Almighty? will he always call upon God?' Delight is a grace; and as faith, desire, and love have God for their object, so hath this; and according to the strength of our delight in the object or end, is the strength of our delight in the means of attainment. When we delight in God as glorious, we shall delight to honour him; when we regard him as good, we shall delight to pursue and enjoy him, and delight in that which brings us to an intercourse with him. He that rejoices in God, will rejoice in every approach to him: 'The joy of the Lord is our strength,' Neh. viii. 10. The more joy in God, the more strength to come to him. The want of this is the reason of our snail-like motion to him. Men have no sweet thoughts of God, and therefore no mind to converse with him. We cannot judge our delight in prayer to be right if we have not a delight in God, for natural men may have a delight in prayer when they have corrupt and selfish ends. They may have a delight in a duty as it is a means, according to their apprehensions, to gain such an end; as Balaam and Balak offered their sacrifices cheerfully, hoping to ingratiate themselves with God, and to have liberty to curse his people.

3. A delight in the precepts and promises of God, which are the ground and rules of prayer. First, David delights in God's testimonies, and then calls upon him with his whole heart. A gracious heart must first delight in precepts and promises before it can turn them into prayers; for prayer is

nothing else but a presenting God with his own promise, desiring to work that in us and for us which he hath promised to us. None was more cheerful in prayer than David, because none was more rejoicing in the statutes of God. God's statutes were his songs, Ps. cxix. 54; and the divine word was sweeter to him than the honey, and honey-comb. If our hearts leap not at divine promises, we are like to have but drowsy souls in desiring them. If our eye be not upon the dainties God sets before us, our desires cannot be strong for him. If we have no delight in the great charters of heaven, the rich legacies of God, how can we sue for them? If we delight not in the covenant of grace, we shall not delight in prayers for grace. It was the hopes of reward made Moses so valiant in suffering; and the joy set before Christ in a promise made him so cheerful in enduring the shame, Heb. xii. 1, 2.

4. A delight in prayer itself. A Christian's heart is in secret ravished into heaven. There is a delight in coming near God, and warming the soul by the fire of his love. The angels are cheerful in the act of praise; their work is their glory. A holy soul doth so delight in this duty, that if there were no command to engage him, no promise to encourage him, he would be stepping into God's courts; he thinks it not a good day that passeth without some intercourse with God. David would have taken up his lodgings in the courts of God, and regards it as the only blessedness, Ps. lxv. 4. And so great a delight he had in being in God's presence, that he envies the birds the happiness of building their nests near his tabernacle. A delight there is in the holiness of prayer; a natural man under some troubles may delight in God's comforting and easing presence, but not in his sanctifying presence; he may delight to pray to God as a storehouse to supply his wants, but not as a refiner's fire to purge away his dross. Prayer, as praise, is a melody to God in the heart, Eph. v. 19; and the soul loves to be fingering the instrument and touching the strings.

5. A delight in the things asked. This heavenly cheerfulness is most in heavenly things. What delight others have in asking worldly goods, that a gracious heart hath in begging the light of God's countenance. That soul cannot be dull in prayer that seriously considers he prays for no less than heaven and happiness, no less than the glory of the great God. A gracious man is never weary of spiritual things, as men are never weary of the sun, but though it is enjoyed every day, yet long for the rising of it again. From this delight in the matter of prayer it is that the saints have redoubled and repeated their petitions, and often double the *Amen* at the end of prayer, to manifest the great affections to those things they have asked. The soul loves to think of those things the heart is set upon, and frequent thoughts express a delight.

6. A delight in those graces and affections which are exercised in prayer. A gracious heart is most delighted with that prayer wherein grace hath been more stirring, and gracious affections have been boiling over. The soul desires not only to speak to God, but to make melody to God; the heart is the instrument, but graces are the strings, and prayer the touching them; and therefore he is more displeased with the flagging of his graces than with missing an answer. There may be a delight in gifts, in a man's own gifts, in the gifts of another, in the pomp and varnish of devotion, but a delight in exercising spiritual graces is an ingredient in this true delight. The pharisees are marked by Christ to make long prayers, vaunting in outward bravery of words, as if they were playing the courtiers with God, and complimenting him; but the publican had a short prayer, but more grace, 'Lord, be merciful to me a sinner.' There is reliance and humility. A gracious heart labours to bring flaming affections, and if he cannot bring flaming grace,

he will bring smoking grace; he desires the preparation of his heart as well as the answer of his prayer, Ps. x. 17.

II. Whence this delight springs.

1. From the Spirit of God. Not a spark of fire upon our own hearth that is able to kindle this spiritual delight. It is the Holy Ghost that breathes such an heavenly heat into our affections. The Spirit is the fire that kindles the soul, the spring that moves the watch, the wind that drives the ship. The swiftest ship with spread sails will be but sluggish in its motion unless the wind fills its sails. Without this Spirit, we are but in a weak and sickly condition, our breath but short, a heavy and troublesome asthma is upon us: Ps. cxxxviii. 3, 'When I cried unto thee, thou didst strengthen me with strength in my soul.' As prayer is the work of the Spirit in the heart, so doth delight in prayer owe itself to the same author. God will make them joyful in his house of prayer, Isa. lvi. 7.

2. From grace. The Spirit kindles, but gives us the oil of grace to make the lamp burn clear. There must not only be wind to drive, but sails to catch it. A prayer without grace is a prayer without wings. There must be grace to begin it. A dead man cannot rejoice in his land, money, or food; he cannot act, and therefore cannot be cheerful in action. Cheerfulness supposeth life; dead men cannot perform a duty (Ps. cxv. 17, 'The dead praise not the Lord'), nor dead souls a cheerful duty. There must not only be grace infused, but grace actuated. No man in a sleep or swoon can rejoice. There must not only be a living principle, but a lively operation. If the sap lurk only in the root, the branches can bring forth no fruit; our best prayers, without the sap of grace diffusing itself, will be but as withered branches. Grace actuated puts heat into performances, without which they are but benumbed and frozen.* Rusty grace, as a rusty key, will not unlock, will not enlarge the heart: there must be grace to maintain it. There is not only need of fire to kindle the lamp, but of oil to preserve the flame; natural men may have their affections kindled in a way of common working, but they will presently faint and die, as the flame of cotton will dim and vanish, if there be no oil to nourish it. There is a temporary joy in hearing the word; and if in one duty, why not in another, why not in prayer? Mat. xiii. 20. Like a fire of thorns that makes a great blaze, but a short stay.

3. From a good conscience. A good heart is a continual feast, Prov. xv. 15. He that hath a good conscience must needs be cheerful in his religious and civil duties. Guilt will come trembling, and with a sad countenance, into the presence of God's majesty. A guilty child cannot with cheerfulness come into a displeased father's presence. A soul smoked with hell cannot with delight approach to heaven. Guilty souls, in regard of the injury they have done to God, will be afraid to come; and in regard of the foot of sin wherewith they are defiled, and the blackness they have contracted, they will be ashamed to come; they know that by their sins they should provoke his anger, not allure his love. A soul under conscience of sin cannot look up to God, Ps. xl. 12; nor will God with favour look down upon it, Ps. lix. 2. It must be a pure heart that must see him with pleasure, Mat. v. 8; and pure hands must be lifted up to him, 1 Tim. ii. 8. Jonah was asleep after his sin, and was outstripped in quickness to pray, even by idolaters. The mariners jog him, but could not get him, that we read of, to call upon that God whom he had offended, Jonah. i. Where there is corruption, the sparks of sin will kindle that tinder, and weaken a

* Reynolds.

spiritual delight. A perfect heart and a willing mind are put together, 1 Chron. xxix. 2. There cannot be willingness without sincerity, nor sincerity without willingness.

4. From a holy and frequent familiarity with God. Where there is a great familiarity, there is a great delight; delight in one another's company, and delight in one another's converse: strangeness contracts, and familiarity dilates the soul. There is more alacrity in going to a God with whom we are acquainted than to a God to whom we are strangers. This doth encourage the soul to go to God. I go to a God whose face I have seen, whose goodness I have tasted, with whom I have often met in prayer. Frequent familiarity makes us more apprehensive of the excellency of another; an excellency apprehended will be beloved, and being beloved, will be delighted in.

5. From hopes of speeding. There is an expectative delight which ariseth from hopes of enjoying: Rom. xii. 12, 'Rejoicing in hope.' There cannot be a pleasant motion where there is a palsy of doubts. How full of delight must that soul be that can plead a promise, and carry God's hand and seal to heaven, and shew him his own bond, when it can be pleaded, not only as a favour to engage his mercy, but in some sense to engage his truth and righteousness! Christ in his prayer, which was his swan-like song, John xvii., pleads the terms of the covenant between his Father and himself: 'I have glorified thee on earth, glorify me with that glory I had with thee before the world was.' This is the case of a delighful approach, when we carry a covenant of grace with us for ourselves, and a promise of security and perpetuity for the church. Upon this account we have more cause of a pleasant motion to God than ancient believers had. Fear acted them under the law, love us under the gospel. He cannot but delight in prayer that hath arguments of God's own framing to plead with God, who cannot deny his own arguments and reasonings. Little comfort can be sucked from a *perhaps;* but when we come to seek covenant mercies, God's faithfulness to his covenant puts the mercy past a *perhaps.* We come to a God sitting upon a throne of grace, upon mount Sion, not on mount Sinai; to a God that desires our presence, more than we desire his assistance.

6. From a sense of former mercies and acceptation. If manna be rained down, it doth not only take off our thoughts from Egyptian garlic, but quickens our desires for a second shower. A sense of God's majesty will make us lose our garishness, and a sense of God's love will make us lose our dumpishness. We may as well come again with a merry heart, when God accepts our prayers, as go away and eat our bread with joy when God accepts our works, Eccles. ix. 7. The doves will readily fly to the windows where they have formerly found shelter, and the beggar to the door where he hath often received an alms: 'Because he hath inclined his ear to hear me, therefore will I call upon him as long as I live,' Ps. cxvi. 2. I have found refuge with God before; I have found my wants supplied, my soul raised, my temptations checked, my doubts answered, and my prayers accepted, therefore I will repeat my addresses with cheerfulness.

I might add, also, other causes: as a love to God, a heavenliness of spirit, a consideration of Christ's intercession, a deep humiliation. The more unpleasant sin is to our relish, the more delightful will God be, and the more cheerful our souls in addresses to him. The more unpleasant sin is to us, the more spiritual our souls are; and the more spiritual our souls, the more spiritual our affections: the more stony, the more lumpish and unapt for motion; the more contrite, the more agile. From a spiritual taste; report of a thing may contribute some pleasure, but a taste greater.

III. Reasons. Without cheerful seeking, we cannot have a gracious answer.

1. God will not give an answer to those prayers that dishonour him. A flat and dumpish temper is not for his honour. The heathens themselves thought their gods should not be put off with a sacrifice dragged to the altar. We read of no lead, that lumpish, earthly metal, employed about the tabernacle or temple, but the purest and most glistering sorts of metals. God will have the most excellent service, because he is the most excellent being; he will have the most delighful service, because he bestows the most delightful and excellent gifts. All sacrifices were to be offered up with fire, which is the quickest and most active element. It is a dishonour to so great, so glorious a majesty, to put him off with such low and dead-hearted services. Those petitions cannot expect an answer which are offered in a manner injurious to the person we address to. It is not for the credit of our great Master, to have his servants dejected in his work; as though his service were an uncomfortable thing; as though God were a wilderness, and the world a paradise.

2. Dull and lumpish prayer doth not reach him, and therefore cannot expect an answer. Such desires are as arrows that sink down at our feet. There is no force to carry them to heaven. The heart is an unbent bow that hath no strength. When God will hear, he makes first a prepared heart, Ps. x. 17. He first strings the instrument, and then receives the sound. An enlarged heart only runs, Ps. cxix. 32; a contracted heart moves slowly, and often faints in the journey.

3. Lumpishness speaks an unwillingness that God should hear us. It speaks a kind of fear that God should grant our petitions. He that puts up a petition to a prince coldly and dully, gives him good reason to think that he doth not care for an answer. The husbandman hath no great mind to a harvest, that is lazy in tilling his ground and sowing his seed. How can we think God should delight to read over our petitions, when we take so little delight in presenting them? God gives not mercy to the unwilling person. The first thing God doth is to make his people willing. Dull spirits seek God as if they did not care for finding him: such tempers either account not God real, or their petitions unnecessary.

4. Without delight we are not fit to receive a mercy. Delight in a mercy wanted makes room for desire, and large desires make room for mercy. If no delight in begging, there will be no delight in enjoying; if there be no cheerfulness to quicken our prayers when we need a blessing, there will be little joy to quicken our praise when we receive a blessing. A weak, sickly stomach is not fit to be seated at a plentiful table. Where there is a dull asking supply, there is none, or a very dull sense of wants. Now, God will not send his mercies but to a soul that will welcome them. The deeper the sense of our wants, the higher the estimation of our supplies. A cheerful soul is fit to receive the least, and fit to receive the greatest mercy. He will more prize a little mercy than a dull petitioner shall prize a greater, because he hath a sense of his wants. Had not Zaccheus had a great joy at the news of Christ's coming by his door, he had not so readily entertained and welcomed him.

IV. *Use*. 1. Of information.

1. There is a great pleasure in the ways of God, if rightly understood. Prayer, which is a duty wherein we express our wants, is delightful. There is more sweetness in a Christian's asking, than in a wicked man's enjoying, blessings.

2. What delight will there be in heaven! If there be such sweetness in desire, what will there be in full fruition! There is joy in seeking; what is there then in finding! Duty hath its sweets, its thousands, but glory its

ten thousands. If the pleasure of the seed-time be so great, what will the pleasure of the harvest be.

3. The miserable condition of those that can delight in anything but prayer. It is an aggravation of our enmity to God, when we can sin cheerfully and pray dully, when duty is more loathsome than iniquity.

Use 2. Of examination. We pray, but how are our hearts? If it be for what concerns our momentary being, is not our running like the running of Ahimaaz? But when for spiritual things, do not our hearts sink within us, like Nabal's? Let us therefore follow our hearts close, suffer them not to give us the slip in our examination of them, resolve not to take the first answer, but search to the bottom.

1. Whether we delight at all in prayer.

1. How do we prize the opportunities of duty? There is an opportunity of an earthly, and an opportunity of an heavenly, gain. Consider which our hearts more readily close with. Can we with much pleasure follow a vain world, and heartlessly welcome an opportunity of duty, delight more with Judas in bags, than in Christ's company? This is sad. But are praying opportunities our festival times? Do we go to the house of God with the voice of joy and praise?

2 Whether we study excuses to waive a present duty, when conscience and opportunity urge and invite us to it. Are our souls more skilful in delays than in performances? Are there no excuses when sin calls us, and studied put-offs when God invites us, like the sluggard, folding our arms yet a little while longer? or do our hearts rise and beat quick against frivolous excuses that step in to hinder us from prayer?

3. How are our hearts affected in prayer? Are we more ready to pray ourselves asleep than into a vigorous frame? Do we enter into it with some life, and find our hearts quickly tire and jade us? Are we more awake when we are up than we were all the time upon our knees? Are our hearts in prayer like withered, sapless things, and very quick afterwards if any worldly business invite us? Are we like logs and blocks in prayer, and like a roe upon the mountains in earthly concerns? Surely what our pulse beats quickest to, is the object most delighted in.

4. What time is it we choose for prayer? Is it not our drowsiest, laziest time, when our nods are as many or more than our petitions, as though the dullest time and the deadest frame were most suitable to a living God? Do we come with our hearts full of the world to pray for heaven? or do we pick out the most lively seasons? Luther chose those hours for prayer and meditation wherein he found himself most lively for study.

5. Do we not often wish a duty over, as those in the prophet that were glad when the Sabbath was over, that they might run to their buying and selling? or are we of Peter's temper, and express Peter's language, 'It is good to be here' with Christ on the mount?

6. Do we prepare ourselves by delightful and enlivening considerations? Do we think of the precept of God, which should spur us, and of the promise of God, which should allure us? Do we rub our souls to heat them? Do we blow them, to kindle them into a flame? Do we send up ejaculations for a quickening spirit? If thoughts of God be a burden, requests to him will not be a pleasure. If we have a coldness in our thoughts of God and duty, we can have no warmth in our desire, no delight in our petitions.

7. Do we content ourselves with dull motions, or do we give check to them? Can we, though our hearts be never so lazy, stroke ourselves at the end, and call ourselves good and faithful servants? Do we take our souls to task afterwards, and examine why they are so lazy, why so heavy? Do

we inquire into the causes of our deadness? A gracious soul is more troubled at its dulness in prayer than a natural conscience is at the omission of prayer. He will complain of his sluggishness, and mend his pace.

2. If we find we have a delight, let us examine whether it be a delight of the right kind.

1. Do we delight in it because of the gifts we have ourselves, or the gifts of others we join with? A man may rejoice in hearing the word, not because of the holiness and spirituality of the matter, but because of the goodness of the dress, and the elegancy of the expression, Ezek. xxxiii. 32. The prophet was unto them as a lovely song, as one that had a pleasant voice. He may upon the same ground delight in prayer. But this is a temper not kindled by the true fire of the sanctuary. Or do we delight in it, not when our tongues are most quick, but our hearts most warm; not because we have the best words, but the most spiritualized affections? We may have angels' gifts in prayer, without an angel's spirit.

2. Is there a delight in all parts of a duty, not only in asking temporal blessings, or some spiritual, as pardoning mercy, but in begging for refining grace? Are we earnest only when we have bosom quarrels and conscience convulsions, but flag when we come to pray for sanctifying mercy? The rise of this is a displacency with the trouble and danger, not with the sin and cause.

3. Doth our delight in prayer and spiritual things outdo our delight in outward things? The psalmist's joy in God was more than his delight in the harvest or vintage, Ps. vii. 4. Are we like ravens, that delight to hover in the air sometimes, but our greatest delight is to feed upon carrion? Though we have, and may have, a sensible delight in worldly things, yet is it as solid and rational as that we have in duty?

4. Is our delight in prayer an humble delight? Is it a rejoicing with humbling? Ps. ii. 11, 'Serve the Lord with gladness, and rejoice before him with trembling.' If our service be right, it will be cheerful, and if truly cheerful, it will be humble.

5. Is our delight in prayer accompanied with a delight in waiting? Do we, like merchants, not only delight in the first launching of a ship, or the setting it out of the haven with a full freight, but also in expectations of a rich return of spiritual mercies? Do we delight to pray, though God for the present doth not delight to give, and wait like David with an owning God's wisdom in delaying? Ps. cxxx. 6; or do we shoot them only as arrows at random, and never look after them where they light, or where to find them?

6. Is our delight in praising God, when mercy comes, answerable to the delight in praying, when a wanted mercy was begged? The ten lepers desired mercy with an equal cheerfulness, in hopes of having their leprosy cured, but his delight that returned only was genuine. As he prayed with a loud voice, so he praised with a loud voice, Luke xvii. 13, 15; and Christ tells him his faith had made him whole. As he had an answer in a way of grace, so he had before a gracious delight in his asking. The others had a natural delight, and so a return in a way of common providence.

Use 3, of exhortation. Let us delight in prayer. God loves a cheerful giver in alms, and a cheerful petitioner in prayer. God would have his children free with him. He takes special notice of a spiritual frame: Jer. xxx. 21, 'Who hath engaged his heart?' The more delight we have in God, the more delight he will have in us. He takes no pleasure in a lumpish service. It is an uncomely sight to see a joyful sinner and a dumpish petitioner. Why should we not exercise as much joy in holy duties as formerly we did in sinful practices? How delightfully will men sit at their games, and spend their days in gluttony and luxury! And shall not a Christian find much more delight in applying himself to God? We should delight that we can, and have hearts to ask, such gifts, that thousands in the world never dream of begging. To be dull is a discontentedness with our own petitions. Delight in prayer is the way to gain assurance. To seek God, and treat him as our chiefest good, endears the soul to him. Delighting in accesses to him will inflame our love; and there is no greater sign of an interest in him than a prevalent estimation of him. God casts off none that affectionately clasp about his throne.

To this purpose,

1. Pray for quickening grace. How often do we find David upon his knees for it! God only gives this grace, and God only stirs this grace.

2. Meditate on the promises you intend to plead. Unbelief is the great root of all dumpishness. It was by the belief of the word we had life at first, and by an exercise of that belief we gain liveliness. What maintains our love will maintain our delight; the amiableness of God and the excellency of the promises are the incentives and fuel both of the one and of the other. Think that they are eternal things you are to pray for, and that you have as much invitation to beg them, and as good promise to attain them, as David, Paul, or any other ever had. How would this awaken our drowsy souls, and elevate our heavy hearts, and open the lazy eyelids to look up! And whatever meditation we find begin to kindle our souls, let us follow it on, that the spark may not go out.

3. Choose the time when your hearts are most revived. Observe when God sends an invitation, and hoist up the sails when the wind begins to blow. There is no Christian but hath one time or another a greater activeness of spirit. Choose none of those seasons which may quench the heat and dull the sprightliness of your affections. Resolve beforehand this, to delight yourselves in the Lord, and thereby you shall gain the desire of your hearts.

A DISCOURSE OF MOURNING FOR OTHER MEN'S SINS.

And the Lord said unto him, Go through the midst of the city, through the midst of Jerusalem, and set a mark upon the foreheads of the men that sigh and that cry for all the abominations that be done in the midst thereof.—EZEKIEL IX. 4.

WHEN God in the former chapter had charged the Jews with their idolatry, and the multiplicity of abominations committed in his temple; and, ver. 18, had passed a resolve that he would not spare them, but deal in fury with them, though they should solicit him with the strongest and most importunate supplications; in this chapter he calls and commissions the executioners of his just decree: ver. 1, 'He cried also in mine ears with a loud voice, saying, Cause them that have charge over the city to draw near, even every man with his destroying weapon in his hand;' and declares whom, and in what manner, he would punish, and whom he would pardon. The executioners of God's vengeance are the Chaldeans, described by the situation of them from Judea, and the direct road from that country to Jerusalem: ver. 2, 'Six men came from the way of the higher gate, which lies towards the north.' Babylon lay north-east from Jerusalem, and this gate was the way of entrance for travellers from those parts. It led also into the court of the priests, which shews from whence the judgment should come, and upon whom it should light.

Six men. A certain number. Whether the Holy Ghost alludes to a particular number of nations, which the Chaldean army might be composed of under their prince, who reigned over several countries; or respects the other chief captains or marshals of his army which are named, Jer. xxxix. 3, or speaks with reference to the other places wherein the city was assaulted by that army, as some think, is uncertain.

And every man a slaughter-weapon in his hand. A hammer of destruction, an instrument of death; the word seems to signify a weapon much like a pole-axe.

And one of them clothed with linen, with a writer's inkhorn by his side. Christ, say the ancients (and so they understood it before, and in Jerome's time), who appears here in his priestly habit, a linen garment being the vestment of the priests, Lev. xvi. 4. White is an emblem of peace. Christ seals his people with his Spirit, the Spirit of peace. Calvin rejects not this interpretation, but rather understands it of an angel whom God commissioned to secure his people in this destroying judgment. And indeed angels have often appeared in the form of men, and clothed with linen; as to Daniel, chap. x. 5; xii. 6, 7. Christ's royal power is founded upon his priestly office, which is the ground of all the spiritual and temporal salvation believers have from God.

Inkhorn. The word is so translated. Though the word, say some, signifies a table, such as they then used to write upon with a pen of iron; or rather it signifies a case to put those pens in wherewith they wrote.

And they went and stood beside the brazen altar. It is uncertain whether this respects the original cause of their punishment, viz., their offering sacrifices to their idols upon that altar which was consecrated to the service of God, or else respects the sacrifices of vengeance, those were instrumentally to offer to God's justice. The judicial punishment of God's enemies is called a sacrifice in Scripture, Isa. xxxiv. 6; a sacrifice in Bozrah; Jer. xlvi. 10, God's day of vengeance is called God's sacrifice in the north country.

Obs. 1. With what a small number, if God please, can he destroy a city or nation. But six mentioned. Almightiness needs not great numbers to effect his will; no, not a man, since he can do it by his immediate hand, and command judgment in a trice.

2. How quick are God's creatures to obey his call for the punishment of a rebellious people. He calls those six men, and they presently appear ready to execute God's pleasure.

3. God doth not bring judgments on a people till their wickedness hath overgrown the goodness of his own children. Six to destroy, but one to preserve; a sixfold work of judgment to one of preservation, intimating that there were six bad to one good in the city.

4. The security of God's people in this world, as well as that to come, depends upon the priestly office of Christ.

Ver. 3. *And the glory of the God of Israel was gone up from the cherub, whereupon he was, to the threshold of the house.* The glory of God, which was in the propitiatory above the cherubims, went from one cherub to another till it came to the threshold; as birds that are leaving their nests leap from one branch to another till they fly quite away.

Obs. 1. God is not fixed to any one place; he hath his temple among his people; discovers himself in his ordinances, but upon provocations departs. The glory of God and his ordinances are not entailed upon any nation longer than they walk worthy of them.

2. The glory of God's ordinances is obscured among a people before judgments come upon them. The glory of God went up from the cherub. 'I will take away the hedge of my vineyard, and it shall be eaten up; and break down the wall thereof, and it shall be trodden down,' Isa. v. 5. The ordinances of God are understood by some interpreters to be the hedge and wall of a people; when God takes away the hedge, the breach is made wide for every wild beast to enter and tread it down. The presence of God in his ordinances, the presence of God in his providences, is the hedge of a people. The temple is forsaken by God, and then polluted, in judgment, by men, ver. 7. God then comes to the man clothed with linen, that had the writer's inkhorn by his side, and said unto him, 'Go through the midst of Jerusalem, and set a mark upon the foreheads of the men that sigh and that cry for all the abominations that be done in the midst thereof,' ver. 4; and ver. 5, he commands the executioners of his wrath to go after him, and smite without any pity both small and great, beginning at his sanctuary. תו; interpreters trouble themselves much what this mark should be, and tell us from Origen, that a believing Jew told him the ancient Samaritan letter called *tau* was written like a cross; but that is a fancy, the ancient Samaritan letter being the same with the Phenician, was not writ in that form. Some say it was the law, because the Hebrew word תורה, signifying the law, begins with that letter, to shew that such were to be marked that were devoted to the observance of the law.* Marked they were, saith Calvin, with a *tau;* because that being the last letter in the alphabet, shews that the people of God are of the lowest account among men, and the offscouring of the world; ת being the first letter of תחיה, *vives*, noted the preservation of them. *On the foreheads.* Alluding to the custom of the eastern countries to mark their servants on the foreheads with the names of their masters;† not on their visible foreheads, but on their invisible consciences. The conscience is the forehead of the soul, as eminent in the heart as a forehead in the body.‡

The blood of Christ upon the conscience is the best mark of distinction, as the blood of the paschal lamb upon the posts was the mark whereby the Israelites were discerned from the Egyptians, and the edge of the angel's destroying sword diverted from them. It was a mark of a special providence of God. The destroying judgments were to follow the sealing angel, and not touch those that were marked by him on the forehead.

Obs. 1. All judgments have their commissions from God, whom to touch, whom to overthrow. God doth not strike at random. The man in the linen garment was to bridle the Chaldeans, and direct their swords to the right objects. God overpowers the natural inclinations of all his creatures, whom he appoints executioners. God hath a hook in the nostrils of leviathan; nothing can be done without the leave of providence, 'man forms the weapons, God gives the edge and directs the stroke.

2. In the highest fury and vengeance, God hath reserves of mercy for his own people. Angels are appointed to be preservers of his children in the midst of the destroying of a people. Invisible angels are joined with visible enemies, to conduct and govern their motions according to the command of

* Vossius de Arte Grammat. lib. i. cap. † Grotius. ‡ Œcolampad.

their great general. God's judgments are dispensed with greater kindness to his people, than desires to take vengeance upon his enemies. He hath a heart of mercy as well as a hand of justice.

3. God is more careful of his people than revengeful against his enemies. He first orders the sealing of the mourners, before he orders the destruction of the rebels; he will first honour his mercy in the protection of the one, before he will glorify his justice in the destruction of the other. The angel hath orders to secure Lot before Sodom was fired. The executioners of his wrath were to march after the securing angel, not before him, nor equal with him, and were only to cut off those whom the angel had passed by.

4. If you take this mark for a mark on the conscience, then observe, that serenity of conscience is a gift of God to his people in the time of severe judgments. As when death is near, the conscience of a good man is most serene, and sings sweetly in his breast the notes of his own integrity. In judgments as well as in death, God sets conscience upon its pleasant notes. But this mark is not properly meant here; the conscience is a mark to ourselves, but this is a mark to the executioners.

5. The places where God hath manifested the glory of his ordinances, are the subjects of his greatest judgments upon their provocations. Go through the city, through Jerusalem; that Jerusalem wherein I have manifested my glory, which I have entrusted with my oracles, which I have protected in the midst of enemies, like a spark in the midst of many waters. Go through that city, into the midst of it, and let not your eye spare.

6. The greatest fury of God in a time of judgment often lights upon the sanctuary, ver. 6. Begin at the sanctuary, defile the house. Not a man of them escaped, as Œcolampadius notes: ver. 7, 'I was left.' He saw not in the vision what was done in the city, but he was left alone in the temple. The whole Sanhedrim, the seventy ancients, had revolted to idolatry, Ezek. viii. 11, and the stroke first lights upon them: ver. 6, 'Then they began at the ancient men which were before the house.'

In the verse observe,

1. God's care in the preserving his people. He commands the angel to go through the midst of the city, and set a mark, a visible mark, upon their foreheads.

2. The qualification of the persons so preserved. He doth not say, all that have not committed idolatry, but such as sigh, which signifies,

1. The intenseness of their grief: 'Sigh and cry,' אנק, notes an intense groaning and sorrow.

2. The extensiveness of the object: 'all the abominations.'

Doct. Lamenting the sins of the times and places wherein we live, is a duty incumbent on us, acceptable to God, and a great means of preservation under public judgments.

There are three branches.

1. It is a duty.

2. A duty acceptable to God. God has his eye particularly upon them that practise it.

3. It is a means of preservation under public judgments.

1. It is a duty. If we are by the prescript of God to bewail in confession the sins of our forefathers, committed before our being in the world, certainly much more are we to lament the sins of the age wherein we live, as well as our own: Lev. xxvi. 40, 'If they shall confess their iniquity, and the iniquity of their fathers. If then their uncircumcised be humbled, then will I remember my covenant.' Posterity are part of the same body with their ancestors, and every member in a nation is part of the body of a nation;

every drop in the sea is a part of the ocean. God made a standing law for an annual fast, wherein they should afflict their souls, the 'tenth day of the seventh month,' answering to our September, and backed it with a severe penalty. 'He whose soul was not afflicted in that day, should be cut off from among his people,' which the Jews understand of 'cutting off by the hand of the Lord,' Lev. xxiii. 27, 29. The particular sin for which they were thus annually to afflict their souls, was that national sin of the golden calf, in the judgment of the Jewish doctors.

It was also the practice of holy men in their private retirements; as Daniel, chap. ix. 5, 6. He bewails the sins of his ancestors; and Nehemiah, chap. i. 6. Much more it is our duty to bewail a present guilt. The church's eyes are compared to the fish-pools of Heshbon, Cant. vii. 4, in her weeping for her own and others' sins. To what purpose has God given us passions, but to honour him withal? And our affections of grief and anger cannot be better employed, than for the interest, nor better bestowed, than for the service of him who implanted those passions in us. Our natural motions should be ordered for the God of nature, and spiritual ordered for the God of grace.

1. This was the practice of believers in all ages. Before the deluge,* Seth called the name of his son, which was born at the time of the profaning the name of God in worship, Enos, which signifies sorrowful or miserable, that he might in the sight of his son have a constant monitor to excite him to an holy grief for the profaneness and idolatry that entered into the worship of God: Gen. iv. 26, 'He called his name Enos: then began men to call upon the name of the Lord;' הוחל, profane it by calling upon it.

The rational and most precious part of Lot was vexed with the unlawful deeds of the generation of Sodom, among whom he lived, 2 Peter ii. 7, 8; he had a horror and torment in his righteous soul at the execrable villanies he saw committed by his neighbours, καταπονούμενον, afflicted under it, as under a grievous burden. It was a rack to him, as the other word, ver. 8, ἐβασάνιζεν, signifies. The meekest man upon earth, with grief and indignation, breaks the tables of the law, when he saw the holiness of it broken by the Israelites, and expresseth more his regret for that, than his honour for the material stones, wherein God had with his own finger engraven the orders of his will. He is more desirous to destroy the idol, than preserve the tables; such an indignation against their sin could not well be without grief for it. David, a man of the greatest goodness upon record, had a deluge of tears, because they kept not God's law: Ps. cxix. 136, 'Rivers of waters run down mine eyes, because they keep not thy law.' Besides his grief, which was not a small one, horror seized upon him upon the same account, Ps. cxix. 53, like a storm that tossed him to and fro. How doth poor Isaiah bewail himself, and the people among whom he lived, as 'men of polluted lips!' Isa. vi. 5. Perhaps such as could hardly speak a word without an oath, or by hypocritical lip service, mocked God in the very temple.

Jeremiah is upon the same practice, Jer. xiii. 17, when his soul should weep in secret for the pride of the people; and, as if he was not satisfied with a few tears, wisheth his head were a full springing fountain to weep for the slain of the daughter of his people; for the sin the cause, as well as the calamity the effect, Jer. ix. 1. He wishes his head to be filled with the vapours from his heart, and become a fountain.

What a transport of sorrow had Ezra, when he heard of the people's sins, and the mingling the holy seed with that of idolaters! A horror ran through

* Broughton, Lives of the Fathers, p. 7. Crit in loc.

his whole soul. His astonishment is twice repeated, Ezra ix. 3, 4. Every faculty was alarmed at the sin of the people.

It is probable John Baptist used himself to those severities which are mentioned, Mat. iii. 4, because of the sinfulness of that generation among whom he lived.

Paul discovers it to be a duty, when he reproves the Corinthians for being puffed up, instead of mourning for that fornication which had been committed by one of their profession, 1 Cor. v. 2. And when he writes of some that made the glorious gospel subservient to their own bellies, he mixes his tears with his ink: Philip. iii. 18, 19, 'I tell you weeping, they are enemies to the cross of Christ. The primitive Christians did much bewail the lapses of their fellows. Celerinus, among the epistles of Cyprian, acquaints Lucian of his great grief for the apostasy of a woman, through fear of persecution, which afflicted him so, that in the time of Easter, the time of their joy in that age, he wept night and day, and was resolved that no delight should enter into his heart, till through the mercy of Christ she should be recovered to the church. And we find the witnesses clothed in sackcloth when they prophesied in a sinful time, to shew their grief for the public abominations, Rev. xi. 3. The kingdom of Satan can be no pleasure to a Christian, and must therefore be a torment.

2. It was our Saviour's practice. As he had the highest love to God, so he must needs have the greatest grief for his dishonour. He sighed in his spirit for the incredulity of that generation, when they asked a sign, after so many had been presented to their eyes: Mark viii. 12, 'He sighed deeply in his spirit.' And the hardness of their hearts at another time raised his grief as well as his indignation, Mark iii. 5. He was sensible of the least dishonour to his Father: Ps. lxix. 9, 'The reproaches of them that reproached thee, fell upon me.' I took them to heart. Christ pleased not himself when his Father was injured; as the apostle descants upon it, when he applies it to Christ, Rom. xv. 3. His soul was more pierced with the wrongs done to God, than the reproaches which were directed against his own person. His grief was inexpressibly greater than can be in any creature, because of the inimitable ardency of his love to God, the nearness of his relation to him, and the unspotted purity of his soul. Christ had a double relation: to man, to God. His compassion to men afflicted him with groans and tears at their bodily distempers; his affection to his Father would make him grieve as much to see him dishonoured, as his love to man made him groan to see man afflicted. This grief for sin was one part of Christ's sacrifice and suffering; for he came to make a full satisfaction to the justice of God by enduring his wrath, to the holiness of God by offering up an infinite sorrow for sin, which it was impossible for a creature to do. We cannot suppose that Christ should only accept the punishment, but not bewail the offence which was the cause of it. A sacrifice for the sins of others, without remorse for those sins, had not been acceptable; it had not been agreeable to the purity of his human nature. He wept at Jerusalem's obstinacy, as well as for her misery, and that in the time of his triumph. The loud hosannas could not silence his grief, and stop the expressions of it, Luke xix. 41. It was like a shower when the sun shined. If Christ as our head was filled with inward sorrow for men's displeasing the holiness of God, it is surely our duty, as his members, to imitate the afflictions of the head. He is unworthy of the name of Christ, who is not afflicted as Christ was, nor can call Christ his master, who doth not imitate his graces, as well as pretend to believe his doctrine; he cannot see that God, who hath distinguished him from the

world, dishonoured, his precepts contemned, but he must have his soul overcast with a gloomy cloud. It is our glory to value the things he esteemed, to despise the things he condemned, to rejoice in that wherein he was delighted, and to grieve for that which was the matter of his sorrow and indignation. Thus was he afflicted, though he had a joy in the assurance of his Father's favour, and the assistance of his Father's power. The highest assurance of God's love in particular to us, ought not to hinder the impressions of grief for the dishonour of his name. Did Christ ever look upon the swinish world without melting into pity? Did he bleed for the sins of the world, and shall not we mourn for them?

3. Angels, as far as they are capable, have their grief for the sins of men. The Jewish doctors often bring in the angels weeping for sin.* And one tells us, that in an ancient Mahomedan book he finds an answer of God to Moses, Even about this throne of mine there stand those, and they are many, that shed tears for the sins of men. But the Scripture tells us they rejoice at the repentance of men, Luke xv. 10. The Lord is glorified by the return of a subject; the subject advantaged by casting down his arms at the feet of his Lord. They do therefore, as far as they are capable, mourn for the revolts of men, *suo modo*, as Beza upon the place. They can scarce rejoice at men's repentance without having a contrary affection for men's profaneness. If they are glad at men's return, because God is thereby glorified, it cannot be conceived but they mourn for, and are angry with their sins, because God is thereby slighted. Unconcernedness at the dishonour of God cannot consist with their shining knowledge and burning love. They cannot behold a God so holy, so glorious, so worthy to be beloved, without having some regret for the neglects and abuses of him by the sons of men. How can they be instruments of God's justice if they are without anger against the deservers of it?

II. It is an acceptable duty to God. Since it is an imitating the copy of our Saviour, it is acceptable to God; nothing can please him more than to see his creatures tread in the steps of his Son.

1. It is a fulfilling the whole law, which consists of love to God and love to our neighbours. It is set down as a character of charity, both as it respects God and man, not to rejoice in iniquity, 1 Cor. xiii. 5, *i.e.* to be mightily troubled at it.

(1.) It is a high testimony of love to God. The nature of true love is to wish all good to them we love, to rejoice when any good we wish doth arrive unto them, to mourn when any evil afflicts them, and that with a respect to the beloved object. Τὸ φιλεῖν, τὸ βούλεσθαί τινι ἃ οἴεται ἀγαθὰ, ἐκείνου ἕνεκα, ἀλλὰ καὶ αὐτοῦ συναλγεῖν τοῖς λυπηροῖς.† Where there is this love, there is a rejoicing at one another's happiness, a grieving at one another's misfortunes. If it be a part of love to rejoice at that whereby God is glorified, it is no less a part of love to mourn for that whereby God is vilified. So strait is the union of affection between God and a righteous soul, that their blessings and injuries, joys and sorrows, are twisted together. The increase of God's glory is the greatest good that can happen to a soul enamoured of him; his dishonour, then, is the greatest misery. A gracious soul is like John Baptist, content to decrease that Christ might increase in the esteem of men. He is like Jonathan, that would rather have the crown upon David's head than his own, as the words intimate, 1 Sam. xxiii. 17, 'Thou shalt be king over Israel, and I shall be next unto thee.' And grieved more for his father's displeasure against David than against himself. So doth a Christian

* Grotius, Luc. xv. 7. Ob peccatum Hebræi angelos flentes inducunt.

† Aristot. Rhetor. lib. i. cap. iv.

grieve more for the wrongs of God than for those of his own liberty, estate, or life.

Joshua was more careful of the name of God than of the safety of the people singly considered: Joshua vii. 9, 'What wilt thou do unto thy great name?' The glory of God is not dear to that man that can without any regret look upon his bespattered name. What affection hath he to his friend, who can see him torn in pieces by dogs, and stand unconcerned at his calamity? God indeed is incapable of suffering; but what rending is to a creature, that is sin to the divine Majesty. Can that man be said to love God, who hath no reflection when he sees others tumbling God from his throne, and setting up the devil in his stead; who can hear the tremendous name of God belched out by polluted lips upon every vile occasion, and made the sport of stage and stews, without any inward resentment?

He only esteems God as his king who cannot see his laws broken without remorse. How loyally did Moses his affection to God work when he heard the name of God blasphemed, and saw a calf usurp the adoration due to the God of heaven! And David felt the stroke of that sword in his own bowels which was directed against the heart of God, Ps. cxxxix. 20–22. The dearer God's name is to any, the more affected they are that God and Christ are loved and honoured less than they desire they should be.

It is hard sometimes to discern this love to God when God's interest and ours are joined, when we would mask our displeasure against some men's offences with a care of God's honour, which is nothing but a hatred of the person sinning, or revenge against him for some conceived injury to us. The apostles' calling for fire from heaven upon the Samaritans when they refused Christ, Luke ix. 53–55, might seem to be a generous concern for their Master's honour, but Christ knew it proceeded much from their natural enmity which the Jews bore to the Samaritans. The best way to judge is, when the interest is purely God's, and hath no fuel of our own discontents to boil up, either grief or anger. Such an affection cannot but be highly acceptable to God, who is affected with the love of the creature, and honours them that honour him, as well as despises those that lightly concern themselves for him.

(2.) Love to our neighbour. Nothing can evidence our love to man more than a sorrowful reflection upon that wickedness which is the ruin of his soul, the disturbance of human society, and unlocks the treasures of God's judgments to fall upon mankind. 'Sin is a reproach to a people,' Prov. xiv. 34. It is always an act of charity to mourn for the reproaches and ruin of a people. It is a gross enmity to others to see them stab themselves to the heart, jest with eternal flames, wish their damnation at every word, run merrily to the bottomless gulf, and all this without bestowing a sigh upon them, and pitying their madness; the greater should be our grief, by how much the further they are from any for their own destruction. If Cain discovered both his enmity to God and also to his brother, in grieving that his brother's works were so good, Abel must needs, in the practice of the contrary duty, manifest his love to Cain in grieving that his works were so bad. Our Saviour's tears for the Jews discovered no less a concern for their misery than for God's dishonour. Anger for sin may have something of revenge in it; grief for sin discovers an affection both to God and the sinner. A duty which respects at once the substance of both the tables cannot but be pleasing to God.

2. It is an imitating return for God's affection. How doth God resent the injuries done to his people, as much as those done to himself? Those sins that immediately strike at his glory are not accompanied with such

quick judgments as those that grate upon his servants. Sharp persecutions that tear the people of God in pieces, have fuller vials of judgment here than volleys of other sins which rend the name of God. When Cain affronted God by his sacrifice, God comes not to a reckoning with him till he had added the murder of his brother to his former crimes against his Maker. A sweeter and more thankful return, and a more affectionate imitation of God, there cannot be, than to resent the injuries done to God more than those done to ourselves. The pinching of his people doth most pierce his heart, a stab to his honour, in gratitude, should most pierce theirs. The four kings that came against Sodom, Gen. xiv. 9, &c., sped well enough in their invasion, gained the victory, and had been in a fair way to have enjoyed the spoil, had they not laid their hands upon Lot, which was the occasion of their disgorging their prey. As God engaged himself in the recovery of Lot, so Lot concerned himself in the honour of God; God's anger is stirred at the captivity of Lot, and Lot's vexation is awakened at the injuries against God. What troubles his children, raises sensible compassion in him to the sufferer, and revenge upon the persecutor. Whatsoever doth blaspheme the name of God, doth at the same time rack a sincere heart. A persecutor cannot injure a believer, but Christ records it as a wrong done to himself; and Christ cannot be dishonoured by men, but a righteous soul doubles his grief. Here is a mutual return of affection and estimation which is highly pleasing.

3. This temper justifies God's law and his justice. David's grief being for man's forsaking the law, testified his choice valuation of it. When we dislike and disapprove of others' sins as well as our own, we acknowledge the glory of the law, that it is just, holy, and good, and set our seal of approbation to it. It justifies the holiness of the law in prohibiting sin, the righteousness of the law in condemning sin; it owns the sovereignty of God in commanding, and the justice of God in punishing. The law requires two things, obedience to it, and suffering for the transgression of it. This frame of heart approves of the obedience the law requires of men as rational creatures, and justifies the sufferings the law inflicts upon men as impenitent sinners. Unless we mourn for the sins of others, and thereby shew our distaste, we cannot give God the glory of his judgments which he sends upon a people. This disowning of sin is very acceptable to God, because by it men honour that law for whose violations they are so troubled, and own God's right of imposing a law upon his creatures, and the creatures' vileness in disgracing that law.

4. It is a sign of such a temper God hath evidenced himself in Scripture much affected with. It is a sign of a heart of flesh, the noblest work of God in the creature. A sign of a contrite heart, the best sacrifice that can smoke upon his altar, next to that of his Son. This he will not despise, because it is a beam of glory dropped down from him, and ascending in a sweet savour to him, Ps. li. 17. Without this, we cannot have a sufficient evidence that we are truly broken-hearted. We may mourn for our own sins for secret by-ends, because they are against our worldly interests, and have reproaches treading upon the heels of them; we may mourn for the sins of our friends, out of a natural compassion to them, and as they are the prognostics of some approaching misery to them; but in sorrowing for the sins of the world, we have not so many and so affecting obligations to divert us from a sound aim in our sorrow. To be affected with the dishonour of God in the sins of others, is a distinguishing character of a spiritual constitution from a natural tenderness. It is both our duty and God's pleasure. No grief is sweeter to God, nor more becoming us.

III. It is a means of preservation from public judgments. Noah did not preach righteousness without a sensible reflection on that unrighteousness he preached against; and he of all the world had the security of an ark for him and his family, when all the rest struggled for life, and sunk in the waters. No mere man ever wore more black for the funeral of God's honour than David, nor was any blessed with more gracious deliverances. The more zeal we have for God (which is an affection made up of grief and anger) the more protection we have from him. 'The steps of a man' (good man, our translation renders it; but the word is גבר, a valiant man) 'are ordered by the Lord, and he delights in his way,' Ps. xxxvii. 23. The more courage we have for God, the more we may expect both his conduct and security. If there be any hope in a time of actual or threatened judgments, it is by laying our mouths in the dust, Lam. iii. 29. If there be any ground of hope, it will shine forth when we are in such a posture. There might be others in Jerusalem who had not complied with the idolatry of that age, but none exempted from the stroke of the six destroyers, but those whose mouths lay in the dust, and whose cries against the common sin ascended to heaven. Only the mourners among the good men are marked by the angel for indemnity from the public punishment.

1. Sincerity always escapes best in common judgments, and this temper of mourning for public sins is the greatest note of it. This is the greatest note of sincerity. We read of an Ahab who put on sackcloth for his own sin, and humbled himself before the Lord; of a Judas sorrowing that he betrayed his master. Self interest might broach their tears, and force out their sorrow; but never an Ahab, or Judas, or any other ungodly person in Scripture, lamented the sins of others. Nay, they were all eminent for holiness that were noted for this frame, whom we have mentioned before: Moses, a non-such for speaking with God face to face; David, who only had that honourable title of a man after God's own heart; Isaiah, who had the fullest prospect of evangelical glory of all the prophets; Ezra, a restorer of his country; Daniel, a man greatly beloved; Christ, the Redeemer of the world; and Paul, the only apostle rapt up in the third heaven; he was also humbled for the sins of the Corinthians, 2 Cor. xii. 21. Ezra hath a mighty character: Ezra vii. 10, he 'prepared his heart to seek the law of the Lord, and to do it, and to teach in Israel statutes and judgments.' And he both mourned for and prayed against the common sin. Lot is not recorded for this without a glorious epithet; the Spirit of God overlooks those sins of his mentioned in Scripture, and speaks not of him by his single name, but 'just Lot,' 'his righteous soul,' 2 Peter ii. 7, 8; a sincere righteousness glittered in his vexation for the wronged interest of God. What a mark of honour doth the Holy Ghost set upon this temper! It is not drunken Lot, or incestuous Lot, with which sins he is taxed in Scripture; this publicly-religious spirit covered those temporary spots in his scutcheon. When all other signs of righteousness may have their exceptions, this temper is the utmost term, which we cannot go beyond in our self-examination. The utmost prospect David had of his sincerity, when he was upon a diligent inquiry after it, was his anger and grief for the sin of others. When he had reached so far, he was at a stand, and knew not what more to add: Ps. cxxxix. 21–24, 'Am I not grieved with those that rise up against thee? I hate them with perfect hatred; I count them mine enemies. Search me, O God, and know my heart; try me, and know my thoughts; and see if there be any wicked way in me.' If there be anything that better can evidence my sincerity than this, Lord, acquaint me with it; 'know my heart,' *i. e.* make me to know it. He whose sorrow is only for matter confined within his own breast, or streams

with it in his life, has reason many times to question the truth of it; but when a man cannot behold sin as sin in another without sensible regret, it is a sign he hath savingly felt the bitterness of it in his own soul. It is a high pitch and growth, and a consent between the Spirit of God and the soul of a Christian, when he can lament those sins in others whereby the Spirit is grieved; when he can rejoice with the Spirit rejoicing, and mourn with the Spirit mourning. This is a clear testimony that we have not self-ends in the service of God; that we take not up religion to serve a turn; that God is our aim, and Christ our beloved. Now, upright persons have special promises for protection: Ps. xxxvii. 18, 19, 'The Lord knows the way of the upright; they shall not be ashamed in an evil time.' They shall not be ashamed in it, though they may be dashed by it; they shall have a blessed inward security, though they may not always have an outward, when the wicked shall consume away as the fat of lambs, and exhale in the smoke. God's eyes are upon them in the worst of straits. If ever he shew himself strong, it is for those that are 'perfect in heart' before him. This is the end of the rolling and running of his 'eyes about the earth,' 2 Chron. xvi. 9. To such he is both a sun and a shield; a sun to comfort them, and a shield to defend them that walk uprightly, Ps. lxxxiv. 11. There may be an uprightness in the heart, when there is an unknown or a negligent crookedness in some particular path; and when men are negligent in reproving others for such sins as open the clouds of judgments, God may be a sun to such, to give them some comfort in a common calamity, but scarce a shield to defend them from it.

2. This frame clears us from the guilt of common sins. He that is not afflicted with them contracts a guilt of those insolences against God by a tacit approbation, or not hindering the torrent by his prayers, tears, endeavours. Sin is not to be viewed without horror; we share in the guilt if we manifest not our detestation of the practice. The Corinthians had not approved themselves clear in the matter of the incestuous person till they had mourned for it, 2 Cor. vii. 11. Jacob was afraid he should be charged by God as a murderer and thief, as well as Simeon and Levi, if he did not profess his loathing of it: Gen. xlix. 6, 'O my soul, come not thou into their secrets; unto their assembly, mine honour, be not thou united! for in their anger they slew a man, and in their self-will they digged down a wall.' His soul should bear a testimony against their secrets; he would count it his dishonour to give their sin any countenance before God or man. David intimates, Ps. ci. 3, that if he did not hate the works of those that turn aside, the guilt of them would cleave to him. If we can patiently bear the dishonour of God without marks of our displeasure, we shall be reckoned in the common infection, as one lump with the greatest sinners. He that is not with Christ is against him; he that is not on the side of God by a holy grief, is on the side of sin by a silent consent. A thorough distaste of sins, upon the account of their abomination to God, frees us from the guilt of them in the sight of God. To mourn for them, and pray against them, is a sign we would have prevented them if it had lain in our power; and where we have contributed to them, we, by those acts, revoke the crime. When we cannot be reformers, all that we can do is to turn mourners, and in our places admonishers and reprovers; and God is righteous not to charge the guilt where it is not contracted or revoked. But where any are infected with common sins, they must expect to taste of some common judgments.* The Israelites did partake of some of the Egyptian sins; and though God was upon their deliverance, yet he inflicteth upon them some of the Egyptian

* Lightfoot, Glean. on Exod. vi. 13.

plagues. The plague of lice, which was the first God brought, without being imitated by the magicians, was common upon the Israelites as well as the Egyptians; for God did not sever Goshen from Egypt till the plague of flies: Exod. viii. 12, 23, 'In that day will I sever the land of Goshen; I will put a division between my people and thy people.' And therefore, in Ps. lxxviii., the psalmist, reckoning those plagues, never mentions the lice, because that was inflicted upon Israel as well as Egypt. This is a way to keep the soul from common infection. It is difficult for a soul to defile itself with the sins of the times, when tears are continually running down the eyes for them. It is an antidote against the sin, and against the plague which follows at the heels of it. If we look not upon them with grief, we are in danger to be snared in the same temptation. Besides, not sorrowing for them is an implicit consent to them; and by consenting to them, we are little better than actors in them. By grieving for them, we enter our dissent, and pass our vote against them. When any sin becomes national, it is imputed to the body of the nation; as, in some transgressions of the law, the whole body of the nation of the Jews was involved; and there is no way for any particular person to remove the guilt from him, but by disowning it before God.

3. A grief for common sins is an endeavour to repair the honour God has lost. It is a paying to God that, by repentance (as much as lies in a creature), which is due from the worst sinner himself; it is to keep up some of God's glory, when so much is trodden down. And when the grief is accompanied with a more exact obedience, it repairs the honour God hath lost by the miscarriage of others. It is an endeavour to wipe off the stains from the robe of the glory of God. And those that bear up God's glory in the world shall find, if need be, the creative, omnipotent power of God stretched out for their defence in as eminent a manner as the cloud by day, which preserved the Israelites from the scorching of the sun, or the flaming fire by night, which prevented their wandering into by-ways and precipices; for upon all the glory shall be a defence, Isa. iv. 5, *i. e.* upon those that bear the mark of his glorious redemption, and bear up his honour among the sons of men. When we concern ourselves for God's honour, God will concern himself for our protection. God never was, or ever will be, behind-hand with his creature in affection. Moses was zealous for God's glory against the golden calf, and God concerned himself for his honour against Aaron and Miriam, Numb. xii., and then against the tumults of the people.

4. The mourners in Sion are humble, and humility is preventive of judgments. To lie flat upon the ground, is a means to avoid the stroke of a cannon-bullet. 'When men are cast down, he shall save the humble person,' Job xxii. 29. They lie lowest in the dust before God, who concern themselves not only with the weight of their own sins, but with that of others. Pride is a preparation for judgment; the higher the tower aspires, the fitter tinder it is for lightning; the bigger anything swells, the nearer it is to bursting; the prouder any man is, the plainer butt he is for an arrow of God's wrath. Pride lifts up itself against God's laws and sovereignty, as much as this frame of spirit acknowledges and submits to him. It was a temper contrary to this caused God to send worms to banquet upon Herod: Acts xii. 23, 'He gave not God the glory.' He was not afflicted with the sin of the people, nor reproved them for ascribing to him the honour of God. A soul affliction for common sins is a bar to judgments. God revives the spirit of the humble, Isa. lvii. 15. They that share in the griefs of the Spirit, shall not want the comforts of the Spirit. God is concerned in honour, by virtue of his promise, not to neglect those whom he hath promised to revive. He dwells with the contrite spirit; who more contrite than he that grieves for

public sins, and family sins, and city sins, as well as his own private? Men do not use to fire their own houses, much less God the house and heart, which is dearer to him than either first or second temple, or local heaven itself. I might add,

5. That such keep covenant with God. The contract runs on God's part to be an enemy to his people's enemies, Exod. xxiii. 22. It must run on our parts to love that which God loves, hate that which God hates, grieve for that which grieves and dishonours him; who can do this by an unconcernedness? Those that keep covenant with God shall not fail of one tittle of it on God's part. 6. Such also fear God's judgments, and fear is a good means to prevent them. The old world feared not God's threatening of the deluge, and that came and swallowed them up. The Sodomites feared not God's judgments, and that hastened the destroying shower. The advice of the angel upon the approach of judgments, is to fear God, and give glory to him, Rev. xiv. 7. And then follows another, ver. 8, with the news of Babylon's fall: 'Babylon is fallen, is fallen.' The fall of Babylon is the preservation of his people.

IV. The use. 1. Reproof for us. Where is the man that hangs his harp upon the willows at the time the temple of God is profaned? A head, a fountain of tears for common sins, is a commodity rare to be found even in hearts otherwise gracious. The mourners have been for number but a few, like the gleanings of the vintage; but the sinners in Sion for multitude, like the weeds in fallow ground. What multitudes of those that disparage God, and trample upon his sovereign commands, rend in pieces the very law of nature, as well as the rights of religion! It were well if there were one to six, as was intimated in the beginning there might be in Jerusalem; but we have reason to fear that one marker for the secret mourners would be too much for an hundred destroyers. I do not question but there are some that sigh for the abominations they see and hear of, and that because they are dishonourable to God, as well as injurious to themselves. But who of us present here can say, we have been deeply enough, and graciously enough, affected with them? Certainly, both you and I may bring a charge against ourselves before the throne of God for this neglect, that we have not been thoroughly humbled for, and frequently bewailed public iniquities, and spread them before God in secret. If we are unconcerned in common sins, can we imagine God will leave us unconcerned in common judgments? If we endeavour not to keep up the glory of God, he will extract glory to himself out of our ashes. If this frame be so little regarded among professors, what shall we say to many others, that have as little remorse for the stabs of God's honour as they would have for the tragedy of an East India prince, nay, for the death of some inconsiderable fly; that have resentments for wrongs done to themselves, and sorrow at command for any worldly loss, but not one spark of regret for affronts offered to God? In this cause their hearts are as dry as heath in a parching summer. Who laments the tearing the name of God in pieces by execrable oaths? Who bewails the impudent uncleanness boasted of by concubines in the face of the sun? Who mourns for so many thousand foreheads bearing the mark of the beast, and so many thousands more preparing to receive it? It reproves, then,

1. Those that make a mock and sport of sin, so far they are from mourning for it. The wise man gives them the title of fools: Prov. xiv. 9, 'Fools make a mock at sin;' which, though it seems too low a character for such abominable works, yet in Scripture it hath a greater import than in our common discourse; it signifies an atheist, Ps. xiv. 1. Prodigious madness!

to make that our sport which is the dishonour of God, the murderer of Christ, the grief of the Spirit, and the destruction of the soul; that which opens the flood-gates of wrath, and brings famines, plagues, wars upon a people! If mourning for others' sins be an affection like that of angels, delighting in others' sins is an affection like that of devils. He is at the greatest distance from Christ that looks pleasantly upon that which Christ could not regard without grief and anger. God seems to seal up such to destruction, as well as the mourners to preservation: Isa. xxii. 12, 13, 'And in that day did the Lord God of hosts call to weeping and mourning, to baldness and girding with sackcloth: and behold joy and gladness, slaying oxen and killing sheep, eating flesh and drinking wine: let us eat and drink, for to-morrow we shall die. And it was revealed in mine ears by the Lord of hosts, Surely this iniquity shall not be purged from you till you die.' They were ranters instead of mourners, and God passes this sentence on them, 'Their iniquity shall not be purged from them till they die.' If we carry ourselves jollily at the sins of others, we evidence that the concerns of God are of little concern to us, that we have slight thoughts of his glory, and cast it at the heels of our own passions.

2. Those that make others' sins the matter of invectives, rather than of lamentations, and bespatter the man without bewailing the sin. We should consider common sins with affection to God, and pity to the offenders, with a desire that they may restore, by a true conversion, the glory they have robbed God of by an accursed rebellion. While we hate the sin, we should evidence that we love the man.* We must never love the wickedness, nor hate the person. We pity a sick man, though we loathe his disease. Sinners are miserable enough without our hatred, and by hating them we make ourselves more miserable, by committing a fault against reason and nature, and do them no good. The more wicked any man is, the more worthy of pity, by how much the more his crime is our hatred. God, who is infinite purity, hates men's sins, because they are enemies to his holiness; but he hath a common affection to their persons, as they are the effects of his goodness and creative power. Our exclamations against common sins ought not to exceed lamentations for them. There ought to be more grief in our hearts, than fire in our tongues. They break the whole law that lament not the crime out of love to the law-maker, and grieve not for the sinner out of love to their neighbour.

3. Those who are imitators of common sins, instead of being mourners for them; as though others did not pilfer God's right fast enough, and were too slow in pulling him from his throne; as if they grieved that others had got the start of them in wickedness. It is a pious sadness, and a blessed grief, to be affected with common sins, without being fettered by them; to mourn for them, without cleaving to them; to be transported with sorrow for them, without being drawn by a love to them.

4. Those that fret against God, instead of fretting against their own foolishness, Prov. xix. 3. The sins of good men are many times provocations to God to draw up the sluice from the hearts of wicked men, and give liberty to their lusts, for the chastening of others; and therefore, in grieving for the sins of others, they implicitly grieve for their own.

5. Those who are more transported against others' sins, as they are, or may be, occasions of hurt to them, than as they are injuries to God. How warm are we often in our own cause, and how cold in God's! We partly satisfy our own discontent by such a carriage, but not our duty.

6. Those who are so far from mourning for common sins, that they never

* Nonnunquam sævituri in culpam sævimus in hominem.—*Prosper.*

truly mourned for their own; who have yet the treasures of wickedness, after the rod of God hath been upon them: Micah vi. 9, 10, 'Are there yet the treasures of wickedness in the house of the wicked?' reflecting upon the rod they had felt. Common sins are but a glass wherein we may see our common nature. The best men have the worst sins in their nature, though, by grace, they have them not in their practice. He that grieves not for other men's sins, more or less, never grieved truly for his own. He that is not concerned for the dishonours of God by others, is little concerned for the dishonour of God by himself. Let us use our eyes for those ends for which God hath given them; they are instruments of sight, and instruments of sorrow.

It is necessary for us to mourn for our own sins. We can never mourn for others' sins unless we mourn for our own. If we sorrow not for our own, the sorrow we may pretend to have for others proceeds not from a right cause. We have that one sin of Adam in our nature, which subjected the whole world to an anathema. Let us not stay in generals; every man will lay the fault upon sin in the bulk, without reflecting on the sin in his own bowels. We can complain particularly of those sins that are common, and why should we rest in generals when we come to our own? *Dolus versatur in universalibus*, it is a deceitful sorrow that is for sin in a heap. Is there not perfidiousness to God, coldness in his ways, too much slighting the gospel, want of bowels and compassion, incorrigibleness under judgments, houses fired and pride not consumed; falseness in resolutions, like oxen moving with the touch of the goad, and presently standing still; deceitful bows, letting the string slip after they have stood fully bent? Hosea x. 4. There may be sins among us that may cause a storm that we little think of; the mariners little suspected Jonah to be the cause of the tempest till he discovered it himself. He that never mourned for his own sins cannot perform this duty so necessary for his preservation, and therefore cannot expect the mark of God in a time of public judgment. He that would rightly mourn for the corruptions of others, must inquire whether he hath not the same in his own bowels, and fling the hardest stone at them. Judah calls for Tamar to the flames for that crime which himself had been a partner and actor in; so apt are we to be severe against others' sins, and indulgent to our own. The best have need to mourn for their own sins in relation to the public; the only good man in the ship was Jonah, and for his sin was the storm sent, and the rest like to be wrecked.

Use 2. Of comfort to such as mourn for common sins. All the carnal world hath not such a writ of protection to shew in the whole strength of nature, as the meanest mourner in Sion hath in his sighs and tears. Christ's mark is above all the shields of the earth; and those that are stamped with it have his wisdom to guard them against folly, his power against weakness, the everlasting Father against man, whose breath is in his nostrils. We see that God doth not strike at random, but reserves a sweetness for his servants in the midst of his fury against his enemies; he hath his messengers to mark as well as his executioners to strike; the issuing the resolute orders of his fury hinders not those of his grace and compassion to his own. He will have a care of his balsam trees that distil this precious liquor, no less than he commanded the Israelites in their sharpest wars to have a care of the 'fruitful trees of a land,' Deut. xx. 19. God in the six verses following the text gives the like charge to the executioners of his judgments, as David did to the army concerning Absalom: 2 Sam. xviii. 5, 'Deal gently with the young man;' Ezek. ix. 6, 'Come not near any man upon whom is the mark.' He makes provision first for the security of those, before he unsheathes his sword against his enemies. The deluge flows not from heaven till Noah be cased in the ark, nor is Sodom on fire till Lot be lodged in the mountain. God will always have a church in the world, and suffer a generation of his own to inhabit the earth. God's attributes shall not interfere one with another; his truth remains firm notwithstanding the provocations of men. When those people were ripe for judgments, God had his mourners among the idolaters, which he marks for preservation. When he had threatened great judgments, Joel ii. 30, 31, the turning the sun into darkness and the moon into blood, he promises a remnant in Jerusalem and Sion: ver. 32, 'And it shall come to pass, that whosoever shall call upon the name of the Lord shall be delivered; for in mount Sion, and in Jerusalem, shall be deliverance, as the Lord hath said, and in the remnant whom the Lord shall call.' Neither the fury of men shall, nor the judgments of God will, extinguish the church; nor the malice of men, because of God's power; nor God himself, because of his truth: 'The Lord hath said.' God will either preserve under judgments, or take away in them to a place of happiness. It is thought by some that the reason Enoch was snatched to heaven in the midst of his life, according to the rate of living in that age, was because he was afflicted with the sins of those among whom he lived. And indeed he could scarce walk with God without grieving that others disdained to walk with him, and acted contrary to him. God would take him from that affliction, as well as from the danger of being corrupted by the age. He will either have his chambers wherein to hide them here till the indignation be overpast, Isa. xxvi. 20, 21; or his mansions to lodge them in for ever with himself. What hurt is it to any to be refused a hiding-place here, that he may be conducted to the possession of a glorious residence for ever? That judgment that takes off the fetters of a wicked man for execution, knocks off the fetters of the godly for a jail delivery; like fire, it consumes the dross and refines the gold. The day of God's wrath is 'a day of gloominess to the wicked,' Joel ii. 2; but as the morning spread upon the mountains to the godly mourners, the dawning of comfort to them. God, out of the same pillar of the cloud, diffused light upon the Israelites, and shot thunders and lightnings upon the Egyptians, to which perhaps the prophet might here allude.

Use 3. Mourn for the sins of the time and place where you live. It is the least dislike we can shew to them. A flood of grief becomes us in a flood of sin. How well would it be if we were as loud in crying for mercy, as our sins at the present are in crying for vengeance! While judgments run to seize our persons, our grief should run to damp the judgments; moist walls choke the bullet. It is far better to mourn for the cause of judgments, than to mourn under them. The jolly blades were the first prey to the enemy: Amos vi. 1–3 to verse 7, 'They that chaunt to the sound of the viol, and drink wine in bowls, shall go captive with the first that go captive.' We of this city have most reason to mourn; the metropolis of a nation is the metropolis usually of sin, and the fairest mark for the arrows of God's indignation. The chief city of a nation is usually threatened in Scripture: Rabbah of the Ammonites, Damascus of Syria, Tyrus of Phenicia, Babylon of the Chaldean empire, Jerusalem of Judea; and, suitably, why not London of England? And let no man think that mourning is a degenerate and effeminate disposition. Doth Solomon ever imprint the same character on mourning as he doth on laughter? Eccles. ii. 2. Doth he ever vilify that with a term of madness, and call the mourners bedlams? How can any, who hath not put off the title and nature of man, behold without amazement and grief men so bold as to pull down the judgments of God upon them, and force his indignation! This temper is a pious embalming Christ's crucified honour; shall any man that professeth Christ have so little love to him, as not to bestow a groan upon him when he sees him freshly dishonoured and abused? If we had not committed any sin in our whole life, there is cause of mourning for the abominations of the world. Christ had an unspotted innocence and an unexpressible grief for Jerusalem's sins and misery: 'O Jerusalem, Jerusalem, how often would I have gathered thee, and thou wouldest not!' Never doth sorrow more appear in love than when it is more for what dishonours God than what pincheth us. Men may pretend a grief for the sins of the times, when it is only for themselves, that they have not those pleasing opportunities of greatening themselves, and that estimation in the world, that stage for pride and covetousness to act upon, which they desire. Our mourning is then right, when we grieve not so much that we, as that God, is a sufferer. It should be proportionable where there are great breaches of God's law; our grief should be as full as, if possible, to fill up the ditch that is digged. The Septuagint in the text implies it, καταστεναζόντων. Paul and Barnabas tore their garments (a sign of a great grief and indignation) when the heathens would have sacrificed to them as gods, Acts xiv. 13. They used not the same expressions in smaller sins; but this was against the nature of God, and a multitude engaged in it. The greater the sin, the greater the sorrow. I need not mention the sins among us; the impudent atheism, contempt of the gospel, putrefying lust, barefaced pride, rending divisions, many sins visible enough to be grieved for, and too many to be spoken of. The sorrow should be universal. Not for one sin which may be against any man's particular interest; but for all, even those that our carnal advantage is not concerned in. God is dishonoured by one as well as by another, and Christ is crucified by one as well as by another. It must be attended with a more strict obedience. It is the highest generosity to wear Christ's livery when others put it off and lay it aside as useless. No doubt but Joseph of Arimathea mourned as well as the rest for the sufferings of our Saviour; but he testified also an heroic affection to him in going boldly to Pilate to beg the body of Jesus for an honourable burial, when none of the other disciples sought after it, but trusted more to the swiftness of their heels for their own security, than concerned themselves for the honour of their Master. While others therefore are defiling the world with their abominations, let us be washing it with our tears, and filling heaven with our cries; that when God marcheth in his fury, we may be secure by his acceptance of our humiliations.

Motives.

1. This is a means to have great tokens of the love of God. No question but Christ in his agony bewailed the sins of the world, and then was an angel sent to comfort him, and assure him of an happy issue. It was just after the testimony of his displeasure against Peter for dissuading him from that death, whereby he was to honour God, and wash off the stain of sin, and repair the violations of the law, whereby he manifested a concern for his Father's honour, that he was transfigured, and had therein the earnest of an heavenly glory, and that transporting voice, 'This is my beloved Son, in whom I am well pleased, hear you him,' Mat. xvi. 23, xvii. 1, 2, &c.

2. It is a means to prevent judgments. Tears cleansed by the blood of Christ are a good means to quench that justice which is a consuming fire. Sin puts a stop to the working of God's bowels, and opens the magazines of wrath; grief for it disarms God's hand of his thunders, and may divert his darts from our hearts. No other defence is often left against the strength of judgments after sin hath made its entrance. A 'holy seed in Jerusalem' is the guard of it in the time of Sennacherib's invasion: Isa. vi. 13, 'The holy seed shall be the substance thereof.' Growth in sin ripens judgments, turns blossoms and buds into fruit, rods into scorpions; grief for it turns scorpions

into rods, lessens a judgment if not wholly prevents it. The water of repentance is the best way to quench the flames of sin and sparks of wrath. If good men fall under a common judgment, it may be often for a defect in this temper. This was Austin's opinion: that many good men are taken away with the wicked in common judgments; because, though they do not commit the same sins, yet they connive at their iniquities, and so are lashed with rods; temporally chastened, but not eternally punished.*

3. It will sweeten judgments. Such may say of judgment as Paul of death, O judgment, where is thy sting! It is a double burden to lie under the weight of common judgments and the weight of common sins; grief for them is a means to remove the guilt, and thereby to ease thee of a judgment. If we are concerned in mourning for sin, we shall be more fit to honour God, if he makes us fall under his stroke. A holy sorrow will bring us into a submissive frame. Aaron had been, without question, humbled for his timorous compliance with the people in the making of the golden calf; and when God came to strike him near in his own children, he held his peace, Lev. x. 3. No doubt but his former humiliation fitted him for his present patience.

4. Our repentance for our own sins was never right, unless we are of this temper. Repentance is a justice towards God, and therefore is conversant about other men's sins in a hatred of them. It is for sin as sin, and sin is sin in whatsoever subject it be, and worthy of hatred according to right reason, and therefore that grace whereby a man hates it in his own person, will engage him to hate it wheresoever it is; and we always grieve for the increase of that which is the object of our hatred. A truly just man hates the injury committed against another as well as that against himself. That filthiness which displeaseth a penitent in his own act, displeaseth him in another's act, there being the same adequate reason, and sin being of the same nature against God in another as in himself. It is all abominations in the text; this is an argument of sincerity. To mourn for one may be from self-interest, to mourn for all must be from a pure affection.

5. It is an argument of a true affection to God. To mourn for sin when it is rare, though gross, is not so much a sign of sincerity as to mourn for it when it is epidemical, when the foundations of godliness are out of course, and the graces contrary to those sins are generally discountenanced; as it is a greater sign of sincerity to love the word when it is generally slighted, than to love it when all admire it. What a noble affection had that lady in Samuel, 1 Sam. iv. 19, &c., that grieved not so much for the loss of her father, husband, friends, but bewailed the departure of the glory of Israel, and, implicitly at least, the sin that occasioned it! How did her affection to God drown all carnal affections! Her sorrow for the ark stifled the sorrow of her travail, and the joy at the birth of her son. She regarded it not. This is an evident token of affection, when we mourn most for the sins which most dishonour God, and the sins of those persons that seem to be nearer to God, and cast most reproaches upon his name.

6. Shall we be outstripped by idolaters? The mourning for others' sins was a custom kept up in Israel after their revolt from God unto Jeroboam. When Naboth was put to death for a pretended crime of blasphemy, a fast was proclaimed, to lament his sin, 1 Kings xxi. 12; and though with a wicked intention, to palliate a murder with the cloak of religion, yet it evidenceth this mourning for the gross sins of others to be a common sentiment among them, and practised upon the like occasions.

7. We have just fears of judgments; we know not whence they will come,

* August. de Civit. Dei. lib. i. cap. ix.

from the north or from the south. God sets up his warnings in the heavens; we behold him frowning and preparing his arrows, and are we careless in what posture we shall meet him? He hath spit in our faces, made us a by-word and reproach; should we not be humbled? Num. xii. 14, 'If her father had spit in her face, should she not be ashamed?' God seems to be departing. He hath, as it were, kept open market a long time; he seems now to be putting up his wares, removing his candlestick, withdrawing the power of his ordinances, recalling his messengers; the light is almost in the socket. The voice of God is received with a deaf ear, the reproofs and admonitions of God have not a kindly operation, the signs of judgment amaze us, and the amazement quite vanishes. We start like a man in a dream, and fall back upon our pillow, and snort out our sleep. Can we expect God to stay? He seems to be upon the threshold of the temple, come down already from the cherubims, and is it not high time to bewail our own sins, and the common abominations that have so polluted the place of his habitation, that we may say we cannot see how God can stay with honour to himself? If we bewail the sins that provoke him to it, God may stay; if he will not, let us at least shew this affection to him at parting. This is not a thing unbecoming the highest Christian. Doth not the Spirit grieve for the sins of others, which play the wantons with the grace of God? Eph. iv. 30, 'Grieve not the Holy Spirit of God.' The Holy Spirit hath no sins of his own to grieve for. Shall we be above that which the Spirit of God thinks himself not above? Shall we refuse mourning for that which goes to the heart of the Holy Ghost? Let us therefore examine what are our own sins, what are the abominations of the times and places wherein we live; make inquisition for the one, that we may drag them out before the Lord, and in our places endeavour to stop and reform the other. As the true fire of love to God will melt us into tears, so it will heat us into zeal. He is no friend that will complain of a toad's being in another's bosom, but not strive to kill it. It will shew either cowardice or falseness. That zeal is wild-fire that is not accompanied with an holy sorrow, and that sorrow is crude which is not accompanied with a godly zeal.

A DISCOURSE FOR THE COMFORT OF CHILD-BEARING WOMEN.

Notwithstanding she shall be saved in child-bearing, if they continue in faith, and charity, and holiness, with sobriety.—1 TIM. II. 15.

I SHALL not take my rise any higher than ver. 12, where the apostle orders that a woman should not teach: 'But I suffer not a woman to teach,' *i.e.* publicly.

Two reasons are rendered.

1. She was last in creation.* 'Adam was first formed, then Eve.'

2. First in defection: ver. 14, 'And Adam was not deceived, but the woman being deceived, was in the transgression.' The fall of man was the fruit of the woman's first doctrine, and therefore she is not suffered to teach

* Hierom.

any more. The woman was deceived by the serpent, and so drew her husband and whole posterity into ruin. Some of the papists bring this place as an argument against women's reading the Scripture; but no reason can conclude it from this place. How can the Spirit of God prohibit their reading the Scripture in private, and the instruction of their families, since women are among those who are commended for reading the Scripture? Acts xvii. 11, 12, where the honourable women are mentioned; and Lois and Eunice are applauded for their instruction of Timothy. Are not women bound, by that command of Peter, to give a reason of their faith to any that shall ask them, unless they would have women Christians without reason? What was the office of those ecclesiastical widows in the primitive times, but to instruct the younger women? But this is not to be charged upon all the papists: Becanus only is the man that Rivet mentions.* And because, upon this declaration of the apostle, some might be dejected by the consideration of the deep hand the woman had in the first fall, in the punishment inflicted upon them for it, the apostle in the text brings in a 'notwithstanding' for their comfort. Notwithstanding her guilt in defection, her punishment in child-bearing, she hath as good a right to salvation as the man; so that the apostle here answers, by way of anticipation, an objection which might be made, whether the guilt contracted by the woman, and the punishment inflicted, might not hinder her eternal salvation. The apostle answers, No. Though she was first in the transgression, and the pain of child-bearing was the punishment of that first sin, yet the woman may arrive to everlasting salvation notwithstanding that pain, if she be adorned with those graces which are necessary for all Christians. Though the punishment remain, yet the believing woman is in the covenant of grace, under the wings of the mediator of that covenant, if she have faith, the condition of the covenant, which works by love and charity, and is attended with holiness and renewal of the heart.

Observe, God hath gracious cordials to cheer up the hearts of believers in their distress, and in the midst of those cases which are sufficient of themselves to cast them down. The apostle here alludes to that curse upon the woman: Gen. iii. 16, 'Unto the woman he said, I will greatly multiply thy sorrow and thy conception: in sorrow thou shalt bring forth children.' The punishment is peculiar to the married woman, besides that punishment which was common to her with the man.

Thy sorrow and thy conception. Hendiadis, say some; the sorrow of thy conception. The word הרנך signifies the whole time of the woman's bearing in the womb, and so includes not only those pains in the very time of labour, but also all those precursory indispositions, as the weakness of the stomach, heaviness of the head, irregular longings, and those other symptoms which accompany conceptions. Though this pain seems to be natural, from the constitution of the body, yet since some other creatures do bring forth with little or no pain,† it would not have been so with the woman in innocency, because all pain, which is a punishment of sin, had not been incident to a sinless and immortal body.

We will consider the words apart.

Saved. It may either note the salvation of the soul, or the preservation of the woman in child-bearing. The first, I suppose, is principally intended; for the apostle here would signify some special comfort to women under that curse. But the preservation of women in child-bearing was a common thing testified by daily experience in the worst, as well as in the best women, and Christianity did not bring the professors of it into a worse estate in those

* Isagog. ad Script. c. xiii. pp. 990, 991.

† Arist. Hist. Animal. l. vii. c. ix.

things which immediately depended upon God, or make the children vipers, not to come into the world without the death of their mothers ; yet a temporal preservation may be included, for when an eternal salvation is promised, temporal salvation is also promised, according to the methods of God's wisdom and goodness in the course of his providence, there being in all such promises a tacit reserve, viz., if God sees it good for us ; and the manner of their preservation also, wherein the preservation of a believer differs from that of an unregenerate person. Others are preserved by God, as a merciful Creator and Governor, in a way of common providence, for the keeping up of the world ; but believers are preserved in the way of promise and covenant, in the exercise of faith, and by the special love of God, as a tender Father, and their God in covenant with them through Christ.

In child-bearing. Διὰ τεκνογονίας, through child-bearing. The preposition δια is often taken for ἐν, as Rom. iv. 11, 'That he might be the Father of all that believe,' though they be not circumcised, πιστευόντων δι' ἀκροβυστίας, believing in uncircumcision, where it notes the state wherein they shall be saved. So it notes here, not the cause of the salvation of the woman, but the state wherein she shall be saved, and amounts to this much : the punishment inflicted upon the woman for her first sin shall not be removed in this life, yet notwithstanding this, there is a certain way of salvation by faith, though she pass through this punishment. For by τεκνογονία is not meant a simple child-bearing, but a child-bearing in such a manner as God hath threatened with sorrow and grief.

If they continue. By *they* is not meant the children, as some imagine, because of the change of the singular to the plural ; the sense then should run thus : she shall be saved, if the children remain in faith, &c. That would be absurd to think that the salvation of the mother should depend upon the faith and grace of the children, when it is sometimes seen that the children of a godly mother may prove as wicked as hell itself. But by *they* is meant the woman. The name *woman* is taken collectively for all women, and therefore the plural number is added. The apostle passes from the singular number to the plural, as he had done from the plural to the singular, ver. 9, 'In like manner let the women adorn themselves' in modesty, where he uses the plural, but ver. 11, reassumes the other number again in his discourse. The graces which are here put as the conditions, are faith, charity, sanctification, sobriety ; where the apostle seems to oppose those to the first causes or ingredients of the defection.

1. Faith opposed to unbelief of the precept of God and the threatening annexed.

2. Charity, opposed to disaffection to God ; as though God were an enemy to their happiness, and commanded a thing which did prejudice their happiness, whereupon must arise ill surmises of God, and an aversion from him.

3. Sanctification. In opposition to this filthiness and pollution brought upon the soul by that first defection, there must therefore be in them an aim and endeavour to attain that primitive integrity and purity they then lost.

4. Sobriety, Σωφροσύνη, temperance. Because the giving the reins to sense, and obeying the longings thereof, was the cause of the fall, Gen. iii. 6. She saw that it was pleasant to the eye. Original sin is called concupiscence, and lusting, and to this is opposed sobriety.

1. *Faith.* This is put first, because it is a fundamental grace. It is the employer of charity, for it works by it ; the root of sanctification, for by faith the heart is purified. By faith is chiefly meant the grace of faith : (1.) faith in the habit, (2.) faith in the exercise.

2. *Charity*. The first sin was an enmity against God, therefore there is now necessary a love to God. The first sin was virtually an enmity to all the posterity of man, which were to come out of his loins, therefore love to mankind is necessary, and faith always infers love to God and man.

3. *Sanctification* is here added, because by that both the truth of faith and love appears to ourselves and others; and justification by faith is thereby ratified, James ii. 24. By sanctification is not here meant a particular holiness or chastity due to the marriage bed, as some of the papists assert, but an universal sanctity of heart and life.

4. *Sobriety*. This is a natural means for preservation. Intemperance makes bodily distempers more dangerous in their assaults. True faith is accompanied with temperance and sobriety in the use of lawful comforts. The papists, though without any good ground, frame an argument from hence to prove marriage to be a sacrament, asserting that those graces of faith and charity, &c., are conferred upon the women by virtue of marriage, and *ex vi institutionis*. How severe a doctrine is it then to engage any in vows of a single life, when they might have a readier way to attain grace with the satisfaction of nature? Are not the virtues mentioned here as necessary to the single as the married Christians? Who ever heard that marriage was appointed to confer those Christian graces which are necessary for men and women in all conditions? Besides, is it probable that that was instituted to confer Christian graces, which was instituted in paradise before Christianity was in being, and had been valid if man had stood in innocency, where there had been no need of a justifying faith?

Obs. 1. The punishment of the woman: 'in child-bearing.'

2. The comfort of the woman: 'she shall be saved.'

3. The condition of the salvation: 'if they continue.' Wherein is implied an exhortation to continue in faith, &c.

Doct. Many observations might be raised.

1. The pain in child-bearing is a punishment inflicted upon the woman for the first sin.

2. The continuance of this punishment after redemption by Christ, doth not hinder the salvation of the woman, if there be the gospel-conditions requisite.

3. The exercise of faith, with other Christian graces, is a peculiar means for the preservation of believers under God's afflicting hand.

I shall sum them up into this one

Doct. The continuance of the punishment inflicted upon the woman for the first sin, doth not prejudice her eternal salvation, nor her preservation in child-bearing, where there are the conditions of faith, and other graces.

Here I shall speak,

I. Concerning the punishment, and the cause of it.

II. The nature of it.

III. It is not prejudicing eternal salvation.

I. Concerning the punishment. Child-bearing itself is not the punishment, but the pain in it. For the blessing, *increase and multiply*, was given in innocency. This punishment is peculiar to the woman, and superadded to that inflicted upon the man, wherein the woman also hath her share, though it lay heaviest upon Adam's shoulders. And because this punishment is the greater, it is disputed in the schools whether Adam's or Eve's sin were the greater. Various opinions there are. We may, I think, safely make these conclusions.

1. In regard of the kind of sin, it was equal in both. They both had an

equal pride, an equal aspiring to be like God; for in all probability, Eve gave not her husband the fruit to eat, without acquainting him with the reasons which moved her to eat it, as also the advantage she expected from it. And God chargeth this aspiring humour upon the man: Gen. iii. 22, 'The man, האדם, is become like one of us.' Both of them, therefore, embraced the temptation as it was directed, and swallowed the fruit, with an expectation to be like, not the angels (as some think, from Gen. iii. 5, 'ye shall be as gods,' Elohim), but like God himself, as appears by ver. 22, in that ironical speech where the Lord God Jehovah saith, 'The man is become like one of us.' They both believed the serpent, both broke the command in eating the fruit, both were guilty of this aspiring ambition. Some indeed think Eve ate twice of the fruit, once before the serpent, and the other time when she gave her husband: Gen. iii. 6, 'She did eat, and gave to her husband with her, and he did eat.'* But that is not so clear in the text.

2. In regard of the first motion to this sin, Eve's sin was the greater. She was the seducer of Adam, which the apostle expresseth in the verse before the text. 'The woman being deceived, was in the transgression.' Where the apostle intimates the woman's in that respect to be greater than the man's. Adam was in it too, but the woman deeper.

3. In regard of the woman's condition, the sin was greater on Adam's part.†

(1.) Because he, being the man, had more power to resist, more strength to argue the case.

(2.) Eve had a stronger and craftier adversary to deal with, the subtlest of all the beasts of the field, Gen. iii. 1, animated and inspired by a craftier devil. The stronger the tempter, the more excusable the sin. Adam was tempted by Eve, but Eve by the serpent.

(3.) Eve had the command of not eating immediately from her husband, which laid not altogether so strong a tie upon her as it did upon him, who had it immediately from the mouth of God, and therefore was more certain of the verity of the precept.

II. Of what nature is this punishment?

1. It is not a punishment in a rigid sense, nor continued as such.

(1.) Because it is not commensurate to the nature of the sin, neither is it that penalty which the law required. Death was due, and death immediately upon the offence; but death was kept off by the interposition of the Mediator, and this which is less than death, inflicted at present. The Mediator or day's-man interposed before this sentence, for the promise of the seed which should bruise the serpent's head preceded the pronouncing of this sentence, Gen. iii. 15, 16. God arms himself against both, but not with those weapons they had deserved. Capital crimes are usually attended with capital punishments, which draw a destruction upon the offender. Where death is deserved, and a lighter punishment inflicted, it is rather an act of clemency than strict justice, and may be called by the name of a partial pardon or reprieve, as well as a punishment. It is indeed a punishment when conscience racks a man with further expectation of torment, when it is but a prologue to everlasting burnings, when through those pains any fall into the place of everlasting horror. It is then more properly a punishment, when it proceeds from an irreconcileable justice, armed with omnipotency in the execution, not when it proceeds from an anger mixed with mildness, and mitigated by the intercessions of a Mediator.

(2.) It is not a reparation of the injury done to God. One reason of the institution of punishment is to repair the damage the person offended sus-

* Mariana in loc.

† Estius in senten.

tains by the malefactor, as far as he is capable. The injury done to God cannot be repaired by any temporary punishment; no, nor indeed actually by an eternal one, though an eternal suffering is all the reparation a finite creature is capable to make to the honour of God. A man is capable of making some kind of amends to his neighbour for an offence done, but God being infinitely our superior, cannot have his honour repaired by anything a creature can do or suffer.

(3.) It is not continued as a part of satisfaction to the justice of God; as though Christ needed the sufferings of the creature to make up the sum which he was to pay for us, and which he hath already paid. It is not, on the account of the death of Christ, purely a vindictive, but a medicinal act to a believer: it is rather to awaken us than to satisfy justice; as we wring a man by the nose who is fallen into a swoon, not to have satisfaction from him for any injury he may have done us, but to fetch him out of his fit. These punishments are to awaken men to a sight of their first sin.

(4.) The proper impulsive cause of punishment is wrath. Though this was the first cause of this sentence, yet it is not inflicted in wrath upon a believer. Though at first it was an effect of God's anger, yet in a believer it is a fruit of God's fatherly anger, wherein he acts with a composition of Judge and Father. In inflicting it, he preserves the authority of a judge; in preserving under it, and pardoning the sin for which it was inflicted, he evidenceth the affection of a Father. Punishment, as such, is only to hurt, and make men reap the fruit of their iniquity; but the end of affliction, in the intention of the person that doth afflict, is oftentimes to benefit.

2. Yet it is in some sort a punishment, and something more than an affliction.

(1.) In respect of the meritorious cause, sin. This is not inflicted *ratione absoluti dominii*, but *ratione meriti;* it is not an act of absolute sovereignty, but a judicial legal act upon the demerit of sin. There are some afflictions which are not punishments, as in the case of the man that was born blind: Christ tells us that it was neither for his own sin, nor for the sins of his parents, but that God might be glorified, John ix. 2, 3, *i. e.* God in inflicting that blindness, respected neither the sin of the man, nor the sin of the parents, but the making him a passive subject of his glory in our Saviour's miraculous cure. But in this case God respected the sin of the woman as the cause and reason of the punishment.

(2.) Because if man had stood in innocency, neither this grief, nor indeed any other, had been. The birth in innocency would have been without sorrow and grief, as the hunger and thirst which would have been in Adam in that state, would have been without that gnawing in the stomach, and that pain which we find in those defects, because a state of integrity and perfect righteousness must needs be without grief. But after the fall, all those pains incident to man or woman are fruits of the curse of sin.

III. This punishment doth not hinder salvation, though it be continued.

I shall lay down these propositions to clear up this matter.

1. God intended not in the acceptance of Christ's mediation to remove in this life all the punishments denounced after the fall. God takes away the eternal, but not the temporal. For this very punishment was threatened after his acceptance of Christ's mediation; and after the compact and covenant between the Father and the Son about the redemption of mankind, because the promise preceded the threatening, and the mediatory covenant preceded the promise. Some parts of Christ's purchase are only payable in another life, and some fruits of redemption God intends for growth only in another soil; such are freedom from pain, diseases, death, and sin. And

therefore the last day, when believers shall be gathered together, is called, by way of excellency, the day of redemption, Eph. iv. 30, as if we had nothing of redemption properly in this life, because we have it not complete. And it is called upon this account, the 'time of refreshing,' and 'the time of the restitution of all things,' Acts iii. 19, 21; when all things shall be restored to their primitive completeness, and we shall have a full refreshment by a removal of all the evils which we suffer by reason of sin; so that the satisfaction made by Christ extends not to a present removal of all the effects of the curse, pains of the body, death of relations, &c. The ground is not restored to its original vigour and fruitfulness, man must still eat his bread in the sweat of his brows, women must still bring forth with sorrow, our lives must waste by a continual invasion of weaknesses and diseases, we must drop one after another into the grave, send some before us, and leave others to come after us; though God in mercy doth mitigate these, in some more, in some less, according to his sovereign pleasure; and though those curses do materially continue, yet they are attended with a blessing, the fruits of Christ's purchase. But the full value of Christ's satisfaction will appear when there shall be a new heaven and a new earth, when the day of redemption shall dawn, and all tears be wiped from believers' eyes. But God never promised the total removal of them in this life to any saint; no, though he should have all the faith and holiness of all the catalogue of saints in the book of life centred in him.

2. Christ never intended, in the payment of the price of our redemption, the present removal of them. He interposed himself before this sentence was pronounced, for the promise preceded the threatening, and therefore shewed himself content that those marks should be set upon that sin, though he prevented by his mediation the dreadful sentence of eternal death. Christ never expected it; for the compact between the Father and the Son did not run in this strain. Christ's enemies were not presently upon his ascension to be made his footstool, whereof death is not the least; but he was to sit at the right hand of God expecting it: neither can we expect to be rid of our burdens till Christ's victory over his enemies be fully complete. He sent, after his ascension, the Spirit to be our comforter, which supposeth a state wherein we should need comfort; and when are we under a greater necessity of comfort than when the punishment of sin is actually inflicted on us? The Spirit was to comfort us in the absence of our Saviour, and consequently in the absence and want of those fruits of redemption which are not yet completed.

3. Christ intended, and did actually take away the curse of those punishments from every believer. As Christ came to take away the guilt of sin, so by consequence he took away the curse of punishment; for as he was not a minister of sin, so he was not a minister of the curse, Gal. ii. 17; for he himself, by taking the curse upon himself, took it off from us; so that though the curse remains materially, yet it doth not formally. As when man fell, his understanding and will were not destroyed, but the purity and healthfulness of those faculties which made up his well-being were lost; so in redemption, the temporal punishment is not removed, but the curse, which is the sting in that punishment, and is indeed the essential part of it, is removed, since the anger of God is pacified by the death of Christ. Death was a curse upon man for sin, yet the death of a believer falls not under that title, because Christ hath taken away the sting: 1 Cor. xv. 55, 56, 'O death, where is thy sting?' &c. And the victory over it, he saith, is given us through our Lord Jesus Christ; whence the apostle puts even death itself, and things present, into the catalogue of privileges, upon the account of Christ: 1 Cor. iii. 22, 'Life, or death, or things present, or things to come, all are yours,

and you are Christ's, and Christ is God's.' Not that death simply in itself is a privilege, but death as conquered, and as attended with consequent blessings, is so to a believer. Now the same reason is for all the other parts of the curse, which were either prologues to, or attendants upon, death. And as Christ destroyed death by raising his own body from the grave, thereby taking from death the power of perpetually retaining man, so in the same manner he hath took away those punishments, that they shall not perpetually remain, though they do for a time; but when death is swallowed up in victory, all the attendants on it shall undergo the same fate. Though the curse was not immediately the work of the devil, yet that which procured it was; and Christ's intention being to take away sin, it was also to take away the curse, which was intentionally the devil's work, his chief aim being to bring men under the curse, by enticing them to sin. The end of his manifestation was to destroy the works of the devil, 1 John iii. 8. Christ therefore bore our infirmities, our natural penal infirmities, though not our natural sinful ones, unless morally, *i.e.* by suffering for them; he bore the infirmity of our nature, though not our personal infirmities. He endured pain, and grief, and death, and greater than we can endure; but he did not bear every particular pain and disease which ariseth from sin, and a particular cause; yet by satisfying the justice of God, which required death, he satisfied for all other pains which were parts of the curse, though he did not formally feel them; so that no longer they remain as a curse, no more than death itself is a curse to a believer. Now, as Christ by his death upon the cross did remove the sting of death from every believer, and sanctify it, though he did not die every kind of death which a man may die; so by enduring pain and grief, and being a man of sorrows, he took away the sting of all those pains which are fruits of the curse, though they were of a different kind from those he hath himself endured. This I have added to prevent an objection that may be made, that Christ endured not this particular pain, and therefore the curse is not taken away.

4. Hence it will follow, that to a believer the very nature of these punishments is altered. Whence ariseth a mighty difference between the same punishments, when suffered by a believer and by an unregenerate man. Though they are materially the same, yet not formally, nor eventually. In the one, the sting remains; in the other, it is pulled out. The one is an earnest of eternal torture, and a sprinkling of hell; the other is in order to salvation, and sanctified by the blood of Christ. Christ by his cross hath made our judgments to become physic, and turned a believer's punishments into purges. The intention of the agent makes a vast difference. There is a great difference between a punishment edged with a prince's wrath, and those which are sweetened with a father's affection; much difference between a chirurgeon's lance, and a tyrant's wound. The cord that binds a malefactor and a patient may be made of the same hemp, and a knife only go between; but it binds the malefactor to execution, the other to a cure. In a believer, they bring forth the peaceable fruits of righteousness, Heb. xii. 11, such fruits of righteousness which engender peace and joy in the soul. That which brings such excellent effects is rather an argument of love in the inflicter, and so cannot come under the full notion of a punishment. God comforts the Israelites that were to go into captivity by a gospel promise: Hosea xiv. 4, 'I will heal their backslidings; I will love them freely, for mine anger is turned away from them.' The punishment was continued, for they never returned into their country in the form of a commonwealth; but the anger was removed, so that the captivity of the believers among them was not the effect of God's wrath as a judge, since they were under his magnificent love as a

Father. The change in our relation to God, makes a change in the nature of the punishment; though the punishment threatened may be inflicted and continued, yet the anger in that punishment may be turned away.

5. Therefore all temporal punishments of original sin, though they remain, do not prejudice a believer's present interest.

(1.) They cut not off his relation to God. A son is as much a son under the rod as in the bosom: neither the father's stroke nor the child's grief dissolve that near relation; nay, a father may shew more of a true paternal affection in his chastisements than in his caresses. The branches which are battered with sticks may be nearer the root than those that flourish at their ease. Christ, while a man of sorrows, was pronounced by God his well-beloved Son, and bore our punishment, not only without forfeiting his Father's affection, but with a high gratification of him; neither doth God's visiting the seed of Christ with stripes cut off their relation to him: Ps. lxxxix. 32, 'Then will I visit their transgressions with rods.' Whose transgressions? Ver. 30, his children. Whose children? Even the children of him whom he would make 'the first-born, higher than the kings of the earth,' ver. 27; which cannot be understood literally of David or his lineal posterity in the Jewish kingdom, who were never higher than the kings of the earth.

(2.) They debar not from the presence of God. God may be and is as near to us in supporting as he is in punishing. It is not the cloud that interposeth between the sun and us that alters the sun's course or obstructs its influences. Christ took not off the badges of original guilt from those disciples which had the greatest interest in his affections; he left them in a sinful world to endure the fruits of sin; he sent them not to ease, pleasure, and a quiet and painless life, but to labour, toil, and sweat, yet promised that he would abide with them, that he and his Father would manifest themselves to them. And he turned that sweat and pain, which was the fruit of sin, by his presence with them, to be instrumental for the glory of God and the good of themselves in the world.

(3.) They break not the covenant. His rod and his stripes, though they seem to break our backs, make no breaches in his covenant, Ps. lxxxix. 32–34; he will visit transgression with rods, but he will not suffer his faithfulness to fail, nor break his covenant. No; they are rather covenant mercies when they break our hearts, and are means by his grace to make our stony hearts more fleshy. He makes even those dispensations which were pronounced for punishment to bring forth covenant mercies, and the rich fruits of his grace to grow upon the sour crab-stock of his judgments. Jacob, in Gen. xlix., is said to bless his children, though he predicts smart afflictions to come upon them; they are ranked among the blessings, because the covenant should remain firm. The lash removes not the inheritance. Austin saith well, *Noli attendere quam pœnam habes in flagello, sed quem locum in testamento.*

6. Add to all this, that the first promise secures a believer under the sufferings of those punishments. God's affection in the promise of bruising the serpent's head was more illustrious in his wrath than the threatening. There are the bowels of a father in the promise, before there was the voice of a judge in the sentence. God brought sugar with his potion, and administered his cordial before he struck with his lance; and therefore that threatening which commenced after the promise can no more prejudice the fruits of the promise to a believer, than the law, which was given four hundred and thirty years after the promise to Abraham, could disannul that and make it of no effect, as the apostle argues in another case, Gal. iii. 17. Much less can the threatening denounced immediately after the promise change the veracity

of God in that which was fresh in his mind at the very time of his threatening.

Obs. But it may be asked, What is the reason these punishments are continued since the redemption wrought by Christ?

Ans. It is frequent with God to inflict a temporal punishment after pardon, not, as the papists assert, in order to satisfaction. Moses his unbelief hindered him from coming unto Canaan, so that when he desired to go over Jordan, God was wroth with him, cut him off short, and commands him silence: Deut. iii. 25, 26, 'Speak to me no more of this matter.'

There are reasons:

1. On God's part. 2. On our part.

1. On God's part.

(1.) It is congruous to the wisdom of God to leave them upon us while we are in the world. Since God created man to gain glory by his actions, but was presently after his creation disgraced and disparaged by him, it seems agreeable to the wisdom of God not immediately to bring him to his former state, but to leave some marks of his displeasure upon man, to mind him of the state whence he was fallen, the misery he contracted, and the necessity of flying to his mercy for succour.

(2.) It is congruous to the holiness of God. God keeps up those punishments as the rector and governor of the world, to shew his detestation of that sin which brought a disorder and deformity upon the creation, and was the first act of dishonour to God, and the first pollution of the creature. It is an high vindication of the holiness and authority of God, and the majesty and purity of his law, to punish sin in them that are dear to him upon another's righteousness, whereby he evidenceth that he hates sin in all, and will not wink at it or approve of it. So he pardoned David; but for the honour of his name, which had been blasphemed by occasion of David's sin, he would leave the smart of it upon his family, 2 Sam. xii. 10, 14.

(3.) It is a declaration of his justice. It is not congruous to the justice of God not to leave some marks of his anger against that sin which caused him to be at the expense of his Son's blood, and is the source of all those evils whereby God is injured, for which the Redeemer bled, and by which the Spirit is grieved, since pardon doth not, neither can, alter the demerit of sin; but that will continue, and what is once meritoriously a capital crime in its own nature can never be otherwise. God may for the demonstration of his justice inflict and continue something upon the creature, though he free him from actual condemnation. We should not be so sensible of the justice of God in the death of Christ, did we not feel some strokes of it upon ourselves, nor what the purchase of our redemption did cost our Saviour. What we hear doth not so much affect as what we feel. That which brought disorder into God's government of the world, and made him change the scene of his providence, may very justly have some signal remark upon it notwithstanding the redemption, especially when the fruits of it are not fully complete; for since man was the immediate end of the creation of this lower world, and since all creatures were made for the service of man, that he might be fit for the service of his righteous Creator, he did by his fall violate the order of the creation, and subjected it to the service of the devil, a corrupt creature, and an enemy to God, the chief Lord of the world, and so did deprave the order of the universe, and endeavoured to frustrate the end of God and the end of all the creatures. It is very rational to think that though God, out of his infinite compassion, would not lose his creature, yet that he should set such a badge upon him that should make him sensible of a depravation he had wrought in the world.

(4.) It is useful to magnify his love. We should not be sensible of what our Saviour suffered, nor how transcendently he loved us, if the punishment of sin had been presently removed upon the first promise. Nay, how then could he have died in the fulness of time, which was necessary to the demonstration of God's love, satisfaction of his justice, and the security of the creature's happiness? God adds the threatening to the promise, as a dark colour to set off and beautify the brighter. As Christ suffered that he might have compassion on us, so are we punished that we might have an estimation of him. When Paul cries out of the body of death, so when we cry out of the punishment of sin, it should raise our thankfulness for redeeming love: 'I thank God through Jesus Christ,' Rom. vii. 24, 25. We never know the worth of mercy till we feel the weight of misery. The sharper the pains of sin, the higher are our valuations of redeeming mercy. In Isa. iv. 2, 'In that day shall the branch of the Lord be beautiful and glorious.' In what day? After great punishments, ver. 1, and in the foregoing chapter. He appears most beautiful to us when we are under the lash for sin. As sin continues in us that the justifying grace of Christ's righteousness might more appear to us, so punishment continues on us that redeeming love might be more prized by us.

2. On our parts. It is useful to us,

1. To make us abhor our first defection and sin. It was great, and is not duly considered by us. This sin of Adam is the worst that ever was committed in the world, extensively, though not intensively, worse than the sin of Judas or the sin against the Holy Ghost,* in respect that those are but the effects of it, and branches of that corrupt root; also because those sins hurt only the persons sinning. But this drew down destruction upon the whole world, and drove thousands into everlasting fire and brimstone. It is not fit that this, which was the murder of all mankind, the disorder of the creation, the disturbing of God's rest in the works of his hands, should be passed over without a scar left upon us to make us sensible of the greatness of the evil. Though the wounds be great upon our souls, yet they do not so much affect us as those strokes upon our bodies. This certainly was one main end of God in this; to what purpose else did he (after the promise of restoration, and giving our first parents the comfort of hearing the head of their great seducer threatened to be bruised by the seed of the woman) order this punishment, but to put them in mind of the cause of it, and stir up a standing abhorrency of it in all ages of the world? Had not this been his intent, he would never have ushered it in by a promise, but *ipso facto* have showered down a destroying judgment upon the world, as he did upon Sodom, without any comfortable word preceding. God inflicts those punishments both to shew his own and excite our detestation of this sin. 'He binds us in those fetters to shew us our work and our transgression wherein we have exceeded,' Job xxxvi. 8, 9.

2. To make us fear to sin, and to purge it out. Sin hath riveted itself so deep, that easy medicines will not displace it. It hath so much of our affections, that gentle means will not divorce us from it. We shall hate it most when we reap the punishment of it. Punishment is inflicted as a guard to the law, and the security of righteousness from the corrupt inclinations of the creature; so it is ἰατρεία ψυχῆς, as Plato calls punishment. As death is continued for the destruction of sin in the body, so are the lesser punishments continued for the restraint of sin in our lives. We need further conversions, closer applications of ourselves to God, more quick walks to him, and fixedness with him. God's smitings are to quicken our turn-

* Kellet Miscel.

ings. As it was the fruit of Jacob's trouble to take away sin, Isa. xxvii. 9, so it is a great end of God in those common punishments of mankind to weaken corruption in a believer by them; therefore, when we have any more remarkable sense of those punishments, let us see what wounds our sin gets thereby; how our hatred of it is increased. If we find such gracious effects we shall have more reason to bless God for it than complain of it. Oh happy troubles, when they repair, not ruin us, when they pinch us and cure us, like thunder, which, though it trouble the air, disperses the infectious vapours mixed with it, or the tide, which, though turning the stream of the river against its natural course, carries away much of the filth with it at its departure.

3. To exercise grace. Punishments of themselves have no power to set any grace on work, but rather excite our corruptions; but the grace of God accompanying them makes them beneficial for such an end. God hath to a believer altered the commission of such punishments; they are to exercise our faith, improve our patience, draw us nearer in acts of recumbency, but he hath given them no order to impair our grace, waste our faith, or deaden our hopes.

(1.) Faith and trust: 1 Tim. v. 5, 'She that is desolate trusts in God.' The lower the state, the greater necessity and greater obligation to trust; such exercises manifest that the condition we are in is sanctified to us. As sin is suffered to dwell in a regenerate man, to occasion the exercise of faith, so is the punishment of sin continued for the same end. The continuance of it is a mighty ground of our confidence in God. We experiment the righteousness of God in his threatening, and it is an evidence he will be the same in his promise. When we bear the marks of his punitive justice, it is an evidence that he will keep up the credit of his mercy in the promise, as well as of his justice in the punishment, both being pronounced at the same time; the good of the one is as sure by God's grace to our faith, as the smart of the other is by our desert to that sin. The continuance, therefore, of those punishments may be used by a believer as a means to fix a stronger confidence in God, for if he were not true to the one, we might suspect his truth in the other; if God should be careless of maintaining the honour of his truth in his threatenings, we should have reason to think that he would be careless of maintaining the honour of it in his promises, and thereupon be filled with despondencies. What comfort could we have in an unrighteous God? The righteousness of God in inflicting punishment is but a branch of that essential righteousness of his nature, which obligeth him to be righteous in the performing his promise too. It is a mighty support to faith, that the righteous God loveth righteousness.

(2.) Obedience in a believer hath a greater lustre by them. It was the glory of Job, that he preserved his integrity under the smartest troubles. To obey a God always smiling, is not so great an act of loyalty as to obey a God frowning and striking. It is the crown of our obedience to follow our God though he visits us with stripes. It is a noble temper to love that hand which strikes us, and cheerfully serve that Father which lasheth us. Our obedience is too low when it must be excited by a succession of favours, and cannot run to God unless he allures it by smiles. It is then a generous and sincere obedience, when we can embrace him with a sword in his hand, trust him though he kill us, love him though he stone us, and, as the Persians did by the sun, adore him when he scorcheth, as well as when he refresheth us. Were these punishments wholly absent, we should not have a rise for so heroic faith and love, and our holiness in this state would want much of its lustre.

(3.) Humility. These punishments are left upon us to allay our pride, and be our remembrancers of our deplorable miscarriage. It had been an occasion of pride in us to be freed from punishment at the first appearance of a mediator. It is reasonable the soul should have occasions to exercise itself in a grace contrary to that first sin, pride, which was the cause of the fall. We affected to be gods, and punishment is left that we may know we are but men, which is the end of judgments: Ps. ix. 20, 'Put them in fear, O Lord, that the nations may know they are but men;' we should otherwise think ourselves gods. We are so inclined to sin that we need strong restraints, and so swelled with a natural pride against God, that we need thorns in the flesh to let out the corrupt matter. The constant hanging the rod over us makes us lick the dust, and acknowledge ourselves to be altogether at the Lord's mercy. Though God hath pardoned us, he will make us wear the halter about our necks to humble us.

(4.) Patience. Were there no punishments, there would be but little occasion for patience. This grace would not have had its extensive exercise, its full formation, without such strokes left upon the creature. Resignation to God, which is the beauty of grace, would not come to its due maturity and stature without such trials. So that in these reasons of the continuance, we see they are rather advantages to salvation than hindrances, by promoting, through the influence of God's grace, those graces in us which are necessary to a happy state.

Use 1. See the infinite mercy of God, who, when upon the defection of our first parents he might have burnt up the whole world as he did Sodom, would upon the Redeemer's account, who stepped in, impose so light a punishment upon that sin; it is but light in comparison of what the nature of sin deserves, every sin being a contempt of the majesty of God, and a slight of his authority, and that sin having greater aggravations attending it. It is a merciful punishment, it might have been everlasting damnation; God might have left us to the first sentence of the law, and made no exchange of eternal death for temporal pains; he might have been deaf to the voice of a mediator, and put his mercy to silence, as he did Moses, 'Speak no more of this matter;' but his bowels pull his justice by the arm, and hinder that fatal stroke, and a Mediator, by his interposition, breaks off the full blow from us by taking it upon himself, and suffers only some few smart drops to light upon us. Oh wonderful mercy, that our punishment should not hinder, but rather further, our everlasting happiness by incomprehensible grace! Let not, then, our punishments for sin hinder our thankfulness. Let our mouths swell with praise, while our bodies crumble away by diseases, and relations drop from us by death. Let us love God's glory, admire his mercy, while we feel his arrows; whatever our punishments are, there is more matter for praise than murmuring.

2. How should we bewail original sin, the first fall of man. It is a great slighting of God not to take notice either of his judicial or fatherly proceedings. As we are to lament any particular sin more especially when the judgments of God, which bear the marks of that sin in their foreheads, are upon a nation or person, so, though we are to bewail the sin of our nature at all times, yet more signally when the strokes of God, the remembrancers of it, are most signally upon us. A child doth more particularly think of his fault when he is under the correcting rod for it. We should scarce think of original sin, if we did not feel original punishment. All the pains of sin should be considered as God's sermon to us, and we should under them be afflicted with that sin, as we may suppose Adam and Eve were when they first heard the punishment denounced in paradise, when they had a sense of

the flourishing condition they had lost for a slight temptation. To turn sorrow for pain into sorrow for our first sin, is to spiritualize our grief, and sanctify our passion.

3. What an argument for patience under punishments is here! The continuance of them doth not hinder our salvation. 'Shall a living man complain, a man for the punishment of his sin?' For such a punishment that doth not hinder his eternal welfare, but by the grace of God, and the exercise of faith, rather promote it. God promised as well as threatened; both his mercy and righteousness directs him to that which is most for his honour and our good. Let us not by any impatience charge infinite wisdom with blindness or unrighteousness. They were punishments at first, but by faith in Christ, the deportment of a judge is changed into that of a father. Drusius hath an observation: Ps. lvi. 10, 'In God will I praise his word; in the Lord will I praise his word.' The first word, *Elohim*, is a name belonging to God as a judge, the second word, *Jehovah*, is a name of mercy; I will praise God, whether he deal with me in a way of justice or in a way of mercy, when he hath thunder in his voice as well as when he hath honey under his tongue. Oh how should we praise God, and pleasure ourselves by such a frame! When our distresses lie hard upon us, we should justify God's holiness. So the psalmist, or rather Christ, in the bearing our punishment, Ps. xxii. 1, 'But thou art holy,' when he expostulates with God why he had forsaken him, justifies God's holiness. Howsoever thou dealest with me, thou art holy in all thy ways. Thou doest me no wrong; why should I complain, when holiness and hatred of sin guides thee in all those actings with me?

4. How earnest should we be to get rid of sin! By pardon, by sanctification. Guilt is the sting of punishment. Sin only embitters trouble. The remission and mortification of sin is the health of the soul. If the arrow's head be out of a wound, the cure will be more easy. 'Look upon my affliction, and my pain, and forgive all my sin,' saith the psalmist, Ps. xxv. 8; forgiveness of sin would mitigate the sharpness of his pain.

5. How should we act faith on God in Christ, before, and under, such a condition of punishment! As we can never love God too much, because he is the highest good, so we can never trust God too much, because he is one of immutable truth. When we are in straits, it is not for want of faithfulness in God, but for want of faith in us, that we are many times not preserved. We distrust God, and this is the cause we fall into many distresses, which otherwise would not come upon us, or be quickly removed from us. Did we grasp the promises closely, and plead them earnestly, we should often find the deliverance we desire. We pray, but we pray not in faith; we cry for deliverance, but not with confidence; we plead God's power, but forget his promise. Many temporal promises are not performed to us, not for want of truth in God, but for want of faith in us. Particular fiduciary acts will draw out the riches of a promise, for want of which we remain poor in the midst of abundance. Some think that the promise made to Josiah of his dying in peace, which phrase is usually meant in Scripture of a peaceable death upon the bed, was not performed, because Josiah was out of the way against the precept of God, and therefore could not act faith requisite to the fulfilling of that promise, for faith is much damped in its actings under present contracted guilt.* This faith in promises for outward preservation is not an absolute, infallible assurance that God will bestow such outward things (because the promises themselves are not absolute), but it is rather an indefinite act of recumbency, and submission, referring it to his good

* Tho. Goodwin.

pleasure towards us. But it is certain we are very much defective in acting faith upon promises for temporal mercies, because it is an epidemical distemper in us to trust God with our souls rather than with our bodies and outward concerns.

1. Exercise faith before such a time. Furnish yourselves with the comforts of the covenant, and the efficacy of the death of Christ. In bodily distempers, our minds are discomposed, and we cannot have that freedom of thoughts and spiritual reflections. This is the way to engage God, who is the best assistant, 'a very present help in time of trouble.'

2. Exercise it in the use of spiritual means. God never commanded us to trust him but in his own methods. That is not trust in God which is attended with any wilful omissions. If we be careful in doing our duty, God will be careful in doing what belongs to him. Prayer is the best means for faith to exercise itself in. A spirit of prayer beforehand is a sign of good success. When the heart is drawn out to cry, it is a sign God stands ready with the mercy in his hand. Times of distress are times of calling upon God: Ps. xviii. 6, 'In my distress I called upon the Lord, and he heard my cry.' God is to be acknowledged in all our ways, Prov. iii. 6: in the beginning by prayer for his direction; in the end, by praises for the success. We are usually more earnest in trouble. We have not at all times an equal fervency. Christ himself (some say) had not; for when he was in his agony, he prayed more earnestly than before, Luke xxii. 44.

3. Act faith upon the relation God bears to you. He is our Father. We trust earthly fathers, and are confident they will not abuse us. How much more ought we to trust our heavenly Father, and not doubt of his sincerity towards us! The greater the trouble, the more we should plead God's relation to us. Our Saviour in the garden, Mat. xxvi. 29, 42, at his entrance into his passion for us, prays to God by the title of *my Father*, whereas at other times he calls God *Father*, without that appropriation. But now he would excite his confidence, and trust in God, and those promises he had made him to assist him in that hour.

4. Act faith upon the attributes of God. There is nothing in God can affright a believer. There is not an attribute but seems fixed in God to encourage our dependence on him in any strait; wisdom, mercy, truth, omniscience, power, justice too (for what comfort could we have to trust an unjust God?). All which attributes are promised to be assistant to a believer in any case of need, in the covenant of grace, where God makes himself over to us as our God, and therefore all that God hath, and is, is promised there for our good. Upon the power of God: God's omnipotence was the ground of our Saviour's prayer to him in his distress, and that which the apostle seems to intimate his eyeing of: Heb. v. 7, 'He offered up prayers unto him that was able to save him from death.' And, Ps. xvi. 1, the psalmist, or rather Christ, pleads the power of God: 'Preserve me, O Lord, for in thee do I put my trust.' אל, ἰσχυρέ. Aquila renders it *strong*. Plead the truth of God in his promise, the promise that preceded the threatening, viz., the bruising the serpent's head, the defeating all his plots and designs, whereof this was one, to bring man into a state of punishment. There is a promise which has been especially tried and made good, though all in the book of God have been found true: Ps. xviii. 30, 'The word of the Lord is tried.' Not one word but the truth of it hath been tried, but especially this word, 'that God is a buckler to them that trust in him,' *i. e.* that he will preserve and defend depending believers.

5. Act faith upon Christ. Hath God delivered Christ to death? It must be for some glorious end, not for destruction of the creature, that might

have been done without the death of his Son, but for remission; if so, there is sufficient ground to trust him for everything else. We have a merciful high Priest, which encourageth us to make our addresses known to him. He cannot but be touched with the feeling of our infirmities, our penal infirmities which he suffered, our sinful infirmities for which he suffered. Where can he shew his mercy but in our misery? Are we under God's strokes? Christ himself felt them, that he might the better pity us. Are we in such cases tempted to despond and distrust? He felt such fiery darts of the devil, that he might the better commiserate us. Run to him and cry out, Blessed Redeemer, compassionate High Priest, let thy pity break out to allay my grief, and support my weakness.

Take a few encouragements to fiduciary acts.

1. Nothing is more pleasing to God. The continuance in faith is the necessary condition of our salvation. Nothing more honours him. We honour his wisdom and goodness, when we acknowledge that he hath a singular care of his creatures, and trust him in his own methods; we own his skill in governing, and his goodness in bringing every thing about to the best end. Christ hath given us the highest example of trust, and highly pleased God in it, in coming into the world to die upon God's bare word and oath. It is all we can do to glorify God. Other graces glorify some particular attribute, but confidence in God glorifies all in the lump; his wisdom, righteousness, faithfulness, mercy, truth, omniscience, and power. There is no attribute but gives a particular encouragement to faith, and there is no attribute but faith returns a revenue of glory to. Despondency disparageth the Father's affection and the Redeemer's love. If we do not trust him, we imply that he hath not either wisdom, or love, or power, or faithfulness enough to be trusted by us, and that his word is of no value.

2. Nothing is more successful. It is the argument the psalmist, or rather Christ, useth, Ps. xvi. 1, 'Preserve me.' Why? 'Because I trust in thee.' Trust in God is a strong argument to prevail with God for preservation. All the ancient fathers were delivered by God upon their trust: Ps. xxii. 4, 5, 'Our fathers trusted in thee: they trusted, and thou didst deliver them. They cried unto thee, and were delivered: they trusted in thee, and were not confounded.' Faith in gospel promises is not a grace of a new date. It is as old as Adam's fall, as old as the patriarchs, and successful in all ages of the world. They were under new-covenant promises, and had new-covenant deliverances before the promises were actually sealed by the blood of Christ. How much stronger ground have we of trust now! Faith draws out the treasures of God, and sets God on work to display both his wisdom, goodness, and power: Ps. xxxi. 19, 'How great is thy goodness which thou hast laid up for them that fear thee, which thou hast wrought for them that trust in thee!' Much more when faith is vigorously acted. Unbelief binds God's hands. Faith then draws forth that power which unbelief locks up. God is first the hope of Israel, and then 'the Saviour thereof in times of trouble,' Jer. xiv. 8, of every one of Israel. Where God inspires with a humble confidence in himself, there is hope of success, for God will not frustrate the expectation of that which he hath been the author of in his creature. David had found such good evidence of this, that he tells God he would make bold with him upon every occasion of fear: Ps. lvii. 3, 'What time I am afraid, I will trust in thee.'

3. Nothing more calms the spirit. A fiduciary reliance on God is the way to live free from fears and anxieties. Faith is an establishing grace. By faith we stand. What storms would be in the minds of poor passengers in a ship, as great as those in the sea, if they had no pilot to direct them!

How soon would the arrival of a skilful steersman, in whom they could confide, and that knew the shelves and rocks upon the coast, calm their disquiets!

Well, then, to sum up all. This very scripture is a letter of comfort, writ only to women in the state of child-bearing; claim it as your right by faith. What comfort is here to appeal from the threatening to the promise, from God as a judge to God as a father, from God angry to God pacified in Christ! How comfortable is this, that when God seems to fight against you with his punishments, you can take off the edge of his weapons by the pleas of his promise! Oh blessed God, who arms a believer against himself, before he arms himself against a believer! You can never be under the curse if you have faith, as long as God is sensible of his own credit in the promise. In the material part of the punishment, there is no difference between a believer and an unbeliever. Jacob is pinched with famine as well as the Canaanite; but Jacob is in covenant, and hath a God in heaven and a Joseph in Egypt to preserve him. God directs every pain in all by his providence, in believers by a particular love; every gripe in all the physic he gives us. He orders even his contendings with his creature in such a measure as the Spirit may not fail before him, Isa. lvii. 16.

A DISCOURSE OF THE SINS OF THE REGENERATE.

Whosoever is born of God doth not commit sin; for his seed remaineth in him: and he cannot sin, because he is born of God.—1 John III. 9.

The apostle, having exhorted the saints to whom he writes in the former chapter to abide in Christ, and to do righteousness, ver. 28, 29, follows on this exhortation with several arguments and demonstrations, that a true Christian is not only bound to do so, but that he indeed doth so.

1. From that hope which hath eternal happiness for its object, ver. 2, 3. Where this hope is truly founded, it will inflame us with a desire and endeavour after holiness, which is a necessary means to attain it. There will be an endeavour to be like that head here, which they hope to be perfectly like hereafter.

2. From the contrariety of sin to the law of God. It is not reasonable, neither can there be such a disingenuous disposition in any to transgress the laws of that person from whom only he expects his highest felicity; and the law of God, being pure and perfect, sin being contrary unto it, must be filthy and unreasonable. A Christian, who is guided by this law, will not transgress it.

3. From the end of Christ's coming, which was to take away sin, ver. 5. And a Christian ought not to endeavour to frustrate the ends of Christ's coming by the nourishment of that which he came to destroy.

4. From the communion they have with Christ. Abiding in him, they sin not. If any man sin, it is an evident sign he hath not the knowledge of Christ, ver 6, nor ever was conformed to that pattern. Where there is a communion with Christ, it is necessary such an one should be righteous, because Christ was so.

5. From the first author of sin, the devil. He that sins hath a communion with the devil, ver. 8, as he that doth righteousness hath a communion with Christ. And to maintain the design and works of the devil is to walk contrary to the end and design of Christ, which was to destroy the works of the devil. Those therefore that indulge themselves in sin, are the seed of the devil.

6. From the new nature of a Christian, which hinders him from sin : ver. 9, 'Whosoever is born of God doth not commit sin,' &c. Various expositions there are of this. The greatest difficulty lies in those words, *doth not commit sin*, and *cannot sin*.

1. He ought not to sin. *Cannot* indeed is sometimes taken for *ought not*, as Acts iv. 20, 'For we cannot but speak the things which we have seen and heard.' They had a physical ability to hold their peace, but morally they could not, because of Christ's precept to them to publish those things. What we cannot lawfully do, we cannot do. *Non possumus quod non jure possumus*, what we cannot honourably do, we are said not to be able to do : Mark vi. 5, 'He could there do no mighty work.' Christ had natural ability to do mighty works there, but morally he could not, honourably he could not, because of their unbelief, which was a moral hindrance; and according to God's methods there was no hope of doing any good among them. Their unbelief was so strong, they gave him no opportunity to do any mighty work. But this is not the meaning of *cannot* here, *ought not* ; for an unrenewed man ought not to sin any more than a regenerate man. But the apostle attributes here something peculiar to the regenerate, adding the reason, 'because he is born of God.' Though it carry in it something of an obligation in a higher manner than upon a mere natural man, he ought not to sin, not only upon the general obligation which lies upon all men not to sin, but upon the more special one of his state, being a son of God, which ought to be counted a moral impossibility by a righteous man. Regeneration gives a man no advantage to sin, no external licence, no internal liberty or ability to sin; for the apostle useth this as an argument to them as well as an establishment not to sin, because they are born of God, which was a more special obligation upon them not to sin than what they had by nature.

2. He cannot sin so easily. It is not impossible but difficult for him to sin, because by receiving grace he receives a principle contrary to sin, and so hath a principle of resistance against it; or because by that grace he is inclined not to sin, and so there is *inchoativè*, an impossibility of sinning, which shall hereafter be perfected ; not a simple impossibility, but *secundum quid*. He endeavours to work as one born of God, and follows the motions of the Spirit against the sin to which he is tempted.

He cannot sin, *i. e.* it is a hard matter for him to sin ; for considering the efficacy of grace, and the assistances attending it, it is a difficult thing for a righteous man to be brought under the power of sin. He may sin easily in respect of the frailty of the flesh, but not so easily in regard of the abiding of the seed in him, which helps him to beware of sin. Grace being a divine habit, hath the nature of a habit, which is to incline the person to acts proper to that habit, and facilitate those acts, as a man that hath the habit of an art or trade can with more ease work in it than any other.

3. He cannot sin *in sensu formali*, as he is regenerate, *ex vi talis nativitatis*. Grace cannot sin, because it can do nothing but what pertains to the nature of it. As the heat cannot cool, unrighteousness cannot do good. Fire doth not moisten *per se*, nor water naturally heat. But it is not said, 'The seed of God cannot sin,' but in the concrete, 'He that is born of God,

and he that hath the seed remaining in him, cannot sin.' A gracious man, as a gracious man, cannot sin, for grace, being a good habit, is not capable of producing acts contrary to its nature. Sin in a regenerate man proceeds not from his grace, but from his corruption. Grace cannot be the principle of evil; but because his grace is imperfect, dwelling among remainders of sin; therefore a man's sins, though his principle in him keeps sin from attaining a full dominion and superiority, yet though he doth sin, his sin is not the proper fruit of the form whereby he is regenerate.

4. He cannot sin *in sensu composito*, as long as he is regenerate, as long as the seed remains in him, as long as he follows the motions of the Spirit and grace, which are able to overcome the motions of concupiscence, but he may give up the grace; as an impregnable tower cannot be taken as long as it is defended by those within, but they may fling away their arms and deliver it up. Grace, *quantum est ex parte sua*, renders a man impeccable as long as it continues in him, as innocency did render Adam immortal as long as he persisted in it; but we may *ex culpâ nostrâ*, lose it by mortal sin, and so perish, as Adam by his own will lost the integrity of his nature, and was thereby made subject to death. This is founded upon a false hypothesis, viz. that grace may be lost; and the text renders the being born of God and the seed remaining in us to be the reason why we cannot sin, not the côndition of our not sinning; for if it remains, and we cannot sin therefore, how can any sin come in to expel that which preserves us from it? A man must cease, according to what the apostle here writes, to be born of God before he can sin in that sense the apostle means.

5. He doth not commit sin, and cannot sin, *i. e. grave peccatum*, the mortal sin, and persist in it. The sin of unbelief, which is called in Scripture, by way of eminency, *sin*, and *the sin*; it is the chief sin the Spirit convinceth of; it is the sin that 'easily besets us:' Heb. xii. 1, 'Let us lay aside every weight, and the sin which doth so easily beset us,' *i. e.* especially unbelief. Though this be true, yet it is not the full meaning and sense of it.

6. He doth not commit sin, and cannot sin, as the devil doth, or as one that is of a diabolical nature, as one that is acted by the devil, which is clear by the antithesis: ver. 8, 'He that commits sin is of the devil, for the devil sins from the beginning.' He cannot set himself against Christ, as the devil doth, as the pharisees did, in which respect our Saviour calls them the children of the devil, for their remarkable and constant opposition to him. He cannot make a practice of sin, and persist in it, as the devil doth, who began to sin presently after the creation, and continueth in it ever since. *He sins*, the present tense noting the continued act of the devil. Sin may be considered two ways, viz., as to,

1. The act of sin. Thus a believer sins.

2. The habit of sin, or custom in it, when a man runs to sin freely, willingly, and is not displeased with it. Thus a believer doth not commit sin, nor cannot sin; he commits it not: *potius patitur quàm facit*, he gives not a full consent to it; he hates it while he cannot escape it. He is not such a committer of it as to be the servant of sin: John viii. 34, 'He that commits sin is the servant of sin,' because he serves with his mind the law of God. He bestows not all his thoughts and labour upon sin, in making 'provision for the flesh,' Rom. xiii. 14, in being a caterer for sin; he yields not up his members as instruments of unrighteousness unto sin; he doth not let sin reign in his mortal body, nor yield a voluntary obedience to it in the lusts thereof, Rom. vi. 12, 13, for, being God's son, he cannot be sin's servant; he cannot sin in such a manner, and so absolutely, as one of the devil's children, one born of the devil.

'His seed remains in him.' *His*, refers to God, or the person born of God. God's seed efficiently, man's seed subjectively.

'Born of God.' Twice repeated: in the first is chiefly intended the declaration of the state; in the second, the disposition, or likeness to God.

Observe, 1. The description of a Christian: 'born of God.'

2. The privilege of this birth, or effects of it.

(1.) Inactivity to sin: he 'doth not' commit it.

(2.) Inability to sin: he 'cannot.'

3. The ground and reasons of those privileges.

(1.) The inward form or principle whereby he is regenerate, which makes him unactive.

(2.) The efficient cause, which makes him unable: 'born of God,' or likeness to God, makes him unable.

4. The latitude of them in regard of the subject: 'whosoever,' every regenerate man. I intend not to run through all the parts of this text, having only chose it as a bar to presumption, which may be occasioned by the former doctrine, upon men's false suppositions of their having grace. There needs not any doctrine from the text; but, if you please, take this:

Doct. There is a mighty difference between the sinning of a regenerate and a natural man. A regenerate man doth not, neither can, commit sin in the same manner as an unregenerate man doth.

That I may not be mistaken, observe, when I use the word *may* sin, I understand it of a *may* of possibility, not a *may* of lawfulness. And when I say a regenerate man *cannot* sin so and so, understand it of a settled, habitual frame; distinguish between passion and surprise, a sudden effort of nature and an habitual and deliberate determination. The sense of this *cannot*, I shall lay down in several propositions.

1. It is not meant exclusively of lesser sins, or sins of infirmity. There are sins of daily incursion, and lighter skirmishes; there are some open, some secret assaults, a multitude of secret faults, Ps. xix. 12, undiscernible and unknown. Every good man is like Jacob; though he hath one thigh sound, he hath another halting. I do not find that ever God intended to free any in this life from the remainders of sin. What he hath not evidenced to have done in any, we may suppose he intended not to do. It is a total apostasy, not a partial fall, that the covenant provides against. Christ, in his last prayer, prays for believers' preservation, and gradual sanctification, not for their present perfection. The very office of advocacy erected in heaven, supposeth sins after regeneration, and during our continuance in the world: 1 John ii. 1, 'My little children, I write unto you, that you sin not; and if any man sin, we have an advocate with the Father.' 'In many things we offend all,' James iii. 2; not only you that are the inferior sort of Christians, but we apostles. *We* is extensive; all offend in many things. It is implied in the Lord's prayer, the daily standing pattern. As we are to pray for our daily bread, so for a daily pardon, and against daily temptations, which supposeth our being subject to the one, and our commission of the other. The brightest sun hath its spots; the clearest moon, her dark parts. The church, in her highest comeliness in this world, hath her blackness of sin, as well as of affliction, because, though sin be dismounted from its throne by grace, it is not expelled out of its residence. It dwells in us, though it doth not rule over us, Rom. vii. 20; and it cannot but manifest itself by its fruits while it remains. Yet those sins do not destroy our adoption. Christ, in his sermon on the mount to his disciples, supposeth the inherency of sin, with the continuance of the relation of children: Mat. vii. 11, 'If,

then, you being evil, know how to give good gifts to your children, how much more shall your Father which is in heaven give good things to them that ask him?' He doth acknowledge them evil while he calls God their father, and gives them the title of children. To sin is to decline from that rectitude in an act which the agent ought to observe. In this respect we sin, according to the tenor of the law, in everything we do, though not according to the tenor of the gospel.

2. A regenerate man cannot live in the customary practice of any known sin, either of omission or commission.

1. Not in a constant omission of known duties. If a good man falls into a gross sin, he doth not totally omit the performance of common duties to God. Not that this attendance on God in his ordinances doth of itself argue a man to be a good man; for many that walk in a constant course of sin may, from natural conscience and education, be as constant in the performing external services as he is. It is a proper note of an hypocrite, that he will not always delight himself in the Almighty, nor always call upon God, Job xxvii. 10, *i.e.* not customarily. Whence it follows, that a delight in God in duties of worship is a property of a regenerate man. An act of sin may impair his liveliness in them, but not cause him wholly to omit them. We need not question but David, in the time of his impenitency, did go to the tabernacle, attend upon the worship of God. It is not likely that for ten months together he should wholly omit it, though no doubt but he was dead-hearted in it, which is intimated when he desires a free spirit, Ps. li., and prays for quickening, Ps. cxliii. 11, one of his penitential psalms. A total neglect of ordinances and duties is a shrewd sign of a total apostasy, and that grace was never in such a man's heart, especially a total omission of prayer. This is an high contempt of God, denying him to be the author of our mercies, depriving him of the prerogative of governing the world, disowning any need of him, any sufficiency in him, declaring we can be our own gods, and subsist of ourselves without him, and that there is no need of his blessing. Grace, though sunk under a sin, will more or less desire its proper nourishment, the milk of the word, and other institutions of God. Nature, though oppressed by a disease, will require food to keep it alive. A good man, in this case, is like the planets, which, though they be turned about daily from east to west, by the motion of the *primum mobile*, yet they still keep up their proper motion from west to east, either slower or quicker.

2. Not in a customary commission of any known sin. To work iniquity, is the proper character of natural men, hence called workers of iniquity: Ps. v. 5, 'Thou hatest all workers of iniquity.' And by the same title are they called by Christ at the day of judgment: 'Depart from me, all you workers of iniquity,' that contrive, lay the platform of it, and work at it as at a trade, or as a curious piece of art. It is one thing to sin, another to commit or do a sin: Ps. cxix. 3, 'They do not iniquity, they walk in his ways;' their usual, constant course is in the way of God; they do not iniquity, they settle not to it, take not pleasure in it as their work, and way of livelihood. So it is the character of an ungodly man to walk in the ways of sin. Walking according to the course of the world, and fulfilling the desires of the flesh, are one and the same thing, Eph. ii. 2, 3. A good man may step into a way of sin, but he walks not in it, to make it either his business or recreation. So walking in sin, and living in sin, are put together. What is called 'walking after the flesh,' Rom. viii. 1, is called 'living after the flesh,' ver. 13, which is the same with committing sin in the text. So ways and doings are joined together, Zech. i. 6. To make sin

our way or walk, is when a man chooses it as a particular trade and way of living. A good man in sin is out of his way; a wicked man in sin is in his way; a good man will not have so much as one way of sin; a wicked hath many ways, for he seeks out many inventions. Not one example of the gross fall of a good man in Scripture will countenance any pretence for a course in sin; for either they were not in a course of sin, or it was not a course of known sins.

Noah was drunk but once, yet that was not a sin of the same hue with that among us. He first found out the fruits of the vine, Gen. ix. 20, knew nothing of the strength of the grape, and therefore might easily be overcome by an unusual liquor.

Lot's incest was but twice, and that unwillingly. He knew not his daughters' lying down or rising, neither time, Gen xix. 33, 35. And for his daughters, some think that they thought there was no man left upon the earth but their father; but that is not clear, for Lot had been in Zoar, and departed thence to the mountain where their fact was committed. His drunkenness admits of some aggravations; it was no fit season for him to swill after so sharp a judgment upon Sodom, so severe a remark of God upon his wife, and so great a deliverance to himself. Yet this was not a course of sin; you read no more of it. There is difference between a man's being drunk, and being a drunkard: the one notes the act, the other the habit and love of it.

Peter denied Christ, yet but three times together; not three times with considerable intervals for a full deliberation. It is probable Peter's faith was so stupefied (as well as the faith of those disciples that were going to Emmaus: Luke xxiv. 21, 'We trusted that it had been he which should have redeemed Israel,' who, and indeed all the disciples in several passages, seemed to expect a temporal kingdom to be erected by him), as therefore not to judge it fit to hazard himself for a person he thought himself so much mistaken in. Howsoever it was, it was not a course of sin, and his repentance overrules the plea for any customary transgression.

And though the Corinthians were charged with fornication, and eating things sacrificed to idols, yet it seems to be out of a corrupt judgment, as appears by the apostles' disputing against the one, 1 Cor. vi. 13–15, and against the other, 1 Cor. viii. And that neither of those were generally judged to be sins by the converted Gentiles, as appears by the decree of the apostles, Acts xv. 28, 29, where they determine against both these; though this was a course of sin, yet not a course of known sins. And after they were informed by the apostle of the sinfulness of them, they abstained; therefore in the second epistle,* writ the year after to them, he charges them not with those former crimes, but comforts them for their being so much cast down with sorrow.

David's sin, though lying upon him for about ten or twelve months, yet it was not a course of sin; and we find a signal repentance afterwards; but of that after. To walk in a road of known sins is the next step to committing sin as sin, and manifests the habit of sin to have a strong and fixed dominion in the will.

I shall confirm this by some reasons, because upon this proposition depend all the following.

1. Regeneration gives not a man a dispensation from the law of God. As Christ came not to destroy the law, but to establish it, so grace doth not dispense with the law, but confirms the authority of it. Habitual grace is

* The first epistle was writ the twenty-fifth year after the death of Christ, and the second epistle, the twenty-sixth year, according to Baronius.

not given us to assist us in the breaches of it, but to enable us to the performance of it. As the grace of God, which hath appeared to all men, teaches the doctrine of holiness, so the grace of God in us enables us to walk in the way of holiness. Grace in a believer embraceth what the grace of God teaches. The moral laws of God are indispensable in themselves, and of eternal verity. Therefore as no rational creature, much less can a regenerate person, be exempted from that obedience to the law, which, as a rational creature, he is bound to observe. The grace of God justifying is never conferred without grace sanctifying. It is certain, where Christ is made righteousness, he is made sanctification. It is not congruous to the divine holiness, to look upon a person as righteous, who hath not a renewed principle in him, no more than it is congruous to the divine justice and holiness to look upon him as righteous, merely for this principle so imperfect.

2. It is not for the honour of God to suffer a custom and course of sin in a renewed man. It is true, a renewed man should not voluntarily, nor doth commit willingly, even sins of lighter infirmities; but God suffers those, because they do not wound the honour of Christianity, though they discover a remoteness from a state of perfection. But they do not customarily fall into great sins; for it seems not congruous to permit such courses commonly in any one which would disgrace religion, and make that despicable in the eyes of the world which God hath designed in all ages to honour. Since he hath delivered his Son to death, to preserve the honour of his law, it seems not to consist with his wisdom to let those who enjoy the fruits of his death walk in a customary contempt of his law. Neither can we think that God would permit that in a believer which is against the very essence of grace, though he may permit that which is against the beauty and accidental perfection of it.

3. It is against the nature of the covenant. In the covenant, we are to take God for our God, *i.e.* for our chief good and last end. But a course of sin is an adoration of the sinful object as the chief good and last end, because a man prefers the creature before God, and loves it supremely, contrary to the will of God. It is essential for one in covenant with God to have an high valuation of God and his will. But a custom of known sins evidenceth that there is not a worthy and practical esteem of God. How can any condition of the covenant consist with a constant practice of sin? How can there be faith, where the precept is not believed? How can there be love, if the pleasure of God be not regarded? How can there be fear, if his authority be wilfully contemned? How can there be a new heart, when there is nothing but an old frame and a diabolical nature? It is a renouncing those conditions upon which a right to heaven is founded; for a worker of iniquity walks in those ways which are prohibited upon pain of not entering into that place of glory, and so doth wilfully refuse the acceptance of the conditions on God's part, and the performance of the conditions on his own part, which are necessary to God's glory and his own interest. It is an invasion of God's right, whereby he refuseth God for his God and Lord, and sets up himself as his own governor; an affecting virtually an equality with God, and independency on him, which, in the common nature of sin, is virtually the same with that of the devil, who sinned from the beginning; and, therefore, a course of sin one that is born of God doth not continue in. Perhaps the apostle, in the text, might have some such respect upon his opposing the believer's not committing sin to the sin of the devil from the beginning, viz., such a course of sin whereby a man declares, as the devil did, that he will be his own governor, as indeed, in every course of sin, a man doth practically declare.

4. It is against the nature of our first repentance and conversion to God. True repentance is 'a breaking off iniquity by righteousness,' Dan. iv. 27, a turning from sin to holiness, from ourselves to God, from our own wills to the will of God; from everything else, as the chief good and last end, to God as both these. Now, though a particular act of sin be against the watchfulness which attends repentance, yet a course of sin is against the nature of it;* the one is against the liveliness of repentance, the other against the life of it. A delightful walking in any known sin, though never so little, is a defiance of God, and therefore contrary to the nature of conversion, and is a virtual embracing of all sin whatsoever; because he that, in his ordinary walk in sin, hath no respect to the will and pleasure of God, though he knows it, and will not be restrained from his delight by any such regard of God, would be restrained from no other sin whatsoever, if he did conceive them as pleasant, advantageous, and suitable to him, as he doth that which is his darling. As he that 'breaks one point of the law is guilty of all,' James ii. 10, because he shews thereby a will and disposition to break all, if the same occasions were offered; so he that commits one known sin wilfully, much more he that walks in a course of sin, is guilty of all sins virtually. For he would boggle at no temptations upon a respect to God; because, if a regard to God doth not prevail upon him against a course in one kind, it will not detain him from a course in all other kinds of sin, if he come under the same circumstances for it. Let me add this too: if he that offends in one point of the law be guilty of all, *i. e.* as much delight and eagerness as he hath in the breach of that one, it is to be supposed that he would have in the breach of all the rest upon the former reason, can then such a disposition, which is in every course of known sin, be consistent with the nature of repentance and conversion?

5. It is against the nature of habitual grace, which is the principle and form of our regeneration. If he doth not commit sin because the seed of God remains in him, then such a course of sin is against the nature of this seed, inconsistent with the birth of God. A crooked and perverse spirit in sin is a sign of a putrefied soul, a spot of a different nature from that of God's children: Deut. xxxii. 5, 'They have corrupted themselves; their spot is not the spot of his children: they are a perverse and crooked generation.' It is a stain peculiar to the children of the devil, not the sons of God. A trade in sin is an evidence of a diabolical nature: 1 John iii. 8, 'He that commits sin is of the devil.' It is not, therefore, consistent with grace, which is a divine nature. The reign of sin is inconsistent with the reign of grace, though the rebellion of sin be not. It is against the nature of regeneration for sin to guide our wills, though it be not against the nature of it for sin to reside in our flesh. To 'walk after the flesh,' Rom. viii. 1, is an inseparable character of a natural man. The apostle, Rom. vii. 25, had been complaining of the law of his members, the serving sin with his flesh. He comforts himself with this, that he obeyed it not, and that they were in Christ, whose ordinary walk was as the Spirit led, not as the flesh allured.† And, indeed, every tree brings forth fruit suitable to its nature. A vine brings not forth thorns; and he that hath the seed of God is under an impossibility of bringing forth the fruits of sin with delight, since he hath a root of righteousness planted in him.

1. It is against the nature of a renewed understanding. A regenerate man hath a new light in his mind, whereby he hath a fairer prospect of God, and a fouler of sin. He was an enemy to God in his mind before, Col. i. 21. He had dishonourable opinions and conceits of God and goodness, and

* Taylor of Repentance, p. 188. † Amyraut. in Joh. viii. 9.

honourable thoughts of sin above its merit; he thought ill of the one and well of the other. But now he is 'renewed in the spirit of his mind,' Eph. iv. 23; and he hath the 'spirit of a sound mind,' 2 Tim. i. 7. His judgment is regulated by the law of God; he judges of sin as it is, in its nature, a transgression of the law. Can we imagine that a man restored to a sound mind, and that hath his natural madness and folly cured, should act, after this cure, as much out of his wits as before? If he hath his constant frenzies and madness as much as before, where is his cure? Can any man in the world act always against his judgment? Though he may be overpowered by the importunity of others, or overruled by a fit of passion, to do something against his judgment, can you expect always to find him in the road of crossing the dictates of his understanding? An unregenerate man hath a natural light in his mind and conscience, and so a judgment of sin; but he hath not a judgment of sin adequate to the object, he doth not judge of sin in the whole latitude of it, he hath not a settled judgment of the contrariety of his beloved sin to God. He looks not upon it in the extent of it, as, *malum injucundum, inhonestum, inutile*. If he looks upon sin as dishonest, he regards it as profitable; if neither as honest or profitable, yet as pleasant; so that the natural light, which is in the understanding when it dictates right, is mated and overruled by some other principle, the pleasure or profit of it, and swayed by the inherent habits of sin in the will. The devil that works in them hath some principle to stir up, or dim this natural light and cast a mist before the eye; and so they direct their course according to that particular judgment which is befriended in its vote by sense.

2. It is against the nature of a renewed will. Grace is the law of God in the heart, and is put in to enable us to walk in the ways of God; and shall it endure such wilful pollutions in the creature, when it is the end of its being there to preserve from them? The Spirit is given in the heart, 2 Cor. i. 22, sent into the heart, Gal. iv. 6; the law put into the heart, Heb. x. 16. Since, therefore, there is an habit of grace in the will, a man cannot frequently and easily launch into sin; because he cannot do it habitually, the remainders of sin being mated with a powerful habit, which watches their motions to resist them. Doth God put such a habit there, such a seed, an abiding seed, to no purpose but to let the soul be wounded by every temptation, to be deserted in every time of need? Grace is an habit superadded to that natural and moral strength which is in the will. Man, by nature's strength merely, or with the assistance of common grace, hath power to avoid the acts of gross sins; for he is master of his own actions, though he is not of the motions tending to them. The devil cannot force a man's will. And when grace, a greater strength, comes in, shall there be no effects of this strength, but the reins be as stiff in the hands of old lust, and the will as much captive to the sinful habit of it, as before? Grace being a new nature, it is as absurd to think that a gracious man should wallow in a course of sin, as it is to think that any creature should constantly and willingly do that which is against its nature. A gracious man 'delights in the law of God': Ps. i. 2, 'His delight is in the law of the Lord, and in his law doth he meditate day and night.' If he delights in it, can he delight to break it? Do men fling that which they delight in every day in the dirt, and trample upon it; or, rather, do they not keep it choicely in their cabinets? If it be also the character of a good man to 'meditate in the law' of God, he must have frequent exercises of faith, reflections upon himself, motions to God, which cannot consist with a course of sin. Grace doth essentially include a contrariety to sin, and a love to God in the will. It is a principle of doing good and eschewing evil; and these being essential properties of grace, are essen-

tial to every regenerate man, and in every one. As a drop of water or one spark of fire hath the essential properties of a great mass of water or a great quantity of fire, so every renewed man hath the same love to God and the same hatred to sin essentially as the most eminent saint, though not in degree; yea, which those in heaven have, though not in the same degree. As a spark of fire will burn, a drop of water will moisten, though not in so eminent a measure. Now, upon the whole, consider whether is it possible to bare reason that a regenerate man should customarily do those things which are against the essential properties of that which is in him, in his will, and doth denominate him a new creature?

Prop. 3. A regenerate man cannot have a fixed resolution to walk in such a way of sin, were the impediments to it removed. Though unregenerate men may actually, as to the outward exercise, abstain from some sins, yet it is usually upon low and mean conditions. If it were not for such or such an obstacle in the way, I would do such and such an act. This temper is not in a good man; he cannot have a fixed and determinate resolution to commit such an act if such bars were taken away. Such resolutions are common in unregenerate men: Jer. xliv. 25, 'We will surely perform our vows which we have vowed, to burn incense to the queen of heaven;' and Isa. lvi. 12, 'We will fill ourselves with strong drink, and to-morrow shall be as this day, and much more abundant;' we will have as merry a meeting as we had to-day. The same character is ascribed to such an one: Ps. xxxvi. 4, 'He deviseth mischief upon his bed. He sets himself in a way that is not good. He abhorreth not evil.' He models out his sinful designs with head and heart; he settles himself as an army settles in their ground when they resolve to fight, ימאס; he abhors not evil; he starts not at such motions, but by a *meiosis*, he hugs and caresseth them with a wonderful delight. Regenerate men fear to sin, wicked men contrive to sin. One would starve it, the other makes provision for it. This temper cannot be in a regenerate man.

1. It is diabolical, and so falls under that in the text. He cannot commit sin as the devil doth. It is a stain of the devil, who is resolved in his way of malice to God, and mischief to man, but for the strait chains God holds him in. His resolution is fixed, though the execution restrained: 'He goes about seeking whom he may devour,' 1 Pet. v. 8, καταπίῃ, to drink at one draught; seeking both for an opportunity and permission. Unwearied searches manifest fixed resolutions. His throat is ready to swallow, if he had a morsel for it.

2. It is a sign of habitual sin, a state of sin. This temper manifests that the will is habituated in sin, though the hand doth not outwardly act it. The inherent power of sin must be great, when a man is greedy to commit that to which he hath no outward allurements, or when those allurements are balanced with contrary considerations; when he hath either no outward temptation to it, or the cross impediments are as strong, or stronger, than the temptation. When men, in the midst of such bars, long for a temptation, it is such a kind of desire in one way as the creature hath in another for the manifestation of the sons of God: Rom. viii. 19, 'For the earnest expectation of the creature waits for the manifestation;' it is ἀποκαραδοκία, a putting out the head to see if he can find any coming to knock off the fetters, not of his sin, but of his forced morality. In this case take two men; one commits a great sin upon a temptation, even as it were overpowered by it, and had no thoughts, no inclinations, before that temptation appeared which began first to spirit him; another commits a lighter sin, or would fain commit it, upon a weak temptation, and many bars

lying in the way, and his heart was hankering and thirsting for some opportunity to commit it; which do you think really is the greater offence in point of heart and affection? The first appears blacker, but it is an invasion; the other is really blacker, because it is an affection, and shews sin to be rooted in the heart as its proper soil, wherein sin delights to grow, and the soil delights to nourish it. The one shews sin to be a stranger and a thief, which hath waylaid him, the other evidenceth sin to be an inmate and intimate friend. Such a man is not obliged to his will for his abstinence from sin, but to the outward hindrances; and the resolving act of the will to commit it, were those impediments removed, is as real an act of sin in the sight of God as any outward act can be in the sight of man, because God measures the greatness of sin by the proportion of the will allowed to it; therefore many sins which may be little in our account may be greater in God's account than the seemingly blacker sins of others, because there may be a greater ingrediency of the heart and affection in them than in the other.

3. It is against the nature of our repentance and first closing with God. Repentance is a change of the purpose of the heart not to commit the same iniquity again, nor any other: Job xxxiv. 32, 'If I have done iniquity, I will do no more.' It is the property of converting grace to make the soul cleave to the Lord with full purpose of heart, Acts xi. 23. This is essential to it, though there may be some startings out by passion and temptation, A pilot's intention stands right for the port, though, by the violence of the wind, he may be forced another way. It alters not his purpose, though it defer his performance. This purpose is a perpetual intent: Ps. cxix. 112, 'I have inclined my heart to keep thy statutes alway, even to the end.' It was an heart-purpose and inclination. It regarded all God's statutes, not for a fit, but perpetually, which he manifests by two words, *always, even to the end*, to shew that the perpetuity of it doth difference it from the resolutions of wicked men, who may indeed have some fits to do good, but not a fixed purpose to cleave to the Lord. These flashy purposes are like the flight of a bird, which seems to touch heaven, and in a moment falls down to the earth; as Saul resolved not to persecute David, but we soon find him again upon his old game and pursuit. Where there is true grace, there is hatred of all sin, for hatred is πρὸς τὸ γένος. Can a man be resolved to commit what he hates? No; for his inward aversion would secure him more against it than all outward obstacles. As this inward purpose of a good man is against all sin, so more particularly against that which doth so easily beset him. David seems in several places to be naturally inclined to lying, but he takes up a particular resolution against it: Ps. xvii. 3, 'I am purposed that my mouth shall not transgress;' זמתי, I have contrived to waylay and intercept the sin of lying when it hath an occasion to approach me. A good man hath not only purposes, but he endeavours to fasten and strengthen those purposes by prayer; so David, ver. 5, 'Hold up my goings in thy paths, that my footsteps slip not.' He strengthens himself by stirring up a liveliness in duty, and by avoiding occasions of sin; ver. 4, 'I have kept me from the paths of the destroyer;' whereas a wicked man neither steps out of the way of a temptation, nor steps up to God for strength against it. Now if all this be true, that in conversion the heart hath a fixed resolution for God and his ways, and that perpetually, against all sin, and particularly against the sin of our natural inclination, and all this backed with strong cries, how can it have a fixed resolution to commit it, if the way were outwardly fair for it?

4. It is absolutely against the terms of the covenant. God requires in

that a giving up ourselves to him to be his people with our whole heart and soul, as he gives himself to us with his whole heart. He will not be a sharer of the heart with sin, much less an underling to it. God will not endure a competitor in the affections. To serve God and mammon are inconsistent, by the infallible axiom of our Saviour, Luke xvi. 13. Now as God cannot be true to his covenant if he had purposes against the articles of it on his part, so neither can we be true to our covenanting with him if we have settled purposes of heart against the conditions of it. Therefore the instability in the covenant ariseth only from the falseness of the heart: Ps. lxxviii. 37, 'Their heart was not right with him, neither were they stedfast in his covenant.' The iniquity of our heels may compass us about, and make us stumble in our walk, yet our fears of being out with God may receive no establishment: Ps. xlix. 5, 'Wherefore should I fear, when the iniquity of my heels shall compass me about?' Whether he means by iniquity the sins of his ordinary walk, or the punishment of them, is all one. But yet if purposes of iniquity settle their residence in the heart, though we never act it, by reason of obstacles, it is a sign we never sincerely closed with God in covenant, nor God with us. The very regards of iniquity in the heart put a bar to the regards of God towards us. It hinders all covenant acts on God's part, because it is a manifest breach of it: Ps. lxvi. 18, 'If I regard iniquity in my heart, the Lord will not hear me,' ראיתי; if I have curiously and intently looked upon iniquity with pleasure in my heart.

5. It is against the nature of regeneration. Regeneration is a change of nature, and consequently of resolutions. A lion chained up hath an inclination to ravage, but a lion changed into the nature of a lamb loses his inclinations with that change of his nature; so that it is as impossible a regenerate man can have the fixed and determinate resolutions that a wicked man hath, as it is impossible that a lamb should have the ravenous disposition of a lion. You know the Scripture makes the change as great. How can any man resolve to do a thing against that law which at the same time he hath an habitual approbation of as holy, just, and good? against a law natural to him, viz. the law of the heart? If a delight in the law of God be a constitutive part of regeneration, then any settled purpose to sin is inconsistent with regeneration, because such a purpose, being a testimony of an inward delight in that which is contrary to the law of God, cannot consist with a delight in that which forbids what his heart is set upon.

Prop. 4. A regenerate man cannot walk in a way doubtful to him, without inquiries whether it be a way of sin or a way of duty, and without admitting of reproofs and admonitions, according to his circumstances. This consists of two parts.

1. He cannot walk in a way doubtful to him, without inquiries whether it be a way of sin or of duty. If the nature of conversion be an inclination of the heart to keep God's statutes always, even to the end, Ps. cxix. 112, the natural result then will be an inquiry what are the statutes of God which the soul is to keep. A natural man, for fear of being disturbed in his sinful pleasure, refuseth to understand the way of the Lord, and delights to be under the power of a wilful darkness: Job xxi. 14, 15, 'We desire not the knowledge of thy ways: what is the Almighty that we should serve him? and what profit should we have if we pray to him?' This unwillingness to know the ways of God arises from a contempt of the Almighty and his service. They judged it not profitable to serve and worship God, and therefore were loath to receive any instruction, for fear any light should spring up in them, by way of conviction, to disturb them. Men love sin, and therefore hate any knowledge which may deprive them of the sweetness of it: Prov.

i. 22, 'The scorners delight in their scorning, and fools hate knowledge.' They delight in sin, and therefore hate any knowledge which may check their delight. And this unwillingness to choose the fear of the Lord is the ground of their hating the knowledge of it: ver. 30, 'For that they hated knowledge, and did not choose the fear of the Lord.' They are afraid to be convinced that the way of their delight is a way of sin; they would have no gall in their conscience to embitter the honey of their lusts. This hatred of knowledge is inconsistent with true conversion, because conversion is an election or choice of the fear of God, and therefore cannot resist any means tending to promote that which is chosen. It is essential to true grace to inquire into the mind and will of God, to understand what is pleasing to him: Job. xxxiv. 32, 'That which I see not, teach thou me: if I have done iniquity, I will do no more.' Inform me in what I know not, and if I understand it is iniquity which I have walked ignorantly in, I will do it no more. He will not return to folly when he shall hear what God the Lord shall speak. It is certainly incompatible to the new nature to act in a contrariety to God. Grace is always attended with an universal desire to know his will, and pleasure him in performing it; hence will follow an inquiry, what behaviour and what acts are most agreeable to him: John xiv. 21, 'He that hath my commandments, and keeps them, he it is that loves me;' Ἐκεῖνός ἐστι. The antithesis is, He that hath no mind to have my commandments, because he would not keep them, hath no love to me. *He it is*, emphatically, exclusively, that is the man, and none else, that loves me. Now if a man be afraid of making inquiry into the lawfulness of a course he is wedded to, for fear his beloved object should appear to be a sin, it is a sign he abstains from what he knows certainly to be a sin out of a servile fear, not out of a generous, divine love, a principle as essential to the new nature as fear is to an enlightened carnalist.

2. A regenerate man cannot despise admonitions and reproofs, which would inform him and withdraw him from a sinful course. If he be in the way of life that keeps instruction, then he that refuseth reproof is in the way of death: Prov. x. 17, 'He is in the way of life that keeps instruction: but he that refuseth reproof erreth.' It is put in a milder expression, but if you observe the opposition, it amounts to the inference I make: so, Prov. xv. 9, 10, 'The Lord loves them that follow after righteousness. Correction is grievous unto them that forsake the way: and he that hates reproof shall die.' Here is a plain opposition made between them that follow after righteousness, which is the character of a regenerate man, who is therefore the object of God's love; and that person that accounts correction grievous, and hates reproof, he is not one that follows after righteousness (to pursue is to embrace it), and therefore not the object of God's love, but the mark of death; so that it is impossible a righteous man should hate reproof. Nay, the hating of reproof, whereby a man might be informed of his duty, is a sign, not of a bare unregeneracy, but of one at the very bottom of it, wallowing in the very dregs and mud of it, farthest from the kingdom of heaven; one that scarce looks like a rational creature: Prov. xii. 1, 'Whoso loves instruction, loves knowledge: but he that hates reproof is brutish.' Whereas Solomon's wise man, which is a regenerate man, will love the reprover for the reproof's sake, and grow wiser by instruction: Prov. ix. 8, 9, 'Reprove not a scorner, lest he hate thee: rebuke a wise man, and he will love thee. Give instruction to a wise man, and he will be yet wiser: teach a just man, and he will increase in learning.' Just men change their intentions upon a discovery of the sinfulness of their way; and though it may not at the first assault of an admonition appear to be a sin, yet it will check somewhat their

violence in it. But where sin hath a dominion, every check and discovery of it doth rather inflame than quench it; and the heart, like a stream, rises the higher for the dam. Judas had an admonition from Christ that informed him of what wickedness he was about, and the danger of it, Mark xiv. 21. He pronounceth a woe against him. Compare this with John xiii. 27, 30, when he gives him the sop, which was at the same time he informed him of the danger, Satan entered into him, and he went more roundly to work to accomplish it; he went immediately out. Observe, by the way, that the Spirit of God enters into a man's heart often upon admonitions from friends, and the devil also more powerfully upon the same occasions than at other times. A good man cannot habitually hate the reprover. There is one example of a good man dealing hardly with a prophet for reproving him in the name of the Lord: 2 Chron. xvi. 10, 'Then Asa was wroth with the seer, and put him into a prison-house; for he was in a rage with him because of this thing;' and partly for the judgment of war against him. But the Scripture gives an allay to it; 'for he was in a rage;' he was in a passion, because of the threatening and the plainness of the speech, 'thou hast done foolishly.' To say such a word to an inferior, would ordinarily now a days swell many a professor to a fury, much more a prince. This very proposition will discover that there are many more pretenders to a regenerate state than possessors of it, so strangely is not only human nature, but the Christian religion, depraved among us.

Prop. 5. A regenerate man cannot have a settled, deliberate love to any one act of sin, though he may fall into it. Thus the devil sins; he loves what he doth. Though a good man may fall into a sin, and even such a sin, which he was much guilty of before his conversion, and which he hath repented of, yet never into a love of it, or the allowance of any one act of it; for by regeneration the soul becomes like God in disposition, and therefore cannot love anything which he hates, whose hatred and love being always just, are unerring rules to the love and hatred of every one of his children. He can never account a sin his ornament, but his fetter; never his delight, but his grief. I add this proposition, because there may be a love of an act of sin where there is not a constant course in it; as a man that hath committed a murder out of revenge, may love afterwards the very thoughts of that revenge, though he never murder any more. And a man that hath committed an act of adultery, may review it with pleasure, though he never commit an act again; but a good man cannot. David is supposed to be inclined to the way of lying and dissembling; though he may falter sometimes, and look that way, and perhaps fall into it, yet never into a love of it; therefore observe, Ps. cxix. 163, 'I hate and abhor lying; but thy law do I love.' A single hatred would not serve the turn; but, 'I hate and abhor.' I have not the least affection to this of any, though I have the greatest natural inclination to it. What was the reason? 'Thy law do I love.' There was another affection planted in his soul, which could not consist with a love to, or allowance either of the habit, or any one act of lying. A good man hath yielded his soul up to the government of Christ, his affections are fully engaged; he cannot see an equal amiableness in any other object, for he cannot lose his eyes again; his enlightened mind cannot be wholly blinded and deceived by Satan; he walks not by the inveiglements of sense, but by the unerring rule of faith; so that, though by some mists before his eyes, he may for a while be deluded, yet as he cannot have a settled false judgment, so he cannot have a settled affection to any one act of sin. It is one thing for a city to surrender itself to the enemy out of affection, and another thing to be forced by them: under a force they may retain their loyalty to their lawful prince. There may be some passionate approbations of an act of sin. Jonah was an advocate for his own passion against God, and made a very peremptory apology for it: Jonah iv. 9, 'I do well to be angry, even to the death.' Yet, if we may judge by his former temper, we cannot think he did afterwards defend it out of judgment, as he did then out of passion; for when the lot fell upon him, Jonah ii. 9, 12, he made no defence for his sin; he very calmly wishes them to cast him into the sea. Where there is a passionate approbation, it cannot be constant in a good man; for when he returns to himself, his abhorrences of the sin, and himself for it, are greater, as if by the greatness of his grief he would endeavour to make some recompence for the folly of his passion.

Observe, by the way, a good man may commit a sin with much eagerness, and yet have a less affection to it in the very act, than another who acts that sin more calmly; because it may arise, not from any particular inclination he hath in his temper to that sin, but from the general violence of his natural temper, which is common to him in that action. This seems to be the case of Jonah, both in this and the former act. But if a man be more violent in that act of sin than he is in other things by his natural temper, there is ground both for himself and others to think, that sin hath got a great mastery over his affections.

Peter seems to be a man of great affections, and of a forward natural temper; he was very hasty to have tabernacles built in the mountain for his Master, Moses, and Elias, and have resided there. He hastily rebukes his Master; he flung himself out of a ship to meet our Saviour walking upon the water; and after his resurrection he leapt into the sea to get to him; so that Peter's denying his Master was not such an evidence of disaffection to him, or love to the sinful act he was then surprised by, as it would have been in John, or any other disciple of a more sedate temper. But this only by the way, as a rule both to judge yourselves by, and to moderate your censures of others; and consider, that such acts of sin are not frequent. The violence of a man's temper, if godly, cannot carry him out into a course of sin, or a love to any one act. As a wicked man may hit upon a good duty, and perform it, but not out of a settled love to God, or habitual obedience to his law; so a good man may by surprise do an evil work, not out of obedience to the law of sin, or any love to the sin itself. What considerations may move a wicked man to a good duty, may in some respect move a good man to a sinful act; yet it is not to be called a duty in the one, no more than it is to be called a sin in the other of the same hue, of the same hue, I say, with that in a natural man.

Prop. 6. A regenerate man cannot commit any sin with a full consent and bent of will. A man may consent to that which he doth not love. Hereby I distinguish it from the former proposition. I mean not that he cannot commit any sin wilfully as sin, for so I believe no man doth; it being against the nature of the creature to do evil, as evil *formaliter*, but under some other notion of it. Some consent of the will I do acknowledge, because the will, as well as the other faculties, is but in part regenerate. As there is not a triumphant light in the understanding, so neither is the grace of the will at present triumphant, but militant; yet it may be rather called the will of sin, than a man's own will. Sometimes a good man is by some sudden motion hurried on to sin, before he can consult law and reason, before he hath his wits well at liberty, before he can compare the temptation or sin with the prohibition of it by the divine law. But generally there is a resistance in him, as well as a provocation in sin; for the two contrary principles exert themselves in some measure. Grace resists, and sin provokes, whereas another, that hath no grace, sins with a full consent, because he hath no spiritual resisting principle in him; for he is flesh, and not spirit, and whatsoever is born of the flesh, is flesh, and wholly flesh. There is a resisting indeed in a natural man, but it is a resistance of natural light, not of grace; a resistance not of the will, but of the conscience; the will is bent to sin, but natural conscience puts rubs in the way. Neither is this resistance in spiritual sins (which is the greatest character I know whereby to distinguish a resistance of natural conscience from a resistance by a principle of grace), which natural conscience doth not so much trouble itself about, as not having light without a spiritual illumination to discern them, but only in gross sins, such as are condemned by common reason; so that if he hath any resistance, it is not in the will of the man, but the will of his interest, will of his credit, or the will of his conscience; not in the rational will, complying with and delighting in the will of God.

A regenerate man cannot commit any sin with,

1. An habitual consent, because he hath a principle of grace within him which opposes that tide of nature which did forcibly carry him down before. This opposite principle doth remain, though the present opposition may not be discerned by reason of the prevalency of the temptation. As in a room warmed by the fire in winter, there is a principle in the air doth resist that heat, and reduce it after the fire is out to its former rawness and coldness. A renewed man being passed into another nature, it cannot be supposed he can do anything with an habitual bent of will against his nature. Grace hath put a stop to that. Paul distinguisheth himself from sin in the acts of it; it is not 'I,' or my will, but 'sin': Rom. vii. 20, 'Now, if I do that I would not, it is no more I that do it, but sin that dwells in me.' Κατεργάζομαι signifies to perfect and complete a work, to work industriously and politely. Had I my will, I should not do thus. There is a divorce made between will and sin, so that sin acts upon a single score. Now, 'it is no more I': a divorce is made between my will and sin. The law of sin is therefore called a law *in* the members, not *of* the members; a law found working there: ver. 21, 'I find a law in my members'; I did not enact it, I placed it not there, I consent not to its being there, but there I find it, and know not how to be rid of it, but it shall never have my will. But the law of grace is called a law *of* the mind, not *in* the mind, a law which is settled there by the consent of the soul, and to whose sovereignty and guidance it yields itself. The law of sin is in the members; the vigour of it is seen in the inferior faculties of the soul, not in the higher, the mind and will; it is a law imposed upon me, not embraced by me; a law of disturbance, not of obedience; a law that troubles me, doth not delight me, ver. 21, 22. It resides as an enemy warring, but hath no intimacy with me as a friend, ver. 23, yet it is an enemy driven to the outworks, to the members; so that where all this is, you cannot suppose an habitual consent to sin when the will is formed into another nature. As the will of the wicked is possessed by habits of sin under the restraints from it, so the will of the godly is possessed by habits of grace even under the rape of a prevailing temptation.

2. Nor an actual consent both antecedent and consequent. The interest of sin may seem to be actually higher and stronger in the soul than the interest of God, though this latter is habitually stronger than the interest of sin. Though there may be an antecedent delight in the motion, a present delight in the action, yet there is not a permanent consequent delight after it; yet the two first are rare. It is seldom that a renewed soul and sin do so friendly conspire together without any spirital reluctancy. Suppose he may have by the suspension of grace a whole actual consent of will to one particular sin

upon some strong provocation, yet he gives not up himself to the will or way of that sin. He is only under a temporary, not a perpetual power of it, as a man in a fight may by a fall be under the power of his enemy, yet in the struggle get up again and reduce him to the same necessity. Though there be not an express dissent at the motion nor in the action, yet there is always after, for it is as much against the terms of the covenant to have a perpetual delight in any sin committed as to commit it often, because this delight in it is an approbation of it, and every act of delight is a new act of approbation, and consequently a recommission of it, and a making a man's self a perpetual accessory to that first act.

(1.) Sometimes he hath an antecedent dissent. A renewed man is troubled and displeased at the first motion to a sin; he is sometimes troubled that any sin should so much as ask him the question to have entertainment in him. It is so many times with a natural man, much more with a regenerate man; yet afterwards, that displicency abating, the sin creeps upon him by degrees and ensnares him. Paul had an act of will against that which he did before he did it; he did that which was preceded by an act of his will nilling it, as there was an act of his will for the doing good preceding his not doing it: Rom. vii. 19, 'The good that I would, I do not, but the evil which I would not, that I do.' The act of his will was present: ver. 18, 'To will is present with me; I have that standing in a readiness to do good, but the executive power is at a distance, I know not how to have it; but how to perform that which is good I find not.' He speaks as a man that was searching for something which he had a great desire to find, and could not meet with it. Many times a good man is tired out with the importunity of a temptation, and is fain to fling down his weapons and sink under the oppression, till he receive a new recruit of strength by exciting and assisting grace.

(2.) Sometimes concomitant in the very commission of a sin. Peter seems to have had some resistance in the very act of denying his master. The Spirit of God blew up some sparks of shame in him at that very time, for after the very first denial he went out into the porch, Mark xiv. 68. By his retirement he discovers some willingness to have avoided a further temptation. There is many times an exercise of displeasure against it while a man cannot avoid it: Rom. vii. 15, 'That which I do, I allow not; that which I hate, that I do.' I hate it even while I do it, and my hatred is excited against it in the very act; he means it of sins of infirmity. The seed of God in the heart cannot consent to sin, but will many times in the very acting of it be shewing its displeasure, weakly or strongly, against it. As a needle touched with a loadstone, if it be disturbed in its standing to the north pole, will shake and tremble while the impediment is upon it.* Some demurrers were made in Peter's heart, but fear overruled the plea; and it is probable his heart was not wholly asleep even in the very act, else it is not likely he should have been so suddenly roused. There is a voice in him: grace speaks for God, but it is overruled and oppressed by a temptation; there are some pull-backs, some spiritual whisperers, even when it presses hard. 'Why art thou cast down, my soul?' Ps. xliii. 5; there is the carnal part stirring in distrust: 'hope thou in God;' there is a spiritual part rising in faith. A neat person may by stumbling be bemired in a dirty hole, but while he stumbles there is a natural impetus which endeavours to keep him upright; and if he doth fall, he struggles till he be delivered; but when a swine falls into a puddle, he lies grunting with pleasure, and grumbles at any that will drag him out. Which leads me to a third thing:

(3.) But there is always a consequent dissent after the fall. He hath many

* Smith on the Creed.

rebukes in his conscience, whereas a natural man's sin is brought up and nurtured with him: Eccles. v. 1, 'They consider not that they do evil;' they lay it not to heart, especially if it break not out in some foul and notorious manner. A renewed man is displeased at the very first motion that clambered up into his heart to entice him to sin: not only the fruit but the root that bears it is odious to him: Ps. li. 5, 'Behold, I was shapen in iniquity. By the same reason that he directs his hatred to the sin of his nature, by the same reason he will do it to the first motion that immediately brought forth that bitter fruit, which a natural man doth not. It is the character of a wicked man to rejoice that he hath done evil, Prov. ii. 14, which I think is never found in a renewed man, for this is indeed to be under the power of Satan, and like their father the devil. But he condemns what he hath committed, and the greater his delight in it the greater will his abhorrency be of it, and the more earnest his cry to be rid of his burden. When he comes to see what contrariety there was in his act to the law of God, it is impossible but his heart should smite him. It cannot be, but that delight in the law of God, which is a constitutive part of a regenerate man, Rom. vii. 22, must revive when the weights which did suspend it are removed, and according to the degrees of his revived delight there will be suitable degrees of displeasure with what was contrary to the object of it, for since a delight in the law of God is essential to a renewed nature, that delight must needs produce an aversion from everything contrary to that law, otherwise it is not a delight. If there be not such workings after a review of sin, I dare pronounce that such a man is not regenerate. But how long he may lie in a sin without acting consideration about it, I cannot determine. He must needs have torment in his soul and a high disaffection to his sin and himself for it, because upon a review he cannot but see how unlike to God it hath made him, how much it hath defiled his soul, and impaired the divine image. No disease can be more grievous to the body than a sin fallen into is to the new nature; it grieves and pains the new creature, which is restless till it be rid of the disease. The new nature is a tender thing. Though he be assured of its pardon, he is in anxiety till he finds it purged: Ps. li. 7, 'Purge me with hyssop, and I shall be clean.' David had been assured of the pardon of his sin by Nathan: that would not quiet him as long as the filth remained; he would not only have the guilt removed, but the stain washed off, as a man fallen in the dirt is desirous not only to be raised up, but to be washed clean from any remainders of the mire. A good man hath a disquietness in his heart, and is as much troubled at his sin as at a stinking wound or a loathsome disease, Ps. xxxviii. 5–8, and his 'sorrow is continually before him,' ver. 17. He is more displeased with that sin than he is pleased at present with all the grace he hath. David's sin was ever before him, Ps. li. 3. Peter brought forth no other fruit immediately after the review of his sin but sorrow, and exercised more grief for that than he did joy at the present for the not failing of his faith, as a man is more troubled with a pain of the tooth or a fit of the gout than pleased with all the health in his vital parts, which is far greater than his pain. Here then is a difference; regenerate men have pain in their sins, natural men pleasure; the one is ashamed of his sin, the other at best but ashamed of his discredit; he condemns himself for it with so much severity, rips his heart open before God, that if a wicked man should hear him praying in his closet after some sin, he would think he did belie himself, or else that he were the vilest villain in the world. He will study no excuses, and present no pleas to God for his sin. If he hath not strength to conquer it, he hath a voice to cry against it: prayers are doubled, one messenger goes to heaven upon the heels of another, and so moderation, which was in his requests before, is turned to an unsatisfied importunity; so that, you see, there is not a plenary consent of will, but the dissent is habitual and actual; if not antecedent or concomitant, yet always consequent.

What, then, doth the regenerate man's sin arise from? It ariseth,

1. Either from a strong passion, which many times bears down the bars both of grace and reason. That is not wholly voluntary which is done by the prevalency of passion, which suspends the determination of the understanding, and consequently the regular and free motion of the will. Such was the accusation of God in his prophet, which David was guilty of: Ps. cxvi. 11, 'I said in my haste, All men are liars.' 'I said,' it is true: 'all men are liars,' even the prophet too, but it was in 'my haste.' And in his haste he accuseth God of the breach of his promises: Ps. xxxi. 22, 'I said in my haste, I am cut off from before thy eyes': God hath either forgot his promise or changed his resolutions, for not one of them will be made good unto me. It was a passion in Moses which made him guilty of that act of unbelief that cost him his exclusion from the land of promise, Num. xx. 8, 10, 11, 12. God commands him to use his tongue, not his rod, on the rock, but the passion the good man was in by the provocation of the people transported him beyond his bounds. Peter's heart was not so full of courage as of loyalty: his zeal was put out of countenance by his fear. A strong fit of passion may make a man as good and meek as Moses fling away both the tables of the law, which otherwise would be as dear to him as the apple of his eye.

2. From inconsiderateness. There cannot be a full consent of will where a deliberate judgment doth not precede. Many a man, through an inconsiderate indulging his appetite, eats that meat which foments his humours into some dangerous disease. Sin creeps upon a good man when the liveliness and activity of his spirit in former duties is in a slumber; but another hath as great inclinations to sin when his understanding is in its strength. Peter had the grace of faith, but he fell into his sin for want of acting it. Upon his repentance it is said, Luke xxii. 6, 'And Peter remembered the words of the Lord.' He had forgot Christ's words, and that made him forget himself and his Master in that act of sin. If our Saviour had cast his eye upon Peter, and excited his slumbering grace before the maid had spoken to him, he might have prevented Peter's fall as well as afterwards recovered him. If God had sent Nathan with a message to David when his corruption began first to put on its arms, to have shewed him the vileness of his intentions, and excited him to a stout resistance, he might have prevented the loss of his innocency, as well as restored him after he had lain in the dust so long. David might have kept his standing, and dismissed those inclinations, as he did his inconsiderate design of murdering Nabal and his family upon Abigail's admonition, for which he blesseth God, 1 Samuel xxv. 32, 33. In short, the motion of a regenerate man to sin is violent, like a stone upward; the motion of an unrenewed man is natural, like a stone downwards. The godly are violently pursued, but the wicked sottishly infatuated by a temptation. And certainly when the strength of the passion is abated, and the free exercise of reason recovered, there will be the exercise of grace again; for it is not conceivable that the habit of grace and repentance should be without the actual exercise of it, when the impediments are removed, and an occasion presented; so that he that doth not recover himself to his former exercise, never had this true seed of God infused into him.*

Prop. 7. Though a regenerate man may fall, and sin have a temporary

* Greenham.

dominion, yet he recovers out of this state, and for the most part returns to his former holiness, and an increase of it, though not always to his former comforts. There are none whose sins are recorded in Scripture, but there are some evidences of their repentance for it, or the acting the contrary grace. David's sin was gross, and his repentance remarkable; he was more tender afterwards in point of blood, 2 Samuel xxiii. 16, 17. When he desired water out of the well of Bethlehem, and it was brought him by three valiant men with the jeopardy of their lives, he would not drink it, because it was the blood of the men that ventured their lives to satisfy his curiosity. Peter's repentance is eminent, his affection is hot, for the truth of which he could appeal to his Master's omnisciency: John xxi. 17, 'Lord, thou knowest all things, thou knowest that I love thee.' His courage is illustrious in asserting his Master's honour in the face of the greatest dangers, in which exercise you find him the foreman of that jury of the twelve apostles before every assembly, Acts ii. 3–5, &c. Though Abraham had discovered a distrust of God in Pharaoh's and Abimelech's courts, yet his faith afterward, in his readiness to sacrifice Isaac, was as glorious as his unbelief had been base, which gave him the title of the father of the faithful. Noah, who was drunk, and thereby exposed to the derision of his son, could not so well have cursed him had he not abhorred the sin as well as the reproach. And Lot, whose righteous soul was vexed with the filthiness of others, could not have a less vexation at his own when he came to know of it. Those that affirm that mortal sins expel grace, yet doubt whether they expel the gifts of the Spirit, one end whereof, say they, is to render the soul pliable and flexible to the motions of the Spirit. If they do not expel the gifts, I know not why they should expel the grace, which is under the manutenancy of the Spirit of God in a particular manner.* The spirit lusts against the flesh, as well as the flesh against the spirit; and the lusting of the spirit will prevail as well as the lusting of the flesh, and more, Gal. v. 17. All natural things that are removed out of their proper place, are restless till they are reduced to their right station. A good man is as water, that though it be turned into a mass of ice, wholly cold in the ways of God, yet still there is a principle in him (as there is in ice) to return to his former form, figure, and activity, upon the warm irruptions of the Spirit of God. There is a powerful voice behind him that brings him back, when he turns either to the right hand or to the left from the ways of God, Isa. xxx. 21. By virtue of this seed within him, and the Spirit of God exciting it, that word which comes home to the soul after a sin becomes efficaciously melting, and raises up springs of penitential motions, which could not arise so suddenly were the spiritual life wholly departed; for a man that hath no habit of grace in him, cannot so suddenly concur with God's proposals, and exercise a repentance. In such an one we see first a stupefaction of mind and an unaptness to faith; no motions of a true repentance, though some preparation to it. But with a regenerate man it is otherwise: David, being admonished by Nathan, was struck to the heart; and Peter, presently upon our Saviour's look, melted into tears. Their grace, like tinder, took fire presently upon those small, but powerful, occasions. Though it did not act at the time of their sin, yet it had an aptness to act upon the removal of the impediments. Though Jonah seems to cast off all regard of God and his command, yet upon the first occasion, in the whale's belly, he brings forth excellent fruits of faith in a moment, Jonah ii. Grace in an instant, upon the first motion of the Spirit, will rise up, and take its place from whence it seems to be deposed. As a natural man under some

* Suarez. de Gratia. lib. xi. cap. iii. num. x. p. 415.

sting of conscience, and flash of a lightning conviction, may be restrained from sin, yet his natural inclination to it remains, though suspended at the present, and may be carried the quite contrary way. As the stream of a river, by the force of the tide, is carried against its natural current, yet slides down its channel with its wonted calmness upon the removal of the force, so a good man, under the violence of some lust, hath not his new nature changed, though at present it is restrained by an extrinsic force. So that as the one, upon the taking off his conviction, returns to his sin, so the other, upon the removal of his fetters, returns to his holiness with a greater spirit and delight. A wicked man may sometimes do a good action, but he continues not in it; as a planet is sometimes retrograde, but soon returns to its direct course. When their conscience pinches them, they awake out of their trance. So a good man may sin through infirmity, but he will revoke it by repentance. The seed of God remains in him, as the sap in the root of a tree, that recovers the leaves the next return of the sun at the spring. He may sink by nature and rise again by grace; but the devil, who sinned at the beginning, fell and never rose more.

Use, of examination.

If you find yourselves in these cases, in a course of known sin, resolution to commit it, were it not for such bars—unwillingness to know God's pleasure and injunction; despising admonitions and reproofs; a settled love of it; a full consent of will, without any antecedent, concomitant, or consequent dissent; tumbling in it without rising by repentance; a circle of sinning and repenting without abhorrence of sin—you may conclude yourselves in an unregenerate state; you sin like the devil, who sinned from the beginning.

A DISCOURSE OF THE PARDON OF SIN.

Blessed is he whose transgression is forgiven, whose sin is covered. Blessed is the man unto whom the Lord imputes not iniquity.—Ps. XXXII. 1, 2.

This psalm, as Grotius thinks, was made to be sung upon the annual day of the Jewish expiation, when a general confession of their sins was made. It is one of David's penitential psalms, supposed to be composed by him after the murder of Uriah, and the pronouncing of his pardon by Nathan, ver. 5, and rather a psalm of thanksgiving. It is called *Maschil*, a psalm of understanding. Maschil is translated *eruditio, intelligentia*, and notes some excellent doctrine in the psalm, not known by the light of nature. Blessed, אשרי, blessednesses. *Ex omni parte beatus.* Three words there are to discover the nature of sin, and three words to discover the nature of pardon.

פשע, *Transgression.* Prevarication. Some understand by it sins of omission and commission.

חטאה, *Sin.* Some understand those inward inclinations, lusts, and motions, whereby the soul swerves from the law of God, and which are the immediate causes of external sins.

עון, *Iniquity.* Notes original sin, the root of all. Three words that note pardon.

נשוי, *Levatus, forgiven, eased,* נשא, signifies to take away, to bear, to carry away. Two words in Scripture are chiefly used to denote remission, כפר, to expiate; נשא, to bear or carry away: the one signifies the manner whereby it is done, viz., atonement; the other the effect of this expiation, carrying away: one notes the meritorious cause, the other the consequent.

כסוי, *Covered.* Alluding to the covering of the Egyptians in the Red Sea. Menochius thinks it alludes to the manner of writing among the Hebrews, which he thinks to be the same with that of the Romans; as writing with a pencil upon wax spread upon tables, which when they would blot out, they made the wax plain, and drawing it over the writing, covered the former letters. And so it is equivalent with that expression of 'blotting out sin,' as in the other allusion it is with 'casting sin into the depths of the sea.'

יחשב, *Impute.* Not charging upon account. As sin is a defection from the law, so it is forgiven; as it is offensive to God's holiness, so it is covered; as it is a debt involving man in a debt of punishment, so it is not imputed; they all note the certainty, and extent, and perfection of pardon: the three words expressing sin here, being the same that are used by God in the declaration of his name, Exod. xxxiv. 7. Here are to be considered,

I. The nature of pardon.

II. The author of it, God.

III. The extent of it, transgression, sin, iniquity.

IV. The manner of it, implied, by faith in Christ.

The apostle quoting this place, Rom. iv. 7, to prove justification by faith; as sin is not imputed, so something is imputed instead of it. Covering implies something wherewith a thing is covered, as well as the act whereby it is covered.

V. The effect of it, blessedness.

I shall not divide them into distinct propositions, but take the words in order as they lie.

I. The nature of pardon.

1. Consider the words, and what notes they will afford to us.

(1.) Covering, as it alludes to the manner of writing, and so is the same with blotting out: Isa. xliii. 25, 'I, even I, am he that blots out thy transgression;' whereby is implied, that sin is a debt, and pardon is the remitting of it. It notes,

[1.] The nullity of the debt. A crossed book will not stand good in law, because the crossing of the book implies the satisfaction of the debt. A debt may be read in our manner of writing in a crossed book, but it cannot be pleaded. God may after pardon read our sins in the book of his omniscience, but not charge them upon us at the bar of his justice.

[2.] God's willingness to pardon. Blots, not razeth. He engraves them not upon marble, he writes them not with a pen of iron, or point of a diamond; writing upon wax is easily made plain.

[3.] The extent of it. Blotting serves for a great debt as well as a small; a thousand pound may as well, and as soon, be dashed out by a blot as a thousand pence.

[4.] The quickness of it upon repentance. It takes more time to write a debt in a book, than to cross it out; one blow would obliterate a great deal of writing upon wax. Sins that have been contracting many years, when God pardons, he blots out in a moment.

(2.) Covering, as it alludes to the drowning the Egyptians, is expressed by casting into the depths of the sea: Micah vii. 19, 'Thou wilt cast all their sins into the depths of the sea.'

This notes also,

[1.] God's willingness to pardon. Casts them, not lays them gently aside, but flings them away with violence, as things that he cannot endure the sight of, and is resolved never to take notice of them more.

[2.] God's reality in pardon. He will cast their sins as far as the arm of his omnipotency can reach; if there be any place further than the depths of the sea, thither they shall be thrown out of the sight of his justice.

[3.] The extent. *All* their sins. The sea covered Egyptian princes as well as the people. The mighty lord, as well as the common soldier, sank like lead in those mighty waters.

[4.] The duration of it. The sea vomits up nothing that it takes into its lower bowels; things cast into the depths of the ocean never appear more. Rivers may be turned and drained, but who can lave out the ocean?

(2.) Not imputing. Not putting upon account, not charging the debt in a legal process. To this is equivalent the expression of not remembering: Isa. xliii. 25, 'I will not remember their sins.' An act of oblivion is passed upon sin. This notes,

(1.) That God will not exact the debt of thee. God doth not absolutely forget sin, for what he knows never slips out of his knowledge. So that his not remembering is rather an act of his will than a defect in his understanding. As when an act of oblivion is passed, the fact committed is not physically forgotten, but legally, because the fear of punishment is removed. God puts them out of the memory of his wrath, though not out of the memory of his knowledge. He doth remember them paternally to chastise thee for them, though not judicially to condemn thee.

(2.) Not upbraid thee. Not with a scornful upbraiding mention them to cast thee off, but with a merciful renewing the remembrance of them upon thy conscience, to excite thy repentance, and keep thee within the due bounds of humility and reverence.

2. More particularly the nature of pardon may be explained in these propositions. We must not think that these expressions, as they denote pardon, do intimate in this act the taking away of the being of sin, nature of sin, or demerit of sin.

1. The being and inherency of sin is not taken away. Though sin be not imputed to us, yet it is inherent in us. The being remains, though the power be dethroned. By pardon God takes away sin, not as it is a pollution of the soul, but as it is an inducement to wrath. Though remission and sanctification are concomitants, yet they are distinct acts, and wrought in a distinct manner.

2. The nature of sin is not taken away. Justification is a relative change of the person, not of the sin; for though God will not by an act of his justice punish the person pardoned, yet by his holiness he cannot but hate the sin, because though it be pardoned, it is still contrary to God, and enmity against him. It is not a change of the native malice of the sin, but a non-imputation of it to the offender. Though the person sinning be free from any indictment, yet sin is not freed from its *malitia*, and opposition to God. For though the law doth not condemn a justified person because he is translated into another state, yet it condemns the acts of sin, though the guilt of those acts doth not redound upon the person, to bring the wrath of God upon him. Though David had the sins of murder and adultery pardoned, yet this pardon did not make David a righteous person in those acts, for it was murder and adultery still, and the change was not in his sin, but in his soul and state.

3. The demerit of sin is not taken away. As pardon doth not alter sin's nature, so neither doth it alter sin's demerit, for to merit damnation belongs to the nature of it; so that we may look upon ourselves as deserving hell, though the sin whereby we deserve it be remitted. Pardon frees us from actual condemnation, but not, as considered in our own persons, from the

desert of condemnation. As when a king pardons a thief, he doth not make the theft to become formally no theft, or to be meritoriously no capital crime. Upon those two grounds of the nature and demerit of sin, a justified person is to bewail it, and I question not but the consideration of this doth add to the triumph and hallelujahs of the glorified souls, whose chief work being to praise God for redemption, they cannot but think of the nature and demerit of that from which they were redeemed, Rev. v. 13.

4. The guilt of sin, or obligation to punishment, is taken away by pardon. Sin committed doth presently, by virtue of the law transgressed, bind over the sinner to death, but pardon makes void this obligation, so that God no longer accounts us persons obnoxious to him. *Peccatum remitti non aliud est quam non imputari ad pœnam.** It is a revoking the sentence of the law against the sinner, and God renouncing, upon the account of the satisfaction made by Christ to his justice, any right to punish a believer, doth actually discharge him, upon his believing, from that sentence of the law under which he lay in the state of unbelief; and also as he parts with this right to punish, so he confers a right upon a believer humbly to challenge it, upon the account of the satisfaction wrought by his surety. God hath not only in his own mind and resolution parted with this right of punishing, but also given an express declaration of his will: 2 Cor. v. 19, 'God was in Christ reconciling the world unto himself,' *i. e.* openly renouncing upon Christ's account the right to punish, whence follows the non-imputation of sin, 'not imputing their trespasses unto them.' The justice of God will not suffer that that sin which is pardoned should be punished, for can that be justice in a prince, to pardon a thief, and yet to bring him to the gallows for that fact? Though the malefactor doth justly deserve it, yet after a pardon and the word passed, it is not justly inflicted. God indeed doth punish for that sin which is pardoned. Though Nathan, by God's commission, had declared David's sin pardoned, yet the sword was to stick in the bowels of his family: 2 Sam. xii. 10, 15, 'The sword shall never depart from thy house.' 'The Lord hath put away thy sin; thou shalt not die.' But,

(1.) It is not a punishment in order to satisfaction, because Christ's satisfaction had no flaw in it, and stood in need of nothing to eke it out; but it is for the vindication of the honour of God's holiness, that he might not be thought an approver of sin; and this was the reason of David's punishment in the death of his child by Bathsheba: 2 Sam. xii. 14, 'Because by this deed thou hast given great occasion to the enemies of the Lord to blaspheme.'

(2.) It is not so much penal as medicinal. A judge commands a hand to be cut off, that is for punishment; a physician and a father order the same, but for the patient's cure, and the preservation of the body. And though God after pardon acts not towards his people in the nature of a judge, yet he never lays aside the authority and affection of a father. We are delivered from a judge's wrath, but not from a father's anger. In that remarkable dumbness inflicted upon Zacharias for his unbelief, Luke i. 18, 20, there was a confirmation of his faith, as well as the chastisement of his incredulity. The angel, upon his unbelieving desire of a sign, gives him a testimony of the truth of his errand, but such an one that should make him feel in some measure the smart of his unbelief.

(3.) If it be penal, it is not the eternal punishment due to sin. It is but temporary, and not embittered by wrath, which is the gall of punishment.

This taking off the obligation to punishment is the true nature of pardon:

* Durand. lib. iv. dict. i. q. 7. For sin to be pardoned is nothing else but not to be imputed in order to punishment.

which will be evident from 2 Sam. xix. 19, 'Let not my lord impute iniquity unto me.' Shimei desires David not to impute iniquity, and not to remember it. It was not in David's power absolutely to forget it, and Shimei's confessing the fact with those circumstances in ver. 20, was enough to recall it to David's memory, if he had forgot it; but he desires David not to bring him to satisfy the penalty of the law for reviling his sovereign.

II. The author of pardon, God. For pardon is the sovereign prerogative of God, whereby he doth acquit a believing sinner from all obligation to satisfactory punishment, upon the account of the satisfaction and righteousness of Christ apprehended by faith.

1. It is God's act. Remission is the creditor's, not the debtor's, act; though the debtor be obliged in justice to pay the debt, yet there is no obligation upon the creditor to demand the debt, because it is at his liberty to renounce or maintain his right to it; and God hath as much power as man to relax his right, provided it be with a salvo to his own honour, and the holiness of his nature, which he cannot deny for the sinner's safety, as the apostle tells us 'God cannot deny himself.' Yet properly, say some, though sin be a debt, God is not to be considered in pardon as a creditor, because sin is not a pecuniary debt, but a criminal, and so God is to be considered as a governor, lawgiver, guardian, and executor of his laws, and so may dispense with the severities of them. If an inferior person tear an indictment, it may be brought again into court, but if the chief magistrate order the casting it out, who can plead it? It is God's act; and if God justifies, who can condemn? Rom. viii. 33, 'Who shall lay any thing to the charge of God's elect? It is God that justifies, who shall condemn?' That God absolves thee that hath power to condemn thee; that God who enacted the law whereby thou art sentenced, proclaims the gospel whereby thou art reconciled. It is an offended God who is a forgiving God: that God whose name thou hast profaned, whose patience thou hast abused, whose laws thou hast violated, whose mercy thou hast slighted, whose justice thou hast dared, and whose glory thou hast stained.

2. It is not only his act, but his prerogative, and he only can do it. God is the party wronged. *Nemo potest remittere de jure alieno*. This prerogative he glories in as peculiar to himself; the thoughts of this honour are so sweet to him, that he repeats it twice, as a title he will not share with another: Isa. xliii. 25, 'I, even I, am he that blots out thy transgressions.' Pardoning offenders is one of a prince's royalties. And this is reckoned among his regalia, as a choice flower and jewel in his crown: Exod. xxxiv. 7, 'Forgiving iniquity, transgressions, and sins.' A prince punisheth by his ministers, but pardons by himself. And, indeed, God is never so glorious as in acts of mercy; justice makes him terrible, but mercy renders him amiable. When Moses desired to see God in his royalty, and best perfections, he displays himself in his goodness: Exod. xxxiii. 18, 'Shew me thy glory.' Ver. 19, 'I will make all my goodness pass before thee; I will be gracious to whom I will be gracious.' And though the apostles had a power of remission and binding, that was only ministerial and declarative, like that prophetical power which Jeremiah had to root up nations and destroy, Jer. i. 10, *i. e.* to declare God's will in such and such judgments, as he should send him to pronounce. Men cannot pardon an infinite wrong done to an infinite justice. Forgiveness belongs to God, as,

(1.) Proprietor. He hath a greater right to us than we have to ourselves.

(2.) Sovereign. He is Lord over us, as we are his creatures.

(3.) Governor of us, as we are parts of the world.

(4.) It is an act of his mercy, not our merit. Though there be a conditional connection between pardon, and repentance, and faith, yet there is no meritorious connection ariseth from the nature of those graces, but remission flows from the gracious indulgence of the promise.

3. It is the very tenderness of mercy, the meltings of the inward bowels: Luke i. 78, 'To give knowledge of salvation, and remission of their sins, through the tender mercies of our God.' σπλαγχνα ἐλέους, an inexhaustible mercy: Ps. lxxxvi. 5, 'Thou, Lord, art ready to forgive, and art plenteous in mercy.' A 'multitude of tender mercies,' Ps. li. 1. What arithmetic can count all the bubblings up of mercy in the breast of God, and all the glances and all the doles of his pardoning grace towards his creatures? And he keeps this mercy by him, as in a treasury, to this purpose: Exod. xxxiv. 7, 'Keeping mercy for thousands, forgiving iniquity,' &c.; and is still as full as ever, as the sun, which hath influenced so many animals and vegetables, and expelled so much darkness and cold, is still as a strong man able to run the same race, and perform by its light and heat the same operations. When mercy shews itself in state with all its train, it is but to usher in pardoning grace, Exod. xxxiv. 6, 7; not a letter, not an attribute that makes up the composition of that name, but is a friend and votary of mercy. And that latter clause a learned man explains of God's clemency; 'He will by no means clear the guilty; visiting the iniquity of the fathers,' &c., which he renders thus: He will not utterly cut off and destroy; but, when he doth visit the sins of the fathers upon the children, it shall be but to the third or fourth generation, not for ever. This name of God is urged by Moses: Num. xiv. 17, 'Now, I beseech thee, let the power of my Lord be great; the Lord is long-suffering, and of great mercy, forgiving iniquity and transgression, and by no means clearing the guilty; visiting the iniquity,' &c. 'Pardon, I beseech thee, the iniquity of this people, according to the greatness of thy mercy.' Where Moses repeats this clause more particularly than he doth the other parts of his name; which surely he would not have done, and pleaded it as a motive to God to pardon Israel, if he had not understood it of God's clemency; for otherwise he had dwelt more upon the argument of justice than upon that of mercy, which had not been proper to edge his present petition with. Nay, it is such pure mercy, the genuine birth of mercy, that it partakes of its very name, as children bear the name of their father: Heb. viii. 12, 'I will be merciful to their iniquity,' which in the prophet, Jer. xxxi. 34, whence the apostle quotes it, is, 'I will forgive their iniquity.'

That it is so, will appear; because

(1.) No attribute could be the first motive of pardon but this. His justice would loudly cry for vengeance, and flame out against ungrateful sinners. His holiness would make him abhor not only the embraces but the very sight of such filthy creatures as we are. His power would attend to receive and execute the commands of his justice and holiness, did not compassion step in to qualify.

(2.) Unconstrained mercy. Men pardon many times, because they are too weak to punish; but God wants not power to inflict judgments, neither doth man want weakness to sink under it: Rom. v. 6, 'When we were without strength, Christ died for us.' God wanted not sufficient reason to justify a severe proceeding, both in the quality of sin, every sin being a contrariety to the law, sovereignty, work, glory, yea, the very being of God. Now for God to pardon that which would pull him out of his throne, hath blemished the creation, robs him of his honour, must be an act of the richest and purest mercy; and in the quantity, multitudes of sins of this cursed quality, as numerous as motes in the sunbeams. It is impossible for the nimblest angel to write down the extravagances of men committed in the space of twenty-four hours, if he could know all the operations of their souls as well as their outward actions; all those God doth see, *simul et semel*, and yet is ready to pardon in the midst of numberless provocations.

(3.) Resolved and designed mercy. It is not through inadvertency and insensibleness of the aggravating circumstances of them; God must needs know the nature and circumstances of all those sins he himself laid upon Christ; yea, God hath an actuated knowledge of all when he is about to pardon, Isa. xliii. 22. God reckons up their sins of omissions; they had been weary of him, and had not brought to him their small cattle; had preferred their lambs and kids before his service; wearied him with their iniquities; endeavoured to tire him out of the government of the world. What could one have expected after this black scroll, but fire-balls of wrath? Yet he blots them out, ver. 25, though all those sins were fresh in his memory. Nay, the name we have profaned becomes our solicitor: Ezek. xxxvi. 22, 'For my holy name's sake which you have profaned.'

(4.) Delightful and pleasant mercy. He delights in pardoning mercy, as a father delights in his children. He is therefore called the Father of mercy: Micah vii. 18, 'He pardons iniquity, and retains not his anger for ever, because he delights in mercy.' Never did we take so much pleasure in sinning as God doth in forgiving; never did any penitent take so much pleasure in receiving, as God doth in giving, a pardon. He so much delights in it that he counts it his wealth: riches of grace, riches of mercy, glorious riches of mercy. No attribute else is called his riches. He sighs when he must draw his sword: Hosea xi. 8, 'How shall I give thee up, O Ephraim!' but when he blots out iniquity, then it is, 'I, even I, am he that blots out your transgressions for my name's sake.' His delight in this is equal to the delight he hath in his name. This is pure mercy, to change the tribunal of justice into a throne of grace, to bestow pardons where he might inflict punishments, and to put on the deportment of a father instead of that of a judge.

4. The act of his justice. Those attributes which seem contrary are joined together to produce forgiveness; yet God is not to be considered in pardon only as *judex*, but *paternus judex*. There is a composition of judge and father in this act; free grace on God's part, but justice upon the account of Christ. That God will accept of a satisfaction, is mercy; that he will not forgive without a satisfaction, is justice. Mercy forgives it in us, though justice did punish it in Christ. Christ by his death paid the debt, and God, by the resurrection of Christ, discharged the debt; and therefore the justice of God is engaged to bestow pardon upon a believer. God set forth Christ as 'a propitiation, that he might be just, and therefore a justifier of him that believes,' Rom. iii. 26. Either the debt is paid or not; if not, then Christ's death is in vain. If it be, then God's justice is so equitable as not to demand a second payment. Therefore another apostle joins *faithful* and *righteous*. It might have been faithful and merciful, faithful and loving, but faithful and righteous, or just, takes in the attribute which is most terrible to man: 1 John i. 9, 'He is faithful and just to forgive us our sins,' δίκαιος. Isaiah joins both together, 'a just God and a Saviour,' Isa. xlv. 21, so that here is unspeakable comfort. That which engaged God formerly to punish man, engageth him now to pardon a believer; that which moved him to punish Christ, doth excite him to forgive thee.

5. The act of his power. It is a sign of a noble and generous mind to pass over offences and injuries. Sick and indigent persons are the most peevish and impatient, and least able to concoct an injury. And when we kindle into a flame upon the least sparks of a wrong, the apostle tells us we

are overcome of evil: Rom. xii. 21, 'Be not overcome of evil.' We become captives to our angry passions. Speedy revenge in us being an act of weakness, the contrary must be an act of power over ourselves. God's not executing the fierceness of his anger, is laid upon his being a God and not man: Hosea xi. 9. God's infinite power gives a rise to pardon: Micah vii. 18, 'Who is a God like to thee, that pardons iniquity?' Junius and Tremellius render it, 'Who is a *strong* God?' and the Hebrew אל will bear it. 'Let the power of my Lord be great,' saith Moses, Num. xiv. 17. The word *jigdal* is written with a great *jod*, to shew, say the Jews, that it is more than an ordinary power to command one's self when injured. Therefore, when God proclaims his pardoning name, he ushers it in with names of power: 'The Lord, the Lord God,' Exod. xxxiv. 6. It is a greater work to forgive than to prevent the commission of sin, as it is a greater work to raise a dead man than to cure a sick man: one is a work of art, the other belongs only to omnipotency.

III. The manner of it. How it is carried on.

1. On God's part by Christ.

(1.) By his death. He is the scape-goat upon whom our sins are laid, Isa. liii. 6. Our sins are made Christ's, and Christ's righteousness is made ours. He is said to be 'made sin for us,' and we are said to be 'made the righteousness of God in him,' 2 Cor. v. 21; a blessed exchange for us. He bore that wrath, endured those torments, suffered those strokes of justice which were due to us. The pardon of sin doth cost us confessions and tears, but it cost Christ blood and unknown pains (as the Greek liturgy, Δι' ἀγνώστων κόπων, have mercy on us).

[1.] Laid upon him by God. God appropriates this work to himself: Zech. iii. 9, 'I will engrave the engraving thereof,' speaking of the stone, which is the same with his servant the branch. As a stone is cut with a chisel, which makes deep furrows in it, so did God deal with Christ, and that in order to the taking away of sin: 'I will remove the iniquity of that land in one day,' viz. the day of Christ's suffering. By that offering of himself, he shall perfectly satisfy me. Therefore it is called 'the will of God,' in order to the taking away sin, Heb. x. 9, 10, compared with ver. 11, 12, 'I come to do thy will, by which will we are sanctified,' which will was to take away sin; for, ver. 11, that was the end of his sacrifice, the legal sacrifices not being able to do it. God did not only consent to it, or give a bare grant, but it was a propense and affectionate motion of his heart: Isa. liii. 10, 'It pleased the Lord to bruise him;' hence did the angels sing at his birth, 'Glory to God in the highest, peace on earth, and good will towards men.' The peace he was to procure was the fruit of God's will towards us.

[2.] Voluntarily undertaken by Christ: Heb. x. 5, 7, 'Lo I come, I delight to do thy will, O my God.' Willingness in the entrance of the work, willingness to take a body, and willingness to lay down that body. He had as it were a fever of affection, a combustion in his bowels till it was finished. In his greatest agonies he did not repent of his undertaking, or desire to give it over. He cried indeed to his Father that this cup might pass from him, but he presently submits: If there be no other way to save sinners, I will pass on through death and hell to do it. When he was afflicted and oppressed, he murmured not at it: Isa. liii. 7, 'He opened not his mouth, he opened not his mouth.' It is twice repeated, to shew his willingness. And God was highly pleased with him for this very reason, because he did 'pour out his soul,' and 'bore the sins of many, and made intercession for the transgressors;' all which expressions denote his earnestness and readiness in it.

(2.) By his resurrection. His death is the payment, his resurrection the discharge: Rom. iv. 25, 'Who was delivered for our offences, and rose again for our justification.' Not that we are formally justified by the resurrection of Christ, but that thereby God declared that whosoever believes in him should be justified upon that believing; for if Christ had not risen, there had been no certainty of the payment of the debt. In his death he pays the sum, as he is our surety; and in his resurrection he hath his *quietus est* out of God's exchequer. God will not have this payment from Christ, which he hath acknowledged himself publicly to be satisfied with, and from believers too; for upon his resurrection he sent him to bless men: Acts iii. 26, 'God having raised up his Son Jesus, sent him to bless you.' How? 'In turning away every one of you from his iniquity,' it being a great encouragement to turn men from sin, when God hath thus declared them pardonable by the resurrection of his Son.

2. On our parts by faith. Faith is as necessary in an instrumental way, as Christ in a meritorious way: Acts xxvi. 18, 'That they may receive forgiveness of sins by faith that is in me.' Christ purchaseth a pardon, but faith only puts us in possession of a pardon; yet it cannot from its own worth challenge forgiveness at the hands of God, but upon the account of Christ, who hath merited forgiveness. Though the king grants a pardon to a condemned malefactor, yet he may be executed unless he pleads it the next assizes, though he hath it lying by him; so unless we sue it out, and accept of it by faith, all Christ's purchase will not advantage us. Faith looks not barely upon the sufferings of Christ, but upon his end and design in it. It looks not upon his passion as a story, but as a testament; and you seldom find the death of Christ mentioned in the New Testament without expressing the end of it. This forgiveness by Christ's death as the meritorious cause, shews,

(1.) God's willingness to pardon. If God did delight in the death of Christ, it was not surely simply in his death; for could a father delight to tear out the bowels of his son? The afflictions of his people go to his heart; much more would the sufferings of his darling. God had more delight in forgiveness than grief at his Son's sufferings; for he never repented it, though our Saviour besought him with tears; and that God who was never deaf to any that called upon him, nor ever will be, would not hear his only Son in the request to take the cup from him, or abate anything of the weight of his sufferings, because it was necessary for the pardon of sin, *necessitate decreti*, if not *naturæ*. God repented of making the world, but never of forgiving sin; so that the pardon of sin is more pleasing to him than the sufferings of his Son were grievous; otherwise whatsoever the Father would have done by instruments, yet surely he himself would not have been the executioner of him. But in this affair there were not only instruments, Judas to betray him, the Jews to accuse him, the disciples to forsake him, Pilate to condemn him, the soldiers to mock and crucify him, and thieves to revile him, but God himself: Isa. liii. 10, 'Yet it pleased the Lord to bruise him; he hath put him to grief: thou shalt make his soul an offering for sin.' His own Father that loved him (as Abraham in the type) puts as it were the knife to the throat of his only Son, which surely God would not have done had not pardon of sin been infinitely pleasing to him. And how great a pleasure must that be, that swallowed up all grief at his Son's sufferings! Yea, he seemed to love our salvation more than he loved the life of his Son, since the end is always more amiable than the means, and the means only lovely as they respect the end.

(2.) The certainty of forgiveness. God must deny Christ's payment before he can deny thy pardon. God will not deny what his Son hath earned so dearly, and what he earned was for us and not for himself. Did God pardon many before Christ died, and will he not pardon believing souls since Christ died? Some were certainly saved before the coming of Christ: upon what account? Not for their own righteousness; that is but a rag, and could not merit infinite grace. Not by the law; that thundered nothing but death, and condemned millions, but never breathed a pardon to one person. Or was it by their vehement supplications? Those could not make an infinite righteousness mutable; justice must be preferred before the cries of malefactors; and if those could have done it, God would not have been at the expense of his Son's blood. Therefore, it must be upon this account, Rom. iii. 25, 'for the remission of sins that are past.' Did God pardon upon trust? and will he not much more upon payment? Did he forgive when there was only a promise of payment, and some thousands of years to run out before it was to be made? and will he not much more forgive, since he hath all the debt paid into his hands? Would God remit sin when Christ had nothing under his hand to shew for it? and now that he hath a public testimony and acquittance, will he not much more do it? Seeing his purging our sins, or expiating them by his death, was the ground of his exaltation to the honour of sitting at the right hand of God in our natures: Heb. i. 3, 'When he had by himself purged our sins, sat down on the right hand of the Majesty on high;' it is a certain evidence of the grant of pardon upon the account of this sacrifice to those that seek it in God's methods, since God hath shewn himself so pleased with it. For it is clear, that because Christ 'loved righteousness and hated iniquity,' *i. e.* kept up the honour of God's justice and holiness by the offering himself to death, that God hath given him a portion above all his fellows.

(3.) The extent of it. Both to original and actual sin: John i. 29, 'Behold the Lamb of God, that takes away the sin of the world;' sin of the world, the sin of human nature, that first sin of Adam. Of this mind is Austin, and others, that original sin is not imputed to any to condemnation since the death of Christ. But howsoever this be, it is certain it is taken away from believers as to its imputation. Christ was 'made sin for us, 2 Cor. v. 21, to bear all sin. It had been an imperfect payment to have paid the interest, and let the principal remain; or to have paid the principal, and let the interest remain. 'There is no condemnation to them that are in Christ Jesus,' Rom. viii. 1, and therefore no damning matter or guilt left in arrear. It had been folly else for the apostle to have published a defying challenge to the whole creation to have brought an indictment against a justified person (Rom. viii. 33, 'Who shall lay any thing to the charge of God's elect?'), if the least crime remained unremitted for the justice of God, the severity of the law, the acuteness of conscience, or the malice of the devil to draw up into a charge. Since the end of his coming was 'to destroy the works of the devil,' whereby he had acquired a power over man, he leaves not therefore any one sin of a believer unsatisfied for, which may continue, and establish the devil's right over him. If the redemption only of the Jews, with the exclusion of the Gentiles, in the first compact seemed to displease him, to shed his blood for small sins only would have been as little to his content. It had been too low a work for so great a Saviour to have undergone those unknown sufferings for debts of a smaller value, and to shed that inestimable blood for the payment of farthings, and leave talents unsatisfied. Certainly, God sent not his Son, but with an intention his blood should be improved to the highest uses for those that perform the covenant conditions, and that Father who would have us honour his Son as we honour himself, will surely honour his Son's satisfaction in the extensive effects of it, as he would honour his own mercy, since they are both so straitly linked together. And it is as much for the glory of Christ's satisfaction, as for the honour of his Father's mercy, to pass by the greatest transgressions.

(4.) The continuance of it. Thou art pardoned, and yet thou sinnest; but Christ hath paid and never runs more upon the score. Thou art pardoned and dost daily forfeit, and needest a daily renewal; but Christ hath purchased, and never sins away his purchase. God exacted a price suitable to the debt he foresaw men would owe him, for he knew how much the sum would amount unto. When he gave Christ, he intended him for the justification of many offences, Rom. v. 16. 'The free gift is of many offences unto justification,' speaking of the gift of God, ver. 15. And therefore since God cannot be mistaken in the greatness of the sum, because of his infinite knowledge, it had been a greater act of wisdom not to provide any remedy at all, than not to do it thoroughly. If the continuance of that imperfect remission of Adam and the patriarchs was drawn out for above three thousand years and more, and the enjoyment of happiness made good to them merely upon Christ's undertaking, surely it will be much more upon his actual performing, Rom. iii. 25. There was then a πάρεσις, now an ἄφεσις; they had a continuance of freedom from punishment by his mediatorship and sponsion, much more shall believers have a continuance of pardon by his actual sacrifice, upon which the validity of all the former mediatory acts did depend, since now there is no more remembrance of sin by the continuance of legal sacrifices, his being so absolutely complete. Therefore God hath erected a standing office of advocacy for Christ, 1 John ii. 1, in heaven, for the representing of his wounds and satisfaction, and bespeaking a continuance of grace to us. He is said to be 'the Lamb that taketh away the sins of the world,' John i. 29; not ὁ ἄρας, hath taken, or ὁ ἀρῶν, will take, but ὁ αἴρων, which notes, *actum perpetuum*, the constant effect of his death. And since, as I said before, Christ hath an higher portion than others, because he loved righteousness, in this portion he hath a joy and gladness; but his joy would certainly be sullied, if pardon should not be continued to those for whom he purchased it.

(5.) The worth of it. That must be of incomparable value that was purchased at so great a price as the blood of God, Acts xx. 28. (So it is called by reason of the union of the divine nature with the human, constituting one person.) It is blood, which all the gold and silver, and the stones and dust of the earth turned into pearls, could not equal. God understood the worth of it, who in justice would require no more of his Son at least than the thing was worth, not a drop of blood more than the value of it. Neither surely would Christ, who could not be mistaken in the just price, have parted with more than was necessary for the purchase of it. It would have beggared the whole creation to have paid a price for it. The prayers and services of a gracious soul, though God delights in them, could not be a sufficient recompence. And the bare mercy of God, without the concurrence of his provoked justice, could not grant it, though his bowels naturally are troubled at the afflictions of his creatures.

IV. Extensiveness, fulness, or perfectness of pardon. 1. In the act; forgiving, covering, not imputing. 2. In the object; iniquities, transgressions, and sins.

1. Perfect in respect of state. God retains no hatred against a pardoned person. He never imputes sin formally, because he no more remembers it, though virtually he may, to aggravate the offence a believer hath fallen into after his justification. So Job possessed the sins of his youth. And Christ tacitly put Peter in remembrance of his denial of him. The grant is com-

plete here, though all the fruits of remission are not enjoyed till the day of judgment, and therefore in Scripture sin is said then to be forgiven. It is a question whether believers' sins will be mentioned at the day of judgment. Some think they will, because all men are to give an account. Methinks there is some evidence to the contrary. Our Saviour never mentioned the unworthy carriage of his disciples to him in his sufferings, and after his resurrection seems to have removed from him all remembrance of it. It is not to be expected, that a loving husband will lay open the faults of his tender spouse upon the day of the public solemnisation of the nuptials. But if it be otherwise, it is not to upbraid them, but to enhance their admirations of his grace. He will discover their graces as well as their sin, and unstop the bottles of their tears, as well as open the book of their transgressions. Our Saviour, upon Mary's anointing him, applauds her affection, but mentions not her former iniquity.

It must needs be perfect.

(1.) All God's actions are suitable to his nature. What God doth, he doth as a God. And is he perfect in his other works, and not in his mercy, which is the choicest flower in his crown? God sees blacker circumstances in our sins, than an enraged conscience or a malicious devil can represent; but God pardons not according to our apprehensions, which though great in a tempestuous conscience, yet are not so high as God's knowledge of it.

(2.) The cause of pardon is perfect. Both the mercy of God and the merits of Christ are immutably perfect. It is for his own glory, his own mercies' sake, that he pardons. He will not dim the lustre of his own crown, by leaving the effect of his glory imperfect, or satisfying the importunities of his mercy by halves. The saints in heaven have not a more perfect righteousness, whereby they continue their standing, than those on earth have; for, though inherent righteousness here is stained, yet imputed, upon which pardon is founded, is altogether spotless. A righteousness that, being infinite in respect of the person, hath a sufficiency for devils, had it a congruity; but it hath both for us, because manifested in our natures.

2. In respect of the objects. Sinful nature, sinful habits, sinful dispositions, pardoned at once, though never so heinous.

(1.) For quality. There was no limitation as to the deepness of the wounds caused by the fiery serpents in the wilderness; the precept of looking upon them, extended to the cure of all, let the sting reach never so deep, the wound be never so wide or sharp, and his sight be never so weak, if he could but cast his eye on the brazen one. The commission Christ gave to his disciples, was to preach the gospel to every creature, Mark xvi. 15, every human creature; the worst as well as the best. Though you meet with monstrous sinners in the likeness of beasts, and devils, except none from sueing out a pardon in the court of mercy. The almightiness of his mercy doth as much transcend our highest iniquities, as it doth our shallowest apprehensions. Our sins, as well as our substance, are but as the dust of the balance, as easily to be blown away by his grace, as the other puffed into nothing by his power. No sin is excepted in the gospel, but that against the Holy Ghost, because it doth not stand with the honour of God to pardon them who wilfully scorn the means, and account the Redeemer no better than an impostor. No man can expect, in reason, he should be saved by mercy, who, by a wilful malice against the Son of God, tramples upon the free offers of grace, and provokes mercy itself to put on the deportment of justice, and call in revenging wrath to its assistance, for the vindication of its despised honour. The infinite grace of God dissolves the greatest mists, as well as the smallest exhalations, and melts the thick clouds of sin, as well as the little icicles.

(2.) The quantity. Hath God ever put a restraint upon his grace and promise, that we shall find mercy if we sin but to such a number, and no more? It is not agreeable to the greatness and majesty of God's mercy, to remit one part of the debt, and to exact the other. It consists not with the motive of pardon, which is his own love, to be both a friend and an enemy at the same time, in pardoning some, and charging others; and thus his grace would rather be a mockery and derision of men. Neither doth it consist with the end of pardon, which is salvation; for to give an half pardon is to give no salvation, since, if the least guilt remains unremitted, it gives justice an unanswerable plea against us. What profit would it be to have some forgiven, and be damned for the remainder? Had any one sin for which Christ was to have made a compensation remained unsatisfied, the Redeemer could not have risen. So if the smallest sin remains unblotted, it will hinder our rising from the power of eternal death, and make the pardon of all the rest as a nullity in law. But it is the glory of God to pass by all: Prov. xix. 31, 'It is his glory to pass over a transgression.' It is the glory of a man to pass by an offence. It is a discovery of an inward principle or property, which is an honour for a man to be known the master of. If it be his glory to pass by a single and small injury, then to pass by the more heinous and numerous offences, is a more transcendent honour, because it evidenceth this property to be in him in a more triumphant strength and power. So that it is a clearer evidence of the illustrious vigour of mercy in God, to pass by mountains and heaped up transgressions, than to forgive only some few iniquities of a lesser guilt: Jer. xxxiii. 8, 'I will cleanse them from all their iniquities, whereby they have sinned against me; and I will pardon all their iniquities, whereby they have sinned against me, and whereby they have transgressed against me.' Therefore, when God tells the Jews that he would give them a general discharge in the fullest terms imaginable, to remove all jealousy from men, either because of the number, or the aggravations of their sins, he knew not how to leave expressing the delight he had in it, and the honour which accrued to him by it: 'It shall be to me a name of joy, a praise and honour before all the nations of the earth.' He would get himself an honourable name by the large riches of his clemency. Mercy is as infinite as any other attribute, as infinite as God himself. And as his power can create incomprehensible multitudes of worlds, and his justice kindle unconceivable hells, so can his mercy remit innumerable sins.

3. Perfect in respect of duration. Because the handwriting of ordinances is taken away: Col. ii. 14, 15, 'Blotting out the handwriting of ordinances that was against us, which was contrary to us, and took it out of the way, nailing it to his cross;' which was the ceremonial law, wherein they did, by their continual presenting sacrifices, and imposition of hands upon them, sign a bill or bond against themselves, whereby a conscience of sin was retained, Heb. x. 2, 3, and a remembrance of sin renewed. They could not settle the conscience in any firm place, Heb. ix. 9; they were compelled to do that every day, whereby they did confess that sin did remain, and want an expiation. Hence is the law called 'a ministration of condemnation,' 2 Cor. iii. 9, because it puts them in mind of condemnation, and compelled the people to do that which testified that the curse was yet to be abolished by virtue of a better sacrifice. This handwriting, which was so contrary to us, was taken away, nailed to his cross, torn in pieces, wholly cancelled, no more to be put in suit. Whence, in opposition to this continual remembrance of sin under the legal administration, we read, under the New Testament, of

God's remembering sin no more, Heb. x. 3, 17. Christ hath so compounded the business with divine justice, that we have the sins remitted, never returning upon us, and the renewal also of remissions upon daily sins, if we truly repent. For though there be a blacker tincture in sins after conversion, as being more deeply stained with ingratitude, yet the covenant of God stands firm, and he will not take away his kindness, Isa. liv. 9, 10. And there is a greater affection in God to his children than to his enemies; for these he loves before their conversion with a love of benevolence, but those with a love of complacency. Will not God be as ready to continue his grace to those that are penitent, as to offer it to offending rebels? Will he refuse it to his friends, when he entreats his enemies? Not that any should think that, because of this duration, they have liberty to sin, and, upon some trivial repentance, are restored to God's favour. No; where Christ is made righteousness, he is made sanctification. His spirit and merit go together. A new nature, and a new state, are concomitants; and he that sins upon presumption of the grand sacrifice, never had any share in it.

V. The effect of pardon. That is blessedness.

1. The greatest evil is taken away, sin, and the dreadful consequents of it. Other evils are temporal, but those know no period in a doleful eternity. There is more evil in sin, than good in all the creatures. Sin stripped the fallen angels of their excellency, and dispossessed them of the seat of blessedness. It fights against God, it disparages all his attributes, it deforms and destroys the creature, Rom. vii. 13. Other evils may have some mixture of good to make them tolerable, but sin being exceedingly sinful, without the mixture of any good, engenders nothing but destruction and endless damnation. Into what miseries, afflictions, sorrows, hath that one sin of Adam hurled all his posterity! what screechings, wounds, pangs, horrors, doth it make in troubled consciences! How did it deface the beauty of the Son of God, that created and upheld the world, with sorrow in his agonies, and the stroke of death on the cross! How many thousands, millions of poor creatures have been damned for sin, and are never like to cease roaring under an inevitable justice! Ask the damned, and their groans, yellings, howlings, will read thee a dreadful lecture of sin's sinfulness, and the punishment of it. And is it not then an inestimable blessedness to be delivered from that which hath wrought such deplorable executions in the world?

2. The greatest blessings are conferred. Pardon is God's family-blessing, and the peculiar mercy of his choicest darlings. He hands out other things to wicked men, but he deals out this only to his children.

(1.) The favour of God. Sin makes thee Satan's drudge, but pardon makes thee God's favourite. We may be sick to death, with Lazarus, and be God's friends; sold to slavery, with Joseph, and yet be dear to him; thrown into a lion's den, with Daniel, and be greatly beloved; poor, with Lazarus, who had only dogs for chirurgeons to dress his sores, and yet have a title to Abraham's bosom. But we can never be beloved if we are unpardoned; no share in his friendship, his love, his inheritance, without a pardon. All created evils cannot make us loathsome in a justified state, nor all created goods make us lovely under guilt. Sin is the only object of God's hatred; while this remains, his holiness cannot but hate us; when this is removed, his righteousness cannot but love us. Remission and favour are inseparable, and can never be disjoined. It is by this he makes us as a diadem upon his head, a bracelet on his arm; it is by this he writes us upon the palms of his hands, makes us his peculiar treasure, even as the apple of his eye, which nature hath so carefully fenced.

(2.) Access to God. A prince may discard a favourite for some guilt, and though he may restore him to his liberty in the commonwealth, yet he may not admit him to the favour of his wonted privacies. But a pardoned man hath an access to God, to a standing and perpetually settled grace: Rom. v. 1, 2, 'Being justified by faith, we have peace with God through our Lord Jesus Christ, by whom also we have access.' Guilt frights us, and makes us loathe the very sight of God; pardon encourageth us to come near to him. Guilt respects him as a judge; pardon, as a friend. Who can confidently or hopefully call upon an angry and condemning God? But who cannot but hopefully call upon a forgiving God? Sin is the partition wall between God and us, and pardon is the demolishing of it. Forgiveness is never bestowed, but the sceptre is held out to invite us to come into God's presence. And what can be more desirable than to have not only the favour of, but a free access at any time to, the Lord of heaven and earth, and at length an everlasting being with him?

(3.) Peace of conscience. There must needs be fair weather when heaven smiles upon us. All other things breed disquietness. Sin was a thorn in David's crown; his throne and sceptre were but miserable comforters, while his guilt overwhelmed him. The glory of the world is no sovereign plaster for a wounded spirit. Other enjoyments may please the sense, but this only can gratify the soul. God's thunder made Moses tremble, Heb. xii. 21; but the probability of a gracious pardon would make a damned soul smile in the midst of tormenting flames. How often hath the sense of it raised the hearts of martyrs, and made the sufferers sing, while the spectators wept! though this, I must confess, is not always an inseparable concomitant. There is much difference between a pardon and the comfort of it; that may pass the seal of the king without the knowledge of the malefactor. Pardon, indeed, always gives the *jus ad rem*, a right to peace of conscience, but not always *jus in re*, the possession of it. There may be an actual separation between pardon and actual peace, but not between pardon and the ground of peace.

(4.) It sweetens all mercies. Other mercies are a ring, but pardon is the diamond in it. A justified person may say, I have temporal mercies and a pardon too; I live in repute in the world, and God's favour too; riches increase, and my peace with God doth not diminish. I have health with a pardon, friends with a pardon, as Job, chap. xxix. 3, 6, 7; among all other blessings this he counts the chiefest, that God's candle shined upon his head. A prisoner for some capital crime may have all outward accommodations for lodging, diet, attendance, without a real happiness, when he expects to be called to his trial before a severe judge, from whom there is no appeal, and that will certainly both pass, and cause to be executed, a sentence of death upon him. So, though a man wallows in all outward contents, he cannot write himself blessed, while the wrath of God hangs over his head, and he knows not how soon he may be summoned before God's tribunal, and hear that terrible voice, 'Go, thou cursed.' What comfort can a man take in houses, land, health, when he considers he owes more than all his estate is worth? So, what comfort can a man have in anything in this world, when he may hourly expect an arrest from God, and a demand of all his debts, and he hath not so much as one farthing of his own, or any interest in a sufficient surety? We may have honour and a curse, wealth and a curse, children and a curse, health and long life and a curse, learning and a curse, but we can never have pardon and a curse. Our outward things may be gifts, but not blessings, without a pardon.

(5.) It sweetens all afflictions. A frown with a pardon is better than a thousand smiles without it. Sin is the sting of crosses, and remission is a taking the sting out of them. A sight of heaven will mitigate a cross on earth. The stones about Stephen's ears did scarce afflict him, when he saw his Saviour open heaven to entertain him. To see death staring us in the face, and an angry and offended God above, ready to charge all our guilt, is a doleful spectacle. 'Look upon my affliction and my pain, and forgive all my sins,' saith the psalmist, Ps. xxv. 18. Sin doth embitter, and adds weight to an affliction, but the removal of sin doth both lighten it and sweeten it.

Use 1. An unpardoned man is a miserable man. Such a state lays you open to all the miseries on earth, and all the torments in hell. The poorest beggar with a pardon is higher than the greatest prince without it. How can we enjoy a quiet hour, if our debt be not remitted, since we owe more than we are able to pay? You may die with a forfeited reputation, and yet be happy; but what happiness, if you die with unpardoned guilt?

(1.) There must either be pardon or punishment. The law doth oblige either to obedience or suffering: the commands of it must be observed, or the penalty endured. God will not relax the punishment without a valuable consideration. If it be not executed, the creature may accuse God of want of wisdom in enacting it, or defect of power in maintaining it. Therefore there must be an exact observance of the law, which no creature after the first deviation is able to do; or an undergoing the penalty of it, which no sinner is able to bear. There must therefore be a remission of this punishment for the good of the creature, and the satisfaction of the law by a surety, for the honour of God's justice. If we have not therefore an interest in the surety, the purchaser of remission, we must lie under the severity of the law in our persons.

(2.) You can call nothing an act of God's love towards you, while you remain unpardoned. What is there you do enjoy, which may not consist with his hatred as well as his love? Have we knowledge? So have devils. Have we riches? So had Nabal and Cain. Have we honour? So had Pharaoh and Herod. Have we sermons? So had Judas, the best that ever were preached. Nothing, nothing but a pardon, is properly a blessing. How can that man take pleasure in anything he hath, when all the threatenings in the book of God are so many arrows directed against him?

(3.) All the time thou livest unpardoned, thy debts mount the higher. Every new sin is an adding a figure to the former sum, and every figure after the three first adds a thousand. Every act of sin adds not only the guilt proper to that single act upon it, but draws a new universal guilt from all the rest committed before, because the persisting in any one sin is a renewed approbation of all the former acts of rebellion committed against God.

(4.) It is that God, who would have pardoned thee if thou wouldst have accepted of it, who will condemn if thou dost utterly refuse it. It is that God thou hast provoked, offended, and dishonoured. That power which would have been manifested in forgiving thee, will be glorified in condemning thee. That justice which would have signed thy absolution, if thou hadst accepted of its terms, will sign the writ of execution upon thy refusal of them. Nay, the mercy that would have saved thee, will have no compassion on thee. The law condemns thee, because thou hast transgressed it, and mercy will reject thee, because thou hast despised it. The gospel, wherein pardon was proclaimed, will acquit others, but condemn thee. God would be false to his own word, if, after thy slighting so many promises of grace and threatenings of wrath, thou shouldst be spared.

Use 2. Of comfort.

Pardon of sin may make thee hope for all other blessings. Hath God done the hardest, and will he stick at the easiest? Hath he overthrown mountains, and shall molehills stop him? It is an easier thing to waft thee to heaven, than it was at first to remit thy guilt: Rom. v. 10, 'For if when we were enemies we were reconciled to God by the death of his Son, much more being reconciled we shall be saved by his life.' To this the death and resurrection of the Son of God was necessary, and there was to be composition and agreement made between mercy and justice. But since this is completed, the Redeemer saves thee by his life; since he hath died for thy remission, there is no need of his dying for thy further salvation. Seeing he hath made manifestation of his pardoning grace unto thee, he will not cease till he hath brought thee into a perfect state. For to what purpose should the creditor forgive the smaller part of the debt, and cast the creditor into prison for an unpayable sum.

(1.) If once pardoned, thou wilt be always pardoned. For the first pardon Christ paid his blood, for the continuance he doth but plead his blood, and we cannot be without a pardon till Christ be without a plea. He merited the continuance as well as the first remission. Will our Saviour be more backward to intercede for pardon, than he was to bleed and pray for it on earth? Would not our dearest Saviour let sin go unremitted, when he was to contest with the Father's wrath? and will he let it go unpardoned when he is only to solicit his Father's mercy? Thou shalt not want the daily renewals of it, since he has only to present his blood in the most holy place, seeing an ignominious and painful death did not scare him from the purchase of it upon the cross. As God's heart is more ready to give than we are to ask forgiveness, so is Christ's heart more ready to plead for the continuance of it, than we are daily to beg it; for he loves his people more than they can love him, or love themselves. Our praying is according to self-love, but Christ's intercession is according to his own infinite love, with a more intense fervency.

(2.) Thou art above the reach of all accusations. Shall the law condemn thee? No. Thou art 'not under the law, but under grace.' And if grace hath forgiven thee, the law cannot sentence thee. Shall conscience? No. Conscience is but the echo of the law within us: that must speak what God speaks. God's Spirit and a believer's spirit are joint witnesses: Rom. viii. 16, 'For the Spirit itself bears witness with our spirits that we are the children of God.' Conscience is sprinkled by the blood of Christ, which quite changeth the tenor of its commission. Will God condemn thee? No. That were to lose the glory of all his pardoning mercy hitherto conferred upon thee; that were to fling away the vast revenue grace hath all this while been gathering for him; yea, it were to deny his own covenant and promise. Shall Christ condemn thee? No. That were to discard all his offices, to undo his death, and belie his merits. Did he sweat and bleed, pray and die for thee, and will he now condemn thee? Hath he been pleading for thee in heaven all this time, and will he now at the upshot cast thee off? Shall we imagine the severity of a judge more pleasing to him than the charity of an advocate, since his primary intention in coming was to save the world, not to condemn it? No. It would not be for his honour to pay the price and to lose the purchase.

(3.) There will be a solemn justification of thee at the last day. Thou art here pardoned in law, and then thou shalt be justified by a final sentence; there is a secret grant here, but a public manifestation of it hereafter. Thy pardon was passed by the Spirit of God in thy own conscience, it will then be passed by the Son of God in thy own hearing. That Saviour that did merit it upon his cross, will pronounce it upon his throne. The book shall be laid out of sight; there shall be no more writing in the book of God's omniscience to charge thee, or of thy conscience to affright thee. His fatherly anger shall for ever cease; and as all disposition to sin, so all paternal correction for it shall be for ever abolished, and forgiveness be fully complete in all the glorious effects of it.

(4.) Faith doth interest us in all this, though it be weak. The grant of a pardon doth not depend upon the strength of faith, though the sense of a pardon doth. A weak faith, as a palsy person, may not so well read a pardon, though it may receive it. As a strong faith gives more glory to God, so it receives more comfort from him. Christ made no difference in his prayer, John xvii., between the feeblest and stoutest believer. His lambs as well as sheep were to be fed by his apostle with gospel comforts; and even those lambs, Isa. xl. 11, he himself carries in his bosom. Strong faith doth not entitle us to it because it is strong, or a feeble faith debar us from it because it is weak; but it is for the sake of a mighty Saviour that we are pardoned. It is the same Christ that justifies thee as well as Abraham, the father of the faithful; it is the same righteousness whereby thou art justified as well as Paul and the most beloved disciple.

Use 3. Of examination.

Consider whether your sins are pardoned. Will you examine whether your estates are sure, and will you not examine whether your souls are sure?

Here I shall, 1, remove false signs whereon men rest, and think themselves pardoned.

(1.) The littleness of sin is no ground of pardon. Oh, some may say, my sins are little; some tricks of youth, some petty oaths, or the like. The Scripture saith that drunkards, fornicators, extortioners, and covetous, shall not enter into the kingdom of heaven; not great drunkards only, but those that are drunk but now and then, as well as those that are drunkards every day.

[1.] Dost thou know the malignity of the least sin? No sin can be called absolutely (though it may comparatively) little. Is it a little God who is offended by sin? Is it a little wrath which is poured down on sin? Is it a little Christ that hath died for sin? Is it a little soul that is destroyed by sin? And is it a little hell that is prepared for sin? Is not the least sin *deicidium*, as much as in a man lieth, a destroying of God? Did not Christ shed his blood for the least as well as for the greatest? Is not hell kindled by the breath of the Lord for the least as well as the greatest sins? Is that little which is God's burden, Christ's wound, the Spirit's grief, the penitent's sorrow, and the devil's hell? Every drop of poison is poison, every drop of hell is hell, every part of sin is sin, and hath the destroying and condemning nature of sin. Can angels expiate the least sin, or can a thousand worlds be a sufficient recompence for the injury that is done to God by the least sin?

[2.] The less thy sin, the less the excuse for thyself. It is the aggravation of their injustice, that they 'sold the righteous for a pair of shoes,' Amos ii. 6. Dost thou undervalue God so as to sell a righteous and eternal God so cheap, for a little sin? Is a little sin dearer to thee than the favour of the great God? Is a little sin dearer to thee than an eternal hell is grievous? To endanger thy soul for a trifle, to lose God for a bubble, is a confounding aggravation of it; as it was of Judas his sin, that he would sell his Saviour for a little silver, for so small a sum. Sin is not little in respect of the formality of it, but in respect of the matter, in respect of the temptation; and this littleness is an aggravation of sin.

[3.] Dost thou know how God hath punished the least sin? A drop of sin may bring a deluge of misery. An atom of sin is strong enough to overturn a world. It was but an apple that poisoned Adam and his whole posterity. Less sins are punished in hell than are pardoned here. God casts off Saul for less sins than he pardoned David for. How many ships have been destroyed upon small sands as well as great rocks!

(2.) Fewness of sins is no argument of pardon. Conceive, if thou canst, the amiableness and lustre of the angels, how far beyond the glory of the sun it was; yet one sin divested them of all their glory. It was but one sin kindled hell for the fallen angels; every sin must receive 'a just recompence of reward,' Heb. ii. 2. Shall one single sin entitle thee to hell, what will millions of sins then entitle thee to? One sin is too much against God. Had thy iniquities been never so few, Christ must have died to answer the pleas of his Father's justice against thee. Every sin is rebellion against God as a sovereign, undutifulness to God as a father,* contempt of God as a governor, and preferring the devil before God; the devil that would damn thee, before God that made thee and preserves thee; a preferring the devil's temptations before God's promises.

(3.) The commonness of sin is no argument of pardon. Many angels combined in the first conspiracy against God; but as they were companions in sin, so are they companions in torments. The commonness of Sodom's sin made the louder cry, and hastened the severer judgment; not one inhabitant escaped, but only righteous Lot and his family. Common sins will have common plagues. It doth rather aggravate thy sin than plead for pardon, when thou wilt rather follow men's example to offend God than conform to God's law to please him. Sin was common in the old world, for 'all flesh had corrupted their ways,' Gen. vi. 12; and all were swept away by the destroying deluge. To walk according to the course of the world, is so far from being a foundation of pardon, that it is made a character of a child of the devil. To walk according to the course of the world, is to walk according to the pattern of the devil, and to be in the number of the children of wrath: Eph. ii. 2, 'Wherein in times past ye walked according to the course of this world, according to the prince of the power of the air.'

(4.) Forbearance of punishment is no argument of pardon: Eccles. viii. 11, 'Because sentence against an evil work is not executed speedily, therefore the heart of the sons of men is fully set in them to do evil.' Forbearance is made use of by men, to make them sin more desperately, more headily. 'Fully set:' all checks silenced and stopped. Forbearance is no acquittance; it argues not God's forgiving the debt; the debt is due, though it be not presently sued for; and the longer the debt remains unpaid, the greater sum will the interest amount to; because the longer God doth forbear punishment, the longer time thou hast for repentance; the account for that time will run high.

That God doth not punish, is an argument of his patience, not of his pardoning mercy. God laughs at sinners; he sees their day is coming, though they may be jocund and confident of a pardon. God's forbearance may be justice; he may be brewing the cup and mixing that which thou art to drink. Prisoners may be reprieved one assize, and executed the next; reprieval of execution is no allowance of the crime, or change of the sentence.

(5.) Prosperity is no sign of pardon. Oh, I am not only borne with, and forborne; but I have a great addition of outward contentments since my sin!

That which you make an argument of pardon, may be an argument of condemnation.

* Burges.

Asaph was much troubled at the prosperity of the wicked; but at last saith, 'Pride compasseth them as a chain, and violence covers them as a garment,' Ps. lxxiii. 6. That kindness which should have made them melt, made them presume; that which should broach thy repentance, inflames thy pride; thy goods may increase thy sins.

(6.) Forgetfulness of thy sin, and commission long ago, is no sign of pardon; and therefore having no checks for them, is no sign of pardon. God doth not forget, though thou dost; no sin slips from the memory of his knowledge, though now he doth cast many sins away from the memory of his justice. In regard of God's eternity, the first sins are accounted as committed this moment; for in that there is no succession of time, and the sins thou hast committed twenty years ago, are as fresh as if thou hadst acted them all since thy coming into the congregation. Joseph's brethren, Gen. xxxvii. 25, laboured to wipe out the thoughts of their late cruelty by their eating and drinking, when the cries and tears of their brother were fresh in their memory, and might have damped their jollity. His affliction troubled them not; his relation to them, his youth, and their father's love to him, could not make them relent. But twenty-two years after, conscience began to fly in their faces, when awakened by a powerful affliction, Gen. xlii. 21. Is not thy conscience oftentimes a remembrancer to thee of thy old forgotten sins, and doth it not turn over the old records thou hadst quite forgot?

(7.) Hopes of God's mercy are no grounds of thy being pardoned. God's mercy is not barely enough, for then Christ needed not have died for sin; nor Christ's death enough, without the condition of that covenant whereby God will make over the interest and merits of his death to thee. God's mercy must be considered, but in God's own way. God is merciful, but his mercy must not abolish his truth. Doth not a judge's mercy consist with condemning a malefactor? God hath been merciful to thee, and thou wouldst not accept of it; thou wouldst not hear mercy speak in a day of grace, why then should not justice speak in a day of vengeance? Thou wouldst not hear a God of mercy when he cried to thee, how then should mercy hear thee when thou comest to beg?

2. Some false grounds why those that are pardoned think themselves not pardoned.

(1.) Great afflictions are not signs of an unpardoned state. Moses had sinned by unbelief, Aaron by making a golden calf; God pardoned their sin, but took vengeance on their inventions: Ps. xcix. 8, 'Thou wast a God that forgavest them, though thou tookest vengeance.' Nathan, in his message to David, brings at once both pardon and punishment. The sin is removed, but the sword must still stick in the bowels of his family: 2 Sam. xii. 13, 14, 'The Lord hath put away thy sin; thou shalt not die. Howbeit, because by this deed thou hast given great occasion to the enemies of the Lord to blaspheme, the child also that is born unto thee shall surely die.' God may afflict temporally, when he resolves not to punish eternally. What! because he will not condemn thee as a judge, will he not chastise thee as a father? We may well bear a scourge in one hand, when we have a pardon sealed in the other. God pardons thy sin, but there is need of affliction to subdue that stout, stubborn heart of thine. God doth visit with rods when he is resolved not utterly to take away his loving-kindness from a people, Ps. lxxxix. 32, 33.

(2.) Terrors of conscience are no sign of an unpardoned state. We find a pardoned David having broken bones and a racked conscience after Nathan had pronounced his pardon, when there was no remorse before, Ps. li. He had the grant of a pardon, but the comfort of a pardon was wanting. God may scorch thy soul when he gives a pardon, not that justice is thereby satisfied, but sin more imbittered to thee. By a pardon thou dost relish his mercy, and by the torments thou mayest have in thy soul, thou wilt understand his justice. He shews thee what he freely gives, but he would have thee know what thou hast fully deserved; he gives thee pardon, but gall and wormwood with it, that thou mayest know what the purchase of it did cost thy Saviour. The physic which heals, causeth pain. That physic which doth not make thee sick, is not like to bring thee health. God pardons thee, that thou mayest be saved; he terrifies thee withal, that thou mayest not be induced by temptations to sin.

(3.) Sense of sin is no argument of an unpardoned state. A pardon may be granted when the poor condemned man expects to be haled out to execution. Mary stands weeping behind her Saviour when Christ was declaring her pardon to Simon; that much was forgiven her, and afterwards Christ turns to her, and cheers her with the news of it, Luke vii. 44–47. He pronounceth her pardon, ver. 48, and the comfort of it: ver. 50, 'Thy faith hath saved thee; go in peace.' The heavens may drop, when now and then the sun may steal a beam through the clouds. There may be a pardon where there are not always the sensible effects of a pardon. We find, after the stilling of a storm, the ragings and rollings of the sea. A penitent's wound may ache afresh when a Saviour's blood drops in mercy.

(4.) The remainders of sin are not a sign of an unpardoned state. Though a disease be mastered by physic, there may be some grudgings of it in a person. Though sin be pardoned, yet the dregs of sin will be remaining, and sometimes stirring. Christ hath enlivened us, not by wholly destroying, but pardoning, sin. Pardon takes away the guilt of sin, grace takes away the power of sin, but neither pardon nor infusion of grace takes away the nature, and all motions of sin; for in purging out an humour, some dregs still remain behind: Col. ii. 13, 'And you hath he quickened together with him, having forgiven you all trespasses.'

3. What are the true signs of a pardoned man?

(1.) Sincerity in our walk. A spirit without guile is made the character of a pardoned man in the text. There may be failings in the life, yet no guile in the heart; such a man is a pardoned man. A heart that hath no mixtures, no pretences or excuses for sin, no private reserves for God; a heart that, as the needle in a compass, stands right for the interest and glory of God, and answers to the profession as an echo to the voice; a heart that would thrust out any sin that harboured there, would not have an atom of any filth odious to the eye of God lurk there. Where this sincerity is, a willingness and readiness to obey God (which is the condition of the covenant), the substance of the covenant is kept, though some particular articles of it may be broken. Grace, the pardoning grace of God, is with them that love Christ in sincerity: Eph. vi. 24, 'Grace be with all them that love Christ Jesus in sincerity.' Not a man excluded that is sincere, though he hath not so sparkling a flame as another, yet, if he be sincere, the crown of pardoning grace, and that of consummating grace, will be set upon his head.

(2.) Mourning for sin. A tender heart is a sign of a pardoned state, when sin discontents thee, because it displeaseth God. What showers of tears did Mary Magdalene weep after a pardon! Love to God, like a gentle fire, sets the soul a-melting. Tears that come from love are never without pardoning mercy. God's bowels do first stir our mournings. It is impossible a gracious heart can read a pardon with dry eyes; it is the least it thinks it can do, as it were, like Mary Magdalene, to wash Christ's feet with its tears, when it hath been washed itself with Christ's blood. The soul cannot enough hate that which God hath been merciful in the pardon of. Forgiveness is like the warmth of the spring; it draws out the sap of the tree, the tears of the soul, which else would scarcely stir. If God hath given thee repentance, it is sure enough that he hath given thee a pardon; for if he did not mean to give thee that, he would never have given thee the other.

(3.) Fearfulness of sin. Whosoever knows the bitterness of sin, and the benefit of a pardon, can never confidently rush into it. A pardoned man will never go about to forfeit that which he hath newly received. Forgiveness from God doth produce fear in the creature: Ps. cxxx. 4, 'But there is forgiveness with thee, that thou mayest be feared.' It is a sign we have repented and got pardon, if we find, after that exercise of repentance and prayer, our hatred of sin increaseth, especially of that sin we were guilty of before.

(4.) Sanctification. God never pardons but he subdues sin: Micah vii. 19, 'He will subdue our iniquity, and thou wilt cast all their sins into the depths of the sea.' Both are put together. In the Lord's prayer, desires to be rid of all evil, and not to be led into any temptation, follow immediately upon the desire of pardon. A justified person and a sanctified nature are inseparable: Rom. viii. 1, 'There is no condemnation to them that are in Christ;' there is pardon, but how shall I know that I am pardoned? If you 'walk not after the flesh, but after the Spirit.' We never sincerely desire pardon, but we desire purging; and God never gives the one, but he bestows the other. If thou hast an interest in a pardoning Christ, thou wilt have the effects of a sanctifying Spirit. Where God's grace forgives all sin, he will give us grace to forsake all sin. It is his covenant to turn away ungodliness, when he takes away the punishment of sin: Rom. xi. 26, 27, 'The Deliverer shall turn away ungodliness from Jacob.' The applications of God's grace to us are attended with the infusions of God's grace into us. When he puts his law into the heart, he remembers sin no more, Jer. xxxi. 33, 34.

(5.) Forgiving others. In the Lord's prayer we pray, 'Forgive us our trespasses, as we forgive them that trespass against us.' Our Saviour comments upon this petition, to shew that pardon cannot be without this condition in Mat. xviii., from ver. 23 to the 35th. Christ makes it at least a *causa sine quâ non* of pardon: Luke xi. 4, 'And forgive us our sins, for we also forgive every one that is indebted to us.'

(6.) Affectionate love to God and Christ. When we desire to glorify him by his grace, as well as be glorified by it. It is the injury done to God by our sins which doth most affect that heart upon which the Spirit of God is poured: Zech. xii. 10, 'They shall mourn over him, or be in bitterness for him.' The soul is more concerned for Christ than for itself. When there is too much of self in our desires for it, God delays the manifestation of it to the heart, that we may come up to purer strains. Christ certainly shed his blood for their remission, who are willing to shed theirs for his glory. Else Christ, whose glory it is to outstrip the hottest affection of his creature, would be behind-hand with him in love. That soul that would spend its all upon Christ, he will not suffer to stand long sobbing before him, Luke vii. 47.

Use 4. Of exhortation.

(1.) To those who are careless of it. Oh, by all means seek it! Will it at last comfort thee to think of thy mirth and pleasures, how honourable, how rich, or how well stored with friends thou hast been? What should take up thy heart, busy thy thoughts, or employ thy endeavours, but this that concerns thy eternal state? Wilt thou sin away the time of God's patience, and thine own happiness? Is it not a time which God hath allotted thee to get a pardon in? What would Cain, Judas, Pilate, Herod, and all the black regiment, give for the very hopes of it? Oh prize that here which thou wilt hereafter esteem infinitely valuable, and call thyself fool and madman a thousand times, for neglecting the opportunity of getting! The anger of a king is as the roaring of a lion; what then are the frowns of an infinite just God? Why is thy strength and affection spent about other things? Would a forlorn malefactor leading to execution listen cheerfully to anything but the news of his prince's clemency? Seek it,

[1.] Earnestly. Pardon is an inestimable blessing, and must not be sought with faint and tired affections.

[2.] Presently. Is it not full time seriously to set about it? Thou hast lost too many days already, and wilt thou be so senseless as to let another slip? How knowest thou but if thou dost refuse it this day, thou mayest be uncapable of it to-morrow? There is but a step, a few minutes, between thee and death, and delays in great emergencies are dangerous.

[3.] Universally. Content not yourselves with seeking a pardon for grisly, staring sins, which fright the conscience with every look, but seek the pardon of your inward secret spiritual sins; while you beg most for the pardon of those, sanctifying grace will come in as well as justifying; the more you pray against the guilt of them, the more you will hate the filth of them.

(2.) To those that seek a pardon, and yet are in doubt of it. Secure sinners, that understand not the evil of sin, think it is an easy thing, and that forgiveness will be granted of course. But those that groan under the burden of their iniquity, imagine it more difficult than indeed it is. Presumption wrongs God in his justice, and every degree of despair or doubting, in his mercy.

[1.] God is willing to pardon. Ephraim doth but desire that God would turn him, and God presently cries out, 'Is Ephraim my dear son? Is he a pleasant child?' Jer. xxxi. 18, 20. 'I have surely heard Ephraim bemoaning himself thus.' A penitent Ephraim is instantly a pleasant child. Ephraim strikes upon his thigh with confession, and God speaks to his heart with affection. God doth, as it were, take the words out of Ephraim's mouth, as though he watched for the first look of Ephraim towards him, or the first breath of a supplication. God is more willing to pardon sin than we are to sin; because we sin with reluctancy, natural conscience checking us, but God hath no check when he goes to pardon. He 'waits to be gracious,' Isa. xxx. 18, 'therefore will the Lord wait, that he may be gracious unto you: and therefore will he be exalted, that he may have mercy upon you.' He hath waited all the time of your sinning, to have an opportunity to shew grace to you; and now you give it him by repenting, will he lose the fruit of his waiting? It is the end of Christ's exaltation, whether it be meant of his being lifted up on the cross, or his exaltation in heaven; it is true of both, that his end is to have mercy upon you.

[2.] God will pardon the greatest sins. His infinite compassion cannot exhaust itself by a frequent remission. Mercy holds proportion to justice; as his justice punisheth little sins as well as great, so doth mercy pass by great sins as well as little. Your highest sins are the sins of men, but the mercy offered is the mercy of a God.

The debt you owe is a vast debt, but Christ's satisfaction is of a greater value; and a king's revenue may well pay a beggar's debts, though she owe many thousands the first day of marriage. Multiplied sins upon repentance shall meet with multiplied pardons: Isa. lv. 7, ירבה לסלות, 'abundantly pardon.' We cannot vie our sins with God's mercy. The grace of God, and the righteousness of Christ, which are necessary for the remission of one sin, are infinite, and no more is requisite for the pardon of the greatest, yea, of the sins of the whole world, if they were upon thy single score. The grace conferred upon Paul was more than would suit his necessity: 1 Tim. i. 14, ὑπερεπλεόνασε, superabound; 'and the grace of our Lord was exceeding abundant,' enough to have pardoned a whole world as well as Paul; like the sun, that emits as much heat in his beams upon one puddle, as is enough not only to exhale the moisture of that, but of a hundred more. Suppose thou art the greatest sinner that ever was yet extant in the world, do not think that God, who hath snatched so many firebrands of hell out of the devil's hands, will neglect such an opportunity to make his grace illustrious upon thy humble soul. If God hath given thee repentance, it is a certain evidence he will follow it with a pardon, though thy sins be of a deeper scarlet than ever yet was seen upon the earth; for if he did not mean to bestow this, he would never have bestowed upon thee the necessary condition of it. Is there not a sinner can equal thee? Then surely God is wiser than to lose the highest opportunity he yet had to evidence his superlative grace. And therefore,

[1.] Continue thy humiliations. There must be a conformity between Christ and thee. He was humbled when he purchased remission, and you must be humbled when you receive it. God will not part with that very cheap, that cost his Son so dear: though thou art not at the expense of the blood of thy soul, thou must be at the expense of the blood of thy sins. When a man comes to be deeply affected with his sin, then God sends a message of peace: Isa. vi. 6, 7, 'Then flew one of the seraphims, and laid a live coal upon his mouth, and said, Thine iniquity is taken away, and thy sin purged.' When, ver. 5, he had cried out, 'Woe is me, for I am undone, because I am a man of unclean lips.' The way to have a debt forgiven is to acknowledge it: Ps. xxxii. 5, 'I said, I will confess my transgressions unto the Lord: and thou forgavest the iniquity of my sin.' God stood as ready to forgive David's unrighteousness, as he was ready to confess it. Mercy will not save a man without making him sensible of, and humbled for, his iniquity. Put thy business, therefore, into Christ's hands, and submit to what terms he will impose upon thee.

[2.] In thy supplications plead his glory. You find this the constant argument the people of God in the Scripture use for the prevailing with God for forgiveness. That argument is most comfortably pleaded, which God loves most, and whereunto he orders all his actions. No stronger motive can be used to him to grant it, than that whereby he excites himself to bestow it. When thou beggest other things, thou mayest dishonour God; but God cannot be a loser of his glory in granting this. Lord, if thou turnest me into hell, where is the glory of thy mercy upon thy creature? Nay, where is the glory of thy justice, my eternal torments not being able to compensate the injury done to thee by sin, so much as the suffering of thy only Son, whose death I desire to share in, and whose terms I am willing to submit to?

(3.) Exhortation to those that are pardoned.

1. Admire this grace of God. To pardon one sin is a greater thing than to create a world; to pardon one sin is greater than to damn a world. God can create a world without the death of a creature; he can damn a world without the death of a creator; but in pardoning there must be the death of the creator, the Son of God.

2. Serve God much. Is the guilt of sin, the cord that bound thee, taken

off? It is fit that when thou art so unfettered, thou shouldst run the ways of God's commandments. A sense of pardon of sin makes the soul willing and ready to run upon God's errands, and to obey his commandments: Isa. vi. 8, 'I heard the voice of the Lord saying, Whom shall I send? Then said I, Here am I.' Then when he had received assurance that his iniquity was taken away, ver. 7, God's pardon set thee upon a new stock, and therefore he expects thou shouldst be full of new clusters.

3. Be more fearful of sin. Dispute with thyself, Hath God pardoned the guilt of sin that it shall not damn me, and shall I wallow in the mire of sin to pollute myself? Oh, thy sins after pardon have a blacker circumstance than the sins of devils, or the sins of wicked men, for theirs are not against pardoning mercy, not against special love. Oh, thaw thy heart every morning with a meditation on pardon, and sin will not so easily freeze it in the day-time. When thou art tempted to sin, consider what thoughts thou hadst when thou wert sueing for pardon, how earnest thou wert for it, what promises and vows thou didst make, and consider the love God shewed thee in pardoning. Do not blur thy pardon, so easily wound thy conscience, or weaken thy faith.

4. Be content with what God gives thee. If he gives thee heaven, will he deny thee earth? He that bestows upon thee the pardon of sin, would surely pour into thy bosom the gold of both the Indies, were it necessary for thee. But thou hast got a greater happiness; for it is not said, Blessed is he that wallows in wealth, honour, and a confluence of worldly prosperity, but, 'Blessed is he whose sin is forgiven, and whose iniquity is covered.'

MAN'S ENMITY TO GOD.

[Thus far is a reprint of the entire contents of the two folio volumes commonly known as 'Charnock's Works,' including the appendix contained in some copies, but not in all. The two sermons that follow were published in 1699, and were reprinted at Leeds in a small 8vo volume in 1817. From that they are now reprinted. It will be remembered that Mr Veel, the author of the following advertisement, was one of the editors of the 'Works.'—Ed.]

AN ADVERTISEMENT TO THE READER.

Good Reader,—Upon the publication of the second volume of Mr Charnock's works, it was much lamented by those that knew him, and had a just value for him, that some sermons he was known to have preached (and which were as worthy of the public view as the rest, and no less useful to the grand design of man's salvation) could not be found among his papers; especially three sermons, which many heard him preach on three several Lord's days, upon 1 Tim. xi. 15, 'Christ Jesus came into the world to save sinners.' But now, beyond expectation, instead of them, the good providence of God hath brought to light the two following treatises, by the unwearied diligence of Mr Ashton, one of the laborious transcribers of the first volume of this author's works, and who, to give him his due, hath raked them out of the ashes, and rescued them from that oblivion to which they seemed condemned, having with great pains and patience transcribed, as well as with great judgment joined together, the several materials he found belonging respectively to each subject, in the many loose papers of Mr Charnock he had by him. The papers I have seen, and, with Mr Ashton's help, have (so far as was needful) compared the transcription with them.

One of these treatises contains the continuation of the author's meditations on 1 Tim. i. 15. And herein he handles a second doctrine, grounded on the last clause of the verse. The text was fruitful, and bore twins, whereof the younger only survives; the other, I fear, is dead without recovery.

But I verily persuade myself that many an honest soul will have occasion to bless the Lord for the birth, shall I say? or the resurrection of this still-born offspring of so worthy a father, being thereby stirred up not only to admire that rich grace of God which so eminently appears in many times calling the chiefest of sinners, but encouraged in the faith of it, and supported under the burden of the greatest guilt which we find so often oppressing, terrifying, and even sinking, awakened sinners into despair, when they look upon their sins as not only above the sins of others, but even above the mercy of God itself, and therefore unpardonable. If secure sinners shall dare to abuse the great truths here declared and set forth, to the strengthening their hands in their evil works, and emboldening themselves to a life of sin because God's grace abounds, at their peril be it, and let them answer for it. But in the mean time, it is pity that such rich and precious cordials should be withheld from those that need them, lest others to whom they do not belong should presumptuously catch at them, and undo themselves by misapplying them. And who knows not that what is a cordial to some may prove poison to others?

As for the other discourse, *Of Man's Enmity against God*, we cannot find when or where it was preached. I have been credibly informed, that the author had a design (had it pleased God to have prolonged his days) to have preached largely about original sin, and then it is not unlikely that he might intend this present treatise as one branch of it. And in it, if the reader can but dispense with one degree less of that accuracy and neatness of style which usually appears in his other writings, he will find as excellent matter, and great things, as in most of them, and indeed the true spirit of the author. He had made great use of the hammer in beating out the truth, but wanted time to apply the file for the more thorough smoothing and polishing of his work, which truly wants nothing but the finishing-stroke. The thread of this discourse is as finely spun as any, though the piece be not altogether so glossy; but whatever is wanting in ornament, is abundantly made up in usefulness. And if one of these treatises may be a glass in which humbled sinners may see the beauty and glory of sovereign grace, the other too may be a glass in which the best of saints may see the face of their own souls, and a lively representation of that inherent wickedness which all that diligently observe and know their own hearts cannot but acknowledge to be natural to them, as having been born with them into the world. I cannot but say that this discourse is an excellent portraiture of the old man; a graphical description of the devil's image impressed upon and deforming the most beautiful part of this lower creation. It shews how much man is debased and degraded by sin, and become a slave to his lusts, who was made at first to be the lord of his fellow-creatures; and so how rueful a legacy our first father has left us, and to what misery he hath entailed us, by communicating so cursed a nature to us. That the blessing of God may be upon these labours of his (long since) deceased but faithful servant, and that they may, by the power of his grace, be made effectual for obtaining the ends designed by the author, is the desire and prayer of him who is, good reader,

Thy soul's well-wisher, and servant for Jesus' sake,

EDW. VEEL.

September 20. 1699.

MAN'S ENMITY TO GOD.

Because the carnal mind is enmity against God: for it is not subject to the law of God, neither indeed can be.—Rom. VIII. 7.

PART I.

A state of nature a state of enmity against God.

In the fourth verse the apostle renews the description of those persons to whom he had proclaimed a jubilee in the first verse: 'There is now no condemnation,' &c. Sanctified persons only have an interest in Christ, and those that have an interest in Christ are not subject to a sentence of death. They are described from their course and conversation: they 'walk not after the flesh,' not after the dictates, wills, desires, importunities of the flesh, but according to the motions, dictates, direction of the Holy Ghost in the gospel.

The note by which we may know whether we walk after the Spirit is laid down: 'They that are after the flesh do mind the things of the flesh; but they that are after the Spirit the things of the Spirit,' ver. 5. Φρονειν signifies,

1. *Affectum*, affection, Rom. xii. 16. Το ἀυτο φρονουντες.

2. *Sensum*, sense or relish. The understanding is the palate of the soul, the taster to the will; it considers what things be good, and under that notion offers them to the will. Spiritual things are as dry chips to a carnal heart, even as carnal things are contemptible to a spiritual mind.

3. *Cogitationem*, thought. So for the most part it is taken, and notes the τὸ ἡγεμονικόν, and is meant of the higher acts of the soul.

Frequent thoughts discover rooted affections. Operations of the mind are the indexes, Κριτήρια, of a regenerate or unregenerate estate. If about carnal [things], they evidence the bent of the heart to be turned that way, and that worldly objects are dearest to them. If about spiritual, they manifest spiritual objects to be the most grateful to the soul. Carnal thoughts are signs of a languishing and feeble frame, but spiritual discover a well-tempered and complexioned soul.

As this is laid down by the apostle, it hath, as some pictures, a double aspect. It is a character and a duty. For the apostle enforces it by the consideration of the danger of the one, and the happiness of the other: 'To be carnally minded is death; to be spiritually minded is life and peace,' ver. 6.

Death and life.

1. *Effectivè*, by way of efficiency. As they deaden and enliven the soul. Carnal principles are spiritual diseases. Spiritual thoughts are healing restoratives.

2. *Consecutivè*, by way of consequence. Revenge and justice attends the one, as grace and mercy accompanies the other.

The proof of this is, ver. 7, it is death, because it is enmity to, and aversion from God, who is the fountain of life. It is the description of a natural estate, and what relation a man considered in his corrupt nature bears to God.

Φρονημα. The most refined and elevated thoughts, which have no other groundwork than nature. The highest flights of an unregenerate soul by the wings of the greatest reason. The wisdom and virtues of the heathen were enmity, therefore translated by some, *sapientia carnis*, the wisdom of the flesh.

Τῆς σαρκὸς. Unregenerate man. Flesh is usually taken in scripture for the unregenerate part of the soul. 'That which is born of the flesh is flesh,' John iii. 6. Εχθρα. Not *enemy*, but *enmity*.

1. Not anger. That is not so bad. It may arise from some distaste; every disgust does not destroy friendship. 2. Not aversion. That may be quickly removed. But, 3. Enmity. How directly opposite is man to God! God is said to be love, and man enmity, both in the abstract. Like that in Ezek. xliv. 6, 'Thou shalt say to the rebellion,' מרד, *rebellion* instead of *rebellious*. Enmity in nature; the nature of God, and that of a corrupt man can never be reconciled.

In the first verse, observe, 1. A proposition. 'The carnal mind,' &c. 2. The proof. 1. Proposition. 1. The state, *enmity*. 2. The object of this enmity, *God*. 3. The subject or seat of it, *mind*. 4. The qualification, *carnal*. 2. The proof, 'It is not subject,' &c.; wherein observe, 1. Wilfulness. 'It is not subject.' The holiness of the law, like the light of the sun, dazzles its eyes, that he cannot endure it. If we be not God's subjects, we must be his enemies, for he that is not with Christ is against him. 2. Weakness. 'Neither indeed can be.' It cannot, *quia non vult*, because it will not, saith Haymo. It is an enemy to it, and therefore will not be subject to its determinations.

1. It cannot be perfectly subject. I may be subject to the material part, and outward bark, not to the spiritual and true intendment of the law. 2. It cannot *qua talis*, as such. Sin cannot be reconciled to God, neither can a sinner as a sinner. It must be some superior power that must conquer an enemy that hath possession of a strong fort.

Doct. I. A state of nature is a state of enmity against God. II. Man is naturally an enemy to the sovereignty and dominion of God. Not subject to the law of God. By law, I mean not here the moral law only, but the whole will and rule of God, which is chiefly discovered in his law.

For the first doctrine, a state of nature is a state of enmity against God. 1. For the explication. 2. The confirmation. 3. The application.

I. The explication; and, 1. What is meant by a natural man, or state of nature?

(1.) By a state of nature is not meant the human nature, or man as a creature consisting of body and soul; then Jesus Christ, who truly and really assumed the human nature, was an enemy to God as well as we. Therefore some that understand those scriptures which speak of the flesh hindering us, of the natural or fleshly body, are much mistaken; for if the flesh as created, and not as corrupted, did impose a necessity upon us of sinning, it would necessarily follow, that God did first place in us a natural enmity, and so is the author of all our sin. And also that Christ could not be free from this black character, if it be owned (as it must be), that he had a nature of the same kind and mould as ours are.

God did not in creation implant in us a principle of contrariety to him; neither could a God of infinite goodness dash any such blot upon man's nature, for he framed him in an exact harmony to his own will, and printed him a fair copy, without any *errata*, according to his own image, which is nothing but holiness and love. But our defection from God puts us into this state, which is maintained by our inherent and tumultuous lusts. In our creation there was an union to God; in our corruption a separation from him, whence ariseth an opposition to him, so that it is not created, but corrupted nature, which is here meant.

(2.) Every profane man is a natural man, and consequently an enemy. Wicked works are *demonstrativè*, demonstratively denials of God. 'In works they deny him,' Titus i. 16. 'Sensual,' and 'having not the Spirit,' are put together, Jude 19. That man that is actuated by sensuality, is not acted by the holy, but by the diabolical spirit. Luxurious persons, that make their belly their God, are termed 'enemies to the cross of Christ,' Phil. iii. 18. And if enemies to the cross of Christ, then enemies to God, who was engaged in the greatest design that ever was upon the stage of heaven and earth, at the time of Christ's being upon the cross. And if enemies to the cross of Christ, then enemies to all those attributes of wisdom, power, holiness, truth, justice, mercy, which God glorified in the death of Christ, and in the most illustrious manner.

(3.) Every unrenewed man, though never so richly endowed with morals, is a natural man. What is called *φρόνημα σαρκὸς* in the text, is called, 1 Cor. ii. 14, *ψυχικος ἄνθρωπος*, one that hath nothing excellent but a rational soul. As *ψυχικὸς* is opposed to *πνευματικὸς*, it is a soul jointured in the richest dowry of nature. And as opposed to *σαρκικὸς*, a fleshly man, it notes a freedom from gross pollutions and defilements without. A *ψυχικὸς ἄνθρωπος*, is one led by the rational dictates of his mind, and *σαρκικος* is a man led by his sensitive affections. Though the one be better than the other, and more agreeable to the order of nature, yet both being corrupted and defiled, are contrary to God.

Suppose a man with the highest endowments of reason, wisdom, understanding, learning, as wise as Solomon, and suppose him as rich in morals as in intellectuals; yet if he be not 'renewed in the spirit of his mind,' Rom. xii. 2, *i. e.* the more spiritual and rational part of his soul, though there be never so fair a frontispiece, colour, and pretences of friendship, yet such a man is an enemy; because by all that strength of nature he cannot have a knowledge of spiritual things, or a faith in God; and without a knowledge of him, he cannot be subject to him; and without faith it is impossible to do any thing to please him.

The most civilised heathens, who disdained those ugly and carnal sins of drunkenness, lust, &c., yet were possessed by the more spiritual legions of pride and vain glory, &c. Though you have not outwardly the impurity of the flesh, yet you may flow with a greater impurity of the spirit. External acts of pollution are more abhorred by reason, because they are more brutish, they degrade the nature of a man, and disgrace his person. But in heart-sins, though there be not so much of discredit, there is more of enmity.

2. What kind of enmity this is. (1.) I understand it of nature, not of

actions only. Every action of a natural man is an enemy's action, but not an action of enmity. A toad doth not envenom every spire of grass it crawls upon, nor poison every thing it toucheth, but its nature is poisonous. Certainly every man's nature is worse than his actions: as waters are purest at the fountain, and poison most pernicious in the mass, so is enmity in the heart. And as waters relish of the mineral vein they run through, so the actions of a wicked man are tinctured with the enmity they spring from, but the mass and strength of this is lodged in his nature. There is in all our natures such a diabolical contrariety to God, that if God should leave a man to the current of his own heart, it would overflow in all kind of wickedness: for the best mere nature has fundamentally and radically as much of this enmity, as the worst; for the disposition is the same, though the effects may be restrained in some men more than in others. No man is any more born with a love to God, than he is with the knowledge of the highest sciences. There is indeed an active power to the attainment of those by the assistance of a good education; but man hath only a passive power to the other, as being a subject passively capable of the grace of God. The inherency of this enmity in our nature the psalmist expresses, when he tells us, 'The wicked are estranged from the womb, they go astray as soon as ever they be born,' Ps. lviii. 3, 4. They go sinfully, before they go naturally. Their poison is like the poison of a serpent, which you know is radically the same in all of the same species.

(2.) It is a state of enmity. Godly men may do an enemy's action, but they are not in a state of enmity. They may be cheated into sin, but they do not dwell in it; they may fall into it as a man into a ditch, but they lie not in it. There may be some jarrings between God and a regenerate man; God may be displeased with him, and he disgusted with God, and jealous of him, as in the case of Jonah, a type of Christ, but there is not a stated war. But a natural man is in a state of universal contrariety.

[1.] All times, it is rooted in the nature of a man. It is called a 'root of bitterness,' planted in a man's disposition: therefore bitterness is a quality essential to it, and inseparable from it: for while it remains a root, it will remain bitter.

You can never suppose a thing to exist, and be without its nature, and the modes and qualities due to such a being; or a man to live, and be without a soul. So you cannot suppose a corrupted creature to be one moment of time without this enmity, no more than a serpent can be imagined to retain its nature without the venom inherent in it, though there is not at all times the discovery of it.

[2.] In every sinful act. Though the interest of particular sins may be contrary to one another, yet they all conspire in a joint league against God. *Scelera dissident.** Sins are in conflict with one another; covetousness and prodigality, covetousness and intemperance, cannot agree, but they are all in an amicable combination against the interest of God. In betraying Christ, Judas was acted by covetousness, the high priest by envy, Pilate by popularity, but all shook hands together in the murdering of Christ.† And those various iniquities were blended together, to make up one lump of enmity. Though in every sin there is not an express hatred of God, yet there is *odium Dei participativè*, some participation of hatred of him. As all virtuous actions partake of the nature of love to the chiefest good, our beloved object; so all vicious actions, which are at a distance from the chief end, are marshalled by, and tinctured with, that inward enmity which lurks in the soul.

[3.] Objectively universal, against all the attributes of God. For sin

* Seneca.

† Jenkin, Jude, part ii. p. 522.

being an opposition to the law of God, is consequently a contrariety to his will, and his understanding, and therefore to all those attributes which flow from his will, as goodness, righteousness, truth; and his understanding, as wisdom, knowledge. Though every law proceeds from the will of the lawgiver, and doth formally consist *in actu voluntatis*, yet it presupposes *actum intellectus*, *i. e.* though it consists in the will of the lawgiver, yet it presupposes the wisdom of the lawgiver to be the fountain. As the understanding of God precedes the act of his will, so every sin being against the will of God, is also against the infinite reason and wisdom of God, which is the foundation of all his laws.

(3.) This enmity against God is habitually seated in the mind. Corruption extends its empire as large as regeneration; but this is seated in the mind, and the most spiritual part of it; 'renewed in the spirit of your mind,' Rom. xii. 2; it does not content itself with the outworks of the affections, but triumphs in the chiefest forts of the soul, and there displays its banners. The great contest between God and the devil is in the understanding and will. The standards are first erected there. As in conversion, the mind is first enlightened by God, and the will first inclined; so in seduction, they are first possessed by Satan.

Hence a natural man is described to be one that fulfils 'the desires of the mind,' as well as 'of the flesh,' Eph. ii. 3. In this part, wherein God placed the most splendid part of his image, does Satan diffuse his poison; and wisdom, the chiefest flower in the rational part of man, is infected with this plague, for that is devilish too, James iii. 15. The mind thus infected, is like those eminent persons that spread the contagion of their vices to all their attendants. If it be thus in the noblest and governing part of the soul, it must be so also in the other faculties, which are directed by it, and observe the dictates of it. The other faculties, like common soldiers in a war, fight for the prey and booty;* but the mind, the sovereign, being filled with principles of a more direct contrariety to God, fights for the superiority, and orders all the motions of the lower rout.

But more particularly, there is *odium aversionis*, as opposed to desire. Thus man hates God, because he turns from him. . Man naturally gives his vote for God's absence, and is so far from loving the practice, that his stomach abhors the knowledge of God's ways; that say unto God, 'Depart from us, for we desire not the knowledge of thy ways,' Job xxi. 14. That 'say unto God.' No creature durst be so bold to say it to God's face; but it is the language of our natures, though not of our tongues, We desire not the knowledge of thy ways. The laws and ways of God, which he commands us to walk in, are too holy, righteous, and spiritual for our corrupted nature.

By sin we stand indebted to God, and therefore have an aversion from him; as debtors hate the sight of their creditors, and are loath to meet them. Adam fled from God when he had run upon God's score: sin is a disease, and so contrary to that physic which would abate the violence of the humour. God's presence and purity is too dazzling a sight for sinful men; and therefore they cannot look upon God, but are like sore eyes that are distempered with the sun.

Again, there is *odium prosecutionis*, which implies a detestation opposite to love and affection. And so there is not only an aversion from God, but an opposition to him. Both those parts of hatred are described: 'And you that were sometime *alienated*, and *enemies* in your minds by wicked works,' Col. i. 21.

Here is *alienation*, which is aversion; and *enmity*, which is opposition;

* Gurnal's Christian Armour, something changed.

and both seated in the mind: though some expound alienation according to outward, enmity according to inward, estate. But the apostle declares hatred to be complete in those two, alienation and enmity, which is both in mind and works; mind as the seat, works as the issues of it. Enemies in disposition and action, principle and execution.

This *odium persecutionis* is, 1, natural, which we call antipathy. And there are steps of this among many creatures: many men have an abhorrency to some kinds of meats, and can never endure the taste, nor the sight; and if unawares they eat any of that disagreeing sort, it breeds a distemper in the body. Some men have had an antipathy at the sight of some creatures, as Germanicus, according to Plutarch's relation, could not endure the crowing of a cock; another the smell or touch of a rose. Antipathies have been observed between some creatures after they are dead. The entrails of a lamb and wolf upon the same instrument can never be tuned; the blood of dragons and eagles can never mix together; some plants will not grow by one another. There is not such a hatred absolutely between God and man, though there be between God and sin; because there may be a reconciliation between God and a sinner, but not between God and sin; for antipathies are irreconcileable.

The enmity between God and a sinner is not founded in nature, but corrupt nature; and this nature may be removed by satisfaction and regeneration. A fundamental reconciliation was the great intendment of God in the death of Christ; for he was in him as in his ambassador, reconciling the world unto himself; and an actual reconciliation is made between God and a particular soul at the first instant of faith; though this reconciliation be made between God and man, yet not between God and the corrupt nature of man; for it would be against God's nature to be reconciled to that, though he be his creature; because since his nature is infinitely good, he cannot but love goodness, as it is a resemblance of himself, and consequently cannot but abhor unrighteousness, as being most distant from the nature; and therefore never will express any dearness or intimacy to man's corrupted nature, but to man justified and regenerate.

But the enmity which is between God and sin is founded in the nature of God, and the nature of sin. Sin being the *summum malum*, the greatest evil, is naturally most opposite to God, who is the *summum bonum*, the greatest good. So that God can never be reconciled to sin, or sin to God; for on the one side God must part with his holiness, or sin with its malice and impurity, and so God cease to be God, or sin cease to be sin.

As God is unchangeably good both in nature and decree, so sin is unchangeably evil. As God can never cease to be good, so sin can never cease to be sin; because the natural imprinted law of God can never cease to be his law, because it is grounded upon eternal principles of righteousness. God's nature is against sin; for if his hating sin were a mere voluntary act, he might then either love it or detest it, which he pleased. But is God unrighteous, to love unrighteousness? No, it is a voluntary, natural* act.

The hatred sin hath to God hath no mixture of love; the hatred a man has to God may have some mixture of a natural love, because of the kindness he knows he receives from God.

2. Acquired hatred, which is grounded upon diversity of interests. Various interests must have contrary means for the attainment of their ends. The interest of a sinner as such, *qua talis*, consists in gratifying the importunities of his lusts, in finding out occasions of pleasures; and the interest of God lies in vindicating the righteousness of his commands, and maintaining the truth of his threatenings.

* Qu. 'not a merely voluntary, but a natural'?—ED.

This is either, 1, direct. When a man burns with a desire of revenge against another for some real or supposed affront, endeavouring to do him all the ill offices in his power. This none but the despairing and malicious devils are guilty of, who know themselves to be under an inevitable sentence. In this, some place the sin against the Holy Ghost, and make it to be a direct and malicious hatred of God. But that will be a question, whether a creature, in a possibility and probability of salvation, and presuming upon mercy, can maliciously take up arms against God as God; for, as I believe, there is no settled opinionative atheism in the world, nor a man ever in any age that did deliberately think there was no God; so I believe there is no settled malice against God.

But there may be a malicious contempt of Christ, such as Julian's was, who in scorn termed him the Galilean: 'They have hated me and my Father also,' John xv. 24; me directly, my Father interpretatively or virtually, through many sins; as when he saith, 'Those that have seen me, have seen my Father also,' John xiv. 9; me plainly, evidently, in my person and works; my Father virtually, as I am his extraordinary ambassador in the world to represent him, and because they have seen the power of my Father acting in and by me in the miracles I have wrought; so that they hated the Father as they had seen him, *i. e.* not directly, but in his agent, our Saviour. Their hatred of God was as their sight of God had been.

2. *Implicitè et interpretativè. Idem velle et nolle est proprium amicorum.* Lovers are said to have but one soul, and therefore but one will. Men love not the things that God loves, and therefore may be said to hate him. A man may be said to hate God, as men are said to wrong their own souls, and love death, and despise their own souls: 'He that sins against me, wrongs his own soul: all they that hate me, love death,' Prov. viii. 36; 'He that refuseth instruction, despiseth his own soul,' Prov. xv. 32. *Consecutivè*, as they do those things that will be an injury unto, and bring death upon, them; as a thief may be said in this sense to hate his own life, because he doth those things which will be the occasion and meritorious cause of his destruction.

For no man formally loves death, as death, or despises his own soul, but in doing those things, the effects whereof are such as a man may be said to contemn himself; so men, acting those things which jostle with God's law, and stand diametrically opposite to his will, are said to hate God. In this respect sin is called a contempt of God, not formal and express, but implicit and interpretative, because by sin the law of God is contemned, and consequently the authority, will, and wisdom of the lawgiver: 'They that despise me shall be lightly esteemed,' 1 Sam. ii. 30.

The nature of hatred being thus explained, let us see what kind of enmity against God this is. *First*, negatively. We hate not God *as God*. It is not the primary intention of a creature to set itself against the nature of God; and indeed it is impossible, because God, absolutely considered, hath all the attractives of love, since the noblest perfections of the creatures are in a more excellent manner united in him as the original. As a man cannot will sin as sin, because it is purely evil, and therefore cannot be the object of the desire, since his will is carried out to things under the notion of good, so we cannot hate God as God, because of the amiableness of his nature; and what we conceive good cannot be the object of contempt. No man can hate truth as truth, or good as good, because the one is the proper object of his understanding, the other of his will, though he may hate them both under an apprehension that they are evil and inconvenient to him.

God in himself, as he is known by an open vision, cannot be a motive to enmity;* no, not to the devils themselves; but as they apprehend his nature destructive of their well-being.

We never yet met with any so monstrously base as to hate a creature as a creature, or man as man; not a toad or a serpent as a creature, but as it is venomous. And though Timon was surnamed μισάνθρωπος, because possessed with a melancholy kind of hatred, yet he professed he hated bad men because of their vices, and good men, because they did not concur with him in so intense and exact a hatred of the enormities of the world. And as it is impossible that we should hate a creature under the notion of a creature, because there is nothing in the simple notion of a creature contrary to us, but in regard of some appropriated nature of this or that creature of a different or contrary stamp to our own, so neither can we hate God as God, because in the general and abstracted notion of God there is nothing contrary to man, no, nor to corrupted man, but he is an infinite mirror of goodness and ravishing loveliness.

Again, we hate not God *as creator and preserver*. Hatred always supposes some injury, either real or imaginary, or at least the fear of some; and our hatred doth evaporate when we find him to be good whom we hated under a conceit of being bad, or when our supposed injuries are recompensed by comforting benefits. What servant can disdain his master for feeding him? or what child hate his father for begetting and maintaining him? This is contrary to the common sparks of ingenuity which are in the natures of men, and against their natural interest. Reason will acquaint men with a first cause, and that their beings are produced and preserved by a power superior to their own. Who can loathe this infinite Sun for the constant refreshment they receive by his beams and influences, any more than a man can hate the created sun for the kindly warmth darted upon him? In this respect natural men, from a common ingenuity, have some starts of love to God, though this is not a love of a right impression, because it respects not the excellency of God's nature, but the agreeableness of his benefits to us, and so is rather a self-love, as terminated principally in our own welfare, sustained and increased by the influence of his providence. Sometimes this love to God, which a wicked man thinks himself endued with, is rather an enmity, when he loves God with an only respect to his own corrupt ends; as when he professes an affection to God for his preservation, that he may the longer continue in the society of his darling lusts; or when he loves God for the wealth he gives him, because he hath thereby the more materials for his luxury and voluptuousness. This is such an affection to God which may be termed an enmity, since it is subordinate to the love of his brutish lusts. It is a love of him for those mercies which he turns into fuel to support his natural contrariety against God.

Secondly, positively.

1. We hate God *as a sovereign*. Man cannot endure a superior; he would be uncontrollable. Pharaoh's principle, that would acknowledge none above him, but proclaimed war against heaven, this dwells naturally in every one: 'Our lips are our own, who is Lord over us?' Ps. xii. 4; 'Who is the Lord, that I should obey his voice to let Israel go? I know not the Lord, neither will I let Israel go,' Exod. v. 2. How contemptibly doth he speak of God, which is the dialect of every man's heart! Who is the Lord, that I should obey his voice, and let my dearest carnal pleasures go? I know not the Lord, neither will I let them depart from me. A desire of being like to God, or equal to him in wisdom, was the first sin of man after the creation, as to be equal to God in authority and power was the first sin of devils, a

* Non potest esse motivum voluntatis ad odium.—*Banet. in* 22 *da. q.* 34. *art.* 2.

renouncing of God's dominion. God, by a positive law, enjoined man not to eat of the forbidden fruit, a thing in itself indifferent, but commanded for the trial of his obedience, to see whether he would own a subjection to God's absolute will, and abstain from things desirable in themselves, because of the mere pleasure of the Creator. But by his transgression he disowned God's right of commanding, and his own duty of obeying.

The devil knows by his own temper what bait man was most like to catch at, since the noblest creature among the animals aims most at superiority and victory. Nebuchadnezzar, who was for this aspiring humour to be accounted and worshipped as a sovereign god, was as deservedly as disgracefully turned a-grazing among the beasts; and the great charge at the last day against the sons of men will be, that they would not have God, or Christ of his appointment, to reign over them.

We hate God *as a lawgiver*, as he is *peccati prohibitor*, Luke xix. 27. It is impossible that man should do otherwise, as considered in the nature wherein he stands, because it is as natural to us to abhor those things which are unsuitable and troublesome, as to please ourselves in things agreeable to our minds and humours. But since man is so deeply in love with sin, accounting it the most estimable good, he cannot but hate the law which checks it, both the external precept and the counterpart of it in his own conscience, because the strictness of the commands molest and shackle him in his agreeable course, and the severity of its threatenings stare him in the face with curses; as the sea foams most, and casts up most mire, when the impetuousness of it is restrained by some rock, or bounded by the shore.

It is not the law that provokes us to sin directly, but accidentally, because of our corruption, contrary to the image of God's purity in the precept; for we look upon God as cruel, and injurious to our liberty and well-being, and commanding those things which in our apprehensions do thwart and contradict our pleasures. This conceit was the hammer whereby the hellish Jael struck the nail into our first parents, which hath conveyed death and damnation, together with the same imagination, to all their posterity: 'God doth know, that in the day you eat thereof, your eyes shall be opened; and you shall be as gods, knowing good and evil,' Gen. iii. 5. Alas! poor soul; God knows what he did when he forbade you that fruit; he was jealous you should be too happy, and it was a cruelty in him to deprive you of a food so pleasant and delicious! It was for this end the law was given with thunderings and lightnings from mount Sinai, to enforce an awe upon men, God well knowing how apt we are to break the hedges, and fly from restraints.

The sum is, man would be as a lamb in a large place, like a heifer sliding from the yoke, Hos. iv. 16, Mal. i. 13. He snuffs at the command of his Lord, and would be subject to no law but his own, and be guided by no will but that of the flesh. Have you not many times wished that there were no law, or that it were not so strict as to check your darling lusts? What is this, but an enmity to the authority of that law you account so burdensome?

2. We hate God *as a judge; as autor legis* and *ultor legis; as peccati prohibitor* and *pœnæ executor*. Fear is often the cause of hatred.* All men have a fear of God, not of offending him, but of being punished by him. Corruption kindles this enmity, but fear, like a bellows, inflames it. When men know they deserve punishment, they must needs fear, and consequently disaffect both the author and the inflicter of it. Guilt makes malefactors tremble at the report of a judge's coming. All the perfections of God, though never so amiable, cannot produce any true spiritual love in a natural man, though he be never so specious in the eye of the world, or good-natured

* 'Ουδεὶς γαρ ὃ φοβεῖται φιλεῖ.—*Arist. Rhetor.* lib. ii. cap. iv.

to his fellow-creatures, while he lies under the apprehensions of wrath, and is in his own sense concluded under an eternal doom. If you should tell a prisoner that his judge is a brave, comely, genteel man, of excellent accomplishments and unspotted innocency, would this commend the person of the judge to the prisoner? No; because he considers him not in his intellectual or moral endowments, but in his political function, as a judge that will try, and condemn, and take away his life.

This hatred of God is stronger or weaker, according as the fear is, and therefore in hell it is in its meridian and maturity, and most proper to the damned spirits; but not so evident in this world, unless a man be brought into such a despairing condition as Spira was, who professed he hated God upon this account; because the acts of God as a judge are remote, and evils at a distance do not so much affect us, because we flatter ourselves with hopes of escape. It is the certainty and approach of judgment that inspires fear. Evils hurt us not by a single apprehension of their nature; for the contemplation may be delightful, as a picture of a storm at sea or a battle on land; but they affect us as they have relation to us; that which was the devil's language to Christ, 'What have we to do with thee, Jesus, thou Son of God? art thou come to torment us before the time?' Mat. viii. 29. This is the dialect of our hearts: 'Depart from us, we desire not the knowledge of thy ways,' Job xxi. 14, of holiness, nor thy ways of justice.

Well, then, did none of you ever rage against God under his afflicting hand? Were you never like wild beasts, ready to tear in pieces those that would take and tame you? Did you never wish that God were so careless, as to enact no law to hurt you; and so unrighteous, as to have no justice to punish you? Did you never wish him stripped of his preceptive will and his revenging arm? Have you not wished sometimes that the law might be as dead a letter in respect of curses as it is in respect of conveying strength for the performance of it? that it might be a silent law, like Eli to his sons, never to correct you?

3. When this fear rises high, or men are under a sense of punishment, they hate *the very being of God*. This rises so high, that it aims at the very essence of God, as in Spira's case, who wished that he could destroy him. Since all men are actuated by a principle of self-preservation, and that this principle is universally natural and predominant, it will move them to take away the life of any person, rather than lose their own life by them. When men look upon God as a judge and punisher of their crimes, if they could by any means, yea, by the undeifying of God himself, rescue themselves from those fears, there is self-love enough, and enmity enough against God in them, to quicken them to it. There is no doubt but the damned, if they could, would pull God out of his throne, to have ease from those dreadful torments they undergo. And whatsoever fearful apprehensions we have of God in this world, are but the lower degrees of that hatred which the damned have in the highest.

But that I may not send you so far as hell for a proof, I will assert that the wishing, nay, the endeavouring the destruction of God, is fundamentally and seminally in every one of our natures. I will appeal to yourselves. Did none of you ever please yourselves sometimes in the thoughts how happy you should be, how free in your lustful pleasures, if there were no God? Have you not one time or other wished there were no law given above to restrain you, no conscience within to check you, no judge hereafter to sentence you? And can God be hated worse than when the destruction of his inseparable perfections, his holiness, righteousness, are thought so desirable? It is a wishing the destruction of his being. Hatred is defined by one to be *appetitus amovendi rem aliquem.** As love is a desire of union, hatred must be a desire of separation. And Aristotle tells us that hatred is an affection of a higher strain than anger, because it desires the τὸ μὴ εἶναι, the very not being, of the hated object.

As the hatred of sin aims at the destruction of sin, and men's hatred of saints would cause their expulsion out of the world, so the hatred of God is a desire to despoil him of his being; and their not doing it is not for want of an innate disposition, but for want of strength; for men hate God more than the best saint doth sin. All hatred includes a virtual murder: 'Whosoever hates his brother is a murderer,' John iii. 15. If he who hates his brother is, in the court of exact judgment, a murderer of his brother, he that hates God is a murderer of God. The more self-love we have, the more we shall hate that which we judge destructive to us; because the more we wish well to ourselves, the more we wish ill to that which we imagine contrary to our well-being. And since we hate those acts of God which flow from the righteousness of his nature, we consequently rise up to a hatred of God's being; because he could not be God unless he loved righteousness, and hated iniquity; and he could not testify his love to the one, or his loathing to the other, but in encouraging goodness, and witnessing his anger against iniquity.

Man would have God at the greatest distance from him, and there is no greater distance from being than not being, Job. xxi. 14, 'who say unto God, Depart from us,' and Ps. xiv. 1, 'The fool hath said in his heart, No God,' as it is in the Hebrew, I wish there were no God; and this is founded upon sin, for the reason rendered is, that 'they are corrupt, and have done abominable works.' Hence is sin by some called *deicidium*, a slaughtering of God, because every sin, being enmity to God, doth virtually include in its nature the destruction of God; and since every man naturally is a child of the devil, and is acted by the diabolical spirit, 'the spirit that now works in the children of disobedience,' Eph. ii. 2, he must necessarily have that nature which his father hath, and the infusion of all that venom which the spirit that acts him is possessed with, though the full discovery of it may be restrained by various circumstances. And this assertion seems to be intimated in the death of Christ, for when we see for the satisfaction of the dishonour done to God, Christ must die for sin, it intimates that if it were possible God should die by sin. If sin can be expiated by no less than the blood of God, it seems to imply that in its own nature it aims at no less than the life of God, because all God's punishments are founded *in lege talionis*, and are highly equitable.

For confirmation that a state of nature is a state of enmity. The very design of Christ's coming into the world being an errand of peace, and the management of this design, both when he was conversant in the world and since his ascension, being to reconcile God and man, to promote by his Spirit an acceptance of this reconciliation, plainly discovers the state man was in, wherein man injured God and was punished by him, for what need of piecing up a friendship if there had not been an antecedent enmity?

There was a moral enmity against God on our parts, which must needs draw a legal enmity on God's part against us; but the apostle in Rom. v. 10 declares it, 'If when we were enemies we were reconciled to God.' If when we were enemies, *we, all of us*; not the best saint on earth, nor the most illustrious glorified saint in heaven, but had once this black character of being God's enemy; not a son of Adam but inherited this abominable character, and had this hostile disposition boiling up against God. Every

* Scaliger Exercit. 316, s. i.

man naturally is like the lake of Sodom, that no holy motion can flutter over it, but falls down dead, being choked by those steams which exhale from the corruption of the heart. 'Haters of God,' Rom. i. 30, Θεοστυγεῖς. Στυγεω signifies to hate a thing as hell; it is derived from Στύξ, one of the poetical rivers of hell, and signifies a more intense and rooted hatred than the expression of the LXX, Ps. cxxxix. 21, μισουντες θεόν. The most desperate enemy God hath now in hell of mankind had not a blacker soul at his nativity than every one of us had at ours, Tit. i. 16. The apostle tells us of some that denied God though they professed they knew him. They knew him notionally and denied him practically, yea, every attribute of his and his very being. Denied God! There are the characters of a Deity engraven upon every man by nature, so deeply in men's consciences that it is impossible for all the malice of the devil to raze it out. But if we make a judgment of men's hearts by the counterpart of them in their lives, and consider men's practices, which are the best indexes of their principles, we shall quickly find by tracing the streams how corrupt the fountain is.

This enmity is against the sovereignty of God. Men will not have God reign over them; they will not have God for their governor nor his law for their rule. Our created arms cannot reach heaven to pull God from his throne, but there is a radical disposition in man to do it, had he ability equivalent to his corruption; for what is the great quarrel between God and man but this, whose will and whose authority shall stand? While we exclude him from being the Lord of our hearts, we would exclude him from being the Lord of the world, for that unjust principle which doth deprive him of the heart would deprive him also of the other, to which God hath no greater right nor no juster title than he hath to our heart, over which we will not let him reign.

Sin is therefore called rebellion, which is a denial of subjection to him as our Lord; it is an act of disloyalty, a breach of allegiance. As the Jews say of every judgment that is upon them, that there is some of the dust of the golden calf, *i. e.* something of the punishment of their first idolatry, so we may say that in every sin there is a taint of that first prodigious ambition of our first parents, which cost them and their posterity so dear, viz. that we would be as gods, we would be God's equals, if not superiors.

PART II.

Enmity against God as a Sovereign.

The enmity against the sovereignty of God is in three things: 1. In the breach of God's laws; 2. In setting up other sovereigns; 3. In usurping God's prerogative.

First, In the breach of God's laws. That servant that doth not perform his master's command doth virtually deny his authority. If obedience be a sign of love, disobedience is an argument of hatred. 'If you love me, keep my commandments,' John xiv. 15. If obedience to God ennobles us with the glorious title of God's friend, John xv. 14, disobedience to God must needs expose us to the unworthy character of his enemies. And indeed the breach of God's laws is not only a discarding his sovereignty, but a casting dirt upon his other attributes; for if his 'command be holy, just, and good,' if it be the image of God's holiness, the transcript of his righteousness, and the efflux of his goodness, then in the breach of it all those attributes are despised. The law is then slighted as it is a medal of God's holiness, as it is equitable in itself, and as it is in its goodness designed for our conveniency and advantage; therefore by the breach of one point of the law we contract virtually the guilt of the contempt of the whole statute-book of God, 'Whosoever shall keep the whole law, and yet offend in one point, he is guilty of all,' James ii. 10, 11, because the will and authority of the lawgiver, which gives the sanction to it, is opposed, also because that the authority of the lawgiver, which is not prevalent with us to restrain us from the breach of one point, would be of as little force with us to restrain us from the breach of all the rest when occasion is offered, because also the breach of any one law declares a want of that love which is the sum and spirit of the whole law.

This enmity to God's law will appear in these ten things.

1. Unwillingness to know the law of God, inquire into it, or think of it. Men affect an ignorance of God's command; they are loath to inform themselves; they hate the light, which would both discover their spots and direct their course.

Hence those expressions, 'Refusing to hearken, and stopping the ears that we should not hear,' Zech. vii. 11; 'None understands; there is none that seeks after God,' Rom. iii. 10. Unwillingness to seek the knowledge of him; yea, though it be the most advantageous and refreshing to their soul, 'yet they would not hear,' Isa. xxviii. 12. When God presses in upon them by inward motions, or outward declarations of his will, they secretly desire God not to trouble them with his laws, though their hearts bear witness to the righteousness of them; 'which say to the prophets, Prophesy not unto us right things: cause the Holy One of Israel to cease from before us,' Isa. xxx. 10, 11. Let not the Holy One of Israel trouble us with any of his laws, but leave us to our sinful labour. Herein God placed their rebellion: 'Rebellious children, that will not hear the law of the Lord,' ver. 9. They would have smooth things prophesied to them; they would partake of his mercy, but would not imitate his holiness.

And when any motion of the Spirit thrusts itself in to enlighten them, they 'exalt themselves against the knowledge of God,' 2 Cor. x. 5, and resist the Holy Ghost; keep their hearts barred, that he may not have admittance. The word ἀντιπίπτετε, Acts vii. 51, is emphatical, to fall against, as a stone or any other ponderous body falls against that which lies in its way. They would dash in pieces or grind to powder that very motion which is made for their instruction; yes, and the Spirit too which makes it; and that not in a fit of passion, but from an habitual enmity always. Whereas a faithful subject or servant, who loves his prince or master, would fain know what his will is, and what laws are ordered, that he may observe them. But when men have a superficial knowledge of God's laws by education, or attendance upon a godly and able ministry, yet they are loath to retain it, negligent in improving it; they easily let it slip from them; their minds have not delight to employ themselves in meditating of it, or to know the spirit of it, which the psalmist fixes as the character of a godly man, Ps. i. 2.

Men are more generally fond of the knowledge of anything than of God's will. Do not the most of men that are intent upon knowledge spend more time, and engage more serious and affectionate thoughts, in the study of some science or trade than in the knowledge of God's will? With what readiness and dexterity will a man discourse about philosophy, mathematics, history, &c.; but any discourse of God begun in company strikes them dead; he is quite at a loss in the knowledge of him and his will, which was the great end of his coming into the world, and the great concern of his soul.

But if a man doth desire to know the law of God, it is many times more out of a curiosity and natural itch to know, than any design to come under the power of it; therefore, many men that can dispute for the principles of religion are ashamed of the practice, and ashamed to discourse much of the practical part of it, which is a contradictory thing; for can the profession be honourable if the practice be vile? If the principles be true and good, and worthy to be known, why are they not practised? If the practice be disgraceful, why are the principles which lead to such practices professed and studied? Whence can this affected ignorance of God's laws, this careless inquiry into his will, arise, but from an enmity against it, for fear they should be disturbed by it in the pursuit of their carnal pleasures? Therefore they account the word of the Lord a reproach to them and their ways, and a trouble to have their consciences set on work by the law that galls them, Jer. vi. 10.

2. Unwillingness to be determined by any law of God. When men cannot escape the convincing knowledge of the law, but it breaks in upon them as the morning light, they set up their carnal resolutions against it. 'As for the word which thou hast spoken to us in the name of the Lord, we will not hearken unto thee,' Jer. xliv. 16; and harden their hearts with 'a stoutness' against God, Mal. iii. 13; 'Refuse to walk in his law,' Ps. lxxviii. 10. Though it be a 'strength to them,' yet they will not, Isa. xxx. 15; they would rather guide themselves to destruction than be under God's conduct to happiness; they would rather be their own rulers than God's subjects. Men naturally affect an unbounded liberty, would not have the bridle of a command to check them, or be hedged in by any law; they think it too slavish a thing to be guided by the will of another; they are well compared to the wild ass, that loves to snuff up the wind at her pleasure in the wilderness; they will take their own course, rather than come under the guidance of God, Jer. ii. 24. Since the law checks the inward operations of the soul, and would keep them from inward as well as outward compliances with sin, they therefore account it a heavy yoke to be so strictly regulated as not to have their secret retirements, and dalliances with sin in their thoughts.

'Let not God speak to us,' say the Jews, Exod. xx. 19, 20, 'lest we die.' One would think it was the terror of the thunder-claps wherewith the law was proclaimed that made them so unwilling to hear God speak to them. But the apostle tells us it was the hatred of the law itself: 'For they could not endure that which was commanded,' Heb. xii. 20; which particle, *for*, shews it to be a reason why they desired the word should not be spoken to them any more. They had a natural unwillingness to be guided by any statute of God's enacting. Had they been only afraid of those terrible lightnings, without any aversion to God himself, methinks they should not so suddenly after have preferred a golden calf, the similitude of the Egyptian idol, and put the name of God upon it, and ascribed to it their deliverance from Egypt, which had been wrought, not by a senseless calf, but an almighty and outstretched arm. Therefore, in the charge God brought against them, 'Because, even because they despised my judgments, and because their soul abhorred my statutes,' Lev. xxvi. 43, he accuseth them not only of despising his judgments, but of a rooted abhorrency of them even in their souls. There is not a law but the heart of man naturally hath a secret and rooted detestation of.

Hence man is said to make void the law of God, Ps. cxix. 126. They have 'made void thy law.' To make it of no obligation to them, as if it were an almanac out of date; which Christ calls a 'making the law of none effect,' Mat. xv. 6, ἠκυρώσατε; you have unlorded the law, put it out of commission, thrown off all the power and dominion of it, which law God values more than he doth the whole world, nay, the least tittle of it is so dear to him, that it shall stand when heaven and earth shall fall. And to vindicate the honour of it, he would have his Son to die for a satisfaction for the breach of it. So that if a man could destroy the whole world, it were not so bad as sin, which is an unlording that which is an act of God's royalty, a copy of his holiness, whereas the making the world was but an act of his wisdom and executive power; nay, God would not be so angry at it, because his power is by that contemned, but in this, his holiness, which is an attribute he doth particularly delight in.

3. The violence man offers to those laws, which God doth most strictly enjoin, and which he doth most delight in the performance of. If a man be willing to be determined by some law of God, it is not because it is his law, but because it doth not run counter to some beloved lust of his. But when God enjoins any thing which is against the beloved interest of the flesh, he flies out in rage against God, and the interest of his corrupt affection excites him to a loathing of that which is truly good. The strictness of the law, which natural men account their band and shackle, is the ground of their quarrel with God, the reason of their rage, and their counsel against God and his Christ: 'Let us break their bands, and cast away their cords from us,' Ps. ii. 3. All this was, ver. 1, 2, for the strictness of his law, which Grotius understands of the law of Moses, and all the rites of it, but meant certainly of the evangelical law of Christ, the psalm being a prophecy of him.

If a man be willing to comply with any law of God, it is as it prohibits some outward carnal sins; but the more spiritual the law, the more averse the heart. The more spiritual the law is, the more doth indwelling sin exercise its power, and endeavour to increase our slavery: 'The law is spiritual, but I am carnal, sold under sin,' Rom. vii. 14. The apostle there intimates that our carnality, our slavery to sin, the enmity of our hearts to God, is best discerned by comparing man with the spirituality of the law. The Jews were much for sacrifices, and very diligent in them, which were but the skirts of the law, and which God did not principally require at their hands; but for holiness, mercy, piety, and other duties most valued by God, they were mere strangers unto them. Men will grant God the lip and the ear, but deny him that which he most calls for, viz. the heart. The more earnestly conscience doth at any time urge the law, the more furiously will the flesh act against it. But 'sin taking occasion by the commandment, wrought in me all manner of concupiscence,' Rom. vii. 8. Like as the boisterous waves, which roar most at that bank or rock which forbids their progress; or like wind, which pent within the narrow compass of the earth, grows more violent.

Had not God commanded some things so strictly, they had not been broken so frequently. God's righteous laws, which are intended to check our corruptions, are occasions to enrage them, as the vapour in a cloud ends in a tearing clap of thunder when it meets with opposition. We shall find our hearts most averse from the observation of those laws which are eternal and essential to righteousness, which God could not but command, as he is a righteous governor; in the observance of which we come nearest to him, and express his image more illustriously. As those laws for an inward and spiritual worship of God, the loving God with all our heart and soul, God cannot, in regard of his holiness and righteousness, command the contrary to this. These our hearts most swell at, those our corruptions most oppose;

whereas those laws that are only morally positive, or those that are only positive, and have no intrinsic righteousness in them, but depend purely upon the will of the lawgiver, and may be changed at pleasure (which the other that have an intrinsic righteousness cannot), such as the ceremonial part of worship, and the ceremonial law among the Jews; these we can comply better with, than with those laws which have an essential righteousness in them, and express more in them the righteousness of God's nature.

4. Man hates his own conscience, when it puts him in mind of the law of God. Man cannot naturally endure a quick and lively practical thought of God and his law, and is an enemy to his own conscience, for putting him in mind of God. This is evidenced by our stifling of conscience, when it doth dictate any practical conclusions from the law, and would stamp suitable impressions upon the soul. As it is an evidence of an enmity in one man against another, when he cannot bear his company, nor endure to hear him speak, so it is an evidence of an enmity to God when a man cannot endure to listen to that which is in himself, and more intimate with him than any friend he hath, for the wholesome and necessary advice it gives him as God's viceroy in him. Which is not an enmity to conscience itself, or to its act of self-reflection, but to the matter of it as it is God's vicegerent and representative, and bears the marks of his authority in it, and presseth the holy law of God upon the mind and heart.

Because in other cases this self-reflecting act of conscience is welcome, and is cherished, where it doth not act in a way of sovereignty derived from God, but suitable to natural affections. As suppose a man hath in a passion struck his child that caused some great mischief to him, his conscience reflecting upon him afterwards will be welcome, and shall work some tenderness in him, which it shall not do in the more spiritual concerns of God, but shall rather be loathed by him as a busy-body. And by such frequent oppositions of conscience, this enmity does so far prevail, that the sovereignty of conscience seems to be quite cashiered, insomuch that it ceaseth with any efficacy to spur on the soul to good, or withdraw it from evil; and being overpowered by sinful habits, its commands grow weak, and it sits labouring like a magistrate that cannot stem the tide of ill manners in a commonwealth; it enjoins as if it had no mind to be observed. It is upon this account that men oftentimes cannot endure to hear any gracious discourses of God, because they excite unwelcome reflections in their own consciences, which, instead of reforming them, do more distemper them, as the sweetest perfumes affect a weak head with aches.

Now, since men hate their own consciences for putting them in mind of God's laws, it is clear that they hate God himself, because conscience is God's officer in them; since they would destroy the memorials and prints of God in the conscience, since they would destroy God's commissioner for doing his work, they would destroy God himself. The apostle therefore calls disobedience to the light of nature a contention: 'To them that are contentious, and obey not the truth,' Rom. ii. 8, ἐξ ἐριθείας, that act out of contention; it must be a contention against conscience, the light of nature, and consequently against God, for the apostle in that chapter speaks of disobedience to the light of nature; they obey not the truth, out of contention against it, and against God, who has published that truth, and had imprinted it on their souls as a guide to them; for God hath put into man a conscience as his deputy, to have a command over him, and to keep up his prerogative as a lawgiver in him.

And as the disowning the principles of the Christian doctrine after a taste and profession is a crucifying of Christ,—'Seeing they crucify to themselves the Son of God afresh, and put him to an open shame,' Heb. vi. 6,—and a real acting that in spirit upon his doctrine, which the Jews did upon his body, it being an accounting him an impostor, and disowning all the excellency of his person and offices, and an implicit assertion that there is nothing in him worthy their desire, and this crucifying, ἑαυτοῖς (it may be *in themselves* as well as *to themselves*), in themselves the common works of Christ upon them was in effect the killing of his person; so by the rule of proportion, every sin against conscience and blotting out common principles, is not only a contention against God, but an interpretative destroying of him and putting God to shame, who is the engraver of those principles and that law of nature in man.

5. Man sets up another law in him in opposition to the law of God. A sinner looks upon God as too severe a taskmaster, and his laws as too hard a yoke, as though God were cruel and injurious to the liberty of his creature, and envied man of well-being and a due pleasure. 'God knows that in the day you eat thereof, your eyes shall be opened,' Gen. iii. 5. It was the old charge the devil brought against God to Eve, and the same impressions he makes still upon the minds of those children of disobedience in whom he works, and fills them with unjust reflections upon God. Man having this conceit wrought in him will be a law to himself, and will frame a rule subservient to his own ends: 'But I see another law in my members, warring against the law of my mind,' Rom. vii. 23, which is called the law of sin, and is set up in a warlike and authoritative opposition against the law of God in the mind, νόμον ἀντιστρατευόμενον. This law of sin is nothing else but the setting up our own corrupt appetite and will against God. As corrupt reason is opposed to gospel, so corrupt will is opposed to law.

Sin having set up this law, makes it the measure and rule of righteousness, and measures also the righteousness of God's law by this law of its own framing, nay, measures the holiness and righteousness of God himself by it. This is horrible, to make God's law no holier than our own, and to square God's holiness and righteousness according to our conceptions, as if God's holiness were to be tried by our measures and judged by our corruption. 'Thou thoughtest I was altogether such a one as thyself,' Ps. l. 21. This men do when they plead for sins as little, as venial, as that which is below God to take notice of; because they themselves think it so, therefore God must think it so too. Man, with a giant-like pride, would climb into the throne of the Almighty, and establish a contradiction to the will of God by making his own will, and not God's, the square and rule of his actions. This principle commenced and took date in paradise, when Adam would not depend upon the will of God revealed to him, but upon himself and his own will, and thereby makes himself as God.

This is the hereditary disease of all his posterity, to affect an independency, and leave God's directions, to be his own guide. And this is the great controversy that has been ever since between God and man, whether he or they shall be God, whether his reason or truths, or their reason, his will or theirs, be of most force, just as the dispute was between Pharaoh and God who should be God, whether the great Jehovah or a petty king of Egypt. And what saith the psalmist? They say of their tongues, 'Our tongues are our own,' who shall control us? But more truly the language of men's hearts, Our wills are our own, who shall check us? This is the thing God condemns in the Jews: 'A rebellious people, that walk after their own thoughts,' Isa. lxv. 2. They would set up their own thoughts above his precepts, as though their vain imaginations were a more just and holy rule than the infinite perfect will of God: 'We will walk after our own devices,' Jer. xviii. 12. We will be a law to ourselves; let God take his way and we will take ours.

It is not perhaps so heinous an idolatry to set up a graven image, a senseless and a sinless stock or stone, as for a man to set up his own sinful corrupt affections, and devote himself to a compliance with them in opposition to the righteous will of God.

6. In being at greater pains and charge to break God's law than is necessary to keep it. How will men rack their heads to study mischief, wear out their time and strength in contrivances to satisfy some base lust, which leaves behind it no other recompense but a momentary pleasure, attended at length with inconceivable horror, and cast off that yoke which is easy and that burden which is light, in the keeping whereof there is great reward: 'Wherewith shall I come before the Lord? Will the Lord be pleased with thousands of rams, or with ten thousands of rivers of oil? Shall I give my first-born for my transgression? the fruit of my body for the sin of my soul?' Micah vi. 7, 8. They in the prophet would be at the expense of one thousand of rams and ten thousands of rivers of oil, offer violence to the principles of nature, give the first-born of their bodies for the sin of their souls rather than to 'do justice, love mercy, or walk humbly with God;' things more easy in the practice than the offerings they wished for.

Thus men would rather be sin's drudges than God's freemen, and neglect that service wherein is perfect freedom for that wherein there is intolerable slavery; they will make a combustion in their consciences, violate the reason of their minds, impair the health of their bodies in contradicting the laws of God, and prefer a sensual satisfaction with toil here and eternal ruin hereafter, before the honour of God, the dignity of their nature, or happiness, or peace and health, which might be preserved with a cheaper expense than they are at to destroy them.

7. In doing that which is just and righteous upon any other consideration rather than of obedience to God's will, when men will indent with God, and obey him so far as may comport with their own ends. Unless God will degrade himself to submit to the conditions of their interest, they will pay him no duty of obedience nor render him a grain of service. What is hypocrisy, a sin so odious to God, but performing duties materially good upon any other consideration rather than that of God's sovereignty?

(1.) Out of respect to some human consideration. When men will practise some points of religion, and walk in the track of some laws of God, not out of conscience to the command, but the agreeableness of it to their honour, constitution, or nature, out of the sway of a natural generosity, the dictate of carnal reason, the bias of secular interest, not from an holy affection to God, an ingenuous sense of his authority, or voluntary submission to his will, as when a man will avoid intoxication, not because God forbids it, but because it is attended with bodily indispositions, or when a man will give alms, not with respect to God's injunction, but to his own natural compassion, or to shew his generosity. This is obedience to his own preservation, the interest of moral virtue, not to God.

Though it may look like virtue, yet when it is done from custom and example, without a due regard to our sovereign, we may in the doing it be rather accounted apes than Christians, or indeed men. This seems to be obedience in the act, but disobedience in the motive, for it is not a respect to God, but to ourselves; at the best it is but the performance of the material part without the spiritual manner, which is most regarded by God. Besides, if we observe any law upon the account of its suitableness to our natural sentiments or carnal designs, we shall as readily disobey when it crosses the purposes of our minds or desires of the flesh, for our obedience will be changeable according to the mutations we find in our own humours. How can that be entitled an affection to God which is as mutable as the interest of an inconstant mind?

'And Esau hated Jacob because of the blessing wherewith his father blessed him: and Esau said in his heart, The days of mourning for my father are at hand; then will I slay my brother Jacob,' Gen. xxvii. 41. So many children that expect at the death of their parents great inheritances, may be very observant of them, not because they respect God's commands in it, but because they would not frustrate their hopes by any disobligement. Esau had no regard of God in decreeing his brother's death, though he was awed by the reverence of his father from a speedy execution. He considered, perhaps, how justly he might lie under the imputation of hastening Isaac's death, by depriving him of a beloved son. But had the old man's head been laid, neither the contrary command of God, nor the nearness of a fraternal relation, could have dissuaded him from the act, any more than they did from the resolution.

Whence it is that many men abstain from gross sin only out of love to their reputation; they act that wickedness privately, which, if seen or taken notice of by others, would overspread their faces with blushing and confusion. He may have his mind in a brothel-house, notwithstanding God's prohibition, but restrain his body for fear of disgrace. He may commit murder in his heart, when the fear of punishment shall tie up his hands. Has not, then, our outward credit more power over us than God? And do we not sooner observe the opinion of the world, which frights us, than the authority of God, which commands us? Is it not a monstrous thing to be swayed by everything but the right motive? to let everything be a chain to bind us to the doing good, or eschewing evil, rather than God's law in his word, or the natural law of reason implanted in us? or to be moved rather by the examples of men that are just, or the customs of the places where we live, than to act in conformity to the righteous nature of God? How great an evidence is this of our enmity to God, or at least a great want of affection!

(2.) Out of affection to some base lust, some cursed end. The pharisees were devout in long prayers, not that God might be honoured, but themselves esteemed by men. Ambition may be the spring and soul of men's devotions. Jehu was ordered to cut off the house of Ahab; the service which he undertook was in itself acceptable, but corrupt nature acted that which holiness and righteousness commanded. God appointed it to magnify his justice, and Jehu acted it to satisfy his revenge or ambition: he did it to fulfil the will of his lust, not the will of his true Lord. Jehu applauds it as zeal, and God abhors it as murder, Hosea i. 4. We may shew our hatred to God, and provoke him, in doing the thing which he particularly enjoins us. This is a compliance with the design of some carnal lust, more than with the authority of the Lawgiver. It is a service not to God for his own sake, but to ourselves for our sin's sake. It is rather a casting down the will of God from commanding, to set our own in its place. Nothing more positively commanded, both in nature's law and the gospel, than to pray and worship God. Men may observe some laws, to have the better convenience to break others. The pharisees were great observers of this; they prayed, and, to outward appearance, devoutly, with a zeal (if zeal may be measured by length), but to what end? Not that God might be honoured, but themselves esteemed; nay, more cursed, to 'devour widows' houses,' that men might be induced, by that appearance of devotion, to make them executors of their wills, and guardians of their children; feoffees in trust for their widows, and so they might get a good share for themselves.

(3.) Out of a slavish fear. In the doing anything out of this principle, men are rather enemies than friends. 'There is no fear in love, but perfect love casteth out fear,' 1 John iv. 18, 'because fear hath torment.' If fear be inconsistent with love, it must be the property of hatred. If perfect love doth cast out fear, then perfect fear doth cast out love, and nourish enmity. If fear be a torment, the effects of it cannot be a pleasure; and the duties flowing from it have a spice of that hatred which is an inseparable companion of that passion, and are done rather to appease their fears than to pleasure their Creator. Just as Pharaoh parted with the Israelites, so do some men with some sins, not out of love to God's law, but for fear of a further wrath, or because of the smart of present judgments. Well then, how can we discharge ourselves from this accusation of enmity to God, when we will be excited to a performance of good, and abstinence from evil, by anything of a less authority, as the presence of a child, the sentiments of the world, the preservation of our own reputation, and the fear of punishment? So that actions materially honest in men, may be rather a fruit of passion than reason; and that which we call our obedience, a product of the bestial part in us, rather than that of the man.

8. In being more observant of the laws of men than of the law of God. The fear of man is a more powerful curb to retain men in their duty, than the fear of God; for men are restrained from breaking human laws for fear of the present penalties annexed to them, but they encourage themselves in the breach of divine by God's forbearance, whereby they attribute a greater right of dominion to a man than they will acknowledge to be in God. They 'willingly walk after the commandment of man,' though in case of idolatry; but like snails creep after the commandment of God, if they move at all. So they made the king glad with their lies, they cheered his heart with their ready obedience to his command for idolatry, against the counsel of God and warnings of the prophets. And they, contrary to the speech of Christ, fear him that can kill the body more than that God who can destroy both body and soul; and are scared more by the frowns of men than the power of God. It is natural in all ages. It was Jerome's complaint, *Timent leges humanas, at non divinas; quasi majora sint imperatorum scuta quam Christi, leges timemus, evangclia contemnimus.**

Without question man is obliged to obey his Creator without consulting whether his commands are agreeable to the institutions of men. For if we obey him because men's laws enjoin the same, we obey not God, but man; human laws being the chief motive of our obedience. This is to vilify God's sovereignty, and lay it under the hatches of men's authority, since we thus slight the duty which in point of right he may demand of us, and pay with ungrateful returns so liberal a benefactor; for men, whose laws we principally regard, were never the principal author of our being; and the instrumental preservation we have by them, is not without the providential influence of that Lord whose authority we subject to theirs. Why should we readily submit to human laws, and stagger at divine? Why should we depose God from his right of governing the world, and value men's laws above our Maker's? Why should we make God's authority of a less concern to us than that of a justice of peace or a petty constable; as though they were God's superiors, and obedience more rightfully due to them than to him? What a contempt of God is this; it is to tell God, I will break the Sabbath,

* Hierom. vol. i. epist ii. p. 11, b.

swear, revile, revel, were it not for the curb of national laws, for all thy precepts to the contrary.

9. In man's unwillingness to have God's laws observed by any. Man would not have God have a loyal subject in the world. What is the reason else of the persecution of those who would be the strictest observers of God's injunctions, as if they were the most execrable persons under the cope of heaven? What is the reason the seed of the serpent hates the seed of the woman with as much vehemency as the holy angels do the most prodigious villains? It is ordinary for profane men to look upon such as would walk before God unto all well-pleasing as strange and abominable monsters: 'Wherein they think it strange that you run not with them to the same excess of riot, speaking evil of you,' 1 Peter iv. 4. 'Speaking evil of you;' βλασφημοῦντες, railing, libelling the whole profession; loading them with many opprobrious epithets, because they will not be as diffusive in sensuality as themselves; because they run not, εἰς ἀσωτίας ἀνάχυσιν; thus censuring those acts of theirs, which were pleasing to God, at the bar of profaneness.

It is not for any wrong done to them that they thus hate them, but because they will not injure God and transgress his laws so much as themselves do. How clear a discovery is this of men's natural unwillingness to suffer God to have the least grain of obedience in the world, when they are angry that any bear a veneration to his laws, and that others will not run into the same career, and be in arms against God as well as they! Hence it is that the holiest persons have been most persecuted: amongst the Jews, Isaiah sawed to death, Jeremiah stoned, Zacharias killed at the altar, Elias put to flight; among the Christians, all the apostles but John put to death. The holiest men have been the greatest sufferers; among the heathen, Socrates condemned to poison. And the reason is, because they have more honourable thoughts of God, and would maintain the interest of God in the world.

10. In the pleasure we take to see his laws broken by others. Sin is the greatest evil that can happen to God; and there is nothing man doth more caress and gratify himself in than to see a creature bemired with it. And indeed sin is the very essence of most of the mirth in the world. Job so well knew it, that he rose every morning to make an atonement for his sons, who he knew could not be without many erratas in their jollities. This indictment the apostle brings among the rest against the Gentiles: 'Not only do the same, but have pleasure in them that do them,' Rom. i. 32. Do not men often make that the object of their laughter, which is the object of God's infinite hatred? Are not other men's sins the subject of our sport and mirth, which should be the subject of our pity and sorrow; pity to the sinner, and sorrow for the sin? What is this but an evidence of a rooted hatred of God in our nature, when we please ourselves with any dishonour done to him by others? For it is put among the noble attributes of love, 1 Cor. xiii. 6, that it 'rejoiceth not in iniquity,' neither its own iniquity nor other men's. To rejoice in it, then, must be an accursed quality belonging to hatred; yet how many are there in the world that cannot see others dishonour God without some sort of satisfaction! They are displeased with his glory, and pleased with his dishonour.

Secondly, We are enemies to God's sovereignty, in setting up other sovereigns in the stead of God. If we did dethrone God to set up an angel, or some virtuous man, it would be a lighter affront; but to place the basest and filthiest thing in his throne is intolerable. What we love better than God, what we sacrifice all our industry to, what we set our hearts most upon, what we grieve most for when we miss of our end, we prefer before God.

1. Idols. Though so palpable idolatry be not committed by us, yet it was natural to mankind, since we know all nations were overrun with it, Joshua xxiv. 2; since the father of the faithful was an idolater before he was a believer, and his posterity, the Jews, who had heard God himself speak to them from mount Sinai, were no sooner departed from the foot of the mountain but they adored a golden calf in his stead, and this sin did run in the blood of all their posterity; since we find God charging them with it through the whole Old Testament, and it was not rooted out till the seventy years' captivity in Babylon. And that the naturalness of it to mankind may further appear, consider what incentives against it the Jews had. They had the greatest appearances of God, particular marks of his favour, his judgments and statutes, which the psalmist, Ps. cxlvii. 19, 20, sets an emphasis upon, that he had not dealt so with every nation, no, not with any nation. They had the visible signs of his presence, the pillar of fire by night, the cloud by day; they were more particularly under his indulgent care; he had altered the course of nature, and wrought miracles for their deliverance, rained manna from heaven to spread their table, carried them in his bosom; yet those wretches were throwing down God to make room for their golden calf.

This idolatry is as absolute a degrading and vilifying of God as hell itself could invent; it is a real calling him by the names of all those loathsome, senseless creatures so odious as images of him. As if God were no better than a stone, a piece of carved brass or wood, of no greater excellency than an image or puppet. This is a denying of God. Job speaketh, that he had not kissed his hand, or made obeisance to idols; for then, saith he, 'I should have denied the God that is above,' Job xxxi. 28. It is called a loathing God, who is the husband of Christians; a loathing of all his authority over them, Ezek. xvi. 45. The giving adoration to an image which belongs to God, is a making it equal to him, if not above him; for by such a veneration they evidence that God is no better in their apprehension than the stock they worship. The heathen world is at this day drenched in this kind of idolatry, and most part of the Christian world are subject to the remains of this pagan sin; as the papists, who adore for their Saviour a little wafer, which perhaps the mice have bitten, and flies have cast their excrements upon.

2. We are enemies to God's sovereignty in setting up self. Man imagined at first that, by eating the forbidden fruit, he should have a knowledge of good and evil as to be independent upon God, and founded upon himself and his own will. This self in us is properly the old Adam, the true offspring of the first corrupted man. This is the greatest antichrist, the great anti-god in us, which sits in the heart, the temple of God, and would be adored as God; would be the chiefest, as the highest end. This is the great usurper in the world, for it invades the right of God; it is the most direct compliance and likeness to the devil, whose actions centre wholly in malicious self-will. In this respect, I suppose, the devil is called 'the god of this world,' because he acts so as if the world should only serve his ends.

Self is the centre of many men's religious actions, while God seems to be the object. Self is the end: 'Did you fast unto me?' Zech. vii. 5. This, being the motive of hypocrisy, makes it more idolatry, and so more odious to God. Other sins subject only the creature to self; but this subjects the soul, and even God himself, to corrupt self. Self-love leads the van: 'Men shall be lovers of their own selves,' 2 Tim. iii. 2. To that black catalogue he seems to speak of that black regiment which march behind it, and is concluded with a 'form of godliness, and denying the power of it;' and a denying the power of godliness is a denying the sovereignty of God. The righteousness a man would establish in opposition to God is called a man's own, a righteousness of his own framing, that hath its rise only from himself: Rom. x. 3, 'Going about to establish their own righteousness.'

Sin and self are all one; what is called a *living in sin* in one place, Rom. vi. 2, is a *living to self* in another: 'That they which live, should not live to themselves,' 2 Cor. v. 15. What a man serves, and directs all his projects, and the whole labour of his life to, that is his god and lord; and that is self. All inferior things act for some superior as their immediate end; this order hath nature constituted; the lesser animals are designed for the greater; the irrational for man, and man for something higher and nobler than himself; for all beings naturally should, in their several stations, tend to the service of the first being. Now to make ourselves the end, and all other things to act for ourselves, is to make ourselves the supreme being, to deny any superior as the centre to which our actions should be directed, and usurp God's place, who alone being the Supreme Being, can be his own end; for if there were anything higher and better than God, his own purity and goodness would cause him to act for that as more noble and worthy.

I appeal to you, whether you have not sometimes secret wishes that you were in the place of God? for where there is a slavish fear of him, there must needs be such wishes, according to the degrees of fear; and so you have wished God undeified, that you might be advanced to the godhead.

This some think to be the sin of the devils, affecting an independency on God by a proud reflection upon their own created excellency, and at least a delightful wish, if not an endeavour, to make themselves the ultimate end of all their actions.

3. We are enemies to God's sovereignty in setting up the world. When we place this in our heart, God's proper seat and chair, we deprive God of his propriety, and do him the greatest wrong, in giving the possession of his right to another. The apostle gives covetousness no better title than that of idolatry, Col. iii. 5; and the psalmist puts the atheist's cap upon the oppressor's head: 'Who eat up my people as they eat bread, and call not upon the Lord,' Ps. xiv. 4. What we make the chief object of our desires, is to us in the place of God. The poor Indians made a very natural and rational consequence, that gold was the Spaniards' god, because they hunted so greedily after it. This is an intolerable dethroning of God, to make that which is God's footstool to climb up into his throne; to bow down to an atom, a little dust and mud of the world, a drop out of the ocean; to set that in thy heart which God hath made even below thyself, and put under thy feet; and to make that which thou tramplest upon to tread down the right God hath to thy heart. Alas! who serves God with that care and with that spirit that he serves the world with?

4. We are enemies to God's sovereignty in setting up sensual pleasures. Love is a commanding affection, and gives the object a power over us; what we chiefly love we readily obey. Now men are said to be *φιλήδονοι μᾶλλον ἢ φιλόθεοι*, 2 Tim. iii. 4; a glutton's belly is said to be his god, because his projects and affections are devoted to the satisfaction of that, and he lays in not for the service of God, but a magazine for lust. If you preferred some honourable thing which might perfect your natures, as learning, wisdom, moral virtues, though this were an indignity to be censured by the Judge of all the world, yet it would be more tolerable; but to consecrate your heart and time to a sordid voluptuousness, and feed it with the cream of your strength, this is an inexcusable contempt, to pay a quick and lively service to an effeminate delight, which is only due to the supreme Lord.

Does not that man dethrone God, and hate him, that will be under the command of a swinish pleasure, and make that the supreme end of his life and actions, rather than to be under the righteous government of God? The greatest excellency in the world is infinitely below our Creator, how much more must a bestial delight be below him, which is so exceedingly disgraceful to, and below the nature of man! If we should love all the creatures in heaven and earth above God, it were more excusable than to degrade him in our affections beneath a brutish pleasure. Why doth any man court an ignoble sensuality, with the displeasure of God, hell, and damnation at the end of it, if he did not value it above God, as well as above his own soul? The more sordid anything is that we set up in the place of God, the greater is the despite done to him, Ezek. viii. 5. When the prophet saw the image of jealousy at the gate, God tells him there were greater abominations than that, which are described, ver. 10, 'Creeping things, and abominable beasts,' viz. the Egyptian idols. The viler the thing is which possesses our heart, the greater slight is put upon God, and the greater the abomination.

5. We are enemies to God's sovereignty in setting up Satan. Every sin is an election of the devil to be our lord. If sin had a voice, it would give its suffrage for such a lord as would favour its interest. As the Spirit dwells in a godly man to guide him, so doth the devil in a natural man, to direct him to evil, Eph. ii. 2, 3, so that every sin is an effect of the devil's government; therefore sins are called his lusts, which natural men (who, being the devil's children, are under his paternal government) fulfil and do with a resolute obedience: 'His lusts you will do,' John viii. 44. If we divide sins into spiritual and carnal, which division comprehends all sin, we shall find that in both; we own the devil's authority either in obeying his commands, or in conforming to his example. Some are said to be his lusts *subjectivè*, as he commits them; others *dispositivè*, as he directs them. In spiritual he is an actor, in carnal a tempter. In carnal, men obey his commands; in spiritual, they model themselves according to his pattern; in the one they are his servants, to do his work, in the other his children, to partake of his nature. In the one we acknowledge him as our master, in the other we own him as our copy. In both we derogate from God's sovereignty over us, whom we are bound to imitate, as well as to obey. Every sin, in its own nature, is a communion or society with Belial, a fighting for the devil against God; it is the end of the act, though it be not the intention of the agent. Every sin is the devil's work, and therefore the choice of it is a preferring his service before God's. The sin of Saul, though in a small matter, and not in any natural, but positive command, is equalled to the sin of witchcraft, which, you know, is a covenanting with the devil to yield obedience to him, 1 Sam. xv. 23.

What a monstrous baseness is this, to advance an impure spirit in the place of infinite purity; to embrace the great ringleader of rebellion above the contriver of our reconciliation, the only enemy God hath in the world, who drew all the rest into the faction against him, before him who is ready to pardon us upon our revolt from his adversary. To affect that destroyer above our preserver and benefactor; to esteem him as the exactest pattern and the greatest lord, as though he had created us, provided for us, and in mercy watched over us all our days. What a prodigious enmity is this, to offend God, to pleasure the devil, and injure our Creator, to gratify our adversary! Have we nothing to prefer before him but the deadliest enemy that both God and our souls have in the world? Must we side with our tormentor against our preserver? Shall he which will fire us for ever be valued above him who would wipe all tears from our eyes? Oh let us blush, if any spark of ingenuity be left; and let our hatred of God change its object, and boil up against ourselves for our abominable ingratitude.

3. In usurping God's prerogative, and exacting those observances which belong to God. We destroy his sovereignty in deifying and rewarding men for things done in opposition to the law of God, in putting glorious titles upon the vilest acts, naming ambition generosity, murder valour, &c. (1.) In challenging titles and acts of worship due only to God. What act of worship is there due to God, but man hath one time or other challenged it as pertaining to him? Darius for thirty days must have all petitions put up to him, as though he could supply the wants of all creatures, Dan. vi. 7–9. Alexander would be worshipped as God; after him Antiochus, whom God calls a vile person. The pope makes up the number in the preface the canonists put to his decrees: *Edictum domini deique nostri.* In men's equalling themselves to God. The first man would know as God. Babel builders would dwell as God. Rabbins tell us, that Eve was told by the devil, that if she ate the forbidden fruit, she should make a world as God. The pope would sit in the temple of God, and pardon sins as God; exalts himself above all that is called God, shewing himself that he is God.

(2.) Usurping God's prerogative, in lording over the consciences and reasons of others. Whence else springs the restless desire in some men, to model all consciences according to their own wills, which belongs to a greater power than man is capable of? Ferdinand's speech was eminent, who when by the persuasion of others, with much reluctancy on his part he had passed an edict against the protestants, &c., said, 'I expected such a thing, when I would take upon me the prerogative of God to be Lord over men's consciences.' We usurp God's prerogative, when we are angry that others are not of our minds and judgments; when they will not be blind servants to our opinion, in endeavouring to have our own fancies, yea, and passions, though never so boisterous and ridiculous, to be a measure to others. When we are pertinacious in any doubtful opinion, and assume to ourselves infallibility of judgment, as if our sentiments were as firm as divine decrees, what is this but an exalting ourselves above all that is called God, to erect an unlimited power over other men's reasons and judgments, as though it were as infallible as God, and all others differing from us under blindness and error?

(3.) Usurping God's prerogative, in prescribing rules of worship, which ought only to be appointed by God. In putting out, or leaving in, what they think fit to be the rule of worship; in prescribing by human laws, what they judge good and right in divine. All the reason under heaven could not have informed us what God was in himself, or what worship he expected of us, without supernatural revelation: therefore, when God hath fixed it, for men to be making alterations in it, and additions to it, is an intolerable invading of his right, at least it is an equalling our own fallible inventions with his infallible oracles, imperiously to obtrude upon people human inventions with as much authority as if they had been signed and sealed in heaven, and were unquestionably warranted by God himself. The prescribing the manner of worship, is a part of God's sovereignty; therefore in the two last chapters of Exodus, where the erecting of the tabernacle is described, those words, '*As the Lord commanded*,' are seventeen times inserted. And to prescribe any thing which God hath not commanded (though he hath not forbidden it) is such an invasion of his prerogative, that he hath punished it by a remarkable judgment. Lev. x. 1. When Nadab and Abihu took strange fire, *i. e.* other fire than what was upon the altar, wherewith to kindle their incense, though God had given no command to the contrary, yet because he had not commanded the offering with strange fire, he cut them off by a terrible judgment.

And it is to be observed, that none are more irreconcileable enemies to the true power and spirit of godliness, than the usurpers of this prerogative of God, the Lord in just judgment leaving them to the dotages of their own minds, and the enmity of their hearts against him, being successors of the pharisees in their judicial blindness, as well as their usurpations of God's authority.

4. In subjecting the truths of God to the trial of reason, or trying God's oracles at the tribunal of our shallow reason. It is a part of God's sovereignty to be the interpreter, as well as maker of his own laws, as it is a right inherent in the legislative power among men. So that it is an invasion of his right to fasten a sense upon his declared will, which doth not naturally flow from the words: for to put any interpretation according to our pleasure upon divine as well as human laws, contrary to the true intent, is a virtual usurpation of this power; because if laws may be interpreted according to our humours, the power of the law would be more in the interpreter than in the legislator. And it is the worse when men try the word not by their reasons, but by their fancies and humours, and put allegories, the brats of crazy or humorous fancy, as the genuine meaning of the word of God.

5. In judging future events, as if we had been of God's privy council when he first undertook any great action in the world.

6. In censuring others' state. It is an intruding into God's judicial authority. 'Who hath made me a judge?' was Christ's plea, Luke xii. 14. Who art thou that judgest another's state, as though thou wert Lord of the heart of thy brother, and God had given over his jurisdiction over the heart to thee; as though he were to stand or fall to thy censure?

PART III.

Enmity against the Attributes of God in general.

II. Enmity to the holiness of God.

This hating his holiness is a virtual depriving him of his being; for if he did not infinitely hate evil, he would not be infinitely good, and consequently would not be God. God can never endure sin, no, not to look upon it; and to cherish that which is so contrary to his purity, is a denial of his holiness. 'Thou art of purer eyes than to behold evil, thou canst not look on iniquity,' Hab. i. 13.

First, In sinning under a pretence of religion. Many resolve upon some ways of wickedness, and then rake the Scripture to find out at least excuses and evasions for it, if not a justification for their crimes. This was the devil's method to Christ, to bring Scripture for self-murder. Saul resolves not to obey God, but would preserve the spoils of the Amalekites, and then thinks to qualify all with offering a few sacrifices; as though God's holiness would not hate sin, that had a religious pretext. Many that have wrung estates from the tears of widows and heart-blood of orphans, think to wipe off all their oppression by some charitable legacies at their death. It is abominable to make charity, the transcript of God's goodness, a covert for sin; and religion, which is to bring us near to God, to patronise our tyranny; when men will speak wickedly and talk deceitfully for God, Job. xiii. 7, *i. e.* will sin for God's glory, and make the honour of his service a stalking-horse to the affront of his holiness.

2. In charging sin upon God. Every man naturally is willing to find he

inducement to sin in another rather than in himself. This is an act of hatred, to bespot the reputation of others, by imputing our crimes to them, and accusing them as the authors or occasions of our transgressions. It is an act of fear, which is the companion of hatred. If men can make God a sinner against his own law, they blemish his holiness, they think they are secure from the punishment they did dread; for we fear not man, who is faulty as well as ourselves.* When men have done all that they can to blot out a sense of a Deity, and see they cannot do it, they will raze out the reverence of it; and if we find a way to lay our sins at God's door when he chargeth them upon us, we think then to escape the rigour of his justice, and that he cannot be unrighteous to punish us for those crimes which he is guilty of as well as ourselves. But it is a foolish consideration; for if we can fancy an unholy God, we have no reason to think him a righteous God. That you may see that this very thing which looks so horrible runs in our blood, take notice of the two first discourses God had with man after his fall, and they will both discover this.

When God examines Adam about his transgression, he excuses himself by laying it upon God: 'The woman whom thou gavest me to be with me, she gave me of the tree, and I did eat,' Gen. iii. 12. Hadst thou not given me the woman, I had not been tempted; and had I not been tempted, I had not sinned; and this sin was committed presently after the woman was given me, as if thou hadst given me this woman to be my immediate tempter, and infused such a love in my heart to her, that it could not resist her allurements; for he seems by the speech to intimate that God gave him a woman on purpose to draw him into sin. The next is Cain. Some think Cain here lays the fault upon God: 'Am I my brother's keeper?' Gen. iv. 9, as if he should have said, Art not thou the keeper and governor of the world? why didst not thou hinder me from killing my brother? David, a holy man, follows him in those steps, and charges a sin of his own contrivance upon the providence of God. When the news of Uriah's death was brought, he wipes his mouth, and saith, 'The sword devours one as well as another.' He fastens that solely on divine providence, which was his own wicked contrivance, 2 Sam. xi. 25.

3. In hating the image of God's holiness in others. The more holy any man is, and the more active in the severest duties of religion, the more is he the object of the scoffs of others; and not only barked at by tippling drunkards on the ale-bench, but by formal and grave judges on the seat of justice. David, though a king, whose example might have been powerful to have brought them to an outward pretended love to holiness, was spoke against by them that sat in the gate, and was the song of the drunkards, and that when he wept, and chastised his soul with fasting, Ps. lxix. 10–12.

Hence nothing is so burdensome as the presence of a sober, religious person, because of that image of God's holiness shining in him, which strikes so full upon his soul, and sets his heart on work in checking and gripping reflections. Now, holiness being the glory of God, the peculiar title of the Deity, and from him derived upon the soul, he that mocks this in a person, derides God himself. He that hates the picture of a prince, hates the prince also, and much more were he in his power. He that hates the stream, hates the fountain; he that hates the beams, hates the sun. The holiness of a creature is but a beam from that infinite sun, a stream from that eternal fountain. If a mixed and imperfect holiness be more the subject of thy scoffs than a great deal of sin, surely thou wouldst more roundly scoff at God himself, should he appear in the unblemished and unspotted holiness of

* Manton on James, p. 92.

his nature, which infinitely shines in him, for thy hatred would be greater, because thy contrariety is so much more against the perfection of holiness than where it is with a mixture. Where there is a hatred of the purity and perfection of any creature, there is a greater reflection upon God, who is the author of that purity.

4. In having debasing notions of the holy nature of God. We invert the creation contrary to God's order in it. God made man according to his own image, and we make God according to ours. We fashion God like ourselves, and fasten our own humours upon him, as the Lacedæmonians were wont to dress their gods after the fashion of their cities, Ps. l. 21. Though men are enemies to the holy majesty of God, yet they can please themselves well enough with him as represented by that idea their corrupt minds have framed of him. We cannot comprehend God; if we could, we should be infinite, not finite; and because we cannot comprehend him, we set up in our fancies strange images of him, and so ungod God in our heart and affections.

(1.) This is an higher affront to God than we imagine. *Vulgi opiniones diis applicare profanum est.*—Epicurus. *De Deo male sentire quam deum esse negare pejus duco.* It is worse to degrade the nature of God in our conceits, and to make him a vicious God, than if in our thoughts we did quite discard any such being; for it is not so gross a crime to deny his being, as to fancy him otherwise than he is. Such imaginations strip him of his perfections, and reduce him to a mere vanity. Plutarch saith, he should account himself less wronged by that man that should deny there ever was such a man as Plutarch, than that they should affirm there was such a man indeed, but he was a choleric clown, a decrepid fellow, a debauched man, and an ignorant fool. This was the general censure of the heathen, that superstition was far worse than atheism, by how much the less evil it was to have no opinion of God, than such as is vile, wicked, derogatory to the pure and holy nature of the divine majesty.

(2.) Carnal imaginations of God, as well as corporeal images, are idolatry. It is a question which idolatry is the greatest, to worship an image of wood or stone, or to entertain monstrous imaginations of God. It provokes a man when we liken him to some inferior creature, and call him a dog or toad. It is not such an affront to a man to call him a creature of such a low rank and *classis*, as to square and model the perfections of the great God according to our limited capacities. We do worse than the heathen (of whom the apostle proclaimed) did in their images: they likened the glory of God to such creatures as were of the lowest form in the creation; we liken God not to corruptible man, but to corrupt man; and worse yet, to the very corruptions of men, and worship a God dressed up according to our own foolish fancies: 'And changed the glory of the incorruptible God into an image made like to corruptible man, and to birds, and four-footed beasts, and creeping things,' Rom. i. 23. If all those several conceptions and ideas men have of God were uncased and discovered, what a monstrous thing would God appear to be, according to the modes the imaginative faculty frames them in!

5. In our unworthy and perfunctory addresses to God. When men come into the presence of God with lusts reeking in their hearts, and leap from sin to duty. God is so holy, that were our services the most refined, as pure as those of the angels, yet we could not serve him suitably to his holy nature, Joshua xxiv. 19; therefore we deny this holiness when we come before him without due preparation, as if God did not deserve the purest thoughts in our applications to him; or as if a blemished and polluted sacrifice were suitable enough to his nature. When we excite not those elevated

frames of spirit, which are due to his greatness and fulness, and think to put him off with cheap and spotted services, we slight the holy majesty of God, and are guilty of a higher presumption than is fitting for us in our access to an earthly prince.

We worship him not according to the excellent holiness of his nature, when we have foolish imaginations creep upon us in the very act of duty, which makes our services erroneous and misguided. When we bring our worldly, carnal, debauched thoughts into his presence, worse than the dogs or slaves we would blush to be attended by in our visits of a great man; when our hearts are turned from God in any duty; while we are speaking with our Creator, to be in our hearts conversing with our sordid sensualities; it is as if we should be raking in a dunghill when we are talking with a king. We do here but defame his holiness, while we pretend to honour it; and profane his name, while we are praying 'Hallowed be thy name.' It would argue more modesty, though less sincerity, to say to our lusts, as Abraham to his servant, 'Tarry here till I go to sacrifice.'

6. In defacing the image of God in our own souls. God, in the first draught of man, conformed him to his own image; because we find that in regeneration this image is rewewed: 'The new man, which after God, κατα Θεὸν, is created in righteousness and true holiness,' Eph. iv. 24. He did not take angels for his pattern in his first polishing the soul, but himself. In defacing this image, therefore, we cast dirt upon the holiness of God, which was his pattern in the framing of us; and rather choose to be conformed to Satan, who is God's great enemy, and to have God's image wiped out of us, and the devil's pictured in us. Therefore natural men, that are guilty of gross sins, are called devils, John vi. 70. It is spoken of Judas; Christ gave it to Peter too, Mat. xvi. 23. And if he gave this title to one of the worst of men, and one of the best of men, it will be no wrong to give it to all men. Men wallow in sin, which is directly contrary to that illustrious image which God did imprint upon them; and perform those actions which are odious to God and his righteousness, and suitable to their corruption. Men glory in that which is their shame; and account that their ornament which is the greatest blot upon their nature, which if it were upon God would make him cease to be God.

III. Enmity to the wisdom of God. Presumptuous sins are called a reproach of God: 'The soul that doth aught presumptuously, the same reproaches the Lord,' Num. xv. 30. All reproaches are either for natural, moral, or intellectual defects; all reproaches of God must be either for wickedness or weakness: if for wickedness, his holiness is denied; if for weakness, his wisdom is blemished.

1. In slighting the laws of God. Since God hath no defect in his understanding, his will must be the best and wisest, and therefore his laws highly rational, as being the orders of the wisest agent. As God's understanding apprehends all things in their true reason, so his will enjoins nothing but what is highly good, and makes for the happiness of his creature; the true means of whose happiness he understands better than men or angels can do. All laws, though they are enforced by sovereignty, yet they are, or ought to be, in the composing of them, founded upon reason, are indeed applications of the law of nature upon this or that particular emergency. The laws of God, then, who is *summa ratio*, are purely founded upon the truest reason, though every one of them may not be so clear to us; therefore they that make alteration in his precepts, either dogmatically or practically, control his wisdom, and charge him with folly. When men will observe one part of his law, and not another, pick and choose where they please, hence it is that

sinners are called fools in Scripture. It is certainly inexcusable folly, to contradict undeniable and infallible wisdom. If infinite prudence hath framed the law, why is not every part of it observed? If it were not made with the best wisdom, why is anything of it observed?

He that receives the promises of God, and the testimony of Christ, 'sets to his seal that God is true,' John iii. 33. It must thence undeniably follow, that he that refuseth obedience to his law, sets to his seal that God is foolish. Men live as though the commands of God were made in sport, not by counsel. If God took counsel in the making man, there is as much need of counsel in the right ordering him.

If the defacing his image by any sin is a defaming his wisdom in the creation, the breaking his law is a disgracing his wisdom in the administration. Were they not rational, God would not enjoin them; and if they are rational, we are enemies to infinite wisdom by not complying with them.

2. In defacing the wise workmanship of God. Every sin is a defacing our own souls, which, as they are the prime creatures in the sensible world, had greater characters of God's wisdom in the fabric of them. But this image of God is ruined and broken by sin. Though the spoiling of it be a scorn of his holiness, it is also an affront to his wisdom; because though his power was the cause of the production of so fair a being, yet his wisdom was the guide of his power, as well as his holiness the exemplar whereby he wrought it. If a man had a curious clock or watch, which had cost him many years' pain, and the strength of his skill to frame; for a man, after he had seen and considered it, to cut, slash, and break all, would argue a contempt of the workman's skill. God hath shewn infinite art in the creation of man, but sin unbeautifies man, and bereaves him of his excellency.

3. Censuring his ways. What is our impatience at any passages of his providence, but a censuring his dealing with us as unjust or unwise; as if we would presume to instruct him better in the management of human affairs? It is to take upon us to be God's judges, to cite him to our tribunal to give an account of his ministration of things. It is a reviling him because he doth manage things according to his own will, and not according to ours. It is a striving with God, and a summoning him to the bar of our reason: 'Woe to him that strives with his Maker! Shall the clay say to him that fashioned it, What makest thou?' Isa. xlv. 9. To quarrel with him, and examine him about his works, why he made them thus, and not thus; it is a reproaching of God, a contending with him, to instruct him: 'Shall he that contendeth with the Almighty instruct him? he that reproves God, let him answer it,' Job xl. 2. A reproof argues a superiority in authority, knowledge, or goodness. It is a playing Absalom's game: Oh that I were king in Israel, I would do this and that man justice; so that it is a virtual wishing, Oh that I were king of the world, the governor of all creatures, things should be disposed more wisely, and more justly.

4. Prescribing rules and methods to God. We presume to be God's tutors, and would sway him according to the dictates of our wisdom; when we would have a mercy in this method which God designs to convey through another channel; when we would have him take his measures from our humours; this was the ground of Jonah's argument with God, 'It displeased Jonah exceedingly; and he was very angry,' Jonah iv. 1. When we make vows to flatter God into a compliance with our design; when we pray imperiously for anything without a due submission to God's will; as if we were his counsellors, and he were bound to follow our humours. Thus would the most glorious of virgins and mothers prescribe to Christ a rule for his miraculous action, Luke ii. 48. His mother said to him, 'Son, why hast thou

thus dealt with us?' John ii. 3, 4. So the Jews who nailed him to the cross, offered to believe on him, if he would submit to their terms, and gratify their curiosity in descending from the cross they had fixed him to. Are not most men Jews in this, to prescribe terms to God, upon the grant whereof he shall have our service of believing in him; as if a child should appoint rules for his father, or an insane patient to his physician; would it not be an injury to their prudence and skill? This presumptuous humour is a hellish offence. Abraham asserts the way of God's appointment by Moses and the prophets, to be the best way for bringing men to repentance and salvation; but the rich man prefers his own judgment, and would have him send one from the dead to preach to them. Abraham saith unto him, 'They have Moses and the prophets;' and he said, 'Nay, father Abraham,' Luke xvi. 27–30. We deal often thus with God, as though we were his counsellors, not his subjects.

IV. Enmity to the sufficiency of God. The preferring any sin before God is a denial of the fulness and content to be had in the enjoyment of God; as though God were inferior to a base lust, and that a vile pleasure had a better relish than the communication of God to the soul. For when God describes what pleasure and peace there is in his ways, what fulness of joy in his presence, what is the refusal of it but equivalent to this language of the sinner: No, I believe no such thing; there is more happiness to be had in sin than in God? And so he values a vapour, an empty bubble, more than infinite fulness. The greater is the scorn of God's sufficiency, by how much the more ignoble, brutish, and contemptible the pleasure is we prefer before him.

1. In secret thoughts of meriting by any religious act. As though God could be indebted to us, and obliged by us. As though our devotions could bring a blessedness to God more than he essentially hath; when indeed 'our goodness extends not to him,' Ps. xvi. 2. Our services of God are rather services to ourselves, and bring a happiness to us, not to God. This secret opinion of merit (though disputed against the papists, yet) is natural to man; and this secret self-pleasing, when we have performed any duty, and upon that account expect some fair compensation from God, as having been profitable to him. God intimates this: 'The wild beasts of the field are mine; if I were hungry I would not tell thee; for the world is mine, and the fulness thereof,' Ps. l. 11, 12. He implies, that they wronged his infinite fulness, by thinking that he stood in need of their sacrifices and services, and that he was beholden to them for their adoration of him. All merit implies a moral or natural insufficiency in the person of whom we merit, and our doing something for him, which he could not, or at least so well do for himself. It is implied in our murmuring at God's dealing with us in a course of cross providences, wherein men think they have deserved better at the hands of God by their service, than to be so cast aside and degraded by him. In our prosperity we are apt to have secret thoughts that our enjoyments were the debts God owed us, rather than gifts freely bestowed upon us. Hence it is that men are more unwilling to part with their righteousness than with their sins, and are apt to challenge salvation as a due, rather than beg it as an act of grace.

2. Trying all ways of helping ourselves, before we come to God. Having hopes to find that in creatures, which is only to be found in an all-sufficient God. When we rather seek an alms from the world than God, as though there were some hidden excellency in the world, which overtopped the excellency of God. When we would rather drink of cisterns than of the fountain; as though the waters in the cistern were fresher and sweeter than

those in the spring. Hence it is that upon any emergency we set our own reason on work, before we crave the assistance of God's power; and scarce seek him till we have modelled the whole contrivance in our own brains, and resolved upon the methods of performance; as though there were not a fulness of reason in God to guide us in our resolves, as well as power to breathe success upon them, 'after vows to make inquiry,' Prov. xx. 25, after resolutions to beg direction in our business. Sometimes men seek out unlawful ways for their delivery, as though there were more sufficiency of help in sin than in God. Did we believe and love the sufficiency of God, that is able to supply our wants, we should not upon every strait be turned from him, and beg help at the door of creatures.

3. In our apostasies from God. When, after fair pretences and devout applications, we grow cold, and thrust him from us, it implies, that God hath not that fulness in him which we expected. Backsliding testifies that there is not that sweetness and satisfactoriness in God which we expected, upon our first approach to him. All apostasy is a denial of God; for it denies him either to be a fountain of all good, or else that he is not true to his promises, but deceives us in our just expectations of good from him. It either speaks him evil or deceitful; it is a greater affront to deny him, after an experience of his sweetness and assistance, than to deny him before any dealing with him, or trial of him. Now, though all apostasy begins in a neglect, yet it quickly ripens into a hatred.

4. In joining something with God to make up our happiness. Though men are willing to have the enjoyment of God, yet they are not content with him alone, but would have something else to eke him out; as though God, who accounts the enjoyment of himself the greatest blessedness, had not also in himself a sufficient blessedness for his creatures, without the additions of anything else. The young man in the Gospel went away sorrowful, because he could not enjoy God and the world both together, Mat. xix. 21, 22. If we would light up candles in a clear day, when the sun shines in its full brightness, what do we imply but that the sun has not light enough in itself to make it day? And when we labour for other things with as much strength and eagerness as we labour for the enjoyment of God, what is it but to deny that there is enough in him without the concurrence of some other good?

V. Against the omniscience of God. Men hate God's omniscience, and could willingly have him stripped of this eminency. For men naturally love not those that dive into their purposes and canvass their thoughts; so neither can men love this attribute of God, whereby he enters into the secret closets of their hearts, and takes an exact measure of every wicked and subtle contrivance. The first speech that Adam spake in paradise after his fall, infringed God's omniscience, 'I heard thy voice in the garden, and I hid myself,' Gen. iii. 10; as if the trees could shelter him from that eye that saw the minutest part of the whole earth. The next speech recorded of the second man, Cain, is to the same purpose; when God put the question to him, 'Where is thy brother?' 'I know not,' Gen. iv. 9; thinking thereby to delude God's omnisciency. He that practically denies God's omnisciency, denies his Godhead: for a man may as well deny that there is a sun, as deny that it shines, and disperseth its light and influence into every corner.*

This appears,

1. When we commit sin upon the ground of secresy. If all hearts, surely then all places, are open to God's eye; no private bench for a drunkard, or secret stew for an adulterer, but is obvious to him. Common modesty before

* See more of this in the Discourse of God's Omnipresence.

man is not practised before God; men are ashamed to have their actions seen by man's eye, but not by God's. *Maxima debetur pueris reverentia,* filthy actions cannot endure the presence of a child's eye, much less of man's. Shall the presence of a child have more power over us than the presence of God, and men's observing more than God's censuring eye? Is not this a denial of him, when the eye of God is of less force to restrain thee than the eye of man, as if men only could see, and God were blind? All the sin thou committest before the eye of the holiest man in the world, cannot make him hate thee so much as God hates thee; because his holiness is infinitely short of God's holiness, and consequently his hatred is infinitely short of God's.

It is an aggravation of a man's sin to be committed in the presence of God, Gen. x. 9, 'a mighty hunter before the Lord.' As it was of Haman's offence, when he lay upon Esther's bed, that he would force the queen 'before the king's face.' It seems to be David's conceit in his sin, that God would not see him; both by Nathan's charge, Wherefore hast thou despised the commandment of the Lord, 'to do evil in his sight?' 2 Sam. ii. 19; and by his own confession, 'This evil have I done in thy sight,' Ps. li. 4. Every penitent takes notice of the wrong he doth to God's all-seeing eye. It is a high provocation for a servant to do ill when his master's eye is upon him, or a thief to cut a purse before the judge's face. God observes all wickedness; wickedness under lock and key. If he registers all thy members in his book, he will also register the sins of those members; what use thou puttest them to, whether to his service or the devil's drudgery; whether thy eye rove about in wanton glances, or thy tongue be let loose in profane language, or thy ear open to ungodly discourse, or thy feet more swift to carry thee to an alehouse than a sermon.

It was once a check a young man gave to a harlot, who had enticed him, and carried him from one room to another for secresy, Oh, saith he, can none see us here? can we be hid from God's eye? Yet sinners in their practice make their boast as they in express words: 'Thick clouds are a covering to him, that he sees not; and he walks in the circuit of heaven,' Job xxii. 14. As though God's eye could not pierce the thick clouds; as though his cares were confined only to celestial things, and earth were too low an orb for his eyes to roll about. If we think a word in the presence of a grave religious man may disgrace us, we are troubled in our minds; but we regard not an injury done to God. We are more cast down if a foolish action of ours comes to the knowledge of men than to the knowledge of God.

2. When men give liberty to inward sins. God often sets forth himself by that expression, that he 'trieth the heart, and searcheth the reins.' The heart hath many valves and ventricles, but God searches all the valves, which cannot be espied and discerned but by a curious eye. God sees all the contrivances of it. The reins are partly hid, most inward, surrounded with fat. The most inward thoughts cannot be hid from God's piercing eye; for all is open before him, like dissected sacrifices when the bowels are ripped up, and all the inwards discovered. God is more within the soul of a creature than any one hidden thought can be, and knows it before the heart that mints it has a full discovery of it. What do the actings of sin in our fancies import, but as though God's eye could not pierce into the remoteness and darkness of our minds?

Manasseh is blamed for setting up strange altars in the house of God; much more may we for setting up strange imaginations in the heart, which should belong to God. This is to deny God's judicial prerogative; this is the attribute which speaks him fit to be a judge, and yet men can possess their hearts with this, that he is defective in this attribute, and so make him incapable of judging the world. Hypocrisy is a plain denial of his omnisciency. When men have a religious lip, and a black soul; an outside swept and garnished, and a legion of devils garrisoned within, this derogates from God, as though his eye were as easily deceived as men's, and outward appearance limited God's observation. Are we not more slight in the performance of private devotions before God, than we are in our attendances in public in the sight of men.

3. When men give way to diversions in a duty, it is a denial of God's omniscience. Love is the cause of fixedness. The angels have a pure affection to God, and therefore they have an uninterrupted attention in his presence. If thou thinkest God does not mind thee, why dost thou pray at all? If thou thinkest he does mind thee, why dost thou not pray more fervently, fixedly, and hear more attentively? This attention consists in the frame of the soul; for bodily exercise is required for our sakes, not for God's. Gesture and speech are to quicken our affections. Christ has given us a short pattern of prayer, and can our hearts be steady upon God in the repetition of it? Duties are visits we pay to God; would it not be an affront if, when we were to visit a prince, we should send a noisome rotten carcase in our stead? Do we not deal so with God, when we come without our heart, as though God were ignorant, and could be put off with anything, the worst in our flocks, as well as the best.

It wrongs the majesty of God's presence, that when he speaks to us, we will not give him so much respect as to regard him; and when we speak to him, we do not regard ourselves. What a vain thing is it to be speaking to a scullion, when the king is in presence? Every careless diversion to a vain object, is a denial of God's presence in the place. It is a wrong to God's excellency, that when we come to God for what we count sweet and desirable, we presently turn our backs, as though our addresses were an act of imprudence and folly; as much as to say, There is no sweetness in him, no beauty that we should desire him.

VI. Enmity to the mercy of God. God is not wronged more in any attribute by devils and men, than in his mercy. Man would deprive God of the honour of his own mercy, of the objects of mercy, when God's mercy to others comes in competition with his self-love and credit. Jonah's pride would null the goodness of God. With what an unreasonable passion doth he fly in the face of God for reprieving the humbled Ninevites! He would rather have had his own credit preserved in the destruction of them according to his prediction, than God's tenderness magnified in their preservation. Some fancy a God made up altogether of mercy, a childish mercy; as if his mercy had nothing else to do but to wrong all his other perfections, to make him belie his truth, extinguish his justice, discard his wisdom, and enslave his power.

This appears, (1.) In the severe and jealous thoughts men have of God. Men are apt to charge God with tyranny, whereby they strip him of the riches of his glorious mercy. The devil's design at first was to belie God to man, that he might have hard and contracted thoughts of God, to think him strait-handed towards his creature. Therefore he is called 'a liar from the beginning,' in urging man to misbelieve his Creator to be an unjust, hard, and cruel master, and that envied him comforts necessary for him, which frightful thoughts of the Deity have haunted man ever since. If man in creation was so ready to entertain jealousies of God, man in corruption, with the load of guilt upon him, is much more prone.

The heathens (by the devil's instigation), as the Indians, have their notions that mercy flows not naturally from God, but must be wrested by a multitude of services, that he will do nothing without the bribe of a sacrifice, which they offer, lest he should hurt them. As if God only created men to make sport with their misery; as if God had no other design in the creation, than to load his creatures with chains, and govern that world by tyranny which he made by an efflux of powerful goodness. The worship of many men is founded upon this conceit, whereby they are frighted into some actions of adoration, not sweetly drawn. This representation of God doth debase the soul, and fills it with that tyrannical passion of fear which is always accompanied with hatred; for we hate what we fear. Thus the devil accuses God to troubled consciences, persuading them that he has no mercy for them, that so he may drive them to despair. This he attained in Cain, who cries in despair, 'My punishment is greater than I can bear,' *i. e.* my sin is greater than can be pardoned, Gen. iv. 13.

When any soul is like to be snatched out of Satan's hands, he makes it interpret those acts wherein God means favour, to be acts of enmity. So that the main work God has to do after conviction, is to persuade the soul to have good thoughts of him. Hence arises that unwillingness in the soul to come to God. How can we approach to him of whom we have such narrow thoughts, and judge of according to our own revengeful humours? How can we do otherwise but hate him, when we represent him as one easily angry, hardly appeased, of a cruel nature; a Minos, a Rhadamanthus, or Phalaris, rather than an infinite mirror of sweetness and love. If we do not think him so, why do we stand off from him? Hence arises our wrong constructions of providence, and sinister interpretations of God's acts, when we attribute to God such ends as have no other foundation but our own foolish fancy. Thus Manoah interprets the angel's coming, which was an act of God's kindness to him, to be an ill-meant providence, Judges xiii. 22. Now, as it is the quality of love to think no evil, so it is the property of hatred to think all evil. And as when a man hates sin, he cannot endure any varnish of an excuse to be put upon it, and cannot speak or think too bad of it; so when a man hates God, he cannot endure to have a good gloss put upon his actions.

(2.) Slighting his mercy, and robbing him of the end of it. The wilful breaking of a prince's laws, upon the observance whereof great rewards are promised, is not only a despising his sovereignty, but a slighting his goodness, in the rewards proffered to the observers. Rebels that stand it out against proclamations of pardon do what in them lies to deprive the prince of any objects to shew his clemency on. So obstinate sinners against mercy would, as far as they are able, deprive God of any subject to magnify his mercy on, especially when they do not only stand it out against so gracious proffers of God, but draw in others to take up arms against him; every sin in this respect is a stealing the glory of this attribute from God, in denying him that tribute of obedience which is due to him for it. Often this enmity rises higher; and whereas men should fear him, because he is ready to forgive, Ps. cxxx. 4, they rather slight him, and presume to sin because he hath mercy to pardon; and so make that which should cherish their obedience to be a spur to their rebellion, and encourage their future offences by that goodness which should excite a fear and holy awe of him in their souls. Because God is gracious, men will be more vicious; hence they are said to 'despise his goodness,' Rom. ii. 4. And that patience which should teach them repentance inflames their hatred, and in this humour they turn grace itself into wantonness, Eccles. viii. 11.

VII. Enmity to the justice of God. When men wish there were no God, they wish this at least, that God were unclothed of those perfections which are averse and dreadful to their guilty consciences; scarce a man but hath flattering fancies that God is not so terrible as he is represented.

This appears, (1.) In not fearing it, but running under the lash of it. Sin is an act of rebellion, and rebels fear not the justice, or else hope to overcome the power of their superior. Would not men be afraid to spit in the face of heaven, did they really believe there was a God who was just and righteous, and would not let any sin go unpunished? The prophet speaks of some that had wearied God with their sins, and made him serve with their iniquities, Isa. xliii. 24, as if God were bound to endure their evil carriage against him with patience, and never to unsheathe the sword of his justice. How often are men upon this account said to have a rocky heart, and iron sinews, that will neither be broken nor bent! Are not the Belshazzars of the world merry, though the handwriting be upon the wall against them. Thus men 'commit sin with greediness, and are past feeling,' Eph. iv. 19, daring the justice of God, and without any sense of revenge due to sin, and say, To-morrow shall be as this day, and much more abundant. Nay, I dare aver, that if a man who had been scorched in hell should again enjoy his wonted pleasures, and have all the while a fresh remembrance of his late torments, were not his will changed by a powerful grace, he would stand it out as stiffly against God as ever, notwithstanding those terrible marks of wrath, and be without a holy fear of that justice which he had felt.

(2.) Sinning under the strokes of justice. Men will not turn to God that smites them, though they have hypocritical howlings upon their beds under God's stroke, Hosea vii. 13, 14, and Isa. ix. 13. They will roar under the stroke, but not submit to the striker. It is the witch of Endor, or the god of Ekron, shall have their addresses, and not the God of heaven.

(3.) In hoping easily to evade it. There are sometimes secret thoughts that a man is able to maintain himself against all the force God can use, which the apostle implies, 'Are we stronger than he?' 1 Cor. x. 22. Do we think to try it out at arms-length with God? Sin implies a mastering God's all-powerful justice. Sometimes men will argue for impiety from their present impunity; and because he keeps silence, think that he will not publish a condemning sentence, Ps. l. 21; and because God forbears, think that he has forgotten to punish: 'God hath forgotten,' Ps. x. 11. Sometimes we fancy God like to ourselves, mutable with every wind, as soon appeased as angry; either unable to resist the force of our prayers, or easily enticed by our good words and praises of him, as though he were to be flattered out of his just anger, his holy and righteous nature: 'They flattered him with their mouth,' Ps. lxxviii. 36. As if he needed our trifles, and rattles, as children do, to appease them; or might be wrought upon as the poor Indians, to give the gold of heaven for a few beads.

They fancy him a god of wax, whom they can bend at their pleasure; either so weak that he cannot, or of so soft a disposition that he will not, be revenged of sin, and that a few sighs will blow away a storm of wrath. Hence men invent ways of pleasing God after they have offended him, and think to expiate the sin of their soul by the offering their substance, or presenting some melancholy devotions, or inflicting some self-chastisements. As if God were to be bribed by the blood of a lamb, or goat, or by some superstitious and formal services, to change his provoked justice into an easy clemency.

VIII. Enmity to the truth of God. Most men live upon trust for their knowledge, and know far more by the relation, and upon the credit of others, than upon certain demonstrations, as that there are such places as China, Peru, and Mexico. And why are men so backward in believing God speaking in his word? It is clear hereby that men have not so great enmity against one another as they have against God.

This appears (1.) in not believing his threatenings. Men believe not either the matter or sudden execution of them. Our faith is more operative upon reports from men than revelations from God. Men will believe stories of danger, so as to avoid the places wherein they be liable to it; yet though God tells them what the issue of sin will be, how certainly it will destroy them, they will walk on in their own way. Men look upon hell as a painted fire, upon the threatenings as scarecrows without a sting, and are not so much affected with them as at the reading of a tragedy. Would men be so stupid as not to stir out of the fire, if they did really believe God were true? They are apt to fear others that threaten inferior punishments, and not to fear God, who threatens everlasting woe, but think to find mercy in the way of sin, though God assures them to the contrary. How soon did the Israelites lose the sense of the thunder, which terrified them when the law was given! Like those sponges that thunder will pass through, such are secure persons, through whom the thunder of God's threatenings will pass without doing any hurt. A contrite heart trembles at the word, Isa. lxvi. 2, because he acknowledges it to be true, whereas a proud heart is like an unmoved rock, that is not daunted at God's threatenings, as imagining them to be false. If a man at first believes them, yet if God delays the execution of them, he thinks they were in jest with him, and takes delays for denials: 'My master delays his coming,' Luke xii. 45. This temper is called a belying of God: 'It is not he, this evil shall not come upon us,' Jer. v. 12. (2.) His promises. Man is more prone to believe God's promises than threatenings, because men are naturally credulous of that which makes for their interest; therefore God made the Jews to say *Amen* to the curses, Deut. xxvii. 26. Not to the blessings, Deut. xxviii, because they were ready to slight threatenings, and snatch at promises. But yet even his words of grace are not credited by men; hence it is that they are not allured by his gracious proffers, which would work upon men if they really believed that God intended as he spake. All the unbelief in the world gives God the lie, the greatest indignity among the sons of men: 'He that believes not God, hath made him a liar,' 1 John v. 10. We believe the promises of a man that is a lie, as the psalmist speaks, and has deceived us, and rely upon a vain creature that fails, rather than upon the true and living God; like the foolish Indians, part with the gold of God's promises for glass and ribbons, brittle and gaudy things. Present things do more affect us than future. It was the present world Demas loved more than a future crown, 2 Tim. iv. 10. Sensible trifles are esteemed more valuable than invisible and external excellency. Men look upon heaven as a poet's elysium, a dream and fancy, and the promise of Christ's coming to be the greatest falsehood: 'Where is the promise of his coming? 2 Peter iii. 4. It is an undervaluing God's veracity to be led by sense, a brutish principle, rather than by God, who is truth itself. Our following the dictates of natural reason against revelation is not so derogatory as the making sense our guide.

IX. Enmity to his providence. By denying his truth, we deny his providence; for as the crediting the truth of one another keeps up commerce in the world, so the veracity of God on his part, and the sincerity of man, keep up an intercourse between God and the world. Some have thought God a sleepy God, as though he never cared how the world moved, so he might rest, Zeph. i. 12. Some thought it below God's majesty to mind sublunary things, as though it were more unworthy for God to govern them than it was to create them. This appears,

1. In ascribing his works to second causes. When we look upon second causes as the authors of benefits we enjoy, and attribute to them what is due to God, and ascribe them to blind chance, or the dexterity of our own wit, and thither return our thank-offerings: 'They sacrifice unto their net, and burn incense to their drag,' Hab. i. 16. Deifying the creature, the instrument, without any or a formal regard to the chief actor. In chastisements we look not upon sin as the meritorious, or God as the efficient cause. Thus Balaam spurred on his ass, and never considered the angel that stood in the way. Many regard instruments, and never consider God, who does all the evil in the city, and thus rob God both of the honour of his mercies, and the obedience required both by him and his chastisements.

2. In the offence we take, and the resistance we make, to his providences, if they cross our will. Sometimes men will charge the providence of God in times of affliction, that he is unjust towards them, and inflicts punishments when they deserve rewards; therefore the Spirit of God gives it as commendation of Job, that 'in all this,' *i. e.* in those many afflictions, he did 'not charge God foolishly,' Job i. 22, a praise scarce to be given to any man in the world. We are apt to murmur, as if God were bound to take care of us, and act all for our good, and neglect the whole world besides, or as though it were fitter for him to govern according to our foolish wills than his own wise and righteous will. Sometimes men will oppose the designs of his providence. The Gadarenes are so startled at the loss of their swine, that with a joint consent they desire Christ to depart from their coasts, having no mind to entertain his person or his doctrine, when they should rather have been moved by his miraculous power and his preaching to have inquired into the gospel which he preached. When the carnal interests of men's grandeur are struck at, they will quarrel at the powerful ways of God. Acts v. 16, 17, the high priests and Sadducees were filled with indignation at the apostles' miracles, which had reason enough to convince them had they not had too much malice to withstand them. Instead of submitting to the rod, we rage against God when he is correcting us, and, like chaff, fly in the face of him that fans us; not like children submitting to a father, but, like rebels, denying his superiority over us.

3. In our misinterpretations of providence. Shimei misinterpreted the providence of God when David fled from Jerusalem upon his son Absalom's rebellion. Oh, saith he, now God will revenge the house of Saul, 2 Sam. xvi. 7, 8. We will put interpretations upon God's acts according to our fancies, humours, and wishes; therefore the Spirit of God takes particular notice that Shimei was of the house of Saul, and therefore according to his own humour accounted this a punishment for his outing the house of Saul from the government. This is a high usurpation of God's prerogative, who is the best interpreter of his own acts as well as his laws.

X. Enmity to his content and pleasure.

1. In his nature. Such an enmity there is in sin, that it strives to make a confusion in God himself, a war in his very nature; for sin put God to his infinite wisdom to satisfy all the perfections of his nature. If he spared the sinner, how could he be just? If he destroyed him, how could he be merciful? What wit of men or angels could contrive a way to compose those attributes, and make truth and righteousness, mercy and justice, to kiss each other, and still those jars which sin endeavoured to make between them? If justice should have its full due, what would become of the creature? If mercy should only act its part, what would become of the righteousness of God's nature? If the creature should be damned by the severity of justice, mercy might sit weeping for want of objects, unless new

ones were created. If mercy should have its contentment in the impunity of the sinner, righteousness and truth might bewail the want of a due satisfaction. The heart of mercy would be broken if sin were punished, and the cry of justice would be perpetual unless the sinner fell under his own demerits. That surely is the greatest enemy, that endeavours to set division in a man's own family and nature.

2. In his works. Men endeavour to disappoint God of his glory, the end of his creation, and the most valuable jewel he reserves for his own use, and will not impart to another. God created all things for himself; and man, by turning them to another use, evidences that he would not let God have the pleasure of his own works, or the rent due to him for them. Sin made him repent that ever he put his hand to the framing that world, which, after the creation, he had pronounced good, Gen. vi. 6, 7, and made God be grieved with his own creatures, which with so much wisdom he made, and so much delight acquiesced in. God requires no more of man for all his benefits than a service; and they deny him this, and endeavour to make him weary of his life, as if we studied how we could most vex and disquiet him: thou hast 'fretted me in all those things,' Ezek. xvi. 43.

God created the world to have a service from his rational creatures; and yet their services naturally, as well as their sins, are a trouble to him, and tire him, and is ready to shake the world in pieces: 'Your appointed feasts my soul hateth: I am weary to bear them; they are a trouble to me,' Isa. i. 14. So that he can have no ease but in the acts of vengeance: 'Ah, I will ease me of my adversaries, and avenge me of mine enemies,' ver. 24. God created the world, not for any need he had of it, but to communicate his own goodness, and made man as a choice vessel to receive it; but man shrinks his soul, that goodness cannot enter upon him, and so endeavours to frustrate God of this end. Can there be a greater contempt than to deny God the satisfaction of his own works?

Now, to sum up all that has been said, suppose, if it were possible, that there were another God to judge, or an indifferent person to judge between God and men of this world, and had a copy of all the laws and promises, records of all God's dealings, would he not judge by the practices of men that God was some cruel Pharaoh, that, notwithstanding all his fair words and promises, minded nothing but the destruction of his creature, and that man had some high provocations from God to act so against the laws of goodness and proposals of eminent rewards; that God had no excellency to make him desirable, but that he were the most despicable, contemptible, unworthy being in the whole world? All the actions and practices of men testify thus much, that he is a weak, impure, cruel, false, empty, shallow, inconsiderable being, and one that hath no authority over him; a pattern not fit to be imitated; one that hath been injurious to him, &c. An indifferent person, that had no knowledge of God, viewing his laws, would have a high opinion of him; but again considering the practices of his creatures, he could not but think that some great provocation was offered by God to men; that he was full of dissimulation. He could not otherwise think that there should be so general a defection from him. But to declare this enmity further, it will be evident, by considering what enmity there is against all that comes from him, both the truths he reveals, and the duties he enjoins.

PART IV.

Enmity against the Truth, &c.

I. First, The carnal mind is enmity against God in his truth. Hating instruction is a part of atheism: 'Seeing thou hatest instruction, and castest my words behind thee,' Ps. l. 17. God complains, in Hos. viii. 12, that the most excellent things were accounted as a strange thing. God had given them the great things of his law, and they esteemed them not.

1. In men's unwillingness to believe any divine truth, or to meditate upon it. Men shun the thoughts of what they do not love. If we will not let truth in, which is a message from heaven, it is a sign we care not for the person from whom it comes.

It is hard to believe moral or divine truths; because they are against the interests of our lusts, and would eject those principles which have got so firm footing in our minds and affections, and would bring them into such a reformed course, which our minds, biassed by such principles, do exceedingly hate; whereas natural or mathematical verities are readily credited and kindly entertained, because they thwart not our principles, as the others do. The more divine and spiritual the object is, the more unwilling we are to close with it; and by how much the nearer any notion of truth is to God, and the more clearly representing him, the more averse are we from it. And if men are enemies to that truth which doth most clearly discover God and his mind, and cannot endure the thoughts of it, much less can they endure the thoughts of God himself. They are loath to entertain anything that may disquiet them. Christ describes this humour as it was in Noah's time, and as it will be towards the end of the world, Mat. xxiv. 38, 39. They were eating and drinking as though the world were their own, and loath to think of a deluge; and at the latter end men will as hardly believe a burning as they did then the drowning of the world. The pharisees derided the soundest doctrine. They derided him, *subsannarunt*; ἐξεμυκτήριζον, they treated him with every mark of the lowest contempt when he declaimed against their covetousness.

If the word lays hold upon a man, he endeavours to shake it off as a man would a serjeant who comes to arrest him. Men 'like not to retain God in their knowledge,' Rom. i. 28. If any truth presses in upon them, they turn it away, as men do importunate beggars: We have nothing for you; do not trouble us; we have no alms to bestow upon you. And the reason is, because men having abortivated and deadened all those relics and natural infusions of God in their soul, any lively truth and apprehension of him proves most unsavoury. As wine and strong waters which have lost their natural spirit become most ungrateful and unpleasant to the stomach, so those innate impressions of God which are so refreshing to a good man, they do what they can to shake off or taint them by mingling with them their own corrupt notions; and when they cannot, they are filled with an irreligious rancour against God. Men keep the truths that rise up in themselves for conviction and instruction in unrighteousness, and quench the motions of the blessed Spirit, killing them in the womb. Have not men often had secret wishes that the Scripture had never mentioned some truths, or that they were blotted out of the Bible; because they face their consciences, damp their pleasures, and cool their boiling lusts, which else they would with eagerness and delight pursue?

When men cannot shake off a truth, but it sticks fasts in them, yet they have no pleasure in the consideration of it, which would be if there were a love to God; for men love to read over the letters which are sent by them to whom they have an affection, and stick them up, or peruse them afterwards at their leisure. As it was an unclean beast that did not chew the cud under the law, so it is a corrupt heart that doth not chew truth by meditation. Hence a natural man is said not to know the things of God; for while he is inclined to a sensual life, he can have no delight in spiritual things, for sensuality hinders the operations of his soul about the choicest objects. Natural men may indeed meditate on a truth, but they do not delight in it; or if they do, it is only as it is knowledge; for we delight in nothing that we desire but upon the same account that we desire it. Now natural men desire to know God and some truths, not out of a sense of his excellency, but from a natural thirst after knowledge, so that they rejoice in the act, not in the object, not to quicken their affections, as idle boys strike fire, not to kindle anything, but please themselves with the sparks; whereas a gracious soul accounts not only his meditation, or the operation of his soul about a thing to be sweet, but he hath a spiritual joy in the object of that meditation. Many have the knowledge of God who have no delight in it; as owls and bats have eyes to perceive the light, but, by reason of the weakness of their sight, have no delight in it to look cheerfully upon it, so neither can a man, by his natural or acquired knowledge, delight in God, or love to look upon him, because of his corruption.

2. In their opposition to it. (1.) This opposition is external. In the first dawning of the gospel, what opposition did the apostles meet with! What persecutions were raised against them! How did the carnal world, like dogs, bark at the shining of the moon! It is as natural for men to persecute the truth, which is against the grain, as it is for them to breathe. When Socrates, upon natural principles, did confute the heathen idolatry, and asserted the unity of God, the whole cry of Athens, a learned university, is against him; and because he opposed the public received religion, he must die: Acts xiii. 45, *contradicting* and *blaspheming* are put together; disputes against the word many times end in blasphemies.

(2.) Their opposition is internal. God's truths cast against a hard heart are like balls thrown against a stone wall, which rebound the further from it; such a resistance there is in man, to beat back all the tenders of grace. Where the grace of God comes in any power, it accidentally stirs up sin in the heart; as when the sun shines upon a noisome dunghill, it becomes more noisome; not that the sun communicates any filthiness or pollution to the dunghill, but by accident in warming it, it makes the stench break forth. Sin, as a garrison in a city, is up in arms upon any alarm from its adversary. A word of God against the great Diana of a man's lust sets the whole soul in an uproar; sin follows the steps of its father the devil, and endeavours to bruise the heel of truth, which would break the head of lust. Men hate the truths of God when they begin to search and tent their beloved corruptions; so Ahab, 1 Kings xxii. 8, 'I hate him, for he doth not prophesy good concerning me, but evil;' John iii. 19, 20, 'lest their deeds should be reproved;' as apes are reported to break the glass, because they would not see their own deformity. The light of speculation may be pleasant, but the light of conviction is grievous; the light strikes too strongly upon their sore eyes, and makes them smart.

3. If men do entertain truth, it is not for truth's sake, but for some other by-end. Truth is scarcely received as truth; there is more of hypocrisy than sincerity in the pale of the church; the dowry makes it more desirable than the beauty. Judas follows Christ for the bag. Sometimes men enter-

tain truth to satisfy their own passions, rather than upon God's account. The religion of many is not the judgment of the man, but the passion of the brute. Many rather entertain the doctrine for the person's sake, than the person for the doctrine, and believe anything that comes from a man they esteem and affect, as if his lips were as canonical as Scripture. You received it 'not as the word of men, but, as it is in truth, the word of God,' 1 Thes. ii. 13; so that many times the very same truth delivered by another is disregarded, which, when coming from the fancy and mouth of their own idol, is cried up for an oracle, whenas, alas! it was the truth of God in the ass's as well as in the angel's mouth. And thus they have the word of God 'with respect of persons,' and receive it not for the sake of the fountain, but of the channel; and though they entertain the truth of God materially, yet not formally as his truth: 'Have not the faith of Christ with respect of persons,' James ii. 1.

4. If men do entertain truth, it is with unsettled affections, and much mixture. If men let in some good notions of God, they let in also much of corruption and error, like sponges that can suck up the foulest water as well as the sweetest wine; they have the unclean beasts enter into the ark of their souls as well as the clean. There is a great levity in the heart of man. The Jews cry Hosanna to Christ one day, and crucify him the next. They have their heart open one day for truth, and the next turn it out of doors. Those truths which are easy to be understood are hard to be impressed; our affections will as soon lose them as our understandings embrace them. Some were willing to rejoice in John's light, which gave a lustre to their minds, not in his heat, which would have given warmth to their affections; for John was a burning and a shining light, and they would rejoice in his light, but not in his heat, and in that too but for a season. We begin in the Spirit, and end in the flesh. We go from God with affections, and quickly grow cold again. Our hearts are like lute strings, changed with every change of weather, with every temptation, and scarce one motion of God in a thousand can prevail upon us.

5. In a carnal improvement of truth. Some endeavour to make truth subservient to lust, and, like spiders, draw cursed poison out of the sweetest flowers; as when men hear of God's willingness to pardon and receive repenting sinners, they will argue from hence for deferring their repentance till they come to die; so, Ps. xciv. 7, God's patience is made a topic whence to argue against his providence. Wicked men father their sins upon God's word. A liar will find his refuge in the rewards God gave the midwives that lied to Pharaoh, for the preservation of the Israelites' children, and Rahab's lie for preserving the spies. Though God rewarded their fidelity, yet we read not that he approved their sin. Some will venture into all kind of wicked company, from Christ's example, who conversed with sinners, when Christ companied with sinners as a physician with diseased persons, to cure them, not to approve them; but these with persons not to communicate holiness to them, but receive infection from them. Thus, like the devil, we have Scripture at our fingers' ends to plead for our lusts. As the sea turns fresh water into salt, so a carnal heart turns divine things to carnal ends. As man subjects the precepts of God to a carnal interest, so they subject the truths of God to carnal fancies; make a humorous and crazy fancy the interpreter of divine oracles, and not the Spirit speaking in the word; this is to rifle truth of its true mind and intent, as it is more to rob a man of his reason, the essential constitutive part of man, than of his estate.

II. Secondly, Enmity against the duties God doth enjoin, as well as against the truths he doth reveal. We are not willing to come to God in duty;

which strangeness took date from the beginning of our nature. We were 'estranged from the womb,' Ps. lviii. 3. I shall instance in prayer, which is one of the greatest duties, and is an immediate speaking to God. And in that duty wherein there is the greatest intimacy with God, there is the greatest aversion, and consequently an enmity against God.

1. Unwillingness to it. Men cannot endure to give God a visit; if they do, it is with such a dulness of spirit, as if they wished themselves out of his company; which testifies that men care not for any correspondence or friendship between God and their souls. Man having an enmity to true holiness, hath from thence an enmity to prayer, because holiness must at least be pretended in prayer, because in that duty there is a real speaking to God, and a communion with him, unto which holiness is required. Now, as wicked men hate the truth of holiness, because it is unsuitable to them, so they are not friends to the pretence of it in that duty, because thy must for some space be diverted from the thoughts of their beloved lusts. I appeal to you, whether you are not more unwilling to practise prayer in your closets than to join with others, as if it were a going to the rack, and rather your penance than privilege. If men do come to God, it is a constrained act, to satisfy conscience; and such are rather servile than son-like performances, and spring from bondage more than affection. If conscience, like a task-master, did not lash them to duty, they would never perform it. If we do come willingly, it is for our own ends, to have some deliverance from some troubles: 'In trouble have they visited thee; they poured out a prayer when thy chastening was upon them,' Isa. xxvi. 16. In trouble they will visit God; in prosperity he shall scarce hear of them. In affliction he finds them kneeling, and in prosperity he finds them kicking. They can pour out a prayer in distress, and scarce drop a prayer when they are delivered. This unwillingness to address God, what slight and low thoughts doth it imply! It is a wrong to his providence, as though we stood not in need of his assistance, but that we can do all our business ourselves.

It is a wrong to his excellency, as though there were no amiableness in him to make his company desirable. This enmity is the greater, by how much God's condescension is the greater to admit us to his presence. It was a part of the devils' hatred; they were loath to have Christ present with them: 'What have we to do with thee, Jesus, thou Son of God?' Mat. viii. 29. Men excuse their neglect of private prayer by their want of opportunity; but, indeed, they want hearts. We no sooner step up to heaven with a whole ejaculation, than step over the threshold about our business. We naturally desire acquaintance with the greatest persons that may advance our interest; but we are ready to bury our interest, rather than be acquainted with God.

2. Slightness in the duty. We are loath to come into God's presence, and when we are come, we are loath to keep with him. When men do not their duty heartily, as to the Lord, they look not upon him as their master, whose work they ought to do, and whose honour they ought to aim at.

(1.) In respect of time. Our dullest and deadest time we think fittest for God; when sleep is ready to close our eyes, we think it a fit time to open our hearts. How few morning sacrifices hath God from men? They leap out of their beds to their pleasures or worldly employments, without asking counsel at God's mouth. As men reserve the dregs of their life, their old age, to offer up their souls to God; so they reserve the dregs of the day, their sleepy times, for the offering their service to God.

(2.) In respect of frame. We think any frame will serve God's turn; which certainly speaks our enmity, and slight thoughts we have of him.

Man naturally performs duty with an unholy heart, whereby it becomes an abomination to God, Prov. xxviii. 9. He that turns away his ear from hearing the law, even 'his prayer shall be an abomination.' God calls for our best sacrifices, and we give him the worst, such which he hates: I hate, I despise your feast days, and I will not smell in your solemn assemblies,' Amos v. 21. They were duties which God commanded, but he hated them for their evil frames, or corrupt ends. God requires works of grace, and we present him not with so much as the work of nature, but the work of corruption. There is not that natural vigour which we have in worldly business: you may often observe a liveliness in man as to that; but change the scene into a motion towards God, and how suddenly does this vigour shrink, and their hearts become sluggish, and freeze with coldness.

Many times we pray as coldly as if we were loath that God should hear us, and take away that lust which conscience forces us to pray against. How flitting are we in divine meditations, how sleepy in spiritual exercises! This proceeds from the aversion of the soul, and its estrangedness from God. But in other exercises we are active. The soul doth not awaken itself, and stir up those animal spirits in religious duties, which it will in bodily recreations and sports; whereby it is evident we prefer the latter before any service to God. Since there is a fulness of animal spirits in us, why might they not be excited in holy duties, as well as in corporeal operations, but that there is a reluctancy in the soul to exercise its supremacy over them in this case?

3. Weariness in it. We are not weary with that dulness, but in the duty itself; our deadness shews a disaffection, our weariness shews a greater; we are loath that God should have so much as a day's service from us, or anything that looks like a service. How tired are we in the performance of spiritual duties, when in the vain triflings of time we have a perpetual motion! How will many force themselves to dance and revel a whole night, when their hearts will flag and jade at the first entrance into a religious service. Some in the prophet wished the Sabbath over: Mal. i. 13, 'Ye said also, Behold what a weariness it is.' Attendance on him is a weariness; God had but a poor polluted service from them, and they were weary of that little they gave him, they grudged him that. This unwieldiness in duty is a sign we receive little satisfaction in God's company, and that there is a great unsuitableness between him and us. When our joy begins when the duty ends, it evidences that there was no affectionate motion to God, but a tired and yawning service. Unwilling servants stay not long at their master's work, neither are cheerful in it. If we did love God, it would be with us as with the needle towards the loadstone, there would be a speedy motion, and a fixed union. Saints in heaven, whose affections and judgments are perfect, behold the face of God five or six thousand years together without weariness; but we naturally are neither willing to come, nor come to stay in his presence.

Objection. Natural men had best not pray, or meditate at all, if even their prayers are acts of enmity.

Answer. Their prayers are not acts of enmity, though the natural enmity be discovered in them. In the mal-performance of the duty there is a denial of his holiness, but in the total omission there is a denial of his sovereignty, who commands it as a natural duty; or his providence, who orders human affairs; of his holiness too, and righteousness in his law which enjoins it.

4. Neglect of expecting answers. Men naturally care not for having the spiritual mercy they pray for of course from God, though they are desirous of any temporal; for the latter they will endeavour, but leave the other

wholly upon God's hands, as if they were careless whether they had them or no. They care not whether their letters come to God's hands or no, and therefore care not much for any returns from him; whereas if we have any love to a person we send to, or value of a thing we send for, we should expect an answer every post. The creature in its natural instinct goes beyond such persons, for there is an ἀποκαραδοκία, 'For the earnest expectation of the creature waits for the manifestation,' &c., Rom. viii. 19. Every creature is in a more waiting posture than a natural man. It is a sign we do not own God for our master, or ourselves for his servants, if we do not wait upon him till he shew mercy to us: 'As the eyes of servants look unto the hands of their master, so our eyes wait upon the Lord our God, until he have mercy upon us,' Ps. cxxiii. 2. It implies that we think God will not hear or cannot hear, or that we have no need of him, and can do well enough without him, or that prayer is no effectual means to procure blessings. If so, why dost thou pray at all? If it be otherwise, why dost thou not wait for an answer? So that there is a disaffection in man to the duty itself, and to God the object of it, or to the subject of it, the thing prayed for; whereas those that love God, and love the spiritual mercy they pray for, watch thereunto with thanksgiving: 'Continue in prayer, and watch in the same with thanksgiving,' Col. iv. 2. They watch for occasion of praise. As we are to be in a praying posture to desire a blessing, so in a waiting posture to meet with it. But a natural man doth not love to be beholden to God if he can help it, and if he doth praise God after any common mercy received, it may proceed from a natural ingenuity or present sense of the mercy itself, not from any affection to the donor; but as for any spiritual mercy, as the stirrings of his affections by any truth, he is so far from praising God for them that he is troubled at them, and quickly quenches them.

5. Desertion of the duty. If God does not answer us, naturally we cast off the duty, and say with those in Job, 'What is the Almighty, that we should serve him? and what profit should we have, if we pray to him?' chap. xxi. 15. They pray not out of conscience of the command, but merely for the profit; and if God makes them wait for it, they will not wait his leisure, but solicit him no longer. There are two things expressed, that God was not worthy of their service, and that the serving of him would not bring them in a good revenue, or an advantage of that kind they expected. It is interest draws men to prayer, and when that is not advanced they will beg no more; like some beggars, if you give them not presently upon their asking, from blessing they turn to cursing, so do men secretly do that which Job's wife advised him to do upon his affliction: 'Dost thou still retain thy integrity? Curse God and die,' chap. ii. 9. What a stir, and pulling, and waiting, and caring is here! Cast off all service, be at daggers-drawing with God! So 'it is vain to serve God, and what profit is it that we have kept his ordinances, or that we have walked mournfully before the Lord of hosts?' Mal. iii. 14. If they have not the benefits they beg, they think God unrighteous, and does them wrong to withhold from them the favours they imagine they have deserved, and if they have not that recompence when they would, they leave off the serving God any more as a vain and unprofitable thing; whereas love moves upon a sense of duty, a natural man that hath an aversion, moves upon a sense of interest. Love is encouraged by answer, but is not dissolved by silence; but a natural man would have God at his beck, and steers his course in duty by the outward profit, not by the inward pleasure.

This enmity might further be evidenced by,

First, Our enmity against Christ. Many that are his own receive him not, John i. 11; his own by privileges, to whom he gave ordinances and spiritual meat from his table; his own by profession, who profess they have made a covenant with him, and yet underhand keep up their ancient agreement with hell. Professions of Christ are no demonstrations of love to him. We may commend another for his parts and perfections, and yet have a secret grudge against him. All the pretended love unrenewed men have to Christ has no better ground than the Turk's love to Mahomet, for it has no higher spring than education; and had their lot been to be born among them, they would have loved Mahomet with as warm a devotion as now they pretend to love Christ, for they love him not formally, but they love that which they were brought up in the profession of, let it be what it will. This enmity against Christ reflects upon God himself. Christ tells us often he was sent by God: an affront to an ambassador is an injury to the majesty he represents. Despising the embassy of an angel is an act of enmity against God, much more the despising the embassy of his own Son.

This is evident in the practices of men. It is hard to convince men of the necessity of Christ. You see what little fruit Christ himself had by all his preaching among the Jews. When men are convinced, they endeavour to stifle those convictions. We are as untamed and unruly heifers, that will not endure the yoke; they will break those cords as if they were the most formidable evils, and shake them off from them as if they were vipers upon their hands. When men cannot stifle their convictions, yet they are loath to come to Christ. 'You will not come to me,' John v. 40. They would bring something of their own to him, for they grudge him the glory of being an entire Saviour; or if they do come to Christ, it is for ease, not for holiness, for when their troubles are ceased they return to their vomit. If men do come, it is a restrained act; men are therefore said to be drawn, and it is the mighty power of God to bring them. Did not God overpower the hearts of his people, but leave them to themselves, they would still stand it out in rebellion against God.

Secondly, Enmity to the saints. When the devil found God above his reach, he set himself against the creatures that were designed more peculiarly for his service. Just after we read of enmity to God in Adam, we read of enmity to the godly in Cain. The Italians, when they say *un Christiano*, commonly mean a blockhead; and our common speech, *a silly Abraham*, imports no better: it will be so to the world's end. 'Despisers of those that are good' are ranked with those that are enemies to God, 2 Tim. iii. 3. It arises from a hatred of holiness itself, and it is enmity to God; for he that would not suffer him to have a holy servant would not suffer him to have a holy throne, a holy sceptre, a holy crown, a holy kingdom. If men hate the children of light, they do by consequence hate the Father of lights. Mr Cotton was convinced of his enmity against God by his enmity to the servants of God.

There are several causes of this enmity:

1. Dissimilitude between God and a natural man. As likeness in nature and inclinations is a cause of love, so dissimilitude and unsuitableness is a cause of hatred. Distance of manners breeds alienation of affection. This dissimilitude depends also upon the opposition between the law and the nature of a sinner; 'The law is spiritual, but I am carnal,' Rom. vii. 14. Hence proceeds all that acting against it; for the apostle says, 'I consent to the law that it is good,' ver. 15, 16, but my flesh, which hath a repugnancy to it, will not comply with it: the spiritual law and the carnal heart do quarrel with one another.

Dissimilitude between God and a natural man is the greatest in respect of nature. God is infinitely holy, man corrupt and filthy. Darkness and light, heaven and hell, are directly contrary, so is Christ and Belial. Let engagements be what they will, so long as men are of different spirits they cannot agree. As in regenerate men this dissimilitude works an abhorrency of themselves, as in Job, so in natural men it engenders a disaffection to God.

This dissimilitude is greatest in respect of ends. There are in God and men different ends. Man's end is to please himself and satisfy the desires of the flesh; God's end is to vindicate his law, and shew himself the righteous governor of the world, which cannot be attained without a contrariety to the corrupt end of man. The remedy then will be to get a renewed nature, the image of God new-formed in the soul.

2. Guilt. Men fly from God out of shame; they consider the debts they owe God are great, and naturally debtors fly from their creditors for fear they should exact or demand anything of them. Adam's guilt was rather attended with a flight from him than with an approach to him. Those Israelites that desired God no more to speak to them but by Moses were afraid of his presence too when his face shone with an heavenly splendour. Terror is essential to guilt, and hatred to a perpetual terror. Their guilt made them fly from that Moses, whom they knew to be their friend, when God had set a signal mark upon him. When men cannot discharge their judgments of the belief of a strict account, and dreadful hell, and perpetual immortality, their hearts are pierced with their sins like so many darts. As they have a thousand sins, so they have a thousand stings all pointed with God's wrath, and returned back with their own hatred, though it is but the just fruit of their own doings. The frequency of iniquity contracts the more implacable contrariety to God, and makes them as incapable of any union to God as of repose in themselves. The remedy then is to labour for justification by the blood of Christ, which is only able to remove that guilt which engenders our hatred.

3. God's crossing the desires and interests of the flesh. Natural qualities increase with the resistance of their contraries, so doth sin. The duties God doth principally love do most of all cross our corruptions, and those are the duties we hate most. Sodomites shew most disaffection to Lot when he opposeth them in the prosecution of their lusts with the angels: 'We will deal worse with thee than with them,' Gen. xix. 9. Had God (as well as Micaiah to Ahab) spoke good to natural men in their own esteem, and held them up in their lust, his truth would not be so much imprisoned in unrighteousness, but be highly adored with men's choicest affections; but his commanding things according to his own holy nature brings into act that habitual hatred which was before in the heart. All hatred arises from an opinion of destructiveness in the object hated. Why do we loathe a thing but because we imagine it inconsistent with our happiness and wishes? And a sinner being possessed that his darling sin is inconsistent with the holiness of God's law, hates God for being of a nature so contrary to that which he loves. The disappointment our corrupt principles find by any truth of God exasperates the heart. The Jews expecting an earthly grandeur by the Messiah, and that they should be made lords paramount of the world, was the cause that they were the more desperate enemies to Christ, when they found his design to be short of their expectations, and that his humility favoured not their pride, and his meekness was not like to raise him from the footstool of the Roman empire to the throne of the world.

The remedy then is, to have a high esteem of the holiness and wisdom of the law of God, and the advantages he aims at for our good in the enjoining of it; to account it better than thousands of gold and silver; to look upon his commands as not grievous, 1 John v. 3.

4. Love of sin. The greater the love of sin, the more must be our hatred of God; because the more we love that which hath an essential enmity against God, the more we signify that it is our chief good and happiness, and consequently we must hate that which is most contrary to it, and would hinder our enjoyment of it; and therefore our hatred of God's holiness grows up equally with our fondness of sin. When by frequent acts the habitual nature is strengthened, all the power of doing contrary is swallowed up in that habit. Hence it is said, 'the carnal mind is enmity to God,' *i. e.* the sensual mind, when sensuality hath got the mastery of the mind, and planted sensual habits, there is enmity to God; and it cannot be subject to the law of God, because that habit wholly acts the mind. Men's reasons side with the precepts of God, and conclude them to be the way to felicity; but the law of the mind is too weak for the powerful and pleasing charms of the flesh, whereby they are drawn into an imaginary paradise, but a real captivity. The hating all the dictates of God our Saviour is put upon this score. Light must be odious when darkness is lovely; God must needs be hated when his enemy is most caressed. As the love of God in the godly is the cause that they hate sin, so the love of sin in the wicked is the cause that they hate God. Every sin being an aversion from God in its own nature, and a conversion to the creature, according to the multiplying the acts of sin, this aversion from God, and conversion to the creature, must needs be increased; and by how much the more love we have to the creature, so much the more love is taken from God. The remedy then is, to endeavour for as great a hatred of sin as thou hast of God; to look upon sin as the greatest evil in itself, the greatest disadvantage to thy happiness.

5. Injury we do to God. It is proper to men *odisse quos læserint;* whereas the person injured might rather hate, yet the person injuring hath often the greatest disaffection. Joseph's mistress first wronged him, and then hated him. Saul first injured David, and then persecuted him; as if David had been the malefactor, and Saul the innocent. Italians have a proverb to this purpose, *Chifa injuria ne pardonna mai.* The reason is, because they think the injured person must needs hate him; and love is not an affection due to an enemy. We have also suspicious thoughts of the person we have provoked to be our enemy. We wrong God, and then we hate him; measuring his affections by human passions; and thinking, that because we have wronged him, he must needs lay aside all the goodness and patience of his own nature, and watch the first opportunity of revenge. Every sin and act of it being enmity to God, the more the habit of any sin is increased, by frequent acts, the more also is the habitual enmity in the heart increased; for as every sin has an immediate tendency to the supply of some lust, so it has a remote and principal tendency to the increase of that enmity. Cain first affronts God in his omniscience and providence, and then departs from his presence; turns his back upon him, and becomes the head of the profane part of the world; 'The presence of the Lord,' Gen. iv. 16, *i. e.* from all the ordinance of God, and communion with him in worship. The remedy then is, to endeavour a conformity to God's holy will; to think with thyself every morning, What shall I do this day to please God? what duty does he require of me? The more thou dost obey his will, the more thou wilt love his holiness.

6. Slavish fear of God. Men are apt to fear a just recompence for an injury done to another, that he will do him one ill turn for another; and fear is the mother of hatred. God being man's superior, and wronged by

him, there follows necessarily a slavish fear of him and his power; and such a fear makes wrathful and embittered thoughts of God, while he considers God armed with an unconquerable and irresistible power to punish him. It is as natural for a man to hate that which he conceives to be against him, as for any animal to hate that whose acts it fears do tend to a dissolution of its being. The devils tremble, James ii. 19, φρίσσουσι; they have a great horror, and their enmity is as great as their fear; nay, heightened by their fear, because they have no hopes of pardon, they do their utmost to oppose God and have companions in misery; it is impossible a man should love God while he is apprehended as an irreconcileable adversary. The stronger the impressions of fear, the quicker the inclinations to hatred. But when the evil feared begins to strike, it makes the hatred shoot out in volleys of curses and blasphemies, which is evident in the damned. God considered as a Judge, is the object not of comforting, but terrifying faith; no man can naturally love that judge who he thinks will condemn him. A fear of God as an inexorable judge, that we have highly wronged, will nourish an enmity against him.

Then, be much in communion with God; strangeness is the mother of fear; we dread men sometimes, because we know not their disposition. The beasts themselves delight in the company of man, when, being familiarised to him, they fancy his disposition, and taste his kindness to them, which, when they were unacquainted with, they would fly from his presence with the greatest speed. Study the reconciling love of God in the gospel; consider much the loveliness and amiableness of his nature, his ardent desire thou wouldest be his friend more than his enemy. A cause of our hating God is our ignorance of him; for if we did but know how good he is, how merciful to man, and to us, if we would but leave our sin, we could not possibly hate him.

7. Pride. Self-denial is absolutely against the pride of reason, and this is the first lesson God teaches us. It is the first letter in the alphabet of the gospel of peace, and therefore we are against him. Men lift up the pride of reason against the truth of God, and the pride of heart against the will of God. Hence it appears that self is the great incendiary of the soul against God. The enmity of Tyre against God is charged upon this foot of account: 'Thy heart is lifted up in the midst of the sea; thou hast set thy heart as the heart of God,' Ezek. xxviii. 2. She would rather have her wisdom admired by God, than God's wisdom admired by her. The sharpest enmities in the world are founded upon this vice. This makes the greatest combustions in commonwealths. Men fear to be overtopped by one another. All other vices desire companions. A drunkard loves his good-fellows; he cares not to drink alone. An unclean person must have his mate. Swearers hate those that come not up to their own pitch; but a proud man would have none keep an equal pace with him; he cannot endure a companion, but would have all others under his feet. Pride is naturally against God, and therefore sin is often called a lifting up of the heart against God, a hardening the heart against him. Then endeavour after humility. Study the humility of God, who is more humble to us than we can be to him. Reflect more upon thy vileness than thy worth.

8. Love of the world. The greater dearness of sensual pleasures, the further our divorce from God. The love of the world is inconsistent with the love of God: 'If any man love the world, the love of the Father is not in him,' 1 John ii. 15. It puts us under an impossibility, while that love remains, to entertain the Spirit of truth: 'The Spirit of truth, whom the world cannot receive,' John xiv. 17; 'Whosoever will be a friend of the

world, is an enemy to God. The friendship of the world is enmity with God;' 'Ye adulterers, know ye not that the friendship of the world is enmity with God?' James iv. 4; know you not it is an unquestionable truth, your own consciences cannot be strangers to it. Indulgence to carnal interests and pleasures mounts up to a fierceness against God: 'Jeshurun waxed fat, and kicked,' Deut. xxxii. 15. The wisdom of the flesh is first earthly, then sensual, then devilish; when once the mind is possessed by an earthly and sensual temper, it will not be long before it grows up to devilishness, and you know that can be no friend of God. What begins in earthliness, earthly principles and ends, and proceeds on to sensuality, will end in devilishness, both principle and practice. Whosoever loves his own pleasure and voluptuousness, must needs hate whatsoever is contrary to it, and would destroy it; this is the great root of anger, revenge in man, and our contempt of God.

The remedy then is, to look upon the world with scorn, to think the soul above it, and that the contentments and pleasures of the world are fitter for beasts, and at best but accommodations for thee as a traveller, not a fit pillow to repose thy soul on. Despise the world, and the devil hath scarce any bait and argument left to move thee to an estrangedness from and an enmity against God.

Now if all the saints that ever were should meet together in a synod, to consult of the truth of this proposition, that the heart of man is enmity against God, they would all bear witness to it *nemine contradicente;* and he that denies it, I may confidently affirm, did never seriously read the Scripture, or cast one practical glance upon his own heart.

PART V.

The Subject improved.

I. The information to be derived from the subject.

1. How desperate is the atheism in every man's heart by nature! What a mass of villany is in the heart of man! What! to make God no God! set up our wills against the will of God! When we say an enemy to God, we must conceive all that may denominate a man base and abominable. What more can be added, than to say, such a man is an enemy to love itself? Sin and God are at direct odds. To harbour a traitor in a house after proclamation, is a capital crime, and comes under the charge of high treason. What then is the harbouring of sin against God, but involving thyself in the same rebellion which every sin includes in its own nature? This enmity to God has this aggravation in it, that it cannot upon any account whatsoever be just.

God himself cannot command a creature not to love him; before he can command this, he must change his nature, cashier his loveliness, cease to be the chief good. God cannot command any thing unjust; but this is intrinsecally unjust, eternally unjust, not to love that which is infinitely amiable. It had been unjust to command an act of the highest disingenuity and ingratitude, to hate the author of our mercies. It had been against the original nature of a rational creature, to be an enemy to that which is its chiefest good. Our loving God doth not arise merely from the command of God enjoining it, but from the nature of God, and the creature's relation to him. None but will confess, that had God never commanded us to love him, it had been highly abominable for a creature to hate his Maker and Benefactor: therefore in the moral law or decalogue, the love of God is not explicitly commanded, but supposed as a fundamental and indispensable principle; from whence all other commands are necessary consequences: so that this enmity against God is not only against his command, but against his very nature, and against the fundamental and indispensable principle of all God's commands, and all the duties which as rational creatures we owe to God.

The desperateness of this natural enmity will appear, (1.) In that it is as bad, and in some respects worse, than atheism. We complain much, and not without cause, of the growing atheism of the times; but we shall find as bad and worse than we complain of in our own nature, and the practices of men. Mirandula says, a speculative atheist is the most prodigious monster in the world, but a practical. An atheist that denies the being of God, does not so much affront him, as a natural man that owns his being, but walks as if there were no God; as if he were not a just and righteous God; as if he made use of his sovereign power to make laws for the prejudice of his creature.

The atheist barely denies God's being, the other mocks him. 'They have turned to me the back, and not the face,' Jer. xxxii. 33. This puts a slight upon him, turning the back upon him, which is an act of disdain, as if God were the most contemptible being in the world. Thou that turnest thy face to thy dog, thy beast, the devil, usest God with more contempt than thou dost thy dog, thy swine, thy ox, thy ass, yea, the devil himself. The atheist that denies God's being, and yet walks according to moral principles, is like the son in the Gospel, that told his father he would not go, and yet did; which Christ commends above the other, which acknowledged his father's authority to command him, and pretended a readiness to obey, but answered not his acknowledgments by the performance of his duty. A profane man, or a hypocrite, is more an atheist than one that professeth himself so, inasmuch as actions, and a continual succession and circle of them, makes a greater discovery of the principles of the heart, than the motions of the tongue. Would not that man who, in his belief of a Deity, doth things which fall under the censure of God's justice, and contrary to his law, and odious among men, though not punishable by man, do things far worse, did not the fear of laws, the anger of his prince, the pain and disgrace of punishment, restrain him? Surely he would: for that principle which carries him against his reason and professed religion in his practices against God, would hurry him further, were there not some powerful limits set to him by human laws. Now what does this evince, but that he honours man more than God, fears man more than God, obeys man more than God, owns the power of man more than the power of God, which he pretends to acknowledge and believe?

The atheist denies God's being, the other his authority. And in denying his authority, virtually denies his being: for it is a contradiction to be God, and not to be sovereign. Does not man imply, by the breaking God's laws, that he would not have God act as a sovereign; that he would have him but a careless God, an unholy and unrighteous God in giving him the reins, and not prohibiting by holy laws any wickedness his heart is inclined unto? What then would become of God's being? His deity cannot outlive the life of his authority and righteousness. If he ceased to be a righteous lawgiver, and a holy maintainer of his laws, he would cease to be a God. So that every breach of the law is a virtual deposing him from his supreme government, and consequently a virtual deposing him from his deity.

(2.) This enmity is of the same nature with the devil's enmity. It is not indeed in the present state, wherein man is, so intense, because his is direct, man's implicit. But yet, [1.] Natural men have a diabolical nature. There are but two seeds, the seed of the woman, and that of the serpent; two natures, the divine and diabolical. Satan is the father of wicked men, and fathers derive their nature to their children. He is not their father by creation, nor by generation, but by a diffusion of his principles into them. 'You are of your father the devil,' John viii. 44. God made man in creation according to his own image; and the devil quickly by corruption brings him into his likeness. In Scripture is not meant by the devil only a particular person, but a nature: so Christ intimates in his rebuke to Peter, 'Get thee behind me, Satan,' Mat. xvi. 23.

Peter, an eminent apostle, who had a little before made an illustrious profession of Christ being the Son of God, vers. 16, 17, is now called devil; not because he was really the person of the devil, but the devil's nature did then exert itself in him; for that advice proceeded not from a divine, but diabolical disposition; for it made directly for the serving the devil's kingdom, which was only to be overthrown by the death of Christ. Hell itself could not produce a more devilish result of its deepest counsels, than the advice which Peter now gave, which would highly have promoted the interest of hell. And do but observe the reason why Christ calls him Satan: 'Thou savourest not the things which be of God,' &c., ver. 23. The things of God, and the things of man, and savouring the things of God, and the things of man, are set in opposition; and a man that savours not the things of God, but the things of man, such a man and Satan are all one and the same in the account of Christ. So by *Christ* sometimes is not meant a particular person, but a nature: 'Christ in you the hope of glory,' Col. i. 27. What in one place is called the divine nature, is by Paul called *Christ;* not the person of Christ, but the nature of Christ; *i. e.* that spiritual principle of grace, or new nature, which is an earnest of your future inheritance, and so a ground of hope. A natural man is wholly carnal, Rom. vii. 18. There is no good thing dwells in him, no good principle; it may lodge a while; but it hath no settled abode; and what is not good, is of the devil. As God is the author of all good, so is the devil of all moral evil. So that a natural man is wholly diabolical.

[2.] Every natural man is a friend to the devil. There are but two sovereigns in the world, one rightful, and the other usurping. If we are enemies to the right sovereign, we must be friends to the usurper; if enemies to God, friends to the devil. He 'works in the children of disobedience,' Eph. ii. 2, 3, not by force, but by consent: for he works in them according to the desires of the flesh, which the apostle implies, 'fulfilling the desires of the flesh,' ver. 3. If the love of the world be enmity to God, 'the friendship of the world is enmity with God,' James iv. 4; then enmity to God must needs be a love of the devil; enmity to God implying a friendship with every thing that hath the same disposition against him. The love of the world, *i.e.* of the sin and unrighteousness of the world, necessarily includes virtually love of the god of the world, which is the devil's title, 2 Cor. iv. 4. And so a man adores Satan as a god, in loving that world the devil is the god of, that wickedness the devil is the head of, above God. Rebellion against God is called 'a covenant with death, and an agreement with hell,' Isa. xxviii. 18 (not with the punishments, but principles of hell); and being a friend of the devil, he must needs be a friend to the grand design of the devil, Isa. xiv. 12–14, and ver. 4, was spoke to the king of Babylon. The knot of friendship in the world is some particular man's design, which both friends agree in, and drive on. Now his design seems to be affecting the throne and authority of God; for God threatening the king of Babylon, and in him, as the type, the great antichrist, compares him to Lucifer, who was not content with his station as a subject, but would mount into the chair of the supreme power.

[3.] Thy enmity against God is in some respect as much, in regard of the actual effects of it, as the devil's is, though not in regard of disposition. We declare our enmity as far as we can: we cannot pull God out of heaven; we cannot nail Christ to the cross again, and pierce his heart; we cannot rail at him to his face as the Jews did; but the despising his laws, disowning his power granted by heaven over us, is the only thing we can do against him; and this we do as much as we can, as much as the gripes of conscience and our interest in the world will give us leave. We virtually deprive him of that which was the reward of his sufferings, viz., his power; of the design of his sufferings, viz., the propagation of his evangelical law in our heart. And he that would destroy the dearest things God and Christ have left in the world, and that which he gave the greatest charge for the preservation of, would act all the villanies against the person of Christ, as well as against what he had in the world, and against the essence of God, were it in his power; thou dost as much in this, as the devil can do. The being of God and the person of Christ are above his reach as well as ours. All that he can do is to trample upon his laws, and list others in rebellion against God, and in this thou dost comply with him. He can do no more, and thou dost as much.

[4.] It is a worse enmity than is in hell. This enmity is more disingenuous than that in hell. Our hatred of God is worse than that of the damned; they despairingly hate him under the inevitable and unavoidable strokes of justice; thou hatest him while thou art hedged in with the expressions of his goodness. They hate him under vials of wrath, and we under showers of mercy; they in terror of damnation, and we under the sense of kindness. They hate him because he inflicts what is hurtful, and we because he commands what is profitable and holy. Our hatred of God is worse than the devils' hatred of him. We hate God, who contrived our redemption, and sent his Son to accomplish it; the devils had not those obligations laid upon them. Christ came not for them, nor shed his blood for their recovery. They hate their Creator, but we our Creator and Redeemer too. The devils hate him that came to torment them and destroy their works; we hate him that came to bless us, and save our souls.

2. Information. God is the greatest evil in the account of every natural man. If there be in us a greater enmity to God and his law than to anything else, it implies that we think him the greatest evil, and the worst of beings. Evil, and not good, is the object of hatred. As love is the propension of the mind to something as good, so hatred is an alienation of the mind from something as evil, either really or supposedly.* We cannot possibly hate good as good, as we cannot possibly love evil as evil. Now, nothing but sin is absolutely evil, and therefore nothing but sin should be the absolute object of our hatred. But seeing that love, which should be set upon God, is set upon sin, and that hatred, which should have only sin for its object, pitches upon God as its object, it is hence clear that we account sin the highest good, and God the greatest evil.

Though a man doth not hate God as God, yet, there being more of his hatred spent against God than against anything else, it is most certain that

* Plutarch's Morals, pp. 536, 537.

God is virtually accounted by us the most detestable being. Do we offend any so much as we do God? Do we love the prosecution of anything which is distasteful to man, as we do that which is an abomination to God? Is there anything in the world we do more rejoice in than that whereby God is prejudiced? Is there anything we do love and pursue with greater violence than that which is hateful and injurious to him? Are we so absolutely contrary to any man, any creature, in our natural inclinations, dispositions, affections, and desires, as unto God? Is it not clearly manifest by our inward and outward carriage, that we imply that God is the greatest evil, and we rank him who is unchangeably good in the place of sin, which is unchangeably bad? As love is carried out in desire for the object beloved, so hatred is a flight from it. As love is accompanied with joy at the presence of a beloved object, so is hatred attended with a detestation. Are we not naturally more desirous of opportunities of sin, than opportunities of service to our Maker? Are we ever so cheerful in the presence of God, and communion with him in religious services, as in our sports, recreations, and sinful practices? What, then, has most of our love; what do we account our supreme happiness, and our worst misery?

3. Information. It justifies God in his acts of punitive justice. (1.) In his severest judgments in the world. Who can blame God for his severities against those that hate him, especially after riches of forbearance? Consider man as his desperate enemy, and you may more admire his clemency than accuse his justice. You may wonder that he does not destroy the whole stock of mankind, as well as send some few drops and hailstones of judgment upon the world. We may rather stand amazed at his patience, that he suffers such creatures to live, than murmur at his judgments, for not a day but we commit many acts which manifest this hatred. For as all actions truly good partake of the nature of love to the chiefest good, so all unworthy actions, which are at a distance from God, the chief end, are marshalled by, and tinctured with, that enmity which lurks in the soul. It is equal God should be a judge to condemn, where he is rejected as a sovereign to rule.

(2.) It justifies God in his judgments upon infants. Indeed, we call infants innocent, and we are startled at the pain and sufferings of babes; but this doctrine is a sufficient curb to any accusations of God in such proceedings. Do we not kill vipers and noxious creatures in the nest? Infants are endued with an inimical and hostile nature against God, though they exert it not by reason of the weakness of their organs. If death reigned over them that had not sinned after the similitude of Adam's transgression, Rom. v. 14, enmity surely reigned over them. The frost which, by congealing a viper, suspends its motion, does not expel its natural venom (which it hath in as great a quantity as the liveliest), though at present it binds up the activity of it, which will shew itself when outward impediments are removed by heat. Neither does the inability of infants exercising this enmity, discharge their nature from an inconceivable mass of it; nay, you may perceive some starts of it even in them. Did you never see envy, passion, sensuality in an infant? We may more wonder that God does not dash them in pieces at their first appearance in the world, as we do young wolves and ravenous creatures, than that he should use his right over them for their original pravity, and take them out of the world.

(3.) It justifies the eternity of punishment. Who can charge God with injustice, for punishing eternally a creature who doth eternally hate him, to keep that person in being to his everlasting damage, that does wish, and, if it were in his power, would accomplish, the destruction of God himself?

Can any punishment be too hard, any duration of it too long, for him that is an enemy to the best of beings; to one infinitely good, and therefore disingenuous; to one infinitely powerful, and therefore intolerably foolish?

4. Information. What an admirable prospect may we take here of God's patience! With what astonishment may we review all the former, as well as the present, age of God's forbearance towards men! that he should preserve such a crew of disingenuous monsters as we all naturally are; 'or despisest thou the riches of his goodness, and forbearance, and longsuffering?' Rom. ii. 4. Had he not had riches of goodness, forbearance, and longsuffering, and infinite riches too, the enmity of man against him had exhausted all before this time; and, being the riches of goodness, as well as longsuffering, it makes our enmity appear the blacker. A grain of goodness is no fit object for hatred, much less riches of it. How many millions of such haters of him breathe every day in his air, are maintained by his bounty, have their tables spread, and their cups filled to the brim, and that in the maddest of their reiterated belchings out of this enmity against him, under sufficient provocations to the highest indignation!

5. Information. Hence we see the root of all sin in the world. What is the reason men row against the stream of their own consciences? What is the reason men of sublimated reason, and clear natural wisdom, are voluntary slaves to their own lusts, which they serve with as delightful, as disgraceful, a drudgery against the light of their own minds? It is from this contrariety to God, seated in their very nature; they could never else so earnestly, so cheerfully, do the devil's work before God's; they could never else be deaf to the loud voice of God, and have their ears open to the least whisper of Satan. Whence proceeds our stupidity, the folly of our thoughts, the levity of our minds, the deadness of our affections, the sleepiness of our souls, our inexcusable carelessness in holy duties, more than anything of a temporal concern, but from this aversion from God! It is this enmity dulls our heart in any service. Though conscience which is in us, to keep up the interest of God's law, spurs us on to duty, yet sin that is within us, that keeps up the quarrel against heaven, hinders us from it, or diverts us in it.

6. Information. Hence follows the necessity of regeneration. This division between God and his creature will not admit of any union without a change of nature. The carnal mind, as such, can never be reconciled to God before this be wrought. The old frame must be demolished, and a new one reared, for a change of state cannot be without a change of nature. It is impossible that this nature, so corrupt and contrary, can ever be reconciled to the pure and holy nature of God; what communion hath light with darkness? We must be God's friends before we can be sin's enemies; the root of bitterness must be taken away, habitual corruption removed, the heart will never else stand right as a compass towards heaven. Who can ever fight against his nature? No man will ever resist the devil without a change; we cannot, without the rooting out this enmity, make a profitable approach to God. What expectation canst thou have of a good look from him, when thou comest to him with all thy natural hatred of him? How canst thou dare to come to him, who knows every circumstance of thy enmity better than thou dost thy name, and is so well acquainted with thy heart? What hopes can you have of any answer from him? If we bring our wickednesses with us to Gilgal, the place of worship, even there in the solemnest duties will God hate us: 'All their wickedness is in Gilgal, for there I hated them,' Hosea ix. 15. If the mind be filled with hostile principles against the purity of God's commands, it must be inexperienced and inactive to every work: 'To every good work reprobate,' Titus i. 16. If the head

be sick, needs must the heart be faint. If the counselling faculty be false, cursed must be all its advice.

7. Information. That is not grace which does not alter nature. Morality therefore is not grace, because it doth not change nature; if it did, many of the heathens were as near to God as the best of Christians; whatsoever may be done by the strength of nature cannot alter it, for no nature can change itself. Poison may be great within the skin, like to a viper's, be we never so speckled with a reformation. Freedom from gross sins argues not a friendship to God. None were so great enemies to Christ as the pharisees, to whom Christ gives no better a title than that of the devil's children, and charges them with the hatred both of himself and his Father, John xv. 24. The enmity may be the greater under a zealous and devout morality. The poor publicans crowded in to Christ, while the self-righteous Jews derided him, and rejected the counsel of God, and put the word of God from them. Luke vii. 30, Acts xiii. 46. It is a foolish thing for men to boast of their own heart, or outward conformity; thou canst not tell how soon that heart thou boastest of may boil out its enmity. The plant which is pleasant to the eye may be poison to the stomach. Boast not, therefore, of thy glossy morality, thy chequered skin, so long as there is a venom in thy nature. Whatsoever excellencies a natural man has are all tainted with this poison; his wisdom, learning, moral virtue, are rather aggravations than excuses.

8. Information. Hence follows the necessity of applying to Christ. As there is a necessity of a change of nature in us, because our enmity to God is a moral enmity, so there is a necessity of a compensation and satisfaction to God for the preservation of God's honour, because it is an unjust enmity, not rising from any injury that ever God did to us; and because his enmity to us, provoked by our disaffection to him, is a legal enmity, his law violated must be satisfied. Our enmity is unjust, and therefore must be parted with; God's enmity against us is just, and therefore must be removed by a satisfaction. And since we are unable to give God a compensation for our wrongs, we must have recourse by faith to that blood which hath given him a complete satisfaction. It is Christ only that satisfies God for us, by the shedding of his blood, and removes our enmity by the operation of his Spirlt.

9. Information. See hence the reason of the difficulty of conversion, and the little success the gospel hath. All the words in the world will not change nature; men strive against the Spirit, and will not come under the power of it if they might have their own will. Can you by exhortations ever reconcile a wolf and a lamb? Can you by rational arguments new mould the nature of a fierce lion, or by moral discourses stop the tide of the sea? Though man be a rational creature, yet corrupt habits in him answer to mere nature in them, and sway and tide us as much against God. Grave discourses can never set a man straight that is born crooked. It is no easy thing for the heart of man, possessed so long by this cursed principle, to surrender itself upon God's summons; men are not so easily reconciled when the hatred hath been hereditary in the family; this has been of as long a standing, within a few hours, as Adam himself. To turn to God in ways of righteousness, is contrary to the stream of corrupt nature, and therefore it must be overpowered by a flood of almighty grace, as the stream of the river is by the tide of the sea.

10. Information. If there be such an enmity against the sovereignty of God in the heart of man, this shews us the excellency of obedience. It is the endeavour of the creature, as much as in him lies, to exalt God, to keep him upon his throne, to preserve the sceptre in his hand, and the crown upon his head. As faith is a setting a seal to the truth of God, so is obedience a

setting a seal to the dominion of God, and subscribing to the righteousness thereof. It is called a confirmation of God's law, an affection to the honour of it: 'Cursed be he that confirms not all the words of this law, to do them,' Deut. xxvii. 26. It is an establishing it as a standing infallible rule, and consequently an establishing the lawgiver, and an applause to the righteousness of his government. God being the highest perfection, and infinitely good, therefore whatsoever rule he gives the creature must be good and amiable, or else it cannot proceed from God. A base and vile thing can never proceed from that which is only excellent. An unreasonable thing can never proceed from that which is altogether reason and regular; therefore the obedience to God's law is an acknowledging the excellent goodness, love, wisdom, righteousness of the lawgiver, and a bearing witness to it in the face of the world.

II. Use is for examination. Examine yourselves by those demonstrations laid down in the first part, whether this enmity be prevalent in you or no. 1. Have you yet a stoutness of heart against hearing the law of God, which crosses the desires of the flesh? 2. Are you unwilling to be determined by divine injunctions? 3. Doth your heart swell most against those laws which are most spiritual, and which God doth most strictly urge? 4. Do you fall out, and quarrel with your own consciences, when they press upon you any command of God? 5. Do you countenance that law in your members, that law of sin, in opposition to the law of your mind? 6. Are you willing to be at more pains and expense to violate God's law, than to observe it and preserve the honour of it? 7. Do you perform things materially righteous because of the agreeableness of them to your humour and constitution, out of respect to your reputation, or, which is worse, out of an affection to some base lust and carnal end, or out of a slavish fear of God? 8. Are the laws of men more valued and feared by you than the laws of God? Do you more readily obey them? 9. Are you desirous and diligent in the drawing men from compliance with God's laws, to be your companions in any sin you are addicted unto? 10. Do you take pleasure in the affronts men offer to God, and make them the matter of your sport and jollity? So much as you find of this temper in any of your souls, so much of enmity there is.

III. Use is for exhortation. 1. To sinners. Lay down thy arms against God. How can you hear these things without saying, Lord, deliver me from this nature? Oh, what, should I be an enemy to so good a God? Did God put enmity between the seed of the woman and the seed of the serpent, and shall I put enmity between God and my soul, and a love between my heart and the serpent? Shall I change this promise of God, and make my dearest affections embrace the serpent's seed, and refuse God himself? Lay down thy cudgels, strip thyself, yield thyself to him upon his own terms. How canst thou sit down at rest in hating God, and being hated by him? While thou art in thy natural condition, thou canst not be a friend to God; for 'they that are in the flesh cannot please him,' Rom. viii. 8. 'How can two walk together, unless they be agreed?' We must change our enmity into friendship if ever we would be happy. We must accept of his terms, to be at peace with him, or feel the bitter fruits of his powerful justice. We may pronounce in the presence of God, that if we henceforward endeavour not to get out of a natural state, it is a resolute maintaining the war against heaven.

Lament this enmity, and be humbled for it. If there be a common ingenuity, it will make thee tremble to think of thy hatred of mercy itself. Every sin is a branch of this enmity, and doth contribute to the increase of it; as acts strengthen habits, and as every part of the sea, according to its quantity and strength, contributes to the roaring and violent eruptions of it. We have robbed God, for as much obedience as we have given to the flesh we have taken from God; therefore rise as high as the fountain in your humiliations, and lie low, not for a particular sin only, but for that enmity in thy nature which is the root of all the sins thou ever didst act. The evil in our actions is transient, but there is a perfect and overflowing fulness of evil in thy nature to animate a thousand acts of the same kind; as the habit of love to God resident in thy soul can command and spirit a thousand acts with its own nature.

2. Use of exhortation. To regenerate persons, such as by the powerful working of the grace of God, and the overruling hand of the Spirit, have been brought out of this state of enmity. Besides those things which you may gather from the former informations as to grow up in all parts of the new creature, to further and advance that regenerate work in your soul, to make frequent applications of the blood of Christ, and to have your heart lifted up in the ways of God, and obedience to him, thereby to bear witness to Christ, the righteousness of God in his administrations in the world. Let me advise to these things.

1. Possess your hearts with great admirations of the grace of God towards you, in wounding this enmity in your hearts and changing your state. The apostle winds up our admirations of the love of Christ upon this peg: 'When we were enemies, we were reconciled to God by the death of his Son; much more being reconciled, we shall be saved by his life,' Rom. v. 10. Our salvation from sin by regeneration is the fruit of his resurrection and life, as our salvation from the guilt of sin by satisfaction was the fruit of his death; and not only so, saith he, but 'we also joy in God through our Lord Jesus Christ, by whom we now receive the atonement,' ver. 11. This reconciliation of us being the fruit of the first promise of breaking the serpent's head, Gen. iii. 15, *i.e.* the projects and designs of the devil, to set God and man at eternal variance, makes it the more admirable; that as soon as man had, immediately after his creation, and being made lord of the rest of the sublunary creatures, cast off his Lord and Creator, that just at that time, under the present sense of that unworthy slight, he should be laying about for the good of fallen man, and make a promise for the dissolving this enmity, and change this resistance of God into a more righteous one, viz. a variance with, and an eternal enmity against, the serpent.

And hath not this been the case of some of our souls, that God hath grappled with us, and changed the current of our wills, even at the very time of the spitting out our venomous disaffection against him? It was Paul's case; and the case of many, I am sure, since that time. If such a circumstance as this did attend thy first conversion, it should, methinks, enlarge thy notes, and wind up thy astonishment to a higher pitch. But howsoever it be, change your complaints into praises for your deliverance, though it be as yet imperfect. A lively and warm sense of it would quicken thy obedience, and spirit thee more in the ways of God than all thy complaints can do. It is to the grace of God that we owe the decays of it; it is a particular assisting grace that keeps it down, and binds it up at any time. If we are sometimes without considerable disturbances by it, it is not for want of the will of the flesh, nor for want of strength enough in the flesh, even in the best of men; but it is staked down, and stopped by the powerful operation of the Spirit, and the working of irresistible grace. To this purpose often reflect upon your former state; it will set a gloss upon the grace of God. The more disingenuous our enmity was, the more illustrious will it make the love of God to appear in our eye.

2. Endeavour to hate sin as much as thou hast hated God. What reason have we to bewail ourselves! None of us have ever yet hated sin so much as naturally we have hated God. Turn this affection now as much upon thy great enemy as thou hast done upon thy best friend. The deeper gashes thou hast given to God, Christ, and his glory, the wider wounds, the harder blows, the sharper stabs give to thy sin; have as great an animosity against it as you have had stoutness of heart against God. Come not under the power of any one; lift up thy hand most against spiritual sins; shew no obedience to the law of sin in thy members.

3. Inflame thy love to God by all the considerations thou canst possibly muster up. Outdo thy former disaffection by a greater ardency of love. Sincerely aim at his glory. Eye his command only in everything thou dost. Delight to please him above thyself. Endeavour by all means to draw others to think well of him and be at peace with him. Take pleasure in the conversion of others to him. Rejoice at any glory he gains in the world. The unjust enmity he receives from others should procure a greater respect from us to God. Oh that we could make up by an intenseness of love the injury he receives by the enmity of others, and balance their hatred by an increase of our affection! Oh that we could delight ourselves in him as much as we have been displeased with him, that he might be as dear to us as he is odious to devils, and that the devils themselves, in the degrees of their detestation of God, might not outstrip us in the degrees of our affection to him.

4. Bewail this enmity. Are the best of us perfect? Are we stripped of all relics of it? Has any man on earth put off the dregs of the flesh, and commenced an angel in purity? Have we got the start of all the saints of old, and expelled it wholly out of us? Have we outstripped the great apostle, who complained of sins dwelling in his flesh? Is there no more need of groans to be delivered from this body of death? Ah, what relics are there! Doth not the best man find it a laborious undertaking to engage against the remainders of nature in him, and to manage a constant and open hostility against the force of the sensual appetite, and the spiritual wickedness in the high places of his soul, though much wounded by the grace of God? It is this gasping body of death in a regenerate man that gives life to those swarms of imperfections in his religious duties. It is this that cripples our obedience, that shackles our feet, when they should run the ways of God's commandments. It is this drags away our heart after unworthy objects in the midst of those services wherein we attempt the nearest approaches to God. It is upon the score of this lurking principle in us that we may charge all the foils we suffer in our strongest wrestling for heaven.

And is not this cause enough to bewail it? One great ingredient in any day's repentance is an acknowledgment of the due demerit of sin, and the righteousness of God in his threatenings and punishment, and this must be the ground of the abhorrency our souls have to his statutes, 'They shall accept of the punishment of their iniquity,' Lev. xxvi. 43, *i. e.* they shall repent of it, and acknowledge my righteousness in it, 'because, even because;' and ver. 40, they were to confess their iniquity and the iniquity of their fathers, *i. e.* the iniquity derived from their fathers, for their actual sins are expressed by 'the trespass they trespassed against God.' Are there not daily starts of this nature in us? Do we not need a daily pardon for it? And is it for God's honour to pardon us without an humble acknowledgment? It is the greatest part of our enmity that we are not more affected with it. Our breaking God's commands is not so much as the inherent contempt of God in us; a man may receive injuries from another, and lightly pass them over, when he knows the person hath no disaffection to him.

It was not so much the act of adultery and murder that Nathan, by God's commission, charges so home upon David, as his despising God's commands and despising God himself: 'Wherefore hast thou despised the command of the Lord?' 2 Sam. xii. 9; and ver. 10, 'Thou hast despised me.' And it is not so much our actual breaches as our natural and indwelling contempt of God, that is most chargeable upon us in our approaches to him and exercises of our repentance before him. If a likeness to Adam's sin be made a ground of the aggravation of actual sin,—'But they like men have transgressed,' Hos. vi. 7, implying that to be the greatest,—then the corruption of nature we derived from him by the means of that sin must be the highest and most lamented.

5. Watch against the daily exertings and exercises of this enmity. When we would be serious in the concerns of God and our own souls, do we not feel some inward assaults against our own resolutions, and some secret adversary within striving against our most spiritual reflection? and is there no need of a watch? Alas! this being a constant adversary, requires our constant care; it being a secret and inward adversary, requires our utmost diligence and prudence. Who is there of us who serves God with that care, and obeys him with that reverence, as he doth his worldly superior? Do we not sometimes hate instruction when it goes against the grain, and cast the words of God behind our backs, and thus kick against the Lawgiver? Do we not many times prefer the flesh before him? (I know in the bent of the heart a godly man doth not, but in some particular acts he may and doth.) Are not our understandings more frequently awakened to anything than that which God doth command? Are not our desires too vehement for those things which have no commerce with the law and mind of God? Have we no doubts of his faithfulness, no murmuring against his sovereign disposal of things, no risings of heart against his law, against his providences, no self-confidence, envy, ambition, revenge? All these are but the branches of this bitter root. And is not our exactest care and constant watchfulness requisite against the workings of this natural cursed disposition? Sure it is, and sure it must be.

IV. Motives. These exhortations.

1. Consider the disingenuity of this enmity. There is no necessity thou shouldest be his enemy: it will not be honourable to thee to stand out. Peter denied Christ when his own life was in danger, and thou hatest God, who would put the life of thy soul out of danger. It is against all the obligations of nature and grace to be an enemy to him to whom thou owest thy being, thy preservation from hell, and recovery from misery, but for thy own fault. Do we not voluntarily subject ourselves to men whom we esteem good, though the loveliness of their persons and the goodness of their nature be infinitely short of God, and are as much below him in alluring qualities as they are in greatness and majesty? What benefits can men bestow upon their servants like those God doth recompense his sincere adorers with? Men may love their friends more than they can help them, but the loving-kindness of God is attended with a power as infinite as itself.

(1.) God hath been good to us. He is love, and we are out of love with love itself, 1 John iv. 8. Is he not our Father? why should we not honour him? Is he not our master? why should we not obey him? Is he not our benefactor? why should we not affect him? Whence have we our mercies, but from his hand? Who besides him maintains our breath this moment? Would he call for our spirits this instant, they must depart from us to attend his command. What, shall his benefits be made weapons of unrighteousness, and the devil's arms against him? Christ died for us while we were enemies, and shall we stand out as enemies still? It will be the least thou canst do to love him at the very time he shews mercy to thee, and that is every minute. There is not a moment wherein thou canst with any ingenuity be an enemy to him, because there is not a moment wherein he is not thy guardian, wherein thou dost not taste of his bounty. God hath let thee have thy swing all this time; thou hast had thy rendezvous at thy pleasure, and he never laid wait for thee but in kindness. He might have dwelt with us, as we do with venomous creatures, and destroyed such a generation of vipers, and crushed the cockatrice in the egg. What a disgraceful thing is it to put off the nature of men for that of devils, to hate God under mercy, as much as the devils do under wrathful anger! Is not God our greatest benefactor, and shall he have nothing but disdains from us for all his benefits? The psalmist cries out, 'What shall I render to the Lord for all his benefits towards me?' But it is the language of our heart, What ill turns shall we render to God for all his mercies unto us? It is his mercy we are not consumed, and shall we spend this mercy upon our lusts? He was compassionate in sparing us, and shall we be ungrateful in hating him? It is the highest disingenuity.

(2.) God hath been importunate in entreaties of us. God offers not only truce, but a peace, and hath been most active in urging a reconciliation. Can he manifest his willingness in clearer methods, than that of sending his Son to reconcile the world to himself? Can he evidence more sincerity than by his repeated and reiterated pressing of our souls to the acceptance of him? God knocks at our hearts, and we are deaf to him; he thunders in our ears, and we regard him not; he waits upon us for our acceptance of his love, and we grow more mad against him; he beseecheth us, and we ungratefully and proudly reject him; he opens his bosom, and we turn our backs; he offers us his pearls, and we tread them under our feet; he would clothe us with pure linen, but we would still wear our foul rags; he would give us angels' bread, and we feed on husks with swine. The wisdom of God shines upon us, and we account it foolishness. The infinite kindness of God courts us, and we refuse it, as if it were the greatest cruelty. Christ calls and begs, and we will not hear him either commanding or entreating. To love God is our privilege, and though it be our indispensable duty, yet it had been a presumption in us to aspire so high as to think the casting our earthly affections upon so transcendent an object should be so dear to him, had he not authorised it by his command, and encouraged it by his acceptance. But it is strange that God should court us by such varieties of kindness to that, wherein not his happiness but our affection does consist; and much stranger, that such pieces of earth and clay should turn their backs upon so adorable an object, and be enemies to him, who displays himself in so many allurements to their souls, and fix their hatred upon that tender God who sues for their affections.

Consider that God is our superior. An inferior should seek to a superior, not a superior to one below him. There is an equality between man and man, but an infinite inequality between God and us. God is also the party wronged, and yet offers a parley. And consider further, that when he could as well damn us as court us, he wants not power to rid his hands of us, but he would rather shew his almightiness in the triumph of his mercy, than the trophies of his justice; he would rather be a refreshing light than a consuming fire.

2. This enmity to God is the greatest folly and madness. The Scripture

tells us, that sin is folly and madness; and certainly had man a clear prospect of this truth, which in his first apostasy he fell from, so that he could examine all his speculations, desires, motions, and actions by that rule, they would appear to him to be acts of a crazy and frantic mind. Therefore, when upon our return to God we have but a glimpse of this truth, how much ashamed is man of the deformity of his actions from that rule; as a man that has been mad is of those pranks he played in his frenzy, after he is brought to his right wits. Hence repentance, which is always accompanied with a shame, is called μετάνοια, a return to our right wits.

1. This enmity to God is in itself irrational; because (1.) God is the most lovely object. He hath in his own nature, as well as in his operations, the highest right to our love; for the more of entity and being anything hath, the more of perfection, and the more lovely it is in itself, the more to be beloved by us. Now God hath the most of being, because other beings were eminently contained in his immense essence, and produced by his infinite power, and were the manifestations of himself, and lines drawn from him, and by him; and therefore he is the most amiable object, because the creature has nothing lovely but only what it hath from God, which is more eminently treasured up in him, and may in him be seen and enjoyed with a greater advantage. The creatures are but pictures, and can no more represent to the full the true amiableness of God, than a few colours, though never so well suited together, can the moral or intellectual loveliness of the soul of man. As God had all the ideas of his creatures in his mind, so he had the virtues of them in his essence. Therefore to love any creature above God, and so to hate him, is the highest piece of unreasonableness.

(2.) God is the chiefest good, and the fountain of all goodness. It is unreasonable to look upon that which comes from the fountain of goodness, to be destructive to our true pleasure; yet men have such hard thoughts of religion and divine commands, as if they were designed for their utter ruin, when they are the effluxes of infinite goodness. All hatred doth arise from an apprehension of the inconsistency of the thing we hate, with something we esteem a part of our happiness; and sinners being possessed with the thoughts of the justice and holiness of God, as inconsistent with their darling sin, hate him for being of a nature so contrary to that which they love; whereas none of God's perfections are repugnant to our being or well-being in themselves; for would we have a God unjust, what comfort could we then take in him? We hate him for being against that which is most against us. We hate him for hating of that which would destroy our souls, and embitter our beings to us to all eternity; we hate him for hating that which, if it were possible, would disquiet his felicity, and destroy his being. What an unreasonable thing is it to quarrel with that law of God, which obligeth you to nothing but what conduceth to the benefit of your souls, and the order of the world! What doth it bound and restrain you from, but that which would bring destruction upon you? Is it not a greater advantage to be carried fettered to heaven, than to run at liberty to hell? Who but a madman would prefer the devil's before God's yoke, and be the captive of a hellish tyrant, rather than the subject of a gracious sovereign? What an unreasonable thing is it to love any sin, a privation better than the best of beings? Can we expect to get as much advantage from him by being his enemies, as by being his friends, since he is of so merciful a disposition?

(3.) God cannot possibly do us wrong. All right hatred is from a real wrong, sense of wrong, or fear of wrong. Either of those is an unjust imputation upon God, who cannot possibly do wrong to his creatures, because he cannot be unrighteous: 'Is God unrighteous who takes vengeance?' Rom. iii. 5. Μὴ γένοιτο. For God is so far from being injurious in the least to us, that he doth cast about, and contrive our happiness in his laws more than we can ourselves, or are willing he should do for us. Men cannot, if they consult but the sparks of reason, but confess the reasonableness of God's commands, and be satisfied in the righteousness of the duties enjoined, and the profitableness of the counsels set out in the gospel, and must needs look upon the felicity promised to be excellent and desirable; and therefore cannot, upon any reasonable account, charge God with doing them any wrong. Or let me argue thus: either God hath wronged us or not. If not, it is unreasonable to disaffect him; if he hath, why should we hate him, seeing if God could do any injustice, he would not have the being of a God? For if it were possible, as soon as ever he should cease to be just and righteous, he would cease to be God, and destroy his own nature; for as every man, in doing an unjust act, is less than a man, and loses the end of his own reason, so God, by doing any injustice, would be less than a God. Nay, our hating him as a judge is highly irrational, because of his equity and righteousness in all his proceedings, and because it is our own act in forcing him to that by our evil practices, which he is not willing to do, but according to his own righteous nature, and for the vindication of his holiness in his law, cannot but do upon our final impenitency, and persisting in our transgressions.

(4.) God cannot be hurt by us. It is a folly among men to shew their enmity where they cannot hurt. What an unreasonable boldness is it for a man to think he can grapple with omnipotence, and enter the lists with the fountain of all strength and power! What is thy enmity, but a small wriggling against God! What disadvantage can accrue to him by thy opposing him! Just as much as the moon receives by the dog's barking at it, which neither stands still, nor alters its course, nor is frighted at the noise. Foolish man, that will not discover an enmity against a superior, but rakes it up in the ashes, and muzzles his anger till he be able to bite, and yet proclaims a war openly against heaven, as if he were too strong for God, and God too weak for him! As the light of God's face is too dazzling to be seen, so the arm of his power is too mighty to be oppressed by us. His almightiness is above the reach of our potsherd strength, as his infiniteness is above the capacity of our purblind understandings. His happiness is too firm to be disturbed by us, as well as his essence too glorious to be comprehended. What force canst thou have to resist the presence of him before whom the rocks melt, and the heavens at length will be shrivelled up as parchment by the last fire?

(5.) But though thou canst not hurt God, yet thou dost mightily wrong thyself. Senseless sinner! God is out of thy gunshot; thy arrows are too short for that mark, but his are long enough for thee; thy shot will fall before it reach him, but his arrows will both reach thy heart and stick in it. Hatred in the world is attended sometimes with outward advantage; but what gain canst thou expect by this enmity? What refreshment is there by thy endeavouring to dry up the fountain? What good by labouring to destroy the original of goodness itself? What harm is it to the sun to shoot up arrows against it? Do they pierce its light, or shatter any of the sparks of it? No, but they fall down upon the archer's head. The opposition of a wicked man against God is much like a man's running his head against a rock to be revenged on it for splitting his ship, whereby he bruiseth not the rock, but dashes out his own brains, and pays his life for a price of his folly. Poor man is like a potsherd, that justles with a rock, and bursts itself; and s not this the highest piece of madness? 'Woe unto him that strives with his Maker! Let the potsherds strive with the potsherds of the earth,' Isa. xlv. 9. Dost thou fight against the Rock of Ages? It will rather blunt thy weapon than be hurt by thy arm; it will make thy sword fly back in pieces upon thy own face. Every wicked man is a greater enemy to himself than the devil is, and wrongs himself more than the devil can do; because he nourishes that sin in him which wars against his soul.

3. Consider the misery of such a state. Thou wilt be miserable with a witness: 'If any man love not the Lord Jesus Christ, let him be anathema,' 1 Cor. xvi. 22. Let all the curses in heaven and earth light upon him; let the mercy, wisdom, power, strength of God appear against him; let him not have an advocate to make any plea for him. Angels, men, devils will all appear against such a person.

(1.) Thou canst not possibly escape vengeance. The Sodomites, whose sins had so long dared God's justice, might have better escaped than thou canst; but, alas! what force hath a puppy or worm in a lion's paw! Thou art no more in his hand than a fly between a giant's fingers. Go, foolish, self-deluding creature, recollect thyself. Can such a bubble, dust, chaff, stubble, worse than nothing and vanity, wrestle with God? Ah, poor worm, wilt thou set thyself in a strutting array against omnipotency, far less in God's hands than a chicken new stripped of its shell in the talons of an eagle? Jacob, a holy man, wrestled with him upon a holy account, and broke his thigh. Take heed in thy wrestling with him upon a sinful account thou dost not break thy neck. If he be thy friend, none can hurt thee; but if thy enemy, none can relieve thee.

He is the best friend when men will love him, but as terrible an enemy as consuming fire when men will hate him. Thou must be subject to him whether thou wilt or no; there is no remedy. If submission to his mercy be not free, subjection to his justice must be forced. We must be under his power whether we will or no; we cannot wrest ourselves out of the compass of his arm. If we go down to hell, he is there; if we dive to the bottom of the deep, thence his hand will fetch us out. We always have been, are still, and for ever must be, within the reach of his almighty power. Whither wilt thou go? Is there any garrison to defend thee, any sanctuary to secure thee, any champion to stand for thee? If all the angels in heaven and devils in hell should rouse up themselves to be thy protectors, thou wouldest be just as happy as if thou hadst the shelter of the dust of the balance, or a drop of a bucket. Can we blind his eye that he should not see, or deafen his ear that he should not hear, or bind his arm that he should not strike? Can we remove his jealousy by increasing it? Can we mitigate everlasting burnings by adding oil to them? Can our sins stand out against his judgments, or our persons successfully combat with his wrath? Before any of those can be done, the Creator must descend into our impotency. What man will confess he is able to do any of those? And yet he will walk in a path of enmity. Wrath will come, though it be slow in coming. It is slow, but sure; the longer it is preparing, the bitterer it will be in enduring. Let all devils and sinners in the world join together, how soon is God able to overthrow them, and turn their Babel-fort to their own confusion, and bury them in the ruins of their own works! 'Though hand join in hand, the wicked shall not go unpunished,' Prov. xi. 21. How would he fling them all into hell, as one of us can a bag of dust or sand into the sea!

(2.) Thou dost even force God to destroy thee for his own content, and as it were provoke him to damn thee for his own ease; if thou wilt not lay down thy arms, thou dost wrest wrath out of his hands: 'Have quieted my spirit,' Zech. vi. 8. He speaks of the angels which he had sent out against Babylon, those black horses which noted death and destruction; and those angels doing their work and duty, are said by himself to quiet his Spirit; so that God can have no rest in his own Spirit but by thy submission or destruction. And the longer thou dost stand out, the more thou dost provoke God to take some course for the easing of himself; for punishment in another place, he calls his ease: 'I will ease me of my adversaries' Isa. l. 24; and the latter words explain it, 'I will avenge me of my enemies.' Is not the honour of God concerned in his laws? And would he not make himself ridiculous to the sons of men, if he did not severely punish their violations of them?

(3.) God cannot save thee without disturbing the happiness of those that love him, and are loved by him. Thou wilt but make a disturbance in heaven by thy contrary disposition, and hinder that exact harmony; thy jarring principles could never agree with that comfort;* thy enmity and division with that union; the repose of the saints would be disquieted, and their pleasure cooled: for if they cared not for thy company in the world, when they had many relics of enmity in themselves, and an imperfect holiness, they can less endure it in heaven, where their holiness is fully ripe, and their hatred against impiety perfectly strong; and God will not bring thee thither with that cursed nature thou hast, to damp their joy, and spoil the order of heaven. A state of wrath must necessarily succeed a state of enmity: for heaven can never be a place suitable to you; it will be as little agreeable to you, as your being there will be to God.

(4.) Thou hast the beginnings of hell in thee already. Enmity is a hellish disposition. As the perfection of love in heaven is a part of heaven's happiness, so the perfection of enmity in hell is a part of the damned's misery. The sight of God in heaven inflames love in saints, so the absence of God from hell enrageth enmity in the devils and damned spirits.

(5.) All thy enmity will certainly be charged upon thee one day. There is a time when all thy acts of enmity shall be set in order before thee: 'I will set them in order before thee,' Ps. l. 21. This is to be understood *more militari*, when sin shall be set in rank and file, in bloody array against thy soul; or *more forensi*, when they shall be set in order as so many indictments for thy rebellion and treason. What sadness will seize upon thee at the last, when God shall fix upon thee out of the crowd, and point at thee: 'But those my enemies, which would not that I should reign over them, bring hither, and slay them before me,' Luke xix. 27. How solemnly will he execute every enemy at the last! They shall be brought out shackled one by one, and Christ will sit and behold it. Lo, here is one of my enemies, I have found him out for all his fair hopes of escape. When men and angels shall say, 'Lo, this is the man that made not God his strength;' this is the man that set up other gods in his heart; that was such a fool as to think his pleasures, riches, strength, honour, to be his god. Ah, fool with a witness, to think that a god could be of thy own making!

* Qu 'concert'?—Ed.

THE CHIEF SINNERS OBJECTS OF THE CHOICEST MERCY.

This is a faithful saying, and worthy of all acceptation, that Christ Jesus came into the world to save sinners; of whom I am chief.—1 Tim. I. 15.

PART I.

The chief of sinners saved.

I. *Obs.* The salvation of sinners was the main design of Christ's coming into the world. II. God often makes the chiefest sinners objects of his choicest mercy.

For the last, that God doth so, observe,

1. God hath formerly made invitations to such. See what a black generation they were, Isa. i. by the scroll of their sins. They were rebels, and rebels against him that had nursed them: 'I have nourished and brought up children, and they have rebelled against me,' ver. 2. And in this respect worse than the beasts they were masters of; the stupid ox and the dull ass outstripped them in ingenuity: 'The ox knoweth his owner, and the ass his master's crib; but Israel doth not know, my people doth not consider,' ver. 3. He calls upon heaven and earth to judge between them, ver. 2. He appeals to men and angels as a jury to give their verdict, whether these people had not been the most disingenuous and ungrateful people in the world. Or if by heavens and earth he meant magistrates and people, as in the prophetic style they are usually taken, God then appeals to themselves to let their own natural consciences, and the common ingenuity their sins had left them, to judge between them. He comes to charge them 'laden with iniquity,' ver. 4. They had such great weights lying upon them that they were not able to stir, or laden with it, as some crabtree is of sour fruit. They had sprouted from a wicked stock; they had corrupted one another by their society and example, as rotten apples putrefy the sound ones that lie near them.

They had been incorrigible under judgments. God had used the rod again and again; but being there was no reformation, he was even weary of whipping them any longer: 'Why should ye be stricken any more? ye will revolt more and more,' ver. 5. They were also so universally infected that there was no sound part about them, but running sores all over; both head and heart were affected; corrupt notions in the one, and corrupt affections in the other. Or if you take it prophetically, *head* signifies the chief magistrate; *heart*, the judges; *feet*, the common people. The fire which had burnt their cities had not consumed their lusts, and dried up their sins: 'Your country is desolate, your cities are burnt with fire, your land strangers devour it in your presence, and it is desolate, as overthrown by strangers,' ver. 7. And had it not been for a small remnant, they had been as bad as Sodom and Gomorrah, ver. 9. Their services were polluted, vain, and an abomination to him, ver. 13; a trouble to him, his soul hated them, he was tired with them, ver. 14, for they came with their bloody murderous hands into God's presence.

Yet though he justly charged them with those horrid crimes, he gives them assurance of entertainment if they would return to him: 'Come now and let us reason together,' ver. 18. He would condescend to debate the case with them, when one would have thought he should have said, I'll have nothing to do with such a crew as they. God loves to discourse with men about this argument of pardon, and he loves that men should hear him speak concerning it. He would dispute them out of their sins into good and right apprehensions of his mercy; so 'Turn ye unto him from whom the children of Israel have deeply revolted,' Isa. xxxi. 6. *Revolted!* there is their sin; *deeply*, there is the aggravation of it; and being also *children of Israel*, a people of much mercy and miracles, there is another aggravation; yet turn unto him against whom you have thus sinned. The great objection of a penitent is, I have sinned, and I know not whether God will receive me. Consider, God knows thy sin better than thou dost, yet he kindly calls to thee, and promiseth thee as good a reception as if thou hadst never sinned.

So 'They say, If a man put away his wife, and she go from him, and become another man's, shall he return unto her again? Shall not that land be greatly polluted? But thou hast played the harlot with many lovers, yet return again to me, saith the Lord,' Jer. iii. 1. Though thou hast been a common adulteress, and made all comers every idle welcome, and been in league with many sins, yet upon thy return I will own thee; and these are God's warrants for encouragement.

2. God hath given examples of it in Scripture. Adam, the ringleader of all rebellions of mankind in the world, had the promise of the seed of the woman to break the serpent's head made to him, and in the genealogy of Christ is called the son of God, Luke iii. 38, not only in respect of creation, for so the devil is the son of God, but in a nearer relation. Yet all that deluge of wickedness which has overflowed the world since the fall, sprang out of his loins; nay, Abraham, the father of the faithful, was probably an idolater in Ur of the Chaldees, and a worshipper of the sun and fire, as his fathers were, Josh. xxiv. 2, yet God makes a particular covenant with this man, presents him with a richer act of grace than any in the world besides him had, even that the Messiah, the great Redeemer of the world, should come from his seed. This man is set up as the pattern of faith to others, and his bosom seems to be a great receptacle of saints in glory, Luke xvi. 22, 23. Israel's sins were as a thick cloud, yet this powerful sun did melt them: 'I have blotted out as a thick cloud thy transgressions, and as a cloud thy sins,' Isa. xliv. 22. A sullen gloomy morning often ends in a well-complexioned noon. Manasseh is an eminent example of this doctrine. His story, 2 Chron. xxxiii., represents him as a black devil, if all the aggravations of his sins be considered.

(1.) It was against knowledge. He had a pious education under a religious father. An education usually leaves some tinctures and impressions of religion. No doubt but the instructions his father Hezekiah had taught him, and the exemplary holiness he had seen in him, were sometimes awakened in his memory, and recoiled upon his conscience.

(2.) His place and station; a king. Sins of kings are like their robes, more scarlet and crimson than the sins of a peasant. Their example usually infects their subjects. As they are not without their attendance in their progresses and recreations, so neither in their vices and virtues.

(3.) Restoration of idolatry. Had he found the worship of the host of heaven derived to him by succession from his father, and the idols set up to his hand, the continuance of them had less of sin, because more of temptation; but he built again those high places and altars to idols, after they had been broken down, ver. 3, and dashed in pieces that reformation his father had completed.

(4.) Affronting God to his very face. He sets up his idols, as it were, to nose God, and built altars in the house of the Lord, and in the two courts of his temple, whereof God had said he would have his name there for ever, ver. 4, 5, 7. He brought in all the stars of heaven to be sharers in that worship which was only due to the God of heaven. What! could he find no other place for his idols but in the very temple of God? Must God be cast out of his house to make room for Baal?

(5.) Murder. Perhaps of his children, which he caused to pass through the fire as an offering to his idol, ver. 6; it may be it was only for purification. But he had the guilt of much innocent blood upon him, the streams whereof ran down in every part of the city: 'Moreover, Manasseh shed innocent blood very much, till he filled Jerusalem with blood from one end to the other,' 2 Kings xxi. 16.

(6.) Covenant with the devil. He used enchantments and witchcraft, and dealt with a familiar spirit, ver. 6, yea, he had acquaintance with more devils than one, and dealt with familiar spirits and wizards, in the plural number.

(7.) His other men's sins. He did not only lead the people by his example, but compelled them by his commands: 'So Manasseh made Judah and the inhabitants of Jerusalem to err, and to do worse than the heathen God had rooted out,' 2 Chron. xxxiii. 9, to make room for them. Hereby he contracted the guilt of the whole nation upon himself.

(8.) Obstinacy against admonitions: 'God spake to him and his people, but they would not hearken, or alter their course,' 2 Kings xxi. 10.

(9.) Continuance in it. He ascended the throne young, at twelve years old, ver. 1. It is uncertain how long he continued in this sin. Torniellus thinks fifteen years; Bellarmine, twenty-seven; Kimchi, fifty years, reckoning but five years of his life after his restoration. What a world of sin, and aggravations of it, were there in this man! and yet God was entreated, ver. 19.

3. The stock whereof Christ came, seems to intimate this: God might have kept the stock whence Christ descended according to the flesh, pure and free from being tainted with any notorious crimes; but we find sins of a crimson dye even among them. There are no women reckoned up in Christ's genealogy, but such as in Scripture are noted for looseness, Mat. i. 3. Tamar, who played the harlot with Judah her father-in-law, Gen. xxviii.; Rahab, ver. 5, the harlot of Jericho; Ruth, ver. 5, a Gentile and a Moabitess, the root of whose generation was Lot's son, by incest with his own daughter; Bathsheba, ver. 6, David's adulteress. He chose these repenting

sinners, out of whose loins Christ was to come, that the greatest sinners might not be afraid to come to him.

Was David, whose son our Saviour is called, much better? It is true, he was a man after God's own heart, but yet very notorious for that act of murder and adultery, and with more aggravating circumstances than usually are met with in acts of the like nature, 2 Sam. xi. Uriah was a godly man, and had a sense of the condition of the church and nation whereof he was a member, ver. 11; and such a man's bed David is not only content to defile, but he pollutes his soul with drunkenness, ver. 13; lays snares for his life, not in a manly, but sly and treacherous manner; for while he doth caress him, and shew him a fair countenance in his palace, he draws up secret instructions to Joab so to order the business, that Uriah might be thrust into his grave, and makes him the post to carry the commission for his own death, ver. 15, 16. After all this, he hath no remorse when he hears of the loss of so godly and valiant a man, but wipes his mouth, and sweeps all the dirt to the door of providence, ver. 25. Now, Christ's stock being thus tainted, was, methinks, an evidence that penitents, though before of the greatest pollutions, might be welcome to him. And that as he picked out such out of whose loins to proceed, so he would pick out such also in whose hearts to reside.

4. It was Christ's employment in the world to court and gain such kind of creatures. The first thing he did, while in the manger, was to snatch some of the devil's prophets out of his service, and take them into his own, Mat. ii. 1, some of the Magi, who were astrologers and idolaters. When he fled from Herod's cruelty, he chose Egypt, the most idolatrous country in the world, for his sanctuary; a place where the people worshipped oxen, crocodiles, cats, garlic, *putida numina*, all kind of riff-raff, to shew that he often comes to sojourn in the blackest souls. The first people he took care to preach to, were the seamen, who usually are the rudest and most debauched sort of men, as gaining the vices, as well as the commodities of those nations they traffic with, Mal. iv. 13. The inhabitants of those sea-coasts are said to sit in darkness, ver. 16; in darkness both of sin and ignorance, just as the Egyptians were not able to stir in that thick darkness which was sent as a plague upon them. And the country, by reason of the vices of the inhabitants, is called the region and shadow of death—a title properly belonging to hell itself. To call sinners to repentance, was the errand of his coming. And he usually delighted to choose such that had not the least pretence to merit, Mark ii. 17: Matthew, a publican; Zaccheus, an extortioner, store of that generation of men and harlots, and very little company besides.

He chose his attendants out of the devil's rabble; and he was more Jesus, a Saviour, among this sort of trash, than among all other sorts of people, for all his design was to get clients out of hell itself. What was that woman that he must needs go out of his way to convert? A harlot, John iv. 18, an idolater; for the Samaritans had a mixed worship, a linsey-woolsey religion, and, upon that account, were hateful to the Jews. She continued in her adultery at the very time Christ spake to her, yet he makes her a monument of his grace; and not only so, but the first preacher of the gospel to her neighbours: 'Is not this the Christ?' ver. 29; and an instrument to conduct them to him, 'Come, see a man which told me all things,' &c. Was any more defiled than Mary Magdalene? Seven devils would make her sooty to purpose, and so many did Christ cast out of her. 'Now, when Jesus was risen early the first day of the week, he appeared first to Mary

Magdalene,' Mark xvi. 9, out of whom he cast seven devils. This lustful devil he turns into a weeping saint.

What was that Canaanitish woman who had so powerful a faith infused? One sprung of a cursed stock, hateful to God, rooted out of the pleasant land, a dog, not a child; she comes a dog, but returns a child. Christ made this crab in a wilderness to bring forth fruit, even the best that heaven could afford, viz., the fruit of faith; and larger and better bunches of it than at that time sprouted out of any branches of the Jewish vine, so well planted, and so often watered by Christ himself. When he comes to act his last part in the world, he saves a thief, who was got to hell-gates, ready to be pushed in by the devil. Do you find examples among the pharisees? No; dunghill sinners take heaven by violence, while the proud pharisees lose it by their own righteousness. Scribes and doctors continue devils in the chair, while harlots commence saints from the stews, and the thief proceeds a convert on the cross.

Since there was but one that in his own person he converted after he went to heaven, what was he? One that had 'breathed out slaughters and threatenings against the church,' Acts ix. 1. To do so was as common with him, and natural to him, as to suck in air, and breathe it out again. This man, galloping to hell as fast as his mad rage and passion could carry him, he stops in his career, ordains a preacher of a persecutor; gives him as large a commission as he had given any of his favourites, for he makes him the chiefest apostle of the Gentiles. What bogs and miry places did Christ drain, and make fruitful gardens! what barren and thorny wildernesses did he change into pleasant paradises! He made subjects of vengeance objects of mercy; he told the woman of Samaria, who lived in fornication, that he was the Messiah; 'The woman saith to him, I know that Messiah cometh, which is called Christ: Jesus saith unto her, I that speak unto thee am he,' John iv. 25, which he never discovered to the self-righteous pharisees, nor indeed in so many words to his disciples, till Peter's confession of him.

5. The commission Christ gave to his apostles was to this purpose. He bids them proclaim the promise free to all; 'Go ye into all the world, and preach the gospel to every creature,' Mark xvi. 15. All the world; every creature. He put no difference between men in this respect, though you meet with them in the likeness of beasts and devils, never so wicked, never so abominable. As long as they are creatures, reach out the cup of salvation to them, if they will drink; open the treasures of grace to them, if they will receive them; indent with them for nothing but faith for justification, and profession of it for their salvation.

This commission is set out by the parable of a king commanding his servants to fetch the maimed, halt, and blind, with their wounds, sores, and infirmities about them: Luke xiv. 21, 23, 'Bring in hither the poor, and the maimed, and the halt, and the blind.' Yea, and go out into the highways and hedges, and those loathsome persons, those dregs of mankind, which you shall find swarming with vermin, and cleaning themselves under every hedge, bring them in.' If they pretend their rags and nastiness, as unsuitable to my rank and quality, compel them, force them against their own natural inclinations and doubts, that my house may be filled. God will have heaven filled with such, when self-righteous persons refuse him. When you come to heaven, to sit down with Abraham, Isaac, and Jacob, you will find some, and a great many, that were once as filthy morally, as these hedge-birds were naturally, who had once as many lusts creeping about them as there were frogs in Egypt. Such a compulsion as this spoken of there was in the primitive times by the power of the Spirit of grace.* Two stage-players, that in their acting scoffed at the Christian religion, were converted, and proved martyrs; one under Diocletian, the other under Julian.

6. The practice of the Spirit after Christ's ascension to lay hold of such persons.

(1.) Some out of the worst families in the world; one out of Herod's: Acts xiii. 1, 'Now there were in the church that was at Antioch certain prophets and teachers, as Barnabas, and Simeon that was called Niger, and Lucius of Cyrene, and Manaen, which had been brought up with Herod the tetrarch, and Saul.' Either Herod Antipas, who derided Christ before Pilate, or Herod Agrippa, who put James to death. Which of these Herods it was, it was not likely that in such a family he should suck in any principles advantageous to the Christian religion; for, being brought up with him, he was either his playfellow when young, or his confidant when grown up; yet out of the family of this wicked prince he calls out one, to make not only an object of his mercy, but an instrument of it to others, contrary to the force of education, which usually roots bad principles deep in the heart. It is likely to this intent the Holy Ghost takes particular notice of the place of Manaen's education, when the families where the rest named with him were bred up are not mentioned. Some rude and rough stones were taken out of Nero's palace, some that were servants to the most abominable tyrant, and the greatest monster of mankind; one that set Rome on fire, and played on his harp while the flames were crackling about the city; ripped up his mother's belly, to see the place where he lay. Would any of the civiller sort of mankind be attendants upon such a devil? Yet some of this monster's servants became saints: Philip. iv. 22, 'All the saints salute you, chiefly they that are of Cæsar's household.' To hear of saints in Nero's family is as great a prodigy as to hear of saints in hell. God before had promised his grace to Egypt, the most idolatrous country; there God would have an altar erected: 'In that day shall five cities in the land of Egypt speak the language of Canaan, and swear to the Lord of hosts; in that day shall there be an altar to the Lord in the midst of the land of Egypt,' Isa. xix. 18–20. And indeed the gospel was famous in Egypt, both at the Christian school at Alexandria, and for many famous lights.

(2.) Some of the worst vices. The Ephesians were as bad as any, such that Paul calls darkness itself; 'For ye were sometimes darkness,' Eph. v. 8. There was not only an eclipse, or a dark mask upon them, but they were changed into the very nature of night. Great idolaters. The temple of Diana, adored and resorted to by all Asia, and the whole world, was in that city: Acts xix. 27, 'That the temple of the great goddess Diana should be despised, and her magnificence should be destroyed, whom all Asia and the world worshippeth.' And they cry up this statue they pretended fell down from Jupiter above Christ, who was preached by Paul. They were given to magic and other diabolical arts;† yet many of these were weaned from their idol and their magic, and of darkness were made light in the Lord; which is more than if you saw a black piece of pitch changed into a clear piece of crystal, or a stone ascend into the nature of a glittering star.

Take a view of another corporation, at Corinth, of as filthy persons as ever you heard of, 'such were some of you,' 1 Cor. vi. 11. After he had drawn out a catalogue of their sins against the light of nature, and made the enumeration so perfect, that very little can be added, he adds, 'such were some of you.' Not all, but some. 'But you are washed,' &c. Not τοιοῦτοι, such sinners; but ταῦτα, such sins. Persons not only committing some few acts

* Grot. in Luke xiv. 23. † Plin. lib. v. cap. xxxvi.

of them, but so habituated in them, that they seemed metamorphosed into the very nature of these sins themselves, so that they were become the very dirt, mud, and rubbish of hell. Yet you see devils he really turned into angels of light. Well, then, how many flinty rocks has God dissolved into a stream of tears! How many hard hearts has he made to bleed and melt! That which is now pure gold has been earthy and polluted.

I shall only add this to the whole. Great sins are made preparations by God to some men's conversion; not in their own nature (that is impossible), but by the wise disposal of God, which Mr Burges illustrates thus: as a child whose coat is but a little dirty has it not presently washed; but when he comes to fall over head and ears in the mire, it is taken off, and washed immediately. The child might have gone many a day with a little dirt, had not such an accident happened. Peter might have had his proud and vainglorious humour still, had he not fallen so foully in the denial of his Master; but when he fell into the jakes and puddle, it promotes his conversion; for so Christ calls it: 'And when thou art converted, strengthen thy brethren,' Luke xxii. 32; it was conversion in a new edition; and you do not find him in the same boasting vanity again.

David's falling into the sin of murder and adultery, is the occasion of the ransacking his soul, which you find him not so hot about another time. He digs all about to the very root: 'Behold, I was shapen in iniquity, and in sin did my mother conceive me,' Ps. li. 5. This sin had stirred and raked up all the mud in his heart, and made him see himself an abominable creature; therefore he desires God to hide his face from his sins, ver. 9. He was so loathsome, he would not have any one look upon him (fling all this mud out of my soul); and prays more earnestly for a new heart and a right spirit. So when a wicked man falls into some grievous sin, which his conscience frowns upon him and lashes him for, he looks out for a shelter, which in all his peaceable wickedness he never did.

II. Why God chooses the greatest sinners, and lets his elect run on so far in sin before he turns them.

1. There is a passive disposition in the greatest sinners, more than in moral or superstitious men, to see their need; because they have not any self-righteousness to boast of. Man's blameless outward carriage, and freedom from the common sins of the times and places wherein they live, many times proves a snare of death to them, and makes them more cold and faint towards Christ; because they possess themselves with imaginations, that Christ cannot but look upon them, though they never so much as set their faces toward him. And because they are not drenched in such villanies as others are, their consciences sit quiet under this moral carriage, and gall them not by any self-reflections; therefore when the threatenings of the law are denounced against such and such sins, these men wipe their mouths, being untainted from those sins that are thus cursed, and vainly glory in their gay and gaudy plumes, and bless God, with the pharisee, that they are not sinners of such a scarlet dye, and that they do such and such duties; and so go on without seeing a necessity of the new birth; and by this means the strength of sin is more compacted and condensed in them.

Superstitious and formal men are hardly reduced to their right wits, partly because of a defect in the reason from whence those extravagances arise, and partly because those false habits and spirit of error possessing their faculties, they are incapable of more generous impressions. Besides, they are more tenacious of the opinions they have sucked in, which have got the empire and command over their souls; such misguided zeal fortifies men against proposals of grace, and fastens them in a more obstinate inflexibleness to any converting motions. This self-righteous temper is like an external heat got into the body, which produceth an hectic fever, and is not easily perceived till it be incurable; and naturally it is a harder matter to part with self-righteousness than to part with gross sins, for that is more deeply rooted upon the stock of self-love, a principle which departs not from us without our very nature; it hath more arguments to plead for it, it hath a natural conscience, a patron of it; whereas a great sinner stands speechless at reproofs, and a faithful monitor has a good second and correspondent of natural conscience within a man's own breast. It was not the gross sins of the Jews against the light of nature, so much as the establishing the idol of their own righteousness, that was the block to hinder them from submitting to the righteousness of God, Rom. x. 3.

Christ 'came to his own, and his own received him not,' John i. 11. Those that seem to have his peculiar stamp and mark upon them, that had their heads in heaven by some kind of resemblance to God in moral righteousness, being undefiled with the common pollutions of the world, these received him not, when publicans and harlots got the start of them, and ran before them, to catch hold of the tenders of grace: 'Publicans and harlots go into the kingdom of heaven before you,' Mat. xxi. 31. Just as travellers that have loitered away their time in an alehouse, being sensible how the darkness of the night creeps upon them, spur on, and outstrip those that were many miles on their way, and get to their stage before them; so these publicans and harlots, which were at a great distance from heaven, arrived there before those who, like the young man, were not far off from it.

Great sinners are most easily convinced of the notorious wickedness of their lives; and reflecting upon themselves because of their horrid crimes against the light of nature, are more inclinable to endeavour an escape from the devil's slavery, and are frighted and shaken by their consciences into a compliance with the doctrine of redemption; whereas those that do by nature the things contained in the law, are so much a law to themselves, that it is difficult to persuade them of the necessity of conforming to another law, and to part with this self-law in matter of justification. As metals of the noblest substance are hardest to be polished, so men of the most generous, natural, and moral endowments are with more difficulty argued into a state of Christianity than those of more drossy conversations. Cassianus speaks very peremptorily in this case: *Frequenter vidimus de frigidis et carnalibus ad spiritualem venisse fervorem; de lepidis et animalibus nunquam.*

2. To shew the insufficiency of nature to such a work as conversion is, that men may not fall down and idolise their own wit and power. A change from acts of sin to moral duties may be done by a natural strength and the prevalency of natural conscience; for the very same motives which led to sin, as education, interest, profit, may, upon a change of circumstances, guide men to an outward morality; but a change to the contrary grace is supernatural.

Two things are certain in nature: (1.) Natural inclinations never change, but by some superior virtue. A loadstone will not cease to draw iron while that attractive quality remains in it. The wolf can never love the lamb, nor the lamb the wolf; nothing but must act suitably to its nature; water cannot but moisten, fire cannot but burn; so likewise the corrupt nature of man, being possessed with an invincible contrariety and enmity to God, will never suffer him to comply with God. And the inclinations of a sinner to sin being more strengthened by the frequency of sinful acts, have as great a power over him, and as natural to him, as any qualities are to natural agents; and being stronger than any sympathies in the world, cannot by a man's own power, or the power of any other nature equal to it, be turned into a contrary channel.

(2.) Nothing can act beyond its own principle and nature. Nothing in the world can raise itself to a higher rank of being than that which nature hath placed it in. A spark cannot make itself a star, though it mount a little up to heaven; nor a plant endue itself with sense, nor a beast adorn itself with reason, nor a man make himself an angel. Thorns cannot bring forth grapes, nor thistles produce figs, because such fruits are above the nature of those plants; so neither can our corrupt nature bring forth grace, which is a fruit above it. *Effectus non excedit virtutem suæ causæ*, grace is more excellent than nature, therefore cannot be the fruit of nature. It is Christ's conclusion, 'How can you, being evil, speak good things?' Mat. xii. 33, 34. Not so much as the buds and blossoms of words, much less the fruit of actions. They can no more change their natures than a viper can cashier his poison. Now, though this I have said be true, yet there is nothing man does more affect in the world than a self-sufficiency and an independency upon any other power but his own. This temper is as much riveted in his nature as any other false principle whatsoever; for man does derive it from his first parents, as the prime legacy bequeathed to his nature. For it was the first thing discovered in man at his fall: he would be as God, independent upon him. Now God, to cross this principle, suffers his elect, like Lazarus, to lie in the grave till they stink, that there may be no excuse to ascribe their resurrection to their own power. If a putrefied rotten carcase should be brought to life, it could never be thought that it inspired itself with that active principle. God lets men run on so far in sin, that they do unman themselves, that he may proclaim to all the world that we are unable to do anything of ourselves at first towards our recovery without a superior principle. The evidence of which will appear if we consider,

1. Man's subjection under sin. He is 'sold under sin,' Rom. vii. 14, and brought into captivity to 'the law of sin,' ver. 23; law of sin, that sin seems to have a legal authority over him; and man is not only a slave to one sin, but divers: Titus i. 3, 'serving divers lusts.' Now, when a man is sold under the power of a thousand lusts, every one of which hath an absolute tyranny over him, and rules him as a sovereign by a law; when a man is thus bound by a thousand laws, a thousand cords and fetters, and carried whither his lords please, against the dictates of his own conscience, and force of natural light; can any man imagine that his own power can rescue him from the strength of these masters that claim such a right to him, and keep such a force upon him, and have so often baffled his own strength, when he offered to turn head against them?

2. Man's affection to them. He doth not only serve them, but he serves them, and every one of them, with delight and pleasure, Titus iii. 3. They were all pleasures as well as lusts, friends as well as lords. Will any man leave his voluptuousness, and such sins that please and flatter his flesh? Will a man ever endeavour to run away from those lords which he serves with affection? having as much delight in being bound a slave to these lusts as the devil hath in binding him. Therefore, when you see a man cast away his pleasures, deprive himself of those contentments to which his soul was once knit, and walk in paths contrary to corrupt nature, you may search for the cause anywhere, rather than in nature itself. No piece of dirty muddy clay can form itself into a neat and handsome vessel; no plain piece of timber can fit itself for the building, much less a crooked one; nor a man that is born blind give himself eyes.

God deals with men in this case as he did with Abraham. He would not give Isaac, while Sarah's womb, in a natural probability, might have borne him; but when her womb was dead, and age had taken away all natural strength of conception, then God gives him, that it might appear that he was not a child of nature, but a child of promise. I have been the larger on these two heads (which I design rather as things premised, than reasons) because these two principles of common honesty and self-sufficiency are the great impediments to conversion, and natural to most men.

PART II.

God's regard for his own glory.

1. The glory of his patience. We wonder, when we see a notorious sinner, how God can let his thunders still lie by him, and his sword rust in his sheath. And, indeed, when such are converted, they wonder themselves that God did not draw his sword out, and pierce their bowels, or shoot one of his arrows into their hearts all this while. But God, by such a forbearance, shews himself to be God indeed, and something in this act infinitely above such a weak creature as man is: 'I will not execute the fierceness of mine anger, I will not return to destroy Ephraim; for I am God, and not man,' Hosea xi. 9. When God had reckoned up their sins before, and they might have expected the sentence after the reading the charge, God tells them, he would not destroy them, he would not execute them, because he was God. If he were not a God, he could not keep himself from pouring out a just vengeance upon them. If a man did inherit all the meekness of all the angels and all the men that ever were in the world, he could not be able to bear with patience the extravagances and injuries done in the world the space of one day; for none but a God, *i. e.* one infinitely longsuffering, can bear with them.

Not a sin passed in the world before the coming of Christ in the flesh, but was a commendatory letter of God's forbearance, 'To declare his righteousness for the remission of sins that are past, through the forbearance of God,' Rom. iii. 25. And not a sin passed before the coming of Christ into the soul, but gives the same testimony, and bears the same record. And the greater number of sins, and great sins are passed, the more trophies there are erected to God's longsuffering; the reason why the grace of the gospel appeared so late in the world, was to testify God's patience. Our apostle takes notice of this long-suffering towards himself in bearing with such a persecutor; 'Howbeit, for this cause I obtained mercy, that in me first Jesus Christ might shew forth all long-suffering, for a pattern to them which should hereafter believe on him,' 1 Tim. i. 16. This was Christ's end in letting him run so far, that he might shew forth not a few mites, grains, or ounces of patience, but all longsuffering, longsuffering without measure, or weight, by wholesale; and this as a pattern to all ages of the world; ὑποτύπωσιν, for a type: a type is but a shadow in respect of the substance. To shew, that all the ages of the world should not waste that patience, whereof he had then manifested but a pattern. A pattern, we know, is less than the whole piece of cloth from whence it is cut; and as an essay is but a short taste of a man's skill, and doth not discover all his art, as the first miracle Christ wrought, of turning water into wine, as a sample of what power he had, was less than those miracles which succeeded; and the first miracle God wrought in Egypt, in turning Aaron's rod into a serpent, was but a sample of his power which would produce greater wonders; so this patience to Paul was but a little essay of his meekness, a little patience cut off from the whole piece, which should always be dealing out to some sinners or other, and would never be cut wholly out till the world had left being. This sample or pattern was but of the extent of a few years; for Paul was but young, the Scripture terms him a young man, Acts vii. 58, about thirty-six years of age,* yet he calls it all longsuffering. Ah, Paul! some since have experienced more of this patience; in some it has reached not only to thirty, but forty, fifty, or sixty years.

2. Grace. It is partly for the admiration of this grace that God intends the day of judgment. It is a strange place: 'When he shall come to be glorified in his saints, and to be admired in all them that believe in that day,' 2 Thes. i. 10. What, has not Christ glory enough in heaven with his Father? Will he come on purpose to seek glory from such worthless creatures as his saints are? What is that which glorifies Christ in them? It is the gracious work he has wrought in them. For the word is, ἐνδοξασθῆναι ἐν ἁγίοις, to be inglorified in his saints, *i. e.* by something within them; for which they glorify Christ *activè* and *objectivè*. As the creatures glorify the wisdom and power of God, by affording matter to men to do so, so does the work of God in saints afford matter of praise to angels, and admiration to devils. The apostle useth two words: *glorified*, that is, the work of angels and saints, who shall sing out his praises for it, as a prince, after a great conquest, receives the congratulations of all his nobility; *admired*, that the very devil and damned shall do; for, though their malice and condition will not suffer them to praise him, yet his inexpressible love in making such black insides so beautiful, shall astonish them.

In this sense those things under the earth shall bow down to that name of Jesus, a Saviour; a name which God gave him at first: 'Wherefore God also hath highly exalted him, and given him a name which is above every name; that at the name of Jesus every knee should bow,' Philip. ii. 9, 1 And upon his exaltation did confirm, Heb. v. 9, when he was made perfect, *i. e.* exalted, he became the author of eternal salvation, and had the power of saving, as well as the name conferred upon him. They shall confess that he is Lord, Philip. ii. 11, *i. e.* that he acted like a Lord, when he prevailed over all the opposition which those great sinners made against him. The whole trial of the saints, and the sentence of their blessedness, shall be finished before that of the damned, Mat. xxv. 35, 44. That the whole scene of his love, and the wonders of the work of faith being laid open, might strike them with a vast amazement. And that this is the design of Christ, to be thus glorified in his grace and power, appears by the apostle's prayer, ver. 11, 12, that the Thessalonians might be in the number of those Christ should be thus glorified in. Therefore he prays, that God would 'fulfil all the good pleasure of his goodness,' *i. e.* that grace he so pleased and delighted to manifest, and carry on the work of faith with power; 'that the name of Christ might be glorified in them,' as well as in the rest of his saints. Ordinary conversion is an act of grace; Barnabas so interprets it, Acts xi. 21, 23, when a great number believed; what abundance of grace then is expended in converting a company of extraordinary sinners!

It is the glory of a man to pass by an offence, Prov. xix. 11, *i. e.* it is a manifestation of a property which is an honour to him to be known to have. If it be thus an honour to pass by an offence simply, then the greater the offence is, and the more the offences are which he passeth by, the greater must the glory needs be, because it is a manifestation of such a quality in greater strength and vigour. So it must argue a more exceeding grace in

* Sanctius in locum.

God to remit many and great sins in man, than to forgive only some few and lesser offences.

(1.) Fulness of his grace. He shews hereby that there is more grace in him than there can be sin in us or the whole world. He lets some sinners run mightily upon his score, to manifest that though they are beggared, yet his grace is not; that though they have spent all their stock upon their swinish lusts, yet they have not drained his treasures; no more than the sun is emptied of its strength by exhaling the ill vapours of so many dung-hills. This was his design in giving the moral law, *finis operis;* that is, the event of the law was to increase the sin; but *finis operantis*, was thereby to glorify his grace; 'Moreover, the law entered, that the offence might abound; but where sin abounded, grace did much more abound,' Rom. v. 20. When the law of nature was out of print, and so blurred that it could scarce be read, God brings the moral law (the counterpart of the law of nature) in a new edition into the world; and thereby sin hath new aggravations, as being rebellion against a clearer light, a swelling and breaking over this mighty bank of the law laid in its way. But this was serviceable to the fulness of his grace, which had more abundant matter hereby to work upon, and a larger field to sow its inexhaustible seed in, ὑπερεπερίσσευσεν, it did super-abound. That grace should rise in its tide higher than sin, and bear it down before it, just as the rolling tide of the sea riseth higher than the streams of the river, and beats them back with all their mud and filth. It was mercy in God to create us; it is abundant mercy to make any new creatures, after they had forfeited their happiness, 1 Pet. i. 3, which, according to his abundant mercy, κατὰ τὸ πολὺ, according to his much mercy. But it was ὑπερπλεονάζουσα χαρις, overflowing, exceeding abundant, more than full grace, to make such deformed creatures new creatures, ver. 14 of this chapter.

(2.) Freeness of grace. None can entertain an imagination that Christ should be a debtor to sin, unless in vengeance, much less a debtor to the worst of sinners. But if Christ should only take persons of moral and natural excellencies, men might suspect that Christ were some way or other engaged to them, and that the gift of salvation were limited to the endowments of nature, and the good exercise and use of a man's own will. But when he puts no difference between persons of the least and those of the greatest demerit, but affecting the foulest monsters of sin, as well as the fairest of nature's children, he builds triumphal arches to his grace upon this rubbish, and makes men and angels admiringly gaze upon these infinitely free compassions, when he takes souls full of disease and misery into his arms. For it is manifest hereby that the God and Lord of nature is no more bound to his servant (as touching the gift of salvation), when she carries it the most smoothly with him, than when she rebels against him with the highest hand; and that Christ is at perfect liberty from any conditions but that of his own, viz. faith; and that he can and will embrace the dirt and mud, as well as the beauty and varnish of nature, if they believe with the like precious faith.

Therefore it is frequently God's method in Scripture, just before the offer of pardon, to sum up the sinner's debts, with their aggravations; to convince them of their insolvency to satisfy so large a score, and also to manifest the freeness and vastness of his grace: 'But thou hast not called upon me, O Jacob, but thou hast been weary of me, O Israel; thou hast not brought me the small cattle of thy burnt-offering, &c., but thou hast made me to serve with thy sins, thou hast wearied me with thine iniquities,' Isa. xliii. 22–24. When he had told them how dirtily they had dealt with him, and would have made him a very slave to their corrupt humours; at the conclusion, when they, nor no creature else, but would have expected fire-balls of wrath to be flung in their faces; and that God should have dipped his pen in gall, and have writ their mittimus to hell, he dips it in honey, and crosses the debt; 'I, even I, am he that blotteth out thy transgressions for mine own sake, and will not remember thy sins,' ver. 25. Could there be anything of merit here, when the criminal, instead of favour, could expect nothing but severity, there being nothing but demerit in him?

It is so free, that the mercy we abuse, the name we have profaned, the name of which we have deserved wrath, opens its mouth with pleas for us; 'But I had pity for mine holy name, which the house of Israel had profaned among the heathen whither they went,' Ezek. xxxvi. 21. Not for their sakes. It should be wholly free; for he repeats their profaning of his name four times. This name he would sanctify, *i. e.* glorify. How? In cleansing them from their filthiness, ver. 25. His name, while it pleads for them, mentions their demerits, that grace might appear to be grace indeed, and triumph in its own freeness. Our sins against him cannot deserve more than our sufferings for him, and even they are not worthy of the glory which shall be revealed, Rom. viii. 18.

(3.) Extent of his grace. The mercy of God is called his riches, and exceeding riches of grace. Now as there is no end of his holiness, which is his honour, neither any limits set to his power, so there is no end of his grace, which is his wealth; no end of his mines; therefore the foulest and greatest sinners are the fittest for Christ to manifest the abundant riches of his graces upon; for it must needs argue a more vast estate to remit great debts, and many thousands of talents, than to forgive some fewer shillings or pence, than to pardon some smaller sins in men of a more unstained conversation. If it were not for turning and pardoning mountainous sinners, we should not know so much of God's estate; we should not know how rich he were, or what he were worth. He pardons iniquities for his name's sake; and who can spell all the letters of his name, and turn over all the leaves in the book of mercy? Who shall say to his grace, as he does to the sea, Hitherto shalt thou go, and no further?

As the heavens are of a vast extension, which, like a great circle, encompass the earth, which lies in the middle like a little atom, in comparison of that vast body of air and ether, so are our sins to the extent of God's mercy; 'For as the heavens are higher than the earth, so are my ways higher than your ways, and my thoughts than your thoughts,' Isa. lv. 9. Men's sins are innumerable, yet they are but ciphers to the vast sums of grace which are every day expended; because they are finite, but mercy is infinite; so that all sins in the world put together cannot be of so large an extent as mercy; because being every one of them finite, if all laid together, cannot amount to infinite.

The gospel is entitled 'good-will to men;' to all sorts of men, with iniquities, transgressions, and sins of all sorts and sizes. God hath stores of mercy lying by him. His exchequer is never empty; 'Keeps mercy for thousands,' Exod. xxxiv. 7, in a readiness to deal it upon thousand millions of sins as well as millions of persons. Abraham, Isaac, and Jacob, and all that were before, have not wasted it; and if God were to proclaim his name again, it is the same still, for his name as well as his essence is unchangeable. His grace is no more tied to one sin than it is to one person; he has mercy on whom he will, and his grace can pardon what sins he will; therefore he tells them, Isa. lv. 7, that he would multiply pardons. He will have mercy to suit every sin of thine, and a salve for every sore. Though thy sin has its heights and depths, yet he will heap mercy upon mercy, till he makes it to overtop thy sin. He will be as good at his merciful arithmetic as thou hast been at thy sinful, if thou dost sincerely repent and reform. Though thou multiply thy sins by thousands, where repentance goes before, remission of sin follows without limitation. When Christ gives the one, he is sure to second it with the other. Though aggravating circumstances be never so many, yet he will multiply his mercies as fast as thou canst the sins thou hast committed.

He hath a cleansing virtue and a pardoning grace for all iniquities and transgressions; 'And I will cleanse them from all their iniquity, whereby they have sinned against me: and I will pardon all their iniquities, whereby they have sinned, and whereby they have transgressed against me,' Jer. xxxiii. 8. It is three times repeated, to shew that his mercy should be as large as their sin, though there was not a more sinful nation upon the earth than they were. His justifying and sanctifying grace should have as vast an extension, for he would both pardon and cleanse them. Why? Ver. 9, that it might be a name of joy and praise, and an honour to him before all the nations of the earth.

It is so great, that self-righteous persons murmur at it, that such swines should be preferred before them; as the eldest son was angry that his father should lavish out his kindness upon the prodigal more than upon himself, Luke xv. 28.

(4.) Compassion of his grace. The formal nature of mercy is tenderness, and the natural effect of it is relief. The more miserable the object, the more compassionate human mercy is, and the more forward to assist. Now that mercy which in man is a quality, in God is a nature. How would the infinite tenderness of his nature be discovered, if there were no objects to draw it forth? It would not be known to be mercy, unless it were shed abroad; nor to be tender mercy, unless it relieved great and oppressing miseries; for mercy is a quality in man that cannot keep at home, and be stowed under a lock and key in a man's own breast; much less in God, in whom it is a nature. Now the greater the disease, the greater is that compassion discovered to be wherewith God is so fully stored.

As his end in letting the devil pour out so many afflictions upon Job was to shew his pity and tender mercy in relieving him; 'You have heard of the patience of Job, and have seen the end of the Lord, that the Lord is very pitiful, and of tender mercy, James v. 11; so, in permitting the devil to draw his elect to so many sins, it is the same end he drives at. And he is more pitiful to help men under sin than under affliction, because the guilt of one sin is a greater misery than the burden of a thousand crosses. If forgiveness be a part of tenderness in man, it is also so in God, who is set, Eph. iv. 32, as a pattern of the compassion we are to shew to others; 'And be ye kind one to another, tender-hearted, forgiving one another, even as God for Christ's sake hath forgiven you.' The lower a man is brought, the more tender is that mercy that relieves him: 'Let thy tender mercies speedily prevent us; for we are brought very low,' Ps. lxxix. 8. To visit them that sit in darkness and the shadow of death, and to pardon their sins, is called mercy, with this epithet of tender; 'Through the tender mercy of our God, whereby the day-spring from on high hath visited us,' Luke i. 77–79. And so it is indeed when he visits the most forlorn sinners.

(5.) Sincerity and pleasure of his grace. Ordinary pardon proceeds from his delight in mercy; 'Who is a God like unto thee, that pardoneth iniquity, and passeth by the transgression of the remnant of his heritage. He retaineth not his anger for ever, because he delighteth in mercy,' Micah vii.

18. Therefore the more of his grace he lays out upon any one, the more excess of delight he hath in it, because it is a larger effect of that grace. If he were not sincere in it, he would never mention men's sins, which would scare them from him rather than allure them to him. If he were not sincere, he would never change the heart of an enemy, and shew kindness to him in the very act of enmity; for the first act of grace upon us is quite against our wills. And man is so far from being active in it, that he is contrary to it. *In primo actionis*, it is thus with a man, though not *in primo actu;* for in the first act of conversion man is willing, though not in the first moment of that act. But for God to bestow his grace upon us against our wills, and when he can expect no suitable recompence from us, evidences the purity of his affection; that when he endured so many contradictions of sinners against himself day by day, yet he is resolved to have them, and does seize upon them, though they struggle and fly in his face, and provoke him to fling them off.

It is so much his delight, that it is called by the very name of his glory: 'The glory of the Lord shall follow thee,' Isa. lviii. 8; *i.e.* the mercy of the Lord shall follow them at the very heels. And when they call, it should answer them; and when they cry, he would, like a watchful guardian servant, cry out, Here I am. So that he never lets a great sinner, when changed into a penitent, wait long for mercy, though he sometimes lets them wait long for a sense of it. This mercy is never so delightful to him as when it is most glorious, and it is most glorious when it takes hold of the worst sinners. For such black spots which mercy wears upon its face, makes it appear more beautiful.

Christ does not care for staying where he has not opportunities to do great cures, suitable to the vastness of his power, Mark vi. 5. When he was in his own country, he could do no great work there, but only laid his hands upon a few sick people. He had not a suitable employment for that glorious power of working miracles. So when men come to Christ with lighter guilt, he has but an under opportunity given him, and with a kind of disadvantage, to manifest the greatness of his charity. Though he has so much grace and mercy, yet he cannot shew more than the nature and exigence of the opportunity will bear; and so his pleasure doth not swell so high as otherwise it would do, for little sins, and few sins, are not so fit an object for a grace that would ride in triumph. Free grace is God's darling, which he loves to advance; and it is never more advanced, than when it beautifies the most misshapen souls.

3. Power. The Scripture makes conversion a most wonderful work, and resembles it to creation, and the resurection of Christ from the dead, &c.

(1.) Creation. Conversion, simply considered, is concluded by divines to be a greater work than creation; for God puts forth more power morally in conversion than he did physically in creation. The world was created by a word; but many words, and many acts, concur to conversion. The heavens are called the works of God's fingers, Ps. viii. 3; but the gospel, in the effects of it, is called the arm of the Lord, Isa. liii. 1. Men put not their arm to a thing but when the work requires more strength than the fingers possess. It is 'the power of God to salvation;' and the faith it works is begun and fulfilled with power, 2 Thes. i. 11. God created the world of nothing; *nothing* could not objectively contribute to his design, as matter does to a workman's intent; yet neither doth it oppose him, because it is nothing. As soon as God spake the word, this nothing brings forth sun, moon, stars, earth, trees, flowers, all the garnish of nature out of its barren womb. But sin is actively disobedient, disputes his commands, slights his power, fortifies itself against his entrance upon the heart, gives not up an inch of ground without a contest. There is not only a passive indisposition, but an active opposition. His creating power drew the world out of nothing, but his converting power frames the new creature out of something worse than nothing.

Naturally there is nothing but darkness and confusion in the soul. We have not the least spark of divine light, no more than the chaos had, when God, who commanded light to shine out of that darkness, 2 Cor. iv. 6, shined in our hearts. To bring a principle of light into the heart, and to set it up in spite of all the opposition that the devil and a man's own corruption makes, is greater than creation. As the power of the sun is more seen in scattering the thickest mists that triumph over the earth, and mask the face of the heavens, than in melting the small clouds compacted of a few vapours, so it must needs argue a greater strength to root out those great sins that were twisted and inlaid with our very nature, and become as dear to us as our right eye and right hand, than a few sins that have taken no deep root. Every man naturally is possessed with a hatred of God, and doth oppose everything which would restore God to his right; and being, since the fall, filled with a desire of independency, which is daily strengthened with new recruits, and loath to surrender himself to the power and direction of another, it is a more difficult thing to tame this unruly disposition in man's heart, I say more difficult, than to annihilate him, and new create him again; as it is more easy oftentimes for an artificer to make a new piece of work, than to repair and patch up an old one that is out of frame.

(2.) Resurrection. Conversion simply is so called: 'Quickened us when we were dead,' Eph. ii. 5. And the power that effects it is the same power that raised Christ from the dead; which was a mighty power, that could remove the stone from the grave, when Christ lay with all the sins of the world upon him, Eph. i. 19, 20; so the greater the stone is upon them, the greater is God's power to remove it. For if it be the power of God simply to regenerate nature, and put a new law into the heart, and to qualify the will with a new bias to comply with this law, and to make them that could not endure any thoughts of grace not to endure any thoughts of sin, it is a greater power sure to raise a man from that death wherein he has lain thirty or forty years rotten and putrefied in the grave; for if conversion in its own nature be creation and resurrection, this must needs be creation and resurrection with an emphasis.

The more malignant any distemper is, and the more fixed in the vital parts, and complicated with other diseases, the greater is the power in curing it; for a disease is more easily checked at the first invasion, than when it has infected the whole mass of blood, and become chronical; so it is more to pull up a sin, or many sins, that have spread their roots deep, and stood against the shock of many blustering winds of threatenings, than that which is but a twig, and newly planted.

(3.) Traction or drawing. Drawing implies a strength. If conversion be a traction, then more strength is required to draw one that is bound to a post by great cables, than one that is only tied by a few pack-threads; one that has millions of weights upon him, than one that hath but a few pounds.

(4.) It is the only miracle Christ hath left standing in the world, and declares him more to be Christ than anything. When John sent to know what he was, Luke vii. 20, he returns no other account but a list of his miracles; and that which brings up the rear as the greatest is, the poor εὐαγγελίζονται, are evangelised. It is not to be taken actively, of the preaching of the gospel; but passively, they were wrought upon by the gospel, and became an evangelised people, transformed into the mould of it; for else it would bear no analogy to the other miracles. The deaf heard, and the dead were raised; they had not only exhortations to hear, but the effects were wrought upon them. So these words import not only the preaching of the gospel to them, but the powerful operation of the gospel in them. It is not so great a work to raise many thousands killed in a battle, as to evangelise one dead soul. It is a miracle of power to transform a ravenous wolf into a gentle lamb, a furious lion into a meek dove, a nasty sink into a clear fountain, a stinking weed into a fragrant rose, a toad or viper into a man endued with rational faculties and moral endowments; and so to transform a filthy swine into a king and priest unto God. In conquests of this nature does divine power appear glorious. It is some strength to polish a rough stone taken out of the quarry, and hew it into the statue of a great prince; but more to make this statue a living man. Worse stones than these doth God make children, not only to Abraham, but to himself, even the Gentiles, who were accounted stones* by the Jews; and are called stones in Scripture for the worshipping idols.

What power must that be which can stop the tide of the sea, and make it suddenly recoil back! What vast power must that be that can change a black cloud into a glorious sun? This and more doth God do in conversion. He doth not only take smooth pieces of the softest matter, but the ruggedest timber full of knots, to plane and shew both his strength and art upon.

4. Wisdom. The work of grace being a new creation, is not only an act of God's power, but of his wisdom, as the natural creation was. As he did in contriving the platform of grace, and bringing Christ upon the stage, so also in particular distributions of it, he acts according to counsel, and that infinite too, even the counsel of his own will, Eph. i. 11. The apostle having discoursed before, ver. 9, of God's making known the mystery of his will in and through Christ, and, ver. 11, of the dispensation of this grace, in bestowing an inheritance, 'being predestinated according to the purpose of him who works all things according to the counsel of his own will,' he doth not say God predestinated us according to the counsel of his own will, but refers it to all he had said before, viz., of his making known the mystery of Christ, and their obtaining an inheritance. And ver. 8, speaking before of the pardon of sin in the blood of Christ, according to the riches of God's grace, wherein, saith he, 'he hath abounded towards us in all wisdom.' As there was abundance of grace set apart to be dealt out, so there was abundance of wisdom, even all God's wisdom, employed in the distribution of it. The restoring of God's image requires at least as much wisdom as the first creating of it. And the application of redemption, and bestowing of pardoning and converting grace, is as much an act of God's prudence as the contrivance of it was of his counsel.

Grace, or a gracious man in respect of his grace, is called God's workmanship, Eph. ii. 10, ποίημα, not ἔργον; work of his art as well as strength, and operation of his mind as well as his hand; his *poem*, not barely a work of omnipotency, but an intellectual spark. A new creature is a curious piece of divine art, fashioned by God's wisdom to set forth the praise of the framer, as a poem is, by a man's reason and fancy, to publish the wit and parts of the composer. It is a great skill of an artificer, with a mixture of a few sands and ashes, by his breath to blow up such a clear and diaphanous body as glass, and frame several vessels of it for several uses. It is not barely his breath that does it, for other men have breath as well as he; but it is breath managed by art. And is it not a marvellous skill in God to make a miry soul so pure and chrystalline on a sudden, to endue an irra-

* Grot. Mat. iii. 9.

tional creature with a divine nature, and by a powerful word to frame so beautiful a model as a new creature is!

The more intricate and knotty any business is, the more eminent is a man's ability in effecting it. The more desperate the wound is, the more honourable is the chirurgeon's ability in the cure. Christ's healing a soul that is come to the last gasp, and given over by all for lost, shews more of art than setting right an ordinary sinner. Our apostle takes notice of the wisdom of God in his own conversion here; for when he relates the history of it, he breaks out into an *Hallelujah*, and sends up a volley of praises to God for the grace he hath obtained. And in that doxology he puts an emphasis on the wisdom of God: 'Now unto the King eternal, immortal, invisible, the only wise God, be honour and glory for ever and ever,' ver. 17. Only wise God; only, which he does not add to any other attribute he there gives him.

This wisdom appears, (1.) In the subjects he chooseth. We will go no further than the example in our text. Our apostle seems to be a man full of heat and zeal. And the church had already felt the smart of his activity, insomuch that they were afraid to come at him after his change, or to admit him into their company, imagining that his fury was not changed, but disguised, and he of an open persecutor turned trepanner, Acts ix. 26. None can express better what a lion he was than he doth himself: 'Many of the saints did I shut up in prison, having received authority from the chief priests; and when they were put to death, I gave my voice against them. And I punished them oft in every synagogue, and compelled them to blaspheme; and being exceedingly mad against them, I persecuted them even unto strange cities,' Acts xxvi. 10, 11. He seems also to have been a man of high and ambitious spirit. This persecuting probably was acted so vigorously by him to ingratiate himself with the chief priests, and as a means to step into preferment, for which he was endued with parts and learning, and would not want zeal and industry to attain it. He seems to be of a proud spirit, by the temptation which he had: 'Lest I should be exalted above measure,' 2 Cor. xii. 7. He speaks it twice in that verse, intimating that his natural disposition led him to be lifted up with any excellency he had; and usually God doth direct his battery to beat down that which is the sin of our constitution.

He was a man of a very honest mind, and was forward in following every point his conscience directed him to; for what he did against Christ, he did according to the dictates of his conscience, as then informed: 'I verily thought with myself,' Acts xxvi. 9, *i. e.* in my conscience, 'that I ought,' not that I might, but that it was his duty. His error commanded with the same power that truth does where it reigns. Now it discovers the wisdom of God to lay hold of this man thus tempered, who had honesty to obey the dictates of a rightly-informed conscience, as well as those of an erroneous one; zeal to execute them, and height of spirit to preserve his activity from being blunted by any opposition, and parts and prudence for the management of all these. I say, to turn these affections and excellencies to run in a heavenly channel, and to guide this natural passion and heat for the service and advancement of that interest which before he endeavoured to destroy, and for the propagation of that gospel which before he persecuted, is an effect of a wonderful wisdom; as it is a rider's skill to order the mettle of a headstrong horse for his own use to carry him on his journey.

(2.) This wisdom appears in the time. As man's wisdom consists as well in timing his actions as contriving the models of them, so doth God's. He lays hold of the fittest opportunities to bring his wonderful providences upon the stage. He hath his set time to deliver his church from her enemies, Ps. cii. 13; and he hath his set time also to deliver every particular soul, that he intends to make a member of his church from the devil. He waits the fittest season to manifest his grace: 'Therefore will the Lord wait, that he may be gracious unto you,' Isa. xxx. 18. Why? 'For the Lord is a God of judgment,' *i. e.* a God of wisdom; therefore will time things to the best advantage, both of his glory and the sinner's good. His timing of his grace was excellent in the conversion of Paul.

[1.] In respect of himself. There could not be a fitter time to glorify his grace than when Paul was almost got to the length of his chain; almost to the sin against the Holy Ghost. For if he had had but a little more light, and done that out of malice which he did out of ignorance, he had been lost for ever. He obtained mercy. Why? Because he did it ignorantly, ver. 13. As I said before, he followed the dictates of his conscience; for if he had had knowledge suitable to his fury, it had been the unpardonable sin. Christ suffered him to run to the brink of hell before he laid hold upon him.

[2.] In respect of others. He is converted at such a time when he went as full of madness as a toad of poison, to spit it out against the poor Christians at Damascus, armed with all the power and credential letters the high priest could give him, who without question promised himself much from his industry; and when he was almost at his journey's end, ready to execute his commission, 'And as he journeyed, he came near Damascus,' Acts ix. 3, about half a mile from the city, as Gulielmus Tyrius thinks,* at this very time Christ grapples with him, and overcomes all his mad principles, secures Paul from hell, and his disciples from their fears of him. Behold the nature of this lion changed, just as he was going to fasten upon his prey. Christ might have converted Paul sooner, either when Paul had heard of some of his miracles, for perhaps Paul was resident at Jerusalem at the time of Christ's preaching in Judea, for he was brought up in Jerusalem at the feet of Gamaliel, Acts xxii. 3, who was one of the council, Acts v. 24. He might have converted him when he heard Stephen make that elegant and convincing oration in his own defence, Acts vii.; or when he saw Stephen's constancy, patience, and charity in his suffering, which might somewhat have startled a moral man as Paul was, and made him look about him.

But Christ omits the doing of it at all these opportunities, and suffers him to kick against the pricks of miracles, admonitions, and arguments of Stephen and others, yet hath his eye upon him all along in a special manner, Acts vii. 58. He is there named when none else are: 'And the witnesses laid their clothes at a young man's feet, named Saul.' And 'Saul was consenting to his death,' Acts viii. 1. Was there none else that had a hand in it? The Spirit of God takes special notice of Saul here. He runs in God's mind, yet God would not stop his fury: 'As for Saul, he made havoc of the church,' Acts viii. 3. Did nobody else shew as much zeal and cruelty as Saul? Sure he must have some instrument with him. Yet we hear none named but Saul: and 'Saul yet breathing,' &c., Acts ix. 1; *yet*, as much as to say, he shall not do so long. I shall have a fit time to meet with him presently.

And was it not a fit time, when the devil hoped to rout the Christians by him, when the high priests assured themselves success from this man's passionate zeal, when the church travailed with throws of fear of him? But Christ sent the devil sneaking away for the loss of such an active instrument, frustrates all the expectations of the high priests, and calms all the stormy fears of his disciples; for Christ sets him first a preaching at Damascus in

* Turin. in loc.

the very synagogues which were to assist him in his cruel design: 'And straightway he preached Christ in the synagogues, that he is the Son of God, and increased the more in strength, and confounded the Jews which dwelt at Damascus, proving that this is very Christ,' Acts ix. 20–22.

Did not Christ shew himself to be a God of judgment here? He sat watching in heaven for this season to turn Paul with the greatest advantage. His wisdom answers many ends at once, and killed so many birds with one stone. He struck dead at one blow Paul's sin, his people's fears, the high priests' expectations, and the devil's hopes. He triumphs over his enemies, secures his friends, saves Paul's soul, and promotes his interest by him; he disappoints the devil of his expectations, and hell of her longing.

(3.) This wisdom appears to keep up the credit of Christ's death. The great excellence of Christ's sacrifice, wherein it transcends the sacrifices under the law, is because it perfectly makes an atonement for all sins; it first satisfies God, and then calms the conscience, which they could not do, Heb. x. 1, 2, for there was a conscience of sin after their sacrifices. The tenor of the covenant of grace which God makes with his people, is upon the account of this sacrifice, 'This is the covenant I will make with them. And their sins and iniquities will I remember no more,' Heb. x. 16, 17. 'Now, where remission of these is, there is no more offering for sin,' ver. 18. This covenant extends not only to little sins, for there is no limitation; great sins are included; therefore Christ satisfied for great sins, or else, if ever they be pardoned, there must be another sacrifice, either of himself or some other, which the apostle, upon the account of this covenant, asserts there need not be, because this sacrifice was complete, otherwise there would be a remembrance of sin; as the covenant implied the completeness of Christ's satisfaction, so the continual fulfilling or application of the tenor of the covenant implies the perpetual favour and force of this sacrifice.

And, indeed, when God delivered him up, he intended it for the greatest sins: 'He was delivered for our offences,' Rom. iv. 25, παραπτωματα, which signifies not stumbling, but falling. Not a light, but a great transgression. Now, if Christ's death be not satisfactory for great debts, Christ must be too weak to perform what God intended by him, and so infinite wisdom was frustrate of its intention, which cannot, nor ought not, to be imagined. Now, therefore, God takes the greatest sinners, to shew,

[1.] First, the value of this sacrifice. If God should only entertain men of a lighter guilt, Christ's death would be suspected to be too low a ransom for monstrous enormities; and that his treasure was sufficient for the satisfaction of smaller debts, but a penury of merit to discharge talents; which had not been a design suitable to the grandeur of Christ, or the infiniteness of that mercy God proclaims in his word. But now the conversion of giant-like sinners does credit to the atonement which Christ made, and is a great renewed approbation of the infinite value of it, and its equivalency to God's demands; for it bears some analogy to the resurrection of Christ, which was God's general acquittance to Christ, to evidence the sufficiency of his payment. And the justification of every sinner is a branch of that acquittance given to Christ at his resurrection; 'Raised again for our justification,' Rom. iv. 25; and a particular acquittance to Christ for that particular soul he had the charge of from his Father.

All that power that works in the first creation of grace, or the progress of regeneration, bears some proportion to the acquitting and approving power manifested in Christ's resurrection: 'And what is the exceeding greatness of his power to us-ward who believe, according to the working of his mighty power, which he wrought in Christ, when he raised him from the dead,' Eph. i. 19, 20. In ver. 17, 18, the apostle prays for the carrying on the work of grace and regeneration begun in them, that they might more clearly understand that power which wrought in Christ, viz., that approving power of what Christ has done, which he exerts daily in conversion, and in the effects of it. For by raising any soul from a death in sin, God doth evidence the particular value of Christ's blood for that soul, as he did, in raising Christ, evidence the general fulness of that satisfaction. And this he will do even to the end of the world; 'raised us up together with Christ;' 'kindness through Christ Jesus,' Eph. ii. 6, 7. All his grace in all ages, even to the end of the world, shall run through this channel, to put credit and honour upon Christ. Now the greater the sin is that is pardoned, and the greater the sinner is that is converted, the more it shews the sufficiency of the price Christ paid.

[2.] The virtue of this sacrifice. He is a 'priest for ever,' Heb. vii. 17; and therefore the virtue as well as the value of his sacrifice remains for ever: he hath 'obtained an eternal redemption,' Heb. ix. 12, *i. e.* a redemption of an eternal efficacy. As long as men receive any venom from the fiery serpent, they may be healed by the antitype of the brazen one, though it were so many years since he was lifted up. And those who were stung all over, as well as those who are bitten but in one part, may, by a believing looking upon him, draw virtue from him as diffusive as their sin.

Now the new conversion of men of extraordinary guilt proclaims to the world, that the fountain of his blood is inexhaustible; that the virtue of it is not spent and drained, though so much hath been drawn out of it for these five thousand years and upwards, for the cleansing of sins past before his coming, and sins since his death. This evidences that his priesthood now is of as much efficacy as his sufferings on earth were valuable; and that his merit is as much in virtue above our iniquity, as his person is in excellency above our nothingness. He can wash the tawny American, as well as the moral heathen; and make the black Ethiopian as white as the most virtuous philosopher. God fastens upon the worst of men sometimes, to adorn the cross of Christ; and maketh them eminent testimonies of the power of Christ's death: 'He made his grave with the wicked,' Isa. liii. 9. Heb. 'He shall give the wicked (not grave), and the rich in his death.' God shall make man, wallowing in sinful pleasures, tied to the blandishments and profits of the world, to come to Christ, and comply with him, to be standing testimonies in all ages of the virtue of his sufferings.

(4.) For the fruitfulness of this grace in the converts themselves. The most rugged souls prove most eminent in grace upon their conversion, as the most orient diamonds in India, which are naturally more rough, are most bright and sparkling when cut and smoothed. Men usually sprout up in stature after shattering agues.

PART III.

The fruits of converting grace, &c.

1. A sense of the sovereignty of grace in conversion, will first increase thankfulness. Converts only are fit to shew forth the praises of Christ: 'That you should shew forth the praises of him who hath called you out of darkness into his marvellous light,' 1 Peter ii. 9; ἀρετὰς, the virtues of

Christ. The end why God sets men at liberty from prisons and dungeons, and from fear of death and condemnation for great sins, is, that they may be fitted, and gain a commodious standing, to publish to the world the virtues of him; *i. e.* the mercy, meekness, patience, bounty, truth, and other royal perfections of Christ.

Men at their first conversion receive the grace of God with astonishment; for it is θαυμαστὸν φῶς, 1 Peter ii. 9, most amazing at the first appearance of it; as the northern nations, that want the sun for some months in the winter, are ready to deify it when it appears in their horizon; for the thickness of the foregoing darkness makes the lustre of the sun more admirable. But suppose a man had been all his lifetime like a mole under ground, and had never seen so much as the light of a candle, and had a view of that weak light at a distance, how would he admire it, when he compares it with his former darkness? But if he should be brought further, to behold the moon with its train of stars, his amazement would increase with the light. But let this person behold the sun, be touched with its warm beams, and enjoy the pleasure of seeing those rarities which the sun discovers, he will bless himself, adore it, and embrace that person that led him to enjoy such a benefit. And the blackness of that darkness he sat in before, will endear the present splendour to him, swell up such a spring-tide of astonishment, as that there shall be no more spirit in him. God lets men sit long in the shadow of death, and run to the utmost of sin, before he stops them, that their danger may enhance their deliverance.

We admire more when we are pulled out of danger, than when we are prevented from running into it. A malefactor will be more thankful for a pardon, when it comes just as he is going to be turned off. If there be degrees of harmony in heaven, without question the convert thief on the cross warbles out louder notes than others, because he had little time to do it on earth; and his engagements are the greater, because Christ took him in his arms when he was hanging over hell.

When Paul writ this epistle to Timothy, he was about fifty-five years of age; and yet those twenty years run out since his conversion had not stifled his admiration nor damped his thankfulness for converting grace. Take a prospect of it in this chapter: 'And I thank Christ Jesus our Lord, who hath enabled me, for that he counted me faithful, putting me into the ministry; who was before a blasphemer, and a persecutor, and injurious,' ver. 12, 13. I thank Christ Jesus our Lord. He seems to set his sin and God's mercy in opposition. I was injurious, but I obtained mercy. I was a blasphemer, but I obtained, &c. I—mercy. Who would imagine but that of all persons he should have passed by me, while he had taken this or that polished pharisee, this or that doctor of morality? But that he should overlook them, and set his eye upon me, so injurious, such a blasphemer, such a persecutor! A great sinner, when he reflects upon his sin, wonders that a butt was not made at him. You find that no apostle gives such epithets to the grace of God as our apostle does; none so seraphical in his admiring expressions. Riches of grace, exceeding riches of grace, abundant grace, riches of glory, unsearchable riches of grace. He never speaks of grace without an emphasis. Single grace and single mercy would not serve his turn.

2. Love and affection. Mary Magdalene, out of whom Christ had cast seven devils, was most early in her affection to bestow her provision of spices upon the dead body of her Saviour. The fire of grace cannot be stifled, but will break out in glory to God. This is such a grace that man in innocency could not have exercised in such a height; because now the sinner is not

only in his own sight unworthy of pardon, but worthy of the greatest hatred and punishment. You scarce find yourselves possessed with greater affection to any, than those who have been instruments to free you from your sinful fetters. How often do you bless them, could pull out your eyes for them, and think all ways too little to manifest the sense of your obligations to them! And does the instrument carry away all? Surely God has the greatest sacrifice of affection when the convert considers that his powerful grace was the principal agent to draw him out of this spiritual mire. As when a present is sent to you, you shew a courtesy to the servant; but the chief part of your kindness is devoted to the master that sent him. What flames of love, raptures of joy, transports of affection, boilings of courage for God in a young convert! The soul is most courageous for God at first conversion; because it is then most stored with comforts, and is so struck into amazement at the marvellous light which darts upon him, that he is ambitious to be a martyr for God presently: 'After that you were illuminated, you endured a great fight of afflictions,' Heb. x. 32. Grace is not only attended with afflictions, but bestows a courage upon a convert to endure them. The soul then thinks it is able to undergo anything for God, who hath bestowed so much grace upon it.

A Christian hath the greatest love to Christ at the first turning to him; for since the horror of all his sins, and the natural ugliness and deformity of that which he has served so long, comes with a full sense upon him, and since the admirable excellency of Christ shines upon him, which is a sight he was never acquainted with before, the greatness of the danger he was in, and the incomparable love which beams upon him from his believing a Saviour, fills his affection with full sails. Thus do men who have been tossed in a dangerous tempest, afflicted with the darkness of the night, as well as their danger, rejoice and welcome the rising sun in the morning, which dispels their tumultuous fears, as well as those gloomy shadows.

God permits a man's sin to abound, that his love after pardon may abound too: 'Her sins, which are many, are forgiven; for she loved much,' Luke vii. 47; *ὅτι, therefore*, it is the consequent, not the cause of remission. And this interpretation agrees best with the following words: 'To whom little is forgiven, the same loves little.' It is more consonant to reason, that where there are greater mercies, there should be greater returns of affection. Remission of sins is the greatest evidence of God's love, and therefore should be the greatest incentive of ours. And indeed Christ never appears to a penitent with a more comely air in his countenance than upon the removal of great judgments or the pardon of great sins: 'In that day shall the branch of the Lord be beautiful and glorious, and the fruit of the earth shall be excellent and comely for them that are escaped of Israel,' Isa. iv. 2. In that day! In what day? After great judgments, ver. 1; and in the foregoing chapter, in purging away great filth, ver. 4. The branch Jesus appears most lovely when he comes laden with the fruit of grace, with the sanctifying juice of his blood, as a ripe bunch of grapes looks pleasantly in a thirsty traveller's eye. This convert Paul was more affectionate to Christ than any of the other apostles; for when he could not look upon him, he is enamoured on his very name, and delights to express it no less than five hundred times, as I remember some have numbered it in his epistles; more, proportionably, than Peter, James, and John did in what they writ.

3. Service and obedience. Such will endeavour to redeem the time, because their former days have been so evil, and recover those advantages of service which they lost by a course of sin. They will labour that the largeness of their sin may be answered by an extension of their zeal. Such will

be almost as much ashamed to do but common service as they are now ashamed of their scarlet sins. As men, the further they go backward, the greater leap they usually take forward. Grace instructs a man in holiness out of gratitude. The grace of God 'teacheth us to deny ungodliness and worldly lusts, that we should live soberly, righteously, and godly in this present world,' Titus ii. 12. Grace teaches us. The greater the grace, the more pressing is the instruction: as it increases gratitude, it increases service.

That Peter, who had been so criminal in denying his Master, and adding perjury to his perfidiousness, was as active in service as he had been in apostasy. He laid the first stone of the Christian church among the Jews after Christ's ascension; he preached the first sermon to them, and charged them home with his Master's murder, Acts ii. He was also the spokesman in all business described in the first six chapters of the Acts. He laid also the first foundation of the Gentile church; for God in a vision revealed to him the calling of the Gentiles, passing by all the other apostles, to whom it was not known but by Peter's relation:* 'Men and brethren, ye know how that a good while ago God made choice among us, that the Gentiles by my mouth should hear the word of the gospel, and believe,' Acts xv. 7. A good while ago, which good while ago refers to the time, Mat. xvi. 18, wherein Christ said, 'Upon this rock will I build my church.' He was chosen by God to this purpose, *i. e.* separated from the rest of the apostles, and adorned with this prerogative. Great sins did not make Christ change his resolution.

Never an apostle that had been bred up under Christ's wing that was so active an instrument as this Paul, who had been so bitter an enemy. He 'laboured more abundantly than all,' 1 Cor. xv. 10. In matters of obedience he would not ask counsel of flesh and blood: 'Immediately I conferred not with flesh and blood,' Gal. i. 16. He was quick in his obedience. He had endeavoured to weaken Christ's kingdom; he now endeavours to list men in his service. He had breathed out threatenings; he now breathes out affections. He could even spend and be spent for the interests of his Saviour. And usually we find converted souls most active in the exercise of that grace which is most contrary to that which was their darling sin.

4. Humility and self-emptiness. Christ 'chose the foolish things of the world to confound the wise, and the weak things of the world to confound the things that are mighty,' 1 Cor. i. 26, 27, that nothing should be attributed to their worth and dignity, but to his grace and mercy. Were the gospel discovered only to the wise, they would look upon it rather as a discovery made by the optics of their own reason. And if God did bestow his grace only upon men of unspotted conversations, they would rather think it a debt God stood obliged to pay them than a free act of grace. As God reveals knowledge to the simplest, Mat. xi. 25, so he does manifest grace to the sinfullest; and as Christ blessed his Father for that, so no doubt but he doth return the same thanks for this. Such great sinners receive all from God, and so have more reason to hang down their heads; others may sometimes cast many a loving look to their own righteousness, and, like Nebuchadnezzar, glory, This is the Babylon which I have built; and boast of their good acts, and freedom from the common pollutions of the world.

But such who were fallen over head and ears in the mire, and were dirty all over, have no cause to boast; for God did not find them, but made them worthy. They brought nothing but dirt and rags, that were not worthy the washing; only God would pick glory out of their worthlessness to his own grace. Such are sensible that God was not their debtor, but they his,

* Cameron Myro. in Acts xv. 7.

and that there was nothing in them to oblige God to bestow the least mite of mercy on them.

Therefore we find not one of these mountainous sinners in Scripture ascribing their conversion to their own strength or merit. As no apostle was so God-magnifying, so none was so self-vilifying as Paul. Though he was the greatest apostle, yet he accounts himself less than the least of all saints: Eph. iii. 8, 'Unto me, who am less than the least of all saints.' Surely he might have put himself equal to the least; it would have been great humility to do so; but he is more humble than so; even less than the least; less even than him who was only fit to be a door-keeper in the house of God. And he esteems himself not only unworthy of the office of an apostle, but of the very name; 'not worthy,' 1 Cor. xv. 9, not only to be, but 'to be called an apostle.' And why? Because of his former sin; 'because I persecuted the church of God.' The remembrance of his great sin before his conversion kept him humble. And in ver. 10, when he had a little boasted of his abundant labour, he checks himself presently; 'Yet not I, but the grace of God.' He attributes his very being as a Christian, as well as his actions, to the same cause, viz. the grace of God; 'By grace I am what I am.' So, Gal. i. 16, how doth Paul attribute to grace; 'pleased by his grace to reveal;' revelation, not acquisition.

5. Bewailing of sin, and self-abhorrence for it. When men are first translated out of darkness into the kingdom of Christ, and begin to know Christ truly, the ways of their former ignorance are very bitter and uncouth things unto them. The very disproportion and unsuitableness of them to the sweetness of that grace which now they taste from the hand of Jesus is an offence to them, and hateful to their thoughts. Therefore the more sin a man hath run into before his return to God, the more he sees the vileness of his own nature, and consequently the more he abhors himself: 'Then shall you remember your iniquities, and shall loathe yourselves,' Ezek. xxxvi. 31. When? Ver. 29, when God had accomplished the promise of saving them from all their uncleanness. They shall remember with abhorrency what was their own, sin, and shall enjoy what is purely God's. The time of pardoning great sins is the time of great self-loathing; such prove the holiest persons, because they have had more experience of the evil of sin.

Such are ashamed of their sins, not only at the instant of their conversion, but afterwards, every time they remember them: 'What fruit had you then in those things whereof you are now ashamed?' Rom. vi. 21. Now, at that time when Paul writ to them, the very shame of their sins stuck upon them, though they had been converted before. The more they grew in the experimental knowledge of God and his goodness, the more a holy shame for sins committed in their natural condition was stirred in their consciences, and they could not but blush every time they considered how dirty they had been towards God. Now the greater the shame, the greater the hatred of the occasion of that shame, and the more exact the watchfulness against it; as a man that hath fallen into some slough by some stumble or oversight, when he travels that way again, he cannot but remember what a pickle he was in, and will be watchful lest he meet with the same mishap. Whose heart was more melted by mercy than Mary Magdalene's? All the pharisees that Christ converted never rained such showers of tears. How she used all her instruments of sin to be servants to her repentance! Her eyes, which had inflamed so many hearts, been snares to catch men, she makes the conduits to convey her penitential tears to her Saviour's feet. Her hair, which had engrossed so much time in the curiosity of dresses, she uses as a towel to wipe them. The ointment she had used for the tricking up herself, to gratify the senses of her lovers, she pours out to embalm her Lord. Her lusts should have no more of her choicest things, but her Saviour should have all. She would keep them not so much for her own use, as his.

6. Faith and dependence. (1.) At present, in the instant of the first act of faith. Great sins make us appear in the court of justification, *sub forma impii*, with a naked faith, when we have nothing to merit it, but much to deserve the contrary: 'Believes on him that justifies the ungodly,' Rom. iv. 5. The more ungodly, the more elevated is that faith which lays hold on God. Thomas's unbelief was very black, for he had refused to give credit to all the testimonies of the disciples concerning Christ's resurrection; but when he was sensible of his crime, and so kindly dealt with by his Saviour, he puts forth a stronger act of faith than any of the rest: 'My Lord, and my God,' John xx. 28. His faith was not satisfied with a single *my*; he gives him more honourable titles, and his heart grasps him more closely and affectionately than any of the rest.

The man that was born blind, and cured by Christ, owns him, acts some faith before the pharisees: 'If this man were not of God, he could do nothing,' John ix. 33; and he said, 'I believe,' ver. 39, and he worshipped him. But when Christ comes to talk with him particularly, vers. 36–38, he believes. When Christ comes to talk with a great sinner, one that hath had diseases naturally incurable, he exerts a stronger faith than others. It is then, *Lord, I believe*, and it is a faith accompanied with an adoration.

(2.) In following occasions. Pardoning such great sins, and converting such great sinners, is the best credential letter Christ brings with him from heaven. Men naturally would scarce believe for his own sake, but for his work's sake they would, because they are more led by sense than faith. This Christ knew, when he bids his disciples believe him for the work's sake that he was sent by God, and that they are unanimous in this work of grace, as well as in other works: 'Believe me, that I am in the Father, and the Father in me, or else believe me for the very work's sake,' John xiv. 11. Therefore those that have been partakers of this converting grace, if they stagger and doubt afterwards, they give the greatest affront to Christ.

For their unbelief is not only against his person, but against its work too. That he has far more reason to say to such than he did to his disciples, 'How long shall I be with you,' &c., Mat. xvii. 17: what should I stay to do such great works as these, and cannot be believed? Such great sins pardoned and escaped, make men take faster hold of Christ afterward. As a man that hath lately got out of a deep lake, wherein there were many serpents, crocodiles, and venomous creatures, which he has escaped, and has no sanctuary to protect him from their fury but by hanging upon a small bough; when he looks down upon them, and sees them gaping for him, and ready to devour him, if he were within their reach, he would summon up all his strength to hold fast that branch. In such a day will the branch of the Lord also be beautiful and glorious.

Certainly when the soul went out to Christ in so desperate a condition, with the load of guilt and discouragement upon it, and resolved to venture upon him, come what would of it, and found success; as it was the boldest adventure, which the Scripture frequently calls boldness, so it is the greatest encouragement to come to Christ upon any occasion whatsoever hereafter. This first act of faith is of so noble and generous a quality, that it is set as the copy of all following acts of faith: 'Beginning of your confidence,' Heb. iii. 14; ἀρχὴν, the primary act of faith, which was the principal act of confidence. Though there was a greater strength in the habit of faith after conversion, yet the first exercise of it upon Christ is the boldest and most vigorous, because it was for the saving the life when the soul saw no recovery any way but in Christ, and the most noble when it was under the discouragements of such mountains of guilt.

It also gave Christ the greatest honour, for it was an act of greater confidence in him than any succeeding act could be. Now if thou didst put forth such a high and daring act of faith when all thy sins hung about thee, and thou hadst neither a Hur nor Aaron to hold up thy hands, with much more confidence mayest thou come now, since thou hast tried how successful thy first faith has been. So when temptations assault thee, and the devil with all his black legions besets thee round, thou art not in a worse condition than at the first, when all thy sins did not only besiege thee, but possess thee. Well may such a soul say, If I acted faith when the devil had all the strongholds in me at the worst, now it is but a start out, and exercise the power of that first faith.

(3.) In case of corruptions likewise and unmastered sins. I have great corruptions, but the power which raised Christ raised me, when I had greater stones upon me wherewith I had even wearied God himself; and now when I have fewer, though they are too great still, shall I despair of that power which wrought greater miracles for me, and threw away my gravestones when I was not able to stir myself?

(4.) So in the case of desertion. I will venture to go to God, let him frown and strike; for I am sure I did once go to him when I was his absolute sworn enemy, and he had not a greater hater of him in the world than I was, and he did receive me. I am not worse now than I was at that time, for I love him, and would do all that I can to please him; therefore I will press into his presence now, and try the success of my first faith. Such men's faith is usually a more generous faith, because they have less of the principle of reason to support it. It is like that of Abraham's, a believing 'in hope against hope,' Rom. iv. 18. A faith against mighty and mountainous opposition of high and mighty sins, that might scare a man from such acts of faith, and establish a diffidence of the promises of God in the soul. God receives no more glory from the faith of any than from those of the greatest sinners through their repentance.

7. Fear and reverence. Such will never despise the riches of that goodness and patience which has been given out to him, Rom. ii. 4, because it has led him to repentance; and he will not provoke that goodness, which is conducting him to the enjoyment of all the fruits of repentance, to throw him off: 'There is forgiveness with thee,' saith David, 'that thou mayest be feared,' or worshipped, Ps. cxxx. 4. If God should set a mark of death upon every iniquity, who could stand in his presence, or have any hope to be heard? but because he is a God of forgiveness, therefore he is reverenced; therefore the more forgiveness he doth expend upon any, the more he is reverenced. After a man's return to God, his fear of God is increased upon a more ingenuous account, for he fears God and his goodness, Hosea iii. 5, whereas before he feared God and his power, God and his justice. And the Jews, of whom he there speaks, shall fear or reverence that goodness the more, because the sin he has pardoned was so great, as the crucifying the Son of God, which, according to their fathers' wish, lay upon the heads of all their posterity.

God's goodness once tasted will make ingenuity afraid to offend him. Self-interest also will make them afraid to provoke that mercy that formally relieved them, to cashier them out of his favour. When the man was in the deep dungeon, where the fetters of sin entered into his very soul, and bound up under the terrors of the law, when mercy stepped in and delivered him, and poured oil into his wounds, he will be afraid to provoke that mercy to leave him in the same condition in which it found him, and from whence it drew him. He will be loath to be numbered amongst the crew of transgressors and bank of galley-slaves from whence he has been redeemed. He that hath tasted the bitterness of sin will fear to commit it; and he that hath felt the sweetness of mercy will fear to offend it.

I might add, for others' sakes, to engage them to come to Christ. Every conversion of a great sinner is a new copy of God's love; it is a repeated proclamation of the transcendency of his grace: 'Even when we were dead in sins, hath quickened us together with Christ,' Eph. ii. 5, 6. God hath quickened those rank sinners that were as black as darkness itself, and hath raised them to a condition of light. Why? Not only for themselves, but that in the ages to come he might shew forth, ὑπερβάλλοντα, transcendent riches of his grace, ver. 7. It was a picture God drew of his own heart, and exposed to the view of the world, that they might know, by the gracious entertainment and high advancement of those sinners, how liberal he is, and would always be, in the distribution of his grace, that penitent sinners of as great stains might be encouraged in all ages to rely upon him. This was his design in Paul's conversion, in this chapter: 'Howbeit for this cause I obtained mercy, that in me first Jesus Christ might shew forth all long-suffering, for a pattern to them which should hereafter believe on him to life everlasting,' ver 16; a pattern to them which should hereafter believe on him. He sets up this apostle as a white flag to invite rebels to treat with him, and return to their loyalty. As every great judgment upon a grand sinner is as the hanging a man in chains, to deter others from the like practice, so every conversion is not only an act of God's mercy to the convert, but an invitation to the spectators.

This is the argument David useth to persuade God to pour into him the joy of his salvation: 'Then will I teach transgressors thy ways,' &c., Ps. li. 12, 13. I will make all Jerusalem ring of it, and sinners, seeing the multitude and long train of thy tender mercies, shall fly into thy arms to be partakers of the same grace. For every great conversion is as a sea-mark to guide others into a safe harbour. And indeed, this he tells God when he had received pardon, that this would be the issue of God's pardon to David, Ps. lii. 5, 6, which is thought to be penned upon the same occasion. Ps. li., when, ver. 5, he had been forgiven, he tells God what the effect upon others would be: 'For this shall every one that is godly,' &c., ver. 6, judging it the fittest time to come when God is dealing out his mercy. Such effects we find when Christ was upon the earth; when Christ called Matthew, Mark ii. 14, the next news we hear, ver. 15, is, that many publicans and sinners sat down with him, and followed him. Many of the same tribe were encouraged by this kindness to one of their fellows to attend upon him.

As when a physician comes into an house where many are sick, and cures one that is desperate, it is an encouragement to the rest to rely upon his skill.

When Christ gives an experiment of his art on any sinner near thee, it is a call from heaven as well to excite thy emulation to come to him, as thy astonishment at it; as the conversion of the Gentiles was to provoke the Jews to jealousy: 'Salvation is come unto the Gentiles, for to provoke,' &c., Rom. xi. 11. Indeed, such conversions may more rationally move men, than any miracle can objectively move the sense, to see such a remarkable change wrought in the soul of a devil, in a diabolical nature. If men believe not in Christ after the sight of such standing miracles, it is an aggravation of their impenitence, as much as any miracle Christ wrought upon the earth was of the Jews' obstinacy, and does put as black a dye upon it: 'Ye, when you had seen it, repented not afterward, that you might believe him,' Mat. xxi. 32. Not any great sinner that thou hast seen take heaven by violence, but is writ down by God as a *yet* upon all thy unbelief. And how many hundred *yets* may Christ bring against thee, upon the account of others converted round about thee. The *yet* set upon Paul may refer to this, Acts ix. 1; because in the foregoing chapter Luke had related the successful progress of the gospel in Samaria and Jerusalem, which was an evidence of the power of this new doctrine; yet Paul proceeded in his persecuting fury, against such clear testimonies.

Had you been in the times of Christ, and seen those miracles he wrought among the Jews, you would all think you should never have been so stupid as they were, but would presently have believed in him upon a sight of those wonders. Let me tell you, the success of Christ's grace upon the souls of men, whereof you have seen many evidences, is a greater miracle, by Christ's own confession, than usually he wrought; for he tells the apostles they should work greater works, John xiv. 12, which he means of their success in converting work. And so thy impenitency has as great aggravations as the Jewish perversity. Let every such conversion of a great sinner be a ground of hope to thee, and a spur in thy side.

Further, such conversions evidence that God's commands are practicable, that his yoke is not burdensome. Men naturally think God a hard master, that his commands are impossible to be performed; but when they see men that had lain soaking in sin many years to have a fresh and fair verdure by grace, to run with delight in the ways of God's commands; when they see men that had the greatest prejudices against the ways of God thoroughly turned, they may think with themselves, Why may not I observe those commands? Is it more impossible for me than such a one? It is natural to men not to believe unless they see miracles: 'Except ye see signs and wonders, ye will not believe,' John iv. 48. Therefore all the standing miracles God hath left in the world are the extraordinary conversions of men, and the worst of men, that men may thereby be convinced of the power of the gospel and the strength of his grace, by seeing the admirable effects of it upon others; for many times conversion begins in admiration.

The use of this subject is,

1. First, Instruction. The doctrine manifests the power of the gospel. Nothing shews more the heavenly authority of the Christian religion, and the divine efficacy of the word, than the sudden conversions of notorious sinners; that a man should enter into a church a tiger, and return a lamb. It is this little stone which is instrumental to lay lusts, more giant-like than Goliath, grovelling in the dust. That Paul, mad with rage against the Christians, should, after an arrest in his journey, embrace a religion he hated; a pharisee changed into a preacher; a persecutor commence a martyr; that one of eminent parts, in favour with the Sanhedrim, should fly from a preferment expected, and patronise a doctrine contemned in the world, and attended with poverty, misery, cruel scourgings, and death; whenever you see such effects, take them as credentials from heaven, to maintain the credit of the word, and to assert the authority of that conclusion Paul lays down, that it is 'the power of God unto salvation,' Rom. i. 16. God gains a reputation to the gospel and the power of Christianity, that can in a moment change persons from beasts to men, from serpents to saints.

2. Groundlessness of despair. Despair not of others, when thou dost reflect upon thy own crimes, and considerest that God never dealt with a baser heart in the world than thine was. Was not Paul as unlike to prove a convert as

any relation of thine that wallows in his blood? Who would have thought that Onesimus should run from his master and be catched in Christ's arms? Neither despair of thyself. Shall any soul in anguish, and covered with penitential blushes, think itself cast out of the riches of God's affectionate grace? Shall any man so much blaspheme the merciful heart of Jesus Christ, as to fly to a knife, a halter, or a deep well for succour? Though thou wert in hell, David tells thee God is with thee, even there in his essential presence, yea, though thou wert hell itself; for where the devil dwells, that is hell; yet if the soul throbs, sighs, groans under it, his infinite grace will break down the door, and come in upon thee. And we know that neither she that had seven devils, nor he that had a legion, were strong enough to keep out Christ.

Secondly, Comfort of this subject. If God has made thee of a great sinner the object of his mercy, thou mayest be assured of, 1, continuance of his love. He pardoned thee when thou wert an enemy, will he leave thee now thou art his friend? He loved thee when thou hadst razed out in a great measure his image and picture which he had set in thy soul, will he hate thee now since he has restored that image, and drawn it with fresh colours? He justified thee when thou wert ungodly, and will he cast thee off since he hath been at such pains about thee, and written in thee a counterpart of his own divine nature in the work of grace? Were his compassions first moved when thou hadst no grace, and will they not sound louder since thou hast grace? Would the father embrace his son when his garments smelled of draff and swine, and will he cast him off after he hath put upon him a royal robe? Will Pharaoh's daughter pity Moses when he was in the ark, and will she scorn him when he is dressed?

2. Supplies of his grace. Thou hadst a rich present of his grace sent thee when thou couldst not pray for it, and will he not much more give thee whatsoever is needful when thou callest upon him? He was found of thee when thou didst not seek him, and will he hide himself from thee when thou art inquiring after him? A wise builder does not begin a work when he is not able to finish it. God considered, before he began with thee, what charge thou wouldst stand him in, both of merit in Christ and grace in thee; so that the grace he hath given thee is not only a mercy to thee, but an obligation on himself, since his credit is engaged to complete it. Thou hast more unanswerable arguments to plead before him than thou hadst, viz. his Son, his truth, his promise, his grace, his name, wherein thou hadst not the least interest. To what purpose has God called thee, and marked thee, if he doth not intend to supply thee with as much grace as shall bring thee to glory? To what purpose should a creditor forgive part of a debt, and lay the debtor in prison for the other part? Has God given thee Christ, and will he detain anything else? Supplies of wants, grants of anything thou desirest, are but as a few grains of pepper that the grocer puts in as an overplus to many pounds.

3. Strength against corruptions. Can molehills stand against him who has levelled mountains? Can a few clouds withstand the melting force of the sun, which has dissolved those black mists that overspread the face of the heavens? No more can the remainders of thy corruption bear head against his power, which has thrown down the great hills of the sins of thy natural condition, and has dissolved the thick fogs of thy unregeneracy. Thou canst neither doubt his strength nor his love; *amor gaudet in maximis;* he has done the greatest, and will he withdraw his hand from doing the least? When Moses slew the Egyptain, it is said that he 'supposed his brethren would have understood, that God intended by his hand to deliver

them,' Acts vii. 25. Moses was a type of Christ: has Christ overthrown a whole army of Egyptians, that did not only pursue thee, but keep thee in slavery? Has he overturned them all in the Red Sea? And wilt thou not take notice thereby, that he intends to be thy deliverer from the scattered troops of them?

Thirdly, Exhortation. 1. To those that God hath dealt so with.

1. Glorify God for his grace. Admiration is all the glory you can give to God for his grace, seeing you can add nothing to his essential glory. Christ will come at the last day to be admired; I pray send your admirations beforehand to attend him at his coming. Who made thee thus to differ from another? Was it not God? Let him, then, have the glory. If he made thee to differ from others in the enjoyment of his mercy, do thou also differ from others in the sounding of his praise. If thou hast an angel's state, it is fit thou shouldest have an angel's note. If David, when he considered the glorious heavens God had made for man, cried out so affectionately, 'What is man, that thou art mindful of him!' Ps. viii. 4; surely when thou considerest that work of grace which God hath wrought in thee, thou mayest with astonishment cry out, Oh, what is man that thou art mindful of him! What is such a vile creature, that thou shouldest take him into thy bosom? For there is not a grace in thee but is more glorious than the sun with all its regiments of stars, and is more like to God than the great fountain of light with all its amazing splendour. It is something of that heaven which is more glorious than all the rest of the heavens, and is above the reach of the natural eye. Oh what is man, that thou art thus mindful of him, to make him, who is a hell by sin, to become heaven by grace! Pardon of but one act of sin, makes us for ever debtors to God; because one sin renders us obnoxious to eternal torments, and every sin includes a hatred of God. What, then, is it to remit such vast sums, if to pardon one be a miracle? To pardon many committed against a suffering Christ that hath invited us, and repeats his invitations, after they have been rejected, is a miracle of the greatest magnitude, something above a miracle!

How should you think Jacob's expression in temporal mercies, a few sheep, too mean, 'I am less than the least of all thy mercies,' Gen. xxxii. 10. Oh I am less, less, less than the least of all this mercy. A great sinner, when converted, should sing a note somewhat above David's 'What shall I render?' Ps. cxvi. 12; and should say, I can render nothing, nothing; but I will render praise, blessing, amazement, astonishment; that is all I can render, and I cannot render enough of that. Had you chosen God first, it had been some ingenuity in God to answer that affection; but God chose you first, and that when there was nothing lovely in you, when he saw you the most deformed creatures in the world. There was no likeness between God and thee. *Similis simile amat*, is a rule in nature; but in this case, *Deus optimus diligit hominem pessimum*.

It is that which does amaze the disciples; they could not tell the reason why Christ should manifest himself to them, John xiv. 22. Perhaps thou art only snatched out of a family; the wrath of God may be fallen upon the rest, and thou only escaped. Has he not lopped down many cedars in morality, and chosen thee, a thorn, a shrub, to deck heaven with? Are not many damned that were not guilty of thy sins?

How wonderful is it that such a black firebrand should be made a statue fit for glory! He might have written thy name as easily in his black book as in his white. Is it not admirable mercy for a God provoked, to take pains with stiff-necked sinners, and to beat down mountains of high imaginations, to rear up a temple to himself? If mercy had knocked once or twice, and no more, thou hadst dropped into hell; but mercy would not leave knocking. Perhaps thy sins were so great, that if thou hadst gone but a little farther, thou hadst been irrecoverable; but God put a stop to the proud waves, saying, 'Hitherto shalt thou go, and no further.'

2. Often call to mind thy former sin. It hath been the custom of the saints of God formerly. When Matthew reckons up the twelve apostles, Mat. x. 3, whereof he was one, he remembers his former state, 'Matthew the publican;' but none of the other evangelists call him so in that enumeration.

(1.) It makes us more humble. Thoughts of pride cannot lodge in us, when the remembrance of our rags, bolts, and fetters is frequently renewed. What was there in thy former life, but misery, to move God to shew mercy to thee? Though Panl had a greater manifestation than any we read of, nay, than Christ himself had (for we do not read that Christ was rapt up into the third heavens), yet how frequently does he remember his sin of persecuting, to keep humiliation in exercise, and stop the growth of pride.

(2.) It will make us thankful. Sense of misery heightens our obligation to mercy. Men at sea are most thankful for deliverance when they consider the danger of the foregoing storm. A long night makes a clear morning more welcome.

(3.) It will make thee more active in the exercise of that grace which is contrary to thy former sin. Christ asked Peter thrice whether he loved him, John xxi., to put him tacitly in mind of his late sin, and to have a threefold exercise of his love, proportionable to his threefold denial.

(4.) It will be a preservative against falling into the same sin again. Perhaps Christ might press that threefold demand of Peter's love, to renew his repentance for his apostasy, as the best antidote against the falling into the same sin; and therefore Peter was grieved when he asked him the third time; not so much, it may be, for the suspicion his Master had of his fidelity, as for the just cause of jealousy his fall had given him. And at this third question, calling to mind his denial, he renewed his grief for his late unworthy carriage. Look back, then, upon thy former sin, but let it be with anger and shame, to strengthen thy detestation, to strangle thy former delight in it, and to magnify the mercy of God, who has delivered thee from it. When the Corinthians were proud of their spiritual gifts, the apostle beats down their swelling plumes, by giving them a review of their accursed state: 'Ye know that ye were Gentiles, carried away unto these dumb idols,' 1 Cor. xii. 2. When a convert frequently considers what he was once in his unregenerate state, he would not for all the honours, profits, and pleasures of the world, return to that state again, so great a delight he takes in the work of the new creature.

The second branch of exhortation is to those that are in a doubting condition. The main objection such make is the greatness of sin. Oh, there was never such a great sinner in the world as I am! If you rake all hell over, you will not find such another. Sure God will never pardon me; my sins are too great to be forgiven. Such language as this does sometimes drop from men, which they are partly urged to by the devil, to disparage that royal prince Jesus, that came to destroy his works, and to keep up an enmity between God and man, in making the creature have jealous thoughts of the Creator; and partly from a man's own conscience, which, acting by those legal principles written in the heart by nature, which are directive, and upon non-observance condemning, but discover nothing of pardoning grace. This was the first act of natural conscience in Adam after he had sinned; he had the least thoughts of forgiveness, for he studied nothing but how he might fly from the presence of God. Such speeches as these discredit thy

Creator if they be persisted in; argue thee to be one of Cain's posterity, who indeed told God to his very face that his 'sin was greater than could be forgiven,' Gen. iv. 13. I will a little argue with such.

But, 1, art thou indeed the greatest sinner? I can hardly believe it. Didst thou ever sin after the rate that Paul did? or wert thou ever possessed with such a fury? Sure there have been some as great sinners as thou art, be thou as bad as bad can be. If thou were to look over the names of all those now in heaven, and ask them all what sins they were guilty of before God shewed mercy to them, I cannot think but thou wouldest find many that would mate thee, yea, and exceed thee too; and thou canst not charge thyself with any black circumstances, but thou wouldest meet with some or other that would cry out presently, Oh, I was in the like condition, and rather worse! What dost thou think of Christ's murderers, who resisted the eloquence of his sermons and the power of his miracles? And when his death had darkened the sun, shook the earth, clave the rocks, rent the veil of the temple in twain, not one heart among that murderous crew had any saving relentings that we read of. And yet were not some of these converted by Peter's sermon, and the pardon of them left upon record by the Spirit of God?

Have not some of God's greatest favourites been the greatest sinners? Did not Adam draw upon him the guilt of all his posterity, and may in some sense be charged with the sins of all those that came out of his loins, even all mankind? Yet to this very person was the first promise of the gospel made, and that before he pronounced any sentence against him for his sin, Gen. iii. 15.

2. Suppose thou art the greatest, is thy staying from Christ the way to make all thy sins less? Art thou so rich as to pay this great debt out of thy own revenue? or hast thou any hopes of another surety? Did any man or angel tell thee they could satisfy for thee? Can complaints of a great load, without endeavouring its removal, ease that back that bears it?

3. Are thy sins the greatest? Is not the staying from Christ a making them greater? Does not God command thee to come to Christ? and is not thy delay a greater act of disobedience than the complaint of thy sinfulness can be of humility? Hast thou not load enough already? but wilt thou add unbelief, which is as black as all thy other sins put together? Is not a refusal of his mercy provocative? Thou art mad if thou thinkest thy sin can decrease by trampling upon Christ's heart, and spurning at his compassion. Thou hast sinned against justice, against wisdom, against common providence. Is not this enough, but wilt thou rob him of an opportunity to shew the riches of his grace, by refusing the blood of his Son, which his wisdom contrived and his love offers? Who is it persuades thee thus to keep off from Christ? Does God? Shew me where is his hand for it? Shew me thy authority in God's warrant. But since thou canst not, I am sure it is thy own corrupt heart and the devil in league together. And mayest thou not say of him far better than Ahab did of Micaiah, 'Thou didst never prophesy good to me'? No, he never did, nor ever will. What, wilt thou more black thyself by following the devil's counsel than obeying God's command? If thy sin be great, let it multiply thy tears, but by no means stop thy progress to Christ.

4. Were thy sins less than they are, thou mightest not so easily believe in Christ, as now thou mayest. If thou wilt not believe while thy sins are great, and thy heart naughty, I dare assure thee, if thy heart were not naught, and thy sins little, thou wouldst not believe; for thou wouldst be apt to believe in thy own heart, and trust in thy own righteousness, rather

than believe in Christ. Great sins and a bad heart felt and bewailed, is rather an advantage; as hunger is an incentive to a man to seek for meat. If men had clean hearts, it is like they would dispose of them otherwise, and rather think Christ should come to them. Men's poverty should rather make them more importunate than more modest. To say, I will not come to Christ, because I have great sins, is as if one should say, I will never have anything to do with happiness if offered, because I have great misery; I will go to no chirurgeon, because my wound is so great; I will eat no bread, because I am so exceeding hungry and like to starve. This is ill logic; and so it is with thee to argue, Because I am unclean, therefore I will not go to the fountain to be washed; or to think to be sanctified before believing. Now since thou hast, as thou confessest, no righteousness to trust in, methinks thou shouldst be the more easily persuaded to cast thyself upon Christ, since there is no other way but that.

If, therefore, thou art afraid of drowning under these mighty floods which roll upon thee, methinks thou shouldst do as men ready to perish in the waters, catch hold of that which is next them, though it be the dearest friend they have; and there is none nearer to thee than Christ, nor any such a friend; catch hold therefore of him.

5. The greatness of thy sin is a ground for a plea. Turn thy sins into arguments, as David doth, 'for it is great,' Ps. xxv. 11; some translate it, 'though it be great;' and the Hebrew word כִּי will bear both. The psalmist useth two arguments, God's name, and the greatness of his sin. And both are as good arguments as they were then. Thou mayest go to God with this language in thy mouth; Lord, my impurity is great, there is more need therefore of thy washing me; my wound is deep, the greater is the necessity of some plaster for a cure. What charitable man in the world would not hasten a medicine, rather than refuse to grant it! What earthly physician would object, The disease is great, therefore there is no necessity of a cure; therefore there is no room left for my skill! And shall God be less charitable than man? Dogs may lay claim to crumbs that fall from the master's table. Thou mayest use also the argument of God's name. Sinners may plead for grace upon the account of God's glory, viz., the glory God will have by it. His wisdom is eminent in serving his own ends by his greatest enemy. His power in conquering sin, his grace in pardoning. Show him his own name, Exod. xxxiv., and see if he will deny any letter of it.

If thy disease were not so great, Christ's glory would not be so illustrious. Pardon of such sins enhanceth the mercy and skill of thy Saviour. The multitude of devils which were in Mary Magdalene, are recorded to shew the power of that Saviour that expelled them, and wrought so remarkable a change. Are thy sins the greatest? God that loves to advance his free grace in the highest manner, will be glad of the opportunity to have so great a sinner follow the chariot of it, and to manifest thereby its uncontrollable power. Use David's argument, Ps. xxxvii. 12, when, ver. 8, he prayed that God would deliver him from his transgressions; ver. 12, he useth this argument, that he was a stranger. I know no reason but it may be thine, for if thy sins be great, thou art more alienated from God than the ordinary rank of men. Lord, thou dost command us to shew kindness to strangers, to love our enemies; and wilt thou not use the same mercy to a stranger that thou commandest others to use, and shew the same love to so great an enemy as I am? The greater my enmity, the more glorious will be thy love.

Plead therefore, 1, the infiniteness of God's mercy. It is strange if thy debts should be so great, that the exchequer of the King of kings cannot discharge them. Why should the apostle say God was 'rich in mercy,' Eph. iv., and call it 'great love,' if it were spent only upon little sins, and if any debts could exhaust it; for surely an infinite God cannot be finitely rich. If God be rich in mercy, he is surely infinitely rich; thou canst not think that any that have got to heaven before thee have drained his treasures, for then it had been finite, not infinite. They were not unsearchable riches, if the sins of all the world could find the bottom of them.

God looks upon his grace as the greatest part of his estate. He calls it his riches, which title he gives not any other attribute. Now riches are not to lie by and rust, but to be laid out and traded with; and the more they are traded with, the more wealth they bring in. God hath not delight to keep these riches by him, and to hoard them up for no use; for *omne bonum est sui diffusivum;* therefore the more goodness anything hath, the more diffusive it is of itself. God loves to distribute his wealth upon his own terms, nd to venture out riches of grace, that he may have returns of riches of glory; so that if you come to God, you have all his estate at your service. Till thou canst be as sinful as God is merciful, as evil as God is good, do not think thy iniquities can check an almighty goodness. Mercy bears the greatest sway in God's name, Exod. xxxiv. 6, 7. There is but one letter of his power, two of his justice, and nine or ten expressions of his mercy. His power attends his mercy as well as his justice, so that on mercy's side against justice there is five to one, which is great odds.

Plead then with God, Lord, it is said in thy word, 'Say not unto thy neighbour, Go, and come again, and to-morrow I will give thee, when it is in the power of thine hand to do it,' Prov. iii. 28. Should a man not refuse to give to his neighbour when he has it by him? and shall the merciful God deny me that mercy which I beg of him upon my knees, when he has it all in store by him? Must I forgive my brother, if he offends seventy-seven times, a double perfect number? and must I be more charitable to man than infinite mercy will be to me? Shall thy justice only speak, and thy mercy be silent, and plead nothing on my behalf? Hast thou not said that thou art he 'that blots out transgressions for thy own sake?' Isa. xliii. 25; that thou dost 'blot out iniquities like a thick cloud?' Isa. xliv. 22. Is there any cloud so thick as to master the melting power of the sun; and shall ever a cloud of sin be so thick as to master the power of thy mercy? Has not thy mercy as much strength and eloquence to plead for me, as thy justice has to declaim against me? Is thy justice better armed with reason than thy kindness with compassions? Have thy compassions no eloquence? Oh, who can resist their pleasing rhetoric!

2. Christ's, and God's intent in his coming, was to discharge great sins. He was called Jesus, a Saviour, because he was to save his people from their sins. And do you think some of his people's sins were not as great as any men's sins in the world? To save only from little iniquities, had not been a work suitable to the glorious name of Jesus. Neither can we conceive how Christ should enter into such strict bonds to his Father to be a surety only for some smaller debts. If this had not been his intent, he would have put some limitation in that prayer he taught his disciples, and not have commanded them to pray, 'Forgive us our trespasses,' but forgive us our little sins, or sins of such a size. He never asked what sins, and how many sins, men were guilty of when they came to him; but upon faith, saith he, 'Thy sins are forgiven thee.' Plead therefore with Christ, and say, Thou didst come to do thy Father's will, which was, that none should be cast off that come unto thee; and thou hast said the same; it is not sufficient for thee to say it merely, and not to do it. Wilt thou draw me

with the cords of a man (for I could not thus come to thee unless thou didst draw me), and shall I be beaten back with a frown?

3. Christ's death was a satisfaction for the greatest sins, both *ex parte facientis*, Christ, and *ex parte acceptantis*, God; for God could not accept any satisfaction but what was infinite. 'One sacrifice for sins for ever,' &c., Heb. x. 12; not *one sin*, but *sins*; not *little sins*, but *sins* without exception. Yea, and it is all sin, 1 John i. 7; and all includes great as well as little. Satan once came to a sick man, and shews him a great catalogue of his sins, concluding from thence his eternal damnation. The sick man, strengthening himself by the word of God, bid the devil write over the catalogue in great letters those words, 1 John i. 7, whereupon the devil presently leaves him.* Can thy sins be greater than Christ's merit? or thine offences than his sacrifice? It is strange if the malignity of thy sin should be as infinite as the virtue of his death. He hath satisfied for all the saints that ever came to heaven; and put thy sins in the balance with theirs, and surely they cannot weigh so much. He was 'a propitiation for the sins of the whole world;' and are thy sins as great as the sins of the whole world? If part of his merits be enough to save ten thousand damned souls in hell, if they had applied it, is it not enough to satisfy God for thy sins, which are far less? Was not Christ charged with as great sins as thine can be when he was upon the cross? Or are thy single sins bigger than all those the prophet means when he saith, 'And the Lord hath laid on him the iniquity of us all'? Isa. liii. 6.

Well, then, plead thy Saviour's death, since it was for his honour to satisfy for sins of so deep a dye. It is said in thy word, it is a joy to a righteous man to perform judgment, and shall it not be much more a joy to the righteous God? Behold, here I offer thee the atonement thy Son and my Saviour has made, and if it be not enough, I am content to perish; but if it be, I desire thee to do me justice with that joy that a righteous man would do it with, and discharge my transgressions. And if thou dost object, that I have flung away this satisfaction, and would not have it, I answer, my Saviour's satisfaction was for such sins as those, otherwise none would be saved; for was there any but refused the proffer of it at first, made demurs before they entertained it? Let thy objections be what they will, Christ shall be my advocate to answer for me.

4. Christ is able to take away great sins. Did he ever let any one that came to him with a great infirmity, go back without a cure, and dishonour himself so much, as that it should be said, it was a distemper too great for the power of Jesus to remedy? And why should there be any sin that he cannot pardon? It is as easy for him to heal the one as the other; for he did with as much ease and delight say, 'Thy sins are forgiven thee;' as say, 'Take up thy bed, and walk.' Hast thou seven devils? Suppose a legion, *i.e.* six thousand six hundred and sixty-six; he did dispossess a body of as many: can he not as easily dispossess a soul? If thou hadst ten thousand legions, I dare say Christ would not lose an opportunity of such a conquest; for it would please him more to do great works than little, and to shew how far his power could reach.

Were it not for such objects, we could not know whether he could 'save to the utmost,' or no, Heb. vii. 25. What has he this ability for? To lie idle? No, surely to be exercised about the most difficult tasks. Suppose the scroll of thy sins were as long as to reach from earth to the highest heavens, would this reach to the utmost of Christ's ability? If thou hadst

* Goulart Tableau de la mort, Tableau 9, p. 131.

sinned as far as any man in the world can sin, yet still thou art not got without the verge of Christ's saving power. That word *utmost* I dare set against all thy objections. If you had the sins of all the damned in hell upon you, you could not put either his free grace or vast power to a nonplus. His blood is of that virtue, that were it poured out upon a devil, it would make him presently commence a glorious angel. What is either a great or a light disease to omnipotence, when with the same word he can cure the greatest as well as the least distempers?

But may the soul say, I do not question his power, but his will. Therefore,

5. Christ's nature leads him to shew mercy to the greatest sinners. Some question whether Christ will pardon them, for they look upon him as a hard master, that will not easily forgive. But Christ gives another character of himself, Mat. xi. 28, 29, when he exhorts men to come to him; he tells them they must not judge him to be of a rugged and implacable nature, but as meek as they are sinful. Meekness is seen in pardoning of injuries, not keeping them in memory, to beget and cherish revenge. Now, the greater the provocation, the more transcendent is that meekness to pass it by. Did he ever upbraid any with their offences, and hit them in the teeth with their former extravagances? Luke vii. 44. Christ makes a narrative of Mary's acts of kindness to him, but not a syllable of her foul transgressions. Are thy sins so great? Surely Christ, who delights in his compassions, will not lose such an opportunity of evidencing both his power and his pity upon such a subject; for if there cannot be so great a sinner as thou art, he is never like to have such a season for it, if he miss of thee.

6. Christ was exalted by God upon this very account: 'Wherefore he is able to save them to the uttermost that come unto God by him,' Heb. vii. 25. How comes Christ to be so able to save to the uttermost? It is 'because he ever lives to make intercession for them.' For whom? For those that come to God by him. What has Christ his life in heaven for, but to intercede? And would his Father's love to him, and the greatness of his interest in God be discovered by granting some small requests, the pardon of a few and little sins? Christ is consecrated priest by the oath of God, Heb. vii. 28; would God put himself to his oath for a light business, a thing of little moment? What is the end of this oath? Compare it with: 'For men verily swear by the greater: and an oath for confirmation is to them an end of all strife. Wherein God, willing more abundantly to shew unto the heirs of promise the immutability of his counsel, confirmed it by an oath,' Heb. vi. 16–18; and all is that you 'might have a strong consolation.' What strong comfort could there be, if only little debts were remitted? What is the end of an oath? Ver. 16, to take away strife. Men do not strive with God, or doubt of his mercy to forgive little sins, for they think that will be done of course. But the great contest men have with God is about his willingness to remit great debts, scarlet sins: upon this account the strife is between God and doubting sinners; therefore, to bring this contest to a period, God hath put himself to his oath, and sworn that Christ should be a priest for ever, to take away all strife between him and believing sinners. For whom is this strong consolation founded upon God's oath? For those that 'fly for refuge,' ver. 18. Now the cities of refuge were not appointed for ordinary crimes, but for blood, to secure the malefactor from the avenger.

Shall I add further, God is best pleased with Christ when he makes intercession for the greatest transgressors. Suppose thou hadst been one of Christ's murderers, and hadst given thy vote against him; perhaps thou wouldst have thought this a more crimson sin than any thou art guilty of. You know Christ prayed for their pardon while he was upon the cross; and God gives this as one reason why he would exalt him: 'He shall divide him,' &c., Isa. liii. 12. Why? 'Because he poured out his soul to death.' What should he bear sin for, if God had no mind to pardon it? And because 'he was numbered among the transgressors,' which the evangelist understands of his being crucified with thieves, Mark xv. 28. And therefore his making intercession for transgressors, must be understood of his prayer upon the cross. And if God did exalt him for this, would God be pleased with him, or would Christ answer the end of his exaltation, if he did cease to make intercession for sinners of the like stamp? Go and tell God, that he sent Christ to bless you, Acts iii. 26, in converting you; and desire Christ to do his office.

7. Christ is entrusted by God to give out his grace to great sinners. Christ is God's Lord-almoner, for the dispensing redemption, and the riches of his grace. To whom? Not to the righteous, they have no need of it; but to sinners, and those that have the greatest necessity. He would be an ill steward, who, when entrusted by his lord to bestow his alms upon the poor, should overlook the most miserable, indigent, and necessitous persons, when they crave it of him, and relieve those that had not so great and crying wants. Christ is a priest for intents of the same nature as the legal typical priests were. They were to have compassion, Heb. v. 2, μετριοπαθεῖν, to measure out their compassion, to order the sacrifice according to the nature of the sin of the person that presented it. So is Christ, by virtue of his office, to measure out his grace according to the greatness of a man's necessity, as manna was to be gathered according to every one's wants.

Well, then, to conclude this exhortation. Embolden thyself to draw near to Christ. It is the apostle's use he makes of all his foregoing doctrine, Heb. x. 19, &c. God requires not a heart without sin, but a heart without guile. Who needs more boldness than great sinners? And the apostle sets no limits to it. Let us, who have been as great sinners as any, resolve to do as they in Jeremiah did, Jer. iii. 22. They had both a command and a promise. 'Return,' there is the command. 'I will heal,' &c., there is the promise. Presently they reply, 'We will come to thee,' &c. They seem to snatch the promise out of God's mouth. How will these quick and ready converts rise up in judgment against thy slowness and dulness! Shall they do this upon one promise; and when thou hast all the promises in the book of God repeated to thee, shall God hear no other answer but this, We will not return, or We dare not come, We dare not believe thee? Did God give but one promise to Adam, and did he embrace it, and live upon it all his life (for we read of no more he had than that of the seed of the woman breaking the serpent's head); and wilt thou not return, when thou hast so many promises, filling every page in the Scripture?

Hast thou not a world of precedents? Did not God take up all his saints from the dunghill with all their rags, and clothe them? Were any of them born princes and sons of heaven? Alas, every man at first sued for a Saviour in the right of a sinner; and all pleaded in the court of heaven *in forma pauperis*. Were they not debtors, and could they do that which might make God cross out one of those sums they owed him? Oh, think not then thou canst dam up that torrent of love that has flowed so freely to the world for so many ages. Though thy disease be grievous, yet it is not irrecoverable, provided thou goest to the physician. He can with a breath burn up thy corruption, as soon as dissolve the creation. Christ can turn the muddiest water into such wine that can please the heart both of God and man. As you have been vessels of sin, if you will be vessels of repentance God will make you brimful of mercy. Plead not, therefore, thy own unworthiness. Man's unworthiness never yet hindered the flowing of God's kindness. It is too weak a bank to stop the current of God's favour. The greater thy unworthiness, the greater advantage has free grace to manifest its uncontrollable excellency. That man dishonours God that sets his sin above God's goodness, or his unworthiness above God's condescension. You cannot do God a greater pleasure than to come to him to be made clean. When he reckons up thy sin, it is not with an upbraiding, but a compassionate sigh, Jer. xiii. 27. He longs for the time of thy returning, and minds thee of thy sin, that thou mayest the sooner seek a remedy, and wonders thou wilt continue in such a filthy condition so long.

Fourthly, The caution which this subject suggests. 1. Think not thy sins are pardoned because they are not so great as those God has pardoned in others. This is *ad suam consolationem aliena numerare vitia.** Consider God cast off Saul for less sins than David committed. Evil angels were cast off for one sin. A few small sands may sink a ship as well as a great rock. Thy sins may be pardoned though as great as others, but then you must have equal qualifications with them. They had great sins, so hast thou; but have you as great a hatred and loathing of sin as they had?

2. Let not this doctrine encourage any person to go on in sin. If thou dost now suck such poison out of this doctrine, and boast of that name God proclaims, Exod. xxxiv. 6, 7, take the cooler along with thee, and remember it is one part of his name 'by no means to clear the guilty.' He never intended those mercies for sinners as sinners, but as penitent. Penitents, as such, are not guilty, because repentance is a moral revocation of a sin, and always supposes faith in Christ. There is 'forgiveness with God,' Ps. cxxx. 4; but it is 'that he may be feared,' not despised. God never intended mercy as a sanctuary to protect sin.

(1.) It is disingenuous to do so. Great love requires great duties, not great sins. Freeness of grace should make us increase holiness in a more cheerful manner. What high ingratitude is it to be inclined to sin because God is inclined to pardon, to have a frozen heart to him because he hath a melting heart to thee! What, to rebel against him because he hath a compassionate heart, and to be wicked because God is good! to turn grace itself into wantonness! Is this to fear his goodness? No, it is to trample on it; to make that which should excite thee to holiness a bawd to thy lust, and God himself a pander to the devil. If thou dost thus slight the design of this mercy, which thou canst never prize at too high a rate, it is certain thou never hadst the least taste of it. If thou hadst, thou couldst not sin so freely; for when grace enters, it makes the soul dead to sin, Rom. vi. 1, 2. The apostle answers such a consequence with a *God forbid!*

(2.) It is foolish so to do. Would any man be so simple as to set his house on fire because he has a great river running by his door, from whence he may have water to quench it; or wound himself, because there is an excellent plaster which has cured several?

(3.) It is dangerous to do so. If thou losest the present time, thou art in danger to lose eternity. There are many in hell never sinned at such a presumptuous rate. He is merciful to the penitent, but he will not be unfaithful to his threatenings. If thou art willing to receive grace, thou mayest have it, but upon God's conditions. He will not pin it upon thy sleeve whether thou wilt or no. This is to make that which is the savour of life to become the savour of death unto thee. See what an answer Paul

* Hieron. in vol. i. p. 114, e.

gives to such an imagination, 'Let us do evil, that good may come; whose damnation is just,' Rom. iii. 8. He takes a handful of hell-fire and flings it in their faces. Let but Deut. xxix. 18, 19, stare thee in the face, and promise thyself peace in this course if thou canst: 'Lest there should be among you a root that beareth gall and wormwood; and it cometh to pass, when he heareth the words of this curse, that he bless himself in his heart, saying, I shall have peace, though I walk in the imagination of mine heart.' As his goodness is great, which thou dost despise; so the wrath will be the hotter thou dost treasure up. Though great sins are occasions of great grace, yet sin doth not necessitate grace. Who can tell whether ever God would have shewn mercy to Paul, had he done that against knowledge which he did ignorantly? Repentance must first be; see the order, 'Repent, and be converted, that your sins may be blotted out,' Acts iii. 19. First, repentance and conversion, then justification. This grace is only given to penitent sinners. You know not whether you shall repent, but you may know, that if you do not repent you shall be damned. As there is infinite grace to pardon you, if you repent; so there is infinite justice to punish you, if you do not repent. The gospel binds us to our good behaviour as much as the law.

INDEX.

SCRIPTURE TEXTS.